Transnational Law
Cases and Materials

■ ■ ■

By

Mathias W. Reimann
Hessel E. Yntema Professor of Law
University of Michigan Law School

James C. Hathaway
James E. and Sarah A. Degan Professor of Law
University of Michigan Law School

Timothy L. Dickinson
Professor from Practice, University of Michigan Law School
Partner, Paul Hastings, Washington, D.C.

Joel H. Samuels
Associate Professor of Law
University of South Carolina School of Law

AMERICAN CASEBOOK SERIES®

WEST.

Mat #40268901

American Casebook Series is a trademark registered in the U.S. Patent and Trademark Office.

© 2013 LEG, Inc. d/b/a West Academic Publishing

610 Opperman Drive
St. Paul, MN 55123
1–800-313-9378

Printed in the United States of America

ISBN: 978–0–314–15450–7

FOREWORD

If there ever was a casebook designed to fill a real gap, it is the present one. In 2001, the University of Michigan Law School introduced "Transnational Law" as a mandatory part of its curriculum, and similar courses have since been implemented by a number of other law schools. Now Michigan has again taken the lead. Since three of the four authors are members of the Ann Arbor faculty and the fourth is a Michigan alumnus, I may be allowed to attribute the project to my own academic home in the United States. The authors have produced a teaching tool designed both to fill the idea of the new course with concrete substance and to make Transnational Law more attractive to teach at a still larger number of law schools.

I may have been a more or less "classic" public international lawyer for the greatest part of my teaching career. But I have always been keenly aware that the traditional stuff of public international law that I offered my students could in and of itself not sufficiently prepare them for their work in the real world out there. Such preparation, however, is precisely what the present book pursues: it introduces the students to the law transcending national boundaries "in her infinite variety" (to use Richard Baxter's expression), because students will encounter such law nowadays in almost all legal careers.

The Casebook provides the basic orientation in highly diversified fields of the law and thus renders its users "literate" in transnational legal issues. While it covers many of the essentials of the classic law of nations, it goes far beyond the traditional paradigm. Not only does it venture into some of the special areas that have developed in the post-WW II era, such as international trade and foreign investment, it also covers basic elements of private international law. Further, as a European with considerable experience teaching in the United States, I am impressed that, despite its extensive coverage of international and American cases, the book also provides more than any competitor a significant sampling of primary sources from other national and regional legal systems, including materials from every continent.

When I arrive in an interesting foreign city, I like to go on a tour in those double-decker buses that one can leave and re-enter at will, to get a first impression of the whole and yet at the same time to have a closer look at things I find more interesting than others. I read the minds of the authors of "Transnational Law" as wanting to offer exactly such a first guided tour. It is important to note that this new book, and with it the course it is to accompany, is not designed to replace the teaching of full-fledged courses in public or private international law as traditionally understood. Rather, the authors intend to offer a first exposure to the field as they understand it, and thereby to whet the appetite of the student for further, more comprehensive or more specialized, courses. I very much hope that this expectation will come true.

In sum, the present book with its novel approach of integrating transnational legal questions hitherto dealt with in separate "boxes", as it were, is a significant achievement. One must hope that it will be widely used.

The Hague,   BRUNO SIMMA
December 2012

> Member of the International Law Commission (1996–2003)
> Judge at the International Court of Justice (2003–2012)
> Judge at the Iran–United States Claims Tribunal (2012–)
> Professor of Law, University of Michigan Law School

PREFACE

This new casebook provides an introduction to the international legal order as it presents itself at the beginning of the 21st century. It does not focus on any of the traditional categories, such as public international law, private international law (conflict of laws), or comparative law. Instead, it strives to transcend these categories because the issues you as students will face in practice typically defy the established divisions.

The book's origins lie in the decision of the University of Michigan Law School to make a course entitled *Transnational Law* mandatory beginning with the class entering in 2001. At the time, Michigan was, as far as we can see, the only law school in the United States to *require* such a course. Back then, Anne-Marie Slaughter called the decision "a historic step," and Supreme Court Justice Sandra Day O'Connor praised it in her keynote address to the American Society of International Law. (See Anne-Marie Slaughter, Notes from the President, American Society of International Law Newsletter, March/April 2002, 1 at 4; Sandra Day O'Connor, Keynote Address, American Society of International Law, Proceedings of the 96th Annual Meeting, March 13–16, 2002,Washington D.C. (2002), 348 at 352.)

The book's pedagogical goal is to provide an overview, i.e., to give you a sense of orientation in transactions and disputes reaching beyond national boundaries. Its objective is decidedly modest: it is designed as a mere introduction which renders you "literate" in transnational issues. Thus, it provides you with the basic knowledge and understanding that every American lawyer should possess today, and it lays the foundations on which more specialized courses can build.

While it covers important elements of public and private international law, it is not intended as a substitute for full-fledged courses in either of these, or other, subjects. In particular, it does not deal with the intricacies of the lawmaking process on the international level nor does it fully engage the theories and critiques of international law. Where the book delves more deeply into particular matters, it does so in order to demonstrate their complexity, not to teach intricacies for their own sake. Students mastering a course built on this book will not be experts in international law but will understand transboundary problems in their overall context, ask the right questions, and know how to conceive answers.

The book's organizational principle is to map the terrain of the world legal order by looking at five major components: the respective *Actors*, the nature of their *Interaction*, the major forms and effects of transnational *Law*, transnational mechanisms of *Dispute Resolution*, and the *Domestic*

Effects of international rules. It approaches the material from an evolutionary perspective and shows how the situation with regard to each of the five topics has changed, especially over the last half-century.

We have included many fewer questions and notes before and after the assigned materials than you will find in most casebooks. This decision reflects our view that a casebook should serve the needs of students to learn the material rather than of the authors to display their learning. We hope that by concentrating on a few questions for each reading, you will be able to perform a more focused analysis on your own and as a consequence engage in a more robust class discussion. In addition, for ease of reading, we have omitted most citations and footnotes from the cases, excerpts and other materials in the casebook. In the cases where we have retained the internal citations and footnotes, we have done so quite intentionally, so you should make sure not to gloss over them, as they have been retained to enhance class discussion and your learning experience more generally.

All four authors have taught (and at times co-taught) Michigan's basic *Transnational Law* course, but we approach the project from very different angles. One of us is a professor from practice whose main career is as a partner in a major international law firm practicing international business law with a focus on foreign investment and foreign corrupt practices issues. The second is an academic working in public international law, who is a leading authority on international and comparative refugee law. The third is an expert in private international and comparative law. And the fourth is an academic who writes on both public and private international law, having entered academia after practicing in those areas at a leading American law firm. While this diversity of perspectives inevitably creates tensions, it also helps us to overcome the boundaries between public and private international law, substantive law and procedure, theoretical analysis and practical experience.

We thank our research assistants, especially Ananda Burra, Ted Kill, Elina Lae, and Nawreen Sattar for their help and suggestions; the excellent library staff at the University of Michigan; Vanessa Byars and Carolyn Russell for their assistance in completing the project; and our colleagues Reuven Avi-Yonah, Michael Barr, Daniel Halberstam, Rob Howse, Steve Ratner and the late Eric Stein, as well as Karima Bennoune and Sonia Rolland, for advice in matters large and small. We are indebted to the University of Michigan Law School and the University of South Carolina School of Law for their support. The usual disclaimer applies.

Many people will find many things wrong with this book. As usual, no one is more keenly aware of its weaknesses than its authors. While we cannot, and indeed would not try, to please everybody, we welcome comments and criticism from all users—teachers and students alike.

Ann Arbor, Michigan & Columbia, South Carolina

MATHIAS W. REIMANN
JAMES C. HATHAWAY
TIMOTHY L. DICKINSON
JOEL H. SAMUELS

April 2013

ACKNOWLEDGED SOURCES

Roger Alford, *Medellin and The Continuation of Deference to International Tribunals*, Opinio Juris, Oct. 11, 2007.

Jose E. Alvarez, *The Internationalization of U.S. Law*, 47 Colum. J. Transnat'l L. 537 (2009). Republished with the permission of the Columbia Journal of Transnational Law, permission conveyed through Copyright Clearance Center.

Anthony Aust, Modern Treaty Law and Practice (2nd Edition 2007). Reprinted with the permission of Cambridge University Press.

Harold Berman, Law and Revolution. Reprinted by Permission of the Publisher from Law and Revolution: The Formation of Western Legal Tradition by Harold J. Berman, pp. 346-348, Cambridge: Mass.: Harvard University Press, Copyright © 1983 by the President and Fellows of Harvard College.

Gary Born, *Reflections on Judicial Jurisdiction in International Cases* 17 Ga. J. Int'l & Comp. L. 1 (1987).

J. L. Brierly, Brierly: The Law of Nations 5th Edition (1955).

Ian Brownlie, Principles of Public International Law, 6th ed. (2003) © Ian Brownlie 2003.

Ian Brownlie, Principles of Public International Law, 7th Edition (2008).

Thomas Buergenthal, *Proliferation of International Courts and Tribunals: Is It Good or Bad?* 14 Leiden J. Int'l L. 267 (2001). Reprinted with the Permission of Cambridge Press.

Antonio Cassese, International Law, 2nd Edition (2005). By Permission of Oxford University Press. © Antonio Cassese 2005.

Enzo Cannizzaro and Paolo Palchetti (eds.), Customary International Law on the Use of Force (2005), M. Nijhoff.

Steve Charnovitz, Non Governmental Organizations and International Law, 100 Am. J. Int'l L. 348 (2006). Republished with the permission of the American Society of International Law, permission conveyed through Copyright Clearance Center.

Christine Chinkin, The Challenge of Soft Law: Development and Change in International Law, 38 Int'l & Comp L.Q. 850 (1989). © British Institute of International and Comparative Law. Reprinted with the Permission of Cambridge University Press.

James Crawford, Creation States in International Law, 2nd Edition (2006).

Thomas M. Franck, *What Happens Now? The United Nations after Iraq*, 97 Am. J. Int'l L. 607 (2003). Republished with the permission of the American Society of International Law, permission conveyed through Copyright Clearance Center.

Leo Gross, The Peace of Westphalia (1948). Republished with the permission of the American Society of International Law, permission conveyed through Copyright Clearance Center.

Jack Goldsmith, *The Self-Defeating International Criminal Court,* 70 U. Chi. L. Rev. 83, 89, 95-99 (2003). Republished with the permission of the University of Chicago Law Review, permission conveyed through Copyright Clearance Center.

James C. Hathaway. *Leveraging Asylum*, 45 Tex. Int'l L. J. 503 (2010).

James C. Hathaway, The Rights of Refugees Under International Law, (2005). © 2005 James C. Hathaway. Reprinted with the Permission of Cambridge University Press.

Mark W. Janis, *Sovereignty and International Law: Hobbes and Grotius, in* Matrinus Nijhoff, Essays in Honour of Wang Tieya (R. St. J. Macdonald ed. 1993), pp. 392-400. Reprinted with kind permission from Springer Science+Business Media B.V.

Benedict Kingsbury, Nico Krisch, Richard B. Stewart, The Emergence of Global Administrative Law, 68 Law and Contemporary Problems 15 (2005). Used with permission of the author.

Frederic L. Kirgis, *Security Council Resolution 1441 on Iraq's Final Opportunity to Comply with Disarmament Obligations* Am. Soc'y Int'l L. Insights (November 2002). Republished with the permission of the American Society of International Law, permission conveyed through Copyright Clearance Center.

John H. Langbein, *Comparative Civil Procedure and the Style of Complex Contracts,* 35 Am. J. Comp. L. 381 (1987).

Joan L. Larsen, *Importing Constitutional Norms from a "Wider Civilization": Lawrence and the Rehnquist Court's Use of Foreign and International Law Domestic Constitutional Interpretation*, 65 Ohio St. L.J. 1283 (2004). Reproduced with permission of the author.

Jessica T. Matthews, Power Shift, 76 Foreign Affairs 50 (Jan-Feb 1997). Reprinted by permission of FOREIGN AFFAIRS, © 1997 by the Council on Foreign Relations, Inc. www.ForeignAffairs.com

Rein Mullerson, *The Continuity and Succession of States, By Reference to the Former USSR and Yugoslavia, By Reference to the Former USSR and*

Yugoslavia, 42 Int'l & Comp Law Quarterly 473 (1993). Reprinted with the permission of Cambridge University Press.

Stephen C. Neff, War and the Law of Nations: A General History. Copyright © 2005 Stephen C. Neff. Reprinted with the Permission of Cambridge University Press.

Daniel Philpott, Revolutions in Sovereignty (2001), Princeton University Press. Reprinted by Permission of Princeton University Press.

Sandra Day O'Connor, *American Society of International Law Proceedings – Keynote Address* (March 16, 2002). Republished with the permission of the American Society of International Law, permission conveyed through Copyright Clearance Center.

Steven R. Ratner, *Corporations and Human Rights: A Theory of Legal Responsibility*, 111 Yale L.J. 443 (2001). Republished with the permission of the Yale Law Journal, permission conveyed through Copyright Clearance Center.

Mathias Reimann, From The Law of Nations to Transnational Law: Why We Need a New Basic Course for the International Curriculum, 22 Penn State Int'l L. J. 397 (2004).

Bruno Simma, *Does the UN Charter Provide an Adequate Legal Basis for Individual or Collective Responses to Violations of Obligations erga omnes?,* The Future of International Law Enforcement (J. Delbrück ed. 1993), pp. 125-26, 130-31. Republished with the permission of Duncker & Humblot GmbH, permission conveyed through Copyright Clearance Center.

Oscar Schachter, International Law in Theory and Practice (1991). Republished with the permission of Springer Publishing, permission conveyed through Copyright Clearance Center.

Malcolm Shaw, International Law. © 2003 Cambridge University Press.

Malcolm Shaw, International Law 6th Ed. © 2009 Malcolm N. Shaw. Reprinted with the Permission of Cambridge University Press.

Gerry Simpson, Great Powers and Outlaw States (2004). © 2004 Gerry Simpson. Reprinted with the permission of Cambridge University Press.

Anne-Marie Slaughter, *The Real New World Order*, 76 Foreign Affairs 183 (Sept-Oct 1997). Reprinted by permission of FOREIGN AFFAIRS, © 1997 by the Council on Foreign Relations, Inc. www.ForeignAffairs.com

Anne-Marie Slaughter, A New World Order, © 2004 Princeton University Press. Reprinted by permission of Princeton University Press.

Eric Stein, *International Integration and Democracy: No Love at First Sight*, 95 Am. J. Int'l L. 489 (2001). Republished with the permission of the American Society of International Law, permission conveyed through Copyright Clearance Center.

Thucydides, History of the Peloponnesian War (Rex Warner translation., Penguin Classics 1954).

William H. Taft IV and Todd F. Buchwald, *Preemption, Iraq, and International Law*, 97 Am. J. Int'l L. 557 (2005) Republished with the permission of the American Society of International Law, permission conveyed through Copyright Clearance Center.

Stefan Talmon, *The Constitutive Theory Versus Declaratory Theory of Recognition: Tertium non Datur?* British Yearbook of International Law v75 BYIL (2004).

Andreas Zimmermann et al., The Statute of the International Court of Justice (2006) By Permission of Oxford University Press.

ICJ Rejects Mexico's Request to Interpret Avena but Finds United States Violated Provisional Measures Order 103 Am. J. Int'l L. 362 (2009). Republished with the permission of the American Society of International Law, permission conveyed through Copyright Clearance Center.

TIMETABLE

1618	Thirty Years War breaks out
1625	Hugo Grotius, *De iure belli ac pacis*
1648	Peace of Westphalia
1651	Thomas Hobbes, Leviathan
1776	Declaration of Independence
1787	U.S. Constitution
1789	French Revolution
1794	Jay Treaty (United States–United Kingdom) (providing for binding arbitration)
1871	Alabama Arbitration
1899	First Hague Peace Conference
1900	Permanent Court of International Arbitration
1907	Second Hague Peace Conference
1914	World War I breaks out (ends in 1918)
1917	Russian Revolution
1919	Versailles Treaty
1920	League of Nations
1928	Kellogg–Briand Pact (Renunciation of War)
1939	World War II breaks out (ends in 1945)
1945	United Nations
1945	"Bretton Woods Institutions" (including International Monetary Fund (IMF) and World Bank)
1945	Circa 30-year period of massive decolonization begins

1947	General Agreement on Tariffs and Trade (GATT)
1948	Universal Declaration of Human Rights
1948	Genocide Convention (in force 1951)
1949	North Atlantic Treaty Organization (NATO)
1950	Korean War breaks out (ends 1953)
1951	Organization of American States (OAS)
1953	European Convention on Human Rights
1955	Warsaw Pact
1957	European Economic Community (EEC)
1958	(UN) New York Convention on Arbitral Awards
1960	Organization for Economic Cooperation and Development (OECD)
1963	Organization of African Unity (OAU)
1965	Convention against Racial Discrimination (in force 1969)
1966	Covenant on Civil and Political Rights (in force 1976)
1966	Covenant on Economic, Social and Cultural Rights (in force 1976)
1969	Vienna Convention on the Law of Treaties (in force 1980)
1979	Convention on the Elimination of All Forms of Discrimination Against Women (in force 1981)
1980	Vienna Convention on the International Sale of Goods (in force 1988)
1989	End of Cold War Period
1989	Convention on the Rights of the Child (in force 1990)
1990	Gulf War (with UN Security Council Approval)
1992	Treaty on European Union (Maastricht Treaty; in force 1993)
1993	International Criminal Tribunal for the former Yugoslavia

1994   International Criminal Tribunal for Rwanda

1994   GATT, GATS and TRIPS (in force 1995)

1995   World Trade Organization (WTO)

1998   Rome Statute of the International Criminal Court (in force 2002)

1999   International Convention for the Suppression of Financing of Terrorism (in force 2002)

2000   African Union (succeeds Organization of African Unity)

2000   UN Trafficking Protocol (in force 2003)

2000   UN Smuggling Protocol (in force 2004)

2001   Terrorist Attacks of September 11

2003   Iraq War

2004   UN Convention against Corruption (in force 2005)

2008   Global Financial Crisis

2011   Arab Spring (wave of democratization in the Middle East)

SUMMARY OF CONTENTS

———

PART 2. EVOLUTION: THE COMPLEXITIES OF THE MODERN ORDER

TABLE OF CONTENTS

TABLE OF CASES

The principal cases are in bold type.

INTRODUCTION

∎ ∎ ∎

1. DOES TRANSNATIONAL LAW MATTER? (AND TO WHOM?)

YOUR BAGS ARE LOST!

Recently, you took a trip to Taipei, Taiwan, on the following itinerary:

You selected these flights:

OUTBOUND	Sun 06 Jan 2013 12:40 PM (DTW) / 9:40 PM (TPE) **1 STOP**				Show Details
Sun 06 Jan 2013	**DEP**	**STOP**	**ARR**	**Flight Time**	**FLIGHT**
DELTA	DTW 06 Jan 12:40pm	NRT Change Planes	TPE 07 Jan 9:40pm	21h 55m	DL 275 Economy (M) View Seats
RETURN	Fri 11 Jan 2013 9:30am (TPE) /12:15pm (DTW) **1 STOP**				Show Details
Fri 11 Jan 2013	**DEP**	**STOP**	**ARR**	**Flight Time**	**FLIGHT**
DELTA	TPE 11 Jan 9:30 am	NRT Change Planes	DTW 12 Jan 12:15pm	16h 40m	DL 276 Economy (M) View Seats

Upon your arrival at home, your checked bags weren't there. Lost. You had some very expensive equipment in your suitcases the total value of which comes to approximately $7,000. The airline representative at the "Lost Baggage" counter tells you that the airline will do its best to locate your bags. He then points out that if the bags cannot be found, the airline will pay at best part of that amount because of international rules limiting its liability. Of course, you say: "What?"

After doing some research once you get home, you come across the following document. What does it tell you about the airline's potential liability to you?

1

CONVENTION FOR THE UNIFICATION OF CERTAIN RULES FOR INTERNATIONAL CARRIAGE BY AIR

(Adopted 1999; in force 2003)

Article 37—Right of recourse against third parties

Chapter IV—Combined Carriage

Article 38—Combined carriage

* * *

Article 1

Scope of application

1. This Convention applies to all international carriage of persons, baggage or cargo performed by aircraft for reward. It applies equally to gratuitous carriage by aircraft performed by an air transport undertaking.

2. For the purposes of this Convention, the expression "international carriage" means any carriage in which, according to the agreement between the parties, the place of departure and the place of destination, whether or not there be a break in the carriage or a transhipment, are situated either within the territories of two States Parties, or within the territory of a single State Party if there is an agreed stopping place within the territory of another State, even if that State is not a State Party. Carriage between two points within the territory of a single State Party without an agreed stopping place within the territory of another State is not international carriage for the purposes of this Convention.

3. Carriage to be performed by several successive carriers is deemed, for the purposes of this Convention, to be one undivided carriage if it has been regarded by the parties as a single operation, whether it had been agreed upon under the form of a single contract or of a series of contracts, and it does not lose its international character merely because one contract or a series of contracts is to be performed entirely within the territory of the same State.

4. This Convention applies also to carriage as set out in Chapter V, subject to the terms contained therein.

* * *

Article 17

Death and injury of passengers—damage to baggage

1. The carrier is liable for damage sustained in case of death or bodily injury of a passenger upon condition only that the accident which caused the death or injury took place on board the aircraft or in the course of any of the operations of embarking or disembarking.

2. The carrier is liable for damage sustained in case of destruction or loss of, or of damage to, checked baggage upon condition only that the event

which caused the destruction, loss or damage took place on board the aircraft or during any period within which the checked baggage was in the charge of the carrier. However, the carrier is not liable if and to the extent that the damage resulted from the inherent defect, quality or vice of the baggage. In the case of unchecked baggage, including personal items, the carrier is liable if the damage resulted from its fault or that of its servants or agents.

3. If the carrier admits the loss of the checked baggage, or if the checked baggage has not arrived at the expiration of twenty-one days after the date on which it ought to have arrived, the passenger is entitled to enforce against the carrier the rights which flow from the contract of carriage.

4. Unless otherwise specified, in this Convention the term "baggage" means both checked baggage and unchecked baggage.

*   *   *

Article 21

Compensation in case of death or injury of passengers

1. For damages arising under paragraph 1 of Article 17 not exceeding 100,000 Special Drawing Rights* for each passenger, the carrier shall not be able to exclude or limit its liability.

2. The carrier shall not be liable for damages arising under paragraph 1 of Article 17 to the extent that they exceed for each passenger 100,000 Special Drawing Rights if the carrier proves that:

   (a) such damage was not due to the negligence or other wrongful act or omission of the carrier or its servants or agents; or

   (b) such damage was solely due to the negligence or other wrongful act or omission of a third party.

Article 22

Limits of liability in relation to delay, baggage and cargo

1. In the case of damage caused by delay as specified in Article 19 in the carriage of persons, the liability of the carrier for each passenger is limited to 4,150 Special Drawing Rights.

2. In the carriage of baggage, the liability of the carrier in the case of destruction, loss, damage or delay is limited to 1,000 Special Drawing Rights for each passenger unless the passenger has made, at the time when the checked baggage was handed over to the carrier, a special declaration of interest in delivery at destination and has paid a sup-

---

* The currency value of "Special Drawing Rights" fluctuates. Currently, one "drawing right" equals about $1.50.

plementary sum if the case so requires. In that case the carrier will be liable to pay a sum not exceeding the declared sum, unless it proves that the sum is greater than the passenger's actual interest in delivery at destination.

*　*　*

Article 33
Jurisdiction

1. An action for damages must be brought, at the option of the plaintiff, in the territory of one of the States Parties, either before the court of the domicile of the carrier or of its principal place of business, or where it has a place of business through which the contract has been made or before the court at the place of destination.

2. In respect of damage resulting from the death or injury of a passenger, an action may be brought before one of the courts mentioned in paragraph 1 of this Article, or in the territory of a State Party in which at the time of the accident the passenger has his or her principal and permanent residence and to or from which the carrier operates services for the carriage of passengers by air, either on its own aircraft or on another carrier's aircraft pursuant to a commercial agreement, and in which that carrier conducts its business of carriage of passengers by air from premises leased or owned by the carrier itself or by another carrier with which it has a commercial agreement.

*　*　*

Does this document tell you whether you have a claim against the airline and, if so, for how much? Which provisions help you to answer those questions?

What is the nature and effect of this document?

The issue of air carrier liability under international agreements has been the subject of frequent litigation in U.S. courts, including two cases in which the Supreme Court has interpreted the Warsaw Convention (which preceded the Montreal Convention). See *Air France v. Saks*, 470 U.S. 392 (1985) and *Olympic Airways v. Husain*, 540 U.S. 644 (2004).

2.　THE MODERN PRACTICE OF TRANSNATIONAL LAW

The international practice of law has changed dramatically over the past fifty years. While international commerce has existed for centuries, it was not until the relatively recent wave of rapid "globalization" that even the private practitioner has faced international legal problems on a regular basis.

Today, it comes as no surprise that if you practice law in New York City, you can face a multitude of transboundary issues, ranging from international banking transactions to cross-border securities listings, and from international commercial arbitration in a forum outside the United States to project finance work in literally any place in the world. While this may be obvious in a large law firm in a big city, a sole practitioner in a small town environment can easily be confronted with international cases as well, be they a child custody dispute with a parent in a foreign country, estate issues involving foreign assets, or a product liability claim by a local resident against an appliance manufacturer in East Asia. As a result, every lawyer entering practice today must be equipped to at least triage such problems. In short, long gone are the days when an understanding of the international dimensions of legal practice was a luxury.

Private practitioners face international legal issues more frequently because international law today encompasses many more topics and penetrates so much more deeply into the domestic legal orders than in the past. As a result, many questions that even a generation ago would have been handled purely under domestic law are now largely subject to international regimes. More importantly, in many international disputes, there simply was no realistic access to law, whereas today the parties can turn to domestic or international tribunals with a fair chance of success. Let us look at five examples to illustrate this development. They are all drawn from the real world and will all be discussed at some length in the materials that follow.

An International Sales Transaction

The first case involves a routine business transaction: one company buys electronic parts from another. Both are incorporated in Delaware. The buyer has its principal place of business in California. While the seller also has California operations, its principal place of business is to the north in British Columbia. Both parties have boilerplate choice-of-law clauses in their general business terms, each providing for the application of the respective home state (or province) law.

A generation ago, this case would have had very little to do with international law. It would have been decided in California state court and under the California version of the Uniform Commercial Code or under the British Columbia Sales Act, depending on who won the battle of forms regarding the choice-of-law clause. In 2001, however, a federal judge in California decided in *Asante Technologies, Inc. v. PMC Sierra, Inc.,* 164 F. Supp. 2d 1142 (N.D. Cal. 2001) that the dispute was not subject to either of these statutes at all. Instead, it was governed by the Convention for the International Sale of Goods (CISG), a treaty drafted under the auspices of the United Nations and ratified by both the United States and Canada.

As a treaty, the CISG is "the supreme Law of the Land" according to Article VI sec. 2 of the U.S. Constitution. Thus it is (just like the Constitution or other federal law) superior to state law. In other words, the CISG trumps the UCC.

International law has come a long way—it can now displace domestic law in routine sales transactions. This raises interesting questions that can easily end up on the desk of even a local practitioner with no international specialization at all. What does it mean for the parties' positions that the contract is not governed by the UCC but rather by a UN Treaty? (It means, for example, that the case falls under the jurisdiction of the federal courts because they can hear all cases "arising under * * * treaties of the United States," 28 U.S.C. § 1331.) Does it make any difference regarding the respective remedies? Who interprets this treaty and where does one find guidance? And perhaps most importantly, can the application of the CISG be avoided if the client (or, for that matter, counsel) wishes to steer clear of such unfamiliar terrain? As it turns out, the parties could have opted out of the CISG but had failed to do so. Why? They probably had not, at the stage of contracting, been aware that it would apply to them—a mistake they would not have made had they studied these materials.

Protecting Foreign Investment

The second dispute never ended up in a court of law and yet provided a remedy almost impossible to imagine fifty years ago. A U.S. company had invested in the transportation of natural gas in Argentina in the context of the privatization program in the gas distribution sector begun there in 1989. Ten years later, however, Argentina was experiencing a significant economic decline. In order to stabilize the situation, the Argentine government enacted laws and regulations that seriously affected the American investor's (and its partner's) license rights and income.

In response to these actions, the investor claimed that the government had effectively expropriated its contract rights. In earlier times, the American company's primary grievance process would have been to negotiate with the Argentine authorities or to turn to its own government for help in the form of exerting political or economic pressure on Argentina. There would have been no recourse to judicial tribunals because the Argentine government enjoyed sovereign immunity both in its own courts and in tribunals abroad.

In the early 21st century, however, the U.S. corporation invoked the Bilateral Investment Treaty (BIT) which entered into force between Argentina and the United States in 1994. This treaty not only protects investors against expropriation and guarantees their "fair and equitable treatment" by the host state, it also provides for international arbitration before the International Center for Settlement of Investment Disputes, an institution operating under the auspices of the World Bank and created by the

ICSID Convention of 1966. It was to this institution that the American company now turned. In the resulting arbitration award, *CMS Gas Transmission Company v. Argentina*, the investor won $133 million plus interest.

Note that more than 2,500 BITs are now in force around the world providing for such arbitration. Also note that the resulting awards are binding and enforceable under yet another treaty, the UN Convention on the Recognition and Enforcement of Foreign Arbitral Awards. In other words, things have evolved from virtually no proper legal recourse to routine arbitration and enforceable awards in international investment disputes—providing, along the way, a lot of work for lawyers. We will also have to consider, however, that enforcing these arbitral awards is often challenging and indeed, at times, practically impossible.

A Child Custody Battle

The third case results from the break-up of a family. For professional reasons, a British husband and his American wife lived in Chile with their infant son. When the parents separated, the Chilean court granted the mother daily care and control of the child and gave the father regular visitation rights. The court also provided the father with a right to consent before the mother could take the child out of Chile (a "ne exeat" right). She nonetheless secretly took the child with her to Texas where the father eventually tracked them down. He sought relief in the Texas courts, but to no avail.

Until a few years earlier, there was little he could have done against this act of abduction. Now, however, the father could (and did) invoke the Hague Convention on the Civil Aspects of International Child Abduction, a treaty ratified by both Chile and the United States (in 1994 and 1998 respectively). Under the treaty, if a child is taken to another country in "breach of rights of custody," that country's authorities "shall order the return of the child forthwith." This raised a question of treaty interpretation: did the Chilean "ne exeat" provision in favor of the father amount to a "right to custody" under the Convention? Looking at the language and purpose of the treaty, as well as at other countries' interpretations of the clause, the United States Supreme Court found in favor of the father. As a result, his son had to be returned to Chile. (*Abbott v. Abbott*, 130 S. Ct. 1983 (2010)).

Corporations and Human Rights

In the fourth example, a U.S. corporation invests with a French company to build a pipeline in a foreign country, teaming up with the host government to complete the project. The foreign government employs its military to protect the workers on the pipeline in regions threatened by local protest and general instability. In the process, the military allegedly enslaves some villagers along the way to perform work on the project and responds to resistance with torture, rape and murder. The victims now seek compensation for their suffering at the hands of the soldiers, but their own country is unwilling to hold the military accountable.

Until about three decades ago, there was no recourse for these victims anywhere in the world. The only potential defendant would have been the victims' own government, and that government enjoyed sovereign immunity in foreign courts. Thus, there was simply no international case to bring. Today, however, there is, as we will see in *Doe v. Unocal Corp.*, 248 F.3d 915 (9th Cir. 2001). In that case, villagers in Myanmar sued a United States-based corporation in federal court in California for aiding and abetting the foreign military's human rights abuses. They did so under the Alien Tort Claims Act (ATCA), which provides that the federal courts shall have "original jurisdiction of any civil action by an alien for a tort only, committed in violation of the law of nations."

To be sure, the statute itself is more than two hundred years old (it dates from 1789), but it had lain dormant until it was rediscovered, so to speak, in 1980; it has since become a popular basis for suits by foreign plaintiffs brought in U.S. courts for human rights abuses in other parts of the world. Note, however, that the revival of the statute alone could not establish the plaintiffs' case. In order to sue the U.S. investor successfully, the plaintiffs had to show not only that they were aliens suing in tort (which was easy) but also that the defendant corporation had acted "in violation of the law of nations."

Doesn't the "law of nations" apply only to states? In other words, could a private business entity be held accountable under "international law"? To the shock of boardrooms across the United States, the Ninth Circuit Court of Appeals held that international law could indeed apply to private businesses. The Court decided that corporations are bound by certain parts of the law of nations such as the prohibition of forced labor (slavery), that they can thus violate it when they participate in certain human rights abuses, and that the defendant could therefore be liable in tort to the local villagers.

Obviously, the impact of international law raises important issues for modern corporations acting, or even merely investing, in foreign countries—issues that their in-house counsel or hired lawyer must confront: how can one protect the company against potentially catastrophic liability? How much due diligence must a passive investor perform? How far can investors be held accountable for the conduct of another corporation or even a government actor? What if you own shares in a foreign company listed on the New York Stock Exchange and read about atrocities in which that company is allegedly involved abroad: could you be at risk of a lawsuit?

International Law on Death Row

Transnational law can also have an impact on domestic criminal law and procedure. Ernesto José Medellín, a Mexican citizen, was convicted and sentenced to death by a Texas state court for the 1993 gang rape and murder of two teenage girls. Mexico found out that Medellín (as well as many other Mexican death row inmates in the United States) had not been informed of his right to contact his consulate (in order to seek assistance in his defense).

Mexico sued the United States in the International Court of Justice (ICJ) in The Hague for breach of the Vienna Convention on Consular Relations. This treaty (to which both the United States and Mexico are parties) provides that upon their arrest, foreign citizens must be informed of the right to contact their consulate. Mexico won the case, *Mexico v. United States* (2001 I.C.J. 1, known as the *Avena* case), and the ICJ ordered the United States to provide review and reconsideration of Medellín's conviction. The United States, however, refused to comply, arguing that whatever procedural remedy Medellín might have had was procedurally "defaulted" because he had failed to invoke it in a timely manner. Note that this procedural failure occurred because Medellín had not known about the right he had—precisely because he had not been informed as required by the Vienna Convention.

The case eventually ended up before the United States Supreme Court. The issue was whether under these circumstances, the ICJ judgment required that Medellín's case be reviewed and reconsidered in the domestic courts. That decision turned on whether the ICJ judgment had direct effect in the domestic legal system. *Medellín v. Texas*, 552 U.S. 491 (2008). While the Supreme Court denied direct effect to the ICJ's judgment, the federal government undertook a major campaign to make local law enforcement agencies aware of a foreign suspect's consular rights.

These five cases illustrate the theme that runs through the materials that follow: the landscape of international law has evolved dramatically since the end of World War II. International law is no longer primarily the domain of government officials, nor is it limited to state-to-state relations. Instead, it matters for tort victims, parents and children, buyers and sellers, corporate investors, death row inmates, and many others not mentioned here—all the time. For practitioners in the early 21st century, understanding the basic rules of this new international game will help avoid embarrassment or worse; it is also imperative in order to be able to serve clients' needs.

Analyzing a Transnational Law Case

To be sure, all this sounds confusing, and it would be misleading to claim that transnational law is simple, because it is not. Yet, this course will give you the tools you need to understand how to approach transnational problems. In fact, the course will analyze the very cases described above (and many others) and, by the end, you will probably find them quite manageable. In particular, this course will help you ask a series of questions that will make it possible to identify the crucial issues and ultimately to resolve them:

1. Is there a transnational component in the problem you are facing? This is, of course, the most important question to raise because if it is skipped—and the transnational dimensions of a case are simply overlooked—fatal mistakes are almost sure to ensue. Studying the materials for this course will make you aware of those dimensions and thus much less likely to miss them altogether. Once you have realized that there is a transnational law problem, you can at minimum seek help from specialists.

2. Which other legal orders (or actors) might be involved? We will survey the most pertinent orders and actors in this course so that you get a sense of who they are, what they do, and how they may affect your case.

3. Are there any transnational law rules that might apply? The course will show you what they may consist of: treaties, customary international law, general principles of international law, international administrative regulations, case law of international or foreign courts, "soft law" (hortatory rules), domestic rules pertaining to transnational events and transactions, etc.

4. What exactly is the force of these rules? In particular, how do they interact with the more familiar domestic law? Can both be reconciled? In case of conflict, which rule wins? We will look at the interplay between the international and domestic levels so that you learn how to sort these things out.

5. How are the rules you find pertinent applied? Is there anything special about the construction of transnational law rules as compared to purely domestic ones? Who has final authority in this regard? International tribunals? Domestic courts? The involved parties themselves? We will study some examples illustrating transnational law in action so that you can get at least a rough feel for the process and its pitfalls.

6. Can the international rules and decisions actually be enforced? If so, how? Through global mechanisms? Through (domestic) courts? With the help of the non-judicial branches of government, e.g., through diplomacy? By applying political, economic or other forms of pressure? We will see that enforcement is often one of the thorniest issues in the transnational context.

3. THE EVOLUTION OF THE INTERNATIONAL LEGAL ORDER: AN OVERVIEW

MATHIAS REIMANN, FROM THE LAW OF NATIONS
TO TRANSNATIONAL LAW:
WHY WE NEED A NEW BASIC COURSE FOR THE
INTERNATIONAL CURRICULUM
22 Penn State Int'l L.J. 397 (2004)

* * *

I.   THE CLASSIC MODEL: THE LAW OF NATIONS

Fifty years ago, interest in international affairs was high after the cataclysm of World War II, the Nuremberg and Tokyo trials, and the foundation of the United Nations. When money from the Ford Foundation began lavishly to fund international legal studies programs, American law schools set out to develop a more substantial international law curriculum.

At that time, international law was conceived of, and taught in, what I call the classic mode. For present purposes, three features of this approach are particularly important. It dealt only with a limited subset of international legal issues. It presented a fairly simple legal order. And it portrayed a field with well-defined boundaries. Let us look at these three features in turn.

The classic approach covered only part of the law beyond national boundaries because it defined the topic in fairly narrow terms. It conceived of international law in a literal, Benthamite, sense: as inter-national law, i.e., the law existing *inter nationes* as sovereigns. Thus, it was primarily concerned with the basic features of the "Westphalian order" as modified over time. Originally, it focused only on the world of sovereign and formally co-equal nation states who make, follow or violate international law, and who sometimes arbitrate or litigate in international tribunals. Around the middle of the 20th century, two additional elements became important: permanent international organizations and international human rights. Despite this addition, however, the coverage of the classic model remained strictly limited to *public international law*. Consequently, it excluded private international law, not only in the narrow sense of conflict of laws but also in the broader sense of all rules pertaining to transboundary transactions and disputes between private parties, be they individuals or business organizations. In other words, international law under the classic model was, at its core, *The Law of Nations* as actors on the world stage.

Second, classic international law presented a relatively uncomplicated and internally consistent picture of the international legal order. By restricting itself to the public law elements, it focused on a limited range of actors, sources, principles, and dispute resolution mechanisms. In terms of actors, it dealt primarily with states and eventually with the United Nations as their principal organization; individuals played a marginal role at best and other actors, such as non-governmental entities, received virtually no attention. The sources considered were those listed in article 38 (1) of the Statute of the International Court of Justice (treaties, customary international law, general principles, judicial decisions, and the opinions of leading scholars) and perhaps soft-law in the form of UN resolutions or the like. As far as the basic principles are concerned, classic public international law typically addressed state sovereignty and its consequences, international comity, and the major bases for international jurisdiction as well as the immunity of states and their representatives. Its coverage of dispute resolution mechanisms centered around the procedure before the International Court of Justice though it often included arbitration of state v. state disputes. While all this amounted to a rather full plate, the whole menu was decisively and intentionally state-centered.

Finally, the classic view saw public international law as a subject with well-defined boundaries. This is particularly true in two regards. First, the approach assumed that there is a clear distinction between public and private international law. As mentioned, it concerned itself only with the former and did not address private transactions and disputes across international boundaries. Second, it presumed a fundamental difference between international and domestic law. Hence it addressed the basic relationship between the two spheres (monism and dualism) and discussed whether and how international law becomes effective within certain domestic legal systems.

At the time, a pretty good case could be made that a public international law course with such contents and characteristics should serve as the basis for the international curriculum.

The most important argument for that proposition is that fifty years ago, the law of nations was probably the single most relevant topic in international legal studies. Most related subjects either had not yet fully developed, as was the case with human rights and international trade, or had yet to come into existence at all, such as European Community law. To be sure, private international law had existed for centuries. Yet, even this area was arguably of lesser importance. Transboundary transactions and disputes among private parties were still relatively rare and most practitioners never faced them. Thus there was no urgent need to train the majority of future attorneys and judges in this regard. It was therefore not unreasonable that international law teaching was aimed at those future lawyers who would have a need for it: lawyers working for governments or international organizations whose primary concern was, of course, not private but public international law.

In addition, public international law was a fairly suitable basis for the international curriculum because it was still a rather limited field that could be covered in reasonable depth in a two- or three-credit-hour course. It also presented a relatively self-contained system that could thus be understood with limited reference to other areas, especially private international and domestic law.

All this has changed in the last fifty years.

II. THE WINDS OF CHANGE: THE EXPANSION AND DIVERSIFICATION OF INTERNATIONAL LAW

It is no longer news that in the last half-century, the global legal order has undergone enormous changes. In the present context, three developments are particularly noteworthy. Numerous fields lying beyond the traditional law of nations have developed, matured, and become important in practice. The world legal order has become more diversified and complex. And the boundaries between public international law and other areas have blurred or broken down. Here, we will simply describe these developments and leave for later to what extent current international law teaching takes them into account.

1. THE RISE OF OTHER AREAS

Of the many areas that have risen to prominence in the last couple of decades, some belong in the realm of public international law, some lie completely outside of it, and some straddle its borders.

Of course, public international law itself has long comprised a number of particular topics, such as the law of the sea, humanitarian law, and the rules pertaining to foreign diplomatic and consular representatives. In the second half of the twentieth century, several additional new specialties have developed. The most prominent examples are, as already mentioned, the law of international organizations and of human rights. More recently, international criminal, environmental, refugee, and trade law have become standard sub-topics of public international law. To be sure, many of these new areas have matured to the point where a thorough understanding requires studying them in their own right, not simply as an appendix to the general law of nations. Yet, they do cluster closely around the classic core.

This cannot be said for private international law which has gained enormous importance in the last few decades. Fifty years ago, transboundary transactions and disputes between private parties were probably exceptional enough to treat them as discreet specialties and to leave them in the hands of a few experts. The phenomenon commonly labeled "globalization" has changed that dramatically. The combined effects of the internationalization of markets, the increased mobility of persons and capital, and the age of electronic communication have turned the private side of international law from a backwater into a vast and highly prominent field of enormous practical importance. At the same time, this field has diversified as well. It is now often divided into international business transactions, corporate law, commercial arbitration, litigation, and other subjects. All these topics lie well beyond the territory of public international law.

There is now a panoply of areas which are impossible to assign to either the public or private international law realm because they contain ingredients of, and begin to transcend, both. Probably the most salient example is European Union law where elements of public international law (international organizations, treaty, supremacy issues, etc.) are inextricably intertwined with the regulation of markets and private relationships as well as administrative and procedural matters. Here, the blending of public and private international law has in fact created a new order which is by now *sui generis*, especially since it has engendered truly supranational law, i.e., law made and enforced by a body above sovereign nation states and binding upon them. Other mixed areas range from the regulation of cyberspace to international investment and intellectual property regimes. At least in terms of their practical relevance, these hybrids no longer linger at the margin of the international law universe but present core transboundary issues.

2. THE GROWING COMPLEXITY OF THE GLOBAL LEGAL ORDER

The rise of these new areas has not only broadened the range of international legal issues, it has also changed the character of the world legal order. In particular, it has rendered this order much more complex than it was even a generation ago. This is most visible in the emergence of new actors, sources, principles, and tribunals.

Legal actors in international law have become more numerous and diverse than ever. This is already true for the two categories considered by classic public international law, i.e., states and international organizations. States have become a much larger and more heterogeneous group as a result of de-colonization and the break-up of former federations such as the Soviet Union and Yugoslavia. Today, third world countries leave the Western industrial states in the minority and present a challenge to the traditional international law regime originally created by the European powers. Intergovernmental organizations have multiplied as well. Fifty years ago, the United Nations and the Bretton Woods institutions were almost the only major actors of that kind on the world stage. Today we have to include at least the North Atlantic Treaty Organization (NATO), the Organization for Economic Cooperation and Development (OECD), and the World Trade Organization (WTO), as well as regional clubs such as the African Union, the Arab League, the European Union (EU), the

Council of Europe, the Organization of American States (OAS) and the Association of South East Asian Nations (ASEAN).

What is even more significant in the present context is the multiplication and rise of non-state actors. Non-Governmental Organizations (NGOs) especially now play a significant role in the international legal process, particularly in lobbying and pressuring governments and in influencing international lawmaking. Individuals have become important players as well. Virtually irrelevant in the classic law of nations, they have advanced from mere objects of protection under humanitarian and human rights law to actors with their own rights (e.g., to petition international human rights bodies) and responsibilities (e.g., for crimes under international law). The latest additions are business corporations. While their status continues to be much disputed, they, too, enjoy rights (e.g., investment protection) and are charged with responsibilities (e.g., for environmental damage or human rights abuses) as actors on the international scene.

The sources that shape international legal issues have multiplied and diversified as well. Again, this is already true for the traditional categories under classic public international law. In particular the number of treaties, both bilateral and multilateral, has grown exponentially. They cover an ever wider spectrum of subjects, ranging from arms control to international sales, from human rights to service of process, and from the protection of biodiversity to foreign investment. In the meantime, customary international law has also continued to develop. And the number of judicial decisions rendered by international tribunals has skyrocketed as has the number of publications on international legal issues.

Yet, there are also many sources that lie outside the traditional public international law catalog. There is now a dense network of regulatory law on the international level, issued by international organizations and agencies such as the IMF and the World Bank, as well as by the European Union. Moreover, as countries have become more internationally involved, they have produced more and more (domestic) law dealing with transboundary issues, addressing matters as far-ranging as export and import control, asylum and refugee status, and the domestic effects of foreign commercial activity. In this process, especially the sources of private international law have become enormously important. We now have a multitude of treaties drafted under the auspices of the Hague Conference of Private International Law, UNCITRAL, and the European Communities addressing substantive private law, choice of law, and private international litigation. Finally, there are the practices and principles governing international business transactions which, as a revived *lex mercatoria*, greatly influence international arbitral proceedings.

The changing nature of international law is also evident in the expansion of jurisdictional claims made by states and their institutions. In addition to the classic paradigms of territoriality and personality, particularly the effects principle has become firmly established and begun to play an enormous role. Today, the main jurisdictional battleground is no longer just the relationship between states as such, i.e., classic public international law territory. Instead, jurisdictional principles are most often invoked (and contested) to justify (or attack) the regulation of transboundary business activities, the exercise of personal jurisdiction in private litigation, and the enforcement of criminal law beyond national borders.

Finally, we have witnessed a tremendous proliferation of international tribunals and dispute resolution mechanisms. Half a century ago, nearly all the emphasis was on the International Court of Justice in The Hague (Netherlands). Today, this court is just one among a host of others. Again, many of the new institutions can be said to belong to the realm of public international law proper. This is true not only for the various human rights tribunals, i.e. the United Nations Commission of Human Rights and the European, Inter-American, and (incipient) African Courts of Human Rights. It is also the case for the International Criminal Court and the UN Tribunals on Rwanda and the former Yugoslavia as well as for the International Tribunal of the Law of the Sea.

Yet, as with the new actors and sources, there are also numerous institutions that lie outside the purview of classic public international law. The most salient examples are the European Court of Justice and the dispute resolution body of the WTO. In addition, there is a thriving regime of international arbitration, both for disputes between investors and states and among private businesses themselves, not to mention ad hoc institutions like the Iran Claims Tribunal. Finally, we must not forget the enormous practical and theoretical importance of the many international cases adjudicated in domestic tribunals around the world, the United States courts prominent among them.

3. THE BLURRING OF BOUNDARIES

In this expanding and increasingly complex world of international law, the lines dividing the various areas have blurred more and more. This has occurred in two major regards.

The boundary between public and private international law has become more uncertain and less meaningful. Fifty years ago, it may have seemed clear that public international law deals with the law applicable among states and intergovernmental organizations, while private international law concerns itself with transboundary relationships between private parties, i.e., individuals and businesses. In theory, this remains today but in practice, the distinction is increasingly pointless. As mentioned before, there are many subject matter areas which escape the traditional classification altogether because they combine public and private international law elements, such as European Union law or the regulation of electronic commerce. Perhaps even more important, we now live in a world in which hybrid issues arise in myriad specific contexts, all the time: a business sues a foreign governmental entity which promptly invokes sovereign immunity but loses because the action is based on a commercial activity; a firm invests private capital in another country, suffers from adverse government regulation, and resorts to ICSID arbitration; a citizen brings a claim for employment discrimination and wins in the European Court of Justice because the rejection of her job application violates European Community law; a defendant sued by a foreign plaintiff moves for dismissal on forum non conveniens grounds but the court denies the motion inter alia because of bilateral treaty obligations. The list of examples is nearly endless.

The boundary between international and domestic law has become less clear and rigid as well. The traditional assumption was that international law exists between (public) international actors, i.e., states and intergovernmental organizations, while domestic law applies (only) within a particular jurisdiction. Of course, things were never quite so simple in the real world. Today, however, the two areas intermingle in so many ways that the traditional division is often outright misleading. Which sphere defines the limits on the exercise of jurisdiction over a foreign corporation in a suit based on acts committed abroad? Are bribes offered to foreign officials forbidden by international or domestic law? How do we answer the question whether the conviction of a foreign national for a serious crime committed in the United States must be reversed because the defendant was not informed of his right to contact his consulate for assistance? Does the recognition of an English judgment turn on the municipal rules of the forum or on international law? Again, these are just examples to which others could be added.

In fact, many cases today straddle both the public-private and the international-domestic boundaries at the same time. If Peruvian citizens sue an American corporation in a US federal court for environmental damage inflicted in their home country, the case involves a (tort) cause of action under private domestic law but it can be brought only if plaintiffs show the violation of public international law required by the Alien Tort Claims Act. Similarly, if a Chinese buyer sues an American seller for breach of contract, we have a private action based on an international treaty which has the rank and effect of federal law. And if an American plaintiff brings a product liability action against a French corporation in Federal District Court, we have private litigation in domestic courts in which the plaintiff's right to obtain documents under the defendant's control depends on the interpretation of an international convention.

To be sure, none of this means that a grasp of the basic distinction between public and private international law and between the international and the domestic legal order is not helpful. In fact, such a grasp may very well be crucial, e.g., in order to gauge the force of particular rules and to understand who has the power to change them. But we must recognize that in practice, these spheres cannot be neatly separated and that many issues cannot be resolved unless we consider how pieces taken from all of them fit together and interact.

* * *

4. WHAT IS TRANSNATIONAL LAW?

What does the term "Transnational Law" really mean? The term was coined by the late Philip Jessup (1897–1986), a professor of international law and diplomacy at Columbia University and later (1961–1970) a judge at the International Court of Justice, in his Storrs Lectures given at Yale in 1956. Here is how he put it:

> I shall use, instead of "international law," the term "transnational law" to include all law which regulates actions or events that transcend national frontiers. Both public and private international law are included, as are other rules which do not wholly fit into such standard categories.

* * *

> Transnational situations, then, may involve individuals, corporations, states, organizations of states, or other groups. A private American citizen, or a stateless person for that matter, whose passport or other travel document is challenged at a European frontier confronts a transnational situation. So does an American oil company doing business in Venezuela; or the New York lawyer who retains French counsel to advise on his client's estate in France; or the United States government when negotiating with the Soviet Union regarding the unification of Germany. So does the United Nations when shipping milk for UNICEF or sending a mediator to Palestine. Equally one could mention the International Chamber of Commerce exercising its privilege of taking part in a conference called by the Economic and Social Council of the United Nations. One is sufficiently aware of the transnational activities of individuals, corporations, and states. When one considers that there are also in existence more than 140 intergovernmental organizations and over 1,100 nongovernmental organizations commonly described as international, one realizes the almost infinite variety of the transnational situation which may arise.

* * *

> Transnational law then includes both civil and criminal aspects, it includes what we know as public and private international law, and

it includes national law, both public and private. There is no inherent reason why a judicial tribunal, whether national or international, should not be authorized to choose from all these bodies of law the rules considered most in conformity with reason and justice for the solution of any particular controversy.

Philip Jessup, TRANSNATIONAL LAW (1956), pp. 2–4, 106.

Jessup thus uses the term in a kitchen-sink fashion: for him, it denotes all law that transcends national boundaries.

For several decades following Jessup's lecture, the term "Transnational Law" was rarely employed. It was simply not considered very useful to have a residual category for all law that is not purely domestic. After all, there were much more precise categories, such as Public International Law, Private International Law, Comparative Law, etc. In the last twenty years, however, this has largely changed. The traditional categories were increasingly regarded as problematic since they suggested boundaries (e.g., between public and private, international and domestic law) that often strained theory and failed to reflect the global realities. As a result, scholars searched for a term that was broad enough to transcend these traditional categories, and "Transnational Law" fit the bill. Today, the term thus enjoys wide currency and even a certain fashionability. Still, it continues to lack a precise meaning, and different people employ it in different ways.

This book uses the term "Transnational Law" in Jessup's original sense, i.e., as an umbrella concept for all law pertaining to issues that transcend national boundaries. Its main attraction, however, is not that it is so broad but that it deemphasizes the traditional categories and divisions.

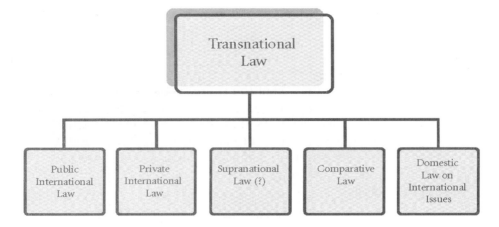

It is still helpful to understand—at least in broad outline—what these more traditional categories mean and thus what "Transnational Law" encompasses. The two core concepts here are Public and Private International Law; Supranational Law is a more recent and less clearly understood term; Domestic Law governing international issues is a subcategory of enormous practical importance; and Comparative Law operates on an entirely different level.

Public International Law is a term originating in the 19th century and is essentially identical with the older term "Law of Nations." It is "international" because in its classical form it is the law applicable (only) between nations ("*inter nationes*"). It thus deals with questions such as statehood and state succession, state rights and responsibilities, treaty making and customary international law, war and peace, diplomatic and consular relations, the law of the sea, international dispute resolution, and many other aspects of international relations.

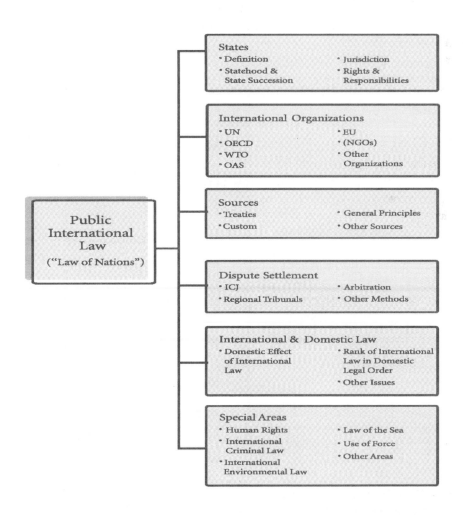

Private International Law addresses international issues arising between private actors, such as individuals and corporations, and is roughly coterminous with "Conflict of Laws." It deals mainly with three questions: Which state (in the international sense) has jurisdiction to hear and decide a dispute between private actors (international civil jurisdiction)? Whose law applies in an international private dispute (choice of law)? Will one state recognize and enforce a judgment rendered in another state (judgments recognition)? (In federal systems with different private law regimes, such as the United States or Canada, these issues also arise on the domestic level, i.e., between the states or provinces. This domestic dimension of Conflict of Laws is taught as a separate course and is not part of this book.) In addition, private international law deals with procedural matters, such as service of process abroad, taking of evidence located in a foreign country, and other issues of international judicial assistance. Beyond this classical description lies the law of international business transactions which, in a sense, is also part of Private International Law.

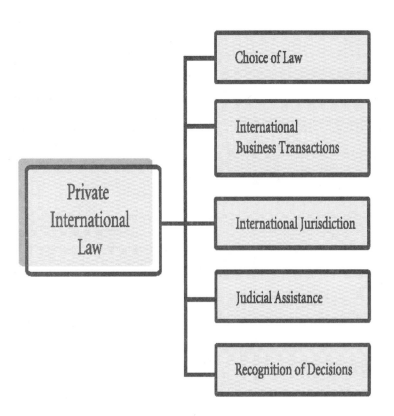

While the terms Public and Private International Law have been commonly used and generally understood for almost two hundred years, the term **Supranational Law** is of more recent origin. Its meaning is less precise and it is sometimes used in various ways. Strictly speaking, it denotes law that is *superior to*, i.e., takes precedence over, national law. Thus understood, there is rather little of it in the world today because there are few institutions which stand truly *above* states in the sense that they themselves can make and enforce law that binds otherwise sovereign nations. A clear case in point is the law of the European Union. And, arguably, decisions made by certain international organizations and bodies, such as the UN Security Council or the World Trade Organization, have supranational character. In any event, it is important not to use the term carelessly and to distinguish it from (Public) International Law, i.e., from the rules applying *between* nations. Thus, the rules contained in a treaty are usually international, not supranational.

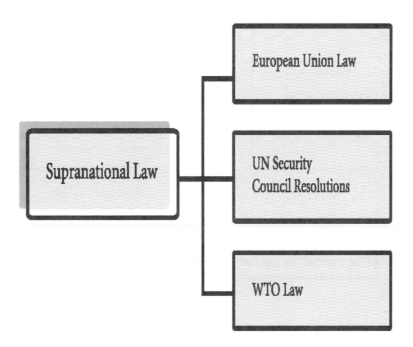

A huge part of transnational activities are governed by **Domestic Law**, i.e., by national rules applicable to international activities or events. This national law sometimes implements international legal obligations (mainly arising from treaties). It covers a wide spectrum of issues: export and import controls; measures against foreign corrupt business practices; rules on citizenship, immigration and asylum; the criminalization of acts beyond national boundaries; taxation of foreign income; treatment of foreign investment; etc.

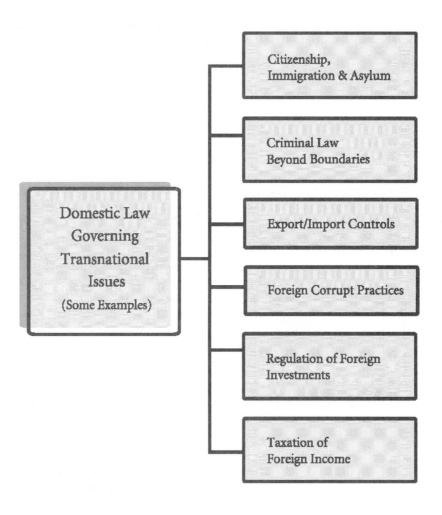

Comparative Law is an entirely different matter. It is not a body of law at all but rather denotes the comparative study of laws (better captured by the French term *droit comparé* or the German expression *Rechtsvergleichung*). On the macro-level it deals with the major legal families in the world (civil law, common law, mixed systems, etc.) and the comparison between them or between national legal systems. On the micro-level, it compares institutions and processes (e.g., courts and their procedures) or individual concepts and rules (e.g., of contract or family law). Much of what parades as Comparative Law is merely the study of foreign law. A comparative understanding of law is often necessary in international business transactions or dispute resolution. It is also indispensable because Comparative Law can provide ideas for domestic law reform, bring to light how legal systems develop and interact, or simply help to understand one's own system and rules better by looking at them in a comparative light.

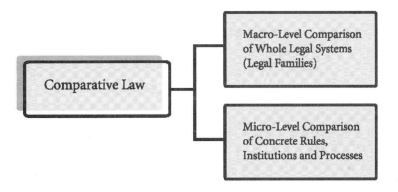

This book focuses mainly on Public and Private International Law as well as on domestic law governing transnational issues, showing how these areas tend to mix and blend today. It discusses the question of Supranational Law in connection with the modern changes in state sovereignty (ch. VII). It does not contain a specific chapter on Comparative Law. Instead, comparative perspectives pervade much of the material, e.g., when we compare various forms of international organizations, consider different styles of contract drafting, or look at alternative attitudes towards the domestic effect of international law.

PART 1

FOUNDATIONS: THE LAW OF NATIONS

■ ■ ■

To lay the foundations for our understanding of the current world legal order, this first part of the course provides an introduction to the classical view of (public) international law: *inter-national* law in the sense of the law between nations. While international law in the 21st century comprises concerns that go well beyond the regulation of interstate disputes, classically conceived public international law still provides the foundation on which the more complex (modern) international legal order has been built. Part One of the book thus seeks to convey an understanding of the (classic, largely interstate) view of international law. Part Two will then introduce the additions to, and variations from, this order.

The classic law of nations presents a relatively straightforward picture with regard to its actors, its concept of (state) interaction (and sovereignty), its sources of law, its dispute resolution mechanisms, and the relationship between international and domestic law. In terms of *actors*, it fully recognized only sovereign states. The *interaction* between states was based on a strong conception of sovereignty that entailed certain rights and privileges, certain duties and responsibilities, and the idea that states should exercise comity (i.e., deference and mutual respect) vis-à-vis each other. International *law* emerged largely from two sources: customs and (mainly bilateral) treaties. *Dispute resolution* beyond diplomacy or war, i.e. through legal proceedings, lacked permanent institutions and had to be organized *ad hoc*, mainly through arbitration. *International and domestic law* were considered fundamentally different matters although opinions differed as to whether they belonged to different spheres (dualism) or were parts of one all-encompassing legal order (monism).

This classic view is a creation of the Western European legal and political culture between the 17th and the early 20th centuries, arising from diplomatic and political practice as well as scholarly writings. It owes much to 17th and 18th century natural law and 19th century positivism and nationalism. Thus it embodies a specific kind of legalism as well as a value system reflecting the heritage of the Western (Greco–Roman, Christian, and Enlightenment) tradition. Like many other features of Western European culture, it was exported to, or forced upon, most other parts and peoples of the globe in the age of European imperialism, mostly regardless of the respective indigenous cultures. For better or worse, it therefore became the foundation of the modern global legal order into the 20th century and beyond.

CHAPTER 1

ACTORS: NATION STATES

■ ■ ■

1. THE WESTPHALIAN ORIGINS

The traditional regime of (public) international law is often called "the Westphalian System" (or "Westphalian Order"). Westphalia is a region in Northern Germany. It gave the traditional international regime its name because it was the location of the Peace Treaty that ended the Thirty Years' War in 1648. The Treaty actually consists of several documents; it is usually called "The Treaty of Münster and Osnabrück" after the two towns in the region where the respective documents were negotiated and signed. It established what came to be known as "The Peace of Westphalia." Over time, the "Westphalian System" became synonymous with the order of nation states from the early modern period to the beginning of the 20th century.

This subchapter contains materials explaining why this Treaty is considered such a signal event and what the main features of the "Westphalian System" are. In order to understand these materials, one has to understand the historical background of the "Westphalian Peace" at least in rough outline.

The medieval European order, emerging first from the ruins of the Western Roman Empire (which disintegrated in the 4th and 5th centuries A.D.) and then from the break-up of the Carolingian Empire (9th century) was characterized by three main features. First, there was the coexistence of spiritual and temporal authority, embodied mainly in the Pope and the Emperor who were engaged in a centuries-long (and ultimately inconclusive) struggle for political supremacy. Second, it was marked by the feudal, i.e., top-down, organization of political power in which authority was delegated from the supreme ruler to the high nobility, then on to the lower nobility, and finally to local office holders, creating "feudal pyramids." Third, the nature of political power was largely personal rather than territorial; as a result, power was defined more by how much loyalty one could command from others than by how much land one controlled.

All this led to an intricate interlacing of alliances and allegiances among the various political actors on all levels: some held power by grant from the emperor but owed allegiance also to a bishop; some owed their land to a king but their ecclesiastical office to the Pope; some acknowledged the emperor as their overlord but claimed independence from the local nobili-ty. As a result, political power was widely dispersed, often overlapping, and constantly contested. The result was a messy world characterized by frequent conflict among the various political actors.

Much like certain conflict regions in the world today, medieval Europe was plagued by political instability, war and internal strife. And much like the United Nations today, no authority—not even the Pope or the Emperor—was strong enough to guarantee lasting international order and peace. As a result, life was often, as Thomas Hobbes famously phrased it in *Leviathan* (1651) half a millennium later, "solitary, poor, nasty, brutish, and short."

During the 13th through 16th centuries, this system became further weakened by several events. On the temporal side, the (Holy Roman) Empire experienced the *Great Interregnum* (1254–73), a civil war period without a universally recognized ruler. It seriously weakened the position of the Emperor. When the dust had settled, he had to yield important powers to the regional princes who thus advanced from inferiors to rivals of the Emperor. In a similar fashion, the church was shaken by the *Great Schism* (1378–1417) during which two rival popes were elected. It suf-fered a second blow during the Reformation (1517 onwards). Together, these developments destroyed most of the papacy's political power on the international level. In addition, the Renaissance, the discovery of the New World, and the invention of the printing press radically reshaped the world in multiple ways.

In the early 17th century, the Thirty Years' War, fueled by both religious and secular ambitions and divisions, finally led to the self-destruction of the old order. After laying waste to much of Central Europe and killing up to half of the population in some areas through war, disease, and famine, it ended in complete exhaustion and, as mentioned, in the Peace of West-phalia of 1648. The 17th century also brought civil war, revolution, and finally a new political settlement to England.

The turbulence of the century was reflected in several seminal works of political thought and jurisprudence. Among them, two books are particu-larly important in our present context: Thomas Hobbes' *Leviathan* (1651) and Hugo Grotius' *De iure belli ac pacis* (On the Law of War and Peace, 1625).

MARK W. JANIS, SOVEREIGNTY AND INTERNATIONAL LAW: HOBBES AND GROTIUS

In ESSAYS IN HONOR OF WANG TIEYA (R. St. J. MacDonald ed. 1993)

* * *

I. HOBBES AND THE SOVEREIGN STATES

In 1651, just three years after the close of the Thirty Years War, Thomas Hobbes published what would become a masterpiece of political philosophy, *Leviathan*. At the time, Hobbes, a 63-year old Englishman, was not himself in a position of power or influence. He was, in fact, in exile in France, a refugee from Cromwell and the English Civil War. The Oxford-educated classicist-turned-philosopher had at one time been tutor to the Earl of Devonshire and then to the young prince who later became Charles II.

Leviathan's eventual philosophic success owed a great deal to a transformation of European politics. In 1648, the Peace of Westphalia ushered in a new period of international relations for which new legal and moral principles were needed. These principles *Leviathan*, a celebration of the sovereign State, supplied.

The Peace of Westphalia legitimated the right of sovereigns to govern their peoples free of outside interference, whether any such external claim to interfere was based on political, legal or religious principles. The two 1648 peace treaties elaborated in great detail which sovereign ruled what. The Peace was a great property settlement for Europe, a quieting of title across the continent. It stilled many of the competitions for land and loyalty that had devastated much of what, otherwise, would have been the prizes of war.

What 1648 most significantly inaugurated (and what Thomas Hobbes most significantly conceptionalised) was the organising principle of the State, particularly the sovereign State. Sovereignty, as a concept, formed the cornerstone of the edifice of international relations that 1648 raised up. Sovereignty was the crucial element in the peace treaties of Westphalia, the international agreements that were intended to end a great war and to promote a coming peace. The treaties of Westphalia enthroned and sanctified sovereigns, gave them powers domestically and independence externally. But what exactly did "sovereignty" mean? How did being a "sovereign" work? Because Hobbes in 1651 provided answers to these questions raised so critically in 1648, *Leviathan* took on the lasting importance it did.

Hobbes crafted and fit a crucial puzzle piece into an emerging picture of the new Europe. Hobbes' lasting contribution was the envisioning, in his own words, of "that great Leviathan, or rather (to speak more reverently) of that *Mortall God,* to which we owe under the *Immortall God,* our peace and defence." Rather than believing in any number of loyalties, Hobbes believed that all men required "a Common Power, to keep them in awe, and to direct their actions to the Common Benefit." This Common Power, the Leviathan, required a single authoritarian State:

> The only way to erect such a Common Power, as may be able to defend them from the invasion of Forraigners, and the injuries of one another, and thereby to secure them in such sort, as that by their owne industrie, and by the fruites of the Earth, they may nourish themselves and live contentedly; is, to conferre all their power and strength upon one Man, or upon one Assembly of men, that may reduce all their Wills, by plurality of voices, unto one Will: which is as much to say, to appoint one Man, or Assembly of men; to beare their Person; and every one to owne, and acknowledge himselfe to be Author of whatsoever he that so beareth their Person, shall Act, or cause to be Acted, in those things which concerne the Common Peace and Safetie; and therein to submit their Wills, everyone to his Will, and their Judgments, to his Judgment.

This "Multitude so united in one Person, is called a Commonwealth in latine Civitas * * * that great Leviathan." The Person, be it one man or an assembly, [is the one in] whom is united the Multitude; Commonwealth, Civitas or Leviathan "is called Soveraigne, and said to have *Soveraigne Power*, and everyone besides, his Subject."

Hobbes' celebration of the Leviathan, the sovereign State, provided a crucial bit of the ideological and diplomatic machinery necessary to operate the structure of world politics crafted at Westphalia. Given the long traditions of loyalty to Church as well as to King, to guild as well as to city, to baron as well as to empire, there needed to be some sort of solvent to dissolve these old ties, some sort of glue to fasten a new and simpler allegiance. Hobbes offered both solvent and glue, proffering the notion that the key actor on the world's stage was the sovereign State to which all loyalty was due internally and which was unrestrained externally.

So successful was the political settlement of Westphalia, so useful was Hobbes' concept of Leviathan and the sovereign State, that they became deeply imbedded in the public consciousness. It is difficult now even to conceive that a world of sovereign States is an intellectual abstraction, a humanly-devised creation, albeit one of tremendous force and utility over more than three centuries.

II. GROTIUS AND THE LAW OF WAR AND PEACE

As Hobbes was the man with a plausible vision of a sovereign State at the right place at the right time, so Hugo Grotius was timely on the same scene with a workable theory of a law and order for inter-state relations. Twenty-six years before *Leviathan*, Grotius' *De Jure Belli Ac Pacis* was published in 1625 in the midst of terrible slaughter. That the excesses of the Thirty Years War motivated Grotius is plain from the book's Prologue:

> I have had many and weighty reasons for undertaking to write upon this subject. Throughout the Christian world I observed a lack of restraint in relation to war, such as even barbarous races should be ashamed of; I observed that men rush to arms for slight causes, or no cause at all, and that when arms have once been taken up there is no longer any respect for law, divine or human; it is as if, in accordance with a general decree, frenzy had openly been let loose for the committing of all crimes.

* * * Grotius had not been by any means the first to write or to speculate about what would become modern international law. The antecedents of the discipline—treaties, diplomacy, arbitration, laws of war—go back thousands of years. Grotius himself was in intellectual debt to a number of sixteenth century Spanish theologians—Vitoria, Suarez and others—who sought to apply the Catholic Church's mediaeval theories of natural law to the new realities of international politics as they urged that the Spanish Crown deal justly with the natives Spain had found and conquered in the Americas.

Some have argued that in light of the Spanish tradition, Grotius' truly distinctive contribution was that he "secularised" international law. Indeed, it may be true that Grotius, unlike the Spaniards, presumed to write outside a single Christian denomination, seeking to fashion a law of nations that could appeal to and bind Catholics and various denominational Protestants alike. However, it is doubtful, given his times and character, that Grotius meant to effect a strictly secular refashioning of the mediaeval Catholic natural law tradition. His approach was very different from a truly secular author like Machiavelli who felt that princes ought to be fundamentally irreligious and faithfully unscrupulous. Machiavelli believed that Christianity was a less desirable religion for princes than the pagan faiths of ancient times because Christianity placed "the supreme happiness in humility, lowliness, and a contempt for worldly objects." * * *

Grotius' ideas were quite different. His basic notion was that there was an authentic law of nations which was based on the "mutual consent" of sovereigns acting in the context of a "great society of States." Though meant to be religiously neutral, Grotius' vision of the law of nations was not secular but was rather a liberal Christian pronouncement. * * *

Grotius used religious citations freely in his text. Acknowledging that "I frequently appeal to the authority of the books which men inspired by God have either written or approved," Grotius went on to say that one must distinguish the laws of the Old and New Testaments from the laws of nature. "The New Testament I use in order to explain—and this cannot be learned from any other source—what is permissible to Christians."

Grotius considered it "as certain that in that most holy law a greater degree of moral perfection is enjoined upon us than the law of nature, alone and by itself, would require."

Grotius believed that sovereigns not only made rules, but were obliged to live with the rules once made. The covenants or contracts of sovereigns were legally and morally binding and not just Machiavellian temporary arrangements of mutual convenience. As men and women could bind themselves together in religious communities and to the law of God, so could sovereigns bind themselves to the law of nations. That there was anything transitory to or hypocritical in commitments made in the law of nations, were notions alien to Grotius:

> [M]ost important of all, in God injustice finds an enemy, justice a protector. He reserves His judgements for the life after this, yet in such a way that He often causes their effects to become manifest even in this life, as history teaches us by numerous examples.

For example, Grotius believed that the law of nature obliged promisors to keep their promises and makers of contracts to honor their commitments.

Compared to private contracts, treaties were a "more excellent kind of agreement" and, though made by the sovereign, binding on the whole of the people. Treaties were to be fulfilled and interpreted in good faith. Even between enemies, good faith, either expressed or implied, was the foundation for all promises. * * *

Not only were the laws of nations legally and morally binding, they were rationally calculated to lead to the long-term advantage of sovereign States. Here again Grotius treated the sovereign State as a person, and a reasonable person at that:

> [T]he national who in his own country obeys its laws is not foolish, even though, out of regard for that law, he may be obliged to forgo certain things advantageous for himself, so that nation is not foolish which does not press its own advantage to the point of disregarding the laws common to nations. The reason in either case is the same. For just as the national, who violates the law of his country in order to obtain an immediate advantage, breaks down that by which the advantages of himself and his posterity are for all future time assured, so the State which transgresses the laws of nature and of nations cuts away also the bulwarks which safeguard its own future peace.

Grotius' argument was based on natural law in the sense that he believed that sovereign States, like individuals, naturally relied upon communities for their well-being. The pacts made within these communities needed to be respected for the benefit of all, even the greatest individual or state. "[L]aw is not founded on expedience alone, there is no State so powerful that it may not some time need the help of others outside itself, either for purposes of trade, or even to ward off the forces of many foreign nations united against it." "[N]o association of men can be maintained without law * * * surely also that association which binds together the human race, or binds many nations together, has need of law."

Grotius, a diplomat as well as a jurist, was no starry-eyed idealist. His approach to international law and order was quite different from the Utopian proposals of the Abbé de Saint-Pierre who, almost a century later, would suggest a peace-keeping league of the principal European powers. Grotius acknowledged that war, as well as law, was a natural feature of human society. His belief was that war and law were inextricably intertwined:

> Least of all should that be admitted which some people imagine, that in war all laws are in abeyance. On the contrary war ought not to be undertaken except for the enforcement of rights: when once undertaken, it should be carried on only within the bounds of law and good faith. Demosthenes well said that war is directed against those who cannot be held in check by judicial processes. For judgements are efficacious against those who feel that they are too weak to resist; against those who are equally strong, or think they are, wars are undertaken. But in order that wars may be justified, they must be carried on with no less scrupulousness than judicial processes are wont to be.

Grotius' ideas, like those of Hobbes, emerged at a critical moment. To settle the Catholic–Protestant disputes underlying the Thirty Years War, the Treaties of Westphalia of 1648 acknowledged the sovereign authority of Europe's individual princes and nations. Not only the authority of the Emperor, but the temporal jurisdiction of the Church, including its power to regulate and moderate wars, were much restricted in theory and practice. If international conflicts were to be controlled, the Emperor and the Church could no longer be counted on as principal instruments of moderation. Rather, sovereign States would have to restrain themselves. Grotius' suggestion that the States could do so with a positive law of nations grounded on moral notions of covenant caught hold in the imagination of those conducting world affairs.

III. HOBBES, GROTIUS AND THE NEW WORLD ORDER

Hobbes in 1651 fashioned a Leviathan, an intellectual perception of a corporate personality called a sovereign State. His Leviathan was empowered by necessarily loyal citizens to rule them and their territory, exclusive of foreign interference and to act freely and forcefully in international affairs. For over three centuries Hobbes' paradigm has provided a working model, however rejuvenated and modified from time to time, for international political organisation. However, Leviathan has never reigned absolutely.

Alongside Hobbes' Leviathan came Grotius' law of nations. Designed for sovereign States, the law of nations juridically described States, defined their powers, spoke of their rights and duties, and made into legal systems their interactions and processes. Concerned as he was with the excesses of the Thirty Years War, Grotius, unlike Hobbes, came only indirectly to the ideas of the State and sovereignty. He explained in his Prolegomena that "in order to determine the differences between public war and private war, we found it necessary to explain the nature of sovereignty—what nations, what kings possess complete sovereignty; who possess sovereignty only in part, who with right of alienation, who otherwise; then it was necessary to speak also concerning the duty of subjects to their superiors."

The apparently inherent conflict between sovereignty and international law was resolved and balanced by notions of contract and covenant. The great contribution of Grotius in 1625 was the elaboration of a consensual theory of international politics that could and was used after 1648 to explain the settlement of the Thirty Years War and the binding effect of the Peace of Westphalia. There was need then to explain a new world order based, not on the Emperor or the Pope, but on independent States, States that were created and protected by treaty. Like Hobbes, Grotius personified States and wrote that, like persons, sovereign States were not only free agents, but also bound by their agreements, *pacta sunt servanda.* Furthermore, States, like persons, could be bound not only by their written contracts but by implicit contracts for States in the form of international custom.

Using theories of covenant, Grotius wove the conflicting notions of sovereignty and international law into a single fabric that has covered international practice more or less for three centuries. Grotius' contractual scheme for the reconciliation of sovereignty and international law was adequate not only for the balance of power politics of the eighteenth and nineteenth centuries but for the global wars, hot and cold, of the twentieth century. The question is whether the Grotian scheme will still do the trick in whatever becomes the new world order of the twenty-first century.

* * *

LEO ROSS, THE PEACE OF WESTPHALIA
42 Am. J. Int'l L. 20 (1948)

* * *

* * * [T]he actual terms of the settlement [of Westphalia], interesting and novel as they may be, would hardly suffice to account for the outstanding place attributed to it in the evolution of international relations. In order to find a more adequate explanation it would seem appropriate to search not so much in the text of the treaties themselves as in their implications, in the broad conceptions on which they rest and the developments to which they provided impetus.

In this order of ideas it has been affirmed that the Peace of Westphalia was the starting point for the development of modern international law. It has also been contended that it constituted "the first faint beginning of an international constitutional law" and the first instance "of deliberate enactment of common regulations by concerted action." In this connection the special merits of the work of Grotius have been stressed. On the one hand it has been argued that "Grotius adapted the (old) Law of Nature to fill the vacuum created by the extinction of the supreme authority of Emperor and Pope." On the other hand it has been affirmed that Grotius developed a system of international law which would equally appeal to, and be approved by, the believers and the atheists, and which would apply to all states irrespective of the character and dignity of their rulers. It can hardly be denied that the Peace of Westphalia marked an epoch in the evolution of international law. It undoubtedly promoted the laicization of international law by divorcing it from any particular religious background, and the extension of its scope so as to include, on a footing of equality, republican and monarchical states. Indeed these two byproducts of the Peace of 1648 would seem significant enough for students of international law and relations to regard it as an event of outstanding and lasting value. It would seem hazardous, however, to regard the Settlement of Westphalia and the work of Grotius as more than stages in the gradual, though by no means uniform, process which antedates and continues beyond the year 1648.

Of even greater importance than any of these particular aspects of developments of the Treaties of Osnabrück and Münster were the general political ideas, the triumph of which they apparently consecrated in the mind of man. The Peace of Westphalia, for better or worse, marks the end of an epoch and the opening of another. It represents the majestic portal which leads from the old into the new world.

In the spiritual field the Treaty of Westphalia was said to be "a public act of disregard of the international authority of the Papacy." In the political field it marked man's abandonment of the idea of a hierarchical structure of society and his option for a new system characterized by the coexistence of a multiplicity of states, each sovereign within its territory, equal to one another, and free from any external earthly authority. The idea of an authority or organization above the sovereign states is no longer. What takes its place is the notion that all states form a world-wide political system or that, at any rate, the states of Western Europe form a single political system. This new system rests on international law and the balance of power, a law operating between rather than above states and a power operating between rather than above states.

* * *

———————

Here is a short excerpt from the very long treaties constituting the "Peace of Westphalia" in a contemporary English translation, reflecting the equally arcane language of the original. What does this excerpt tell you about the old order on which the treaties were based? Consider in particular the first (long) paragraph. Who is agreeing with whom about exactly what? Consider in particular the issue of religion and how it is being resolved. Where does the excerpt touch on emerging notions of modern statehood and sovereignty?

TREATY OF OSNABRÜCK

A Treaty of Peace between the Empire *and* Sweden, *concluded and sign'd at* Osnabrug *the* 24th *of* October, 1648. *The* King *of* France *was comprehended in this Treaty as an Ally of* Sweden.

BE it known to all and singular whom it does concern, or whom it may in any manner concern, That after the Differences and Troubles which began several years ago in the *Roman* Empire, had come to such a height, that not only all *Germany,* but likewise some neighbouring Kingdoms, especially *Sweden* and *France,* found themselves so involv'd in them, that from thence there arose a long and cruel War; in the first place, between the most Serene and most Potent Prince and Lord, *Ferdinand* III. of Glorious Memory, chosen Emperor of the *Romans,* always August, King of *Germany, Hungary, Bohemia, Dalmatia, Croatia, Sclavonia,* &c. Archduke of *Austria,* Duke of *Burgundy, Brabant, Stiria, Carinthia* and *Carniola,* Marquiss of *Moravia,* Duke of *Luxemburg,* of the *Upper* and *Lower Silesia, Wirtemberg* and *Teck,* Prince of *Swabia,* Count of *Hapsburg, Tirol, Kyburg* and *Goricia,* Landtgrave of *Alsatia,* Marquiss of the Sacred Empire, *Burgovia,* the *Upper* and *Lower Lusatia,* Lord of the *Sclavonick* Borders, Port *Naon* and *Salines,* his Confederates and Adherents on the one side; and the most Serene and most Potent Prince and Lord *Gustavus Adolphus,* King of *Sweden,* of the *Goths* and *Vandals,* Great Prince of *Finland,* Duke of *Esthonia* and *Carelia,* and Lord of *Ingria,* likewise of Glorious Memory, the Kingdom of *Sweden,* its Allies and Confederates on the other side: And after his Decease, between the most Serene and most Potent Prince and Lord *Ferdinand* III. elected Emperor of the *Romans,* always August, *&c.* with his Allies and Adherents on the one side; and the most Serene and most Potent Princess and Lady *Christina,* Queen of *Sweden,* &c. her Allies and Adherents on the other side; upon which ensu'd a great Effusion of Christian Blood, and Devastation of several Provinces. At last it fell out by an Effect of the Divine Bounty, that both sides turn'd their Thoughts towards the means of making Peace, and that by a mutual Agreement made at *Hamburg* the 25th of *December* N. S. or the 15th O. S. 1641. between the Parties, the 11th N. S. or the 1st O. S. 1643. was by common Consent appointed for beginning the Assembly or Congress of Plenipotentiaries at *Osnabrug,* and at *Munster* in *Westphalia.* . . .

. . . . After having in-
vok'd the Affiftance of God, and reciprocally exchang'd
the Originals of their refpective full Powers, they tranfacted and agreed among themfelves, to the Glory of
God, and Safety of the Chriftian World (the Electors,
Princes and States of the Sacred *Roman* Empire being
prefent, approving and confenting) the Articles of Peace
and Amity, whereof the Tenour follows.

The Re-efta-   I. That there be a Chriftian, univerfal
blifhment of   and perpetual Peace, and a true and fincere
Peace and A-   Friendfhip and Amity between his Sacred
mity.   Imperial Majefty, the Houfe of *Auftria,*
                 and all his Allies and Adherents, and the
Heirs and Succeffors of each of them, chiefly the King
of *Spain,* and the Electors, Princes and States of the Empire, of the one fide ; and her Sacred Royal Majefty,
and the Kingdom of *Sweden,* her Allies and Adherents,
and the Heirs and Succeffors of each of them, efpecially
the moft Chriftian King, the refpective Electors, Princes
and States of the Empire, of the other fide ; and that this
Peace be obferv'd and cultivated fincerely and ferioufly,
fo that each Party may procure the Benefit, Honour and
Advantage of one another, and thereby the Fruits of this
Peace and Amity may be feen to grow up and flourifh a-
new, by a fure and reciprocal maintaining of a good
and faithful Neighbourhood between the *Roman* Empire
and the Kingdom of *Sweden* reciprocally.

. . . .

Point of Eccle-   V. Now whereas the Grievances of the
fiaftical Grie- one and the other Religion, which were
vances, or of   debated amongft the Electors, Princes and
Religion.   States of the Empire, have been partly
                  the Caufe and Occafion of the prefent
War, it has been agreed and tranfacted in the following
manner.

Confirmation of   I. That the Tranfaction fettled at *Paf-*
the Pacification *fau* in the Year 1552. and follow'd in the
of Paffau, and Year 1555. with the Peace of Religion,
that of Reli-   according as it was confirm'd in the Year
gion.   1556. at *Augsburg,* and afterwards in di-
                  vers other Diets of the facred *Roman* Em-
pire, in all its Points and Articles agreed and concluded
by the unanimous Confent of the Emperor and Electors,
Princes and States of both Religions, fhall be maintain'd
in its Force and Vigour, and facredly and inviolably obferv'd. But thofe things that are appointed by this Treaty with Confent of both Parties, touching certain Articles in the faid Tranfaction which are troublefom and liti-
gious, fhall be look'd upon to have been obferv'd in Judgment and otherwife, as a perpetual Declaration of the
faid Pacification, until the Matter of Religion can, by
the Grace of God, be agreed upon, and that without
ftopping fhort for the Contradiction and Proteftation of

any one whatſoever, Ecclefiaſtical or Secular, either within or without the Empire, in any time whatſoever : all which Oppoſitions are by virtue of theſe Preſents declar'd null and void. And as to all other things, That there be an exact and reciprocal Equality amongſt all the Electors, Princes and States of both Religions, conformably to the State of the Commonweal, the Conſtitutions of the Empire, and the preſent Convention : ſo that what is juſt of one ſide ſhall be ſo of the other, all Violence and Force between the two Parties being for ever prohibited.

VIII. And in order to prevent for the future all Differences in the Political State, all and every the Electors, Princes, and States of the *Roman* Empire ſhall be ſo eſtabliſh'd and confirm'd in their antient Rights, Prerogatives, Liberties, Privileges, free Exerciſe of their Territorial Right, as *The Re-eſtablifhment of the Eſtates of the Empire to their antient Rights.* well in Spirituals and Temporals, Seigneuries, Regalian Rights, and in the poſſeſſion of all theſe things, by virtue of the preſent Tranſaction, that they may not be moleſted at any time in any manner, under any pretext whatſoever.

I. That they enjoy without contradiction the Right of Suffrage in all Deliberations touching the Affairs of the Empire, eſpecially in the matter of interpreting Laws, reſolving upon a War, impoſing Taxes, ordering Levies and quartering of Soldiers, building for the publick Uſe new Fortreſſes in the Lands of the States, and reinforcing old Gariſons, making of Peace and Alliances, and treating of other ſuch-like Affairs ; ſo that none of thoſe or the like things ſhall be done or receiv'd afterwards, without the Advice and Conſent of a free Aſſembly of all the States of the Empire : That, above all, each of the Eſtates of the Empire ſhall freely and for ever enjoy the Right of making Alliances among themſelves, or with Foreigners, for the Preſervation and Security of every one of them : provided neverthleſs that theſe Alliances be neither againſt the Emperor nor the Empire, nor the publick Peace, nor againſt this Tranſaction eſpecially ; and that they be made without prejudice in every reſpect to the Oath whereby every one of them is bound to the Emperor and the Empire.

* * * *

XVI. So ſoon as the Treaty of Peace ſhall have been ſubſcrib'd and ſign'd by the Plenipotentiaries and Ambaſſadors, all Acts *Ceſſation of Hoſtilities.* of Hoſtility ſhall ceaſe, and whatever things have been agreed above, ſhall at the ſame time be executed and perform'd on both ſides.

* * * *

2. THE CRITERIA OF STATEHOOD

The system of sovereign nation states that arose after the Peace of Westphalia rests, necessarily, on entities called states. International law has long defined the criteria of statehood (as well as the rights and duties of states, at least vis-à-vis each other). Despite the considerable changes in the number, make-up and position of states in the global legal order, these criteria have—perhaps surprisingly—changed very little over the last century.

The Montevideo Convention on the Rights and Duties of States sets forth what is widely considered to be the definitive statement of the criteria of statehood. While the Convention itself was only signed by nineteen states (all of the Americas, since it was drafted at a conference of states of the Western hemisphere), the document is now understood to be the clearest statement of the criteria of statehood. The various criteria have always been interpreted in a flexible fashion, and much depends on the circumstances and the (political) context in which the question comes up whether an entity counts as a state.

According to the criteria set forth below, is Michigan a state? The Vatican? The Russian Federation? The European Union?

MONTEVIDEO CONVENTION ON THE RIGHTS AND DUTIES OF STATES
(Adopted 1933; in force 1934)

Article 1

The state as a person of international law should possess the following qualifications:

(a) a permanent population;

(b) a defined territory;

(c) government; and

(d) capacity to enter into relations with the other states.

Article 2

The federal state shall constitute a sole person in the eyes of international law.

Article 3

The political existence of the state is independent of recognition by the other states. Even before recognition the state has the right to defend its integrity and independence, to provide for its conservation and prosperity, and consequently to organize itself as it sees fit, to legislate upon its interests, administer its services, and to define the jurisdiction and competence of its courts. The exercise of these rights has no other limitation than the exercise of the rights of other states according to international law.

Article 4

States are juridically equal, enjoy the same rights, and have equal capacity in their exercise. The rights of each one do not depend upon the power which it possesses to assure its exercise, but upon the simple fact of its existence as a person under international law.

* * *

———————

The following excerpt provides a commentary on the criteria of statehood. In practice, these criteria are applied by states to one another. Thus, political factors often play a considerable role in their interpretation and application.

JAMES CRAWFORD, THE CREATION OF STATES IN INTERNATIONAL LAW
(2006)

* * *

[There is] considerable disagreement as to the definition of both "State" and "Nation" and their relationship. As we shall see, to refer merely to statehood "for the purposes of international law" assumes that a State for one purpose is necessarily also a State for another. * * * Many legal issues subsumed under the rubric of "statehood" may be able to be resolved in their own terms—often this will take the form of interpretation of a treaty or other document. But at a basic level and for many purposes it still makes a great difference whether an entity is or is not a State.

* * *

2.2 THE CLASSICAL CRITERIA FOR STATEHOOD: *EX FACTIS JUS ORITUR*

The best known formulation of the basic criteria for statehood is that laid down in Article 1 of the Montevideo Convention on the Rights and Duties of States, 1933: "The State as a person of international law should possess the following qualifications: (a) a permanent population; (b) a defined territory; (c) government; and (d) capacity to enter into relations with other States."

* * *

(1) DEFINED TERRITORY

Evidently, States are territorial entities. "Territorial sovereignty * * * involves the exclusive right to display the activities of a State." Conversely, the right to be a State is dependent at least in the first instance upon the exercise of full governmental powers with respect to some area of territory. But, although a State must possess some territory, there appears to be no rule prescribing the minimum area of that territory. States may occupy an extremely small area, provided they are independent in the sense to be explained. The ten smallest States at present are as set out in Table 1.

Table 1. Areas of Some Small States

Vatican City	0.4 sq km
Monaco	1.5
Nauru	21
Tuvalu	26
San Marino	61
Liechtenstein	160
Marshall Islands	181
St. Kitts & Nevis	267
Maldives	298
Malta	315

Nor is there any rule requiring contiguity of the territory of the State. The separation of East Prussia from Germany between 1919 and 1945, of East Pakistan from West Pakistan before 1971, or of Alaska from the "lower Forty-Eight," cast no doubt on the statehood of Germany, Pakistan or the United States. Some archipelagic States—e.g., the Federated States of Micronesia, the Marshall Islands, São Tomé e Príncipe—consist of minute areas of land territory separated by wide expanses of ocean, the ocean nonetheless legally under the aegis of the land. Little bits of States can be enclaved within other States. Sovereignty comes in all shapes and sizes.* * *

(2) PERMANENT POPULATION

If States are territorial entities, they are also aggregates of individuals. A permanent population is thus necessary for statehood, though, as in the case of territory, no minimum limit is apparently prescribed. The ten smallest States by population are set out in Table 2.

Table 2. Populations of Some Small States.

Vatican City	768
Tuvalu	9,743
Nauru	11,218
Palau	21,092
San Marino	30,472
Monaco	33,084
Liechtenstein	34,927
St. Kitts & Nevis	39,601
Marshall Islands	54,313
Andorra	68,584

Of States with very small populations only the Vatican City raises any question on this ground, and this more because of the ecclesiastical character of its population than its size.

The criterion under discussion requires States to have a permanent population: it is not a rule relating to the nationality of that population.* * *

(3) GOVERNMENT

The requirement that a putative State have an effective government might be regarded as central to its claim to statehood. "Government" or "effective government" is evidently a basis for the other central criterion of independence. Moreover, international law defines "territory" not by adopting private law analogies of real property but by reference to the extent of governmental power exercised, or capable of being exercised, with respect to some territory and population. Territorial sovereignty is not ownership of but governing power with respect to territory. There is thus a good case for regarding government as the most important single criterion of statehood, since all the others depend upon it. This is true equally for external as internal affairs. Governmental authority is the basis for normal inter-State relations; what is an act of a State is defined primarily by reference to its organs of government—legislative, executive or judicial.

The difficulty is, however, that the criteria for statehood are nominal and exclusionary. Their concern is not with the clear undoubted cases but with the borderline ones. Hence the application of the criterion of government in practice is much less simple than this analysis might suggest.* * *

The following conclusions suggest themselves. First, to be a State, an entity must possess a government or a system of government in general control of its territory, to the exclusion of other entities not claiming through or under it.

Second, international law lays down no specific requirements as to the nature and extent of this control, except that it include some degree of maintenance of law and order and the establishment of basic institutions.

Third, in applying the general principle to specific cases, the following must be considered:

whether the statehood of the entity is opposed under title of international law: if so, the requirement of effectiveness is likely to be more strictly applied;

whether the government claiming authority, if it does not effectively control the territory in question, has obtained authority by consent of the previous sovereign and exercises a certain degree of control;

there is a distinction between the creation of a new State on the one hand and the subsistence or extinction of an established State on the other. In the former situation, the criterion of effective government may be applied more strictly.* * *

(4) CAPACITY TO ENTER INTO RELATIONS WITH OTHER STATES

Capacity to enter into relations with States at the international level is no longer, if it ever was, an exclusive State prerogative. True, States preeminently possess that capacity, but this is a consequence of statehood, not a criterion for it—and it is not constant but depends on the situation of particular States. It might still be said that *capacity* to enter into the full range of international relations is a useful criterion, since such capacity is independent of its recognition by other States and of its exercise by the entity concerned. * * *

But capacity, competence or "ability" in this sense depends partly on the power of internal government of a territory, without which international obligations may not be carried into effect, and partly on the entity concerned being separate for the purpose of international relations so that no other entity both carries out and accepts responsibility for them. In other words, capacity to enter into relations with other States, in the sense in which it might be a useful criterion, is a conflation of the requirements of government and independence. To the latter we must now turn.

(5) INDEPENDENCE

Independence is the central criterion for statehood. As Judge Huber stated in the *Island of Palmas* arbitration:

> "Sovereignty in the relations between States signifies independence. Independence in regard to a portion of the globe is the right to exercise therein, to the exclusion of any other State, the functions of a State. The development of the national organization of States during the last few centuries, and, as a corollary, the development of international law, have established this principle of the exclusive competence of the State in regard to its own territory in such a way as to make it the point of departure in settling most questions that concern international relations."

In more than one sense it has been a "point of departure," since the difficulty of applying independence as a criterion leads in many cases to assumptions, based on little or no argument as to the independence or otherwise of an entity. The claim of international law to determine questions of statehood is squarely in issue.

As usual, the problem is partly one of determining the purposes for which and the context within which the question is asked. Different legal consequences may be attached to lack of independence in specific cases. Lack of independence may be so complete that the entity concerned is not a State but an internationally indistinguishable part of another dominant State. A grant of "independence" may, in certain circumstances, be a legal nullity, or even an act engaging the responsibility of the grantor, as with so-called "puppet States." Or an entity may be independent in some basic sense but act in a specific matter under the control of another State so that the relation becomes one of agency, and the responsibility of the latter State is attracted for acts of the former. Moreover, although our concern is with independence as the basic element of statehood in international law, in other contexts the term can have other meanings. In particular it is important to distinguish independence as an initial qualification for statehood and as a condition for continued existence. A new State attempting to secede will have to demonstrate substantial independence, both formal and real, from the State of which it formed part before it will be regarded as definitively created. On the other hand, the independence of an existing State is protected by international law rules against unlawful invasion and annexation, so that the State may, even for a considerable time, continue to exist as a legal entity despite lack of effectiveness. The context in which the claim to independence or to loss of independence is made is thus highly significant. * * *

(6) SOVEREIGNTY

The term "sovereignty" is sometimes used in place of independence as a basic criterion for statehood. However, it has another more satisfactory meaning as an incidence or consequence of statehood, namely, the plenary competence that States prima facie possess. Since the two meanings are distinct, it is better to use the term "independence" to denote the prerequisite for statehood and "sovereignty" the legal incident.

* * *

_____

Under the Montevideo Convention criteria, the status of most states in the world today is unquestioned. However, the status of a handful of entities remains disputed. Perhaps the most enduring example is Taiwan, which we will analyze in greater depth in Chapter VI.1. Another prominent example is Palestine, which we will also consider then. For now, take a minute to reflect on whether Taiwan and Palestine meet the criteria as laid out in the Convention and as explained by Crawford.

EXERCISE ON STATEHOOD

In 1967, a British family occupied an offshore platform in the North Sea seven miles off the coast of Britain. It had been built by the British as a defense base in World War II and subsequently abandoned. The occupiers raised a flag and declared the foundation of the "Principality of Sealand." Later, they even adopted a coat of arms and a national anthem. They are presently considering forming a national rugby team. For more information, go to "Sealand's" website at www.sealandgov.org. According to the materials you have just read, is "Sealand" a sovereign state?

CHAPTER 2

INTERACTION: STATES IN THE CLASSICAL SYSTEM

∎ ∎ ∎

This chapter addresses the manner in which states in the classical system interacted with one another. Their interaction was based on their view of each other as self-reliant, closed entities endowed with "sovereignty." As the bedrock principle of classic (public) international law, the sovereignty of nation states dates back to the Westphalian Treaties of 1648. Note that, strictly speaking, sovereignty is not a legal term. Rather, it is a political concept from which legal consequences (rights and responsibilities of nation states) were derived.

In order to get a better sense of the notion of sovereignty, we begin by asking what it really means under the classical approach. Next, we look at the rights of states emanating from the traditional understanding of sovereignty and then turn to some of the major obligations it entails. Finally, we consider "comity" as a concept that lies beyond legal rights and obligations but that nonetheless shapes the interaction between nation states in important ways.

1. WHAT DOES SOVEREIGNTY MEAN?

The following three texts—two excerpted from books and the third from case law—deal with the meaning of sovereignty. How do they define the concept?

DAN PHILPOTT, REVOLUTIONS IN SOVEREIGNTY

(2001)

* * *

Sovereignty, then, is a type of legitimate authority; it is not power, and today it is prescribed by law. But this is still too broad: a police chief, a priest, or a corporate executive could all qualify as sovereigns. Are there other traits that will narrow the concept, yet allow us to capture sovereignty's many colors? In fact, sovereignty has always comprised a certain other ingredient: supremacy. In the chain of authority by which I look up to higher authority, who looks up to yet a higher one, and so on, the holder of sovereignty is highest; this person or institution has final authority.

49

A police chief may have authority over me, but he is not sovereign. This is not to say that the sovereign need be an individual. Supreme authority might lie in a triumvirate, a committee, a constitution, or, in Rousseau's version, in the united will of the people. In all cases, nobody may question the sovereign; nobody may legitimately oppose it.

A final important ingredient in sovereignty's definition is territoriality: the people over whom the holder of sovereignty rules are defined by virtue of their location within borders, not by some other principle such as kinship or religious belief. In the high Middle Ages, when sovereignty did not exist, neither supremacy nor territoriality characterized political authorities, in precise contrast to modern international relations, whose sovereign states have been compared by scholars to private property, in which one person or body of law is supreme within a demarcated piece of turf. * * *

Absolute and *nonabsolute* are useful distinguishing terms. Helpful too are *internal* and *external*, which do not denote distinct types of sovereignty, but rather complementary, always coexistent, aspects of sovereignty. Supreme authority within a territory means not only sovereignty within borders, but also implies immunity from external interference. Such interference, were it legitimate, would make the sovereign less than supreme. Since the Peace of Westphalia of 1648, the state has been the chief holder of external sovereignty; then it became illegitimate to interfere in other states to influence their governance of religion or of anything else. The external sovereignty of the state is what international lawyers have in mind when they speak of sovereignty, and it is what the UN charter means by "political independence and territorial integrity." If the state is private property, its external sovereignty is a no-trespassing law.

The external sovereignty of the state is also what lawyers and political scientists mean when they speak of international relations as anarchy, a notion that means not necessarily chaos, riot, and violence, but simply the lack of a government, the absence of a higher authority that has claims upon those who live under it. The external sovereignty of the state is also compatible with a variety of holders of internal sovereignty—a monarch, the people, and a constitution can each represent the state within borders and be immune from external intervention. Compared with internal sovereignty, external sovereignty has remained relatively constant—not unrevised (otherwise international revolutions in sovereignty would make little sense), but steady like a suit of armor whose plates and hinges are only occasionally updated and restructured, while the personality inside changes often, from reform to reform, from revolution to revolution.

* * *

Sovereignty is not an entirely fixed concept, and many sophisticated thinkers have conceived of it differently. How does this short excerpt from Brierly contrast with what Philpott had to say? And what is the difference between internal sovereignty and external sovereignty?

J. L. BRIERLY, THE LAW OF NATIONS
(5th ed. 1955)

* * *

§ 2. THE MODERN "SOVEREIGN" STATE

* * *

Starting in Bodin as a formal juristic concept, the attribute of a personal monarch entrusted by the constitution with supreme authority over the ordinary laws of the state, sovereignty, under the impulsion of the historical developments which took place in the character of European governments, came to be regarded as power absolute and above the law, and eventually, when it had become impossible to fix the location of such power in any definite person or organ within the state, as the attribute of the personified state itself. The doctrine was developed for the most part by political theorists who were not interested in, and paid little regard to, the relations of states with one another, and in its later forms it not only involved a denial of the possibility of states being subject to any kind of law, but became an impossible theory for a world which contained more states than one.

Writers on international law have attempted in many ingenious ways to reconcile the existence of their subject with the doctrine of the absolute sovereignty of states, but all these devices are in effect variations of the theory of the auto-limitation of sovereignty which is referred to later in this chapter. One formula, for example, is to say that international law is a law of *co-ordination* but not of *subordination*.

* * *

[S]overeignty, however much it may need reformulating as a political doctrine, does stand today for something in the relations of states which is both true and very formidable. It expresses, though in a misleading way, the claims that states habitually make to act as seems good to them without restraint on their freedom. An American Commission which was formed during the last war to study the organization of peace has summarized these claims conveniently.

"A sovereign state," says the Commission's report, "at the present time claims the power to judge its own controversies, to enforce its own conception of its rights, to increase its armaments without limit, to treat its own nationals as it sees fit, and to regulate its economic life without regard to the effect of such regulations upon its neighbours. These attributes of sovereignty must be limited."

Thus for the practical purposes of the international lawyer sovereignty is not a metaphysical concept, nor is it part of the essence of statehood; it is merely a term which designates an aggregate of particular and very extensive claims that states habitually make for themselves in their relations with other states.

Having seen how two scholars conceive of sovereignty, let us turn to one of the classic cases to shape our understanding of the concept.

Max Huber, the sole arbitrator in the case below, was a major force in shaping international law during the first part of the 20th century. A Swiss national, he sat as a judge on the Permanent Court of International Justice (PCIJ) from 1922 to 1939 and was that Court's President from 1925 to 1927. The opinion below was authored while he was also serving as President of the International Committee of the Red Cross. According to the excerpts below, what are the main attributes of sovereignty? What does it take to exercise (and maintain) it? What if a state fails to do so?

THE ISLAND OF PALMAS
Permanent Court of Arbitration
2 U.N. Rep. Int'l Arb. Awards 829 (1928)

[The question was whether the Island of Palmas (or Miangas), which geographically is part of the archipelago of the Philippines, belonged to the United States or to the Netherlands. The United States argued that it had acquired the Island from Spain in the (Peace) Treaty of Paris of 1898 which ended the Spanish–American War. Since the United States' claim was thus derivative of Spain's, it depended on whether Spain had title to the Island in 1898. The United States alleged that it did because Spain had first discovered the island. In contrast, the Netherlands claimed the island by virtue of the fact that it (not Spain) had "possessed and exercised rights of sovereignty from 1677 or probably from a date prior even to 1648, to the present day." The question thus became: does a territory belong to the first discoverer even if it never exercises any authority for centuries thereafter, or does it belong to the state which actually exercises sovereignty over it (over a long period of time).]

HUBER, Sole Arbitrator:

* * *

The *United States*, as successor to the rights of Spain over the Philippines, bases its title in the first place on discovery. The existence of sovereignty thus acquired is, in the American view, confirmed not merely by the most reliable cartographers and authors, but also by treaty, in particular by the Treaty of Münster, of 1648, to which Spain and the Netherlands are themselves Contracting Parties. As, according to the same argument, nothing has occurred of a nature, in international law, to cause the acquired title to disappear, this latter title was intact at the moment when, by the Treaty of December 10th, 1898, Spain ceded the Philippines to the United States. In these circumstances, it is, in the American view, unnecessary to establish facts showing the actual display of sovereignty precisely over the Island of Palmas (or Miangas). The United States Government finally maintains that Palmas (or Miangas) forms a geographical part of the Philippine group and in virtue of the principle of contiguity belongs to the Power having the sovereignty over the Philippines.

* * *

Sovereignty in the relation between States signifies independence. Independence in regard to a portion of the globe is the right to exercise therein, to the exclusion of any other State, the functions of a State. The development of the national organisation of States during the last few centuries and, as a corollary, the development of international law, have established this principle of the exclusive competence of the State in regard to its own territory in such a way as to make it the point of departure in settling most questions that concern international relations. * * *

Titles of acquisition of territorial sovereignty in present-day international law are either based on an act of effective apprehension, such as occupation or conquest, or, like cession, presuppose that the ceding and the cessionary Power or at least one of them, have the faculty of effectively disposing of the ceded territory. In the same way natural accretion can only be conceived of as an accretion to a portion of territory where there exists an actual sovereignty capable of extending to a spot which falls within its sphere of activity. It seems therefore natural that an element which is essential for the constitution of sovereignty should not be lacking in its continuation. So true is this, that practice, as well as doctrine, recognizes—though under different legal formulae and with certain differences as to the conditions required—that the continuous and peaceful display of territorial sovereignty (peaceful in relation to other States) is as good as a title. The growing insistence with which international law, ever since the middle of the 18th century, has demanded that the occupation shall be effective would be inconceivable, if effectiveness were required only for the act of acquisition and not equally for the maintenance of the right. * * *

Territorial sovereignty, as has already been said, involves the exclusive right to display the activities of a State. That right has as corollary a duty: the obligation to protect within the territory the rights of other States, in particular their right to integrity and inviolability in peace and in war,

to be sovereign, must be able to fulfill obligations to other states

together with the rights which each State may claim for its nationals in foreign territory. Without manifesting its territorial sovereignty in a manner corresponding to circumstances, the State cannot fulfill this duty. Territorial sovereignty cannot limit itself to its negative side, i.e., to excluding the activities of other States; for it serves to divide between nations the space upon which human activities are employed, in order to assure them at all points the minimum of protection of which international law is the guardian.

* * *

The principle that continuous and peaceful display of the functions of a State within a given region is a constituent element of territorial sovereignty is not only based on the conditions of the formation of independent States and their boundaries (as shown by the experience of political history) as well as on an international jurisprudence and doctrine widely accepted; this principle has further been recognized in more than one federal State, where a jurisdiction is established in order to apply, as need arises, rules of international law to the interstate relations of the States members. * * *

Manifestations of territorial sovereignty assume, it is true, different forms, according to conditions of time and place. Although continuous in principle, sovereignty cannot be exercised in fact at every moment on every point of territory. The intermittence and discontinuity compatible with the maintenance of the right necessarily differ according as inhabited or uninhabited regions are involved, or regions enclosed within territories in which sovereignty is incontestably displayed or again regions accessible from, for instance, the high seas. It is true that neighbouring States may by convention fix limits to their own sovereignty, even in regions such as the interior of scarcely explored continents where such sovereignty is scarcely manifested, and in this way each may prevent the other from any penetration of its territory. The delimitation of hinterland may also be mentioned in this connection.

* * *

The *title alleged by the United States of America* as constituting the immediate foundation of its claim is that of *cession*, brought about by the Treaty of Paris, which cession transferred all rights of sovereignty which Spain may have possessed in the region indicated in Article III of the said Treaty and therefore also those concerning the Island of Palmas (or Miangas).

It is evident that Spain could not transfer more rights than she herself possessed. * * *

[Huber found that the Island of Palmas belonged to the Netherlands.]

Whose argument prevails here, and why? What values are advanced by each party's position? What incentives do these positions entail?

2. RIGHTS AND PRIVILEGES

Overview: Rights of Sovereign States

This subchapter explores some of the rights and privileges nations enjoy by virtue of their status as sovereign states. We limit our attention here to the traditional rights and privileges even a non-specialist in public international law should know about: the right to equality with all other sovereign states and, as a consequence, the right to be free from outside interference; the power to exercise jurisdiction (i.e., governmental authority) over the state's territory and its nationals; and the immunity from jurisdiction in each others' courts. Beyond these examples, states have many other rights and privileges not examined here in any detail. Among them are control over a state's airspace and territorial seas; the right to enter into treaties and to participate in the making of customary international law (see Ch. III.2. and 3.); the right to become a full-fledged member of international organizations (see Ch. VI.2.) and to claim reparations for violations of international law (see infra. 3.D.); the right to establish diplomatic and consular relations with other states; and, within certain limits, even the right to wage war. This catalog is not exhaustive. In fact, there can really be no complete list of sovereign rights because sovereignty is a default rule of power: as most famously illustrated by the *Lotus* case, which we will consider in this Chapter, sovereignty means that a state can do whatever it pleases as long as it does not violate rules of international law by which it is bound.

A. SOVEREIGN EQUALITY

GERRY SIMPSON, GREAT POWERS AND OUTLAW STATES

(2004)

* * *

It is a commonplace in international law that states are equal or, at least, that they possess something called sovereign equality. This form of equality is a foundational principle of the international legal order. There is a mass of support—doctrinal, jurisprudential and scholarly—for at least some variant of the principle. Re-assertions of the doctrine tend to be accompanied by claims for its centrality, its existence in the face of material, cultural, intellectual and military differences, and its long lineage in international law.* * *

In 1825, in the *Antelope Case*, Chief Justice Marshall of the United States Supreme Court remarked that: "No principle of general law is more universally acknowledged than the perfect equality of nations." In a classic statement from his treatise, Oppenheim elaborated on this:

> The equality before International Law of all member States of the Family of Nations is an invariable equality derived from their international personality. Whatever inequality may exist between states as regards their size, power, degree of civilisation, wealth and other qualities, they are nevertheless equals as international persons.

In 1951, President Basdevant of the International Court of Justice put the matter even more bluntly: "Before this Court, there are no great or small states * * *."

The major textbooks are in broad agreement with these dicta. Doctrinally, the significance of sovereign equality is made explicit in the United Nations Charter at Article 2(1) (the Organisation is "based" on the principle of sovereign equality) and in the 1970 Declaration on Friendly Relations. The Preamble of the United Charter refers to the equality of "nations large and small" and many writers claim the principle falls within the category of norms of jus cogens.

The orthodoxy on sovereign equality assumes that the international system contains a plurality of states and that these states are both similar and different, i.e., capable of enjoying equality in some domains but distinct in others. States enjoying sovereign equality are often said to possess internal sovereignty (e.g. a monopoly of legitimate legal authority within a certain territory and jurisdictional primacy in that area) and external sovereignty (e.g. a right to territorial integrity, immunity from suits in the courts of another state). The core idea (of both sovereignty and equality) is that no state is legally superior to another—*par in parem non habet imperium*. The separate opinion of Judge Anzilotti in the *Customs Union Case* is usually viewed as a standard definition of "independence" but much of the language employed concerns hierarchy and equality. State equality requires the absence of formal superiority and subordination in the legal relations between states. So no state can sit in judgement on another state or sign treaties on behalf of another state. Nor can a state procure the consent of another state to an agreement or treaty through the use of physical coercion. States recognise only one legal superior and that is international law itself. In addition states are said to be bound only by those rules to which they have agreed to be bound. This is the principle of consent.

The principle of sovereign equality also provides the basis for a network of rights and duties found in many substantive areas of international law. In the law on the use of force, both the right to territorial integrity (Article 2(4)) and the right to self-defence (Article 51) are derived from sovereign equality. Even the possession and threatened use of nuclear weapons can be justified as a concomitant of sovereign equality. This, indeed, was a consideration in Judge Fleischhauer's Separate Opinion in *The Legality of Nuclear Weapons,* where he states:

> To end the matter with the simple statement that recourse to nuclear weapons would be contrary to international law applicable in armed conflict, and in particular the principles and rules of humanitarian law, would have meant that the law applicable in armed conflict, and in particular the humanitarian law was given precedence over the inherent right of individual or collective self-defence which every State possesses as a matter of sovereign equality and which is expressly preserved in Article 51 of the Charter.

On the other hand, the prohibition on the use of force (except in self-defence and collective security) secures implementation of the sovereign equality norm. While this norm purports to constrain the application of sovereign authority, it also confirms the importance of state equality by mitigating the effects of superior military force and placing states on a level footing in relation to the unilateral use of force.

At other times, the principle provides a basis for specific treaty or customary rights:

> [the] community of interest in a navigable river becomes the basis of a common legal right, the essential features of which are the perfect equality of all riparian States in the use of the whole course of the river and the exclusion of any preferential privilege of any one riparian State in relation to the others.

Finally * * * the element of sovereign equality I characterise as existential equality encompasses states' rights to organise their communities on any basis they wish. Sovereign equality is a guarantee of state autonomy in the domestic sphere and pluralism and diversity in the international system as a whole.

* * *

Today, the principle of sovereign equality is enshrined in the United Nations Charter.

CHARTER OF THE UNITED NATIONS

(Adopted 1945; in force 1945)

* * *

Article 2

The Organization and its Members, in pursuit of the Purposes stated in Article 1, shall act in accordance with the following Principles.

1. The Organization is based on the principle of the sovereign equality of all its Members.

2. All Members, in order to ensure to all of them the rights and benefits resulting from membership, shall fulfill in good faith the obligations assumed by them in accordance with the present Charter.

3. All Members shall settle their international disputes by peaceful means in such a manner that international peace and security, and justice, are not endangered.

4. All Members shall refrain in their international relations from the threat or use of force against the territorial integrity or political independence of any state, or in any other manner inconsistent with the Purposes of the United Nations.

* * *

––––––––––

The following text is a little more specific. What rights does it purport to extend to states? What are the corollary duties?

UN GENERAL ASSEMBLY DECLARATION 2625 (XXV)

October 24, 1970

Declaration on Principles of International Law concerning Friendly Relations and Co-operation among States in accordance with the Charter of the United Nations.

* * *

THE PRINCIPLE OF SOVEREIGN EQUALITY OF STATES

All States enjoy sovereign equality. They have equal rights and duties and are equal members of the international community, notwithstanding differences of an economic, social, political, or other nature.

In particular, sovereign equality includes the following elements:

(a) States are juridically equal;

(b) Each State enjoys the rights inherent in full sovereignty;

(c) Each State has the duty to respect the personality of other States;

(d) The territorial integrity and political independence of the State are inviolable;

(e) Each State has the right freely to choose and develop its political, social, economic, and cultural systems;

(f) Each State has the duty to comply fully and in good faith with its international obligations and to live in peace with other states.

*   *   *

The equality of sovereign nation states is an appealing idea, but does it have any real traction? In other words, does formal equality really matter in light of the huge discrepancies in the UN member states' size, population, and political, economic, and military power? How would you expect the equality of members to manifest itself within the UN itself?

B. PROTECTION AGAINST OUTSIDE INTERFERENCE

LASSA OPPENHEIM, INTERNATIONAL LAW, VOL. I
(9th ed. 1992)

*   *   *

All states are under an international legal obligation not to commit any violation of the independence, or territorial or personal authority, of any other state. In consequence of its external independence a state can, unless restricted by customary law or by treaty, manage its international affairs according to discretion; thus, for example, it can enter into alliances and conclude other treaties, and send and receive diplomatic envoys.
*   *   *

The duty of every state itself to abstain, and to prevent its agents and, in certain cases, nationals, from committing any violation of another state's independence or territorial integrity or personal authority is correlative to the corresponding right possessed by other states. In the *Lotus* case the Permanent Court of International Justice stated that "the first and foremost restriction imposed by international law upon a State is that, failing the existence of a permissive rule to the contrary, it may not exercise its power in any form in the territory of another State;" and in the *Corfu Channel* case the International Court of Justice observed that "between independent States, respect for territorial sovereignty is an essential foundation of international relations."

However, not all acts performed by one state in the territory of another involve a violation of sovereignty. Thus no violation of the territorial state's sovereignty is involved if another state buys a house there, or concludes a commercial transaction there. Such acts are unlikely to involve the exercise of a state's sovereign authority or derogate from the sovereign authority of the territorial state. Similarly, even if a state does exercise its sovereign authority in another state, if that other state consents there will be no derogation from its sovereign authority and thus no violation of its territorial authority.

It is not feasible to enumerate all such actions as might constitute a breach of a state's duty not to violate another state's independence or territorial or personal authority. But it is useful to give some illustrative examples. Thus, in the absence of treaty provisions to the contrary, a state is not allowed to intervene in the management of the internal or international affairs of other states, or to prevent them from doing or to compel them to do certain acts in their domestic relations or international intercourse. A state is not allowed to send its troops, its warships, or its police forces into or through foreign territory, or its aircraft over it, or to carry out official investigations on foreign territory or to let its agents conduct clandestine operations there, or to exercise an act of administration or jurisdiction on foreign territory, without permission. Thus it will normally be a violation of the territorial sovereignty of a state for the police or military forces of another state to pursue criminals or rebel forces who flee over the frontier of a neighbouring state; and it is nonetheless a violation if the police or military forces are acting on the basis of "hot pursuit" analogous to that accepted in maritime matters, for in that context the right of "hot pursuit" involves no violation of territorial sovereignty since it ceases at the outer limit of another state's territorial sea. The violation of the territorial sovereignty of the neighbouring state into which the pursuers enter may occasionally be justified on grounds of self-defence or by the failure or inability of the invaded state to fulfil the duties of control over its territory which are the corollary of its rights to territorial sovereignty. Such pursuit on land is, however, a form of self-help which is now mostly unlawful. It is also a breach of international law for a state without permission to send its agents into the territory of another state to apprehend persons accused of having committed a crime. Where this has happened, the offending state should—and often does—hand over the person in question to the state in whose territory he was apprehended. But states do not always do this, and the fugitive may be brought to trial in the courts of the state whose agents have seized him. The question then arises whether those courts should decline jurisdiction because of the violation of international law involved in his seizure. National courts have generally not declined to exercise jurisdiction over an accused who has been brought within their power by means of a seizure in violation of international law.

Having regard to the personal authority of other states, a state is not allowed to naturalise aliens residing on its territory without their consent, nor to prevent them from returning home for the purpose of fulfilling military service.

* * *

In the late 1940s the question of protection against outside interference came before the International Court of Justice (ICJ) in a case between the United Kingdom and Albania involving events in the so-called Corfu Channel off the Albanian coast. The litigation was complex. Here, we focus only on the aspects of territorial integrity; later in this Chapter, we will revisit the case in the context of state responsibility.

In this case, we encounter the ICJ for the first time in this book. The ICJ is the principal judicial organ of the UN (often called the "World Court"). Throughout this course, we will see more than a dozen further decisions of the ICJ. We will look at the Court's jurisdiction, structure and decision-making process in some detail in Chapter IX. For now, it suffices to understand that the ICJ is the judicial organ of the United Nations; the Court has its seat in The Hague, Netherlands; only states can be parties before the ICJ; and the Court has jurisdiction only on the basis of the litigants' consent (which can come in various forms). The *Corfu Channel Case* led to one of the ICJ's earliest judgments and has become a landmark decision.

THE CORFU CHANNEL CASE
(UNITED KINGDOM V. ALBANIA)

International Court of Justice
1949 I.C.J. 4

[The Corfu Channel is a narrow strait between the Island of Corfu (which belongs to Greece) and the mainland of Albania. The boundary between Greece and Albania runs through the middle of the strait, and the strait is so narrow that there are no international waters. All of the waters in the channel are part of the territory of either Greece or Albania.

Claiming a right to innocent passage under (customary) international law, in October 1948, several British warships passed through the Channel (which the British Royal Navy had previously swept). Two of the ships struck mines, resulting in heavy damage to the ships and 86 casualties (44 dead and 42 injured). The United Kingdom claimed that Albania was responsible for the mining, which Albania denied. We will deal with this aspect of the case later in this Chapter. In response to the incident, the British Navy again swept the Channel for mines. Albania (counter-)

claimed that this amounted to a violation of its territorial sovereignty. The ICJ discussed Albania's claim as follows, asking whether the U.K. had violated Albanian sovereignty by passing through the channel or by conducting the minesweeping operation.]

* * *

[The minesweeping operation] took place on November 12th and 13th. * * * The area swept was in Albanian territorial waters. * * *

The United Kingdom Government does not dispute that [the minesweeping operation] was carried out against the clearly expressed wish of the Albanian Government. It recognizes that the operation had not the consent of the international mine clearance organizations, that it could not be justified as the exercise of a right of innocent passage, and lastly that, in principle, international law does not allow a State to assemble a large number of warships in the territorial waters of another State and to carry out minesweeping in those waters. The United Kingdom Government states that the operation was one of extreme urgency, and that it considered itself entitled to carry it out without anybody's consent.

* * *

[The U.K. argued that the sweeping was justified because the U.K. had to obtain evidence to establish liability for the explosions that had occurred on October 22, 1946. According to the U.K., this was] a new and special application of the theory of intervention, by means of which the State intervening would secure possession of evidence in the territory of another State, in order to submit it to an international tribunal and thus facilitate its task.

The Court cannot accept such a line of defence. The Court can only regard the alleged right of intervention as the manifestation of a policy of force, such as has, in the past, given rise to most serious abuses and such as cannot, whatever be the present defects in international organization, find a place in international law. Intervention is perhaps still less admissible in the particular form it would take here; for, from the nature of things, it would be reserved for the most powerful States, and might easily lead to perverting the administration of international justice itself.

The United Kingdom Agent, in his speech in reply, has further classified "Operation Retail" among methods of self-protection or self-help. The Court cannot accept this defence either. Between independent States, respect for territorial sovereignty is an essential foundation of international relations. The Court recognizes that the Albanian Government's complete failure to carry out its duties after the explosions, and the dilatory nature of its diplomatic notes, are extenuating circumstances for the action of the United Kingdom Government. But to ensure respect for international law, of which it is the organ, the Court must declare that the action of the British Navy constituted a violation of Albanian sovereignty.

This declaration is in accordance with the request made by Albania through her Counsel, and is in itself appropriate satisfaction.

* * *

C. JURISDICTION

"The jurisdiction of courts is a branch of that which is possessed by the nation as an independent sovereign power."

The Schooner Exchange v. *McFaddon*, 11 U.S. 116 (1812)

From a lawyer's point of view, perhaps the most important element of sovereignty is that states have "jurisdiction." By "jurisdiction" here we mean a sovereign state's power to act through law. To be sure, this jurisdiction can take on different forms, e.g., the power to make law ("legislative" or "prescriptive" jurisdiction), to adjudicate cases ("judicial" jurisdiction) or to execute decisions ("jurisdiction to enforce"), etc., and these forms are subject to somewhat different rules. For present purposes, however, we need not distinguish between them. Instead, we pursue only the question of what international law has to say generally about sovereign states' power to act through law. Where does this power come from? What are its limits? On what bases can it be exercised?

THE BASIC RULE: THE *LOTUS* PRESUMPTION

The Case of the S.S. *Lotus* would be on every international lawyer's top ten list of the most important court decisions in international law because it is the foundation of our understanding of a sovereign state's jurisdiction.

Before turning to the decision itself, some background information may be useful to put it into context. After the end of World War I, the Treaty of Versailles established the League of Nations (1919), the predecessor to the United Nations (1945). In 1922, the League instituted a tribunal for the peaceful settlement of disputes between states called the Permanent Court of International Justice (PICJ), the predecessor of the current International Court of Justice (ICJ). Thus when the PICJ decided the *Lotus* Case in 1926, it spoke as the "World Court."

At the time, Turkey was a new state. After the decline and fall of the Ottoman Empire and a war of independence against various allies, Turkey emerged as an independent republic in 1922. It was internationally recognized in an agreement between Turkey and the allies (the United Kingdom, France, Italy, Japan, Greece, and Romania). The agreement was signed in Lausanne, Switzerland, and hence came to be known as the Lausanne Treaty of 1923. Article 15 of this Treaty provided that "all questions of jurisdiction shall, as between Turkey and the other contracting Powers, be decided in accordance with the principles of international law." In the *Lotus* case (between France and Turkey), this required the PCIJ to determine what these principles are.

THE CASE OF THE S.S. LOTUS
(FRANCE V. TURKEY)

Permanent Court of International Justice
1927 P.C.I.J. (ser. A) No. 10

* * *

THE FACTS

[13] According to the statements submitted to the Court by the Parties' Agents in their Cases and in their oral pleadings, the facts in which the affair originated are agreed to be as follows:

[14] On August 2nd, 1926, just before midnight, a collision occurred between the French mail steamer Lotus, proceeding to Constantinople, and the Turkish collier Boz–Kourt, between five and six nautical miles to the north of Cape Sigri (Mitylene). The Boz–Kourt, which was cut in two, sank, and eight Turkish nationals who were on board perished. After having done everything possible to succour the shipwrecked persons, of whom ten were able to be saved, the Lotus continued on its course to Constantinople, where it arrived on August 3rd.

[15] At the time of the collision, the officer of the watch on board the Lotus was Monsieur Demons, a French citizen, lieutenant in the merchant service and first officer of the ship, whilst the movements of the Boz–Kourt were directed by its captain, Hassan Bey, who was one of those saved from the wreck.

[16] As early as August 3rd the Turkish police proceeded to hold an enquiry into the collision on board the Lotus; and on the following day, August 4th, the captain of the Lotus handed in his master's report at the French Consulate–General, transmitting a copy to the harbour master.

[17] On August 5th, Lieutenant Demons was requested by the Turkish authorities to go ashore to give evidence. The examination, the length of which incidentally resulted in delaying the departure of the Lotus, led to the placing under arrest of Lieutenant Demons without previous notice being given to the French Consul–General—and Hassan Bey, amongst others. This arrest, which has been characterized by the Turkish Agent as arrest pending trial (arrestation preventive), was effected in order to ensure that the criminal prosecution instituted against the two officers, on a charge of manslaughter, by the Public Prosecutor of Stamboul, on the

complaint of the families of the victims of the collision, should follow its normal course.

[18] The case was first heard by the Criminal Court of Stamboul on August 28th. On that occasion, Lieutenant Demons submitted that the Turkish Courts had no jurisdiction; the Court, however, overruled his objection. When the proceedings were resumed on September 11th, Lieutenant Demons demanded his release on bail: this request was complied with on September 13th, the bail being fixed at 6,000 Turkish pounds.

[19] On September 15th, the Criminal Court delivered its judgment, the terms of which have not been communicated to the Court by the Parties. It is, however, common ground, that it sentenced Lieutenant Demons to eighty days' imprisonment and a fine of twenty-two pounds, Hassan Bey being sentenced to a slightly more severe penalty.

[20] It is also common ground between the Parties that the Public Prosecutor of the Turkish Republic entered an appeal against this decision, which had the effect of suspending its execution until a decision upon the appeal had been given; that such decision has not yet been given; but that the special agreement of October 12th, 1926, did not have the effect of suspending "the criminal proceedings * * * now in progress in Turkey."

[21] The action of the Turkish judicial authorities with regard to Lieutenant Demons at once gave rise to many diplomatic representations and other steps on the part of the French Government or its representatives in Turkey, either protesting against the arrest of Lieutenant Demons or demanding his release, or with a view to obtaining the transfer of the case from the Turkish Courts to the French Courts.

[22] As a result of these representations, the Government of the Turkish Republic declared on September 2nd, 1926, that "it would have no objection to the reference of the conflict of jurisdiction to the Court at The Hague."

[23] The French Government having, on the 6th of the same month, given "its full consent to the proposed solution," the two Governments appointed their plenipotentiaries with a view to the drawing up of the special agreement to be submitted to the Court; this special agreement was signed at Geneva on October 12th, 1926, as stated above, and the ratifications were deposited on December 27th, 1926.

* * *

THE LAW

* * *

[30] 5.—The prosecution was instituted in pursuance of Turkish legislation. The special agreement does not indicate what clause or clauses of

that legislation apply. No document has been submitted to the Court indicating on what article of the Turkish Penal Code the prosecution was based; the French Government however declares that the Criminal Court claimed jurisdiction under Article 6 of the Turkish Penal Code, and far from denying this statement, Turkey, in the submissions of her Counter-Case, contends that that article is in conformity with the principles of international law. It does not appear from the proceedings whether the prosecution was instituted solely on the basis of that article.

[31] Article 6 of the Turkish Penal Code runs as follows: [Translation]

"Any foreigner who * * * commits an offence abroad to the prejudice of Turkey or of a Turkish subject, for which offence Turkish law prescribes a penalty involving loss of freedom for a minimum period of not less than one year, shall be punished in accordance with the Turkish Penal Code provided that he is arrested in Turkey. The penalty shall however be reduced by one third and instead of the death penalty, twenty years of penal servitude shall be awarded. * * * "

* * *

II.   [VIOLATED PRINCIPLES OF INTERNATIONAL LAW]

[33] Having determined the position resulting from the terms of the special agreement, the Court must now ascertain which were the principles of international law that the prosecution of Lieutenant Demons could conceivably be said to contravene.

[34] It is Article 15 of the Convention of Lausanne of July 24th, 1923, respecting conditions of residence and business and jurisdiction, which refers the contracting Parties to the principles of international law as regards the delimitation of their respective jurisdiction.

[35] This clause is as follows:

"Subject to the provisions of Article 16, all questions of jurisdiction shall, as between Turkey and the other contracting Powers, be decided in accordance with the principles of international law."

* * *

III.   [FUNDAMENTAL PRINCIPLES OF INTERNATIONAL LAW]

[41] The Court, having to consider whether there are any rules of international law which may have been violated by the prosecution in pursuance of Turkish law of Lieutenant Demons, is confronted in the first place by a question of principle which, in the written and oral arguments of the two Parties, has proved to be a fundamental one. The French Government contends that the Turkish Courts, in order to have jurisdiction, should be able to point to some title to jurisdiction recognized by international law in favour of Turkey. On the other hand, the Turkish Government takes

the view that Article 15 allows Turkey jurisdiction whenever such jurisdiction does not come into conflict with a principle of international law.

[42] The latter view seems to be in conformity with the special agreement itself, No. I of which asks the Court to say whether Turkey has acted contrary to the principles of international law and, if so, what principles. According to the special agreement, therefore, it is not a question of stating principles which would permit Turkey to take criminal proceedings, but of formulating the principles, if any, which might have been violated by such proceedings.

[43] This way of stating the question is also dictated by the very nature and existing conditions of international law.

[44] International law governs relations between independent States. The rules of law binding upon States therefore emanate from their own free will as expressed in conventions or by usages generally accepted as expressing principles of law and established in order to regulate the relations between these co-existing independent communities or with a view to the achievement of common aims. Restrictions upon the independence of States cannot therefore be presumed.

[45] Now the first and foremost restriction imposed by international law upon a State is that—failing the existence of a permissive rule to the contrary—it may not exercise its power in any form in the territory of another State. In this sense jurisdiction is certainly territorial; it cannot be exercised by a State outside its territory except by virtue of a permissive rule derived from international custom or from a convention.

[46] It does not, however, follow that international law prohibits a State from exercising jurisdiction in its own territory, in respect of any case which relates to acts which have taken place abroad, and in which it cannot rely on some permissive rule of international law. Such a view would only be tenable if international law contained a general prohibition to States to extend the application of their laws and the jurisdiction of their courts to persons, property and acts outside their territory, and if, as an exception to this general prohibition, it allowed States to do so in certain specific cases. But this is certainly not the case under international law as it stands at present. Far from laying down a general prohibition to the effect that States may not extend the application of their laws and the jurisdiction of their courts to persons, property and acts outside their territory, it leaves them in this respect a wide measure of discretion, which is only limited in certain cases by prohibitive rules; as regards other cases, every State remains free to adopt the principles which it regards as best and most suitable.

[47] This discretion left to States by international law explains the great variety of rules which they have been able to adopt without objections or complaints on the part of other States; it is in order to remedy the diffi-

culties resulting from such variety that efforts have been made for many years past, both in Europe and America, to prepare conventions the effect of which would be precisely to limit the discretion at present left to States in this respect by international law, thus making good the existing lacunæ in respect of jurisdiction or removing the conflicting jurisdictions arising from the diversity of the principles adopted by the various States. In these circumstances all that can be required of a State is that it should not overstep the limits which international law places upon its jurisdiction; within these limits, its title to exercise jurisdiction rests in its sovereignty.

[48] It follows from the foregoing that the contention of the French Government to the effect that Turkey must in each case be able to cite a rule of international law authorizing her to exercise jurisdiction, is opposed to the generally accepted international law to which Article 13 of the Convention of Lausanne refers. Having regard to the terms of Article 15 and to the construction which the Court has just placed upon it, this contention would apply in regard to civil as well as to criminal cases, and would be applicable on conditions of absolute reciprocity as between Turkey and the other contracting Parties; in practice, it would therefore in many cases result in paralysing the action of the courts, owing to the impossibility of citing a universally accepted rule on which to support the exercise of their jurisdiction.

[49] Nevertheless, it has to be seen whether the foregoing considerations really apply as regards criminal jurisdiction, or whether this jurisdiction is governed by a different principle: this might be the outcome of the close connection which for a long time existed between the conception of supreme criminal jurisdiction and that of a State, and also by the especial importance of criminal jurisdiction from the point of view of the individual.

[50] Though it is true that in all systems of law the principle of the territorial character of criminal law is fundamental, it is equally true that all or nearly all these systems of law extend their action to offences committed outside the territory of the State which adopts them, and they do so in ways which vary from State to State. The territoriality of criminal law, therefore, is not an absolute principle of international law and by no means coincides with territorial sovereignty.

[51] This situation may be considered from two different standpoints corresponding to the points of view respectively taken up by the Parties. According to one of these standpoints, the principle of freedom, in virtue of which each State may regulate its legislation at its discretion, provided that in so doing it does not come in conflict with a restriction imposed by international law, would also apply as regards law governing the scope of jurisdiction in criminal cases. According to the other standpoint, the exclusively territorial character of law relating to this domain constitutes a

principle which, except as otherwise expressly provided, would, ipso facto, prevent States from extending the criminal jurisdiction of their courts beyond their frontiers; the exceptions in question, which include for instance extraterritorial jurisdiction over nationals and over crimes directed against public safety, would therefore rest on special permissive rules forming part of international law.

* * *

IV. [PROHIBITION OF PROSECUTION UNDER INTERNATIONAL LAW]

[55] The Court will now proceed to ascertain whether general international law, to which Article 15 of the Convention of Lausanne refers, contains a rule prohibiting Turkey from prosecuting Lieutenant Demons.

[56] For this purpose, it will in the first place examine the value of the arguments advanced by the French Government, without however omitting to take into account other possible aspects of the problem, which might show the existence of a restrictive rule applicable in this case.

[57] The arguments advanced by the French Government, other than those considered above, are, in substance, the three following:

(1) International law does not allow a State to take proceedings with regard to offences committed by foreigners abroad, simply by reason of the nationality of the victim; and such is the situation in the present case because the offence must be regarded as having been committed on board the French vessel.

* * *

[58] As regards the first argument, the Court feels obliged in the first place to recall that its examination is strictly confined to the specific situation in the present case, for it is only in regard to this situation that its decision is asked for.

[59] As has already been observed, the characteristic features of the situation of fact are as follows: there has been a collision on the high seas between two vessels flying different flags, on one of which was one of the persons alleged to be guilty of the offence, whilst the victims were on board the other.

[60] This being so, the Court does not think it necessary to consider the contention that a State cannot punish offences committed abroad by a foreigner simply by reason of the nationality of the victim. For this contention only relates to the case where the nationality of the victim is the only criterion on which the criminal jurisdiction of the State is based. Even if that argument were correct generally speaking—and in regard to this the Court reserves its opinion—it could only be used in the present case if international law forbade Turkey to take into consideration the

fact that the offence produced its effects on the Turkish vessel and consequently in a place assimilated to Turkish territory in which the application of Turkish criminal law cannot be challenged, even in regard to offences committed there by foreigners. But no such rule of international
law exists. No argument has come to the knowledge of the Court from
which it could be deduced that States recognize themselves to be under
an obligation towards each other only to have regard to the place where
the author of the offence happens to be at the time of the offence. On the
contrary, it is certain that the courts of many countries, even of countries
which have given their criminal legislation a strictly territorial character,
interpret criminal law in the sense that offences, the authors of which at
the moment of commission are in the territory of another State, are nevertheless to be regarded as having been committed in the national territory, if one of the constituent elements of the offence, and more especially
its effects, have taken place there. French courts have, in regard to a variety of situations, given decisions sanctioning this way of interpreting
the territorial principle. Again, the Court does not know of any cases in
which governments have protested against the fact that the criminal law
of some country contained a rule to this effect or that the courts of a country construed their criminal law in this sense. Consequently, once it is
admitted that the effects of the offence were produced on the Turkish vessel, it becomes impossible to hold that there is a rule of international law
which prohibits Turkey from prosecuting Lieutenant Demons because of
the fact that the author of the offence was on board the French ship.
Since, as has already been observed, the special agreement does not deal
with the provision of Turkish law under which the prosecution was instituted, but only with the question whether the prosecution should be regarded as contrary to the principles of international law, there is no reason preventing the Court from confining itself to observing that, in this
case, a prosecution may also be justified from the point of view of the so-
called territorial principle.

[61] Nevertheless, even if the Court had to consider whether Article 6 of
the Turkish Penal Code was compatible with international law, and if it
held that the nationality of the victim did not in all circumstances constitute a sufficient basis for the exercise of criminal jurisdiction by the State
of which the victim was a national, the Court would arrive at the same
conclusion for the reasons just set out. For even were Article 6 to be held
incompatible with the principles of international law, since the prosecution might have been based on another provision of Turkish law which
would not have been contrary to any principle of international law, it follows that it would be impossible to deduce from the mere fact that Article
6 was not in conformity with those principles, that the prosecution itself
was contrary to them. The fact that the judicial authorities may have
committed an error in their choice of the legal provision applicable to the
particular case and compatible with international law only concerns mu-

nicipal law and can only affect international law in so far as a treaty provision enters into account, or the possibility of a denial of justice arises.

* * *

Dissenting Opinion by M. Loder (the Netherlands) [Translation]

[95] Turkey, having arrested, tried and convicted a foreigner for an offence which he is alleged to have committed outside her territory, claims to have been authorized to do so by reason of the absence of a prohibitive rule of international law.

[96] Her defence is based on the contention that under international law everything which is not prohibited is permitted.

[97] In other words, on the contention that, under international law, every door is open unless it is closed by treaty or by established Custom.

[98] The Court in its judgment holds that this view is correct, well-founded, and in accordance with actual facts.

[99] I regret that I am unable to concur with the opinion of the Court.

* * *

[104] The family of nations consists of a collection of different sovereign and independent States.

[105] The fundamental consequence of their independence and sovereignty is that no municipal law, in the particular case under consideration no criminal law, can apply or have binding effect outside the national territory.

[106] This fundamental truth, which is not a custom but the direct and inevitable consequence of its premise, is a logical principle of law, and is a postulate upon which the mutual independence of States rests.

[107] The criminal law of a State applies in the first place to all persons within its territory, whether nationals or foreigners, because the right of jurisdiction over its own territory is an attribute of its sovereignty.

[108] The criminal law of a State may extend to crimes and offences committed abroad by its nationals, since such nationals are subject to the law of their own country; but it cannot extend to offences committed by a foreigner in foreign territory, without infringing the sovereign rights of the foreign State concerned, since in that State the State enacting the law has no jurisdiction.

[109] Nor can such a law extend in the territory of the State enacting it to an offence committed by a foreigner abroad should the foreigner happen to be in this territory after the commission of the offence, because the guilty act has not been committed within the area subject to the jurisdic-

tion of that State and the subsequent presence of the guilty person cannot have the effect of extending the jurisdiction of the State.

[110] It seems to me clear that such is the logical consequence of the fundamental principle above enunciated.

* * *

[117] It will appear from the foregoing that I am of opinion that for this reason alone, Turkey must be held to have acted in contravention of the principles of international law.

* * *

[121] Turkey argues from these facts that M. Demons, officer of the watch on board the Lotus, is guilty of manslaughter and that he is responsible for the death of the persons above mentioned.

[122] She argues that this offence took place on board the Boz–Kourt because it was there that the effects of the alleged negligence were felt.

[123] She therefore contends that the wrongful act having taken place on board the Turkish ship, its author is amenable to the jurisdiction of the Turkish Courts.

[124] If this argument be sound, in point of fact the deduction made from it is correct and the accusation of having acted contrary to the principles of international law at once falls to the ground, because every State is entitled to prosecute and sentence any foreigner who commits an offence within its territory. And the vessel Boz–Kourt must be regarded as Turkish territory.

[125] The question of the localization of the offence is therefore of capital importance for the purposes of the decision of the dispute before the Court.

[126] It is clear that the place where an offence has been committed is necessarily that where the guilty person is when he commits the act. The assumption that the place where the effect is produced is the place where the act was committed is in every case a legal fiction. It is, however justified where the act and its effect are indistinguishable, when there is a direct relation between them; for instance, a shot fired at a person on the other side of a frontier; a parcel containing an infernal machine intended to explode on being opened by the person to whom it is sent. The author of the crime intends in such cases to inflict injury at a place other than that where he himself is.

[127] But the case which the Court has to consider bears no resemblance to these instances. The officer of the Lotus, who had never set foot on board the Boz–Kourt, had no intention of injuring anyone, and no such

intention is imputed to him. The movements executed in the navigation of a vessel are only designed to avoid an accident.

[128] Only an investigation by naval experts into the circumstances can show whether the manner in which the ship was navigated is to be regarded as contrary to the regulations or negligent in some respect, or whether some unforeseen movement by the other vessel contributed to the accident—and this investigation is a matter solely for the naval authorities of the country of the person responsible for navigating the ship.

[129] In these circumstances, it seems to me that the legal fiction whereby the act is held to have been committed at the place where the effect is produced must be discarded.

* * *

[Five additional judges dissented on a variety of grounds, each writing a separate opinion.]

———————————

Eleven permanent judges participated in the *Lotus* case. In addition, Turkey was allowed to appoint an ad hoc judge to sit in the case, since one of the permanent judges was a French national. As you might guess, the specially appointed Turkish judge voted in favor of Turkey, while the French judge voted in favor of France. Without the ad hoc appointment of the Turkish judge, Turkey would have lost, 6–5.

Instead, the final vote tally was 6–6. The President, Judge Max Huber of Switzerland (whom we have met as the author of the *Island of Palmas* opinion), cast the deciding vote in favor of Turkey.

———————————

Now that you've read the case, what *is* the *Lotus* presumption? What are its effects for our thinking about the (international) jurisdiction of states? Doesn't the Court create a laissez faire regime (the late David Bederman, a prominent international law scholar, called it a "Wild West") in which states get away with pretty much everything? What, if anything, is going to restrain them?

Today, the specific issue litigated in the *Lotus* case is addressed by treaty. Article 97(1) of the United Nations Convention on the Law of the Sea (UNCLOS), provides that "[i]n the event of a collision or any other incident of navigation concerning a ship on the high seas, involving the penal or disciplinary responsibility of the master or of any other person in the service of the ship, no penal or disciplinary proceedings may be instituted against such person except before the judicial or administrative authorities either of the flag State or of the State of which such person is a national." Assuming that the Treaty applied to both France and Turkey, how would the *Lotus* case have been resolved under UNCLOS?

The logical consequence of the *Lotus* presumption is that states do not need to assert positive bases for jurisdiction; it is enough to stay out of prohibited territory. Yet positive bases of jurisdiction do play a role—and an important one at that—in international law. The two bases clearly recognized under the classical law of nations were territoriality and nationality (of the defendant). We take a look at both below.

Ask yourself what a state gets out of relying on one of these positive bases of jurisdiction. In other words, why don't states just rely on the *Lotus* presumption plain and simple?

Territoriality

As *Lotus* indicates, a state can exercise jurisdiction based on the territoriality principle, i.e., on the ground that it has (exclusive) sovereign power within its geographical boundaries. What exactly is the basis for the exercise of jurisdiction in the following case?

CARRICK V. HANCOCK
Queen's Bench (United Kingdom)
12 T.L.R. 59 (1895)

This was an action brought upon a foreign judgment. The facts were not in dispute, and the jury were consequently discharged. The plaintiff was an Englishman domiciled in Sweden. The defendant was likewise an Englishman, but resided and carried on his business at Newcastle. The action the judgment in which was now sued upon was commenced by the plaintiff in the Municipal Court of Gothenburg [Sweden] in the year 1889. It was brought to recover a sum of £900, more or less, which was the amount of commissions alleged to be due to the plaintiff under an agreement of February 9, 1888, whereby the plaintiff, on consideration of receiving a commission, undertook to transact business for the defendant in Sweden as his agent. The writ in this action was served upon the defendant during a short visit he was paying to that country, and he duly appeared to the writ. Though he did not himself remain in Sweden he was represented throughout the subsequent proceedings. He put in a defense and counterclaim, and on three separate occasions took his opponent to the Court of Appeal at Gota [Sweden]. The proceedings lasted till June, 1894, when final judgment was pronounced in favour of the plaintiff for £900, the amount claimed in the present action. The defendant pleaded that he was not at any time in the course of the action in which the plaintiff obtained the judgment a subject of or resident or domiciled in the kingdom of Sweden, but while temporarily present therein was served with process, and only appeared under pressure duress and compulsion of law; and that the said judgment was therefore void and inoperative, and contrary to natural justice, and ought not be enforced in this country.

* * *

The LORD CHIEF JUSTICE, at the close of the arguments, said that as the matter was now fully before him there would be nothing gained by his reserving his judgment, and he at once proceeded to deliver judgment in favour of the plaintiff. Having reviewed the cause of action and its various stages while before the Courts in Sweden and dealt with the arguments of the respective counsel, he observed that the jurisdiction of a Court was based upon the principle of territorial dominion, and that all persons within any territorial dominion owe their allegiance to its sovereign power and obedience to all its laws and to the lawful jurisdiction of its Courts. In his opinion that duty of allegiance was correlative to the protection given by a State to any person within its territory. This relationship and its inherent rights depended upon the fact of the person being within its territory. It seemed to him that the question of the time the person was actually in the territory was wholly immaterial. This being so it was quite clear that under the facts of this case it was properly and lawfully initiated, and all its subsequent proceedings were lawful and valid, and that the Swedish Courts had ample jurisdiction to enforce the plaintiff's claim against the defendant. Under these circumstances he held that both upon the principles of the comity of nations and that a foreign judgment creating a legal obligation upon a person will be enforced by these Courts, the plaintiff was here entitled to judgment for the same amount as had been awarded him by the Swedish Court of Appeal—viz., for £900—but if it was desired by the defendant he would grant a stay, but only upon the terms that security was given for the full debt and costs.

In *Burnham v. Superior Court*, 495 U.S. 604 (1990), the United States Supreme Court considered (personal) jurisdiction (to adjudicate) based on service of process within the state to be constitutional under the Due Process Clause of the Fourteenth Amendment, albeit in a purely domestic case. Is exercising jurisdiction over a defendant based solely on handing him a piece of paper in the forum state compatible with international law?

The Restatement (Third) of Foreign Relations says no:

> "Tag" jurisdiction, i.e., jurisdiction based on service of process on a person only transitorily in the territory of the state is not generally acceptable under international law. [While jurisdiction over a person can be based on "presence" in the forum, that] does not include merely transitory presence, such as while changing planes at an airport, coming on shore from a cruise ship, or a few days sojourn unconnect-

ed with the activity giving rise to rise to the claim. Restatement (Third) of Foreign Relations (1986), § 421 cmt. e.

The Restatement does not cite much support for this view. Is it convincing under the approach in *Lotus*?

Establishing personal jurisdiction by service of process in the forum state—i.e., by the sheer exercise of (temporary) territorial power over the defendant—is a common and longstanding practice, particularly in common law countries. It is by and large unknown and disfavored in civil law countries. Most civil law systems consider it an unjustified ("exorbitant") basis of jurisdiction. For example, such service of process is on the blacklist of "bad" forms of jurisdiction under EU law; member states are not forbidden from using it, but judgments based on it are not entitled to recognition (what an American lawyer would call "full faith and credit") in other member states. In short, if you, as an American plaintiff's lawyer, foresee that you may have to execute an American judgment in a foreign jurisdiction (because that is where the defendant's assets are), then beware how you establish personal jurisdiction in a U.S. court.

How does Justice Holmes, writing for the Supreme Court, employ the territoriality principle in the following case?

AMERICAN BANANA COMPANY V. UNITED FRUIT COMPANY

United States Supreme Court
213 U.S. 347 (1909)

JUSTICE HOLMES:

This is an action brought to recover threefold damages under the act to protect trade against monopolies. The circuit court dismissed the complaint upon motion, as not setting forth a cause of action. This judgment was affirmed by the circuit court of appeals, and the case then was brought to this court by writ of error.

The allegations of the complaint may be summed up as follows: The plaintiff is an Alabama corporation, organized in 1904. The defendant is a New Jersey corporation, organized in 1899. Long before the plaintiff was formed, the defendant, with intent to prevent competition and to control and monopolize the banana trade, bought the property and business of several of its previous competitors, with provision against their resuming the trade, made contracts with others, including a majority of the most important, regulating the quantity to be purchased and the price to be paid, and acquired a controlling amount of stock in still others. For the same purpose it organized a selling company, of which it held the stock, that by agreement sold at fixed prices all the bananas of the combining parties. By this and other means it did monopolize and restrain the trade and maintained unreasonable prices. * * *

As a result of the defendant's acts the plaintiff has been deprived of the use of the plantation, and the railway, the plantation, and supplies have been injured. The defendant also, by outbidding, has driven purchasers out of the market and has compelled producers to come to its terms, and it has prevented the plaintiff from buying for export and sale. This is the substantial damage alleged. There is thrown in a further allegation that the defendant has "sought to injure" the plaintiff's business by offering positions to its employees, and by discharging and threatening to discharge persons in its own employ who were stockholders of the plaintiff. But no particular point is made of this. It is contended, however, that, even if the main argument fails and the defendant is held not to be answerable for acts depending on the co-operation of the government of Costa Rica for their effect, a wrongful conspiracy resulting in driving the plaintiff out of business is to be gathered from the complaint, and that it was entitled to go to trial upon that.

It is obvious that, however stated, the plaintiff's case depends on several rather startling propositions. In the first place, the acts causing the damage were done, so far as appears, outside the jurisdiction of the United States, and within that of other states. It is surprising to hear it argued that they were governed by the act of Congress.

No doubt in regions subject to no sovereign, like the high seas, or to no law that civilized countries would recognize as adequate, such countries may treat some relations between their citizens as governed by their own law, and keep, to some extent, the old notion of personal sovereignty alive. They go further, at times, and declare that they will punish anyone, subject or not, who shall do certain things, if they can catch him, as in the case of pirates on the high seas. In cases immediately affecting national interests they may go further still and may make, and, if they get the chance, execute, similar threats as to acts done within another recognized jurisdiction. An illustration from our statutes is found with regard to criminal correspondence with foreign governments. And the notion that English statutes bind British subjects everywhere has found expression in modern times and has had some startling applications. But the general and almost universal rule is that the character of an act as lawful or unlawful must be determined wholly by the law of the country where the act is done. This principle was carried to an extreme in *Milliken v. Pratt*, 125 Mass. 374, 28 Am. Rep. 241. For another jurisdiction, if it should happen to lay hold of the actor, to treat him according to its own notions rather than those of the place where he did the acts, not only would be unjust, but would be an interference with the authority of another sovereign, contrary to the comity of nations, which the other state concerned justly might resent.

* * *

The foregoing considerations would lead, in case of doubt, to a construction of any statute as intended to be confined in its operation and effect to the territorial limits over which the lawmaker has general and legitimate power. "All legislation is prima facie territorial." Words having universal scope, such as "every contract in restraint of trade," "every person who shall monopolize," etc., will be taken, as a matter of course, to mean only everyone subject to such legislation, not all that the legislator subsequently may be able to catch. In the case of the present statute, the improbability of the United States attempting to make acts done in Panama or Costa Rica criminal is obvious, yet the law begins by making criminal the acts for which it gives a right to sue. We think it entirely plain that what the defendant did in Panama or Costa Rica is not within the scope of the statute so far as the present suit is concerned. Other objections of a serious nature are urged, but need not be discussed.

* * *

Further reasons might be given why this complaint should not be upheld, but we have said enough to dispose of it and to indicate our general point of view.

Judgment affirmed.

What if the parties in *American Banana* had been from Costa Rica but had committed the acts in the United States? Apparently, the statute would apply. Would such an application violate international law?

The traditional rule that federal statutes apply only within the territorial jurisdiction of the United States unless a contrary Congressional intent is clear was resoundingly affirmed by the Supreme Court in *EEOC v. Arabian–American Oil Co.*, 499 U.S. 244 (1991). The Court held that Title VII of the Civil Rights Act of 1964 did not apply extraterritorially to prohibit employment discrimination against an American citizen in Saudi Arabia. Congress promptly amended the statute so that Title VII now does apply to some discrimination in foreign countries as well. We will discuss the limits of extraterritorial application of U.S. laws in greater detail in Chapter VII.5.

In civil law nations, the principles of jurisdiction are generally found in civil and criminal codes (legislation) rather than in case law. How does the French approach compare to the American ground rules we have just seen?

PENAL CODE (FRANCE)

* * *

Article 113–2

French criminal law is applicable to all offenses committed within the territory of the French Republic.

An offense is deemed to have been committed within the territory of the French Republic where one of its constituent elements was committed within that territory.

Article 113–3

French criminal law is applicable to offenses committed on board ships flying the French flag, or committed against such ships, wherever they may be. It is the only applicable law in relation to offenses committed on board ships of the national navy, or against such ships, wherever they may be.

Article 113–4

French criminal law is applicable to offenses committed on board aircraft registered in France, or committed against such aircraft, wherever they may be. It is the only applicable law in relation to offenses committed on board French military aircraft, or against such aircraft, wherever they may be.

Article 113–5

French criminal law is applicable to any person who, within the territory of the French Republic, is guilty as an accomplice to a felony or misdemeanor committed abroad if the felony or misdemeanor is punishable both by French law and the foreign law, and if it was established by a final decision of the foreign court.

* * *

Nationality

A second uncontroversial basis for the exercise of jurisdiction is the nationality of the wrongdoer. According to the opinion below, what is the justification for this form of power? Does it matter that Mr. Blackmer had been residing abroad for many years?

BLACKMER V. UNITED STATES

United States Supreme Court
284 U.S. 421 (1932)

CHIEF JUSTICE HUGHES:

The petitioner, Harry M. Blackmer, a citizen of the United States resident in Paris, France, was adjudged guilty of contempt of the Supreme Court of the District of Columbia for failure to respond to subpoenas served upon him in France and requiring him to appear as a witness on behalf of the United States at a criminal trial in that court. Two subpoenas were issued, for appearances at different times, and there was a separate proceeding with respect to each. The two cases were heard together, and a fine of $30,000 with costs was imposed in each case, to be satisfied out of the property of the petitioner which had been seized by order of the court. The decrees were affirmed by the Court of Appeals of the District, and this Court granted writs of certiorari.

The subpoenas were issued and served, and the proceedings to punish for contempt were taken, under the provisions of the Act of July 3, 1926. The statute provided that whenever the attendance at the trial of a criminal action of a witness abroad, who is "a citizen of the United States or domiciled therein," is desired by the Attorney General, or any assistant or district attorney acting under him, the judge of the court in which the action is pending may order a subpoena to issue, to be addressed to a consul of the United States and to be served by him personally upon the witness with a tender of traveling expenses. Upon proof of such service and of the failure of the witness to appear, the court may make an order requiring the witness to show cause why he should not be punished for contempt, and, upon the issue of such an order, the court may direct that property belonging to the witness and within the United States may be seized and held to satisfy any judgment which may be rendered against him in the proceeding. Provision is made for personal service of the order upon the witness and also for its publication in a newspaper of general circulation in the district where the court is sitting. If, upon the hearing, the charge is sustained, the court may adjudge the witness guilty of contempt and impose upon him a fine not exceeding $100,000, to be satisfied by a sale of the property seized. This statute and the proceedings against the petitioner are assailed as being repugnant to the Constitution of the United States.

* * *

While it appears that the petitioner removed his residence to France in the year 1924, it is undisputed that he was, and continued to be, a citizen of the United States. He continued to owe allegiance to the United States. By virtue of the obligations of citizenship, the United States retained its authority over him, and he was bound by its laws made applicable to him in a foreign country. Thus, although resident abroad, the petitioner remained subject to the taxing power of the United States. For disobedience to its laws through conduct abroad, he was subject to punishment in the courts of the United States. With respect to such an exercise of authority, there is no question of international law, but solely of the purport of the municipal law which establishes the duties of the citizen in relation to his own government. While the legislation of the Congress, unless the contrary intent appears, is construed to apply only within the territorial jurisdiction of the United States, the question of its application, so far as citizens of the United States in foreign countries are concerned, is one of construction, not of legislative power. *American Banana Co. v. United Fruit Co.*, 213 U.S. 347, 357. Nor can it be doubted that the United States possesses the power inherent in sovereignty to require the return to this country of a citizen, resident elsewhere, whenever the public interest requires it, and to penalize him in case of refusal. What in England was the prerogative of the sovereign in this respect pertains under our constitutional system to the national authority which may be exercised by the Congress by virtue of the legislative power to prescribe the duties of the citizens of the United States. It is also beyond controversy that one of the duties which the citizen owes to his government is to support the administration of justice by attending its courts and giving his testimony whenever he is properly summoned. And the Congress may provide for the performance of this duty and prescribe penalties for disobedience.

* * *

Doesn't issuing a subpoena to a resident of Paris and subsequently seizing his property constitute a violation of the sovereignty of France? What if the property seized had been located in Paris?

What if Congress added a proviso to the antitrust statutes, making them applicable to acts committed by U.S. citizens or corporations abroad? Would such a rule violate international law? What if the acts were committed by foreigners (abroad)?

Does international law permit the United States to convict an eighteen-year-old American citizen for having sex with a seventeen-year-old Dutch girl for compensation during a trip to Amsterdam? Would your answer be different if the defendant were a U.S. permanent resident alien who is a citizen of Belgium? (See 18 U.S.C. § 2423(c), § 2423(f)(2) and 18 U.S.C. § 1591(c).) What if the act is not criminalized in the Netherlands?

Consider the French approach illustrated below. What would the result have been in *Blackmer* had the roles been reversed with a French court analyzing its power over a French citizen residing in the United States?

PENAL CODE (FRANCE)

* * *

Article 113–6

French criminal law is applicable to any felony committed by a French national outside the territory of the French Republic.

It is applicable to misdemeanors committed by French nationals outside the territory of the French Republic if the conduct is punishable under the legislation of the country in which it was committed.

The present article applies even if the offender has acquired French nationality after the commission of the offense of which he is accused.

* * *

NOTE ON CITIZENSHIP

In principle, every state determines for itself and under its own law whom it considers a citizen, and states differ widely in that regard. Citizenship is mostly acquired by birth. Some states grant citizenship through descent from one's parents (by "blood," *ius sanguinis*), others to all those born on its soil (*ius soli*), some recognize both grounds. Citizenship can also be acquired by naturalization. States impose varying requirements for naturalization, and some make it relatively easy (e.g., the United States for permanent resident aliens) while others make it extremely difficult (e.g., Japan). In addition, some countries allow dual citizenship, others forbid it. All this is generally left to domestic law.

International law comes into play mainly in two regards. First, it establishes a regime dealing with persons who are, for one reason or another, without any recognized citizenship, i.e., stateless. Since such persons cannot count on the protection of any state, international law provides a minimum of protection for them.

Second, international law determines whether the citizenship granted to an individual by a state is entitled to recognition by other states. This question can arise, for example, when one state exercises its right to protect its "citizen" against another state (or seeks compensation for injury to its "citizen" from another state), but that other state refuses to accept the person's asserted citizenship. The International Court of Justice tackled exactly that issue in the famous *Nottebohm* case between Liechtenstein and Guatemala.

Frederic Nottebohm was born in Hamburg, Germany in 1881 and was a German citizen. But he had spent virtually all his adult life and had all his business activities in Guatemala. Shortly after the outbreak of World War II, Nottebohm went briefly to Liechtenstein (where his brother lived), applied for citizenship and essentially bought it. He then returned to Guatemala. When Guatemala began to treat him as a German enemy alien in 1943 (e.g., by not letting him back into the country after a trip abroad), he invoked his Liechtenstein citizenship (Liechtenstein being a neutral country). Guatemala refused to recognize Nottebohm's Liechtenstein citizenship, and Liechtenstein brought suit against Guatemala in the ICJ after the war. The ICJ decided that Nottebohm lacked a genuine "bond of attachment" to Liechtenstein and held therefore that Guatemala did not have to recognize his naturalization by Liechtenstein. (*Liechtenstein v. Guatemala*, 1955 I.C.J. 4.)

What if Mr. Blackmer had been born in the United States to French parents during a brief vacation in New York (thus becoming a U.S. citizen by virtue of his birth on United States soil), had never claimed his U.S. citizenship, had never visited or maintained any ties with the United States, and always held himself out as a French citizen? Would the action taken against him by the federal district court (and upheld by the Supreme Court) in *Blackmer* violate international law?

We will later see that, today, citizenship is also an issue with regard to multinational corporations when they have ties with more than one state, e.g., through incorporation, headquarters, business operations or ownership (see Chapter VI.5.).

EXERCISE IN INTERNATIONAL JURISDICTION

Pierre, a Parisian (from France), sues Diallo, a Dakarian (from Senegal) in the *Tribunal de Grande Instance* in Paris for breach of a contract negotiated, made, and to be performed in Senegal. The court claims jurisdiction under art. 14 of the French *Code Civil*, which provides (in translation):

> A foreigner, even if not resident in France, may be called before the French courts for the execution of obligations resulting from contracts made in France with a Frenchman; he may be called before the courts of France for obligations resulting from contracts abroad with a Frenchman.

Diallo never appears before the French court and suffers a default judgment. Since he has no assets in France but a sizable bank account in New York, Pierre seeks to execute the French judgment there. It is a generally established rule that in order to be recognized, a (foreign) judgment must be based on proper jurisdiction. Diallo argues that the French courts lacked jurisdiction under international law. Pierre invokes the *Lotus* presumption and challenges Diallo to show a positive prohibition of French jurisdiction under international law. Who is right? If there is no violation of international law, could the United States still refuse to recognize the French judgment?

D. JURISDICTIONAL IMMUNITY

The classic American source on sovereign immunity is the Supreme Court's opinion in *The Schooner Exchange*. It also demonstrates one of the most important benefits of sovereignty—immunity in the courts of other states. What are the reasons for this privilege? What are the effects?

THE SCHOONER EXCHANGE v. McFADDON

United States Supreme Court
11 U.S. 116 (1812)

CHIEF JUSTICE MARSHALL:

THIS being a cause in which the sovereign right claimed by NAPOLEON, the reigning emperor of the French, and the political relations between the United States and France, were involved, it was, upon the suggestion of the Attorney General, ordered to a hearing in preference to other causes which stood before it on the docket. It was an appeal from the sentence of the Circuit Court of the United States, for the district of Pennsylvania, which reversed the sentence of the District Court, and ordered the vessel to be restored to the libellants.

The case was this—on the 24th of August, 1811, *John M'Faddon & William Greetham*, of the State of Maryland, filed their libel in the District Court of the United States, for the District of Pennsylvania, against the *Schooner Exchange*, setting forth that they were her sole owners, on the 27th of October, 1809, when she sailed from Baltimore, bound to St. Sebastians, in Spain. That while lawfully and peaceably pursuing her voyage, she was on the 30th of December, 1810, violently and forcibly taken by certain persons, acting under the decrees and orders of NAPOLEON, *Emperor of the French*, out of the custody of the libellants, and of their captain and agent, and was disposed of by those persons, or some of them, in violation of the rights of the libellants, and of the law of nations in that behalf. That she had been brought into the port of Philadelphia, and was then in the jurisdiction of the court, in possession of a certain *Dennis M. Begon*, her reputed captain or master. That no sentence or decree of condemnation had been pronounced against her, by any court of competent jurisdiction; but that the property of the libellants in her, remained unchanged and in full force. They therefore prayed the usual process of the court, to attach the vessel, and that she might be restored to them.

* * *

The jurisdiction of *courts* is a branch of that which is possessed by the nation as an independent sovereign power.

The jurisdiction of the nation within its own territory is necessarily exclusive and absolute. It is susceptible of no limitation not imposed by itself. Any restriction upon it, deriving validity from an external source, would imply a diminution of its sovereignty to the extent of the restriction, and an investment of that sovereignty to the same extent in that power which could impose such restriction.

All exceptions, therefore, to the full and complete power of a nation within its own territories, must be traced up to the consent of the nation itself. They can flow from no other legitimate source.

This consent may be either express or implied. In the latter case, it is less determinate, exposed more to the uncertainties of construction; but, if understood, not less obligatory.

The world being composed of distinct sovereignties, possessing equal rights and equal independence, whose mutual benefit is promoted by intercourse with each other, and by an interchange of those good offices which humanity dictates and its wants require, all sovereigns have consented to a relaxation in practice, in cases under certain peculiar circumstances, of that absolute and complete jurisdiction within their respective territories which sovereignty confers.

This consent may, in some instances, be tested by common usage, and by common opinion, growing out of that usage.

A nation would justly be considered as violating its faith, although that faith might not be expressly plighted, which should suddenly and without previous notice, exercise its territorial powers in a manner not consonant to the usages and received obligations of the civilized world.

This full and absolute territorial jurisdiction being alike the attribute of every sovereign, and being incapable of conferring extra-territorial power, would not seem to contemplate foreign sovereigns nor their sovereign rights as its objects. One sovereign being in no respect amenable to another; and being bound by obligations of the highest character not to degrade the dignity of his nation, by placing himself or its sovereign rights within the jurisdiction of another, can be supposed to enter a foreign territory only under an express license, or in the confidence that the immunities belonging to his independent sovereign station, though not expressly stipulated, are reserved by implication, and will be extended to him.

This perfect equality and absolute independence of sovereigns, and this common interest impelling them to mutual intercourse, and an interchange of good offices with each other, have given rise to a class of cases in which every sovereign is understood to wave [sic] the exercise of a part of that complete exclusive territorial jurisdiction, which has been stated to be the attribute of every nation.

1st. One of these is admitted to be the exemption of the person of the sovereign from arrest or detention within a foreign territory.

* * *

2d. A second case, standing on the same principles with the first, is the immunity which all civilized nations allow to foreign ministers.

* * *

3d. A third case in which a sovereign is understood to cede a portion of his territorial jurisdiction is, where he allows the troops of a foreign prince to pass through his dominions.

* * *

But the rule which is applicable to armies, does not appear to be equally applicable to ships of war entering the ports of a friendly power. The injury inseparable from the march of an army through an inhabited country, and the dangers often, indeed generally, attending it, do not ensue from admitting a ship of war, without special license, into a friendly port. A different rule therefore with respect to this species of military force has been generally adopted. If, for reasons of state, the ports of a nation generally, or any particular ports be closed against vessels of war generally, or the vessels of any particular nation, notice is usually given of such determination. If there be no prohibition, the ports of a friendly nation are considered as open to the public ships of all powers with whom it is at peace, and they are supposed to enter such ports and to remain in them while allowed to remain, under the protection of the government of the place.

* * *

To the Court, it appears, that where, without treaty, the ports of a nation are open to the private and public ships of a friendly power, whose subjects have also liberty without special license, to enter the country for business or amusement, a clear distinction is to be drawn between the rights accorded to private individuals or private trading vessels, and those accorded to public armed ships which constitute a part of the military force of the nation.

* * *

When private individuals of one nation spread themselves through another as business or caprice may direct, mingling indiscriminately with the inhabitants of that other, or when merchant vessels enter for the purposes of trade, it would be obviously inconvenient and dangerous to society, and would subject the laws to continual infraction, and the government to degradation, if such individuals or merchants did not owe temporary and local allegiance, and were not amenable to the jurisdiction of the country. Nor can the foreign sovereign have any motive for wishing such exemption. His subjects thus passing into foreign countries, are not employed by him, nor are they engaged in national pursuits. Consequently there are powerful motives for not exempting persons of this description from the jurisdiction of the country in which they are found, and no one motive for requiring it. The implied license, therefore, under which they enter can never be construed to grant such exemption.

But in all respects different is the situation of a public armed ship. She constitutes a part of the military force of her nation; acts under the immediate and direct command of the sovereign; is employed by him in national objects. He has many and powerful motives for preventing those objects from being defeated by the interference of a foreign state. Such interference cannot take place without affecting his power and his dignity. The implied license therefore under which such vessel enters a friendly port, may reasonably be construed, and it seems to the Court, ought to be construed, as containing an exemption from the jurisdiction of the sovereign, within whose territory she claims the rites of hospitality.

Upon these principles, by the unanimous consent of nations, a foreigner is amenable to the laws of the place; but certainly in practice, nations have not yet asserted their jurisdiction over the public armed ships of a foreign sovereign entering a port open for their reception.

* * *

Without indicating any opinion on this question, it may safely be assumed, that there is a manifest distinction between the private property of the person who happens to be a prince, and that military force which supports the sovereign power, and maintains the dignity and the independence of a nation. A prince, by acquiring private property in a foreign country, may possibly be considered as subjecting that property to the territorial jurisdiction; he may be considered as so far laying down the prince, and assuming the character of a private individual; but this he cannot be presumed to do with respect to any portion of that armed force, which upholds his crown, and the nation he is entrusted to govern.

* * *

It seems then to the Court, to be a principle of public law, that national ships of war, entering the port of a friendly power open for their reception, are to be considered as exempted by the consent of that power from its jurisdiction.

Without doubt, the sovereign of the place is capable of destroying this implication. He may claim and exercise jurisdiction either by employing force, or by subjecting such vessels to the ordinary tribunals. But until such power be exerted in a manner not to be misunderstood, the sovereign cannot be considered as having imparted to the ordinary tribunals a jurisdiction, which it would be a breach of faith to exercise. Those general statutory provisions therefore which are descriptive of the ordinary jurisdiction of the judicial tribunals, which give an individual whose property has been wrested from him, a right to claim that property in the courts of the country, in which it is found, ought not, in the opinion of this Court, to be so construed as to give them jurisdiction in a case, in which the sovereign power has impliedly consented to wave [sic] its jurisdiction.

The arguments in favor of this opinion which have been drawn from the general inability of the judicial power to enforce its decisions in cases of this description, from the consideration, that the sovereign power of the nation is alone competent to avenge wrongs committed by a sovereign, that the questions to which such wrongs give birth are rather questions of policy than of law, that they are for diplomatic, rather than legal discussion, are of great weight, and merit serious attention. But the argument has already been drawn to a length, which forbids a particular examination of these points.

The principles which have been stated, will now be applied to the case at bar.

In the present state of the evidence and proceedings, the Exchange must be considered as a vessel, which was the property of the Libellants, whose claim is repelled by the fact, that she is now a national armed vessel, commissioned by, and in the service of the emperor of France. The evidence of this fact is not controverted. But it is contended, that it constitutes no bar to an enquiry into the validity of the title, by which the emperor holds this vessel. Every person, it is alleged, who is entitled to property brought within the jurisdiction of our Courts, has a right to assert his title in those Courts, unless there be some law taking his case out of the general rule. It is therefore said to be the right, and if it be the right, it is the duty of the Court, to enquire whether this title has been extinguished by an act, the validity of which is recognized by national or municipal law.

If the preceding reasoning be correct, the Exchange, being a public armed ship, in the service of a foreign sovereign, with whom the government of the United States is at peace, and having entered an American port open for her reception, on the terms on which ships of war are generally permitted to enter the ports of a friendly power, must be considered as having come into the American territory, under an implied promise, that while necessarily within it, and demeaning herself in a friendly manner, she should be exempt from the jurisdiction of the country.

What is the legal basis for sovereign immunity in Justice Marshall's view? International Law? Domestic (U.S.) law? Mere voluntary deference to a foreign sovereign?

What can Mr. M'Faddon and Mr. Greetham, the (former?) owners of the ship do now? Can they sue France (or Napoleon) somewhere else?

What if the United States had been at war with France (on the British side—admittedly unlikely in 1812)?

3. OBLIGATIONS

Even the traditional concept of sovereignty never meant that a state could do whatever it wanted to whomever it wanted, even within its own borders. While statehood bestows rights and privileges, as indicated in the *Island of Palmas* arbitration, it also entails duties and responsibilities under international law. The list of these duties and responsibilities is long, but we will, again, only consider a few items that are so important that every lawyer should be aware of them.

A. PROTECTION OF DIPLOMATIC AND CONSULAR PERSONNEL AND PREMISES

The next case arose from a political crisis triggered by the storming of the U.S. embassy in Iran in 1979. That event followed a tumultuous period in Iran and a change not only in leadership, but also in the fundamental nature of the Iranian state itself.

Shah Mohammed Reza Pahlavi ruled Iran from 1941 until 1979, at times heavily supported by the United States. From October 1977 until January 1979, protests and strikes expanded throughout the country until the Shah went into exile in January 1979. Soon thereafter, Ayatollah Khomeini returned to Iran, and his supporters overthrew the monarchy. On April 1, 1979, by referendum, Iranians voted to become an Islamic Republic, and Ayatollah Khomeini was installed as Supreme Leader later that same year. Exiled to Egypt, the Shah ended up in the United States for medical treatment in the fall of 1979 against the strong objections of the Khomeini government. He later returned to Egypt where he died.

In November 1979, while the Shah was in the United States, a group of Iranian demonstrators (made up largely of students and militants) violently took over the United States embassy in Tehran. By the time the crisis had ended, they had held 52 Americans hostage for 444 days. Eventually, the crisis was resolved through a treaty regime known as the Algiers Accords, signed in January 1981.

The case below was brought by the United States against Iran in the International Court of Justice immediately after the hostage crisis began. As Iran did not formally appear in the case, the ICJ—acting in accordance with its Statute—sought to ensure that the claims made by the United States were supported by both facts and law. What does the excerpt below tell you about Iran's obligations to the United States?

CASE CONCERNING UNITED STATES DIPLOMATIC AND CONSULAR STAFF IN TEHRAN (UNITED STATES V. IRAN)

International Court of Justice
1980 I.C.J. 3

* * *

56. The principal facts material for the Court's decision on the merits of the present case have been set out earlier in this Judgment. Those facts have to be looked at by the Court from two points of view. First, it must determine how far, legally, the acts in question may be regarded as imputable to the Iranian State. Secondly, it must consider their compatibility or incompatibility with the obligations of Iran under treaties in force or under any other rules of international law that may be applicable. The events, which are the subject of the United States' claims, fall into two phases which it will be convenient to examine separately.

57. The first of these phases covers the armed attack on the United States Embassy by militants on 4 November 1979, the overrunning of its premises, the seizure of its inmates as hostages, the appropriation of its property and archives and the conduct of the Iranian authorities in the face of those occurrences. The attack and the subsequent overrunning, bit by bit, of the whole Embassy premises, was an operation which continued over a period of some three hours without any body of police, any military unit or any Iranian official intervening to try to stop or impede it from being carried through to its completion. The result of the attack was considerable damage to the Embassy premises and property, the forcible opening and seizure of its archives, the confiscation of the archives and other documents found in the Embassy and, most grave of all, the seizure by force of its diplomatic and consular personnel as hostages, together with two United States nationals.

58. No suggestion has been made that the militants, when they executed their attack on the Embassy, had any form of official status as recognized "agents" or organs of the Iranian State. Their conduct in mounting the attack, overrunning the Embassy and seizing its inmates as hostages cannot, therefore, be regarded as imputable to that State on that basis. Their conduct might be considered as itself directly imputable to the Iranian State only if it were established that, in fact, on the occasion in question the militants acted on behalf of the State, having been charged by some competent organ of the Iranian State to carry out a specific operation. The information before the Court does not, however, suffice to establish with the requisite certainty the existence at that time of such a link between the militants and any competent organ of the State.

* * *

61. The conclusion just reached by the Court, that the initiation of the attack on the United States Embassy on 4 November 1979, and of the attacks on the Consulates at Tabriz and Shiraz the following day, cannot be considered as in itself imputable to the Iranian State does not mean that Iran is, in consequence, free of any responsibility in regard to those attacks; for its own conduct was in conflict with its international obligations. By a number of provisions of the Vienna Conventions of 1961 and 1963, Iran was placed under the most categorical obligations, as a receiving State, to take appropriate steps to ensure the protection of the United States Embassy and Consulates, their staffs, their archives, their means of communication and the freedom of movement of the members of their staffs.

62. Thus, after solemnly proclaiming the inviolability of the premises of a diplomatic mission, Article 22 of the 1961 Convention continues in paragraph 2:

> *"The receiving State is under a special duty to take all appropriate steps to protect the premises of the mission against* any intrusion or damage and to prevent any disturbance of the peace of the mission or impairment of its dignity." (Emphasis added.)

So, too, after proclaiming that the person of a diplomatic agent shall be inviolable, and that he shall not be liable to any form of arrest or detention, Article 29 provides:

> "The receiving State shall treat him with due respect and *shall take all appropriate steps to prevent any attack on his person, freedom or dignity.*" (Emphasis added.)

The obligation of a receiving State to protect the inviolability of the archives and documents of a diplomatic mission is laid down in Article 24, which specifically provides that they are to be "inviolable at any time and wherever they may be." Under Article 25 it is required to "accord full facilities for the performance of the functions of the mission," under Article 26 to "ensure to all members of the mission freedom of movement and travel in its territory," and under Article 27 to "permit and protect free communication on the part of the mission for all official purposes." Analogous provisions are to be found in the 1963 Convention regarding the privileges and immunities of consular missions and their staffs (Art. 31, para. 3, Arts. 40, 33, 28, 34 and 35). In the view of the Court, the obligations of the Iranian Government here in question are not merely contractual obligations established by the Vienna Conventions of 1961 and 1963, but also obligations under general international law.

63. The facts set out in paragraphs 14 to 27 above establish to the satisfaction of the Court that on 4 November 1979 the Iranian Government failed altogether to take any "appropriate steps" to protect the premises, staff and archives of the United States' mission against attack by the mil-

itants, and to take any steps either to prevent this attack or to stop it before it reached its completion. They also show that on 5 November 1979
the Iranian Government similarly failed to take appropriate steps for the
protection of the United States Consulates at Tabriz and Shiraz. In addition they show, in the opinion of the Court, that the failure of the Iranian
Government to take such steps was due to more than mere negligence or
lack of appropriate means.

* * *

66. As to the actual conduct of the Iranian authorities when faced with
the events of 4 November 1979, the information before the Court establishes that, despite assurances previously given by them to the United
States Government and despite repeated and urgent calls for help, they
took no apparent steps either to prevent the militants from invading the
Embassy or to persuade or to compel them to withdraw. Furthermore,
after the militants had forced an entry into the premises of the Embassy,
the Iranian authorities made no effort to compel or even to persuade them
to withdraw from the Embassy and to free the diplomatic and consular
staff whom they had made prisoner.

67. This inaction of the Iranian Government by itself constituted clear
and serious violation of Iran's obligations to the United States under the
provisions of Article 22, paragraph 2, and Articles 24, 25, 26, 27 and 29 of
the 1961 Vienna Convention on Diplomatic Relations, and Articles 5 and
36 of the 1963 Vienna Convention on Consular Relations. Similarly, with
respect to the attacks on the Consulates at Tabriz and Shiraz, the inaction of the Iranian authorities entailed clear and serious breaches of its
obligations under the provisions of several further articles of the 1963
Convention on Consular Relations. So far as concerns the two private
United States nationals seized as hostages by the invading militants, that
inaction entailed, albeit incidentally, a breach of its obligations under Article II, paragraph 4, of the 1955 Treaty of Amity, Economic Relations,
and Consular Rights which, in addition to the obligations of Iran existing
under general international law, requires the parties to ensure "the most
constant protection and security" to each other's nationals in their respective territories.

68. The Court is therefore led inevitably to conclude, in regard to the first
phase of the events which has so far been considered, that on 4 November
1979 the Iranian authorities:

   (a) were fully aware of their obligations under the conventions in force
       to take appropriate steps to protect the premises of the United
       States Embassy and its diplomatic and consular staff from any at-
       tack and from any infringement of their inviolability, and to ensure
       the security of such other persons as might be present on the said
       premises;

(b) were fully aware, as a result of the appeals for help made by the United States Embassy, of the urgent need for action on their part;

(c) had the means at their disposal to perform their obligations;

(d) completely failed to comply with these obligations.

Similarly, the Court is led to conclude that the Iranian authorities were equally aware of their obligations to protect the United States Consulates at Tabriz and Shiraz, and of the need for action on their part, and similarly failed to use the means which were at their disposal to comply with their obligations.

69. The second phase of the events which are the subject of the United States' claims comprises the whole series of facts which occurred following the completion of the occupation of the United States Embassy by the militants, and the seizure of the Consulates at Tabriz and Shiraz. The occupation having taken place and the diplomatic and consular personnel of the United States' mission having been taken hostage, the action required of the Iranian Government by the Vienna Conventions and by general international law was manifest. Its plain duty was at once to make every effort, and to take every appropriate step, to bring these flagrant infringements of the inviolability of the premises, archives and diplomatic and consular staff of the United States Embassy to a speedy end, to restore the Consulates at Tabriz and Shiraz to United States control, and in general to re-establish the status quo and to offer reparation for the damage.

70. No such step was, however, taken by the Iranian authorities. At a press conference on 5 November the Foreign Minister, Mr. Yazdi, conceded that "according to international regulations the Iranian Government is duty bound to safeguard the life and property of foreign nationals." But he made no mention of Iran's obligation to safeguard the inviolability of foreign embassies and diplomats; and he ended by announcing that the action of the students "enjoys the endorsement and support of the government, because America herself is responsible for this incident." As to the Prime Minister, Mr. Bazargan, he does not appear to have made any statement on the matter before resigning his office on 5 November.

71. In any event expressions of approval of the take-over of the Embassy, and indeed also of the Consulates at Tabriz and Shiraz, by militants came immediately from numerous Iranian authorities, including religious, judicial, executive, police and broadcasting authorities. Above all, the Ayatollah Khomeini himself made crystal clear the endorsement by the State both of the take-over of the Embassy and Consulates and of the detention of the Embassy staff as hostages. At a reception in Qom on 5 November, the Ayatollah Khomeini left his audience in no doubt as to his approval of the action of the militants in occupying the Embassy, to which he said they had resorted "because they saw that the shah was allowed in Ameri-

ca." Saying that he had been informed that the "centre occupied by our young men * * * has been a lair of espionage and plotting," he asked how the young people could be expected "simply to remain idle and witness all these things." Furthermore he expressly stigmatized as "rotten roots" those in Iran who were "hoping we would mediate and tell the young people to leave this place." The Ayatollah's refusal to order "the young people" to put an end to their occupation of the Embassy, or the militants in Tabriz and Shiraz to evacuate the United States Consulates there, must have appeared the more significant when, on 6 November, he instructed "the young people" who had occupied the Iraqi Consulate in Kermanshah that they should leave it as soon as possible. The true significance of this was only reinforced when, next day, he expressly forbade members of the Revolutionary Council and all responsible officials to meet the special representatives sent by President Carter to try and obtain the release of the hostages and evacuation of the Embassy.

72. At any rate, thus fortified in their action, the militants at the Embassy at once went one step farther. On 6 November they proclaimed that the Embassy, which they too referred to as "the U.S. centre of plots and espionage," would remain under their occupation, and that they were watching "most closely" the members of the diplomatic staff taken hostage whom they called "U.S. mercenaries and spies."

73. The seal of official government approval was finally set on this situation by a decree issued on 17 November 1979 by the Ayatollah Khomeini. His decree began with the assertion that the American Embassy was "a centre of espionage and conspiracy" and that "those people who hatched plots against our Islamic movement in that place do not enjoy international diplomatic respect." He went on expressly to declare that the premises of the Embassy and the hostages would remain as they were until the United States had handed over the former Shah for trial and returned his property to Iran. This statement of policy the Ayatollah qualified only to the extent of requesting the militants holding the hostages to "hand over the blacks and the women, if it is proven that they did not spy, to the Ministry of Foreign Affairs so that they may be immediately expelled from Iran." As to the rest of the hostages, he made the Iranian Government's intentions all too clear:

> "The noble Iranian nation will not give permission for the release of the rest of them. Therefore, the rest of them will be under arrest until the American Government acts according to the wish of the nation."

74. The policy thus announced by the Ayatollah Khomeini, of maintaining the occupation of the Embassy and the detention of its inmates as hostages for the purpose of exerting pressure on the United States Government was complied with by other Iranian authorities and endorsed by them repeatedly in statements made in various contexts. The result of that pol-

icy was fundamentally to transform the legal nature of the situation created by the occupation of the Embassy and the detention of its diplomatic and consular staff as hostages. The approval given to these facts by the Ayatollah Khomeini and other organs of the Iranian State, and the decision to perpetuate them, translated continuing occupation of the Embassy and detention of the hostages into acts of that State. The militants, authors of the invasion and jailers of the hostages, had now become agents of the Iranian State for whose acts the State itself was internationally responsible. On 6 May 1980, the Minister for Foreign Affairs, Mr. Ghotbzadeh, is reported to have said in a television interview that the occupation of the United States Embassy had been "done by our nation." Moreover, in the prevailing circumstances the situation of the hostages was aggravated by the fact that their detention by the militants did not even offer the normal guarantees which might have been afforded by police and security forces subject to the discipline and the control of official superiors.

* * *

76. The Iranian authorities' decision to continue the subjection of the premises of the United States Embassy to occupation by militants and of the Embassy staff to detention as hostages, clearly gave rise to repeated and multiple breaches of the applicable provisions of the Vienna Conventions even more serious than those which arose from their failure to take any steps to prevent the attacks on the inviolability of these premises and staff.

77. In the first place, these facts constituted breaches additional to those already committed of paragraph 2 of Article 22 of the 1961 Vienna Convention on Diplomatic Relations which requires Iran to protect the premises of the mission against any intrusion or damage and to prevent any disturbance of its peace or impairment of its dignity. Paragraphs 1 and 3 of that Article have also been infringed, and continue to be infringed, since they forbid agents of a receiving State to enter the premises of a mission without consent or to undertake any search, requisition, attachment or like measure on the premises. Secondly, they constitute continuing breaches of Article 29 of the same Convention which forbids any arrest or detention of a diplomatic agent and any attack on his person, freedom or dignity. Thirdly, the Iranian authorities are without doubt in continuing breach of the provisions of Articles 25, 26 and 27 of the 1961 Vienna Convention and of pertinent provisions of the 1963 Vienna Convention concerning facilities for the performance of functions, freedom of movement and communications for diplomatic and consular staff, as well as of Article 24 of the former Convention and Article 33 of the latter, which provide for the absolute inviolability of the archives and documents of diplomatic missions and consulates. This particular violation has been made manifest to the world by repeated statements by the militants oc-

cupying the Embassy, who claim to be in possession of documents from the archives, and by various government authorities, purporting to specify the contents thereof. Finally, the continued detention as hostages of the two private individuals of United States nationality entails a renewed breach of the obligations of Iran under Article II, paragraph 4, of the 1955 Treaty of Amity, Economic Relations, and Consular Rights.

* * *

90. On the basis of the foregoing detailed examination of the merits of the case, the Court finds that Iran, by committing successive and continuing breaches of the obligations laid upon it by the Vienna Conventions of 1961 and 1963 on Diplomatic and Consular Relations, the Treaty of Amity, Economic Relations, and Consular Rights of 1955, and the applicable rules of general international law, has incurred responsibility towards the United States. As to the consequences of this finding, it clearly entails an obligation on the part of the Iranian State to make reparation for the injury thereby caused to the United States. Since however Iran's breaches of its obligations are still continuing, the form and amount of such reparation cannot be determined at the present date.

* * *

The court found, inter alia, that Iran must "make reparation for the injury * * * caused to the United States," but it left the form and amount open. Once an amount is determined, what can the United States do if Iran simply doesn't pay? Send the Marines?

B. THE PROTECTION OF ALIENS

JAMES HATHAWAY, THE RIGHTS OF REFUGEES UNDER INTERNATIONAL LAW
(2005)

* * *

The emergence of nation-states in the sixteenth century provided the context within which to formalize [the] ad hoc pattern of special rights granted to traders by various European rulers. Governments undertook the bilateral negotiation of treaties in which safe passage and basic civil rights were mutually guaranteed to merchants and others wishing to do business or to travel in the partner state. By the late nineteenth century, a network of "friendship, commerce, and navigation" treaties consistently guaranteed certain critical aspects of human dignity to aliens admitted to most trading states. Because these agreements were pervasively implemented in the domestic laws of state parties, certain human rights universally guaranteed to aliens were identified as general principles of law. These included recognition of the alien's juridical personality, respect for life and physical integrity, and personal and spiritual liberty within socially bearable limits. Aliens were afforded no political rights, though resident aliens were subject to reasonable public duties. In the economic sphere, there was a duty of non-discrimination among categories of aliens where they were allowed to engage in commercial activity. There was also an obligation to provide adequate compensation for denial of property rights where aliens were allowed to acquire private property. Finally, aliens were to be granted access to a fair and non-discriminatory judicial system to enforce these basic rights.

* * *

The general principles that emerged from the network of interstate arrangements on the protection of aliens do not, however, endow aliens themselves with rights and remedies. International aliens law was conceived very much within the traditional contours of international law: the rights created are the rights of national states, enforced at their discretion under the rules of diplomatic protection and international arbitration. While injured aliens may benefit indirectly from the assertion of claims by their national state, they can neither require action to be taken to vindicate their loss, nor even compel their state to share with them whatever damages are recovered in the event of a successful claim. The theory underlying international aliens law is not the need to restore the alien to a pre-injury position. As summarized by Brierly, the system reflects "the plain truth that the injurious results of a denial of justice are not, or at any rate are not necessarily, confined to the individual sufferer or his family, but include such consequences as the mistrust and lack of safety felt by other foreigners similarly situated."

* * *

As Hathaway explains, it has long been recognized in international law that states have an obligation to protect aliens on their territory, at least against some forms of harm. It has also long been recognized that in case of a breach of this obligation, an alien's country of nationality has a right to bring a claim against the offending state. This is known as the right of diplomatic protection (or espousal). The case below is an example of such a claim. Who is suing whom here? Why didn't Roberts sue in Mexican courts?

THE UNITED STATES OF AMERICA ON BEHALF OF HARRY ROBERTS, CLAIMANT V. THE UNITED MEXICAN STATES

General Claims Commission—United States and Mexico
4 U.N. Rep. Intl. Arb. Awards 77 (1926)

1. This claim is presented by the United States of America in behalf of Harry Roberts, an American citizen who, it is alleged in the memorial, was arbitrarily and illegally arrested by Mexican authorities, who held him prisoner for a long time in contravention of Mexican law and subjected him to cruel and inhumane treatment throughout the entire period of confinement.

2. From the memorial filed by the Government of the United States and accompanying documents, the allegations upon which the claim is based are briefly stated as follows: Harry Roberts, together with a number of other persons, was arrested by Mexican Federal troops on May 12, 1922, in the vicinity of Ocampo, Tamaulipas, Mexico, charged with having taken part in an assault on the house of E. F. Watts, near Ebano, San Luis Potosi, Mexico, on the night of May 5, 1922. The claimant was taken prisoner and brought to Tampico, whence he was taken to Ciudad Valles, San Luis Potosi, where he was held under detention, until he was placed at liberty on December 16, 1923, a period of nearly nineteen months. It is alleged that there were undue delays in the prosecution of the trial of the accused which was not instituted within one year from the time of his arrest, as required by the Constitution of Mexico. These delays were brought to the notice of the Government of Mexico, but no corrective measures were taken. During the entire period of imprisonment, he was subjected to rude and cruel treatment from which he suffered great physical pain and mental anguish.

3. The United States asks that an indemnity be paid by the Government of Mexico in the sum of $10,000.00 for the wrongful treatment of the accused. It is stated in the memorial that Roberts earned prior to the time of his arrest $350.00 a month; that he would have earned $6,650.00 during the nineteen months that he was under arrest; and that he spent $1,000.00 in fees paid to a lawyer resident in the United States to assist in obtaining his release. A total indemnity is asked in the sum of $17,650.00 together with a proper allowance of interest.

* * *

5. It does not appear from this evidence that the Mexican authorities had not serious grounds for apprehending Roberts and his companions. * * *

6. The Commission is not called upon to reach a conclusion whether Roberts committed the crime with which he was charged. The determination of that question rested with the Mexican judiciary, and it is distinct from the question whether the Mexican authorities had just cause to arrest Roberts and to bring him to trial. Aliens of course are obliged to submit to

proceedings properly instituted against them in conformity with local laws. In the light of the evidence presented in the case the Commission is of the opinion that the Mexican authorities had ample grounds to suspect that Harry Roberts had committed a crime and to proceed against him as they did. The Commission therefore holds that the claim is not substantiated with respect to the charge of illegal arrest.

7. In order to pass upon the complaint with reference to an excessive period of imprisonment, it is necessary to consider whether the proceedings instituted against Roberts while he was incarcerated exceeded reasonable limits within which an alien charged with crime may be held in custody pending the investigation of the charge against him. Clearly there is no definite standard prescribed by international law by which such limits may be fixed. Doubtless an examination of local laws fixing a maximum length of time within which a person charged with crime may be held without being brought to trial may be useful in determining whether detention has been unreasonable in a given case. The Mexican Constitution of 1917, provides by its Article 20, section 8, that a person accused of crime "must be judged within four months if he is accused of a crime the maximum penalty for which may not exceed two years' imprisonment, and within one year if the maximum penalty is greater." From the judicial records presented by the Mexican Agent it clearly appears that there was a failure of compliance with this constitutional provision, since the proceedings were instituted on May 17, 1922, and that Roberts had not been brought to trial on December 16, 1923, the date when he was released. * * *

8. With respect to the charge of ill-treatment of Roberts, it appears from evidence submitted by the American Agency that the jail in which he was kept was a room thirty-five feet long and twenty feet wide with stone walls, earthen floor, straw roof, a single window, a single door and no sanitary accommodations, all the prisoners depositing their excrement in a barrel kept in a corner of the room; that thirty or forty men were at times thrown together in this single room; that the prisoners were given no facilities to clean themselves; that the room contained no furniture except that which the prisoners were able to obtain by their own means; that they were afforded no opportunity to take physical exercise; and that the food given them was scarce, unclean and of the coarsest kind. The Mexican Agency did not present evidence disproving that such conditions existed in the jail. It was stated by the Agency that Roberts was accorded the same treatment as that given to all other persons, and with respect to the food Roberts received, it was observed in the answer that he was given "the food that was believed necessary, and within the means of the municipality." All of the details given by Roberts in testimony which accompanies the memorial with respect to the conditions of the jail are corroborated by a statement of the American Consul at Tampico who visited the jail. Facts with respect to equality of treatment of aliens and nation-

als may be important in determining the merits of a complaint of mistreatment of an alien. But such equality is not the ultimate test of the propriety of the acts of authorities in the light of international law. That test is, broadly speaking, whether aliens are treated in accordance with ordinary standards of civilization. We do not hesitate to say that the treatment of Roberts was such as to warrant an indemnity on the ground of cruel and inhumane imprisonment.

9. The respondent Government has not denied that, under the convention of September 8, 1923, acts of authorities of San Luis Potosi may give rise to claims against the Government of Mexico. The Commission is of the opinion that claims can be predicated on such acts.

10. As has been stated, the Commission holds that damages may be assessed on two of the grounds asserted in the American memorial, namely, (1) excessively long imprisonment—with which the Mexican Government is clearly chargeable for a period of seven months, and (2) cruel and inhumane treatment suffered by Roberts in jail during nineteen months. After careful consideration of the facts of the case and of similar cases decided by international tribunals, the Commission is of the opinion that a total sum of $8,000.00 is a proper indemnity to be paid in satisfaction of this claim.

DECISION

11. For the reasons stated above the Commission decides that the Government of the United Mexican States must pay to the Government of the United States of America on behalf of Harry Roberts $8,000.00 (eight thousand dollars) without interest.

Done at Washington, D. C, this 2nd day of November, 1926.

C. Van Vollenhoven,

Presiding Commissioner.

Fred K. Nielsen,

Commissioner,

G. Fernández MacGregor,

Commissioner.

———————

Who gets the money awarded for Mexico's violations against Roberts? What are Mexico's obligations to Roberts, and what sources of law do the commissioners turn to in identifying those obligations? What do the commissioners who drafted this opinion suggest that Mexico will have to do if it wants to detain aliens in the future in compliance with international law?

C. PREVENTION OF ENVIRONMENTAL HARM TO OTHER STATES

The question of whether a state is under an international obligation to refrain from causing environmental damage to other states is one of the most salient issues in the world today. Although, more often than not, the issue arises in the diplomatic and regulatory contexts, the decision below, rendered by an arbitral tribunal two generations ago, is widely considered the starting point of international environmental law. In reading the following document notice that it has two distinct parts—an excerpt from a bilateral treaty and an excerpt from an arbitral decision rendered under the treaty.

TRAIL SMELTER ARBITRATION (UNITED STATES V. CANADA)
Trail Smelter Arbitration Tribunal
3 U.N. Rep. Intl. Arb. Awards 1905 (1938 & 1941)

CONVENTION FOR SETTLEMENT OF DIFFICULTIES ARISING FROM OPERATION OF SMELTER AT TRAIL, B.C.

Signed at Ottawa, April 15, 1935; ratifications exchanged Aug. 3, 1935

The President of the United States of America, and His Majesty the King of Great Britain, Ireland and the British dominions beyond the Seas, Emperor of India, in respect of the Dominion of Canada.

Considering that the Government of the United States has complained to the Government of Canada that fumes discharged from the smelter of the Consolidated Mining and Smelting Company at Trail, British Columbia, have been causing damage in the State of Washington, and

Considering further that the International Joint Commission, established pursuant to the Boundary Waters Treaty of 1909, investigated problems arising from the operation of the smelter at Trail and rendered a report and recommendations thereon, dated February 28, 1931, and

Recognizing the desirability and necessity of effecting a permanent settlement,

Have decided to conclude a convention for the purposes aforesaid * * *

Article III

The Tribunal shall finally decide the questions, hereinafter referred to as "the Questions," set forth hereunder, namely:

(1) Whether damage caused by the Trail Smelter in the State of Washington has occurred since the first day of January, 1932, and, if so, what indemnity should be paid therefor?

(2) In the event of the answer to the first part of the preceding Question being in the affirmative, whether the Trail Smelter should be required to refrain from causing damage in the State of Washington in the future and, if so, to what extent?

(3) In the light of the answer to the preceding Question, what measures or regime, if any, should be adopted or maintained by the Trail Smelter?

(4) What indemnity or compensation, if any, should be paid on account of any decision or decisions rendered by the Tribunal pursuant to the next two preceding Questions?

* * *

ARBITRAL DECISION

* * *

The second question under Article III of the Convention is as follows:

> In the event of the answer to the first part of the preceding question being in the affirmative, whether the Trail Smelter should be required to refrain from causing damage in the State of Washington in the future and, if so, to what extent?

Damage has occurred since January 1, 1932, as fully set forth in the previous decision. To that extent, the first part of the preceding question has thus been answered in the affirmative. [The Tribunal discussed a Swiss decision and several American cases.]

* * *

The Tribunal, therefore, finds that the above decisions, taken as whole, constitute an adequate basis for its conclusions, namely, that, under the principles of international law, as well as of the law of the United States, no State has the right to use or permit the use of its territory in such a manner as to cause injury by fumes in or to the territory of another or the properties or persons therein, when the case is of serious consequence and the injury is established by clear and convincing evidence.

* * *

Considering the circumstances of the case, the Tribunal holds that the Dominion of Canada is responsible in international law for the conduct of the Trail Smelter. Apart from the undertakings in the convention, it is, therefore, the duty of the Government of the Dominion of Canada to see to it that this conduct should be in conformity with the obligation of the Dominion under international law as herein determined.

The Tribunal, therefore, answers Question No. 2 as follows: (2) So long as the present conditions in the Columbia River Valley prevail, the Trail

Smelter shall be required to refrain from causing any damage through fumes in the State of Washington, the damage herein referred to and its extent being such as would be recoverable under the decisions of the courts of the United States in suits between private individuals. The indemnity for such damage should be fixed in such manner as the Governments, acting under Article XI of the Convention, should agree upon.

* * *

According to this decision, when is a state under an international obligation to avoid damage to a neighboring (or other) state? Who should decide whether the standards announced here are met? According to what criteria?

D. RESPONSIBILITY FOR BREACHES OF INTERNATIONAL LAW

The modern foundations of state responsibility for breaches of international law were laid in litigation between Germany and Poland before the Permanent Court of International Justice (PCIJ) in the late 1920s. The story is complex, but for our present purpose, the bare essentials suffice.

In the aftermath of World War I, Poland acquired some formerly German territory in a region called Upper Silesia, including the town of Chorzów. In this context, Poland took over a German-owned factory, which was of considerable strategic importance. Germany complained that this takeover violated certain provisions of the Versailles Treaty as well as a particular Convention concluded between Germany and Poland in Geneva in 1922. Germany eventually sued Poland for compensation in the PCIJ. The litigation generated several judgments.

In a decision issued in 1927, the Court formulated the fundamental principle of state responsibility in language which has been quoted innumerable times:

> It is a principle of international law that the breach of an engagement involves an obligation to make reparation in an adequate form. Reparation therefore is the indispensable complement of a failure to apply a convention, and there is no necessity for this to be stated in the convention itself.

Factory at Chorzów (*Germany v. Poland*) 1927 P.C.I.J. (ser. A) No. 9, at 21.

In a later decision, the Court explained this principle in greater detail. What does the excerpt below add to this general statement?

CASE CONCERNING THE FACTORY AT CHORZÓW
(GERMANY V. POLAND)

Permanent Court of International Justice
1928 P.C.I.J. (ser. A) No. 17

* * *

It is a principle of international law that the reparation of a wrong may consist in an indemnity corresponding to the damage which the nationals of the injured State have suffered as a result of the act which is contrary to international law. This is even the most usual form of reparation; it is the form selected by Germany in this case and the admissibility of it has not been disputed. The reparation due by one State to another does not however change its character by reason of the fact that it takes the form of an indemnity for the calculation of which the damage suffered by a private person is taken as the measure. The rules of law governing the reparation are the rules of international law in force between the two States concerned, and not the law governing relations between the State which has committed a wrongful act and the individual who has suffered damage. Rights or interests of an individual the violation of which rights causes damage are always in a different plane to rights belonging to a State, which rights may also be infringed by the same act. The damage suffered by an individual is never therefore identical in kind with that which will be suffered by a State; it can only afford a convenient scale for the calculation of the reparation due to the State.

* * *

The essential principle contained in the actual notion of an illegal act—a principle which seems to be established by international practice and in particular by the decisions of arbitral tribunals—is that reparation must, as far as possible, wipe out all the consequences of the illegal act and re-establish the situation which would, in all probability, have existed if that act had not been committed. Restitution in kind, or, if this is not possible, payment of a sum corresponding to the value which a restitution in kind would bear; the award, if need be, of damages for loss sustained which would not be covered by restitution in kind or payment in place of it—such are the principles which should serve to determine the amount of compensation due for an act contrary to international law.

* * *

———————

State responsibility under international law also played a central role in the first case heard in the International Court of Justice (ICJ). The case arose from events in the Corfu Channel in the fall of 1948 in the early stages of the Cold War.

THE CORFU CHANNEL CASE
(UNITED KINGDOM V. ALBANIA)

International Court of Justice
1949 I.C.J. 4

[To remind yourself of the basic facts leading to this litigation, go back to sub-chapter 2.B. where we first encountered the *Corfu Channel Case*. Remember that the United Kingdom claimed that Albania was responsible for the mines that had damaged the British warships. Britain further maintained that, at a minimum, Albania must have known of the mines and had failed to warn the approaching British ships. The United Kingdom thus sued Albania for £875,000 in damages.

Most of the case brought by the United Kingdom is concerned with evidentiary issues, i.e., with burdens and requisite levels of proof. Ultimately, it remained unclear exactly who had laid the mines. The ICJ concluded, however, that Albania must at least have known of their existence. According to the ICJ, what obligations did Albania have to Great Britain as result?]

* * *

The obligations incumbent upon the Albanian authorities consisted in notifying, for the benefit of shipping in general, the existence of a minefield in Albanian territorial waters and in warning the approaching British warships of the imminent danger to which the minefield exposed them. Such obligations are based, not on the Hague Convention of 1907, No. VIII, which is applicable in time of war, but on certain general and well-recognized principles, namely: elementary considerations of humanity, even more exacting in peace than in war; the principle of the freedom of maritime communication; and every State's obligation not to allow knowingly its territory to be used for acts contrary to the rights of other States.

In fact, Albania neither notified the existence of the minefield, nor warned the British warships of the danger they were approaching.

* * *

In fact, nothing was attempted by the Albanian authorities to prevent the disaster. These grave omissions involve the international responsibility of Albania.

The Court therefore reaches the conclusion that Albania is responsible under international law for the explosions which occurred on October 22nd, 1946, in Albanian waters, and for the damage and loss of human life which resulted from them, and that there is a duty upon Albania to pay compensation to the United Kingdom.

* * *

—————————

The ICJ eventually awarded the United Kingdom £843,947 (at the time more than $2,000,000) in damages against Albania. What does the *Corfu Channel Case* tell you about state responsibility under international law?

Today, the basics of state responsibility under international law are codified, albeit in non-binding form, in the Articles on Responsibility of States for Internationally Wrongful Acts. The Articles were drafted by the International Law Commission (ILC), a UN-chartered body with the mission of developing and codifying principles of international law. Like the American Law Institute's drafting of Restatements of Law which aggregate and distill the common law principles prevailing in the United States, the ILC's work focuses on themes and principles in the field of international law. Just as the ALI uses Reporters to draft the content of the Restatement, the ILC uses a Drafting Committee.

There is no need to memorize these rules in detail. However, think about and be ready to explain in class which of these articles would apply (and how) in the three decisions by the World Court in this Chapter, i.e., (1) *The Tehran Embassy Case*, (2) *The Chorzów Factory Case*, and (3) The *Corfu Channel Case*. Which articles would apply in the *Harry Roberts Case*? To what extent could these cases be "solved" by applying the Articles below?

ARTICLES ON RESPONSIBILITY OF STATES FOR INTERNATIONALLY WRONGFUL ACTS

International Law Commission (2001)

Part One

The Internationally Wrongful Act of a State

Chapter I

General principles

Article 1

Responsibility of a State for its internationally wrongful acts

Every internationally wrongful act of a State entails the international responsibility of that State.

Article 2

Elements of an internationally wrongful act of a State

There is an internationally wrongful act of a State when conduct consisting of an action or omission:

(a) is attributable to the State under international law; and

(b) constitutes a breach of an international obligation of the State.

Article 3

Characterization of an act of a State as internationally wrongful

The characterization of an act of a State as internationally wrongful is governed by international law. Such characterization is not affected by the characterization of the same act as lawful by internal law.

CHAPTER II

Attribution of conduct to a State

Article 4

Conduct of organs of a State

1. The conduct of any State organ shall be considered an act of that State under international law, whether the organ exercises legislative, executive, judicial or any other functions, whatever position it holds in the organization of the State, and whatever its character as an organ of the central government or of a territorial unit of the State.

2. An organ includes any person or entity which has that status in accordance with the internal law of the State.

Article 5

Conduct of persons or entities exercising elements of governmental authority

The conduct of a person or entity which is not an organ of the State under article 4 but which is empowered by the law of that State to exercise elements of the governmental authority shall be considered an act of the State under international law, provided the person or entity is acting in that capacity in the particular instance.

Article 6

Conduct of organs placed at the disposal of a State by another State

The conduct of an organ placed at the disposal of a State by another State shall be considered an act of the former State under international law if the organ is acting in the exercise of elements of the governmental authority of the State at whose disposal it is placed.

Article 7

Excess of authority or contravention of instructions

The conduct of an organ of a State or of a person or entity empowered to exercise elements of the governmental authority shall be considered an act of the State under international law if the organ, person or entity acts in that capacity, even if it exceeds its authority or contravenes instructions.

Article 8

Conduct directed or controlled by a State

The conduct of a person or group of persons shall be considered an act of a State under international law if the person or group of persons is in fact acting on the instructions of, or under the direction or control of, that State in carrying out the conduct.

Article 9

Conduct carried out in the absence or default of the official authorities

The conduct of a person or group of persons shall be considered an act of a State under international law if the person or group of persons is in fact exercising elements of the governmental authority in the absence or default of the official authorities and in circumstances such as to call for the exercise of those elements of authority.

Article 10

Conduct of an insurrectional or other movement

1. The conduct of an insurrectional movement which becomes the new government of a State shall be considered an act of that State under international law.

2. The conduct of a movement, insurrectional or other, which succeeds in establishing a new State in part of the territory of a pre-existing State or in a territory under its administration shall be considered an act of the new State under international law.

3. This article is without prejudice to the attribution to a State of any conduct, however related to that of the movement concerned, which is to be considered an act of that State by virtue of articles 4 to 9.

Article 11

Conduct acknowledged and adopted by a State as its own

Conduct which is not attributable to a State under the preceding articles shall nevertheless be considered an act of that State under international law if and to the extent that the State acknowledges and adopts the conduct in question as its own.

* * *

Part Two

Content of the International Responsibility of a State

Chapter I

General principles

Article 28

Legal consequences of an internationally wrongful act

The international responsibility of a State which is entailed by an internationally wrongful act in accordance with the provisions of Part One involves legal consequences as set out in this Part.

Article 29

Continued duty of performance

The legal consequences of an internationally wrongful act under this Part do not affect the continued duty of the responsible State to perform the obligation breached.

Article 30

Cessation and non-repetition

The State responsible for the internationally wrongful act is under an obligation:

(a) to cease that act, if it is continuing;

(b) to offer appropriate assurances and guarantees of non-repetition, if circumstances so require.

Article 31

Reparation

1. The responsible State is under an obligation to make full reparation for the injury caused by the internationally wrongful act.

2. Injury includes any damage, whether material or moral, caused by the internationally wrongful act of a State.

Article 32

Irrelevance of internal law

The responsible State may not rely on the provisions of its internal law as justification for failure to comply with its obligations under this Part.

Article 33

Scope of international obligations set out in this Part

1. The obligations of the responsible State set out in this Part may be owed to another State, to several States, or to the international com-

munity as a whole, depending in particular on the character and content of the international obligation and on the circumstances of the breach.

2. This Part is without prejudice to any right, arising from the international responsibility of a State, which may accrue directly to any person or entity other than a State.

Chapter II

Reparation for injury

Article 34

Forms of reparation

Full reparation for the injury caused by the internationally wrongful act shall take the form of restitution, compensation and satisfaction, either singly or in combination, in accordance with the provisions of this chapter.

Article 35

Restitution

A State responsible for an internationally wrongful act is under an obligation to make restitution, that is, to re-establish the situation which existed before the wrongful act was committed, provided and to the extent that restitution:

(a) is not materially impossible;

(b) does not involve a burden out of all proportion to the benefit deriving from restitution instead of compensation.

Article 36

Compensation

1. The State responsible for an internationally wrongful act is under an obligation to compensate for the damage caused thereby, insofar as such damage is not made good by restitution.

2. The compensation shall cover any financially assessable damage including loss of profits insofar as it is established.

Article 37

Satisfaction

1. The State responsible for an internationally wrongful act is under an obligation to give satisfaction for the injury caused by that act insofar as it cannot be made good by restitution or compensation.

2. Satisfaction may consist in an acknowledgement of the breach, an expression of regret, a formal apology or another appropriate modality.

3. Satisfaction shall not be out of proportion to the injury and may not take a form humiliating to the responsible State.

Article 38

Interest

1. Interest on any principal sum due under this chapter shall be payable when necessary in order to ensure full reparation. The interest rate and mode of calculation shall be set so as to achieve that result.

2. Interest runs from the date when the principal sum should have been paid until the date the obligation to pay is fulfilled.

Article 39

Contribution to the injury

In the determination of reparation, account shall be taken of the contribution to the injury by wilful or negligent action or omission of the injured State or any person or entity in relation to whom reparation is sought.

* * *

4. BEYOND LEGAL OBLIGATIONS: COMITY

As the *Schooner Exchange* case indicates, sovereignty does not necessarily imply ruthless pursuit of immediate self-interest. Instead, international relations work better with a dose of altruism and a certain amount of goodwill among sovereigns, which may well lie outside (and go beyond) legal obligations. This element is often called "comity" and is explained by the leading American legal scholar of the early 19th century as follows:

JOSEPH STORY, COMMENTARIES ON THE CONFLICT OF LAWS

(1834)

* * *

§ 33. It has been thought by some jurists, that the term, "comity," is not sufficiently expressive of the obligation of nations to give effect to foreign laws, when they are not prejudicial to their own rights and interests.* * *

§ 35. The true foundation, on which the administration of international law must rest, is, that the rules, which are to govern, are those, which arise from mutual interest and utility, from a sense of the inconveniences, which would result from a contrary doctrine, and from a sort of moral necessity to do justice, in order that justice may be done to us in return. * * *

§ 36. But of the nature, and extent, and utility of this recognition of foreign laws, respecting the state and condition of persons, every nation must judge for itself, and certainly is not bound to recognise them, when they would be prejudicial to its own interests. The very terms, in which the doctrine is commonly enunciated, carry along with them this necessary qualification and limitation of it. Mutual utility presupposes, that the interest of all nations is consulted, and not that of one only. Now, this demonstrates, that the doctrine owes its origin and authority to the voluntary adoption and consent of nations. It is, therefore, in the strictest sense, a matter of the comity of nations, and not of absolute paramount obligation, superseding all discretion on the subject.

* * *

§ 37. * * * It is not the comity of the courts, but the comity of the nation which is administered, and ascertained in the same way by which all other principles of the municipal law are ascertained and guided.

* * *

If something is not a matter of legal obligation but of "comity," how does that help a party to an international dispute in practice? What is the significance of the "comity" argument in the following case?

CANADA SOUTHERN RAILWAY COMPANY V. GEBHARD

United States Supreme Court
109 U.S. 527 (1883)

[The facts of this case are complicated; for our purposes the following description of what happened will suffice: A railway company was formed in Canada. It issued negotiable bonds. Investors in New York bought some of these bonds, which were payable in New York. When the railway company ran into financial trouble and was unable to pay the money owed under the bonds, the Canadian parliament passed an "Arrangement Act." The Act allowed the Company to reschedule its debts by issuing new securities instead of the old ones, thus extending and changing its obligations. The New York investors had no say in that decision. They eventually brought suit in New York on the bonds (and past due coupons). The railway company presented the arrangement under the Canadian Act as a defense to suit, and the plaintiffs disagreed.]

CHIEF JUSTICE WAITE:

* * *

Two questions are presented for our consideration: (1) Whether the "arrangement act" is valid in Canada, and had the effect of binding non-assenting bondholders within the dominion by the terms of the scheme;

and, (2) whether, if it did have that effect in Canada, the courts of the United States should give it the same effect as against citizens of the United States whose rights accrued before its passage.

* * *

That the laws of a country have no extraterritorial force is an axiom of international jurisprudence, but things done in one country under the authority of law may be of binding effect in another country. The obligor of the bonds and coupons here sued on was a corporation created for a public purpose, that is to say, to build, maintain, and work a railway in Canada. It had its corporate home in Canada, and was subject to the exclusive legislative authority of the Dominion parliament. * * * A corporation "must dwell in the place of its creation, and cannot migrate to another sovereignty," though it may do business in all places where its charter allows and the local laws do not forbid. But wherever it goes for business it carries its charter, as that is the law of its existence, and the charter is the same abroad that it is at home. Whatever disabilities are placed upon the corporation at home it retains abroad, and whatever legislative control it is subjected to at home must be recognized and submitted to by those who deal with it elsewhere. A corporation of one country may be excluded from business in another country, but, if admitted, it must, in the absence of legislation equivalent to making it a corporation of the latter country, be taken, both by the government and those who deal with it, as a creature of the law of its own country, and subject to all the legislative control and direction that may be properly exercised over it at the place of its creation. Such being the law, it follows that every person who deals with a foreign corporation impliedly subjects himself to such laws of the foreign government, affecting the powers and obligations of the corporation with which he voluntarily contracts, as the known and established policy of that government authorizes. To all intents and purposes, he submits his contract with the corporation to such a policy of the foreign government, and whatever is done by that government in furtherance of that policy which binds those in like situation with himself, who are subjects of the government, in respect to the operation and effect of their contracts with the corporation, will necessarily bind him. He is conclusively presumed to have contracted with a view to such laws of that government, because the corporation must of necessity be controlled by them, and it has no power to contract with a view to any other laws with which they are not in entire harmony. It follows, therefore, that anything done at the legal home of the corporation, under the authority of such laws, which discharges it from liability there, discharges it everywhere.

* * *

* * * Under these circumstances the true spirit of international comity requires that schemes of this character, legalized at home, should be recognized in other countries. The fact that the bonds made in Canada were payable in New York is unimportant, except in determining by what law the parties intended their contract should be governed; and every citizen of a country, other than that in which the corporation is located, may protect himself against all unjust legislation of the foreign government by refusing to deal with its corporations

On the whole, we are satisfied that the scheme of arrangement bound the defendants in error, and that these actions cannot be maintained. The same result was reached by the Court of Queen's Bench in the Province of Ontario, when passing on a similar statute in *Jones v. The Canada Central Railway Company.*

The judgments are reversed and the causes remanded, with instructions to enter judgment on the facts found in favor of the railway company in each of the cases.

* * *

MR. JUSTICE HARLAN, dissenting.

* * *

> "The laws of other governments have no force beyond their territorial limits; and if permitted to operate in other States, it is upon a principle of comity, and only when neither the State nor its citizens would suffer any inconvenience from the application of the foreign law." 2 Kent, 406.

Story announces the same doctrine in the following language:

> "And even in relation to a discharge according to the laws of the place where the contract is made, there are (as we have seen) some necessary limitations and exceptions ingrafted upon the general doctrine which every country will enforce, whenever those laws are manifestly unjust, or are injurious to the fair rights of its own citizens. It has been said by a learned judge with great force: "As the laws of foreign countries are not admitted *ex proprio vigore*, but merely *ex comitate*, the judicial power will exercise a discretion with respect to the laws which they may be called upon to sanction; for should they be manifestly unjust, or calculated to injure their own citizens, they ought to be rejected." Thus, if any State should enact that its citizens should be discharged from all debts due to creditors living without the State, such a provision would be so contrary to the common principles of justice that the most liberal spirit of comity would not require its adoption in any other State."

In [Burgess' Commentaries on Colonial and Foreign Laws, vol. 1, p. 5], the author says:

"It is established as a principle of international jurisprudsence that effect should be given to the laws of another State whenever the rights of a litigant before its tribunals are derived from, or are dependent on, those laws, and when such recognition is not prejudicial to its own interests or the rights of its own subjects."

The same view is thus expressed by another American author:

"It [the State] must consult sound morals and the interests and public policy of its own people, and if to enforce the laws of another State or country would lead to their infringement, it would be treacherous to its own duties to lend aid to their execution." 1 Daniel on Negotiable Instruments, § 866.

* * *

The case, then, before us is one in which a foreign railway corporation pleads in discharge of its liability to pay its negotiable securities, held by citizens of the United States, and which were delivered and are payable in this country, not that it had paid such securities; not that there had been a composition in bankruptcy embracing these claims; not that any court had given its sanction to the scheme in question; but that a statute of a foreign country, without the consent of those who did not approve such scheme, and without giving an opportunity before any authorized tribunal to show that such scheme ought not to be ratified, had absolved it from liability to meet its contract engagements. This defence my brethren feel obliged, upon grounds of international comity, to sustain. Thus an American court denies to American holders of foreign railway securities what an English court would not deny to English holders of American railway securities. An English court would not permit the rights of Englishmen, growing out of a contract between them and a foreign corporation, which is to be performed in England, to be injuriously affected by foreign laws in violation of the terms of that contract. I fully concur in what the circuit judge said:

"If any of our own States had passed such an act as the one under consideration, it would have been the duty of the courts of that State to treat it as an unlawful exercise of power; and certainly it cannot be expected that this court will tolerate legislation by a foreign State which it would not sanction if passed here, and which, if allowed to operate, would seriously prejudice the rights of a citizen of this State. Comity can ask no recognition of such unjust foreign legislation, and the case falls under the qualifications of a general rule, which prescribes that when the foreign law is repugnant to the fundamental principle of the *lex fori*, it will be ignored."

* * *

As I do not think that a foreign railway corporation is entitled, upon principles of international comity, to have the benefit, in our courts—to the prejudice of our own people and in violation of their contract and property rights—of a foreign statute which could not be sustained had it been enacted by Congress or by any one of the United States, with reference to the negotiable securities of an American railway corporation; and, as I do not agree that an American court should accord to a foreign railway corporation the privilege of repudiating its contract obligations to American citizens, when it must deny any such privilege, under like circumstances, to our own railway corporations, I dissent from the opinion and judgment of the court.

Both the majority opinion and the dissent invoke the concept of "international comity." Why do the majority opinion and the dissent reach different results applying the same principle? What views of "comity" underlie their differences?

CHAPTER 3

LAW: TREATIES, CUSTOM, AND GENERAL PRINCIPLES

■ ■ ■

The origins and nature of (public) international law have been intensely debated by scholars for many decades. An introduction to transnational law is not the place to delve deeply into the philosophical underpinnings and theories of international law. Still, a rough sense of the major views is important to put the traditional sources of international law into perspective.

It has often been doubted whether the "law of nations" is "real" law at all. The classic negative view was famously expressed by the English jurist John Austin, the founder of analytical jurisprudence, in the early 19th-century. According to Austin (and, following him, many 19th- and even 20th-century jurists) law is essentially the command of a sovereign to its subjects which can be enforced by coercion. Since one of the defining features of the Westphalian system was that sovereigns themselves did not recognize any authority above them, they were, by definition, not subject to any binding commands issued and enforced from high above. Therefore, there could be no real "law" between nations: "The so called law of nations consists of opinions or sentiments current among nations generally. It is therefore not law so properly called." (John Austin, THE PROVINCE OF JURISPRUDENCE DETERMINED (1832) (Wilfred E. Rumble ed. 1995), p. 124). While Austin's view may have adequately reflected the nature of international law in his time, today it is generally considered too narrow. Most jurists have come to recognize that law consists of much more than just sovereign commands to subjects. It may include self-imposed rules that are followed out of a sense of legal obligation, and the coercion backing them up may come not only from a superior authority, but also from within the context of co-equal (state) actors.

If the law of nations is "real" law, however, the question remains: what are its true origins and nature? If, under the classical regime of co-equal sovereign nation states, law could not originate in (legislative, executive, or judicial) commands from above, where did it ultimately come from? Two main answers have been given to that question; they were aptly summarized in an introduction to international law widely used around the middle of the 20th century, which you see below.

117

J. L. BRIERLY, THE LAW OF NATIONS
(5th ed., 1955)

* * *

Traditionally there are two rival doctrines which attempt to answer the question why states should be bound to observe the rules of international law.

The doctrine of "fundamental rights" is a corollary of the doctrine of the "state of nature," in which men are supposed to have lived before they formed themselves into political communities or states; for states, not having formed themselves into a super-state, are still supposed by the adherents of this doctrine to be living in such a condition. It teaches that the principles of international law, or the primary principles upon which the others rest, can be deduced from the essential nature of the state. Every state, by the very fact that it is a state, is endowed with certain fundamental, or inherent, or natural, rights. Writers differ in enumerating what these rights are, but generally five rights are claimed, namely self-preservation, independence, equality, respect, and intercourse. It is obvious that the doctrine of fundamental rights is merely the old doctrine of the natural rights of man transferred to states. That doctrine has played a great part in history; Locke justified the English Revolution by it, and from Locke it passed to the leaders of the American Revolution and became the philosophical basis of the Declaration of Independence.

The doctrine of positivism, on the other hand, teaches that international law is the sum of the rules by which states have *consented* to be bound, and that nothing can be law to which they have not consented. This consent may be given expressly, as in a treaty, or it may be implied by a state acquiescing in a customary rule. But the assumption that international law consists of nothing save what states have consented to is an inadequate account of the system as it can be seen in actual operation, and even if it were a complete account of the contents of the law, it would fail to explain why the law is binding.

* * *

Hugo Grotius, to whom you were introduced before, wrote that "[t]he law of nations is that 'which is common to many Nations or Rulers of Nations, whether derived from Nature, or instituted by Divine Commands, or introduced by Custom and tacit Consent.'" Hugo Grotius, I De Jure Belli ac Pacis, The Preliminary Discourse 75 (The Liberty Fund, Indianapolis 2005). William Blackstone, by contrast, wrote that "[s]ince 'none of these states will acknowledge a superiority in the other, * * * [the law of nations] depends entirely upon the rules of natural law, or upon mutual compacts, treaties, leagues, and agreements between these several communities.'" William Blackstone, I Commentaries on the Laws of England 43 (Oxford 1765).

How do these two observations fit with the position explained by Brierly?

———————

The dichotomy between a "natural law" and a "positivist" conception of international law may be theoretically fascinating, but does it have any practical impact? In other words, does it make a difference in real cases? How do these respective views shape the discourse on international law? What are their respective advantages and disadvantages?

How does Justice Story address natural law in *La Jeune Eugenie*? What is Justice Marshall's position in *The Antelope*? How do their respective positions affect the outcomes of these cases?

UNITED STATES V. LA JEUNE EUGENIE

Circuit Court of Massachusetts
26 F. Cas. 832 (1822)

JUSTICE STORY:

This is a libel brought against the schooner *La Jeune Eugenie*, which was seized by Lieut. Stockton, on the coast of Africa, for being employed in the slave trade. The allegation asserts the offence in two forms: first, as against the slave trade acts of the United States; and, secondly, as against the general law of nations. A claim has been given in by the French consul, in behalf of the claimants, who are subjects of France, resident in Basseterre, in the island of Guadaloupe, as owners of the schooner; and there is also a protest filed by the French consul against the jurisdiction of the court, upon the ground, that this is a French vessel, owned by French subjects, and, as such, exclusively liable to the jurisdiction of the French tribunals, if she shall turn out, upon the evidence, to have been engaged in this dishonourable traffic.

* * *

It is contended, on behalf of the plaintiffs, that this court has a right to entertain jurisdiction, and is bound to reject the claim of the defendants: First, because the African slave trade is repugnant to the law of nations, secondly, because it is prohibited by the municipal laws of France. On the other side it is contended, that the trade is not repugnant to the law of nations; and if prohibited by the laws of France, it is a municipal regulation, which the tribunals of France are alone competent to inquire into and punish.

* * *

Having adverted to these preliminary considerations, I may now be permitted to proceed to the great points in controversy. And the first question naturally arising out of the asserted facts is, whether the African slave trade be prohibited by the law of nations; for, if it be so, it will not, I presume, be denied, that confiscation of the property ought to follow; for that is the proper penalty denounced by that law for any violation of its precepts; and the same reasons, which enforce that penalty ordinarily, apply with equal force to employment in this trade.

* * * It would be unbecoming in me here to assert, that the state of slavery cannot have a legitimate existence, or that it stands condemned by the unequivocal testimony of the law of nations. But this concession carries us but a very short distance towards the decision of this cause. It is not, as the learned counsel for the government have justly stated, on account of the simple fact, that the traffic necessarily involves the enslavement of human beings, that it stands reprehended by the present sense of nations; but that it necessarily carries with it a breach of all the moral duties, of all the maxims of justice, mercy and humanity, and of the admitted rights, which independent Christian nations now hold sacred in their intercourse with each other. * * *

Now in respect to the African slave trade, such as it has been described to be, and in fact is, in its origin, progress, and consummation, it cannot admit of serious question, that it is founded in a violation of some of the first principles, which ought to govern nations. It is repugnant to the great principles of Christian duty, the dictates of natural religion, the obligations of good faith and morality, and the eternal maxims of social justice. When any trade can be truly said to have these ingredients, it is impossible, that it can be consistent with any system of law, that purports to rest on the authority of reason or revelation. And it is sufficient to stamp any trade as interdicted by public law, when it can be justly affirmed, that it is repugnant to the general principles of justice and humanity. Now there is scarcely a single maritime nation of Europe, that has not in the most significant terms, in the most deliberate and solemn conferences, acts, or treaties, acknowledged the injustice and inhumanity of this trade; and pledged itself to promote its abolition. * * * [A]t the present moment the traffic is vindicated by no nation, and is admitted by almost all commercial nations as incurably unjust and inhuman. It appears to me, therefore, that in an American court of judicature, I am bound to consider the trade an offence against the universal law of society and in all cases, where it is not protected by a foreign government, to deal with it as an offence carrying with it the penalty of confiscation. * * *

* * * I have come to the conclusion, that the slave trade is a trade prohibited by universal law, and by the law of France, and that, therefore, the claim of the asserted French owners must be rejected. That claim being rejected, I feel myself at perfect liberty, with the express consent of our

own government, to decree, that the property be delivered over to the consular agent of the king of France, to be dealt with according to his own sense of duty and right. * * *

THE ANTELOPE

United States Supreme Court
23 U.S. 66 (1825)

CHIEF JUSTICE MARSHALL:

* * *

The *Antelope*, a vessel unquestionably belonging to Spanish subjects, was captured while receiving a cargo of Africans on the coast of Africa, by the *Arraganta*, a privateer which was manned in Baltimore, and is said to have been then under the flag of the Oriental republic. Some other vessels, said to be Portuguese, engaged in the same traffic, were previously plundered, and the slaves taken from them, as well as from another vessel then in the same port, were put on board the *Antelope*, of which vessel the *Arraganta* took possession, landed her crew, and put on board a prize master and prize crew. Both vessels proceeded to the coast of Brazil, where the *Arraganta* was wrecked, and her captain and crew either lost or made prisoners.

The *Antelope*, whose name was changed to the *General Ramirez*, after an ineffectual attempt to sell the Africans on board at Surinam, arrived off the coast of Florida, and was hovering on that coast, near that of the United States, for several days. Supposing her to be a pirate, or a vessel wishing to smuggle slaves into the United States, Captain Jackson, of the revenue cutter *Dallas*, went in quest of her, and finding her laden with slaves, commanded by officers who were citizens of the United States, with a crew who spoke English, brought her in for adjudication.

She was libelled by the Vice Consuls of Spain and Portugal, each of whom claim that portion of the slaves which were conjectured to belong to the subjects of their respective sovereigns; which claims are opposed by the United States on behalf of the Africans.

* * *

In prosecuting this appeal, the United States asserts no property in themselves. It appears in the character of guardians, or next friends, of these Africans, who are brought, without any act of their own, into the bosom of our country, insist on their right to freedom, and submit their claim to the laws of the land, and to the tribunals of the nation.

The Consuls of Spain and Portugal, respectively, demand these Africans as slaves, who have, in the regular course of legitimate commerce, been acquired as property by the subjects of their respective sovereigns, and claim their restitution under the laws of the United States.

* * *

That the course of opinion on the slave trade should be unsettled, ought to excite no surprise. The Christian and civilized nations of the world, with whom we have most intercourse, have all been engaged in it. However abhorrent this traffic may be to a mind whose original feelings are not blunted by familiarity with the practice, it has been sanctioned in modern times by the laws of all nations who possess distant colonies, each of whom has engaged in it as a common commercial business which no other could rightfully interrupt. It has claimed all the sanction which could be derived from long usage, and general acquiescence. That trade could not be considered as contrary to the law of nations which was authorized and protected by the laws of all commercial nations; the right to carry on which was claimed by each, and allowed by each.

* * *

That it is contrary to the law of nature will scarcely be denied. That every man has a natural right to the fruits of his own labour, is generally admitted; and that no other person can rightfully deprive him of those fruits, and appropriate them against his will, seems to be the necessary result of this admission. But from the earliest times war has existed, and war confers rights in which all have acquiesced. Among the most enlightened nations of antiquity, one of these was, that the victor might enslave the vanquished. This, which was the usage of all, could not be pronounced repugnant to the law of nations, which is certainly to be tried by the test of general usage. That which has received the assent of all, must be the law of all.

* * *

Whatever might be the answer of a moralist to this question, a jurist must search for its legal solution, in those principles of action which are sanctioned by the usages, the national acts, and the general assent, of that portion of the world of which he considers himself as a part, and to whose law the appeal is made. If we resort to this standard as the test of international law, the question, as has already been observed, is decided in favour of the legality of the trade. Both Europe and America embarked in it; and for nearly two centuries, it was carried on without opposition, and without censure. A jurist could not say, that a practice thus supported was illegal, and that those engaged in it might be punished, either personally, or by deprivation of property.

In this commerce, thus sanctioned by universal assent, every nation has an equal right to engage. How is this right to be lost? Each may renounce it for its own people; but can this renunciation affect others?

If it be neither repugnant to the law of nations, nor piracy, it is almost superfluous to say in this Court, that the right of bringing in for adjudication in time of peace, even where the vessel belongs to a nation which has prohibited the trade, cannot exist. The Courts of no country execute the penal laws of another; and the course of the American government on the subject of visitation and search, would decide any case in which that right had been exercised by an American cruiser, on the vessel of a foreign nation, not violating our municipal laws, against the captors.

It follows, that a foreign vessel engaged in the African slave trade, captured on the high seas in time of peace, by an American cruiser, and brought in for adjudication, would be restored.

[After considering the claims of each party and finding insufficient support for the Portuguese claim, the Court concluded:]

We think, then, that all the Africans, now in possession of the Marshal for the District of Georgia, and under the control of the Circuit Court of the United States for that District, which were brought in with the *Antelope*, otherwise called the *General Ramirez*, except those which may be designated as the property of the Spanish claimants, ought to be delivered up to the United States, to be disposed of according to law.

* * *

1. THE TRADITIONAL CATALOG

Article 38 of the Statute of the International Court of Justice (on which more in Chapter IX.1.) is the classic list of sources of public international law. Read it *carefully*! Compare it with Section 103 of the Restatement (Third) on Foreign Relations (which is, of course, not binding). In Article 38, Section 1, what is the difference between (a)–(c) on the one hand and (d) on the other hand?

STATUTE OF THE INTERNATIONAL
COURT OF JUSTICE

* * *

Article 38

(1) The Court, whose function is to decide in accordance with international law such disputes as are submitted to it, shall apply:

(a) international conventions, whether general or particular, establishing rules expressly recognized by the contesting states;

(b) international custom, as evidence of a general practice accepted as law;

(c) the general principles of law recognized by civilized nations;

(d) subject to the provisions of Article 59, judicial decisions and the teachings of the most highly qualified publicists of the various nations, as subsidiary means for the determination of rules of law.

(2) This provision shall not prejudice the power of the Court to decide a case *ex aequo et bono*, if the parties agree thereto.

* * *

RESTATEMENT (THIRD) OF FOREIGN RELATIONS LAW OF THE UNITED STATES
American Law Institute (1987)

* * *

§ 102. Sources of International Law

(1) A rule of international law is one that has been accepted as such by the international community of states:

(a) in the form of customary law;

(b) by international agreement; or

(c) by derivation from general principles common to the major legal systems of the world.

(2) Customary international law results from a general and consistent practice of states followed by them from a sense of legal obligation.

(3) International agreements create law for the states parties thereto and may lead to the creation of customary international law when such agreements are intended for adherence by states generally and are in fact widely accepted.

(4) General principles common to the major legal systems, even if not incorporated or reflected in customary law or international agreement, may be invoked as supplementary rules of international law where appropriate.

§ 103. Evidence of International Law

(1) Whether a rule has become international law is determined by evidence appropriate to the particular source from which that rule is alleged to derive (§ 102).

(2) In determining whether a rule has become international law, substantial weight is accorded to

    (a) judgments and opinions of international judicial and arbitral tribunals;

    (b) judgments and opinions of national judicial tribunals;

    (c) the writings of scholars;

    (d) pronouncements by states that undertake to state a rule of international law, when such pronouncements are not seriously challenged by other states.

* * *

How do these lists of sources compare with the traditional list of sources of domestic law? What explains the difference?

How do you ascertain a rule of domestic law versus a rule of international law?

2. TREATIES

Treaties are arguably the most important source of public international law (and play a major role in private international law as you will see in Chapter VIII.1.). This subchapter deals with three aspects of treaties. It first provides some background information, especially about the treaty making process. It then presents excerpts from the most fundamental rules about them, which are codified in the Vienna Convention on the Law of Treaties (VCLT). Finally, it turns to treaty interpretation issues that are illustrated by two major decisions of the United States Supreme Court.

David Bederman, International Law Frameworks
(3d ed. 2010)

* * *

Popular understanding notwithstanding, there is no legal difference between various kinds of international instruments because of the name they are given. In other words, "treaties," "pacts," "protocols," "conventions," "covenants," and "declarations" are all terms to convey international agreements. Some of these terms may connote more or less solemnity or formality, but it does not matter for purposes of characterizing an accord as an international agreement, binding under international law. (You should know, however, that the term "treaty" *does* have a particular meaning in U.S. constitutional law * * *.)

Much ink has been spilt by international law academics in trying to distinguish various kinds of treaties, depending on some essential characteristics or subject-matters. This has largely been futile. Most international agreements defy easy categorization. For example, some scholars have attempted to identify treaties that are more like *contracts* between nations, and those that have more the flavor of *legislation*, definitively establishing rules of conduct between countries. Many international agreements have aspects of both properties: they try to settle relations between nations, while also ordaining rules. The contracts–legislation duality is a significant one, and it does explain the peculiar problems that international lawyers face in interpreting and applying treaties. But it does not serve as a reliable guidepost for categorizing international agreements.

Likewise, some writers have tried to differentiate treaties that purport to write down existing rules of customary international law ("codification"), as opposed to freshly legislating rules of international conduct ("progressive development"). This distinction is supposed to explain whether a new treaty is likely to garner sufficient international support. It rarely does. Treaty projects that "merely" codify existing law are among the most contentious in modern diplomatic history. (Just ask the International Law Commission (ILC), the UN body that had deliberated rules of State Responsibility for over 50 years!) On the other hand, the international community can often mobilize substantial support for entirely novel forms of law-making—if the circumstances are compelling enough.

The only sensible typology of international agreements is the simple distinction between *bilateral* treaties (made between two nations) and *multilateral* treaties (concluded between three or more countries). This distinction will need to be kept in mind when conducting treaty research, whether in historical collections of treaties made before 1919 (like Parry's and Marten's), international collections (like the League of Nations Treaty Series (LNTS) or the UN Treaty Series (now available on-line)), or national treaty sources (for the United States, "U.S. Treaties and Other International Agreements" (U.S.T.) or "Treaties and Other International Acts Series" (T.I.A.S.)).

That leaves the question of what actually defines an international agreement. Fortunately, international law provides an answer in the 1969 Vienna Convention on the Law of Treaties (VCLT). The VCLT is, quite literally, a treaty on treaties. Almost every question of treaty law is settled in that document, and it is an essential bit of reading for every international lawyer. (Just as the Uniform Commercial Code (UCC) and the Convention on International Sale of Goods (CISG) are the "bibles" for commercial litigators in the U.S.) In any event, VCLT article 2 thoughtfully provides that an international agreement is one "concluded between States in written form and governed by international law."

* * *

After many years of work, the International Law Commission adopted the draft of a convention on treaties in 1966. Building on that document, the Vienna (UN) Conference concluded what came to be known as the Vienna Convention on the Law of Treaties in 1969. The Convention entered into force in 1980. Most countries in the world are parties to the Convention. While the United States is not (so that general treaty issues between it and other countries continue to be governed by customary international law), it has routinely agreed that the Vienna Convention by and large reflects customary international law.

At some point in his or her education or career, every lawyer should read through the most important parts of the Vienna Convention on the Law of Treaties at least once—if for no other reason than just to know what it is all about. The Convention is a near-comprehensive codification of the international law on treaties. Yet, when you look at Articles 1 through 3, you can see that it does not cover all treaties. What kinds of treaties are excluded?

As you are reading through the treaty excerpts below, consider some additional questions as a guide to give context to these provisions: To what extent does the Convention deal with treaties essentially as contracts between states? Which of the rules sound familiar from contract law and which strike you as surprising or hard to understand?

VIENNA CONVENTION ON THE LAW OF TREATIES
(Adopted 1969; in force 1980)

Preamble

The States Parties to the present Convention,

Considering the fundamental role of treaties in the history of international relations,

Recognizing the ever-increasing importance of treaties as a source of international law and as a means of developing peaceful cooperation among nations, whatever their constitutional and social systems,

Noting that the principles of free consent and of good faith and the *pacta sunt servanda* rule are universally recognized,

Affirming that disputes concerning treaties, like other international disputes, should be settled by peaceful means and in conformity with the principles of justice and international law,

Recalling the determination of the peoples of the United Nations to establish conditions under which justice and respect for the obligations arising from treaties can be maintained,

Having in mind the principles of international law embodied in the Charter of the United Nations, such as the principles of the equal rights and self-determination of peoples, of the sovereign equality and independence of all States, of non-interference in the domestic affairs of States, of the prohibition of the threat or use of force and of universal respect for, and observance of, human rights and fundamental freedoms for all,

Believing that the codification and progressive development of the law of treaties achieved in the present Convention will promote the purposes of the United Nations set forth in the Charter, namely, the maintenance of international peace and security, the development of friendly relations and the achievement of cooperation among nations,

Affirming that the rules of customary international law will continue to govern questions not regulated by the provisions of the present Convention,

Have agreed as follows:

Part I: Introduction

Article 1

Scope of the present Convention

The present Convention applies to treaties between States.

Article 2

Use of terms

1. For the purposes of the present Convention:

    (a) "treaty" means an international agreement concluded between States in written form and governed by international law, whether embodied in a single instrument or in two or more related instruments and whatever its particular designation;

    (b) "ratification," "acceptance," "approval" and "accession" mean in each case the international act so named whereby a State establishes on the international plane its consent to be bound by a treaty;

    (c) "full powers" means a document emanating from the competent authority of a State designating a person or persons to represent the State for negotiating, adopting or authenticating the text of a treaty, for expressing the consent of the State to be bound by a treaty, or for accomplishing any other act with respect to a treaty;

    (d) "reservation" means a unilateral statement, however phrased or named, made by a State, when signing, ratifying, accepting, approving or acceding to a treaty, whereby it purports to exclude or to modify the legal effect of certain provisions of the treaty in their application to that State;

(e) "negotiating State" means a State which took part in the drawing up and adoption of the text of the treaty;

(f) "contracting State" means a State which has consented to be bound by the treaty, whether or not the treaty has entered into force;

(g) "party" means a State which has consented to be bound by the treaty and for which the treaty is in force;

(h) "third State" means a State not a party to the treaty;

(i) "international organization" means an intergovernmental organization.

2. The provisions of paragraph 1 regarding the use of terms in the present Convention are without prejudice to the use of those terms or to the meanings which may be given to them in the internal law of any State.

Article 3

International agreements not within the scope of the Present Convention

The fact that the present Convention does not apply to international agreements concluded between States and other subjects of international law or between such other subjects of international law, or to international agreements not in written form, shall not affect:

(a) the legal force of such agreements;

(b) the application to them of any of the rules set forth in the present Convention to which they would be subject under international law independently of the Convention;

(c) the application of the Convention to the relations of States as between themselves under international agreements to which other subjects of international law are also parties.

Article 4

Non-retroactivity of the present Convention

Without prejudice to the application of any rules set forth in the present Convention to which treaties would be subject under international law independently of the Convention, the Convention applies only to treaties which are concluded by States after the entry into force of the present Convention with regard to such States.

Article 5

Treaties constituting international organizations and treaties adopted within an international organization

The present Convention applies to any treaty which is the constituent instrument of an international organization and to any treaty adopted within an international organization without prejudice to any relevant rules of the organization.

Part II: Conclusion and Entry Into Force of Treaties

Section 1. Conclusion of Treaties

Article 6

Capacity of States to conclude treaties

Every State possesses capacity to conclude treaties.

* * *

Article 9

Adoption of the text

1. The adoption of the text of a treaty takes place by the consent of all the States participating in its drawing up except as provided in paragraph 2.

2. The adoption of the text of a treaty at an international conference takes place by the vote of two-thirds of the States present and voting, unless by the same majority they shall decide to apply a different rule.

* * *

Article 11

Means of expressing consent to be bound by a treaty

The consent of a State to be bound by a treaty may be expressed by signature, exchange of instruments constituting a treaty, ratification, acceptance, approval or accession, or by any other means if so agreed.

* * *

Article 16

Exchange or deposit of instruments of ratification, acceptance, approval or accession

Unless the treaty otherwise provides, instruments of ratification, acceptance, approval or accession establish the consent of a State to be bound by a treaty upon:

(a) their exchange between the contracting States;

(b) their deposit with the depositary; or

(c) their notification to the contracting States or to the depositary, if so agreed.

* * *

Article 18

Obligation not to defeat the object and purpose of a treaty prior to its entry into force

A State is obliged to refrain from acts which would defeat the object and purpose of a treaty when:

(a) it has signed the treaty or has exchanged instruments constituting the treaty subject to ratification, acceptance or approval, until it shall have made its intention clear not to become a party to the treaty; or

(b) it has expressed its consent to be bound by the treaty, pending the entry into force of the treaty and provided that such entry into force is not unduly delayed.

Section 2. Reservations

[We will study these provisions in Chapter VIII.1.]

Section 3. Entry into Force and Provisional Application of Treaties

Article 24

Entry into force

1. A treaty enters into force in such manner and upon such date as it may provide or as the negotiating States may agree.

2. Failing any such provision or agreement, a treaty enters into force as soon as consent to be bound by the treaty has been established for all the negotiating States.

3. When the consent of a State to be bound by a treaty is established on a date after the treaty has come into force, the treaty enters into force for that State on that date, unless the treaty otherwise provides.

4. The provisions of a treaty regulating the authentication of its text, the establishment of the consent of States to be bound by the treaty, the manner or date of its entry into force, reservations, the functions of the depositary and other matters arising necessarily before the entry into force of the treaty apply from the time of the adoption of its text.

* * *

Part III: Observance, Application and Interpretation of Treaties

Section 1. Observance of Treaties

Article 26

Pacta sunt servanda

Every treaty in force is binding upon the parties to it and must be performed by them in good faith.

Article 27

Internal law and observance of treaties

A party may not invoke the provisions of its internal law as justification for its failure to perform a treaty. This rule is without prejudice to article 46.

Section 2. Application of Treaties

* * *

Section 3. Interpretation of Treaties

Article 31

General rule of interpretation

1. A treaty shall be interpreted in good faith in accordance with the ordinary meaning to be given to the terms of the treaty in their context and in the light of its object and purpose.

2. The context for the purpose of the interpretation of a treaty shall comprise, in addition to the text, including its preamble and annexes:

    (a) any agreement relating to the treaty which was made between all the parties in connexion with the conclusion of the treaty;

    (b) any instrument which was made by one or more parties in connexion with the conclusion of the treaty and accepted by the other parties as an instrument related to the treaty.

3. There shall be taken into account, together with the context:

    (a) any subsequent agreement between the parties regarding the interpretation of the treaty or the application of its provisions;

    (b) any subsequent practice in the application of the treaty which establishes the agreement of the parties regarding its interpretation;

    (c) any relevant rules of international law applicable in the relations between the parties.

4. A special meaning shall be given to a term if it is established that the parties so intended.

Article 32

Supplementary means of interpretation

Recourse may be had to supplementary means of interpretation, including the preparatory work of the treaty and the circumstances of its conclusion, in order to confirm the meaning resulting from the application of article 31, or to determine the meaning when the interpretation according to article 31:

(a) leaves the meaning ambiguous or obscure; or

(b) leads to a result which is manifestly absurd or unreasonable.

Article 33

Interpretation of treaties authenticated in two or more languages

1. When a treaty has been authenticated in two or more languages, the text is equally authoritative in each language, unless the treaty provides or the parties agree that, in case of divergence, a particular text shall prevail.

2. A version of the treaty in a language other than one of those in which the text was authenticated shall be considered an authentic text only if the treaty so provides or the parties so agree.

3. The terms of the treaty are presumed to have the same meaning in each authentic text.

4. Except where a particular text prevails in accordance with paragraph 1, when a comparison of the authentic texts discloses a difference of meaning which the application of articles 31 and 32 does not remove, the meaning which best reconciles the texts, having regard to the object and purpose of the treaty, shall be adopted.

Section 4. Treaties and Third States

* * *

Article 38

Rules in a treaty becoming binding on third States through international custom

Nothing in articles 34 to 37 precludes a rule set forth in a treaty from becoming binding upon a third State as a customary rule of international law, recognized as such.

Part IV: Amendment and Modification of Treaties

[Omitted here; we will study these provisions in Chapter VIII.1.]

* * *

Part V: Invalidity, Termination and Suspension of the Operation of Treaties

* * *

Section 2. Invalidity of Treaties

Article 46

Provisions of internal law regarding competence to conclude treaties

1. A State may not invoke the fact that its consent to be bound by a treaty has been expressed in violation of a provision of its internal law regarding competence to conclude treaties as invalidating its consent unless that violation was manifest and concerned a rule of its internal law of fundamental importance.

2. A violation is manifest if it would be objectively evident to any State conducting itself in the matter in accordance with normal practice and in good faith.

Article 47

Specific restrictions on authority to express the consent of a State

If the authority of a representative to express the consent of a State to be bound by a particular treaty has been made subject to a specific restriction, his omission to observe that restriction may not be invoked as invalidating the consent expressed by him unless the restriction was notified to the other negotiating States prior to his expressing such consent.

Article 48

Error

1. A State may invoke an error in a treaty as invalidating its consent to be bound by the treaty if the error relates to a fact or situation which was assumed by that State to exist at the time when the treaty was concluded and formed an essential basis of its consent to be bound by the treaty.

2. Paragraph 1 shall not apply if the State in question contributed by its own conduct to the error or if the circumstances were such as to put that State on notice of a possible error.

3. An error relating only to the wording of the text of a treaty does not affect its validity; article 79 then applies.

Article 49

Fraud

If a State has been induced to conclude a treaty by the fraudulent conduct of another negotiating State, the State may invoke the fraud as invalidating its consent to be bound by the treaty.

Article 50

Corruption of a representative of a State

If the expression of a State's consent to be bound by a treaty has been procured through the corruption of its representative directly or indirectly by another negotiating State, the State may invoke such corruption as invalidating its consent to be bound by the treaty.

Article 51

Coercion of a representative of a State

The expression of a State's consent to be bound by a treaty which has been procured by the coercion of its representative through acts or threats directed against him shall be without any legal effect.

Article 52

Coercion of a State by the threat or use of force

A treaty is void if its conclusion has been procured by the threat or use of force in violation of the principles of international law embodied in the Charter of the United Nations.

Article 53

Treaties conflicting with a peremptory norm of general international law ("jus cogens")

A treaty is void if, at the time of its conclusion, it conflicts with a peremptory norm of general international law. For the purposes of the present Convention, a peremptory norm of general international law is a norm accepted and recognized by the international community of States as a whole as a norm from which no derogation is permitted and which can be modified only by a subsequent norm of general international law having the same character.

Section 3. Termination and Suspension of the Operation of Treaties

Article 54

Termination of or withdrawal from a treaty under its provisions or by consent of the parties

The termination of a treaty or the withdrawal of a party may take place:

(a) in conformity with the provisions of the treaty; or

(b) at any time by consent of all the parties after consultation with the other contracting States.

* * *

Article 56

Denunciation of or withdrawal from a treaty containing no provision regarding termination, denunciation or withdrawal

1. A treaty which contains no provision regarding its termination and which does not provide for denunciation or withdrawal is not subject to denunciation or withdrawal unless:

   (a) it is established that the parties intended to admit the possibility of denunciation or withdrawal; or

   (b) a right of denunciation or withdrawal may be implied by the nature of the treaty.

2. A party shall give not less than twelve months' notice of its intention to denounce or withdraw from a treaty under paragraph 1.

* * *

Article 60

Termination or suspension of the operation of a treaty as a consequence of its breach

1. A material breach of a bilateral treaty by one of the parties entitles the other to invoke the breach as a ground for terminating the treaty or suspending its operation in whole or in part.

2. A material breach of a multilateral treaty by one of the parties entitles:

   (a) the other parties by unanimous agreement to suspend the operation of the treaty in whole or in part or to terminate it either:

      (i) in the relations between themselves and the defaulting State, or

      (ii) as between all the parties;

   (b) a party specially affected by the breach to invoke it as a ground for suspending the operation of the treaty in whole or in part in the relations between itself and the defaulting State;

   (c) any party other than the defaulting State to invoke the breach as a ground for suspending the operation of the treaty in whole or in part with respect to itself if the treaty is of such a character that a material breach of its provisions by one party radically changes the position of every party with respect to the further performance of its obligations under the treaty.

3. A material breach of a treaty, for the purposes of this article, consists in:

   (a) a repudiation of the treaty not sanctioned by the present Convention; or

   (b) the violation of a provision essential to the accomplishment of the object or purpose of the treaty.

4. The foregoing paragraphs are without prejudice to any provision in the treaty applicable in the event of a breach.

5. Paragraphs 1 to 3 do not apply to provisions relating to the protection of the human person contained in treaties of a humanitarian character, in particular to provisions prohibiting any form of reprisals against persons protected by such treaties.

Article 61

Supervening impossibility of performance

1. A party may invoke the impossibility of performing a treaty as a ground for terminating or withdrawing from it if the impossibility results from the permanent disappearance or destruction of an object indispensable for the execution of the treaty. If the impossibility is temporary, it may be invoked only as a ground for suspending the operation of the treaty.

2. Impossibility of performance may not be invoked by a party as a ground for terminating, withdrawing from or suspending the operation of a treaty if the impossibility is the result of a breach by that party either of an obligation under the treaty or of any other international obligation owed to any other party to the treaty.

Article 62

Fundamental change of circumstances

1. A fundamental change of circumstances which has occurred with regard to those existing at the time of the conclusion of a treaty, and which was not foreseen by the parties, may not be invoked as a ground for terminating or withdrawing from the treaty unless:

   (a) the existence of those circumstances constituted an essential basis of the consent of the parties to be bound by the treaty; and

   (b) the effect of the change is radically to transform the extent of obligations still to be performed under the treaty.

2. A fundamental change of circumstances may not be invoked as a ground for terminating or withdrawing from a treaty:

   (a) if the treaty establishes a boundary; or

(b) if the fundamental change is the result of a breach by the party invoking it either of an obligation under the treaty or of any other international obligation owed to any other party to the treaty.

3. If, under the foregoing paragraphs, a party may invoke a fundamental change of circumstances as a ground for terminating or withdrawing from a treaty it may also invoke the change as a ground for suspending the operation of the treaty.

Article 63

Severance of diplomatic or consular relations

The severance of diplomatic or consular relations between parties to a treaty does not affect the legal relations established between them by the treaty except insofar as the existence of diplomatic or consular relations is indispensable for the application of the treaty.

Article 64

Emergence of a new peremptory norm of general international law ("jus cogens")

If a new peremptory norm of general international law emerges, any existing treaty which is in conflict with that norm becomes void and terminates.

Section 4. Procedure

* * *

Section 5. Consequences of the Invalidity, Termination or Suspension of the Operation of a Treaty

* * *

Article 71

Consequences of the invalidity of a treaty which conflicts with a peremptory norm of general international law

1. In the case of a treaty which is void under article 53 the parties shall:

(a) eliminate as far as possible the consequences of any act performed in reliance on any provision which conflicts with the peremptory norm of general international law; and

(b) bring their mutual relations into conformity with the peremptory norm of general international law.

2. In the case of a treaty which becomes void and terminates under article 64, the termination of the treaty:

(a) releases the parties from any obligation further to perform the treaty;

(b) does not affect any right, obligation or legal situation of the parties created through the execution of the treaty prior to its termination, provided that those rights, obligations or situations may thereafter be maintained only to the extent that their maintenance is not in itself in conflict with the new peremptory norm of general international law.

Article 72

Consequences of the suspension of the operation of a treaty

1. Unless the treaty otherwise provides or the parties otherwise agree, the suspension of the operation of a treaty under its provisions or in accordance with the present Convention:

   (a) releases the parties between which the operation of the treaty is suspended from the obligation to perform the treaty in their mutual relations during the period of the suspension;

   (b) does not otherwise affect the legal relations between the parties established by the treaty.

2. During the period of the suspension the parties shall refrain from acts tending to obstruct the resumption of the operation of the treaty.

Part VI: Miscellaneous Provisions

* * *

Article 74

Diplomatic and consular relations and the conclusion of treaties

The severance or absence of diplomatic or consular relations between two or more States does not prevent the conclusion of treaties between those States. The conclusion of a treaty does not in itself affect the situation in regard to diplomatic or consular relations.

Part VII: Depositaries, Notifications, Corrections and Registration

* * *

Part VIII: Final Provisions

Article 81

Signature

The present Convention shall be open for signature by all States Members of the United Nations or of any of the specialized agencies or of the International Atomic Energy Agency or parties to the Statute of the International Court of Justice, and by any other State invited by the General Assembly of the United Nations to become a party to the Convention, as follows: until 30 November 1969, at the Federal Ministry for Foreign Affairs of the Republic of Austria, and subsequently, until 30 April 1970, at United Nations Headquarters, New York.

Article 82

Ratification

The present Convention is subject to ratification. The instruments of ratification shall be deposited with the Secretary–General of the United Nations.

Article 83

Accession

The present Convention shall remain open for accession by any State belonging to any of the categories mentioned in article 81. The instruments of accession shall be deposited with the Secretary–General of the United Nations.

Article 84

Entry into force

1. The present Convention shall enter into force on the thirtieth day following the date of deposit of the thirty-fifth instrument of ratification or accession.

2. For each State ratifying or acceding to the Convention after the deposit of the thirty-fifth instrument of ratification or accession, the Convention shall enter into force on the thirtieth day after deposit by such State of its instrument of ratification or accession.

Article 85

Authentic texts

The original of the present Convention, of which the Chinese, English, French, Russian and Spanish texts are equally authentic, shall be deposited with the Secretary–General of the United Nations.

IN WITNESS WHEREOF the undersigned Plenipotentiaries, being duly authorized thereto by their respective Governments, have signed the present Convention.

DONE at Vienna, this twenty-third day of May, one thousand nine hundred and sixty-nine.

In order to understand the status of a treaty—in particular, what force it has (and between whom)—one must understand the treaty-making process, including its specific nomenclature. What do "adoption," "ratification," and "entry into force" mean, and what are the legal consequences of these steps? The following text, which is the standard book on modern treaty law, explains these basic terms.

ANTHONY AUST, MODERN TREATY LAW AND PRACTICE
(2d ed. 2007)

* * *

ADOPTION

Once the negotiations are complete, it is necessary for the states which took part in drawing up the treaty to adopt the text. This is the first decisive stage in the conclusion of a treaty. Then the text has to be authenticated (see below). Thereafter, states can express their consent to be bound by the treaty.

The term adoption is not defined in the Convention, but is the formal act by which the form and content of the treaty are settled; and, a state which takes part in the drawing up and adoption of the text is known as a "negotiating state" (Article 2(1)(e)). Unless the circumstances suggest otherwise, the act of adoption does *not* amount to the authentication of, or consent to be bound by, the treaty, or that the treaty has entered into force. However, as will be explained, in the case of bilateral treaties these stages are sometimes run together.

The rules on adoption in Article 9 embody the classic principle that, unless otherwise agreed, adoption needs the consent of all the states which participated in drawing up the text. Until recent times this was the norm. The article, however, recognises that, since the Second World War, in drawing up treaties in large international conferences or within international organisations, the practice had been for adoption by the affirmative vote of a specified majority of the states. The pre-War unanimity rule is now restricted to the adoption of bilateral treaties or treaties drawn up by only a few states (plurilateral treaties). However, consensus is now frequently sought for multilateral treaties, though it is not always attainable (see below).

* * *

RATIFICATION

Ratification is defined by the Convention as "the international act so named whereby a State establishes on the international plane its consent to be bound by a treaty" (Article 2(1)(b)), although, as already explained, it is not the only way in which a state can express its consent to be bound. The most common misconception about ratification is that it is a constitutional process. It is not. As the definition makes clear, it is an "international" act carried out on the "international" plane. Although parliamentary approval of a treaty may well be required—and be referred to, most misleadingly, as "ratification"—that is a quite different (and entirely domestic) process.

Ratification consists of (1) the execution of an *instrument of ratification* by the executive and (2) either its exchange for the instrument of ratification of the other state (bilateral treaty) or its lodging with the depositary (multilateral treaty).

The normal reason for requiring ratification is that after the adoption and signature of a treaty one or more of the negotiating states will need time before it can give its consent to be bound. There can be various reasons for this. First, the treaty may require legislation. This should always be done before the treaty enters into force for the state, otherwise it risks being in breach of its treaty obligations. Sometimes a state will ratify before the necessary legislation has been enacted. This may be done so that it can say that it has been one of the first to ratify, and thereby gain kudos at home and abroad. Although the stratagem may also have the beneficial effect of encouraging other states to ratify early, it is inherently risky since the treaty might enter into force before the state has enacted the legislation. Secondly, even if no legislation is needed, the constitution may require parliamentary approval of the treaty, or some other procedure, like publication, before the state can ratify. Thirdly, even if no legislative or other constitutional process has to be gone through, the state may need time to consider the implications of the treaty. That a state has taken part—even an active part—in the negotiations does not necessarily mean that it is enthusiastic about the subject or the text which was finally agreed, or there may be a change of government. The breathing space provided by the ratification process allows time for reflection.

Most bilateral treaties now provide either that they shall be subject to ratification, or dispense with it by providing that they shall enter into force on signature, upon a specified date or event, or, rarely, on a date to be agreed. These days even less formal instruments, such as exchanges of notes, can have similar, though simpler, ratification provisions. * * * But the need for ratification is generally much greater for multilateral treaties.

* * *

It is another common misconception that once a treaty has been ratified it is then legally binding on the ratifying state. The situation is quite different from the coming into force of legislation. Expressing consent to be bound does, in itself, not make the treaty binding on the state. *The treaty also has to enter into force for that state.* When that happens the state becomes a "party" to the treaty (Article 2(l)(g)). Whether, and when, ratification will bring the treaty into force for the state will depend on the provisions of the treaty.

* * *

NO OBLIGATION TO RATIFY

Signature of a treaty imposes no obligation to ratify, though a state should refrain from signature if it has little intention of ratifying.

PERIOD FOR RATIFICATION

It is not usual to set a deadline for ratification, and some multilateral treaties are ratified (or more usually acceded to) many years later. The United States did not ratify the Genocide Convention 1948 until 1988. Following the break-up of the Soviet Union, the Baltic States (not regarding themselves as successor states to the Soviet Union) acceded to many treaties, including some nearly fifty years old. Libya and the United Kingdom acceded to the Hague Convention on the Pacific Settlement of Disputes 1907 some sixty-five and eighty years, respectively, later.

* * *

RIGHTS AND OBLIGATIONS PRIOR TO ENTRY INTO FORCE

In the period prior to the entry into force of a treaty, the acts of adopting, signing and consenting to be bound will create certain rights and obligations for the negotiating and contracting states, and for any depositary. The most obvious relate to those matters which have to be attended to so that the treaty can enter into force. As from the moment the text is adopted, the provisions on depositary functions, authentication, consent to be bound, reservations and other matters necessarily arising before entry into force will apply (Article 24(4)). Other rights and obligations will arise during the interim period if the Convention or the treaty in question so provides, such as in relation to a preparatory commission.

OBLIGATION NOT TO DEFEAT THE OBJECT AND PURPOSE OF A TREATY PRIOR TO ITS ENTRY INTO FORCE

Article 18 requires a state "to refrain from acts which would defeat the object and purpose of a treaty" when:

(a) it has signed the treaty * * * subject to ratification, until it shall have made its intention clear not to become a party to the treaty; or

(b) it has expressed its consent to be bound by the treaty, pending the entry into force of the treaty and provided that such entry into force is not unduly delayed.

It is sometimes argued (especially by law students) that a state which has not yet even ratified a treaty must, in accordance with Article 18, nevertheless comply with it, or, at least, do nothing inconsistent with its provisions. This is clearly wrong, since the act of ratification would then have little or no purpose, the obligation to perform the treaty being then not dependent on ratification and entry into force.

When a treaty enters into force on the signature of the negotiating states signing at the same time, the legal effect of their signature is established at that point. However, if the treaty enters into force only after all (or a minimum number of) states have signed (which is only likely to occur with a plurilateral treaty), it is possible that a state could "withdraw" its signature before it enters into force. Although, withdrawal of signature could not be done physically, a diplomatic note to the depositary that the signature of the state "shall be considered as having been withdrawn" would have the same legal effect as the withdrawal of an instrument of ratification before entry into force. Another way in which the legal effect of signature might be nullified would be if the act of signature were invalid, though the chances of that occurring are likely to be extremely rare.

* * *

ENTRY INTO FORCE

* * *

[The] suggestion that *all* states are bound by a (multilateral) treaty once it has entered into force is a common misconception, even among diplomats. When a treaty has entered into force, it binds *only* those states which have consented to be bound by it. A treaty is much closer to a contract. But if the treaty reflects (or comes to reflect) rules of customary international law, a non-party can be bound by those rules, though only as customary law.

Each of the states for which a treaty is in force is a "party" (Article 2(1)(g)). Thereafter it should never be referred to by the—uninformative and misleading—term "signatory." But it must also be remembered that when a state expresses its consent to be bound it does not necessarily mean that the treaty will enter into force for it then: it will depend on whether the treaty is already in force for the states which have already consented to be bound, or whether further consents are needed to bring it into force. A state's consent may of course have the effect of bringing the treaty into force if it is the last one needed to do that.

* * *

EXPRESS PROVISIONS

A treaty enters into force in such manner and on such date as provided for in the treaty or as the negotiating states may agree (Article 24(1)).

* * *

NO PROVISION OR AGREEMENT ON ENTRY INTO FORCE

If the treaty has no express provision on entry into force, and there is no agreement about it between the negotiating states, the treaty will enter into force as soon as all those states have consented to be bound (Article. 24(2)).

* * *

DATE OF ENTRY INTO FORCE

In the case of *multilateral* treaties it is usual to provide that the *date* of entry into force will be a specified number of days, weeks or months following the deposit of the last instrument of ratification which is needed to bring the treaty into force (see, e.g., Article 84(1) of the Vienna Convention itself). The period may be of any length, but the normal range is from thirty days to twelve months. This breathing space gives the depositary time to notify the contracting states of the forthcoming entry into force. In addition, contracting states may need time to bring into effect implementing legislation which they have previously enacted (or even to enact it). It also allows time for other necessary preparations.

* * *

EXERCISE ON TREATY ANALYSIS

[The following is based on an actual case, but we have changed some of the facts, such as the inclusion of the payment of undisclosed sums, to make the exercise better suited to issues raised in this Chapter of the book.] The American–Russian Cultural Cooperation Foundation (the Foundation), an entity organized by the United States federal government, negotiated an agreement with the Organizing Committee for the Goodwill Mission (the Organizing Committee), a group under the auspices of the Russian Ministry of Culture. Under the agreement, the Russian Royal Jewels of the Romanov (Tsar) family were going to be shown in various museums in the United States.

Following several preliminary agreements, members of the American Foundation flew to Moscow to negotiate the final deal with the Russian Organizing Committee. The American side was advised by American lawyers from the Moscow office of a major Washington, D.C. law firm; the Russians did not consider the consultation of lawyers necessary and relied on the expertise of government officials and museum personnel. The agreement was signed in Moscow.

While in Moscow, two of the Foundation's representatives secretly paid undisclosed sums of money to key government officials in the Russian Ministry of Culture to secure their cooperation.

After the first exhibition of the Jewels in the United States, the Russian side was unhappy with several of its features. They considered security insufficient, some displays flawed, and the distribution of the proceeds too favorable to the American side. They requested re-negotiation of the agreement, but the Americans responded that "a deal is a deal."

The Russians then wanted to walk away from the agreement and claimed that it was never validly made. Even if the agreement was valid, the Russians declared that they "terminated" it effective immediately.

Look at the Vienna Convention on the Law of Treaties and discuss whether it applies and, if so, whether under its rules the Russians were free of their obligations.

———————

Like all legal texts, treaties have to be interpreted. Here are two (American) examples of a treaty interpretation by the U.S. Supreme Court. How does the Court in *Asakura* interpret the Treaty of Friendship, Commerce and Navigation (FCN) between the United States and Japan? What criteria does the Court consider? Even though the decision predates the VCLT, ask yourself whether the Court's approach comports with VCLT principles of treaty interpretation.

ASAKURA V. CITY OF SEATTLE

United States Supreme Court
265 U.S. 332 (1924)

JUSTICE BUTLER:

Plaintiff in error is a subject of the emperor of Japan, and since 1904 has resided in Seattle, Wash. Since July, 1915, he has been engaged in business there as a pawnbroker. The city passed an ordinance, which took effect July 2, 1921, regulating the business of pawnbroker, and repealing former ordinances on the same subject. It makes it unlawful for any person to engage in the business unless he shall have a license, and the ordinance provides "that no such license shall be granted unless the applicant be a citizen of the United States." Violations of the ordinance are punishable by fine or imprisonment or both. Plaintiff in error brought this suit in the superior court of King County, Wash., against the city, its comptroller, and chief of police, to restrain them from enforcing the ordinance against him. He attacked the ordinance on the ground that it violates the treaty between the United States and the empire of Japan, proclaimed April 5, 1911 (37 Stat. 1504); violates the Constitution of the state of Washington, and also the due process and equal protection clauses of the Fourteenth Amendment of the Constitution of the United States. He declared his willingness to comply with any valid ordinance relating to the business of pawnbroker. It was shown that he had about $5,000 invested in his business, which would be broken up and destroyed by the enforcement of the ordinance. The superior court granted the relief prayed. On appeal, the Supreme Court of the state held the ordinance valid and reversed the decree. The case is here on writ of error under section 237 of the Judicial Code (Comp. St. § 1214).

Does the ordinance violate the treaty? Plaintiff in error invokes and relies upon the following provisions:

> "The citizens or subjects of each of the high contracting parties shall have liberty to enter, travel and reside in the territories of the other to carry on trade, wholesale and retail, to own or lease and occupy houses, manufactories, warehouses and shops, to employ agents of their choice, to lease land for residential and commercial purposes, and generally to do anything incident to or necessary for trade upon the same terms as native citizens or subjects, submitting themselves to the laws and regulations there established. * * * The citizens or subjects of each * * * shall receive, in the territories of the other, the most constant protection and security of their persons and property. * * * "

A treaty made under the authority of the United States—

> "shall be the supreme law of the land; and the judges in every state shall be bound thereby, anything in the Constitution or laws of any state to the contrary notwithstanding." Constitution, art. 6, § 2.

* * * The treaty was made to strengthen friendly relations between the two nations. As to the things covered by it, the provision quoted establishes the rule of equality between Japanese subjects while in this country and native citizens. Treaties for the protection of citizens of one country residing in the territory of another are numerous, and make for good understanding between nations. The treaty is binding within the state of Washington. The rule of equality established by it cannot be rendered nugatory in any part of the United States by municipal ordinances or state laws. It stands on the same footing of supremacy as do the provisions of the Constitution and laws of the United States. It operates of itself without the aid of any legislation, state or national; and it will be applied and given authoritative effect by the courts.

* * *

It remains to be considered whether the business of pawnbroker is "trade" within the meaning of the treaty. Treaties are to be construed in a broad and liberal spirit, and, when two constructions are possible, one restrictive of rights that may be claimed under it and the other favorable to them, the latter is to be preferred. The ordinance defines "pawnbroker" to "mean and include every person whose business or occupation it is to take and receive by way of pledge, pawn or exchange, goods, wares or mer-

chandise, or any kind of personal property whatever, for the repayment or
security of any money loaned thereon, or to loan money on deposit or personal property," and defines "pawnshop" to "mean and include every place
at which the business of pawnbroker is carried on." The language of the
treaty is comprehensive. The phrase "to carry on trade" is broad. That it
is not to be given a restricted meaning is plain. The clauses, "to * * * own
or lease * * * shops, * * * to lease land * * * for * * * commercial purposes,
and generally to do anything incident to or necessary for trade," and
"shall receive * * * the most constant protection and security of their * * *
property, * * * " all go to show the intention of the parties that the citizens or subjects of either shall have liberty in the territory of the other to
engage in all kinds and classes of business that are or reasonably may be
embraced within the meaning of the word "trade" as used in the treaty.

By definition contained in the ordinance, pawnbrokers are regarded as
carrying on a "business." A feature of it is the lending of money upon the
pledge or pawn of personal property which, in case of default, may be sold
to pay the debt. While the amounts of the loans made in that business are
relatively small and the character of property pledged as security is different, the transactions are similar to loans made by banks on collateral
security. The business of lending money on portable securities has been
carried on for centuries. In most of the countries of Europe, the pledge
system is carried on by governmental agencies; in some of them the business is also carried on by private parties. In England, as in the United
States, the private pledge system prevails. In this country, the practice of
pledging personal property for loans dates back to early colonial times,
and pawnshops have been regulated by state laws for more than a century. We have found no state legislation abolishing or forbidding the business. * * * There is nothing in the character of the business of pawnbroker which requires it to be excluded from the field covered by the above-
quoted provision, and it must be held that such business is "trade" within
the meaning of the treaty. The ordinance violates the treaty. The question
in the present case relates solely to Japanese subjects who have been admitted to this country. We do not pass upon the right of admission or the
construction of the treaty in this respect, as that question is not before us
and would require consideration of other matters with which it is not now
necessary to deal. We need not consider other grounds upon which it is
attacked.

Decree reversed.

––––––––––

In *Asakura* the Court interpreted the meaning of a specific provision. As
you will see, in the next case the Court is confronted with a different
problem. What exactly is that problem in *Alvarez-Machain*? Does the
VCLT help to resolve it?

How does the majority in *Alvarez-Machain* read the U.S.–Mexican Extradition Treaty? Does that reading conform to the VCLT? Why does the dissent read the Treaty very differently? What is at the core of their disagreement?

Who has the better arguments? What are the long-term implications of these different readings, especially with regard to future treaty drafting and to cooperation between the United States and its treaty partners?

UNITED STATES V. ALVAREZ–MACHAIN

United States Supreme Court
504 U.S. 655 (1992)

CHIEF JUSTICE REHNQUIST delivered the opinion of the Court, in which JUSTICES WHITE, SCALIA, KENNEDY, SOUTER, and THOMAS joined. JUSTICE STEVENS filed a dissenting opinion, in which JUSTICES BLACKMUN and O'CONNOR joined.

The issue in this case is whether a criminal defendant, abducted to the United States from a nation with which it has an extradition treaty, thereby acquires a defense to the jurisdiction of this country's courts. We hold that he does not, and that he may be tried in federal district court for violations of the criminal law of the United States.

Respondent, Humberto Alvarez-Machain, is a citizen and resident of Mexico. He was indicted for participating in the kidnap and murder of United States Drug Enforcement Administration (DEA) special agent Enrique Camarena-Salazar and a Mexican pilot working with Camarena, Alfredo Zavala-Avelar. The DEA believes that respondent, a medical doctor, participated in the murder by prolonging Agent Camarena's life so that others could further torture and interrogate him. On April 2, 1990, respondent was forcibly kidnaped from his medical office in Guadalajara, Mexico, to be flown by private plane to El Paso, Texas, where he was arrested by DEA officials. The District Court concluded that DEA agents were responsible for respondent's abduction, although they were not personally involved in it.

Respondent moved to dismiss the indictment, claiming that his abduction constituted outrageous governmental conduct, and that the District Court lacked jurisdiction to try him because he was abducted in violation of the extradition treaty between the United States and Mexico. The District Court rejected the outrageous governmental conduct claim, but held that it lacked jurisdiction to try respondent because his abduction violated the Extradition Treaty. The District Court discharged respondent and ordered that he be repatriated to Mexico.

The Court of Appeals affirmed the dismissal of the indictment and the repatriation of respondent, relying on its decision in *United States v. Ver-*

dugo-Urquidez. In *Verdugo*, the Court of Appeals held that the forcible abduction of a Mexican national with the authorization or participation of the United States violated the Extradition Treaty between the United States and Mexico.[3] Although the Treaty does not expressly prohibit such abductions, the Court of Appeals held that the purpose of the Treaty was violated by a forcible abduction, which, along with a formal protest by the offended nation, would give a defendant the right to invoke the Treaty violation to defeat jurisdiction of the District Court to try him. The Court of Appeals further held that the proper remedy for such a violation would be dismissal of the indictment and repatriation of the defendant to Mexico.

In the instant case, the Court of Appeals affirmed the District Court's finding that the United States had authorized the abduction of respondent, and that letters from the Mexican Government to the United States Government served as an official protest of the Treaty violation. Therefore, the Court of Appeals ordered that the indictment against respondent be dismissed and that respondent be repatriated to Mexico. We granted certiorari and now reverse.

Although we have never before addressed the precise issue raised in the present case, we have previously considered proceedings in claimed violation of an extradition treaty and proceedings against a defendant brought before a court by means of a forcible abduction. We addressed the former issue in *United States v. Rauscher*, 119 U.S. 407 (1886); more precisely, the issue whether the Webster–Ashburton Treaty of 1842, which governed extraditions between England and the United States, prohibited the prosecution of defendant Rauscher for a crime other than the crime for which he had been extradited. Whether this prohibition, known as the doctrine of specialty, was an intended part of the treaty had been disputed between the two nations for some time. Justice Miller delivered the opinion of the Court, which carefully examined the terms and history of the treaty; the practice of nations in regards to extradition treaties; the case law from the States; and the writings of commentators, and reached the following conclusion:

> "[A] person who has been brought within the jurisdiction of the court *by virtue of proceedings under an extradition* treaty, can only be tried for one of the offences described in that treaty, and for the offence with which he is charged in the proceedings for his extradition, until a reasonable time and opportunity have been given him, after his release or trial upon such charge, to return to the country from whose asylum he had been forcibly taken under those proceedings." Id., at 430 (emphasis added).

---

[3] Rene Martin Verdugo-Urquidez was also indicted for the murder of Agent Camarena. In an earlier decision, we held that the Fourth Amendment did not apply to a search by United States agents of Verdugo-Urquidez' home in Mexico. *United States v. Verdugo-Urquidez*, 494 U.S. 259 (1990).

In addition, Justice Miller's opinion noted that any doubt as to this interpretation was put to rest by two federal statutes which imposed the doctrine of specialty upon extradition treaties to which the United States was a party. Unlike the case before us today, the defendant in *Rauscher* had been brought to the United States by way of an extradition treaty; there was no issue of a forcible abduction.

In *Ker v. Illinois*, 119 U.S. 436 (1886), also written by Justice Miller and decided the same day as *Rauscher*, we addressed the issue of a defendant brought before the court by way of a forcible abduction. Frederick Ker had been tried and convicted in an Illinois court for larceny; his presence before the court was procured by means of forcible abduction from Peru. A messenger was sent to Lima with the proper warrant to demand Ker by virtue of the extradition treaty between Peru and the United States. The messenger, however, disdained reliance on the treaty processes, and instead forcibly kidnaped Ker and brought him to the United States. We distinguished Ker's case from *Rauscher*, on the basis that Ker was not brought into the United States by virtue of the extradition treaty between the United States and Peru, and rejected Ker's argument that he had a right under the extradition treaty to be returned to this country only in accordance with its terms. We rejected Ker's due process argument more broadly, holding in line with "the highest authorities" that "such forcible abduction is no sufficient reason why the party should not answer when brought within the jurisdiction of the court which has the right to try him for such an offence, and presents no valid objection to his trial in such court."

* * *

In construing a treaty, as in construing a statute, we first look to its terms to determine its meaning. The Treaty says nothing about the obligations of the United States and Mexico to refrain from forcible abductions of people from the territory of the other nation, or the consequences under the Treaty if such an abduction occurs. Respondent submits that Article 22(1) of the Treaty, which states that it "shall apply to offenses specified in Article 2 [including murder] committed before and after this Treaty enters into force," evidences an intent to make application of the Treaty mandatory for those offenses. However, the more natural conclusion is that Article 22 was included to ensure that the Treaty was applied to extraditions requested after the Treaty went into force, regardless of when the crime of extradition occurred.

More critical to respondent's argument is Article 9 of the Treaty, which provides:

"1. Neither Contracting Party shall be bound to deliver up its own nationals, but the executive authority of the requested Party shall, if not prevented by the laws of that Party, have the power to deliver them up if, in its discretion, it be deemed proper to do so.

"2. If extradition is not granted pursuant to paragraph 1 of this Article, the requested Party shall submit the case to its competent authorities for the purpose of prosecution, provided that Party has jurisdiction over the offense."

According to respondent, Article 9 embodies the terms of the bargain which the United States struck: If the United States wishes to prosecute a Mexican national, it may request that individual's extradition. Upon a request from the United States, Mexico may either extradite the individual or submit the case to the proper authorities for prosecution in Mexico. In this way, respondent reasons, each nation preserved its right to choose whether its nationals would be tried in its own courts or by the courts of the other nation. This preservation of rights would be frustrated if either nation were free to abduct nationals of the other nation for the purposes of prosecution. More broadly, respondent reasons, as did the Court of Appeals, that all the processes and restrictions on the obligation to extradite established by the Treaty would make no sense if either nation were free to resort to forcible kidnapping to gain the presence of an individual for prosecution in a manner not contemplated by the Treaty.

We do not read the Treaty in such a fashion. Article 9 does not purport to specify the only way in which one country may gain custody of a national of the other country for the purposes of prosecution. In the absence of an extradition treaty, nations are under no obligation to surrender those in their country to foreign authorities for prosecution. Extradition treaties exist so as to impose mutual obligations to surrender individuals in certain defined sets of circumstances, following established procedures. The Treaty thus provides a mechanism which would not otherwise exist, requiring, under certain circumstances, the United States and Mexico to extradite individuals to the other country, and establishing the procedures to be followed when the Treaty is invoked.

The history of negotiation and practice under the Treaty also fails to show that abductions outside of the Treaty constitute a violation of the Treaty. As the Solicitor General notes, the Mexican Government was made aware, as early as 1906, of the *Ker* doctrine, and the United States' position that it applied to forcible abductions made outside of the terms of the United States–Mexico Extradition Treaty. Nonetheless, the current version of the Treaty, signed in 1978, does not attempt to establish a rule that would in any way curtail the effect of *Ker*.[12] Moreover, although language which would grant individuals exactly the right sought by respondent had been considered and drafted as early as 1935 by a prominent

---

[12] The parties did expressly include the doctrine of specialty in Article 17 of the Treaty, notwithstanding the judicial recognition of it in *United States v. Rauscher*.

group of legal scholars sponsored by the faculty of Harvard Law School, no such clause appears in the current Treaty.[13]

Thus, the language of the Treaty, in the context of its history, does not support the proposition that the Treaty prohibits abductions outside of its terms. The remaining question, therefore, is whether the Treaty should be interpreted so as to include an implied term prohibiting prosecution where the defendant's presence is obtained by means other than those established by the Treaty.

Respondent contends that the Treaty must be interpreted against the backdrop of customary international law, and that international abductions are "so clearly prohibited in international law" that there was no reason to include such a clause in the Treaty itself. The international censure of international abductions is further evidenced, according to respondent, by the United Nations Charter and the Charter of the Organization of American States. Respondent does not argue that these sources of international law provide an independent basis for the right respondent asserts not to be tried in the United States, but rather that they should inform the interpretation of the Treaty terms.

* * *

* * * [T]he difficulty with the support respondent garners from international law is that none of it relates to the practice of nations in relation to extradition treaties. In *Rauscher*, we implied a term in the Webster–Ashburton Treaty because of the practice of nations with regard to extradition treaties. In the instant case, respondent would imply terms in the Extradition Treaty from the practice of nations with regards to international law more generally. Respondent would have us find that the Treaty acts as a prohibition against a violation of the general principle of international law that one government may not "exercise its police power in the territory of another state." There are many actions which could be taken by a nation that would violate this principle, including waging war, but it cannot seriously be contended that an invasion of the United States by Mexico would violate the terms of the Extradition Treaty between the two nations.

In sum, to infer from this Treaty and its terms that it prohibits all means of gaining the presence of an individual outside of its terms goes beyond established precedent and practice. * * * The general principles cited by

---

[13] In Article 16 of the Draft Convention on Jurisdiction with Respect to Crime, the Advisory Committee of the Research in International Law proposed:

"In exercising jurisdiction under this Convention, no State shall prosecute or punish any person who has been brought within its territory or a place subject to its authority by recourse to measures in violation of international law or international convention without first obtaining the consent of the State or States whose rights have been violated by such measures." Harvard Research in International Law, 29 Am.J. Int'l L. 442 (Supp. 1935).

respondent simply fail to persuade us that we should imply in the United States–Mexico Extradition Treaty a term prohibiting international abductions.

Respondent and his amici may be correct that respondent's abduction was "shocking," and that it may be in violation of general international law principles. Mexico has protested the abduction of respondent through diplomatic notes, and the decision of whether respondent should be returned to Mexico, as a matter outside of the Treaty, is a matter for the Executive Branch.[16] We conclude, however, that respondent's abduction was not in violation of the Extradition Treaty between the United States and Mexico, and therefore the rule of *Ker v. Illinois* is fully applicable to this case. The fact of respondent's forcible abduction does not therefore prohibit his trial in a court in the United States for violations of the criminal laws of the United States.

The judgment of the Court of Appeals is therefore reversed, and the case is remanded for further proceedings consistent with this opinion.

So ordered.

JUSTICE STEVENS, with whom JUSTICE BLACKMUN and JUSTICE O'CONNOR join, dissenting.

The Court correctly observes that this case raises a question of first impression. The case is unique for several reasons. It does not involve an ordinary abduction by a private kidnaper, or bounty hunter, as in *Ker v. Illinois*; nor does it involve the apprehension of an American fugitive who committed a crime in one State and sought asylum in another, as in *Frisbie v. Collins*. Rather, it involves this country's abduction of another country's citizen; it also involves a violation of the territorial integrity of that other country, with which this country has signed an extradition treaty.

A Mexican citizen was kidnaped in Mexico and charged with a crime committed in Mexico; his offense allegedly violated both Mexican and American law. Mexico has formally demanded on at least two separate occasions that he be returned to Mexico and has represented that he will be prosecuted and, if convicted, punished for his offense. It is clear that Mexico's demand must be honored if this official abduction violated the 1978 Extradition Treaty between the United States and Mexico. In my opinion, a fair reading of the treaty in light of our decision in *United States v. Rauscher*, and applicable principles of international law, leads inexorably to the conclusion that the District Court, *United States v. Caro-Quintero*, and the Court of Appeals for the Ninth Circuit correctly construed that instrument.

---

[16] The Mexican Government has also requested from the United States the extradition of two individuals it suspects of having abducted respondent in Mexico, on charges of kidnaping.

I

The extradition treaty with Mexico is a comprehensive document containing 23 articles and an appendix listing the extraditable offenses covered by the agreement. The parties announced their purpose in the preamble: The two governments desire "to cooperate more closely in the fight against crime and, to this end, to mutually render better assistance in matters of extradition."[4] From the preamble, through the description of the parties' obligations with respect to offenses committed within as well as beyond the territory of a requesting party, the delineation of the procedures and evidentiary requirements for extradition, the special provisions for political offenses and capital punishment, and other details, the Treaty appears to have been designed to cover the entire subject of extradition. Thus, Article 22, entitled "Scope of Application," states that the "Treaty shall apply to offenses specified in Article 2 committed before and after this Treaty enters into force," and Article 2 directs that "[e]xtradition shall take place, subject to this Treaty, for willful acts which fall within any of [the extraditable offenses listed in] the clauses of the Appendix." Moreover, as noted by the Court, Article 9 expressly provides that neither contracting party is bound to deliver up its own nationals, although it may do so in its discretion, but if it does not do so, it "shall submit the case to its competent authorities for purposes of prosecution."

The Government's claim that the Treaty is not exclusive, but permits forcible governmental kidnaping, would transform these, and other, provisions into little more than verbiage. For example, provisions requiring "sufficient" evidence to grant extradition (Art. 3), withholding extradition for political or military offenses (Art. 5), withholding extradition when the person sought has already been tried (Art. 6), withholding extradition when the statute of limitations for the crime has lapsed (Art. 7), and granting the requested Country discretion to refuse to extradite an individual who would face the death penalty in the requesting country (Art. 8), would serve little purpose if the requesting country could simply kidnap the person. As the Court of Appeals for the Ninth Circuit recognized in a related case, "[e]ach of these provisions would be utterly frustrated if a kidnapping were held to be a permissible course of governmental con-

---

[4] In construing a treaty, the Court has the "responsibility to give the specific words of the treaty a meaning consistent with the shared expectations of the contracting parties." *Air France v. Saks*, 470 U.S. 392, 399 (1985). It is difficult to see how an interpretation that encourages unilateral action could foster cooperation and mutual assistance—the stated goals of the Treaty. See also Presidential Letter of Transmittal attached to Senate Advice and Consent 3 (Treaty would "make a significant contribution to international cooperation in law enforcement").

Extradition treaties prevent international conflict by providing agreed-upon standards so that the parties may cooperate and avoid retaliatory invasions of territorial sovereignty. * * *

The object of reducing conflict by promoting cooperation explains why extradition treaties do not prohibit informal consensual delivery of fugitives, but why they do prohibit state-sponsored abductions. See Restatement (Third) of Foreign Relations (Restatement) § 432, and Comments a–c (1987).

duct." *United States v. Verdugo-Urquidez*, 939 F.2d 1341, 1349 (1991). In addition, all of these provisions "only make sense if they are understood as *requiring* each treaty signatory to comply with those procedures whenever it wishes to obtain jurisdiction over an individual who is located in another treaty nation." *Id.*, at 1351.

It is true, as the Court notes, that there is no express promise by either party to refrain from forcible abductions in the territory of the other nation. Relying on that omission, the Court, in effect, concludes that the Treaty merely creates an optional method of obtaining jurisdiction over alleged offenders, and that the parties silently reserved the right to resort to self-help whenever they deem force more expeditious than legal process.[11] If the United States, for example, thought it more expedient to torture or simply to execute a person rather than to attempt extradition, these options would be equally available because they, too, were not explicitly prohibited by the Treaty.[12] That, however, is a highly improbable interpretation of a consensual agreement,[13] which on its face appears to have been intended to set forth comprehensive and exclusive rules concerning the subject of extradition.[14] In my opinion, "the manifest scope and object of the treaty itself," *Rauscher*, 119 U.S., at 422, plainly imply a mutual undertaking to respect the territorial integrity of the other contracting party. That opinion is confirmed by a consideration of the "legal context" in which the Treaty was negotiated.[15]

* * *

---

[11] To make the point more starkly, the Court has, in effect, written into Article 9 a new provision, which says: "Notwithstanding paragraphs 1 and 2 of this Article, either Contracting Party can, without the consent of the other, abduct nationals from the territory of one Party to be tried in the territory of the other."

[12] It is ironic that the United States has attempted to justify its unilateral action based on the kidnaping, torture, and murder of a federal agent by authorizing the kidnaping of respondent, for which the American law enforcement agents who participated have now been charged by Mexico. This goes to my earlier point, that extradition treaties promote harmonious relations by providing for the orderly surrender of a person by one state to another, and without such treaties, resort to force often followed.

[13] This Court has previously described a treaty as generally "in its nature a contract between two nations," *Foster v. Neilson*, 2 Pet. 253, 314, (1829); see *Rauscher*, 119 U.S., at 418,; it is also in this country the law of the land. 2 Pet., at 314; 119 U.S., at 418–419.

[14] Mexico's understanding is that "[t]he extradition treaty governs comprehensively the delivery of all persons for trial in the requesting state 'for an offense committed outside the territory of the requesting Party.' " Brief for United Mexican States as *Amicus Curiae*. And Canada, with whom the United States also shares a large border and with whom the United States also has an extradition treaty, understands the treaty to be "the exclusive means for a requesting government to obtain * * * a removal" of a person from its territory, unless a nation otherwise gives its consent. Brief for Government of Canada as *Amicus Curiae*.

[15] The United States has offered no evidence from the negotiating record, ratification process, or later communications with Mexico to support the suggestion that a different understanding with Mexico was reached. See Bassiouni, International Extradition: United States Law and Practice, ch. 2, § 4.3, at 82 ("Negotiations, preparatory works, and diplomatic correspondence are an integral part of th[e] surrounding circumstances, and [are] often relied on by courts in ascertaining the intentions of the parties").

III

A critical flaw pervades the Court's entire opinion. It fails to differentiate between the conduct of private citizens, which does not violate any treaty obligation, and conduct expressly authorized by the Executive Branch of the Government, which unquestionably constitutes a flagrant violation of international law, and in my opinion, also constitutes a breach of our treaty obligations. Thus, at the outset of its opinion, the Court states the issue as "whether a criminal defendant, abducted to the United States from a nation with which it has an extradition treaty, thereby acquires a defense to the jurisdiction of this country's courts." That, of course, is the question decided in *Ker v. Illinois*; it is not, however, the question presented for decision today.

* * *

IV

As the Court observes at the outset of its opinion, there is reason to believe that respondent participated in an especially brutal murder of an American law enforcement agent. That fact, if true, may explain the Executive's intense interest in punishing respondent in our courts. Such an explanation, however, provides no justification for disregarding the Rule of Law that this Court has a duty to uphold. That the Executive may wish to reinterpret the Treaty to allow for an action that the Treaty in no way authorizes should not influence this Court's interpretation. Indeed, the desire for revenge exerts "a kind of hydraulic pressure * * * before which even well settled principles of law will bend," *Northern Securities Co. v. United States*, 193 U.S. 197, 401 (1904) (Holmes, J., dissenting), but it is precisely at such moments that we should remember and be guided by our duty "to render judgment evenly and dispassionately according to law, as each is given understanding to ascertain and apply it." *United States v. Mine Workers*, 330 U.S. 258, 342 (1947) (Rutledge, J., dissenting). The way that we perform that duty in a case of this kind sets an example that other tribunals in other countries are sure to emulate.

The significance of this Court's precedents is illustrated by a recent decision of the Court of Appeal of the Republic of South Africa. Based largely on its understanding of the import of this Court's cases—including our decision in *Ker*—that court held that the prosecution of a defendant kidnaped by agents of South Africa in another country must be dismissed. The Court of Appeal of South Africa—indeed, I suspect most courts throughout the civilized world—will be deeply disturbed by the "monstrous" decision the Court announces today. For every nation that has an interest in preserving the Rule of Law is affected, directly or indirectly, by a decision of this character. As Thomas Paine warned, an "avidity to punish is always dangerous to liberty" because it leads a nation "to stretch, to misinterpret, and to misapply even the best of laws." To counter that tendency, he reminds us:

> "He that would make his own liberty secure must guard even his enemy from oppression; for if he violates this duty he establishes a precedent that will reach to himself."

I respectfully dissent.

3. CUSTOMARY INTERNATIONAL LAW

DAVID BEDERMAN, INTERNATIONAL LAW FRAMEWORKS
(3d. ed. 2010)

* * *

Custom is a source unique for public international law. It also presents special problems of interpretation and methodology. Most of these problems stem from the fact that in most mature legal systems, lawyers typically assume that the only binding rules are those made by legislatures (or, by delegation, to administrative agencies or bureaucrats) or by courts. We tend to forget that law can also be made by the consent of communities of people, without any formal enactment by governmental entities. Indeed, such customs or practices are sometimes not even written down. Think of a group of businesspeople who formulate their own rules for conducting certain types of transactions. (We call these "usages of trade.") Or imagine that the standard of care exercised within a certain community for a particular activity becomes the relevant basis for determining negligence. Although we do not tend to think of custom as a legitimate source of law, we do know that industry customs are enforced in commercial disputes, just as an industry benchmark can be held up as the standard of negligence.

So custom remains a powerful, if subliminal, source of law, even in "mature" legal systems. But public international law is not a mature legal system at all—it remains strikingly primitive. And customary international law is a source of signal strength and flexibility for international law. It allows international legal actors to informally develop rules of behavior, without the necessity of resorting to more formal and difficult means of law-making (like treaties). * * *

There are two key elements in the formation of a customary international law rule. They are elegantly and succinctly expressed in Article 38 of the ICJ Statute. Custom is "evidence of a general practice accepted as law." To show a rule of customary international law, one must prove to the satisfaction of the relevant decision-maker (whether it be an international tribunal, domestic court, or government or inter-governmental actor) that the rule has (1) been followed as a "general practice," *and* (2) has been "accepted as law." Although this formulation has been subject to criticism as being too simplistic (or not reflecting the complex realities of international legal negotiations), it remains a useful paradigm of analysis.

The first part of the equation (the general practice element) is an objective inquiry: have international actors really followed the rule? has the practice been consistent? has the practice been followed for a sufficient period of time? The second part of the equation (the "accepted as law" element) has often been called a subjective, or even psychological, inquiry. It asks *why* an international actor has observed a particular practice. This is specifically known as *opinio juris sive necessitatus* (or just "*opinio juris*"), and it attempts to ascertain whether a practice is observed out of a sense of legal obligation or necessity, or rather, merely out of courtesy, neighborliness, or expediency.

* * *

The Paquete Habana is *the* classic American case dealing with customary international law. It is a long opinion—but for a good reason. What rule does the Supreme Court find in customary international law? How does the Court ascertain customary international law? In particular, what sources does it rely on? What problem does the *Young Jacob* case create?

THE PAQUETE HABANA
THE LOLA

United States Supreme Court
20 S. Ct. 290 (1900)

* * *

JUSTICE GRAY:

These are two appeals from decrees of the district court of the United States for the southern district of Florida condemning two fishing vessels and their cargoes as prize of war.

Each vessel was a fishing smack, running in and out of Havana, and regularly engaged in fishing on the coast of Cuba; sailed under the Spanish flag; was owned by a Spanish subject of Cuban birth, living in the city of Havana; was commanded by a subject of Spain, also residing in Havana; and her master and crew had no interest in the vessel, but were entitled to shares, amounting in all to two thirds, of her catch, the other third belonging to her owner. Her cargo consisted of fresh fish, caught by her crew from the sea, put on board as they were caught, and kept and sold alive. Until stopped by the blockading squadron she had no knowledge of the existence of the war or of any blockade. She had no arms or ammunition on board, and made no attempt to run the blockade after she knew of its existence, nor any resistance at the time of the capture.

The Paquete Habana was a sloop, 43 feet long on the keel, and of 25 tons burden, and had a crew of three Cubans, including the master, who had a fishing license from the Spanish government, and no other commission or license. She left Havana March 25, 1898; sailed along the coast of Cuba to Cape San Antonio, at the western end of the island, and there fished for twenty-five days, lying between the reefs off the cape, within the territorial waters of Spain; and then started back for Havana, with a cargo of about 40 quintals of live fish. On April 25, 1898, about 2 miles off Mariel, and 11 miles from Havana, she was captured by the United States gunboat Castine.

The Lola was a schooner, 51 feet long on the keel, and of 35 tons burden, and had a crew of six Cubans, including the master, and no commission or license. She left Havana April 11, 1898, and proceeded to Campeachy sound, off Yucatan, fished there eight days, and started back for Havana with a cargo of about 10,000 pounds of live fish. On April 26, 1898, near Havana, she was stopped by the United States steamship Cincinnati, and was warned not to go into Havana, but was told that she would be allowed to land at Bahia Honda. She then changed her course, and put for Bahia Honda, but on the next morning, when near that port, was captured by the United States steamship Dolphin.

Both the fishing vessels were brought by their captors into Key West. A libel for the condemnation of each vessel and her cargo as prize of war was there filed on April 27, 1898; a claim was interposed by her master on behalf of himself and the other members of the crew, and of her owner; evidence was taken, showing the facts above stated; and on May 30, 1898, a final decree of condemnation and sale was entered, "the court not being satisfied that as a matter of law, without any ordinance, treaty, or proclamation, fishing vessels of this class are exempt from seizure."

Each vessel was thereupon sold by auction; the Paquete Habana for the sum of $490; and the Lola for the sum of $800. There was no other evidence in the record of the value of either vessel or of her cargo.

* * *

We are then brought to the consideration of the question whether, upon the facts appearing in these records, the fishing smacks were subject to capture by the armed vessels of the United States during the recent war with Spain.

By an ancient usage among civilized nations, beginning centuries ago, and gradually ripening into a rule of international law, coast fishing vessels, pursuing their vocation of catching and bringing in fresh fish, have been recognized as exempt, with their cargoes and crews, from capture as prize of war.

This doctrine, however, has been earnestly contested at the bar; and no complete collection of the instances illustrating it is to be found, so far as we are aware, in a single published work although many are referred to and discussed by the writers on international law, notable in 2 Ortolan, Règles Internationales et Diplomatie de la Mer (4th ed.) lib. 3, chap. 2, pp. 51–56; in 4 Calvo, Droit International (5th ed.) §§ 2367–2373; in De Boeck, Propriété Privée Ennemie sous Pavillon Ennemi, §§ 191–196; and in Hall, International Law (4th ed.) § 148. It is therefore worth the while to trace the history of the rule, from the earliest accessible sources, through the increasing recognition of it, with occasional setbacks, to what we may now justly consider as its final establishment in our own country and generally throughout the civilized world.

The earliest acts of any government on the subject, mentioned in the books, either emanated from, or were approved by, a King of England.

In 1403 and 1406 Henry IV. issued orders to his admirals and other officers, entitled "Concerning Safety for Fishermen–*De Securitate pro Piscatoribus.*" By an order of October 26, 1403, reciting that it was made pursuant to a treaty between himself and the King of France; and for the greater safety of the fishermen of either country, and so that they could be, and carry on their industry, the more safely on the sea, and deal with each other in peace; and that the French King had consented that English fishermen should be treated likewise,—it was ordained that French fishermen might, during the then pending season for the herring fishery, safely fish for herrings and all other fish, from the harbor of Gravelines and the island of Thanet to the mouth of the Seine and the harbor of Hautoune. And by an order of October 5, 1406, he took into his safe conduct and under his special protection, guardianship, and defense, all and singular the fishermen of France, Flanders, and Brittany, with their fishing vessels and boats, everywhere on the sea, through and within his dominions, jurisdictions, and territories, in regard to their fishery, while sailing, coming, and going, and, at their pleasure, freely and lawfully fishing, delaying, or proceeding, and returning homeward with their catch of fish, without any molestation or hindrance whatever; and also their fish, nets, and other property and goods soever; and it was therefore ordered that such fishermen should not be interfered with, provided they should comport themselves well and properly, and should not, by color of these presents, do or attempt, or presume to do or attempt, anything that could prejudice the King, or his Kingdom of England, or his subjects. 8 Rymer's Foedera, 336, 451.

The treaty made October 2, 1521, between the Emperor Charles V. and Francis I. of France, through their ambassadors, recited that a great and fierce war had arisen between them, because of which there had been, both by land and by sea, frequent depredations and incursions on either side, to the grave detriment and intolerable injury of the innocent subjects of each; and that a suitable time for the herring fishery was at hand, and, by reason of the sea being beset by the enemy, the fishermen did not dare to go out, whereby the subject of their industry, bestowed by heaven to allay the hunger of the poor, would wholly fail for the year, unless it were otherwise provided,—*Quo fit, ut piscaturoe commoditas, ad pauperum levandam famen a coelesti numine concessa, cessare hoc anno cmnino debeat, nisi aliter provideatur.* And it was therefore agreed that the subjects of each sovereign, fishing in the sea, or exercising the calling of fishermen, could and might, until the end of the next January, without incurring any attack, depredation, molestation, trouble, or hindrance soever, safely and freely, everywhere in the sea, take herrings and every other kind of fish, the existing war by land and sea notwithstanding; and, further, that during the time aforesaid no subject of either sovereign should commit, or attempt or presume to commit, any depredation, force, violence, molestation, or vexation to or upon such fishermen or their vessels, supplies, equipments, nets, and fish, or other goods soever truly appertaining to fishing. The treaty was made at Calais, then an English possession. It recites that the ambassadors of the two sovereigns met there at the earnest request of Henry VIII. and with his countenance, and in the presence of Cardinal Wolsey, his chancellor and representative. And towards the end of the treaty it is agreed that the said King and his said representative, "by whose means the treaty stands concluded, shall be conservators of the agreements therein, as if thereto by both parties elected and chosen." 4 Dumont, Corps Diplomatique, pt. 1, pp. 352, 353.

The herring fishery was permitted, in time of war, by French and Dutch edicts in 1536. Bynkershoek, Quaestiones Juris Publicae, lib. 1, chap. 3; 1 Emerigon des Assurances, chap. 4, § 9; chap. 12, § 19, § 8.

France, from remote times, set the example of alleviating the evils of war in favor of all coast fishermen. In the compilation entitled "Us et Coutumes de la Mer," published by Cleirac in 1661, and in the third part thereof, containing "Maritime or Admiralty Jurisdiction,—*la Jurisdiction de la Marine ou d' Admirauté*—as well in time of peace, as in time of war," article 80 is as follows: "The admiral may in time of war accord fishing truces—*tresves pescheresses*—to the enemy and to his subjects; provided that the enemy will likewise accord them to Frenchmen." Cleirac, 544. Under this article, reference is made to articles 49 and 79 respectively of the French ordinances concerning the admiralty in 1543 and 1584, of which it is but a reproduction. 4 Pardessus, Collection de Lois Maritimes, 319; 2 Ortolan, 51. And Cleirac adds, in a note, this quotation from Froissart's Chronicles: "Fishermen on the sea, whatever war there were in France and England, never did harm to one another; so they are friends, and help one another at need,—*Pescheurs sur mer, quelque guerre qui soit en France et Angleterre, jamais ne se firent mal l'un a l'autre; aincois sont amis, et s'aydent l'un a l'autre au besoin."*

The same custom would seem to have prevailed in France until towards the end of the seventeenth century. For example, in 1675, Louis XIV. and the States General of Holland by mutual agreement granted to Dutch and French fishermen the liberty, undisturbed by their vessels of war, of fishing along the coast of France, Holland, and England. D'Hauterive et De Cussy, Traites de Commerce, pt. 1, vol. 2, p. 278. But by the ordinances of 1681 and 1692 the practice was discontinued, because, Valin says, of the faithless conduct of the enemies of France, who, abusing the good faith with which she had always observed the treaties, habitually carried off her fishermen, while their own fished in safety. 2 Valin sur l'Ordonnance de la Marine (1776) 689, 690; 2 Ortolan, 52; De Boeck, § 192.

The doctrine which exempts coast fishermen, with their vessels and cargoes, from capture as prize of war, has been familiar to the United States from the time of the War of Independence.

On June 5, 1779, Louis XVI., our ally in that war, addressed a letter to his admiral, informing him that the wish he had always had of alleviating, as far as he could, the hardships of war, had directed his attention to that class of his subjects which devoted itself to the trade of fishing, and had no other means of livelihood; that he had thought that the example which he should give to his enemies, and which could have no other source than the sentiments of humanity which inspired him, would determine them to allow to fishermen the same facilities which he should consent to grant; and that he had therefore given orders to the commanders of all his ships not to disturb English fishermen, nor to arrest their vessels laden with fresh fish, even if not caught by those vessels; provided they had no offensive arms, and were not proved to have made any signals creating a suspicion of intelligence with the enemy; and the admiral was directed to communicate the King's intentions to all officers under his control. By a royal order in council of November 6, 1780, the former orders were confirmed; and the capture and ransom, by a French cruiser, of *The John and Sarah*, an English vessel, coming from Holland, laden with fresh fish, were pronounced to be illegal. 2 Code des Prises (ed. 1784) 721, 901, 903.

Among the standing orders made by Sir James Marriott, Judge of the English High Court of Admiralty, was one of April 11, 1780, by which it was "ordered that all causes of prize of fishing boats or vessels taken from the enemy may be consolidated in one monition, and one sentence or interlocutory, if under 50 tons burthen, and not more than 6 in number." Marriott's Formulary, 4. But by the statements of his successor, and of both French and English writers, it appears that England, as well as France, during the American Revolutionary War, abstained from interfering with the coast fisheries. *The Young Jacob and Johanna*, 1 C. Rob. 20; 2 Ortolan, 53; Hall, § 148.

In the treaty of 1785 between the United States and Prussia, article 23 (which was proposed by the American Commissioners, John Adams, Benjamin Franklin, and Thomas Jefferson, and is said to have been drawn up by Franklin), provided that, if war should arise between the contracting parties, "all women and children, scholars of every faculty, cultivators of the earth, artisans, manufacturers, and fishermen, unarmed and inhabiting unfortified towns, villages, or places, and in general all others whose occupations are for the common subsistence and benefit of mankind, shall be allowed to continue their respective employments, and shall not be molested in their persons, nor shall their houses or goods be burnt or otherwise destroyed, nor their fields wasted by the armed force of the enemy, into whose power, by the events of war, they may happen to fall; but if anything is necessary to be taken from them for the use of such armed force, the same shall be paid for at a reasonable price." 8 Stat. at L. 96; 1 Kent, Com. 91, note; Wheaton, History of the Law of Nations, 306, 308. Here was the clearest exemption from hostile molestation or seizure of the persons, occupations, houses, and goods of unarmed fishermen inhabiting unfortified places. The article was repeated in the later treaties between the United States and Prussia of 1799 and 1828. And Dana, in a note to his edition of Wheaton's International Laws, says: "In many treaties and decrees, fishermen catching fish as an article of food are added to the class of persons whose occupation is not to be disturbed in war." Wheaton, International Law (8th ed.) § 345, note 168.

Since the United States became a nation, the only serious interruptions, so far as we are informed, of the general recognition of the exemption of coast fishing vessels from hostile capture, arose out of the mutual suspicions and recriminations of England and France during the wars of the French Revolution.

In the first years of those wars, England having authorized the capture of French fishermen, a decree of the French National Convention of October 2, 1793, directed the executive power "to protest against this conduct, theretofore without example; to reclaim the fishing boats seized; and, in case of refusal, to resort to reprisals." But in July, 1796, the Committee of Public Safety ordered the release of English fishermen seized under the former decree, "not considering them as prisoners of war." *La Nostra Segnora de la Piedad* (1801) cited below; 2 De Cussy, Droit Maritime, 164, 165; 1 Massé, Droit Commercial (2d ed.) 266, 267.

On January 24, 1798, the English government by express order instructed the commanders of its ships to seize French and Dutch fishermen with their boats. 6 Martens, Recueil des Traités (2d ed.) 505; 6 Schoell, Histoire des Traités, 119; 2 Ortolan, 53. After the promulgation of that order, Lord Stowell (then Sir William Scott) in the High Court of Admiralty of

England condemned small Dutch fishing vessels as prize of war. In one case the capture was in April, 1798, and the decree was made November 13, 1798. *The Young Jacob and Johanna*, 1 C. Rob. 20. In another case the decree was made August 23, 1799. *The Noydt Gedacht*, 2 C. Rob. 137, note.

For the year 1800 the orders of the English and French governments and the correspondence between them may be found in books already referred to. 6 Martens, 503–512; 6 Schoell, 118–120; 2 Ortolan, 53, 54. The doings for that year may be summed up as follows: On March 27, 1800, the French government, unwilling to resort to reprisals, re-enacted the orders given by Louis XVI. in 1780, above mentioned, prohibiting any seizure by the French ships of English fishermen, unless armed or proved to have made signals to the enemy. On May 30, 1800, the English government, having received notice of that action of the French government, revoked its order of January 24, 1798. But soon afterward the English government complained that French fishing boats had been made into fireboats at Flushing, as well as that the French government had impressed and had sent to Brest, to serve in its flotilla, French fishermen and their boats, even those whom the English had released on condition of their not serving; and on January 21, 1801, summarily revoked its last order, and again put in force its order of January 24, 1798. On February 16, 1801, Napoleon Bonaparte, then First Consul, directed the French commissioner at London to return at once to France, first declaring to the English government that its conduct, "contrary to all the usages of civilized nations, and to the common law which governs them, even in time of war, gave to the existing war a character of rage and bitterness which destroyed even the relations usual in a loyal war," and "tended only to exasperate the two nations, and to put off the term of peace;" and that the French government, having always made it "a maxim to alleviate as much as possible the evils of war, could not think, on its part, of rendering wretched fishermen victims of a prolongation of hostilities, and would abstain from all reprisals."

On March 16, 1801, the Addington Ministry, having come into power in England, revoked the orders of its predecessors against the French fishermen; maintaining, however, that "the freedom of fishing was nowise founded upon an agreement, but upon a simple concession;" that "this concession would be always subordinate to the convenience of the moment," and that "it was never extended to the great fishery, or to commerce in oysters or in fish." And the freedom of the coast fisheries was again allowed on both sides. 6 Martens, 514; 6 Schoell, 121; 2 Ortolan, 54; Manning, Law of Nations (Amos's ed.) 206.

Lord Stowell's judgment in *The Young Jacob and Johanna*, 1 C. Rob. 20, above cited, was much relied on by the counsel for the United States, and deserves careful consideration.

The vessel there condemned is described in the report as "a small Dutch fishing vessel taken April, 1798, on her return from the Dogger bank to Holland;" and Lord Stowell, in delivering judgment, said: "In former wars it has not been usual to make captures of these small fishing vessels; but this rule was a rule of comity only, and not of legal decision; it has prevailed from views of mutual accommodation between neighboring countries, and from tenderness to a poor and industrious order of people. In the present war there has, I presume, been sufficient reason for changing this mode of treatment; and as they are brought before me for my judgment they must be referred to the general principles of this court; they fall under the character and description of the last class of cases; that is, of ships constantly and exclusively employed in the enemy's trade." And he added: "It is a further satisfaction to me, in giving this judgment, to observe that the facts also bear strong marks of a false and fraudulent transaction."

Both the capture and the condemnation were within a year after the order of the English government of January 24, 1798, instructing the commanders of its ships to seize French and Dutch fishing vessels, and before any revocation of that order. Lord Stowell's judgment shows that his decision was based upon the order of 1798, as well as upon strong evidence of fraud. Nothing more was adjudged in the case.

But some expressions in his opinion have been given so much weight by English writers that it may be well to examine them particularly. The opinion begins by admitting the known custom in former wars not to capture such vessels; adding, however, "but this was a rule of comity only, and not of legal decision." Assuming the phrase "legal decision" to have been there used, in the sense in which courts are accustomed to use it, as equivalent to "judicial decision," it is true that, so far as appears, there had been no such decision on the point in England. The word "comity" was apparently used by Lord Stowell as synonymous with courtesy or goodwill. But the period of a hundred years which has since elapsed is amply sufficient to have enabled what originally may have rested in custom or comity, courtesy or concession, to grow, by the general assent of civilized nations, into a settled rule of international law. As well said by Sir James Mackintosh: "In the present century a slow and silent, but very substantial, mitigation has taken place in the practice of war; and in proportion as that mitigated practice has received the sanction of time it is raised from the rank of mere usage, and becomes part of the law of nations." Discourse on the Law of Nations, 38; 1 Miscellaneous Works, 360.

The French prize tribunals, both before and after Lord Stowell's decision, took a wholly different view of the general question. In 1780, as already mentioned, an order in council of Louis XVI. had declared illegal the capture by a French cruiser of *The John and Sarah*, an English vessel coming from Holland, laden with fresh fish. And on May 17, 1801, where a

Portuguese fishing vessel, with her cargo of fish, having no more crew than was needed for her management and for serving the nets, on a trip of several days, had been captured in April, 1801, by a French cruiser, 3 leagues off the coast of Portugal, the Council of Prizes held that the capture was contrary to "the principles of humanity and the maxims of international law," and decreed that the vessel, with the fish on board, or the net proceeds of any that had been sold, should be restored to her master. *La Nostra Segnora de la Piedad*, 25 Merlin, Jurisprudence, Prise Maritime, § 3, arts. 1, 3; *S. C.* 1 Pistoye et Duverdy, Prises Maritimes, 331; 2 De Cussy, Droit Maritime, 166.

The English government, soon afterwards, more than once unqualifiedly prohibited the molestation of fishing vessels employed in catching and bringing to market fresh fish. On May 23, 1806, it was "ordered in council that all fishing vessels under Prussian and other colors, and engaged for the purpose of catching fish and conveying them fresh to market, with their crews, cargoes, and stores, shall not be molested on their fishing voyages and bringing the same to market; and that no fishing vessels of this description shall hereafter be molested. And the Right Honorable the Lords Commissioners of His Majesty's Treasury, the Lords Commissioners of the Admiralty, and the Judge of the High Court of Admiralty, are to give the necessary directions herein as to them may respectively appertain." 5 C. Rob. 408. Again, in the order in council of May 2, 1810, which directed that "all vessels which shall have cleared out from any port so far under the control of France or her allies as that British vessels may not freely trade thereat, and which are employed in the whale fishery, or other fishery of any description, save as hereinafter excepted, and are returning, or destined to return either to the port from whence they cleared, or to any other port or place at which the British flag may not freely trade, shall be captured and condemned together with their stores and cargoes, as prize to the captors," there were excepted "vessels employed in catching and conveying fish fresh to market, such vessels not being fitted or provided for the curing of fish." Edw. Adm. appx. L.

Wheaton, in his Digest of the Law of Maritime Captures and Prizes, published in 1815, wrote: "It has been usual in maritime wars to exempt from capture fishing boats and their cargoes, both from views of mutual accommodation between neighboring countries, and from tenderness to a poor and industrious order of people. This custom, so honorable to the humanity of civilized nations, has fallen into disuse; and it is remarkable that both France and England mutually reproach each other with that breach of good faith which has finally abolished it." Wheaton, Captures, chap. 2, § 18.

This statement clearly exhibits Wheaton's opinion that the custom had been a general one, as well as that it ought to remain so. His assumption that it had been abolished by the differences between France and England at the close of the last century was hardly justified by the state of things when he wrote, and has not since been borne out.

During the wars of the French Empire, as both French and English writers agree, the coast fisheries were left in peace. 2 Ortolan, 54; De Boeck, § 193; Hall, § 148. De Boeck quaintly and truly adds, "and the incidents of 1800 and of 1801 had no morrow,—*n'eurent pas de lendemain.*"

In the war with Mexico, in 1846, the United States recognized the exemption of coast fishing boats from capture. In proof of this, counsel have referred to records of the Navy Department, which this court is clearly authorized to consult upon such a question. *Jones v. United States*, 137 U. S. 202, 34 L. ed. 691, 11 Sup. Ct. Rep. 80; *Underhill v. Hernandez*, 168 U. S. 250, 253, 42 L. ed. 456, 457, 18 Sup. Ct. Rep. 83.

By those records it appears that Commodore Conner, commanding the Home Squadron blockading the east coast of Mexico, on May 14, 1846, wrote a letter from the ship Cumberland, off Brazos Santiago, near the southern point of Texas, to Mr. Bancroft, the Secretary of the Navy, inclosing a copy of the commodore's "instructions to the commanders of the vessels of the Home Squadron, showing the principles to be observed in the blockade of the Mexican ports," one of which was that "Mexican boats engaged in fishing on any part of the coast will be allowed to pursue their labors unmolested;" and that on June 10, 1846, those instructions were approved by the Navy Department, of which Mr. Bancroft was still the head, and continued to be until he was appointed Minister to England in September following. Although Commodore Conner's instructions and the Department's approval thereof do not appear in any contemporary publication of the government, they evidently became generally known at the time, or soon after; for it is stated in several treatises on international law (beginning with Ortolan's second edition, published in 1853) that the United States in the Mexican war permitted the coast fishermen of the enemy to continue the free exercise of their industry. 2 Ortolan (2d ed.) 49, note; (4th ed.) 55; 4 Calvo (5th ed.) § 2372; De Boeck, § 194; Hall (4th ed.) § 148.

As qualifying the effect of those statements, the counsel for the United States relied on a proclamation of Commodore Stockton, commanding the Pacific Squadron, dated August 20, 1846, directing officers under his command to proceed immediately to blockade the ports of Mazatlan and San Blas, on the west coast of Mexico, and saying to them, "All neutral vessels that you may find there you will allow twenty days to depart; and you will make the blockade absolute against all vessels, except armed vessels of neutral nations. You will capture all vessels under the Mexican flag that you may be able to take." Navy Reports of 1846, pp. 673, 674. But there is nothing to show that Commodore Stockton intended, or that the government approved, the capture of coast fishing vessels.

On the contrary, General Halleck, in the preface to his work on International Law, or Rules Regulating the Intercourse of States in Peace and War, published in 1861, says that he began that work, during the war between the United States and Mexico, "while serving on the staff of the commander of the Pacific Squadron" and "often required to give opinions on questions of international law growing out of the operations of the war." Had the practice of the blockading squadron on the west coast of Mexico during that war, in regard to fishing vessels, differed from that approved by the Navy Department on the east coast, General Halleck could hardly have failed to mention it, when stating the prevailing doctrine upon the subject as follows:

"Fishing boats have also, as a general rule, been exempted from the effects of hostilities. As early as 1521, while war was raging between Charles V. and Francis, ambassadors from these two sovereigns met at Calais, then English, and agreed that, whereas the herring fishery was about to commence, the subjects of both belligerents engaged in this pursuit should be safe and unmolested by the other party, and should have leave to fish as in time of peace. In the war of 1800, the British and French governments issued formal instructions exempting the fishing boats of each other's subjects from seizure. This order was subsequently rescinded by the British government, on the alleged ground that some French fishing boats were equipped as gunboats, and that some French fishermen who had been prisoners in England had violated their parole not to serve, and had gone to join the French fleet at Brest. Such excuses were evidently mere pretexts; and after some angry discussions had taken place on the subject the British restriction was withdrawn, and the freedom of fishing was again allowed on both sides. French writers consider this exemption as an established principle of the modern law of war, and it has been so recognized in the French courts, which have restored such vessels when captured by French cruisers." Halleck (1st ed.) chap. 20, § 23.

That edition was the only one sent out under the author's own auspices, except an abridgment, entitled "Elements of International Law and the Law of War," which he published in 1866, as he said in the preface, to supply a suitable text-book for instruction upon the subject, "not only in our colleges, but also in our two great national schools,—the Military and Naval Academies." In that abridgment the statement as to fishing boats was condensed as follows: "Fishing boats have also, as a general rule, been exempted from the effects of hostilities. French writers consider this exemption as an established principle of the modern law of war, and it has been so recognized in the French courts, which have restored such vessels when captured by French cruisers." Halleck's Elements, chap. 20, § 21.

In the treaty of peace between the United States and Mexico, in 1848, were inserted the very words of the earlier treaties with Prussia, already quoted, forbidding the hostile molestation or seizure in time of war of the persons, occupations, houses, or goods of fishermen. 9 Stat. at L. 939, 940.

Wharton's Digest of the International Law of the United States, published by authority of Congress in 1886 and 1887, embodies General Halleck's fuller statement, above quoted, and contains nothing else upon the subject. 3 Whart. Int. Law Dig. § 345, p. 315; 2 Halleck (Eng. eds. 1873 and 1878) p. 151.

France in the Crimean war in 1854, and in her wars with Italy in 1859 and with Germany in 1870, by general orders, forbade her cruisers to trouble the coast fisheries, or to seize any vessel or boat engaged therein, unless naval or military operations should make it necessary. Calvo, § 2372; Hall, § 148; 2 Ortolan (4th ed.) 449; 10 Revue de Droit International (1878) 399. Revue de Droit International (1878) 399.

Calvo says that, in the Crimean War, "notwithstanding her alliance with France and Italy, England did not follow the same line of conduct; and that her cruisers in the Sea of Azof destroyed the fisheries, nets, fishing implements, provisions, boats, and even the cabins of inhabitants of the coast." Calvo, § 2372. And a Russian writer on prize law remarks that those depredations, "having brought ruin on poor fishermen and inoffensive traders, could not but leave a painful impression on the minds of the population, without impairing in the least the resources of the Russian government." Katchenovsky (Pratt's ed.) 148. But the contemporaneous reports of the English naval officers put a different face on the matter, by stating that the destruction in question was part of a military measure, conducted with the co-operation of the French ships, and pursuant to instructions of the English admiral "to clear the seaboard of all fish stores, all fisheries and mills, on a scale beyond the wants of the neighboring population, and indeed of all things destined to contribute to the maintenance of the enemy's army in the Crimea;" and that the property destroyed consisted of large fishing establishments and storehouses of the Russian government, numbers of heavy launches, and enormous quantities of nets and gear, salted fish, corn, and other provisions intended for the supply of the Russian army. United Service Journal of 1855, pt. 3, pp. 108–112.

Since the English orders in council of 1806 and 1810, before quoted, in favor of fishing vessels employed in catching and bringing to market fresh fish, no instance has been found in which the exemption from capture of private coast fishing vessels honestly pursuing their peaceful industry has been denied by England or by any other nation. And the Empire of Japan (the last state admitted into the rank of civilized nations), by an ordinance promulgated at the beginning of its war with China in August, 1894, established prize courts, and ordained that "the following enemy's vessels are exempt from detention," including in the exemption "boats engaged in coast fisheries," as well as "ships engaged exclusively on a voyage of scientific discovery, philanthrophy, or religious mission." Takahashi, International Law, 11, 178.

International law is part of our law, and must be ascertained and administered by the courts of justice of appropriate jurisdiction as often as questions of right depending upon it are duly presented for their determination. For this purpose, where there is no treaty and no controlling executive or legislative act or judicial decision, resort must be had to the customs and usages of civilized nations, and, as evidence of these, to the works of jurists and commentators who by years of labor, research, and experience have made themselves peculiarly well acquainted with the subjects of which they treat. Such works are resorted to by judicial tribunals, not for the speculations of their authors concerning what the law ought to be, but for trustworthy evidence of what the law really is. *Hilton v. Guyot*, 159 U. S. 113, 163, 164, 214, 215.

Wheaton places among the principal sources [of] international law "text-writers of authority, showing what is the approved usage of nations, or the general opinion respecting their mutual conduct, with the definitions and modifications introduced by general consent." As to these he forcibly observes: "Without wishing to exaggerate the importance of these writers, or to substitute, in any case, their authority for the principles of reason, it may be affirmed that they are generally impartial in their judgment. They are witnesses of the sentiments and usages of civilized nations, and the weight of their testimony increases every time that their authority is invoked by statesmen, and every year that passes without the rules laid down in their works being impugned by the avowal of contrary principles." Wheaton, International Law (8th ed.), § 15.

Chancellor Kent says: "In the absence of higher and more authoritative sanctions, the ordinances of foreign states, the opinions of eminent statesmen, and the writings of distinguished jurists, are regarded as of great consideration on questions not settled by conventional law. In cases where the principal jurists agree, the presumption will be very great in favor of the solidity of their maxims; and no civilized nation that does not arrogantly set all ordinary law and justice at defiance will venture to disregard the uniform sense of the established writers on international law." 1 Kent, Com. 18.

It will be convenient, in the first place, to refer to some leading French treatises on international law, which deal with the question now before us, not as one of the law of France only, but as one determined by the general consent of civilized nations.

"Enemy ships," say Pistoye and Duverdy, in their Treatise on Maritime Prizes, published in 1855, "are good prize. Not all, however; for it results from the unanimous accord of the maritime powers that an exception should be made in favor of coast fishermen. Such fishermen are respected by the enemy so long as they devote themselves exclusively to fishing." 1 Pistoye et Duverdy, tit. 6, chap. 1, p. 314.

De Cussy, in his work on the Phases and Leading Cases of the Maritime Law of Nations,–*Phases et Causes Célèbres du Droit Maritime des Nations*,—published in 1856, affirms in the clearest language the exemption from capture of fishing boats, saying, in lib. 1, tit. 3, § 36, that "in time of war the freedom of fishing is respected by belligerents; fishing boats are considered as neutral; in law, as in principle, they are not subject either to capture or to confiscation;" and that in lib. 2, chap. 20, he will state "several facts and several decisions which prove that the perfect freedom and neutrality of fishing boats are not illusory." 1 De Cussy, p. 291. And in the chapter so referred to, entitled *De la Liberte et de la Neutralite Parfaite de la Peche*, besides references to the edicts and decisions in France during the French Revolution, is this general statement: "If one consulted only positive international law,"—*le droit des gens positif*,—(by which is evidently meant international law expressed in treaties, decrees, or other public acts, as distinguished from what may be implied from custom or usage) "fishing boats would be subject, like all other trading vessels, to the law of prize; a sort of tacit agreement among all European nations frees them from it, and several official declarations have confirmed this privilege in favor of 'a class of men whose hard and ill-rewarded labor, commonly performed by feeble and aged hands,' is so foreign to the operations of war."

Ortolan, in the fourth edition of his Règles Internationales et Diplomatie de la Mer, published in 1864, after stating the general rule that the vessels and cargoes of subjects of the enemy are lawful prize, says: "Nevertheless, custom admits an exception in favor of boats engaged in the coast fishery; these boats, as well as their crews, are free from capture and exempt from all hostilities. The coast-fishing industry is, in truth, wholly pacific, and of much less importance in regard to the national wealth that it may produce than maritime commerce or the great fisheries. Peaceful and wholly inoffensive, those who carry it on, among whom women are often seen, may be called the harvesters of the territorial seas, since they confine themselves to gathering in the products thereof; they are for the most part poor families who seek in this calling hardly more than the means of gaining their livelihood." 2 Ortolan, 51. Again, after observing that there are very few solemn public treaties which make mention of the immunity of fishing boats in time of war, he says: "From another point of view the custom which sanctions this immunity is not so general that it can be considered as making an absolute international rule; but it has been so often put in practice, and, besides, it accords so well with the rule in use in wars on land, in regard to peasants and husbandmen, to whom coast fishermen may be likened, that it will doubtless continue to be followed in maritime wars to come." 2 Ortolan, 55.

No international jurist of the present day has a wider or more deserved reputation than Calvo, who, though writing in French, is a citizen of the Argentine Republic, employed in its diplomatic service abroad. In the fifth edition of his great work on international law, published in 1896, he observes, in § 2366, that the international authority of decisions in particular cases by the prize courts of France, of England, and of the United States is lessened by the fact that the principles on which they are based are largely derived from the internal legislation of each country; and yet the peculiar character of maritime wars, with other considerations, gives to prize jurisprudence a force and importance reaching beyond the limits of the country in which it has prevailed. He therefore proposes here to group together a number of particular cases proper to serve as precedents for the solution of grave questions of maritime law in regard to the capture of private property as prize of war. Immediately, in § 2367, he goes on to say: "Notwithstanding the hardships to which maritime wars subject private property, notwithstanding the extent of the recognized rights of belligerents, there are generally exempted, from seizure and capture, fishing vessels." In the next section he adds: "This exception is perfectly justiciable,—*Cette exception est parfaitement justiciable,*"—that is to say, belonging to judicial jurisdiction or cognizance. Littre, Dist. *voc. Justiciable*; *Hans v. Louisiana,* 134 U. S. 1, 15. Calvo then quotes Ortolan's description, above cited, of the nature of the coast-fishing industry; and proceeds to refer, in detail, to some of the French precedents, to the acts of the French and English governments in the times of Louis XVI. and of the French Revolution, to the position of the United States in the war with Mexico, and of France in later wars, and to the action of British cruisers in the Crimean war. And he concludes his discussion of the subject, in § 2373, by affirming the exemption of the coast fishery, and pointing out the distinction in this regard between the coast fishery and what he calls the great fishery, for cod, whales, or seals, as follows: "The privilege of exemption from capture, which is generally acquired by fishing vessels plying their industry near the coasts, is not extended in any country to ships employed on the high sea in what is called the great fishery, such as that for the cod, for the whale or the sperm whale, or for the seal or sea calf. These ships are, in effect, considered as devoted to operations which are at once commercial and industrial,—*Ces navires sont en effect considérés comme adonnés à des opérations à la fois commerciales et industrielles.*" The distinction is generally recognized. 2 Ortolan, 54; De Boeck, § 196; Hall, § 148. See also *The Susa,* 2 C. Rob. 251; *The Johan,* Edw. Adm. 275, and appx. L.

The modern German books on international law, cited by the counsel for the appellants, treat the custom by which the vessels and implements of coast fishermen are exempt from seizure and capture as well established by the practice of nations. Heffter, § 137; 2 Kalterborn, § 237, p. 480; Bluntschli, § 667; Perels, § 37, p. 217.

De Boeck, in his work on Enemy Private Property under Enemy's Flag,— *De la Propriété Privée Ennemie sous Pavillon Ennemi*,—published in 1882, and the only continental treatise cited by the counsel for the United States, says in § 191: "A usage very ancient, if not universal, withdraws from the right of capture enemy vessels engaged in the coast fishery. The reason of this exception is evident; it would have been too hard to snatch from poor fishermen the means of earning their bread. * * * The exemption includes the boats, the fishing implements, and the cargo of fish." Again, in § 195: "It is to be observed that very few treatises sanction in due form this immunity of the coast fishery. * * * There is, then, only a custom. But what is its character? Is it so fixed and general that it can be raised to the rank of a positive and formal rule of international law?" After discussing the statements of other writers, he approves the opinion of Ortolan (as expressed in the last sentence above quoted from his work), and says that, at bottom, it differs by a shade only from that formulated by Calvo and by some of the German jurists, and that "it is more exact, without ignoring the imperative character of the humane rule in question,—*elle est plus exacte, sans meconnaitre le caractere imperatif de la regle d'humanite dont il s'agit.*" And in § 196 he defines the limits of the rule as follows: "But the immunity of the coast fishery must be limited by the reasons which justify it. The reasons of humanity and of harmlessness—*les raisons d'humanite et d'innocuite*—which militate in its favor do not exist in the great fishery, such as the cod fishery; ships engaged in that fishery devote themselves to truly commercial operations, which employ a large number of seamen. And these same reasons cease to be applicable to fishing vessels employed for a warlike purpose, to those which conceal arms, or which exchange signals of intelligence with ships of war; but only those taken in the fact can be rigorously treated; to allow seizure by way of preventive would open the door to every abuse, and would be equivalent to a suppression of the immunity."

Two recent English text-writers cited at the bar (influenced by what Lord Stowell said a century since) hesitate to recognize that the exemption of coast fishing vessels from capture has now become a settled rule of international law. Yet they both admit that there is little real difference in the views, or in the practice, of England and of other maritime nations; and that no civilized nation at the present day would molest coast fishing vessels so long as they were peaceably pursuing their calling and there was no danger that they or their crews might be of military use to the enemy. Hall, in § 148 of the fourth edition of his Treatise on International Law, after briefly sketching the history of the positions occupied by France and England at different periods, and by the United States in the Mexican war, goes on to say: "In the foregoing facts there is nothing to show that much real difference has existed in the practice of the maritime countries. England does not seem to have been unwilling to spare fishing vessels so long as they are harmless, and it does not appear that any state has accorded them immunity under circumstances of inconvenience to itself. It is likely that all nations would now refrain from molesting them as a general rule, and would capture them so soon as any danger arose that they or their crews might be of military use to the enemy; and it is also likely that it is impossible to grant them a more distinct exemption." So, T. J. Lawrence, in § 206 of his Principles of International Law, says: "The difference between the English and the French view is more apparent than real; for no civilized belligerent would now capture the boats of fishermen plying their avocation peaceably in the territorial waters of their own state; and no jurist would seriously argue that their immunity must be respected if they were used for warlike purposes, as were the smacks belonging to the northern ports of France when Great Britain gave the order to capture them in 1800."

But there are writers of various maritime countries, not yet cited, too important to be passed by without notice.

Jan Helenus Ferguson, Netherlands Minister to China, and previously in the naval and in the colonial service of his country, in his Manual of International Law for the Use of Navies, Colonies, and Consulates, published in 1882, writes: "An exception to the usage of capturing enemy's private vessels at sea is the coast fishery. * * * This principle of immunity from capture of fishing boats is generally adopted by all maritime powers, and in actual warfare they are universally spared so long as they remain harmless." 2 Ferguson, § 212.

Ferdinand Attlmayr, captain in the Austrian Navy, in his Manual for Naval Officers, published at Vienna in 1872 under the auspices of Admiral Tegetthoff, says: "Regarding the capture of enemy property, an exception must be mentioned, which is a universal custom. Fishing vessels which belong to the adjacent coast, and whose business yields only a necessary livelihood, are, from considerations of humanity, universally excluded from capture." 1 Attlmayr, 61.

Ignacio de Negrin, First Official of the Spanish Board of Admiralty, in his Elementary Treatise on Maritime International Law, adopted by royal order as a text-book in the naval schools of Spain, and published at Madrid in 1873, concludes his chapter "Of the lawfulness of prizes" with these words: "It remains to be added that the custom of all civilized peoples excludes from capture and from all kind of hostility the fishing vessels of the enemy's coasts, considering this industry as absolutely inoffensive, and deserving, from its hardships and usefulness, of this favorable exception. It has been thus expressed in very many international conventions, so that it can be deemed an incontestable principle of law, at least among enlightened nations." Negrin, tit. 3, chap. 1, § 310.

Carlos Testa, captain in the Portugese Navy and professor in the naval school at Lisbon, in his work on Public International Law, published in French at Paris in 1886, when discussing the general right of capturing enemy ships, says: "Nevertheless, in this, customary law establishes an exception of immunity in favor of coast fishing vessels. Fishing is so peaceful an industry, and is generally carried on by so poor and so hard-working a class of men, that it is likened, in the territorial waters of the enemy's country, to the class of husbandmen who gather the fruits of the earth for their livelihood. The examples and practice generally followed establish this humane and beneficent exception as an international rule, and this rule may be considered as adopted by customary law and by all civilized nations." Testa, pt. 3, chap. 2, in 18 Bibliotheque International et Diplomatique, pp. 152, 153.

No less clearly and decisively speaks the distinguished Italian jurist, Pasquale Fiore, in the enlarged edition of his exhaustive work on Public International Law, published at Paris in 1885–6, saying: "The vessels of fishermen have been generally declared exempt from confiscation, because of the eminently peaceful object of their humble industry, and of the principles of equity and humanity. The exemption includes the vessel, the implements of fishing, and the cargo resulting from the fishery. This usage, eminently humane, goes back to very ancient times; and although the immunity of the fishery along the coasts may not have been sanctioned by treaties, yet it is considered to-day as so definitely established that the inviolability of vessels devoted to that fishery is proclaimed by the publicists as a positive rule of international law, and is generally respected by the nations. Consequently we shall lay down the following rule: (*a*) Vessels belonging to citizens of the enemy state, and devoted to fishing along the coasts, cannot be subject to capture; (*b*) Such vessels, however, will lose all right of exemption, when employed for a warlike purpose; (*c*) there may, nevertheless, be subjected to capture vessels devoted to the great fishery in the ocean, such as those employed in the whale fishery, or in that for seals or sea calves." 3 Fiore, § 1421.

This review of the precedents and authorities on the subject appears to us abundantly to demonstrate that at the present day, by the general consent of the civilized nations of the world, and independently of any express treaty or other public act, it is an established rule of international law, founded on considerations of humanity to a poor and industrious order of men, and of the mutual convenience of belligerent states, that coast fishing vessels, with their implements and supplies, cargoes and crews, unarmed and honestly pursuing their peaceful calling of catching and bringing in fresh fish, are exempt from capture as prize of war.

The exemption, of course, does not apply to coast fishermen or their vessels if employed for a warlike purpose, or in such a way as to give aid or information to the enemy; nor when military or naval operations create a necessity to which all private interests must give way.

Nor has the exemption been extended to ships or vessels employed on the high sea in taking whales or seals or cod or other fish which are not brought fresh to market, but are salted or otherwise cured and made a regular article of commerce.

This rule of international law is one which prize courts administering the law of nations are bound to take judicial notice of, and to give effect to, in the absence of any treaty or other public act of their own government in relation to the matter.

Calvo, in a passage already quoted, distinctly affirms that the exemption of coast fishing vessels from capture is perfectly justiciable, or, in other words, of judicial jurisdiction or cognizance. Calvo, § 2368. Nor are judicial precedents wanting in support of the view that this exemption, or a somewhat analogous one, should be recognized and declared by a prize court.

By the practice of all civilized nations, vessels employed only for the purposes of discovery or science are considered as exempt from the contingencies of war, and therefore not subject to capture. It has been usual for the government sending out such an expedition to give notice to other powers; but it is not essential. 1 Kent, Com. 91, note; Halleck, chap. 20, § 22; Calvo, § 2376; Hall, § 138.

* * *

Upon the facts proved in either case, it is the duty of this court, sitting as the highest prize court of the United States, and administering the law of nations, to declare and adjudge that the capture was unlawful and without probable cause; and it is therefore, in each case,—

Ordered, that the decree of the District Court be reversed, and the proceeds of the sale of the vessel, together with the proceeds of any sale of her cargo, be restored to the claimant, with damages and costs.

MR. CHIEF JUSTICE FULLER, with whom concurred MR. JUSTICE HARLAN and MR. JUSTICE MCKENNA, dissenting:

The district court held these vessels and their cargoes liable because not "satisfied that as a matter of law, without any ordinance, treaty, or proclamation, fishing vessels of this class are exempt from seizure."

This court holds otherwise, not because such exemption is to be found in any treaty, legislation, proclamation, or instruction granting it, but on the ground that the vessels were exempt by reason of an established rule of international law applicable to them, which it is the duty of the court to enforce.

I am unable to conclude that there is any such established international rule, or that this court can properly revise action which must be treated as having been taken in the ordinary exercise of discretion in the conduct of war.

* * *

_____

The Court here finds a rule of customary *international* law—why would that rule bind a *domestic* court?

What impact does this decision of the United States Supreme Court have on other national or international tribunals facing the same issue?

MALCOLM SHAW, INTERNATIONAL LAW
(2003)

* * *

* * * [W]hat is state practice? Does it cover every kind of behaviour initiated by the state, or is it limited to actual, positive actions? To put it more simply, does it include such things as speeches, informal documents and governmental statements or is it restricted to what states actually do?

It is how states behave in practice that forms the basis of customary law, but evidence of what a state does can be obtained from numerous sources. A state is not a living entity, but consists of governmental departments and thousands of officials, and state activity is spread throughout a whole range of national organs. There are the state's legal officers, legislative institutions, courts, diplomatic agents and political leaders. Each of these engages in activity which relates to the international field and therefore one has to examine all such material sources and more in order to discover evidence of what states do.

The obvious way to find out how countries are behaving is to read the newspapers, consult historical records, listen to what governmental authorities are saying and peruse the many official publications. There are also memoirs of various past leaders, official manuals on legal questions, diplomatic interchanges and the opinions of national legal advisors. All these methods are valuable in seeking to determine actual state practice.

* * *

OPINIO JURIS

Once one has established the existence of a specified usage, it becomes necessary to consider how the state views its own behaviour. Is it to be regarded as a moral or political or legal act or statement? The *opinio juris,* or belief that a state activity is legally obligatory, is the factor which turns the usage into a custom and renders it part of the rules of international law. To put it slightly differently, states will behave a certain way because they are convinced it is binding upon them to do so.

* * *

The great problem connected with the *opinio juris* is that if it calls for behaviour in accordance with law, how can new customary rules be created since that obviously requires action different from or contrary to what until then is regarded as law? If a country claims a three-mile territorial sea in the belief that this is legal, how can the rule be changed in customary law to allow claims of, for example, twelve miles, since that cannot also be in accordance with prevailing law? Obviously if one takes a restricted view of the psychological aspects, then logically the law will become stultified and this demonstrably has not happened.

Thus, one has to treat the matter in terms of a process whereby states behave in a certain way in the belief that such behaviour is law or is becoming law. It will then depend upon how other states react as to whether this process of legislation is accepted or rejected. It follows that rigid definitions as to legality have to be modified to see whether the legitimating stamp of state activity can be provided or not. If a state proclaims a twelve-mile limit to its territorial sea in the belief that although the three-mile limit has been accepted law, the circumstances are so altering that a twelve-mile limit might now be treated as becoming law, it is vindicated if other states follow suit and a new rule of customary law is established. If other states reject the proposition, then the projected rule withers away and the original rule stands, reinforced by state practice and common acceptance. As the Court itself noted in the *Nicaragua* case, "[r]eliance by a State on a novel right or an unprecedented exception to the principle might, if shared in principle by other States, tend towards a modification of customary international law." The difficulty in this kind of approach is that it is sometimes hard to pinpoint exactly when one rule supersedes another, but that is a complication inherent in the nature of custom. Change is rarely smooth but rather spasmodic.

* * *

However, states must be made aware that when one state takes a course of action, it does so because it regards it as within the confines of international law, and not as, for example, purely a political or moral gesture. There has to be an aspect of legality about the behaviour and the acting state will have to confirm that this is so, so that the international community can easily distinguish legal from non-legal practices. This is essential to the development and presentation of a legal framework amongst the states.

* * *

Isn't this whole customary international law business an exercise in legal indeterminacy? How is one to ascertain (not to mention agree on) "state practice" if that practice isn't uniform, if so many elements (even mere claims!) can be considered, and if what states do varies over time? How is one to come to grips with "opinio juris," if states have (as they often do) mixed motives, if they may do things beyond recognized law (pushing for a new custom), and if the whole test is admittedly "subjective" to boot? Doesn't all of this mean that either states agree on what custom is—in which case there is no conflict and we don't really need a rule—or they don't—in which case finding a rule is at best enormously burdensome and indeterminate?

4. GENERAL PRINCIPLES OF LAW

Beyond treaties and custom, the third traditional source of international law is general principles of law recognized by civilized nations. Below, Shaw explains what functions these principles fulfill. What is their role in international adjudication? He also hints at various conceptions of such principles. How do they differ?

MALCOLM SHAW, INTERNATIONAL LAW
(2d ed. 2006)

* * *

In any system of law, a situation may very well arise where the court in considering a case before it realises that there is no law covering exactly that point, neither parliamentary statute nor judicial precedent. In such instances the judge will proceed to deduce a rule that will be relevant, by analogy from already existing rules or directly from the general principles that guide the legal system, whether they be referred to as emanating from justice, equity or considerations of public policy. Such a situation is perhaps even more likely to arise in international law because of the relative underdevelopment of the system in relation to the needs with which it is faced.

There are fewer decided cases in international law than in a municipal system and no method of legislating to provide rules to govern new situations. It is for such a reason that the provision of "the general principles of law recognised by civilised nations" was inserted into article 38 [of the ICJ Statute] as a source of law, to close the gap that might be uncovered in international law and solve this problem which is known legally as *non liquet*. The question of gaps in the system is an important one. It is important to appreciate that while there may not always be an immediate and obvious rule applicable to every international situation, every international situation is capable of being determined *as a matter of law.*

There are various opinions as to what the general principles of law concept is intended to refer. Some writers regard it as an affirmation of Natural Law concepts, which are deemed to underlie the system of international law and constitute the method for testing the validity of the positive (i.e. man-made) rules. Other writers, particularly positivists, treat it as a sub-heading under treaty and customary law and incapable of adding anything new to international law unless it reflects the consent of states. Soviet writers like Tunkin subscribed to this approach and regarded the "general principles of law" as reiterating the fundamental precepts of international law, for example, the law of peaceful co-existence, which have already been set out in treaty and custom law.

Between these two approaches, most writers are prepared to accept that the general principles do constitute a separate source of law but of fairly limited scope, and this is reflected in the decisions of the Permanent Court of International Justice and the International Court of Justice. It is not clear, however, in all cases, whether what is involved is a general principle of law appearing in municipal systems or a general principle of international law. But perhaps this is not a terribly serious problem since both municipal legal concepts and those derived from existing international practice can be defined as falling within the recognised catchment area.

While the reservoir from which one can draw contains the legal operations of 190 or so states, it does not follow that judges have to be experts in every legal system. There are certain common themes that run through the many different orders. Anglo–American common law has influenced a number of states throughout the world, as have the French and Germanic systems. There are many common elements in the law in Latin America, and most Afro–Asian states have borrowed heavily from the European experience in their efforts to modernise the structure administering the state and westernise economic and other enterprises.

* * *

———————————

This text still leaves a lot of questions open. Which are the "civilized nations"? Must they all recognize such principles or does a majority suffice?

To what extent must they recognize the principles? How specific do they have to be? (The principle "to give each his due" would probably be so vague as to be meaningless.)

While general principles have often played a role in international decisions, relatively few cases have turned exclusively on them. Below is an example of a case that did.

GENTINI CASE
(ITALY V. VENEZUELA)

Mixed Claims Commission
10 U.N. Rep. Int'l Arb. Awards 551 (1903)

RALSTON, UMPIRE:

In this case, referred to the umpire upon difference of opinion between the honorable Commissioners for Italy and Venezuela, it appears that the claimant, an Italian, was, in 1871, a resident of Trujillo, when, as it is said, his store was closed temporarily and business injured by the presence of a large number of soldiers, the claimant sent to prison on the order of the jefe [chief], his establishment plundered, and later on forced loans were imposed upon him under threat of imprisonment. The proofs were taken the following year, and from that time till the past month nothing appears to have been done with the claim, it not having even been called to the attention of the royal Italian legation. The claim is for the sum of 3,900 bolivars.

It is submitted on behalf of Venezuela that this claim is barred by prescription, although it is admitted that no national statute can be invoked against it.

On the other hand, it is insisted for Italy that prescription can not be recognized in international tribunals * * *.

The Permanent Court of Arbitration has never denied the principle of prescription, a principle well recognized in international law, and it is fair to believe it will never do so. Such denial would tend to upset all government, since power over fixed areas depends upon possession sanctified by prescription, although the circumstances of its origin and the time it must run may vary with each case. The expressions of many international law writers upon this point, including Wheaton, Vattel, Phillimore, Hall, Polson, Calvo, Vico, Grotius, Taparelli, Sala, Coke, Sir Henry Maine, Brocher, Domat, Burke, Wharton, and Markby, are collated in the case of Williams v. Venezuela, Venezuelan–American Claims Commission of 1888, cited at length in 4 Moore, page 4181.

* * *

But it remains true that the international law writers have referred almost invariably to that form of prescription involved in the taking and possession of property known at one time as usucaption, and we are left to examine whether the general principles of prescription should be applied to claims for money damages as between nations.

* * *

On examining the general subject we find that by all nations and from the earliest period has it been considered that as between individuals an end to disputes should be brought about by the efflux of time. Early in the history of the Roman law this feeling received fixity by legislative sanction. In every country have periods been limited beyond which actions could not be brought. In the opinion of the writer these laws of universal application were not the arbitrary acts of power, but instituted because of the necessities of mankind, and were the outgrowth of a general feeling that equity demanded their enactment; for very early it was perceived that with the lapse of time the defendant, through death of witnesses and destruction of vouchers, became less able to meet demands against him, and the danger of consequent injustice increased, while no hardship was imposed upon the claimant in requiring him within a reasonable time to institute his suit. In addition, another view found its expression with relation to the matter in the maxim *"Interest republica ut sit finis litium."*

* * *

Additionally, however, we may refer to the position taken by courts of equity in England and the United States with reference to statutes of prescription.

* * *

Further, the fact will not be lost sight of that the presentation of a claim to competent authority within proper time will interrupt the running of prescription.

The qualifications above referred to, and others which might be imagined, cannot, however, have any application to the present case, in which for thirty-one years after proof had been prepared the case does not appear to have been presented in any manner, the royal Italian legation, even, until very recently, having been in ignorance of its existence. Of this conduct on the part of the claimant no explanation is offered.

The umpire, while disallowing the claim, expresses no opinion as to the number of years constituting sufficient prescription to defeat claims against governments in an international court. Each must be decided according to its especial conditions. He calls attention to the fact that under varying circumstances the civil-law period is ten, twenty, and thirty years; in England, for many years—for contracts, six years; in the United

States, on contracts with the Government, six years, and in the several States, on personal actions, from three to ten years.

It is sufficient to say that in the present case the claimant had so long neglected his supposed rights as to justify a belief in their nonexistence.

A judgment of dismissal will be signed.

Formulate the general principle on which the umpire relies. Do you believe that this principle is "recognized by civilized nations"? All? Most? Some? What if the time lag between the events and the complaint had been five years instead of 31?

5. EVIDENCE OF INTERNATIONAL LAW: JUDICIAL DECISIONS

Article 38 sec. I of the Statute of the International Court of Justice provides that the ICJ shall (inter alia) apply, "subject to the provisions of Article 59, judicial decisions * * * as subsidiary means for the determination of rules of law." This suggests that "judicial decisions" are not themselves sources of (international) law but just a means to determine its rules. In addition, Article 59 provides:

> The decision of the Court has no binding force except between the parties and in respect of that particular case.

According to these provisions, there is, strictly speaking, no binding force of precedent, nor a rule of *stare decisis*, in international law. This may surprise a common law student or practitioner. Two primary reasons explain this feature of classic international law.

First, the lack of a principle of precedent is a heritage of the (so-called) civil law system prevailing in continental Europe (as well as, today, in Latin America and much of East Asia). In the early-modern period, the civil law tradition shaped much of classic public international law, through the works of Grotius and other leading scholars. In that tradition, at least in theory, courts have not had the power to make law. Instead, their role was limited, at least in theory, to interpreting the law that had been made by the legislator. Second, given the co-equal status of states and the fact that the ICJ's jurisdiction is strictly consent-based (as we will see in Chapter IX), the Court simply does not have the power to make law beyond the parties that appear before it. To hold otherwise would be in effect to suggest that its decisions could bind parties that have not consented to its jurisdiction.

In practice, however, previous ICJ decisions do matter in cases before the Court. In the case below, we see an example of how the ICJ treats its prior decisions. The *Gulf of Maine* case involved "the course of the single maritime boundary that divides the continental shelf and fisheries zones" of Canada and the United States. The initial dispute concerned rights to resources as exploration of petroleum began in the 1960s. Both states subsequently delineated an exclusive 200-mile fishery zone off their respective coasts and instituted regulations about the limits of the zone and continental shelf they claimed. In a complex and technical decision, aiming to ensure equitable results, the International Court of Justice resolved the dispute by drawing the boundary according to its own neutral criteria.

In reading the excerpts below, keep in mind Article 59 of the ICJ Statute.

CASE CONCERNING THE DELIMITATION OF THE MARITIME BOUNDARY IN THE GULF OF MAINE AREA (CANADA V. UNITED STATES)

International Court of Justice
1984 I.C.J. 247

JUDGMENT:

* * *

91. Following this review of the implications for the present problem of the endeavour made in 1958 to codify the subject, it will now be appropriate to consider the bearing on the same problem of the Court's Judgment of 20 February 1969 in the *North Sea Continental Shelf* cases. That Judgment, while well known to have attributed more marked importance to the link between the legal institution of the continental shelf and the physical fact of the natural prolongation than has subsequently been given to it, is nonetheless the judicial decision which has made the greatest contribution to the formation of customary law in this field. From this point of view, its achievements remain unchallenged. Rehearsing the historical development of general international law on the subject, that Judgment begins by considering the Truman Proclamation of 28 September 1945, which stated that, for the United States and its neighbours, the delimitation of lateral boundaries between the continental shelves of adjacent States should be decided by mutual agreement and "in accordance with equitable principles." "These two concepts" the Court noted, "have underlain all the subsequent history of the subject." Turning to the work of the International Law Commission, the 1969 Judgment notes that, according to the Commission, concepts such as that of proximity and its corollaries, and other alleged principles variously advanced, do not comprise mandatory rules of international law. After this the Judgment restates and endorses the dual principle "that delimitation must be the object of agreement between the States concerned, and that such agreement must be arrived at in accordance with equitable principles." From this it deduces the dual obligation for these States to "enter into negotiations with a

view to arriving at an agreement" and to "act in such a way that, in the particular case, and taking all the circumstances into account, equitable principles are applied," no matter what methods are used for this purpose.

92. Subsequently, the Court of Arbitration's Decision of 30 June 1977 on the delimitation of the continental shelf between France and the United Kingdom confirms on this point the Court's conclusions in the *North Sea Continental Shelf* cases and enunciates as follows the general rule of customary international law on the matter: "failing agreement, the boundary between States abutting on the same continental shelf is to be determined on equitable principles."

93. The next relevant decision is the Court's Judgment of 24 February 1982 in the case concerning the *Continental Shelf (Tunisia/Libyan Arab Jumahiriya)*. In that case, it should be recalled, the Court had to render a judgment on the basis of a Special Agreement which, besides requesting the Court to determine "the principles and rules of international law" applicable to the delimitation, further requested that the Court take account of "equitable principles and the relevant circumstances which characterize the area, as well as the recent trends admitted at the Third Conference on the Law of the Sea." Referring back to the earlier Judgment in the North Sea Continental Shelf cases, and to the proceedings and conclusions of the Third Conference, the 1982 Judgment stresses the importance of "the satisfaction of equitable principles * * * in the delimitation process."

* * *

Separate [Concurring] Opinion of JUDGE SCHWEBEL [United States]:

* * *

Where I disagree with the Chamber is in its placement of the dividing line. Its line substantially departs from the line which would result from the application of the Chamber's methodology if the Chamber did not, as I see it, err in one key respect.

There was much dispute between the Parties over the extent of the coasts of the Bay of Fundy to be regarded as coasts of the Gulf of Maine area for purposes of calculations of proportionality. That is understandable, because the impact of the treatment of those coasts could be anticipated to affect, and, in the event, does most materially affect, the placement of the line of delimitation.

The Judgment disposes of this dispute by holding that the coasts of the Bay of Fundy should be included up to the point where the Bay so narrows that it contains "only maritime areas lying no further than 12 miles from the low water mark." But the Judgment does not show why this is a determinative or even relevant consideration.

It is instructive to recall (as the Chamber does not) that, as recently as 1982, the International Court of Justice rejected a calculation of proportionality which would have taken into account the legal status of waters of the Gulf of Gabes *(Continental Shelf (Tunisia/Libyan Arab Jamahiriya), Judgment)*. As the late distinguished counsel of Canada, Professor Antonio Malintoppi, reminded the Chamber, at the hearing of 5 May 1984 (afternoon):

> "* * * the legal status of the waters off the Coast in question is not a relevant factor when deciding whether or not these coasts should be included in the calculation of coast-ratios for the purpose of the proportionality test. The *Tunisia/Libya* case is quite clear on this point."

* * *

———————

Doesn't the Court use its own prior decisions just like an American court uses precedent? How does the following text answer that question?

ANDREAS ZIMMERMANN ET AL., THE STATUTE OF THE INTERNATIONAL COURT OF JUSTICE

(2006)

* * *

That international law does not recognize the binding force of precedent nor the principle of stare decisis is correct in legal theory, but the reality is different. The ICJ, like every court, hesitates to overrule former pronouncements; quite to the contrary, it often refers to previous decisions and to reasons developed in such decisions, whether these reasons have been essential for that decision or are only *obiter dicta*. In many judgments of the ICJ, the Court quotes extensively its own pronouncements in former cases with different parties. Even advisory opinions, which are formally not binding for any State or even for the international organ having requested the opinion, are often quoted in later advisory opinions and judgments.

Article 38, para. 1(d) of the Statute recognizes * * * subject to the provisions of Article 59, "judicial decisions * * * as subsidiary means for the determination of rules of law." Governments, other courts and writers usually refer in other cases to judgments of the Court in order to support a legal opinion. Pronouncements of the Court are not *de lege lata* but in fact sources of international law. A commentary on Art. 59 is not the right place for explaining or justifying in detail this well-known experience; only a few remarks can be made.

Judgments of any court or tribunal are only, in simple cases, nothing more than the logical application of legal norms to given facts. In all other cases they contain a law-creating element; the courts apply and create the law, in national as well as in international law. If a judgment, especially of the highest court, has pronounced legal rules and principles, legal certainty requires adherence to these rules and principles in other cases, unless compelling reasons militate in favour of changing the case law. As seven judges put it in a joint declaration to the Court's judgment in the *Kosovo* case:

> [The Court] must ensure consistency with its own past case law in order to provide predictability. Consistency is the essence of judicial reasoning. This is especially true in different phases of the same case or with regard to closely connected cases.

Therefore, it is not only the experience, but a necessity that earlier case law is in principle respected in later decisions and in practice. Article 59 and Art. 38, para. 1(d) reflect this truth: the Statute does not recognize the binding force of a judgment beyond the individual case, but the Court can and should apply the law as developed in judicial decisions.

* * *

Of the roughly 150 decisions handed down by the ICJ so far, more than three quarters contain references to prior decisions of the Court. In addition, virtually all of the decisions that do not refer to earlier cases contained only orders but not full judgments or came in the first few years of the Court's existence. What does this tell you about the value in practice of ICJ judgments?

6. EVIDENCE OF INTERNATIONAL LAW: THE TEACHINGS OF THE MOST HIGHLY QUALIFIED PUBLICISTS

According to the following text, is the work of international law scholars a source of international law? What is the basis for the (alleged) "authority" of scholars? Is that basis sufficient to make the views of scholars a legitimate source of international law?

ANTHONY D'AMATO, COLLECTED LEGAL PAPERS, VOL. III
(1995)

* * *

A scholar of public international law has a unique place among legal academicians. There is no other field of law where the writings of a respected scholar constitute an actual source of law. The Statute of the International Court of Justice, lists as a subsidiary means for the determination of rules of international law "the teaching of the most highly qualified publicists of the various nations." The term "highly qualified publicists," of course, is synonymous with what I've called "respected scholars."

People unfamiliar with international law might look at the quoted language and quickly assume that it denotes nothing more than the way American courts use treatise writers or the various restatements. Many courts will cite as "authority" for their decisions a text-writer such as Prosser on Torts or Wigmore on Evidence. Even more frequently they will cite the Restatement of Contracts or the Restatement of the Foreign Relations Law of the United States. They might wonder whether such citations are not at least equivalent to the way the International Court of Justice might use the teachings of publicists as a subsidiary means for determining rules of law.

There is, however, an important and subtle difference. Wigmore's text on evidence is only as good as the case authority he uses to back it up. A Restatement of the law is only as good as its accuracy in restating black-letter rules from judicial opinions. These texts can be, and are, impeached in adversary debate by argumentation over their accuracy. In such arguments, the ultimate reference is not to the text itself, but to the cases marshaled in its support.

To be sure, there is another factor that, over time, validates normal, domestic texts. Consider a section in a Restatement that is an "advance" over present law—such as Section 90 of the First Restatement of Contracts, on "promissory estoppel." If that Section is cited (and not rejected) in judicial opinions, soon it becomes authoritative *because* it was cited in those judicial opinions. The Section then begins to live a life of its own. Indeed, this is true of any successful text. If a paragraph of Wigmore on Evidence is cited by many courts, pretty soon the paragraph itself becomes a statement of the law, and there is no need to look behind it to the original supporting case law.

Certainly an international law text can be used in the same way. One consults the book to find a general statement of an international norm; then repairs to the footnote to see what authority supports the statement. But with this similarity the resemblance to domestic legal texts ends. There is a wholly different and added meaning and use for the "teachings of publicists" in international law that is not true of writers of domestic texts.

The difference, I believe, is that in a sense an international publicist is a judge. He or she writes a book that is like an extended judicial opinion, adjudicating thousands of international incidents and events and coming up with a consistent doctrine to explain them. These thousands of incidents that make up the stuff of customary international law are not themselves immediately available to others: digging them out requires extensive research. The research sometimes takes the publicist into materials that have hardly ever been looked at by anyone else—voluminous correspondence between foreign offices housed in diplomatic archives, old cases in forgotten library collections, newspaper reports on microfilm, and so on. Perhaps if all these materials were indexed and retrievable on computers, the status of the writings of international publicists as a source of law would diminish.

The status of their writings would only diminish to an extent, however. The writings of publicists would still be a subsidiary source of law because of the authoritativeness the publicist enjoys by virtue of having made judgments about all the raw material of international practice. Being exposed to thousands of hotly-debated incidents, events, and cases tends to make the publicists disinterested and neutral. The jigsaw puzzle of fitting all these events into coherent rules, principles, and generalizations becomes training in objectivity. And it is this objectivity that ultimately lends a status of authority to the work of the international publicist such that it can be used as a subsidiary source of international law.

To be sure, some writers never become objective. They see everything through nationalistic eyeglasses, and their work merely apologizes for their own country's policies. The mere fact that one is an international "scholar" by no means assures personal objectivity. Yet there is a safety valve: the work of such "scholars" does not attain general acceptance in the world community. Such persons are *not* the "most highly qualified publicists" in the words of Article 38. The term "most highly qualified" selects from the class of scholars those whose writings have commended themselves, through objectivity of reporting and judgment to the international legal community.

* * *

Courts often cite scholarly works on international law, just like they cite books and law review articles on other subjects, but at least in the United States, they have often refused to be told by academics how to decide an international case. The two following examples address slightly different aspects of the issue. Exactly which proposition does the Second Circuit

Court of Appeals reject in *Yousef*? Why does the Court refuse to listen to scholars in *Flores*?

UNITED STATES V. YOUSEF

United States Circuit Court
327 F.3d 56 (2d Cir. 2003)

* * *

* * * [A]ccording to the Statute of the International Court of Justice and the writings of leading publicists themselves, publicists' writings are not true "sources" of international law, though they may be useful in explicating or clarifying an established legal principle or body of law. Nor do the writings of any particular publicists necessarily constitute strong evidence of a proposition of international law or of any State's consent thereto. Rather, as Professor Parry of Cambridge University observed, the writings of publicists are an acceptable additional source to shed light on a particular question of international law only when "*recourse must also be had*" beyond the "opinions," "decisions," and "acts" of States, and only then "to a lesser degree" than to more authoritative evidence, such as the State's own "declarations," "laws," and "instructions" to its agents.

Some contemporary international law scholars assert that they themselves are an authentic source of customary international law, perhaps even more relevant than the practices and acts of States. The most candid and aggressive formulation of the unfounded claim to legal suzerainty by the international law professoriate has been made by the eminent Louis B. Sohn, the emeritus Bemis Professor of International Law at the Harvard Law School, who stated:

> I submit that states really never make international law on the subject of human rights. *It is made by the people that care,* the professors, the writers of textbooks and casebooks, and the authors of articles in the leading international law journals. * * * This is the way international law is made, *not by states, but by "silly" professors writing books*[.]

Louis B. Sohn, *Sources of International Law*, 25 Ga. J. Int'l & Comp. L. 399, 399, 401 (1996) (emphasis added). This notion—that professors of international law enjoy a special competence to prescribe the nature of customary international law wholly unmoored from legitimating territorial or national responsibilities, the interests and practices of States, or (in countries such as ours) the processes of democratic consent—may not be unique, but it is certainly without merit.

Put simply, and despite protestations to the contrary by some scholars (or "publicists" or "jurists"), a statement by the most highly qualified scholars that international law is *x* cannot trump evidence that the treaty practice or customary practices of States is otherwise, much less trump a statute or constitutional provision of the United States at variance with *x*. This is only to emphasize the point that scholars do not *make* law, and that it would be profoundly inconsistent with the law-making processes within and between States for courts to permit scholars to do so by relying upon their statements, standing alone, as sources of international law. In a system governed by the rule of law, no private person—or group of men and women such as comprise the body of international law scholars—*creates* the law. Accordingly, instead of relying primarily on the works of scholars for a statement of customary international law, we look primarily to the formal lawmaking and official actions of States and only secondarily to the works of scholars as evidence of the established practice of States.

* * *

FLORES V. SOUTHERN PERU COPPER CORPORATION

United States Circuit Court
343 F.3d 140 (2d Cir. 2003)

* * *

5.   EXPERT AFFIDAVITS SUBMITTED BY PLAINTIFFS

Plaintiffs submitted to the District Court several affidavits by international law scholars in support of their argument that strictly *intranational* pollution violates customary international law. After careful consideration, the District Court declined to afford evidentiary weight to these affidavits. It determined that the affidavits "are even less probative [than plaintiffs' documentary evidence] of the existence of universal norms, especially considering the vigorous academic debate over the content of international law." It explained further:

> The Second Circuit in *Filartiga* stated that courts should determine whether a rule is well-established and universally recognized by consulting, among other sources, " 'the works of jurists, writing professedly on public law.' " *Filartiga*, 630 F.2d at 880, *quoting United States v. Smith*, 18 U.S. (5 Wheat.) 153, 160–61 (1820). In this case, plaintiffs and defendant have submitted multiple affidavits by professors, explaining why or why not plaintiffs' claims are supported by customary international law. The affidavits serve essentially as supplemental briefs, providing arguments and citations which for the most part also appear in the parties' main briefs. I doubt that such academic exercises in advocacy are the sort of scholarly writings the Second Circuit had in mind when it identified the sources that could serve as evidence of customary international law.

Plaintiffs argue on appeal that the District Court did not accord proper weight to the statements of their experts. They maintain that "the authority of scholars, [and] jurists * * * has long been recognized by the Supreme Court and this Court as *authoritative sources* for determining the content of international law." In support of this assertion, they rely upon the Supreme Court's decision in *The Paquete Habana*, 175 U.S. 677, 700 (1900), as well as Article 38 of the ICJ Statute.

In its seminal decision in *Paquete Habana*, the Supreme Court designated "the works of jurists [*i.e.*, scholars] and commentators" as a possible source of customary international law. *Paquete Habana*, 175 U.S. at 700. However, the Court expressly stated that such works "are resorted to by judicial tribunals, *not for the speculations of their authors concerning what the law ought to be*, but for trustworthy evidence of what the law *really is.*" *Id.* (emphasis added), *quoted in Filartiga*, 630 F.2d at 881. Accordingly, under *Paquete Habana*, United States judicial tribunals may only "resort[ ] to" the works of "jurists and commentators" insofar as such works set forth the current law as it "*really is.*" 175 U.S. at 700 (emphasis added). Conversely, courts may not entertain as evidence of customary international law "speculations" by "jurists and commentators" about "what the law ought to be." *Id.*

Similarly, Article 38 of the ICJ Statute does *not* recognize the writings of scholars as primary or independent sources of customary international law. Section 1(d) of Article 38 provides in pertinent part that courts may consult "the teachings of the most highly qualified publicists [*i.e.*, scholars or "jurists"] of the various nations, *as subsidiary means for the determination of rules of law.*" ICJ Statute, June 26, 1945, art. 38(1)(d), 59 Stat. 1055 (emphasis added). Here, the word "subsidiary" assigns to the works of scholars a distinctly secondary role—to assist in discovering the authoritative principles of law, rather than to create or supplement them. The other three categories of evidence enumerated in Article 38 constitute primary sources of customary international law, but the works of scholars constitute subsidiary or secondary sources that may only be consulted "for trustworthy evidence" of what customary international law "really *is.*" *Paquete Habana*, 175 U.S. at 700; *see United States v. Yousef*, 327 F.3d 56, 102–03 (2d Cir. 2003).

The acknowledgment in *Paquete Habana* and Article 38 of the works of scholars as subsidiary or secondary sources of customary international law stems from the fact that, as noted above, the primary evidence of customary international law is widely dispersed and generally unfamiliar to lawyers and judges. The Supreme Court and the drafters of Article 38 recognized the value of the role traditionally played by scholars in identifying and recording the practices of States and thereby revealing the development of customary international law rules. But neither *Paquete Habana* nor Article 38 recognizes as a source of customary international law the policy-driven or theoretical work of advocates that comprises a substantial amount of contemporary international law scholarship. Nor do these authorities permit us to consider personal viewpoints expressed in the affidavits of international law scholars. In sum, although scholars may provide accurate descriptions of the *actual* customs and practices and legal obligations of States, only the courts may determine whether these customs and practices give rise to a rule of customary international law.

We have reviewed the affidavits submitted by plaintiffs and agree with the District Court's conclusion that they are not competent evidence of customary international law.

* * *

What is the lesson a practitioner can learn from these cases regarding the forensic use of international law scholarship?

NOTE ON THE ROLE OF INTERNATIONAL LAW SCHOLARS IN CIVIL LAW JURISDICTIONS

In other countries, especially in civil law jurisdictions (e.g., in continental Europe and Latin America), courts are often more deferential to international law scholarship, for three main reasons. First, in the civil law orbit, legal scholars have enjoyed greater prestige and influence than in the common law tradition. Whereas the latter may be called a "law of judges," the former was largely shaped as a "law of professors." Second, legal scholarship in general, and international law scholarship in particular, is more neutral and sober in the civil law than in the common law tradition. The contrast is particularly striking between the civil law position on the one hand and the United States on the other: in the former, a scholar can easily discredit him- or herself by advocating a particular position, whereas in the United States such advocacy is often considered the very point of legal scholarship. As a result, courts in civil law jurisdictions have greater trust in the objectivity of legal scholarship. Third, in forensic proceedings, experts in civil law jurisdictions are selected and appointed by the court, not by the parties; thus their primary obligation is to help the judges to ascertain the law, not to support the position of the litigant that hired them.

7. INTEGRATING THE SOURCES

DAVID BEDERMAN, INTERNATIONAL LAW FRAMEWORKS

(3d ed. 2010)

* * *

It is important for every international lawyer to realize that there is a strong synergy between the various sources of international legal obligation. Understanding how these sources interact is vital to seeing how rules and doctrines evolve and change over time, and thus how decisions and outcomes are achieved in international relations.

To best illustrate this dynamic in the creation of international law, consider the formation of rules for international environmental law * * *. Before the 1920's or 1930's there was simply no law on this subject. One would have looked in vain for State practice, treaties, case law, or even academic writings on this subject. Necessity is the mother of invention, though, and the exigency of creating law on this subject was impelled by a single dispute: the 1941 *Trail Smelter* Arbitration between the U.S. and Canada. This case featured a claim by the U.S. that an ore smelter in Trail, British Columbia, was belching such quantities of air pollution as to be causing substantial damage in Washington state. In the absence of any international law, the arbitrators were obliged to derive a rule from the domestic jurisprudence of States with federal systems (like the U.S. and Switzerland) that one entity should not use its territory in such a way as to injure the rights of another jurisdiction's territory. From this insight—a general principle of law recognized by a sufficient number of civilized nations—the arbitration concluded that Canada owed the United States a duty to prevent and minimize air pollution emanating from the smelter and to compensate for past damages.

From this kernel of a general principle grew the shoots of State practice, slowly at first, but then later with growing rapidity. Nations began to adjust more and more disputes regarding shared resources (including boundary lakes and rivers) or environmental concerns. In the 1950's, 1960's, and 1970's customary international law began to crystalize around a small group of rules of international environmental law: avoidance of transboundary pollution, liability and compensation for environmental damage, and substantive standards to protect wildlife and prevent harmful emissions. Indeed, this process was almost exclusively customary— there were exceedingly few treaties (either bilateral or multilateral) on this subject. At some point in this process there was a sufficient "critical mass" of State practice, combined with a realization that these norms had a binding and legal character (*opinio juris*) so that they were confirmed as customary international law.

Beginning in 1972, with the Stockholm Declaration on the Human Environment, treaty-making began slowly to occupy this field of international law. Again, the process began slowly as exclusively a manifestation of codification—organizing and rationalizing the body of customary norms. Codification did not, however, end the role of customary international law. Just as a tree that has been pruned continues to grow, so, too, a codified rule of custom will continue to be affected by subsequent State conduct. Indeed, customary practices might continue to exert an influence and change the treaty rule. That might occur through the development of new rules, or, more typically, through the process of treaty interpretation in which treaty provisions are gradually given certain well-established meanings.

Treaty-making in international environmental law quickly advanced from a footing of codifying custom to one of affirmatively legislating new rules of international conduct—"progressive development." The 1980's and 1990's saw a literal explosion in the number, variety, and complexity of treaties on international environmental law. Conventions were concluded on atmospheric issues, including ozone depletion, acid rain, and global warming. Many treaties were focused on habitat protection, rational management of common resources (like fisheries), preservation of wildlife and flora, and trade restrictions to promote these goals. Often these "legislative" treaties began as "framework conventions," merely sketching out the course of future negotiations. But, like much "soft" international law, vague guidelines hardened into explicit norms and then into elaborately-detailed regulatory regimes, with rules periodically updated by the parties through expedited or tacit amendment procedures. Some commentators have complained that international environmental law has become too "congested" with convention regimes and treaty-drafting, so that effective observance, compliance and enforcement of existing rules have been ignored.

In less than 70 years we have seen one very significant field in international law go from a literal vacuum (with no rules of international conduct *at all*) to incredibly sophisticated regimes featuring detailed rules of behavior and complex institutional machinery to enforce those rules. This would have been impossible without general principles "jump-starting" the process of international law formation (by effective borrowing from domestic legal systems), and the dynamic of customary international law (which allowed the quick accretion of State practice in response to pressing needs), and the processes of treaty-making (which permitted both the codification and progressive development of these rules).

It is this kind of synergy which explains the unique sources and methods of international law—and also the inherent strength of the international legal system. It also accounts for the special skills and aptitudes that an international lawyer must bring to bear in understanding the evolution of rules of international conduct, as well as constructing arguments and transactions on behalf of parties and clients.

* * *

EXERCISE ON THE TRADITIONAL SOURCES OF INTERNATIONAL LAW

In the case of the "American–Russian Cultural Cooperation Foundation" (the Foundation) and the "Organizing Committee for the Goodwill Mission" (the Organizing Committee), which we discussed earlier in this Chapter, the main Russian argument for invalidating the agreement was that bribery was itself a violation of international law.

Is the argument correct? Using this book as well as what you can find on the Internet on bribery and corruption in international law, consider all the relevant sources and then put together the best argument you can make for either side.

In particular, is there a treaty that applies to this dispute? Is there a customary international law basis, and what would you have to show to establish it? Is there a general principle that bribery is prohibited? Would any domestic law apply here?

It would be useful in this exercise to trace the evolution of anti-corruption law on a timeline using the kinds of sources we have discussed (i.e., treaties, custom, general principles, judicial opinions, scholarship, domestic law, etc.).

Anti-corruption law is one of many areas of international legal practice that has developed through a patchwork of sources. Taken one by one, these sources may not carry the day, but when good lawyers combine them, a decision-maker sometimes can be persuaded to find a legal obligation where none existed before. We will see an example of this in the context of the prohibition of torture in the case of *Filartiga v. Peña–Irala* (Ch. VIII.2.B.).

CHAPTER 4

DISPUTE RESOLUTION:
AD HOC APPROACHES

∎ ∎ ∎

What does international dispute resolution look like under the traditional, "law of nations," approach? Let us, first, take a historical look at dispute resolution in public international law among the then-almost-sole players—states. But let us also consider where private parties could take international cases, such as disputes arising out of transnational business relationships.

1. AMONG SOVEREIGN STATES

"States do not plead their cause before a tribunal;
war alone is their way of bringing suit."

Immanuel Kant, On Perpetual Peace (Second Definitive Article, Article, 1795)

As a lawyer, it is easy—but dangerous—to lose sight of two important facts. First, the vast majority of actors comply with the law in the vast majority of instances. Contrary to widely held belief, this is also true for nation states. As Louis Henkin, one of the 20th century's most prominent international lawyers, famously concluded several decades ago, "almost all nations observe almost all principles and almost all of their obligations almost all of the time." (Louis Henkin, HOW NATIONS BEHAVE 47 (2d ed. 1979).) Today, this is widely accepted, although scholars still struggle to explain why that is so. For an in-depth discussion, see Harold H. Koh, Why Do Nations Obey International Law?, 106 Yale L.J. 2599 (1997); for a challenge to the orthodoxy, see Jack Goldsmith and Eric Posner, THE LIMITS OF INTERNATIONAL LAW (2005).

Second, as lawyers we tend to overlook that when disputes do arise, they are usually settled outside of courts and tribunals. Again, this is true for nation states as well. In the majority of instances, they have resolved their international disputes through political and diplomatic means. To be sure, in their negotiations, legal arguments often play a significant role, but they do so only as part of a much larger concert of considerations, and the result is not a legal decision in the sense of an outcome dictated by law.

But what if diplomacy and political negotiation have failed? The following materials illustrate the major options for dispute resolution under the traditional approach, ranging from the use of force (war) and its gradual containment through law to peaceful legal processes (ad hoc arbitration).

A. WAR

The Melian Dialogue

About two-and-a-half millennia ago, the Athenians had a prolonged argument with the Spartans which Thucydides (c. 460–400 B.C.), himself a general on the Athenian side, chronicled in his History of the Peloponnesian War. The following excerpts describe a famous episode known as the Melian Dialogue, which took place in 416 B.C. In reading it, ask yourself: How did this "international dispute" arise? How did the parties try to "resolve" it? How did they actually resolve it? What view of international law underlies their attitudes and arguments?

THUCYDIDES, HISTORY OF THE PELOPONNESIAN WAR
(Rex Warner transl., Penguin Classics 1954)

* * *

The Athenians also made an expedition against the island of Melos. They had thirty of their own ships, six from Chios, and two from Lesbos; 1,200 hoplites, 300 archers, and twenty mounted archers, all from Athens; and about 1,500 hoplites from the allies and the islanders.

The Melians are a colony from Sparta. They had refused to join the Athenian empire like the other islanders, and at first had remained neutral without helping either side; but afterwards, when the Athenians had brought force to bear on them by laying waste to their land, they had become open enemies of Athens.

Now the generals Cleomedes, the son of Lycomedes, and Tisias, the son of Tisimachus, encamped with the above force in Melian territory and, before doing any harm to the land, first of all sent representatives to negotiate. The Melians did not invite these representatives to speak before the people, but asked them to make the statement for which they had come in front of the governing body and the few. The Athenian representatives then spoke as follows:

"So we are not to speak before the people, no doubt in case the mass of the people should hear once and for all and without interruption an argument from us which is both persuasive and incontrovertible, and should so be led astray. This, we realize, is your motive in bringing us here to speak before the few. Now suppose that you who sit here should make assurance doubly sure. Suppose that you, too, should refrain from dealing with every point in detail in a set speech, and should instead interrupt us whenever we say something controversial and deal with that before going on to the next point? Tell us first whether you approve of this suggestion of ours."

The Council of the Melians replied as follows:

"No one can object to each of us putting forward our own views in a calm atmosphere. That is perfectly reasonable. What is scarcely consistent with such a proposal is the present threat, indeed the certainty, of your making war on us. We see that you have come prepared to judge the argument yourselves, and that the likely end of it all will be either war, if we prove that we are in the right, and so refuse to surrender, or else slavery."

Athenians: If you are going to spend the time in enumerating your suspicions about the future, or if you have met here for any other reason except to look the facts in the face and on the basis of these facts to consider how you can save your city from destruction, there is no point in our going on with this discussion. If, however, you will do as we suggest, then we will speak on.

Melians: It is natural and understandable that people who are placed as we are should have recourse to all kinds of arguments and different points of view. However, you are right in saying that we are met together here to discuss the safety of our country and, if you will have it so, the discussion shall proceed on the lines that you have laid down.

Athenians: Then we on our side will use no fine phrases saying, for example, that we have a right to our empire because we defeated the Persians, or that we have come against you now because of the injuries you have done us—a great mass of words that nobody would believe. And we ask you on your side not to imagine that you will influence us by saying that you, though a colony of Sparta, have not joined Sparta in the war, or that you have never done us any harm. Instead we recommend that you should try to get what it is possible for you to get, taking into consideration what we both really do think; since you know as well as we do that, when these matters are discussed by practical people, the standard of justice depends on the equality of power to compel and that in fact the strong do what they have the power to do and the weak accept what they have to accept.

* * *

Melians: And how could it be just as good for us to be the slaves as for you to be the masters?

Athenians: You, by giving in, would save yourselves from disaster; we, by not destroying you, would be able to profit from you.

Melians: So you would not agree to our being neutral, friends instead of enemies, but allies of neither side?

Athenians: No, because it is not so much your hostility that injures us; it is rather the case that, if we were on friendly terms with you, our subjects would regard that as a sign of weakness in us, whereas your hatred is evidence of our power.

Melians: Is that your subjects' idea of fair play—that no distinction should be made between people who are quite unconnected with you and people who are mostly your own colonists or else rebels whom you have conquered?

Athenians: So far as right and wrong are concerned they think that there is no difference between the two, that those who still preserve their independence do so because they are strong, and that if we fail to attack them it is because we are afraid. So that by conquering you we shall increase not only the size but the security of our empire. We rule the sea and you are islanders, and weaker islanders too than the others; it is therefore particularly important that you should not escape.

* * *

Melians: Then surely, if such hazards are taken by you to keep your empire and by your subjects to escape from it, we who are still free would show ourselves great cowards and weaklings if we failed to face everything that comes rather than submit to slavery.

Athenians: No, not if you are sensible. This is no fair fight, with honour on one side and shame on the other. It is rather a question of saving your lives and not resisting those who are far too strong for you.

* * *

Melians: It is difficult, and you may be sure that we know it, for us to oppose your power and fortune, unless the terms be equal. Nevertheless we trust that the gods will give us fortune as good as yours, because we are standing for what is right against what is wrong; and as for what we lack in power, we trust that it will be made up for by our alliance with the Spartans, who are bound, if for no other reason, then for honour's sake, and because we are their kinsmen, to come to our help. Our confidence, therefore, is not so entirely irrational as you think.

Athenians: So far as the favour of the gods is concerned, we think we have as much right to that as you have. Our aims and our actions are perfectly consistent with the beliefs men hold about the gods and with the principles which govern their own conduct. Our opinion of the gods and our knowledge of men lead us to conclude that it is a general and necessary law of nature to rule whatever one can. This is not a law that we made ourselves, nor were we the first to act upon it when it was made. We found it already in existence, and we shall leave it to exist for ever among those who come after us. We are merely acting in accordance with it, and we know that you or anybody else with the same power as ours would be acting in precisely the same way. And therefore, so far as the gods are concerned, we see no good reason why we should fear to be at a disadvantage. But with regard to your views about Sparta and your confidence that she, out of a sense of honour, will come to your aid, we must say that we congratulate you on your simplicity but do not envy you your folly. In matters that concern themselves or their own constitution the Spartans are quite remarkably good; as for their relations with others, that is a long story, but it can be expressed shortly and clearly by saying that of all people we know the Spartans are most conspicuous for believing that what they like doing is honourable and what suits their interests is just. And this kind of attitude is not going to be of much help to you in your absurd quest for safety at the moment.

* * *

The Athenians then withdrew from the discussion. The Melians, left to themselves, reached a conclusion which was much the same as they had indicated in their previous replies. Their answer was as follows:

"Our decision, Athenians, is just the same as it was at first. We are not prepared to give up in a short moment the liberty which our city has enjoyed from its foundation for 700 years. We put our trust in the fortune that the gods will send and which has saved us up to now, and in the help of men—that is, of the Spartans; and so we shall try to save ourselves. But we invite you to allow us to be friends of yours and enemies to neither side, to make a treaty which shall be agreeable to both you and us, and so to leave our country."

The Melians made this reply, and the Athenians, just as they were breaking off the discussion, said:

"Well, at any rate, judging from this decision of yours, you seem to us quite unique in your ability to consider the future as something more certain than what is before your eyes, and to see uncertainties as realities, simply because you would like them to be so. As you have staked most on and trusted most in Spartans, luck, and hopes, so in all these you will find yourselves most completely deluded."

The Athenian representatives then went back to the army, and the Athenian generals, finding that the Melians would not submit, immediately commenced hostilities and built a wall completely round the city of Melos, dividing the work out among the various states. Later they left behind a garrison of some of their own and some allied troops to blockade the place by land and sea, and with the greater part of their army returned home. The force left behind stayed on and continued with the siege.

* * *

[After several months of siege, the Melians surrendered unconditionally. The Athenians killed the Melian men of military age and sold the women and children as slaves.]

B. "JUST WAR"

U.S. NATIONAL ANTHEM

Then conquer we must, when our cause it is just,
And this be our motto: "In God is our trust."

> Francis Scott Key, The Star Spangled Banner
> (Fourth Stanza, 1814)

Two thousand years later, Hugo Grotius (often considered the father of modern public international law) pondered the question whether, and, if so, under what conditions, war could be just. Had the two millennia since the Peloponnesian War brought progress? If so, how?

HUGO GROTIUS, THE RIGHTS OF WAR AND PEACE, BOOK I
(Liberty Fund 2005 (orig. 1625))

* * *

WHETHER 'TIS EVER LAWFUL TO MAKE WAR.

Having viewed the Sources of Right, let us proceed to the first and most general Question, which is Whether any War be Just, or, Whether 'tis ever Lawful to make War?

* * *

IV. By the Law of Nature then, which may also be called the Law of Nations, it is plain, that every Kind of War is not to be condemned. History, and the Laws and Customs of all People, fully inform us, that War is not disallowed of by the Voluntary Law of Nations: Nay, *Hermogenianus* declares, that Wars were introduced by the Law of Nations, which I think ought to be interpreted somewhat different from what it generally is, *viz.* That the Law of Nations has established a certain Manner of making War; so that those Wars which are conformable to it, have, by the Rules of that Law, certain peculiar Effects: Whence arises that Distinction which we shall hereafter make use of, between a *solemn War*, which is also called Just, (that is, regular and compleat) and a *War not solemn*, which yet does not therefore cease to be just, that is, agreeable to Right. For tho' the Law of Nations does not authorize Wars *not solemn*, yet it does not condemn them, (provided the Cause be just) as shall hereafter be more fully explained. *By the Law of Nations*, (says *Livy*) *it is allowed to repel Force by Force*. And *Floretinus* declares it *to be allowed by the Law of Nations to repel Violence and Wrong, and to defend our Lives.*

* * *

STEPHEN C. NEFF, WAR AND THE LAW OF NATIONS: A GENERAL HISTORY

(2005)

* * *

Once the hurdle of Christian pacifism had been overcome, the intellectual path was open towards an elaboration of a theory of just wars * * * Its essence may be stated with the utmost brevity: a just war was a war waged for the enforcement of right and the eradication of evil. In approximately the period between 1050 and 1300, a number of European writers, mostly theologians, proceeded to construct a detailed doctrine on this basic conceptual foundation, which stands as one of the most impressive intellectual achievements of medieval thought. There were naturally disagreements about many of the specific aspects of just-war doctrine; but essential elements of it were broadly agreed. In particular, it was usually agreed that five main principles or criteria were necessary in order for a war to be just in the strict sense.

The first was *auctoritas*: the proposition that a just war could be waged only by the command of a sovereign. This principle reflected the pacifist view underlying just-war theory as a whole, according to which a just war was one waged in defence of others rather than of oneself—with the direct implication that the just warrior had to hold a commission from his community (i.e., from his ruler) to justify the shedding of blood. A notable feature of *auctoritas* was that it was commonly held to be necessary on *both* sides of the conflict, and not on the just side only. This requirement had the effect of excluding domestic law-enforcement operations against bandits, pirates and the like from the category of just wars.

The second criterion of a just war was *personae*. This meant that only certain categories of persons were allowed to engage in armed conflict. Some, such as women, children and the aged or infirm, were excluded by the dictates of nature. Another important excluded category was ecclesiastics, whose professional calling was held to be incompatible with the shedding of blood. (Clerics, incidentally, were forbidden to practise surgery on the same ground.) Some writers, with a practical bent, extended this principle to conclude that clergy were also entitled to exemption from taxes levied for war purposes.

The third principle was known as *res*. Meaning literally "thing," it really meant a thing in contention, the object of the quarrel, the *casus belli*. This concept meant, in effect, that a just war must have a well-defined objective. The *res* might take a corporeal form, such as a territory whose title was disputed. But it could also take an incorporeal form such as a demand for compensation for an injury inflicted. An important implication of this principle was the exclusion of endemic conflict from the category of just war—that is, it meant the rejection by Europeans of any doctrine like the Muslim one of the *Dar al-Islam* versus the *Dar al-Harb*.

The fourth principle was of the highest importance: the requirement of a just cause, or *justa causa*. This meant that, in order for a war to be permissible, it had to be waged in the pursuit of a valid legal claim. *Res* and *justa causa* had an intimate relation, with res referring to the claim that was being made and *justa causa* to the legal validity of that claim in the eyes of the law and, more broadly, to the permissibility of resorting to force to obtain the res. This principle of *justa causa* is what most persons would intuitively regard as the very heart of just-war theory. It may therefore come as something of a surprise that relatively little attention was given to it by medieval writers, who typically confined themselves to the most general comments on this topic. Augustine, for example, stated that a just war was "one that avenges wrongs, when a nation or state has to be punished for refusing to make amends for the wrongs inflicted by its subjects or to restore what it has seized unjustly." This broad formulation was endorsed verbatim by Thomas Aquinas in the thirteenth century.

A very important point about *justa causa* was that it was strictly an objective question. That is to say, the legal claim on which a war was waged must actually be valid in order for the war to be just. A sincere, but erroneous, belief in the rightness of one's legal cause would not suffice. Consequently, a war could not be just on both sides, any more than both parties to a lawsuit could have the law supporting their respective claims. That meant that a ruler should take the greatest care before resorting to war to be sure that the law was actually in his favour. To this end, it was advisable that the ruler should consult with legal experts, who in turn should give their advice conscientiously, without fear or favour. It should be appreciated, however, that *justa causa* was not a narrowly legalistic principle, referring only to the validity of the legal claim without regard to the broader context of the dispute. Prudential elements played a part as well. One of these was a requirement of necessity—that a war would not be just if an alternative and non-forcible way of resolving the crisis was available. There was also, if only implicitly, a requirement of proportionality—that a war should not be waged if the good which was expected to flow from it was outweighed by the evils that it would entail.

The final criterion was *animus*: "rightful intention." This was a require-ment that a just war be waged not out of hatred but out of love, for the purpose of correcting evil and bringing the enemy to the path of right-eousness. *Animus* may be thought of as a sort of subjective or mental counterpart of *justa causa*. *Justa causa* determined whether an action as such was permissible in principle; while *animus* concerned the extent to which the actor's soul was endangered by performing that act. *Justa causa* was therefore the natural realm of the lawyer, and *animus* of the theologian. Of all of the elements of the just-war schema, this was the most distinctively Christian one, since it functioned as the key means of reconciling the Christian duty of universal love with the resort to force. It is perhaps not surprising, then, that animus received rather more atten-tion from the theologians than *justa causa* did. To Augustine, nothing was more reprehensible than the love of violence for its own sake, or the quest for personal glory or booty. "The real evils in war," he warned, "are love of violence, revengeful cruelty, fierce and implacable enmity, wild re-sistance, and the lust of power, and such like." Aquinas was very careful to stress that the lack of the correct *animus* would make a war unjust, even if the requisite objective *justa causa* was present.

A clear implication of this principle of *animus* was to exclude personal hatred from the sphere of just war-making. There must be hatred only of the wrong-doing that had made the war necessary, but not of the wrong-doer. Augustine stressed that war must be waged, if at all, with reluc-tance, out of regrettable necessity and "with a certain benevolent severi-ty." Aquinas agreed, insisting that a just war must be motivated solely by a desire for "the advancement of good or the avoidance of evil" with no element of "private animosity." Indeed, to wage a just war was actually to confer a positive benefit onto the misguided enemy, by preventing his sin-ful enterprise from succeeding and thereby imperilling his soul. Augus-tine made an analogy with a father applying corporal punishment to a son for corrective purposes, with a motive of love. The fourteenth-century clerical writer, Honore de Bonet, echoed this view by likening a just war to the administration of medicine to the sick—painful and unpleasant in the short term, but done for the good of the patient himself. It may be noted, in this connection, that Aquinas's discussion of warfare appeared in the section of his great *Summa Theologica* that dealt with charity. The waging of war with the correct *animus* was therefore a means by which a Christian could be true to the gospel command to return kindness for ha-tred, to love one's enemy as one's friend.

* * *

C. NO WAR?

How does the following document approach the question whether war can ever be "just"?

THE KELLOGG–BRIAND PACT
(Adopted 1928; in force 1929)

The President of the German Reich, the President of the United States of America, His Majesty the King of the Belgians, the President of the French Republic, His Majesty the King of Great Britain Ireland and the British Dominions Beyond the Seas, Emperor of India, His Majesty the King of Italy, His Majesty the Emperor of Japan, the President of the Republic of Poland the President of the Czechoslovak Republic,

Deeply sensible of their solemn duty to promote the welfare of mankind;

Persuaded that the time has come when a frank renunciation of war as an instrument of national policy should be made to the end that the peaceful and friendly relations now existing between their peoples may be perpetuated;

Convinced that all changes in their relations with one another should be sought only by pacific means and be the result of a peaceful and orderly process, and that any signatory Power which shall hereafter seek to promote its national interests by resort to war should be denied the benefits furnished by this Treaty;

Hopeful that, encouraged by their example, all the other nations of the world will join in this humane endeavor and by adhering to the present Treaty as soon as it comes into force bring their peoples within the scope of its beneficent provisions, thus uniting the civilized nations of the world in a common renunciation of war as an instrument of their national policy;

Have decided to conclude a Treaty * * * [and agreed on the following articles through their representatives]:

Article I

The High Contracting Parties solemnly declare in the names of their respective peoples that they condemn recourse to war for the solution of international controversies, and renounce it, as an instrument of national policy in their relations with one another.

Article II

The High Contracting Parties agree that the settlement or solution of all disputes or conflicts of whatever nature or of whatever origin they may be, which may arise among them, shall never be sought except by pacific means.

Article III

The present Treaty shall be ratified by the High Contracting Parties named in the Preamble in accordance with their respective constitutional requirements, and shall take effect as between them as soon as all their several instruments of ratification shall have been deposited at Washington.

This Treaty shall, when it has come into effect as prescribed in the preceding paragraph, remain open as long as may be necessary for adherence by all the other Powers of the world. Every instrument evidencing the adherence of a Power shall be deposited at Washington and the Treaty shall immediately upon such deposit become effective as; between the Power thus adhering and the other Powers parties hereto.

* * *

IN FAITH WHEREOF the respective Plenipotentiaries have signed this Treaty in the French and English languages both texts having equal force, and hereunto affix their seals.

DONE at Paris, the twenty seventh day of August in the year one thousand nine hundred and twenty-eight.

———————

In light of subsequent events in world history, how would you evaluate the success of the Kellogg-Briand Pact?

D. AD HOC ARBITRATION

In the 19th century, there was no established general institution in which states could resolve their international disputes. Since the late middle ages, the papacy had occasionally arbitrated disputes among European rulers and nation states. That, however, required that all involved recognized themselves as members of the (Christian) world community, and that they were willing to submit their case to an ecclesiastical authority. As nation states outside of Europe increasingly entered the world stage, and as secularism advanced in the 19th century, these conditions were more and more rarely fulfilled. Nations seeking to resolve disputes through a legal process thus had no choice but to set up their own mechanism.

Modern international arbitration is usually said to have its origins in the *Treaty of Amity, Commerce and Navigation* concluded between the United States and Great Britain in 1794 (8 Stat. 116). In fact, however, there was already an arbitration clause in the Treaty of Carlowitz between the Austro–Hungarian and the Ottoman Empires, concluded in 1699.

The agreement between the United States and Great Britain, generally known as *Jay's Treaty* (because it was negotiated by United States Supreme Court Chief Justice John Jay), settled a number of issues between the newly independent country and its former colonial master. Articles V–VII provided that several questions were to be settled by joint commissions, consisting of one or two representatives of both governments who were then to choose a neutral third or fifth member. The treaty also outlined the basic rules under which these commissions were to proceed.

The text of the agreement below (drafted pursuant to Articles V–VII) was designed to resolve a dispute that had arisen between the two parties to the Treaty. As you read it, think about how the two sides agreed to settle the matter. Who set up the tribunal? Who made the rules according to which the Tribunal should decide? Who paid the cost of it?

TREATY ON THE ALABAMA ARIBTRATION
(Adopted 1871, in force 1871)

[During the Civil War, the Confederacy had a raider, the *Alabama*, built in Britain. The Union urged the British government to prevent the ship from leaving port as the rules of neutrality required. The British government hesitated and requested further proof of the Union allegations. When it finally decided to seize the *Alabama* it was too late—the ship had already left port. It then interrupted Union trade all over the oceans and sunk, burned, and ransomed close to 70 Union ships before it was sunk in June of 1864. After the war, the United States claimed damages from Britain. Relations between the two countries were extremely tense. In 1871, the parties finally concluded the following agreement (143 Consolidated Treaty Series 146) which may have prevented another war.]

HER Britannic Majesty and the United States of America, being desirous to provide for an amicable settlement of all causes of difference between the two countries, have for that purpose appointed their respective Plenipotentiaries * * *.

And the said Plenipotentiaries, after having exchanged their full powers, which were found to be in due and proper form have agreed to and concluded the following Articles:

Art. I. "Whereas differences have arisen between the Government of The United States and the Government of Her Britannic Majesty, and still exist, growing out of the acts committed by the several vessels which have given rise to the claims generically known as the *Alabama* claims:

And whereas Her Britannic Majesty has authorised Her High Commissioners and Plenipotentiaries to express, in a friendly spirit, the regret felt by Her Majesty's Government for the escape, under whatever circumstances, of the *Alabama* and other vessels from British ports, and for the depredations committed by those vessels:

Now, in order to remove and adjust all complaints and claims on the part of The United States, and to provide for the speedy settlement of such claims, which are not admitted by Her Britannic Majesty's Government, the High Contracting Parties agree that all the said claims, growing out of acts committed by the aforesaid vessels, and generically known as the *Alabama* claims, shall be referred to a Tribunal of Arbitration to be composed of 5 Arbitrators to be appointed in the following manner, that is to say one shall be named by Her Britannic Majesty; one shall be named by the President of The United States; His Majesty the King of Italy shall be requested to name one; the President of the Swiss Confederation shall be requested to name one; and His Majesty the Emperor of Brazil shall be requested to name one.

* * *

Art. II.   The Arbitrators shall meet at Geneva, in Switzerland, at the earliest convenient day after they shall have been named, and shall proceed impartially and carefully to examine and decide all questions that shall be laid before them on the part of the Governments of Her Britannic Majesty and The United States respectively. All questions considered by the Tribunal, including the final award, shall be decided by a majority of all the Arbitrators.

Each of the High Contracting Parties shall also name one person to attend the Tribunal as its Agent to represent it generally in all matters connected with the arbitration.

* * *

Art. VI.   In deciding the matters submitted to the Arbitrators they shall be governed by the following 3 rules, which are agreed upon by the High Contracting Parties as rules to be taken as applicable to the case, and by such principles of international law not inconsistent therewith as the Arbitrators shall determine to have been applicable to the case.

RULES

A neutral Government is bound—

First. To use due diligence to prevent the fitting out, arming, or equipping, within its jurisdiction, of any vessel which it has reasonable ground to believe is intended to cruise or to carry on war against a Power with which it is at peace; and also to use like diligence to prevent the departure from its jurisdiction of any vessel intended to cruise or carry on war as above, such vessel having been specially adapted, in whole or in part, within such jurisdiction, to warlike use.

Secondly. Not to permit or suffer either belligerent to make use of its ports or waters as the base of naval operations against the other, or for the purpose of the renewal or augmentation of military supplies or arms, or the recruitment of men.

Thirdly. To exercise due diligence in its own ports and waters, and, as to all persons within its jurisdiction, to prevent any violation of the foregoing obligations and duties.

Her Britannic Majesty has commanded her High Commissioners and Plenipotentiaries to declare that Her Majesty's Government can not assent to the foregoing roles as a statement of principles of International Law which were in force at the time when the claims mentioned in Article I arose, but that Her Majesty's Government, in order to evince its desire of strengthening the friendly relations between the two countries and of making satisfactory provision for the future, agrees that, in deciding the questions between the two countries arising out of those claims, the Arbitrators should assume that Her Majesty's Government had undertaken to act upon the principles set forth in these rules.

And the High Contracting Parties agree to observe these rules as between themselves in future, and to bring them to the knowledge of other maritime Powers and to invite them to accede to them.

Art. VII. The decision of the Tribunal shall, if possible, be made within 3 months from the close of the argument on both sides.

It shall be made in writing and dated, and shall be signed by the Arbitrators who may assent to it.

The said Tribunal shall first determine as to each vessel separately whether Great Britain has, by any act or omission, failed to fulfil any of the duties set forth in the foregoing three rules, or recognized by the principles of international law not inconsistent with such rules, and shall certify such fact as to each of the said vessels. In case the Tribunal finds that Great Britain has failed to fulfil any duty or duties as aforesaid, it may, if it think proper, proceed to award a sum in gross to be paid by Great Britain to The United States for all the claims referred to it; and in such case the gross sum so awarded shall be paid in coin by the Government of Great Britain to the Government of The United States at Washington within twelve months after the date of the award.

The award shall be in duplicate, one copy whereof shall be delivered to the Agent of Great Britain for his Government, and the other copy shall be delivered to the Agent of The United States for his Government.

* * *

The tribunal finally awarded the United States $15,500,000 in damages. What if the Government of Great Britain was outraged and refused to pay? Could the United States enforce the award? If so, how?

NOTE ON THE PERMANENT COURT OF ARBITRATION

In 1899, the Hague Convention for the Pacific Settlement of International Disputes established a Permanent Court of Arbitration (PCA). The name is misleading because it is not a permanent Court at all. Instead, it consists merely of an institutional framework and a mechanism for establishing arbitral tribunals for concrete disputes. When parties submit a dispute to the institution, they each pick two arbitrators from the panel who then pick a fifth member. In other words, the actual panels are still established ad hoc. The PCA played a moderately important role in international dispute settlement in the first third of the 20th century but then fell into disuse. Since the beginning of the 21st century, however, it has seen renewed activity. The PCA deals with different categories of cases. A few cases involve traditional state-to-state arbitration; other cases involve investment disputes between states and private parties; still other cases involve disputes entirely between private businesses.

2. AMONG PRIVATE PARTIES

Under the classic law-of-nations view of the world, where could private parties turn to resolve international disputes?

Interestingly, in the middle ages, there was a regime of private international dispute resolution. A look at it is important—not because it is important from an historical point of view but because it can be seen, and is often cited, as a precursor of, and model for, developments in our own time, especially the "new lex mercatoria" (Chapter VIII.4.) and modern international commercial arbitration (Chapter IX.3.).

HAROLD BERMAN, LAW AND REVOLUTION: THE FORMATION OF THE WESTERN LEGAL TRADITION
(1983)

* * *

PARTICIPATORY ADJUDICATION: COMMERCIAL COURTS

[In the high and late middle ages] Commercial courts included courts of markets and fairs, courts of merchant guilds, and urban courts. Although guild and urban courts were not concerned exclusively with commercial matters, their commercial jurisdiction was sufficiently extensive to warrant their being treated as commercial courts.

Market and fair courts, like seignorial and manorial courts, were non-professional community tribunals; the judges were elected by the merchants of markets or fairs from among their numbers. Guild courts were also nonprofessional tribunals, usually consisting simply of the head of the guild or his representative, but often he chose two or three merchant members of the guild to sit as assessors in mercantile cases. Occasionally, a professional jurist would sit with the merchant assessors. Professional notaries often acted as clerks to take care of legal formalities. Urban mercantile courts, too, often consisted of merchants elected by their fellows. * * *

Various other types of commercial courts developed in the course of time in various parts of the West. In England, Wales, and Ireland, so-called courts of the staple were established in the fourteen towns through which the flourishing English trade in certain "staple" products, chiefly wool, leather, and lead, was channeled. Italian, Flemish, and German merchants and bankers handled much of this business. The English offered protection to "merchant strangers" in the staple towns, and under the Statute of the Staple of 1353 the merchants of each staple town, as well as their servants and the members of their households, were to be "ruled by the law merchant [in] all things touching the staple, and not by the common law of the land, nor by the usage of cities, boroughs, or other towns." They were subject to the jurisdiction of the staple court, whose presiding officer was to be the mayor of the town, elected for a one-year term "by the commonalty of merchants, as well of strangers as of denizens." Thus foreign merchants participated in the elections of the mayors of English towns! The mayor was required to have "knowledge of the law merchant" and to judge according to it. Trials involving both a merchant stranger and an Englishman required a mixed jury composed half of foreigners and half of English subjects. Appeals could be taken to the chancellor and the king's council.

Another type of commercial court was the local maritime court in seaport towns, with jurisdiction over both commercial and maritime causes involving carriage of goods by sea. These courts called admiralty courts would sit on the seashore "from tide to tide."

In all types of commercial courts the procedure was marked by speed and informality. Time limits were narrow: in the fair courts justice was to be done while the merchants' feet were still dusty, in the maritime courts it was to be done "from tide to tide," in guild and town courts "from day to day." Often appeals were forbidden. Not only were professional lawyers generally excluded but also technical legal argumentation was frowned upon. The court was to be "ruled by equity * * * wherein every man will be received to tell his facts * * * and to say the best he can" in his defense. A typical statute of a merchant guild provided that commercial cases "are to be decided *ex aequo et bono*; it is not meet to dispute on the subtleties of the law." These procedural characteristics sharply distinguished commercial law from the formalistic procedure of urban and royal courts and also from the written procedure of the canon law in ordinary cases. * * *

In England, the speed of merchant justice was stressed by Bracton, who wrote that there were certain classes of people "who ought to have swift justice, such as merchants, to whom justice is given in the Court Pepoudrous" (the "piepowder" or "dusty feet" courts of fairs and markets).

The principle of speedy, informal, and equitable procedure in the commercial courts was, of course, a response to mercantile needs. That response could only be made, however, because of the communal, or participatory, character of commercial adjudication. Like the other characteristics of mercantile law its objectivity, universality, reciprocity of rights, integration, growth the communal character of commercial adjudication (that is, the participation of merchants in the resolution of mercantile disputes) may be viewed as a principle of abstract justice, a legal ideal. From that point of view it may be evaluated negatively as well as positively, for while it contributed to equitable solution of individual commercial cases it also helped to insulate commercial law from ecclesiastical, royal, and even urban control and to preserve mercantile privileges. But the system of participatory adjudication of commercial cases must also be viewed in historical terms as an aspect of the relative autonomy of the mercantile class and of its law in the formative era of the Western legal tradition, an autonomy relative to the overarching unity of Western law with its interaction of spiritual and secular authorities and within the secular, or feudal, manorial, commercial, urban, and royal legal systems.

* * *

The rise of the nation state in the early modern period entailed a concentration of adjudicatory power in the hands of the sovereign and its officials. Eventually, the sovereign state claimed, and acquired, a jurisdictional monopoly which left no room for institutions like the medieval merchant courts.

Of course, private parties could still, like states, arbitrate. But until more recently, private international arbitration was a cumbersome business. There was no established framework which the parties could use; ad hoc arbitration was logistically difficult and costly to organize; and there were few guarantees that an award would actually be enforced. Thus, private international arbitration was rarely used. As we will see later (Chapter IX.3.), this has changed dramatically in the last few decades.

The following case illustrates where and how an international private dispute was resolved in the late 19th century. What were the advantages, and what the downsides, of suing in the domestic courts of one of the involved countries? Why did the plaintiffs sue in France rather than in the United States?

The case is also the foundational decision on the recognition of foreign judgments in the United States. What are the basic positions on which law governs the issue (and which position wins)? What is the Supreme Court's basic attitude towards foreign judgments? Which requirements for recognition of a foreign judgment does the majority establish? Why?

HILTON V. GUYOT
United States Supreme Court
159 U.S. 113 (1895)

JUSTICE GRAY:

The first of these two cases was an action at law, brought December 18, 1885, in the circuit court of the United States for the Southern District of New York, by Gustave Bertin Guyot, as official liquidator of the firm of Charles Fortin & Co., and by the surviving members of that firm, all aliens and citizens of the republic of France, against Henry Hilton and William Libbey, citizens of the United States and of the state of New York, and trading as copartners, in the cities of New York and Paris, and elsewhere, under the firm name of A. T. Stewart & Co. The action was upon a judgment recovered in a French court at Paris, in the republic of France, by the firm of Charles Fortin & Co., all of whose members were French citizens, against Hilton & Libbey, trading as copartners as aforesaid, and citizens of the United States and of the State of New York.

The complaint alleged that in 1886, and since, during the time of all the transactions included in the judgment sued on, Hilton and Libbey, as successors to Alexander T. Stewart and Libbey, under the firm name of A. T. Stewart & Co., carried on a general business as merchants in the cities of New York and Paris and elsewhere, and maintained a regular store and place of business at Paris; that during the same time Charles Fortin & Co. carried on the manufacture and sale of gloves at Paris, and the two firms had there large dealings in that business, and controversies arose in the adjustment of accounts between them.

* * *

The defendants, in their answer, set forth in detail the original contracts and transactions in France between the parties, and the subsequent dealings between them, modifying those contracts; and alleged that the plaintiffs had no just claim against the defendants, but that, to the contrary, the defendants, upon a just settlement of the accounts, were entitled to recover large sums from the plaintiffs.

The answer admitted the proceedings and judgments in the French courts; and that the defendants gave up their business in France before the judgment on appeal, and had no property within the jurisdiction of France out of which that judgment could be collected.

* * *

The answer further alleged that, without any fault or negligence on the part of the defendants, there was not a full and fair trial of the controversies before the arbitrator, in that no witness was sworn or affirmed; in that Charles Fortin was permitted to make, and did make, statements not under oath, containing many falsehoods; in that the privilege of cross-examination of Fortin and other persons who made statements before the arbitrator was denied to the defendants; and in that extracts from printed newspapers, the knowledge of which was not brought home to the defendants, and letters and other communications in writing between Fortin & Co. and third persons, to which the defendants were neither privy nor party, were received by the arbitrator; that without such improper evidence the judgment would not have been obtained; and that the arbitrator was deceived and misled by the false and fraudulent accounts introduced by Fortin & Co., and by the hearsay testimony given without the solemnity of an oath and without cross-examination, and by the fraudulent suppression of the books and papers.

* * *

"Defendants, further answering, allege that it is contrary to natural justice, that the judgment hereinbefore mentioned should be enforced without an examination of the merits thereof; that by the laws of the Republic of France, to wit, article 181 of the Royal Ordinance of June 15, 1629, it is provided, namely: 'Judgments rendered, contracts or obligations recognized, in foreign kingdoms and sovereignties, for any cause whatever, shall give rise to no lien or execution in our kingdom. Thus the contracts shall stand for simple promises, and notwithstanding such judgments our subjects against whom they have been rendered may contest their rights anew before our own judges.'

* * *

* * * [T]hat the tribunals of the Republic of France give no force and effect, within the jurisdiction of the said country, to the duly rendered judgments of courts of competent jurisdiction of the United States against citizens of France after proper personal service of the process of said courts is made thereon in this country."

* * *

The records of the judgments of the French courts, put in evidence by the plaintiffs, showed that all the matters now relied on to show fraud were contested in and considered by those courts.

The plaintiffs objected to all the evidence offered by the defendants, on the grounds that the matters offered to be proved were irrelevant, immaterial, and incompetent; that, in respect to them, the defendants were concluded by the judgment sued on and given in evidence; and that none of those matters, if proved, would be a defense to this action upon that judgment.

The court declined to admit any of the evidence so offered by the defendants, and directed a verdict for the plaintiffs in the sum of $277,775.44, being the amount of the French judgment and interest. The defendants, having duly excepted to the rulings and direction of the court, sued out a writ of error.

* * *

International law, in its widest and most comprehensive sense—including not only questions of right between nations, governed by what has been appropriately called the law of nations; but also questions arising under what is usually called private international law, or the conflict of laws, and concerning the rights of persons within the territory and dominion of one nation, by reason of acts, private or public, done within the dominions of another nation—is part of our law, and must be ascertained and administered by the courts of justice, as often as such questions are presented in litigation between man and man, duly submitted to their determination.

The most certain guide, no doubt, for the decision of such questions is a treaty or a statute of this country. But when, as is the case here, there is no written law upon the subject, the duty still rests upon the judicial tribunals of ascertaining and declaring what the law is, whenever it becomes necessary to do so, in order to determine the rights of parties to suits regularly brought before them. In doing this, the courts must obtain such aid as they can from judicial decisions, from the works of jurists and commentators, and from the acts and usages of civilized nations.

No law has any effect, of its own force, beyond the limits of the sovereignty from which its authority is derived. The extent to which the law of one nation, as put in force within its territory, whether by executive order, by legislative act, or by judicial decree, shall be allowed to operate within the dominion of another nation, depends upon what our greatest jurists have been content to call "the comity of nations." Although the phrase has been often criticised, no satisfactory substitute has been suggested.

"Comity," in the legal sense, is neither a matter of absolute obligation, on the one hand, nor of mere courtesy and good will, upon the other. But it is the recognition which one nation allows within its territory to the legislative, executive or judicial acts of another nation, having due regard both to international duty and convenience, and to the rights of its own citizens or of other persons who are under the protection of its laws.

* * *

In view of all the authorities upon the subject, and of the trend of judicial opinion in this country and in England, following the lead of Kent and Story, we are satisfied that, where there has been opportunity for a full and fair trial abroad before a court of competent jurisdiction, conducting the trial upon regular proceedings, after due citation or voluntary appearance of the defendant, and under a system of jurisprudence likely to secure an impartial administration of justice between the citizens of its own country and those of other countries, and there is nothing to show either prejudice in the court, or in the system of laws under which it was sitting, or fraud in procuring the judgment, or any other special reason why the comity of this nation should not allow it full effect, the merits of the case should not, in an action brought in this country upon the judgment, be tried afresh, as on a new trial or an appeal, upon the mere assertion of the party that the judgment was erroneous in law or in fact. The defendants, therefore, cannot be permitted, upon that general ground, to contest the validity or the effect of the judgment sued on.

But they have sought to impeach that judgment upon several other grounds, which require separate consideration.

It is objected that the appearance and litigation of the defendants in the French tribunals were not voluntary, but by legal compulsion, and therefore that the French courts never acquired such jurisdiction over the defendants, that they should be held bound by the judgment.

Upon the question what should be considered such a voluntary appearance, as to amount to a submission to the jurisdiction of a foreign court, there has been some difference of opinion in England.

* * *

The present case is not one of a person traveling through or casually found in a foreign country. The defendants, although they were not citizens or residents of France, but were citizens and residents of the State of New York, and their principal place of business was in the city of New York, yet had a storehouse and an agent in Paris, and were accustomed to purchase large quantities of goods there, although they did not make sales in France. Under such circumstances, evidence that their sole object in appearing and carrying on the litigation in the French courts was to prevent property, in their storehouse at Paris, belonging to them, and within the jurisdiction, but not in the custody, of those courts, from being taken in satisfaction of any judgment that might be recovered against them, would not, according to our law, show that those courts did not acquire jurisdiction of the persons of the defendants.

It is next objected that in those courts one of the plaintiffs was permitted to testify not under oath, and was not subjected to cross-examination by the opposite party, and that the defendants were, therefore, deprived of safeguards which are by our law considered essential to secure honesty and to detect fraud in a witness; and also that documents and papers were admitted in evidence, with which the defendants had no connection, and which would not be admissible under our own system of jurisprudence. But it having been shown by the plaintiffs, and hardly denied by the defendants, that the practice followed and the method of examining witnesses were according to the laws of France, we are not prepared to hold that the fact that the procedure in these respects differed from that of our own courts is, of itself, a sufficient ground for impeaching the foreign judgment.

* * *

It must, however, always be kept in mind that it is the paramount duty of the court, before which any suit is brought, to see to it that the parties have had a fair and impartial trial, before a final decision is rendered against either party.

When an action is brought in a court of this country, by a citizen of a foreign country against one of our own citizens, to recover a sum of money adjudged by a court of that country to be due from the defendant to the plaintiff, and the foreign judgment appears to have been rendered by a competent court, having jurisdiction of the cause and of the parties, and upon due allegations and proofs, and opportunity to defend against them, and its proceedings are according to the course of a civilized jurisprudence, and are stated in a clear and formal record, the judgment is *prima facie* evidence, at least, of the truth of the matter adjudged; and it should be held conclusive upon the merits tried in the foreign court, unless some special ground is shown for impeaching the judgment, as by showing that it was affected by fraud or prejudice, or that, by the principles of international law, and by the comity of our own country, it should not be given full credit and effect.

There is no doubt that both in this country, as appears by the authorities already cited, and in England, a foreign judgment may be impeached for fraud.

* * *

Under what circumstances this may be done does not appear to have ever been the subject of judicial investigation in this country.

* * *

In the case at bar, the defendants offered to prove, in much detail, that the plaintiffs presented to the French court of first instance and to the arbitrator appointed by that court, and upon whose report its judgment was largely based, false and fraudulent statements and accounts against the defendants, by which the arbitrator and the French courts were deceived and misled, and their judgments were based upon such false and fraudulent statements and accounts. This offer, if satisfactorily proved, would, according to the decisions of the English Court of Appeal in *Abouloff v. Oppenheimer*, *Vadala v. Lawes*, and *Crozat v. Brogden*, above cited, be a sufficient ground for impeaching the foreign judgment, and examining into the merits of the original claim.

But whether those decisions can be followed in regard to foreign judgments, consistently with our own decisions as to impeaching domestic judgments for fraud, it is unnecessary in this case to determine, because there is a distinct and independent ground upon which we are satisfied that the comity of our nation does not require us to give conclusive effect to the judgments of the courts of France; and that ground is the want of reciprocity, on the part of France, as to the effect to be given to the judgments of this and other foreign countries.

* * *

Mr. Justice Story said: "If a civilized nation seeks to have the sentences of its own courts held of any validity elsewhere, they ought to have a just regard to the rights and usages of other civilized nations, and the principles of public and national law in the administration of justice."

Mr. Justice Woodbury said that judgments *in personam*, rendered under a foreign government, "are, *ex comitate*, treated with respect, according to the nature of the judgment, and the character of the tribunal which rendered it, and the reciprocal mode, if any, in which that government treats our judgments;" and added, "Nor can much comity be asked for the judgments of another nation which, like France, pays no respect to those of other countries."

Mr. Justice Cooley said: "True comity is equality; we should demand nothing more and concede nothing less."

Mr. Wheaton said: "There is no obligation, recognized by legislators, public authorities, and publicists, to regard foreign laws; but their application is admitted only from considerations of utility and the mutual convenience of states (*ex comitate, ob reciprocam utilitatem*)." "The general comity, utility and convenience of nations have, however, established a usage among most civilized States, by which the final judgments of foreign courts of competent jurisdiction are reciprocally carried into execution."

Since Story, Kent, and Wheaton wrote their commentaries, many books and essays have been published upon the subject of the effect to be allowed by the courts of one country to the judgments of another, with references to the statutes and decisions in various countries. * * * For the reasons stated at the outset of this opinion, we have not thought it important to state the conflicting theories of continental commentators and essayists as to what each may think the law ought to be; but have referred to their works only for evidence of authoritative declarations, legislative or judicial, of what the law is.

By the law of France, settled by a series of uniform decisions of the Court of Cassation, the highest judicial tribunal, for more than half a century, no foreign judgment can be rendered executory in France without a review of the judgment *au fond*—to the bottom, including the whole merits of the cause of action on which the judgment rests.

* * *

It appears, therefore, that there is hardly a civilized nation on either continent, which, by its general law, allows conclusive effect to an executory foreign judgment for the recovery of money. In France, and in a few smaller states—Norway, Portugal, Greece, Monaco, and Haiti—the merits of the controversy are reviewed, as of course, allowing to the foreign judgment, at the most, no more effect than of being *prima facie* evidence of the justice of the claim. In the great majority of the countries on the continent of Europe—in Belgium, Holland, Denmark, Sweden, Germany, in many cantons of Switzerland, in Russia and Poland, in Roumania, in Austria and Hungary, (perhaps in Italy) and in Spain—as well as in Egypt, in Mexico, and in a great part of South America, the judgment rendered in a foreign country is allowed the same effect only as the courts of that country allow to the judgments of the country in which the judgment in question is sought to be executed.

The prediction of Mr. Justice Story (in section 618 of his Commentaries on the Conflict of Laws, already cited) has thus been fulfilled, and the rule of reciprocity has worked itself firmly into the structure of international jurisprudence.

The reasonable, if not the necessary, conclusion appears to us to be that judgments rendered in France, or in any other foreign country, by the laws of which our own judgments are reviewable upon the merits, are not entitled to full credit and conclusive effect when sued upon in this country, but are *prima facie* evidence only of the justice of the plaintiffs' claim.

In holding such a judgment, for want of reciprocity, not to be conclusive evidence of the merits of the claim, we do not proceed upon any theory of retaliation upon one person by reason of injustice done to another; but upon the broad ground that international law is founded upon mutuality and reciprocity, and that by the principles of international law recognized in most civilized nations, and by the comity of our own country, which it is our judicial duty to know and to declare, the judgment is not entitled to be considered conclusive.

* * *

For these reasons, in the action at law, *the Judgment is reversed, and the cause remanded to the Circuit Court with directions to set aside the verdict and to order a new trial.*

* * *

CHIEF JUSTICE FULLER, dissenting.

Plaintiffs brought their action on a judgment recovered by them against the defendants in the courts of France, which courts had jurisdiction over person and subject-matter, and in respect of which judgment no fraud was alleged, except in particulars contested in and considered by the French courts. The question is whether under these circumstances, and in the absence of a treaty or act of Congress, the judgment is reexaminable upon the merits. This question I regard as one to be determined by the ordinary and settled rule in respect of allowing a party who has had an opportunity to prove his case in a competent court, to retry it on the merits, and it seems to me that the doctrine of *res judicata* applicable to domestic judgments should be applied to foreign judgments as well, and rests on the same general ground of public policy that there should be an end of litigation.

This application of the doctrine is in accordance with our own jurisprudence, and it is not necessary that we should hold it to be required by some rule of international law. The fundamental principle concerning judgments is that disputes are finally determined by them, and I am unable to perceive why a judgment *in personam* which is not open to question on the ground of want of jurisdiction, either intrinsically or over the parties, or of fraud, or on any other recognized ground of impeachment, should not be held *inter partes* though recovered abroad, conclusive on the merits.

Judgments are executory while unpaid, but in this country execution is not given upon a foreign judgment as such, it being enforced through a new judgment obtained in an action brought for that purpose.

The principle that requires litigation to be treated as terminated by final judgment properly rendered, is as applicable to a judgment proceeded on in such an action, as to any other, and forbids the allowance to the judgment debtor of a retrial of the original cause of action, as of right, in disregard of the obligation to pay arising on the judgment and of the rights acquired by the judgment creditor thereby.

That any other conclusion is inadmissible is forcibly illustrated by the case in hand. Plaintiffs in error were trading copartners in Paris as well as in New York, and had a place of business in Paris at the time of these transactions and of the commencement of the suit against them in France. The subjects of the suit were commercial transactions, having their origin, and partly performed, in France under a contract there made, and alleged to be modified by the dealings of the parties there; and one of the claims against them was for goods sold to them there. They appeared generally in the case, without protest, and by counterclaims relating to the same general course of business, a part of them only connected with the claims against them, became actors in the suit, and submitted to the courts their own claims for affirmative relief, as well as the claims against them. The courts were competent and they took the chances of a decision in their favor. As traders in France they were under the protection of its laws and were bound by its laws, its commercial usages and its rules of procedure. The fact that they were Americans and the opposite parties were citizens of France is immaterial, and there is no suggestion on the record that those courts proceeded on any other ground than that all litigants, whatever their nationality, were entitled to equal justice therein. If plaintiffs in error had succeeded in their cross suit and recovered judgment against defendants in error, and had sued them here on that judgment, defendants in error would not have been permitted to say that the judgment in France was not conclusive against them. As it was, defendants in error recovered, and I think plaintiffs in error are not entitled to try their fortune anew before the courts of this country on the same matters voluntarily submitted by them to the decision of the foreign tribunal. We are dealing with the judgment of a court of a civilized country, whose laws and system of justice recognize the general rules in respect to property and rights between man and man prevailing among all civilized peoples. Obviously the last persons who should be heard to complain are those who identified themselves with the business of that country, knowing that all their transactions there would be subject to the local laws and modes of doing business.

* * *

I cannot yield my assent to the proposition that because by legislation and judicial decision in France that effect is not there given to judgments recovered in this country which, according to our jurisprudence, we think should be given to judgments wherever recovered, (subject, of course, to the recognized exceptions), therefore we should pursue the same line of conduct as respects the judgments of French tribunals. The application of the doctrine of *res judicata* does not rest in discretion; and it is for the government, and not for its courts, to adopt the principle of retorsion, if deemed under any circumstances desirable or necessary.

* * *

Today, the rules on recognition of foreign money judgments are codified in a uniform law. An older version, the *Uniform Foreign Money Judgments Recognition Act* (1962) was adopted by 31 states and the District of Columbia. Its successor, the *Uniform Foreign–Country Judgments Recognition Act* (2005), has, as of last count, been adopted by 17 states and the District of Columbia. It differs from the earlier version only with regard to details that need not concern us here.

So, whose rules ultimately govern the recognition of foreign money judgments in the United States? How do the *Act's* rules compare to the ones laid down by the majority in *Hilton*? In particular, what is added and what is missing in the *Act*? Is the *Act* more or less permissive than *Hilton*?

UNIFORM FOREIGN–COUNTRY MONEY JUDGMENTS RECOGNITION ACT OF 2005

* * *

SECTION 2. DEFINITIONS. In this [act]:

(1) "Foreign country" means a government other than:

   (A) the United States;

   (B) a state, district, commonwealth, territory, or insular possession of the United States; or

   (C) any other government with regard to which the decision in this state as to whether to recognize a judgment of that government's courts is initially subject to determination under the Full Faith and Credit Clause of the United States Constitution.

(2) "Foreign-country judgment" means a judgment of a court of a foreign country.

SECTION 3. APPLICABILITY.

(a) Except as otherwise provided in subsection (b), this [act] applies to a foreign-country judgment to the extent that the judgment:

   (1) grants or denies recovery of a sum of money; and

   (2) under the law of the foreign country where rendered, is final, conclusive, and enforceable.

(b) This [act] does not apply to a foreign-country judgment, even if the judgment grants or denies recovery of a sum of money, to the extent that the judgment is:

   (1) a judgment for taxes;

(2) a fine or other penalty; or

(3) a judgment for divorce, support, or maintenance, or other judgment rendered in connection with domestic relations.

(c) A party seeking recognition of a foreign-country judgment has the burden of establishing that this [act] applies to the foreign-country judgment.

SECTION 4. STANDARDS FOR RECOGNITION OF FOREIGN–COUNTRY JUDGMENT.

(a) Except as otherwise provided in subsections (b) and (c), a court of this state shall recognize a foreign-country judgment to which this [act] applies.

(b) A court of this state may not recognize a foreign-country judgment if:

(1) the judgment was rendered under a judicial system that does not provide impartial tribunals or procedures compatible with the requirements of due process of law;

(2) the foreign court did not have personal jurisdiction over the defendant; or

(3) the foreign court did not have jurisdiction over the subject matter.

(c) A court of this state need not recognize a foreign-country judgment if:

(1) the defendant in the proceeding in the foreign court did not receive notice of the proceeding in sufficient time to enable the defendant to defend;

(2) the judgment was obtained by fraud that deprived the losing party of an adequate opportunity to present its case;

(3) the judgment or the [cause of action] [claim for relief] on which the judgment is based is repugnant to the public policy of this state or of the United States;

(4) the judgment conflicts with another final and conclusive judgment;

(5) the proceeding in the foreign court was contrary to an agreement between the parties under which the dispute in question was to be determined otherwise than by proceedings in that foreign court;

(6) in the case of jurisdiction based only on personal service, the foreign court was a seriously inconvenient forum for the trial of the action;

(7) the judgment was rendered in circumstances that raise substantial doubt about the integrity of the rendering court with respect to the judgment; or

(8) the specific proceeding in the foreign court leading to the judgment was not compatible with the requirements of due process of law.

(d) A party resisting recognition of a foreign-country judgment has the burden of establishing that a ground for nonrecognition stated in subsection (b) or (c) exists.

* * *

SECTION 6. PROCEDURE FOR RECOGNITION OF FOREIGN–COUNTRY JUDGMENT.

(a) If recognition of a foreign-country judgment is sought as an original matter, the issue of recognition shall be raised by filing an action seeking recognition of the foreign-country judgment.

(b) If recognition of a foreign-country judgment is sought in a pending action, the issue of recognition may be raised by counterclaim, crossclaim, or affirmative defense.

SECTION 7. EFFECT OF RECOGNITION OF FOREIGN–COUNTRY JUDGMENT.

If the court in a proceeding under Section 6 finds that the foreign-country judgment is entitled to recognition under this [act] then, to the extent that the foreign-country judgment grants or denies recovery of a sum of money, the foreign-country judgment is:

(1) conclusive between the parties to the same extent as the judgment of a sister state entitled to full faith and credit in this state would be conclusive; and

(2) enforceable in the same manner and to the same extent as a judgment rendered in this state.

* * *

SECTION 9. STATUTE OF LIMITATIONS.

An action to recognize a foreign-country judgment must be commenced within the earlier of the time during which the foreign-country judgment is effective in the foreign country or 15 years from the date that the foreign-country judgment became effective in the foreign country.

The basic approach to foreign judgment recognition in *Hilton* and the Uniform Act, i.e., the ground rule of recognition and the list of reasons for refusal, is fairly standard in the world today, with some exceptions and variations. Compare the German rules in the Code of Civil Procedure (Zivilprozessordnung) with the American approach presented above.

CODE OF CIVIL PROCEDURE (GERMANY)

Art. 328

(1) The recognition of a foreign judgment is excluded:

1. if the courts of the state to which the foreign court belongs are not competent according to German law;

2. if the defendant, who has not participated in the proceedings and raises this plea, has not been served with the written pleadings initiating the proceedings in the regular way or in a timely manner, so that he was not in a position to defend himself;

3. if the judgment is inconsistent with a judgment issued here or with an earlier foreign judgment. * * *

4. if the recognition of the judgment would give rise to a result which is manifestly incompatible with the basic principles of German law, especially if the recognition would be inconsistent with the constitution;

5. if reciprocity is not assured.

Art. 722

(1) The judgment of a foreign court shall only be executed if its admissibility is pronounced by an enforceable [German] judgment.

* * *

Art. 723

(1) The execution judgment shall be given without examination of the legality of the [foreign] decision.

* * *

EXERCISE ON INTERNATIONAL DISPUTE RESOLUTION

The year is 1900. Assume you are the surviving spouse of a sailor on a U.S. merchant marine vessel sunk by *The Alabama*. You want to bring a claim for damages both against the British government and the (privately owned) shipyard that built *The Alabama*. Outline the possible venues for each claim as well as all issues that you would expect to face.

CHAPTER 5

DOMESTIC EFFECT: MONISM AND DUALISM

■ ■ ■

The traditional relationship between international and domestic law is best explored in two steps. First, one must understand whether international law is (perhaps automatically) considered part of the domestic legal order or rather outside of it. Second, to the extent that international law *is* part of the domestic legal order, one must ascertain its place in the hierarchy of legal sources. Does it trump ordinary legislation? Even the constitution? This is the question of its rank within the domestic legal system.

1. THE TRADITIONAL DICHOTOMY: MONISM AND DUALISM

The relationship between international and domestic law (often called "municipal law" in Europe) has been much debated for decades. While it is a favorite issue of international lawyers, an introductory course is not the place for lengthy theoretical discussions of the matter. It is quite sufficient here to understand the two basic positions: Monism and Dualism.

Monism assumes that there is but one legal universe of which both international and domestic law are parts. Since there is no dividing line between them, international law is automatically effective within the domestic legal order. The most important practical consequence is that international law can be invoked before, and directly applied by, domestic courts without any further ado. As mentioned, its actual rank and concrete effect within the domestic order are separate matters, but many adherents of Monism assume that international law is also superior to purely domestic law.

Dualism assumes that international and domestic law are separate spheres and must, by and large, be kept apart. International law regulates the relationships among sovereign nation states (and, today, a variety of other inherently international issues) while domestic law addresses the relationship between the state and its citizens as well as among these citizens themselves. As a result of this separateness, international law remains largely outside of the domestic legal order and has no direct effect within it. It assumes such an effect only if it is transformed into domestic law, e.g., by legislation implementing a treaty. Thus, domestic courts do not apply international law itself but rather the domestic rules that "incorporate" it. Note that the issue of rank essentially vanishes— international law as such has no place and therefore no rank in the domestic legal order; its effect turns on the rank of the incorporating act (if any). Note also that under Dualism, international and domestic law can easily diverge, e.g., if a binding international law rule is not duly incorporated and, as a result, is ignored by domestic courts. In that circumstance, a domestic decision may put the respective states in question in breach of their international obligations.

It is tempting to ask which of the two approaches is "better," but the question cannot be answered in the abstract. Monism gives international law more (direct) force and is thus often preferred by those who put trust in it, such as many human rights advocates. Dualism provides more clarity because there is less confusion about what law domestic courts have to apply.

Whether Monism or Dualism prevails depends on the individual national legal system, usually on its (written or unwritten) constitutional law. Each country decides for itself whether to let international law (quasi automatically) in, so to speak, or to keep it out (unless it is incorporated). The world's legal systems differ substantially in that regard. While some (mainly in the civil law tradition) tend towards Monism, others (e.g., most of the former British Commonwealth members) take a more dualist stance.

When looking at a legal system's attitudes towards international law, one has to bear in mind that Monism and Dualism are what Max Weber called "ideal-types," i.e., artificially unequivocal constructs. Like "democracy" and "dictatorship," they are models marking the opposite ends of a spectrum: just as real political systems are more or less democratic or dictatorial, real legal systems are more or less monist or dualist.

Look at the following samples and identify the monist and dualist elements. What else complicates the picture here?

CONSTITUTION OF THE KINGDOM OF THE NETHERLANDS
(1983, as amended 1995)

* * *

Art. 93

Provisions of treaties and of resolutions by international institutions, which may be binding on all persons by virtue of their contents, shall become binding after they have been published.

Art. 94

Statutory regulations in force within the Kingdom shall not be applicable if such application is in conflict with provisions of treaties that are binding on all persons or of resolutions by international institutions.

* * *

CONSTITUTION OF GERMANY (BASIC LAW)
(1949)

* * *

Art. 25

The general rules of public international law shall be an integral part of federal law. They shall take precedence over the laws and directly create rights and duties for the inhabitants of the federal territory.

* * *

GREAT BRITAIN
From Ian Brownlie, PRINCIPLES OF PUBLIC INTERNATIONAL LAW (6th ed. 2003)

(a) Customary International Law. The dominant principle, normally characterized as the doctrine of incorporation, is that customary rules are to be considered part of the law of the land and enforced as such, with the qualification that they are incorporated only so far as it is not inconsistent with Acts of Parliament or prior judicial decision of final authority. This principle is supported by a long line of authority and represents a practical rather than theoretical policy in the courts. * * *

However, the cases decided since 1876 are interpreted by some authorities in such a way as to displace the doctrine of incorporation by that of transformation, viz.: customary international law is part of the law of the England *only in so far* as the rules have been clearly adopted and made part of the law of England by legislation, judicial decision, or established usage. * * * [Brownlie then discusses these cases.] The authorities, taken as a whole, support the doctrine of incorporation, and the less favourable dicta are equivocal to say the least. Commonwealth decisions reflect the English accent on incorporation.

(b) Treaties. In England, and also it seems in most Commonwealth countries, the conclusion and ratification of treaties are within the prerogative of the Crown (or its equivalent), and if a transformation doctrine were not applied, the Crown could legislate for the subject without parliamentary consent. As a consequence treaties are only part of English law if an enabling Act of Parliament has been passed. This rule applies to treaties which affect private rights or liabilities, result in a charge on public

funds, or require modification of the common law or statute for their enforcement in the courts. The rule does not apply to treaties relating to the
conduct of war or treaties of cession. In any case, the words of a subsequent Act of Parliament will prevail over the provision of a prior treaty in
case of inconsistency between the two.

* * *

CONSTITUTION OF THE REPUBLIC OF SOUTH AFRICA
(1996)

Art. 231
International agreements

* * *

(4) Any international agreement becomes law in the Republic when it is
enacted into law by national legislation; but a self-executing provision of
an agreement that has been approved by Parliament is law in the Republic unless it is inconsistent with the Constitution or an Act of Parliament.

Art. 232
Customary international law

Customary international law is law in the Republic unless it is inconsistent with the Constitution or an Act of Parliament.

Art. 233
Application of international law

When interpreting any legislation, every court must prefer any reasonable interpretation of the legislation that is consistent with international
law over any alternative interpretation that is inconsistent with international law.

* * *

CONSTITUTION OF THE ARGENTINE NATION
(1994)

* * *

Section 75—*Congress is empowered:*

* * *

22. To approve or reject treaties concluded with other nations and international organizations, and concordats with the Holy See. Treaties and
concordats have a higher hierarchy than laws.

The American Declaration of the Rights and Duties of Man; the Universal Declaration of Human Rights; the American Convention on Human Rights; the International Pact on Economic, Social and Cultural Rights; the International Pact on Civil and Political Rights and its empowering Protocol; the Convention on the Prevention and Punishment of Genocide; the International Convention on the Elimination of all Forms of Racial Discrimination; the Convention on the Elimination of all Forms of Discrimination against Women; the Convention against Torture and other Cruel, Inhuman or Degrading Treatments or Punishments; the Convention on the Rights of the Child; in the full force of their provisions, they have constitutional hierarchy, do not repeal any section of the First Part of this Constitution and are to be understood as complementing the rights and guarantees recognized herein. They shall only be denounced, in such event, by the National Executive Power after the approval of two-thirds of all the members of each House.

In order to attain constitutional hierarchy, the other treaties and conventions on human rights shall require the vote of two-thirds of all the members of each House, after their approval by Congress.

* * *

CONSTITUTION OF THE FEDERATION OF BOSNIA AND HERZEGOVINA
(1995)

* * *

Art. II.2.
International Standards

The rights and freedoms set forth in the European Convention for the Protection of Human Rights and Fundamental Freedoms and its Protocols shall apply directly in Bosnia and Herzegovina. These shall have priority over all other law.

* * *

UNITED STATES CONSTITUTION
(1787)

* * *

Art. 6 § 2

This Constitution, and the Laws of the United States which shall be made in Pursuance thereof, and all Treaties made, or which shall be made, under Authority of the United States, shall be the supreme Law of the Land;

and the Judges in every State shall be bound thereby, any Thing in the Constitution or Laws of any state to the Contrary notwithstanding.

* * *

Looking at the short excerpt from the U.S. Constitution above, would you describe the United States as a monist or dualist state? Does the following case change your mind?

FOSTER V. NEILSON
United States Supreme Court
27 U.S. 253 (1829)

CHIEF JUSTICE MARSHALL:

[The parties fought about title to a certain tract of land. The issue turned on whether title to the land had been confirmed by a treaty between the United States and Spain, concluded in 1819. In the crucial part of his opinion, Justice Marshall wrote:]

* * *

Whatever difference may exist respecting the effect of the ratification, in whatever sense it may be understood, we think the sound construction of the eighth article will not enable this Court to apply its provisions to the present case. The words of the article are, that

> "all the grants of land made before the 24th of January 1818, by His Catholic Majesty, &c. shall be ratified and confirmed to the persons in possession of the lands, to the same extent that the same grants would be valid if the territories had remained under the dominion of His Catholic Majesty."

Do these words act directly on the grants, so as to give validity to those not otherwise valid; or do they pledge the faith of the United States to pass acts which shall ratify and confirm them?

A treaty is in its nature a contract between two nations, not a legislative act. It does not generally effect, of itself, the object to be accomplished, especially so far as its operation is intra-territorial; but is carried into execution by the sovereign power of the respective parties to the instrument.

In the United States a different principle is established. Our Constitution declares a treaty to be the law of the land. It is, consequently, to be regarded in courts of justice as equivalent to an act of the legislature, whenever it operates of itself without the aid of any legislative provision. But when the terms of the stipulation import a contract, when either of the parties engages to perform a particular act, the treaty addresses itself to the political, not the judicial department; and the legislature must execute the contract before it can become a rule for the Court.

The article under consideration does not declare that all the grants made by His Catholic Majesty before the 24th of January 1818, shall be valid to the same extent as if the ceded territories had remained under his dominion. It does not say that those grants are hereby confirmed. Had such been its language, it would have acted directly on the subject, and would have repealed those acts of congress which were repugnant to it; but its language is that those grants shall be ratified and confirmed to the persons in possession, &c. By whom shall they be ratified and confirmed? This seems to be the language of contract; and if it is, the ratification and confirmation which are promised must be the act of the legislature. Until such act shall be passed, the Court is not at liberty to disregard the existing laws on the subject. Congress appears to have understood this article as it is understood by the Court. Boards of commissioners have been appointed for East and West Florida, to receive claims for lands; and on their reports titles to lands not exceeding _____ acres have been confirmed, and to a very large amount.

* * *

————————

Thus was born the distinction between (later so-called) "self-executing" and "non-self-executing" treaties. What does it mean in plain English if a treaty is self-executing? Non-self-executing? Is the distinction helpful? What are the advantages or disadvantages of viewing a treaty as self-executing or non-self-executing?

How does one know whether a treaty is "self-executing" or not? Look at the International Covenant on Civil and Political Rights (ICCPR) [http://www2.ohchr.org/english/law/ccpr.htm], to which the United States became a party in 1992. Is the ICCPR self-executing?

Four years after *Foster and Elam*, in *United States v. Percheman*, 32 U.S. 51 (1833), the Supreme Court had reason to review the same treaty in the context of a different land dispute. On the second pass through the treaty, Chief Justice Marshall took a close look at the Spanish version, which he had not reviewed in *Foster* since he had not been made aware of it. As a result of this review, he reached a different conclusion on the self-executing nature of the treaty, observing that:

> The treaty was drawn up in the Spanish as well as in the English language. Both are originals, and were unquestionably intended by the parties to be identical. The Spanish has been translated, and we now understand that the article, as expressed in that language, is,

that the grants "shall remain ratified and confirmed to the persons in possession of them, to the same extent, &c.,"—thus conforming exactly to the universally received doctrine of the law of nations.

If the English and the Spanish parts can, without violence, be made to agree, that construction which establishes this conformity ought to prevail.

No violence is done to the language of the treaty by a construction which conforms the English and Spanish to each other. * * *

In the case of "[*Elam*]" this court considered these words as importing contract. The Spanish part of the treaty was not then brought to our view, and we then supposed that there was no variance between them. We did not suppose that there was even a formal difference of expression in the same instrument, drawn up in the language of each party. Had this circumstance been known, we believe it would have produced the construction which we now give to the article.

Percheman, 32 U.S. at 88–89. Chief Justice Marshall therefore concluded that the treaty was self-executing after all. What does this teach us about how to approach the question of whether a treaty is self-executing or not?

Article VI, Section 2 of the U.S. Constitution, *Foster and Elam*, and *Percheman* deal only with treaties. On the subject of customary international law, the Supreme Court made a statement in *The Paquete Habana* which has been reiterated hundreds of times over the past century:

International law is part of our law, and must be ascertained and administered by the courts of justice of appropriate jurisdiction as often as questions of right depending upon it are duly presented for their determination. For this purpose, where there is no treaty and no controlling executive or legislative act or judicial decision, resort must be had to the customs and usages of civilized nations, and, as evidence of these, to the works of jurists and commentators who by years of labor, research, and experience have made themselves peculiarly well acquainted with the subjects of which they treat. Such works are resorted to by judicial tribunals, not for the speculations of their authors concerning what the law ought to be, but for trustworthy evidence of what the law really is.

The Paquete Habana, 175 U.S. 677, 700. What basic approach does this excerpt from *The Paquete Habana* reflect?

Should customary international law be directly applicable in U.S. courts (given how it was made)?

2. THE RANK OF INTERNATIONAL LAW IN THE U.S. DOMESTIC LEGAL ORDER

To the extent international law is part of the domestic legal order, how does it relate to other legal sources? Look at the constitutional provisions in the previous subchapter. How do they decide that question?

A. TREATIES

Article VI, Section 2 of the United States Constitution calls treaties, just like the Constitution and the "Laws of the United States," the "supreme law of the land." This "supremacy clause" tells us that treaties rank with federal law and thus prevail over state law. But it does not tell us what happens if a treaty conflicts with other federal law, e.g., with a federal statute. Such a conflict is a serious matter.

In 1804, the United States Supreme Court faced the question whether a ship bearing the enticing name *The Charming Betsy* had been justly "condemned" by the United States under an Act that sought to suspend all commerce with France and its dependencies. The case turned in large part on the construction of this Act.

MURRAY V. SCHOONER CHARMING BETSY

United States Supreme Court
6 U.S. 64 (1804)

* * *

CHIEF JUSTICE MARSHALL:

* * *

1st. Is the *Charming Betsy* subject to seizure and condemnation for having violated a law of the *United States*?

The libel claims this forfeiture under the act passed in *February*, 1800, further to suspend the commercial intercourse between the *United States* and *France* and the dependencies thereof.

That act declares "that all commercial intercourse," &c. [sic] It has been very properly observed, in argument, that the building of vessels in the *United States* for sale to neutrals, in the islands, is, during war, a profitable business, which Congress cannot be intended to have prohibited, unless that intent be manifested by express words or a very plain and necessary implication.

It has also been observed that an act of Congress ought never to be construed to violate the law of nations if any other possible construction remains, and consequently can never be construed to violate neutral rights, or to affect neutral commerce, further than is warranted by the law of nations as understood in this country.

These principles are believed to be correct, and they ought to be kept in view in construing the act now under consideration.

* * *

It is therefore the opinion of the court, that the *Charming Betsy*, with her cargo, being at the time of her recapture the *bona fide* property of a *Danish* burgher, is not forfeitable, in consequence of her being employed in carrying on trade and commerce with a *French* island.

* * *

The maxim that domestic laws ought to be construed in a manner consistent with international law unless contrary Congressional intent is clear became known as the *Charming Betsy* principle, and it has been applied in many cases since. For a recent example, see Justice Scalia's dissenting opinion in *Hartford Fire Insurance Co. v. California*, 509 U.S. 764 (1993). (See Chapter VII.5.)

Interpreting domestic law in light of international law is a fairly common practice in other legal systems as well. An example is *Mabo v. Queensland* (No 2) (1992) 175 C.L.R. 1, one of the most famous decisions by the High Court of Australia. The case involved aboriginal land rights and raised the issue of how the common law background rules should be interpreted. In a famous passage, Justice Brennan (of the Australian High Court) wrote:

> Whatever the justification advanced in earlier days for refusing to recognize the rights and interests in land of the indigenous inhabitants of settled colonies, an unjust and discriminatory doctrine of that kind can no longer be accepted. The expectations of the international community accord in this respect with the contemporary values of the Australian people. The opening up of international remedies to individuals pursuant to Australia's accession to the Optional Protocol to the International Covenant on Civil and Political Rights brings to bear on the common law the powerful influence of the Covenant and the international standards it imports. The common law does not necessarily conform with international law, but international law is a legitimate and important influence on the development of the common law, especially when international law declares the existence of universal human rights. A common law doctrine founded on unjust discrimination in the enjoyment of civil and political rights demands reconsideration. It is contrary both to international standards and to

the fundamental values of our common law to entrench a discriminatory rule which, because of the supposed position on the scale of social organization of the indigenous inhabitants of a settled colony, denies them a right to occupy their traditional lands.

Note that the principle articulated by the High Court of Australia in *Mabo* is slightly narrower than the *Charming Betsy* principle: it focuses on only the common law whereas the *Charming Betsy* principle requires courts to interpret all national law, including statutes, in accordance with international law.

What difference does that make with regard to the rule's rationale and effect?

The *Charming Betsy* principle can defuse many conflicts between domestic and international law. But what if a conflict between a treaty and a congressional statute is plainly unavoidable?

WHITNEY V. ROBERTSON
United States Supreme Court
124 U.S. 190 (1888)

JUSTICE FIELD:

The plaintiffs are merchants, doing business in the city of New York, and in August, 1882, they imported a large quantity of "centrifugal and molasses sugars," the produce and manufacture of the island of San Domingo. These goods were similar in kind to sugars produced in the Hawaiian Islands, which are admitted free of duty under the treaty with the king of those islands, and the act of Congress, passed to carry the treaty into effect. They were duly entered at the custom house at the Port of New York, the plaintiffs claiming that by the treaty with the Republic of San Domingo the goods should be admitted on the same terms, that is, free of duty, as similar articles, the produce and manufacture of the Hawaiian Islands. The defendant, who was at the time collector of the port, refused to allow this claim, treated the goods as dutiable articles under the acts of Congress, and extracted duties on them to the amount of $21,936. The plaintiffs appealed from the collector's decision to the Secretary of the Treasury, by whom the appeal was denied, They then paid under protest the duties exacted, and brought this present action to recover the amount.

* * *

The treaty with the king of the Hawaiian Islands [of January 30, 1875] provides for the importation into the United States, free of duty, of various articles, the produce and manufacture of those islands, in consideration, among other things, of like exemption on duty, on the importation into that country, of sundry specified articles which are the produce and manufacture of the United States. The language of the first two articles of the treaty, which recite the reciprocal engagements of the two countries, declares that they are made in consideration "of the rights and privileges" and "as an equivalent therefor," which one concedes to the other.

The plaintiffs rely for a like exemption of the sugars imported by them from San Domingo upon the 9th article of the treaty with the Dominican Republic [of February 8, 1867], which is as follows: "No higher or other duty shall be imposed on the importation into the United States of any article of the growth, produce, or manufacture of the Dominican Republic, or of her fisheries; and no higher or other duty shall be imposed on the importation into the Dominican Republic of any article the growth, produce, or manufacture of the United States, or their fisheries, than are or shall be payable on the like articles the growth, produce, or manufacture of any other foreign country, or its fisheries."

* * *

But * * * there is [a] complete answer to the pretensions of the plaintiffs. The Act of Congress under which the duties were collected authorized their exaction. It is of general application, making no exceptions in favor of goods of any country. It was passed after the Treaty with the Dominican Republic; and if there be any conflict between the stipulations of the Treaty and the requirements of the law the latter must control. * * * By the Constitution a treaty is placed on the same footing, and made of like obligation, with an act of legislation. Both are declared by that instrument to be the supreme law of the land, and no superior efficacy is given to either over the other. When the two relate to the same subject, the courts will always endeavor to construe them so as to give effect to both, if that can be done without violating the language of either; but if the two are inconsistent, the one last in date will control the other, provided always the stipulation on the treaty is self-executing. If the country with which the treaty is made is dissatisfied with the action of the legislative department, it may present its complaint to the executive head of the government, and take such other measures as it may deem essential for the protection of its interests. The courts can afford no redress. Whether the complaining nation has just cause of complaint, or our country was justified in its legislation, are not matters for judicial cognizance.

Judgment affirmed.

State the rule established in this case in one (brief) sentence.

The Court says that the rule is valid "provided always the stipulation on the treaty is self-executing." What if it is not? If you were a lawyer for the plaintiffs what could you do now to help your client?

An even more dramatic divergence between treaty obligations and congressional legislation was at issue in the *Chinese Exclusion Case*. A treaty between the United States and China (ratified in 1869) granted Chinese citizens the right freely to migrate to the United States (and the equivalent right to U.S. citizens to migrate to China), and this treaty had been duly implemented by Congress. In 1888, however, Congress enacted legislation to control the size of the Chinese workforce in the U.S. labor market. Under the later federal statute, even Chinese laborers permanently living in the United States, who had travelled abroad with a valid re-entry certificate before the passing of the law, were barred from re-entering the United States. As a result, 20,000 Chinese immigrants were left stranded—away from their families and property in the United States.

CHAE CHAN PING V. UNITED STATES
United States Supreme Court
130 U.S. 581 (1889)

JUSTICE FIELD:

* * *

The validity of this legislative release from the stipulations of the treaties was, of course, not a matter for judicial cognizance. The question whether our government is justified in disregarding its engagements with another nation is not one for the determination of the courts. This subject was fully considered by Mr. Justice CURTIS, while sitting at the circuit, in *Taylor v. Morton*, 2 Curt. 454, 459, and he held that, while it would always be a matter of the utmost gravity and delicacy to refuse to execute a treaty, the power to do so was prerogative, of which no nation could be deprived without deeply affecting its independence; but whether a treaty with a foreign sovereign had been violated by him, whether the consideration of a particular stipulation of a treaty had been voluntarily withdrawn by one party so as to no longer be obligatory upon the other, and whether the views and acts of a foreign sovereign, manifested through his representative, had given just occasion to the political departments of our government to withhold the execution of a promise contained in a treaty or to act in direct contravention of such promise, were not judicial questions; that the power to determine them has not been confided to the judiciary, which has no suitable means to execute it, but to the executive and legislative departments of the government; and that it belongs to diplomacy and legislation, and not to the administration of existing laws. And the learned justice added, as a necessary consequence of these conclusions, that if congress has this power it is wholly immaterial to inquire whether it has, by the statute complained of, departed from the treaty or not; or, if it has, whether such departure was accidental or designed; and, if the latter, whether the reasons therefor were good or bad. These views were re-asserted and fully adopted by this court in *Whitney v. Robertson*. And we may add, to the concluding observation of the learned justice, that, if the power mentioned is vested in congress, any reflection upon its motives, or the motives of any of its members in exercising it, would be entirely un-called for. This court is not a censor of the morals of other departments of the government; it is not invested with any authority to pass judgment upon the motives of their conduct. When once it is established that con-gress possesses the power to pass an act, our province ends with its con-struction and its application to cases as they are presented for determina-tion.

* * *

Can this decision be reconciled with *Asakura* (supra III.2.) where the Court had found a Seattle City Ordinance invalid because it violated a treaty with Japan—although the Ordinance had also been passed *after* the ratification of the treaty?

Do the excluded Chinese workers have any remedy? Can their own gov-ernment help them?

As we have seen, (self-executing) treaties, as "the supreme law of the land," have the rank and effect of a federal statute. As such, they trump not only an earlier federal statute but also all state law. Treaties, in other words, are powerful instruments of federal legislation. This makes it im-portant, especially from the perspective of the states, to determine how far the federal treaty-making power goes.

On the one hand, one might think that in our federal system, which, in Article I of the Constitution, ascribes carefully limited legislative powers to the Congress, the federal treaty making power can go no farther than the regular legislative power. On the other hand, treaties are not made just like federal statutes, i.e., by both Houses of Congress. Instead, Article II, Section 2 of the U.S. Constitution provides:

> [The President] shall have Power, by and with the Advice and Con-sent of the Senate, to make Treaties, provided that two thirds of the Senators present consent * * *.

In short, treaties are made by the President, as the head of the executive branch and the authority primarily in charge of the country's foreign rela-tions, together with a supermajority in the Senate. The House of Repre-sentatives is not involved at all.

So, is the treaty-making power coterminous with general federal legislative power? If so, treaties about subjects not covered by Article I of the Constitution would be unconstitutional infringements of the states' rights under the Tenth Amendment. This issue came before the United States Supreme Court in 1920. How did the Court resolve it? Are the reasons given convincing? What are the consequences for the balance of power between the federal government and the states in international matters?

STATE OF MISSOURI V. HOLLAND

United States Supreme Court
252 U.S. 416 (1920)

JUSTICE HOLMES:

This is a bill in equity brought by the State of Missouri to prevent a game warden of the United States from attempting to enforce the Migratory Bird Treaty Act of July 3, 1918, and the regulations made by the Secretary of Agriculture in pursuance of the same. The ground of the bill is that the statute is an unconstitutional interference with the rights reserved to the States by the Tenth Amendment, and that the acts of the defendant done and threatened under that authority invade the sovereign right of the State and contravene its will manifested in statutes. The State also alleges a pecuniary interest, as owner of the wild birds within its borders and otherwise, admitted by the Government to be sufficient, but it is enough that the bill is a reasonable and proper means to assert the alleged quasi sovereign rights of a State.

On December 8, 1916, a treaty between the United States and Great Britain was proclaimed by the President. It recited that many species of birds in their annual migrations traversed many parts of the United States and of Canada, that they were of great value as a source of food and in destroying insects injurious to vegetation, but were in danger of extermination through lack of adequate protection. It therefore provided for specified closed seasons and protection in other forms, and agreed that the two powers would take or propose to their lawmaking bodies the necessary measures for carrying the treaty out. The above mentioned act of July 3, 1918, entitled an Act to give effect to the convention, prohibited the killing, capturing or selling any of the migratory birds included in the terms of the treaty except as permitted by regulations compatible with those terms, to be made by the Secretary of Agriculture. Regulations were proclaimed on July 31, and October 25, 1918. It is unnecessary to go into any details, because, as we have said, the question raised is the general one whether the treaty and statute are void as an interference with the rights reserved to the States.

To answer this question it is not enough to refer to the Tenth Amendment, reserving the powers not delegated to the United States, because by Article II, § 2, the power to make treaties is delegated expressly, and by Article 6 treaties made under the authority of the United States, along with the Constitution and laws of the United States made in pursuance thereof, are declared the supreme law of the land. If the treaty is valid there can be no dispute about the validity of the statute under Article 1, § 8, as a necessary and proper means to execute the powers of the Government. The language of the Constitution as to the supremacy of treaties being general, the question before us is narrowed to an inquiry into the ground upon which the present supposed exception is placed.

It is said that a treaty cannot be valid if it infringes the Constitution, that there are limits, therefore, to the treaty-making power, and that one such limit is that what an act of Congress could not do unaided, in derogation of the powers reserved to the States, a treaty cannot do. An earlier act of Congress that attempted by itself and not in pursuance of a treaty to regulate the killing of migratory birds within the States had been held bad in the District Court. Those decisions were supported by arguments that migratory birds were owned by the States in their sovereign capacity for the benefit of their people, and that under cases like *Geer v. Connecticut*, this control was one that Congress had no power to displace. The same argument is supposed to apply now with equal force.

Whether the two cases cited were decided rightly or not, they cannot be accepted as a test of the treaty power. Acts of Congress are the supreme law of the land only when made in pursuance of the Constitution, while treaties are declared to be so when made under the authority of the United States. It is open to question whether the authority of the United States means more than the formal acts prescribed to make the convention. We do not mean to imply that there are no qualifications to the treaty-making power; but they must be ascertained in a different way. It is obvious that there may be matters of the sharpest exigency for the national well being that an act of Congress could not deal with but that a treaty followed by such an act could, and it is not lightly to be assumed that, in matters requiring national action, "a power which must belong to and somewhere reside in every civilized government" is not to be found. What was said in that case with regard to the powers of the States applies with equal force to the powers of the nation in cases where the States individually are incompetent to act. We are not yet discussing the particular case before us but only are considering the validity of the test proposed. With regard to that we may add that when we are dealing with words that also are a constituent act, like the Constitution of the United States, we must realize that they have called into life a being the development of which could not have been foreseen completely by the most gifted of its begetters. It was enough for them to realize or to hope that they had created an organism; it has taken a century and has cost their successors much sweat and blood to prove that they created a nation. The case before us must be considered in the light of our whole experience and not merely in that of what was said a hundred years ago. The treaty in question does not contravene any prohibitory words to be found in the Constitution. The only question is whether it is forbidden by some invisible radiation from the general terms of the Tenth Amendment. We must consider what this country has become in deciding what that amendment has reserved.

* * *

As most of the laws of the United States are carried out within the States and as many of them deal with matters which in the silence of such laws the State might regulate, such general grounds are not enough to support Missouri's claim. Valid treaties of course "are as binding within the territorial limits of the States as they are elsewhere throughout the dominion of the United States." *Baldwin v. Franks*, 120 U. S. 678, 683. No doubt the great body of private relations usually fall within the control of the State, but a treaty may override its power. * * *

Here a national interest of very nearly the first magnitude is involved. It can be protected only by national action in concert with that of another power. The subject matter is only transitorily within the State and has no permanent habitat therein. But for the treaty and the statute there soon might be no birds for any powers to deal with. We see nothing in the Constitution that compels the Government to sit by while a food supply is cut off and the protectors of our forests and our crops are destroyed. It is not sufficient to rely upon the States. The reliance is vain, and were it otherwise, the question is whether the United States is forbidden to act. We are of opinion that the treaty and statute must be upheld.

Decree affirmed.

JUSTICE VAN DEVANTER and JUSTICE PITNEY dissent.

If the treaty-making power is not confined to the areas of federal lawmaking power, what are its limits? Does the importance of the subject matter of the treaty have to be, in Holmes' words, "a national interest of very nearly the first magnitude"? If the protection of migratory birds is in that category, what isn't?

Holmes argues that the "treaty in question does not contravene any prohibitory words to be found in the Constitution." What if a treaty does? What counts as "prohibitory words" if the Tenth Amendment does not? Is the treaty-making power not even limited by the Bill of Rights?

The problem underlying *Missouri v. Holland* is not unique to the United States but is inherent in all systems in which the power to make treaties and the power to make laws is allocated to different constitutional actors; it is especially acute where treaties are generally not self-executing and thus often require implementing legislation. This is most pronounced in the British Commonwealth tradition where the executive (or Crown) makes treaties but only parliament can legislate. It is no surprise, then, that the High Court of Australia had to face this problem as well.

In *Koowarta v. Bjelke-Petersen* (1982) 153 C.L.R. 168, the Court took a position very similar to the United States Supreme Court's in *Missouri v. Holland*. Australia had become a party to the International Convention on Elimination of All Forms of Racial Discrimination, and it subsequently enacted the Racial Discrimination Act 1975 to implement the treaty domestically. When the legislative competence of the parliament to enact that statute was challenged, the High Court held that the statute was a constitutional exercise of the external affairs power. The dissenting justices, however, expressed concern that if the Parliament's external affairs power was as broad as the executive's treaty power, the Parliament's legislative mandate would be rendered practically limitless.

Missouri and *Koowarta* seem to suggest that there are no effective constitutional limits on the treaty making power. What does the following case say?

REID V. COVERT
United States Supreme Court
354 U.S. 1 (1957)

JUSTICE BLACK announced the judgment of the Court and delivered an opinion, in which THE CHIEF JUSTICE, JUSTICE DOUGLAS, and JUSTICE BRENNAN join.

* * *

* * * Mrs. Clarice Covert killed her husband, a sergeant in the United States Air Force, at an airbase in England. Mrs. Covert, who was not a member of the armed services, was residing on the base with her husband at the time. She was tried by a court-martial for murder under Article 118 of the Uniform Code of Military Justice (UCMJ). The trial was on charges preferred by Air Force personnel and the court-martial was composed of Air Force officers. The court-martial asserted jurisdiction over Mrs. Covert under Article 2(11) of the UCMJ, which provides:

"The following persons are subject to this code:

* * *

(11) Subject to the provisions of any treaty or agreement to which the United States is or may be a party or to any accepted rule of international law, all persons serving with, employed by, or accompanying the armed forces without the continental limits of the United States * * *."

* * *

II.

At the time of Mrs. Covert's alleged offense, an executive agreement was in effect between the United States and Great Britain which permitted United States' military courts to exercise exclusive jurisdiction over offenses committed in Great Britain by American servicemen or their dependents. For its part, the United States agreed that these military courts would be willing and able to try and to punish all offenses against the laws of Great Britain by such persons. In all material respects, the same situation existed in Japan when Mrs. Smith killed her husband. Even though a court-martial does not give an accused trial by jury and other Bill of Rights protections, the Government contends that article 2(11) of UCMJ, insofar as it provides for the military trial of dependents accompanying the armed forces in Great Britain and Japan, can be sustained as legislation which is necessary and proper to carry out the United States' obligations under the international agreements made with those countries. The obvious and decisive answer to this, of course, is that no agreement with a foreign nation can confer power on the Congress, or on any other branch of Government, which is free from the restraints of the Constitution.

Article VI, the Supremacy Clause of the Constitution, declares:

> "This Constitution, and the Laws of the United States which shall be made in Pursuance thereof; and all Treaties made, or which shall be made, under the Authority of the United States, shall be the supreme Law of the Land; * * *."

There is nothing in this language which intimates that treaties and laws enacted pursuant to them do not have to comply with the provisions of the Constitution. Nor is there anything in the debates which accompanied the drafting and ratification of the Constitution which even suggests such a result. These debates as well as the history that surrounds the adoption of the treaty provision in Article VI make it clear that the reason treaties were not limited to those made in "pursuance" of the Constitution was so that agreements made by the United States under the Articles of Confederation, including the important peace treaties which concluded the Revolutionary War, would remain in effect. It would be manifestly contrary to the objectives of those who created the Constitution, as well as those who were responsible for the Bill of Rights—let alone alien to our entire constitutional history and tradition—to construe Article VI as permitting the United States to exercise power under an international agreement without observing constitutional prohibitions. In effect, such construction would permit amendment of that document in a manner not sanctioned by Article V. The prohibitions of the Constitution were designed to apply to all branches of the National Government and they cannot be nullified by the Executive or by the Executive and the Senate combined.

* * *

[The dissenting opinion of JUSTICE CLARK, in which JUSTICE BURTON joined, has been omitted.]

Note that the opposite outcome would have an interesting effect: since virtually all treaties to which the United States is a party were made *after* the Constitution was adopted (constitutional amendments excepted), they would almost invariably prevail. In other words, the age of the Constitution would allow treaties to undermine it.

Does *Reid v. Covert* mean that the United States cannot enter into an international agreement at odds with the Constitution? What would be the effect of the Supreme Court holding a duly ratified treaty unconstitutional? What does Article 27 of the Vienna Convention on the Law of Treaties (supra III.2.) have to say about that?

NOTE ON ALTERNATIVE FORMS OF INTERNATIONAL AGREEMENTS IN THE UNITED STATES

If you read *Reid v. Covert* closely, you may have noticed that the case involved an "executive agreement" between the United States and Great Britain. It was not a "treaty" in the domestic (constitutional) sense, i.e., not approved by a two-thirds majority of the Senate. Instead, the agreement was made by the President alone (in his capacity as the commander-in-chief of the armed forces).

The requirement that treaties be approved by two thirds of the Senate can be a formidable hurdle since that usually requires bipartisan support. Treaties have often lingered in the Senate for years on end before all political and legal issues were resolved to the satisfaction of such a supermajority. Obviously, this can create serious problems for the country's foreign relations, which often require much greater flexibility and much quicker reaction. For this and other reasons, so-called *Executive Agreements* have developed and become generally accepted although they are not mentioned in the Constitution. There are several types of *Executive Agreements* although the terminology used is not always entirely uniform.

A *Congressional Executive Agreement* is made by the President and then passed by both houses of Congress just like a statute, i.e., by simple majority. This can avoid blockage by the Senate (so long as more than half, even if less than two-thirds, support the agreement). A *Congressional Executive Agreement* can also prove useful because it ensures more broadly based majority support in the legislature, which can be particularly important if implementing legislation is needed. For example, both the North American Free Trade Agreement (NAFTA) and the United States' accession to the World Trade Organization were accomplished by *Congressional Executive Agreement*.

A *Sole Executive Agreement* is made by the President alone—as in *Reid v. Covert*. The President has the authority to make such agreements either if there is prior authorization in a treaty or statute or if he acts within the powers given to him by the Constitution. For example, since the President may "receive Ambassadors and other Public Ministers" (Article II, Section 3 of the U.S. Constitution), he can enter into agreements concerning diplomatic relations. We will encounter a prominent example of such an agreement in the Algiers Accords of 1981 in Chapter IX.3.D.

Today, the practical importance of such executive agreements is enormous. They constitute the vast majority of international agreements entered into by the United States. At least in terms of numbers, they have relegated treaties in the sense of Article II, Section 2 of the U.S. Constitution to the status of exceptions. According to Oona Hathaway, from 1980 to 2000, the United States made over three thousand executive agreements, of which only a "handful" (she identified nine) were *Congressional Executive Agreements*. The vast majority, in total 3,876 agreements, were *Sole Executive Agreements*, where the President acted alone—based on congressional authority, an authorization in a pre-existing Article II treaty, or the President's inherent constitutional powers. The most common subject-matter areas of executive agreements were defense, trade, scientific cooperation, postal matters and debts. By contrast, between 1980 and 2000 the United States entered into 375 Article II treaties. In other words, *Executive Agreements* outnumbered such treaties ten to one. See Oona Hathaway, *Presidential Power over International Law: Restoring the Balance*, 119 Yale L. J., 140 (2009).

Note that while executive agreements are not treaties in the domestic sense, i.e., of Article II, Section 2 and Article VI, Section 2 of the U.S. Constitution, they may still be treaties in the international sense, e.g., as defined by the Vienna Convention on the Law of Treaties. It is important to distinguish the domestic from the international law dimension. How the United States arranges the process of entering into international agreements internally is a matter of its own constitutional law; it may call what it enters into "treaties," "executive agreements" or something else and allocate the power to make them as it sees fit. International law, by contrast, governs the making and effect of international agreements among the states (or other international actors) involved, their validity, interpretation, etc. Its legal term for such agreements is (normally) treaty, but as we have seen, the actual instruments may be called a variety of other names such as convention, covenant, pact, or even protocol or statute. The name ascribed has no impact on the treaty's status at international law.

B. CUSTOMARY INTERNATIONAL LAW

In *The Paquete Habana*, the Supreme Court wrote that customary international law is "part of our law." But what is its *rank* in the domestic legal order? It is widely acknowledged that customary international law has federal rank (like treaties), and thus prevails over state law. (For a contrary view, see Curtis Bradley and Jack Goldsmith, Customary International Law as Federal Common Law: A Critique of the Modern Position, 110 Harv. L. Rev. 815, 1997.)

It also seems clear that if a treaty loses to the Constitution as well as to subsequent federal statutes, so must customary international law. But can customary international law, again like a treaty, trump *earlier* congressional legislation? Does the excerpt from *The Paquete Habana* in Chapter III answer that question?

Should customary international law be able to supersede an earlier Congressional act? What if customary international law were to reach a point where it required the recognition of same sex marriages? Would that override the (federal) *Defense of Marriage Act* of 1996, which denies such recognition?

C. JUDICIAL DECISIONS

The rank and effect of decisions rendered by international tribunals, especially the International Court of Justice, in the domestic legal order is a can of worms in its own right. Are such decisions binding on federal and state courts in the United States (and perhaps even the legislative and the executive branches) because ICJ judgments are authoritative pronouncements on the meaning of international law? Do they at least bind the organs of the states that are parties to the particular case? Or do they bind only the states as such, without having any internal effect? Until very recently, there was little authority on these issues and the matter is so complex (and in part still so unsettled) that it is better postponed for now. We will discuss this question later in the context of a concrete story involving the ICJ, the U.S. Supreme Court, and state courts and officials.

EXERCISE ON THE RELATIONSHIP BETWEEN INTERNATIONAL LAW AND DOMESTIC LAW

Assume that the United States is negotiating a multilateral treaty about the recognition of foreign judgments. The current draft provides, inter alia, that foreign judgments must be recognized by American courts whenever the foreign tribunal had jurisdiction according to its own rules, as long as the defendant was given proper notice and an opportunity to defend. Note that the U.S. Supreme Court has consistently held that a judgment rendered by a court without proper jurisdiction is null and void (and thus not entitled to recognition and execution anywhere).

The State of Michigan has adopted the Uniform Foreign Country Money Judgments Recognition Act. One of the Senators from Michigan wonders whether, in case the treaty gets adopted, she should vote for it in the United States Senate. She is worried that French creditors might use the treaty to force Michigan courts to recognize French judgments against Michigan citizens in cases where French jurisdiction was predicated purely on the nationality of the plaintiff (see Exercise in Chapter II.2.C.), which would clearly not pass muster as proper jurisdiction under the U.S. Constitution. Please write a brief memorandum to the Senator explaining whether her worries are justified.

PART 2

EVOLUTION: THE COMPLEXITIES OF THE MODERN ORDER

■ ■ ■

Introduction

The world legal order has undergone profound changes since the middle of the 20th century. It must be emphasized that these changes have rendered the classical view of the international legal order neither wrong nor obsolete. To the contrary, the traditional regime still forms the bedrock of the current international system. There is much continuity with the past, and many modern developments have deep roots in the 19th century or even earlier periods. Still, the changes over the last two generations have forced the system to evolve in important ways.

Some scholars have seen a move from an "international law of coexistence" to an "international law of cooperation," although whether cooperation has become the norm is open to debate. Be that as it may, there has been an expansion of international law, both horizontally and vertically, so to speak. On the horizontal axis, new actors have emerged; on the vertical axis, international law has expanded to regulate many new areas. This development has broadened the range of issues at stake, added new elements to the mix, and occasionally eroded erstwhile ironclad principles. In this second part of the materials, we will re-visit all the basic themes of the first part, one by one, in order to understand the evolution of the international legal order and its results.

To begin, there are many more actors on the international scene than there were half a century ago. There are many more states (almost 200, about a threefold increase), and they are much more diverse, representing all corners and cultures of the world. State clubs, i.e., international organizations, especially the United Nations, have become major players. In addition, non-state actors now perform important functions. Non-governmental organizations are quite influential. Individuals are recognized as bearers of rights and duties under international law. Most recently, business enterprises have taken on a more prominent role on the international stage.

The interaction among states has also changed in at least two ways. One change is the gradual erosion of traditional notions of sovereignty: states are more willing to delegate some of their core powers to international organizations and also more reluctant to grant complete sovereign immunity to other states. The other development is the expansion of extraterritorial jurisdiction: states attempt to regulate (and perhaps adjudicate) more and more matters beyond their boundaries, which often leads to clashes between competing jurisdictional claims. In addition, private international law has come to play a much more prominent role, mainly as a result of the globalization of markets and of the increased mobility of people and goods.

The sources of international law have also greatly diversified. A new generation of multilateral treaties has emerged; some of these treaties purport to set up quasi-constitutional regimes while others deal with issues of private international law, including transboundary litigation. International organizations and other players have created an immense amount of regulatory norms. In addition, there are innumerable non-binding sources, often called "soft law," e.g., UN declarations, guidelines, and principles in quasi-Restatement form drafted and published by various public and private institutions.

If the classic world of (public) international law provided precious few institutionalized dispute resolution mechanisms, the modern global legal order provides perhaps too many. There has been a veritable proliferation of international tribunals over the last half-century or so, ranging from human rights monitoring bodies to arbitral institutions and, lately, criminal tribunals. Many provide access not only to states and international organizations but to private actors as well. This has led to a staggering expansion of case law rendered by these tribunals, the effects of which have yet to be sorted out.

Finally, there has been a blurring of lines that were traditionally considered clearly drawn. With both state and private actors all over the international scene, with sources addressing both public and private legal issues, and with the regulation of markets becoming ever more global, public and private international law have become so closely intertwined in many regards that the distinction between them has become increasingly senseless. In a similar vein, international and domestic law have interpenetrated to a point where the old debate between "monism" and "dualism" looks more simplistic than ever. Many disputes today contain and mix elements of public and private, international and domestic law, in a multitude of combinations.

CHAPTER 6

ACTORS:
STATE CLUBS AND NON–STATE PLAYERS

■ ■ ■

In Chapter I, we saw that the classical regime regarded states as the only full-fledged actors in (public) international law. It looked at the world order as a society of (legally co-equal) sovereign nation states. These states could enter into international agreements (or not), form alliances (or not), and do pretty much whatever they wanted as long as they did not violate established rules of international law. Moreover, they were to have complete power over their domestic affairs because these affairs were not a concern of international law. Such an approach left virtually no room for other actors, especially private individuals or organizations.

This chapter demonstrates how things have changed. While states continue to play the dominant role in (public) international law, they are no longer alone on the stage. We begin by briefly revisiting the question of statehood in order to discuss some of the issues that came to the fore in the last few decades, and then review the crowd that now competes with states for influence and attention. In later chapters, we will see how the new actors have changed the nature of the game—e.g., the catalog of relevant sources of law, the system of basic principles, the world of international dispute resolution, and the relationship between international and domestic law.

1. THE PROLIFERATION OF NATION STATES: STATEHOOD REVISITED

Over the past fifty years, the number of sovereign nation states in the world has skyrocketed as a result of two (more or less successive) developments. The break-up of colonial empires created a large number of newly independent states. More recently, the disintegration of existing states has also multiplied the number of nations in the world.

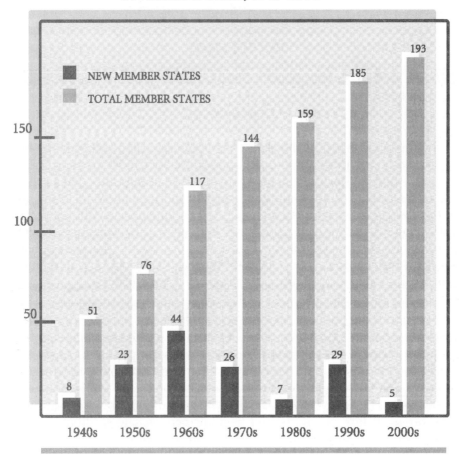

UN Member States, 1945-2011

These developments have raised important issues of state identity and succession. The former problem is exemplified by Taiwan, the latter by the breakup of the Soviet Union.

A. STATE RECOGNITION: TAIWAN

In Chapter I.2., we considered the criteria of statehood under the Montevideo Convention. In the vast majority of cases, the recognition of states is not an issue. For example, in July 2011, South Sudan became a new state, was recognized by other states as such, and was almost immediately admitted to the United Nations and other international organizations. Sometimes, however, the statehood of an entity is in doubt. Is Taiwan a "state" in the international law sense?

JAMES CRAWFORD, CREATION OF STATES IN INTERNATIONALLAW

(2006)

* * *

Taiwan (formerly known as Formosa) became part of the Chinese Empire in 1683 and remained so, despite internal vicissitudes, until the Treaty of Shimonoseki of 17 April 1895, by Article 2(b) and (c) of which "Formosa and the Pescadores" were ceded to Japan. The Japanese authorities were obliged to take possession by force because of local opposition. The islands remained Japanese until 1945. In the Cairo Declaration of 1 December 1943 the Allies declared their "purpose * * * that all the territories Japan has stolen from the Chinese, such as Manchuria, Formosa and the Pescadores, shall be restored to the Republic of China." Paragraph (8) of the Potsdam Proclamation of 26 July 1945 affirmed that "The terms of the Cairo Declaration shall be carried out and Japanese sovereignty shall be limited to the islands of Honshu, Hokkaido, Kyushu, Shikuku, and such minor islands as we determine." In the Instrument of Surrender of 2 September 1945, Japan undertook to carry out the provisions of the Potsdam Proclamation. The Japanese forces in Taiwan thereafter surrendered to the Commander-in-Chief of the Republic of China.

Civil war within China between the Government of the Republic and the proclaimed People's Republic under Mao Tse Tung had been continuing since 1928. On 8 December 1949 the Republic of China's forces retreated to Taiwan, establishing there the provisional capital of that government. With certain exceptions other States remained neutral during the war, and it is clear that the People's Republic was a genuine revolutionary government, not a "puppet" of any other State.

The position of Formosa at this time was stated by the United Kingdom Government to be as follows:

> In 1943 Formosa was a part of the territories of the Japanese Empire and His Majesty's Government consider Formosa is still de jure part of that territory * * * On October 25th, 1945, as a result of an order issued on the basis of consultation and agreement between the Allied Powers concerned, the Japanese forces in Formosa surrendered to Chiang Kai-shek. Thereupon with the consent of the Allied Powers, administration of Formosa was undertaken by the Government of the Republic of China.

On 25 June 1950 the Korean War broke out. Official Chinese participation in that war dated from November 1950. As an immediate result of the hostilities, President Truman ordered the Seventh Fleet to patrol the Taiwan Straits and to prevent attacks by either government on the other. This unilateral action involved an intervention in the still continuing though consolidated civil war between the two Chinese governments, although its justification appears to have been not collective self-defence of Taiwan but individual action in a case of threats to the international peace and security of the Pacific area. Meanwhile negotiations for a peace treaty with Japan were proceeding. The Peace Treaty was in fact signed on 8 September 1951 by Japan and forty-eight Allied Powers (excluding the USSR and China). By Article 2(b) of the Treaty Japan renounced "all right, title and claim to Formosa and the Pescadores," in whose favour was not stated. Secretary of State Dulles said at the time that "the differences of opinion are such that [the disposal of Formosa] could not be definitively dealt with by a Japanese peace treaty to which the Allied powers, as a whole, are parties. Therefore the treaty merely takes Japan formally out of the Formosa picture, leaving the position otherwise unchanged."

In a separate peace treaty with the Republic of China (hereafter RoC), Japan "recognized" its renunciation of title to Formosa without further specification. The treaty was stated to apply to "all the territories under the control of the Government of the Republic of China." A Joint Declaration of 1956 between Japan and the USSR ended the formal state of war between them, without referring to the problems of territorial disposition. In 1954 a Mutual Defence Treaty was signed between the United States and the RoC, providing for collective self-defence of the Pacific territories of the two parties; the territory of the Republic was defined to mean Formosa and the Pescadores, with provision for extension to other territories by agreement.

Thus by the mid-1950s, even though both parties continued to assert a right to use force in pursuit of a final settlement to the civil war, a territorial status quo had been reached between the RoC on Taiwan and the PRC. This status quo has endured, and the dispute between them limited in practice mostly to pacific means, though profoundly affected by a continuing PRC threat to reunify China by force in the event of a unilateral secession by Taiwan. Meanwhile major changes in the relations between Taiwan and third States have nonetheless occurred, tending to turn the RoC from a failed general government of China into a successful and democratic government of Taiwan.

*　*　*

————————

Crawford looks at the issue of statehood from the perspective of public international law. But that may not be the only perspective that matters. If you ask yourself whether an entity is a "state," what other aspects would you consider? For example, does it matter that Taiwan (sometimes referred to as "Chinese Taipei") has its own flag? That it issues its own passports and visas? That it has its own Olympic team?

In looking at the materials that follow, ask yourself whether Taiwan is a "state" under the traditional rules of public international law, or otherwise. The first document involves Taiwan's ongoing efforts to join the United Nations. Doesn't it seem that Taiwan fulfills the fundamental criteria of statehood? If so, why has Taiwan been unable to gain UN membership?

United Nations	**A/61/194**
General Assembly	Dist.: General
	11 August 2006

Original: English

Question of the Representation and Participation of the 23 Million People of Taiwan in the United Nations

Letter dated 10 August 2006 from the representatives of Belize, Burkina Faso, El Salvador, the Gambia, Honduras, Malawi, the Marshall Islands, Nauru, Nicaragua, Palau, Saint Kitts and Nevis, Saint Vincent and the Grenadines, Sao Tome and Principe, Solomon Islands, Swaziland and Tuvalu to the United Nations addressed to the Secretary–General.

Upon the instruction of our respective Governments, we have the honour to request, pursuant to rule 14 of the rules of procedure of the General Assembly, the inclusion in the agenda of the sixty-first session of a supplementary item entitled "Question of the representation and participation of the 23 million people of Taiwan in the United Nations." Pursuant to rule 20 of the rules of procedure of the General Assembly, we attach an explanatory memorandum (annex I) and a draft resolution (annex II).

* * *

ANNEX I

EXPLANATORY MEMORANDUM

The Republic of China (hereinafter referred to as Taiwan) is a free and peace-loving sovereign State, and its democratically elected Government is the sole legitimate government that can represent the interests and wishes of the people of Taiwan in the United Nations. However, the rights and interests of the 23 million people of Taiwan, which is excluded from the United Nations, are not upheld and protected by the United Nations. Today, for the following reasons, there is an urgent need to further examine this particular situation and to redress this mistaken omission.

1.   UNIVERSALITY IS A CORE PRINCIPLE OF THE UNITED NATIONS

The Preamble to the Charter of the United Nations states that the mission of the United Nations is "to reaffirm faith in fundamental human rights, in the dignity and worth of the human person, in the equal rights of men and women and of nations, large and small."

This commitment to the principle of universality, for all peoples and all nations, is at the centre of the international system established by the founding fathers of the United Nations in 1945. Furthermore, Article 4 of the Charter invites "all other peace-loving States" to join the Organization.

Since the end of the cold war and with the advent of globalization, the work of the United Nations has become increasingly important, and the realization of the principle of universality has taken on a new urgency. With the admission of Timor–Leste, Switzerland and Montenegro, almost all the countries of the world have become members of this ever more truly global Organization—all expect one, Taiwan. After all that the United Nations has achieved towards realizing the principle of universality, the complete exclusion of Taiwan from the United Nations poses a moral and legal challenge to the international community. The United Nations must cease senselessly enforcing a policy of political apartheid against the 23 million people of Taiwan.

2.   GENERAL ASSEMBLY RESOLUTION 2758 (XXVI) HAS NOT RESOLVED THE
     ISSUE OF THE REPRESENTATION OF THE PEOPLE OF TAIWAN

From 1949 to 1971, the question of the representation of China in the United Nations had been continuously disputed. The General Assembly finally adopted resolution 2758 (XXVI) on 25 October 1971, by which it admitted the People's Republic of China to the United Nations. This resolution, however, did not address the issue of the representation and participation of the 23 million people of Taiwan in the United Nations. Unfortunately, resolution 2758 (XXVI) has subsequently been misused to justify Taiwan's exclusion from the United Nations system. With a view to examining its falsehood, we cite the pivot statement of the aforesaid resolution, by which the General Assembly:

Decides to restore all its rights to the People's Republic of China and to recognize the representatives of its Government as the only legitimate representatives of China to the United Nations, and to expel forthwith the representatives of Chiang Kai-shek from the place which they unlawfully occupy at the United Nations and in all the organizations related to it.

It should be noted especially that resolution 2758 (XXVI) addressed only the issue of the representation of the People's Republic of China in the United Nations and all related organizations. It did not determine that

Taiwan is a part of the People's Republic of China, nor did it confer on the People's Republic of China the right to represent Taiwan or the people of Taiwan in the United Nations and its related organizations. Taiwan has no intention of competing with the People's Republic of China for the so-called "representation of China." Taiwan has transformed into a fully fledged modern democracy after a series of political reforms, further illustrating that the above-mentioned resolution does not reflect the objective reality that both sides of the Taiwan Strait have separate ruling Governments and are not subject to each other's jurisdiction. It also fails to reflect the depth of democracy developed by the people of Taiwan. The United Nations should look squarely at the fact that it is regrettable that the resolution also fails to safeguard the legal right of the 23 million people of Taiwan to participate in the United Nations.

3.   TAIWAN IS A SOVEREIGN STATE AND A CONSTRUCTIVE MEMBER OF THE INTERNATIONAL COMMUNITY

With a population of 23 million, making it the forty-seventh largest population in the world, and a territory consisting of the islands of Taiwan, Penghu, Kinmen and Matsu, Taiwan enjoys an efficient Government and solid institutions that have proven their capacity to conduct friendly and constructive international relations with many States throughout the world. For example, Taiwan maintains full diplomatic relations with the Holy See and 23 States Members of the United Nations. Taiwan has set up more than 120 embassies, consulates general, representative offices or offices around the world, fully demonstrating that Taiwan is a sovereign country. Moreover, through its full membership, Taiwan plays an active role in several international organizations, including the World Trade Organization, the Asian Development Bank and Asia-Pacific Economic Cooperation.

Taiwan has never been a local government or province of the People's Republic of China. On the contrary, ever since the establishment of the People's Republic of China on 1 October 1949, the two sides of the Taiwan Strait have been governed separately, with neither side having any control or jurisdiction over the other. The fact that international visitors to Taiwan apply for visas at Taiwan's representative institutions, and that China's diplomatic missions cannot provide any visa assistance whatsoever, is an obvious example.

4.   TAIWAN IS A VIBRANT DEMOCRATIC SOCIETY AND AN ACTIVE INTERNATIONAL PARTNER

In his report entitled "In larger freedom: towards development, security and human rights for all," United Nations Secretary–General Kofi Annan pointed out correctly, "The right to choose how they are ruled, and who rules them, must be the birthright of all people, and its universal achievement must be a central objective of an Organization devoted to the cause of larger freedom." Accordingly, the international community should respect public opinion in Taiwan. Taiwan's achievements in deepening democracy are worthy of the active support of the United Nations.

Following the end of four decades of authoritarian rule in Taiwan in 1987, the profound constitutional reforms undertaken made it possible for Taiwan to hold its very first general parliamentary elections in 1992, followed by the first direct presidential election in 1996. In 2000, the second presidential election paved the way to the first peaceful transfer of power from one political party to another. The third direct presidential election of 2004 further demonstrates Taiwan's commitment to genuine democratization.

Taiwan has succeeded in its transition to democracy and in its unrelenting efforts to promote human rights. In his inaugural speech in 2000, President Chen Shui-bian emphasized the importance of democracy and peace for the people of Taiwan: "With our sacred votes, we have proved to the world that freedom and democracy are indisputable universal values, and that peace is the highest goal of humanity." In his inaugural speech in 2004, he reiterated Taiwan's firm belief and determination: "Taiwan stands ready to continue in its role as an active participant and contributor to international society—this is the right of Taiwan's 23 million people; likewise, it is our duty as citizens of the world community."

In recent years, in view of defending and promoting the universal values of freedom, democracy and human rights, Taiwan initiated the founding of the Pacific Democratic Union, established the Taiwan Foundation for Democracy, and actively participates in the activities of related nongovernmental organizations. Taiwan's democratic institutions, open society and respect for human rights are achievements recognized the world over.

Taiwan serves as an excellent model for all those countries that seek to embrace democracy, human rights and the norms and values of our international community. Taiwan deserves to be taken seriously and accepted by the United Nations. * * *

———————————

The General Assembly did not vote on Taiwan's membership. Any decision would have been purely hortatory anyway because according to Article 4(2) of the UN Charter, the admission of new members by the General Assembly requires a recommendation by the Security Council (which China would obviously veto).

Leaving aside membership in the United Nations, why would it be important for Taiwan to be recognized internationally as a state?

The documents that follow involve Taiwan's effort to join another important international organization. What is the result here, and what may explain it?

WORLD TRADE ORGANIZATION

WT/L/433
23 November 2001
(01-5986)

ACCESSION OF THE SEPARATE CUSTOMS TERRITORY OF TAIWAN, PENGHU, KINMEN AND MATSU

Decision of 11 November 2001

The Ministerial Conference,

Having regard to paragraph 2 of Article XII and paragraph 1 of Article IX of the Marrakesh Agreement Establishing the World Trade Organization, and the Decision-Making Procedures under Articles IX and XII of the Marrakesh Agreement Establishing the World Trade Organization agreed by the General Council (WT/L/93),

Taking note of the application of the Separate Customs Territory of Taiwan, Penghu, Kinmen and Matsu for accession to the Marrakesh Agreement Establishing the World Trade Organization dated 7 December 1995,

Noting the results of the negotiations directed toward the establishment of the terms of accession of the Separate Customs Territory of Taiwan, Penghu, Kinmen and Matsu to the Marrakesh Agreement Establishing the World Trade Organization and having prepared a Protocol on the Accession of the Separate Customs Territory of Taiwan, Penghu, Kinmen and Matsu,

Decides as follows:

The Separate Customs Territory of Taiwan, Penghu, Kinmen and Matsu may accede to the Marrakesh Agreement Establishing the World Trade Organization on the terms and conditions set out in the Protocol annexed to this Decision.

PROTOCOL OF ACCESSION OF THE SEPARATE CUSTOMS TERRITORY OF TAIWAN, PENGHU, KINMEN AND MATSU

The World Trade Organization (hereinafter referred to as the "WTO"), pursuant to the approval of the General Council of the WTO accorded under Article XII of the Marrakesh Agreement Establishing the World Trade Organization (hereinafter referred to as the "WTO Agreement"), and the Separate Customs Territory of Taiwan, Penghu, Kinmen and Matsu (hereinafter referred to as "Chinese Taipei"),

Taking note of the Report of the Working Party on the Accession of Chinese Taipei to the WTO Agreement reproduced in document WT/ACC/TPKM/18, dated 5 October 2001 (hereinafter referred to as the "Working Party Report"),

Having regard to the results of the negotiations on the accession of Chinese Taipei to the WTO Agreement,

Agree as follows:

PART I—GENERAL

1.   Upon entry into force of this Protocol pursuant to paragraph 10, Chinese Taipei accedes to the WTO Agreement pursuant to Article XII of that Agreement and thereby becomes a Member of the WTO.

* * *

In the domestic American context, Taiwan's status is governed primarily by the Taiwan Relations Act of 1979. What aspects of statehood does it address, and how does it treat Taiwan?

TAIWAN RELATIONS ACT
22 U.S.C. §§ 3301–3314 (1979)

§ 3301.   CONGRESSIONAL FINDINGS AND DECLARATION OF POLICY

(a) Findings. The President having terminated governmental relations between the United States and the governing authorities on Taiwan recognized by the United States as the Republic of China prior to January 1, 1979, the Congress finds that the enactment of this Act is necessary—

(1) to help maintain peace, security, and stability in the Western Pacific; and

(2) to promote the foreign policy of the United States by authorizing the continuation of commercial, cultural, and other relations between the people of the United States and the people on Taiwan.

(b) Policy. It is the policy of the United States—

  (1) to preserve and promote extensive, close, and friendly commercial, cultural, and other relations between the people of the United States and the people on Taiwan, as well as the people on the China mainland and all other peoples of the Western Pacific area;

  (2) to declare that peace and stability in the area are in the political, security, and economic interests of the United States, and are matters of international concern;

  (3) to make clear that the United States decision to establish diplomatic relations with the People's Republic of China rests upon the expectation that the future of Taiwan will be determined by peaceful means; (4) to consider any effort to determine the future of Taiwan by other than peaceful means, including by boycotts or embargoes, a threat to the peace and security of the Western Pacific area and of grave concern to the United States;

  (5) to provide Taiwan with arms of a defensive character; and

  (6) to maintain the capacity of the United States to resist any resort to force or other forms of coercion that would jeopardize the security, or the social or economic system, of the people on Taiwan.

(c) Human rights. Nothing contained in this Act shall contravene the interest of the United States in human rights, especially with respect to the human rights of all the approximately eighteen million inhabitants of Taiwan. The preservation and enhancement of the human rights of all the people on Taiwan are hereby reaffirmed as objectives of the United States.

§ 3302. IMPLEMENTATION OF UNITED STATES POLICY WITH REGARD
         TO TAIWAN

(a) Defense articles and services. In furtherance of the policy set forth in section 2 of this Act [22 USCS § 3301], the United States will make available to Taiwan such defense articles and defense services in such quantity as may be necessary to enable Taiwan to maintain a sufficient self-defense capability.

(b) Determination of Taiwan's defense needs. The President and the Congress shall determine the nature and quantity of such defense articles and services based solely upon their judgment of the needs of Taiwan, in accordance with procedures established by law. Such determination of Taiwan's defense needs shall include review by United States military authorities in connection with recommendations to the President and the Congress

(c) United States response to threats to Taiwan or dangers to United States interests. The President is directed to inform the Congress promptly of any threat to the security or the social or economic system of the people on Taiwan and any danger to the interests of the United States arising therefrom. The President and the Congress shall determine, in accordance with constitutional processes, appropriate action by the United States in response to any such danger.

§ 3303.   APPLICATION TO TAIWAN OF LAWS AND INTERNATIONAL
            AGREEMENTS

(a) Application of United States laws generally. The absence of diplomatic relations or recognition shall not affect the application of the laws of the United States with respect to Taiwan, and the laws of the United States shall apply with respect to Taiwan in the manner that the laws of the United States applied with respect to Taiwan prior to January 1, 1979.

* * *

(c) Treaties and other international agreements. For all purposes, including actions in any court in the United States, the Congress approves the continuation in force of all treaties and other international agreements, including multilateral conventions, entered into by the United States and the governing authorities on Taiwan recognized by the United States as the Republic of China prior to January 1, 1979, and in force between them on December 31, 1978, unless and until terminated in accordance with law.

* * *

§ 3305.   THE AMERICAN INSTITUTE IN TAIWAN

(a) Conduct of programs, transactions, or other relations with respect to Taiwan. Programs, transactions, and other relations conducted or carried out by the President or any agency of the United States Government with respect to Taiwan shall, in the manner and to the extent directed by the President, be conducted and carried out by or through—

   (1) The American Institute in Taiwan, a nonprofit corporation incorporated under the laws of the District of Columbia, or

   (2) such comparable successor nongovernmental entity as the President may designate, (hereafter in this Act referred to as the "Institute").

(b) Agreements or transactions relative to Taiwan entered into, performed, and enforced. Whenever the President or any agency of the United States Government is authorized or required by or pursuant to the laws of the United States to enter into, perform, enforce, or have in force an agreement or transaction relative to Taiwan, such agreement or transaction shall be entered into, performed, and enforced, in the manner and to the extent directed by the President, by or through the Institute.

* * *

§ 3309. TAIWAN INSTRUMENTALITY

(a) Establishment of instrumentality. Presidential determination of necessary authority. Whenever the President or any agency of the United States Government is authorized or required by or pursuant to the laws of the United States to render or provide to or to receive or accept from Taiwan, any performance, communication, assurance, undertaking, or other action, such action shall, in the manner and to the extent directed by the President, be rendered or provided to, or received or accepted from, an instrumentality established by Taiwan which the President determines has the necessary authority under the laws applied by the people on Taiwan to provide assurances and take other actions on behalf of Taiwan in accordance with this Act.

(b) Offices and personnel. The President is requested to extend to the instrumentality established by Taiwan the same number of offices and complement of personnel as were previously operated in the United States by the governing authorities on Taiwan recognized as the Republic of China prior to January 1, 1979.

(c) Privileges and immunities. Upon the granting by Taiwan of comparable privileges and immunities with respect to the Institute and its appropriate personnel, the President is authorized to extend with respect to the Taiwan instrumentality and its appropriate personnel, such privileges and immunities * * as may be necessary for the effective performance of their functions.

* * *

§ 3314. DEFINITIONS

For purposes of this Act—

(1) the term "laws of the United States" includes any statute, rule, regulation, ordinance, order, or judicial rule of decision of the United States or any political subdivision thereof; and

(2) the term "Taiwan" includes, as the context may require, the islands of Taiwan and the Pescadores, the people on those islands, corporations and other entities and associations created or organized under the laws applied on those islands, and the governing authorities on Taiwan recognized by the United States as the Republic of China prior to January 1, 1979, and any successor governing authorities (including political subdivisions, agencies, and instrumentalities thereof).

* * *

If a corporation sues Taiwan in a U.S. federal court and Taiwan claims sovereign immunity (from jurisdiction), should the court grant Taiwan the protections which would be accorded to a state?

Consider the case of Palestine. How does the issue of statehood there differ from the case of Taiwan?

Palestine is not a full member of the United Nations. On November 29, 2012, Palestine was granted "non-member state" status in the United Nations (the same status that the Vatican possesses) in a politically charged vote of the UN General Assembly with 138 in favor, nine opposed and 41 abstentions. Note that the General Assembly could not award Palestine full membership status because that requires a recommendation from the Security Council (Art. 4 (2) UN Charter). In the Security Council, however, the United States, which has consistently opposed Palestinian statehood, holds veto power as one of the five permanent members.

Still, Palestine has made significant progress on the march towards recognition as a full member. One prominent stage in that process occurred on October 31, 2011, when the United Nations Educational, Scientific and Cultural Organization (UNESCO), a United Nations specialized agency, admitted Palestine as a full member with 107 votes in favor, 14 against and 52 abstentions. The UNESCO General Conference voted on a draft resolution to admit Palestine which set forth a short statement of the basis for Palestinian membership.

REQUEST FOR THE ADMISSION OF PALESTINE TO UNESCO
(October 29, 2011)

The General Conference,

Considering the request for admission of Palestine to UNESCO submitted in 1989, and reiterated at each session of the General Conference,

Having noted that Palestine accepts UNESCO's Constitution and is ready to fulfil the obligations which will devolve upon it by virtue of its admission and to contribute towards the expenses of the Organization,

Also having noted that in 187 EX/Decision 40 the Executive Board recommended the admission of Palestine to membership of UNESCO,

Decides to admit Palestine as a Member of UNESCO.

The United States and Israel immediately protested the UNESCO decision. The U.S. State Department issued a statement that explained its position:

> Today's vote by the member states of UNESCO to admit Palestine as a member is regrettable, premature, and undermines our shared goal of a comprehensive, just, and lasting peace in the Middle East. The United States remains steadfast in its support for the establishment of an independent and sovereign Palestinian state, but such a state can only be realized through direct negotiations between the Israelis and Palestinians.
>
> The United States also remains strongly committed to robust multilateral engagement across the UN system. However, Palestinian membership as a state in UNESCO triggers longstanding legislative restrictions which will compel the United States to refrain from making contributions to UNESCO.[1]

Subsequently, the United States cut off its 80 million dollars in annual dues to UNESCO, arguing that it was required to do so by congressional legislation. The United States' contribution amounted to 22% of UNESCO's annual budget.

The Israeli foreign ministry also immediately criticized UNESCO's actions:

> This is a unilateral Palestinian maneuver which will bring no change on the ground but further removes the possibility for a peace agreement. * * * The Palestinian move at Unesco, as with similar such steps with other UN bodies, is tantamount to a rejection of the international community's efforts to advance the peace process.[2]

In a May 2011 *New York Times* opinion piece[3], Palestinian president Mahmoud Abbas claimed that the Palestinian territories met the Montevideo Convention criteria for statehood as of 2011. Palestine has a permanent population in the form of the Palestinian people. Its territory, demarcated by the 1967 borders, is recognized internationally, albeit currently under Israeli control. Palestinian territories are also self-governed (with significant caveats). In addition, the presence of Palestinian embassies and missions in more than 100 countries demonstrates its capacity to enter into relations with other states. Should Palestine therefore be considered a state notwithstanding the strong objections of several states?

Do the theories laid out below help to explain and understand the cases for or against Taiwanese and Palestinian statehood?

---

[1] http://www.translations.state.gov

[2] http://www.mfa.gov.il/MFA/About+the+Ministry/MFA+Spokesman/2011/UNESCO_vote_harms_peace_negotiation_31-Oct-2011

[3] http://www.nytimes.com/2011/05/17/opinion/17abbas.html?pagewanted=print

STEFAN TALMAN, THE CONSTITUTIVE THEORY VERSUS DECLARATORY THEORY OF RECOGNITION: TERTIUM NON DATUR?

LXXV BRITISH YEARBOOK OF INTERNATIONAL LAW 101 (2004)

* * *

II. CONSTITUTIVE EFFECT

According to the constitutive theory, only recognition makes a State a State, and thus a subject of international law. In Oppenheim's words: "A state is, and becomes, an International Person through recognition only and exclusively." Recognition is therefore a matter within States' discretion. The constitutive theory is an expression of an outdated, positivist view of international law as a purely consensual system, where legal relations can only arise with the consent of those concerned. From this point of view, fulfilling the conditions for statehood alone does not suffice to render an entity a subject of international law, thus leaving the non-recognized State without rights and obligations vis-à-vis the non-recognizing States; in other words, international law does not apply between them. Accordingly, non-recognition of a factually existing State is possible. The non-recognition of a new State does not pose a problem for constitutive theorists; because recognition is seen as *status-creating*, non-recognition (or, more precisely, the non-occurrence of recognition), has *status-preventing* effect.

The most compelling argument against the constitutive theory is that it leads to a relativity of the "State" as subject of international law. What one State may consider to be a State may, for another, be a non-entity under international law. States are *natural-born*, i.e. absolute, subjects of international law and are not relative subjects of international law *treated* by existing States as, for example, international organizations. The idea of one State deciding upon another State's personality in international law is at odds with the fundamental principle of the sovereign equality of States. Furthermore, constitutive theory is incapable of explaining the responsibility of non-recognized States under international law. Not being subjects of international law, they are not only without rights in international law, but are also free from all international legal obligations. How, then, was it possible for the international community to ascribe responsibility to Rhodesia for acts of aggression, or other violations of international law, if it did not exist as a subject of international law? If the non-recognized State can violate international law, it must also (at least partially) be a subject of that law. * * * Contemporary authors, with few exceptions, rightly reject the constitutive theory. Non-recognition, therefore, cannot be accorded a status-preventing effect.

III. DECLARATORY EFFECT

I.   CONFIRMATION OF THE OBJECTIVE LEGAL SITUATION

The now predominant view in the literature is that recognition merely establishes, confirms or provides evidence of the objective legal situation, that is, the existence of a State. Alphonse Rivier stated in 1896 that: "The existence of the sovereign State is independent of its recognition by the other States." The Institut de Droit International shared that view. In Art. 1 of its Brussels Resolutions Concerning the Recognition of New States and New Governments of 23 April 1936, it recorded: "Recognition has a declaratory effect; The existence of a new State with all the juridical effects which are attached to that existence, is not affected by the refusal of recognition by one or more States." Thus, the international legal personality of a State and its concomitant rights and obligations solely depend on it being able to satisfy the criteria for statehood. Although that may be a contentious issue, it does not mean that all States' views are equally correct and that consequently, in applying the constitutive theory, the question of statehood is answered by looking to the views of individual States. It merely means that there is still no central authority that can decide on the question of statehood, its determination being binding for all. However, that is not a problem particular to statehood, but a general problem of international law. States, like natural persons in municipal law, attain legal personality at birth; that is, they are "born" subjects of international law. The declaratory theory has its roots in the natural law view of international law, which considers international law as an objective legal order based on a nature-like community of States.

The declaratory theory is supported by treaties, declarations of States, and especially by jurisprudence. Of particular value are the opinions of the Arbitration Commission of the Hague Conference on Yugoslavia ("Badinter Commission"), established under the auspices of European Political Co-operation (EPC). Its purpose was to consider questions relating to the recognition of new States and State succession, which arose as a result of the dismemberment of the Socialist Federal Republic of Yugoslavia (SFRY). In its first Opinion 29 November 1991, the Commission stated that:

> the principles of public international law [* * *] serve to define the conditions on which an entity constitutes a State; that in this respect, the existence [* * *] of the State is a question of fact; that the effects of recognition by other States are purely declaratory.

Consequently, in its Opinion No. 10, the Commission concluded that the Federal Republic of Yugoslavia (Serbia and Montenegro) (FRY) was a "new State." This was the case although it had neither received nor requested recognition, claiming to be the sole successor to the SFRY. Opinion No. 11 also shows that the question of when a State emerges does not depend on recognition. In this Opinion, the Commission decided on the date of emergence and thus the moment of succession for each successor State to the SFRY: that date was 8 October 1991 for Croatia and Slovenia; 17 November 1991 for Macedonia; 6 March 1992 for Bosnia and Herzegovina and 27 April 1992 for the Federal Republic of Yugoslavia. In all these cases, the date of emergence preceded recognition by other States by several months or even, in some cases, several years. The date of emergence was not always identical to the date when independence was declared. The Member States of the European Union, for example, recognized Croatia and Slovenia on 15 January 1992, Bosnia–Herzegovina on 7 April 1992, and Macedonia on 8 April 1993. They did not recognize the Federal Republic of Yugoslavia until April 1996.

If recognition has *status-confirming* effect, it only corroborates the objective legal situation, i.e. the existence of a State. * * *

B. STATE SUCCESSION: THE BREAK–UP OF THE USSR

The break-up of empires in the second half of the 20th century (especially the British, French and other European powers' colonial empires and the dissolution of the USSR and Yugoslavia) not only led to a proliferation of states, but also brought a crucial question of international law to the fore: what are the legal consequences of the birth and death of states? This question is usually discussed under the label of "state succession." It is helpful to break it up into two issues. One issue is the status of new-born states: do they enter the world of international law free of all obligations or do they inherit all, or at least some, of the obligations of their former masters? The other problem is the status of the (former) center, especially in the case of Russia: is the new (reduced) Russia to be treated as the old Soviet Union (USSR)? Its successor? A new entity?

In the text below, Antonio Cassese, an Italian international law scholar and judge, provides a general overview of the issues and basic rules (to the extent that they exist). Next, you will find an article by Rein Mullerson addressing the break-up of the Soviet Union and the complex practical questions of the treatment of post-Soviet Russia. Sketch out the fundamental situations discussed in the two texts, ranging from a mere change of government to the birth of an entirely new state. In doing so, ask yourself which factors should be considered in evaluating a situation and why it matters how the situation is characterized.

ANTONIO CASSESE, INTERNATIONAL LAW
(2d ed. 2005)

* * *

How do changes in the life or existence of States affect their legal personality? A revolutionary change in the government does not have any major impact on this personality. The principal problem that may arise in the case of revolutionary change following a civil war is whether acts performed by a government are binding upon a State if that government is succeeded by another one. In *Tinoco Concessions (GB* v. *Costa Rica)* the arbitrator Taft satisfactorily clarified the matter in 1923.

In 1917, Tinoco, a political leader, overthrew the government of Costa Rica and proclaimed a new constitution. In 1919 the Tinoco Government was toppled and the old authorities reinstated. In 1922 the government passed legislation quashing all the rights Tinoco had granted by contract to a number of British companies. The arbitrator held that, as Tinoco "was in actual and peaceable administration without resistance or conflict or contest by anyone until a few months before the time when he retired and resigned" (RIAA. i, at 379), those contracts were binding on Costa Rica.

In short, revolutionary or extra-constitutional changes in the government do not have any bearing on the identity of a State and consequently States are bound by international acts performed by previous governments.

In contrast, changes in the territory of a State may affect its legal personality. This happens when a State becomes extinct as a result of its break-up *(dismemberment),* or of its *merger* with one or more States (in which case all the merging States become extinct and at the same time give birth to a new legal subject), or when a State *incorporates* another one which, as a consequence, becomes extinct. In contrast, in case of *secession* of a part of the State's population and territory, the State continues to exist as a legal subject, but the seceding part may acquire international statehood.

Whenever on a territory a State replaces another one, the problem arises of whether there is a State succession, namely whether the rights and obligations of the former State are transferred to the other international subject (or subjects, in case of dismemberment) that has (or have) de facto replaced the old State, or part of it, in its control over the territory and the population living there.

The question is far from academic, as is shown by the merger of Egypt and Syria into the United Arab Republic in 1958 (which lasted until 1961), the merger of Tanganyika and Zanzibar to form Tanzania in 1964, the secession of Bangladesh from Pakistan in 1970, the merger of the two

Yemens in 1990, the incorporation of the German Democratic Republic into the Federal Republic of Germany in 1990, the acquisition (or, rather, the re-acquisition) of independence from the Soviet Union of the three Baltic States (Estonia and Latvia in 1990 and Lithuania in 1991), the break-up of the Soviet Union in 1991, of Yugoslavia in 1991, and Czechoslovakia in 1992.

This matter is regulated by a number of customary rules, to some extent codified in two treaties: the 1978 Vienna Convention on Succession of States in respect of Treaties, and the 1983 Vienna Convention on Succession of States in respect of State property, Archives and Debts (the latter is not yet in force).

Let us first consider the question of succession to *treaties*. In short, under customary law a distinction must be made between various categories of treaties. The first are the so-called *localized treaties,* which impose obligations and confer rights with regard to specific territories (for instance, regulate frontier matters, lay down a right of transit over certain specific areas, demilitarize a territory, establish fishing rights in certain waters or rights of navigation in specific rivers, etc.). Since these treaties attach to a specific territory, for the sake of international stability they are not affected by the mere fact of State succession; in other words, those treaties bind the new entity (see the 1978 Vienna Convention. Art. 12).

With regard to *non-localized treaties* customary law, as codified in the 1978 Vienna Convention, provides for a differentiated legal regime. For "newly independent States" (namely successor States "the territory of which immediately before the date of the succession of States was a dependent territory for the international relations of which the predecessor State was responsible," 1978 Vienna Convention, Art. 2.1), the "clean slate" principle applies, namely the principle whereby the new States are not bound by the treaties in force for the territory at the date of succession. This "anti-colonialist" approach has been clearly dictated by the necessity to take into account the legal condition and the specific needs of States resulting from the decolonization process.

By contrast, with regard to other States, the need to ensure international stability has pushed to uphold the principle of continuity, whereby normally treaties binding on the predecessor State also apply to the successor State (see the 1978 Vienna Convention, Articles 34 and 35, which however do not correspond to customary law, that is instead based on the "clean slate" rule, subject to the exception of localized treaties).

For a particular category of treaties, namely those *on human rights,* it would seem that a *general* rule has gradually evolved whereby the successor State (whether or not it belongs to the category of "newly independent States") must respect them. The rationale for this rule is that human rights treaties are intended to protect and benefit individuals vis-à-vis the central authorities; hence, whatever the nature, character, and political allegiance of these authorities, what matters is that individuals should continue to be protected even after a change in sovereignty over a particular territory. In addition, human rights are now considered so essential that it would be inconsistent with the whole thrust of the present world community to discontinue protecting them only because one State has replaced another in operating as the governing entity responsible for the international relations of a particular territory.

The question of succession also arises with regard to: (i) State assets and debts; (ii) State archives; (iii) membership of international organizations. It would seem that the content of the customary rules regulating these matters is still uncertain.

As for *State property,* the definition of what belongs to a State must be drawn from the relevant national law applicable at the moment of succession, as is laid down in Article 8 of the Vienna Convention of 1983 and was restated by the Arbitration Commission on Yugoslavia in its Opinion no. 14 on *State Succession* (at 732). Once it has been established whether the assets are public, it may normally be held that the State that wields control over the territory where the assets are located succeeds the previous territorial State with regard to ownership. The same holds true for *State archives.*

The question of succession with regard to *public debts* (that is, debts owed by the State) is more difficult, also because State practice is rather confusing. Under Article 40 of the 1983 Vienna Convention, when a State breaks up and new entities come into being, unless they otherwise agree the State debt of the predecessor State passes to the successor States "in an equitable proportion."

With regard to membership in *international organizations,* it is rational to believe that, if two member States merge thereby creating a new State, this State should apply for admission to the Organization. However, in UN practice, no admission has been required (this happened in 1958, when Egypt and Syria merged to form the United Arab Republic, and in 1990, when North Yemen and South Yemen merged). Furthermore, if a member State breaks up into two or more States, all of them must apply for membership (this happened in 1992–3, after the dissolution of Yugoslavia and the birth of six Yugoslav Republics; five were admitted immediately thereafter while the Federal Republic of Yugoslavia (Serbia and Montenegro) applied for, and gained, membership in 2000). An exception may be admitted for the one component that may successfully claim to be a continuation of the old State, as far as membership is concerned (this happened in 1990, when the Soviet Union broke up, and all newly born republics had to apply for admission, except for the Russian Federation which was considered a continuation of the Soviet Union, and Byelorussia and Ukraine which were already members of the UN in their own right). If a new State-like entity comes into being as a result of secession from a member State, it too must apply for membership.

* * *

REIN MULLERSON, THE CONTINUITY AND SUCCESSION OF STATES, BY REFERENCE TO THE FORMER USSR AND YUGOSLAVIA
42 Int'l & Comp. Law Quarterly 473 (1993)

I.   INTRODUCTION

The birth and death of States involving issues of succession do not occur every day or even every year. After a wave of emergence of new States (with Latin American States at the beginning of the 19th century, Eastern European States after the First World War, decolonisation in the 1960s, the dissolution of the USSR and Yugoslavia in the 1990s) there are usually long periods during which no State emerges or disappears. And every wave is unique in its nature. The rarity of such events, which occur in different political contexts, accounts for the existence both of different and mutually exclusive theories and, even more so, of contradictory practice.

* * *

IV.   RUSSIA—SUCCESSOR STATE TO THE SOVIET UNION OR ITS CONTINUATION?

In the case of the dissolution of the Soviet Union, one of the important legal and practical questions is whether the dissolution was a dismemberment of the former State or whether there were secessions from it while it continued to exist—albeit consisting of a different territory and with a different population. As Professor J. Crawford writes:

> there is a fundamental distinction between State continuity and State succession: that is to say, between cases where the "same" State can be said to continue to exist, despite changes of government, territory, or population, and cases where one State can be said to have replaced another with respect to certain territory.

This differentiation between cases of State succession and continuation of States, notwithstanding changes in territory, population and authority, is especially important in the light of uncertainties in the law of State succession.

Certainly, from the point of view of politics, changes in the economy and social structures still in process of development in the erstwhile Soviet Union constitute a deep social revolution. The communist ideology and policy are being replaced by a free market economy and liberal ideas;

democratic reforms are under way in different parts of the former communist empire. But notwithstanding efforts of Soviet diplomacy and legal doctrine to show that social (particularly socialist) revolutions disrupt the existence of States so that there is effectively no State succession in such cases, this approach has been supported by neither legal doctrine nor practice. Consequently, even deep social changes are irrelevant in determining whether or not a State continues to exist.

To determine whether, from the point of view of international law, there was a dismemberment of the Soviet Union (so that it has ceased to exist and there are only successor States) or whether one of the former Soviet republics continues its existence, it is necessary to take into account objective as well as subjective factors. These factors tend to indicate that an analysis of the international legal personality of States existing in place of the former Soviet Union supports the separation of parts of its territory while its core—Russia—continues to exist as a continuation of the Union. What are these factors?

First, even after the dissolution of the Union, Russia remains much bigger than the other States—the former Soviet republics—when all taken together. Although the 14 republics have separated, and from the political point of view we can speak of the dissolution of the Union, geographically and demographically Russia remains one of the largest States in the world. Second, Soviet Russia after 1917, and especially the Soviet Union after 1922, were treated as continuing the same State as existed under the Russian Empire. In a sense, current changes are more profound than changes after the 1917 revolution. Although the socialist revolution changed the nature of Czarist Russia in many respects, it did not abolish its imperial character. Even the national anthem of the Soviet Union began with the words: "Unbreakable Union of free republics united for ever by Great Russia * * * ."

These are factors of an objective character. But as Crawford correctly observes: "Where there are substantial changes in the entity concerned, continuity may depend upon recognition (as in the case of India after 1947)." This means that in such cases subjective factors become important. Whilst Crawford implies recognition by other States, I think that the manner in which the State concerned considers itself is of equal importance. In cases of substantial changes in the State concerned, when there are doubts as to its continuous existence, it seems to me that the State's behaviour *and* recognition by third States are relevant.

The Foreign Minister of the Russian Federation has said that "Russia, as a continuing state of the USSR, intends to promote in every possible way the strengthening of the United Nations." In his letter of 24 December 1991 to the Secretary–General of the United Nations, President Yeltsin stated that "the membership of the Union of the Soviet Socialist Republics in the United Nations, including the Security Council and all other organs and organisations of the United Nations system, is being continued by the Russian Federation (RSFSR) with the support of the Commonwealth of Independent States." Further, in the Decision of the Council of Heads of State of the Commonwealth of Independent States of 21 December 1991, it was held that "the States of the Commonwealth support Russia's continuance of the membership of the Union of Soviet Socialist Republics in the United Nations, including permanent membership of the Security Council, and other international organisations." No State or organisation objected to this continuance by Russia. Consequently, Russia—as a continuing State of the Soviet Union—was not obliged to apply for membership of these organisations, while other former Soviet republics, considered to be successor States, had to go through the usual procedures of application for membership.

The question of UN membership in this case was resolved in exactly the same manner as the question of Indian and Pakistani membership in 1947 following the dissolution of India into two States: India and Pakistan. In 1947 the UN acted on the basis of the Secretariat's legal opinion, issued on 8 August, which concluded that "from the point of view of international law, the situation is one in which a part of an existing State breaks off and becomes a new State." This had no effect on the international status of India, which continued to be a UN member; but "the territory which breaks off, Pakistan, will be a new State; it will not have the treaty rights and obligations of the old State, and will not, of course, have membership in the United Nations." Here I do not comment on the absence of any treaty rights and obligations of a new State. But certainly there is no question of succession to membership of international organisations. This may be considered as a customary norm governing matters of State succession. Therefore if a State, despite substantial changes, retains membership of international organisations, it has not succeeded to the membership of a predecessor State but has instead continued the existing membership of that State. In this sense Russia in fact continues the existence of the Soviet Union, although with less extensive boundaries and a diminished population.

Russia's approach to issues concerning Soviet armed forces stationed outside the Commonwealth of Independent States (CIS) also indicates that Russia considers itself to be a continuation of the former Soviet Union. Furthermore, other States either expressly recognise it or acquiesce in it. This is for reasons of a different and in part non-legal nature, yet the consequences of such recognition or acquiescence are legally important. For example, the permanent members of the Security Council did not want to open up discussion concerning permanent membership. Moreover, the Baltic countries were content that there should be a body which would be in charge of armed forces of the former Soviet Union stationed in their territories and with which it would be possible to negotiate their withdrawal, etc. Generally speaking, recognition of Russia as a continuation of the erstwhile Soviet Union, even if this was to an extent a legal fiction, made the lives of existing States less complicated. In legal terms this implied that Russia assumed all the treaty and other international obligations as well as the rights of the Soviet Union.

Though Russia is a continuing State of the Soviet Union and generally continues to hold the Union's rights and obligations, this is not to say that these rights and obligations remain intact: a substantial change of circumstances leads to certain adjustments of them. For example, Russia (unlike the Soviet Union) is not able to fulfil all the treaty obligations of the former Soviet Union concerning delimitation of or co-operation in the Baltic Sea because its Baltic coastline has greatly diminished. Later, I will consider in more depth the implications of the doctrine of *rebus sic stantibus* in cases of State succession. Here I wish to stress only that though—as Crawford writes—"acquisition or loss of territory does not *per se* affect the continuity of the State" and this "may be so even where the territory acquired or lost is substantially greater in area than the original or remaining State territory," substantial territorial and demographic changes require the use of the *rebus sic stantibus* doctrine to adjust the State's international legal relations.

That said, it is necessary to make some qualifications. Russia's continuation of the Soviet Union does not mean that other former republics have nothing to do with the Soviet Union's rights and obligations. They are successor States to the Soviet Union and this affects also Russia's international rights and obligations. The CIS countries have signed a series of agreements and taken decisions at the level of heads of State and government on issues of State succession.

On 4 December 1991, i.e. before the dissolution of the Soviet Union, eight republics signed (all republics were invited to sign) a Treaty on Succession to the Soviet Union's State Debt and Assets. On 30 December 1991 the heads of the CIS countries agreed that "each of them has the right to an appropriate, fair and ascertained share of the property of the former Soviet Union abroad."

On 20 March 1992 a Decision of the Council of Heads of State of the CIS members was adopted in Kiev on the complex of issues relating to succession to treaties, having mutual interest, State property, State archives, and assets and liabilities of the former Soviet Union. In this document the heads of State decided to recognise that all CIS member States are successors to the rights and obligations of the former Soviet Union. They also decided to establish a commission of representatives with full powers to negotiate and prepare proposals on issues of State succession.

* * *

In the treaty on succession to the Soviet Union's assets and liabilities of 4 December 1991, the future CIS countries had already agreed on their respective shares: Russia 61.34 per cent, Ukraine 16.37 per cent, etc. On 6 July 1992 the CIS heads of State signed an agreement on the division of the property of the former Soviet Union abroad, using the same percentages. Later an understanding was reached between Russia and the other CIS member States, apart from Ukraine, that Russia would take over international liabilities as well as assets. Ukraine accepted 16.37 per cent of these, but at the beginning of January 1993 announced that it would not continue with a deal concluded with Russia in November on sharing debt repayments.

* * *

VIII. Conclusion

The practice of State succession after the dissolution of the Soviet Union and Yugoslavia has clarified some issues. It supports the making of a distinction between succession of States and continuation of States notwithstanding substantial changes in territory, population or political regime. This practice has also highlighted the concern of the international community of States to preserve the stability of international legal relations and also the acceptance by successor States of the obligations of their predecessors. At the same time, however, this practice also confirms that automatic acceptance of the obligations of predecessor States (except universal treaties) is not always possible. Negotiation and adjustment are necessary. The practice also indicates that much depends on fortuitous circumstances. Very often new States do not have sufficiently qualified personnel to differentiate between, say, succession to the obligations of the predecessor State and adherence to the same treaties. Often it is difficult for them to take competent decisions, especially under the time constraints they face. In this context, therefore, the attitude and position of other States (and especially their concerted actions) as well as the stance of international organisations become very important.

I consider that the practice relating to the dissolution of Yugoslavia and the Soviet Union in terms of State succession indicates that even if new States do not consider themselves to be automatically bound by all their predecessors' treaties, they cannot simply unilaterally renounce their predecessors' obligations. Rather, they must negotiate in good faith the readjustment of these obligations. This applies, above all, to very complex arms limitation treaties, since the circumstances existing at their conclusion will usually have significantly changed as a result of the events which produce questions of State succession. However, the application of *rebus sic stantibus* here does not mean that successor States should have nothing to do with such treaties. In this interdependent world, stability of international relations is of such a high value that the world community of States cannot afford to have these relations broken as the result of the dissolution or secession of States.

As to universal human rights instruments, the practice of new States—though not unequivocal—and the position of third States and different international bodies, as well as doctrinal findings, seem to indicate that there is a tendency for new States to accept their predecessors' obligations in order to be accepted as members of the international community. New States are born not only into general customary international law but also into those universal human rights treaties which were obligatory for their predecessors.

According to Mullerson, what are the main criteria for answering the question whether a state is identical with, or rather a successor to, a former entity? What are the factors that influence the determination? Who ultimately makes the decision?

The following texts document the break-up of the Soviet Union and the establishment of the Commonwealth of Independent States (CIS), as discussed in the Mullerson excerpt you have just read. What do these documents tell you about the issue of state continuity and succession in this instance? What is the primary purpose of the Agreements Establishing the CIS? How do the joint statement and the Agreement itself accomplish that purpose?

AGREEMENTS ESTABLISHING THE COMMONWEALTH OF INDEPENDENT STATES

Armenia—Azerbaijan—Belarus—Kazakhstan—Kyrgyzstan—Moldova—Russian Federation—Tajikistan—Turkmenistan—Uzbekistan—Ukraine
Done at Minsk, December 8, 1991, and done at Alma Alta, December 21, 1991

[I.L.M. BACKGROUND/CONTENT SUMMARY

On December 24, 1991, the Secretary–General of the United Nations informed the member states that he had received a letter from the Permanent Representative of the Union of Soviet Socialist Republics transmitting a letter from the President of the Russian Federation (RSFSR). The letter stated that "the membership of the Union of the Soviet Socialist Republics in the United Nations, including the Security Council and all other organs and organizations of the United Nations system, is being continued by the Russian Federation (RSFSR) with the support of the countries of the Commonwealth of Independent States."

As of February 7, 1992, the United Nations Security Council had received applications for admission to the United Nations from Armenia, Azerbaijan, Kazakhstan, Kyrgyzstan, Moldova, Tajikistan, Turkmenistan, and

Uzbekistan. Applications are referred to the Committee on the Admission of New Members for examination and report. The Security Council then acts on the recommendation of the Committee and by resolution recommends to the General Assembly that the country be admitted to membership in the United Nations. U.N. membership was recommended in all cases. Belarus and the Ukraine have been U.N. members since 1945.

On September 17, 1991, Estonia, Latvia and Lithuania were admitted as new members to the United Nations General Assembly. The Baltic States and the ten former Soviet Republics have also become participants in the Conference on Security and Co-operation in Europe, with the Baltic States being admitted on September 10, 1991, and the others on January 30, 1992. Russia assumed the seat held by the former Soviet Union.]

Declaration by the Heads of State of the Republic of Belarus, the RSFSR and Ukraine

We, the leaders of the Republic of Belarus, the RSFSR and Ukraine,

Noting that the talks on the drafting of a new Soviet Treaty have become deadlocked and that the de facto process of withdrawal of republics from the Union of Soviet Socialist Republics and the formation of independent States has become a reality,

Noting that the short-sighted policy of the centre has led to a profound economic and political crisis, to the breakdown of production and to a catastrophic drop in the living standards of practically all strata of society,

Bearing in mind the growing social tension in many regions of the former Union of Soviet Socialist Republics, which has led to conflicts between nationalities with a heavy toll of victims,

Recognizing our responsibility to our peoples and the world community and the pressing need for the practical implementation of political and economic reforms,

Proclaim the establishment of the Commonwealth of Independent States concerning which the parties have signed an agreement on 8 December 1991.

The Commonwealth of Independent States comprising the Republic of Belarus, the RSFSR and Ukraine is open for accession by all States members of the Union of Soviet Socialist Republics, as well as by other States sharing the purposes and principles of this agreement.

The States members of the Commonwealth intend to pursue a policy of strengthening international peace and security. They undertake to discharge the international obligations incumbent on them under treaties and agreements entered into by the former Union of Soviet Socialist Republics, and are making provision for joint control over nuclear weapons and for their non-proliferation.

S. SHUSHKEVICH Chairman of the Supreme Soviet of the Republic of Belarus

B. YELTSIN President of the RSFSR

L. KRAVCHUK President of Ukraine

Minsk, 8 December 1991

AGREEMENT ESTABLISHING THE COMMONWEALTH OF INDEPENDENT STATES

We, the Republic of Belarus, the Russian Federation (RSFSR) and Ukraine, as founder States of the Union of Soviet Socialist Republics and signatories of the Union Treaty of 1922, hereinafter referred to as the High Contracting Parties, hereby declare that the Union of Soviet Socialist Republics as a subject of international law and a geopolitical reality no longer exists.

On the basis of the historical commonality of our peoples and the ties that have developed between them, and bearing in mind the bilateral agreements concluded between High Contracting Parties,

Desirous of setting up lawfully constituted democratic States,

Intending to develop our relations on the basis of mutual recognition of and respect for State sovereignty, the inalienable right to self-determination, the principles of equality and non-intervention in internal affairs, of abstention from the use of force and from economic or other means of applying pressure and of settling controversial issues through agreement, and other universally recognized principles and norms of international law,

Considering that the further development and strengthening of relations of friendship, good-neighbourliness and mutually advantageous cooperation between our States are in accord with the vital national interests of their peoples and serve the cause of peace and security,

Confirming our adherence to the purposes and principles of the Charter of the United Nations, the Helsinki Final Act and the other documents of the Conference on Security and Cooperation in Europe,

Undertaking to abide by the universally recognized international norms relating to human and peoples' rights,

We have agreed as follows:

Article 1

The High Contracting Parties hereby establish the Commonwealth of Independent States.

Article 2

The High Contracting Parties guarantee to their citizens, regardless of their nationality or other differences, equal rights and freedoms. Each of the High Contracting Parties guarantees to the citizens of the other Parties, and also to stateless persons resident in their territory, regardless of national affiliation or other differences, civil, political, social, economic and cultural rights and freedoms in accordance with the universally recognized international norms relating to human rights.

* * *

Article 7

The High Contracting Parties recognize that the sphere of their joint activity, conducted on an equitable basis through common coordinating institutions of the Commonwealth, embraces:

- coordination of foreign policy;
- cooperation in the formation and development of a common economic space and Europe-wide and Eurasian markets and in the field of customs policy;
- cooperation in developing the transport and communications systems;
- cooperation in the protection of the environment and participation in establishing a comprehensive international system of environmental security;
- issues of migration policy;
- combating organized crime.

* * *

Article 12

The High Contracting Parties undertake to discharge the international obligations incumbent on them under treaties and agreements entered into by the former Union of Soviet Socialist Republics.

Article 13

This Agreement shall not affect the obligations of the High Contracting Parties towards third States.

This Agreement is open for accession by all States members of the former Union of Soviet Socialist Republics, and also by other States sharing the purposes and principles of this Agreement.

Article 14

The official location of the coordinating organs of the Commonwealth shall be the city of Minsk.

The activities of organs of the former Union of Soviet Socialist Republics in the territories of the States members of the Commonwealth are hereby terminated.

Done at Minsk on 8 December 1991 in three copies, each in the Byelorussian, Russian and Ukrainian languages, the three texts being equally authentic.

For the Republic of Belarus:	S. SHUSHKEVICH, B. KEBICH
For the RSFSR:	B. YELTSIN, G. BURBULIS
For Ukraine:	L. KRAVCHUK, V. FOKIN

2. INTERGOVERNMENTAL ORGANIZATIONS

Intergovernmental Organizations (also called, more generally, International Organizations) are not an invention of the post-World War II period. They go back at least to the mid- and late-19th century, witness, e.g., the International Telecommunications Union (1865), the Universal Postal Union (founded in 1874), and the Hague Conference on Private International Law (founded in 1895). Yet for many decades, they were few in number, had narrowly circumscribed purposes, and thus played no major role in shaping the world legal order. The only pre-World War II organization intended to play such a role, the League of Nations (founded in 1920), was by and large a failure. It has only been since 1945 that intergovernmental organizations have grown in number exponentially and become powerful players on the international scene, rivaling, and in some respects even overshadowing, states.

In the second half of the 20th century, the number of intergovernmental organizations has skyrocketed—exactly how much is difficult to ascertain as the numbers given in the literature vary widely. According to one count, the number of IOs has risen from 123 (in 1951) to 251 (in 1999), though according to the 2010/2011 Yearbook of International Organizations, a decade later, there were 7,544 IOs.[4] They come in many forms, shapes, and sizes.

Some are global, such as the United Nations (UN, with headquarters in New York, and regional headquarters in Geneva, Vienna, and Nairobi), the Organization for Economic Co-operation and Development (OECD, headquartered in Paris), and the World Trade Organization (WTO, Geneva) which are considered in more detail below. Other IGOs on the global level include various specialized agencies of the UN, such as the International Civil Aeronautics Organization (ICAO, Montreal), which we have encountered in the Introduction, the International Labor Organization

---

[4] Eric Stein, *International Integration and Democracy: No Love at First Sight*, 95 AJIL 489 (2001); Union of International Associations, YEARBOOK OF INTERNATIONAL ORGANIZATIONS 2010/2011, 33–35 (Walter DeGruter ed., 2010).

(ILO, Geneva), the International Monetary Fund (IMF, Washington, D.C.), the United National Educational, Scientific and Cultural Organization (UNESCO, Paris), the World Bank Group (often just called the World Bank, Washington, D.C.), the World Health Organization (WHO, Geneva), and the World Intellectual Property Organization (WIPO, Geneva).

Many IOs are regional. Most notable in Europe are the European Union (EU, Brussels) and the Council of Europe (Strasbourg); in the Americas, the Organization of American States (OAS, Washington D.C.) and the Mercado Commun del Sur (MERCOSUR, Montevideo); in Asia, the Association of South East Asian Nations (ASEAN, Jakarta); in the Middle East, the Arab League (Cairo), and in Africa, the African Union (AU, Addis Ababa) and the L'Organisation pour l'Harmonization en Afrique du Droit des Affaires (OHADA, Abidjan). Many of them have originally held only a specialized portfolio, especially the promotion of regional trade, but have since become more encompassing political unions; the prime example is the development from the European Economic Community (EEC) via the European Community (EC) to the European Union (EU), which we study later (Chapter VII.2.).

Some intergovernmental organizations have also expanded their geographic range. For example, the North Atlantic Treaty Organization (NATO, Brussels) began as a Western defense agreement specifically against the Warsaw Pact on the other side of the Iron Curtain in 1955. It has since pursued broader purposes of a more global reach with troops active far beyond its original zone of interest, such as in Afghanistan and Libya.

A. THE UNITED NATIONS

As the largest, most prominent, and possibly even the most powerful international organization today, the UN is worth knowing something about in its own right—at least with regard to its background, purpose, structure, and major organs.

While the 20th century is usually credited with the idea of a *League of Nations* (1919) or *United Nations* (1945), the notion of an international organization of universal scope was earlier suggested by the German philosopher Immanuel Kant at the end of the 18th century. Kant draws heavily on natural law concepts. According to him, why exactly is a "league of peace" necessary?

IMMANUEL KANT, ON PERPETUAL PEACE

(1795)

* * *

Second Definitive Article for a Definitive Peace

"The Law of Nations Shall be Founded on a Federation of Free States;"

Peoples, as states, like individuals, may be judged to injure one another merely by their coexistence in the state of nature (i.e., while independent of external laws). Each of them, may and should for the sake of its own security demand that the others enter with it into a constitution similar to the civil constitution, for under such a constitution each can be secure in his right. This would be a league of nations, but it would not have to be a state consisting of nations. That would be contradictory, since a state implies the relation of a superior (legislating) to an inferior (obeying), i.e., the people, and many nations in one state would then constitute only one nation. This contradicts the presupposition, for here we have to weigh the rights of nations against each other so far as they are distinct states and not amalgamated into one. * * *

When we consider the perverseness of human nature which is nakedly revealed in the uncontrolled relations between nations * * *, we may well be astonished that the word "law" has not yet been banished from war politics as pedantic, and that no state has yet been bold enough to advocate this point of view. Up to the present, Hugo Grotius, Pufendorf, Vattel, and many other irritating comforters have been cited in justification of war, though their code, philosophically or diplomatically formulated, has not and cannot have the least legal force, because states as such do not stand under a common external power. There is no instance on record that a state has ever been moved to desist from its purpose because of arguments backed up by the testimony of such great men. But the homage which each state pays (at least in words) to the concept of law proves that there is slumbering in man an even greater moral disposition to become master of the evil principle in himself (which he cannot disclaim) and to hope for the same from others. * * *

For these reasons there must be a league of a particular kind, which can be called a league of peace *(foedus pacificum),* and which would be distinguished from a treaty of peace *(pactum pacis)* by the fact that the latter terminates only one war, while the former seeks to make an end of all wars forever. This league does not tend to any dominion over the power of the state but only to the maintenance and security of the freedom of the state itself and of other states in league with it, without there being any need for them to submit to civil laws and their compulsion, as men in a state of nature must submit.

* * *

The League of Nations (1919–1946)

The first attempt to realize Kant's idea of a permanent "league" of peace on a global level was the League of Nations, the predecessor to the United Nations.

The League of Nations was created by the Paris Peace Conference that ended World War I and established by Part I of the Treaty of Versailles in 1919. Its principal goal was to maintain world peace, in particular to prevent another world war, through a combination of collective security and disarmament, and to promote the settlement of international disputes in a peaceful manner through negotiation, arbitration, and adjudication. The League did not have its own armed forces, but relied instead on its members to provide military contingents to execute its decisions.

Its Covenant was originally signed by 44 nations, and by 1934, its membership had grown to 58 countries (then the vast majority in the world). While U.S. President Woodrow Wilson was among its most determined sponsors (he was awarded the Nobel Peace Prize for his efforts in October 1919), the U.S. Senate ultimately refused to ratify the founding treaty, and the United States never joined the League. This deprived the League of Nations of the cooperation of a key player and emerging superpower.

The League's principal organs were the Assembly (of member states), the Council (consisting of both permanent and rotating non-permanent members), a Permanent Secretariat (with its own administrative staff), and the Permanent Court of International Justice (PCIJ), the forerunner of the current International Court of Justice.

For about 15 years, the League operated in a fairly successful manner. It provided the platform for the peaceful resolution of various (mainly regional) disputes, aided the de-colonization of many parts of the world (inter alia by administering a system of "Mandates"—such as the British Mandate in Palestine), provided aid to refugees and stateless persons, and protected ethnic minorities in certain countries.

By the mid-1930s, however, it became clear that due both to structural weaknesses and the lack of participation by the United States, the League could not contain the increasingly aggressive behavior of a number of states. This was particularly obvious with regard to the axis powers, i.e., Italy, Japan and Germany, all of whom withdrew from the League, along with a number of other nations. In addition, the League could not prevent the Soviet aggression against Finland, although it reacted by expelling the Soviet Union in 1939. Finally, in the late 1930s, Britain and France, the strongest remaining members, abandoned the League's system of collective security in favor of a policy of appeasement of the aggressors.

The outbreak of World War II was the ultimate proof of the League's failure in its principal mission. The League lay dormant during the war and was dissolved in 1946 after the foundation of the United Nations.

The Creation of the UN

ANTONIO CASSESE, INTERNATIONAL LAW
(2d ed. 2005)

* * *

As the US Secretary of State, Cordell Hull, recalled, "[f]rom the moment when Hitler's invasion of Poland revealed the bankruptcy of all existing methods to preserve peace, it became evident * * * that we must begin almost immediately to plan the creation of a new system."

The USA and the British did most of the planning. Two grand designs soon emerged, one advocated by the Americans, the other by the British. The former, strongly championed by Cordell Hull and President Roosevelt, hinged on a few main points: (1) resort to military force in international relations must be banned; (2) the traditional system of unilateral action, of military and political alliances, of spheres of influence and balance of power ought to be removed; all these mechanisms and practices must be replaced by a universal organization set up by peace-loving nations; (3) in this organization a major role was to be given to the most powerful allies fighting against the Axis Powers, namely the USA, the USSR, as well as Britain and France (which still had huge colonial empires), and China, which was to be associated with them. They were to be allotted the role of world policemen, responsible for enforcing peace; (4) economic and social co-operation was to be promoted so as to ensure economic progress and better working conditions with a view to forestalling future armed conflict resulting from dramatic economic inequalities; (5) colonial empires were to be dismantled, particularly if they belonged to "weak nations," on three grounds: (a) for ideological reasons, that is, in order to realize the principle of self-determination of peoples throughout the world; (b) for political reasons, namely to avert future clashes and conflicts resulting from the existence in the world of over one billion "brown people" resenting the domination of white minorities; (c) for economic reasons: colonial empires distorted equality and free trade on the world market, one of the primary goals of the US neo-liberal approach; indeed, the colonial Powers had access to cheap labour and cheap primary commodities in their colonies. However, the break up of the colonial system must not be abrupt but gradual: an international trusteeship system was to gradually bring about the demise of that system. * * *

The British scheme, relentlessly propounded by Churchill, accepted the idea of banning force and promoting economic and social co-operation, but also hinged on (1) the notion that world security could be safeguarded by the setting up of regional councils under a world council; (2) the maintenance of colonial empires or, alternatively, their gradual change into self-governing entities.

As the USA was by far the more powerful country, and had indeed become the most industrialized and militarily powerful State in the world, it easily gained the upper hand. However, it had to compromise with Britain over the question of colonialism, the more so because another future "policeman," France, although temporarily "defeated," very much clung to its colonial empire.

The Soviet Union played a relatively minor role in the establishment of the universal organization, the UN, and was primarily vocal on some political issues such as the veto power in the Security Council (SC), the proposed participation in the founding of the Organization of all 16 Soviet republics (eventually accepted by the Western allies only for Byelorussia and the Ukraine) and the upholding of the principle of self-determination.

The fundamental tenets of the future UN Charter were gradually agreed upon. This was done first in the Atlantic Charter, drafted by the USA and Britain in 1941, then by the three victorious Powers (the USA, Britain, and the Soviet Union) plus China, in a string of summits: at Moscow (October 1943), at Dumbarton Oaks (an estate in Washington DC, from 21 August to 7 October 1944), at Yalta (4–11 February 1945, without the participation of China). When the diplomatic conference designed to work out and approve the UN Charter was held (San Francisco, 25 April–26 June 1945), it was presented with a text elaborated by the Great Powers.

To this text amendments, requiring a two-thirds majority, were technically permitted, although politically they were allowed only on relatively minor points. The 50 States gathered at San Francisco (most States of the world: the four convening Powers, the 42 States (including India, not yet independent) that had declared war either on Germany or on Japan, plus Argentina, Denmark, Byelorussia, and the Ukraine, the last two not yet recognized as independent States) could not but accept the key provisions of the Charter. Among these were: the provision on the establishment of a central organ consisting of a few countries, dominated by the five permanent members with veto power, and responsible for the maintenance of international peace and security; and the provision on domestic jurisdiction, corresponding to the present Article 2.7, which was closely intertwined with the traditional principle on non-interference in the internal affairs of States (see below). However, small and medium-sized countries were able to contribute on some points, chiefly: (1) the laying down, in Article 51 (* * *) of the right to individual and collective self-defence; (2)

the expansion of the competence of the General Assembly (GA) (the collective body where every member State had one seat and one vote), which was empowered both to discuss any matter within the scope of the Charter and to make recommendations on questions concerning peace and security not being dealt with by the SC (see Articles 10 and 12); (3) the elevation of the Economic and Social Council, ECOSOC (the body charged with promoting cooperation on economic, social, cultural, educational, health, and related matters) to the rank of one of the principal organs of the new Organization; (4) the laying down of provisions on colonial matters (such as the Declaration regarding non-self-governing territories, contained in Article 73, and the provisions on the trusteeship system); (5) the insertion of a provision establishing the prevalence of obligations imposed by the UN Charter over conflicting obligations, if any, deriving from other treaties (Article 103). A point of some contention was the principle of non-intervention, which was dear to the hearts of Latin American and other small countries (as was pointed out by a distinguished commentator: "there was a widespread conviction among the middle and lesser States that some formal safeguard against intervention in their internal affairs was needed in an Organization in which the great Powers were to play a dominant role"). This principle was intended to be put into what became Article 2.4 (banning the use of force); the motion of Latin American and other countries had enough support to be inserted by a divided vote. However, in the end, the compromise (probably a perverse one) was to put it into Article 2.7 (safeguarding member States' "domestic jurisdiction" from undue interference by the Organization).

It must be stressed that from the outset the new Organization was envisaged as a political body dominated by the Great Powers. They had taken upon themselves the task of safeguarding peace and security on behalf and in the interest of all nations of the world, but did not intend to make major concessions to small nations on matters they regarded as of crucial importance. In this connection, an exchange of views between Stalin, Churchill, and Roosevelt that occurred on 4 February 1945, at Yalta, is illuminating. While discussing the issue of voting procedures in the SC, Stalin noted that "he would never agree to having any action of any of the Great Powers submitted to the judgment of the small powers." The other two leaders substantially agreed.

Furthermore, the new Organization was to be a political entity pursuing political objectives, albeit within a legal framework. In its action it was not to be trammelled by legal technicalities, let alone by judicial restraints: efforts to make disputes on the interpretation of the Charter subject to the mandatory jurisdiction of its principal judicial organ, the ICJ, were rejected at San Francisco (they secured majority support but not the requisite two-thirds majority). * * *

In the view of the founding fathers, the new Organization was to pursue a number of fundamental purposes: (1) to maintain peace and security (Article 1.1); (2) to bring about by peaceful means the adjustment or settlement of international disputes or situations which might lead to a breach of the peace (Article 1.1); (3) to develop friendly relations among nations based on respect for the principle of equal rights and self-determination of peoples (Article 1.2); in short, to promote, if not yet the gradual and internationally organized demise of colonial systems, at least the slow awakening of colonial countries to self-government; (4) to foster economic and social cooperation (Articles 1.3, 55); (5) to promote respect for human rights and fundamental freedoms for all persons (Articles 1.3, 55).

Other purposes of the Organization, clearly considered of minor importance by the founding fathers, were: (6) to promote disarmament and the regulation of armaments (Article 11.1); (7) to further respect for international law (Preamble) and encourage the progressive development of international law and its codification (Article 13.l.b).

Plainly, maintenance of peace and security was the crucial goal of the new entity. In 1939–45 the tension between force and law—endemic in the international community, as in any human grouping—had been magnified by the war. It had become clear that unless serious restraints were put on violence, the world would be heading for catastrophe. One should not believe, however, that the leaders were so naive as to think that in 1945 one could radically break with the approach so forcefully set forth by Bismarck in the nineteenth century, when he reportedly said that "the questions of our time will not be settled by resolutions and majority votes, but by blood and iron." Perhaps it was rather thought that, faced with two radically opposed methods for settling friction and disagreement, "bullets" or "words" (as Camus put it in 1947), one ought bravely to endeavour opting as much as possible for the latter, while however being aware that the former would continue to be used.

Let us take a quick glance at the structure of the new Organization and how the various organs were to pursue the goals set by the founding fathers (and mothers).

The SC and the GA are the two principal organs. The GA, consisting of all member States, each having one vote, was granted a very broad competence: it was authorized to discuss and pronounce upon any matter within the province of the Organization (subject to some procedural restraints whenever a question relating to peace and security is being handled by the SC: see Article 12). Its decisions "on important questions" (listed in Article 18.2) are made by a two-thirds majority of the members present and voting; others are taken instead by a majority of the members present and voting (Article 18.3). Its resolutions (recommendations, Declarations, etc.) may not be legally binding per se (except for decisions concerning the "internal life" of the Organization, such as those apportioning UN expenses among the member States (see Article 17.2), adopting rules of procedure (Article 21), establishing subsidiary organs (Article 22), electing members of the various other bodies, such as the SC, ECOSOC, etc., appointing the Secretary–General (Article 97), electing members of the ICJ) pursuant to Article 8 of the Court Statute, etc.).

The SC consists of 15 members, some permanent (the so-called Big Five: China, France, the UK, Russia, and the USA), others elected every two years by the GA. Its competence is "limited" to the maintenance of peace and security. Its decisions, except for those on procedural matters and on the election of members of the ICJ, may only be taken with an affirmative vote (or at least the abstention) of the five permanent members (hence, if one of the five votes against, the resolution may not be adopted; this is the so-called veto power: see Article 27.3). They are taken by a vote of nine members (those on the election of judges of the ICJ may be taken by a vote of eight members: see Article 10 of the ICJ Statute, requiring the absolute majority of members of the SC). They may either be recommendatory in nature, or legally binding, pursuant to Article 25. The SC was to be assisted and advised by the Military Staff Committee, consisting of the Chiefs of Staff of the permanent members; this body was to be responsible "under the SC" for the strategic direction of any armed forces placed at the disposal of the SC. What is even more important, the military contingents that under Articles 43–5 member States were to put at the disposal of the SC for enforcement action in case of threats to the peace, breaches of the peace or aggression, were to act under SC control.

These two organs are at the top of the Organization. Their principal instrumentality was to be the Secretariat, headed by a Secretary–General, appointed by the GA upon the recommendation of the SC (Article 97). Three other main organs were to fulfil specialized functions: in the field of economic and social co-operation, the Economic and Social Council (ECOSOC), in some colonial matters, the Trusteeship Council, and in matters concerning international legal disputes, the ICJ.

ECOSOC consists of 54 member States elected by the GA for three years: its main task is to discuss, propose, recommend, promote studies, co-ordinate the action of specialized agencies (such as the International Labour Organization (ILO), UNESCO, the Food and Agriculture Organization (FAO) the World Health Organization (WHO), etc.), set up subsidiary bodies (such as the Commission on Human Rights, established in 1946 on the strength of Article 68), etc. in the fields within its competence. * * *

The ICJ is the principal judicial organ of the UN, authorized to settle legal disputes between States by binding judgments, or to issue Advisory Opinions at the request of the principal organs of the UN, that is the SC, the GA, or any other organ or specialized agency authorized by the GA. The ICJ consists of 15 judges elected by the GA and the SC.

* * *

Admittedly, the UN Charter does not make for exciting reading. But since it is arguably the most important international law document of the 20th century (and the closest thing we have to a world constitution) you should force yourself to read it carefully at least once in your life (i.e., now). In doing so, you may want to compare it to a domestic constitution. What strikes you as familiar, and what strikes you as surprising? What is the basic structure of the United Nations and how is decision-making power distributed and allocated, i.e., who really calls the shots?

CHARTER OF THE UNITED NATIONS

(Adopted 1945; in force 1945)

PREAMBLE

WE THE PEOPLES OF THE UNITED NATIONS DETERMINED

to save succeeding generations from the scourge of war, which twice in our lifetime has brought untold sorrow to mankind, and

to reaffirm faith in fundamental human rights, in the dignity and worth of the human person, in the equal rights of men and women and of nations large and small, and

to establish conditions under which justice and respect for the obligations arising from treaties and other sources of international law can be maintained, and

to promote social progress and better standards of life in larger freedom,

AND FOR THESE ENDS

to practice tolerance and live together in peace with one another as good neighbors, and

to unite our strength to maintain international peace and security, and

to ensure by the acceptance of principles and the institution of methods, that armed force shall not be used, save in the common interest, and

to employ international machinery for the promotion of the economic and social advancement of all peoples,

HAVE RESOLVED TO COMBINE OUR EFFORTS TO ACCOMPLISH THESE AIMS.

Accordingly, our respective Governments, through representatives assembled in the city of San Francisco, who have exhibited their full powers found to be in good and due form, have agreed to the present Charter of the United Nations and do hereby establish an international organization to be known as the United Nations.

CHAPTER 1

Purposes and Principles

Article 1

The Purposes of the United Nations are:

1. To maintain international peace and security, and to that end: to take effective collective measures for the prevention and removal of threats to the peace, and for the suppression of acts of aggression or other breaches of the peace, and to bring about by peaceful means, and in conformity with the principles of justice and international law, adjustment or settlement of international disputes or situations which might lead to a breach of the peace;

2. To develop friendly relations among nations based on respect for the principle of equal rights and self-determination of peoples, and to take other appropriate measures to strengthen universal peace;

3. To achieve international cooperation in solving international problems of an economic, social, cultural, or humanitarian character, and in promoting and encouraging respect for human rights and for fundamental freedoms for all without distinction as to race, sex, language, or religion; and

4. To be a center for harmonizing the actions of nations in the attainment of these common ends.

Article 2

The Organization and its Members, in pursuit of the Purposes stated in Article 1, shall act in accordance with the following Principles.

1. The Organization is based on the principle of the sovereign equality of all its Members.

2. All Members, in order to ensure to all of them the rights and benefits resulting from membership, shall fulfill in good faith the obligations assumed by them in accordance with the present Charter.

3. All Members shall settle their international disputes by peaceful means in such a manner that international peace and security, and justice, are not endangered.

4. All Members shall refrain in their international relations from the threat or use of force against the territorial integrity or political inde-

pendence of any state, or in any other manner inconsistent with the Purposes of the United Nations.

5. All Members shall give the United Nations every assistance in any action it takes in accordance with the present Charter, and shall refrain from giving assistance to any state against which the United Nations is taking preventive or enforcement action.

6. The Organization shall ensure that states which are not Members of the United Nations act in accordance with these Principles so far as may be necessary for the maintenance of international peace and security.

7. Nothing contained in the present Charter shall authorize the United Nations to intervene in matters which are essentially within the domestic jurisdiction of any state or shall require the Members to submit such matters to settlement under the present Charter; but this principle shall not prejudice the application of enforcement measures under Chapter VII.

CHAPTER II

Membership

Article 3

The original Members of the United Nations shall be the states which, having participated in the United Nations Conference on International Organization at San Francisco, or having previously signed the Declaration by United Nations of January 1, 1942, sign the present Charter and ratify it in accordance with Article 110.

Article 4

1. Membership in the United Nations is open to all other peace-loving states which accept the obligations contained in the present Charter and, in the judgment of the Organization, are able and willing to carry out these obligations.

2. The admission of any such state to membership in the United Nations will be effected by a decision of the General Assembly upon the recommendation of the Security Council.

* * *

CHAPTER III

Organs

Article 7

1. There are established as the principal organs of the United Nations: a General Assembly, a Security Council, an Economic and Social Coun-

cil, a Trusteeship Council, an International Court of Justice, and a Secretariat.

2. Such subsidiary organs as may be found necessary may be established in accordance with the present Charter.

* * *

CHAPTER IV

The General Assembly

Article 9

Composition

1. The General Assembly shall consist of all the Members of the United Nations.

2. Each member shall have not more than five representatives in the General Assembly.

Functions and Powers

Article 10

The General Assembly may discuss any questions or any matters within the scope of the present Charter or relating to the powers and functions of any organs provided for in the present Charter, and, except as provided in Article 12, may make recommendations to the Members of the United Nations or to the Security Council or to both on any such questions or matters.

Article 11

1. The General Assembly may consider the general principles of cooperation in the maintenance of international peace and security, including the principles governing disarmament and the regulation of armaments, and may make recommendations with regard to such principles to the Members or to the Security Council or to both.

2. The General Assembly may discuss any questions relating to the maintenance of international peace and security brought before it by any Member of the United Nations, or by the Security Council, or by a state which is not a Member of the United Nations in accordance with Article 35, paragraph 2, and, except as provided in Article 12, may make recommendations with regard to any such questions to the state or states concerned or to the Security Council or to both. Any such question on which action is necessary shall be referred to the Security Council by the General Assembly either before or after discussion.

3. The General Assembly may call the attention of the Security Council to situations which are likely to endanger international peace and security.

4. The powers of the General Assembly set forth in this Article shall not limit the general scope of Article 10.

Article 12

1. While the Security Council is exercising in respect of any dispute or situation the functions assigned to it in the present Charter, the General Assembly shall not make any recommendation with regard to that dispute or situation unless the Security Council so requests.

2. The Secretary–General, with the consent of the Security Council, shall notify the General Assembly at each session of any matters relative to the maintenance of international peace and security which are being dealt with by the Security Council and shall similarly notify the General Assembly, or the Members of the United Nations if the General Assembly is not in session, immediately the Security Council ceases to deal with such matters.

Article 13

1. The General Assembly shall initiate studies and make recommendations for the purpose of: a. promoting international co-operation in the political field and encouraging the progressive development of international law and its codification; b. promoting international co-operation in the economic, social, cultural, educational, and health fields, and assisting in the realization of human rights and fundamental freedoms for all without distinction as to race, sex, language, or religion.

2. The further responsibilities, functions and powers of the General Assembly with respect to matters mentioned in paragraph 1 (b) above are set forth in Chapters IX and X.

* * *

Article 17

1. The General Assembly shall consider and approve the budget of the Organization.

2. The expenses of the Organization shall be borne by the Members as apportioned by the General Assembly.

3. The General Assembly shall consider and approve any financial and budgetary arrangements with specialized agencies referred to in Article 57 and shall examine the administrative budgets of such specialized agencies with a view to making recommendations to the agencies concerned.

Article 18

Voting

1. Each member of the General Assembly shall have one vote.

2. Decisions of the General Assembly on important questions shall be made by a two-thirds majority of the members present and voting. These questions shall include: recommendations with respect to the maintenance of international peace and security, the election of the non-permanent members of the Security Council, the election of the members of the Economic and Social Council, the election of members of the Trusteeship Council in accordance with paragraph 1(c) of Article 86, the admission of new Members to the United Nations, the suspension of the rights and privileges of membership, the expulsion of Members, questions relating to the operation of the trusteeship system, and budgetary questions.

3. Decisions on other questions, including the determination of additional categories of questions to be decided by a two-thirds majority, shall be made by a majority of the members present and voting.

* * *

CHAPTER V

The Security Council

Article 23

1. The Security Council shall consist of fifteen Members of the United Nations. The Republic of China, France, the Union of Soviet Socialist Republics, the United Kingdom of Great Britain and Northern Ireland, and the United States of America shall be permanent members of the Security Council. The General Assembly shall elect ten other Members of the United Nations to be non-permanent members of the Security Council, due regard being specially paid, in the first instance to the contribution of Members of the United Nations to the maintenance of international peace and security and to the other purposes of the Organization, and also to equitable geographical distribution.

2. The non-permanent members of the Security Council shall be elected for a term of two years. In the first election of the non-permanent members after the increase of the membership of the Security Council from eleven to fifteen, two of the four additional members shall be chosen for a term of one year. A retiring member shall not be eligible for immediate re-election.

3. Each member of the Security Council shall have one representative.

Article 24

Functions and Powers

1. In order to ensure prompt and effective action by the United Nations, its Members confer on the Security Council primary responsibility for the maintenance of international peace and security, and agree that in

carrying out its duties under this responsibility the Security Council acts on their behalf.

2. In discharging these duties the Security Council shall act in accordance with the Purposes and Principles of the United Nations. The specific powers granted to the Security Council for the discharge of these duties are laid down in Chapters VI, VII, VIII, and XII.

3. The Security Council shall submit annual and, when necessary, special reports to the General Assembly for its consideration.

Article 25

The Members of the United Nations agree to accept and carry out the decisions of the Security Council in accordance with the present Charter.

* * *

Article 27

Voting

1. Each member of the Security Council shall have one vote.

2. Decisions of the Security Council on procedural matters shall be made by an affirmative vote of nine members.

3. Decisions of the Security Council on all other matters shall be made by an affirmative vote of nine members including the concurring votes of the permanent members; provided that, in decisions under Chapter VI, and under paragraph 3 of Article 52, a party to a dispute shall abstain from voting.

* * *

CHAPTER VI

Pacific Settlement of Disputes

Article 33

1. The parties to any dispute, the continuance of which is likely to endanger the maintenance of international peace and security, shall, first of all, seek a solution by negotiation, enquiry, mediation, conciliation, arbitration, judicial settlement, resort to regional agencies or arrangements, or other peaceful means of their own choice.

2. The Security Council shall, when it deems necessary, call upon the parties to settle their dispute by such means.

* * *

CHAPTER VII

Action with Respect to Threats to the Peace, Breaches of the Peace, and Acts of Aggression

Article 39

The Security Council shall determine the existence of any threat to the peace, breach of the peace, or act of aggression and shall make recommendations, or decide what measures shall be taken in accordance with Articles 41 and 42, to maintain or restore international peace and security.

* * *

Article 41

The Security Council may decide what measures not involving the use of armed force are to be employed to give effect to its decisions, and it may call upon the Members of the United Nations to apply such measures. These may include complete or partial interruption of economic relations and of rail, sea, air, postal, telegraphic, radio, and other means of communication, and the severance of diplomatic relations.

Article 42

Should the Security Council consider that measures provided for in Article 41 would be inadequate or have proved to be inadequate, it may take such action by air, sea, or land forces as may be necessary to maintain or restore international peace and security. Such action may include demonstrations, blockade, and other operations by air, sea, or land forces of Members of the United Nations.

* * *

Article 51

Nothing in the present Charter shall impair the inherent right of individual or collective self-defense if an armed attack occurs against a Member of the United Nations, until the Security Council has taken measures necessary to maintain international peace and security. Measures taken by Members in the exercise of this right of self-defense shall be immediately reported to the Security Council and shall not in any way affect the authority and responsibility of the Security Council under the present Charter to take at any time such action as it deems necessary in order to maintain or restore international peace and security.

CHAPTER VIII

Regional Arrangements

Article 52

1. Nothing in the present Charter precludes the existence of regional arrangements or agencies for dealing with such matters relating to the maintenance of international peace and security as are appropriate for regional action, provided that such arrangements or agencies and their activities are consistent with the Purposes and Principles of the United Nations.

* * *

CHAPTER IX

International Economic and Social Co-operation

Article 55

With a view to the creation of conditions of stability and well-being which are necessary for peaceful and friendly relations among nations based on respect for the principle of equal rights and self-determination of peoples, the United Nations shall promote:

a. higher standards of living, full employment, and conditions of economic and social progress and development;

b. solutions of international economic, social, health, and related problems; and international cultural and educational co-operation; and

c. universal respect for, and observance of, human rights and fundamental freedoms for all without distinction as to race, sex, language, or religion.

* * *

CHAPTER X

The Economic and Social Council

Article 61

Composition

1. The Economic and Social Council shall consist of fifty-four Members of the United Nations elected by the General Assembly.

* * *

Article 62

Functions and Powers

1. The Economic and Social Council may make or initiate studies and reports with respect to international economic, social, cultural, educational, health, and related matters and may make recommendations with respect to any such matters to the General Assembly, to the Members of the United Nations, and to the specialized agencies concerned.

2. It may make recommendations for the purpose of promoting respect for, and observance of, human rights and fundamental freedoms for all.

3. It may prepare draft conventions for submission to the General Assembly, with respect to matters falling within its competence.

4. It may call, in accordance with the rules prescribed by the United Nations, international conferences on matters falling within its competence.

* * *

Article 71

The Economic and Social Council may make suitable arrangements for consultation with non-governmental organizations which are concerned with matters within its competence. Such arrangements may be made with international organizations and, where appropriate, with national organizations after consultation with the Member of the United Nations concerned.

* * *

CHAPTER XIV

The International Court of Justice

Article 92

The International Court of Justice shall be the principal judicial organ of the United Nations. It shall function in accordance with the annexed Statute which is based upon the Statute of the Permanent Court of International Justice and forms an integral part of the present Charter.

Article 93

1. All Members of the United Nations are ipso facto parties to the Statute of the International Court of Justice.

2. A state which is not a Member of the United Nations may become a party to the Statute of the International Court of Justice on conditions to be determined in each case by the General Assembly upon the recommendation of the Security Council.

Article 94

1. Each Member of the United Nations undertakes to comply with the decision of the International Court of Justice in any case to which it is a party.

2. If any party to a case fails to perform the obligations incumbent upon it under a judgment rendered by the Court, the other party may have recourse to the Security Council, which may, if it deems necessary, make recommendations or decide upon measures to be taken to give effect to the judgment.

Article 95

Nothing in the present Charter shall prevent Members of the United Nations from entrusting the solution of their differences to other tribunals by virtue of agreements already in existence or which may be concluded in the future.

Article 96

1. The General Assembly or the Security Council may request the International Court of Justice to give an advisory opinion on any legal question.

2. Other organs of the United Nations and specialized agencies, which may at any time be so authorized by the General Assembly, may also request advisory opinions of the Court on legal questions arising within the scope of their activities.

CHAPTER XV

The Secretariat

Article 97

The Secretariat shall comprise a Secretary–General and such staff as the Organization may require. The Secretary–General shall be appointed by the General Assembly upon the recommendation of the Security Council. He shall be the chief administrative officer of the Organization.

* * *

CHAPTER XVI

Miscellaneous Provisions

* * *

Article 103

In the event of a conflict between the obligations of the Members of the United Nations under the present Charter and their obligations under any other international agreement, their obligations under the present Charter shall prevail.

Article 104

The Organization shall enjoy in the territory of each of its Members such legal capacity as may be necessary for the exercise of its functions and the fulfillment of its purposes.

Article 105

1. The Organization shall enjoy in the territory of each of its Members such privileges and immunities as are necessary for the fulfillment of its purposes.

2. Representatives of the Members of the United Nations and officials of the Organization shall similarly enjoy such privileges and immunities as are necessary for the independent exercise of their functions in connection with the Organization.

3. The General Assembly may make recommendations with a view to determining the details of the application of paragraphs 1 and 2 of this Article or may propose conventions to the Members of the United Nations for this purpose.

* * *

CHAPTER XIX

Ratification and Signature

Article 110

1. The present Charter shall be ratified by the signatory states in accordance with their respective constitutional processes.

2. The ratifications shall be deposited with the Government of the United States of America, which shall notify all the signatory states of each deposit as well as the Secretary–General of the Organization when he has been appointed.

3. The present Charter shall come into force upon the deposit of ratifications by the Republic of China, France, the Union of Soviet Socialist Republics, the United Kingdom of Great Britain and Northern Ireland, and the United States of America, and by a majority of the other signatory states. A protocol of the ratifications deposited shall thereupon be drawn up by the Government of the United States of America which shall communicate copies thereof to all the signatory states.

4. The states signatory to the present Charter which ratify it after it has come into force will become original Members of the United Nations on the date of the deposit of their respective ratifications.

Article 111

The present Charter, of which the Chinese, French, Russian, English, and Spanish texts are equally authentic, shall remain deposited in the archives of the Government of the United States of America. Duly certified copies thereof shall be transmitted by that Government to the Governments of the other signatory states.

IN FAITH WHEREOF the representatives of the Governments of the United Nations have signed the present Charter.

DONE at the city of San Francisco the twenty-sixth day of June, one thousand nine hundred and forty-five.

What did the United States do 41 days after signing a treaty calling for "international cooperation * * * in promoting and encouraging respect for human rights" (Article 1(3)) and requiring that its members "shall settle their international disputes by peaceful means" (Article 2(3))? How does that action square with the purpose and principles of the UN Charter?

What does the following decision tell us about the character of the United Nations? It is generally considered a landmark decision. Why?

REPARATION FOR INJURIES SUFFERED IN THE SERVICE OF THE UNITED NATIONS (ADVISORY OPINION)

International Court of Justice
1949 I.C.J. 174

THE COURT gives the following advisory opinion:

On December 3rd, 1948, the General Assembly of the United Nations adopted the following Resolution:

Whereas the series of tragic events which have lately befallen agents of the United Nations engaged in the performance of their duties raises, with greater urgency than ever, the question of the arrangements to be made by the United Nations with a view to ensuring to its agents the fullest measure of protection in the future and ensuring that reparation be made for the injuries suffered; and

Whereas it is highly desirable that the Secretary–General should be able to act without question as efficaciously as possible with a view to obtaining any reparation due; therefore

The General Assembly

Decides to submit the following legal questions to the International Court of Justice for an advisory opinion:

I.   In the event of an agent of the United Nations in the performance of his duties suffering injury in circumstances involving the responsibility of a State, has the United Nations, as an Organization, the capacity to bring an international claim against the responsible de jure or de facto government with a view to obtaining the reparation due in respect of the damage caused (a) to the United Nations, (b) to the victim or to persons entitled through him?

II.   In the event of an affirmative reply on point I (b), how is action by the United Nations to be reconciled with such rights as may be possessed by the State of which the victim is a national?

* * *

The first question asked of the Court is as follows:

"In the event of an agent of the United Nations in the performance of his duties suffering injury in circumstances involving the responsibility of a State, has the United Nations, as an Organization, the capacity to bring an international claim against the responsible de jure or de facto government with a view to obtaining the reparation due in respect of the damage caused (a) to the United Nations, (b) to the victim or to persons entitled through him?"

It will be useful to make the following preliminary observations:

(a) The Organization of the United Nations will be referred to usually, but not invariably, as "the Organization."

(b) Questions I (a) and I (b) refer to "an international claim against the responsible de jure or de facto government." The Court understands that these questions are directed to claims against a State, and will, therefore, in this opinion, use the expression "State" or "defendant State."

(c) The Court understands the word "agent" in the most liberal sense, that is to say, any person who, whether a paid official or not, and whether permanently employed or not, has been charged by an organ of the Organization with carrying out, or helping to carry out, one of its functions—in short, any person through whom it acts.

(d) As this question assumes an injury suffered in such circumstances as to involve a State's responsibility, it must be supposed, for the purpose of this Opinion, that the damage results from a failure by the State to perform obligations of which the purpose is to protect the agents of the Organization in the performance of their duties.

(e) The position of a defendant State which is not a member of the Organization is dealt with later, and for the present the Court will assume that the defendant State is a Member of the Organization.

* * *

The questions asked of the Court relate to the "capacity to bring an international claim;" accordingly, we must begin by defining what is meant by that capacity, and consider the characteristics of the Organization, so as to determine whether, in general, these characteristics do, or do not, include for the Organization a right to present an international claim.

Competence to bring an international claim is, for those possessing it, the capacity to resort to the customary methods recognized by international law for the establishment, the presentation and the settlement of claims. Among these methods may be mentioned protest, request for an enquiry, negotiation, and request for submission to an arbitral tribunal or to the Court in so far as this may be authorized by the Statute.

This capacity certainly belongs to the State; a State can bring an international claim against another State. Such a claim takes the form of a claim between two political entities, equal in law, similar in form, and both the direct subjects of international law. It is dealt with by means of negotiation, and cannot, in the present state of the law as to international jurisdiction, be submitted to a tribunal, except with the consent of the States concerned.

When the Organization brings a claim against one of its Members, this claim will be presented in the same manner, and regulated by the same procedure. It may, when necessary, be supported by the political means at the disposal of the Organization. In these ways the Organization would find a method for securing the observance of its rights by the Member against which it has a claim.

But, in the international sphere, has the Organization such a nature as involves the capacity to bring an international claim? In order to answer this question, the Court must first enquire whether the Charter has given the Organization such a position that it possesses, in regard to its Members, rights which it is entitled to ask them to respect. In other words, does the Organization possess international personality? This is no doubt a doctrinal expression, which has sometimes given rise to controversy. But it will be used here to mean that if the Organization is recognized as having that personality, it is an entity capable of availing itself of obligations incumbent upon its Members.

To answer this question, which is not settled by the actual terms of the Charter, we must consider what characteristics it was intended thereby to give to the Organization.

The subjects of law in any legal system are not necessarily identical in their nature or in the extent of their rights, and their nature depends upon the needs of the community. Throughout its history, the development of international law has been influenced by the requirements of international life, and the progressive increase in the collective activities of States has already given rise to instances of action upon the international plane by certain entities which are not States. This development culminated in the establishment in June 1945 of an international organization whose purposes and principles are specified in the Charter of the United Nations. But to achieve these ends the attribution of international personality is indispensable.

The Charter has not been content to make the Organization created by it merely a centre "for harmonizing the actions of nations in the attainment of these common ends" (Article I, para. 4). It has equipped that centre with organs, and has given it special tasks. It has defined the position of the Members in relation to the Organization by requiring them to give it every assistance in any action undertaken by it (Article 2, para. 5), and to accept and carry out the decisions of the Security Council; by authorizing the General Assembly to make recommendations to the Members; by giving the Organization legal capacity and privileges and immunities in the territory of each of its Members; and by providing for the conclusion of agreements between the Organization and its Members. Practice—in particular the conclusion of conventions to which the Organization is a party—has confirmed this character of the Organization, which occupies a position in certain respects in detachment from its Members, and which is under a duty to remind them, if need be, of certain obligations. It must be added that the Organization is a political body, charged with political tasks of an important character, and covering a wide field namely, the maintenance of international peace and security, the development of friendly relations among nations, and the achievement of international co-operation in the solution of problems of an economic, social, cultural or humanitarian character (Article 1); and in dealing with its Members it employs political means. The "Convention on the Privileges and Immunities of the United Nations" of 1946 creates rights and duties between each of the signatories and the Organization (see, in particular, Section 35). It is difficult to see how such a convention could operate except upon the international plane and as between parties possessing international personality.

In the opinion of the Court, the Organization was intended to exercise and enjoy, and is in fact exercising and enjoying, functions and rights which can only be explained on the basis of the possession of a large measure of international personality and the capacity to operate upon an international plane. It is at present the supreme type of international organization, and it could not carry out the intentions of its founders if it was devoid of international personality. It must be acknowledged that its Members, by entrusting certain functions to it, with the attendant duties and responsibilities, have clothed it with the competence required to enable those functions to be effectively discharged.

Accordingly, the Court has come to the conclusion that the Organization is an international person. That is not the same thing as saying that it is a State, which it certainly is not, or that its legal personality and rights and duties are the same as those of a State. Still less is it the same thing as saying that it is "a super-State," whatever that expression may mean. It does not even imply that all its rights and duties must be upon the international plane, any more than all the rights and duties of a State must be upon that plane. What it does mean is that it is a subject of international law and capable of possessing international rights and duties, and that it has capacity to maintain its rights by bringing international claims.

The next question is whether the sum of the international rights of the Organization comprises the right to bring the kind of international claim described in the Request for this Opinion. That is a claim against a State to obtain reparation in respect of the damage caused by the injury of an agent of the Organization in the course of the performance of his duties. Whereas a State possesses the totality of international rights and duties recognized by international law, the rights and duties of an entity such as the Organization must depend upon its purposes and functions as specified or implied in its constituent documents and developed in practice. The functions of the Organization are of such a character that they could not be effectively discharged if they involved the concurrent action, on the international plane, of fifty-eight or more Foreign Offices, and the Court concludes that the Members have endowed the Organization with capacity to bring international claims when necessitated by the discharge of its functions.

* * *

Question I (b) is as follows:

* * * "has the United Nations, as an Organization, the capacity to bring an international claim * * * in respect of the damage caused. * * * (b) to the victim or to persons entitled through him?"

The traditional rule that diplomatic protection is exercised by the national State does not involve the giving of a negative answer to Question I (b).

* * *The Court is here faced with a new situation. The questions to which it gives rise can only be solved by realizing that the situation is dominated by the provisions of the Charter considered in the light of the principles of international law.

The question lies within the limits already established; that is to say it presupposes that the injury for which the reparation is demanded arises from a breach of an obligation designed to help an agent of the Organization in the performance of his duties. It is not a case in which the wrongful act or omission would merely constitute a breach of the general obligations of a State concerning the position of aliens; claims made under this head would be within the competence of the national State and not, as a general rule, within that of the Organization.

The Charter does not expressly confer upon the Organization the capacity to include, in its claim for reparation, damage caused to the victim or to persons entitled through him. The Court must therefore begin by enquiring whether the provisions of the Charter concerning the functions of the Organization, and the part played by its agents in the performance of those functions, imply for the Organization power to afford its agents the limited protection that would consist in the bringing of a claim on their behalf for reparation for damage suffered in such circumstances. Under international law, the Organization must be deemed to have those powers which, though not expressly provided in the Charter, are conferred upon it by necessary implication as being essential to the performance of its duties. This principle of law was applied by the Permanent Court of International Justice to the International Labour Organization in its Advisory Opinion No. 13 of July 23rd, 1926 (Series B., No. 13, p. 18), and must be applied to the United Nations.

Having regard to its purposes and functions already referred to, the Organization may find it necessary, and has in fact found it necessary, to entrust its agents with important missions to be performed in disturbed parts of the world. Many missions, from their very nature, involve the agents in unusual dangers to which ordinary persons are not exposed. For the same reason, the injuries suffered by its agents in these circumstances will sometimes have occurred in such a manner that their national State would not be justified in bringing a claim for reparation on the ground of diplomatic protection, or, at any rate, would not feel disposed to do so. Both to ensure the efficient and independent performance of these missions and to afford effective support to its agents, the Organization must provide them with adequate protection.

This need of protection for the agents of the Organization, as a condition of the performance of its functions, has already been realized, and the Preamble to the Resolution of December 3rd, 1948 (supra, p. 175), shows that this was the unanimous view of the General Assembly.

For this purpose, the Members of the Organization have entered into certain undertakings, some of which are in the Charter and others in complementary agreements. The content of these undertakings need not be described here; but the Court must stress the importance of the duty to render to the Organization "every assistance" which is accepted by the Members in Article 2, paragraph 5, of the Charter. It must be noted that the effective working of the Organization—the accomplishment of its task, and the independence and effectiveness of the work of its agents—require that these undertakings should be strictly observed. For that purpose, it is necessary that, when an infringement occurs, the Organization should be able to call upon the responsible State to remedy its default, and, in particular, to obtain from the State reparation for the damage that the default may have caused to its agent.

In order that the agent may perform his duties satisfactorily, he must feel that this protection is assured to him by the Organization, and that he may count on it. To ensure the independence of the agent, and, consequently, the independent action of the Organization itself, it is essential that in performing his duties he need not have to rely on any other protection than that of the Organization (save of course for the more direct and immediate protection due from the State in whose territory he may be). In particular, he should not have to rely on the protection of his own State. If he had to rely on that State, his independence might well be compromised, contrary to the principle applied by Article 100 of the Charter. And lastly, it is essential that—whether the agent belongs to a powerful or to a weak State; to one more affected or less affected by the complications of international life; to one in sympathy or not in sympathy with the mission of the agent—he should know that in the performance of his duties he is under the protection of the Organization. This assurance is even more necessary when the agent is stateless.

Upon examination of the character of the functions entrusted to the Organization and of the nature of the missions of its agents, it becomes clear that the capacity of the Organization to exercise a measure of functional protection of its agents arises by necessary intendment out of the Charter.

The obligations entered into by States to enable the agents of the Organization to perform their duties are undertaken not in the interest of the agents, but in that of the Organization. When it claims redress for a breach of these obligations, the Organization is invoking its own right, the right that the obligations due to it should be respected. On this ground, it asks for reparation of the injury suffered, for "it is a principle of international law that the breach of an engagement involves an obligation to make reparation in an adequate form;" as was stated by the Permanent Court in its Judgment No. 8 of July 26th, 1927 (Series A., No. 9, p. 21). In claiming reparation based on the injury suffered by its agent, the Organization does not represent the agent, but is asserting its own right, the right to secure respect for undertakings entered into towards the Organization.

Having regard to the foregoing considerations, and to the undeniable right of the Organization to demand that its Members shall fulfil the obligations entered into by them in the interest of the good working of the Organization, the Court is of the opinion that, in the case of a breach of these obligations, the Organization has the capacity to claim adequate reparation, and that in assessing this reparation it is authorized to include the damage suffered by the victim or by persons entitled through him.

* * *

The question remains whether the Organization has "the capacity to bring an international claim against the responsible de jure or de facto government with a view to obtaining the reparation due in respect of the damage caused (a) to the United Nations, (b) to the victim or to persons entitled through him" when the defendant State is not a member of the Organization.

In considering this aspect of Question I (a) and (b), it is necessary to keep in mind the reasons which have led the Court to give an affirmative answer to it when the defendant State is a Member of the Organization. It has now been established that the Organization has capacity to bring claims on the international plane, and that it possesses a right of functional protection in respect of its agents. Here again the Court is authorized to assume that the damage suffered involves the responsibility of a State, and it is not called upon to express an opinion upon the various ways in which that responsibility might be engaged. Accordingly the question is whether the Organization has capacity to bring a claim against the defendant State to recover reparation in respect of that damage or whether, on the contrary, the defendant State, not being a member, is justified in raising the objection that the Organization lacks the capacity to bring an international claim. On this point, the Court's opinion is that fifty States, representing the vast majority of the members of the international community, had the power, in conformity with international law, to bring into being an entity possessing objective international personality, and not merely personality recognized by them alone, together with capacity to bring international claims.

Accordingly, the Court arrives at the conclusion that an affirmative answer should be given to Question I (a) and (b) whether or not the defendant State is a Member of the United Nations.

* * *

Question II is as follows:

"In the event of an affirmative reply on point I (b), how is action by the United Nations to be reconciled with such rights as may be possessed by the State of which the victim is a national?"

The affirmative reply given by the Court on point I (b) obliges it now to examine Question II. When the victim has a nationality, cases can clearly occur in which the injury suffered by him may engage the interest both of his national State and of the Organization. In such an event, competition between the State's right of diplomatic protection and the Organization's right of functional protection might arise, and this is the only case with which the Court is invited to deal.

In such a case, there is no rule of law which assigns priority to the one or to the other, or which compels either the State or the Organization to refrain from bringing an international claim. The Court sees no reason why the parties concerned should not find solutions inspired by goodwill and common sense, and as between the Organization and its Members it draws attention to their duty to render "every assistance" provided by Article 2, paragraph 5, of the Charter.

Although the bases of the two claims are different, that does not mean that the defendant State can be compelled to pay the reparation due in respect of the damage twice over. International tribunals are already familiar with the problem of a claim in which two or more national States are interested, and they know how to protect the defendant State in such a case.

The risk of competition between the Organization and the national State can be reduced or eliminated either by a general convention or by agreements entered into in each particular case. There is no doubt that in due course a practice will be developed, and it is worthy of note that already certain States whose nationals have been injured in the performance of missions undertaken for the Organization have shown a reasonable and co-operative disposition to find a practical solution.

* * *

The question of reconciling action by the Organization with the rights of a national State may arise in another way; that is to say, when the agent bears the nationality of the defendant State.

The ordinary practice whereby a State does not exercise protection on behalf of one of its nationals against a State which regards him as its own national, does not constitute a precedent which is relevant here. The action of the Organization is in fact based not upon the nationality of the victim but upon his status as agent of the Organization. Therefore it does not matter whether or not the State to which the claim is addressed regards him as its own national, because the question of nationality is not pertinent to the admissibility of the claim.

In law, therefore, it does not seem that the fact of the possession of the nationality of the defendant State by the agent constitutes any obstacle to a claim brought by the Organization for a breach of obligations towards it occurring in relation to the performance of his mission by that agent.

* * *

NOTE ON THE "CERTAIN EXPENSES" CASE

In 1962, the International Court of Justice issued another important opinion concerning the status of the UN, this time vis-à-vis its member states: Certain Expenses of the United Nations, 1962 I.C.J. 151.

In 1960, the General Assembly (rather than the Security Council) had deployed peacekeeping forces in the Congo and in the Middle East. France and the Soviet Union argued that the General Assembly lacked the power to do so under the Charter and thus refused to pay their allotted share of the expenses. In an advisory opinion, the ICJ stated that the General Assembly did have that power and that the member states thus had to pay.

Particularly important in the current context was the Court's view that member states could not challenge UN activities merely based on the *internal power allocation rules* (e.g., General Assembly v. Security Council). They could only argue that an activity was completely *ultra vires* of the organization as a whole, i.e., beyond the scope of the Charter.

In essence that means that once a state has joined the UN, it has no right to refuse to cooperate because it disagrees with a UN decision—even if it thinks that the decision was taken by the wrong organ. To put it more bluntly: once you've joined, you have to go along (or, perhaps, get out).

What are the implications of the *Certain Expenses* case for traditional conceptions of sovereignty?

B. THE PURPOSES, STRUCTURES, AND POWERS OF INTERNATIONAL ORGANIZATIONS: COMPARING THE UN, OECD AND WTO

The objective of this subchapter is to convey a broader sense of international organizations (IOs) by comparing a few of them—the UN, the OECD and the WTO—on the basis of their founding documents. The exercise of reading through these treaties may feel cumbersome, but the ability to work with such documents is among the skill sets you are learning in this course. It is also necessary in order to compare these documents, i.e., to identify the similarities and differences among them. In doing so, ask yourself the following questions:

1. Why do we have IOs? What is their purpose? (See UN Art. 1; OECD Preamble, Art. 1; WTO Preamble, Art. III)

2. Why do states and other entities join them and what are the costs of joining?

3. How do IOs come into being and what is their legal status? (See UN Arts. 104, 110; OECD Art. 19; WTO Art. VIII)

4. Who can be a member of these IOs? Is membership defined globally, regionally, by subject matter, or by a combination of these (and other?) criteria? (See UN Arts. 3, 4; OECD Arts. 4, 16; WTO Arts. XI, XII)

5. What are the principal organs? Is there a standard pattern? (See UN Art. 7; OECD Arts. 7–11; WTO Arts. IV, VI)

6. How do IOs make decisions? By (qualified?) majority? Consensus? How do votes count? Are IOs (internally) "democratic"? (See UN Arts. 18, 27; OECD Art. 6; WTO Art. IX)

7. What underlying facts and considerations do the voting structures and procedures reflect?

The Organization for Economic Cooperation and Development (OECD)

The OECD, founded in 1961, was originally established to further the political and economic reconstruction of a stable international order after World War II. More recently, the focus has shifted to furthering economic progress in the developing world. The OECD provides a forum for policy discussion, makes policy recommendations and conducts research in areas within its mandate including economic, environmental, and educational issues.

The OECD has more than 30 members, including the United States, most of the countries of continental Europe and the United Kingdom, as well as Australia, Canada, Chile, Israel, Japan, Korea, Mexico, New Zealand, and Turkey. Notably, several of the most powerful emerging economies are not members of the OECD, though Brazil, China, India, Indonesia, and South Africa are states with which the OECD has a program of "enhanced engagement." The OECD focuses primarily on fostering economic development through a broad range of incentive programs and various forms of technical assistance. In the area of international law making, a major achievement of the OECD is the Anti-Bribery Convention of 1997. In addition, the OECD has been active in fighting corruption and money laundering on an international scale.

CONVENTION ON THE ORGANISATION FOR ECONOMIC CO–OPERATION AND DEVELOPMENT
(Adopted 1960; in force 1961)

THE GOVERNMENTS of the Republic of Austria, the Kingdom of Belgium, Canada, the Kingdom of Denmark, the French Republic, the Federal Republic of Germany, the Kingdom of Greece, the Republic of Iceland, Ireland, the Italian Republic, the Grand Duchy of Luxembourg, the Kingdom of the Netherlands, the Kingdom of Norway, the Portuguese Republic, Spain, the Kingdom of Sweden, the Swiss Confederation, the Turkish

Republic, the United Kingdom of Great Britain and Northern Ireland, and the United States of America;

CONSIDERING that economic strength and prosperity are essential for the attainment of the purposes of the United Nations, the preservation of individual liberty and the increase of general well-being;

BELIEVING that they can further these aims most effectively by strengthening the tradition of co-operation which has evolved among them;

RECOGNISING that the economic recovery and progress of Europe to which their participation in the Organisation for European Economic Co-operation has made a major contribution, have opened new perspectives for strengthening that tradition and applying it to new tasks and broader objectives;

CONVINCED that broader co-operation will make a vital contribution to peaceful and harmonious relations among the peoples of the world;

RECOGNISING the increasing interdependence of their economies;

DETERMINED by consultation and co-operation to use more effectively their capacities and potentialities so as to promote the highest sustainable growth of their economies and improve the economic and social well-being of their peoples;

BELIEVING that the economically more advanced nations should co-operate in assisting to the best of their ability the countries in process of economic development;

RECOGNISING that the further expansion of world trade is one of the most important factors favouring the economic development of countries and the improvement of international economic relations; and

DETERMINED to pursue these purposes in a manner consistent with their obligations in other international organisations or institutions in which they participate or under agreements to which they are a party;

HAVE THEREFORE AGREED on the following provisions for the re-constitution of the Organisation for European Economic Co-operation as the Organisation for Economic Co-operation and Development:

Article 1

The aims of the Organisation for Economic Co-operation and Development (hereinafter called the "Organisation") shall be to promote policies designed:

(a) to achieve the highest sustainable economic growth and employment and a rising standard of living in Member countries, while maintaining financial stability, and thus to contribute to the development of the world economy;

(b) to contribute to sound economic expansion in Member as well as non-member countries in the process of economic development; and

(c) to contribute to the expansion of world trade on a multilateral, non-discriminatory basis in accordance with international obligations.

Article 2

In the pursuit of these aims, the Members agree that they will, both individually and jointly:

(a) promote the efficient use of their economic resources;

(b) in the scientific and technological field, promote the development of their resources, encourage research and promote vocational training;

(c) pursue policies designed to achieve economic growth and internal and external financial stability and to avoid developments which might endanger their economies or those of other countries;

(d) pursue their efforts to reduce or abolish obstacles to the exchange of goods and services and current payments and maintain and extend the liberalisation of capital movements; and

(e) contribute to the economic development of both Member and non-member countries in the process of economic development by appropriate means and, in particular, by the flow of capital to those countries, having regard to the importance to their economies of receiving technical assistance and of securing expanding export markets.

Article 3

With a view to achieving the aims set out in Article 1 and to fulfilling the undertakings contained in Article 2, the Members agree that they will:

(a) keep each other informed and furnish the Organisation with the information necessary for the accomplishment of its tasks;

(b) consult together on a continuing basis, carry out studies and participate in agreed projects; and

(c) co-operate closely and where appropriate take co-ordinated action.

Article 4

The Contracting Parties to this Convention shall be Members of the Organisation.

Article 5

In order to achieve its aims, the Organisation may:

(a) take decisions which, except as otherwise provided, shall be binding on all the Members;

(b) make recommendations to Members; and

(c) enter into agreements with Members, non-member States and international organisations.

Article 6

1. Unless the Organisation otherwise agrees unanimously for special cases, decisions shall be taken and recommendations shall be made by mutual agreement of all the Members.

2. Each Member shall have one vote. If a Member abstains from voting on a decision or recommendation, such abstention shall not invalidate the decision or recommendation, which shall be applicable to the other Members but not to the abstaining Member.

3. No decision shall be binding on any Member until it has complied with the requirements of its own constitutional procedures. The other Members may agree that such a decision shall apply provisionally to them.

Article 7

A Council composed of all the Members shall be the body from which all acts of the Organisation derive. The Council may meet in sessions of Ministers or of Permanent Representatives.

Article 8

The Council shall designate each year a Chairman, who shall preside at its ministerial sessions, and two Vice-Chairmen. The Chairman may be designated to serve one additional consecutive term.

Article 9

The Council may establish an Executive Committee and such subsidiary bodies as may be required for the achievement of the aims of the Organisation.

Article 10

1. A Secretary–General responsable to the Council shall be appointed by the Council for a term of five years. He shall be assisted by one or more Deputy Secretaries–General or Assistant Secretaries–General appointed by the Council on the recommendation of the Secretary–General.

2. The Secretary–General shall serve as Chairman of the Council meeting at sessions of Permanent Representatives. He shall assist the Council in all appropriate ways and may submit proposals to the Council or to any other body of the Organisation.

Article 11

1. The Secretary–General shall appoint such staff as the Organisation may require in accordance with plans of organisation approved by the Council. Staff regulations shall be subject to approval by the Council.

2. Having regard to the international character of the Organisation, the Secretary–General, the Deputy or Assistant Secretaries–General and the staff shall neither seek nor receive instructions from any of the Members or from any Government or authority external to the Organisation.

Article 12

Upon such terms and conditions as the Council may determine, the Organisation may:

(a) address communications to non-member States or organisations;

(b) establish and maintain relations with non-member States or organisations; and

(c) invite non-member Governments or organisations to participate in activities of the Organisation.

Article 13

Representation in the Organisation of the European Communities established by the Treaties of Paris and Rome of 18th April, 1951, and 25th March, 1957, shall be as defined in Supplementary Protocol No. 1 to this Convention.

Article 14

1. This Convention shall be ratified or accepted by the Signatories in accordance with their respective constitutional requirements.

2. Instruments of ratification or acceptance shall be deposited with the Government of the French Republic, hereby designated as depositary Government.

3. This Convention shall come into force:

   (a) before 30th September, 1961, upon the deposit of instruments of ratification or acceptance by all the Signatories; or

   (b) on 30th September, 1961, if by that date fifteen Signatories or more have deposited such instruments as regards those Signatories; and thereafter as regards any other Signatory upon the deposit of its instrument of ratification or acceptance;

   (c) after 30th September, 1961, but not later than two years from the signature of this Convention, upon the deposit of such instruments by fifteen Signatories, as regards those Signatories; and thereafter as regards any other Signatory upon the deposit of its instrument of ratification or acceptance.

4. Any Signatory which has not deposited its instrument of ratification or acceptance when the Convention comes into force may take part in the activities of the Organisation upon conditions to be determined by agreement between the Organisation and such Signatory.

Article 15

When this Convention comes into force the reconstitution of the Organisation for European Economic Co-operation shall take effect, and its aims, organs, powers and name shall thereupon be as provided herein. The legal personality possessed by the Organisation for European Economic Co-operation shall continue in the Organisation, but decisions, recommendations and resolutions of the Organisation for European Economic Co-operation shall require approval of the Council to be effective after the coming into force of this Convention.

Article 16

The Council may decide to invite any Government prepared to assume the obligations of membership to accede to this Convention. Such decisions shall be unanimous, provided that for any particular case the Council may unanimously decide to permit abstention, in which case, notwithstanding the provisions of Article 6, the decision shall be applicable to all the Members. Accession shall take effect upon the deposit of an instrument of accession with the depositary Government.

Article 17

Any Contracting Party may terminate the application of this Convention to itself by giving twelve months' notice to that effect to the depositary Government.

Article 18

The Headquarters of the Organisation shall be in Paris, unless the Council agrees otherwise.

Article 19

The legal capacity of the Organisation and the privileges, exemptions, and immunities of the Organisation, its officials and representatives to it of the Members shall be as provided in Supplementary Protocol No. 2 to this Convention.

Article 20

1. Each year, in accordance with Financial Regulations adopted by the Council, the Secretary–General shall present to the Council for approval an annual budget, accounts, and such subsidiary budgets as the Council shall request.

2. General expenses of the Organisation, as agreed by the Council, shall be apportioned in accordance with a scale to be decided upon by the Council. Other expenditure shall be financed on such basis as the Council may decide.

Article 21

Upon the receipt of any instrument of ratification, acceptance or accession, or of any notice of termination, the depositary Government shall give notice thereof to all the Contracting Parties and to the Secretary– General of the Organisation.

IN WITNESS WHEREOF, the undersigned Plenipotentiaries, duly empowered, have appended their signatures to this Convention.

DONE in Paris, this fourteenth day of December, Nineteen Hundred and Sixty, in the English and French languages, both texts being equally authentic, in a single copy which shall be deposited with the depositary Government, by whom certified copies will be communicated to all the Signatories.

The World Trade Organization

The World Trade Organization (WTO) is an international organization established in 1995 to reduce barriers to international trade and promote economic growth and development. The WTO aims to achieve its mission in three ways. First, it provides a forum for governments to build consensus and negotiate new trade agreements. Second, the WTO monitors member state trade laws and regulations to ensure proper implementation of existing trade agreements, and it scrutinizes trade policies and practices of member states. Finally, the WTO has a dispute settlement system where member state governments can resolve trade disputes.

The WTO administers three multilateral trade agreements regarding goods (the GATT), services (the GATS), and intellectual property (the TRIPS), among numerous other specialized regimes. The effectiveness of a multilateral trade regime increases as more countries sign on, and the WTO has been expanding rapidly. Today more than three quarters of the states in the world are members. The WTO estimates that 97% of the world's trade occurs among its member states.

Agreement Establishing the World Trade Organization

(Adopted 1994; in force 1995)

The *Parties* to this Agreement,

Recognizing that their relations in the field of trade and economic endeavour should be conducted with a view to raising standards of living, ensuring full employment and a large and steadily growing volume of real income and effective demand, and expanding the production of and trade in goods and services, while allowing for the optimal use of the world's resources in accordance with the objective of sustainable development, seeking both to protect and preserve the environment and to enhance the means for doing so in a manner consistent with their respective needs and concerns at different levels of economic development,

Recognizing further that there is need for positive efforts designed to ensure that developing countries, and especially the least developed among them, secure a share in the growth in international trade commensurate with the needs of their economic development,

Being desirous of contributing to these objectives by entering into reciprocal and mutually advantageous arrangements directed to the substantial reduction of tariffs and other barriers to trade and to the elimination of discriminatory treatment in international trade relations,

Resolved, therefore, to develop an integrated, more viable and durable multilateral trading system encompassing the General Agreement on Tariffs and Trade, the results of past trade liberalization efforts, and all of the results of the Uruguay Round of Multilateral Trade Negotiations,

Determined to preserve the basic principles and to further the objectives underlying this multilateral trading system,

Agree as follows:

Article I

Establishment of the Organization

The World Trade Organization (hereinafter referred to as "the WTO") is hereby established.

Article II

Scope of the WTO

1. The WTO shall provide the common institutional framework for the conduct of trade relations among its Members in matters related to the agreements and associated legal instruments included in the Annexes to this Agreement.

2. The agreements and associated legal instruments included in Annexes 1, 2 and 3 (hereinafter referred to as "Multilateral Trade Agreements") are integral parts of this Agreement, binding on all Members.

3. The agreements and associated legal instruments included in Annex 4 (hereinafter referred to as "Plurilateral Trade Agreements") are also part of this Agreement for those Members that have accepted them, and are binding on those Members. The Plurilateral Trade Agreements do not create either obligations or rights for Members that have not accepted them.

4. The General Agreement on Tariffs and Trade 1994 as specified in Annex 1A (hereinafter referred to as "GATT 1994") is legally distinct from the General Agreement on Tariffs and Trade, dated 30 October 1947, annexed to the Final Act Adopted at the Conclusion of the Second Session of the Preparatory Committee of the United Nations Conference on Trade and Employment, as subsequently rectified, amended or modified (hereinafter referred to as "GATT 1947").

Article III

Functions of the WTO

1. The WTO shall facilitate the implementation, administration and operation, and further the objectives, of this Agreement and of the Multilateral Trade Agreements, and shall also provide the framework for the implementation, administration and operation of the Plurilateral Trade Agreements.

2. The WTO shall provide the forum for negotiations among its Members concerning their multilateral trade relations in matters dealt with under the agreements in the Annexes to this Agreement. The WTO may also provide a forum for further negotiations among its Members concerning their multilateral trade relations, and a framework for the implementation of the results of such negotiations, as may be decided by the Ministerial Conference.

3. The WTO shall administer the Understanding on Rules and Procedures Governing the Settlement of Disputes (hereinafter referred to as the "Dispute Settlement Understanding" or "DSU") in Annex 2 to this Agreement.

4. The WTO shall administer the Trade Policy Review Mechanism (hereinafter referred to as the "TPRM") provided for in Annex 3 to this Agreement.

5. With a view to achieving greater coherence in global economic policy-making, the WTO shall cooperate, as appropriate, with the International Monetary Fund and with the International Bank for Reconstruction and Development and its affiliated agencies.

Article IV

Structure of the WTO

1. There shall be a Ministerial Conference composed of representatives of all the Members, which shall meet at least once every two years. The Ministerial Conference shall carry out the functions of the WTO and take actions necessary to this effect. The Ministerial Conference shall have the authority to take decisions on all matters under any of the Multilateral Trade Agreements, if so requested by a Member, in ac-

cordance with the specific requirements for decision-making in this Agreement and in the relevant Multilateral Trade Agreement.

2. There shall be a General Council composed of representatives of all the Members, which shall meet as appropriate. In the intervals between meetings of the Ministerial Conference, its functions shall be conducted by the General Council. The General Council shall also carry out the functions assigned to it by this Agreement. The General Council shall establish its rules of procedure and approve the rules of procedure for the Committees provided for in paragraph 7.

3. The General Council shall convene as appropriate to discharge the responsibilities of the Dispute Settlement Body provided for in the Dispute Settlement Understanding. The Dispute Settlement Body may have its own chairman and shall establish such rules of procedure as it deems necessary for the fulfilment of those responsibilities.

4. The General Council shall convene as appropriate to discharge the responsibilities of the Trade Policy Review Body provided for in the TPRM. The Trade Policy Review Body may have its own chairman and shall establish such rules of procedure as it deems necessary for the fulfilment of those responsibilities.

5. There shall be a Council for Trade in Goods, a Council for Trade in Services and a Council for Trade-Related Aspects of Intellectual Property Rights (hereinafter referred to as the "Council for TRIPS"), which shall operate under the general guidance of the General Council. The Council for Trade in Goods shall oversee the functioning of the Multilateral Trade Agreements in Annex 1A. The Council for Trade in Services shall oversee the functioning of the General Agreement on Trade in Services (hereinafter referred to as "GATS"). The Council for TRIPS shall oversee the functioning of the Agreement on Trade-Related Aspects of Intellectual Property Rights (hereinafter referred to as the "Agreement on TRIPS"). These Councils shall carry out the functions assigned to them by their respective agreements and by the General Council. They shall establish their respective rules of procedure subject to the approval of the General Council. Membership in these Councils shall be open to representatives of all Members. These Councils shall meet as necessary to carry out their functions.

6. The Council for Trade in Goods, the Council for Trade in Services and the Council for TRIPS shall establish subsidiary bodies as required. These subsidiary bodies shall establish their respective rules of procedure subject to the approval of their respective Councils.

7. The Ministerial Conference shall establish a Committee on Trade and Development, a Committee on Balance-of-Payments Restrictions and a Committee on Budget, Finance and Administration, which shall carry out the functions assigned to them by this Agreement and by the Mul-

tilateral Trade Agreements, and any additional functions assigned to them by the General Council, and may establish such additional Committees with such functions as it may deem appropriate. As part of its functions, the Committee on Trade and Development shall periodically review the special provisions in the Multilateral Trade Agreements in favour of the least-developed country Members and report to the General Council for appropriate action. Membership in these Committees shall be open to representatives of all Members.

8. The bodies provided for under the Plurilateral Trade Agreements shall carry out the functions assigned to them under those Agreements and shall operate within the institutional framework of the WTO. These bodies shall keep the General Council informed of their activities on a regular basis.

Article V

Relations with Other Organizations

* * *

Article VI

The Secretariat

1. There shall be a Secretariat of the WTO (hereinafter referred to as "the Secretariat") headed by a Director–General.

2. The Ministerial Conference shall appoint the Director–General and adopt regulations setting out the powers, duties, conditions of service and term of office of the Director–General.

3. The Director–General shall appoint the members of the staff of the Secretariat and determine their duties and conditions of service in accordance with regulations adopted by the Ministerial Conference.

4. The responsibilities of the Director–General and of the staff of the Secretariat shall be exclusively international in character. In the discharge of their duties, the Director–General and the staff of the Secretariat shall not seek or accept instructions from any government or any other authority external to the WTO. They shall refrain from any action which might adversely reflect on their position as international officials. The Members of the WTO shall respect the international character of the responsibilities of the Director–General and of the staff of the Secretariat and shall not seek to influence them in the discharge of their duties.

* * *

Article VIII

Status of the WTO

1. The WTO shall have legal personality, and shall be accorded by each of its Members such legal capacity as may be necessary for the exercise of its functions.

2. The WTO shall be accorded by each of its Members such privileges and immunities as are necessary for the exercise of its functions.

3. The officials of the WTO and the representatives of the Members shall similarly be accorded by each of its Members such privileges and immunities as are necessary for the independent exercise of their functions in connection with the WTO.

4. The privileges and immunities to be accorded by a Member to the WTO, its officials, and the representatives of its Members shall be similar to the privileges and immunities stipulated in the Convention on the Privileges and Immunities of the Specialized Agencies, approved by the General Assembly of the United Nations on 21 November 1947.

5. The WTO may conclude a headquarters agreement.

Article IX

Decision–Making

1. The WTO shall continue the practice of decision-making by consensus followed under GATT 1947.[1] Except as otherwise provided, where a decision cannot be arrived at by consensus, the matter at issue shall be decided by voting. At meetings of the Ministerial Conference and the General Council, each Member of the WTO shall have one vote. Where the European Communities exercise their right to vote, they shall have a number of votes equal to the number of their member States[2] which are Members of the WTO. Decisions of the Ministerial Conference and the General Council shall be taken by a majority of the votes cast, unless otherwise provided in this Agreement or in the relevant Multilateral Trade Agreement.[3]

* * *

---

[1] The body concerned shall be deemed to have decided by consensus on a matter submitted for its consideration, if no Member, present at the meeting when the decision is taken, formally objects to the proposed decision.

[2] The number of votes of the European Communities and their member States shall in no case exceed the number of the member States of the European Communities.

[3] Decisions by the General Council when convened as the Dispute Settlement Body shall be taken only in accordance with the provisions of paragraph 4 of Article 2 of the Dispute Settlement Understanding.

Article XI

Original Membership

1. The contracting parties to GATT 1947 as of the date of entry into force of this Agreement, and the European Communities, which accept this Agreement and the Multilateral Trade Agreements and for which Schedules of Concessions and Commitments are annexed to GATT 1994 and for which Schedules of Specific Commitments are annexed to GATS shall become original Members of the WTO.

2. The least-developed countries recognized as such by the United Nations will only be required to undertake commitments and concessions to the extent consistent with their individual development, financial and trade needs or their administrative and institutional capabilities.

Article XII

Accession

1. Any State or separate customs territory possessing full autonomy in the conduct of its external commercial relations and of the other matters provided for in this Agreement and the Multilateral Trade Agreements may accede to this Agreement, on terms to be agreed between it and the WTO. Such accession shall apply to this Agreement and the Multilateral Trade Agreements annexed thereto.

2. Decisions on accession shall be taken by the Ministerial Conference. The Ministerial Conference shall approve the agreement on the terms of accession by a two-thirds majority of the Members of the WTO.

3. Accession to a Plurilateral Trade Agreement shall be governed by the provisions of that Agreement.

* * *

Article XIV

Acceptance, Entry into Force and Deposit

1. This Agreement shall be open for acceptance, by signature or otherwise, by contracting parties to GATT 1947, and the European Communities, which are eligible to become original Members of the WTO in accordance with Article XI of this Agreement. Such acceptance shall apply to this Agreement and the Multilateral Trade Agreements annexed hereto. This Agreement and the Multilateral Trade Agreements annexed hereto shall enter into force on the date determined by Ministers in accordance with paragraph 3 of the Final Act Embodying the Results of the Uruguay Round of Multilateral Trade Negotiations and shall remain open for acceptance for a period of two years following that date unless the Ministers decide otherwise. An acceptance follow-

ing the entry into force of this Agreement shall enter into force on the 30th day following the date of such acceptance.

* * *

Article XV

Withdrawal

1. Any Member may withdraw from this Agreement. Such withdrawal shall apply both to this Agreement and the Multilateral Trade Agreements and shall take effect upon the expiration of six months from the date on which written notice of withdrawal is received by the Director–General of the WTO.

2. Withdrawal from a Plurilateral Trade Agreement shall be governed by the provisions of that Agreement.

Article XVI

Miscellaneous Provisions

* * *

DONE at Marrakesh this fifteenth day of April one thousand nine hundred and ninety-four, in a single copy, in the English, French and Spanish languages, each text being authentic.

———————

Article IX of the WTO Agreement envisages decision-making "by consensus." Is that realistic in a state club with more than 150 members—and huge differences among them in terms of political and economic power? Why would powerful states, such as the United States, ever agree to this?

NOTE ON INTERNATIONAL STANDARD SETTING ORGANIZATIONS

In addition to the more typical International Organizations consisting of member states, there are also various international standard-setting bodies to which member states or national organizations send delegates. An important example is the International Organization for Standardization (ISO), which was founded in 1947 and has its seat in Geneva. The ISO is a voluntary organization and consists of representatives of the national standard setting bodies of currently over 160 countries. Employing more than 2,700 subcommittees, it generates (mainly) technical standards that make products and their use internationally compatible. Another example is the International Accounting Standards Board based in London. While such global norm setters do not produce rules that are in and of themselves binding law, they often have such a strong influence on standards used by industry and commerce worldwide that they have been called the "new global rulers." (Tim

Büthe and Walter Mattli, THE NEW GLOBAL RULERS: THE PRIVATIZATION OF REGULATION IN THE WORLD ECONOMY, 2011). We will encounter some of their activities when we look at international administrative law in Chapter VIII.

3. NON–GOVERNMENTAL ORGANIZATIONS

In the 20th century, especially in its latter half, non-governmental organizations (NGOs) have become important players on the international scene. While it is clear that their number has risen dramatically in recent decades, the exact numbers in the literature vary widely, in part due to disagreement over what counts as an NGO and who does the counting. According to some sources the number has risen from 832 in 1951 to 43,958 in 1999 and to 55,853 in 2009.[5] But to get a sense of the wide variations, according to a 2009 article from the *Indian Express*, citing an Indian government study, there were 3.3 million NGOs in India alone in that year. The influence of NGOs on international law and politics has also dramatically increased.[6]

The following text gives you an overview and highlights some of the challenges raised by the existence and activities of NGOs. According to Charnovitz, what are the most important functions of NGOs? What can they contribute to international law creation and decision-making? What are the most salient criticisms and concerns?

STEVE CHARNOVITZ, NON GOVERNMENTAL ORGANIZATIONS AND INTERNATIONAL LAW
100 Am. J. Int'l L. 348 (2006)

Nongovernmental organizations (NGOs) have exerted a profound influence on the scope and dictates of international law. NGOs have fostered treaties, promoted the creation of new international organizations (IOs), and lobbied in national capitals to gain consent to stronger international rules. A decade ago, Antonio Donini, writing about the United Nations, declared that "the Temple of States would be a rather dull place without nongovernmental organisations." His observation was apt and is suggestive of a more general thesis: had NGOs never existed, international law would have a less vital role in human progress.

Often it has been crusading NGOs that led the way for states to see the international dimension of what was previously regarded as a purely domestic matter. As new issues arose in international affairs, interested NGOs formed federations or networks with organizations in different

---

[5] Eric Stein, *International Integration and Democracy: No Love at First Sight*, 95 AJIL 489 (2001); Union of International Associations, YEARBOOK OF INTERNATIONAL ORGANIZATIONS 2010/2011, 33–35 (Walter DeGruter ed., 2010).

[6] Archna Shukla, *First Official Estimate: An NGO for Every 400 People in India*, THE INDIAN EXPRESS (New Dehli, India), July 7, 2010.

countries. This transnationalism has served as a source of strength for NGOs in their various interactions with governments. NGOs act as a solvent against the strictures of sovereignty.

The contribution of NGOs to the vibrancy of international law is a puzzle because, doctrinally, international law is understood to be a product of state positivism. The key to the puzzle lies in the nature of NGOs. Like the state, the NGO is composed of individuals, but unlike the state, the NGO enjoys a relationship with the individual that is voluntary. Individuals join and support an NGO out of commitment to its purpose. That purpose plus organization gives NGOs whatever "authority" they have, and it will be moral authority rather than legal authority.

The self-actuated nature of NGOs distinguishes them from typical IOs, whose mandates are agreed to and limited by states. NGOs do not gain their influence from delegation by states. Rather, whatever influence they have is achieved through the attractiveness of their ideas and values. No NGO is guaranteed influence, not even the most venerable of NGOs, the Red Cross movement. Influence must constantly be earned.

NGOs can change the behavior of states, but very often NGOs fail to do so. Measuring NGO success has become more complicated because for many important issues, competing NGOs have been positioned on all sides of any debate. Years ago, the most involved NGOs were reliable advocates of a stronger world public order. Today, overwhelming NGO support for the international rule of law can no longer be assumed. NGOs follow their own stars.

* * *

I.   WHO NGOS ARE AND WHAT THEY DO

THE IDENTITY OF NGOS

The NGOs that are the subject of this article are groups of persons or of societies, freely created by private initiative, that pursue an interest in matters that cross or transcend national borders and are not profit seeking. Such NGOs are usually international in the sense of drawing members from more than one country. Although profit-seeking business entities are not NGOs, associations of business entities can be, such as the International Chamber of Commerce.

Everything about nongovernmental organizations is contested, including the meaning of the term. In his 1963 treatise on NGOs, J. J. Lador-Lederer observed that the semantic negation neglects the most significant part of the organizations, which is that their strength comes from "their capacity at continuous existence and development." Recently, Philip Alston took note of the widespread use of "nongovernmental organization" and "nonstate actor," and remarked that the insistence upon defining actors "in terms of what they are not combines impeccable purism in terms of traditional international legal analysis with an unparalleled capacity to marginalize a significant part of the international human rights regime." During the past two decades, the term "civil society organization" has gained popularity in some circles as an alternative to "NGO." Recognizing the longtime usage of the NGO acronym, some commentators have suggested keeping it, but changing its meaning to "Necessary to Governance Organization." That clever wordplay has not caught on.

The UN system continues to use the term "NGO," and the chief reason for doing so may be because Article 71 of the UN Charter states, "The Economic and Social Council may make suitable arrangements for consultation with non-governmental organizations which are concerned with matters within its competence." The Charter, however, does not define NGO.

* * *

The traditional distinction between an NGO and an IO is that IOs are established by intergovernmental agreements and NGOs via cooperation of individuals. That distinction holds even when IOs provide formal institutional roles for NGOs. For example, the treaties establishing the International Labour Organization (ILO) and the World Tourism Organization provide for nongovernmental roles in organizational governance. So do the charters of the Joint United Nations Programme on HIV/AIDS (UN-AIDS) and the Arctic Council.

NGO FUNCTIONS IN INTERNATIONAL LAW

* * *

NGOs may be most prolific when new fields of law are initiated or new treaties drafted. An early example concerns the rights of women. In 1928, after women's groups journeyed to the sixth Pan–American Conference, the governments agreed to hold a plenary session to hear the women's representatives, and accepted their proposal to create the Inter–American Commission of Women. Another major milestone occurred when NGOs advanced language on human rights for the UN Charter and then aided the diplomats drafting the Universal Declaration of Human Rights. Advocacy by NGOs and indigenous groups has been similarly instrumental in achieving new international protections for indigenous peoples. In recent years, networks of NGOs worked to inspirit negotiations for the International Criminal Court.

Another function engaged in by NGOs is the interpretation of international law. For example, NGOs helped to develop the "Siracusa Principles" in 1984, on the meaning and scope of the derogation and limitation provisions of the International Covenant on Civil and Political Rights. Theodor Meron has noted that by championing a broad construction of the Fourth Geneva Convention, the International Committee of the Red

Cross (ICRC) clarified that rape is a crime under international humanitarian law.

NGOs seek to contribute to international adjudication by making friend-of-the-court submissions to tribunals. Typically, an NGO initiates action by requesting leave from a court to submit a brief. In an authoritative study of NGO participation, Dinah Shelton found that major international tribunals, except the International Court of Justice (ICJ), had developed procedures to enable NGOs to submit information or statements on pending cases. Since the publication of Shelton's study in 1994, the trends she documented have continued apace. For example, organs of the International Criminal Tribunal for the Former Yugoslavia and the International Criminal Tribunal for Rwanda have requested amicus submissions in some cases and received them from individual jurists and NGOs. On the other hand, NGOs have not yet sought to submit an amicus brief to the International Tribunal for the Law of the Sea.

Although the ICJ remains closed to NGO participation, a useful step toward greater openness was taken in 2004. The ICJ adopted Practice Direction XII, which provides that, in an advisory proceeding, when an international NGO submits a statement or document on its own initiative, it will be placed in a designated location in the Peace Palace. The paper will not be considered part of the case file but will be treated as a readily available publication and may be referred to by states and IOs in the same manner as publications in the public domain.

Over the past decade, amicus curiae briefs have been admitted into trade and investment adjudication. Although no explicit provision in the Agreement Establishing the World Trade Organization (WTO) permits amicus briefs, the Appellate Body ruled in 1998 that WTO panels had discretion to accept unsolicited briefs, and it ruled in 2000 that it could accept such briefs. That development appeared to influence investor-state arbitration under the North American Free Trade Agreement (NAFTA) where, to the surprise of many observers, in 2001 the tribunal in *Methanex* held that it had the power to accept written amicus submissions. Thereafter, the intergovernmental NAFTA Free Trade Commission issued a statement officially recommending a procedure that investor-state tribunals could adopt to guide such private submissions. When the *Methanex* tribunal issued its final award in August 2005, the decision contained a reference to the "carefully reasoned Amicus submission." Following *Methanex*, two other investment arbitration tribunals ruled that they had the power to accept amicus briefs. These developments are significant because amicus submissions in investment arbitration were unknown before 2001.

Despite the initial fanfare regarding NGO opportunities at the WTO, neither the Appellate Body nor the panels have made substantive use of the information in amicus curiae submissions. The Appellate Body's early procedural decisions continue to be criticized by many governments as *ultra vires*, and consequently, any NGO briefs accepted by WTO panels and the Appellate Body are kept in juristic quarantine away from the proceeding. In some instances, panels have exercised their discretion not to accept an NGO brief. For example, in the *Softwood Lumber* litigation, a WTO panel rejected a brief from an environmental NGO "in light of the absence of consensus among WTO Members on the question of how to treat *amicus* submissions."

In contrast to their participation as amici, the ability of NGOs to initiate cases is less extensive. One tribunal that has been open to NGOs is the African Commission on Human and Peoples' Rights, which has allowed states, individuals, and NGOs with observer status to submit communications alleging a violation of the African Charter. The European Court of Human Rights permits an NGO to bring a case if the NGO itself claims to be a victim. Other opportunities present themselves in international administrative entities that permit NGOs to bring complaints. For example, the World Bank Inspection Panel entertains requests for inspection from an organization, association, society, or other grouping of two or more individuals that believes it is likely to be adversely affected as a result of the Bank's violation of its own policies and procedures.

NGOs are now often engaged in the review and promotion of state compliance with international obligations. Oscar Schachter, a keen observer, detected this budding development in 1960, and in the following decades, the NGO role flowered in the monitoring of human rights, humanitarian, and environmental law. In their 1995 book *The New Sovereignty*, Abram Chayes and Antonia Chayes devoted a chapter to the impact of NGOs on treaty compliance, and pointed out that, "[i]n a real sense, [NGOs] supply the personnel and resources for managing compliance that states have become increasingly reluctant to provide." In the decade since that book was published, the NGO role has continued to expand. For example, the parties to the Aarhus Convention agreed to allow NGOs with observer status to nominate candidates for the Convention's Compliance Committee. NGOs can also play an important role within a domestic political system in pressing the government to meet its obligations under a ratified treaty.

The last NGO function to be noted is assistance to collective enforcement efforts. For example, in a 1992 resolution regarding the former Yugoslavia, the UN Security Council called on states "and, as appropriate, international humanitarian organizations to collate substantiated information" relating to violations of humanitarian law. In a 2003 resolution regarding Sierra Leone, the Security Council called on "States, international organizations and non-governmental organizations to continue to support the National Recovery Strategy of the Government of Sierra Leone."

II.   LEGAL STATUS OF NGOS

The analysis in this part examines the legal status of NGOs in two senses—their legal personality and the special capacity they can gain to take part in intergovernmental decision making. Regarding personality, this analysis puts aside the doctrinal question often posed about individuals and NGOs—namely, whether they are "subjects" of international law. As Edwin Borchard wrote in this *Journal*, "Whether the individual is or is not a subject of international law is a matter of concepts, and hardly justifies the metaphysical discussion the question has engendered." Decades later, Rosalyn Higgins reached a parallel conclusion, "that it is not particularly helpful, either intellectually or operationally, to rely on the subject-object dichotomy that runs through so much of the writings."

NGO PERSONALITY

Legal personality is a key factor in determining the rights and immunities of an NGO and its standing before courts. In general, an NGO enjoys legal personality only in municipal law, not in international law. Yet because NGOs so often operate in more than one country, they face potential problems of being subject to conflicting laws and of inability to carry their legal status from one country to another.

* * *

Transnational NGOs have learned how to maneuver without formal international personality. In some instances, the crucial role that an NGO plays has led governments to accord rights to it that are typically granted only to IOs. For example, the ICRC and the International Federation of Red Cross and Red Crescent Societies have signed headquarters agreements with numerous states that provide for certain privileges and immunities.

Over the years, the efforts to achieve an international legal personality for NGOs have exposed some unresolved tensions. On the one hand, providing such recognition may help prevent interstate conflicts and, in the words of the 1923 draft convention, may further "the general interest of the international community to encourage the development of non profit-making international associations." On the other hand, states have worried that granting international recognition to NGOs may reduce governmental control over them, and NGOs have worried that such recognition might entail a loss of autonomy. With the increased attention to NGO (mis)behavior in recent years, a new treaty would more likely impose regulation on NGOs than facilitate freedom of association.

NGOs AS CONSULTATION PARTNERS

In the absence of international NGO law as such, Article 71 of the UN Charter has served de facto as a charter for NGO activities. The legal capacity of the NGO under Article 71 might be termed a consultation partner. Although Article 71 establishes consultative opportunities for the NGOs granted status by the UN Economic and Social Council (ECOSOC), an individual NGO does not have a treaty-based right to be consulted in a particular situation.

* * *

Nevertheless, Article 71 soon took on an importance far broader than its own text and, for that reason, the status attained by NGOs through Article 71 became a foundation stone for their efforts to strengthen international law. Even though Article 71 refers only to ECOSOC, a consultative role for NGOs gradually became an established practice throughout the UN system. Article 71 was implemented comprehensively by ECOSOC in 1950 (the 1950 NGO Rule) in a resolution that was superseded by a new resolution in 1968, and then again in 1996 by the resolution now in place (the 1996 NGO Rule).

Although many of these ECOSOC rules have remained constant, some have changed significantly. First, the 1950 NGO Rule required that an NGO be of "recognized standing" *and* that it "represent a substantial proportion of the organized persons within the particular field in which it operates." By contrast, the 1996 Rule dispenses with this two-part requirement. Now the NGO must "be of recognized standing within the particular field of its competence *or* of a representative character." Second, the preference in the 1950 Rule for international, rather than national, NGOs has now been eliminated. Third, the 1996 Rule adds a requirement that an NGO given status "have a democratically adopted constitution" and that it "have a representative structure and possess appropriate mechanisms of accountability to its members, who shall exercise effective control over its policies and actions through the exercise of voting rights or other appropriate democratic and transparent decision-making processes." This attention to internal NGO governance reflects the growing concerns in the early 1990s about the legitimacy and accountability of NGOs.

The 1996 NGO Rule codified the existing practice of suspending or withdrawing consultative status from NGOs that no longer meet the eligibility requirements or that misbehave as perceived by ECOSOC's Committee on Non-governmental Organizations. For example, engaging in "unsubstantiated or politically motivated acts" against UN member states can be grounds for losing status. An NGO challenged by the government-only ECOSOC committee is to be given written reasons and accorded an opportunity to present its response.

The work of the committee in granting and reviewing accreditation of NGOs has been criticized for overpoliticization and lack of due process. At present, no judicial review is available for a refusal by ECOSOC to grant an NGO consultative status. In my view, ECOSOC could increase the committee's credibility by permitting some NGOs to serve as members.

The consultation norms underlying Article 71 have influenced institutional developments outside the United Nations. For example, in 1999 the Organization of American States (OAS) adopted the Guidelines for the Participation of Civil Society Organizations in OAS Activities. In 2001 the Constitutive Act of the African Union called for the establishment of an advisory Economic, Social and Cultural Council composed of different social and professional groups of the member states. Another example of mimesis is the Antarctic Treaty consultative process where designated NGOs, such as the International Association of Antarctica Tour Operators, are permitted to participate.

In the early twenty-first century, NGOs are pervasive. No policy issues are off-limits for government-NGO consultations. As Alexandre Kiss and Dinah Shelton have observed, "Today, purely inter-state development of norms is probably non-existent in most fields of international law." This circumstance has been appreciated by the U.S. Congress, which in a November 2005 appropriation defined an "international conference" as a "conference attended by representatives of the United States Government and representatives of foreign governments, international organizations, or nongovernmental organizations."

* * *

IV. THE LEGITIMACY OF NGO PARTICIPATION

* * * In part IV, I address this ongoing debate and, in particular, whether it is legitimate for democratic states, acting in IOs or international negotiations, to consult with NGOs or otherwise give them an opportunity to be heard. No systematic exposition has come to my attention of why such a state practice should be considered illegitimate. Various assertions to that effect, however, have been made and are discussed below.

In the 1996 ICJ *Nuclear Weapons* cases, Judges Gilbert Guillaume and Shigeru Oda separately expressed concerns about the propriety of NGO influence on governments. Judge Guillaume, while agreeing to comply with the request by the UN General Assembly, issued a separate opinion saying that the Court could have dismissed that request (as well as the request by the World Health Organization) as inadmissible because it had originated in a campaign conducted by associations and groups. In that regard, he opined: "I dare to hope that Governments and intergovernmental institutions still retain sufficient independence of decision to resist the powerful pressure groups which besiege them today with the support of the mass media." Judge Oda dissented from the Court's decision to comply with the General Assembly's request and stated several reasons. One was that "[t]he idea behind the resolution * * * had previously been advanced by a handful of non-governmental organizations (NGOs)." Neither judge explained why the influential NGO involvement was problematic or why IOs (or the ICJ) should be impermeable to influence from NGOs

The clearest argument for the illegitimacy of intergovernmental attention to NGO advocacy is the "second bite at the apple" thesis. Before he joined the Bush administration's diplomatic team, John Bolton was a leading critic of NGOs. In 2000 Bolton argued that NGO "detachment from governments" was troubling for democracies because civil society "provides a second opportunity for intrastate advocates to reargue their positions, thus advantaging them over their opponents who are unwilling or unable to reargue their cases in international fora." Furthermore, he claimed that "[c]ivil society's 'second bite at the apple' raises profoundly troubling questions of democratic theory that its advocates have almost entirely elided." This thesis might be summarized as saying that governmental receptivity to input from NGOs should occur only in domestic fora, not in international fora.

Kenneth Anderson and David Rieff have offered a more detailed analysis of the legitimacy of NGO advocacy. In part, they object to the inflated rhetoric asserting that internationally active NGOs make up "global civil society" and that, as such, speak for the people(s) of the world. Yet their deeper concern involves what they contend are flawed analogies between domestic and international NGO advocacy with regard to both the role of NGOs and the setting for their activities. In domestic democratic society, they say, NGOs are able to "play the role of single-minded advocates * * * precisely because they are not, and are not seen as being, 'representative' in the sense of democratic representation." Yet in the international realm, they say, NGOs (perceiving themselves as global civil society) aspire to quite different roles, including both representativeness and standing between the people of the world and various transnational institutions. Anderson and Rieff also object to the analogy between domestic democratic society and the international community, saying: "Because, plainly, international society is not democratic, international NGOs are deprived of the democratic context in which their (disanalogous) domestic counterparts act." A central argument in Anderson and Rieff's analysis is that, as the international system is assigned more and more "intrusive" tasks by leading states, "the ever more diluted legitimacy that passes upwards from nation state to international system is inevitably far too attenuated to satisfy the requirements of those new tasks." The gravamen of their argument is that international NGOs cannot fill in any missing legitimacy.

In my view, an NGO cannot justify its own activist role on the claim that it represents the public. So Anderson and Rieff are right to criticize the pretentious assertions of some NGOs. Nevertheless, their argument misses the possibility that more open and inclusive processes of decision making can help to overcome the allegedly attenuated democratic legitimacy of international governance.

* * *

Intergovernmental consultations with NGOs can enhance the legitimacy of international decision making, but it is the consultation itself that makes the contribution, not the quantity of NGO support obtained. Thus, I disagree in part with what Thomas Franck has stated:

> If you continue indefinitely to transfer authority over really important issues that affect people's interests to institutions that do not even have a pretense of representativeness, you will have the seeds of self-destruction. Not only do NGOs not address that problem because they are in no sense a substitute for some direct form of representation of people in the process which normally one thinks of as parliamentary representation * * * NGOs are irrelevant, they do not in any sense legitimate the decision-making process. They may make it better, sometimes they may make it worse, but the legitimacy deficit is not addressed by them. * * *

In my view, Franck does not give enough consideration to the ways that NGOs can improve international decision making. My more serious disagreement, however, is with the arguments by Anderson, Rieff, and Bolton that the democratic context in which NGOs operate internationally differs significantly from the context in which NGOs operate domestically.

Those arguments are wrong because they ignore political reality. Individuals and NGOs must operate in the world as it is. As Florentino Feliciano pointed out several decades ago, our world is "a graduated series of community contexts—each exhibiting a public order system-of varying territorial scope." Every territorial context can be relevant and legitimate for use by an NGO motivated by an international mission. Indeed, the most successful NGOs operate at many levels in localities, national capitals, and international arenas. They play multilevel games.

Because binding international decisions are made by either consensus or prescribed majorities, an individual seeking international collective action wants the assent not only of the government with direct authority over him, but also of many other governments. An NGO can help to amplify the voice of an individual in seeking the support (or opposition) of governments that the individual has no role in electing. For example, an activist NGO in the Federated States of Micronesia concerned about global warming will not rest simply because it has convinced the Micronesian government to ratify the Kyoto Protocol. Since continuing globalization will require frequent intergovernmental decision making, the difficulty of achieving legitimacy is a challenge to be overcome, not a valid justification for avoiding international commitments.

How is legitimacy attained? A study by Daniel Bodansky, focusing on international environmental law, posits three bases of legitimacy—state consent, procedural fairness, and the substantive outcomes achieved. A study by Robert O. Keohane and Joseph S. Nye Jr., focusing on the WTO, suggests that legitimacy at the international level depends on both the procedures followed ("inputs") and the results obtained ("outputs"). Keohane and Nye call attention to existing mechanisms for "nonelectoral accountability" through a "communicative environment" that may involve "global publics" such as NGOs, even when there is no "global community." They conclude that "some form of NGO representation in the institutions involved in multilateral governance * * * could help to maintain their legitimacy." In a more recent study on the sources of normative legitimacy of multilateral decision making, Keohane contends that in the twenty-first century, only democratic principles, appropriately adopted, can confer legitimacy.

Whether NGO participation adds to, or detracts from, the legitimacy of international decision making can be explored through an analysis of inputs and outputs. The input is the process of decision making. The output is the effectiveness of the decisions reached.

NGOs facilitate input legitimacy in several ways. One is to promote accountability by monitoring what government delegates say and do in the IO and to communicate that information to elected officials and the public. Another is to help assure that decision makers are aware of the sympathies and interests of the people who will be affected by intergovernmental decisions.

The contribution of NGOs to input legitimacy may depend on several factors. One is the independence and integrity of the NGO. During the past decade, many analysts have pointed to the need for NGOs to be transparent and accountable. Another factor is whether a consultation process assures a fair balance of NGOs from different parts of the world. Over the past twenty years, NGOs have joined together more often in large coalitions, a practice that can overcome narrow-minded perspectives.

NGOs can contribute to output legitimacy in several ways. One is to offer their specialized expertise to enable more informed decisions. NGOs can often be sources of information that governments may not have. Another is to raise the quality of policy deliberations so that the choices available are better understood.

Of course, NGO participation does not necessarily improve the outputs from IOs or multilateral negotiations. Consultation with NGOs takes time, which can exact a cost. Moreover, while inviting the NGOs in makes the entire process more transparent to the public, such transparency can lead to different results than would ensue if governments arrived at agreements behind closed doors. Sometimes the involvement of NGOs in negotiations has led governments to formulate impractical agreements.

Given the many NGO contributions noted above, there are logical reasons for governments acting together to consult NGOs and to perceive such actions as legitimate. Whether or not these reasons are the motivating force behind current state practice I doubt anyone can know. Perhaps the underlying motivation is that government officials deciding whether to consult NGOs believe that such consultation is good politics.

* * *

NOTE ON NGO INFLUENCE: THE CAMPAIGN AGAINST THE DEATH PENALTY

In recent decades, NGOs have played a particularly prominent role in promoting human rights. This is illustrated by NGO efforts to fight the death penalty.

Drawing on pioneering work by Amnesty International in the 1960s to prevent the execution of prisoners of conscience, specialized NGOs with a mandate to fight the death penalty have now been established in various regions. For example, The Death Penalty Project, a UK-based NGO, represents prisoners facing capital punishment in Africa and the Caribbean. When there is reason to believe that cases involve human rights violations, The Death Penalty Project files complaints with international and regional human rights tribunals, such as the Inter–American Court of Human Rights, the UN Human Rights Committee, and the African Commission on Human and People's Rights.

In *Boyce v. Barbados* (Int. Am. H.R. Ct. 2007), the Death Penalty Project represented four prisoners who were facing death sentences in Barbados, in a proceeding before the Inter–American Court of Human Rights in Costa Rica. The Court held that the mandatory imposition of a death sentence on everyone who committed murder in Barbados violated the right to life as guaranteed under the American Convention on Human Rights. Two years later, Barbados submitted a compliance report to the Court, showing that it had abolished the mandatory death penalty. This example demonstrates the impact that NGOs can have through the litigation of individual cases.

NGOs combatting the death penalty have also begun to form coalitions in order to bolster their impact. This collaborative effort is part of a trend that has recently become noticeable for NGOs more generally—NGOs working for the same cause have started to form alliances in dealing with international organizations and governments. For example, the World Coalition Against the Death Penalty is an alliance of more than 120 NGOs, associations, local authorities, and unions. The Coalition lobbies international organizations and states, persistently pushing for the abolition of the death penalty where it still remains in force. According to Amnesty International, at least 20 countries carried out executions in 2011. The majority of those executions were carried out in China, Iran, Iraq, Saudi Arabia and the United States. Among Western countries, the United States was virtually alone in that regard; Belarus was the only European country to carry out executions in 2011.

The Coalition also promotes international law-making, for example by campaigning for ratification of the Second Optional Protocol to the ICCPR (adopted 1989), requiring the abolition of the death penalty by all states that are parties to the ICCPR. The Second Protocol has been ratified recently by Benin and Mongolia, arguably due to the persistent efforts of the Coalition. In one of its biggest achievements, after a two-year campaign by the Coalition, Latvia abolished the death penalty completely in 2012.

Is it properly the role of NGOs without formal democratic legitimacy to pressure national governments (and legislatures) to change laws made by the duly elected representatives of the people of Latvia (or of any other country)?

————————————

As indicated by Charnovitz, on occasion, the WTO (among other IOs) has admitted amicus briefs from NGOs to its dispute settlement process, a decision that remains controversial. This in turn, has led the WTO to make rules about the submission and acceptance of such *amicus* briefs. What problems are they trying to solve? Do they provide an effective solution?

ADDITIONAL PROCEDURE ADOPTED UNDER RULE 16(1) OF THE WORKING PROCEDURES FOR APPELLATE REVIEW, EUROPEAN COMMUNITIES—*MEASURES AFFECTING ASBESTOS AND ASBESTOS–CONTAINING PRODUCTS*

World Trade Organization
WT/DS135 (April 5, 2001)

To All Participants and Third Participants:

1. In the interests of fairness and orderly procedure in the conduct of this appeal, the Division hearing this appeal has decided to adopt, pursuant to Rule 16(1) of the *Working Procedures for Appellate Review*, and after consultations with the parties and third parties to this dispute, the following additional procedure for purposes of this appeal only.

2. Any person, whether natural or legal, other than a party or a third party to this dispute, wishing to file a written brief with the Appellate

Body, must apply for leave to file such a brief from the Appellate Body *by noon* on Thursday, *16 November 2000.*

3. An application for leave to file such a written brief shall:

   (a) be made in writing, be dated and signed by the applicant, and include the address and other contact details of the applicant;

   (b) be in no case longer than three typed pages;

   (c) contain a description of the applicant, including a statement of the membership and legal status of the applicant, the general objectives pursued by the applicant, the nature of the activities of the applicant, and the sources of financing of the applicant;

   (d) specify the nature of the interest the applicant has in this appeal;

   (e) identify the specific issues of law covered in the Panel Report and legal interpretations developed by the Panel that are the subject of this appeal, as set forth in the Notice of Appeal (WT/DS135/8) dated 23 October 2000, which the applicant intends to address in its written brief;

   (f) state why it would be desirable, in the interests of achieving a satisfactory settlement of the matter at issue, in accordance with the rights and obligations of WTO Members under the DSU and the other covered agreements, for the Appellate Body to grant the applicant leave to file a written brief in this appeal; and indicate, in particular, in what way the applicant will make a contribution to the resolution of this dispute that is not likely to be repetitive of what has been already submitted by a party or third party to this dispute; and

   (g) contain a statement disclosing whether the applicant has any relationship, direct or indirect, with any party or any third party to this dispute, as well as whether it has, or will, receive any assistance, financial or otherwise, from a party or a third party to this dispute in the preparation of its application for leave or its written brief.

4. The Appellate Body will review and consider each application for leave to file a written brief and will, without delay, render a decision whether to grant or deny such leave.

5. The grant of leave to file a brief by the Appellate Body does not imply that the Appellate Body will address, in its Report, the legal arguments made in such a brief.

6. Any person, other than a party or a third party to this dispute, granted leave to file a written brief with the Appellate Body, must file its brief with the Appellate Body Secretariat *by noon* on *Monday, 27 November 2000.*

7. A written brief filed with the Appellate Body by an applicant granted leave to file such a brief shall:

   (a) be dated and signed by the person filing the brief;

(b) be concise and in no case longer than 20 typed pages, including any appendices; and

(c) set out a precise statement, strictly limited to legal arguments, supporting the applicant's legal position on the issues of law or legal interpretations in the Panel Report with respect to which the applicant has been granted leave to file a written brief.

8. An applicant granted leave shall, in addition to filing its written brief with the Appellate Body Secretariat, also serve a copy of its brief on all the parties and third parties to the dispute *by noon* on *Monday, 27 November 2000*.

9. The parties and the third parties to this dispute will be given a full and adequate opportunity by the Appellate Body to comment on and respond to any written brief filed with the Appellate Body by an applicant granted leave under this procedure.

———————

What is the practical impact of these rules from the perspective of an NGO? Which NGOs are likely to be able to comply with the time limits and to commit the requisite resources?

NOTE ON THE SPECIAL CASE OF THE RED CROSS

The Red Cross, in a sense the oldest NGO in the world, was founded in 1863 by Henry Dunant, a Swiss diplomat. He had cared for wounded soldiers at the battle of Solferino in northern Italy in 1859—one of the bloodiest battles of the 19th century, leaving over 40,000 wounded and 6,000 dead. During the wars that flared up around Europe in the 1860s and 1870s, the Red Cross established itself as a neutral humanitarian intermediary protecting and assisting victims in armed conflict and other situations of violence. The original emblem is a red cross on a white background—the Swiss flag with the colors reversed; the Red Crescent, in use since 1876, and the Red Crystal, since 2005, are alternative official emblems of the organization.

The mandate of the Red Cross is now codified in the four Geneva Conventions of 1949, which cover protection of the wounded and the sick on the battlefield, victims of war at sea, prisoners of war, and civilians living under enemy control. Two protocols, added to the conventions in 1977, specifically address the protection of victims of international armed conflicts (Protocol I) and of internal armed conflicts (Protocol II) respectively. All states in the world are parties to the Geneva Conventions, and three-fourths of states are also parties to the Additional Protocols. The Geneva Conventions and Protocols are the modern foundation of international humanitarian law (*jus in bello*).

Article 81 of the First Additional Protocol makes perhaps the strongest statement with regard to the role of the Red Cross. It calls for the Parties to the conflict and the High Contracting Parties (to the Conventions and Protocols) to "facilitate in every possible way the assistance which Red Cross (Red

Crescent, Red Lion and Sun) organizations and the League of Red Cross Societies extend to the victims of conflicts." It also mandates that the parties to any conflict "grant to the International Committee of the Red Cross all facilities, within their power, so as to enable it to carry out the humanitarian functions assigned to it by the Conventions and this Protocol in order to ensure protection and assistance to the victims of conflicts."

Likewise, the Third and Fourth Conventions specify that the "special position of the International Committee of the Red Cross in this field shall be recognized and respected at all times." In more concrete terms, the Conventions and protocols state that "Red Cross personnel, medical facilities, and medical transports are to be 'respected and protected,' and 'immune from attack.'" The assistance they provide is not to be regarded as "interference" in a conflict, and Red Cross personnel are not to be detained or deemed prisoners of war. In addition, the Red Cross is to be granted access and provided with transportation to any facility where prisoners of war are held. Even Red Cross relief parcels are to be "protected" until they reach their intended destinations.

Even though the original Red Cross organization, the International Committee of the Red Cross (ICRC), is organized under Swiss law and still headquartered in Geneva, the Red Cross quickly gained international presence. The first National Red Cross Society was established as early as 1863, the same year that the organization was founded. The ICRC accepts new National Red Cross Societies for membership; they coordinate action through the League of Red Cross Societies.

The American Red Cross is not a full-fledged NGO but rather a quasi-governmental organization. It is a congressionally chartered non-profit corporation with special status under federal law: it is an instrumentality of the federal government with specific, delegated responsibilities. These responsibilities include fulfilling U.S. obligations under the Geneva Conventions and assisting the U.S. military in various ways, such as facilitating emergency communications between military personnel and their family members. Fraudulent use of the Red Cross emblem is criminalized, with a penalty of up to six months' imprisonment.

The unique relationship between the American Red Cross and the U.S. government—and the unique status of national Red Cross societies in the international order—brings with it a mix of advantages and disadvantages. Importantly, although NGOs typically do not have international legal personality, the Geneva Conventions confer upon national Red Cross societies a treaty-based right to respect and protection while carrying out their mission in conflict situations. While the American Red Cross—like other NGOs—must earn its credibility and influence, the nature of its relationship with the federal government has created a presumption of credibility in the United States.

4. INDIVIDUALS

Today, individuals are recognized as subjects of international law in many important contexts. While they do not stand on an equal footing with states, individuals do have rights and responsibilities under international law. The most important area of the former are the international human rights regimes; the most visible form of the latter is criminal and, more lately, even civil responsibility for breaches of certain core norms of international law.

A. RIGHTS (PROTECTIONS)

The origins of the modern human rights regimes lie in the Minority Treaties of the earlier 20th century. In what sense were they already similar to our current approach? How were they different?

JAMES HATHAWAY, THE RIGHTS OF REFUGEES UNDER INTERNATIONAL LAW

(2005)

* * *

Like aliens law, the Minorities Treaties which emerged after the First World War were intended to advance the interests of states. Their specific goal was to require vanquished states to respect the human dignity of resident ethnic and religious minorities, in the hope of limiting the potential for future international conflict:

> We are trying to make a peaceful settlement, that is to say, to eliminate those elements of disturbance, so far as possible, which may interfere with the peace of the world * * * The chief burden of the war fell upon the greater Powers, and had it not been for their action, their military action, we would not be here to settle these questions. And, therefore, we must not close our eyes to the fact that, in the last analysis, the military and naval strength of the Great Powers will be the final guarantee of the peace of the world * * * Nothing, I venture to say, is more likely to disturb the peace of the world than the treatment which might in certain circumstances be meted out to minorities. And, therefore, if the Great Powers are to guarantee the peace of the world in any sense, is it unjust that they should be satisfied that the proper and necessary guarantee has been given?[1]

The Minorities Treaties marked a major advance over the conceptual framework of international aliens' law. Whereas the concern under aliens' law had been simply to set standards for the treatment abroad of a state's

---

[1] Speech by United States President Wilson to the Peace Conference, May 31, 1919, cited in L. John and T. Buergenthal, INTERNATIONAL PROTECTION OF HUMAN RIGHTS (1973), at 216–217.

own nationals, the Minorities Treaties provided for external scrutiny of the relationship between foreign citizens and their own government. Minorities were guaranteed an extensive array of basic civil and political entitlements, access to public employment, the right to distinct social, cultural, and educational institutions, language rights, and an equitable share of public funding. The duty to respect these rights was imposed on the governments of defeated states as a condition precedent to the restoration of sovereign authority over their territories. While no formal international standing was granted to minority citizens themselves, enforcement of interstate obligations relied heavily on information garnered from petitions and other information provided by concerned individuals and associations. The welfare of particular human beings was thereby formally recognized as a legitimate matter of international attention.

Beyond their conceptual importance as limitations on state sovereignty over citizens, the Minorities Treaties also broke new ground in procedural terms. After the 1878 Treaty of Berlin, complaints had been made that victorious states took advantage of their right to supervise the protection of minorities to intervene oppressively in the vanquished states' internal affairs. Rather than overseeing the conduct of the defeated states directly, the Great Powers which emerged from the First World War therefore opted to establish the first international system of collectivized responsibility for the enforcement of human rights. The Great Powers requested the Council of the just-established League of Nations to serve as guarantor of the human rights obligations set by the Minorities Treaties. Once ratified, the treaties were submitted to the Council, which then resolved formally to take action in response to any risk of violation of the stipulated duties. The League of Nations went on to establish an elaborate petition system to ensure that Council members had the benefit of the views of both minorities and respondent governments before taking action in a particular case.

This system was in no sense a universal mechanism to protect human rights. It was applicable only to states forced to accept minority rights provisions as part of the terms of peace, and to a smaller number of states that made general declarations to respect minority rights as a condition of admission to the League of Nations. Nor did the Minorities Treaties system challenge the hegemony of states as the only parties able to make and enforce international law. Petitions from minorities were a source of critical information to the League's Council, but did not enfranchise individuals or collectivities as participants in the enforcement process.

The minorities system nonetheless contributed in important ways to the evolution of * * * international human rights law * * *. The Minorities Treaties firmly established the propriety of international legal attention to the human rights of at-risk persons inside sovereign states. Whereas aliens' law considered harms against individuals merely as evidence in

the adjudication of competing claims by states, the system of minorities'
protection reversed the equation. The focus of concern became the well-
being of the minorities themselves, albeit a concern driven by the desire
to avoid consequential harm to the peace and security of the international
community.

Equally important, the Minorities Treaties provided the context for collec-
tivization of international responsibility for supervision of human rights.
They showed the viability of an enforcement process vested in the community of states, yet open to the voices of particular individuals and collectivities. In contrast to aliens' law, the minorities system did not condition enforcement on the initiative of a particular state, but established a
direct role for the international community itself in the assertion of human rights claims.

* * *

The Emergence of the Global Human Rights Framework

The following texts illustrate the evolution of the post-World War II human rights regime. They make for pretty hard reading because they consist mainly of blackletter rules, but they are among the pillars of the current world legal order. Try to understand the development they embody.
Pay particular attention to the character and effect of the documents. Are
they binding? On whom? What kind of remedies do they provide? For
whom?

Also, consider the kinds of human rights these documents seek to guarantee. What sort of rights does the Universal Declaration list? Which of
these rights strike you as unusual?

UNIVERSAL DECLARATION OF HUMAN RIGHTS
G.A. Res. 217 (III) (1948)

PREAMBLE

Whereas recognition of the inherent dignity and of the equal and inalienable rights of all members of the human family is the foundation of freedom, justice and peace in the world,

Whereas disregard and contempt for human rights have resulted in bar-
barous acts which have outraged the conscience of mankind, and the advent of a world in which human beings shall enjoy freedom of speech and
belief and freedom from fear and want has been proclaimed as the highest
aspiration of the common people,

Whereas it is essential, if man is not to be compelled to have recourse, as a last resort, to rebellion against tyranny and oppression, that human rights should be protected by the rule of law,

Whereas it is essential to promote the development of friendly relations between nations,

Whereas the peoples of the United Nations have in the Charter reaffirmed their faith in fundamental human rights, in the dignity and worth of the human person and in the equal rights of men and women and have determined to promote social progress and better standards of life in larger freedom,

Whereas Member States have pledged themselves to achieve, in cooperation with the United Nations, the promotion of universal respect for and observance of human rights and fundamental freedoms,

Whereas a common understanding of these rights and freedoms is of the greatest importance for the full realization of this pledge,

Now, therefore,

The General Assembly,

Proclaims this Universal Declaration of Human Rights as a common standard of achievement for all peoples and all nations, to the end that every individual and every organ of society, keeping this Declaration constantly in mind, shall strive by teaching and education to promote respect for these rights and freedoms and by progressive measures, national and international, to secure their universal and effective recognition and observance, both among the peoples of Member States themselves and among the peoples of territories under their jurisdiction.

Article 1

All human beings are born free and equal in dignity and rights. They are endowed with reason and conscience and should act towards one another in a spirit of brotherhood.

Article 2

Everyone is entitled to all the rights and freedoms set forth in this Declaration, without distinction of any kind, such as race, colour, sex, language, religion, political or other opinion, national or social origin, property, birth or other status.

Furthermore, no distinction shall be made on the basis of the political, jurisdictional or international status of the country or territory to which a person belongs, whether it be independent, trust, non-self-governing or under any other limitation of sovereignty.

Article 3

Everyone has the right to life, liberty and security of person.

Article 4

No one shall be held in slavery or servitude; slavery and the slave trade shall be prohibited in all their forms.

Article 5

No one shall be subjected to torture or to cruel, inhuman or degrading treatment or punishment.

Article 6

Everyone has the right to recognition everywhere as a person before the law.

Article 7

All are equal before the law and are entitled without any discrimination to equal protection of the law. All are entitled to equal protection against any discrimination in violation of this Declaration and against any incitement to such discrimination.

Article 8

Everyone has the right to an effective remedy by the competent national tribunals for acts violating the fundamental rights granted him by the constitution or by law.

Article 9

No one shall be subjected to arbitrary arrest, detention or exile.

Article 10

Everyone is entitled in full equality to a fair and public hearing by an independent and impartial tribunal, in the determination of his rights and obligations and of any criminal charge against him.

Article 11

1. Everyone charged with a penal offence has the right to be presumed innocent until proved guilty according to law in a public trial at which he has had all the guarantees necessary for his defence.

2. No one shall be held guilty of any penal offence on account of any act or omission which did not constitute a penal offence, under national or international law, at the time when it was committed. Nor shall a heavier penalty be imposed than the one that was applicable at the time the penal offence was committed.

Article 12

No one shall be subjected to arbitrary interference with his privacy, family, home or correspondence, nor to attacks upon his honour and reputation. Everyone has the right to the protection of the law against such interference or attacks.

Article 13

1. Everyone has the right to freedom of movement and residence within the borders of each State.

2. Everyone has the right to leave any country, including his own, and to return to his country.

Article 14

1. Everyone has the right to seek and to enjoy in other countries asylum from persecution.

2. This right may not be invoked in the case of prosecutions genuinely arising from non-political crimes or from acts contrary to the purposes and principles of the United Nations.

Article 15

1. Everyone has the right to a nationality.

2. No one shall be arbitrarily deprived of his nationality nor denied the right to change his nationality.

Article 16

1. Men and women of full age, without any limitation due to race, nationality or religion, have the right to marry and to found a family. They are entitled to equal rights as to marriage, during marriage and at its dissolution.

2. Marriage shall be entered into only with the free and full consent of the intending spouses.

3. The family is the natural and fundamental group unit of society and is entitled to protection by society and the State.

Article 17

1. Everyone has the right to own property alone as well as in association with others.

2. No one shall be arbitrarily deprived of his property.

Article 18

Everyone has the right to freedom of thought, conscience and religion; this right includes freedom to change his religion or belief, and freedom, either alone or in community with others and in public or private, to manifest his religion or belief in teaching, practice, worship and observance.

Article 19

Everyone has the right to freedom of opinion and expression; this right includes freedom to hold opinions without interference and to seek, receive and impart information and ideas through any media and regardless of frontiers.

Article 20

1. Everyone has the right to freedom of peaceful assembly and association.

2. No one may be compelled to belong to an association.

Article 21

1. Everyone has the right to take part in the government of his country, directly or through freely chosen representatives.

2. Everyone has the right to equal access to public service in his country.

3. The will of the people shall be the basis of the authority of government; this will shall be expressed in periodic and genuine elections which shall be by universal and equal suffrage and shall be held by secret vote or by equivalent free voting procedures.

Article 22

Everyone, as a member of society, has the right to social security and is entitled to realization, through national effort and international cooperation and in accordance with the organization and resources of each State, of the economic, social and cultural rights indispensable for his dignity and the free development of his personality.

Article 23

1. Everyone has the right to work, to free choice of employment, to just and favourable conditions of work and to protection against unemployment.

2. Everyone, without any discrimination, has the right to equal pay for equal work.

3. Everyone who works has the right to just and favourable remuneration ensuring for himself and his family an existence worthy of human dignity, and supplemented, if necessary, by other means of social protection.

4. Everyone has the right to form and to join trade unions for the protection of his interests.

Article 24

Everyone has the right to rest and leisure, including reasonable limitation of working hours and periodic holidays with pay.

Article 25

1. Everyone has the right to a standard of living adequate for the health and well-being of himself and of his family, including food, clothing, housing and medical care and necessary social services, and the right to security in the event of unemployment, sickness, disability, widowhood, old age or other lack of livelihood in circumstances beyond his control.

2. Motherhood and childhood are entitled to special care and assistance. All children, whether born in or out of wedlock, shall enjoy the same social protection.

Article 26

1. Everyone has the right to education. Education shall be free, at least in the elementary and fundamental stages. Elementary education shall be compulsory. Technical and professional education shall be made generally available and higher education shall be equally accessible to all on the basis of merit.

2. Education shall be directed to the full development of the human personality and to the strengthening of respect for human rights and fundamental freedoms. It shall promote understanding, tolerance and friendship among all nations, racial or religious groups, and shall further the activities of the United Nations for the maintenance of peace.

3. Parents have a prior right to choose the kind of education that shall be given to their children.

Article 27

1. Everyone has the right freely to participate in the cultural life of the community, to enjoy the arts and to share in scientific advancement and its benefits.

2. Everyone has the right to the protection of the moral and material interests resulting from any scientific, literary or artistic production of which he is the author.

Article 28

Everyone is entitled to a social and international order in which the rights and freedoms set forth in this Declaration can be fully realized.

Article 29

1. Everyone has duties to the community in which alone the free and full development of his personality is possible.

2. In the exercise of his rights and freedoms, everyone shall be subject only to such limitations as are determined by law solely for the purpose of securing due recognition and respect for the rights and freedoms of others and of meeting the just requirements of morality, public order and the general welfare in a democratic society.

3. These rights and freedoms may in no case be exercised contrary to the purposes and principles of the United Nations.

Article 30

Nothing in this Declaration may be interpreted as implying for any State, group or person any right to engage in any activity or to perform any act aimed at the destruction of any of the rights and freedoms set forth herein.

The Universal Declaration of Human Rights (UDHR) was not intended to create binding law; indeed, since the General Assembly lacks general lawmaking authority, the UDHR could not be binding. The UDHR is nonetheless impressive for its breadth—covering traditional Western-inspired civil and political rights, the socioeconomic rights of particular importance to the Soviet Union and its allies, and even (in Article 28) the notion of a "third generation" right to development later championed by states of the less developed world.

To enable all states to sign onto at least some human rights treaties, the project to design a single treaty was abandoned in favor of two separate treaties—the International Covenant on Civil and Political Rights (ICCPR) and the International Covenant on Economic, Social, and Cultural Rights (ICESCR), each of which was adopted in 1966 and entered into force in 1976. In the end, most countries are parties to both (the United States, which still has not ratified the ICESCR, being an important exception). In reading the extract from the ICCPR below, consider the extent to which the rights diverge from, or are comparable to, rights guaranteed in the United States under the Bill of Rights, or by statute.

INTERNATIONAL COVENANT ON CIVIL AND POLITICAL RIGHTS
(Adopted 1966, in force 1976)

* * *

Article 2

1. Each State Party to the present Covenant undertakes to respect and to ensure to all individuals within its territory and subject to its jurisdiction the rights recognized in the present Covenant, without distinction

of any kind, such as race, colour, sex, language, religion, political or other opinion, national or social origin, property, birth or other status.

2. Where not already provided for by existing legislative or other measures, each State Party to the present Covenant undertakes to take the necessary steps, in accordance with its constitutional processes and with the provisions of the present Covenant, to adopt such laws or other measures as may be necessary to give effect to the rights recognized in the present Covenant.

3. Each State Party to the present Covenant undertakes:

   (a) To ensure that any person whose rights or freedoms as herein recognized are violated shall have an effective remedy, notwithstanding that the violation has been committed by persons acting in an official capacity;

   (b) To ensure that any person claiming such a remedy shall have his right thereto determined by competent judicial, administrative or legislative authorities, or by any other competent authority provided for by the legal system of the State, and to develop the possibilities of judicial remedy;

   (c) To ensure that the competent authorities shall enforce such remedies when granted.

Article 3

The States Parties to the present Covenant undertake to ensure the equal right of men and women to the enjoyment of all civil and political rights set forth in the present Covenant.

Article 4

1. In time of public emergency which threatens the life of the nation and the existence of which is officially proclaimed, the States Parties to the present Covenant may take measures derogating from their obligations under the present Covenant to the extent strictly required by the exigencies of the situation, provided that such measures are not inconsistent with their other obligations under international law and do not involve discrimination solely on the ground of race, colour, sex, language, religion or social origin.

2. No derogation from articles 6, 7, 8 (paragraphs 1 and 2), 11, 15, 16 and 18 may be made under this provision.

3. Any State Party to the present Covenant availing itself of the right of derogation shall immediately inform the other States Parties to the present Covenant, through the intermediary of the Secretary–General of the United Nations, of the provisions from which it has derogated and of the reasons by which it was actuated. A further communication

shall be made, through the same intermediary, on the date on which it terminates such derogation.

* * *

Article 6

1. Every human being has the inherent right to life. This right shall be protected by law. No one shall be arbitrarily deprived of his life.

2. In countries which have not abolished the death penalty, sentence of death may be imposed only for the most serious crimes in accordance with the law in force at the time of the commission of the crime and not contrary to the provisions of the present Covenant and to the Convention on the Prevention and Punishment of the Crime of Genocide. This penalty can only be carried out pursuant to a final judgement rendered by a competent court.

3. When deprivation of life constitutes the crime of genocide, it is understood that nothing in this article shall authorize any State Party to the present Covenant to derogate in any way from any obligation assumed under the provisions of the Convention on the Prevention and Punishment of the Crime of Genocide.

4. Anyone sentenced to death shall have the right to seek pardon or commutation of the sentence. Amnesty, pardon or commutation of the sentence of death may be granted in all cases.

5. Sentence of death shall not be imposed for crimes committed by persons below eighteen years of age and shall not be carried out on pregnant women.

6. Nothing in this article shall be invoked to delay or to prevent the abolition of capital punishment by any State Party to the present Covenant.

Article 7

No one shall be subjected to torture or to cruel, inhuman or degrading treatment or punishment. In particular, no one shall be subjected without his free consent to medical or scientific experimentation.

Article 8

1. No one shall be held in slavery; slavery and the slave-trade in all their forms shall be prohibited.

2. No one shall be held in servitude.

3. (a) No one shall be required to perform forced or compulsory labour;

   (b) Paragraph 3(a) shall not be held to preclude, in countries where imprisonment with hard labour may be imposed as a punishment for a crime, the performance of hard labour in pursuance of a sentence to such punishment by a competent court;

* * *

Article 9

1. Everyone has the right to liberty and security of person. No one shall be subjected to arbitrary arrest or detention. No one shall be deprived of his liberty except on such grounds and in accordance with such procedure as are established by law.

2. Anyone who is arrested shall be informed, at the time of arrest, of the reasons for his arrest and shall be promptly informed of any charges against him.

3. Anyone arrested or detained on a criminal charge shall be brought promptly before a judge * * * and shall be entitled to trial within a reasonable time or to release. * * *

4. Anyone who is deprived of his liberty by arrest or detention shall be entitled to take proceedings before a court, in order that that court may decide without delay on the lawfulness of his detention and order his release if the detention is not lawful.

5. Anyone who has been the victim of unlawful arrest or detention shall have an enforceable right to compensation.

* * *

Article 14

1. All persons shall be equal before the courts and tribunals. In the determination of any criminal charge against him, or of his rights and obligations in a suit at law, everyone shall be entitled to a fair and public hearing by a competent, independent and impartial tribunal established by law. The press and the public may be excluded from all or part of a trial for reasons of morals, public order (ordre public) or national security in a democratic society, or when the interest of the private lives of the parties so requires, or to the extent strictly necessary in the opinion of the court in special circumstances where publicity would prejudice the interests of justice; but any judgement rendered in a criminal case or in a suit at law shall be made public except where the interest of juvenile persons otherwise requires or the proceedings concern matrimonial disputes or the guardianship of children.

2. Everyone charged with a criminal offence shall have the right to be presumed innocent until proved guilty according to law.

3. In the determination of any criminal charge against him, everyone shall be entitled to the following minimum guarantees, in full equality:

    (a) To be informed promptly and in detail in a language which he understands of the nature and cause of the charge against him;

(b) To have adequate time and facilities for the preparation of his defence and to communicate with counsel of his own choosing;

(c) To be tried without undue delay;

(d) To be tried in his presence, and to defend himself in person or through legal assistance of his own choosing; to be informed, if he does not have legal assistance, of this right; and to have legal assistance assigned to him, in any case where the interests of justice so require, and without payment by him in any such case if he does not have sufficient means to pay for it;

(e) To examine, or have examined, the witnesses against him and to obtain the attendance and examination of witnesses on his behalf under the same conditions as witnesses against him;

(f) To have the free assistance of an interpreter if he cannot understand or speak the language used in court;

(g) Not to be compelled to testify against himself or to confess guilt.

4. In the case of juvenile persons, the procedure shall be such as will take account of their age and the desirability of promoting their rehabilitation.

5. Everyone convicted of a crime shall have the right to his conviction and sentence being reviewed by a higher tribunal according to law.

6. When a person has by a final decision been convicted of a criminal offence and when subsequently his conviction has been reversed or he has been pardoned on the ground that a new or newly discovered fact shows conclusively that there has been a miscarriage of justice, the person who has suffered punishment as a result of such conviction shall be compensated according to law, unless it is proved that the non-disclosure of the unknown fact in time is wholly or partly attributable to him.

7. No one shall be liable to be tried or punished again for an offence for which he has already been finally convicted or acquitted in accordance with the law and penal procedure of each country.

* * *

Article 17

1. No one shall be subjected to arbitrary or unlawful interference with his privacy, family, home or correspondence, nor to unlawful attacks on his honour and reputation.

2. Everyone has the right to the protection of the law against such interference or attacks.

Article 18

1. Everyone shall have the right to freedom of thought, conscience and religion. This right shall include freedom to have or to adopt a religion or belief of his choice, and freedom, either individually or in community with others and in public or private, to manifest his religion or belief in worship, observance, practice and teaching.

2. No one shall be subject to coercion which would impair his freedom to have or to adopt a religion or belief of his choice.

3. Freedom to manifest one's religion or beliefs may be subject only to such limitations as are prescribed by law and are necessary to protect public safety, order, health, or morals or the fundamental rights and freedoms of others.

4. The States Parties to the present Covenant undertake to have respect for the liberty of parents and, when applicable, legal guardians to ensure the religious and moral education of their children in conformity with their own convictions.

Article 19

1. Everyone shall have the right to hold opinions without interference.

2. Everyone shall have the right to freedom of expression; this right shall include freedom to seek, receive and impart information and ideas of all kinds, regardless of frontiers, either orally, in writing or in print, in the form of art, or through any other media of his choice.

3. The exercise of the rights provided for in paragraph 2 of this article carries with it special duties and responsibilities. It may therefore be subject to certain restrictions, but these shall only be such as are provided by law and are necessary:

    (a) For respect of the rights or reputations of others;
    (b) For the protection of national security or of public order (ordre public), or of public health or morals.

Article 20

1. Any propaganda for war shall be prohibited by law.

2. Any advocacy of national, racial or religious hatred that constitutes incitement to discrimination, hostility or violence shall be prohibited by law.

* * *

Article 26

All persons are equal before the law and are entitled without any discrimination to the equal protection of the law. In this respect, the law shall prohibit any discrimination and guarantee to all persons equal and effective protection against discrimination on any ground such as race, colour, sex, language, religion, political or other opinion, national or social origin, property, birth or other status.

* * *

Article 28

1. There shall be established a Human Rights Committee (hereafter referred to in the present Covenant as the Committee). It shall consist of eighteen members and shall carry out the functions hereinafter provided.

2. The Committee shall be composed of nationals of the States Parties to the present Covenant who shall be persons of high moral character and recognized competence in the field of human rights, consideration being given to the usefulness of the participation of some persons having legal experience.

3. The members of the Committee shall be elected and shall serve in their personal capacity.

* * *

Article 40

1. The States Parties to the present Covenant undertake to submit reports on the measures they have adopted which give effect to the rights recognized herein and on the progress made in the enjoyment of those rights:

    (a) Within one year of the entry into force of the present Covenant for the States Parties concerned;

    (b) Thereafter whenever the Committee so requests.

2. All reports shall be submitted to the Secretary–General of the United Nations, who shall transmit them to the Committee for consideration. Reports shall indicate the factors and difficulties, if any, affecting the implementation of the present Covenant.

3. The Secretary–General of the United Nations may, after consultation with the Committee, transmit to the specialized agencies concerned copies of such parts of the reports as may fall within their field of competence.

4. The Committee shall study the reports submitted by the States Parties to the present Covenant. It shall transmit its reports, and such general comments as it may consider appropriate, to the States Parties. The Committee may also transmit to the Economic and Social Council the-

se comments along with the copies of the reports it has received from States Parties to the present Covenant.

5. The States Parties to the present Covenant may submit to the Committee observations on any comments that may be made in accordance with paragraph 4 of this article.

* * *

What kind of remedy does the First Optional Protocol to the ICCPR provide?

FIRST OPTIONAL PROTOCOL TO THE INTERNATIONAL COVENANT ON CIVIL AND POLITICAL RIGHTS
(Adopted 1966, in force 1976)

The States Parties to the present Protocol,

Considering that in order further to achieve the purposes of the International Covenant on Civil and Political Rights (hereinafter referred to as the Covenant) and the implementation of its provisions it would be appropriate to enable the Human Rights Committee set up in part IV of the Covenant (hereinafter referred to as the Committee) to receive and consider, as provided in the present Protocol, communications from individuals claiming to be victims of violations of any of the rights set forth in the Covenant.

Have agreed as follows:

Article 1

A State Party to the Covenant that becomes a Party to the present Protocol recognizes the competence of the Committee to receive and consider communications from individuals subject to its jurisdiction who claim to be victims of a violation by that State Party of any of the rights set forth in the Covenant. No communication shall be received by the Committee if it concerns a State Party to the Covenant which is not a Party to the present Protocol.

Article 2

Subject to the provisions of article 1, individuals who claim that any of their rights enumerated in the Covenant have been violated and who have exhausted all available domestic remedies may submit a written communication to the Committee for consideration.

Article 3

The Committee shall consider inadmissible any communication under the present Protocol which is anonymous, or which it considers to be an abuse of the right of submission of such communications or to be incompatible with the provisions of the Covenant.

Article 4

1. Subject to the provisions of article 3, the Committee shall bring any communications submitted to it under the present Protocol to the attention of the State Party to the present Protocol alleged to be violating any provision of the Covenant.

2. Within six months, the receiving State shall submit to the Committee written explanations or remedy, if any, that may have been taken by that State.

Article 5

1. The Committee shall consider communications received under the present Protocol in the light of all written information made available to it by the individual and by the State Party concerned.

2. The Committee shall not consider any communication from an individual unless it has ascertained that:

   (a) The same matter is not being examined under another procedure of international investigation or settlement;

   (b) The individual has exhausted all available domestic remedies. This shall not be the rule where the application of the remedies is unreasonably prolonged.

3. The Committee shall hold closed meetings when examining communications under the present Protocol.

4. The Committee shall forward its views to the State Party concerned and to the individual.

Article 6

The Committee shall include in its annual report under article 45 of the Covenant a summary of its activities under the present Protocol.

Article 7

Pending the achievement of the objectives of resolution 1514(XV) adopted by the General Assembly of the United Nations on 14 December 1960 concerning the Declaration on the Granting of Independence to Colonial Countries and Peoples, the provisions of the present Protocol shall in no way limit the right of petition granted to these peoples by the Charter of the United Nations and other international conventions and instruments under the United Nations and its specialized agencies.

Article 8

1. The present Protocol is open for signature by any State which has signed the Covenant.

2. The present Protocol is subject to ratification by any State which has ratified or acceded to the Covenant. Instruments of ratification shall be deposited with the Secretary–General of the United Nations.

3. The present Protocol shall be open to accession by any State which has ratified or acceded to the Covenant.

4. Accession shall be effected by the deposit of an instrument of accession with the Secretary–General of the United Nations.

5. The Secretary–General of the United Nations shall inform all States which have signed the present Protocol or acceded to it of the deposit of each instrument of ratification or accession.

The following case shows the UN Human Rights Committee (HRC) at work. What arguments does Toonen present, and how does the "state" respond? What does the HRC decide? Why? What remedies does it provide? How will the decision be enforced?

TOONEN V. AUSTRALIA

Human Rights Committee
Communication No. 488/1992 (April 4, 1994)

Having concluded its consideration of communication No. 488/1992, submitted to the Human Rights Committee by Mr. Nicholas Toonen under the Optional Protocol to the International Covenant on Civil and Political Rights,

Having taken into account all written information made available to it by the author of the communication and the State party,

Adopts its views under article 5, paragraph 4, of the Optional Protocol.

1. The author of the communication is Nicholas Toonen, an Australian citizen born in 1964, currently residing in Hobart in the state of Tasmania, Australia. He is a leading member of the Tasmanian Gay Law Reform Group and claims to be a victim of violations by Australia of articles 2, paragraph 1; 17; and 26 of the International Covenant on Civil and Political Rights.

THE FACTS AS SUBMITTED BY THE AUTHOR

2.1 The author is an activist for the promotion of the rights of homosexuals in Tasmania, one of Australia's six constitutive states. He challenges two provisions of the Tasmanian Criminal Code, namely, sections 122 (a) and (c) and 123, which criminalize various forms of sexual contact between men, including all forms of sexual contact between consenting adult homosexual men in private.

2.2 The author observes that the above sections of the Tasmanian Criminal Code empower Tasmanian police officers to investigate intimate aspects of his private life and to detain him, if they have reason to believe that he is involved in sexual activities which contravene the above sections. He adds that the Director of Public Prosecutions announced, in August 1988, that proceedings pursuant to sections 122 (a) and (c) and 123 would be initiated if there was sufficient evidence of the commission of a crime.

2.3 Although in practice the Tasmanian police has not charged anyone either with "unnatural sexual intercourse" or "intercourse against nature" (section 122) nor with "indecent practice between male persons" (section 123) for several years, the author argues that because of his long-term relationship with another man, his active lobbying of Tasmanian politicians and the reports about his activities in the local media, and because of his activities as a gay rights activist and gay HIV/AIDS worker, his private life and his liberty are threatened by the continued existence of sections 122 (a) and (c) and 123 of the Criminal Code.

2.4 Mr. Toonen further argues that the criminalization of homosexuality in private has not permitted him to expose openly his sexuality and to publicize his views on reform of the relevant laws on sexual matters, as he felt that this would have been extremely prejudicial to his employment. In this context, he contends that sections 122 (a) and (c) and 123 have created the conditions for discrimination in employment, constant stigmatization, vilification, threats of physical violence and the violation of basic democratic rights.

2.5 The author observes that numerous "figures of authority" in Tasmania have made either derogatory or downright insulting remarks about homosexual men and women over the past few years. These include statements made by members of the Lower House of Parliament, municipal councillors (such as "representatives of the gay community are no better than Saddam Hussein" and "the act of homosexuality is unacceptable in any society, let alone a civilized society"), of the church and of members of the general public, whose statements have been directed against the integrity and welfare of homosexual men and women in Tasmania (such as "[g]ays want to lower society to their level;" "You are 15 times more likely to be murdered by a homosexual than a heterosexual * * * "). In some public meetings, it has been suggested that all Tasmanian homosexuals should be rounded up and "dumped" on an uninhabited island, or be subjected to compulsory sterilization. Remarks such as these, the author affirms, have had the effect of creating constant stress and suspicion in what ought to be routine contacts with the authorities in Tasmania.

2.6 The author further argues that Tasmania has witnessed, and continues to witness, a "campaign of official and unofficial hatred" against homosexuals and lesbians. This campaign has made it difficult for the Tasmanian Gay Law Reform Group to disseminate information about its activities and advocate the decriminalization of homosexuality. Thus, in September 1988, for example, the Group was refused permission to put up a stand in a public square in the city of Hobart, and the author claims that he, as a leading protester against the ban, was subjected to police intimidation.

2.7 Finally, the author argues that the continued existence of sections 122 (a) and (c) and 123 of the Criminal Code of Tasmania continue to have profound and harmful impacts on many people in Tasmania, including himself, in that it fuels discrimination and violence against and harassment of the homosexual community of Tasmania.

THE COMPLAINT

3.1 The author affirms that sections 122 and 123 of the Tasmanian Criminal Code violate articles 2, paragraph 1; 17; and 26 of the Covenant because:

(a) They do not distinguish between sexual activity in private and sexual activity in public and bring private activity into the public domain. In their enforcement, these provisions result in a violation of the right to privacy, since they enable the police to enter a household on the mere suspicion that two consenting adult homosexual men may be committing a criminal offence. Given the stigma attached to homosexuality in Australian society (and especially in Tasmania), the violation of the right to privacy may lead to unlawful attacks on the honour and the reputation of the individuals concerned;

(b) They distinguish between individuals in the exercise of their right to privacy on the basis of sexual activity, sexual orientation and sexual identity;

(c) The Tasmanian Criminal Code does not outlaw any form of homosexual activity between consenting homosexual women in private and only some forms of consenting heterosexual activity between adult men and women in private. That the laws in question are not currently enforced by the judicial authorities of Tasmania should not be taken to mean that homosexual men in Tasmania enjoy effective equality under the law.

3.2 For the author, the only remedy for the rights infringed by sections 122 (a) and (c) and 123 of the Criminal Code through the criminalization of all forms of sexual activity between consenting adult homosexual men in private would be the repeal of these provisions.

3.3 The author submits that no effective remedies are available against sections 122 (a) and (c) and 123. At the legislative level, state jurisdictions have primary responsibility for the enactment and enforcement of criminal law. As the Upper and Lower Houses of the Tasmanian Parliament have been deeply divided over the decriminalization of homosexual activities and reform of the Criminal Code, this potential avenue of redress is said to be ineffective. The author further observes that effective administrative remedies are not available, as they would depend on the support of a majority of members of both Houses of Parliament, support which is lacking. Finally, the author contends that no judicial remedies for a violation of the Covenant are available, as the Covenant has not been incorporated into Australian law, and Australian courts have been unwilling to apply treaties not incorporated into domestic law.

THE STATE PARTY'S INFORMATION AND OBSERVATIONS

4.1 The State party did not challenge the admissibility of the communication on any grounds, while reserving its position on the substance of the author's claims.

* * *

5.2 On 5 November 1992, therefore, the Committee declared the communication admissible inasmuch as it appeared to raise issues under articles 17 and 26 of the Covenant.

THE STATE PARTY'S OBSERVATIONS ON THE MERITS AND AUTHOR'S COMMENTS THEREON

6.1 In its submission under article 4, paragraph 2, of the Optional Protocol, dated 15 September 1993, the State party concedes that the author has been a victim of arbitrary interference with his privacy, and that the legislative provisions challenged by him cannot be justified on public health or moral grounds. It incorporates into its submission the observations of the government of Tasmania, which denies that the author has been the victim of a violation of the Covenant.

6.2 With regard to article 17, the Federal Government notes that the Tasmanian government submits that article 17 does not create a "right to privacy" but only a right to freedom from arbitrary or unlawful interference with privacy, and that as the challenged laws were enacted by democratic process, they cannot be an unlawful interference with privacy. The Federal Government, after reviewing the travaux préparatoires of article 17, subscribes to the following definition of "private": "matters which are individual, personal, or confidential, or which are kept or removed from public observation." The State party acknowledges that based on this definition, consensual sexual activity in private is encompassed by the concept of "privacy" in article 17.

6.3 As to whether sections 122 and 123 of the Tasmanian Criminal Code "interfere" with the author's privacy, the State party notes that the Tasmanian authorities advised that there is no policy to treat investigations or the prosecution of offences under the disputed provisions any differently from the investigation or prosecution of offences under the Tasmanian Criminal Code in general, and that the most recent prosecution under the challenged provisions dates back to 1984. The State party acknowledges, however, that in the absence of any specific policy on the part of the Tasmanian authorities not to enforce the laws, the risk of the provisions being applied to Mr. Toonen remains, and that this risk is relevant to the assessment of whether the provisions "interfere" with his privacy. On balance, the State party concedes that Mr. Toonen is personally and actually affected by the Tasmanian laws.

6.4 As to whether the interference with the author's privacy was arbitrary or unlawful, the State party refers to the travaux préparatoires of article 17 and observes that the drafting history of the provision in the Commission on Human Rights appears to indicate that the term "arbitrary" was meant to cover interferences which, under Australian law, would be covered by the concept of "unreasonableness." * * *

6.5 The State party does not accept the argument of the Tasmanian authorities that the retention of the challenged provisions is partly motivated by a concern to protect Tasmania from the spread of HIV/AIDS, and that the laws are justified on public health and moral grounds. This assessment in fact goes against the National HIV/AIDS Strategy of the Government of Australia, which emphasizes that laws criminalizing homosexual activity obstruct public health programmes promoting safer sex. The State party further disagrees with the Tasmanian authorities' contention that the laws are justified on moral grounds, noting that moral issues were not at issue when article 17 of the Covenant was drafted.

6.6 None the less, the State party cautions that the formulation of article 17 allows for some infringement of the right to privacy if there are reasonable grounds, and that domestic social mores may be relevant to the reasonableness of an interference with privacy. The State party observes that while laws penalizing homosexual activity existed in the past in other Australian states, they have since been repealed with the exception of Tasmania. Furthermore, discrimination on the basis of homosexuality or sexuality is unlawful in three of six Australian states and the two self-governing internal Australian territories. The Federal Government has declared sexual preference to be a ground of discrimination that may be invoked under ILO Convention No. 111 (Discrimination in Employment or Occupation Convention), and has created a mechanism through which complaints about discrimination in employment on the basis of sexual preference may be considered by the Australian Human Rights and Equal Opportunity Commission.

6.7 On the basis of the above, the State party contends that there is now a general Australian acceptance that no individual should be disadvantaged on the basis of his or her sexual orientation. Given the legal and social situation in all of Australia except Tasmania, the State party acknowledges that a complete prohibition on sexual activity between men is unnecessary to sustain the moral fabric of Australian society. On balance, the State party "does not seek to claim that the challenged laws are based on reasonable and objective criteria."

6.8 Finally, the State party examines, in the context of article 17, whether the challenged laws are a proportional response to the aim sought. It does not accept the argument of the Tasmanian authorities that the extent of interference with personal privacy occasioned by sections 122 and 123 of the Tasmanian Criminal Code is a proportional response to the perceived threat to the moral standards of Tasmanian society. * * *

6.9 In respect of the alleged violation of article 26, the State party seeks the Committee's guidance as to whether sexual orientation may be subsumed under the term " * * * or other status" in article 26. In this context, the Tasmanian authorities concede that sexual orientation is an "other status" for the purposes of the Covenant. The State party itself, after review of the travaux préparatoires, the Committee's general comment on articles 2 and 26 and its jurisprudence under these provisions, contends that there "appears to be a strong argument that the words of the two articles should not be read restrictively." The formulation of the provisions "without distinction of any kind, such as" and "on any ground such as" support an inclusive rather than exhaustive interpretation. While the travaux préparatoires do not provide specific guidance on this question, they also appear to support this interpretation.

6.10 The State party continues that if the Committee considers sexual orientation as "other status" for purposes of the Covenant, the following issues must be examined:

(a) Whether Tasmanian laws draw a distinction on the basis of sex or sexual orientation;

(b) Whether Mr. Toonen is a victim of discrimination;

(c) Whether there are reasonable and objective criteria for the distinction;

(d) Whether Tasmanian laws are a proportional means to achieve a legitimate aim under the Covenant.

6.11 The State party concedes that section 123 of the Tasmanian Criminal Code clearly draws a distinction on the basis of sex, as it prohibits sexual acts only between males. * * *

6.12 As to whether the author is a victim of discrimination, the State party concedes, as referred to in paragraph 6.3 above, that the author is actually and personally affected by the challenged provisions, and accepts the general proposition that legislation does affect public opinion. However, the State party contends that it has been unable to ascertain whether all instances of anti-homosexual prejudice and discrimination referred to by the author are traceable to the effect of sections 122 and 123.

* * *

7.1 In his comments, the author welcomes the State party's concession that sections 122 and 123 violate article 17 of the Covenant but expresses concern that the argumentation of the Government of Australia is entirely based on the fact that he is threatened with prosecution under the aforementioned provisions and does not take into account the general adverse effect of the laws on himself. * * *

7.5 The author urges the Committee to take account of the fact that the State party has consistently found that sexual orientation is a protected status in international human rights law and, in particular, constitutes an "other status" for purposes of articles 2, paragraph 1, and 26. The author notes that a precedent for such a finding can be found in several judgements of the European Court of Human Rights.

* * *

7.9 Mr. Toonen explains that since lodging his complaint with the Committee, he has continued to be the subject of personal vilification and harassment. This occurred in the context of the debate on gay law reform in Tasmania and his role as a leading voluntary worker in the Tasmanian community welfare sector. He adds that more importantly, since filing his complaint, he lost his employment partly as a result of his communication before the Committee.

7.10 In this context, he explains that when he submitted the communication to the Committee, he had been employed for three years as General Manager of the Tasmanian AIDS Council (Inc.). His employment was terminated on 2 July 1993 following an external review of the Council's work which had been imposed by the Tasmanian government, through the Department of Community and Health Services. When the Council expressed reluctance to dismiss the author, the Department threatened to withdraw the Council's funding unless Mr. Toonen was given immediate notice. Mr. Toonen submits that the action of the Department was motivated by its concerns over his high profile complaint to the Committee and his gay activism in general. He notes that his complaint has become a source of embarrassment to the Tasmanian government, and emphasizes that at no time had there been any question of his work performance being unsatisfactory.

* * *

EXAMINATION OF THE MERITS

8.1 The Committee is called upon to determine whether Mr. Toonen has been the victim of an unlawful or arbitrary interference with his privacy, contrary to article 17, paragraph 1, and whether he has been discriminated against in his right to equal protection of the law, contrary to article 26.

8.2 In so far as article 17 is concerned, it is undisputed that adult consensual sexual activity in private is covered by the concept of "privacy," and that Mr. Toonen is actually and currently affected by the continued existence of the Tasmanian laws. The Committee considers that sections 122 (a) and (c) and 123 of the Tasmanian Criminal Code "interfere" with the author's privacy, even if these provisions have not been enforced for a decade. In this context, it notes that the policy of the Department of Public Prosecutions not to initiate criminal proceedings in respect of private homosexual conduct does not amount to a guarantee that no actions will be brought against homosexuals in the future, particularly in the light of undisputed statements of the Director of Public Prosecutions of Tasmania in 1988 and those of members of the Tasmanian Parliament. The continued existence of the challenged provisions therefore continuously and directly "interferes" with the author's privacy.

8.3 The prohibition against private homosexual behaviour is provided for by law, namely, sections 122 and 123 of the Tasmanian Criminal Code. As to whether it may be deemed arbitrary, the Committee recalls that pursuant to its general comment 16 (32) on article 17, the "introduction of the concept of arbitrariness is intended to guarantee that even interference provided for by the law should be in accordance with the provisions, aims and objectives of the Covenant and should be, in any event, reasonable in the circumstances." The Committee interprets the requirement of reasonableness to imply that any interference with privacy must be proportional to the end sought and be necessary in the circumstances of any given case.

8.4 While the State party acknowledges that the impugned provisions constitute an arbitrary interference with Mr. Toonen's privacy, the Tasmanian authorities submit that the challenged laws are justified on public health and moral grounds, as they are intended in part to prevent the spread of HIV/AIDS in Tasmania, and because, in the absence of specific limitation clauses in article 17, moral issues must be deemed a matter for domestic decision.

8.5 As far as the public health argument of the Tasmanian authorities is concerned, the Committee notes that the criminalization of homosexual practices cannot be considered a reasonable means or proportionate measure to achieve the aim of preventing the spread of AIDS/HIV. The Government of Australia observes that statutes criminalizing homosexual activity tend to impede public health programmes "by driving underground many of the people at the risk of infection." Criminalization of homosexual activity thus would appear to run counter to the implementation of effective education programmes in respect of the HIV/AIDS prevention. Secondly, the Committee notes that no link has been shown between the continued criminalization of homosexual activity and the effective control of the spread of the HIV/AIDS virus.

8.6 The Committee cannot accept either that for the purposes of article 17 of the Covenant, moral issues are exclusively a matter of domestic concern, as this would open the door to withdrawing from the Committee's scrutiny a potentially large number of statutes interfering with privacy. It further notes that with the exception of Tasmania, all laws criminalizing homosexuality have been repealed throughout Australia and that, even in Tasmania, it is apparent that there is no consensus as to whether sections 122 and 123 should not also be repealed. Considering further that these provisions are not currently enforced, which implies that they are not deemed essential to the protection of morals in Tasmania, the Committee concludes that the provisions do not meet the "reasonableness" test in the circumstances of the case, and that they arbitrarily interfere with Mr. Toonen's right under article 17, paragraph 1.

8.7 The State party has sought the Committee's guidance as to whether sexual orientation may be considered an "other status" for the purposes of article 26. The same issue could arise under article 2, paragraph 1, of the Covenant. The Committee confines itself to noting, however, that in its view, the reference to "sex" in articles 2, paragraph 1, and 26 is to be taken as including sexual orientation.

9. The Human Rights Committee, acting under article 5, paragraph 4, of the Optional Protocol to the International Covenant on Civil and Political Rights, is of the view that the facts before it reveal a violation of articles 17, paragraph 1, juncto 2, paragraph 1, of the Covenant.

10. Under article 2, paragraph 3 (a), of the Covenant, the author, as a victim of a violation of articles 17, paragraph 1, juncto 2, paragraph 1, of the Covenant, is entitled to a remedy. In the opinion of the Committee, an effective remedy would be the repeal of sections 122 (a) and (c) and 123 of the Tasmanian Criminal Code.

11. Since the Committee has found a violation of Mr. Toonen's rights under articles 17, paragraph 1, and 2, paragraph 1, of the Covenant requiring the repeal of the offending law, the Committee does not consider it necessary to consider whether there has also been a violation of article 26 of the Covenant.

12. The Committee would wish to receive, within 90 days of the date of the transmittal of its views, information from the State party on the measures taken to give effect to the views.

Individual opinion submitted by Mr. Bertil Wennergren under rule 94, paragraph 3, of the rules of procedure of the Human Rights Committee

I do not share the Committee's view in paragraph 11 that it is unnecessary to consider whether there has also been a violation of article 26 of the Covenant, as the Committee concluded that there had been a violation of Mr. Toonen's rights under articles 17, paragraph 1, and 2, paragraph 1, of the Covenant. In my opinion, a finding of a violation of article 17, paragraph 1, should rather be deduced from a finding of violation of article 26. * * *

In December 1998, the State of Tasmania passed new anti-discrimination protections that included sexual orientation, making Tasmanian arguably the most protective of gay rights in Australia at the time. Not only was the prohibition on sodomy eliminated, but the new law prohibited both discrimination and incitement of hatred or severe ridicule of sexual orientation.

As under the ICCPR, the right of *individuals* to bring cases against states in international tribunals often depends on the state's consent, which is typically the subject of an additional protocol or declaration. In *Yogogombaye v. Republic of Senegal*, the first decision handed down by the African Court on Human and Peoples' Rights, the court held that it lacked jurisdiction to hear a case brought by an individual against the Government of Senegal, because Senegal had not submitted the requisite declaration accepting such claims. *Yogogombaye v. Republic of Senegal*, App. No. 001/2008, Judgment (Afr. Ct. Hum. & Peoples' Rts. Dec. 15, 2009).

The European Convention on Human Rights

The European human rights regime is a regional, as opposed to a global system. It operates under the control of the Council of Europe, an international organization made up of more than 40 countries. The Council of Europe should not be confused with the European Union, to which we will turn in Chapter VII.2.C.

Looking at the excerpts from the European Convention for the Protection of Human Rights and Fundamental Freedoms and at the decisions of the European Court of Human Rights (ECHR), what are the main differences between this regional system and the global human rights regime established by the Covenants and more specialized human rights treaties?

EUROPEAN CONVENTION FOR THE PROTECTION OF HUMAN RIGHTS AND FUNDAMENTAL FREEDOMS

(Adopted 1950; in force 1953)

The Governments signatory hereto, being members of the Council of Europe,

Considering the Universal Declaration of Human Rights proclaimed by the General Assembly of the United Nations on 10th December 1948;

Considering that this Declaration aims at securing the universal and effective recognition and observance of the Rights therein declared;

Considering that the aim of the Council of Europe is the achievement of greater unity between its members and that one of the methods by which that aim is to be pursued is the maintenance and further realisation of human rights and fundamental freedoms;

Reaffirming their profound belief in those fundamental freedoms which are the foundation of justice and peace in the world and are best maintained on the one hand by an effective political democracy and on the other by a common understanding and observance of the human rights upon which they depend;

Being resolved, as the governments of European countries which are likeminded and have a common heritage of political traditions, ideals, freedom and the rule of law, to take the first steps for the collective enforcement of certain of the rights stated in the Universal Declaration,

Have agreed as follows:

Article 1

Obligation to respect human rights

The High Contracting Parties shall secure to everyone within their jurisdiction the rights and freedoms defined in Section I of this Convention.

Section I

Rights and Freedoms

Article 2

Right to Life

1. Everyone's right to life shall be protected by law. No one shall be deprived of his life intentionally save in the execution of a sentence of a court following his conviction of a crime for which this penalty is provided by law.

2. Deprivation of life shall not be regarded as inflicted in contravention of this Article when it results from the use of force which is no more than absolutely necessary:

(a) in defence of any person from unlawful violence;

(b) in order to effect a lawful arrest or to prevent the escape of a person lawfully detained;

(c) in action lawfully taken for the purpose of quelling a riot or insurrection.

Article 3

Prohibition of torture

No one shall be subjected to torture or to inhuman or degrading treatment or punishment.

Article 4

Prohibition of slavery and forced labour

1. No one shall be held in slavery or servitude.

2. No one shall be required to perform forced or compulsory labour.

* * *

Article 5

Right to liberty and security

1. Everyone has the right to liberty and security of person. No one shall be deprived of his liberty save in the following cases and in accordance with a procedure prescribed by law:

   (a) the lawful detention of a person after conviction by a competent court;

   (b) the lawful arrest or detention of a person for noncompliance with the lawful order of a court or in order to secure the fulfilment of any obligation prescribed by law;

   (c) the lawful arrest or detention of a person effected for the purpose of bringing him before the competent legal authority on reasonable suspicion of having committed an offence or when it is reasonably considered necessary to prevent his committing an offence or fleeing after having done so;

   (d) the detention of a minor by lawful order for the purpose of educational supervision or his lawful detention for the purpose of bringing him before the competent legal authority;

   (e) the lawful detention of persons for the prevention of the spreading of infectious diseases, of persons of unsound mind, alcoholics or drug addicts or vagrants;

(f) the lawful arrest or detention of a person to prevent his effecting an unauthorised entry into the country or of a person against whom action is being taken with a view to deportation or extradition.

* * *

Article 6

Right to a fair trial

1. In the determination of his civil rights and obligations or of any criminal charge against him, everyone is entitled to a fair and public hearing within a reasonable time by an independent and impartial tribunal established by law. Judgment shall be pronounced publicly but the press and public may be excluded from all or part of the trial in the interests of morals, public order or national security in a democratic society, where the interests of juveniles or the protection of the private life of the parties so require, or to the extent strictly necessary in the opinion of the court in special circumstances where publicity would prejudice the interests of justice.

2. Everyone charged with a criminal offense shall be presumed innocent until proven guilty according to law.

* * *

Article 8

Right to respect for private and family life

1. Everyone has the right to respect for his private and family life, his home and his correspondence.

2. There shall be no interference by a public authority with the exercise of this right except such as is in accordance with the law and is necessary in a democratic society in the interests of national security, public safety or the economic well-being of the country, for the prevention of disorder or crime, for the protection of health or morals, or for the protection of the rights and freedoms of others.

Article 9

Freedom of thought, conscience and religion

* * *

Article 10

Freedom of expression

* * *

Article 11

Freedom of assembly and association

* * *

Article 12

Right to marry

* * *

Article 13

Right to an effective remedy

Everyone whose rights and freedoms as set forth in this Convention are violated shall have an effective remedy before a national authority notwithstanding that the violation has been committed by persons acting in an official capacity.

Article 14

Prohibition of discrimination

The enjoyment of the rights and freedoms set forth in this Convention shall be secured without discrimination on any ground such as sex, race, colour, language, religion, political or other opinion, national or social origin, association with a national minority, property, birth or other status.

Article 15

Derogation in time of emergency

1. In time of war or other public emergency threatening the life of the nation any High Contracting Party may take measures derogating from its obligations under this Convention to the extent strictly required by the exigencies of the situation, provided that such measures are not inconsistent with its other obligations under international law.

2. No derogation from Article 2, except in respect of deaths resulting from lawful acts of war, or from Articles 3, 4 [forced labor] (paragraph 1) and 7 [no punishment without law] shall be made under this provision.

3. Any High Contracting Party availing itself of this right of derogation shall keep the Secretary General of the Council of Europe fully informed of the measures which it has taken and the reasons therefor. It shall also inform the Secretary General of the Council of Europe when such measures have ceased to operate and the provisions of the Convention are again being fully executed.

* * *

Section II

European Court of Human Rights

Article 19

Establishment of the Court

To ensure the observance of the engagements undertaken by the High Contracting Parties in the Convention and the protocols thereto, there shall be set up a European Court of Human Rights, hereinafter referred to as "the Court." It shall function on a permanent basis.

* * *

Article 26

Single-judge formation, Committees, Chambers and Grand Chamber

1. To consider cases brought before it, the Court shall sit in a single-judge formation, in committees of three judges, in Chambers of seven judges and in a Grand Chamber of seventeen judges. The Court's Chambers shall set up committees for a fixed period of time.

* * *

Article 32

Jurisdiction of the Court

1. The jurisdiction of the Court shall extend to all matters concerning the interpretation and application of the Convention and the protocols thereto which are referred to it as provided in Articles 33, 34 and 47.

2. In the event of a dispute as to whether the Court has jurisdiction, the Court shall decide.

Article 33

Inter–State cases

Any High Contracting Party may refer to the Court any alleged breach of the provisions of the Convention and the Protocols thereto by another High Contracting Party.

Article 34

Individual applications

The Court may receive applications from any person, non-governmental organisation or group of individuals claiming to be the victim of a violation by one of the High Contracting Parties of the rights set forth in the Convention or the protocols thereto. The High Contracting Parties undertake not to hinder the effective exercise of this right.

Article 35

Admissibility criteria

1. The Court may only deal with the matter after all domestic remedies have been exhausted, according to the generally recognised rules of international law, and within a period of six months from the date on which the final decision was taken.

2. The Court shall not deal with any application submitted under Article 34 that

   (a) is anonymous; or

   (b) is substantially the same as a matter that has already been examined by the Court or has already been submitted to another procedure of international investigation or settlement and contains no relevant new information.

3. The Court shall declare inadmissible any individual application submitted under Article 34 if it considers that:

   (a) the application is incompatible with the provisions of the Convention or the protocols thereto, manifestly ill-founded, or an abuse of the right of application;

* * *

4. The Court shall reject any application which it considers inadmissible under this Article. It may do so at any stage of the proceedings.

* * *

Article 38

Examination of the case

If the Court declares the application admissible, it shall pursue the examination of the case, together with the representatives of the parties, and if need be, undertake an investigation, for the effective conduct of which the States concerned shall furnish all necessary facilities.

Article 39

Friendly settlements

1. At any stage of the proceedings, the Court may place itself at the disposal of the parties concerned with a view to securing a friendly settlement of the matter on the basis of respect for human rights as defined in the Convention and the Protocols thereto.

2. Proceedings conducted under paragraph 1 shall be confidential.

3. If a friendly settlement is effected, the Court shall strike the case out of its list by means of a decision which shall be confined to a brief statement of the facts and of the solution reached.

4. This decision shall be transmitted to the Committee of Ministers, which shall supervise the execution of the terms of the friendly settlement as set out in the decision.

* * *

Article 41

Just satisfaction

If the Court finds that there has been a violation of the Convention or the protocols thereto, and if the internal law of the High Contracting Party concerned allows only partial reparation to be made, the Court shall, if necessary, afford just satisfaction to the injured party.

* * *

Article 43

Referral to the Grand Chamber

1. Within a period of three months from the date of the judgment of the Chamber, any party to the case may, in exceptional cases, request that the case be referred to the Grand Chamber.

2. A panel of five judges of the Grand Chamber shall accept the request if the case raises a serious question affecting the interpretation or application of the Convention or the Protocols thereto, or a serious issue of general importance.

3. If the panel accepts the request, the Grand Chamber shall decide the case by means of a judgment.

Article 44

Final judgments

1. The judgment of the Grand Chamber shall be final.

2. The judgment of a Chamber shall become final

   (a) when the parties declare that they will not request that the case be referred to the Grand Chamber; or

   (b) three months after the date of the judgment, if reference of the case to the Grand Chamber has not been requested; or

   (c) when the panel of the Grand Chamber rejects the request to refer under Article 43.

3. The final judgment shall be published.

* * *

Article 46

Binding force and execution of judgments

1. The High Contracting Parties undertake to abide by the final judgment of the Court in any case to which they are parties.

2. The final judgment of the Court shall be transmitted to the Committee of Ministers, which shall supervise its execution.

* * *

Article 47

Advisory opinions

1. The Court may, at the request of the Committee of Ministers, give advisory opinions on legal questions concerning the interpretation of the Convention and the Protocols thereto.

2. Such opinions shall not deal with any question relating to the content or scope of the rights or freedoms defined in Section I of the Convention and the Protocols thereto, or with any other question which the Court or the Committee of Ministers might have to consider in consequence of any such proceedings as could be instituted in accordance with the Convention.

3. Decisions of the Committee of Ministers to request an advisory opinion of the Court shall require a majority vote of the representatives entitled to sit on the committee.

* * *

In reading the following case, pay close attention to the structure of the Court's argument. What are the various steps in which the Court proceeds?

SMITH AND GRADY V. THE UNITED KINGDOM

European Court of Human Rights
Application nos. 33985/96 and 33986/96
September 27, 1999

* * *

I.   THE CIRCUMSTANCES OF THE CASE

A.   THE FIRST APPLICANT

11. On 8 April 1989 Ms Jeanette Smith (the first applicant) joined the Royal Air Force to serve a nine-year engagement (which could be extended) as an enrolled nurse. She subsequently obtained the rank of senior aircraft woman. From 1991 to 1993 she was recommended for promotion. A promotion was dependent on her becoming a staff nurse and in 1992 she was accepted for the relevant conversion course. Her final exams were to take place in September 1994.

12. On 12 June 1994 the applicant found a message on her answering machine from an unidentified female caller. The caller stated that she had informed the air force authorities of the applicant's homosexuality. On 13 June 1994 the applicant did not report, as required, for duty. On that day a woman telephoned the air force Provost and Security Service ("the service police") stating, *inter alia*, that the applicant was homosexual and was sexually harassing the caller.

13. On 15 June 1994 the applicant reported for duty. She was called to a pre-disciplinary interview because of her absence without leave. In explaining why she did not report for duty, she referred to the anonymous telephone message and admitted that she was homosexual. She also confirmed that she had a previous and current homosexual relationship. Both relationships were with civilians and the current relationship had begun eighteen months previously. The assistance of the service police was requested, a unit investigation report was opened and an investigator from the service police was appointed.

14. The applicant was interviewed on the same day by that investigator and another officer (female) from the service police. The interview lasted approximately thirty-five minutes. She was cautioned that she did not have to say anything but that anything she did say could be given in evidence. The applicant later confirmed that her solicitor had advised her not to say anything but she agreed that she would answer simple questions but not the "nitty gritty." She was told that she might be asked questions which could embarrass her and that if she felt embarrassed she should say so. It was also explained that the purpose of the questions was to verify that her admission was not an attempt to obtain an early discharge from the service.

The applicant confirmed that, while she had had "thoughts" about her sexual orientation for about six years, she had her first lesbian relationship during her first year in the air force. She was asked how she came to realise that she was lesbian, the names of her previous partners (she refused to give this information) and whether her previous partners were in the service (this question was put a number of times). She was questioned about how she had met her current partner and the extent of her relationship with that partner but she would not respond at first, at which stage her interviewer queried how else he was to substantiate her homosexuality. The applicant then confirmed that she and her partner had a full sexual relationship.

She was also asked whether she and her partner had a sexual relationship with their foster daughter (16 years old). The applicant indicated that she knew the consequences of her homosexuality being discovered and, while she considered herself just as capable of doing the job as another, she had come to terms with what was going to happen to her. The interviewers also wanted to know whether she had taken legal advice, who was her solicitor, what advice he had already given her and what action she proposed to take after the interview. She was also asked whether she had thought about HIV, whether she was being "careful," what she did in her spare time and whether she was into "girlie games" like hockey and netball. The applicant agreed that her partner, who was waiting outside during the interview, could be interviewed for "corroboration" purposes.

15. The report prepared by the interviewers dated 15 June 1994 described the subsequent interview of the applicant's partner. The latter confirmed that she and the applicant had been involved in a full sexual relationship for about eighteen months but she declined to elaborate further.

16. The investigation report was sent to the applicant's commanding officer who, on 10 August 1994, recommended the applicant's administrative discharge. On 16 November 1994 the applicant received a certificate of discharge from the armed forces. An internal air force document dated 17 October 1996 described the applicant's overall general assessment for trade proficiency and personal qualities as very good and her overall conduct assessments as exemplary.

B.   THE SECOND APPLICANT

17. On 12 August 1980 Mr Graeme Grady (the second applicant) joined the Royal Air Force at the rank of aircraftman serving as a trainee administrative clerk. By 1991 he had achieved the rank of sergeant and worked as a personnel administrator, at which stage he was posted to Washington at the British Defence Intelligence Liaison Service (North America)—"BDILS(NA)." He served as chief clerk and led the BDILS(NA)

support staff team. In May 1993 the applicant, who was married with two children, told his wife that he was homosexual.

18. The applicant's general assessment covering the period June 1992 to June 1993 gave him 8 out of a maximum of 9 marks for trade proficiency, supervisory ability and personal qualities. His ability to work well with all rank levels, with Canadian and Australian peers and with his senior officer contacts was noted, his commanding officer concluding that the applicant was highly recommended for promotion (a special recommendation being noted as well within his reach) and that he was particularly suited for "PS [personal assistant]/SDL [special duties list]/Diplomatic duties."

19. Following disclosures to the wife of the head of the BDILS(NA) by their nanny, the head of the BDILS(NA) reported that it was suspected that the applicant was homosexual. A unit investigation report was opened and a service police officer nominated as investigator.

20. On 12 May 1994 the applicant's security clearance was replaced with a lower security clearance. On 17 May 1994 he was relieved of his duties by the head of the BDILS(NA) and was informed that he was being returned to the United Kingdom pending investigation of a problem with his security clearance. On the same day the applicant was brought to his home to pack his belongings and was required to leave Washington for the United Kingdom. He was then required to remain at the relevant air force base in the United Kingdom.

21. On 19 May 1994 the head of the BDILS(NA) advised two service police investigators, who had by then arrived in Washington, that his own wife, their nanny, the applicant's wife and another (female) employee of the BDILS(NA), together with the latter's husband, should be interviewed.

22. The nanny detailed in a statement how, through her own involvement in the homosexual community, she had come to suspect that the applicant was homosexual. The wife of the head of the BDILS(NA) revealed in interview confidences made to her by the applicant's wife about the applicant's marriage difficulties and sex life and informed investigators about a cycling holiday taken by the applicant with a male colleague. It was decided by the investigators that her statement would serve no useful purpose. The applicant's colleague and the latter's husband also spoke of the applicant's marriage difficulties, the sleeping arrangements of the applicant and his wife and the applicant's cycling holiday with a male colleague. These persons were also asked about the possibility of the applicant having had an extra-marital relationship and of being involved in the homosexual community. The investigators later reported that these friends were clearly loyal to the applicant and not to be believed.

23. The applicant's wife was then interviewed. The case progress report dated 22 May 1994 describes the interview in detail. It was explained to

the applicant's wife that the interview related to the applicant's security clearance and that her husband had been transferred to the United Kingdom at short notice in accordance with standard procedure. She agreed to talk to the investigators and, further to questioning, outlined in some detail their financial position, the course of and the current state of their marriage, their sexual habits and the applicant's relationship with his two children. She confirmed that her husband's sexual tendencies were normal and indicated that her husband had gone on his own on the cycling holiday in question.

24. On 23 May 1994 the applicant's lower security clearance was suspended.

25. On 25 May 1994 the applicant was required to attend an interview with the same two investigators who had returned from the United States. It began at 2.35 p.m. and was conducted under caution with an observer (also from the air force) present at the applicant's request. The applicant was informed that an allegation had been made regarding his sexual orientation (the terms "queen" and "out and out bender" were used) and it was made clear that the investigators had been to Washington and had spoken to a number of people, one or two of whom thought he was gay.

The applicant denied he was homosexual. He was asked numerous questions about his work, his relationship with the head of the BDILS(NA), his cycling holiday and about his female colleague. He was told that his wife had been interviewed in detail and he was informed from time to time by the interviewers if his answers matched those of his wife. He was asked to tell the interviewers about the break-up of his marriage, whether he had extra-marital affairs, about his and his wife's sex life including their having protected sex and about their financial situation. He was also questioned on the cycling holiday, about a male colleague and the latter's sexual orientation. They asked the applicant who he was calling since he had returned to the United Kingdom and how he was telephoning. He was told that he would be asked to supply his electronic diary which contained names, addresses and telephone numbers and was told that the entries would be verified for homosexual contacts. They informed the applicant that they had a warrant if he did not agree to a search of his accommodation. The applicant agreed to the search. The applicant also requested time to think and to take legal advice. The interview was adjourned at 3.14 p.m.

26. The applicant then took advice from a solicitor and his accommodation was searched. The interview recommenced at 7.44 p.m. with the applicant's solicitor and an observer present. Despite being pressed with numerous questions, the applicant answered "no comment" to most of the questions posed. Given the applicant's responses, his lawyer was asked

what advice had been given to the applicant. The applicant's digital diary was taken from him. He was asked whether he realised the security implications of the investigation and that his career was on the line if the allegations against him were proved. One of the investigators then asked him:

> " * * * if you wish to change your mind and want to speak to me, while I'm still here, before I go back to Washington; because I'm going back to Washington. Because I'm going to see the Colonel tomorrow, that is the one in London, who is then going to see the General and we're going to get permission to speak to the Americans * * * and I shall stay out there, Graeme, until I have spoken to all Americans that you know. Expense is not a problem. Time is not a problem * * *"

The detailed evidence given by his wife to the investigators was put to the applicant, including information about his relationship with his son, his daughter and his mother-in-law, about matters relating to the family home of which the applicant was not aware and about his having protected sex with his wife. The interviewer returned again to the subject of the applicant having previously grown cold towards his wife but now declaring his love for her. The applicant continued to respond "no comment." It was explained to the applicant's solicitor that the service attitude in relation to investigations involving acts of alleged homosexuality did not warrant the provision of legal advice and that the applicant's solicitor was only delaying matters. The investigators also mentioned that it was a security matter which they would not detail further since his solicitor did not have security clearance, but that the applicant should not be surprised if some counter-intelligence people came to talk to him and that there would be no legal advice for that.

The applicant requested time to speak to his lawyer and the interview was interrupted at 8.10 p.m. The applicant then spoke to his lawyer and asked to think about matters overnight.

27. The interview recommenced at 3.27 p.m. on 26 May 1994 with the same investigators and an observer, but the applicant did not require a solicitor. The applicant admitted his homosexuality almost immediately and confirmed that the reason he denied it at first was that he was not clear about the position as regards the retention of certain accumulated benefits on discharge and he was concerned about his family's financial position in that eventuality. However, he had since discovered that his discharge would be administrative and that he would get his terminal benefits, so he could be honest.

The applicant was questioned further about a person called "Randy," whether his wife knew he was homosexual, whether a male colleague was homosexual and when he had "come out." He was asked whether he was a practising homosexual, but he declined to give the name of his current partner, at which stage it was explained to him that the service had to verify his admission of homosexuality to avoid fraudulent attempts at early discharge. He was then questioned about his first homosexual relationship (he confirmed that it began in October 1993), his homosexual partners (past and present), who they were, where they worked, how old they were, how the applicant met them and about the nature of his relationship with them, including the type of sex they had.

During this interview, the personal items taken from the applicant were produced and the applicant was questioned about, *inter alia*, the contents of his digital diary, a photograph, a torn envelope and a letter from the applicant to his current partner. He was questioned further about when he first realised he was homosexual, who knew about his sexual orientation, his relationship with his wife (including their sexual relationship), what his wife thought about his homosexuality, his HIV status and again about the nature of his sexual relationships with his homosexual partners. The interview terminated at 4.10 p.m.

28. The investigators prepared a report on 13 June 1994. In his certificate of qualifications and reference on discharge dated 12 October 1994, the applicant was described as a loyal serviceman and a conscientious and hard worker who could be relied upon to achieve the highest standards. It was also noted that he had displayed sound personal qualities and integrity throughout his service and had enjoyed the respect of his superiors, peers and subordinates alike. The applicant was administratively discharged with effect from 12 December 1994.

    C.   THE APPLICANTS' JUDICIAL REVIEW PROCEEDINGS (*R. V. MINISTRY OF DEFENCE, EX PARTE SMITH AND OTHERS* 2 WEEKLY LAW REPORTS 305)

* * *

II.   RELEVANT DOMESTIC LAW AND PRACTICE

    A.   DECRIMINALISATION OF HOMOSEXUAL ACTS

44. By virtue of section 1(1) of the Sexual Offences Act 1967, homosexual acts in private between two consenting adults (at the time meaning 21 years or over) ceased to be criminal offences. However, such acts continued to constitute offences under the Army and Air Force Acts 1955 and the Naval Discipline Act 1957 (Section 1(5) of the 1967 Act). Section 1(5) of the 1967 Act was repealed by the Criminal Justice and Public Order Act 1994 (which Act also reduced the age of consent to 18 years). However, section 146(4) of the 1994 Act provided that nothing in that section prevented a homosexual act (with or without other acts or circumstances) from constituting a ground for discharging a member of the armed forces.

* * *

C.   THE MINISTRY OF DEFENCE POLICY ON HOMOSEXUAL PERSONNEL
     IN THE ARMED FORCES

49. As a consequence of the changes made by the Criminal Justice and
Public Order Act 1994, updated Armed Forces' Policy and Guidelines on
Homosexuality ("the Guidelines") were distributed to the respective service directorates of personnel in December 1994. The Guidelines provided,
inter alia, as follows:

> "Homosexuality, whether male or female, is considered incompatible
> with service in the armed forces. This is not only because of the close
> physical conditions in which personnel often have to live and work,
> but also because homosexual behaviour can cause offence, polarise
> relationships, induce ill-discipline and, as a consequence, damage
> morale and unit effectiveness. If individuals admit to being homosex-
> ual whilst serving and their Commanding Officer judges that this
> admission is well-founded they will be required to leave the services.
> * * *
>
> The armed forces' policy on homosexuality is made clear to all those
> considering enlistment. If a potential recruit admits to being homo-
> sexual, he/she will not be enlisted. Even if a potential recruit admits
> to being homosexual but states that he/she does not at present nor in
> the future intend to engage in homosexual activity, he/she will not be
> enlisted. * * * "

                              * * *

50. The affidavit of Air Chief Marshal Sir John Frederick Willis KCB,
CBE, Vice Chief of the Defence Staff, Ministry of Defence dated 4 September 1996, which was submitted to the High Court in the case of *R. v.
Secretary of State for Defence, ex parte Perkins* (13 July 1998), read, in so
far as relevant, as follows:

> "The policy of the Ministry of Defence is that the special nature of
> homosexual life precludes the acceptance of homosexuals and homo-
> sexuality in the armed forces. The primary concern of the armed
> forces is the maintenance of an operationally effective and efficient
> force and the consequent need for strict maintenance of discipline.
> [The Ministry of Defence] believes that the presence of homosexual
> personnel has the potential to undermine this.
>
> The conditions of military life, both on operations and within the ser-
> vice environment, are very different from those experienced in civil-
> ian life. * * * The [Ministry of Defence] believes that these conditions,
> and the need for absolute trust and confidence between personnel of
> all ranks, must dictate its policy towards homosexuality in the armed
> forces. It is not a question of a moral judgement, nor is there any
> suggestion that homosexuals are any less courageous than hetero-

sexual personnel; the policy derives from a practical assessment of
the implications of homosexuality for fighting power."

* * *

I.   ALLEGED VIOLATION OF ARTICLE 8 OF THE CONVENTION

69. The applicants complained that the investigations into their homosexuality and their subsequent discharge from the Royal Air Force on the
sole ground that they were homosexual, in pursuance of the Ministry of
Defence's absolute policy against homosexuals in the British armed forces, constituted a violation of their right to respect for their private lives
protected by Article 8 of the Convention. That Article, in so far as is relevant, reads as follows:

> "1. Everyone has the right to respect for his private * * * life. * * *
>
> 2. There shall be no interference by a public authority with the exer-
> cise of this right except such as is in accordance with the law and is
> necessary in a democratic society in the interests of national security,
> * * * for the prevention of disorder * * * "

A.   WHETHER THERE WAS AN INTERFERENCE

* * * [T]he Court is of the view that the investigations by the military police into the applicants' homosexuality, which included detailed inter-
views with each of them and with third parties on matters relating to
their sexual orientation and practices, together with the preparation of a
final report for the armed forces' authorities on the investigations, constituted a direct interference with the applicants' right to respect for their
private lives. Their consequent administrative discharge on the sole
ground of their sexual orientation also constituted an interference with
that right (see the Dudgeon v. the United Kingdom judgment of 22 October 1981, Series A no. 45, pp. 18–19, § 41, and, *mutatis mutandis*, the
Vogt v. Germany judgment of 26 September 1995, Series A no. 323, p. 23,
§ 44).

B.   WHETHER THE INTERFERENCES WERE JUSTIFIED

72. Such interferences can only be considered justified if the conditions of
the second paragraph of Article 8 are satisfied. Accordingly, the interferences must be "in accordance with the law," have an aim which is legitimate under this paragraph and must be "necessary in a democratic society" for the aforesaid aim (see the Norris v. Ireland judgment of 26 October
1988, Series A no. 142, p. 18, § 39).

1.   "IN ACCORDANCE WITH THE LAW"

73. The parties did not dispute that there had been compliance with this
element of Article 8 § 2 of the Convention. * * *

2.   LEGITIMATE AIM

74. The Court observes that the essential justification offered by the Government for the policy and for the consequent investigations and discharges is the maintenance of the morale of service personnel and, consequently, of the fighting power and the operational effectiveness of the armed forces (see paragraph 95 below). The Court finds no reason to doubt that the policy was designed with a view to ensuring the operational effectiveness of the armed forces or that investigations were, in principle, intended to establish whether the person concerned was a homosexual to whom the policy was applicable. To this extent, therefore, the Court considers that the resulting interferences can be said to have pursued the legitimate aims of "the interests of national security" and "the prevention of disorder."

Reasoning

The Court has more doubt as to whether the investigations continued to serve any such legitimate aim once the applicants had admitted their homosexuality. However, given the Court's conclusion at paragraph 111 below, it does not find it necessary to decide whether this element of the investigations pursued a legitimate aim within the meaning of Article 8 § 2 of the Convention.

3.   "NECESSARY IN A DEMOCRATIC SOCIETY"

75. It remains to be determined whether the interferences in the present cases can be considered "necessary in a democratic society" for the aforesaid aims.

* * *

(C) THE COURT'S ASSESSMENT

(i) APPLICABLE GENERAL PRINCIPLES

87. An interference will be considered "necessary in a democratic society" for a legitimate aim if it answers a pressing social need and, in particular, is proportionate to the legitimate aim pursued.

Given the matters at issue in the present case, the Court would underline the link between the notion of "necessity" and that of a "democratic society," the hallmarks of the latter including pluralism, tolerance and broadmindedness (see the Vereinigung demokratischer Soldaten Österreichs and Gubi judgment cited above, p. 17, § 36, and the Dudgeon judgment cited above, p. 21, § 53).

88. The Court recognises that it is for the national authorities to make the initial assessment of necessity, though the final evaluation as to whether the reasons cited for the interference are relevant and sufficient is one for this Court. A margin of appreciation is left to Contracting States in the context of this assessment, which varies according to the

nature of the activities restricted and of the aims pursued by the restrictions (see the Dudgeon judgment cited above, pp. 21 and 23, §§ 52 and 59).

89. Accordingly, when the relevant restrictions concern "a most intimate part of an individual's private life," there must exist "particularly serious reasons" before such interferences can satisfy the requirements of Article 8 § 2 of the Convention (see the Dudgeon judgment cited above, p. 21, § 52).

When the core of the national security aim pursued is the operational effectiveness of the armed forces, it is accepted that each State is competent to organise its own system of military discipline and enjoys a certain margin of appreciation in this respect (see the Engel and Others judgment cited above, p. 25, § 59). The Court also considers that it is open to the State to impose restrictions on an individual's right to respect for his private life where there is a real threat to the armed forces' operational effectiveness, as the proper functioning of an army is hardly imaginable without legal rules designed to prevent service personnel from undermining it. However, the national authorities cannot rely on such rules to frustrate the exercise by individual members of the armed forces of their right to respect for their private lives, which right applies to service personnel as it does to others within the jurisdiction of the State. Moreover, assertions as to a risk to operational effectiveness must be "substantiated by specific examples" (see, *mutatis mutandis*, the Vereinigung demokratischer Soldaten Österreichs and Gubi judgment cited above, p. 17, §§ 36 and 38, and the Grigoriades judgment cited above, pp. 2589–90, § 45).

(ii) APPLICATION TO THE FACTS OF THE CASE

90. It is common ground that the sole reason for the investigations conducted and for the applicants' discharge was their sexual orientation. Concerning as it did a most intimate aspect of an individual's private life, particularly serious reasons by way of justification were required (see paragraph 89 above). In the case of the present applicants, the Court finds the interferences to have been especially grave for the following reasons.

91. In the first place, the investigation process (see the Guidelines at paragraph 49 above and the Government's submissions at paragraph 80) was of an exceptionally intrusive character.

* * *

92. Secondly, the administrative discharge of the applicants had, as Sir Thomas Bingham MR described, a profound effect on their careers and prospects.

* * *

The Court notes, in this respect, the unique nature of the armed forces (underlined by the Government in their pleadings before the Court) and, consequently, the difficulty in directly transferring essentially military qualifications and experience to civilian life. * * *

93. Thirdly, the absolute and general character of the policy which led to the interferences in question is striking (see the Dudgeon judgment cited above, p. 24, § 61, and the Vogt judgment cited above, p. 28, § 59). The policy results in an immediate discharge from the armed forces once an individual's homosexuality is established and irrespective of the individual's conduct or service record. * * *

94. Accordingly, the Court must consider whether, taking account of the margin of appreciation open to the State in matters of national security, particularly convincing and weighty reasons exist by way of justification for the interferences with the applicants' right to respect for their private lives.

95. The core argument of the Government in support of the policy is that the presence of open or suspected homosexuals in the armed forces would have a substantial and negative effect on morale and, consequently, on the fighting power and operational effectiveness of the armed forces. The Government rely in this respect on the report of the HPAT and, in particular, on Section F of the report.

* * *

96. Even accepting that the views on the matter which were expressed to the HPAT may be considered representative, the Court finds that the perceived problems which were identified in the HPAT report as a threat to the fighting power and operational effectiveness of the armed forces were founded solely upon the negative attitudes of heterosexual personnel towards those of homosexual orientation. The Court observes, in this respect, that no moral judgment is made on homosexuality by the policy, as was confirmed in the affidavit of the Vice Chief of the Defence Staff filed in the Perkins' proceedings (see paragraph 50 above). It is also accepted by the Government that neither the records nor conduct of the applicants nor the physical capability, courage, dependability and skills of homosexuals in general are in any way called into question by the policy.

97. The question for the Court is whether the above-noted negative attitudes constitute sufficient justification for the interferences at issue.

The Court observes from the HPAT report that these attitudes, even if sincerely felt by those who expressed them, ranged from stereotypical expressions of hostility to those of homosexual orientation, to vague expressions of unease about the presence of homosexual colleagues. To the extent that they represent a predisposed bias on the part of a heterosexual majority against a homosexual minority, these negative attitudes cannot, of themselves, be considered by the Court to amount to sufficient justification for the interferences with the applicants' rights outlined above any more than similar negative attitudes towards those of a different race, origin or colour.

98. The Government emphasised that the views expressed in the HPAT report served to show that any change in the policy would entail substantial damage to morale and operational effectiveness. The applicants considered these submissions to be unsubstantiated.

99. The Court notes the lack of concrete evidence to substantiate the alleged damage to morale and fighting power that any change in the policy would entail. Thorpe LJ in the Court of Appeal found that there was no actual or significant evidence of such damage as a result of the presence of homosexuals in the armed forces (see paragraph 40 above), and the Court further considers that the subsequent HPAT assessment did not, whatever its value, provide evidence of such damage in the event of the policy changing. * * *

100. However, in the light of the strength of feeling expressed in certain submissions to the HPAT and the special, interdependent and closely knit nature of the armed forces' environment, the Court considers it reasonable to assume that some difficulties could be anticipated as a result of any change in what is now a long-standing policy. Indeed, it would appear that the presence of women and racial minorities in the armed forces led to relational difficulties of the kind which the Government suggest admission of homosexuals would entail (see paragraphs 63 and 64 above).

101. The applicants submitted that a strict code of conduct applicable to all personnel would address any potential difficulties caused by negative attitudes of heterosexuals. The Government, while not rejecting the possibility out of hand, emphasised the need for caution given the subject matter and the armed forces context of the policy and pointed out that this was one of the options to be considered by the next Parliamentary Select Committee in 2001.

102. The Court considers it important to note, in the first place, the approach already adopted by the armed forces to deal with racial discrimination and with racial and sexual harassment and bullying (see paragraphs 63–64 above). The January 1996 Directive, for example, imposed both a strict code of conduct on every soldier together with disciplinary rules to deal with any inappropriate behaviour and conduct. This dual approach was supplemented with information leaflets and training programmes, the army emphasising the need for high standards of personal conduct and for respect for others.

* * *

The Government maintained that homosexuality raised problems of a type and intensity that race and gender did not. However, even if it can be assumed that the integration of homosexuals would give rise to problems not encountered with the integration of women or racial minorities, the Court is not satisfied that the codes and rules which have been found to be effective in the latter case would not equally prove effective in the former. The "robust indifference" reported by the HPAT of the large number of British armed forces' personnel serving abroad with allied forces to homosexuals serving in those foreign forces serves to confirm that the perceived problems of integration are not insuperable (see paragraph 59 above).

103. The Government highlighted particular problems which might be posed by the communal accommodation arrangements in the armed forces. Detailed submissions were made during the hearing, the parties disagreeing as to the potential consequences of shared single-sex accommodation and associated facilities.

The Court notes that the HPAT itself concluded that separate accommodation for homosexuals would not be warranted or wise and that substantial expenditure would not, therefore, have to be incurred in this respect. Nevertheless, the Court remains of the view that it has not been shown that the conduct codes and disciplinary rules referred to above could not adequately deal with any behavioural issues arising on the part either of homosexuals or of heterosexuals.

104. The Government, referring to the relevant analysis in the HPAT report, further argued that no worthwhile lessons could be gleaned from the relatively recent legal changes in those foreign armed forces which now admitted homosexuals. The Court disagrees. It notes the evidence before the domestic courts to the effect that the European countries operating a blanket legal ban on homosexuals in their armed forces are now in a small minority. It considers that, even if relatively recent, the Court cannot overlook the widespread and consistently developing views and associated legal changes to the domestic laws of Contracting States on this issue (see the Dudgeon judgment cited above, pp. 23–24, § 60).

105. Accordingly, the Court concludes that convincing and weighty reasons have not been offered by the Government to justify the policy against homosexuals in the armed forces or, therefore, the consequent discharge of the applicants from those forces.

* * *

110. In such circumstances, the Court considers that the Government have not offered convincing and weighty reasons justifying the continued investigation of the applicants' sexual orientation once they had confirmed their homosexuality to the air force authorities.

111. In sum, the Court finds that neither the investigations conducted into the applicants' sexual orientation, nor their discharge on the grounds of their homosexuality in pursuance of the Ministry of Defence policy, were justified under Article 8 § 2 of the Convention.

112. Accordingly, there has been a violation of Article 8 of the Convention.

* * *

FOR THESE REASONS, THE COURT UNANIMOUSLY

1. *Holds* that there has been a violation of Article 8 of the Convention;

* * *

The Court then found that there "had been no violation of Article 3 of the Convention taken alone or in conjunction with Article 14," but that there "had been a violation of Article 13 of the Convention."

In a later judgment, the Court awarded Ms. Smith £59,000 for pecuniary, and £19,000 for non-pecuniary damages; it awarded Mr. Grady £40,000 and £19,000 respectively. It also ordered the United Kingdom to pay the applicants £32,000 for litigation costs.

Note that the Court accords the "respondent State" a "margin of appreciation" (paragraphs 88, 89, 94 etc.). What exactly is that? And why does that not help the State at the end of the day? What arguments or evidence would the United Kingdom have had to present in order to win the case?

Smith and Grady concerned an essentially intra-state issue, i.e., how the United Kingdom treats members of its armed forces. While the next case also originated in the United Kingdom, it involves the law and situation in another country, namely the United States—which is not even a member of the European human rights system. What rights does the European Convention on Human Rights and Fundamental Freedoms give Soering that he would not have otherwise had?

Soering v. United Kingdom

European Court of Human Rights
161 Eur. Ct. H.R. (ser. A) (1989)

Facts

[Jens Soering, a German national born in 1966, came to the United States with his parents at age eleven. His father was a German diplomat. Soering enrolled at the University of Virginia in 1984, where he started dating Elizabeth Haysom during his freshman year. She was a fellow student, two years his senior and a Canadian national. According to the judgment of the ECHR, Haysom was a "powerful, persuasive and disturbed young woman," and the relationship between Soering and Haysom became "symbiotic," with Haysom calling the shots. Haysom's parents were opposed to the relationship; ultimately, Soering and Haysom decided to kill her parents so that they could remain together.

Soering and Haysom fled to Europe soon after the killing. They were arrested in the United Kingdom several months later on charges of check fraud. While under arrest in the United Kingdom, a Virginia grand jury returned an indictment charging Soering and Haysom with capital murder. The United States requested their extradition under a treaty with the United Kingdom. Haysom was extradited, pled guilty, and was sentenced to 90 years in prison.

Soering contested his extradition. He argued that his psychiatric condition should have reduced the charge against him to manslaughter. This argument was rejected as irrelevant to the question of extradition. In addition, he argued that under the extradition treaty, a state party could refuse extradition if the law of the arresting state had no death penalty for the offense for which the extradition is sought, unless the state seeking extradition gave satisfactory assurances to the treaty partner that the death penalty would not be carried out. Even though the prosecutor in Virginia had provided a statement with precisely that assurance, Soering argued that this should not be considered satisfactory. The United Kingdom rejected Soering's argument and ordered his extradition.

Thereafter, Soering filed a petition with the European Commission of Human Rights, expressing his belief that, notwithstanding the assurances provided by U.S. authorities, he might still be sentenced to death if extradited to the United States. While Articles 2(1) (right to life) and 3 (prohibition of inhuman punishment) of the European Convention of Human Rights had not been interpreted to prohibit the death penalty *per se*, Soering argued that the exceptional delay in carrying out the execution if he were sentenced to death (the *death row phenomenon*) would be inhuman punishment.]

LEGAL ANALYSIS

* * *

86. Article 1 of the Convention, which provides that "the High Contracting Parties shall secure to everyone within their jurisdiction the rights and freedoms defined in Section I," sets a limit, notably territorial, on the reach of the Convention. In particular, the engagement undertaken by a Contracting State is confined to "securing" ("reconnaître" in the French text) the listed rights and freedoms to persons within its own "jurisdiction." Further, the Convention does not govern the actions of States not

Parties to it, nor does it purport to be a means of requiring the Contracting States to impose Convention standards on other States. Article 1 cannot be read as justifying a general principle to the effect that, notwithstanding its extradition obligations, a Contracting State may not surrender an individual unless satisfied that the conditions awaiting him in the country of destination are in full accord with each of the safeguards of the Convention. Indeed, as the United Kingdom Government stressed, the beneficial purpose of extradition in preventing fugitive offenders from evading justice cannot be ignored in determining the scope of application of the Convention and of Article 3 in particular.

In the instant case it is common ground that the United Kingdom has no power over the practices and arrangements of the Virginia authorities which are the subject of the applicant's complaints. It is also true that in other international instruments cited by the United Kingdom Government—for example the 1951 United Nations Convention relating to the Status of Refugees (Article 33), the 1957 European Convention on Extradition (Article 11) and the 1984 United Nations Convention against Torture and Other Cruel, Inhuman and Degrading Treatment or Punishment (Article 3)—the problems of removing a person to another jurisdiction where unwanted consequences may follow are addressed expressly and specifically.

These considerations cannot, however, absolve the Contracting Parties from responsibility under Article 3 for all and any foreseeable consequences of extradition suffered outside their jurisdiction.

87. In interpreting the Convention regard must be had to its special character as a treaty for the collective enforcement of human rights and fundamental freedoms. Thus, the object and purpose of the Convention as an instrument for the protection of individual human beings require that its provisions be interpreted and applied so as to make its safeguards practical and effective. In addition, any interpretation of the rights and freedoms guaranteed has to be consistent with "the general spirit of the Convention, an instrument designed to maintain and promote the ideals and values of a democratic society."

88. Article 3 makes no provision for exceptions and no derogation from it is permissible under Article 15 in time of war or other national emergency. This absolute prohibition of torture and of inhuman or degrading treatment or punishment under the terms of the Convention shows that Article 3 enshrines one of the fundamental values of the democratic societies making up the Council of Europe. It is also to be found in similar terms in other international instruments such as the 1966 International Covenant on Civil and Political Rights and the 1969 American Convention on Human Rights and is generally recognised as an internationally accepted standard.

The question remains whether the extradition of a fugitive to another State where he would be subjected or be likely to be subjected to torture or to inhuman or degrading treatment or punishment would itself engage the responsibility of a Contracting State under Article 3. That the abhorrence of torture has such implications is recognised in Article 3 of the United Nations Convention Against Torture and Other Cruel, Inhuman or Degrading Treatment or Punishment, which provides that "no State Party shall * * * extradite a person where there are substantial grounds for believing that he would be in danger of being subjected to torture." The fact that a specialised treaty should spell out in detail a specific obligation attaching to the prohibition of torture does not mean that an essentially similar obligation is not already inherent in the general terms of Article 3 of the European Convention. It would hardly be compatible with the underlying values of the Convention, that "common heritage of political traditions, ideals, freedom and the rule of law" to which the Preamble refers, were a Contracting State knowingly to surrender a fugitive to another State where there were substantial grounds for believing that he would be in danger of being subjected to torture, however heinous the crime allegedly committed. Extradition in such circumstances, while not explicitly referred to in the brief and general wording of Article 3, would plainly be contrary to the spirit and intendment of the Article, and in the Court's view this inherent obligation not to extradite also extends to cases in which the fugitive would be faced in the receiving State by a real risk of exposure to inhuman or degrading treatment or punishment proscribed by that Article.

* * *

91. In sum, the decision by a Contracting State to extradite a fugitive may give rise to an issue under Article 3, and hence engage the responsibility of that State under the Convention, where substantial grounds have been shown for believing that the person concerned, if extradited, faces a real risk of being subjected to torture or to inhuman or degrading treatment or punishment in the requesting country. The establishment of such responsibility inevitably involves an assessment of conditions in the requesting country against the standards of Article 3 of the Convention. Nonetheless, there is no question of adjudicating on or establishing the responsibility of the receiving country, whether under general international law, under the Convention or otherwise. In so far as any liability under the Convention is or may be incurred, it is liability incurred by the extraditing Contracting State by reason of its having taken action which has as a direct consequence the exposure of an individual to proscribed ill-treatment.

B.   APPLICATION OF ARTICLE 3 IN THE PARTICULAR CIRCUMSTANCES
OF THE PRESENT CASE

    1.   WHETHER THE APPLICANT RUNS A REAL RISK OF A DEATH
SENTENCE AND HENCE OF EXPOSURE TO THE "DEATH ROW
PHENOMENON"

93. The United Kingdom Government, contrary to the Government of the
Federal Republic of Germany, the Commission and the applicant, did not
accept that the risk of a death sentence attains a sufficient level of likelihood to bring Article 3 into play. Their reasons were fourfold.

Firstly, as illustrated by his interview with the German prosecutor where
he appeared to deny any intention to kill, the applicant has not acknowledged his guilt of capital murder as such.

Secondly, only a prima facie case has so far been made out against him.
In particular, in the United Kingdom Government's view the psychiatric
evidence is equivocal as to whether Mr. Soering was suffering from a disease of the mind sufficient to amount to a defence of insanity under Virginia law.

Thirdly, even if Mr. Soering is convicted of capital murder, it cannot be
assumed that in the general exercise of their discretion the jury will recommend, the judge will confirm and the Supreme Court of Virginia will
uphold the imposition of the death penalty. The United Kingdom Government referred to the presence of important mitigating factors, such as
the applicant's age and mental condition at the time of commission of the
offence and his lack of previous criminal activity, which would have to be
taken into account by the jury and then by the judge in the separate sentencing proceedings.

Fourthly, the assurance received from the United States must at the very
least significantly reduce the risk of a capital sentence either being imposed or carried out.

At the public hearing the Attorney General nevertheless made clear his
Government's understanding that if Mr. Soering were extradited to the
United States there was "some risk," which was "more than merely negli-
gible," that the death penalty would be imposed.

94. As the applicant himself pointed out, he has made to American and
British police officers and to two psychiatrists admissions of his participation in the killings of the Haysom parents, although he appeared to re-
tract those admissions somewhat when questioned by the German prosecutor. It is not for the European Court to usurp the function of the Virginia courts by ruling that a defence of insanity would or would not be available on the psychiatric evidence as it stands. The United Kingdom Government are justified in their assertion that no assumption can be made
that Mr. Soering would certainly or even probably be convicted of capital

murder as charged. Nevertheless, as the Attorney General conceded on their behalf at the public hearing, there is "a significant risk" that the applicant would be so convicted.

* * *

99. The Court's conclusion is therefore that the likelihood of the feared exposure of the applicant to the "death row phenomenon" has been shown to be such as to bring Article 3 into play.

* * *

2. WHETHER IN THE CIRCUMSTANCES THE RISK OF EXPOSURE TO THE "DEATH ROW PHENOMENON" WOULD MAKE EXTRADITION A BREACH OF ARTICLE 3

(a) GENERAL CONSIDERATIONS

* * *

101. Capital punishment is permitted under certain conditions by Article 2 § 1 of the Convention, which reads:

> "Everyone's right to life shall be protected by law. No one shall be deprived of his life intentionally save in the execution of a sentence of a court following his conviction of a crime for which this penalty is provided by law."

In view of this wording, the applicant did not suggest that the death penalty per se violated Article 3. He, like the two Government Parties, agreed with the Commission that the extradition of a person to a country where he risks the death penalty does not in itself raise an issue under either Article 2 or Article 3. On the other hand, Amnesty International in their written comments argued that the evolving standards in Western Europe regarding the existence and use of the death penalty required that the death penalty should now be considered as an inhuman and degrading punishment within the meaning of Article 3.

* * *

103. The Convention is to be read as a whole and Article 3 should therefore be construed in harmony with the provisions of Article 2. On this basis Article 3 evidently cannot have been intended by the drafters of the Convention to include a general prohibition of the death penalty since that would nullify the clear wording of Article 2 § 1.

Subsequent practice in national penal policy, in the form of a generalised abolition of capital punishment, could be taken as establishing the agreement of the Contracting States to abrogate the exception provided for under Article 2 § 1 and hence to remove a textual limit on the scope for evolutive interpretation of Article 3. However, Protocol No. 6, as a subsequent written agreement, shows that the intention of the Contracting Parties as recently as 1983 was to adopt the normal method of amendment of the text in order to introduce a new obligation to abolish capital punishment in time of peace and, what is more, to do so by an optional instrument allowing each State to choose the moment when to undertake such an engagement. In these conditions, notwithstanding the special character of the Convention, Article 3 cannot be interpreted as generally prohibiting the death penalty.

104. That does not mean however that circumstances relating to a death sentence can never give rise to an issue under Article 3. The manner in which it is imposed or executed, the personal circumstances of the condemned person and a disproportionality to the gravity of the crime committed, as well as the conditions of detention awaiting execution, are examples of factors capable of bringing the treatment or punishment received by the condemned person within the proscription under Article 3. Present-day attitudes in the Contracting States to capital punishment are relevant for the assessment whether the acceptable threshold of suffering or degradation has been exceeded.

(b) THE PARTICULAR CIRCUMSTANCES

105. The applicant submitted that the circumstances to which he would be exposed as a consequence of the implementation of the Secretary of State's decision to return him to the United States, namely the "death row phenomenon," cumulatively constituted such serious treatment that his extradition would be contrary to Article 3. He cited in particular the delays in the appeal and review procedures following a death sentence, during which time he would be subject to increasing tension and psychological trauma; the fact, so he said, that the judge or jury in determining sentence is not obliged to take into account the defendant's age and mental state at the time of the offence; the extreme conditions of his future detention on "death row" in Mecklenburg Correctional Center, where he expects to be the victim of violence and sexual abuse because of his age, colour and nationality; and the constant spectre of the execution itself, including the ritual of execution. He also relied on the possibility of extradition or deportation, which he would not oppose, to the Federal Republic of Germany as accentuating the disproportionality of the Secretary of State's decision.

The Government of the Federal Republic of Germany took the view that, taking all the circumstances together, the treatment awaiting the applicant in Virginia would go so far beyond treatment inevitably connected with the imposition and execution of a death penalty as to be "inhuman" within the meaning of Article 3.

On the other hand, the conclusion expressed by the Commission was that the degree of severity contemplated by Article 3 would not be attained.

The United Kingdom Government shared this opinion. In particular, they disputed many of the applicant's factual allegations as to the conditions on death row in Mecklenburg and his expected fate there.

i.   LENGTH OF DETENTION PRIOR TO EXECUTION

106. The period that a condemned prisoner can expect to spend on death row in Virginia before being executed is on average six to eight years. This length of time awaiting death is, as the Commission and the United Kingdom Government noted, in a sense largely of the prisoner's own making in that he takes advantage of all avenues of appeal which are offered to him by Virginia law. The automatic appeal to the Supreme Court of Virginia normally takes no more than six months. The remaining time is accounted for by collateral attacks mounted by the prisoner himself in habeas corpus proceedings before both the State and Federal courts and in applications to the Supreme Court of the United States for certiorari review, the prisoner at each stage being able to seek a stay of execution. The remedies available under Virginia law serve the purpose of ensuring that the ultimate sanction of death is not unlawfully or arbitrarily imposed.

Nevertheless, just as some lapse of time between sentence and execution is inevitable if appeal safeguards are to be provided to the condemned person, so it is equally part of human nature that the person will cling to life by exploiting those safeguards to the full. However well-intentioned and even potentially beneficial is the provision of the complex of post-sentence procedures in Virginia, the consequence is that the condemned prisoner has to endure for many years the conditions on death row and the anguish and mounting tension of living in the ever-present shadow of death.

ii.   CONDITIONS ON DEATH ROW

107. As to conditions in Mecklenburg Correctional Center, where the applicant could expect to be held if sentenced to death, the Court bases itself on the facts which were uncontested by the United Kingdom Government, without finding it necessary to determine the reliability of the additional evidence adduced by the applicant, notably as to the risk of homosexual abuse and physical attack undergone by prisoners on death row.

The stringency of the custodial regime in Mecklenburg, as well as the services (medical, legal and social) and the controls (legislative, judicial and administrative) provided for inmates, are described in some detail above. In this connection, the United Kingdom Government drew attention to the necessary requirement of extra security for the safe custody of prisoners condemned to death for murder. Whilst it might thus well be justifiable in principle, the severity of a special regime such as that operated on death row in Mecklenburg is compounded by the fact of inmates being subject to it for a protracted period lasting on average six to eight years.

iii. THE APPLICANT'S AGE AND MENTAL STATE

108. At the time of the killings, the applicant was only 18 years old and there is some psychiatric evidence, which was not contested as such, that he "was suffering from [such] an abnormality of mind * * * as substantially impaired his mental responsibility for his acts."

Unlike Article 2 of the Convention, Article 6 of the 1966 International Covenant on Civil and Political Rights and Article 4 of the 1969 American Convention on Human Rights expressly prohibit the death penalty from being imposed on persons aged less than 18 at the time of commission of the offence. Whether or not such a prohibition be inherent in the brief and general language of Article 2 of the European Convention, its explicit enunciation in other, later international instruments, the former of which has been ratified by a large number of States Parties to the European Convention, at the very least indicates that as a general principle the youth of the person concerned is a circumstance which is liable, with others, to put in question the compatibility with Article 3 of measures connected with a death sentence.

It is in line with the Court's case-law to treat disturbed mental health as having the same effect for the application of Article 3.

109. Virginia law, as the United Kingdom Government and the Commission emphasised, certainly does not ignore these two factors. Under the Virginia Code account has to be taken of mental disturbance in a defendant, either as an absolute bar to conviction if it is judged to be sufficient to amount to insanity or, like age, as a fact in mitigation at the sentencing stage. Additionally, indigent capital murder defendants are entitled to the appointment of a qualified mental health expert to assist in the preparation of their submissions at the separate sentencing proceedings. These provisions in the Virginia Code undoubtedly serve, as the American courts have stated, to prevent the arbitrary or capricious imposition of the death penalty and narrowly to channel the sentencer's discretion. They do not however remove the relevance of age and mental condition in relation to the acceptability, under Article 3, of the "death row phenomenon" for a given individual once condemned to death.

Although it is not for this Court to prejudge issues of criminal responsibility and appropriate sentence, the applicant's youth at the time of the offence and his then mental state, on the psychiatric evidence as it stands, are therefore to be taken into consideration as contributory factors tending, in his case, to bring the treatment on death row within the terms of Article 3.

iv. POSSIBILITY OF EXTRADITION TO THE FEDERAL RE-
PUBLIC OF GERMANY

110. For the United Kingdom Government and the majority of the Commission, the possibility of extraditing or deporting the applicant to face
trial in the Federal Republic of Germany, where the death penalty has
been abolished under the Constitution, is not material for the present
purposes. Any other approach, the United Kingdom Government submitted, would lead to a "dual standard" affording the protection of the Convention to extraditable persons fortunate enough to have such an alternative destination available but refusing it to others not so fortunate.

This argument is not without weight. Furthermore, the Court cannot
overlook either the horrible nature of the murders with which Mr. Soering is charged or the legitimate and beneficial role of extradition arrangements in combating crime. The purpose for which his removal to the
United States was sought, in accordance with the Extradition Treaty between the United Kingdom and the United States, is undoubtedly a legitimate one. However, sending Mr. Soering to be tried in his own country
would remove the danger of a fugitive criminal going unpunished as well
as the risk of intense and protracted suffering on death row. It is therefore a circumstance of relevance for the overall assessment under Article
3 in that it goes to the search for the requisite fair balance of interests
and to the proportionality of the contested extradition decision in the particular case.

(c) CONCLUSION

111. For any prisoner condemned to death, some element of delay between imposition and execution of the sentence and the experience of severe stress in conditions necessary for strict incarceration are inevitable.
The democratic character of the Virginia legal system in general and the
positive features of Virginia trial, sentencing and appeal procedures in
particular are beyond doubt. The Court agrees with the Commission that
the machinery of justice to which the applicant would be subject in the
United States is in itself neither arbitrary nor unreasonable, but, rather,
respects the rule of law and affords not inconsiderable procedural safeguards to the defendant in a capital trial. Facilities are available on death
row for the assistance of inmates, notably through provision of psychological and psychiatric services.

However, in the Court's view, having regard to the very long period of
time spent on death row in such extreme conditions, with the ever present and mounting anguish of awaiting execution of the death penalty,
and to the personal circumstances of the applicant, especially his age and
mental state at the time of the offence, the applicant's extradition to the
United States would expose him to a real risk of treatment going beyond
the threshold set by Article 3. A further consideration of relevance is that

in the particular instance the legitimate purpose of extradition could be achieved by another means which would not involve suffering of such exceptional intensity or duration.

Accordingly, the Secretary of State's decision to extradite the applicant to the United States would, if implemented, give rise to a breach of Article 3.

This finding in no way puts in question the good faith of the United Kingdom Government, who have from the outset of the present proceedings demonstrated their desire to abide by their Convention obligations, firstly by staying the applicant's surrender to the United States authorities in accord with the interim measures indicated by the Convention institutions and secondly by themselves referring the case to the Court for a judicial ruling.

[The Court held unanimously that a decision by the Secretary of State of the United Kingdom to extradite the applicant to the United States would be a violation of Article 3, and ordered the U.K. to pay the applicant's legal expenses.]

CONCURRING OPINION OF JUDGE DE MEYER

The applicant's extradition to the United States of America would not only expose him to inhuman or degrading treatment or punishment. It would also, and above all, violate his right to life.

Indeed, the most important issue in this case is not "the likelihood of the feared exposure of the applicant to the 'death row phenomenon'," but the very simple fact that his life would be put in jeopardy by the said extradition.

The second sentence of Article 2 § 1 of the Convention, as it was drafted in 1950, states that "no one shall be deprived of his life intentionally save in the execution of a sentence of a court following his conviction of a crime for which this penalty is provided by law."

In the circumstances of the present case, the applicant's extradition to the United States would subject him to the risk of being sentenced to death, and executed, in Virginia for a crime for which that penalty is not provided by the law of the United Kingdom.

When a person's right to life is involved, no requested State can be entitled to allow a requesting State to do what the requested State is not itself allowed to do.

If, as in the present case, the domestic law of a State does not provide the death penalty for the crime concerned, that State is not permitted to put the person concerned in a position where he may be deprived of his life for that crime at the hands of another State.

That consideration may already suffice to preclude the United Kingdom from surrendering the applicant to the United States.

There is also something more fundamental.

The second sentence of Article 2 § 1 of the Convention was adopted, nearly forty years ago, in particular historical circumstances, shortly after the Second World War. In so far as it still may seem to permit, under certain conditions, capital punishment in time of peace, it does not reflect the contemporary situation, and is now overridden by the development of legal conscience and practice.

Such punishment is not consistent with the present state of European civilisation.

De facto, it no longer exists in any State Party to the Convention.

Its unlawfulness was recognised by the Committee of Ministers of the Council of Europe when it adopted in December 1982, and opened for signature in April 1983, the Sixth Protocol to the Convention, which to date has been signed by sixteen, and ratified by thirteen, Contracting States.

No State Party to the Convention can in that context, even if it has not yet ratified the Sixth Protocol, be allowed to extradite any person if that person thereby incurs the risk of being put to death in the requesting State.

Extraditing somebody in such circumstances would be repugnant to European standards of justice, and contrary to the public order of Europe.

The applicant's surrender by the United Kingdom to the United States could only be lawful if the United States were to give absolute assurances that he will not be put to death if convicted of the crime he is charged with.

No such assurances were, or can be, obtained.

The Federal Government of the United States is unable to give any undertaking as to what may or may not be decided, or done, by the judicial and other authorities of the Commonwealth of Virginia.

In fact, the Commonwealth's Attorney dealing with the case intends to seek the death penalty and the Commonwealth's Governor has never commuted a death sentence since the imposition of the death penalty was resumed in 1977.

In these circumstances there can be no doubt whatsoever that the applicant's extradition to the United States would violate his right to life.

––––––––––––

Consider the effect of the Court's decision on the United States. Does the decision amount to a *de facto* extraterritorial application of the Convention?

Does the Court's decision put the United Kingdom between a rock and a hard place because the United Kingdom cannot fulfil its obligations under both treaties? Or is there a way to follow the Court's decision here without violating the bilateral extradition treaty?

Eventually, the United Kingdom received the necessary assurances from the United States that the death penalty would not be imposed, and Soering was extradited. He was convicted of first-degree murder in Virginia and sentenced to two consecutive life sentences.

The Inter–American Human Rights System

The Inter–American Human Rights System is a network of regional institutions and documents that safeguard human rights under the auspices of the Organization of American States (OAS) in the Western Hemisphere.

This regional human rights system has two foundational norms:

1. The American Declaration on the Rights and Duties of Man (American Declaration) was adopted in 1948. It calls for respect for basic human rights in much the same fashion as the Universal Declaration of Human Rights would some six months later, but it also establishes certain duties incumbent upon all individuals. All OAS member states, including the United States, have agreed to treat the American Declaration as authoritative.

2. The American Convention on Human Rights (American Convention) was adopted in 1969. It stakes out a more extensive and detailed list of protected rights, and establishes two principal institutions to ensure their observance: the Inter–American Commission on Human Rights and the Inter–American Court of Human Rights. The United States is not a member of the American Convention.

The Inter–American system operates through these two major institutions:

1. The Inter–American Commission, established in 1959, consists of seven members tasked with promoting respect for and defending human rights in OAS Member States. The Commission is empowered to produce reports, request information from governments and, most importantly, receive complaints from individual citizens and organizations regarding specific human rights abuses. If the State alleged to have violated an individual's rights is a party to the American Convention, the Commission will review the State's actions for consistency with the terms of the Convention. If the State in question is not a party to the American Convention, the Commission's investigation is limited to those rights protected in the American Declaration. The Commission may submit individual cases

to the Inter–American Court, but the Court will only issue an advisory opinion if the Respondent State has accepted the jurisdiction of the Court.

The Commission's competence to hear complaints lodged against the United States was initially questioned since the United States is not a party to the American Convention that established the Commission. Nevertheless, in a 1981 ruling on the admissibility of a case brought on behalf of an aborted fetus, the Commission established that the American Declaration had binding force on the United States under the OAS Charter and that the Commission had jurisdiction to monitor observance of the American Declaration by the United States. See *White and Potter v. United States*, Case 2141, Inter–Am. C.H.R., Report No. 23/81, OEA/Ser.L/V/II.54, doc. 9, rev. 1 (1980–81). Since then, the United States has participated in the Commission's proceedings without objection, and the Commission has been relatively active in investigating human rights abuses in the United States. In 2006, the Commission declared four claims against the United States admissible, and in many previous cases, the Commission has reprimanded the United States for violating human rights, even declaring that the U.S. practice of the juvenile death penalty violated a *jus cogens* norm of international law. See *Domingues v. United States*, Case 12.285, Inter–Am. C. H. R., Report No. 62/02 para. 85 (1999).

2. The Inter–American Court of Human Rights, established in 1978, sits in San José, Costa Rica. The Court's contentious jurisdiction, like that of the ICJ, is limited to states that voluntarily appear before the Court. The Court's advisory jurisdiction, however, is broader than the ICJ's, extending to all questions referred to it by the Inter–American Commission and all OAS Member States. Individuals may not petition the Court directly. Although the United States is not a party to the American Convention and has not voluntarily submitted to the Court's contentious jurisdiction, the Court has pronounced upon the consistency of U.S. actions with international human rights standards under its advisory jurisdiction. The Court's rulings in advisory opinions, however, have no binding effect on the parties.

The following decision was rendered by the Inter–American Commission on Human Rights (not by the Inter–American Court of Human Rights). What are the principal arguments by the petitioner and by the United States, and how does the Commission respond?

WILLIAM ANDREWS V. UNITED STATES

Inter–American Commission on Human Rights
Case No. 11.139 OEA/Ser.L/II.95, doc 7 rev. at 57 (1997)

I.   ALLEGATIONS IN PETITION DATED JULY 28, 1992

1. On July 27, 1992, the Commission received a fax communication informing it of the pending execution of Mr. William Andrews by the State

of Utah on July 29, 1992, for three counts of Murder, and briefly outlined the petitioners' allegations.

2. On July 28, 1992 the Commission received a petition filed by Steven W. Hawkins of the LDF Capital Punishment Project; Richard J. Wilson, Director, International Human Rights Clinic, Washington College of Law, American University; and Bartram S. Brown of Chicago–Kent College of Law, on behalf of William Andrews which alleged that he was an African–American male born in Jonesboro, Louisiana, was now a prisoner on death row in Draper Correctional Institution, Draper, Utah, and was scheduled to be executed at or about 12:01 a.m. on July 30, 1992. The petition alleged that in 1974, Mr. Andrews was convicted of three counts of first degree murder and two counts of aggravated robbery in the State of Utah, and that he was subsequently sentenced to death on all three counts by the same jury which convicted him.

3. The petitioners further alleged that both the victims and the jurors were Caucasian, and the sole black member of the jury pool was stricken peremptorily by the prosecution during jury selection. Mr. Andrews had left the premises prior to the offenses, and that his co-defendant, fatally shot the victims. His co-defendant, also African–American was executed by the State of Utah in 1987.

4. It is further alleged that a napkin (note) was found among the jurors during a recess of the trial, which stated "Hang the Nigger's" and that Mr. Andrews' attorney requested a mistrial and a right to question jurors concerning the note, but this request was denied by the trial judge. Instead the trial judge admonished the jurors to "ignore communications from foolish people." [It is alleged that] the denial of the right to question the jury about the note and the mistrial coupled with the known racist Mormon Church doctrine was ground for a mistrial and [that,] at minimum, a further inquiry into the authorship, and source of the note, exposure of the note to members of the jury or their response to it [should have been conducted].

[In Davis County, Utah, where the petitioner was tried, 73.9% of the community was Mormon at the time of the trial. The trial judge presiding over the case and at least some of the jurors were Mormon. The petitioner presented evidence of the formal policy of racial discrimination by the Mormon Church at the time of the trial. In 1969, only five years before Andrews' trial, the First President of the Mormon Church had stated to the congregation: "The seeming discrimination by the Church toward the Negro is not something that originated with man; but goes back to the beginning with God." In addition, the petitioner showed that polls conducted in Utah only three years before the trial showed that over 70 percent of all Mormons believed that God had cursed black people to a life in hell.]

5. Mr. Andrews filed several appeals and habeas corpus petitions before the State and Federal courts in Utah, including the United States Supreme Court, and the Utah Supreme Court, raising a number of issues which included the matters raised in this petition, and collateral attacks, and sought clemency from the Board of Pardons. All his appeals, and habeas corpus petitions were denied, the final denial was on July 29, 1992.

6. The petitioners requested precautionary measures, and requested an immediate stay of the execution proceedings against Mr. Andrews due to the urgency of this matter, the immediacy of the execution and to avoid irreparable damage. The petitioners stated further that the case was admissible, as a result of a final appeal, and that the United States Government violated Articles of the Organization of American States Charter and the American Declaration of the Rights and Duties of Man.

* * *

V.   ISSUES TO BE DECIDED ON THE MERITS OF PETITION

143. Did the action of the United States in trying, convicting, sentencing, and executing William Andrews on July 30, 1992 constitute violations of the American Declaration of the Rights and Duties of Man, in particular, Article I, the right to life, liberty and personal security, Article II, the right to equality before the law and Article XXVI, the right to an impartial hearing, and not to receive cruel, infamous or unusual punishment?

* * *

A.   DID MR. ANDREWS HAVE A FAIR AND IMPARTIAL HEARING?

147. Article XXVI of the American Declaration, paragraph 2 provides: "Every person accused of an offense has the right to be given an impartial and public hearing, and to be tried by courts previously established in accordance with pre-existing laws, and not to receive cruel, infamous or unusual punishment." * * *

148. * * * [T]he Commission will address the * * * right "every person accused of an offense has the right to be given an impartial and public hearing," first. * * * Upon examining all arguments, documentary and testimonial evidence including exhibits submitted to it, the Commission notes that: Mr. Andrews was tried, convicted, sentenced, and executed by the State of Utah on three counts of first degree murder, and two counts of aggravated robbery, which occurred after he participated in the robbery of a radio store. He was tried in the State of Utah where the teaching of the Mormon church doctrine prevailing at the time of his trial, was that all black people were damned to death by God and were inferior beings. This doctrine was changed after the trial and conviction of the victim, Mr. Andrews.

* * *

[The Commission reviewed the evidence submitted by the petitioner and by the government as well as the relevant federal and state law on jury bias.]

e) THE INTERNATIONAL STANDARD ON IMPARTIALITY

159. The international standard on the issue of "judge and juror impartiality" employs an objective test based on "reasonableness, and the appearance of impartiality." The United Nations Committee to Eliminate Racial Discrimination has held that a reasonable suspicion of bias is sufficient for juror disqualification, and stated that: "it is incumbent upon national judicial authorities to investigate the issue and to disqualify the juror if there is a suspicion that the juror might be biased."

160. In the case of *Remli v. France* the European Court of Human Rights referred to the principles laid down in its case-law concerning the independence and impartiality of tribunals, which applied to jurors as they did to professional and lay judges and found that there had been a violation of Article 6(1) of the European Convention For the Protection of Human Rights and Fundamental Freedoms. That Article provides that: "In the determination of his civil rights and obligations or of any criminal charge against him, everyone is entitled to a fair and public hearing * * * by an independent and impartial tribunal established by law. * * * "

* * *

162. The Commission has noted the United States Government's argument that the admonishment by the trial court to the jury to disregard communications from foolish people was appropriate. It has also noted its argument that the jury was not racist because Mr. Andrews' co-defendant, Keith Roberts, who was African American, and whose counsel was African American and also charged with murder, was not convicted of murder, nor sentenced to death; and the attorneys for the other two co-defendants were not African American. The Commission finds that these factors are not dispositive of whether the United States violated the Articles of the American Declaration as pertaining to Mr. William Andrews' right to an "impartial hearing." The Commission has also noted that Mr. Andrews' other co-defendant who was African American was convicted and sentenced to death by the State of Utah, and executed in 1987. * * *

165. The Commission finds that in assessing the totality of the facts in an objective and reasonable manner the evidence indicates that Mr. Andrews did not receive an impartial hearing because there was a reasonable appearance of "racial bias" by some members of the jury, and the omission of the trial court to voir dire the jury tainted his trial and resulted in him being convicted, sentenced to death and executed. The record before the Commission reflects ample evidence of "racial basis [sic]."

166. First, Mr. Andrews was a black male, and was tried by an all white jury some of whom were members of the Mormon Church and adhered to its teachings that black people were inferior beings. The transcript reveals that the bailiff testified that when the juror told him he had some evidence for him, both the bailiff and some of the other jurors thought that it was one of the juror's jokes which they were humoring and there was discussion among the jurors concerning the "napkin."

167. Second, was the conduct and manner, in which the note was handed to the bailiff by the juror. (See trial transcript, the bailiff thought he was humoring a joke.) The note depicts racial words "hang the nigger's," written on the napkin that was given to the Court. (See the opinions of Justices Brennan and Marshall.) The trial transcript states "Hang the Niggers," and the drawing on the napkin was described by the bailiff as "a gallows and a stick figure hanging therefrom." The transcript refers to express language by the bailiff, that the jurors who were immediate to the left and the right of Mr. Weaver, (the juror who found the napkin) would have had to have seen it. The jurors asked the bailiff, if it would affect their present situation and what the court may do about it. The bailiff himself stated under oath that it was possible that one of the jurors could have drawn that note because "that small amount, that much time could have elapsed."

168. Third, the admonishment by the trial court to the jury was inadequate. The trial judge at the very least if he did not want to grant a mistrial, should have conducted an evidentiary hearing of the jury members to ascertain whether some of them had seen the note and they had been influenced by it. The trial judge instead, warned them against foolish people, and questioned the bailiff and left such an important and fundamental issue for the bailiff, whom he instructed to admonish the juror who found the note. The trial judge appeared to be more concerned to continue the trial with the same members of the jury without questioning them, as to whether they had seen the note, and denied both motions to sequester the jury and for a mistrial.

169. Fourth, in addition to the note being found, there is language in the trial transcript which indicates the concern expressed by the defense attorneys, that two things had occurred during the trial, "the talk in the hallway, and the note," which would influence the jury members in their deliberations and in making their decisions, and which language had become accumulative.

170. It should be noted that while it is not the function of the Inter–American Commission on Human Rights to act as a quasi-judicial fourth instance court and to review the holdings of the domestic courts of the OAS member states, it is mandated by its Statute and its Regulations to examine petitions alleging violations of human rights under the American

Declaration against member States who are not parties to the American Convention.

171. The Commission finds that Mr. Andrews did not receive an impartial trial because there was evidence of "racial bias" present during his trial, and because the trial court failed to conduct an evidentiary hearing of the jury in order to ascertain whether members of the jury found the napkin as the juror claimed or whether the jurors themselves wrote and drew the racial words on the napkin. If the note did not originate from the jurors and was "found" by the juror then the trial court could have inquired of the jurors by conducting an evidentiary hearing as to whether they would be influenced or their judgment impaired by the napkin depicting the racial words and drawing so that they would be unable to try the case impartially. Had the Court conducted the hearing it would have had the possibility of remedying, if it had proved necessary so to do, a situation contrary to the requirements of the American Declaration.

172. Therefore, the Commission finds the United States in violation of Article XXVI, paragraph 2, of the American Declaration, because Mr. Andrews had the right to receive an impartial hearing as provided by the Article, and he did not receive an impartial trial in United States Courts. In capital punishment cases, the States Parties have an obligation to observe rigorously all the guarantees for an impartial trial.

   B.   DID MR. ANDREWS RECEIVE EQUAL TREATMENT WITHOUT DISTINCTION AS TO RACE?

[The Commission found that the United States had violated Article II of the American Declaration which provides that everyone has the right to equal protection of the law without discrimination.]

   C.   WAS MR. ANDREWS' RIGHT TO LIFE VIOLATED?

175. With regard to the petitioner's claim that the United States violated Article I of the American Declaration, Article I provides: "Every human being has the right to life, liberty and the security of his person." Article I is silent on the issue of the death penalty. However, when the definitive draft of the "Project of Declaration of the International Rights and Duties of Man, formulated by the Inter–American Juridical Committee," was presented for consideration by the Ninth International Conference of American States in 1948, the original Article I, provided:

> Every person has the right to life. This right extends to the right to life from the moment of conception; to the right to life of incurables, imbeciles and the insane. Capital punishment may only be applied in cases in which it has been prescribed by pre-existing law for crimes of exceptional gravity.

176. The explanation given for the amendment of the last part of Article I was stated by the Committee as follows:

The Committee is not taking sides in favor of the death penalty but rather admitting the fact that there is a diversity of legislation in this respect, recognizes the authority of each State to regulate this question.

The Committee must note that several constitutions of America based on generous humanitarian conceptions, forbid the legislator to impose the said penalty.

177. Thus, the construction of Article I of the Right to Life of the American Declaration does not define nor sanction capital punishment by a member State of the OAS. However, it provides that a member State can impose capital punishment if it is prescribed by pre-existing law for crimes of exceptional gravity. Therefore, inherent in the construction of Article I, is a requirement that before the death penalty can be imposed and before the death sentence can be executed, the accused person must be given all the guarantees established by pre-existing laws, which includes guarantees contained in its Constitution, and its international obligations, including those rights and freedoms enshrined in the American Declaration. These guarantees include, the right to life, and not to be arbitrarily deprived of one's life, the right to due process of law, the right to an impartial and public hearing, the right not to receive cruel, infamous, or unusual punishment, and the right to equality at law. Evidence produced to the Commission was sufficient to prove that Mr. Andrews did not receive an impartial trial because the trial court failed to grant Mr. Andrews an evidentiary hearing for the reasons discussed above. The Commission therefore finds, that Mr. Andrews' right to life was violated because he was tried by an impartial and incompetent court which did not provide him with equal treatment at law. Therefore, the Commission finds for the reasons discussed above that Mr. Andrews' right to life was violated by the United States pursuant to Article I of the American Declaration.

   D.   DID MR. ANDREWS RECEIVE CRUEL, INFAMOUS OR UNUSUAL
        PUNISHMENT?

178. With regard to the question whether Mr. Andrews received cruel, infamous, or unusual punishment, the Commission finds that in this case the death penalty was not rendered by an impartial and competent court for the reasons discussed above. It was rendered by the same jury who found Mr. Andrews guilty. Mr. Andrews did not receive equal treatment at law, and his right to life was violated. He spent eighteen years on death row, and was not allowed to leave his cell for more than a few hours a week. During that time he received notice of at least eight execution dates and was executed by the State of Utah in July of 1992 on the basis of the jury's decision which was tainted because of evidence of "racial biasness" on their part. Therefore, for the reasons discussed above, the

Commission finds that the United States violated Mr. Andrews' right not to receive cruel, infamous or unusual punishment pursuant to Article XXVI of the American Declaration.

* * *

THEREFORE THE INTER–AMERICAN COMMISSION FINDS THAT:

184. The United States violated William Andrews right [to] life pursuant to Article I of the American Declaration.

185. The United States violated William Andrews right to equality at law pursuant to Article II of the American Declaration.

186. The United States violated William Andrews right to an impartial hearing pursuant to Article XXVI of the American Declaration.

187. The United States violated William Andrews right not to receive cruel, infamous, or unusual punishment pursuant to Article XXVI of the American Declaration.

THE COMMISSION RECOMMENDS THAT:

188. The United States must provide adequate compensation to Mr. William Andrews' next of kin for the violations referred to in paragraphs 184 to 187 above.

VII. PUBLICATION:

189. On January 22, 1997, the Commission wrote to the Government of the United States of America and enclosed a copy of this Report, and requested that it "inform the Commission as to the measures that have been adopted to comply with the recommendations made to resolve the situation denounced within two months."

190. On March 14, 1997, the United States of America replied by letter to the Commission's request, and informed it *inter alia* that Mr. Andrews received an impartial trial free of racial bias, and stated that for the reasons stated in its letter and its prior detailed submissions, that it "cannot agree with the Commission's findings, or carry out its recommendations."

191. The Commission, considering that the United States of America has not complied with its recommendations, decides to ratify its conclusions and recommendations contained in this Report; and also decides that this Report be published in accordance with Article 54(5) of its Regulations in its Annual Report to the General Assembly.

———————————

The Commission did not issue its opinion until more than six years had passed since William Andrews' execution. Does this indicate that the Inter–American human rights system is ineffective? Was the United States' response to the decision of the Committee appropriate?

The African Human Rights System

The African human rights system began to take shape with the African Charter on Human and People's Rights (known as the Banjul Charter), which was adopted in 1981 and entered into force in 1986. As the foundational document of the African human rights system, the Banjul Charter established the African Commission on Human and People's Rights, the first major pan-African human rights institution empowered to interpret the Banjul Charter and uphold human rights in member states of the Organization of African Unity (OAU) (and subsequently African Union) across the continent. (The OAU was dissolved on July 9, 2002 and the African Union (AU) was launched to take its place as the key pan-African regional international organization.) Although it is not a court, the Commission has quasi-judicial authority to receive human rights complaints. It can also independently investigate human rights violations and collect information on these issues across the continent. While the Commission can hear individual complaints, a key weakness is that its decisions are not binding on states.

A major development in the evolution of the African human rights system occurred in June 1998 when the African Court on Human and People's Rights (ACHPR) was established by OAU member states to create legal accountability for human rights abuses in Africa. Despite this ambitious goal, fewer than half of OAU member states ratified the Protocol establishing the Court.

The ACHPR finally began accepting cases in June 2008. It has broad jurisdiction over disputes concerning the interpretation and application of the Charter and other human rights instruments ratified by the AU states. It can also issue advisory opinions at the request of AU member states, the AU and its organs, and African organizations recognized by the AU. One of the unique features of the Court is that, unlike other regional human rights institutions in Europe and the Americas, it has broad powers to enforce socio-economic and group rights enumerated in the African Charter of Human and People's Rights. Thus, its scope is not limited to civil and political rights.

In 2008, AU states agreed to establish the African Court of Justice and Human Rights by merging the African Court of Justice (the nascent judicial organ of the AU) with the African Court of Human and People's Rights. This new court is designed to be the primary judicial organ of the AU. It has two sections. The general section will oversee disputes over AU powers and treaty obligations of AU states. The human rights section will basically adopt the mandate of the ACHPR. The agreement establishing the new court is now open for ratification. After a sufficient number of AU states ratify it, the new court will replace the current court.

Partly because of the delay in establishing the Court, a number of sub-regional courts and judicial institutions have been established over the years, such as the Court of Justice of the Economic Community of West African States (ECOWAS), the East African Court of Justice (EACJ), and the Tribunal of the Southern African Development Community (SADC). This multitude has led to complex jurisdictional disputes and forum shopping.

ECOWAS is a regional international organization made up of 15 member states. It was founded in 1975 with a mission of economic integration. The Community Court of Justice is the judicial organ of ECOWAS. It was established through a Supplementary Protocol to the ECOWAS treaty in 1991, but the Court was not functional until 2001. Originally only member states, heads of states, and the community as a whole could bring cases to the Court. In January 2005, a Supplementary Protocol empowered individuals and corporate bodies to bring cases against member states and expanded the jurisdiction of the Court to include human rights violations in all member states. The Court's decisions are legally binding on ECOWAS member states. With regard to human rights cases, the Court applies, inter alia, all international human rights instruments ratified by State(s) party to the case.

What are the primary complaints made by the applicant in the case below against her home country, the Republic of Niger? Which of her complaints does the court accept, and why does it reject others? What sources of law does the court rely on?

KORAOU V. NIGER[7]

ECOWAS Community Court of Justice
ECW/CCJ/JUD/06/08 (2008)

JUDGMENT

1. The applicant, Mrs. Hadijatou Mani Koraou, of Nigerien nationality, is a citizen of the ECOWAS Community.

* * *

3. The defendant, the Republic of Niger, is a Member State of the ECOWAS Community.

* * *

---

[7] Unofficial English translation by Inter Rights (London), an international human rights organization that represented Ms. Koraou.

PRESENTATION OF THE FACTS AND THE PROCEDURE

8. In 1996, while she was only twelve years old, the applicant, Mrs. Hadijatou Mani Koraou, of the Bouzou custom was sold to the tribe chief, Mr. El Hadj Souleymane Naroua, of the Haoussa custom, aged 46 years old, for two hundred and forty thousand CFA francs.

9. This transaction occurred in the name of the *"Wahiya,"* a current practice in Niger consisting of acquiring a young girl, generally a slave, to work as a servant as well as a concubine. The slave woman who is bought under these conditions is called *"Sadaka"* or fifth wife, i.e. a wife who is not one of the legally married wives, the number of which cannot exceed four, according to Islam's Recommendations.

10. In general the *"Sadaka"* does housework and is at the *"master*'s*"* service. He can, at any time, day or night, have sexual relations with her.

11. One day, as she was working in her master's field, he came and surprised her and then abused her. This first forced sexual act was imposed in these conditions while she was less than 13 years old. Thus the applicant was often the victim of acts of violence on the part of her master, as a result of genuine or supposed rebelliousness.

12. For about nine years, Hadijatou Mani Koraou was a servant in El Hadj Souleymane Naroua's household, doing all sorts of housework and serving as a concubine. Four children were born out of relations with her master, two of whom survived.

13. On the 18 August 2005, El Hadj Souleymane Naroua gave Hadijatou Mani Koraou a liberation certificate from slavery. This certificate was signed by the beneficiary, the master and countersigned by the chief of the village who stamped it.

14. Following this liberation act, the applicant decided to leave the house of her former master. He refused, on the ground that she was and remained his wife. Nevertheless, under the pretext of a visit to her mother who was ill, Hadijatou Mani Koraou left El Hadj Souleymane Naroua's house never to go back.

15. On 14 February 2006, Hadijatou Mani Koraou brought a complaint before the civil and customary tribunal of Konni, to have her desire to be totally free and live her life elsewhere recognised.

16. The civil and customary tribunal of Konni, in judgment No. 06 of 20 March 2006, found "that the applicant and El Hadj Souleymane Naroua were never properly married, since the dowry was never paid for, there was no religious ceremony and Hadijatou Mani Koraou remains free to live her own life with the person of her choice."

17. El Hadj Souleymane Naroua lodged an appeal of this judgment before the Court of First Instance of Konni, which by decision No. 30 of 16 June 2006 quashed the first judgment.

18. The applicant took her case to the final court of appeal before the Judicial Chamber of the Supreme Court of Niamey, to request "application of the law against slavery and slavery-like practices."

19. On 28 December 2006, the Supreme Court, by judgment No. 06/06/cout. quashed and invalidated the Court of First Instance of Konni's decision, on the ground of violation of Article 5(4) of Law 2004–50 of 22 July 2004 relating to the Judicial Organisation in Niger, without pronouncing on the issue of Hadijatou Mani Koraou's slave status. The matter was remitted for review to the same court with a different composition.

[Ms. Koraou returned to her father's family and married Mr. Ladan Rabo. Mr. Naroua filed a criminal complaint for bigamy against them which resulted in a sentence of imprisonment for Ms. Koraou, her brother and Mr. Rabo. Ms. Koraou appealed, but she and her brother were imprisoned. The Court of Appeals eventually ruled for their temporary release pending outcome of concurrent divorce related proceedings.]

* * *

24. On 17 May 2007, while Hadijatou Mani Koraou was still in detention * * * her counsel, filed a complaint against Souleymane Naroua before the public prosecutor at the Court of First Instance of Konni for slavery in accordance with Article 270.2 and 3 of the criminal code * * *

28. On 14 December 2007, Hadijatou Mani Koraou filed a submission before the ECOWAS Community Court of Justice on the basis of Articles 9.4 and 10.d) of Supplementary Protocol A/SP.1/01/05 of 19 January 2005 amending Protocol A/P.1/7/91 of 6 July 1991 relating to the Court, seeking to:

a) Condemn the Republic of Niger for violation of Articles 1, 2, 3, 5, 6 and 18(3) of the African Charter of Human and Peoples' Rights;

b) Request Niger authorities to adopt legislation that effectively protects women against discriminatory customs relating to marriage and divorce;

c) Ask Niger authorities to revise the legislation relating to Courts and Tribunals in order to enable justice to fully play its part in order to safeguard victims of slavery;

d) Urge the Republic of Niger to abolish harmful customs and practices founded on the idea of women's inferiority;

e) Grant Hadijatou Mani Koraou a fair reparation for the wrong she was victim of during the 9 years of her captivity.

29. The defendant presented preliminary objections on admissibility to say that:

a) The complaint is not admissible because domestic remedies have not been exhausted;

b) The complaint is not admissible because the case brought before the present Court is still pending before Nigerien domestic courts.

30. The ECOWAS Court of Justice, in applying Art. 87(5) of its Rules of Procedure merged the preliminary objections to the merits, to render one, and single, judgment.

* * *

EXAMINATION OF THE PARTIES' ARGUMENTS

   1.   ON THE PRELIMINARY OBJECTIONS

35. The Republic of Niger argued *in limine litis* inadmissibility on the grounds of non-exhaustion of domestic remedies on the one hand, and of the fact that the matter brought before the ECOWAS Court of Justice was still pending before domestic courts on the other hand.

ON NON EXHAUSTION OF DOMESTIC REMEDIES

* * *

39. While subsidiarity of human rights protection by international mechanisms is longstanding, this principle has evolved over time. As a result, interpretation of the rule of exhaustion of domestic remedies has been very flexible. That is what the European Court of Human Rights said in its judgment De Wilde, Ooms and Versyp v Belgium of 18 June 1971 when it ruled that *"there is nothing to prevent States from waiving the benefit of the rule of exhaustion of domestic remedies (* * *) There exists on this subject a long established international practice"*,

40. The ECOWAS Community legislature must have answered that call when it decided not to make the rule of exhaustion of domestic remedies a condition of admissibility before the Court. Waiving [of] such a rule applies to all ECOWAS Member States, and the Republic of Niger shall not depart from it.

* * *

ON THE MERITS

57. The applicant presented several grounds of violation of her human rights. First of all, she claimed that the defendant did not take appropri-

ate measures to ensure rights and freedoms proclaimed in the African Charter of Human and Peoples' Rights, thus violating Article 1 of the Charter. She argued that this violation derives from other violations enshrined in other arguments submitted to this Court, since Article 1 of the African Charter gives Member States the obligation to respect those rights, and that under Article 1, "The Member States * * * shall recognize the rights, duties and freedoms enshrined in this Charter and shall undertake to adopt legislative or other measures to give effect to them."

58. Additionally, the applicant argued that according to Nigerien legislation, "the Republic of Niger respects the rule of law; it assures equality before the law, without any distinction on the grounds of gender, social, racial, ethnic or religious origin to all" (1996 Constitution, Article 11). "No one shall be submitted to torture or other cruel, inhuman or degrading treatment or punishment (1996 Constitution, Article 12). "Any person * * * who would be responsible for acts of torture, * * * or cruel, inhuman or degrading treatment * * * will be punished in accordance with the law" (Constitutions of 1989 and 1992, Art. 14).

59. The applicant claims that despite this legislation, she was victim of discrimination on gender and social origin grounds since she was held in slavery for nearly 9 years; that after her liberation she could not enjoy her freedom despite her lawsuits; that she was detained and that all these actions contributed to the deprivation of her fundamental rights. Therefore she requests condemnation of the defendant for violating the aforementioned articles of the African Charter of Human and Peoples' Rights and urges adoption of new laws that better protect women's rights against discriminatory customs.

60. On this first ground, the Court affirms that its role is not to examine Community Member States' laws *in abstracto*, but rather to ensure protection of people's rights when they are victims of violations of those rights and that it must do so by examining concrete cases brought before it.

* * *

ON THE DISCRIMINATION

62. The applicant claimed that she was a victim of discrimination on gender and social origin grounds, in violation of Articles 2 and 18(3) of the African Charter of Human and Peoples' Rights. She further argued that she did not enjoy *equal protection of the law and equality before the law* as provided for by Article 3 of the Charter. More precisely, she said that the *Sadaka* or the sale of a woman to a man to serve as a *concubine* is a practice that affects women only and therefore constitutes discrimination based on gender. Moreover, the fact that she could not consent freely to marriage or divorce represents discrimination based on her social origin.

* * *

[The Court held that the discrimination claim was ineffective because Mr. Naroua, rather than the state of Niger, was responsible for it. It was Mr. Naroua who refused to observe civil and customary marriage requirements and did not set Ms. Koraou free despite the liberation certificate.]

WAS THE APPLICANT HELD IN SLAVERY?

72. The applicant claims that she was held in slavery in violation of Article 5 of the African Charter of Human and Peoples' Rights as well as other international human rights instruments that provide for the absolute prohibition of slavery.

She declared that her parents were slaves themselves and she was always treated as such in her former master El Hadj Souleymane Naroua's household.

73. The defendant for its part rebutted the slavery argument and argues that the applicant, despite her slave status, was El Hadj Souleymane Naroua's wife, with whom she lived * * * more or less in happiness as any couple.

74. According to Article 1 of Geneva Slavery Convention of 1926, "*Slavery is the status or condition of a person over whom any or all of the powers attaching to the right of ownership are exercised.*"

* * *

75. Slavery is considered as a serious violation of human dignity and is formally prohibited by all international human rights instruments. Other instruments, such as the European Convention of Human Rights (Art.1 para. 1), the American Convention of Human Rights (Art. 6), and the International Covenant on Civil and Political Rights (Art. Para. 1.2 ratified by the Republic of Niger) make prohibition of slavery an inviolable right, that is to say an absolute and non-derogable right.

Similarly, the Nigerien criminal code, as revised by Law No 2003–05 of 13 June 2003, provides for a definition and punishment of the crime of slavery in its former Article 270.1 to 5.

76. According to the above, it is well established that Mrs. Hadijatou Mani Koraou was transferred in exchange for money at the age of twelve by El hadji Ghousmane Abdourahmane for the sum of two hundred forty thousands CFA francs to El Hadj Souleymane Naroua. She was brought to her purchaser. She was subject for nearly a decade to psychological pressure characterised by submission, sexual exploitation, hard labour in the house and the fields, physical violence, insults, humiliation and the permanent control of her movements by her purchaser who issued, on 18 August 2005, a document entitled "*liberation certificate (of slave),*" men-

tioning that from the date of signature of the act *"she (the applicant) was
free and was nobody's slave."*

77. These elements characterise the applicant's slave situation and show
all the indicators of the slavery definition contained in Article 1 of the
1926 Geneva Convention, as interpreted by the International Criminal
Tribunal for ex-Yugoslavia (ICTY) Appeals Chamber in Prosecutor v
Dragoljub Kunarac, Radomir Kovac and Vukovic Zoran Case, Judgment
of 12 June 2000, paragraph 119.

* * *

80. The Court notes that in the present case, apart from the material acts
well established, the moral element of enslavement lies in El Hadj Souleymane Naroua's intention to exercise the powers attached to the right of
ownership over the applicant, even after the liberation act.

Consequently, there is no doubt that the applicant, Hadijatou Mani
Koraou, was held in slavery for nearly nine years in violation of the legal
prohibition of this practice.

81. Under Nigerien criminal law, as in international instruments, the
prohibition and repression of slavery are absolute and of public order. As
stated by the International Court of Justice in the Barcelona Traction
judgment (5 February 1970), "the outlawing of slavery is an obligation
erga omnes imposed on all State's organs."

82. Therefore, the national judge, when having to rule on a matter relating to the state of persons, as in the case of Mrs. Hadijatou Mani Koraou
before the Court of First Instance of Konni, should deal with this slavery
case of its own volition and initiate the punishment procedure.

83. In conclusion, on this point, the Court observes that the national
judge, having to rule on Mrs. Hadijatou Mani Koraou's application
against Mr. El Hadj Souleymane Naroua, instead of denouncing the applicant's slave status with its own motion as being a violation of Article
270.1 to 5 of the Nigerien criminal code as modified by Law No. 2003–025
of 13 June 2003, stated that "the marriage of a free man with a slave
woman is lawful, as long as he cannot afford to marry a free woman and if
he fears to fall into fornication * * * "

84. The Court considers that recognising the slave status of Mrs. Hadijatou Mani Koraou without denouncing this situation is a form of acceptance, or at least, tolerance of this crime or offence. The national judge
had the obligation to bring a criminal prosecution or punish this crime or
offence as need be.

85. Furthermore, the Court considers that the slavery situation of the applicant, although it was due to a particular individual acting in a so-called

customary or individual context, gave her the right to be protected by the Nigerien authorities, be they administrative or judicial.

Consequently, the defendant becomes responsible under international as well as national law for any form of human rights violations of the applicant founded on slavery because of its tolerance, passivity, inaction and abstention with regard to this practice.

86. When failing to deal with a prohibited offence of its own volition and failing to take adequate measures to ensure punishment, the national judge did not assume its duty of protecting Hadijatou Mani Koraou's human rights and therefore, engaged the defendant's responsibility as the administrative authority's one when it declared: "listen, I cannot do anything, you must leave."

[The Court also held that Ms. Koraou's arrest and detention were not arbitrary because these actions were implementing a judicial decision of the criminal court. Thus, there was adequate legal basis for the state's actions in this regard.]

* * *

IS THE APPLICANT ENTITLED TO REPARATION?

92. In her brief of 07 April 2008, the applicant claims the payment by the Republic of Niger of the sum of fifty millions francs as reparation for the harm she suffered.

93. In response, the defendant says that it is a new argument and invokes Article 37.2 of the Rules of Procedure of the Court and concludes that the reparation claim is inadmissible.

94. The Court recalls that the inadmissibility provided for in Article 37.2 of the Rules of Procedures is about new arguments invoked by a party during the proceedings. In this particular case, the quantification of the requested reparation does not amount to a new argument but rather is a detailed quantification of the reparation request contained in the initial submission.

Therefore, the defendant's argument is rejected.

* * *

CONSEQUENTLY

* * *

2. The *wahiya* or *sadaka* practice founded on social origin considerations put the applicant in a disadvantageous situation and excluded her from the benefits of the equal dignity recognised to all citizens. Thus she was

discriminated because of her social origin. However this discrimination is not attributable to the Republic of Niger.

3. The Court notes that the Republic of Niger did not sufficiently protect the applicant's rights against the practice of slavery.

4. This slavery situation caused the applicant physical, psychological and moral harm.

5. For this reason, the applicant is entitled to an all-inclusive compensation for the harm caused by slavery.

ON THESE GROUNDS

The ECOWAS Community Court of Justice, ruling in public, in the presence of the parties involved, on human rights matters, in the first instance and last resort,

* * *

ON THE MERITS

1. Says that the discrimination to which Mrs. Hadijatou Mani Koraou was subject is not attributable to the Republic of Niger;

2. Says that Mrs. Hadijatou Mani Koraou was victim of slavery and that the Republic of Niger is responsible because of its administrative and judicial authorities' inaction;

3. Accepts Mrs. Hadijatou Mani Koraou's request for reparation for the harm[ ] suffered and grants an all-inclusive compensation of ten millions CFA francs;

4. Rules the payment of this sum to Mrs. Hadijatou Mani Koraou by the Republic of Niger;

5. Rejects all others grounds presented by Mrs. Hadijatou Mani Koraou;

6. Says the Republic of Niger has to pay the expenses, in accordance with Article 66.2 of the Court's Rules of Procedure.

———————

How does the ECOWAS court's decision in *Koraou* compare to the decisions from the ECHR above in terms of format, style, reasoning and result?

B. RESPONSIBILITIES

According to some commentators, the turning point in the relationship between individuals and international law occurred on August 8, 1945, when the United States, France, Great Britain and the Soviet Union signed the agreement forming the International Military Tribunal at Nuremberg.

After reading Malcolm Shaw's overview of the development of 20th century international criminal law, look at the Charter of the Nuremberg Tribunal and in particular at Articles 6, 7 and 8. In light of the traditional concept of international law discussed in the first part of this course, what was unusual about these rules? What did they add to criminal law on the domestic level?

MALCOLM SHAW, INTERNATIONAL LAW
(5th ed. 2008)

* * *

The evolving subject of international individual criminal responsibility marks the coming together of elements of traditional international law with human rights law and humanitarian law, and involves consideration of domestic as well as international enforcement mechanisms. As far as obligations are concerned, international law has imposed direct responsibility upon individuals in certain specified matters. In the cases of piracy and slavery, offenders are guilty of a crime against international society and can thus be punished by international tribunals or by any state at all. Jurisdiction to hear the charge is not confined to, for example, the state on whose territory the act took place, or the national state of the offender.

The Treaty of Versailles, 1919 noted that the German government recognised the right of the Allied and Associated Powers to bring individuals accused of crimes against the laws and customs of war before military tribunals (article 228) and established the individual responsibility of the Kaiser (article 227). In the event, only a few trials were held before German courts in Leipzig. A variety of other international instruments were also relevant in the establishment of individual responsibility with regard to specific issues.

The Charter annexed to the Agreement for the Prosecution and Punishment of the Major War Criminals, 1945 provided specifically for individual responsibility for crimes against peace, war crimes and crimes against humanity. The Nuremberg Tribunal pointed out that "international law imposes duties and liabilities upon individuals as well as upon states." This was because "crimes against international law are committed by men, not by abstract entities, and only by punishing individuals who commit such crimes can the provisions of international law be enforced." Included in the relevant category for which individual responsibility was posited were crimes against peace, war crimes and crimes against humanity.

The provisions of the Nuremberg Charter can now be regarded as part of international law, particularly since the General Assembly in 1946 affirmed the principles of this Charter and the decision of the Tribunal. The Assembly also stated that genocide was a crime under international law bearing individual responsibility. This was reaffirmed in the Genocide Convention of 1948, while the International Convention on the Suppression and Punishment of the Crime of Apartheid of 1973 declares apartheid to be an international crime involving direct individual criminal responsibility.

Individual responsibility has also been confirmed with regard to grave breaches of the four 1949 Geneva Red Cross Conventions and 1977 Additional Protocols I and II dealing with armed conflicts. It is provided specifically that the High Contracting Parties undertake to enact any legislation necessary to provide effective penal sanctions for persons committing or ordering to be committed any of a series of grave breaches. Such grave breaches include wilful killing, torture or inhuman treatment, extensive destruction and appropriation of property not justified by military necessity and carried out unlawfully and wantonly, unlawful deportation or transfer of protected persons and the taking of hostages. Protocol I of 1977 extends the list to include, for example, making the civilian population the object of attack and launching an attack against works or installations containing dangerous forces in the knowledge that such attack will cause excessive loss of life or damage to civilians or their property when committed wilfully and causing death or serious injury; other activities such as transferring civilian population from the territory of an occupying power to that of an occupied area or deporting from an occupied area, apartheid and racial discrimination and attacking clearly recognised historic monuments, works of art or places of worship, may also constitute grave breaches when committed wilfully. Any individual, regardless of rank or governmental status, would be personally liable for any war crimes or grave breaches committed, while the principle of command (or superior) responsibility means that any person in a position of authority ordering the commission of a war crime or grave breach would be as accountable as the subordinate committing it. This would also cover the situation where a commander fails to exercise sufficient control over forces that proceed to commit such offences. Military necessity may not be pleaded as a defence and the claim of superior orders will not provide a defence, although it may be taken in mitigation depending upon the circumstances.

The International Law Commission in 1991 provisionally adopted a Draft Code of Crimes Against the Peace and Security of Mankind, which was revised in 1996. The 1996 Draft Code provides for individual criminal responsibility with regard to aggression, genocide, a crime against humanity, a crime against United Nations and associated personnel and war crimes. The fact that an individual may be responsible for the crimes in question is deemed not to affect the issue of state responsibility.

The Security Council in two resolutions on the Somali situation in the early 1990s unanimously condemned breaches of humanitarian law and stated that the authors of such breaches or those who had ordered their commission would be held "individually responsible" for them.

Events in the former Yugoslavia in particular impelled a renewal of interest in the establishment of an international criminal court, which had long been under consideration. In 1994, the International Law Commission adopted a Draft Statute for an International Criminal Court. This draft provided the basis for the work which culminated in the adoption of the Rome Statute in 1998 at an international conference. The Statute provides that the jurisdiction of the International Criminal Court is limited to the "most serious crimes of concern to the international community as a whole," being genocide, crimes against humanity, war crimes and aggression, and that a person who commits a crime within the jurisdiction of the Court "shall be individually responsible and liable for punishment" in accordance with the Statute. The Yugoslav experience and the Rwanda massacres of 1994 also led to the establishment of two specific war crimes tribunals by the use of the authority of the UN Security Council to adopt decisions binding upon all member states of the organisation under Chapter VII of the Charter, rather than by an international conference as was to be the case with the International Criminal Court. This method was used in order both to enable the tribunal in question to come into operation as quickly as possible and to ensure that the parties most closely associated with the subject-matter of the war crimes alleged should be bound in a manner not dependent upon their consent (as would be necessary in the case of a court established by international agreement).

* * *

CHARTER OF THE NUREMBERG TRIBUNAL
(1945)

Agreement by the government of the United States of America, the provisional government of the French Republic, the government of the United Kingdom of Great Britain and Northern Ireland and the government of the Union of Soviet Socialist Republics for the prosecution and punishment of the major war criminals of the European Axis.

WHEREAS the United Nations have from time to time made declarations of their intention that War Criminals shall be brought to justice;

AND WHEREAS the Moscow Declaration of the 30th October 1943 on German atrocities in Occupied Europe stated that those German Officers and men and members of the Nazi Party who have been responsible for or have taken a consenting part in atrocities and crimes will be sent back to the countries in which their abominable deeds were done in order that they may be judged and punished according to the laws of these liberated countries and of the free Governments that will be created therein:

AND WHEREAS this Declaration was stated to be without prejudice to the case of major criminals whose offenses have no particular geographical location and who will be punished by the joint decision of the Governments of the Allies;

NOW THEREFORE the Government of the United States of America, the Provisional Government of the French Republic, the Government of the United Kingdom of Great Britain and Northern Ireland and the Government of the Union of Soviet Socialist Republics (hereinafter called "the Signatories") acting in the interests of all the United Nations and by their representatives duly authorized thereto have concluded this Agreement.

* * *

II.   JURISDICTION AND GENERAL PRINCIPLES

Article 6

The Tribunal established by the Agreement referred to in Article 1 hereof for the trial and punishment of the major war criminals of the European Axis countries shall have the power to try and punish persons who, acting in the interests of the European Axis countries, whether as individuals or as members of organizations, committed any of the following crimes.

The following acts, or any of them, are crimes coming within the jurisdiction of the Tribunal for which there shall be individual responsibility:

(a) CRIMES AGAINST PEACE: namely, planning, preparation, initiation or waging of a war of aggression, or a war in violation of international treaties, agreements or assurances, or participation in a common plan or conspiracy for the accomplishment of any of the foregoing;

(b) WAR CRIMES: namely, violations of the laws or customs of war. Such violations shall include, but not be limited to, murder, ill-treatment or deportation to slave labor or for any other purpose of civilian population of or in occupied territory, murder or ill-treatment of prisoners of war or persons on the seas, killing of hostages, plunder of public or private property, wanton destruction of cities, towns or villages, or devastation not justified by military necessity;

(c) CRIMES AGAINST HUMANITY: namely, murder, extermination, enslavement, deportation, and other inhuman acts committed against any civilian population, before or during the war; or persecutions on political, racial or religious grounds in execution of or in connection with any crime within the jurisdiction of the Tribunal, whether or not in violation of the domestic law of the country where perpetrated.

Leaders, organizers, instigators and accomplices participating in the formulation or execution of a common plan or conspiracy to commit any of the foregoing crimes are responsible for all acts performed by any persons in execution of such plan.

Article 7

The official position of defendants, whether as Heads of State or responsible officials in Government Departments, shall not be considered as freeing them from responsibility or mitigating punishment.

Article 8

The fact that the Defendant acted pursuant to order of his Government or of a superior shall not free him from responsibility, but may be considered in mitigation of punishment if the Tribunal determines that justice so requires.

Article 9

At the trial of any individual member of any group or organization the Tribunal may declare (in connection with any act of which the individual may be convicted) that the group or organization of which the individual was a member was a criminal organization.

After the receipt of the Indictment the Tribunal shall give such notice as it thinks fit that the prosecution intends to ask the Tribunal to make such declaration and any member of the organization will be entitled to apply to the Tribunal for leave to be heard by the Tribunal upon the question of the criminal character of the organization. The Tribunal shall have power to allow or reject the application. If the application is allowed, the Tribunal may direct in what manner the applicants shall be represented and heard.

Article 10

In cases where a group or organization is declared criminal by the Tribunal, the competent national authority of any Signatory shall have the right to bring individuals to trial for membership therein before national, military or occupation courts. In any such case the criminal nature of the group or organization is considered proved and shall not be questioned.

Article 11

Any person convicted by the Tribunal may be charged before a national, military or occupation court, referred to in Article 10 of this Charter, with a crime other than of membership in a criminal group or organization and such court may, after convicting him, impose upon him punishment independent of and additional to the punishment imposed by the Tribunal for participation in the criminal activities of such group or organization.

Article 12

The Tribunal shall have the right to take proceedings against a person charged with crimes set out in Article 6 of this Charter in his absence, if he has not been found or if the Tribunal, for any reason, finds it necessary, in the interests of justice, to conduct the hearing in his absence.

Article 13

The Tribunal shall draw up rules for its procedure. These rules shall not be inconsistent with the provisions of this Charter.

* * *

The International Criminal Court

The International Criminal Court (ICC), established by the Rome Statute in 1998, is the first permanent international criminal tribunal. The ICC has jurisdiction over the most serious crimes under international law, including genocide, war crimes and crimes against humanity. It is an international organization in its own right, not an organ of the United Nations and gets the bulk of its funding from the state parties to the Rome Statute (more than 120 in number). The ICC started operating in 2002. Proceedings have involved acts that occurred in Libya, Sudan, Uganda, Congo, Central African Republic and Côte d'Ivoire.

Even in the limited set of criminal cases that can be brought before it, the ICC only has jurisdiction under certain circumstances. As a general rule, the jurisdiction of the ICC is largely subsidiary to that of national courts; i.e., if a national court takes jurisdiction, the ICC stands back. However, even that rule has exceptions. If the national proceedings have been deemed a sham or the local courts have shielded the suspect from criminal liability, the ICC prosecutor may proceed with an investigation and potentially indict suspects under the Rome Statute. In addition, the state parties themselves and the United Nations Security Council can initiate ICC proceedings.

Individuals who are direct victims of crimes that are being investigated can participate in the proceedings personally or through legal representatives and can request reparations for physical and emotional injury and property damage. Under certain circumstances, organizations and institutions can be considered victims as well.

The ICC is made up of eighteen judges who are elected by the state parties for a nine-year term. The head of the Office of the Prosecutor of the

ICC is also elected by state parties for a nine-year term. The court has its permanent seat in The Hague, the Netherlands, and it operates in six official languages (English, French, Arabic, Chinese, Russian and Spanish). The Court made its own rules of evidence and criminal procedure, drawing on the traditions of several leading legal systems in the world.

In reading the ICC's foundational statute below, compare it to the Charter of the Nuremberg Tribunal. What are the primary similarities and differences? What is the heart of the Rome Statute?

ROME STATUTE OF THE INTERNATIONAL CRIMINAL COURT
(Adopted 1998, in force 2002)

Part 1. Establishment of the Court

Article 1

The Court

An International Criminal Court ("the Court") is hereby established. It shall be a permanent institution and shall have the power to exercise its jurisdiction over persons for the most serious crimes of international concern, as referred to in this Statute, and shall be complementary to national criminal jurisdictions. The jurisdiction and functioning of the Court shall be governed by the provisions of this Statute.

Article 2

Relationship of the Court with the United Nations

The Court shall be brought into relationship with the United Nations through an agreement to be approved by the Assembly of States Parties to this Statute and thereafter concluded by the President of the Court on its behalf.

Article 3

Seat of the Court

1. The seat of the Court shall be established at The Hague in the Netherlands ("the host State").

* * *

Article 4

Legal status and powers of the Court

1. The Court shall have international legal personality. It shall also have such legal capacity as may be necessary for the exercise of its functions and the fulfilment of its purposes.

2. The Court may exercise its functions and powers, as provided in this Statute, on the territory of any State Party and, by special agreement, on the territory of any other State.

Part 2. Jurisdiction, Admissibility and Applicable Law

Article 5

Crimes within the jurisdiction of the Court

1. The jurisdiction of the Court shall be limited to the most serious crimes of concern to the international community as a whole. The Court has jurisdiction in accordance with this Statute with respect to the following crimes:

   (a) The crime of genocide;

   (b) Crimes against humanity;

   (c) War crimes;

   (d) The crime of aggression.

* * *

Article 6

Genocide

For the purpose of this Statute, "genocide" means any of the following acts committed with intent to destroy, in whole or in part, a national, ethnical, racial or religious group, as such:

   (a) Killing members of the group;

   (b) Causing serious bodily or mental harm to members of the group;

   (c) Deliberately inflicting on the group conditions of life calculated to bring about its physical destruction in whole or in part;

   (d) Imposing measures intended to prevent births within the group;

   (e) Forcibly transferring children of the group to another group.

[Articles 7 and 8 define respective crimes in great detail. These definitions have been omitted.]

Article 7

Crimes against humanity

1. For the purpose of this Statute, "crime against humanity" means any of the following acts when committed as part of a widespread or systematic attack directed against any civilian population, with knowledge of the attack:

   (a) Murder;

   (b) Extermination;

(c) Enslavement;

(d) Deportation or forcible transfer of population;

(e) Imprisonment or other severe deprivation of physical liberty in violation of fundamental rules of international law;

(f) Torture;

(g) Rape, sexual slavery, enforced prostitution, forced pregnancy, enforced sterilization, or any other form of sexual violence of comparable gravity;

(h) Persecution against any identifiable group or collectivity on political, racial, national, ethnic, cultural, religious, gender as defined in paragraph 3, or other grounds that are universally recognized as impermissible under international law, in connection with any act referred to in this paragraph or any crime within the jurisdiction of the Court;

(i) Enforced disappearance of persons;

(j) The crime of apartheid;

(k) Other inhumane acts of a similar character intentionally causing great suffering, or serious injury to body or to mental or physical health.

* * *

Article 8

War crimes

1. The Court shall have jurisdiction in respect of war crimes in particular when committed as part of a plan or policy or as part of a large-scale commission of such crimes.

* * *

Article 12

Preconditions to the exercise of jurisdiction

1. A State which becomes a Party to this Statute thereby accepts the jurisdiction of the Court with respect to the crimes referred to in article 5.

2. In the case of article 13, paragraph (a) or (c), the Court may exercise its jurisdiction if one or more of the following States are Parties to this Statute or have accepted the jurisdiction of the Court in accordance with paragraph 3:

(a) The State on the territory of which the conduct in question occurred or, if the crime was committed on board a vessel or aircraft, the State of registration of that vessel or aircraft;

(b) The State of which the person accused of the crime is a national.

Article 13

Exercise of jurisdiction

The Court may exercise its jurisdiction with respect to a crime referred to in article 5 in accordance with the provisions of this Statute if:

(a) A situation in which one or more of such crimes appears to have been committed is referred to the Prosecutor by a State Party in accordance with article 14;

(b) A situation in which one or more of such crimes appears to have been committed is referred to the Prosecutor by the Security Council acting under Chapter VII of the Charter of the United Nations; or

(c) The Prosecutor has initiated an investigation in respect of such a crime in accordance with article 15.

* * *

Article 17

Issues of Admissibility

1. Having regard to paragraph 10 of the Preamble and article 1, the Court shall determine that a case is inadmissible where:

   (a) The case is being investigated or prosecuted by a State which has jurisdiction over it, unless the State is unwilling or unable genuinely to carry out the investigation or prosecution;

   (b) The case has been investigated by a State which has jurisdiction over it and the State has decided not to prosecute the person concerned, unless the decision resulted from the unwillingness or inability of the State genuinely to prosecute;

   (c) The person concerned has already been tried for conduct which is the subject of the complaint, and a trial by the Court is not permitted under article 20, paragraph 3;

   (d) The case is not of sufficient gravity to justify further action by the Court.

2. In order to determine unwillingness in a particular case, the Court shall consider, having regard to the principles of due process recognized by international law, whether one or more of the following exist, as applicable:

(a) The proceedings were or are being undertaken or the national decision was made for the purpose of shielding the person concerned from criminal responsibility for crimes within the jurisdiction of the Court referred to in article 5;

(b) There has been an unjustified delay in the proceedings which in the circumstances is inconsistent with an intent to bring the person concerned to justice;

(c) The proceedings were not or are not being conducted independently or impartially, and they were or are being conducted in a manner which, in the circumstances, is inconsistent with an intent to bring the person concerned to justice.

3. In order to determine inability in a particular case, the Court shall consider whether, due to a total or substantial collapse or unavailability of its national judicial system, the State is unable to obtain the accused or the necessary evidence and testimony or otherwise unable to carry out its proceedings.

* * *

Part 3. General Principles of Criminal Law

* * *

Article 25

Individual criminal responsibility

1. The Court shall have jurisdiction over natural persons pursuant to this Statute.

2. A person who commits a crime within the jurisdiction of the Court shall be individually responsible and liable for punishment in accordance with this Statute.

3. In accordance with this Statute, a person shall be criminally responsible and liable for punishment for a crime within the jurisdiction of the Court if that person:

(a) Commits such a crime, whether as an individual, jointly with another or through another person, regardless of whether that other person is criminally responsible;

(b) Orders, solicits or induces the commission of such a crime which in fact occurs or is attempted;

(c) For the purpose of facilitating the commission of such a crime, aids, abets or otherwise assists in its commission or its attempted commission, including providing the means for its commission;

(d) In any other way contributes to the commission or attempted commission of such a crime by a group of persons acting with a common purpose. Such contribution shall be intentional and shall either:

   (i) Be made with the aim of furthering the criminal activity or criminal purpose of the group, where such activity or purpose involves the commission of a crime within the jurisdiction of the Court; or

   (ii) Be made in the knowledge of the intention of the group to commit the crime;

(e) In respect of the crime of genocide, directly and publicly incites others to commit genocide;

(f) Attempts to commit such a crime by taking action that commences its execution by means of a substantial step, but the crime does not occur because of circumstances independent of the person's intentions. However, a person who abandons the effort to commit the crime or otherwise prevents the completion of the crime shall not be liable for punishment under this Statute for the attempt to commit that crime if that person completely and voluntarily gave up the criminal purpose.

4. No provision in this Statute relating to individual criminal responsibility shall affect the responsibility of States under international law.

* * *

Article 27

Irrelevance of official capacity

1. This Statute shall apply equally to all persons without any distinction based on official capacity. In particular, official capacity as a Head of State or Government, a member of a Government or parliament, an elected representative or a government official shall in no case exempt a person from criminal responsibility under this Statute, nor shall it, in and of itself, constitute a ground for reduction of sentence.

2. Immunities or special procedural rules which may attach to the official capacity of a person, whether under national or international law, shall not bar the Court from exercising its jurisdiction over such a person.

Article 28

Responsibility of commanders and other superiors

In addition to other grounds of criminal responsibility under this Statute for crimes within the jurisdiction of the Court:

(a) A military commander or person effectively acting as a military commander shall be criminally responsible for crimes within the jurisdiction of the Court committed by forces under his or her effective command and control, or effective authority and control as the case may be, as a result of his or her failure to exercise control properly over such forces, where:

   (i) That military commander or person either knew or, owing to the circumstances at the time, should have known that the forces were committing or about to commit such crimes; and

   (ii) That military commander or person failed to take all necessary and reasonable measures within his or her power to prevent or repress their commission or to submit the matter to the competent authorities for investigation and prosecution.

(b) With respect to superior and subordinate relationships not described in paragraph (a), a superior shall be criminally responsible for crimes within the jurisdiction of the Court committed by subordinates under his or her effective authority and control, as a result of his or her failure to exercise control properly over such subordinates, where:

   (i)   The superior either knew, or consciously disregarded information which clearly indicated, that the subordinates were committing or about to commit such crimes;

   (ii) The crimes concerned activities that were within the effective responsibility and control of the superior; and

   (iii) The superior failed to take all necessary and reasonable measures within his or her power to prevent or repress their commission or to submit the matter to the competent authorities for investigation and prosecution.

* * *

Part 6. The Trial

Article 62

Place of trial

Unless otherwise decided, the place of the trial shall be the seat of the Court.

Article 63

Trial in the presence of the accused

1. The accused shall be present during the trial.

2. If the accused, being present before the Court, continues to disrupt the trial, the Trial Chamber may remove the accused and shall make provision for him or her to observe the trial and instruct counsel from outside the courtroom, through the use of communications technology, if required. Such measures shall be taken only in exceptional circumstances after other reasonable alternatives have proved inadequate, and only for such duration as is strictly required.

* * *

Article 66

Presumption of innocence

1. Everyone shall be presumed innocent until proved guilty before the Court in accordance with the applicable law.

2. The onus is on the Prosecutor to prove the guilt of the accused.

3. In order to convict the accused, the Court must be convinced of the guilt of the accused beyond reasonable doubt.

Article 67

Rights of the accused

1. In the determination of any charge, the accused shall be entitled to a public hearing, having regard to the provisions of this Statute, to a fair hearing conducted impartially, and to the following minimum guarantees, in full equality:

   (a) To be informed promptly and in detail of the nature, cause and content of the charge, in a language which the accused fully understands and speaks;

   (b) To have adequate time and facilities for the preparation of the defence and to communicate freely with counsel of the accused's choosing in confidence;

   (c) To be tried without undue delay;

   (d) Subject to article 63, paragraph 2, to be present at the trial, to conduct the defence in person or through legal assistance of the accused's choosing, to be informed, if the accused does not have legal assistance, of this right and to have legal assistance assigned by the Court in any case where the interests of justice so require, and without payment if the accused lacks sufficient means to pay for it;

   (e) To examine, or have examined, the witnesses against him or her and to obtain the attendance and examination of witnesses on his or her behalf under the same conditions as witnesses against him or her. The accused shall also be entitled to raise defences and to present other evidence admissible under this Statute;

(f) To have, free of any cost, the assistance of a competent interpreter and such translations as are necessary to meet the requirements of fairness, if any of the proceedings of or documents presented to the Court are not in a language which the accused fully understands and speaks;

(g) Not to be compelled to testify or to confess guilt and to remain silent, without such silence being a consideration in the determination of guilt or innocence;

(h) To make an unsworn oral or written statement in his or her defence; and

(i) Not to have imposed on him or her any reversal of the burden of proof or any onus of rebuttal.

2. In addition to any other disclosure provided for in this Statute, the Prosecutor shall, as soon as practicable, disclose to the defence evidence in the Prosecutor's possession or control which he or she believes shows or tends to show the innocence of the accused, or to mitigate the guilt of the accused, or which may affect the credibility of prosecution evidence. In case of doubt as to the application of this paragraph, the Court shall decide.

* * *

Article 74

Requirements for the decision

1. All the judges of the Trial Chamber shall be present at each stage of the trial and throughout their deliberations. The Presidency may, on a case-by-case basis, designate, as available, one or more alternate judges to be present at each stage of the trial and to replace a member of the Trial Chamber if that member is unable to continue attending.

2. The Trial Chamber's decision shall be based on its evaluation of the evidence and the entire proceedings. The decision shall not exceed the facts and circumstances described in the charges and any amendments to the charges. The Court may base its decision only on evidence submitted and discussed before it at the trial.

3. The judges shall attempt to achieve unanimity in their decision, failing which the decision shall be taken by a majority of the judges.

4. The deliberations of the Trial Chamber shall remain secret.

5. The decision shall be in writing and shall contain a full and reasoned statement of the Trial Chamber's findings on the evidence and conclusions. The Trial Chamber shall issue one decision. When there is no unanimity, the Trial Chamber's decision shall contain the views of the

majority and the minority. The decision or a summary thereof shall be delivered in open court.

* * *

Part 7. Penalties

Article 77

Applicable penalties

1. Subject to article 110, the Court may impose one of the following penalties on a person convicted of a crime referred to in article 5 of this Statute:

   (a) Imprisonment for a specified number of years, which may not exceed a maximum of 30 years; or

   (b) A term of life imprisonment when justified by the extreme gravity of the crime and the individual circumstances of the convicted person.

2. In addition to imprisonment, the Court may order:

   (a) A fine under the criteria provided for in the Rules of Procedure and Evidence;

   (b) A forfeiture of proceeds, property and assets derived directly or indirectly from that crime, without prejudice to the rights of bona fide third parties

* * *

In 2010, the state parties amended the Rome Statute expanding the ICC's jurisdiction to cover the crime of aggression. The amendments are scheduled to become effective, at the earliest, in 2017 subject to a two-thirds vote by the state parties to the Statute. The crime of aggression can be prosecuted upon the initiative of the United Nations Security Council or of any state party. In the event that a state party initiates such a prosecution, the Security Council can block the proceeding if it considers the initiation of proceedings inappropriate.

As you will see later, even though the United States participated in the drafting of the Rome Statute in 1998 and signed the treaty at that time, it later announced the intent of the United States not to become party to the statute, thereby "unsigning" it. Was the U.S. announcement consistent with international law? Remember that under Article 18 of the Vienna Convention on the Law of Treaties, after signing, a country is obliged to refrain from acts that would defeat the object and purpose of the treaty until the country makes clear its intent not to become a party to the treaty. (Recall that the United States is not a party to the VCLT.)

In the following case, we see the ICC in action, producing the first conviction in its history. Note that it took nearly a decade from the entry into force of the Rome Statute to reach that point. The following excerpts present a very small part of the opinion and focus only on one particular aspect of it; the full decision consists of 593 pages, 1,364 paragraphs, and includes 3,651 footnotes. As you read the excerpts below, think about what might explain the length and complexity of the decision. What does the Court hold with regard to the defendant's responsibility for employing child soldiers?

SITUATION IN THE DEMOCRATIC REPUBLIC OF THE CONGO CASE OF PROSECUTOR v. THOMAS LUBANGA DYILO

International Criminal Court
Case No. ICC–01/04–01/06–2842 Judgment (March 14, 2012)

* * *

X.   CONSCRIPTION AND ENLISTMENT OF CHILDREN UNDER THE AGE OF 15 OR USING THEM TO PARTICIPATE ACTIVELY IN HOSTILITIES (ARTICLE 8(2)(E)(VII) OF THE STATUTE)

A.   THE LAW

* * *

569. Article 8(2)(e)(vii) of the Statute, the first treaty to include these offences as war crimes, provides:

2. [* * *]

(e) Other serious violations of the laws and customs applicable in armed conflicts not of an international character, within the established framework of international law, namely, any of the following acts:

[* * *]

(vii) Conscripting or enlisting children under the age of fifteen years into armed forces or groups or using them to participate actively in hostilities;

[* * *]

The corresponding Elements of Crimes read as follows:

The perpetrator conscripted or enlisted one or more persons into an armed force or group or used one or more persons to participate actively in hostilities.

Such person or persons were under the age of 15 years.

The perpetrator knew or should have known that such person or persons were under the age of 15 years.

The conduct took place in the context of and was associated with an armed conflict not of an international character.

The perpetrator was aware of the factual circumstances that established the existence of an armed conflict.

570. The Chamber's conclusions on Elements 3 and 5 are addressed separately in the context of Section XI(A)(5). The Chamber has also discussed the definition of an "[organised] armed group" elsewhere in this judgment.

571. The Elements of Crimes require that the relevant "conduct took place in the context of and was associated with an armed conflict not of an international character." Given the plain and ordinary meaning of this provision, it is unnecessary to discuss its interpretation in detail: it is sufficient to show that there was a connection between the conscription, enlistment or use of children under 15 and an armed conflict that was not international in character. The remaining Elements and the relevant applicable law are analysed below.

* * *

2.   THE CHAMBER'S ANALYSIS AND CONCLUSIONS
* * *

601. The Appeals Chamber has established that the interpretation of the Statute is governed by the Vienna Convention on the Law of Treaties, as follows:

> The rule governing the interpretation of a section of the law is its wording read in context and in light of its object and purpose. The context of a given legislative provision is defined by the particular sub-section of the law read as a whole in conjunction with the section of an enactment in its entirety. Its objects may be gathered from the chapter of the law in which the particular section is included and its purposes from the wider aims of the law as may be gathered from its preamble and general tenor of the treaty.

602. The Appeals Chamber has also decided that Article 21(3) of the Statute "makes the interpretation as well as the application of the law applicable under the Statute subject to internationally recognised human rights. It requires the exercise of the jurisdiction of the Court in accordance with internationally recognized human rights norms."

* * *

604. Article 4(3)(c) of Additional Protocol II to the 1949 Geneva Conventions includes an absolute prohibition against the recruitment and use of children under the age of 15 in hostilities (in the context of an armed conflict not of an international character):

> children who have not attained the age of fifteen years shall neither be recruited in the armed forces or groups nor allowed to take part in hostilities;

In addition, the Convention on the Rights of the Child, a widely ratified human rights treaty, requires the State Parties to "take all feasible measures to ensure that persons who have not attained the age of fifteen years do not take a direct part in hostilities," and to "refrain from recruiting any person who has not attained the age of fifteen years into their armed forces" in all types of armed conflicts ("armed conflicts which are relevant to the child").

605. These provisions recognise the fact that "children are particularly vulnerable [and] require privileged treatment in comparison with the rest of the civilian population." The principal objective underlying these prohibitions historically is to protect children under the age of 15 from the risks that are associated with armed conflict, and first and foremost they are directed at securing their physical and psychological well-being. This includes not only protection from violence and fatal or non-fatal injuries during fighting, but also the potentially serious trauma that can accompany recruitment (including separating children from their families, interrupting or disrupting their schooling and exposing them to an environment of violence and fear).

* * *

a) ENLISTMENT AND CONSCRIPTION

607. The Chamber accepts the approach adopted by the Pre-Trial Chamber that "conscription" and "enlistment" are both forms of recruitment in that they refer to the incorporation of a boy or a girl under the age of 15 into an armed group, whether coercively (conscription) or voluntarily (enlistment). The word "recruiting," which is used in the Additional Protocols and in the Convention on the Rights of the Child, was replaced by "conscripting" and "enlisting" in the Statute. Whether a prohibition against voluntary enrolment is included in the concept of "recruitment" is irrelevant to this case, because it is proscribed by Article 8.

608. This interpretation gives the relevant provisions of the Statute their plain and ordinary meaning. It is to be noted that "enlisting" is defined as "to enrol on the list of a military body" and "conscripting" is defined as "to enlist compulsorily." Therefore, the distinguishing element is that for conscription there is the added element of compulsion. Whether this distinction is of relevance in this case is considered below.

* * *

610. The expert witness, Elisabeth Schauer (CHM-0001), suggested in her report and during her evidence before the Chamber that from a psychological point of view children cannot give "informed" consent when joining an armed group, because they have limited understanding of the consequences of their choices; they do not control or fully comprehend the structures and forces they are dealing with; and they have inadequate knowledge and understanding of the short- and long-term consequences of their actions. Ms. Schauer (CHM-0001) concluded that children lack the capacity to determine their best interests in this particular context.

611. In her written submissions, Ms. Coomaraswamy (CHM-0003) notes that it can be difficult to differentiate between a conscripted and an enlisted child:

> The recruitment and enlisting of children in [the] DRC is not always based on abduction and the brute use of force. It also takes place in the context of poverty, ethnic rivalry and ideological motivation. Many children, especially orphans, join armed groups for survival to put food in their stomachs. Others do so to defend their ethnic group or tribe and still others because armed militia leaders are the only seemingly glamorous role models they know. They are sometimes encouraged by parents and elders and are seen as defenders of their family and community.
>
> [* * *]
>
> Children who "voluntarily" join armed groups mostly come from families who were victims of killing and have lost some or all of their family or community protection during the armed conflict.

612. The Special Representative (CHM-0003) further suggests that "the line between voluntary and forced recruitment is therefore not only legally irrelevant but practically superficial in the context of children in armed conflict."

613. The Chamber endorses the conclusions of the expert witnesses, in the sense that it will frequently be the case that girls and boys under the age of 15 will be unable to give genuine and informed consent when enlisting in an armed group or force.

614. Against that background, the Chamber addresses the issue of whether the valid and informed consent of a child under 15 years of age provides the accused with a defence in these circumstances.

615. In Ms. Coomaraswamy's expert testimony before the Chamber she suggested that since children under the age of 15 cannot reasonably give

consent, the accused should not be able to rely on the voluntary nature of their enlistment into an armed force or group as a defence.

* * *

617. In all the circumstances, the Chamber is persuaded that the Statute in this regard is aimed at protecting vulnerable children, including when they lack information or alternatives. The manner in which a child was recruited, and whether it involved compulsion or was "voluntary," are circumstances which may be taken into consideration by the Chamber at the sentencing or reparations phase, as appropriate. However, the consent of a child to his or her recruitment does not provide an accused with a valid defence.

618. Therefore, the Chamber agrees with the Pre-Trial Chamber that under the provisions set out above, the offences of conscripting and enlisting are committed at the moment a child under the age of 15 is enrolled into or joins an armed force or group, with or without compulsion. In the circumstances of this case, conscription and enlistment are dealt with together, notwithstanding the Chamber's earlier conclusion that they constitute separate offences. These offences are continuous in nature. They end only when the child reaches 15 years of age or leaves the force or group.

* * *

B.   The Facts

* * *

6.   Overall Conclusions as regards conscription, enlistment and use of children under the age of 15 within the UPC/FPLC

909. It is alleged that the accused conscripted and enlisted children under the age of 15 years into the armed forces of the UPC/FPLC and that he used them to participate actively in hostilities between 1 September 2002 and 13 August 2003.

910. The Chamber has already set out its conclusion that the UPC/FPLC was an armed group.

a) Conscription and enlistment in the UPC/FPLC

911. The Chamber finds that between 1 September 2002 and 13 August 2003, the armed wing of the UPC/FPLC was responsible for the widespread recruitment of young people, including children under the age of 15, on an enforced as well as a "voluntary" basis. The evidence of witnesses P-00055, P-0014 and P-0017, coupled with the documentary evidence establishes that during this period certain UPC/FPLC leaders, including

Thomas Lubanga, Chief Kahwa, and Bosco Ntaganda, and Hema elders such as Eloy Mafuta, were particularly active in the mobilisation drives and recruitment campaigns that were directed at persuading Hema families to send their children to serve in the UPC/FPLC army.

912. P-0014, P-0016, P-0017, P-0024, P-0030, P-0038, P-0041, P-0046 and P-0055 testified credibly and reliably that children under 15 were "voluntarily" or forcibly recruited into the UPC/FPLC and sent to either the headquarters of the UPC/FPLC in Bunia or its training camps, including at Rwampara, Mandro, and Mongbwalu. Video evidence introduced during the testimony of P-0030 clearly shows recruits under the age of 15 in the camp at Rwampara. The letter of 12 February 2003, (EVD-OTP-00518) further corroborates other evidence that there were children under the age of 15 within the ranks of the UPC.

913. The evidence of P-0016, P-0014 and P-0017 demonstrates that children in the camps endured a harsh training regime and they were subjected to a variety of severe punishments. The evidence of P-0055, P-0017 and P-0038 establishes that children, mainly girls, were used for domestic work for the UPC commanders. The Chamber heard evidence from witnesses P-0046, P-0016, P-0055 and P-0038 that girl soldiers were subjected to sexual violence and rape. P-0046 and P-0038 specifically referred to girls under the age of 15 who were subjected to sexual violence by UPC commanders. As discussed above, in the view of the Majority, sexual violence does not form part of the charges against the accused, and the Chamber has not made any findings of fact on the issue, particularly as to whether responsibility is to be attributed to the accused.

914. In all the circumstances, the evidence has established beyond reasonable doubt that children under the age of 15 were conscripted and enlisted into the UPC/FPLC forces between 1 September 2002 and 13 August 2003.

* * *

XI. INDIVIDUAL CRIMINAL RESPONSIBILITY OF THOMAS LUBANGA (ARTICLE 25(3)(A) OF THE STATUTE)

A. THE LAW

1. THE MODE OF LIABILITY CHARGED

917. The prosecution charged Thomas Lubanga as a co-perpetrator under Article 25(3)(a) of the Statute, and the Pre-Trial Chamber confirmed the charges on this basis.

Article 25 Individual criminal responsibility

1. The Court shall have jurisdiction over natural persons pursuant to this Statute.

2.   A person who commits a crime within the jurisdiction of the Court shall be individually responsible and liable for punishment in accordance with this Statute.

3.   In accordance with this Statute, a person shall be criminally responsible and liable for punishment for a crime within the jurisdiction of the Court if that person:

> (a) Commits such a crime, whether as an individual, *jointly with another* or through another person, regardless of whether that other person is criminally responsible; (emphasis added)

* * *

5.   ANALYSIS

a) THE OBJECTIVE REQUIREMENTS

976. In the view of the Majority, both the Romano Germanic and the Common Law legal systems have developed principles about modes of liability. However, at their inception, neither of these systems was intended to deal with the crimes under the jurisdiction of this Court, *i.e.* the most serious crimes of concern to the international community as a whole. The Statute sets out the modes of liability in Articles 25 and 28 and, they should be interpreted in a way that allows properly expressing and addressing the responsibility for these crimes.

977. Articles 25(3)(a) to (d) establish the modes of individual criminal responsibility under the Statute, other than the "[r]esponsibility of commanders and other superiors," which is addressed in Article 28. Under Article 25(3)(a), an individual can be convicted of committing a crime: (i) individually; (ii) jointly with another; or (iii) through another person. Under Articles 25(3)(b) to (d), an individual can be convicted of: (i) ordering, soliciting or inducing a crime; (ii) acting as an accessory to a crime; or (iii) contributing to a crime committed by a group acting with a common purpose.

978. The Pre-Trial Chamber decided, pursuant to Article 61(7) of the Statute, there was sufficient evidence to establish substantial grounds to believe that Mr. Lubanga committed the crimes charged, under Article 25(3)(a), as a direct co-perpetrator. The Chamber will limit its analysis of Mr. Lubanga's responsibility to this mode of liability.

979. In considering the scope of liability under Article 25(3)(a) of the Rome Statute, the Chamber notes, as set out above, that the Appeals Chamber has stated that the provisions of the Statute are to be interpreted in conformity with Article 31(1) of the Vienna Convention on the Law of Treaties. Hence, the relevant elements of Article 25(3)(a) of the Statute, that the individual "commits such a crime [* * *] jointly with another [* * *] person," must be interpreted in good faith in accordance with the

ordinary meaning to be given to the language of the Statute, bearing in mind the relevant context and in light of its object and purpose.

(1) THE COMMON PLAN OR AGREEMENT

980. Article 25(3)(a) stipulates that a crime can be committed not only by an individual acting by himself or through another person, but also by an individual who acts jointly with another. To establish liability as a co-perpetrator under Article 25(3)(a), it is necessary there are at least two individuals involved in the commission of the crime. This is evident from the use of terms "jointly with another" in Article 25(3)(a).

981. As the Pre-Trial Chamber concluded, co-perpetration requires the existence of an agreement or common plan between the co-perpetrators. This provides for a sufficient connection between the individuals who together commit the crime and it allows responsibility to be established on a "joint" basis.

* * *

b) THE MENTAL ELEMENT

* * *

i) knows that his or her actions or omissions will bring about the objective elements of the crime, and ii) undertakes such actions or omissions with the concrete intent to bring about the objective elements of the crime (also known as *dolus directus* of the first degree)

* * *

4. OVERALL CONCLUSIONS

1351. The accused and his co-perpetrators agreed to, and participated in, a common plan to build an army for the purpose of establishing and maintaining political and military control over Ituri. This resulted, in the ordinary course of events, in the conscription and enlistment of boys and girls under the age of 15, and their use to participate actively in hostilities.

1352. As indicated in an earlier section of this Judgment, the Chamber has concluded that from late 2000 onwards, Thomas Lubanga acted with his co-perpetrators, who included Floribert Kisembo, Bosco Ntaganda, Chief Kahwa, and commanders Tchaligonza, Bagonza and Kasangaki. * * *

1355. The Chamber is satisfied beyond reasonable doubt that as a result of the implementation of the common plan to build an army for the purpose of establishing and maintaining political and military control over Ituri, boys and girls under the age of 15 were conscripted and enlisted into the UPC/FPLC between 1 September 2002 and 13 August 2003. Similarly, the Chamber is satisfied beyond reasonable doubt that the UPC/FPLC used children under the age of 15 to participate actively in hostilities, including during battles. They were also used, during the relevant period, as soldiers and as bodyguards for senior officials, including the accused.

1356. Thomas Lubanga was the President of the UPC/FPLC, and the evidence demonstrates that he was simultaneously the Commander-in-Chief of the army and its political leader. He exercised an overall coordinating role over the activities of the UPC/FPLC. He was informed, on a substantive and continuous basis, of the operations of the FPLC. He was involved in planning military operations, and he played a critical role in providing logistical support, including as regards weapons, ammunition, food, uniforms, military rations and other general supplies for the FPLC troops. He was closely involved in making decisions on recruitment policy and he actively supported recruitment initiatives, for instance by giving speeches to the local population and the recruits. In his speech at the Rwampara camp, he encouraged children, including those under the age of 15 years, to join the army and to provide security for the populace once deployed in the field following their military training. Furthermore, he personally used children below the age of 15 amongst his bodyguards and he regularly saw guards of other UPC/FPLC members of staff who were below the age of 15. The Chamber has concluded that these contributions by Thomas Lubanga, taken together, were essential to a common plan that resulted in the conscription and enlistment of girls and boys below the age of 15 into the UPC/FPLC and their use to actively participate in hostilities.

1357. The Chamber is satisfied beyond reasonable doubt, as set out above, that Thomas Lubanga acted with the intent and knowledge necessary to establish the charges (the mental element required by Article 30). He was aware of the factual circumstances that established the existence of the armed conflict. Furthermore, he was aware of the nexus between those circumstances and his own conduct, which resulted in the enlistment, conscription and use of children below the age of 15 to participate actively in hostilities.

* * *

If the Court goes into this much detail and produces such lengthy opinions, how many cases can it reasonably be expected to decide on an annual basis? Doesn't that limit the numbers to an extent that renders the Court virtually useless as an institution that tries international crimes? Or does the Court serve other valuable functions? What additional concerns does Goldsmith raise in the article below?

JACK GOLDSMITH, THE SELF–DEFEATING INTERNATIONAL CRIMINAL COURT

70 U. Chi. L. Rev. 89 (2003)

* * *

Great expectations greeted the opening of the International Criminal Court (ICC) on July 1, 2002. Kofi Annan captured these expectations when he expressed the hope that the new ICC would "deter future war criminals and bring nearer the day when no ruler, no state, no junta and no army anywhere will be able to abuse human rights with impunity." Chris Patten, the European Union Commissioner for External Relations, echoed this theme when he stated that the new Court's purpose was to "ensure that genocide and other such crimes against humanity should no longer go unpunished." Scores of other world officials, human rights activists, and international law experts made similar predictions.

These are unrealistic dreams. They are unrealistic for many reasons. But perhaps the most salient reason is that the ICC as currently organized is, and will remain, unacceptable to the United States. This is important because the ICC depends on U.S. political, military, and economic support for its success. An ICC without U.S. support—and indeed, with probable U.S. opposition—will not only fail to live up to its expectations. It may well do actual harm by discouraging the United States from engaging in various human rights-protecting activities. And this, in turn, may increase rather than decrease the impunity of those who violate human rights.

* * *

II. PERVERSITY

I now turn to consider how the ICC might actually diminish human rights protections. This perverse result could occur because the ICC's actions may have a chilling effect on U.S. human rights-related activities.

The main reason why the United States opposes the ICC is the fear that its unique international policing responsibilities will expose it to politically motivated prosecutions before an unaccountable court. To be sure, the ICC's safeguards to prevent rogue prosecutions are all ultimately subject to ICC interpretation. The most notable safeguard is complementarity. Complementarity requires that the ICC dismiss a case under investigation "unless the State is unwilling or unable genuinely to carry out the investigation or prosecution." But the ICC has the final word on what counts as a "genuine" investigation based on its judgment whether the domestic proceedings are "inconsistent with an intent to bring the person concerned to justice." The perceived efficacy of complementarity and other ICC safeguards turns on the level of trust a nation has toward the ICC.

The United States has little. This lack of trust is magnified by the ICC's assertion of jurisdiction over non-signatory nations and the more favorable immunities the ICC provides to signatory nations (most notably, the option for a seven-year immunity from war crimes prosecution).

These are genuine bases for U.S. concern, but they strike me as secondary. The real concern is that the indeterminateness of international criminal law makes it easy to imagine the ICC and the United States having genuine, principled disagreements about whether a particular act is an international crime.

The most likely basis of disagreement relevant to the United States concerns war crimes arising from military strikes. The ICC has jurisdiction, for example, over a military strike that causes incidental civilian injury (or damage to civilian objects) "clearly excessive in relation to the concrete and direct overall military advantage anticipated." Such proportionality judgments are almost always contested. The prosecutor for the NATO-dominated ICTY, for example, seriously considered prosecuting U.S. and NATO officials for (among other things) high-altitude bombings in Kosovo that accidentally killed civilians. The prosecutor's staff apparently advised her to pursue these charges, and her memorandum declining to do so seems tendentious because it takes all of NATO's factual assertions, in their best light, as true. Especially during a war in which irregular combatants hide among civilians, it is easy to imagine a prosecution on this basis. And who knows what might be included in the prohibitions on "severe deprivation of physical liberty in violation of fundamental rules of international law," or on "[d]estroying or seizing the enemy's property unless * * * imperatively demanded by the necessities of war," or on "inhumane acts of a similar character [to crimes against humanity that] intentionally caus[e] great suffering, or serious injury to body or to mental or physical health."

There are many other bases for prosecution of U.S. officials. Nonetheless, the ICC's procedural safeguards, when combined with the threat of U.S. retaliation, make it unlikely that a U.S. official will actually end up in the ICC dock. Why, then, is the United States so worried about the ICC? How can an institution that will have little effect on rogue nations affect the calculations of the world's most powerful nation?

There are two plausible answers. First, U.S. troops do not hide behind U.S. borders. Hundreds of thousands of them are spread across the globe and can much more readily be nabbed and whisked away to The Hague. The possibility of capture is thus much more salient for U.S. troops or officials. Even a remote chance that one of them may be prosecuted will understandably concern U.S. leaders. Second, even if no U.S. official ends up in The Hague, the ICC can affect the United States by merely investigating alleged crimes and engaging in official public criticism and judgment of U.S. military actions.

Whatever the source of U.S. opposition, the fact that opposition runs deep is clear. The otherwise-internationalist Clinton administration opposed the treaty that emerged from Rome, and although Clinton nonetheless signed the treaty on the last day possible, he also called it flawed and advised President Bush not to send it to the Senate for ratification. In the spring of 2002, the U.S. officially informed the UN that "the United States does not intend to become a party to the treaty" and that "[a]ccordingly, the United States has no legal obligations arising from its signature on December 31, 2000." The Bush administration has openly opposed the treaty since then. Most notably, in the summer of 2002, it played a game of chicken with the UN over the exposure of UN peacekeepers to ICC jurisdiction. The game was resolved when the Security Council, in the face of significant criticism from ICC supporters, exercised its prerogative under the ICC treaty to immunize UN peacekeepers from ICC investigation for twelve months.

Just as important, the Senate has been steadfastly opposed to the ICC since the July 1998 vote to create it. Few senators have expressed support for the treaty that emerged from Rome, and most, including prominent Democrats such as Tom Daschle, Hillary Rodham Clinton, and Joseph Biden, have opposed it. The House is, if anything, less supportive. In 2002, Congress enacted the American Servicemembers' Protection Act (ASPA). ASPA is sometimes dubbed "The Hague Invasion Act" because it authorizes the President to use "all means necessary and appropriate" to bring about the release from captivity of U.S. or Allied personnel detained or imprisoned by or on behalf of the Court. ASPA also prohibits any cooperation with (including financial support for) the ICC. It bars military aid to nations that support the ICC (except for NATO countries and other major allies). And it requires the President to certify that U.S. forces that participate in peacekeeping will be safe from ICC prosecution. ASPA also gives the President a number of options to waive its requirements.

We can now finally begin to see the perverse effects of the ICC. The first component of the central ICC compromise leaves in place international human rights' dependence on United States political support, funding, and military might. The second component of the fatal compromise exposes the United States, a non-signatory nation, to liability for crimes committed in signatory nations or in non-signatory nations that temporarily invoke Article 12(3). But this latter part of the compromise will lead the United States to limit its human rights enforcement activities. And the first enforcement activities to go will be ones involving human rights crises that lack a powerful U.S. welfare-enhancing justification.

We have already seen these perverse effects in the United States' threat to pull out of UN peacekeeping missions unless U.S. troops receive immunity before the ICC. However this is resolved, peacekeeping will suffer at least at the margin. To the extent that ad hoc international tribunals have been important in protecting human rights, they too have suffered, and will continue to suffer, from a general U.S. withdrawal for reasons already canvassed. But perhaps the greatest effect will be on U.S. humanitarian and quasi-humanitarian interventions, such as in Haiti, Kosovo, Bosnia, and Somalia. Human rights advocates increasingly view such interventions as legitimate and necessary to protect human rights. It is hard enough to generate domestic support in the United States for these interventions when there is no threat of liability. U.S. intervention will now be much harder. Such interventions invariably involve combat against irregular forces interspersed in civilian populations and thus invariably run the risk of war crime accusations. The fatal compromise appears to expose the only nation practically able to intervene to protect human rights to the greatest potential liability for human rights violations.

So in the end the ICC will likely have two ironic consequences. It will affect the generally human-rights-protecting, but globally active, United States more than rogue human rights abusers who hide behind national walls and care little about world opinion or international legitimacy. And it will have the greatest chill on U.S. military action not when important U.S. strategic interests are at stake (as they are now in Afghanistan), but rather in quasi-humanitarian situations (such as in Kosovo) where the strategic benefits of military action are lower and thus a remote possibility of prosecution weighs more heavily.

* * *

While criminal responsibility of individuals under international law has been firmly established for some time now, civil liability (for damages) is a more recent phenomenon. The following case has set the stage for addressing that phenomenon in the United States.

Strictly speaking, the decision presented here deals only with the question whether the federal courts have subject matter jurisdiction, i.e., whether they are empowered to hear this case. Since federal courts are not courts of general jurisdiction, they need a specific (statutory) grant of subject matter jurisdiction. In this case, such a grant may come from two federal statutes: the Alien Tort Statute (ATS, sometimes also called the Alien Tort Claims Act, ATCA) and the Torture Victim Protection Act (TVPA). The question is whether one or the other (or both) are applicable here. The two statutes must be carefully distinguished because they pose different requirements. The court discusses them one after the other. They do raise a common issue, though, which is therefore at the heart of the opinion. What is that issue? How does the court decide it? And what does the decision tell you, more generally, about the responsibility of individuals under international law?

KADIC V. KARADZIC
DOE V. KARADZIC

United States Circuit Court
70 F.3d 232 (2d Cir. 1995)

CHIEF JUDGE NEWMAN:

Most Americans would probably be surprised to learn that victims of atrocities committed in Bosnia are suing the leader of the insurgent Bosnian–Serb forces in a United States District Court in Manhattan. Their claims seek to build upon the foundation of this Court's decision in *Filártiga v. Peña-Irala*, which recognized the important principle that the venerable Alien Tort Act, 28 U.S.C. § 1350 (1988), enacted in 1789 but rarely invoked since then, validly creates federal court jurisdiction for suits alleging torts committed anywhere in the world against aliens in violation of the law of nations. The pending appeals pose additional significant issues as to the scope of the Alien Tort Act: whether some violations of the law of nations may be remedied when committed by those not acting under the authority of a state; if so, whether genocide, war crimes, and crimes against humanity are among the violations that do not require state action; and whether a person, otherwise liable for a violation of the law of nations, is immune from service of process because he is present in the United States as an invitee of the United Nations.

These issues arise on appeals by two groups of plaintiffs-appellants from the November 19, 1994, judgment of the United States District Court for the Southern District of New York, dismissing, for lack of subject-matter jurisdiction, their suits against defendant-appellee Radovan Karadžić, President of the self-proclaimed Bosnian–Serb republic of "Srpska." For the reasons set forth below, we hold that subject-matter jurisdiction exists, that Karadžić may be found liable for genocide, war crimes, and crimes against humanity in his private capacity and for other violations in his capacity as a state actor, and that he is not immune from service of process. We therefore reverse and remand.

BACKGROUND

The plaintiffs-appellants are Croat and Muslim citizens of the internationally recognized nation of Bosnia–Herzegovina, formerly a republic of Yugoslavia. Their complaints, which we accept as true for purposes of this appeal, allege that they are victims, and representatives of victims, of various atrocities, including brutal acts of rape, forced prostitution, forced impregnation, torture, and summary execution, carried out by Bosnian–Serb military forces as part of a genocidal campaign conducted in the course of the Bosnian civil war. Karadžić, formerly a citizen of Yugoslavia and now a citizen of Bosnia–Herzegovina, is the President of a three-man presidency of the self-proclaimed Bosnian–Serb republic within Bosnia–Herzegovina, sometimes referred to as "Srpska," which claims to exercise lawful authority, and does in fact exercise actual control, over large parts of the territory of Bosnia–Herzegovina. In his capacity as President, Karadžić possesses ultimate command authority over the Bosnian–Serb military forces, and the injuries perpetrated upon plaintiffs were committed as part of a pattern of systematic human rights violations that was directed by Karadžić and carried out by the military forces under his command. The complaints allege that Karadžić acted in an official capacity either as the titular head of Srpska or in collaboration with the government of the recognized nation of the former Yugoslavia and its dominant constituent republic, Serbia.

* * *

In the District Court, Karadžić moved for dismissal of both actions on the grounds of insufficient service of process, lack of personal jurisdiction, lack of subject-matter jurisdiction, and nonjusticiability of plaintiffs' claims. However, Karadžić submitted a memorandum of law and supporting papers only on the issues of service of process and personal jurisdiction, while reserving the issues of subject-matter jurisdiction and nonjusticiability for further briefing, if necessary. The plaintiffs submitted papers responding only to the issues raised by the defendant.

Without notice or a hearing, the District Court by-passed the issues briefed by the parties and dismissed both actions for lack of subject-matter jurisdiction. In an Opinion and Order, the District Judge preliminarily noted that the Court might be deprived of jurisdiction if the Executive Branch were to recognize Karadžić as the head of state of a friendly nation, and that this possibility could render the plaintiffs' pending claims requests for an advisory opinion. The District Judge recognized that this consideration was not dispositive but believed that it "militates against this Court exercising jurisdiction."

Turning to the issue of subject-matter jurisdiction under the Alien Tort Act, the Court concluded that "acts committed by non-state actors do not violate the law of nations." Finding that "[t]he current Bosnian–Serb warring military faction does not constitute a recognized state," and that "the members of Karadžić's faction do not act under the color of any recognized state law," the Court concluded that "the acts alleged in the instant action[s], while grossly repugnant, cannot be remedied through [the Alien Tort Act]." The Court did not consider the plaintiffs' alternative claim that Karadžić acted under color of law by acting in concert with the Serbian Republic of the former Yugoslavia, a recognized nation.

The District Judge also found that the apparent absence of state action barred plaintiffs' claims under the Torture Victim Act, which expressly requires that an individual defendant act "under actual or apparent authority, or color of law, of any foreign nation," Torture Victim Act § 2(a). With respect to plaintiffs' further claims that the law of nations, as incorporated into federal common law, gives rise to an implied cause of action over which the Court would have jurisdiction pursuant to section 1331, the Judge found that the law of nations does not give rise to implied rights of action absent specific Congressional authorization, and that, in any event, such an implied right of action would not lie in the absence of state action. Finally, having dismissed all of plaintiffs' federal claims, the Court declined to exercise supplemental jurisdiction over their state-law claims.

DISCUSSION

Though the District Court dismissed for lack of subject-matter jurisdiction, the parties have briefed not only that issue but also the threshold issues of personal jurisdiction and justiciability under the political question doctrine. Karadžić urges us to affirm on any one of these three grounds. We consider each in turn.

I.   SUBJECT–MATTER JURISDICTION

Appellants allege three statutory bases for the subject-matter jurisdiction of the District Court—the Alien Tort Act, the Torture Victim Act, and the general federal-question jurisdictional statute.

A.   THE ALIEN TORT ACT

1.   GENERAL APPLICATION TO APPELLANTS' CLAIMS

The Alien Tort Act provides:

> The district courts shall have original jurisdiction of any civil action by an alien for a tort only, committed in violation of the law of nations or a treaty of the United States. 28 U.S.C. § 1350 (1988).

Our decision in *Filártiga* established that this statute confers federal subject-matter jurisdiction when the following three conditions are satisfied: (1) an alien sues (2) for a tort (3) committed in violation of the law of nations (i.e., international law). The first two requirements are plainly satisfied here, and the only disputed issue is whether plaintiffs have pleaded violations of international law.

Because the Alien Tort Act requires that plaintiffs plead a "violation of the law of nations" at the jurisdictional threshold, this statute requires a more searching review of the merits to establish jurisdiction than is required under the more flexible "arising under" formula of section 1331.

Thus, it is not a sufficient basis for jurisdiction to plead merely a colorable violation of the law of nations. There is no federal subject-matter jurisdiction under the Alien Tort Act unless the complaint adequately pleads a violation of the law of nations (or treaty of the United States).

Filártiga established that courts ascertaining the content of the law of nations "must interpret international law not as it was in 1789, but as it has evolved and exists among the nations of the world today." We find the norms of contemporary international law by " 'consulting the works of jurists, writing professedly on public law; or by the general usage and practice of nations; or by judicial decisions recognizing and enforcing that law.' " *Filártiga*, 630 F.2d at 880 (quoting *United States v. Smith*, 18 U.S. (5 Wheat) 153, 160–61 (1820)). If this inquiry discloses that the defendant's alleged conduct violates "well-established, universally recognized norms of international law," as opposed to "idiosyncratic legal rules," then federal jurisdiction exists under the Alien Tort Act.

Karadžić contends that appellants have not alleged violations of the norms of international law because such norms bind only states and persons acting under color of a state's law, not private individuals. In making this contention, Karadžić advances the contradictory positions that he is not a state actor, even as he asserts that he is the President of the self-proclaimed Republic of Srpska. For their part, the Kadic appellants also take somewhat inconsistent positions in pleading defendant's role as President of Srpska, and also contending that "Karadžić is not an official of any government."

We do not agree that the law of nations, as understood in the modern era, confines its reach to state action. Instead, we hold that certain forms of conduct violate the law of nations whether undertaken by those acting under the auspices of a state or only as private individuals. An early example of the application of the law of nations to the acts of private individuals is the prohibition against piracy. In *The Brig Malek Adhel*, 43 U.S. (2 How.) 210, 232 (1844), the Supreme Court observed that pirates were "hostis humani generis" (an enemy of all mankind) in part because they acted "without * * * any pretense of public authority." Later examples are prohibitions against the slave trade and certain war crimes.

The liability of private persons for certain violations of customary international law and the availability of the Alien Tort Act to remedy such violations was early recognized by the Executive Branch in an opinion of Attorney General Bradford in reference to acts of American citizens aiding the French fleet to plunder British property off the coast of Sierra Leone in 1795. The Executive Branch has emphatically restated in this litigation its position that private persons may be found liable under the Alien Tort Act for acts of genocide, war crimes, and other violations of international humanitarian law.

The Restatement (Third) of the Foreign Relations Law of the United States (1986) proclaims: "Individuals may be held liable for offenses against international law, such as piracy, war crimes, and genocide." The Restatement is careful to identify those violations that are actionable when committed by a state, *Restatement (Third)* § 702,[5] and a more limited category of violations of "universal concern," *id.* § 404,[6] partially overlapping with those listed in section 702. Though the immediate focus of section 404 is to identify those offenses for which a state has jurisdiction to punish without regard to territoriality or the nationality of the offenders, *cf. id.* § 402(1)(a), (2), the inclusion of piracy and slave trade from an earlier era and aircraft hijacking from the modern era demonstrates that the offenses of "universal concern" include those capable of being committed by non-state actors. * * *

Karadžić disputes the application of the law of nations to any violations committed by private individuals, relying on *Filártiga* and the concurring opinion of Judge Edwards in *Tel-Oren v. Libyan Arab Republic. Filártiga* involved an allegation of torture committed by a state official. Relying on the United Nations' Declaration on the Protection of All Persons from Being Subjected to Torture (hereinafter "Declaration on Torture"), as a definitive statement of norms of customary international law prohibiting states from permitting torture, we ruled that "official torture is now prohibited by the law of nations." *Filártiga*, 630 F.2d at 884. We had no occasion to consider whether international law violations other than torture are actionable against private individuals, and nothing in *Filártiga* purports to preclude such a result.

* * *

2.   SPECIFIC APPLICATION OF ALIEN TORT ACT TO APPELLANTS' CLAIMS

[The court then held that individuals could be liable under international law for genocide and war crimes even in the absence of state action. Lia-

---

[5] Section 702 provides:

A state violates international law if, as a matter of state policy, it practices, encourages, or condones

(a) genocide,

(b) slavery or slave trade,

(c) the murder or causing the disappearance of individuals,

(d) torture or other cruel, inhuman, or degrading treatment or punishment,

(e) prolonged arbitrary detention,

(f) systematic racial discrimination, or

(g) a consistent pattern of gross violations of internationally recognized human rights.

[6] Section 404 provides:

A state has jurisdiction to define and prescribe punishment for certain offenses recognized by the community of nations as of universal concern, such as piracy, slave trade, attacks on or hijacking of aircraft, genocide, war crimes, and perhaps certain acts of terrorism, even where [no other basis of jurisdiction] is present.

bility for torture and summary execution, however, does require state action in principle. Yet, the case could proceed against Karadžić even in this regard: "It suffices to hold at this stage that the alleged atrocities are actionable under the Alien Tort Act without regard to state action, to the extent that they were committed in pursuit of genocide or war crimes, and otherwise may be pursued against Karadžić to the extent that he is shown to be a state actor."]

* * *

3. THE STATE ACTION REQUIREMENT FOR INTERNATIONAL LAW VIOLATIONS

In dismissing plaintiffs' complaints for lack of subject-matter jurisdiction, the District Court concluded that the alleged violations required state action and that the "Bosnian–Serb entity" headed by Karadžić does not meet the definition of a state. Appellants contend that they are entitled to prove that Srpska satisfies the definition of a state for purposes of international law violations and, alternatively, that Karadžić acted in concert with the recognized state of the former Yugoslavia and its constituent republic, Serbia.

(A) DEFINITION OF A STATE IN INTERNATIONAL LAW.

The definition of a state is well established in international law:

> Under international law, a state is an entity that has a defined territory and a permanent population, under the control of its own government, and that engages in, or has the capacity to engage in, formal relations with other such entities.

Although the Restatement's definition of statehood requires the *capacity* to engage in formal relations with other states, it does not require recognition by other states. See *Restatement (Third)* § 202 cmt. b ("An entity that satisfies the requirements of § 201 is a state whether or not its statehood is formally recognized by other states."). Recognized states enjoy certain privileges and immunities relevant to judicial proceedings, but an unrecognized state is not a juridical nullity. Our courts have regularly given effect to the "state" action of unrecognized states.

The customary international law of human rights, such as the proscription of official torture, applies to states without distinction between recognized and unrecognized states. It would be anomalous indeed if nonrecognition by the United States, which typically reflects disfavor with a foreign regime—sometimes due to human rights abuses—had the perverse effect of shielding officials of the unrecognized regime from liability for those violations of international law norms that apply only to state actors.

Appellants' allegations entitle them to prove that Karadžić's regime satisfies the criteria for a state, for purposes of those international law violations requiring state action. Srpska is alleged to control defined territory, control populations within its power, and to have entered into agreements with other governments. It has a president, a legislature, and its own currency. These circumstances readily appear to satisfy the criteria for a state in all aspects of international law. Moreover, it is likely that the state action concept, where applicable for some violations like "official" torture, requires merely the semblance of official authority. The inquiry, after all, is whether a person purporting to wield official power has exceeded internationally recognized standards of civilized conduct, not whether statehood in all its formal aspects exists.

(B) ACTING IN CONCERT WITH A FOREIGN STATE.

Appellants also sufficiently alleged that Karadžić acted under color of law insofar as they claimed that he acted in concert with the former Yugoslavia, the statehood of which is not disputed. * * *

B.   THE TORTURE VICTIM PROTECTION ACT

The Torture Victim Act, enacted in 1992, provides a cause of action for official torture and extrajudicial killing:

> An individual who, under actual or apparent authority, or color of law, of any foreign nation—
>
> (1) subjects an individual to torture shall, in a civil action, be liable for damages to that individual; or
>
> (2) subjects an individual to extrajudicial killing shall, in a civil action, be liable for damages to the individual's legal representative, or to any person who may be a claimant in an action for wrongful death.

Torture Victim Act § 2(a). The statute also requires that a plaintiff exhaust adequate and available local remedies, *id.* § 2(b), imposes a ten-year statute of limitations, *id.* § 2(c), and defines the terms "extrajudicial killing" and "torture," *id.* § 3.

By its plain language, the Torture Victim Act renders liable only those individuals who have committed torture or extrajudicial killing "under actual or apparent authority, or color of law, of any foreign nation." Legislative history confirms that this language was intended to "make[ ] clear that the plaintiff must establish some governmental involvement in the torture or killing to prove a claim," and that the statute "does not attempt to deal with torture or killing by purely private groups." In construing the terms "actual or apparent authority" and "color of law," courts are instructed to look to principles of agency law and to jurisprudence under 42 U.S.C. § 1983, respectively.

* * *

CONCLUSION

The judgment of the District Court dismissing appellants' complaints for lack of subject-matter jurisdiction is reversed, and the cases are remanded for further proceedings in accordance with this opinion.

Ultimately, plaintiffs won (an aggregate) $275,000,000 in compensatory and $480,000,000 in punitive damages. How much good does this judgment do?

The state action requirement is a central issue in the case. Exactly why does it matter under these statutes? What if the court had decided that Karadzic was not a state actor? Would the TVPA apply? Would the ATS apply?

Kadic is just one of many cases brought since 1980 by foreign victims of human rights abuses under the ATS in United States courts. The federal courts have developed a rich jurisprudence in this area but have also disagreed in important regards on the proper interpretation of the hoary statute.

The following case is the sequel to the Supreme Court's decision in *United States v. Alvarez-Machain* 504 U.S. 655 (1992), where the Court had found that the defendant's government-orchestrated abduction from his Mexican home did not prevent his criminal prosecution in U.S. courts (Chapter III.3.). There, Justice Rehnquist had admitted that the defendant's abduction may have been "shocking," and that it may "be in violation of general international law principles." While that availed the defendant nothing in that context, these statements can be read as inviting Alvarez-Machain to bring an entirely separate lawsuit on those grounds. When he sued his abductors under the ATS as well as the U.S. government under the Federal Tort Claims Act (FTCA) for damages, he was successful in both the District Court and in the Ninth Circuit Court of Appeals, albeit over a strong dissent en banc. The case then came before the Supreme Court.

In reading the following case, be sure you understand precisely what the issues are. In particular, how does the Court read the ATS? Does the ATS permit claims for violations of international law developed post-1945? If so, under what circumstances? How does the Court's reading impact Alvarez-Machain's claim?

SOSA V. ALVAREZ–MACHAIN

United States Supreme Court
542 U.S. 692 (2004)

JUSTICE SOUTER delivered the opinion of the Court, Parts I and III of which were unanimous, Part II of which was joined by CHIEF JUSTICE REHNQUIST and JUSTICES STEVENS, O'CONNOR, SCALIA, KENNEDY, and THOMAS and Part IV of which was joined by JUSTICES STEVENS, O'CONNOR, KENNEDY, GINSBURG, and BREYER. JUSTICE SCALIA filed an opinion concurring in part and concurring in the judgment, in which CHIEF JUSTICE REHNQUIST and JUSTICE THOMAS joined. JUSTICE GINS-BURG filed an opinion concurring in part and concurring in the judgment, in which JUSTICE BREYER joined. JUSTICE BREYER filed an opinion concurring in part and concurring in the judgment.

[Time out! So, who is agreeing, concurring, disagreeing with whom on what? And what does it all amount to in the end? Fortunately, you will be spared the grief of having to figure it out. We are concerned here only with the Court's decision on the ATS. With regard to *that* set of problems (Part III), the decision is unanimous, except for some concurring remarks by Justice Scalia et al. (Part IV). We thus omit the decision concerning the Federal Tort Claims Act (Part II) where the Court is all over the place.]

The two issues are whether respondent Alvarez-Machain's allegation that the Drug Enforcement Administration instigated his abduction from Mexico for criminal trial in the United States supports a claim against the Government under the Federal Tort Claims Act (FTCA or Act), 28 U.S.C. § 1346(b)(1), §§ 2671–2680, and whether he may recover under the Alien Tort Statute (ATS), 28 U.S.C. § 1350. We hold that he is not entitled to a remedy under either statute.

I

We have considered the underlying facts before, *United States v. Alvarez-Machain,* 504 U.S. 655 (1992). In 1985, an agent of the Drug Enforcement Administration (DEA), Enrique Camarena-Salazar, was captured on assignment in Mexico and taken to a house in Guadalajara, where he was tortured over the course of a 2-day interrogation, then murdered. Based in part on eyewitness testimony, DEA officials in the United States came to believe that respondent Humberto Alvarez-Machain (Alvarez), a Mexican physician, was present at the house and acted to prolong the agent's life in order to extend the interrogation and torture.

In 1990, a federal grand jury indicted Alvarez for the torture and murder of Camarena-Salazar, and the United States District Court for the Central District of California issued a warrant for his arrest. The DEA asked the Mexican Government for help in getting Alvarez into the United States, but when the requests and negotiations proved fruitless, the DEA approved a plan to hire Mexican nationals to seize Alvarez and bring him to the United States for trial. As so planned, a group of Mexicans, including petitioner Jose Francisco Sosa, abducted Alvarez from his house, held him overnight in a motel, and brought him by private plane to El Paso, Texas, where he was arrested by federal officers.

Once in American custody, Alvarez moved to dismiss the indictment on the ground that his seizure was "outrageous governmental conduct," *Alvarez-Machain,* 504 U.S., at 658, and violated the extradition treaty between the United States and Mexico. The District Court agreed, the Ninth Circuit affirmed, and we reversed, *id.,* at 670, holding that the fact of Alvarez's forcible seizure did not affect the jurisdiction of a federal court. The case was tried in 1992, and ended at the close of the Government's case, when the District Court granted Alvarez's motion for a judgment of acquittal.

In 1993, after returning to Mexico, Alvarez began the civil action before us here. He sued Sosa, Mexican citizen and DEA operative Antonio Garate-Bustamante, five unnamed Mexican civilians, the United States, and four DEA agents. So far as it matters here, Alvarez sought damages from the United States under the FTCA, alleging false arrest, and from Sosa under the ATS, for a violation of the law of nations. * * * The former statute authorizes suit "for * * * personal injury * * * caused by the negligent or wrongful act or omission of any employee of the Government while acting within the scope of his office or employment." 28 U.S.C. § 1346(b)(1). The latter provides in its entirety that "the district courts shall have original jurisdiction of any civil action by an alien for a tort only, committed in violation of the law of nations or a treaty of the United States." § 1350.

The District Court granted the Government's motion to dismiss the FTCA claim, but awarded summary judgment and $25,000 in damages to Alvarez on the ATS claim. A three-judge panel of the Ninth Circuit then affirmed the ATS judgment, but reversed the dismissal of the FTCA claim.

A divided en banc court came to the same conclusion. As for the ATS claim, the court called on its own precedent, "that [the ATS] not only provides federal courts with subject matter jurisdiction, but also creates a cause of action for an alleged violation of the law of nations." The Circuit then relied upon what it called the "clear and universally recognized norm prohibiting arbitrary arrest and detention," to support the conclusion that Alvarez's arrest amounted to a tort in violation of international law. On the FTCA claim, the Ninth Circuit held that, because "the DEA had no authority to effect Alvarez's arrest and detention in Mexico," the United States was liable to him under California law for the tort of false arrest.

We granted certiorari in these companion cases to clarify the scope of both the FTCA and the ATS. *540 U.S. 1045, 157 L. Ed. 2d 692, 124 S. Ct. 807 (2003)*. We now reverse in each.

II

The Government seeks reversal of the judgment of liability under the FTCA on two principal grounds. It argues that the arrest could not have been tortious, because it was authorized by 21 U.S.C. § 878, setting out the arrest authority of the DEA, and it says that in any event the liability asserted here falls within the FTCA exception to waiver of sovereign immunity for claims "arising in a foreign country," 28 U.S.C. § 2680(k). We think the exception applies and decide on that ground. * * *

III

Alvarez has also brought an action under the ATS against petitioner, Sosa, who argues (as does the United States supporting him) that there is no relief under the ATS because the statute does no more than vest federal courts with jurisdiction, neither creating nor authorizing the courts to recognize any particular right of action without further congressional action. Although we agree the statute is in terms only jurisdictional, we think that at the time of enactment the jurisdiction enabled federal courts to hear claims in a very limited category defined by the law of nations and recognized at common law. We do not believe, however, that the limited, implicit sanction to entertain the handful of international law *cum* common law claims understood in 1789 should be taken as authority to recognize the right of action asserted by Alvarez here.

A

Judge Friendly called the ATS a "legal Lohengrin," *IIT v. Vencap, Ltd.*, 519 F.2d 1001, 1015 (CA2 1975); "no one seems to know whence it came," *ibid.*, and for over 170 years after its enactment it provided jurisdiction in only one case. The first Congress passed it as part of the Judiciary Act of 1789, in providing that the new federal district courts "shall also have cognizance, concurrent with the courts of the several States, or the circuit courts, as the case may be, of all causes where an alien sues for a tort only in violation of the law of nations or a treaty of the United States." Act of Sept. 24, 1789, ch. 20, § 9(b), 1 Stat. 79.

The parties and *amici* here advance radically different historical interpretations of this terse provision. Alvarez says that the ATS was intended not simply as a jurisdictional grant, but as authority for the creation of a new cause of action for torts in violation of international law. We think that reading is implausible. * * * In sum, we think the statute was intended as jurisdictional in the sense of addressing the power of the courts to entertain cases concerned with a certain subject.

But holding the ATS jurisdictional raises a new question, this one about the interaction between the ATS at the time of its enactment and the ambient law of the era. Sosa would have it that the ATS was stillborn because there could be no claim for relief without a further statute expressly authorizing adoption of causes of action. *Amici* professors of federal jurisdiction and legal history take a different tack, that federal courts could entertain claims once the jurisdictional grant was on the books, because torts in violation of the law of nations would have been recognized within the common law of the time. We think history and practice give the edge to this latter position.

* * *

[Detailed historical discussion omitted.]

Still, the history does tend to support two propositions. First, there is every reason to suppose that the First Congress did not pass the ATS as a jurisdictional convenience to be placed on the shelf for use by a future Congress or state legislature that might, some day, authorize the creation of causes of action or itself decide to make some element of the law of nations actionable for the benefit of foreigners. The anxieties of the preconstitutional period cannot be ignored easily enough to think that the statute was not meant to have a practical effect. * * *

The second inference to be drawn from the history is that Congress intended the ATS to furnish jurisdiction for a relatively modest set of actions alleging violations of the law of nations. Uppermost in the legislative mind appears to have been offenses against ambassadors; violations of safe conduct were probably understood to be actionable, and individual actions arising out of prize captures and piracy may well have also been contemplated. But the common law appears to have understood only those three of the hybrid variety as definite and actionable, or at any rate, to have assumed only a very limited set of claims. As Blackstone had put it, "offences against this law [of nations] are principally incident to whole states or nations," and not individuals seeking relief in court. * * *

The sparse contemporaneous cases and legal materials referring to the ATS tend to confirm both inferences, that some, but few, torts in violation of the law of nations were understood to be within the common law. * * *

In sum, although the ATS is a jurisdictional statute creating no new causes of action, the reasonable inference from the historical materials is that the statute was intended to have practical effect the moment it became law. The jurisdictional grant is best read as having been enacted on the understanding that the common law would provide a cause of action for the modest number of international law violations with a potential for personal liability at the time.

IV

We think it is correct, then, to assume that the First Congress understood that the district courts would recognize private causes of action for certain torts in violation of the law of nations, though we have found no basis to suspect Congress had any examples in mind beyond those torts corresponding to Blackstone's three primary offenses: violation of safe conducts, infringement of the rights of ambassadors, and piracy. We assume, too, that no development in the two centuries from the enactment of § 1350 to the birth of the modern line of cases beginning with *Filartiga v. Pena-Irala*, 630 F.2d 876 (CA2 1980), has categorically precluded federal courts from recognizing a claim under the law of nations as an element of common law; Congress has not in any relevant way amended § 1350 or limited civil common law power by another statute. Still, there are good reasons for a restrained conception of the discretion a federal court should exercise in considering a new cause of action of this kind. Accordingly, we think courts should require any claim based on the present-day law of nations to rest on a norm of international character accepted by the civilized world and defined with a specificity comparable to the features of the 18th-century paradigms we have recognized. This requirement is fatal to Alvarez's claim.

A

A series of reasons argue for judicial caution when considering the kinds of individual claims that might implement the jurisdiction conferred by the early statute. * * *

[The discussion of the first and second reasons is omitted.]

Third, this Court has recently and repeatedly said that a decision to create a private right of action is one better left to legislative judgment in the great majority of cases. The creation of a private right of action raises issues beyond the mere consideration whether underlying primary conduct should be allowed or not, entailing, for example, a decision to permit enforcement without the check imposed by prosecutorial discretion. Accordingly, even when Congress has made it clear by statute that a rule applies to purely domestic conduct, we are reluctant to infer intent to provide a private cause of action where the statute does not supply one expressly. While the absence of congressional action addressing private rights of action under an international norm is more equivocal than its failure to provide such a right when it creates a statute, the possible collateral consequences of making international rules privately actionable argue for judicial caution.

Fourth, the subject of those collateral consequences is itself a reason for a high bar to new private causes of action for violating international law, for the potential implications for the foreign relations of the United States of recognizing such causes should make courts particularly wary of impinging on the discretion of the Legislative and Executive Branches in managing foreign affairs. It is one thing for American courts to enforce constitutional limits on our own State and Federal Governments' power, but quite another to consider suits under rules that would go so far as to claim a limit on the power of foreign governments over their own citizens, and to hold that a foreign government or its agent has transgressed those limits. Yet modern international law is very much concerned with just such questions, and apt to stimulate calls for vindicating private interests in § 1350 cases. Since many attempts by federal courts to craft remedies for the violation of new norms of international law would raise risks of adverse foreign policy consequences, they should be undertaken, if at all, with great caution.

The fifth reason is particularly important in light of the first four. We have no congressional mandate to seek out and define new and debatable violations of the law of nations, and modern indications of congressional understanding of the judicial role in the field have not affirmatively encouraged greater judicial creativity. It is true that a clear mandate appears in the Torture Victim Protection Act of 1991, 106 Stat. 73, providing authority that "establishes an unambiguous and modern basis for" federal claims of torture and extrajudicial killing, H. R. Rep. No. 102–367, pt. 1, p. 3 (1991). But that affirmative authority is confined to specific subject matter, and although the legislative history includes the remark that § 1350 should "remain intact to permit suits based on other norms that already exist or may ripen in the future into rules of customary international law," *id.*, at 4, Congress as a body has done nothing to promote such suits. Several times, indeed, the Senate has expressly declined to give the federal courts the task of interpreting and applying international human rights law, as when its ratification of the International Covenant on Civil and Political Rights declared that the substantive provisions of the document were not self-executing. 138 Cong. Rec. 8071 (1992).

* * *

C

We must still, however, derive a standard or set of standards for assessing the particular claim Alvarez raises, and for this case it suffices to look to the historical antecedents. Whatever the ultimate criteria for accepting a cause of action subject to jurisdiction under § 1350, we are persuaded that federal courts should not recognize private claims under federal common law for violations of any international law norm with less definite content and acceptance among civilized nations than the historical paradigms familiar when § 1350 was enacted. This limit upon judicial recognition is generally consistent with the reasoning of many of the courts and judges who faced the issue before it reached this Court. See *Filartiga, supra,* at 890 ("For purposes of civil liability, the torturer has become—like the pirate and slave trader before him—*hostis humani generis,* an enemy of all mankind"); *Tel-Oren, supra,* at 781 (Edwards, J., concurring) (suggesting that the "limits of section 1350's reach" be defined by "a handful of heinous actions—each of which violates definable, universal and obligatory norms"); see also *In re Estate of Marcos Human Rights Litigation,* 25 F.3d 1467, 1475 (CA9 1994) ("Actionable violations of international law must be of a norm that is specific, universal, and obligatory"). And the determination whether a norm is sufficiently definite to support a cause of action[20] should (and, indeed, inevitably must) involve an element of judgment about the practical consequences of making that cause available to litigants in the federal courts.

Thus, Alvarez's detention claim must be gauged against the current state of international law, looking to those sources we have long, albeit cautiously, recognized.

To begin with, Alvarez cites two well-known international agreements that, despite their moral authority, have little utility under the standard set out in this opinion. He says that his abduction by Sosa was an "arbitrary arrest" within the meaning of the Universal Declaration of Human Rights (Declaration). And he traces the rule against arbitrary arrest not only to the Declaration, but also to article nine of the International Covenant on Civil and Political Rights (Covenant),[22] to which the United States is a party, and to various other conventions to which it is not. But the Declaration does not of its own force impose obligations as a matter of international law. See Humphrey, The UN Charter and the Universal Declaration of Human Rights, in The International Protection of Human Rights 39, 50 (E. Luard ed. 1967) (quoting Eleanor Roosevelt calling the Declaration " 'a statement of principles * * * setting up a common standard of achievement for all peoples and all nations' " and " 'not a treaty or international agreement * * * imposing legal obligations' "). And, although the Covenant does bind the United States as a matter of international law, the United States ratified the Covenant on the express understanding that it was not self-executing and so did not itself create obligations enforceable in the federal courts. Accordingly, Alvarez cannot say that the Declaration and Covenant themselves establish the relevant and applicable rule of international law. He instead attempts to show that

---

[20] A related consideration is whether international law extends the scope of liability for a violation of a given norm to the perpetrator being sued, if the defendant is a private actor such as a corporation or individual. Compare *Tel-Oren v. Libyan Arab Republic,* 726 F.2d 774, 791–795 (CADC 1984) (Edwards, J., concurring) (insufficient consensus in 1984 that torture by private actors violates international law), with *Kadic v. Karadzic,* 70 F.3d 232, 239–241 (CA2 1995) (sufficient consensus in 1995 that genocide by private actors violates international law).

[22] Article nine provides that "no one shall be subjected to arbitrary arrest or detention," that "no one shall be deprived of his liberty except on such grounds and in accordance with such procedure as are established by law," and that "anyone who has been the victim of unlawful arrest or detention shall have an enforceable right to compensation."

prohibition of arbitrary arrest has attained the status of binding customary international law.

Here, it is useful to examine Alvarez's complaint in greater detail. As he presently argues it, the claim does not rest on the cross-border feature of his abduction. Although the District Court granted relief in part on finding a violation of international law in taking Alvarez across the border from Mexico to the United States, the Court of Appeals rejected that ground of liability for failure to identify a norm of requisite force prohibiting a forcible abduction across a border. Instead, it relied on the conclusion that the law of the United States did not authorize Alvarez's arrest, because the DEA lacked extraterritorial authority under 21 U.S.C. § 878, and because Federal Rule of Criminal Procedure 4(d)(2) limited the warrant for Alvarez's arrest to "the jurisdiction of the United States." It is this position that Alvarez takes now: that his arrest was arbitrary and as such forbidden by international law not because it infringed the prerogatives of Mexico, but because no applicable law authorized it.

Alvarez thus invokes a general prohibition of "arbitrary" detention defined as officially sanctioned action exceeding positive authorization to detain under the domestic law of some government, regardless of the circumstances. Whether or not this is an accurate reading of the Covenant, Alvarez cites little authority that a rule so broad has the status of a binding customary norm today.[27] He certainly cites nothing to justify the federal courts in taking his broad rule as the predicate for a federal lawsuit, for its implications would be breathtaking. His rule would support a cause of action in federal court for any arrest, anywhere in the world, unauthorized by the law of the jurisdiction in which it took place, and would create a cause of action for any seizure of an alien in violation of the Fourth Amendment, supplanting the actions under 42 U.S.C. § 1983 and *Bivens v. Six Unknown Fed. Narcotics Agents*, that now provide damages remedies for such violations. It would create an action in federal court for arrests by state officers who simply exceed their authority; and for the violation of any limit that the law of any country might place on the authority of its own officers to arrest. And all of this assumes that Alvarez could establish that Sosa was acting on behalf of a government when he made the arrest, for otherwise he would need a rule broader still.

---

[27] Specifically, he relies on a survey of national constitutions, Bassiouni, *Human Rights in the Context of Criminal Justice: Identifying International Procedural Protections and Equivalent Protections in National Constitutions*, 3 Duke J. Comp. & Int'l L. 235, 260–261 (1993); a case from the International Court of Justice, *United States* v. *Iran,* 1980 I. C. J. 3, 42; and some authority drawn from the federal courts. None of these suffice. The Bassiouni survey does show that many nations recognize a norm against arbitrary detention, but that consensus is at a high level of generality. The *Iran* case, in which the United States sought relief for the taking of its diplomatic and consular staff as hostages, involved a different set of international norms and mentioned the problem of arbitrary detention only in passing; the detention in that case was, moreover, far longer and harsher than Alvarez's. And the authority from the federal courts, to the extent it supports Alvarez's position, reflects a more assertive view of federal judicial discretion over claims based on customary international law than the position we take today.

Alvarez's failure to marshal support for his proposed rule is underscored by the Restatement (Third) of Foreign Relations Law of the United States, which says in its discussion of customary international human rights law that a "state violates international law if, as a matter of state policy, it practices, encourages, or condones * * * prolonged arbitrary detention." *Id.,* § 702. Although the Restatement does not explain its requirements of a "state policy" and of "prolonged" detention, the implication is clear. Any credible invocation of a principle against arbitrary detention that the civilized world accepts as binding customary international law requires a factual basis beyond relatively brief detention in excess of positive authority. Even the Restatement's limits are only the beginning of the enquiry, because although it is easy to say that some policies of prolonged arbitrary detentions are so bad that those who enforce them become enemies of the human race, it may be harder to say which policies cross that line with the certainty afforded by Blackstone's three common law offenses. In any event, the label would never fit the reckless policeman who botches his warrant, even though that same officer might pay damages under municipal law.

Whatever may be said for the broad principle Alvarez advances, in the present, imperfect world, it expresses an aspiration that exceeds any binding customary rule having the specificity we require. Creating a private cause of action to further that aspiration would go beyond any residual common law discretion we think it appropriate to exercise. It is enough to hold that a single illegal detention of less than a day, followed by the transfer of custody to lawful authorities and a prompt arraignment, violates no norm of customary international law so well defined as to support the creation of a federal remedy.

The judgment of the Court of Appeals is

Reversed.

JUSTICE SCALIA, with whom CHIEF JUSTICE REHNQUIST and JUSTICE THOMAS join, concurring in part and concurring in the judgment.

There is not much that I would add to the Court's detailed opinion, and only one thing that I would subtract: its reservation of a discretionary power in the Federal Judiciary to create causes of action for the enforcement of international-law-based norms. Accordingly, I join Parts I, II, and III of the Court's opinion in these consolidated cases. Although I agree with much in Part IV, I cannot join it because the judicial lawmaking role it invites would commit the Federal Judiciary to a task it is neither authorized nor suited to perform.

* * *

Formulate the three major rules of this case. Why does Alvarez-Machain lose under these rules? Isn't there a clear violation of international law when the United States authorizes the abduction of a Mexican national from Mexican territory? What sources of law does the Court look to in addressing these questions? Would the result have been the same if Alvarez-Machain had insisted that the gist of the wrong was his abduction from Mexico to the United States, i.e., across an international border?

Would *Kadic* have to be decided differently today, i.e., after *Sosa*?

In this section, you have seen human rights disputes decided by a variety of tribunals: the UN Human Rights Committee (in *Toonen*), the European Court of Human Rights (in *Smith and Grady* and in *Soering*), the Inter–American Commission on Human Rights (in *Andrews*), the ECOWAS Community Court of Justice (in *Koraou*). In the criminal law context, you have seen the Nuremberg Tribunal (Nazi criminals) and the International Criminal Court (in *Lubanga*). Finally, you have seen various U.S. federal courts (in *Kadic* and *Sosa*) weighing in on the rights and responsibilities of individuals for human rights violations. What functions do these global, regional, and national tribunals serve? Are they suited, by their institutional design, to fulfill their objectives? If you had to represent a victim of human rights abuses and had a choice among the various tribunals we have seen in this Chapter, where would you take your case, and why?

5. INTERNATIONAL BUSINESS ENTITIES

A. RIGHTS

Traditionally, business entities (like individuals) had no standing in international law and, by and large, could only be represented by states. As long as such entities remained primarily within one state, i.e., were incorporated, headquartered and active there, they had a clear home, so to speak. It was this home state which had the right to represent them on the international stage. In the post-World War II period, however, two major developments disturbed that fairly simple picture: business entities became more international so that their "home" often became less clear; and they acquired their own rights under certain treaties so that they became less dependent on state protection in the individual case. The following materials look at these two developments in turn.

In 1970, the International Court of Justice handed down its judgment in the *Barcelona Traction* case. It soon became one of the ICJ's most well-known decisions. This was in part because the judgment touched on several intricate questions of international law, such as the so-called *erga omnes* obligations (which we will discuss in Chapter VII.4.D.). But it was also because the Court decided an issue of fundamental importance for international business entities. What was the central problem in the case, and how did the Court resolve it?

CASE CONCERNING THE BARCELONA TRACTION, LIGHT AND POWER COMPANY, LIMITED (BELGIUM V. SPAIN)

International Court of Justice
1970 I.C.J. 3

[Barcelona Traction was a power company incorporated and headquartered in Canada but with extensive operations in Spain. It had issued bonds payable in Spain. Payment was suspended during the Spanish Civil War and was going to be resumed in 1940. The Spanish government, however, refused to authorize the necessary transfer of funds from Canada to Spain in order for Barcelona Traction to be able to pay interest on the bonds. In 1948, Spanish bondholders sued Barcelona Traction for nonpayment, and a Spanish court declared the company bankrupt. Eventually, Belgium sued Spain in the International Court of Justice, essentially for ruining the company. Belgium brought suit because a very substantial percentage of the shares had for some time been owned by Belgian nationals, and these shares had now become worthless.]

* * *

32. In these circumstances it is logical that the Court should first address itself to what was originally presented as the subject-matter of the third preliminary objection: namely the question of the right of Belgium to exercise diplomatic protection of Belgian shareholders in a company which is a juristic entity incorporated in Canada, the measures complained of having been taken in relation not to any Belgian national but to the company itself.

33. When a State admits into its territory foreign investments or foreign nationals, whether natural or juristic persons, it is bound to extend to them the protection of the law and assumes obligations concerning the treatment to be afforded them. These obligations, however, are neither absolute nor unqualified. In particular, an essential distinction should be drawn between the obligations of a State towards the international community as a whole, and those arising vis-à-vis another State in the field of diplomatic protection. By their very nature the former are the concern of all States. In view of the importance of the rights involved, all States can be held to have a legal interest in their protection; they are obligations *erga omnes*.

34. Such obligations derive, for example, in contemporary international law, from the outlawing of acts of aggression, and of genocide, as also from the principles and rules concerning the basic rights of the human

person, including protection from slavery and racial discrimination. Some of the corresponding rights of protection have entered into the body of general international law (Reservations to the Convention on the Prevention and Punishment of the Crime of Genocide, Advisory Opinion, I.C.J. Reports 1951, p. 23); others are conferred by international instruments of a universal or quasi-universal character.

35. Obligations the performance of which is the subject of diplomatic protection are not of the same category. It cannot be held, when one such obligation in particular is in question, in a specific case, that all States have a legal interest in its observance. In order to bring a claim in respect of the breach of such an obligation, a State must first establish its right to do so, for the rules on the subject rest on two suppositions:

> "The first is that the defendant State has broken an obligation towards the national State in respect of its nationals. The second is that only the party to whom an international obligation is due can bring a claim in respect of its breach."

In the present case it is therefore essential to establish whether the losses allegedly suffered by Belgian shareholders in Barcelona Traction were the consequence of the violation of obligations of which they were the beneficiaries. In other words: has a right of Belgium been violated on account of its nationals' having suffered infringement of their rights as shareholders in a company not of Belgian nationality?

36. Thus it is the existence or absence of a right, belonging to Belgium and recognized as such by international law, which is decisive for the problem of Belgium's capacity.

* * *

39. Seen in historical perspective, the corporate personality represents a development brought about by new and expanding requirements in the economic field, an entity which in particular allows of operation in circumstances which exceed the normal capacity of individuals. As such it has become a powerful factor in the economic life of nations. Of this, municipal law has had to take due account, whence the increasing volume of rules governing the creation and operation of corporate entities, endowed with a specific status. These entities have rights and obligations peculiar to themselves.

* * *

41. Municipal law determines the legal situation not only of such limited liability companies but also of those persons who hold shares in them. Separated from the company by numerous barriers, the shareholder cannot be identified with it. The concept and structure of the company are founded on and determined by a firm distinction between the separate

entity of the company and that of the shareholder, each with a distinct set of rights. The separation of property rights as between company and shareholder is an important manifestation of this distinction. So long as the company is in existence the shareholder has no right to the corporate assets.

* * *

48. The Belgian Government claims that shareholders of Belgian nationality suffered damage in consequence of unlawful acts of the Spanish authorities and, in particular, that the Barcelona Traction shares, though they did not cease to exist, were emptied of all real economic content. It accordingly contends that the shareholders had an independent right to redress, notwithstanding the fact that the acts complained of were directed against the company as such. Thus the legal issue is reducible to the question of whether it is legitimate to identify an attack on company rights, resulting in damage to shareholders, with the violation of their direct rights.

* * *

86. Hence the Belgian Government would be entitled to bring a claim if it could show that one of its rights had been infringed and that the acts complained of involved the breach of an international obligation arising out of a treaty or a general rule of law. The opinion has been expressed that a claim can accordingly be made when investments by a State's nationals abroad are thus prejudicially affected, and that since such investments are part of a State's national economic resources, any prejudice to them directly involves the economic interest of the State.

87. Governments have been known to intervene in such circumstances not only when their interests were affected, but also when they were threatened. However, it must be stressed that this type of action is quite different from and outside the field of diplomatic protection. When a State admits into its territory foreign investments or foreign nationals it is, as indicated in paragraph 33, bound to extend to them the protection of the law. However, it does not thereby become an insurer of that part of another State's wealth which these investments represent. Every investment of this kind carries certain risks. The real question is whether a right has been violated, which right could only be the right of the State to have its nationals enjoy a certain treatment guaranteed by general international law, in the absence of a treaty applicable to the particular case.
* * *

88. It follows from what has already been stated above that, where it is a question of an unlawful act committed against a company representing foreign capital, the general rule of international law authorizes the national State of the company alone to make a claim.

* * *

96. The Court considers that the adoption of the theory of diplomatic protection of shareholders as such, by opening the door to competing diplomatic claims, could create an atmosphere of confusion and insecurity in international economic relations. The danger would be all the greater inasmuch as the shares of companies whose activity is international are widely scattered and frequently change hands. It might perhaps be claimed that, if the right of protection belonging to the national States of the shareholders were considered as only secondary to that of the national State of the company, there would be less danger of difficulties of the kind contemplated. However, the Court must state that the essence of a secondary right is that it only comes into existence at the time when the original right ceases to exist. As the right of protection vested in the national State of the company cannot be regarded as extinguished because it is not exercised, it is not possible to accept the proposition that in case of its non-exercise the national States of the shareholders have a right of protection secondary to that of the national State of the company.

* * *

State the rule established by this decision in one sentence. What are the Court's justifications for this rule?

According to the Court's rule, Canada could have exercised diplomatic protection of its corporation by suing Spain in the ICJ. Canada showed no interest in doing so. Why might that be? What are the larger, long-term consequences of the decision from the perspective of an international business entity deciding where to incorporate?

If Belgium cannot help the Belgian investors in the ICJ, where else can the investors turn to seek compensation for the loss of the value of their shares? Could they sue in the Spanish civil courts? In the Belgian courts?

Over the last 50 years, business entities have begun to acquire their own rights under various treaties. The most important manifestation of this development is the proliferation of Bilateral Investment Treaties (BITs). There are more than 2,500 such treaties in the world today, and the United States alone has concluded them with about 50 countries (often to succeed the older Treaties of Friendship, Commerce, and Navigation, FCNs). Most BITs follow roughly the same model, although they vary considerably in detail, of course. Here is a typical example. You do not have to read it with complete attention to detail. But you should understand what rights it creates for business entities. Pay special attention to Articles II,

IV, V, VII, and XII. When reading the treaty, also pay attention to its structure.

TREATY BETWEEN THE UNITED STATES OF AMERICA AND THE ARGENTINE REPUBLIC CONCERNING THE RECIPROCAL ENCOURAGEMENT AND PROTECTION OF INVESTMENT

(Adopted 1991; in force 1994)

The United States of America and the Argentine Republic, hereinafter referred to as the Parties;

Desiring to promote greater economic cooperation between them, with respect to investment by nationals and companies of one Party in the territory of the other Party;

Recognizing that agreement upon the treatment to be accorded such investment will stimulate the flow of private capital and the economic development of the Parties;

Agreeing that fair and equitable treatment of investment is desirable in order to maintain a stable framework for investment and maximum effective use of economic resources;

Recognizing that the development of economic and business ties can contribute to the well-being of workers in both Parties and promote respect for internationally recognized worker rights; and

Having resolved to conclude a Treaty concerning the encouragement and reciprocal protection of investment;

Have agreed as follows:

Article I

1. For the purposes of this Treaty,

    (a) "investment" means every kind of investment in the territory of one Party owned or controlled directly or indirectly by nationals or companies of the other Party, such as equity, debt, and service and investment contracts; and includes without limitation:

        (i) tangible and intangible property, including rights, such as mortgages, liens and pledges;

        (ii) a company or shares of stock or other interests in a company or interests in the assets thereof;

        (iii) a claim to money or a claim to performance having economic value and directly related to an investment;

        (iv) intellectual property which includes, inter alia, rights relating to: literary and artistic works, including sound recordings, inventions in all fields of human endeavor, industrial designs, semiconductor mask works, trade secrets, know-how, and confidential business information, and trademarks, service marks, and trade names; and

(v) any right conferred by law or contract, and any licenses and permits pursuant to law;

* * *

2. Each Party reserves the right to deny to any company of the other Party the advantages of this Treaty if (a) nationals of any third country, or nationals of such Party, control such company and the company has no substantial business activities in the territory of the other Party, or (b) the company is controlled by nationals of a third country with which the denying Party does not maintain normal economic relations.

3. Any alteration of the form in which assets are invested or reinvested shall not affect their character as investment.

Article II

1. Each Party shall permit and treat investment, and activities associated therewith, on a basis no less favorable than that accorded in like situations to investment or associated activities of its own nationals or companies, or of nationals or companies of any third country, whichever is the more favorable, subject to the right of each Party to make or maintain exceptions falling within one of the sectors or matters listed in the Protocol to this Treaty. * * *

2. (a) Investment shall at all times be accorded fair and equitable treatment, shall enjoy full protection and security and shall in no case be accorded treatment less than that required by international law.

(b) Neither Party shall in any way impair by arbitrary or discriminatory measures the management, operation, maintenance, use, enjoyment, acquisition, expansion, or disposal of investments. For the purposes of dispute resolution under Articles VII and VIII, a measure may be arbitrary or discriminatory notwithstanding the opportunity to review such measure in the courts or administrative tribunals of a Party.

(c) Each Party shall observe any obligation it may have entered into with regard to investments.

3. Subject to the laws relating to the entry and sojourn of aliens, nationals of either Party shall be permitted to enter and to remain in the territory of the other Party for the purpose of establishing, developing, administering or advising on the operation of an investment to which they, or a company of the first Party that employs them, have committed or are in the process of committing a substantial amount of capital or other resources.

4. Companies which are legally constituted under the applicable laws or regulations of one Party, and which are investments, shall be permitted to engage top managerial personnel of their choice, regardless of nationality.

5. Neither Party shall impose performance requirements as a condition of establishment, expansion or maintenance of investments, which require or enforce commitments to export goods produced, or which specify that goods or services must be purchased locally, or which impose any other similar requirements.

6. Each Party shall provide effective means of asserting claims and enforcing rights with respect to investments, investment agreements, and investment authorizations.

7. Each Party shall make public all laws, regulations, administrative practices and procedures, and adjudicatory decisions that pertain to or affect investments.

8. The treatment accorded by the United States of America to investments and associated activities of nationals and companies of the Argentine Republic under the provisions of this Article shall in any State, Territory or possession of the United States of America be no less favorable than the treatment accorded therein to investments and associated activities of nationals of the United States of America resident in, and companies legally constituted under the laws and regulations of, other States, Territories or possessions of the United States of America.

9. The most favored nation provisions of this Article shall not apply to advantages accorded by either Party to nationals or companies of any third country by virtue of that Party's binding obligations that derive from full membership in a regional customs union or free trade area, whether such an arrangement is designated as a customs union, free trade area, common market or otherwise.

Article III

This Treaty shall not preclude either Party from prescribing laws and regulations in connection with the admission of investments made in its territory by nationals or companies of the other Party or with the conduct of associated activities, provided, however, that such laws and regulations shall not impair the substance of any of the rights set forth in this Treaty.

Article IV

1. Investments shall not be expropriated or nationalized either directly or indirectly through measures tantamount to expropriation or nationalization ("expropriation") except for a public purpose; in a non-discriminatory manner; upon payment of prompt, adequate and effec-

tive compensation; and in accordance with due process of law and the general principles of treatment provided for in Article II(2). Compensation shall be equivalent to the fair market value of the expropriated investment immediately before the expropriatory action was taken or became known, whichever is earlier; be paid without delay; include interest at a commercially reasonable rate from the date of expropriation; be fully realizable; and be freely transferable at the prevailing market rate of exchange on the date of expropriation.

2. A national or company of either Party that asserts that all or part of its investment has been expropriated shall have a right to prompt review by the appropriate judicial or administrative authorities of the other Party to determine whether any such expropriation has occurred and, if so, whether such expropriation, and any compensation therefor, conforms to the provisions of this Treaty and the principles of international law.

3. Nationals or companies of either Party whose investments suffer losses in the territory of the other Party owing to war or other armed conflict, revolution, state of national emergency, insurrection, civil disturbance or other similar events shall be accorded treatment by such other Party no less favorable than that accorded to its own nationals or companies or to nationals or companies of any third country, whichever is the more favorable treatment, as regards any measures it adopts in relation to such losses.

Article V

1. Each Party shall permit all transfers related to an investment to be made freely and without delay into and out of its territory. Such transfers include: (a) returns; (b) compensation pursuant to Article IV; (c) payments arising out of an investment dispute; (d) payments made under a contract, including amortization of principal and accrued interest payments made pursuant to a loan agreement directly related to an investment; (e) proceeds from the sale or liquidation of all or any part of an investment; and (f) additional contributions to capital for the maintenance or development of an investment.

* * *

Article VI

The Parties agree to consult promptly, on the request of either, to resolve any disputes in connection with the Treaty, or to discuss any matter relating to the interpretation or application of the Treaty.

Article VII

1. For purposes of this Article, an investment dispute is a dispute between a Party and a national or company of the other Party arising out

of or relating to (a) an investment agreement between that Party and such national or company; (b) an investment authorization granted by that Party's foreign investment authority (if any such authorization exists) to such national or company; or (c) an alleged breach of any right conferred or created by this Treaty with respect to an investment.

2. In the event of an investment dispute, the parties to the dispute should initially seek a resolution through consultation and negotiation. If the dispute cannot be settled amicably, the national or company concerned may choose to submit the dispute for resolution:

    (a) to the courts or administrative tribunals of the Party that is a party to the dispute; or

    (b) in accordance with any applicable, previously agreed dispute-settlement procedures; or

    (c) in accordance with the terms of paragraph 3.

3. (a) Provided that the national or company concerned has not submitted the dispute for resolution under paragraph 2(a) or (b) and that six months have elapsed from the date on which the dispute arose, the national or company concerned may choose to consent in writing to the submission of the dispute for settlement by binding arbitration:

    (i) to the International Centre for the Settlement of Investment Disputes ("Centre") established by the Convention on the Settlement of Investment Disputes between States and Nationals of other States, done at Washington, March 18, 1965 ("ICSID Convention"), provided that the Party is a party to such Convention; or

    (ii) to the Additional Facility of the Centre, if the Centre is not available; or

    (iii) in accordance with the Arbitration Rules of the United Nations Commission on International Trade Law (UNICTRAL); or

    (iv) to any other arbitration institution, or in accordance with any other arbitration rules, as may be mutually agreed between the parties to the dispute.

    (b) Once the national or company concerned has so consented, either party to the dispute may initiate arbitration in accordance with the choice so specified in the consent.

4. Each Party hereby consents to the submission of any investment dispute for settlement by binding arbitration in accordance with the choice specified in the written consent of the national or company under paragraph 3. Such consent, together with the written consent of the national or company when given under paragraph 3 shall satisfy the requirement for:

(a) written consent of the parties to the dispute for purposes of Chapter II of the ICSID Convention (Jurisdiction of the Centre) and for purposes of the Additional Facility Rules; and

(b) an "agreement in writing" for purposes of Article II of the United Nations Convention on the Recognition and Enforcement of Foreign Arbitral Awards, done at New York, June 10, 1958 ("New York Convention").

5. Any arbitration under paragraph 3(a)(ii), (iii) or (iv) of this Article shall be held in a state that is a party to the New York Convention.

6. Any arbitral award rendered pursuant to this Article shall be final and binding on the parties to the dispute. Each Party undertakes to carry out without delay the provisions of any such award and to provide in its territory for its enforcement.

* * *

Article VIII

1. Any dispute between the Parties concerning the interpretation or application of the Treaty which is not resolved through consultations or other diplomatic channels, shall be submitted, upon the request of either Party, to an arbitral tribunal for binding decision in accordance with the applicable rules of international law. In the absence of an agreement by the Parties to the contrary, the arbitration rules of the United Nations Commission on International Trade Law (UNCITRAL), except to the extent modified by the Parties or by the arbitrators, shall govern.

2. Within two months of receipt of a request, each Party shall appoint an arbitrator. The two arbitrators shall select a third arbitrator as Chairman, who is a national of a third State. The UNCITRAL Rules for appointing members of three member panels shall apply mutatis mutandis to the appointment of the arbitral panel except that the appointing authority referenced in those rules shall be the Secretary General of the Permanent Court of Arbitration.

* * *

Article IX

The provisions of Article VII and VIII shall not apply to a dispute arising (a) under the export credit, guarantee or insurance programs of the Export–Import Bank of the United States or (b) under other official credit, guarantee or insurance arrangements pursuant to which the Parties have agreed to other means of settling disputes.

Article X

This Treaty shall not derogate from:

(a) laws and regulations, administrative practices or procedures, or administrative or adjudicatory decisions of either Party;

(b) international legal obligations; or

(c) obligations assumed by either Party, including those contained in an investment agreement or an investment authorization, that entitle investments or associated activities to treatment more favorable than that accorded by this Treaty in like situations.

Article XI

This Treaty shall not preclude the application by either Party of measures necessary for the maintenance of public order, the fulfillment of its obligations with respect to the maintenance or restoration of international peace or security, or the protection of its own essential security interests.

Article XII

1. With respect to its tax policies, each Party should strive to accord fairness and equity in the treatment of investment of nationals and companies of the other Party.

2. Nevertheless, the provisions of this Treaty, and in particular Article VII and VIII, shall apply to matters of taxation only with respect to the following:

(a) expropriation, pursuant to Article IV;

(b) transfers, pursuant to Article V; or

(c) the observance and enforcement of terms of an investment agreement or authorization as referred to in Article VII(1)(a) or (b), to the extent they are not subject to the dispute settlement provisions of a Convention for the avoidance of double taxation between the two Parties, or have been raised under such settlement provisions and are not resolved within a reasonable period of time.

Article XIII

This Treaty shall apply to the political subdivisions of the Parties.

Article XIV

1. This Treaty shall enter into force thirty days after the date of exchange of instruments of ratification. It shall remain in force for a period of ten years and shall continue in force unless terminated in accordance with paragraph 2 of this Article. It shall apply to investments existing at the time of entry into force as well as to investments made or acquired thereafter.

2. Either Party may, by giving one year's written notice to the other Party, terminate this Treaty at the end of the initial ten year period or at any time thereafter.

3. With respect to investments made or acquired prior to the date of termination of this Treaty and to which this Treaty otherwise applies, the provisions of all of the other Articles of this Treaty shall thereafter continue to be effective for a further period of ten years from such date of termination.

4. The Protocol shall form an integral part of the Treaty.

IN WITNESS WHEREOF, the respective plenipotentiaries have signed this Treaty.

DONE in duplicate at Washington on the fourteenth day of November, 1991, in the English and Spanish languages, both texts being equally authentic.

* * *

———————————

Can a corporation rely directly on the provisions of this treaty? If so, exactly what rights does it acquire? From the perspective of the states involved what are the benefits and downsides of agreeing to these provisions? Consider in particular the perspective of the economically weaker partner.

Corporations can also have rights under multilateral human rights treaties as the following decision by the European Court of Human Rights illustrates. What rights does the Court accord to corporations here? How are they viewed? Does this push the concept of human rights too far?

Société Colas Est v. France

European Court of Human Rights
Application No. 37971/97 (2002)

1. The case originated in an application (no. 37971/97) against the French Republic lodged with the European Commission of Human Rights ("the Commission") under former Article 25 of the Convention for the Protection of Human Rights and Fundamental Freedoms ("the Convention") by three French companies, Colas Est, Colas Sud-Ouest and Sacer ("the applicant companies"), based in Colmar, Mérignac and Boulogne–Billancourt respectively, on 2 December 1996.

* * *

THE FACTS

I.   THE CIRCUMSTANCES OF THE CASE

8. Following complaints from the National Union of Finishing Contractors
* * * that large construction firms were engaging in certain illegal practices, France's central government authorities instructed the National
Investigations Office ["the DGCCRF"] to carry out a large-scale administrative investigation into the conduct of public-works contractors.

* * *

10. On 19 November 1985 inspectors from the DGCCRF carried out sim-
ultaneous raids on fifty-six companies without authorisation from the
companies' management and seized several thousand documents. At a
later date, on 15 October 1986, they conducted further inquiries with a
view to obtaining statements.

11. On each occasion the inspectors entered the applicant companies'
premises under the provisions of Ordinance no. 45-1484 of 30 June 1945,
which did not require any judicial authorisation. While carrying out the
raids, the inspectors seized various documents containing evidence of unlawful agreements relating to certain contracts that did not appear in the
list of contracts concerned by the investigation.

12. On 14 November 1986, on the basis of those documents, the Minister
for Economic Affairs, Finance and Privatisation asked the Competition
Commission * * * to investigate certain acts which, in his opinion,
amounted to collusion between separate firms, artificial competition between firms belonging to one and the same group in local tendering procedures for roadworks contracts, and agreements restricting competition
in the operation of mixing plants.

* * *

14. In a decision of 25 October 1989, published in the Official Bulletin on
Competition, Consumer Affairs and Fraud Prevention (* * * "the
BOCCRF"), the Competition Council, finding evidence of practices outlawed by the ordinance of 30 June 1945 and the ordinance of 1 December
1986, fined the first applicant company 12,000,000 French francs (FRF),
the second FRF 4,000,000 and the third FRF 6,000,000.

15. In a judgment of 4 July 1990 published in the BOCCRF, the Paris
Court of Appeal upheld all those penalties. The applicant companies appealed on points of law.

16. In a judgment of 6 October 1992, likewise published in the BOCCRF,
the Commercial Division of the Court of Cassation quashed the judgment
of the Paris Court of Appeal, on the ground that its calculation of turn-
over and its assessment of the amount of the fines had had no basis in

law. It remitted the case to the Paris Court of Appeal sitting with different judges.

17. At the retrial in the Court of Appeal, the applicant companies contested the lawfulness of the searches and seizures carried out by the inspectors, without any judicial authorisation, under the 1945 ordinance. They relied on Article 8 of the Convention.

* * *

III. CASE–LAW OF THE COURT OF JUSTICE OF THE EUROPEAN COMMUNITIES AND OF THE COURT OF FIRST INSTANCE

26. In its judgment of 21 September 1989 in *Hoechst v. Commission*, the Court of Justice of the European Communities (CJEC) held:

* * *

"19. * * * [I]n all the legal systems of the Member States, any intervention by the public authorities in the sphere of private activities of any person, whether natural or legal, must have a legal basis and be justified on the grounds laid down by law, and, consequently, those systems provide, albeit in different forms, protection against arbitrary or disproportionate intervention. The need for such protection must be recognised as a general principle of Community law. In that regard, it should be pointed out that the Court has held that it has the power to determine whether measures of investigation taken by the Commission under the ECSC Treaty are excessive."

* * *

THE LAW

I. ALLEGED VIOLATION OF ARTICLE 8 OF THE CONVENTION

28. The applicant companies considered that the raids carried out by official inspectors on 19 November 1985 and 15 October 1986, without any supervision or restrictions, had infringed their right to respect for their home. They relied on Article 8 of the Convention, the relevant parts of which provide:

"1. Everyone has the right to respect for * * * his home and his correspondence.

2. There shall be no interference by a public authority with the exercise of this right except such as is in accordance with the law and is necessary in a democratic society * * * for the prevention of * * * crime * * * or for the protection of the rights and freedoms of others."

* * *

A.   PRINCIPLES ESTABLISHED UNDER ARTICLE 8 OF THE CONVENTION
     AND THEIR APPLICABILITY TO THE "HOMES" OF JURISTIC PERSONS

40. The Court notes at the outset that the present case differs from * * *
[previous cases] in that the applicants are juristic persons alleging a violation of their right to respect for their "home" under Article 8 of the Convention. However, the Court would point out that, as it has previously
held, the word "*domicile*" (in the French version of Article 8) has a broader connotation than the word "home" and may extend, for example, to a
professional person's office.

* * *

41. The Court reiterates that the Convention is a living instrument which
must be interpreted in the light of present-day conditions. As regards the
rights secured to companies by the Convention, it should be pointed out
that the Court has already recognised a company's right under Article 41
to compensation for non-pecuniary damage sustained as a result of a violation of Article 6 § 1 of the Convention (see *Comingersoll v. Portugal*
[GC], no. 35382/97, §§ 33–35, ECHR 2000–IV). Building on its dynamic
interpretation of the Convention, the Court considers that the time has
come to hold that in certain circumstances the rights guaranteed by Article 8 of the Convention may be construed as including the right to respect
for a company's registered office, branches or other business premises.

42. In the instant case, the Court observes that during a large-scale administrative investigation, officials from the DGCCRF went to the applicant companies' head offices and branches in order to seize several thousand documents. It notes that the Government did not dispute that there
had been interference with the applicant companies' right to respect for
their home, although they argued that the companies could not claim a
right to the protection of their business premises "with as much force as
an individual could in relation to his professional or business address"
and that, consequently, the entitlement to interfere "might well be more
far-reaching."

The Court must therefore determine whether the interference with the
applicant companies' right to respect for their home satisfied the requirements of paragraph 2 of Article 8.

B.   REQUIREMENT OF A MEASURE "IN ACCORDANCE WITH THE LAW"

* * *

In the instant case, the searches and seizures of documents by DGCCRF
inspectors fell within the scope of the powers granted to them by sections
15 and 16(2) of the ordinance of 30 June 1945 governing their investiga-
tive powers for the detection of economic offences relating to competition.

The Court therefore concludes that the interference was "in accordance with the law."

C. LEGITIMATE AIM

44. The purpose of the interference with the applicant companies' right to respect for their premises was to obtain evidence of unlawful agreements between public-works contractors in the award of roadworks contracts. The interference was manifestly in the interests of both "the economic well-being of the country" and "the prevention of crime."

It remains to be determined whether the interference appears proportionate and may be regarded as necessary for achieving those aims.

D. "NECESSARY IN A DEMOCRATIC SOCIETY"

45. The Court notes that the Government submitted that, in accordance with the 1945 ordinance, the officials had exercised only a general right of inspection, supplemented by a power of seizure, and that no "house searches" or "general searches" had been carried out. Although the exercise of the inspectors' powers had not been subject to prior authorisation by a judge, it had been reviewed *ex post facto* by the courts. The Government considered that the interference did not appear disproportionate, and they relied on the State's margin of appreciation, which could be more far-reaching where business premises or professional activities were concerned.

* * *

47. Admittedly, the Court has consistently held that the Contracting States have a certain margin of appreciation in assessing the need for interference, but it goes hand in hand with European supervision. The exceptions provided for in paragraph 2 of Article 8 are to be interpreted narrowly, and the need for them in a given case must be convincingly established.

48. The Court considers that although the scale of the operations that were conducted—as the Government pointed out—in order to prevent the disappearance or concealment of evidence of anti-competitive practices justified the impugned interference with the applicant companies' right to respect for their premises, the relevant legislation and practice should nevertheless have afforded adequate and effective safeguards against abuse.

49. The Court observes, however, that that was not so in the instant case. At the material time * * * the relevant authorities had very wide powers which, pursuant to the 1945 ordinance, gave them exclusive competence to determine the expediency, number, length and scale of inspections. Moreover, the inspections in issue took place without any prior warrant being issued by a judge and without a senior police officer being present.

That being so, even supposing that the entitlement to interfere may be more far-reaching where the business premises of a juristic person are concerned, the Court considers, having regard to the manner of proceeding outlined above, that the impugned operations in the competition field cannot be regarded as strictly proportionate to the legitimate aims pursued.

50. In conclusion, there has been a violation of Article 8 of the Convention.

If the Court's extension of Article 8 protection to "homes" of business entities seems surprising, consider the *Comingersoll v. Portugal* decision referenced above in paragraph 41. After waiting for over 17 years for a final decision on a pending matter, a Portuguese corporation brought a case under Article 6 § 1 of the Convention, which guarantees a timely hearing by a tribunal. Ruling in favor of the corporation's claim against Portugal, the Court awarded compensation for non-pecuniary damages to the corporation (under Article 41). The Court explicitly denied the Portuguese government's contention that,

> the purpose of awarding compensation for non-pecuniary damage for an alleged violation of the right to a hearing within a reasonable time was to provide reparation for anxiety, the mental stress of having to wait for the outcome of the case and uncertainty * * * [and] that such feelings were peculiar to natural persons * * * [that] could under no circumstances entitle a juristic person to compensation.

The *Comingersoll* decision is an important milestone in the ECHR's corporate rights jurisprudence. It holds that like natural persons, corporations can also be awarded non-pecuniary damages as reparation for "mental stress" and "uncertainty" caused by unreasonably delayed adjudication.

B. RESPONSIBILITIES

Much as corporations have rights in international law, so too, they have responsibilities. This section explores some of these responsibilities. Where do these obligations come from? How do they compare to the responsibilities of individuals?

STEVEN R. RATNER, CORPORATIONS AND HUMAN RIGHTS: A THEORY OF LEGAL RESPONSIBILITY

111 Yale L.J. 443 (2001)

The last decade has witnessed a striking new phenomenon in strategies to protect human rights: a shift by global actors concerned about human rights from nearly exclusive attention on the abuses committed by governments to close scrutiny of the activities of business enterprises, in particular multinational corporations. Claims that various kinds of corporate activity have a detrimental impact on human welfare are at least as old as Marxism, and have always been a mantra of the political left worldwide. But today's assertions are different both in their origin and in their content. They emanate not from ideologues with a purportedly redistributive agenda, but from international organizations composed of states both rich and poor; and from respected nongovernmental organizations, such as Amnesty International and Human Rights Watch, whose very credibility turns on avoidance of political affiliation. Equally importantly, these groups do not seek to delegitimize capitalism or corporate economic power itself, but have criticized certain corporate behavior for impinging on clearly accepted norms of human rights law based on widely ratified treaties and customary international law.

Consider the following small set of claims challenging private business activity and the arenas in which they occur:

* The United Nations Security Council condemns illegal trade in diamonds for fueling the civil war in Sierra Leone and asks private diamond trading associations to cooperate in establishing a regime to label diamonds of legitimate origin.

* The European Parliament, concerned about accusations against European companies of involvement in human rights abuses in the developing world, calls upon the European Commission to develop a "European multilateral framework governing companies' operations worldwide" and to include in it a binding code of conduct.

* In response to public concern that American companies and their agents are violating the rights of workers in the developing world, the U.S. government endorses and oversees the creation of a voluntary code of conduct for the apparel industry.

* The South African Truth and Reconciliation Commission, in a searching study of apartheid, devotes three days of hearings and a chapter of its final report to the involvement of the business sector in the practices of apartheid.

* Human Rights Watch establishes a special unit on corporations and human rights; in 1999, it issues two lengthy reports, one accusing the Texas-based Enron Corporation of "corporate complicity in human

rights violations" by the Indian government, and another accusing Shell, Mobil, and other international oil companies operating in Nigeria of cooperating with the government in suppressing political opposition.

* Citizens of Burma and Indonesia sue Unocal and Freeport–McMoRan in United States courts under the Alien Tort Claims Act and accuse the companies of violating the human rights of people near their operations. The corporations win both suits without a trial.

* Holocaust survivors sue European banks, insurance companies, and industries for complicity in wartime human rights violations, and, with the aid of the U.S. government, achieve several multimillion-dollar settlements.

The creation of a new target for human rights advocates is a product of various forces encompassed in the term globalization: the dramatic increase in investment by multinational companies in the developing world; the sense that the economic might of some corporations has eroded the power of the state; the global telecommunications revolution, which has brought worldwide attention to the conditions of those living in less developed countries and has increased the capacity of NGOs to mobilize public opinion; the work of the World Trade Organization (WTO) and International Monetary Fund (IMF) in requiring states to be more hospitable to foreign investors; and the well-documented accounts of the activities of a handful of corporations. These advocacy efforts build on earlier attempts by concerned actors to focus attention on private business activity, ranging from the trials of leading German industrialists for war crimes after World War II to campaigns in the United States in the 1970s and 1980s to encourage divestment from corporations doing business in South Africa. All are based on the view that business enterprises should be held accountable for human rights abuses taking place within their sphere of operations. Corporations, for their part, have responded in numerous ways, from denying any duties in the area of human rights to accepting voluntary codes that could constrain their behavior.

But is there an objective standard by which to appraise both the claims that various business activities are illegitimate from the perspective of international human rights and the corresponding responses of business actors? For example, are corporations responsible for human rights abuses if they simply invest in a repressive society? What if they know that the government will violate human rights in order to make an investment project succeed? What if they share with the government information on suspected troublemakers? What if, illegally, but with the tacit consent of the government, they pay a very low wage or provide bad working conditions?

Any answer not depending exclusively on diverse and possibly parochial national visions of human rights and enterprise responsibility must come from international law. International law offers a process for appraising, and in the end resolving, the demands that governments, international organizations, and nongovernmental organizations are now making of private enterprises. Without some international legal standards, we will likely continue to witness both excessive claims made against such actors for their responsibility and counterclaims by corporate actors against such accountability. Decisionmakers considering these claims—whether legislatures or international organizations contemplating regulation, courts facing suits, or officials deciding whether to intervene in a dispute involving business and human rights—will respond in an ad hoc manner, driven by domestic priorities or by legal frameworks that are likely to differ significantly across the planet. The resultant atmosphere of uncertainty will be detrimental to both the protection of human rights and the economic wealth that private business activity has created worldwide.

* * *

II. WHY CORPORATE RESPONSIBILITY?

Protecting human rights solely through obligations on governments seems rather uncontroversial if host states represented the only threat to human dignity, or if states could be counted on to restrain conduct within their borders effectively. However, a system in which the state is the sole target of international legal obligations may not be sufficient to protect human rights. In this Part, I justify the need for corporate responsibility first by examining the shortcomings of placing human rights duties solely on states, the primary holders of international legal obligations. Corporations are powerful global actors that some states lack the resources or will to control. Other states may go as far as soliciting corporations to cooperate in impinging human rights. These realities make reliance on state duties inadequate. * * *

International human rights law principally contemplates two sets of actors who may be held liable for abuses—states, through the concept of state (primarily civil) responsibility, and individuals, through the concept of individual (primarily criminal) responsibility. States are dutyholders for the full range of human rights, whether defined in treaties or customary law. Individual responsibility applies to a far smaller range of abuses, principally characterized by the gravity of their physical or spiritual assault on the individual.

* * *

The inadequacy of state responsibility stems fundamentally from trends in modern international affairs confirming that corporations may have as much or more power over individuals as governments. In analyzing the power of TNEs [i.e., transnational enterprises] today, Susan Strange emphasizes the need to conceptualize power beyond political power to include economic power and accordingly concludes that markets matter more than states. Whether or not the "retreat of the state" is as great as she states, corporations clearly exercise significant power over individuals in the most direct sense of controlling their well-being. Of course, corporations have always wielded significant power over their employees; and governments have to enforce their own laws as well as to protect the human rights of their citizens. So why does such power require moving beyond state responsibility?

First, the desire of many less developed states to welcome foreign investment means that some governments have neither the interest nor the resources to monitor corporate behavior, either with respect to the TNEs' employees or with respect to the broader community. Their views on investment might lead them to assist companies in violations, for instance, through deployments of security forces. In extreme cases, governments actually grant corporations de facto control over certain territories. For instance, whatever one may believe of the merits of claims against Freeport–McMoRan of human rights abuses in Irian Jaya or against Texaco in the Colombian rainforest, there seems little doubt that those entities exercise significant power in certain regions, often with little interference by the government.

Second, regardless of its position on foreign investment, the government might also use various corporate resources in its own abuses of human rights. The South African experience represents the epitome in recent times of such nefarious cooperation between public and private sectors. Because repressive governments (or opposition movements) may need to rely on businesses to supply them with material for various unacceptable activities, corporations may work in tandem with governments in abusing human rights.

Third, as firms have become more international, they have also become ever more independent of government control. Many of the largest TNEs have headquarters in one state, shareholders in others, and operations worldwide. If the host state fails to regulate the acts of the company, other states, including the state of the corporation's nationality, may well choose to abstain from regulation based on the extraterritorial nature of the acts at issue. Corporations can also shift activities to states with fewer regulatory burdens, including human rights regulations. Recognition of duties on corporations under international law could encourage home states to regulate this conduct or permit others to do so; at the very least, it would suggest a baseline standard of conduct for corporations themselves that could be monitored by interested constituencies.

If private entities might be contributing to a deleterious human rights situation, then those concerned with the behavior of such enterprises are left with three options—to continue to focus exclusively on the state, encouraging it eventually to control such enterprises; to enforce obligations against individuals (the limits of which I discuss below); or to identify and prescribe new obligations upon those private entities in international law and develop a regime of responsibility for violations they might commit.

Indeed, multinational enterprises are themselves recognizing the limits of duties on states. Unocal, for instance, has stated publicly that "human rights are not just a matter for governments." In 2000, the United Kingdom's Prince of Wales Business Leaders Forum and Amnesty International teamed up to issue Human Rights: Is It Any of Your Business?, a glossy 144-page human rights guide for senior corporate policymakers. The publication notes: "While a company is not legally obliged under international law to comply with [human rights] standards, those companies who have violated them have found, to their cost, that society at large will condemn them." And, as discussed in Section VII.A below, corporate-initiated codes of conduct represent clear evidence that normative expectations of all relevant actors—not just NGOs or governments—are now shifting.

In this sense, the need for corporate responsibility parallels the evolution of the existing corpus of law beyond state liability to cover individual responsibility, under which individuals are criminally responsible for exceptionally serious human rights abuses. Individual responsibility emerged primarily from the sense of governments and nonstate actors that holding states accountable proved inadequate to address those acts. Unlike state responsibility, accountability for individual violators might provide victims of atrocities with a sense of justice and a possibility to put the past behind them (the amorphous notion of closure). It might also help deter future abuses more effectively, send a powerful message of moral condemnation of heinous offenses, and help a society traumatized by massive human rights violations to identify perpetrators and thereby promote national reconciliation. In its ability to advance these goals, individual responsibility has become a promising alternative along a continuum of enforcement mechanisms for international human rights or international humanitarian law.

Some of the reasons for the inadequacy of state responsibility for individual human rights abuses—for example, the impact on victims of identifying and punishing their individual perpetrators (as opposed to merely blaming the state)—differ from the reasons for its inadequacy for corporate actions. But the deterrence rationale remains common to both contexts and points to the need to place obligations on entities that have the resources to violate human rights and whose conduct cannot properly be policed by the state where they operate. If international law provided for a regime whereby the corporations had duties themselves and incurred some penalty for violations of them, it would place the incentives on the party with the greatest ability and interest in addressing corporate conduct.

In one historically significant instance, the justifications for individual accountability and business accountability, and the corresponding limits of state responsibility, all came together—international efforts to outlaw the slave trade. The slave trade represented, in a sense, the worst form of private enterprise abuse of human rights. To end it, abolitionists eschewed sole reliance upon state responsibility, both because traders operated on the high seas and because many states tolerated the practice. Instead, they convinced governments to conclude a series of treaties that allowed states to seize vessels and required them to punish slave traders. Thus the first true example of international human rights law was a response to commercially oriented violations of rights.

Beyond these three reasons lies a fourth and, for some readers, I suspect, more compelling reason. Even if one believes that the state should be the sole object of obligations regarding the behavior of businesses operating on its soil based on its unique competence to control private behavior within its borders, one would still need to determine which acts of corporations render the state liable. As discussed in the following Subsection, international human rights courts and other bodies have begun to hold states responsible for failing to prevent private activity that violates human rights. In order to hold states accountable for corporate conduct in a coherent fashion, however, one would still need a theory of understanding when a corporation's violation of human rights rises to such a level that the state is responsible for preventing or suppressing it.

If a legal regime regulating corporations, rather than only states or individuals, is necessary to address the nature of corporations as actors in the human rights field, a final step must be taken before seeking to offer a theory. This step entails examining international practice to see whether states, international organizations, and other key participants are, in a sense, ready for such an enterprise. In reviewing recent trends, one discovers that international law has already effectively recognized duties of corporations.

As an initial matter, it bears brief mention that international law doctrine poses no significant impediment to recognition of duties beyond those of states. Some writers insist that private persons cannot, in general, be liable under international law because the state is a "screen" between them and international law; or that only states are full subjects of international law (with so-called legal personality) because only they can enjoy the full range of legal rights and duties and make claims for violations of rights. Yet the orthodoxy now accepts that nonstate entities may enjoy forms of international personality. For a half-century it has been clear that the United Nations may make claims against states for violations of their obligations to it. International lawyers have argued about the extent of personality enjoyed by individuals and corporations in light of treaties allowing victims of human rights to sue states in regional courts or permitting foreign investors to sue states in the International Centre for the Settlement of Investment Disputes. And the corpus of international criminal law makes clear that actors other than states have duties under international law. The question is not whether nonstate actors have rights and duties, but what those rights and duties are.

The lack of an international court in which businesses can be sued does not alter this conclusion. Of course, mechanisms for compliance—or, as the New Haven School puts it, control mechanisms—are central, for law cannot exist without them. But in most areas of the law, states have obligations without either the possibility or probability that they might be called before an international court. Instead, the diverse methods of enforcement include self-restraint based on states' reluctance to create adverse precedents, reciprocal action, protest, diplomatic responses, nonforcible sanctions, and, in highly limited circumstances, recourse to force. In the human rights area, the presence of a court holding states responsible has never been the linchpin of the obligation itself. The International Covenant on Civil and Political Rights (ICCPR) contains no provisions granting either individuals or interested states the right to take a violating state to the ICJ or any other court. Instead, many states and regional organizations take human rights into account in their foreign policy, and the United Nations has other mechanisms (of varying degrees of effectiveness) for putting pressure on violators.

* * *

A.   CORPORATE–INITIATED CODES OF CONDUCT

The most basic starting point for implementing the above theory is through a form of self-regulation. Indeed, many businesses have adopted formal policies and practices in order to avoid any form of external regulation. In many cases, they may be responding to market pressures from consumers or demands of key shareholders. Ideally, self-regulation based on acceptance of duties from the theory, coupled with transparency, would best address the overall issue. In the end, for optimal effect, corporations will need to internalize such norms in their decisionmaking. This point resonates with the key insight from international relations theorists and others that internalization is critical to successful implementation of international norms, whether in human rights or other areas of the law.

The corporate-initiated code of conduct represents industry's most public response to the claims leveled against corporations in the area of human rights. These codes are voluntary commitments made by companies, business associations, or other entities, which put forth standards and principles for business activities. Although such codes date back at least to the beginning of the twentieth century, they have proliferated in the last twenty years due to shareholder and consumer interest in corporate behavior, and now number in the hundreds. One recent study found that these codes focused on labor and environmental issues and that many included consumer protection, bribery, competition, and information disclosure. The codes typically address a limited range of human rights issues—forced labor, child labor, conditions of employment, and the right to unionize. One offshoot of the corporate code of conduct is social labeling, whereby industry groups agree, often in cooperation with NGOs, to certify products as resulting from processes that do not involve certain deleterious practices (e.g., "dolphin-safe" tuna and the Rugmark label on carpets from the Indian subcontinent that are not produced with child labor).

Inclusion of a larger set of human rights commitments within corporate codes of conduct could have a positive impact on corporate behavior. Many corporations are now ensuring that their internal decisionmaking processes, including their relations with contractors, reflect the commitments undertaken in their codes. At the same time, business groups are reluctant to accept uniform standards of behavior, claiming that each industry must develop its own set of guidelines. And the voluntary nature of corporate codes of conduct creates the clear potential for some TNEs to treat them as purely a public relations exercise, leading human rights NGOs to downplay their effectiveness. NGOs and labor unions have pressed corporations to address this shortcoming by including procedures for independent monitoring. Yet this effort has fallen short, as many TNEs resist such provisions; and while some monitoring provisions have clearly improved conditions of workers, even those codes with monitoring provisions have fallen prey to industry capture. The overall impact of such codes on corporate behavior is thus unclear, with different companies and industries adopting stronger or weaker codes, each of which is observed with varying degrees of seriousness.

The route of corporate-initiated codes of conduct nonetheless seems useful in the process of addressing violations of human rights, as it will at least raise corporate awareness of these issues and permit the possibility of monitoring (either by independent monitors paid by the industry or by NGOs). Undoubtedly, corporations will adopt various, even inconsistent, codes as a substantive matter, and human rights NGOs will object to that inconsistency. But the process of international lawmaking often begins with such private codes, which create expectations of appropriate conduct among diverse actors and can lead over time to other forms of lawmaking.

B. NGO SCRUTINY

NGOs have already demonstrated their interest in monitoring corporate activity and recognized it as a priority for future work. They should consider the adoption of more detailed norms for business enterprises than have been developed to date, and seek to ground their scrutiny of corporate behavior in those principles. In addition, to the extent other institutions develop law regarding corporate duties, NGOs can help with the monitoring process—just as they do regarding state obligations in the area of human rights. They remain central actors in mobilizing shame upon violators, leading to the termination of offensive conduct. At the same time, NGOs have clear responsibilities in light of their lack of accountability to anyone other than their members or donors. Though organizations like Amnesty International and Human Rights Watch are accustomed to making arguments based on legal principles and insisting on high standards of accuracy in reporting, other NGOs seem to fall prey to a visceral anti-TNE bias that only arouses suspicions by TNEs of the bona fides of the human rights agenda.

C. NATIONAL LEGAL REGIMES

If self-regulation and NGO scrutiny prove insufficient, decisionmakers will need to consider the expansion of domestic public and private legal regimes to create duties upon businesses along the model specified above. National regimes would take advantage of the state's power over its territory and respond to those critics who might view corporate responsibility as an abdication of the role of the state. By developing a regulatory scheme through statutes, regulations, and policy directives, governments could monitor corporate human rights activity in the same way they monitor corporate environmental, anticompetitive, securities, or bribery-related activity. Indeed, parts of this model could be incorporated into existing labor laws. Companies violating their duties could face sanctions ranging from mere publication of a list of companies whose practices appear to fall below acceptable standards, to loss of particular benefits, such as preferential loans for overseas investments or permits for the import or export of commodities, up to criminal fines. Although private litigation might prove a cumbersome way to enforce such duties, legislatures or courts could also develop law recognizing private rights of action for victims of human rights abuses.

* * *

D. SOFT INTERNATIONAL LAW

Shifting to interstate arenas of lawmaking, international organizations could elaborate corporate duties through soft law instruments. To identify the appropriate fora for the development of such law, and for harder forms as well, one must consider the views of states, international organizations, corporations, and human rights NGOs as to an institution's legitimacy or authority in this area. This, in turn, will depend on its ability to represent the views of key participants and garner their acceptance, as well as its expertise on the subject.

* * *

E.   THE TREATY PROCESS—A BINDING CODE OF CONDUCT

States could promote uniformity of regulation of TNEs for activities with human rights implications through a multilateral instrument recognizing certain obligations upon corporations. The OECD's Bribery Convention and the various environmental conventions noted earlier represent the clearest examples of multilateral efforts to regulate corporate activity. And the World Health Organization's ongoing efforts to draft a Framework Convention on Tobacco Control evidence further moves in this direction. Such a convention could obligate enterprises based on the theory above; it could also work through the framework of state responsibility by imposing duties on states to regulate corporate conduct, as is the case with much international labor law.

* * *

———————————

As Ratner explains, one way to control corporate behavior in the international arena is through codes of conduct that are not legally binding but create moral obligations vis-à-vis the public to forego certain practices. Below, you find an example: the "UN Global Compact."

The UN Global Compact

In 1999, the United National Global Compact was initiated by Kofi Annan, Secretary–General of the UN at the time. In a speech at the World Economic Forum, Annan invited business leaders to enter into a global compact with the United Nations to promote "shared values and principles, [and to] give a human face to the global market." According to Annan, corporations shared, with the UN, interest in promoting human rights, higher labor standards, and better environmental practices. By joining the compact, corporations hope to gain goodwill by demonstrating their commitment to corporate citizenship, while the UN is establishing a line of communication with the international business community, which had been previously beyond the scope of the UN.

Participants in the Global Compact endorse ten principles derived from the Universal Declaration of Human Rights (1948), the International Labour Organization's Declaration on Fundamental Principles and Rights at Work (1998), and the Rio Declaration on Environment and Development (1992).

Corporations can join the Compact by sending a letter of participation to the UN Secretary–General. Civil society organizations and other non-business organizations also may join the Global Compact, and they play an important role in the policy dialogue among participants. All participants are listed on the website of the Compact in a searchable database. Participants may provide reports on projects completed in promotion of the principles. For example, in one featured project, Volkswagen developed a program to combat HIV/AIDS among its employees in Brazil. The company initiated free testing and established a special healthcare assistance program while ensuring privacy.

In a short time, the Global Compact has become the world's largest corporate responsibility initiative: over 6,000 businesses from 140 countries have signed on.

The Global Compact signatories are required to disclose in their annual reports the progress they have made in implementing the ten principles. Failure by a participant to provide such communication results in expulsion from the Global Compact. The bulk of the funding for the Global Compact comes from governments, but participants are encouraged to make donations through a special foundation set up to support its operations.

As you are reading through the principles, consider whether they strike you as meaningful or not, and why.

UNITED NATIONS GLOBAL COMPACT
THE TEN PRINCIPLES
(Launched on July 26, 2000)

The Global Compact's ten principles in the areas of human rights, labour, the environment and anti-corruption enjoy universal consensus and are derived from:

- The Universal Declaration of Human Rights
- The International Labour Organization's Declaration on Fundamental Principles and Rights at Work
- The Rio Declaration on Environment and Development
- The United Nations Convention Against Corruption

The Global Compact asks companies to embrace, support and enact, within their sphere of influence, a set of core values in the areas of human rights, labour standards, the environment, and anti-corruption:

Human Rights

- Principle 1: Businesses should support and respect the protection of internationally proclaimed human rights; and

- Principle 2: make sure that they are not complicit in human rights abuses.

Labour Standards

- Principle 3: Businesses should uphold the freedom of association and the effective recognition of the right to collective bargaining;
- Principle 4: the elimination of all forms of forced and compulsory labour;
- Principle 5: the effective abolition of child labour; and
- Principle 6: the elimination of discrimination in respect of employment and occupation.

Environment

- Principle 7: Businesses should support a precautionary approach to environmental challenges;
- Principle 8: undertake initiatives to promote greater environmental responsibility; and
- Principle 9: encourage the development and diffusion of environmentally friendly technologies

Anti–Corruption

- Principle 10: Businesses should work against all forms of corruption, including extortion and bribery.

Is this approach to regulating corporate conduct promising at all? What, if anything, suggests that such "soft law" might actually change the way multinational corporations behave? What are the main weaknesses of such an approach? If you were the general counsel of a major international corporation active in regions where the human rights situation is precarious, would you advise your CEO and board of directors to pay attention to such norms? If so, why?

Can multinational enterprises be liable for damages under international law—just like Radovan Karadzic? Note that this would require more than UN-sponsored "principles." It would mean that international law creates *legally binding* obligations for corporations as well. Is the decision of the Ninth Circuit Court of Appeals in this regard convincing? If you were a clerk for a judge who disagreed with the majority and were asked to draft a dissent, what would you write?

DOE V. UNOCAL CORP.

United States Circuit Court
395 F.3d 932 (9th Cir. 2002)

JUDGE PREGERSON:

This case involves human rights violations that allegedly occurred in Myanmar, formerly known as Burma. Villagers from the Tenasserim region in Myanmar allege that the Defendants directly or indirectly subjected the villagers to forced labor, murder, rape, and torture when the Defendants constructed a gas pipeline through the Tenasserim region. The villagers base their claims on the Alien Tort Claims Act, 28 U.S.C. § 1350, and the Racketeer Influenced and Corrupt Organizations Act, 18 U.S.C. § 1961 et seq., as well as state law.

The District Court, through dismissal and summary judgment, resolved all of Plaintiffs' federal claims in favor of the Defendants. For the following reasons, we reverse in part and affirm in part the District Court's rulings.

I.   FACTUAL AND PROCEDURAL BACKGROUND

A.   UNOCAL'S INVESTMENT IN A NATURAL GAS PROJECT IN MYANMAR

Burma has been ruled by a military government since 1958. In 1988, a new military government, Defendant–Appellee State Law and Order Restoration Council ("the Myanmar Military"), took control and renamed the country Myanmar. The Myanmar Military established a state owned company, Defendant–Appellee Myanmar Oil and Gas Enterprise ("Myanmar Oil"), to produce and sell the nation's oil and gas resources.

In 1992, Myanmar Oil licensed the French oil company Total S.A. ("Total") to produce, transport, and sell natural gas from deposits in the Yadana Field off the coast of Myanmar ("the Project"). Total set up a subsidiary, Total Myanmar Exploration and Production ("Total Myanmar"), for this purpose. The Project consisted of a Gas Production Joint Venture, which would extract the natural gas out of the Yadana Field, and a Gas Transportation Company, which would construct and operate a pipeline to transport the natural gas from the coast of Myanmar through the interior of the country to Thailand.

Also in 1992, Defendant–Appellant Unocal Corporation and its wholly owned subsidiary Defendant–Appellant Union Oil Company of California, collectively referred to below as "Unocal," acquired a 28% interest in the Project from Total. Unocal set up a wholly owned subsidiary, the Unocal Myanmar Offshore Company ("the Unocal Offshore Co."), to hold Unocal's 28% interest in the Gas Production Joint Venture half of the Project. Similarly, Unocal set up another wholly owned subsidiary, the Unocal International Pipeline Corporation ("the Unocal Pipeline Corp."), to hold Unocal's 28% interest in the Gas Transportation Company half of the Project. Myanmar Oil and a Thai government entity, the Petroleum Authority of Thailand Exploration and Production, also acquired interests in the Project. Total Myanmar was appointed Operator of the Gas Production Joint Venture and the Gas Transportation Company. As the Operator, Total Myanmar was responsible, *inter alia*, for "determin[ing] * * * the selection of * * * employees [and] the hours of work and the compensation to be paid to all * * * employees" in connection with the Project.

B. UNOCAL'S KNOWLEDGE THAT THE MYANMAR MILITARY WAS PROVIDING SECURITY AND OTHER SERVICES FOR THE PROJECT

It is undisputed that the Myanmar Military provided security and other services for the Project, and that Unocal knew about this. The pipeline was to run through Myanmar's rural Tenasserim region. The Myanmar Military increased its presence in the pipeline region to provide security and other services for the Project. A Unocal memorandum documenting Unocal's meetings with Total on March 1 and 2, 1995 reflects Unocal's understanding that "four battalions of 600 men each will protect the [pipeline] corridor" and "fifty soldiers will be assigned to guard each survey team." A former soldier in one of these battalions testified at his deposition that his battalion had been formed in 1996 specifically for this purpose. In addition, the Military built helipads and cleared roads along the proposed pipeline route for the benefit of the Project.

There is also evidence sufficient to raise a genuine issue of material fact whether the Project *hired* the Myanmar Military, through Myanmar Oil, to provide these services, and whether Unocal knew about this. * * *

C. UNOCAL'S KNOWLEDGE THAT THE MYANMAR MILITARY WAS ALLEGEDLY COMMITTING HUMAN RIGHTS VIOLATIONS IN CONNECTION WITH THE PROJECT

Plaintiffs are villagers from Myanmar's Tenasserim region, the rural area through which the Project built the pipeline. Plaintiffs allege that the Myanmar Military forced them, under threat of violence, to work on and serve as porters for the Project. For instance, John Doe IX testified that he was forced to build a helipad near the pipeline site in 1994 that was then used by Unocal and Total officials who visited the pipeline during its planning stages. John Doe VII and John Roe X, described the construction of helipads at Eindayaza and Po Pah Pta, both of which were near the pipeline site, were used to ferry Total/Unocal executives and materials to the construction site, and were constructed using the forced labor of local villagers, including Plaintiffs. John Roes VIII and IX, as well as John Does I, VIII and IX testified that they were forced to work on building roads leading to the pipeline construction area. Finally, John Does V and IX, testified that they were required to serve as "pipeline porters"— workers who performed menial tasks such as such as hauling materials and cleaning the army camps for the soldiers guarding the pipeline construction.

Plaintiffs also allege in furtherance of the forced labor program just described, the Myanmar Military subjected them to acts of murder, rape, and torture. For instance, Jane Doe I testified that after her husband, John Doe I, attempted to escape the forced labor program, he was shot at by soldiers, and in retaliation for his attempted escape, that she and her baby were thrown into a fire, resulting in injuries to her and the death of the child. Other witnesses described the summary execution of villagers who refused to participate in the forced labor program, or who grew too weak to work effectively. Several Plaintiffs testified that rapes occurred as part of the forced labor program. For instance, both Jane Does II and III testified that while conscripted to work on pipeline-related construction projects, they were raped at knife-point by Myanmar soldiers who were members of a battalion that was supervising the work. Plaintiffs finally allege that Unocal's conduct gives rise to liability for these abuses.

The successive military governments of first Burma and now Myanmar have a long and well-known history of imposing forced labor on their citizens. See, e.g., Forced labour in Myanmar (Burma): Report of the Commission of Inquiry appointed under article 26 of the Constitution of the International Labour Organization to examine the observance by Myanmar of the Forced Labour Convention, 1930 (No. 29) Parts III. 8, V. 14(3) (1998) (describing several inquiries into forced labor in Myanmar conducted between 1960 and 1992 by the International Labor Organization, and finding "abundant evidence * * * showing the pervasive use of forced labour imposed on the civilian population throughout Myanmar by the authorities and the military"). As detailed below, even before Unocal invested in the Project, Unocal was made aware—by its own consultants and by its partners in the Project—of this record and that the Myanmar Military might also employ forced labor and commit other human rights violations in connection with the Project. And after Unocal invested in the Project, Unocal was made aware—by its own consultants and employees, its partners in the Project, and human rights organizations—of allegations that the Myanmar Military was actually committing such violations in connection with the Project.

* * *

ANALYSIS

    A.   LIABILITY UNDER THE ALIEN TORT CLAIMS ACT

        1.   INTRODUCTION

The Alien Tort Claims Act confers upon the federal district courts "original jurisdiction of any civil action by an alien for a tort only, committed in violation of the law of nations." 28 U.S.C. § 1350. We have held that the

ATCA also provides a cause of action, as long as "plaintiffs * * * allege a violation of 'specific, universal, and obligatory' international norms as part of [their] ATCA claim." Plaintiffs allege that Unocal's conduct gave rise to ATCA liability for the forced labor, murder, rape, and torture inflicted on them by the Myanmar Military.

The District Court granted Unocal's motion for summary judgment on Plaintiffs' ATCA claims. We review a grant of summary judgment *de novo*. We must determine whether, viewing the evidence in the light most favorable to the nonmoving party, there are any genuine issues of material fact and whether the district court correctly applied the relevant substantive law.

One threshold question in *any* ATCA case is whether the alleged tort is a violation of the law of nations. We have recognized that torture, murder, and slavery are *jus cogens* violations and, thus, violations of the law of nations. Moreover, forced labor is so widely condemned that it has achieved the status of a *jus cogens* violation. *See, e.g.*, Universal Declaration of Human Rights, G.A. Res. 217(A) III (1948) (banning forced labor); Agreement for the Prosecution and Punishment of the Major War Criminals of the European Axis, and Charter of the International Military Tribunal, Aug. 8, 1945, art. 6 (making forced labor a war crime). Accordingly, all torts alleged in the present case are *jus cogens* violations and, thereby, violations of the law of nations.

Another threshold question in any ATCA case *against a private party*, such as Unocal, is whether the alleged tort requires the private party to engage in state action for ATCA liability to attach, and if so, whether the private party in fact engaged in state action. In his concurrence in *Tel-Oren v. Libyan Arab Republic*, 726 F.2d 774 (D.C. Cir. 1984), Judge Edwards observed that while most crimes require state action for ATCA liability to attach, there are a "handful of crimes," including slave trading, "to which the law of nations attributes *individual liability*," such that state action is not required. 726 F.2d at 794–95 (Edwards, J., concurring) (emphasis added). More recently, the Second Circuit adopted and extended this approach in *Kadic*. The Second Circuit first noted that genocide and war crimes—like slave trading—do not require state action for ATCA liability to attach. See 70 F.3d at 242–243. The Second Circuit went on to state that although "acts of rape, torture, and summary execution," like most crimes, "are proscribed by international law only when committed by state officials or under color of law" to the extent that they were committed *in isolation*, these crimes "are actionable under the Alien Tort [Claims] Act, without regard to state action, to the extent that they were committed *in pursuit of genocide or war crimes.*" Thus, under *Kadic*, even crimes like rape, torture, and summary execution, which by themselves require state action for ATCA liability to attach, do *not* require state action when committed in furtherance of other crimes like slave trading, genocide or war crimes, which by themselves do not require state action for ATCA liability to attach. We agree with this view and apply it below to Plaintiffs' various ATCA claims.

2.   FORCED LABOR

a.   FORCED LABOR IS A MODERN VARIANT OF SLAVERY TO WHICH THE LAW OF NATIONS ATTRIBUTES INDIVIDUAL LIABILITY SUCH THAT STATE ACTION IS NOT REQUIRED.

Our case law strongly supports the conclusion that forced labor is a modern variant of slavery. Accordingly, forced labor, like traditional variants of slave trading, is among the "handful of crimes * * * to which the law of nations attributes *individual liability,*" such that state action is not required.

* * *

b.   UNOCAL MAY BE LIABLE UNDER THE ATCA FOR AIDING AND ABETTING THE MYANMAR MILITARY IN SUBJECTING PLAINTIFFS TO FORCED LABOR

Plaintiffs argue that Unocal aided and abetted the Myanmar Military in subjecting them to forced labor. We hold that the standard for aiding and abetting under the ATCA is, as discussed below, knowing practical assistance or encouragement that has a substantial effect on the perpetration of the crime. We further hold that a reasonable factfinder could find that Unocal's conduct met this standard.

The District Court found that "[t]he evidence * * * suggest[s] that Unocal knew that forced labor was being utilized and that the Joint Venturers benefitted from the practice." The District Court nevertheless held that Unocal could not be liable under the ATCA for forced labor because Unocal's conduct did not rise to the level of "active participation" in the forced labor. The District Court incorrectly borrowed the "active participation" standard for liability from war crimes cases before Nuremberg Military Tribunals involving the role of German industrialists in the Nazi forced labor program during the Second World War. The Military Tribunals applied the "active participation" standard in these cases only to overcome the defendants' "necessity defense." In the present case, Unocal did not invoke—and could not have invoked—the necessity defense. The District Court therefore erred when it applied the "active participation" standard here.

We however agree with the District Court that in the present case, we should apply international law as developed in the decisions by international criminal tribunals such as the Nuremberg Military Tribunals for the applicable substantive law. "The law of nations 'may be ascertained by consulting the works of jurists, writing professedly on public law; or by the general usage and practice of nations; *or by judicial decisions recognizing and enforcing that law.*'" *Filartiga v. Pena-Irala,* 630 F.2d 876, 880 (2d Cir. 1980) (quoting *United States v. Smith,* 18 U.S. (5 Wheat.) 153, 160–61 (1820)) (emphasis added). It is "well settled that the law of nations is part of federal common law."

* * *

International human rights law has been developed largely in the context of criminal prosecutions rather than civil proceedings. But what is a crime in one jurisdiction is often a tort in another jurisdiction, and this distinction is therefore of little help in ascertaining the standards of international human rights law. Moreover, as mentioned above in note 23 and further discussed later in this section, the standard for aiding and abetting in international criminal law is similar to the standard for aiding and abetting in domestic tort law, making the distinction between criminal and tort law less crucial in this context. Accordingly, District Courts are increasingly turning to the decisions by international *criminal* tribunals for instructions regarding the standards of international human rights law under our *civil* ATCA. *See, e.g., Cabello Barrueto v. Fernandez Larios,* 205 F. Supp. 2d 1325, 1333 (S.D. Fla. 2002) (concluding on the basis of, *inter alia,* the statute of and a decision by the International Criminal Tribunal for the former Yugoslavia that defendants "may be held liable under the ATCA for * * * aiding and abetting the actions taken by [foreign] military officials"); *Mehinovic v. Vuckovic,* 198 F. Supp. 2d 1322 (N.D. Ga. 2002) (noting that among "various contemporary sources" for ascertaining the norms of international law as they pertain to the ATCA, "the statutes of the [International Criminal Tribunal for the former Yugoslavia] and the International Criminal Tribunal for Rwanda * * * and recent opinions of these tribunals are particularly relevant"). We agree with this approach. We find recent decisions by the International Criminal Tribunal for the former Yugoslavia and the International Criminal Tribunal for Rwanda especially helpful for ascertaining the current standard for aiding and abetting under international law as it pertains to the ATCA.

* * *

As for the *mens rea* of aiding and abetting, the International Criminal Tribunal for the former Yugoslavia held that what is required is actual or constructive (i.e., "reasonable") "knowledge that [the accomplice's] actions will assist the perpetrator in the commission of the crime." Thus, "it is not necessary for the accomplice to share the *mens rea* of the perpetrator, in the sense of positive intention to commit the crime." In fact, it is not even necessary that the aider and abettor knows the precise crime that the principal intends to commit. Rather, if the accused "is aware that one of a number of crimes will probably be committed, and one of those crimes is in fact committed, he has intended to facilitate the commission of that crime, and is guilty as an aider and abettor."

Similarly, for the *mens rea* of aiding and abetting, the International Criminal Tribunal for Rwanda required that "the accomplice knew of the assistance he was providing in the commission of the principal offence." The accomplice does not have to have had the intent to commit the principal offense. It is sufficient that the accomplice "knew or had reason to know" that the principal had the intent to commit the offense.

The *Furundzija* standard for aiding and abetting liability under international criminal law can be summarized as knowing practical assistance, encouragement, or moral support which has a substantial effect on the perpetration of the crime. At least with respect to assistance and encouragement, this standard is similar to the standard for aiding and abetting under domestic tort law. Thus, the Restatement of Torts states: "For harm resulting to a third person from the tortious conduct of another, one is subject to liability if he * * * (b) knows that the other's conduct constitutes a breach of duty and gives *substantial assistance or encouragement* to the other so to conduct himself. * * * " *Restatement (Second) of Torts* § 876 (1979) (emphasis added). Especially given the similarities between the *Furundzija* international criminal standard and the Restatement domestic tort standard, we find that application of a slightly modified *Furundzija* standard is appropriate in the present case. In particular, given that there is—as discussed below—sufficient evidence in the present case that Unocal gave assistance and encouragement to the Myanmar Military, we do not need to decide whether it would have been enough if Unocal had only given moral support to the Myanmar Military. Accordingly, we may impose aiding and abetting liability for knowing practical assistance or encouragement which has a substantial effect on the perpetration of the crime, leaving the question whether such liability should also be imposed for moral support which has the required substantial effect to another day.

First, a reasonable factfinder could conclude that Unocal's alleged conduct met the *actus reus* requirement of aiding and abetting as we define it today, i.e., practical assistance or encouragement which has a substantial effect on the perpetration of the crime of, in the present case, forced labor.

Unocal's weak protestations notwithstanding, there is little doubt that the record contains substantial evidence creating a material question of fact as to whether forced labor was used in connection with the construction of the pipeline. Numerous witnesses, including a number of Plaintiffs, testified that they were forced to clear the right of way for the pipeline and to build helipads for the project before construction of the pipeline began. * * *

This assistance, moreover, had a "substantial effect" on the perpetration of forced labor, which "most probably would not have occurred in the same way" without someone hiring the Myanmar Military to provide security, and without someone showing them where to do it. This conclusion is supported by the admission of Unocal Representative Robinson that "our assertion that [the Myanmar Military] has not *expanded and amplified its usual methods* around the pipeline *on our behalf* may not withstand much scrutiny," and by the admission of Unocal President Imle that "if forced labor goes hand and glove with the military yes there will be *more forced labor.*" (Emphasis added.)

Second, a reasonable factfinder could also conclude that Unocal's conduct met the *mens rea* requirement of aiding and abetting as we define it today, namely, actual or constructive (i.e., reasonable) knowledge that the accomplice's actions will assist the perpetrator in the commission of the crime. The District Court found that "the evidence does suggest that Unocal knew that forced labor was being utilized and that the Joint Venturers benefited from the practice." Moreover, Unocal knew or should reasonably have known that its conduct—including the payments and the instructions where to provide security and build infrastructure—would assist or encourage the Myanmar Military to subject Plaintiffs to forced labor.

Viewing the evidence in the light most favorable to Plaintiffs, we conclude that there are genuine issues of material fact whether Unocal's conduct met the *actus reus* and *mens rea* requirements for liability under the ATCA for aiding and abetting forced labor. Accordingly, we reverse the District Court's grant of Unocal's motion for summary judgment on Plaintiffs' forced labor claims under the ATCA.

3.   MURDER, RAPE, AND TORTURE

a.   BECAUSE PLAINTIFFS TESTIFIED THAT THE ALLEGED ACTS OF MURDER, RAPE, AND TORTURE OCCURRED IN FURTHERANCE OF FORCED LABOR, STATE ACTION IS NOT REQUIRED TO GIVE RISE TO LIABILITY UNDER THE ATCA

Plaintiffs further allege that the Myanmar military murdered, raped or tortured a number of the plaintiffs. In section II.A.1., we adopted the Second Circuit's conclusion that "acts of rape, torture, and summary execution," like most crimes, "are proscribed by international law only when committed by state officials or under color of law" to the extent that they were committed *in isolation*. We, however, also adopted the Second Circuit's conclusion that these crimes "are actionable under the Alien Tort [Claims] Act, without regard to state action, to the extent that they were committed *in pursuit of genocide or war crimes,"* i.e., in pursuit of crimes, such as slavery, which never require state action for ATCA liability to attach. According to Plaintiffs' deposition testimony, all of the acts of murder, rape, and torture alleged by Plaintiffs occurred in furtherance of the forced labor program. As discussed above in section II.A 2.a, forced labor is a modern variant of slavery and does therefore never require state action to give rise to liability under the ATCA. Thus, under *Kadic*, state action is also not required for the acts of murder, rape, and torture which allegedly occurred in furtherance of the forced labor program.

> b.   UNOCAL MAY BE LIABLE UNDER THE ATCA FOR AIDING
>   AND ABETTING THE MYANMAR MILITARY IN SUBJECTING
>   PLAINTIFFS TO MURDER AND RAPE, BUT UNOCAL IS NOT
>   SIMILARLY LIABLE FOR TORTURE

In section II.A.2.b, we adopted "knowing practical assistance [or] encouragement * * * which has a substantial effect on the perpetration of the crime," from *Furundzija*, as a standard for aiding and abetting liability under the ATCA. The same reasons that convinced us earlier that Unocal may be liable under this standard for aiding and abetting the Myanmar Military in subjecting Plaintiffs to forced labor also convince us now that Unocal may likewise be liable under this standard for aiding and abetting the Myanmar Military in subjecting Plaintiffs to murder and rape. We conclude, however, that as a matter of law, Unocal is not similarly liable for torture in this case.

Initially we observe that the evidence in the record creates a genuine question of material fact as to whether Myanmar soldiers engaged in acts of murder and rape involving Plaintiffs. For instance, Jane Doe I testified that after her husband, John Doe I, attempted to escape the forced labor program, he was shot at by soldiers, and in retaliation for his attempted escape, that she and her baby were thrown into a fire, resulting in injuries to her and the death of the child. Other witnesses described the summary execution of villagers who refused to participate in the forced labor program, or who grew too weak to work effectively. Several Plaintiffs testified that rapes occurred as part of the forced labor program. For instance, both Jane Does II and III testified that while conscripted to work on pipeline-related construction projects, they were raped at knifepoint by Myanmar soldiers who were members of a battalion that was supervising the work. The record does not, however, contain sufficient evidence to establish a claim of torture (other than by means of rape) involving Plaintiffs. Although a number of witnesses described acts of extreme physical abuse that might give rise to a claim of torture, the allegations all involved victims other than Plaintiffs. As this is not a class action, such allegations cannot serve to establish the Plaintiffs' claims of torture here.

* * *

Soon after this decision, the Ninth Circuit ordered that the case be re-heard en banc. It further ordered that the three-judge panel opinion above not be cited as precedent. The case was never heard en banc. When the Supreme Court granted certiorari in *Sosa v. Alvarez-Machain* (supra 4.B.), the Court of Appeals deferred the hearing. After the Supreme Court decided *Sosa* in 2004, the parties in *Unocal* reached a settlement, the terms of which are confidential.

After *Sosa*, do the plaintiffs still have a viable prima facie case against Unocal? In particular, do the violations of international law alleged against Unocal fulfill the requirements set out by the Supreme Court in *Sosa*?

NOTE ON CHALLENGES TO THE ALIEN TORT STATUTE: KIOBEL *AND* EXXON MOBIL

In recent years, the scope of the Alien Tort Statute has been the subject of extensive judicial and academic debate. In addition to the issues covered by the materials above, two major questions have taken center stage in recent litigation before the U.S. Supreme Court: the territorial reach of the statute, and the application of the statute to corporations. At the time of publication of this book, both of these issues are pending before the Supreme Court in *Kiobel v. Royal Dutch Petroleum*, the case summarized below.

On the question of the territorial reach of the statute, U.S. courts had taken for granted that the statute applies to acts and events in foreign countries. That position was suddenly cast into doubt when the Supreme Court, during oral argument on February 28, 2012, questioned that assumption. The point was re-argued on October 1, 2012. The territorial scope of the statute is a crucial threshold issue. All cases we have considered in this context—as well as virtually all other cases decided under the statute in the last three dec-ades—involved acts and events abroad. If the statute does not apply in such cases, there will be virtually nothing left of the ATS—except perhaps occa-sional cases involving acts on the high seas. In other words, the statute will become essentially irrelevant in practice.

The second major question is whether the Alien Tort Statute can provide ju-risdiction over corporations. For many years, U.S. courts had proceeded on this assumption as well in the wake of the *Unocal* case. In 2011, however, courts suddenly began to diverge sharply on this issue. This created a classic split among the circuits that prompted the Supreme Court to grant certiorari in order to decide the issue authoritatively. The Supreme Court is also con-sidering the related question of whether the Torture Victim Protection Act allows for lawsuits against defendants other than natural persons, such as corporations or, as in another case pending before the Supreme Court, the Palestine Liberation Organization (PLO). See *Mohamad v. Rajoub*, 634 F.3d 604 (D.C. Cir. 2011), *cert. granted*, 132 S. Ct. 454, 181 L. Ed. 2d 292 (U.S. 2011).

Below are summaries drafted by the casebook authors of two cases on corporate liability in actions based on the ATS, pointing in opposite directions.

KIOBEL V. ROYAL DUTCH PETROLEUM CO.

621 F.3d 111 (2d Cir. 2010), *reh'g denied*, 642 F.3d 268 (2d Cir. 2011), *cert. denied*, 132 S. Ct. 248 (2011), *cert. granted*, 132 S. Ct. 472 (2011)

[A group of Nigerian citizens and residents sued Royal Dutch Petroleum Company ("Royal Dutch"), incorporated in the Netherlands, and Shell Transport and Trading Company PLC ("Shell"), incorporated in the United Kingdom, under the Alien Tort Claims Act for aiding and abetting the Nigerian government in extrajudicial killing; crimes against humanity; torture or cruel, inhuman, and degrading treatment; arbitrary arrest and detention; violation of the rights to life, liberty, security, and association; forced exile; and property destruction directed at plaintiffs. All defendants were corporate entities.

The claim arose from a long-term oil exploration project by the named companies in Nigeria: Royal Dutch and Shell had been exploring and producing oil in the Ogoni region of Nigeria since 1958. Residents of the Ogoni region had, in opposition to the environmental effects of the oil exploration, organized an environmental activist group named the "Movement for Survival of Ogoni People." Plaintiffs allege that defendants responded by hiring the Nigerian government to suppress the Ogoni resistance—Ogoni residents were shot and killed, and Ogoni villages were attacked. The Nigerian military forces, with the assistance of the defendants, beat, raped, and arrested residents and destroyed property in the villages 1993–1994. The defendants allegedly provided transportation, food and compensation to the Nigerian military forces involved in the attacks.

The court held that corporations could not be liable under customary international law so that there was no subject-matter jurisdiction under the ATCA.

First, the Second Circuit determined that customary international law applies to the question whether corporations can be liable under the ATCA. The court cited *Sosa* for the proposition that the norm of customary international law establishing ATCA liability should be "specific, universal, and obligatory." Then, the court cited article 38 of the Statute of the International Court of Justice as an authoritative list of sources of international law and conducted a review of decisions of the major international tribunals, treaties, general principles of law and most qualified publicists. The Second Circuit concluded that the London Charter establishing the Nuremberg Tribunal only granted jurisdiction over natural persons. Even though the court had the power to declare certain organizations criminal, the organizations themselves were never prosecuted.

Similarly, the International Criminal Tribunal for the Former Yugoslavia and the International Criminal Tribunal for Rwanda only have jurisdiction to prosecute individuals. Most recently, when the International Criminal Court was established, international criminal liability of corporations was considered and rejected.

Next, the majority analyzed treaties that imposed liability on corporations. The majority noted that even though such treaties, in fact, exist, they concerned specific, narrow subject-matter areas, such as oil pollution, nuclear damage or collective bargaining, and could not be used as grounds to establish a general rule. Even though there could be a trend towards corporate liability, it had not yet been crystallized by the great amount of treaties on that subject matter.

Third, the majority analyzed "general principles of law recognized by civilized nations." The majority noted that even though there is some degree of consensus among European nations on the issue, such consensus had not been reached as a matter of customary international law.

Finally, the court looked at works of "most highly qualified publicists of the various nations" which constitute a subsidiary source for ascertaining the rules of international law. Two respected international law scholars, Professor Crawford and Judge Greenwood, had presented opinions that customary international law does not apply to corporations. The majority noted that even the proponents of corporate criminal liability have remarked that such liability is currently a matter of a goal rather than reality.

After this analysis, the Second Circuit court dismissed the complaint for lack of subject-matter jurisdiction.

Judge Leval filed a separate opinion, concurring in the judgment. In his opinion, the plaintiffs had failed to describe with sufficient precision the conduct that allegedly gave rise to liability, but he found corporate liability possible in principle. Leval criticized the majority for their failure to appreciate differences in criminal and civil liability of corporations. While international criminal tribunals had never imposed criminal liability on corporations, this could be, according to Leval, for the reasons that criminal punishments generally require a finding of criminal intent and aim at deterring future crimes of the convicted. Furthermore, little can be inferred from the practice of these international criminal tribunals, according to Leval, as to whether liability for civil damages exists under international law. It is true that tribunals have not imposed civil damages on corporations, but this is no different from their treatment of individual defendants. International criminal tribunals simply have limited their jurisdiction to imposing criminal sanctions, and have never imposed liability for civil damages on any defendant, individual or corporate.

Leval also provided various lower court decisions and two attorney general opinions supporting corporate liability for civil damages, cited a statement by the Chairman of the Rome Statute Drafting Committee, two treatises on the ATCA and the International Commission of Jurists report on "Corporate Complicity and Legal Accountability," all confirming that corporations can be liable for civil damages under international law. Leval noted that the statements by Professor Crawford and Judge Greenwood were made in support of the corporate defendant in other litigation and could not account for unbiased statements of the current state of international law.

Judge Leval's opinion focused mainly on why denying corporate liability for civil damages would be unwise. Perplexingly, he did not present the argument that corporate civil liability could very well constitute a general principle of law common to all civilized nations. This method has been used at least by the Permanent Court of Arbitration in the *Gentini* case (of a general nature) (*Italy v. Venezuela*, Reports of International Arbitral Awards, Vol. X, 551–561), where the arbitrators construed an international rule of statute of limitations because such a rule existed in the national legal systems of most countries. General principles of law were used also by ICJ Justice Simma in his separate opinion in the *Oil Platforms* case where he attempted to construct an international rule of joint tortfeasor liability because such a rule existed in the national legal systems of many Western countries.]

JOHN DOE VIII v. EXXON MOBIL CORP.

United States Circuit Court
654 F.3d 11 (D.C. Cir. 2011)

[Exxon Mobil Corp. ("Exxon"), a United States corporation, operated a large natural gas extraction and processing facility in the Aceh province of Indonesia under contract with the Indonesian government in 2000–2001. Eleven Indonesian villagers from Aceh filed a complaint in 2001 alleging that Exxon's security forces had committed acts of murder, torture, sexual assault, battery and false imprisonment in violation of the Alien Tort Statute ("ATS") and the Torture Victim Protection Act ("TVPA"), as well as several common law torts. Four other villagers claimed in 2007 that Exxon committed various common law torts as well. All fifteen plaintiff-appellants claimed that actions by Exxon in the U.S. as well as in Indonesia resulted in their injuries.

The plaintiffs alleged that although Exxon was aware of the human rights violations committed by the Indonesian army in Aceh, it still hired members of the army as guards for the natural gas facility. The Indonesian army's subsequent misdeeds could be attributed to Exxon because they were committed by soldiers assigned to the Aceh facility administered by Exxon and the corporation controlled the soldiers. Moreover, it profited from the operation of the Aceh facility.

Exxon raised three justiciability objections to these claims: first, it called for the dismissal of the complaint in deference to the foreign policy views of the Executive Branch; second, it argued that the plaintiffs' claims interfered with a peace agreement supported by the United States; and finally, it claimed that the case threatened comity with Indonesia.

The district court dismissed all of the plaintiffs' claims. In particular, it ruled that aiding and abetting violation of human rights was not actionable under the ATS. Plaintiffs appealed and Exxon cross appealed arguing that customary international law does not recognize corporate liability for human rights violations.

The D.C. Circuit Court of Appeals reversed the district court's decision with regard to the ATS claims (among others) and remanded the case to the district court. Focusing on the ATS related arguments, it held that, first, aiding and abetting violations of human rights did constitute a violation of customary international law and the ATS. The court also found historical support for the inference that Congress intended the ATS to apply extraterritorially. Additionally, it pointed out that modern ATS litigation has focused mainly on torts committed abroad, and the facts of the case fit that line of precedent. The law of nations also supports holding those who aid and abet human rights violations responsible for their actions. This principle was upheld in the Nuremberg trials and subsequently affirmed by international criminal courts such as the ICTY and ICTR. The court mentioned that both the Second and Eleventh Circuits have held that actors can be held liable under ATS for aiding and abetting human rights violations.

Second, the court held that corporations can be liable under the ATS. Historically, corporate liability was both consistent with the purposes of the ATS and the understanding of agency law in 1789. Moreover, Congress never gave any special immunity to corporations. The Supreme Court has also observed that the ATS does not make distinctions among classes of defendants (citing *Argentine Republic v. Amerada Hess Shipping Corp.,* 488 U.S. 428, 438 (1989)). The court additionally pointed out that contrary to the opinion in *Kiobel,* a German corporation *was* held responsible for supporting the Nazi war effort because corporate liability exists under customary international law. Also, given that corporate liability is a "universal feature of the world's legal system," it is a general principle of international law that directly favors the plaintiffs.]

NOTE ON THE CHEVRON V. ECUADOR LITIGATION

Even beyond the ATCA context, corporate responsibility is a major issue in international law. This point is illustrated by ongoing litigation arising out of

Texaco's oil exploration in Ecuador that took place from the 1970s through 1992. The litigation quickly became multifaceted and multi-jurisdictional. The point of summarizing it here is simply to give you a sense of the resulting complexity of such cases in which both fundamental rights and big money are at stake, and private litigants and public actors are involved.

The case started in 1993 when residents of Oriente, Ecuador, sued Texaco in a U.S. federal district court for environmental damage caused by Texaco's drilling operations in Ecuador. Plaintiffs were suffering from various illnesses as a result of the environmental harm. Texaco admitted that its operations did in fact cause the damage, but argued that it had already carried out a cleanup agreement with the Ecuadoran government and that all remedial measures had been completed by 1998. According to Texaco, the cleanup agreement released Texaco from any claims related to its Ecuadoran operations. Before the case in the United States reached the merits, the court dismissed the claim on the grounds of *forum non conveniens*, i.e., the court found that Ecuador was a more appropriate forum for the litigation.

The plaintiffs then refiled the case in Ecuador. The Ecuadoran judge awarded the plaintiffs $9 billion in compensatory damages and added another $9 billion in punitive damages because Chevron (which had purchased Texaco in 2001) failed to publicly apologize for the environmental damage it had caused within fourteen days of the Ecuadoran court's judgment. Chevron appealed, alleging that the judgment was a product of fraud and corruption, and that the plaintiffs' representatives had written parts of the court opinion. An Ecuador appeals court affirmed the judgment, rejecting all of Chevron's arguments.

In response to the judgment in Ecuador, Chevron initiated litigation against the plaintiffs' attorneys under U.S. racketeering laws, alleging that the $18 billion judgment was based on fabricated evidence. A U.S. federal district court granted a preliminary injunction preventing enforcement of the Ecuadoran judgment, but an appellate court vacated that order. The enforceability of the Ecuadoran judgment has not yet been definitively adjudicated, but enforcement in the United States is barred pending the resolution of the racketeering charges.

In 2009, Chevron also initiated arbitration against Ecuador under a bilateral investment treaty, alleging that the government of Ecuador had improperly intervened in the litigation in Ecuador. Ecuador has petitioned to stay the arbitration proceeding, arguing that initiation of arbitration was in breach of the original *forum non conveniens* ruling by the U.S. district court. The Second Circuit Court of Appeals rejected Ecuador's arguments and let the arbitration proceed, holding that the arbitration was not incompatible with the pending Ecuadoran litigation. In early 2012, the arbitration panel, administered by the Permanent Court of Arbitration in The Hague, decided that it has jurisdiction to hear Chevron's claims on the merits. A final decision by the panel is expected in 2014.

Even though the Ecuadoran judgment against Chevron stands, and has risen to $19 billion because of the accruing interest and additional court costs, plaintiffs have not yet seen a dollar of the potential recovery. This is because Chevron, whose market capitalization is nearly $200 billion, has no assets in Ecuador.

Plaintiffs are pursuing other avenues, trying to reach any of Chevron's assets where it currently has operations. In May 2012, the plaintiffs sued Chevron in Canada to enforce the Ecuadoran judgment. Under Canadian law, that judgment will be enforced only if it satisfies due process and is free of fraud. Chevron has argued that its Canadian subsidiary is an independent corporate entity, the operations of which are separate from the parent company. Therefore, the Canadian subsidiary should not be liable for the judgment against the parent company. The Canadian litigation is still pending; similar litigation is also pending in Brazil.

CHAPTER 7

INTERACTION: STATES IN THE CONTEMPORARY GLOBAL CONTEXT

■ ■ ■

As we saw in Part One, the classic approach to (public) international law built on a strong notion of state sovereignty. States were considered to have complete control over internal affairs and to have nearly full freedom regarding their relationships with other sovereign states. This strong notion of sovereignty had several important consequences. States were subject to international law only on the basis of some form of consent; for example, they were under no general obligation to settle disputes peacefully and to refrain from waging war. States also enjoyed almost complete sovereign immunity on each other's soil, especially in each other's courts. At the same time, respect for the sovereignty of other states also curtailed a state's jurisdiction: they claimed jurisdiction over their territory and their nationals, but hesitated to go beyond these limits.

Since the middle of the 20th century, the perception of sovereignty has changed in several respects. First, international lawyers have increasingly taken a critical view of sovereignty and its consequences, roughly along the lines of the excerpt from J.L. Brierly we saw in Chapter II.1. In a famous article, Louis Henkin, one of the most prominent public international law scholars of the post-World War II era, "blame[d] the delusions and mythology of sovereignty for the failure of states to collaborate more extensively." Louis Henkin, *That "S" Word: Sovereignty, and Globalization, and Human Rights, Et Cetera*, 68 Fordham L. Rev. 1, 3 (1999). "Sovereignty," Henkin opined, "does not encourage cooperation; it breeds 'going it alone.'" *Id.*

Perhaps more importantly, Henkin and many other observers have noted an "erosion of sovereignty" in the second half of the 20th century. This erosion began largely in response to the cataclysms of World War II and the Holocaust, then grew in response to human rights violations by totalitarian regimes around the world. As Henkin noted, "it took Hitler and the Holocaust to achieve that. Since 1945, how a state treats its own citizens, how it behaves even in its own territory, has no longer been its own business; it has become a matter of international concern, of international politics, and of international law." *Id.* at 4.

While there is much debate about the nature and extent of the post-World War II "erosion of sovereignty," two trends are quite clear.

On the one hand, sovereignty is no longer considered absolute because states have come to accept limits on their sovereign freedom. As we will see in this Chapter, this has happened in three major ways. First, states may find themselves bound by certain fundamental norms of international law (preemptory norms, or *jus cogens*) whether they like it or not. Second, and more importantly, they have established various regimes under which their sovereignty is curtailed.[1] On the global level, this has occurred most notably by entering into a system of collective security under the UN Charter, which limits the right to wage war. We will also take a(nother) look at the WTO in order to learn about an even more integrated global regime. Finally, we will turn to the regional level, where those states that have become members of the European Union have gone much farther in ceding important elements of their sovereignty to a supranational body, including much of their lawmaking power. Third, states are no longer willing to grant each other complete immunity in their courts; in particular, such immunity is no longer accorded if states act commercially rather than in their sovereign capacity.

On the other hand, we will see that states have sought to extend their sovereign powers by expanding their jurisdictional claims beyond the territoriality and personality principle. They now frequently exercise jurisdiction even over acts committed by foreigners abroad if such acts have an effect on their territory (or market). In addition, other jurisdictional bases have become more widely employed, such as the passive personality principle, the protective principle, and the universality principle. In short, it has become quite common for several states to claim jurisdiction over the same matter. As a result, states increasingly step on each other's jurisdictional toes. This has sometimes led to outright clashes of jurisdiction and created a need for restraint through the concept of comity (i.e., mutual respect) and, perhaps paradoxically, a revival of the territoriality paradigm.

1. PREEMPTORY NORMS (*JUS COGENS*)

The strong, classic, concept of sovereignty entailed the idea that, on the international level, states could do whatever they wanted unless they had (in one form or another) promised other states to refrain from certain behavior. As a result, the classic approach saw public international law as a system under which a state was bound only by what it had agreed to. Thus, a state could (at least theoretically) avoid an international obligation by refusing to consent to a particular norm.

---

[1] We have seen this already in the human rights context, especially under the European Convention of Human Rights, Chapter VI.4.A.

In recent decades, however, it has become widely accepted that there are some international law norms that are absolutely binding in the sense that, once such norms have been established, individual states cannot escape them. This is the concept of peremptory norms, also known as *jus cogens* (a Latin term for "binding law"). Today, the most prominent expression of the concept is contained in Article 53 of the Vienna Convention on the Law of Treaties. How does the provision define a *jus cogens* norm? What is the effect of such a norm?

VIENNA CONVENTION ON THE LAW OF TREATIES
(Adopted 1969; in force 1980)

* * *

Article 53

Treaties Conflicting with a Peremptory Norm of General International Law

(Jus Cogens)

A treaty is void if, at the time of its conclusion, it conflicts with a peremptory norm of general international law. For the purposes of the present Convention, a peremptory norm of general international law is a norm accepted and recognized by the international community of States as a whole as a norm from which no derogation is permitted and which can be modified only by a subsequent norm of general international law having the same character.

* * *

_____

The concept of *jus cogens* can easily be, and indeed often is, misunderstood as a blank check for invoking super norms of international law that are more or less generally independent of state consent. As the following text explains, that is a bad mistake.

JAMES HATHAWAY, THE RIGHTS OF REFUGEES UNDER INTERNATIONAL LAW
(2005)

* * *

Properly conceived, the idea of *jus cogens* or higher, peremptory law, is a helpful way of bringing order to international law without feigning the existence of supranational authority. *Jus cogens* is a general principle of law based on the near-universal commitment of national legal systems to insulating certain basic norms from derogation. It sanctions the establishment of an outer limit to the range of subjects on which states may legitimately contract, enforced by the invalidation of conflicting treaties. The *jus cogens* principle is recognized in the Vienna Convention on the Law of Treaties as the basis for giving precedence to any treaty that embodies "a norm accepted and recognized by the international community of States as a whole as a norm from which no derogation is permitted."

Jus cogens is not, therefore, a source of law. It is rather a hierarchical designation that attaches to laws that have come into existence by the usual modes of international lawmaking. The attribution of status as "higher law" derives from the intersection of such a freestanding law with the general principle of law prohibiting agreements that are inconsistent with the most basic values of the international community. *Jus cogens* is best understood as a means of giving greater enforceability to norms that have already acquired the status of universal law by operation of general principles or custom (including custom interacting with treaty). Human rights that are matters of *jus cogens* are therefore "super rights" that trump conflicting claims. It is not possible, however, for a right to have force as *jus cogens* without first acquiring status as law through one of the recognized modes of international lawmaking.

The challenge is to ensure that *jus cogens* is defined in a way that ensures evolution away from its parochial origins in natural law and which advances respect for the consensual premise of international lawmaking. In a world of diverse values, the most useful approach would be to build upon the accepted formalities of international lawmaking. There should be evidence that the putative *jus cogens* norm occupies a privileged position in the context of accepted traditional sources of international law. Thus, for example, where custom and treaty law intersect, it may be reasonable to suggest that common normative standards may be said to be fundamental to transnational community values. One might similarly attribute privileged stature to a pervasively subscribed treaty, or to customary norms or general principles that have shown their durability through application to varied circumstances over time and across cultures. The uniting principle suggested here respects state control over international law, in that "higher law" evolves as a function of the extent and degree of affirmation by states. It similarly acknowledges the truly exceptional nature of defining any standards to be matters of "high illegality" in an essentially coordinative body of law.

At present, however, the utility of the *jus cogens* doctrine is threatened by a range of politically expedient actions. On the one hand, there is an unhealthy tendency on the part of some scholars in powerful states to equate hegemonic political or ideological traditions with universal values. This "character defined" approach to *jus cogens*, impliedly endorsed by the renovation of general principles previously outlined, fails to recognize the impossibility in a pluralist world of defining peremptory norms based on particularized notions of which rights are intrinsic and undeniable. Common human rights standards will be agreed to for varied reasons, and taking account of diverging world views. If there is to be a recognition of standards that trump other norms, the defining characteristic of these *jus cogens* principles must itself be accepted by all those it purports to bind.

Conversely, there are those in the less developed world who see *jus cogens* as a way to override international law established without their full participation, thereby accelerating the pace of global institutional and normative reform. Recognizing the numerical strength of the less developed world in the General Assembly, there have been efforts to characterize its resolutions as constitutive of *jus cogens*. But this approach runs afoul of the principle, described above, that *jus cogens* is not a source of law, but is rather a label that attaches to an otherwise validly conceived law because of its centrality to collective consensus on basic standards. Because the General Assembly and its subordinate bodies have no general lawmaking authority, their resolutions are not usually binding. There is therefore no law to which the *jus cogens* designation can adhere. The only exceptions would be where the resolution is simply the codification of a preexisting custom or general principle of law, or where it has achieved such status over time since passage of the resolution.

It is, of course, perfectly legitimate to argue for the replacement of traditional modes of international lawmaking by a more parliamentary, community-based system of supranational authority. It is, however, duplicitous to pretend that there is presently agreement in favor of such a shift. It is doubly dishonest to argue that the *jus cogens* rule, designed to bring order to established forms of law, can be relied upon to assert the existence of an order of authority superior to standards devised through the three established modes of lawmaking.

* * *

_____

What kinds of norms are actually "peremptory"? In the *Nicaragua Case*, which involved the use of force by the United States against Nicaragua, the ICJ found that the parties actually seemed to agree with regard to at least one such norm:

> The International Law Commission, in the course of its work on the codification of the law of treaties, expressed the view that "the law of the Charter concerning the prohibition of the use of force in itself constitutes a conspicuous example of a rule in international law hav-

ing the character of *jus cogens*." Nicaragua in its Memorial on the Merits submitted in the present case states that the principle prohibiting the use of force embodied in Article 2 paragraph 4, of the Charter of the United Nations "has come to be recognized as *jus cogens*." The United States, in its Counter-Memorial on the questions of jurisdiction and admissibility, found it material to quote the views of scholars that this principle is a "universal norm," a "universal international law," a "universally recognized principle of international law," and a "principle of *jus cogens*." (*Nicaragua v. United States*, 1986 I.C.J. 14, Merits, section 190.)

What other norms would have the rank of *jus cogens*? There is basic agreement that the prohibition of particularly heinous acts, such as genocide, enslavement and torture is included although people may contest what each of these concepts entails. As one moves away from this core, the *jus cogens* character of norms becomes more debatable and debated. What about the principle of racial equality? Gender equality? The duty to pay just compensation for expropriation? Note that the disagreement here is not about the importance of these norms, but about whether they are absolutely non-derogable.

―――――――――

What are the practical consequences of considering a norm *jus cogens*? The International Law Commission addressed some of them in its *Articles on States Responsibility*. What is the basic message of these provisions?

ARTICLES ON RESPONSIBILITY OF STATES FOR INTERNATIONALLY WRONGFUL ACTS

International Law Commission (2001)

* * *

Chapter III

Serious breaches of obligations under peremptory norms of general international law

Article 40

Application of this chapter

1. This chapter applies to the international responsibility which is entailed by a serious breach by a State of an obligation arising under a peremptory norm of general international law.

2. A breach of such an obligation is serious if it involves a gross or systematic failure by the responsible State to fulfil the obligation.

Article 41

Particular consequences of a serious breach of an obligation under this chapter

1. States shall cooperate to bring to an end through lawful means any serious breach within the meaning of article 40.

2. No State shall recognize as lawful a situation created by a serious breach within the meaning of article 40, nor render aid or assistance in maintaining that situation.

* * *

Article 41(1) sounds rather hortatory, and whether Article 41(2) will have much of a practical impact remains to be seen. Beyond all that, what use can a litigant make of *jus cogens*, say, in pursuing an action under the Alien Tort Claims Act? Does it help a plaintiff if the international law norm allegedly violated is accepted (either generally or at least by the particular court) as a peremptory norm? Look at the *Unocal* case again (Chapter VI.5.B.) where the court actually made reference to the concept of *jus cogens*. Does the *jus cogens* argument advance the ball for the plaintiffs? If so, how?

2. THE DELEGATION OF SOVEREIGN POWERS

Perhaps the most important change regarding state sovereignty that has taken place since the middle of the 20th century has been the voluntary delegation of sovereign powers from states to international organizations. This has occurred across a wide spectrum involving dozens, if not hundreds, of such organizations, both on the global and on the regional level. Here, we look only at three contexts, which are, however, arguably the most notable and important ones: the UN System of Collective Security, the World Trade Organization, and the European Union.

In these (and many other) contexts, one can say that states have given up part of their sovereign power. Yet the very participation in multilateral organizations and treaties is itself an exercise of such power. Almost a century ago, the Permanent Court of International Justice famously opined (in a case involving the Versailles Treaty):

> The Court declines to see in the conclusion of any Treaty by which a State undertakes to perform or refrain from performing a particular act an abandonment of sovereignty. No doubt any convention creating an obligation of this kind places a restriction upon the exercise of sovereign rights of the State in the sense that it requires them to be exercised in a certain way. But the right of entering into internation-

al engagements is an attribute of State sovereignty. (*Case of the S.S. Wimbledon (United Kingdom, France, Italy, and Japan v. Germany)*, 1923 P.C.I.J. (Ser. A) No. 1.)

In all three contexts addressed below, ask yourself exactly what powers states gave up, how much control they lost over such powers, and what they (hope to) get out of it.

A. WAGING WAR: THE UNITED NATIONS SYSTEM OF COLLECTIVE SECURITY

In the summer of 1945, after the failed attempt to ban war outright in the Kellogg–Briand Pact of 1928 and the trauma of World War II, the victors tried to establish a more peaceful world order through the United Nations Charter. The pivotal provisions of the instrument are Article 2(3), which calls on all UN members "to settle their international disputes by peaceful means," and Article 2(4), which provides that they "shall refrain in their international relations from the threat or use of force against the territorial integrity or political independence of any state, or in any other manner inconsistent with the Purpose of the United Nations."

DAVID BEDERMAN, INTERNATIONAL LAW FRAMEWORKS
(3d ed. 2010)

* * *

If Article 2(4)'s proscription of use of force is the "prime directive" of modern international law, it is only natural that States will struggle to establish the outer limits of that obligation and any potential exceptions. While the U.N. Charter's legal approach for controlling conflict has been intensely criticized, it does reflect a notable improvement on the League of Nations' model. The United Nations' legal controls on its Members' resort to armed conflict can only be as successful as the underlying collective security regime that the U.N. manages. States will only refrain from aggression if they have the certain knowledge that breaches of the peace will be the subject of immediate economic sanctions and, much more importantly, decisive military response by the wider international community.

The key to the United Nation's collective security regime is the Security Council, the 15-member body consisting of 5 permanent members (Britain, China, France, Russia and the United States) and 10 non-permanent members that each serve a rotating 2-year term. Any permanent member can wield a veto of any substantive action. To order any response to a breach of the peace or an act of aggression requires 9 votes, including the concurrences of the permanent members. (An abstention by a permanent member does not stand as a veto, but it does not count for the needed 9 votes.) Thus to order any credible response to aggression requires a high level of political will by the members of the Security Council, and either the support or silent acquiescence of each of the permanent members. (Proposals to expand the membership of the Security Council to reflect modern international relations, including granting permanent membership (and veto power) to such nations as Japan, India and Brazil, have been inconclusive.)

The original intent of the Charter system was to prevent or suppress dangerous regional powers from militarizing and challenging the authority of the Great Powers. The system of collective security under the Charter was never intended to address Great Power conflict or rivalries acted out between the proxies of the Security Council's permanent members. The Charter's plan was that the Security Council would, in the face of an act of aggression, declare a violation of the Charter under Article 39 and then order all Member States of the U.N. to impose economic sanctions or other penalties. The Security Council's actions with respect to imposition of economic sanctions are to be followed unquestioningly by Member States of the United Nations, although recent decisions have put this in doubt in cases where anti-terrorism measures were imposed against suspects without due process. The Security Council has also gone as far as to modify or "adapt" the treaty obligations of Member States, in order to promote international peace and security. While this has some support in U.N. Charter Article 103 (which places Members' duties to the United Nations above "their obligations under any other international agreement"), this practice remains controversial.

If such sanctions are ineffectual in reversing the unlawful conduct, then the Council can, under Article 42, order the mobilization of air, sea or land forces. U.N. Members are obliged not to give any support to the outlaw nation. Under Charter Article 43, States were supposed to have negotiated agreements with the U.N. to provide military contingents for the U.N.'s use under the command of the Security Council and its Military Staff Committee. No such agreements have ever been concluded, and thus on those few occasions where the U.N. has ordered an enforcement action under Chapter VII of the Charter (as with the response to Iraq's invasion of Kuwait in 1990), ad hoc coalitions of forces have been assembled for the task.

It is fair to say that the entire collective security mechanism of the U.N. Charter was nullified during the Cold War. The Security Council literally could not act against aggressor nations because, almost inevitably, each one was a proxy of either the United States or Soviet Union, and thus the Americans (and their allies) or the Soviets could be counted upon to veto any responsive resolution. The only exception to this Security Council gridlock was the serendipitous action taken by the U.N. at the beginning of the Korean War. The Soviets had been boycotting the Council and thus were not there to cast the necessary veto of the enforcement action. (Since that occurrence, no permanent member representative has ever failed to attend a meeting of the Council!)

The grid-lock on Security Council action profoundly disappointed the international community in the 1950's and 1960's. In response, the U.N. General Assembly began to assert its authority to be able to order certain kinds of actions without Security Council approval. Thus was born the use of U.N. peacekeeping forces, authorized under Chapter VI of the Charter. Developed by the dynamic U.N. Secretary General, Dag Hammarskjöld of Sweden, the first uses of peacekeepers occurred in the aftermath of the Middle East Suez Crisis in 1956 and the 1960–63 Katanga Rebellion in Congo. Essential to the creation of the U.N. Emergency Force for the Sinai (UNEF) and the U.N. Force for the Congo (ONUC)—U.N. peacekeeping forces are inevitably given unwieldy acronyms—was permission for their deployment by the host States. Unlike enforcement actions against malefactor countries, which can only be ordered by the Security Council acting under Chapter VII, peacekeeping forces are consensual (with the permission of the host State) and can thus be established and funded by the General Assembly under Chapter VI of the Charter. In a significant decision, the World Court upheld the right of the General Assembly to create such forces and also to require that all Member States pay their share of the expenses.

Peacekeeping has become a central mission of the United Nations. Oftentimes, however, the ultimate goals of such operations have been frustrated. In many situations, the U.N. peacekeeping force was inserted as a buffer between warring States. Regrettably, the presence of the U.N. peacekeepers often does not promote the negotiation of a final political settlement. U.N. peacekeepers have been stationed on the Indian–Pakistan border since 1947, in Cyprus since 1975, and in southern Lebanon from the early 1980's to the mid-1990's. More recently, U.N. peacekeepers have been used for a task very different from merely separating bickering nations. U.N. forces have been successfully used for election monitoring in El Salvador, East Timor and Namibia, although to little or no effect in Angola and Western Sahara. In a wider sense, U.N. peacekeepers might be enlisted for "democracy and nation building" in parts of the world ravaged by conflict. U.N. forces in the Balkans and in Cambodia have certainly played that role.

Iraq's invasion of Kuwait in August 1990 revived Chapter VII's collective security regime which had been moribund for over 40 years. The combination of factors that led to the United Nations' response was extraordinary. The Cold War was over, and both Russia and China were anxious to let the U.N. operate to its full potential. Iraq was a dangerous, mid-sized power, precisely the regional bully that the Security Council was intended to discipline. Iraq had no allies on the Council. Lastly, and no less important, Iraq's invasion of small, helpless Kuwait was so audacious and unlawful that even the most jaded and callous of diplomats or leaders could not help being appalled.

Within hours of the invasion, the U.N. Security Council met and began to adopt a series of resolutions imposing various diplomatic, economic, trade and transport sanctions against Iraq. From the very beginning, the Council signaled its intent to invoke Chapter VII and follow it to its logical, and necessary, conclusion. Finally, after waiting nearly 4 months for the Iraqis to withdraw from Kuwait, the Council adopted Resolution 678 which "authorized Member States co-operating with the Government of Kuwait * * * to use all necessary means" to eject Iraq from Kuwait, unless Iraq withdrew by January 15, 1991. When the deadline passed, the Gulf War began. Within a few months it was over, and Iraq was compelled to accept a peace imposed by the Council in its Resolution 687, including mandatory disarmament and payment of reparations to Kuwait and other countries injured by Iraq's aggression (managed through a body known as the U.N. Compensation Commission (UNCO)).

The Gulf War was hailed as, at long last, the ultimate vindication of the United Nation's collective security mandate. But such enthusiasm was unwarranted. Since 1991, there has been little political will to respond to violations of international peace and security. U.N. action in the Balkans was ineffectual, and in Rwanda may have actually contributed to a genocide claiming nearly a million lives. The U.N. has also tended to defer to regional security organizations in undertaking enforcement action, as occurred in Liberia and Sierra Leone in West Africa. Lastly, NATO's usurpation of the Security Council's role in fashioning a response to Serbian outrages in Kosovo may have also been indicative of a "new" Cold War mentality.

Ironically, it has even been suggested that the U.N. Security Council has become too powerful and needs to be legally restrained. It has been seriously suggested that the World Court should exercise a form of "judicial review" over Council determinations that certain acts constitute a "threat to the peace, breach of the peace, or act of aggression" within the meaning of Charter Article 39, which is the "trigger" for Chapter VII enforcement actions.

* * *

International law controls on armed conflict will thus continue to reflect a mix of customary international law principles, interpretations of the U.N. Charter's clarion commands of Articles 2(4) and 51, the "constitutional" law of the U.N. as the chief guarantor of international peace and security, and the political reality of States pursuing different national objectives. Make no mistake, the question of when it is appropriate for a nation to resort to war, as well as the mechanisms for collective security, are today more and more regulated by legal considerations.

* * *

Chapter VII of the UN Charter is the heart of the so-called system of collective security. According to the articles below, how does it operate? In particular, what is the process set up by Articles 39–42? What is the role of Article 51 in this context?

You have already seen Article 2 of the Charter. How does Chapter VII interact with Article 2?

CHARTER OF THE UNITED NATIONS
(Adopted 1945; in force 1945)

* * *

Article 2

The Organization and its Members, in pursuit of the Purposes stated in Article 1, shall act in accordance with the following Principles.

1. The Organization is based on the principle of the sovereign equality of all its Members.

2. All Members, in order to ensure to all of them the rights and benefits resulting from membership, shall fulfill in good faith the obligations assumed by them in accordance with the present Charter.

3. All Members shall settle their international disputes by peaceful means in such a manner that international peace and security, and justice, are not endangered.

4. All Members shall refrain in their international relations from the threat or use of force against the territorial integrity or political independence of any state, or in any other manner inconsistent with the Purposes of the United Nations.

5. All Members shall give the United Nations every assistance in any action it takes in accordance with the present Charter, and shall refrain from giving assistance to any state against which the United Nations is taking preventive or enforcement action.

6. The Organization shall ensure that states which are not Members of the United Nations act in accordance with these Principles so far as may be necessary for the maintenance of international peace and security.

7. Nothing contained in the present Charter shall authorize the United Nations to intervene in matters which are essentially within the domestic jurisdiction of any state or shall require the Members to submit such matters to settlement under the present Charter; but this principle shall not prejudice the application of enforcement measures under Chapter Vll.

* * *

Chapter VII

Action with Respect to Threats to the Peace, Breaches of the Peace, and Acts of Aggression

Article 39

The Security Council shall determine the existence of any threat to the peace, breach of the peace, or act of aggression and shall make recommendations, or decide what measures shall be taken in accordance with Articles 41 and 42, to maintain or restore international peace and security.

Article 40

In order to prevent an aggravation of the situation, the Security Council may, before making the recommendations or deciding upon the measures provided for in Article 39, call upon the parties concerned to comply with such provisional measures as it deems necessary or desirable. Such provisional measures shall be without prejudice to the rights, claims, or position of the parties concerned. The Security Council shall duly take account of failure to comply with such provisional measures.

Article 41

The Security Council may decide what measures not involving the use of armed force are to be employed to give effect to its decisions, and it may call upon the Members of the United Nations to apply such measures. These may include complete or partial interruption of economic relations and of rail, sea, air, postal, telegraphic, radio, and other means of communication, and the severance of diplomatic relations.

Article 42

Should the Security Council consider that measures provided for in Article 41 would be inadequate or have proved to be inadequate, it may take such action by air, sea, or land forces as may be necessary to maintain or restore international peace and security. Such action may include demonstrations, blockade, and other operations by air, sea, or land forces of Members of United Nations.

Article 43

1. All Members of the United Nations, in order to contribute to the maintenance of international peace and security, undertake to make available to the Security Council, on its call and in accordance with a special agreement or agreements, armed forces, assistance, and facilities, including rights of passage, necessary for the purpose of maintaining international peace and security.

2. Such agreement or agreements shall govern the numbers and types of forces, their degree of readiness and general location, and the nature of the facilities and assistance to be provided.

3. The agreement or agreements shall be negotiated as soon as possible on the initiative of the Security Council. They shall be concluded between the Security Council and Members or between the Security Council and groups of Members and shall be subject to ratification by the signatory states in accordance with their respective constitutional processes.

* * *

Article 46

Plans for the application of armed force shall be made by the Security Council with the assistance of the Military Staff Committee.

* * *

Article 48

1. The action required to carry out the decisions of the Security Council for the maintenance of international peace and security shall be taken by all the Members of the United Nations or by some of them, as the Security Council may determine.

2. Such decisions shall be carried out by the Members of the United Nations directly and through their action in the appropriate international agencies of which they are members.

Article 49

The Members of the United Nations shall join in affording mutual assistance in carrying out the measures decided upon by the Security Council.

Article 50

If preventive or enforcement measures against any state are taken by the Security Council, any other state, whether a Member of the United Nations or not, which finds itself confronted with special economic problems arising from the carrying out of those measures shall have the right to consult the Security Council with regard to a solution of those problems.

Article 51

Nothing in the present Charter shall impair the inherent right of individual or collective self-defence if an armed attack occurs against a Member of the United Nations, until the Security Council has taken measures necessary to maintain international peace and security. Measures taken by Members in the exercise of this right of self-defence shall be immediately reported to the Security Council and shall not in any way affect the authority and responsibility of the Security Council under the present Charter to take at any time such action as it deems necessary in order to maintain or restore international peace and security.

The 2003 Invasion of Iraq

Operation Iraqi Freedom, the 2003 invasion of Iraq led by the United States and its allies (most notably the United Kingdom, but also including Australia, Denmark and Poland) presents some of the major issues that exist under the UN System of Collective Security.

In the 1990s, the UN implemented a system of sanctions against, and inspectors in, Iraq to monitor Iraqi disarmament after the first Gulf War and to ensure that Iraq wasn't producing what the United States called "weapons of mass destruction." The system was not very successful, largely because Iraq failed to cooperate. The attacks of September 11, 2001 provided the second Bush administration with the necessary impetus to suggest replacing the international program with its own policy of "regime change" in Iraq. Following a year of broadly supported military action in Afghanistan, President Bush addressed the UN General Assembly in September of 2002. In his speech, Bush stated that al Qaeda terrorists were known to be in Iraq, that Iraq had attempted to acquire aluminum tubes for the construction of a nuclear weapon, and that if Iraq were to acquire fissile material it could build a nuclear weapon within a year. On November 8, 2002 the Security Council unanimously adopted Resolution 1441 which decided that Iraq was in material breach of its obligations under previous resolutions and afforded Iraq a "final opportunity to comply with its disarmament obligations."

When UN inspectors finally were able to enter Iraq, they could not find conclusive evidence that Iraq possessed weapons of mass destruction. However, the teams found that Iraq still was unable to account for some weapons caches and that Iraq did not seem to accept all of its disarmament obligations. At a Security Council meeting convened on February 6, 2003 to discuss Iraqi compliance under Resolution 1441, U.S. Secretary of State Colin Powell presented satellite photographs which he claimed proved that Iraq was in possession of prohibited weapons; in addition, he presented other intelligence purporting to show Iraq's non-compliance. Powell also accused Iraq of harboring Abu Musab Al-Zarqawi, whom Powell identified as "an associated collaborator of Osama bin Laden and his al Qaeda lieutenants." Colin Powell,

Presentation to the U.N. Security Council: A Threat to International Peace and Security in THE IRAQ WAR READER: HISTORY, DOCUMENTS, OPINIONS 465, 475 (Micah L. Sifry and Christopher Cerf eds. 2003). Although Iraq had denied any association with al Qaeda, Powell stated that the "denials are simply not credible." *Id.*

In the following month, the United States, Britain and Spain intensified efforts to pass a new resolution authorizing the use of force if President Saddam Hussein did not leave Iraq by March 17, 2003. Other members of the Security Council, in particular Russia and France (as well as non-permanent member Germany), however, rejected the resolution and cautioned against military intervention absent further action by the Security Council. Despite the failure to secure a new resolution, the United States and its "coalition of the willing" announced on March 17 that Saddam Hussein had 48 hours to leave Iraq or face military action. When Hussein ignored the ultimatum, Operation Iraqi Freedom began with an air strike on a location where U.S. officials believed Hussein was meeting with his advisors.

The legality of the invasion of Iraq has been much debated. It turns largely on the respective provisions of the UN Charter and on the (interpretation of) the following four Security Council Resolutions which reflect the developments from the Iraqi invasion of Kuwait in August of 1990 to the eve of the U.S.-led invasion of Iraq in March of 2003.

For each resolution, identify the date on which is was passed, the voting arrangements, the UN Charter provisions invoked by the Security Council, and the operative provisions that form the heart of the resolution itself. Pay particular attention to how the situation keeps changing over more than a decade and how the Security Council reacts to that.

UNITED NATIONS SECURITY COUNCIL RESOLUTION 660

[Adopted by the Security Council at its 2932nd meeting, on 2 August 1990 by 14 votes to none. One SC member, Yemen, did not participate in the voting.]

The Security Council,

Alarmed by the invasion of Kuwait on 2 August 1990 by the military forces of Iraq,

Determining that there exists a breach of international peace and security as regards the Iraqi invasion of Kuwait,

Acting under Articles 39 and 40 of the Charter of the United Nations,

1. *Condemns* the Iraqi invasion of Kuwait;

2. *Demands* that Iraq withdraw immediately and unconditionally all its forces to the positions in which they were located on 1 August 1990;

3. *Calls upon* Iraq and Kuwait to begin immediately intensive negotiations for the resolution of their differences and supports all efforts in this regard, and especially those of the League of Arab States;

4. *Decides* to meet again as necessary to consider further steps to ensure compliance with the present resolution.

UNITED NATIONS SECURITY COUNCIL RESOLUTION 678

[Adopted by the Security Council at its 2963rd meeting on 29 November 1990, by 12 votes to 2 (Cuba and Yemen) and with 1 abstention (China).]

The Security Council,

Recalling, and reaffirming its resolutions 660 (1990) of 2 August 1990, 661 (1990) of 6 August 1990, 662 (1990) of 9 August 1990, 664 (1990) of 18 August 1990, 665 (1990) of 25 August 1990, 666 (1990) of 13 September 1990, 667 (1990) of 16 September 1990, 669 (1990) of 24 September 1990, 670 (1990) of 25 September 1990, 674 (1990) of 29 October 1990 and 677 (1990) of 28 November 1990,

Noting that, despite all efforts by the United Nations, Iraq refuses to comply with its obligation to implement resolution 660 (1990) and the above-mentioned subsequent relevant resolutions, in flagrant contempt of the Security Council,

Mindful of its duties and responsibilities under the Charter of the United Nations for the maintenance and preservation of international peace and security,

Determined to secure full compliance with its decisions,

Acting under Chapter VII of the Charter,

1. *Demands* that Iraq comply fully with resolution 660 (1990) and all subsequent relevant resolutions, and decides, while maintaining all its decisions, to allow Iraq one final opportunity, as a pause of goodwill, to do so;

2. *Authorizes* Member States co-operating with the Government of Kuwait, unless Iraq on or before 15 January 1991 fully implements, as set forth in paragraph 1 above, the above-mentioned resolutions, to use all necessary means to uphold and implement resolution 660 (1990) and all subsequent relevant resolutions and to restore international peace and security in the area;

3. *Requests* all States to provide appropriate support for the actions undertaken in pursuance of paragraph 2 above;

4. *Requests* the States concerned to keep the Security Council regularly informed on the progress of actions undertaken pursuant to paragraphs 2 and 3 above;

5. *Decides* to remain seized of the matter.

UNITED NATIONS SECURITY COUNCIL
RESOLUTION 687

[Adopted by the Security Council at its 2981st meeting, on 3 April 1991 by 12 votes to 1 (Cuba) and 2 abstentions (Ecuador, Yemen).]

The Security Council,

Recalling its resolutions 660 (1990) of 2 August 1990, 661 (1990) of 6 August 1990, 662 (1990) of 9 August 1990, 664 (1990) of 18 August 1990, 665 (1990) of 25 August 1990, 666 (1990) of 13 September 1990, 667 (1990) of 16 September 1990, 669 (1990) of 24 September 1990, 670 (1990) of 25 September 1990, 674 (1990) of 29 October 1990, 677 (1990) of 28 November 1990, 678 (1990) of 29 November 1990 and 686 (1991) of 2 March 1991,

Welcoming the restoration to Kuwait of its sovereignty, independence and territorial integrity and the return of its legitimate Government,

Affirming the commitment of all Member States to the sovereignty, territorial integrity and political independence of Kuwait and Iraq, and noting the intention expressed by the Member States cooperating with Kuwait under paragraph 2 of resolution 678 (1990) to bring their military presence in Iraq to an end as soon as possible consistent with paragraph 8 of resolution 686 (1991),

Reaffirming the need to be assured of Iraq's peaceful intentions in the light of its unlawful invasion and occupation of Kuwait,

* * *

Conscious of the need for demarcation of the [Iraq–Kuwait] boundary,

Conscious also of the statements by Iraq threatening to use weapons in violation of its obligations under the Protocol for the Prohibition of the Use in War of Asphyxiating, Poisonous or Other Gases, and of Bacteriological Methods of Warfare, signed at Geneva on 17 June 1925, and of its prior use of chemical weapons, and affirming that grave consequences would follow any further use by Iraq of such weapons,

* * *

Aware of the use by Iraq of ballistic missiles in unprovoked attacks and therefore of the need to take specific measures in regard to such missiles located in Iraq,

Concerned by the reports in the hands of Member States that Iraq has attempted to acquire materials for a nuclear-weapons programme contrary to its obligations under the Treaty on the Non-Proliferation of Nuclear Weapons of 1 July 1968,

Recalling the objective of the establishment of a nuclear-weapons-free zone in the region of the Middle East,

Conscious of the threat that all weapons of mass destruction pose to peace and security in the area and of the need to work towards the establishment in the Middle East of a zone free of such weapons,

Conscious also of the objective of achieving balanced and comprehensive control of armaments in the region,

* * *

Taking note with grave concern of the reports of the Secretary–General of 20 March and 28 March 1991, and conscious of the necessity to meet urgently the humanitarian needs in Kuwait and Iraq,

Bearing in mind its objective of restoring international peace and security in the area as set out in recent resolutions of the Security Council,

Conscious of the need to take the following measures acting under Chapter VII of the Charter,

1. *Affirms* all thirteen resolutions noted above, except as expressly changed below to achieve the goals of this resolution, including a formal cease-fire;

A

2. *Demands* that Iraq and Kuwait respect the inviolability of the international boundary and the allocation of islands set out in the "Agreed Minutes Between the State of Kuwait and the Republic of Iraq Regarding the Restoration of Friendly Relations, Recognition and Related Matters" * * *;

3. *Calls upon* the Secretary–General to lend his assistance to make arrangements with Iraq and Kuwait to demarcate the boundary between Iraq and Kuwait * * *;

4. *Decides* to guarantee the inviolability of the above-mentioned international boundary and to take, as appropriate, all necessary measures to that end in accordance with the Charter of the United Nations;

B

* * *

6. *Notes* that as soon as the Secretary–General notifies the Security Council of the completion of the deployment of the United Nations ob-

server unit, the conditions will be established for the Member States cooperating with Kuwait in accordance with resolution 678 (1990) to bring their military presence in Iraq to an end consistent with resolution 686 (1991);

C

* * *

8. *Decides* that Iraq shall unconditionally accept the destruction, removal, or rendering harmless, under international supervision, of:

(a) All chemical and biological weapons and all stocks of agents and all related subsystems and components and all research, development, support and manufacturing facilities;

(b) All ballistic missiles with a range greater than one hundred and fifty kilometers, and related major parts and repair and production facilities;

9. *Decides*, for the implementation of paragraph 8, the following:

(a) Iraq shall * * * agree to urgent, on-site inspection as specified below;

(b) The Secretary–General * * * shall develop * * * a plan calling for the completion of the following acts * * *:

(i) The forming of a Special Commission, which shall carry out immediate on-site inspection of Iraq's biological, chemical and missile capabilities * * *;

(ii) The yielding by Iraq of possession to the Special Commission for destruction, removal or rendering harmless, taking into account the requirements of public safety, of all items specified under paragraph 8(a) above, including items at the additional locations designated by the Special Commission under paragraph 9(b)(i) above and the destruction by Iraq, under the supervision of the Special Commission, of all its missile capabilities, including launchers, as specified under paragraph 8(b) above;

* * *

10. *Decides* that Iraq shall unconditionally undertake not to use, develop, construct or acquire any of the items specified in paragraphs 8 and 9 above and requests the Secretary–General, in consultation with the Special Commission, to develop a plan for the future ongoing monitoring and verification of Iraq's compliance with this paragraph, to be submitted to the Security Council for approval within one hundred and twenty days of the passage of this resolution;

* * *

12. *Decides* that Iraq shall unconditionally agree not to acquire or develop nuclear weapons or nuclear-weapon-usable material or any subsystems or components or any research, development, support or manufacturing facilities related to the above; * * * [and] to accept, in accordance with the arrangements provided for in paragraph 13 below, urgent on-site inspection and the destruction, removal or rendering harmless as appropriate of all items specified above; and to accept the plan discussed in paragraph 13 below for the future ongoing monitoring and verification of its compliance with these undertakings;

* * *

14. *Takes note* that the actions to be taken by Iraq in paragraphs [8–13] of the present resolution represent steps towards the goal of establishing in the Middle East a zone free from weapons of mass destruction and all missiles for their delivery and the objective of a global ban on chemical weapons;

* * *

H

32. *Requires* Iraq to inform the Council that it will not commit or support any act of international terrorism or allow any organization directed towards commission of such acts to operate within its territory and to condemn unequivocally and renounce all acts, methods and practices of terrorism;

I

33. *Declares* that, upon official notification by Iraq to the Secretary–General and to the Security Council of its acceptance of the above provisions, a formal cease-fire is effective between Iraq and Kuwait and the Member States cooperating with Kuwait in accordance with resolution 678 (1990);

34. *Decides* to remain seized of the matter and to take such further steps as may be required for the implementation of the present resolution and to secure peace and security in the area.

UNITED NATIONS SECURITY COUNCIL RESOLUTION 1441

[Adopted unanimously on 8 November 2002 at the 4644th meeting of the Security Council.]

The Security Council,

Recalling all its previous relevant resolutions, in particular its resolutions 661 (1990) of 6 August 1990, 678 (1990) of 29 November 1990, 686 (1991) of 2 March 1991, 687 (1991) of 3 April 1991, 688 (1991) of 5 April 1991, 707 (1991) of 15 August 1991, 715 (1991) of 11 October 1991, 986 (1995) of 14 April 1995, and 1284 (1999) of 17 December 1999, and all the relevant statements of its President;

* * *

Recognizing the threat Iraq's noncompliance with Council resolutions and proliferation of weapons of mass destruction and long-range missiles poses to international peace and security,

Recalling that its resolution 678 (1990) authorized Member States to use all necessary means to uphold and implement its resolution 660 (1990) of 2 August 1990 and all relevant resolutions subsequent to Resolution 660 (1990) and to restore international peace and security in the area;

* * *

Deploring the fact that Iraq has not provided an accurate, full, final, and complete disclosure, as required by resolution 687 (1991), of all aspects of its programmes to develop weapons of mass destruction and ballistic missiles with a range greater than one hundred and fifty kilometres, and of all holdings of such weapons, their components and production facilities and locations, as well as all other nuclear programmes, including any which it claims are for purposes not related to nuclear-weapons-usable material,

Deploring further that Iraq repeatedly obstructed immediate, unconditional, and unrestricted access to sites designated by the United Nations Special Commission (UNSCOM) and the International Atomic Energy Agency (IAEA), failed to cooperate fully and unconditionally with UNSCOM and IAEA weapons inspectors, as required by resolution 687 (1991), and ultimately ceased all cooperation with UNSCOM and the IAEA in 1998,

Deploring the absence, since December 1998, in Iraq of international monitoring, inspection, and verification, as required by relevant resolutions, of weapons of mass destruction and ballistic missiles, in spite of the Council's repeated demands that Iraq provide immediate, unconditional, and unrestricted access to the United Nations Monitoring, Verification and Inspection Commission (UNMOVIC), established in resolution 1284 (1999) as the successor organization to UNSCOM, and the IAEA, and regretting the consequent prolonging of the crisis in the region and the suffering of the Iraqi people,

Deploring also that the Government of Iraq has failed to comply with its commitments pursuant to resolution 687 (1991) with regard to terrorism, pursuant to resolution 688 (1991) to end repression of its civilian population and to provide access by international humanitarian organizations to all those in need of assistance in Iraq * * *,

Recalling that in its resolution 687 (1991) the Council declared that a ceasefire would be based on acceptance by Iraq of the provisions of that resolution, including the obligations on Iraq contained therein,

* * *

Reaffirming the commitment of all Member States to the sovereignty and territorial integrity of Iraq, Kuwait, and the neighbouring States,

* * *

Determined to secure full compliance with its decisions,

Acting under Chapter VII of the Charter of the United Nations,

1. *Decides* that Iraq has been and remains in material breach of its obligations under relevant resolutions, including resolution 687 (1991), in particular through Iraq's failure to cooperate with United Nations inspectors and the IAEA * * *;

2. *Decides*, while acknowledging paragraph 1 above, to afford Iraq, by this resolution, a final opportunity to comply with its disarmament obligations under relevant resolutions of the Council * * *;

3. *Decides* that, in order to begin to comply with its disarmament obligations, in addition to submitting the required biannual declarations, the Government of Iraq shall provide to UNMOVIC, the IAEA, and the Council, not later than 30 days from the date of this resolution, a currently accurate, full, and complete declaration of all aspects of its programmes to develop chemical, biological, and nuclear weapons, ballistic missiles, and other delivery systems such as unmanned aerial vehicles and dispersal systems designed for use on aircraft, including any holdings and precise locations of such weapons, components, subcomponents, stocks of agents, and related material and equipment, the locations and work of its research, development and production facilities, as well as all other chemical, biological, and nuclear programmes, including any which it claims are for purposes not related to weapon production or material;

4. *Decides* that false statements or omissions in the declarations submitted by Iraq pursuant to this resolution and failure by Iraq at any time to comply with, and cooperate fully in the implementation of, this resolution shall constitute a further material breach of Iraq's obligations and will be reported to the Council for assessment in accordance with paragraphs 11 and 12 below * * *;

* * *

9. *Requests* the Secretary General immediately to notify Iraq of this resolution, which is binding on Iraq; demands that Iraq confirm within
seven days of that notification its intention to comply fully with this
resolution; and demands further that Iraq cooperate immediately, unconditionally, and actively with UNMOVIC and the IAEA * * *;

* * *

11. *Directs* the Executive Chairman of UNMOVIC and the Director General of the IAEA to report immediately to the Council any interference
by Iraq with inspection activities, as well as any failure by Iraq to
comply with its disarmament obligations, including its obligations regarding inspections under this resolution;

12. *Decides* to convene immediately upon receipt of a report in accordance
with paragraphs 4 or 11 above, in order to consider the situation and
the need for full compliance with all of the relevant Council resolutions in order to secure international peace and security;

13. *Recalls*, in that context, that the Council has repeatedly warned Iraq
that it will face serious consequences as a result of its continued violations of its obligations;

14. *Decides* to remain seized of the matter.

The major arguments for and against the legality of the invasion of Iraq
are laid out in the following articles.

In reading Frederic Kirgis' analysis, you will be called on to think about
how Security Council resolutions differ from other sources of international law that we have studied so far. We will look at these sources again in
Chapter VIII; for now, consider how the nature of these resolutions fits
into Kirgis' analysis. What shortcomings can you see with each of the two
major points raised by him?

FREDERIC L. KIRGIS, SECURITY COUNCIL RESOLUTION 1441 ON IRAQ'S FINAL OPPORTUNITY TO COMPLY WITH DISARMAMENT OBLIGATIONS

American Soc'y Int'l Law Insights (November 2002)

The United Nations Security Council, in Resolution 1441 (November 8,
2002), unanimously deplored Iraq's lack of compliance with Resolution
687 (1991) on inspection, disarmament and renunciation of terrorism in
Iraq, and went on to make several decisions under Chapter VII of the
U.N. Charter. Resolution 687, like Resolution 1441, was adopted under
Chapter VII. Chapter VII gives the Council the authority to determine

the existence of a threat to the peace, breach of the peace or act of aggression, and to take action accordingly.

In paragraph 1 of Resolution 1441, the Council decided that "Iraq has been and remains in material breach of its obligations" under relevant resolutions, including Resolution 687, in particular through Iraq's failure to cooperate with authorized inspectors and its failure to disarm in several respects, including destroying all chemical and biological weapons and placing all of its nuclear-weapons-usable materials under the control of the International Atomic Energy Agency (IAEA). The Council decided to afford Iraq "a final opportunity to comply with its disarmament obligations under relevant resolutions." Resolution 1441 then sets up an enhanced inspection regime and orders Iraq to submit "a currently accurate, full, and complete declaration of all aspects of its programmes to develop chemical, biological, and nuclear weapons, ballistic missiles, and other delivery systems * * *."

* * *

The U.N. Charter obligates all member states to comply with Security Council resolutions adopted under Chapter VII. Consequently, such resolutions are similar to (but not exactly the same as) multilateral treaties in that they are binding instruments under international law. The language of "material breach" in Resolution 1441 is keyed to Article 60 of the Vienna Convention on the Law of Treaties, which is the authoritative statement of international law regarding material breaches of treaties. Under Article 60 of the Vienna Convention, a material breach is an unjustified repudiation of a treaty or the violation of a provision essential to the accomplishment of the object or purpose of a treaty. Article 60 provides that a party specially affected by a material breach of a multilateral treaty may invoke it as a ground for suspending the operation of the treaty in whole or in part in the relations between itself and the defaulting state. Article 60 also provides that any non-breaching party may suspend the operation of a multilateral treaty if the treaty is of such a character that a material breach by one party "radically changes the position of every party with respect to the further performance of its obligations under the treaty."

When the Security Council asserted in paragraph 1 of Resolution 1441 that Iraq is in material breach of its obligations under relevant resolutions, including Resolution 687, it appears to have treated those resolutions as being sufficiently like multilateral treaties to be subject to Article 60 of the Vienna Convention. Alternatively, since the U.N. Charter says that Security Council decisions embodied in Chapter VII resolutions are binding on all members, a material breach of such a resolution by a U.N. member state (such as Iraq) would be a material breach of the Charter itself. Since the Charter is a multilateral treaty, Article 60 of the Vienna Convention would apply directly to any material breach of it.

Security Council Resolution 687, adopted at the end of the Gulf War, includes a provision declaring a formal cease-fire between Iraq, Kuwait and the member states (such as the United States) cooperating with Kuwait in accordance with Resolution 678 (1990). Resolution 678 authorized member states to use all necessary means to restore international peace and security in the area, and thus provided the basis under international law for the allies' military action in the Gulf War. The determination in Resolution 1441 that Iraq is already in material breach of its obligations under Resolution 687 provides a basis for the decision in paragraph 4 (above) of Resolution 1441 that any further lack of cooperation by Iraq will be a further material breach. If Iraq, having confirmed its intention to comply with Resolution 1441, then fails to cooperate fully with the inspectors, it would open the way to an argument by any specially affected state that it could suspend the operation of the cease-fire provision in Resolution 687 and rely again on Resolution 678. It might also invite an argument that any party to the U.N. Charter could suspend the operation of the cease-fire provision because the material breach would pose a threat to international peace and security and would therefore radically change the position of all U.N. member states under Resolution 687. The argument would point out that the breach would relate to weapons or materials capable of mass destruction that, if put to use, could have an impact not just on regional security, but on worldwide security.

The United States could argue that it is a specially affected state because it is the most prominent target of terrorism, and Iraq's noncooperation presumably would stem from its intent to develop or retain terrorist capabilities that would likely be directed at U.S. interests. Some other states could be expected to argue, though, that Resolutions 678 and 687 were aimed primarily at neutralizing any viable threat of Iraqi military action directed against other Middle Eastern states, so a violation of Resolution 687 and related resolutions would not "specially affect" the United States. But if the violation poses a broad threat to international peace and security, the United States (and any other like-minded state) might assert that every U.N. member state's position under Resolution 687 has been radically changed, as outlined above. The counter-argument would be that even if the breach constitutes a threat to the peace, it would not radically change the position of "every party" to the U.N. Charter with respect to its obligations under the resolution.

In any event, the terms of Resolution 1441, paragraph 4 (above), make it clear that a failure of Iraq to cooperate, if reported to the Security Council, would not justify either the United States' or any other state's unilateral suspension of the cease-fire provision without giving the Security Council an opportunity to consider the situation and to act under paragraph 12. Resolution 1441, however, does not specify what is to happen if the Security Council convenes under paragraph 12, but does not take action or only takes action that some states, in particular a specially affected state, do not consider adequate under the circumstances. Nor does Resolution 1441 specify what is to happen if a specially affected state at some point concludes that Iraq is not cooperating fully, but the inspectors disagree and thus do not at that point contemplate making a report to the Council under paragraph 4. In such circumstances, the United States and its allies could argue that a material breach has occurred and nothing stands in the way of their suspension of the cease-fire that was based on Resolution 687. They would further argue that, since Resolution 678 (the resolution that authorized member states to take action against Iraq in the first place) has never been rescinded, it provides continuing authority to use "all necessary means to restore international peace and security in the area."

Other states could argue that since the Security Council has decided in Resolution 1441 that certain conduct by Iraq amounts to a material breach, but the Council did not at the same time suspend its own cease-fire and instead decided to give Iraq another chance to comply with its obligations under Resolution 687, only the Council can decide later that Iraq has not cooperated fully in the implementation of Resolution 1441 and that the cease-fire consequently is no longer in force. For example, the representative of Mexico (a current member of the Security Council) said after the vote on Resolution 1441 that the use of force is only valid as a last resort and with prior, explicit authorization from the Council. Mexico does not stand alone in taking that position. It is based on the Charter-based principle that disputes should be settled peacefully, and that only the Security Council can determine when there is a need for coercion. It would be argued that, in light of the emphasis in the Charter on peaceful dispute settlement, Resolution 678 could not be used as an authorization for the use of force after twelve years of cease fire, unless the Security Council says so.

There is some support for the position of Mexico and like-minded states, stemming from the negotiating history of Resolution 1441. The U.S. draft resolution, in paragraph 12 on the reconvening of the Security Council upon receipt of a report of Iraqi noncompliance, said that the purpose would be "to restore international peace and security." As noted above, paragraph 12 as adopted by the Council says that the purpose is "to secure international peace and security." The substitution of "secure" for "restore" departs not only from the language proposed by the United States, but also from the language quoted above from Resolution 678. It could imply that the situation now is not the same as it was in 1990, when Resolution 678 was adopted.

The position of Mexico and like-minded states does not regard paragraph 13 of Resolution 1441 (repeating the Council's warnings to Iraq that it will face "serious consequences" as a result of its continued violations of its obligations) as an explicit authorization of the use of force. The United States might reply that paragraph 13 does authorize the use of force if the Security Council fails to achieve its goals in Iraq, because of the widespread understanding of what is meant by "serious consequences." Paragraph 13, however, is in the form of a reminder rather than an authorization for action.

Finally, the United States government has argued, wholly apart from Resolution 1441, that it has a right of pre-emptive self defense to protect itself from terrorism fomented by Iraq. For discussion of pre-emptive self-defense in the terrorism context, see the ASIL Insight, "Pre-emptive Action to Forestall Terrorism" (June 2002).

———————

The following two articles tackle more specific substantive questions pertaining to the legality of the U.S.-led invasion. What are the main issues? What arguments do William Taft and Todd Buchwald present? How does Thomas Franck respond?

WILLIAM H. TAFT IV & TODD F. BUCHWALD, PREEMPTION, IRAQ, AND INTERNATIONAL LAW

97 Am. J. Intl'l Law 557 (2005)

Preemption comes in many forms and what we think of it depends on the circumstances. One state may not strike another merely because the second might someday develop an ability and desire to attack it. Yet few would criticize a strike in the midst of an ongoing war against a second state's program to develop new types of weapons. Between these two examples lie countless fact patterns.

In the end, each use of force must find legitimacy in the facts and circumstances that the state believes have made it necessary. Each should be judged not on abstract concepts, but on the particular events that gave rise to it. While nations must not use preemption as a pretext for aggression, to be for or against preemption in the abstract is a mistake. The use of force preemptively is sometimes lawful and sometimes not.[2]

———————

[2] The National Security Strategy of the United States of America 15 (Sept. 17, 2002), *available at* <http://www.whitehouse.gov/nsc/nss.pdf>. The notion of preemption is inherent in the right of self-defense, recognizing the need to adapt the concept of imminence to the capabilities and objectives of today's adversaries. The use of force preemptively in self-defense is the right of each state and does not require Security Council action. In calculating whether the test of imminence has been met, it would be irresponsible to ignore that these adversaries "rely on acts of terror and, potentially, the use of weapons of mass destruction—weapons that can be *easily concealed, delivered covertly, and used without warning*." *Id.* (emphasis added). In the case of Iraq,

Operation Iraqi Freedom has been criticized as unlawful because it constitutes preemption. This criticism is unfounded. Operation Iraqi Freedom was and is lawful. An otherwise lawful use of force does not become unlawful because it can be characterized as preemption. Operation Iraqi Freedom was conducted in a specific context that frames the way it should be analyzed. This context included the naked aggression by Iraq against its neighbors, its efforts to obtain weapons of mass destruction, its record of having used such weapons, Security Council action under Chapter VII of the United Nations Charter, and continuing Iraqi defiance of the Council's requirements.

On August 2, 1990, Iraq invaded Kuwait. It is easy to forget the wantonness of Iraq's invasion, which was unprovoked and carried out with particular cruelty, and the horror with which the world received news of it. That invasion rightly shaped, forever after, the way the world would look at Saddam Hussein's Iraq; and the United States, its allies and friends, and the international community as a whole came to realize that this was a menace from which the world needed special protection. In the midst of over a dozen years of an essentially ongoing conflict, conducted at different times at different levels of intensity, the Iraqi regime committed itself to comply with conditions that would have brought the story to a close. But it could never bring itself to fulfill its commitments.

Virtually immediately, the Security Council adopted UN Security Council Resolution 660, the first of many resolutions condemning Iraq's actions and demanding withdrawal from Kuwait. Additional Council actions were designed to apply further pressure and bring about Iraq's withdrawal.[3] The Council's actions paralleled steps taken by the United States and others pursuant to the inherent right of collective self-defense recognized in Article 51 of the UN Charter. The United States moved forces to the

---

President Bush made clear that the United States could always proceed in the exercise of its inherent right of self-defense recognized in Article 51 of the United Nations Charter. *See* Report in Connection with Presidential Determination Under Public Law 107–243, *reprinted in* 149 Cong. Rec. H1957, H1958 (daily ed. Mar. 19, 2003) (on resolution authorizing use of force against Iraq).

[3] Among other things, Resolution 661 (Aug. 6, 1990), 29 ILM 1326 (1990), imposed broad sanctions on Iraq; Resolution 662 (Aug. 9, 1990), 29 ILM 1327, decided that Iraq's annexation of Kuwait was "null and void" and demanded that Iraq rescind its actions purporting to annex it; Resolution 664 (Aug. 18, 1990), 29 ILM 1328, reaffirmed those decisions, demanded that Iraq rescind its order that foreign diplomatic and consular missions in Kuwait be closed, facilitate departure and consular access for nationals of third states, and take no action to jeopardize their safety, security, or health; Resolution 665 (Aug. 25, 1990), 29 ILM 1329, called upon member states to use such measures commensurate to the specific circumstances as may be necessary to ensure implementation of trade restrictions; Resolution 667 (Sept. 16, 1990), 29 ILM 1332, demanded that Iraq release foreign nationals that it had abducted; Resolution 670 (Sept. 25, 1990), 29 ILM 1334, imposed restrictions on air traffic; Resolution 674 (Oct. 29, 1990), 29 ILM 1561, invited states to collate and make available to the Council information on grave breaches committed by Iraq; and Resolution 677 (Nov. 28, 1990), 29 ILM 1564, condemned Iraqi attempts to alter Kuwait's demographic composition and destroy the civil records of the legitimate government of Kuwait.

Persian Gulf and then commenced maritime interdiction efforts in response to the Iraqi attack. But Iraq was intransigent.

Eventually, in November 1990, the Council adopted Resolution 678, which authorized the use of "all necessary means" to uphold and implement Resolution 660 and subsequent relevant resolutions, and to restore international peace and security in the area. The resolution provided Iraq with "one final opportunity" to comply with the Council's earlier decisions and authorized the use of force "unless Iraq on or before 15 January 1991 fully implements" the Council's resolutions. It specifically invoked the authority of Chapter VII of the Charter, which permits the Security Council to respond to either a threat to, or a breach of, the peace by authorizing the use of force to maintain or restore international peace and security.

Iraq refused to comply with the resolutions by the January 15 deadline, and coalition forces commenced military operations the next day. Significantly, the Security Council did not make a further determination prior to January 15 as to whether or not Iraq had taken advantage of the "one final opportunity" it had been given two months earlier. Member states made that judgment themselves and relied on the Security Council's November decision as authority to use force.

On April 3, 1991, the Council adopted Resolution 687. That resolution did not return the situation to the status quo ante, the situation that might have existed if Iraq had never invaded Kuwait or if the Council had never acted. Rather, Resolution 687 declared that, upon official Iraqi acceptance of its provisions, a formal cease-fire would take effect, and it imposed several conditions on Iraq, including extensive obligations related to the regime's possession of weapons of mass destruction (WMD). As the Council itself subsequently described it, Resolution 687 provided the "conditions essential to the restoration of peace and security."[7]

The Council's conclusion that these WMD-related conditions were essential is neither surprising in the wake of the history of aggression by the Iraqi regime against its neighbors nor irrelevant to the legal situation faced by the coalition when Operation Iraqi Freedom began in March 2003. The Iraqi regime had demonstrated a willingness to use weapons of mass destruction, including by inflicting massive deaths against civilians in large-scale chemical weapons attacks against its own Kurdish population in the late 1980s, killing thousands. On at least ten occasions, the regime's forces had attacked Iranian and Kurdish targets with combinations of mustard gas and nerve agents through the use of aerial bombs,

---

[7] *See, e.g.*, SC Res. 707 (Aug. 15, 1991). The use of the term "cease-fire" itself carries the connotation that one party is not bound to observe it in the face of violations by the other. Even a more formal armistice is subject to the same qualification, as specifically reflected in Article 40 of the 1907 Hague Regulations Respecting the Laws and Customs of War on Land, annexed to Convention Respecting the Laws and Customs of War on Land, Oct. 18, 1907, 36 Stat. 2277, 1 Bevans 631, which states that "[a]ny serious violation of the armistice by one of the parties gives the other party the right of denouncing it."

rockets, and conventional artillery shells. There was no question that such weapons in the hands of such a regime posed dangers to the countries in the region and elsewhere, including the United States, because of the possibility both of their use by Iraq and of their transfer for use by others. After considering the nature of the threat posed by Iraq, the Council, acting under its Chapter VII authority, established a special set of rules to protect against it.

As a legal matter, a material breach of the conditions that had been essential to the establishment of the cease-fire left the responsibility to member states to enforce those conditions, operating consistently with Resolution 678 to use all necessary means to restore international peace and security in the area. On numerous occasions in response to Iraqi violations of WMD obligations, the Council, through either a formal resolution or a statement by its president, determined that Iraq's actions constituted material breaches, understanding that such a determination authorized resort to force. Indeed, when coalition forces—American, British, and French[10]—used force following such a presidential statement in January 1993, then Secretary–General Boutros-Ghali stated that the

> raid was carried out in accordance with a mandate from the Security Council under resolution 678 (1991), and the motive for the raid was Iraq's violation of that resolution, which concerns the cease-fire. As Secretary–General of the United Nations, I can tell you that the action taken was in accordance with the resolutions of the Security Council and the Charter of the United Nations.[11]

It was on this basis that the United States under President Clinton concluded that the Desert Fox campaign against Iraq in December 1998, following repeated efforts by the Iraqi regime to deny access to weapons inspectors, conformed with the Council's resolutions. To be sure, that campaign did not lack critics, who raised questions about whether further Council action was required to authorize it specifically. Some said that, in the absence of a Council determination that a material breach had occurred, an individual member state or group of states could not decide that a particular set of circumstances constituted a material breach, and there was debate about whether language that the Council had used in the period leading to Desert Fox was equivalent to a determination of material breach.[12] The U.S. view was that whether there had been a materi-

---

[10] Notwithstanding its subsequent challenge to the legality of Operation Iraqi Freedom in 2003, France not only supported the rationale, but authorized its planes to engage as active participants in the 1993 strikes. R. W. Apple, *U.S. and Allied Planes Hit Iraq, Bombing Missile Sites in South in Reply to Hussein's Defiance*, N.Y. Times, Jan. 14, 1993, at A1.

[11] Transcript of Press Conference by Secretary–General, Boutros Boutros-Ghali, Following Diplomatic Press Club Luncheon in Paris on 14 January, UN Doc. SG/SM/4902/Rev.1, at 1 (1993).

[12] Among other things, in March 1998, Resolution 1154 (Mar. 2, 1998), 37 ILM 503 (1998), had warned Iraq that continued violations of its disarmament obligations "would have severest

al breach was an objective fact, and it was not necessary for the Council to so determine or state.[13] The debate about whether a material breach had occurred and who should determine this, however, should not obscure a more important point: all agreed that a Council determination that Iraq had committed a material breach would authorize individual member states to use force to secure compliance with the Council's resolutions.

This was well understood in the negotiations leading to the adoption of Resolution 1441 on November 8, 2002, and, indeed, the importance attached to the use of the phrase "material breach" was the subject of wide public discussion. The understanding of the meaning of the phrase was also reflected in the structure of Resolution 1441 itself. Thus, the preamble contained specific language recognizing the threat that Iraq's noncompliance and proliferation posed to international peace and security, recalling that Resolution 678 had authorized member states to use "all necessary means" to uphold the relevant resolutions and restore international peace and security, and further recalling that Resolution 687 had imposed obligations on Iraq as a necessary step for achieving the stated objective of restoring international peace and security.

After recounting and deploring Iraq's violations at some length, the resolution in operative paragraph 1 removed any doubt that Iraq's actions had constituted material breaches. Specifically, paragraph 1 stated that "Iraq has been and remains in material breach of its obligations under relevant resolutions, including resolution 687 (1991), in particular through Iraq's failure to cooperate with United Nations inspectors and the IAEA, and to complete the actions required under [the WMD and missile provisions] of resolution 687." In adopting the "material breach" language, the resolution established that Iraq's violations of its obligations had crossed the threshold that earlier practice had established for coalition forces to use force consistently with Resolution 678.

---

consequences"; and in November of that year, Resolution 1205 (Nov. 5, 1998), 38 ILM 252 (1999), characterized Iraq's failure to cooperate with inspectors as a "flagrant violation."

[13] The United States noted at the time that previous Council findings removed any doubt that Iraq's actions constituted material breaches. For example, the chargé d'affaires of the U.S. Mission to the United Nations stated:

> Following the liberation of Kuwait from Iraqi occupation in 1991, the Security Council, in its resolution 687 (1991) of 3 April 1991, mandated a ceasefire; but it also imposed a number of essential conditions on Iraq, including the destruction of Iraqi weapons of mass destruction and acceptance by Iraq of United Nations inspections.
>
> * * *
>
> * * * Iraq has repeatedly taken actions which constitute flagrant, material breaches of these provisions. On a number of occasions, the Council has affirmed that similar Iraqi actions constituted such breaches, as well as a threat to international peace and security. *In our view, the Council need not state these conclusions on each occasion.*

Letter Dated 16 December 1998 from the Chargé d'Affaires a.i. of the United States Mission, to the United Nations, UN Doc. S/1998/1181, at 1-2 (emphasis added).

Following this decision that Iraq was in material breach, operative paragraph 2 stated the Council's decision, "while acknowledging paragraph 1 above, to afford Iraq, by this resolution, a final opportunity to comply with its disarmament obligations under relevant resolutions of the Council." The resolution then required Iraq to submit, by December 8, 2002, "a currently accurate, full, and complete declaration" that, among other things, would include information on "all aspects of its programmes to develop chemical, biological, and nuclear weapons, ballistic missiles, and other delivery systems." At the same time, the resolution established a reinforced program of weapons inspections, and demanded that Iraq cooperate "immediately, unconditionally, and actively with UNMOVIC and the IAEA."

Operative paragraph 4 stated the Council's decision that "false statements or omissions in the declarations submitted by Iraq pursuant to this resolution and failure by Iraq at any time to comply with, and cooperate fully in the implementation of, this resolution shall constitute a further material breach of Iraq's obligations." The Council in effect decided that, in view of the past behavior of Iraq, the threat it posed to others, and the fact that the opportunity it was being given to remedy its breaches was a final one, any such violations by Iraq would mean that the use of force to address this threat was consistent with Resolution 678.

No serious argument was put forward in the period following the adoption of Resolution 1441 either that the declaration submitted by Iraq was "currently accurate, full, and complete" or that Iraq had complied with and cooperated fully in the implementation of the resolution.[17] Under Resolution 1441, the Council had already decided that any such failure to cooperate would constitute a further material breach by Iraq.

Even at this point, however, the United States returned the issue to the Council for further consideration. This course was consistent with Resolution 1441, which contemplated certain steps regarding the reporting of violations and consideration by the Council; * * *

Violations of paragraph 4 were in fact reported to the Council, including by Secretary Colin L. Powell, whose comprehensive reports drew on human intelligence, communications intercepts, and overhead imagery regarding Iraq's ongoing efforts to pursue WMD and missile programs and conceal them from United Nations inspectors. And the Council did convene and did consider the situation, as provided by paragraph 12.[21]

---

[17] *See* Report in Connection with Presidential Determination Under Public Law 107–243, *supra* note 1; *see also* note 21 *infra*.

[21] *See, e.g.*, UN Docs. S/PV.4701 (2003), S/PV.4714 (2003). Although reports from the weapons inspectors were not required for the Council to convene and consider the situation under paragraph 12, UNMOVIC Director Blix did report Iraq's failure to comply and cooperate. See the following reports by Hans Blix to the Security Council: UN Doc. S/PV.4692, at 3 (2003) ("Iraq appears not to have come to a genuine acceptance—not even today—of the disarmament that

The Council held numerous formal sessions on this issue. However, nothing in Resolution 1441 required the Council to adopt any further resolution, or other form of approval, to establish the occurrence of the material breach that was the predicate for coalition forces to resort to force. The very careful wording of paragraph 12 reflected this fact clearly. Paragraph 12 contemplated that the Council would "consider" the matter, but specifically stopped short of suggesting a requirement for a further decision. As the British attorney general stated on this point, "Resolution 1441 would in terms have provided that a further decision of the Security Council to sanction force was required if that had been intended. Thus, all that resolution 1441 requires is reporting to and discussion by the Security Council of Iraq's failures, but not an express further decision to authorise force."[22]

The language in paragraph 12 contrasts sharply with language on this point in earlier texts circulated among Council members that would have provided for the Council "to convene immediately, upon reception of a report in accordance with paragraph 8 above, in order to *decide* any measure to ensure full compliance of all its relevant resolutions" (emphasis added). The fact that this language was not included in Resolution 1441 as ultimately adopted shows that the Council decided only that it would consider the matter, but not that it would be necessary for it, or even its purpose, to make a further decision. Rather, the Council had already made the decision that violations described in paragraph 4—"false statements or omissions in the declarations submitted by Iraq pursuant to this resolution and failure by Iraq at any time to comply with, and cooperate fully in the implementation of, this resolution"—would constitute a material breach of Iraq's obligations, and thus authorize the use of force to secure Iraqi compliance with its disarmament obligations.

The similarities in this regard between Resolution 1441 and Resolution 678 are striking. Using the same terminology that it later adopted in Resolution 1441, the Council in Resolution 678 decided to allow Iraq a "final opportunity" to comply with the obligations that the Council had established in previous resolutions. The Council then authorized member states to use force "unless Iraq on or before 15 January 1991 fully implement[ed]" those resolutions. It was clear then that coalition members

---

was demanded of it and that it needs to carry out to win the confidence of the world and to live in peace"); *id.* at 6 (noting that Iraq's declaration included a document from which it had excised a table showing the import of bacterial growth media, and concluding that "absence of this table would appear to be deliberate, as the pages of the resubmitted document were renumbered"); UN Doc. S/PV.4714, at 5 (2003) (Iraqi initiatives in weeks prior to Operation Iraqi Freedom "cannot be said to constitute immediate cooperation, nor do they necessarily cover all areas of relevance").

[22] Lord Goldsmith, *Legal Basis for Use of Force Against Iraq* (Mar. 17, 2003) (statement by UK attorney general in answer to a parliamentary question), *available at* <http://www.labour.org.uk/legalbasis>.

were not required to return for a further Council decision that Iraq had
failed to comply; nor did they do so before commencing military operations. The language of Resolution 1441 tracked the language of Resolution 678, and the resolution operated in the same way to authorize coalition forces to bring Iraq into compliance with its obligations.

What does all this tell us about Iraq and the preemptive use of force? Was
Operation Iraqi Freedom an example of preemptive use of force? Viewed
as the final episode in a conflict initiated more than a dozen years earlier
by Iraq's invasion of Kuwait, it may not seem so. However, in the context
of the Security Council's resolutions, preemption of Iraq's possession and
use of weapons of mass destruction was a principal objective of the coalition forces. A central consideration, at least from the U.S. point of view,
was the risk embodied in allowing the Iraqi regime to defy the international community by pursuing weapons of mass destruction. But do U.S.
actions show a disregard for international law? The answer here is clearly
no. Both the United States and the international community had a firm
basis for using preemptive force in the face of the past actions by Iraq and
the threat that it posed, as seen over a protracted period of time. Preemptive use of force is certainly lawful where, as here, it represents an episode in an ongoing broader conflict initiated—without question—by the
opponent and where, as here, it is consistent with the resolutions of the
Security Council.

THOMAS M. FRANCK, WHAT HAPPENS NOW?
THE UNITED NATIONS AFTER IRAQ
97 Am. J. Int'l Law 607 (2003)

* * *

V.   DID THE IRAQ INVASION VIOLATE THE CHARTER?

Any prognosis regarding the future of world order must begin by addressing the question whether recent events have indeed had a transformative
effect on the law of the international system and, if so, what that transformation portends. As in 1970, one must begin by making a clear-eyed
appraisal of what has been happening. If the invasion of Iraq was nothing
but an act of self-defense by the United States and its allies, or merely an
exercise of police power previously authorized by the Security Council,
these events would serve only to verify the continued efficacy of the Charter system. There would have been no violation of the cardinal principle of
Article 2(4), as that no-first-use pledge is always subordinate to both the
right of self-defense recognized by Article 51 and the right of the Security
Council, under Chapter VII, to authorize action against a threat to the
peace. If, however, the invasion cannot thus be reconciled with the rules

of the Charter, does the invasion of Iraq constitute a simple violation of the rules—one of many and thus of no more legal significance than a holdup of the neighborhood grocery—or should it be celebrated as a deliberate and salutary move toward UN reform? Or should these recent events be understood, more apocalyptically, as the final burial of the Charter's fundamental rules? At this point in our analysis of the systemic significance of these events, it becomes essential to focus not only on facts but also on motives for action. Needless to say, this is swampy terrain; but one must try.

The invasion of Iraq can be positioned in each of these explanatory contexts, but just barely. It can be argued that the invasion was lawful (and thus neither violative nor transformative of the Charter). It can also be argued that, while the attack on Iraq may have been technically illegal, its transformative effect on the law has been wholly benevolent. Finally, it can be argued that these events have repealed a legal regime far beyond its prime and, at last, have ushered in a new doctrine of preventive use of force that is far more responsive to the real dangers of our times.

The argument that recent events have not challenged, or have violated only *de minimis*, the Charter law pertaining to recourse to force is very difficult to sustain, although it enjoys the enthusiastic support of some American academics and the rather less enthusiastic support of State Department lawyers. Abroad, it has been advanced only by the British attorney general, supported by a prominent academic lawyer. As enunciated by Legal Adviser William Howard Taft IV of the Department of State, the argument has two prongs. The first is that the president may, "of course, always use force under international law in self-defense." The problem with that rationale is that, even if it were agreed that the right of self-defense "against an armed attack" (Charter, Art. 51) had come, through practice, to include a right of action against an imminent (as opposed to an actual) armed attack, the facts of the situation that existed in March 2003 are hard to fit within *any* plausible theory of imminence. This was a time, after all, when UN and International Atomic Energy Agency inspectors were actively engaged in situ in an apparently unrestricted search for weapons of mass destruction (WMDs) undertaken with full authorization by the Security Council. Whatever the inspectors did or did not learn about Iraqi WMDs, nothing in their reports lends any credibility to the claim of an imminent threat of armed aggression against anyone. Indeed, the memorandum of the attorney general of the United Kingdom, while supporting the right to use force, wisely omits all reference to this rationale for its exercise.

The second prong of the *de minimis* argument is more sophisticated than the plea to have acted in self-defense. It avers that the attack led by Britain and the United States had already been sanctioned by the Security Council. Essential to the success of this assertion is a creative, and ultimately unsustainable, reading of three Security Council resolutions—678, 687, and 1441—and of their "legislative history." According to Legal Adviser Taft, Resolution 678:

> was the authorization to use force for the Gulf War in January 1991. In April of that year, the Council imposed a series of conditions on Iraq, including most importantly extensive disarmament obligations, as a condition of the ceasefire declared under UNSCR 687. Iraq has "materially breached" these disarmament obligations, and force may again be used under UNSCR 678 to compel Iraqi compliance.

> * * * Just last November, in resolution 1441, the Council unanimously decided that Iraq has been and remains in material breach of its obligation. 1441 then gave Iraq a "final opportunity" to comply, but stated specifically that violations of the obligations, including the obligation to cooperate fully, under 1441 would constitute a further material breach. Iraq has clearly committed such violations and, accordingly, the authority to use force to address Iraq's material breaches is clear.

The British government developed this same thesis, claiming that, by Resolution 678 the Security Council had authorized "Member States to use all necessary means to restore international peace and security in the area" and that, while that authorization "was suspended but not terminated by Security Council resolution (SCR) 687 (1991)," it was "revived by SCR 1441 (2002)."

This version of the meaning and intent of these three resolutions is highly problematic, and appears to have caused the resignation, on a matter of principle, of the deputy legal adviser of the British Foreign Office. Resolution 678 culminated a series of resolutions by the Security Council that condemned Iraq's invasion of Kuwait, called for the immediate withdrawal of the aggressor, imposed mandatory sanctions on Iraq until Kuwaiti sovereignty was restored, and declared the Iraqi annexation of Kuwait to be null and void. In each instance, the purpose of the resolution was solely to liberate Kuwait. Only when these measures failed to secure Iraqi withdrawal did the Council in Resolution 678, citing Chapter VII of the Charter, "authorize[ ] Member States co-operating with the Government of Kuwait * * * to use all necessary means to uphold and implement resolution 660 (1990) and all subsequent relevant resolutions and to restore international peace and security in the area."

This sequence readily demonstrates that the restoration of Kuwaiti sovereignty was the leitmotif of Council action. That the authorization of collective measures by Resolution 678 additionally refers to the restoration of "international peace and security in the area" does not connote some expansive further mandate for contingent action against Iraq at the discretion of any individual member of the coalition of the willing. President

George Bush Sr. acknowledged as much in explaining why the American military had not pursued Saddam Hussein's defeated forces to Baghdad. They were not authorized to do so.

The resolution, however, certainly does signal that Iraq was to be subject to further post-conflict intrusive controls: those imposed by the Council in Resolution 687, as part of the cease-fire. These additional obligations are made binding by reference to Chapter VII of the Charter and they were designed, implemented, and meant to be monitored by the Security Council as a whole, not by any individual member acting at its own pleasure. Resolution 687, sometimes referred to as the "mother of all cease-fires," is not only a binding decision of the Security Council, but also an international agreement between the United Nations and Iraq, made effective only "upon official notification by Iraq to the Secretary–General and to the Security Council of its acceptance" of the provisions set out therein. In legal form, then, as also in substance, this proviso manifests that it is the Security Council and the United Nations, and not individual members, who are the parties, with Iraq, to the cease-fire agreement. It is they who are entitled in law to determine whether Iraq is complying with its commitments to the Council, how long these are to remain in effect, and what is to be done in the event of their violation.

The obligations imposed by Resolution 687 are certainly onerous, and encompass everything that Iraq, thereafter, has been accused of failing to do. Baghdad had to agree to the verified destruction of its weapons of mass destruction and any industrial capacity to produce them, as well as of its medium and long-range delivery systems. Monitoring of compliance, both by a special commission to be created by the Secretary–General and by inspectors of the International Atomic Energy Agency, became mandatory. Baghdad was also required "to inform the Security Council that it will not commit or support any act of international terrorism or allow any organization directed towards commission of such acts to operate within its territory." What if Iraq failed to carry out these commitments to the Council and the United Nations? Clearly, this determination was to be made by the collective security process of the Organization. To ensure such follow-up, the Council, in Resolution 687, was "to remain seized of the matter and to take such further steps as may be required for the implementation of the present resolution and to secure peace and security in the area." *It* would take further steps, *not* individual member states acting without further authorization.

Neither the text nor the debates on the adoption of Resolution 687 reveal the slightest indication that the Council intended to empower any of its members, by themselves, to determine that Iraq was in material breach. Much less can the resolution be read to authorize any state to decide unilaterally to resume military action against Iraq, save in the event of an armed attack. That deduction is supported by the architecture of the

Charter. For the Council to have made a prospective grant of unilateral discretion to states to deploy armed force, in the absence of an actual (or imminent) armed attack, would have been an unprecedented derogation from the strictures of Article 2(4). At the least, to be plausible, such a derogation would have had to be explicit. Moreover, such a delegation of unlimited discretion to individual states cannot be assumed because it could not have been implemented alongside the Council's institution of an extensive system of inspections under *its* authority and control.

The UK attorney general cannot overcome these objections by an unsupported averral that a "material breach of resolution 687 revives the authority to use force under resolution 678." As we have noted, the authority to use force under Resolution 678 extended exclusively to the liberation of Kuwait and to restoring peace and security in the region. In March 2003, the peace and security of the region did not require recourse to force, and the Council plainly did not think otherwise. What the Council thought is crucial. Resolution 687 would not have explicitly reserved sole discretion to the Council "to take such further steps as may be required for [its] implementation" if the Council had simultaneously intended to delegate that function to the sole discretion of member states.

* * *

Perhaps to its credit, the Taft statement does not tread this tortuous path. Instead, it argues that since the Council had recognized several times that Iraq had committed a "material breach" of Resolution 687, recourse to force rested within the sole discretion of each Council member in accordance with the provision of the law of treaties on the consequences of such a "material" violation of obligations. This tack moves the argument away from a parsing of Council resolutions to the Vienna Convention on the Law of Treaties. But it is the United Nations, not the United States, that is the offended "party" to Resolution 687, and thus it is the Council, not the United States, that has the option under the Convention to regard the resolution as voided by Iraq's material breaches. Additionally, even if the United States were regarded as a "party" to the commitments made by Iraq in agreeing to Resolution 687, a material breach would not release Washington, as the offended party, from the obligation under the Vienna Convention "to fulfil any obligation embodied in the treaty to which it would be subject under international law independently of the [materially breached] treaty." That provision, it would appear, places the United States squarely back under the obligation of Charter Article 2(4), which, in the absence of any provision in Resolution 687 to the contrary, must be regarded as an essential part of its legal context and which requires states to abstain from the use of force in the absence either of an armed attack or of prior authorization by the Security Council.

These British and U.S. justifications do not fare well under close examination, however benevolent their intent to demonstrate compliance with the Charter. Consequently, the effect of those nations' unauthorized recourse to force against Iraq must be seen as either revising or undermining the provisions limiting the discretion of states to resort to force.

* * *

———————

Considering the relevant articles of the UN Charter and Security Council Resolutions 660, 678, 687, and 1441, can the invasion of Iraq be justified as a matter of (collective) self-defense? Consider this question in light of the discussion of the *Caroline* Incident below. Can the invasion be justified on the basis that it was authorized by the UN Security Council? Can it be justified as an act of humanitarian intervention?

NOTE ON THE CAROLINE INCIDENT AND THE RIGHT TO ANTICIPATORY SELF-DEFENSE

It is contested whether Article 51 of the UN Charter leaves room for any *anticipatory* self-defense. States have often claimed that it does and have engaged in pre-emptive strikes, and at least sometimes, other states have acquiesced. If there is a right to anticipatory self-defense, however, it is narrowly circumscribed. The conditions were formulated by U.S. Secretary of State Daniel Webster in 1842.

In the late 1830s and early 1840s, Canadian rebels fought the British (then still the governing authority of Canada). The Canadian rebels were helped by some Americans who used a small steamship, the *Caroline*, to bring supplies across the Niagara River. At some point, the *Caroline* was docked on the U.S. side, and a British raiding party crossed the river, set the ship ablaze and sent it adrift over Niagara Falls, killing an American citizen in the process.

The U.S. government protested, but the British claimed that they had acted in self-defense. U.S. Secretary of State Daniel Webster rejected this claim and stated that any (anticipatory) self-defense can be justified only in cases in which its necessity "is instant, overwhelming, and leaving no choice of means and no moment of deliberation." The British government acquiesced, and Webster's formula became widely accepted in international law. (Some scholars argue that it applies to *all* self-defense.)

———————

What does an analysis of the legality of "Operation Iraqi Freedom" tell us more broadly about the strengths and weaknesses of the UN System of Collective Security? Should the system be reformed? In what direction? A

2004 Report published under the auspices of the United Nations tackled, inter alia, those very questions.

A more secure world:
Our shared responsibility

Report of the High-level Panel on Threats Challenges and Change

United Nations 2004

* * *

IX. USING FORCE: RULES AND GUIDELINES

183. The framers of the Charter of the United Nations recognized that force may be necessary for the "prevention and removal of threats to the peace, and for the suppression of acts of aggression or other breaches of the peace." Military force, legally and properly applied, is a vital component of any workable system of collective security, whether defined in the traditional narrow sense or more broadly as we would prefer. But few contemporary policy issues cause more difficulty, or involve higher stakes, than the principles concerning its use and application to individual cases.

184. The maintenance of world peace and security depends importantly on there being a common global understanding, and acceptance, of when the application of force is both legal and legitimate. One of these elements being satisfied without the other will always weaken the international legal order—and thereby put both State and human security at greater risk.

A. THE QUESTION OF LEGALITY

185. The Charter of the United Nations, in Article 2.4, expressly prohibits Member States from using or threatening force against each other, allowing only two exceptions: self-defence under Article 51, and military measures authorized by the Security Council under Chapter VII (and by extension for regional organizations under Chapter VIII) in response to "any threat to the peace, breach of the peace or act of aggression."

186. For the first 44 years of the United Nations, Member States often violated these rules and used military force literally hundreds of times, with a paralysed Security Council passing very few Chapter VII resolutions and Article 51 only rarely providing credible cover. Since the end of

the cold war, however, the yearning for an international system governed by the rule of law has grown. There is little evident international acceptance of the idea of security being best preserved by a balance of power, or by any single—even benignly motivated—superpower.

187. But in seeking to apply the express language of the Charter, three particularly difficult questions arise in practice: first, when a State claims the right to strike preventively, in self-defence, in response to a threat which is not imminent; secondly, when a State appears to be posing an external threat, actual or potential, to other States or people outside its borders, but there is disagreement in the Security Council as to what to do about it; and thirdly, where the threat is primarily internal, to a State's own people.

    1.   ARTICLE 51 OF THE CHARTER OF THE UNITED NATIONS AND SELF-DEFENCE

188. The language of this article is restrictive: "Nothing in the present Charter shall impair the inherent right of individual or collective self-defense if an armed attack occurs against a member of the United Nations, until the Security Council has taken measures to maintain international peace and security." However, a threatened State, according to long established international law, can take military action as long as the threatened attack is *imminent,* no other means would deflect it and the action is proportionate. The problem arises where the threat in question is not imminent but still claimed to be real: for example the acquisition, with allegedly hostile intent, of nuclear weapons-making capability.

189. Can a State, without going to the Security Council, claim in these circumstances the right to act, in anticipatory self-defence, not just pre-emptively (against an imminent or proximate threat) but preventively (against a non-imminent or non-proximate one)? Those who say "yes" argue that the potential harm from some threats (e.g., terrorists armed with a nuclear weapon) is so great that one simply cannot risk waiting until they become imminent, and that less harm may be done (e.g., avoiding a nuclear exchange or radioactive fallout from a reactor destruction) by acting earlier.

190. The short answer is that if there are good arguments for preventive military action, with good evidence to support them, they should be put to the Security Council, which can authorize such action if it chooses to. If it does not so choose, there will be, by definition, time to pursue other strategies, including persuasion, negotiation, deterrence and containment—and to visit again the military option.

191. For those impatient with such a response, the answer must be that, in a world full of perceived potential threats, the risk to the global order and the norm of non-intervention on which it continues to be based is simply too great for the legality of unilateral preventive action, as distinct

from collectively endorsed action, to be accepted. Allowing one to so act is to allow all.

192. We do not favour the rewriting or reinterpretation of Article 51.

2. CHAPTER VII OF THE CHARTER OF THE UNITED NATIONS AND EXTERNAL THREATS

193. In the case of a State posing a threat to other States, people outside its borders or to international order more generally, the language of Chapter VII is inherently broad enough, and has been interpreted broadly enough, to allow the Security Council to approve any coercive action at all, including military action, against a State when it deems this "necessary to maintain or restore international peace and security." That is the case whether the threat is occurring now, in the imminent future or more distant future; whether it involves the State's own actions or those of non-State actors it harbours or supports; or whether it takes the form of an act or omission, an actual or potential act of violence or simply a challenge to the Council's authority.

194. We emphasize that the concerns we expressed about the legality of the preventive use of military force in the case of self-defence under Article 51 are not applicable in the case of collective action authorized under Chapter VII. In the world of the twenty-first century, the international community does have to be concerned about nightmare scenarios combining terrorists, weapons of mass destruction and irresponsible States, and much more besides, which may conceivably justify the use of force, not just reactively but preventively and before a latent threat becomes imminent. The question is not whether such action can be taken: it can, by the Security Council as the international community's collective security voice, at any time it deems that there is a threat to international peace and security. The Council may well need to be prepared to be much more proactive on these issues, taking more decisive action earlier, than it has been in the past.

195. Questions of legality apart, there will be issues of prudence, or legitimacy, about whether such preventive action *should* be taken: crucial among them is whether there is credible evidence of the reality of the threat in question (taking into account both capability and specific intent) and whether the military response is the only reasonable one in the circumstances. We address these issues further below.

196. It may be that some States will always feel that they have the obligation to their own citizens, and the capacity, to do whatever they feel they need to do, unburdened by the constraints of collective Security Council process. But however understandable that approach may have been in the cold war years, when the United Nations was manifestly not operating as an effective collective security system, the world has now changed and expectations about legal compliance are very much higher.

197. One of the reasons why States may want to bypass the Security Council is a lack of confidence in the quality and objectivity of its decision-making. The Council's decisions have often been less than consistent, less than persuasive and less than fully responsive to very real State and human security needs. But the solution is not to reduce the Council to impotence and irrelevance: it is to work from within to reform it, including in the ways we propose in the present report.

198. The Security Council is fully empowered under Chapter VII of the Charter of the United Nations to address the full range of security threats with which States are concerned. The task is not to find alternatives to the Security Council as a source of authority but to make the Council work better than it has.

3.   CHAPTER VII OF THE CHARTER OF THE UNITED NATIONS, INTERNAL THREATS AND THE RESPONSIBILITY TO PROTECT

199. The Charter of the United Nations is not as clear as it could be when it comes to saving lives within countries in situations of mass atrocity. It "reaffirm(s) faith in fundamental human rights" but does not do much to protect them, and Article 2.7 prohibits intervention "in matters which are essentially within the jurisdiction of any State." There has been, as a result, a long-standing argument in the international community between those who insist on a right to intervene in man-made catastrophes and those who argue that the Security Council, for all its powers under Chapter VII to "maintain or restore international security," is prohibited from authorizing any coercive action against sovereign States for whatever happens within their borders.

200. Under the Convention on the Prevention and Punishment of the Crime of Genocide (Genocide Convention), States have agreed that genocide, whether committed in time of peace or in time of war, is a crime under international law which they undertake to prevent and punish. Since then it has been understood that genocide anywhere is a threat to the security of all and should never be tolerated. The principle of non-intervention in internal affairs cannot be used to protect genocidal acts or other atrocities, such as large-scale violations of international humanitarian law or large-scale ethnic cleansing, which can properly be considered a threat to international security and as such provoke action by the Security Council.

201. The successive humanitarian disasters in Somalia, Bosnia and Herzegovina, Rwanda, Kosovo and now Darfur, Sudan, have concentrated attention not on the immunities of sovereign Governments but their responsibilities, both to their own people and to the wider international community. There is a growing recognition that the issue is not the "right to intervene" of any State, but the "responsibility to protect" of *every* State when it comes to people suffering from avoidable catastrophe—mass

murder and rape, ethnic cleansing by forcible expulsion and terror, and deliberate starvation and exposure to disease. And there is a growing acceptance that while sovereign Governments have the primary responsibility to protect their own citizens from such catastrophes, when they are unable or unwilling to do so that responsibility should be taken up by the wider international community—with it spanning a continuum involving prevention, response to violence, if necessary, and rebuilding shattered societies. The primary focus should be on assisting the cessation of violence through mediation and other tools and the protection of people through such measures as the dispatch of humanitarian, human rights and police missions. Force, if it needs to be used, should be deployed as a last resort.

202. The Security Council so far has been neither very consistent nor very effective in dealing with these cases, very often acting too late, too hesitantly or not at all. But step by step, the Council and the wider international community have come to accept that, under Chapter VII and in pursuit of the emerging norm of a collective international responsibility to protect, it can always authorize military action to redress catastrophic internal wrongs if it is prepared to declare that the situation is a "threat to international peace and security," not especially difficult when breaches of international law are involved.

203. We endorse the emerging norm that there is a collective international responsibility to protect, exercisable by the Security Council authorizing military intervention as a last resort, in the event of genocide and other large-scale killing, ethnic cleansing or serious violations of international humanitarian law which sovereign Governments have proved powerless or unwilling to prevent.

* * *

It is easy to agree that it would be desirable, as the panel report puts it, "to make the [Security] Council work better than it has." The real problem, however, is that there are few reasons for optimism in this regard.

Would it help to abolish the veto of the permanent members? Note that if any permanent member's position is determined mainly by its national interest (rather than the global interest in international peace and security), that member can still block any Security Council action and thus virtually disable the System of Collective Security. Would it be better if the Council could decide measures under Chapter VII of the Charter simply by a (perhaps qualified) majority?

Go back and look at Article 2 of the UN Charter. If adopted, how would the last recommendation (Paragraph 203) affect Article 2?

B. REGULATING TRADE:
THE WORLD TRADE ORGANIZATION

SONIA E. ROLLAND, WTO LAW:
AN OVERVIEW[*]

This section offers an introduction to the multilateral trade law regime established around the World Trade Organization (WTO). It first describes the WTO's main features and places the regime in its historical context. This section then presents the cornerstone provisions of WTO law through excerpts of the main governing treaties (with the exception of dispute settlement procedures that are addressed separately in Chapter IX), followed by excerpts of the seminal *"Shrimp–Turtles"* case.

Trade law has developed its own terminology, which sometimes differs from that of general public international law. In fact, the General Agreement on Tariffs and Trade (GATT), the precursor to the current trade system, had initially been thought by some to be a stand-alone and altogether separate regime, and there was a debate whether general international law rules, such as the law of treaties, applied to its interpretation. Today, it is settled that the basic principles of public international law and customary rules of treaty interpretation hold true with respect to WTO law as well.

WHAT DOES THE WORLD TRADE ORGANIZATION DO?

The main objective of the World Trade Organization (WTO) is to reduce impediments to international trade on a multilateral basis by providing a forum for negotiations, a set of binding treaties, and a mandatory and exclusive dispute settlement system.

In the aftermath of World War II, political leaders sought to create an international system that would do away with the economic protectionism witnessed during the 1930s. During that inter-war period, states had enacted trade rules making it very costly to import foreign products. After World War II, this came to be seen as politically and economically harmful, not only to individual countries but also to the international community as a whole. Much as the United Nations Charter envisioned a system of collective security, the Bretton Woods conference of 1944 established a collective economic system with the creation of a network of international economic organizations (the World Bank and the International Monetary Fund in particular). An International Trade Organization for trade, economic development and employment was negotiated in the late 1940s. Its normative underpinnings largely reflected the Keynesian approach to macro-economic governance. It was abandoned, however, after the U.S. Congress failed to ratify its founding treaty as political attention in the

---

[*] This overview was written specifically for inclusion in this casebook.

United States and elsewhere moved to the emerging Cold War. As a substitute, 23 signatory countries devised a multilateral treaty, the General Agreement on Tariffs and Trade (GATT) as a temporary agreement that took effect in 1948, pending the future renegotiation of a multilateral trade organization.

The GATT (which did not create an international organization) enabled member states to negotiate reductions in customs duties (a tax levied on products upon their import as a percentage of their value, generally known as a tariff) and other barriers to trade such as quotas on imports and exports. The GATT remains in effect to this day and has been the cornerstone of the international trading system over the past half century. The basic principle of the GATT was to ban quotas completely and thus to force member states to consolidate all the trade restrictions they wanted to impose into tariffs. "Tariffed" trade restrictions would be relatively transparent and quantifiable, which would allow comparison of the level of trade barriers of different member states. The tariffs could then be negotiated down in an effort to achieve free trade between GATT members. Members could initially impose the level of tariffs they deemed appropriate. The countries that were the most important suppliers of a particular product then negotiated with the main importing countries to reduce the tariff on that product (called a tariff line).

The number of state parties to the GATT (called Contracting Parties) grew quickly, with former colonies joining when they gained their independence in the 1960s and most former Soviet republics joining in the early 1990s. The scope of products and activities regulated by the GATT and related treaties also expanded during that period.

From 1986 to 1994, an extensive round of negotiations (the Uruguay Round) between parties to the GATT (92 in 1986 and 128 by the end of the Round in 1994) resulted in the creation of the World Trade Organization. The WTO is an international organization with a mandatory dispute settlement institution (the Dispute Settlement Body); it acts as an umbrella organization administering a series of treaties. The breadth of matters regulated by the WTO, compounded by its near-global membership, is momentous and possibly unprecedented in international law. The WTO legal system incorporates not only the preexisting GATT but also other treaties regulating various aspects of trade into a consolidated regime. Some of these treaties (like the GATT) are mandatory for all WTO members; others are not. Beyond the traditional areas of trade in goods, the WTO has expanded its ambit to trade in services, and regulation of other domains affecting international trade such as intellectual property, investment and competition, sanitary and phytosanitary measures, and government procurement. Because virtually any type of international activity intersects with trade, it is hotly contested whether the WTO is the appropriate forum for regulating matters such as labor issues, environmental protection, and competition (antitrust). More generally, practitioners and scholars alike have asked where the boundaries of the WTO's regulatory ambit should lie. In these matters, rich, industrialized states and developing countries often find themselves at odds.

First and foremost, the WTO provides a forum for negotiation by its members (currently over 150 countries, including all industrialized states except Russia, almost all developing countries, and two thirds of the UN-listed Least-Developed Countries). However, unlike the United Nations, the organization's own resources, personnel and powers are very limited. Decision-making and participation belong exclusively to the member states acting as a group in the various WTO bodies, especially in the Ministerial Conference and the General Council. Thus, the WTO is often referred to as a "members-driven" organization. With the WTO becoming politically prominent, the organization has begun to move away from its traditionally secretive process meant to protect confidentiality of negotiations towards giving at least some access to non-state actors such as non-governmental organizations. In particular, in the aftermath of the "Shrimp–Turtles" case presented below, the Dispute Settlement Body made it possible for NGOs to submit *amicus* briefs and has even opened some hearings to the public.

Structure of the WTO Agreements and Main Bodies

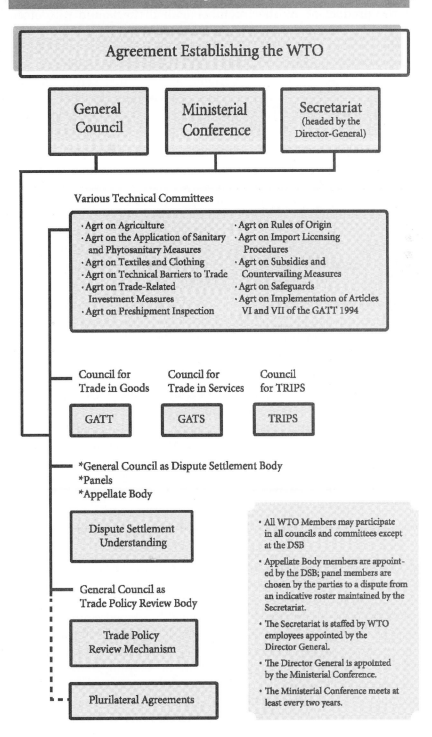

Agreement Establishing the WTO

General Council

Ministerial Conference

Secretariat (headed by the Director-General)

Various Technical Committees

- Agrt on Agriculture
- Agrt on the Application of Sanitary and Phytosanitary Measures
- Agrt on Textiles and Clothing
- Agrt on Technical Barriers to Trade
- Agrt on Trade-Related Investment Measures
- Agrt on Preshipment Inspection
- Agrt on Rules of Origin
- Agrt on Import Licensing Procedures
- Agrt on Subsidies and Countervailing Measures
- Agrt on Safeguards
- Agrt on Implementation of Articles VI and VII of the GATT 1994

Council for Trade in Goods

Council for Trade in Services

Council for TRIPS

GATT

GATS

TRIPS

*General Council as Dispute Settlement Body
*Panels
*Appellate Body

Dispute Settlement Understanding

General Council as Trade Policy Review Body

Trade Policy Review Mechanism

Plurilateral Agreements

- All WTO Members may participate in all councils and committees except at the DSB
- Appellate Body members are appointed by the DSB; panel members are chosen by the parties to a dispute from an indicative roster maintained by the Secretariat.
- The Secretariat is staffed by WTO employees appointed by the Director General.
- The Director General is appointed by the Ministerial Conference.
- The Ministerial Conference meets at least every two years.

The GATT is based on two core principles. The first is the "most favored nation" mechanism. It means that the lowest tariff granted by one member to the product of another member (called the bound rate of duty) is automatically extended to all other GATT members exporting that product to the granting country. This mechanism essentially vests a bilateral negotiation with multilateral effects. Alternatively, members occasionally agree on formulas for tariff reductions to be applied across the board to all products in a given round of trade negotiations. In 1948 the average tariff on industrial goods worldwide was over 40%; today, it is 4.7%. Similarly, quotas on imports and exports largely have been dismantled. The other fundamental principle underpinning the GATT is the "national treatment" obligation. It means that imported products are treated on an equal basis with domestically-produced goods with respect to taxes, regulations and other domestic measures; it thus amounts to a non-discrimination provision for products once they are imported into a country. Most-favored nation and national treatment provisions are found not only in the GATT but also in the General Agreement on Trade in Services (GATS), the Agreement on Trade-Related Aspects of Intellectual Property Rights (TRIPS), and other WTO agreements.

Although the most-favored nation and the national treatment principles are the ground rules on which WTO law operates, several types of exceptions from these principles are built into the system. First, some agreements (the GATT and the GATS) establish a set of general exceptions available to any party to the treaty (see GATT Article XX below).

Second, countries that are part of a regional trade organization (such as the European Union or the North American Free Trade Agreement) may, under certain circumstances, extend more favorable trade conditions to other members of the regional trade organization without having to offer these advantages to other WTO members. (This right accorded to members of regional trade agreements represents a derogation from the most-favored nation clause.) At present, hundreds of such regional trade agreements exist, only some of which meet the conditions to qualify for the derogation, which raises a major challenge to the multilateral trading system.

Third, developing countries have benefited from exceptions and derogations from a number of obligations under the agreements covered by the WTO treaty. The source for these derogations is the so-called Enabling Clause made permanent in 1979. It allows developed countries to extend more favorable access to their market (called trade preferences and consisting in lower tariffs, more favorable quotas, etc.) to developing countries (often former colonies); it also allows developing countries to extend preferences to each other. The usefulness, adequacy and fairness of these exceptions for developing members and many other measures called "special and differential treatment" have increasingly come under criticism, particularly in the current Doha "Development" Round of negotiations initiated in 2001. Other exceptions allow members to take measures in response to particular (and often temporary) economic problems, such as a sudden imbalance of payments or a sudden surge of imported goods at prices lower than fair value (dumping).

As you read the following excerpts from some of the WTO's founding documents, consider how they relate to each other and refer to the organizational chart above. According to the WTO Agreement, what is the object and purpose of the organization and what are the boundaries of its regulatory authority?

AGREEMENT ESTABLISHING THE WORLD TRADE ORGANIZATION
(Adopted 1994; in force 1995)

The *Parties* to this Agreement,

Recognizing that their relations in the field of trade and economic endeavour should be conducted with a view to raising standards of living, ensuring full employment and a large and steadily growing volume of real income and effective demand, and expanding the production of and trade in goods and services, while allowing for the optimal use of the world's resources in accordance with the objective of sustainable development, seeking both to protect and preserve the environment and to enhance the means for doing so in a manner consistent with their respective needs and concerns at different levels of economic development,

Recognizing further that there is need for positive efforts designed to ensure that developing countries, and especially the least developed among them, secure a share in the growth in international trade commensurate with the needs of their economic development,

Being desirous of contributing to these objectives by entering into reciprocal and mutually advantageous arrangements directed to the substantial reduction of tariffs and other barriers to trade and to the elimination of discriminatory treatment in international trade relations,

Resolved, therefore, to develop an integrated, more viable and durable multilateral trading system encompassing the General Agreement on Tariffs and Trade, the results of past trade liberalization efforts, and all of the results of the Uruguay Round of Multilateral Trade Negotiations,

Determined to preserve the basic principles and to further the objectives underlying this multilateral trading system,

Agree as follows:

Article I

Establishment of the Organization

The World Trade Organization (hereinafter referred to as "the WTO") is hereby established.

Article II

Scope of the WTO

1. The WTO shall provide the common institutional framework for the conduct of trade relations among its Members in matters related to the agreements and associated legal instruments included in the Annexes to this Agreement.

* * *

Article IX

Decision–Making

1. The WTO shall continue the practice of decision-making by consensus followed under GATT 1947.[1] Except as otherwise provided, where a decision cannot be arrived at by consensus, the matter at issue shall be decided by voting. At meetings of the Ministerial Conference and the General Council, each Member of the WTO shall have one vote. Where the European Communities exercise their right to vote, they shall have a number of votes equal to the number of their member States which are Members of the WTO. Decisions of the Ministerial Conference and the General Council shall be taken by a majority of the votes cast, unless otherwise provided in this Agreement or in the relevant Multilateral Trade Agreement.

2. The Ministerial Conference and the General Council shall have the exclusive authority to adopt interpretations of this Agreement and of the Multilateral Trade Agreements. In the case of an interpretation of a Multilateral Trade Agreement in Annex 1, they shall exercise their authority on the basis of a recommendation by the Council overseeing the functioning of that Agreement. The decision to adopt an interpretation shall be taken by a three-fourths majority of the Members. This paragraph shall not be used in a manner that would undermine the amendment provisions in Article X.

* * *

---

[1] The body concerned shall be deemed to have decided by consensus on a matter submitted for its consideration, if no Member, present at the meeting when the decision is taken, formally objects to the proposed decision.

The basic WTO agreement establishes the principle of making decisions by consensus. How does that affect the traditional understanding of "pacta sunt servanda"? Is silence sufficient to bind states?

A decision taken by consensus by the General Council in 1995 extends the consensus procedure to decisions on waivers and on accessions that were previously subject to vote only. Is this decision compatible with Article IX.2?

THE GENERAL AGREEMENT ON TARIFFS AND TRADE (GATT)

(Adopted 1994; in force 1995)

Article I

General Most–Favoured–Nation Treatment

1. With respect to customs duties and charges of any kind imposed on or in connection with importation or exportation or imposed on the international transfer of payments for imports or exports, and with respect to the method of levying such duties and charges, and with respect to all rules and formalities in connection with importation and exportation, and with respect to all matters referred to in paragraphs 2 and 4 of Article III, any advantage, favour, privilege or immunity granted by any contracting party to any product originating in or destined for any other country shall be accorded immediately and unconditionally to the like product originating in or destined for the territories of all other contracting parties.

* * *

Article III

National Treatment on Internal Taxation and Regulation

1. The contracting parties recognize that internal taxes and other internal charges, and laws, regulations and requirements affecting the internal sale, offering for sale, purchase, transportation, distribution or use of products, and internal quantitative regulations requiring the mixture, processing or use of products in specified amounts or proportions, should not be applied to imported or domestic products so as to afford protection to domestic production.

2. The products of the territory of any contracting party imported into the territory of any other contracting party shall not be subject, directly or indirectly, to internal taxes or other internal charges of any kind in excess of those applied, directly or indirectly, to like domestic products.

Moreover, no contracting party shall otherwise apply internal taxes or other internal charges to imported or domestic products in a manner contrary to the principles set forth in paragraph 1.

* * *

4. The products of the territory of any contracting party imported into the territory of any other contracting party shall be accorded treatment no less favourable than that accorded to like products of national origin in respect of all laws, regulations and requirements affecting their internal sale, offering for sale, purchase, transportation, distribution or use. The provisions of this paragraph shall not prevent the application of differential internal transportation charges which are based exclusively on the economic operation of the means of transport and not on the nationality of the product.

5. No contracting party shall establish or maintain any internal quantitative regulation relating to the mixture, processing or use of products in specified amounts or proportions which requires, directly or indirectly, that any specified amount or proportion of any product which is the subject of the regulation must be supplied from domestic sources. Moreover, no contracting party shall otherwise apply internal quantitative regulations in a manner contrary to the principles set forth in paragraph 1.

* * *

Article XI

General Elimination of Quantitative Restrictions

1. No prohibitions or restrictions other than duties, taxes or other charges, whether made effective through quotas, import or export licences or other measures, shall be instituted or maintained by any contracting party on the importation of any product of the territory of any other contracting party or on the exportation or sale for export of any product destined for the territory of any other contracting party.

* * *

Article XX

General Exceptions

Subject to the requirement that such measures are not applied in a manner which would constitute a means of arbitrary or unjustifiable discrimination between countries where the same conditions prevail, or a disguised restriction on international trade, nothing in this Agreement shall be construed to prevent the adoption or enforcement by any contracting party of measures:

(a) necessary to protect public morals;

(b) necessary to protect human, animal or plant life or health;

(c) relating to the importations or exportations of gold or silver;

(d) necessary to secure compliance with laws or regulations which are not inconsistent with the provisions of this Agreement, including those relating to customs enforcement, the enforcement of monopolies operated under paragraph 4 of Article II and Article XVII, the protection of patents, trade marks and copyrights, and the prevention of deceptive practices;

(e) relating to the products of prison labour;

(f) imposed for the protection of national treasures of artistic, historic or archaeological value;

(g) relating to the conservation of exhaustible natural resources if such measures are made effective in conjunction with restrictions on domestic production or consumption;

(h) undertaken in pursuance of obligations under any intergovernmental commodity agreement which conforms to criteria submitted to the Contracting Parties and not disapproved by them or which is itself so submitted and not so disapproved;

(i) involving restrictions on exports of domestic materials necessary to ensure essential quantities of such materials to a domestic processing industry during periods when the domestic price of such materials is held below the world price as part of a governmental stabilization plan; *Provided* that such restrictions shall not operate to increase the exports of or the protection afforded to such domestic industry, and shall not depart from the provisions of this Agreement relating to non-discrimination;

(j) essential to the acquisition or distribution of products in general or local short supply * * *.

* * *

The Most-Favored Nation (MFN) and the National Treatment provisions are similar in the GATT, GATS, and TRIPS. How do they operate? The United States, China and India are all parties to the GATT. If the United States wants to foster special trade relations with China and decides to reduce the usual tariff on textile imports only from China, but not from India, does India have a claim against the United States?

GENERAL AGREEMENT ON TRADE IN SERVICES (GATS)

(Adopted 1994; in force 1995)

PART I SCOPE AND DEFINITION

Article I

Scope and Definition

1. This Agreement applies to measures by Members affecting trade in services.

2. For the purposes of this Agreement, trade in services is defined as the supply of a service:

    (a) from the territory of one Member into the territory of any other Member;

    (b) in the territory of one Member to the service consumer of any other Member;

    (c) by a service supplier of one Member, through commercial presence in the territory of any other Member;

    (d) by a service supplier of one Member, through presence of natural persons of a Member in the territory of any other Member.

3. * * *

    (b) "services" includes any service in any sector except services supplied in the exercise of governmental authority;

    (c) "a service supplied in the exercise of governmental authority" means any service which is supplied neither on a commercial basis, nor in competition with one or more service suppliers.

PART II GENERAL OBLIGATIONS AND DISCIPLINES

Article II

Most–Favoured Nation Treatment

1. With respect to any measure covered by this Agreement, each Member shall accord immediately and unconditionally to services and service suppliers of any other Member treatment no less favourable than that it accords to like services and service suppliers of any other country.

* * *

Article XIV

General Exceptions

Subject to the requirement that such measures are not applied in a manner which would constitute a means of arbitrary or unjustifiable discrimination between countries where like conditions prevail, or a disguised restriction on trade in services, nothing in this Agreement shall be construed to prevent the adoption or enforcement by any Member of measures:

(a) necessary to protect public morals or to maintain public order;[5]

(b) necessary to protect human, animal or plant life or health;

(c) necessary to secure compliance with laws or regulations which are not inconsistent with the provisions of this Agreement including those relating to:

  (i) the prevention of deceptive and fraudulent practices or to deal with the effects of a default on services contracts;

  (ii) the protection of the privacy of individuals in relation to the processing and dissemination of personal data and the protection of confidentiality of individual records and accounts;

  (iii) safety;

(d) inconsistent with Article XVII, provided that the difference in treatment is aimed at ensuring the equitable or effective imposition or collection of direct taxes in respect of services or service suppliers of other Members;

(e) inconsistent with Article II, provided that the difference in treatment is the result of an agreement on the avoidance of double taxation or provisions on the avoidance of double taxation in any other international agreement or arrangement by which the Member is bound.

PART III SPECIFIC COMMITMENTS

Article XVI

Market Access

1. With respect to market access through the modes of supply identified in Article I, each Member shall accord services and service suppliers of any other Member treatment no less favourable than that provided for under the terms, limitations and conditions agreed and specified in its Schedule.

2. In sectors where market-access commitments are undertaken, the measures which a Member shall not maintain or adopt either on the basis of a regional subdivision or on the basis of its entire territory, unless otherwise specified in its Schedule, are defined as:

(a) limitations on the number of service suppliers whether in the form of numerical quotas, monopolies, exclusive service suppliers or the requirements of an economic needs test;

---

[5] The public order exception may be invoked only where a genuine and sufficiently serious threat is posed to one of the fundamental interests of society.

(b) limitations on the total value of service transactions or assets in the form of numerical quotas or the requirement of an economic needs test;

(c) limitations on the total number of service operations or on the total quantity of service output expressed in terms of designated numerical units in the form of quotas or the requirement of an economic needs test;

(d) limitations on the total number of natural persons that may be employed in a particular service sector or that a service supplier may employ and who are necessary for, and directly related to, the supply of a specific service in the form of numerical quotas or the requirement of an economic needs test;

(e) measures which restrict or require specific types of legal entity or joint venture through which a service supplier may supply a service; and

(f) limitations on the participation of foreign capital in terms of maximum percentage limit on foreign shareholding or the total value of individual or aggregate foreign investment.

Article XVII

National Treatment

1. In the sectors inscribed in its Schedule, and subject to any conditions and qualifications set out therein, each Member shall accord to services and service suppliers of any other Member, in respect of all measures affecting the supply of services, treatment no less favourable than that it accords to its own like services and service suppliers.

2. A Member may meet the requirement of paragraph 1 by according to services and service suppliers of any other Member, either formally identical treatment or formally different treatment to that it accords to its own like services and service suppliers.

3. Formally identical or formally different treatment shall be considered to be less favourable if it modifies the conditions of competition in favour of services or service suppliers of the Member compared to like services or service suppliers of any other Member.

* * *

—————————

Note that under the GATS, all WTO members are bound by the general obligations, but they are bound by so-called "specific commitments" only for the service sectors they agree to liberalize. For example, the United States can decide not to allow any foreign lawyer to practice law in the United States. However, if it does allow a Canadian national to practice law, then it must allow nationals from other WTO members to do so as well (Most Favored Nation).

If the United States agrees to liberalize the sector of legal services, it becomes subject to the "specific commitment" of Part III. Hence, the United States will not be able to impose additional exams for foreign nationals beyond those required of U.S. nationals on the bar exam (National Treatment). While the United States could notify other states of certain restrictions at the time of liberalizing the service sector (under Article XVI.1.), the United States would not be able to subsequently adopt any additional restrictive measures that violate Article XVI.2.

The Shrimp–Turtles Case

The "Shrimp–Turtles" case is one of the early disputes adjudicated at the WTO. It has become a landmark decision due to its interpretation of GATT Article XX, its position on the interaction between WTO law and public international law (in particular environmental law), and its impact on the opportunity for participation by civil society in WTO dispute proceedings.

Note that the following excerpt, while still long, is heavily edited. The panel decision was over a thousand pages long. Appellate body reports tend to run one hundred to three hundred pages.

In reading the excerpts below focus on two aspects—one of form and the other of substance.

In terms of form, this case is seminal because of the numerous references that the Appellate Body makes to international law provisions external to WTO law in order to interpret GATT obligations. This is a testimony to the integration of trade law into the broader field of public international law. What sources of international law does the Appellate Body refer to in this case?

With regard to substance, the basic dispute involves the consistency between the GATT and a U.S. law imposing certain requirements on the method of catching shrimp that are imported into the United States. What WTO rules are at stake in this dispute? Why does the U.S. law violate the GATT according to the complainants (appellees India, Malaysia, Pakistan and Thailand)? What defense does the United States invoke?

WORLD TRADE ORGANIZATION
APPELLATE BODY

United States— **Import Prohibition of Certain Shrimp** **and Shrimp Products**	AB-1998-4
	Present:
United States, *Appellant* India, Malaysia, Pakistan, Thailand, *Appellees*	Feliciano, Presiding Member Bacchus, Member Lacarte-Muró, Member
Australia, Ecuador, the European Communities, Hong Kong, China, Mexico and Nigeria, *Third Participants*	

I.   INTRODUCTION: STATEMENT OF THE APPEAL

1. This is an appeal by the United States from certain issues of law and legal interpretations in the Panel Report, *United States—Import Prohibition of Certain Shrimp and Shrimp Products*. Following a joint request for consultations by India, Malaysia, Pakistan and Thailand on 8 October 1996, Malaysia and Thailand requested in a communication dated 9 January 1997, and Pakistan asked in a communication dated 30 January 1997, that the Dispute Settlement Body (the "DSB") establish a panel to examine their complaint regarding a prohibition imposed by the United States on the importation of certain shrimp and shrimp products by Section 609 of Public Law 101–162 ("Section 609") and associated regulations and judicial rulings. On 25 February 1997, the DSB established two panels in accordance with these requests and agreed that these panels would be consolidated into a single Panel, pursuant to Article 9 of the *Understanding on Rules and Procedures Governing the Settlement of Disputes* (the "DSU"), with standard terms of reference. On 10 April 1997, the DSB established another panel with standard terms of reference in accordance with a request made by India in a communication dated 25 February 1997, and agreed that this third panel, too, would be merged into the earlier Panel established on 25 February 1997. The Report rendered by the consolidated Panel was circulated to the Members of the World Trade Organization (the "WTO") on 15 May 1998.

2. The relevant factual and regulatory aspects of this dispute are set out in the Panel Report, in particular at paragraphs 2.1–2.16. Here, we outline the United States measure at stake before the Panel and in these appellate proceedings. The United States issued regulations in 1987 pursu-

ant to the Endangered Species Act of 1973 requiring all United States shrimp trawl vessels to use approved Turtle Excluder Devices ("TEDs") or tow-time restrictions in specified areas where there was a significant mortality of sea turtles in shrimp harvesting. These regulations, which became fully effective in 1990, were modified so as to require the use of approved TEDs at all times and in all areas where there is a likelihood that shrimp trawling will interact with sea turtles, with certain limited exceptions.

3. Section 609 was enacted on 21 November 1989. Section 609(a) calls upon the United States Secretary of State, in consultation with the Secretary of Commerce, *inter alia*, to "initiate negotiations as soon as possible for the development of bilateral or multilateral agreements with other nations for the protection and conservation of sea turtles" and to "initiate negotiations as soon as possible with all foreign governments which are engaged in, or which have persons or companies engaged in, commercial fishing operations which, as determined by the Secretary of Commerce, may affect adversely such species of sea turtles, for the purpose of entering into bilateral and multilateral treaties with such countries to protect such species of sea turtles; * * *." Section 609(b)(1) imposed, not later than 1 May 1991, an import ban on shrimp harvested with commercial fishing technology which may adversely affect sea turtles. Section 609(b)(2) provides that the import ban on shrimp will not apply to harvesting nations that are certified. * * *

7. In the Panel Report, the Panel reached the following conclusions:

> In the light of the findings above, we conclude that the import ban on shrimp and shrimp products as applied by the United States on the basis of Section 609 of Public Law 101–162 is not consistent with Article XI:1 of GATT 1994, and cannot be justified under Article XX of GATT 1994.

and made this recommendation:

> The Panel *recommends* that the Dispute Settlement Body request the United States to bring this measure into conformity with its obligations under the WTO Agreement.

8. On 13 July 1998, the United States notified the DSB of its decision to appeal certain issues of law covered in the Panel Report and certain legal interpretations developed by the Panel.* * *

IV. ISSUES RAISED IN THIS APPEAL

98. The issues raised in this appeal by the appellant, the United States, are the following:

* * *

(b) whether the Panel erred in finding that the measure at issue constitutes unjustifiable discrimination between countries where the same conditions prevail and thus is not within the scope of measures permitted under Article XX of the GATT 1994.

* * *

VI. APPRAISING SECTION 609 UNDER ARTICLE XX OF THE GATT 1994

111. We turn to the second issue raised by the appellant, the United States, which is whether the Panel erred in finding that the measure at issue constitutes unjustifiable discrimination between countries where the same conditions prevail and, thus, is not within the scope of measures permitted under Article XX of the GATT 1994.

* * *

123. Having reversed the Panel's legal conclusion that the United States measure at issue "is not within the scope of measures permitted under the chapeau of Article XX," we believe that it is our duty and our responsibility to complete the legal analysis in this case in order to determine whether Section 609 qualifies for justification under Article XX. * * *

B. ARTICLE XX(G): PROVISIONAL JUSTIFICATION OF SECTION 609

125. In claiming justification for its measure, the United States primarily invokes Article XX(g). Justification under Article XX(b) is claimed only in the alternative; that is, the United States suggests that we should look at Article XX(b) only if we find that Section 609 does not fall within the ambit of Article XX(g). We proceed, therefore, to the first tier of the analysis of Section 609 and to our consideration of whether it may be characterized as provisionally justified under the terms of Article XX(g).

126. Paragraph (g) of Article XX covers measures:

relating to the conservation of exhaustible natural resources if such measures are made effective in conjunction with restrictions on domestic production or consumption;

1. "EXHAUSTIBLE NATURAL RESOURCES"

127. We begin with the threshold question of whether Section 609 is a measure concerned with the conservation of "exhaustible natural resources" within the meaning of Article XX(g). The Panel, of course, with its "chapeau-down" approach, did not make a finding on whether the sea turtles that Section 609 is designed to conserve constitute "exhaustible natural resources" for purposes of Article XX(g). In the proceedings before the Panel, however, the parties to the dispute argued this issue vigorously and extensively. India, Pakistan and Thailand contended that a "reasonable interpretation" of the term "exhaustible" is that the term refers to "finite resources such as minerals, rather than biological or renewable

resources." In their view, such finite resources were exhaustible "because there was a limited supply which could and would be depleted unit for unit as the resources were consumed." Moreover, they argued, if "all" natural resources were considered to be exhaustible, the term "exhaustible" would become superfluous. They also referred to the drafting history of Article XX(g), and, in particular, to the mention of minerals, such as manganese, in the context of arguments made by some delegations that "export restrictions" should be permitted for the preservation of scarce natural resources. For its part, Malaysia added that sea turtles, being living creatures, could only be considered under Article XX(b), since Article XX(g) was meant for "nonliving exhaustible natural resources." It followed, according to Malaysia, that the United States cannot invoke both the Article XX(b) and the Article XX(g) exceptions simultaneously.

128. We are not convinced by these arguments. Textually, Article XX(g) is *not* limited to the conservation of "mineral" or "non-living" natural resources. The complainants' principal argument is rooted in the notion that "living" natural resources are "renewable" and therefore cannot be "exhaustible" natural resources. We do not believe that "exhaustible" natural resources and "renewable" natural resources are mutually exclusive. One lesson that modern biological sciences teach us is that living species, though in principle, capable of reproduction and, in that sense, "renewable," are in certain circumstances indeed susceptible of depletion, exhaustion and extinction, frequently because of human activities. Living resources are just as "finite" as petroleum, iron ore and other non-living resources.

129. The words of Article XX(g), "exhaustible natural resources," were actually crafted more than 50 years ago. They must be read by a treaty interpreter in the light of contemporary concerns of the community of nations about the protection and conservation of the environment. While Article XX was not modified in the Uruguay Round, the preamble attached to the *WTO Agreement* shows that the signatories to that Agreement were, in 1994, fully aware of the importance and legitimacy of environmental protection as a goal of national and international policy. The preamble of the *WTO Agreement*—which informs not only the GATT 1994, but also the other covered agreements—explicitly acknowledges "the objective of *sustainable development*" * * *

130. From the perspective embodied in the preamble of the *WTO Agreement*, we note that the generic term "natural resources" in Article XX(g) is not "static" in its content or reference but is rather "by definition, evolutionary." It is, therefore, pertinent to note that modern international conventions and declarations make frequent references to natural resources as embracing both living and non-living resources.

131. Given the recent acknowledgement by the international community of the importance of concerted bilateral or multilateral action to protect living natural resources, and recalling the explicit recognition by WTO Members of the objective of sustainable development in the preamble of the *WTO Agreement*, we believe it is too late in the day to suppose that Article XX(g) of the GATT 1994 may be read as referring only to the conservation of exhaustible mineral or other non-living natural resources. Moreover, two adopted GATT 1947 panel reports previously found fish to be an "exhaustible natural resource" within the meaning of Article XX(g). We hold that, in line with the principle of effectiveness in treaty interpretation, measures to conserve exhaustible natural resources, whether *living* or *non-living*, may fall within Article XX(g).

132. We turn next to the issue of whether the living natural resources sought to be conserved by the measure are "exhaustible" under Article XX(g). That this element is present in respect of the five species of sea turtles here involved appears to be conceded by all the participants and third participants in this case. The exhaustibility of sea turtles would in fact have been very difficult to controvert since all of the seven recognized species of sea turtles are today listed in Appendix 1 of the Convention on International Trade in Endangered Species of Wild Fauna and Flora. The list in Appendix 1 includes "all species *threatened with extinction* which are or may be affected by trade." (emphasis added)

133. Finally, we observe that sea turtles are highly migratory animals, passing in and out of waters subject to the rights of jurisdiction of various coastal states and the high seas. In the Panel Report, the Panel said:

> * * * Information brought to the attention of the Panel, including documented statements from the experts, tends to *confirm the fact that sea turtles, in certain circumstances of their lives, migrate through the waters of several countries and the high sea.* * * * (emphasis added)

The sea turtle species here at stake, i.e., covered by Section 609, are all known to occur in waters over which the United States exercises jurisdiction. Of course, it is not claimed that *all* populations of these species migrate to, or traverse, at one time or another, waters subject to United States jurisdiction. Neither the appellant nor any of the appellees claims any rights of exclusive ownership over the sea turtles, at least not while they are swimming freely in their natural habitat—the oceans. We do not pass upon the question of whether there is an implied jurisdictional limitation in Article XX(g), and if so, the nature or extent of that limitation. We note only that in the specific circumstances of the case before us, there is a sufficient nexus between the migratory and endangered marine populations involved and the United States for purposes of Article XX(g).

134. For all the foregoing reasons, we find that the sea turtles here involved constitute "exhaustible natural resources" for purposes of Article XX(g) of the GATT 1994.

2. "RELATING TO THE CONSERVATION OF [EXHAUSTIBLE NATURAL RESOURCES]"

135. Article XX(g) requires that the measure sought to be justified be one which "relat[es] to" the conservation of exhaustible natural resources. In making this determination, the treaty interpreter essentially looks into the relationship between the measure at stake and the legitimate policy of conserving exhaustible natural resources. It is well to bear in mind that the policy of protecting and conserving the endangered sea turtles here involved is shared by all participants and third participants in this appeal, indeed, by the vast majority of the nations of the world. None of the parties to this dispute question the genuineness of the commitment of the others to that policy.

* * *

137. In the present case, we must examine the relationship between the general structure and design of the measure here at stake, Section 609, and the policy goal it purports to serve, that is, the conservation of sea turtles.

* * *

141. In its general design and structure, therefore, Section 609 is not a simple, blanket prohibition of the importation of shrimp imposed without regard to the consequences (or lack thereof) of the mode of harvesting employed upon the incidental capture and mortality of sea turtles. Focusing on the design of the measure here at stake, it appears to us that Section 609, *cum* implementing guidelines, is not disproportionately wide in its scope and reach in relation to the policy objective of protection and conservation of sea turtle species. The means are, in principle, reasonably related to the ends. The means and ends relationship between Section 609 and the legitimate policy of conserving an exhaustible, and, in fact, endangered species, is observably a close and real one, a relationship that is every bit as substantial as that which we found in *United States–Gasoline* between the EPA baseline establishment rules and the conservation of clean air in the United States.

142. In our view, therefore, Section 609 is a measure "relating to" the conservation of an exhaustible natural resource within the meaning of Article XX(g) of the GATT 1994.

3.   "IF SUCH MEASURES ARE MADE EFFECTIVE IN CONJUNCTION
     WITH RESTRICTIONS ON DOMESTIC PRODUCTION OR CON-
     SUMPTION"

143. In *United States–Gasoline*, we held that the above-captioned clause
of Article XX(g),

> * * * is appropriately read as a requirement that the measures con-
> cerned impose restrictions, not just in respect of imported gasoline
> but also with respect to domestic gasoline. The clause is a require-
> ment of *even-handedness* in the imposition of restrictions, in the
> name of conservation, upon the production or consumption of ex-
> haustible natural resources.

In this case, we need to examine whether the restrictions imposed by Section 609 with respect to imported shrimp are also imposed in respect of
shrimp caught by United States shrimp trawl vessels.

144. We earlier noted that Section 609, enacted in 1989, addresses the
mode of harvesting of imported shrimp only. However, two years earlier,
in 1987, the United States issued regulations pursuant to the Endangered
Species Act requiring all United States shrimp trawl vessels to use approved TEDs, or to restrict the duration of tow-times, in specified areas
where there was significant incidental mortality of sea turtles in shrimp
trawls. These regulations became fully effective in 1990 and were later
modified. They now require United States shrimp trawlers to use approved TEDs "in areas and at times when there is a likelihood of inter-
cepting sea turtles," with certain limited exceptions. Penalties for violation of the Endangered Species Act, or the regulations issued thereunder,
include civil and criminal sanctions. The United States government currently relies on monetary sanctions and civil penalties for enforcement.
The government has the ability to seize shrimp catch from trawl vessels
fishing in United States waters and has done so in cases of egregious violations. We believe that, in principle, Section 609 is an even-handed
measure.

145. Accordingly, we hold that Section 609 is a measure made effective in
conjunction with the restrictions on domestic harvesting of shrimp, as required by Article XX(g).

C.   THE INTRODUCTORY CLAUSES OF ARTICLE XX: CHARACTERIZING
     SECTION 609 UNDER THE CHAPEAU'S STANDARDS

* * *

147. Although provisionally justified under Article XX(g), Section 609, if it
is ultimately to be justified as an exception under Article XX, must also
satisfy the requirements of the introductory clauses—the "chapeau"—of
Article XX, that is,

Article XX

General Exceptions

Subject to the requirement that such measures are *not applied in a manner which would constitute a means of arbitrary or unjustifiable discrimination between countries where the same conditions prevail, or a disguised restriction on international trade*, nothing in this Agreement shall be construed to prevent the adoption or enforcement by any Member of measures: (emphasis added)

We turn, hence, to the task of appraising Section 609, and specifically the manner in which it is applied under the chapeau of Article XX; that is, to the second part of the two-tier analysis required under Article XX.

1.   GENERAL CONSIDERATIONS

148. We begin by noting one of the principal arguments made by the United States in its appellant's submission. The United States argues:

> In context, *an alleged "discrimination between countries where the same conditions prevail" is not "unjustifiable" where the policy goal of the Article XX exception being applied provides a rationale for the justification.* If, for example, a measure is adopted for the purpose of conserving an exhaustible natural resource under Article XX(g), it is relevant whether the conservation goal justifies the discrimination. In this way, the Article XX chapeau guards against the misuse of the Article XX exceptions for the purpose of achieving indirect protection.

> * * *

> [A]n evaluation of whether a measure constitutes "unjustifiable discrimination [between countries] where the same conditions prevail" should take account of *whether differing treatment between countries relates to the policy goal of the applicable Article XX exception. If a measure differentiates between countries based on a rationale legitimately connected with the policy of an Article XX exception*, rather than for protectionist reasons, *the measure does not amount to an abuse of the applicable Article XX exception.* (emphasis added)

149. We believe this argument must be rejected. The policy goal of a measure at issue cannot provide its rationale or justification under the standards of the chapeau of Article XX. The legitimacy of the declared policy objective of the measure, and the relationship of that objective with the measure itself and its general design and structure, are examined under Article XX(g), and the treaty interpreter may then and there declare the measure inconsistent with Article XX(g). If the measure is not held provisionally justified under Article XX(g), it cannot be ultimately justified under the chapeau of Article XX. On the other hand, it does not follow from the fact that a measure falls within the terms of Article XX(g)

that that measure also will necessarily comply with the requirements of the chapeau. To accept the argument of the United States would be to disregard the standards established by the chapeau.

150. We commence the second tier of our analysis with an examination of the ordinary meaning of the words of the chapeau. The precise language of the chapeau requires that a measure not be applied in a manner which would constitute a means of "arbitrary or unjustifiable discrimination between countries where the same conditions prevail" or a "disguised restriction on international trade." There are three standards contained in the chapeau: first, arbitrary discrimination between countries where the same conditions prevail; second, unjustifiable discrimination between countries where the same conditions prevail; and third, a disguised restriction on international trade. In order for a measure to be applied in a manner which would constitute "arbitrary or unjustifiable discrimination between countries where the same conditions prevail," three elements must exist. First, the application of the measure must result in *discrimination*. As we stated in *United States–Gasoline*, the nature and quality of this discrimination is different from the discrimination in the treatment of products which was already found to be inconsistent with one of the substantive obligations of the GATT 1994, such as Articles I, III or XI. Second, the discrimination must be *arbitrary* or *unjustifiable* in character. We will examine this element of *arbitrariness* or *unjustifiability* in detail below. Third, this discrimination must occur *between countries where the same conditions prevail*. In *United States–Gasoline*, we accepted the assumption of the participants in that appeal that such discrimination could occur not only between different exporting Members, but also between exporting Members and the importing Member concerned. Thus, the standards embodied in the language of the chapeau are not only different from the requirements of Article XX(g); they are also different from the standard used in determining that Section 609 is violative of the substantive rules of Article XI:1 of the GATT 1994.

151. In *United States–Gasoline*, we stated that "the purpose and object of the introductory clauses of Article XX is generally the prevention of 'abuse of the exceptions of [Article XX]'." * * *

156. Turning then to the chapeau of Article XX, we consider that it embodies the recognition on the part of WTO Members of the need to maintain a balance of rights and obligations between the right of a Member to invoke one or another of the exceptions of Article XX, specified in paragraphs (a) to (j), on the one hand, and the substantive rights of the other Members under the GATT 1994, on the other hand. Exercise by one Member of its right to invoke an exception, such as Article XX(g), if abused or misused, will, to that extent, erode or render naught the substantive treaty rights in, for example, Article XI:1, of other Members. Similarly, because the GATT 1994 itself makes available the exceptions of

Article XX, in recognition of the legitimate nature of the policies and interests there embodied, the right to invoke one of those exceptions is not to be rendered illusory. The same concept may be expressed from a slightly different angle of vision, thus, a balance must be struck between the *right* of a Member to invoke an exception under Article XX and the *duty* of that same Member to respect the treaty rights of the other Members. To permit one Member to abuse or misuse its right to invoke an exception would be effectively to allow that Member to degrade its own treaty obligations as well as to devalue the treaty rights of other Members. If the abuse or misuse is sufficiently grave or extensive, the Member, in effect, reduces its treaty obligation to a merely facultative one and dissolves its juridical character, and, in so doing, negates altogether the treaty rights of other Members. The chapeau was installed at the head of the list of "General Exceptions" in Article XX to prevent such far-reaching consequences.

* * *

158. The chapeau of Article XX is, in fact, but one expression of the principle of good faith. This principle, at once a general principle of law and a general principle of international law, controls the exercise of rights by states. One application of this general principle, the application widely known as the doctrine of *abus de droit*, prohibits the abusive exercise of a state's rights and enjoins that whenever the assertion of a right "impinges on the field covered by [a] treaty obligation, it must be exercised bona fide, that is to say, reasonably." An abusive exercise by a Member of its own treaty right thus results in a breach of the treaty rights of the other Members and, as well, a violation of the treaty obligation of the Member so acting. Having said this, our task here is to interpret the language of the chapeau, seeking additional interpretative guidance, as appropriate, from the general principles of international law.

* * *

160. With these general considerations in mind, we address now the issue of whether the *application* of the United States measure, although the measure itself falls within the terms of Article XX(g), nevertheless constitutes "a means of arbitrary or unjustifiable discrimination between countries where the same conditions prevail" or "a disguised restriction on international trade." We address, in other words, whether the application of this measure constitutes an abuse or misuse of the provisional justification made available by Article XX(g). We note, preliminarily, that the application of a measure may be characterized as amounting to an abuse or misuse of an exception of Article XX not only when the detailed operating provisions of the measure prescribe the arbitrary or unjustifiable activity, but also where a measure, otherwise fair and just on its face, is actually

applied in an arbitrary or unjustifiable manner. The standards of the chapeau, in our view, project both substantive and procedural requirements.

2. "UNJUSTIFIABLE DISCRIMINATION"

161. We scrutinize first whether Section 609 has been applied in a manner constituting "unjustifiable discrimination between countries where the same conditions prevail." Perhaps the most conspicuous flaw in this measure's application relates to its intended and actual coercive effect on the specific policy decisions made by foreign governments, Members of the WTO. Section 609, in its application, is, in effect, an economic embargo which requires *all other exporting Members*, if they wish to exercise their GATT rights, to adopt *essentially the same* policy (together with an approved enforcement program) as that applied to, and enforced on, United States domestic shrimp trawlers. As enacted by the Congress of the United States, the *statutory* provisions of Section 609(b)(2)(A) and (B) do not, in themselves, *require* that other WTO Members adopt *essentially the same* policies and enforcement practices as the United States. Viewed alone, the statute appears to permit a degree of discretion or flexibility in how the standards for determining comparability might be applied, in practice, to other countries. However, any flexibility that may have been intended by Congress when it enacted the statutory provision has been effectively eliminated in the implementation of that policy through the 1996 Guidelines promulgated by the Department of State and through the practice of the administrators in making certification determinations.

* * *

163. The actual *application* of the measure, through the implementation of the 1996 Guidelines and the regulatory practice of administrators, *requires* other WTO Members to adopt a regulatory program that is not merely *comparable*, but rather *essentially the same*, as that applied to the United States shrimp trawl vessels. Thus, the effect of the application of Section 609 is to establish a rigid and unbending standard by which United States officials determine whether or not countries will be certified, thus granting or refusing other countries the right to export shrimp to the United States. Other specific policies and measures that an exporting country may have adopted for the protection and conservation of sea turtles are not taken into account, in practice, by the administrators making the comparability determination.

164. We understand that the United States also applies a uniform standard throughout its territory, regardless of the particular conditions existing in certain parts of the country. * * * It may be quite acceptable for a government, in adopting and implementing a domestic policy, to adopt a single standard applicable to all its citizens throughout that country.

However, it is not acceptable, in international trade relations, for one WTO Member to use an economic embargo to *require* other Members to adopt essentially the same comprehensive regulatory program, to achieve a certain policy goal, as that in force within that Member's territory, *without* taking into consideration different conditions which may occur in the territories of those other Members.

165. Furthermore, when this dispute was before the Panel and before us, the United States did not permit imports of shrimp harvested by commercial shrimp trawl vessels using TEDs comparable in effectiveness to those required in the United States if those shrimp originated in waters of countries not certified under Section 609. In other words, *shrimp caught using methods identical to those employed in the United States* have been excluded from the United States market solely because they have been caught in waters of *countries that have not been certified by the United States.* The resulting situation is difficult to reconcile with the declared policy objective of protecting and conserving sea turtles. * * * We believe that discrimination results not only when countries in which the same conditions prevail are differently treated, but also when the application of the measure at issue does not allow for any inquiry into the appropriateness of the regulatory program for the conditions prevailing in those exporting countries.

166. Another aspect of the application of Section 609 that bears heavily in any appraisal of justifiable or unjustifiable discrimination is the failure of the United States to engage the appellees, as well as other Members exporting shrimp to the United States, in serious, across-the-board negotiations with the objective of concluding bilateral or multilateral agreements for the protection and conservation of sea turtles, before enforcing the import prohibition against the shrimp exports of those other Members. * * *

172. Clearly, the United States negotiated seriously with some, but not with other Members (including the appellees), that export shrimp to the United States. The effect is plainly discriminatory and, in our view, unjustifiable. * * * As we have emphasized earlier, the policies relating to the necessity for use of particular kinds of TEDs in various maritime areas, and the operating details of these policies, are all shaped by the Department of State, without the participation of the exporting Members. The system and processes of certification are established and administered by the United States agencies alone. The decision-making involved in the grant, denial or withdrawal of certification to the exporting Members, is, accordingly, also unilateral. The unilateral character of the application of Section 609 heightens the disruptive and discriminatory influence of the import prohibition and underscores its unjustifiability.

173. The application of Section 609, through the implementing guidelines together with administrative practice, also resulted in other differential

treatment among various countries desiring certification. Under the 1991 and 1993 Guidelines, to be certifiable, fourteen countries in the wider Caribbean/western Atlantic region had to commit themselves to require the use of TEDs on all commercial shrimp trawling vessels by 1 May 1994. These fourteen countries had a "phase-in" period of three years during which their respective shrimp trawling sectors could adjust to the requirement of the use of TEDs. With respect to all other countries exporting shrimp to the United States (including the appellees, India, Malaysia, Pakistan and Thailand), on 29 December 1995, the United States Court of International Trade directed the Department of State to apply the import ban on a world-wide basis not later than 1 May 1996. On 19 April 1996, the 1996 Guidelines were issued by the Department of State bringing shrimp harvested in *all* foreign countries within the scope of Section 609, effective 1 May 1996. Thus, all countries that were not among the fourteen in the wider Caribbean/western Atlantic region had only four months to implement the requirement of compulsory use of TEDs. We acknowledge that the greatly differing periods for putting into operation the requirement for use of TEDs resulted from decisions of the Court of International Trade. Even so, this does not relieve the United States of the legal consequences of the discriminatory impact of the decisions of that Court. The United States, like all other Members of the WTO and of the general community of states, bears responsibility for acts of all its departments of government, including its judiciary.

* * *

175. Differing treatment of different countries desiring certification is also observable in the differences in the levels of effort made by the United States in transferring the required TED technology to specific countries. Far greater efforts to transfer that technology successfully were made to certain exporting countries—basically the fourteen wider Caribbean/western Atlantic countries cited earlier—than to other exporting countries, including the appellees. * * *

176. When the foregoing differences in the means of application of Section 609 to various shrimp exporting countries are considered in their cumulative effect, we find, and so hold, that those differences in treatment constitute "unjustifiable discrimination" between exporting countries desiring certification in order to gain access to the United States shrimp market within the meaning of the chapeau of Article XX.

3.   "ARBITRARY DISCRIMINATION"

177. We next consider whether Section 609 has been applied in a manner constituting "arbitrary discrimination between countries where the same conditions prevail." We have already observed that Section 609, in its application, imposes a single, rigid and unbending requirement that coun-

tries applying for certification under Section 609(b)(2)(A) and (B) adopt a comprehensive regulatory program that is essentially the same as the United States' program, without inquiring into the appropriateness of that program for the conditions prevailing in the exporting countries. Furthermore, there is little or no flexibility in how officials make the determination for certification pursuant to these provisions. In our view, this rigidity and inflexibility also constitute "arbitrary discrimination" within the meaning of the chapeau.

178. Moreover, the description of the administration of Section 609 provided by the United States in the course of these proceedings highlights certain problematic aspects of the certification processes applied under Section 609(b). With respect to the first type of certification, under Section 609(b)(2)(A) and (B), the 1996 Guidelines set out certain elements of the procedures for acquiring certification, including the requirement to submit documentary evidence of the regulatory program adopted by the applicant country. This certification process also generally includes a visit by United States officials to the applicant country.

* * *

180. * * * [W]ith respect to neither type of certification under Section 609(b)(2) is there a transparent, predictable certification process that is followed by the competent United States government officials. The certification processes under Section 609 consist principally of administrative *ex parte* inquiry or verification by staff of the Office of Marine Conservation in the Department of State with staff of the United States National Marine Fisheries Service. With respect to both types of certification, there is no formal opportunity for an applicant country to be heard, or to respond to any arguments that may be made against it, in the course of the certification process before a decision to grant or to deny certification is made. Moreover, no formal written, reasoned decision, whether of acceptance or rejection, is rendered on applications for either type of certification, whether under Section 609(b)(2)(A) and (B) or under Section 609(b)(2)(C). Countries which are granted certification are included in a list of approved applications published in the Federal Register; however, they are not notified specifically. Countries whose applications are denied also do not receive notice of such denial (other than by omission from the list of approved applications) or of the reasons for the denial. No procedure for review of, or appeal from, a denial of an application is provided.

181. The certification processes followed by the United States thus appear to be singularly informal and casual, and to be conducted in a manner such that these processes could result in the negation of rights of Members. There appears to be no way that exporting Members can be certain whether the terms of Section 609, in particular, the 1996 Guidelines, are being applied in a fair and just manner by the appropriate governmental

agencies of the United States. It appears to us that, effectively, exporting Members applying for certification whose applications are rejected are denied basic fairness and due process, and are discriminated against, *vis-à-vis* those Members which are granted certification.

182. The provisions of Article X:3 of the GATT 1994 bear upon this matter. In our view, Section 609 falls within the "laws, regulations, judicial decisions and administrative rulings of general application" described in Article X:1. Inasmuch as there are due process requirements generally for measures that are otherwise imposed in compliance with WTO obligations, it is only reasonable that rigorous compliance with the fundamental requirements of due process should be required in the application and administration of a measure which purports to be an exception to the treaty obligations of the Member imposing the measure and which effectively results in a suspension *pro hac vice* of the treaty rights of other Members.

183. It is also clear to us that Article X:3 of the GATT 1994 establishes certain minimum standards for transparency and procedural fairness in the administration of trade regulations which, in our view, are not met here. The non-transparent and *ex parte* nature of the internal governmental procedures applied by the competent officials in the Office of Marine Conservation, the Department of State, and the United States National Marine Fisheries Service throughout the certification processes under Section 609, as well as the fact that countries whose applications are denied do not receive formal notice of such denial, nor of the reasons for the denial, and the fact, too, that there is no formal legal procedure for review of, or appeal from, a denial of an application, are all contrary to the spirit, if not the letter, of Article X:3 of the GATT 1994.

184. We find, accordingly, that the United States measure is applied in a manner which amounts to a means not just of "unjustifiable discrimination," but also of "arbitrary discrimination" between countries where the same conditions prevail, contrary to the requirements of the chapeau of Article XX. The measure, therefore, is not entitled to the justifying protection of Article XX of the GATT 1994. Having made this finding, it is not necessary for us to examine also whether the United States measure is applied in a manner that constitutes a "disguised restriction on international trade" under the chapeau of Article XX.

185. In reaching these conclusions, we wish to underscore what we have *not* decided in this appeal. We have *not* decided that the protection and preservation of the environment is of no significance to the Members of the WTO. Clearly, it is. We have *not* decided that the sovereign nations that are Members of the WTO cannot adopt effective measures to protect endangered species, such as sea turtles. Clearly, they can and should. And we have *not* decided that sovereign states should not act together

bilaterally, plurilaterally or multilaterally, either within the WTO or in other international fora, to protect endangered species or to otherwise protect the environment. Clearly, they should and do.

186. What we *have* decided in this appeal is simply this: although the measure of the United States in dispute in this appeal serves an environmental objective that is recognized as legitimate under paragraph (g) of Article XX of the GATT 1994, this measure has been applied by the United States in a manner which constitutes arbitrary and unjustifiable discrimination between Members of the WTO, contrary to the requirements of the chapeau of Article XX. * * *

VII. FINDINGS AND CONCLUSIONS

187. For the reasons set out in this Report, the Appellate Body:

* * *

(b) reverses the Panel's finding that the United States measure at issue is not within the scope of measures permitted under the chapeau of Article XX of the GATT 1994, and

(c) concludes that the United States measure, while qualifying for provisional justification under Article XX(g), fails to meet the requirements of the chapeau of Article XX, and, therefore, is not justified under Article XX of the GATT 1994.

The Appellate Body *recommends* that the DSB request the United States to bring its measure found in the Panel Report to be inconsistent with Article XI of the GATT 1994, and found in this Report to be not justified under Article XX of the GATT 1994, into conformity with the obligations of the United States under that Agreement.

––––––––––––––––

Although the conclusions of the Panel and Appellate Body are formally called "recommendations," they become binding on the parties to the dispute when the Panel and Appellate Body reports are adopted by the Dispute Settlement Body (DSB). The DSB is made up of all of the WTO members and adopts decisions by "reverse consensus." Specifically, a decision is adopted unless all members agree by consensus not to adopt it. Since the party that won the dispute would break the consensus not to adopt, this procedure means that reports are always adopted.

In the *Shrimp–Turtles* case, there is a fundamental difference between the approaches taken by the United States on the one hand and by the Appellate Body on the other. What are those approaches? Do they boil down to unilateralism versus multilateralism? What is the impact of the decision on the sovereignty of the states joining the WTO?

The *Shrimp–Turtles* case also was a turning point in the debate about the role of non-state entities in the WTO's dispute settlement process (as discussed in Chapter VI.3.). In this case, three environmental NGOs submitted briefs, which argued generally in favor of the U.S. measure. A number of WTO members, including India, Malaysia, Thailand and Pakistan, urged the Panel not to consider them. Why do you think they opposed NGO participation?

The issue came to a head with the *Asbestos* case in 2001, which we saw in Chapter VI, where the Appellate Body decided for the first time to invite amicus submissions by any interested party (*European Communities—Measures Affecting Asbestos and Asbestos-Containing Products*, WT/DS135/R, WT/DS135/AB/R (2001)). In more recent years, some dispute settlement proceedings have even been opened to the public, a major departure from the strictly "closed doors" approach of the past six decades.

C. MAKING LAW: THE EUROPEAN UNION

In 1957, six countries (Belgium, France, Germany, Italy, Luxembourg, and the Netherlands) founded the European Economic Community (EEC) in the Treaty of Rome. (In part, they built on earlier associations, especially the European Coal and Steel Community founded in 1953 in the Treaty of Paris.) Their immediate goal was to create a common market; the larger motivation was to establish a basis for friendship and cooperation among Western European states that would prevent another war. In the half century since, the Community has succeeded beyond its founders' expectations, leading to the EU receiving the Nobel Peace Prize in 2012. The organization has grown substantially in four major respects.

First, the original treaty regime has been amended, enlarged and in part replaced by a series of further accords, most importantly the Single European Act of 1987 and the treaties of Maastricht (also called the Treaty of European Union, 1992), Amsterdam (1997), Nice (2000), and Lisbon (2009)[2]. Together, these documents have gradually assumed quasi-constitutional character. The Treaty of Lisbon also includes a binding Charter of Fundamental Rights.[3]

---

[2] The treaty of Lisbon is a "reform treaty" which does not provide an independent text but rather amends previous treaties, in particular the Rome Treaty (Treaty on the European Communities, TEC) and the Maastricht Treaty (Treaty on the European Union, TEU); the Rome Treaty was renamed Treaty on the Functioning of the European Union (TFEU). The entire regime of successive treaties is extremely confusing to outsiders. It helps to make European (Union) Law a field that is both enormously important and very difficult to enter. Confusion is further increased by the fact that consecutive treaties have sometimes renumbered the treaty articles so that references in the older cases and literature no longer match the current numbering.

[3] In 2002, a drafting committee began to work on a "Constitution of Europe" (officially named Treaty Establishing a Constitution for Europe) which, however, became a compilation of existing treaties and other law rather than a new, foundational, document like the U.S. Constitution. The project was completed in 2004. It was spectacularly defeated by popular referenda in

Second, the concept and name of the organization have changed. The Community advanced from the original concept of a merely *economic* community, i.e., a common market, to a much more encompassing *political* union whose goals include, inter alia, common consumer protection, environmental policies, monetary matters and cooperation in the police, judicial, and foreign relations sectors. Reflecting its growing competences, its title changed from European Economic Community (EEC) in 1987 to European Community (EC), and to European Union (which is the term exclusively used since 2009).[4]

Third, the organization has become increasingly integrated. It has grown together in part through the delegation of more and more law-making power from the member states to (first) the Community and (then) the Union, in part through the production of a vast amount of genuine Community/Union law.

Union law consists of six major categories: treaty provisions (often difficult to sort out), regulations (quasi statutes which are directly applicable in the member states), directives (quasi-statutory guidelines which the member states must implement), binding decisions of EU bodies, case law of the European Court of Justice, and "general principles" recognized by that court emanating from the common legal tradition of the member states.

An important element, as well as a symbol, of this integration was the introduction of a common currency (the *Euro*) in 1999–2001, although not all member states have introduced it. That European integration has its limits is also obvious in regard to the Union's external relations: it still has no completely common foreign policy nor does it command a common military force.

Fourth, the number of member states grew steadily from the original six to twenty-seven at present. Since most of the new members are located in Central and Eastern Europe, this has entailed a significant expansion eastwards. The vast majority of European countries are EU members, although Switzerland, Norway and some of the Balkan states remain outside of it. The growth in member state numbers has, of course, led to a growth in total population and market size. The EU's total population is now about 500 million, and in terms of GNP, the EU is the largest economic force in the world today, easily surpassing the United States.

---

two key countries, France and the Netherlands, in 2005 and subsequently abandoned. The defeat reflected the growing unease of Europe's populations with an increasingly centralized, heavily bureaucratized, and ever more intrusive organization lacking transparency, accountability, and, some argued, democratic legitimacy.

[4] From 1994 to 2009, the European Union actually coexisted with the European Community, the former being an umbrella organization (without legal personality) encompassing, inter alia, the latter. The Treaty of Lisbon eliminates the separation between "Union" and "Community," subsuming everything under a single "European Union" with legal personality.

The EU is governed by four major organs. They fit the classic model of separation of powers (legislature, executive, and judiciary) only imperfectly. The *Council of Ministers*[5] consists of member state delegates on the ministerial level and meets in Brussels; it is the major policy-making body and was originally the Community's sole legislative organ. Today, it shares legislative power with the *European Parliament*, which consists of representatives chosen by direct popular election and meets alternately in Brussels and Strasbourg. The *Commission* is a multi-division bureaucracy staffed by officials appointed by the Council in cooperation with the Parliament; it has its seat in Brussels and is best characterized as the EU's executive-political branch. It is, so to speak, the Community's civil service. Its main responsibilities are to propose legislation and to ensure the member states' compliance with EU law. Last, but not least, there is the *Court of Justice of the European Union* (formerly the *European Court of Justice*), which consists of judges from all member states and sits in Luxembourg.[6]

Of all these organs, the Court of Justice has probably been the most influential in promoting the integration of Europe through law. The Court has no general appellate jurisdiction. Instead, its jurisdiction is limited to specific roles listed in the respective treaties. Among the most important categories is the reference procedure provided in the following treaty.

Art. 177 of the Treaty of Rome (Now Article 267 TFEU)

The Court of Justice shall have jurisdiction to give preliminary rulings concerning:

(a) the interpretation of this Treaty

(b) the validity and interpretation of acts of the institutions of the Community;

(c) the interpretation of the statutes of bodies established by an act of the Council, where those statutes so provide.

---

[5] The Council of Ministers must be carefully distinguished from other institutions. One is the European Council which is an organ of the EU and consists of the heads of state or government of the Member States. It has no formal lawmaking power but provides important policy guidelines for the EU. The other institution is the Council of Europe. It is not an organ of the EU at all but rather an international organization much larger than the EU. It is, among other things, the body that created the European Convention of Human Rights. There is some connection, however, between the Council of Europe and the EU: membership in the Council of Europe (and thus in the European Convention of Human Rights) is a minimum requirement for membership in the EU.

[6] Until 1989, i.e., during the period when the decisions reproduced below were rendered, there was only one institution, the European Court of Justice. In 1989, a European Court of First Instance was added. Today, there is a larger entity called the Court of Justice of the European Union. It consists of the General Court (the former Court of First Instance), a Civil Service Tribunal (for internal personnel matters), and the main protagonist, the European Court of Justice (ECJ) as a higher instance. This, again, makes EU law more confusing because now one always has to consider which court decided what and how that relates to earlier decisions when a simpler structure prevailed.

> Where such a question is raised before any court or tribunal of a Member State, that court or tribunal may, if it considers that decision on the question is necessary to enable it to give judgment, request the Court of Justice to give a ruling thereon.
>
> Where any such question is raised in a case pending before a court of tribunal of a Member State, against whose decisions there is no judicial remedy under national law, that court or tribunal shall bring the matter before the Court of Justice.

It was mainly through such "preliminary rulings" that the Court of Justice established the relationship between EC/EU and member state law. The three decisions excerpted below represent three major steps in that process. In reading them, keep in mind that the only article speaking directly to the relationship between EC/EU and member state law was (at the time):

Art. 10 of the Treaty of Rome:

> Member States shall take all appropriate measures, whether general or particular, to ensure fulfilment of the obligations arising out of this Treaty or resulting from action taken by the institutions of the Community. They shall facilitate the achievement of the Community's tasks.
>
> They shall abstain from any measure which could jeopardize the attainment of the objectives of this Treaty.

More than thirty years ago, in a justly celebrated essay, Eric Stein, the principal founder of European Community law as a field of legal scholarship in the United States, wrote:

> Tucked away in the fairyland Duchy of Luxembourg and blessed, until recently, with benign neglect by the powers that be and the mass media, the Court of Justice of the European Communities has fashioned a constitutional framework for a federal-type structure in Europe. From its inception a mere quarter century ago, the Court has construed the European Community Treaties in a constitutional mode rather than employing the traditional international law methodology. Eric Stein, Lawyers, Judges, and the Making of a Transnational Constitution, 75 Am. J. Int'l L. 1 (1981).

It all started with a rather harmless looking dispute in the Netherlands in the early 1960s—*Van Gend & Loos v. Nederlandse administratie der belastingen.*

Van Gend & Loos was importing chemicals from Germany into the Netherlands. When the EEC Treaty entered into force on January 1, 1958, these chemicals were subject to an import duty of 3%. In 1960, the Netherlands ratified a bilateral treaty with Belgium according to which Dutch regulations changed and the import duty rose to 8%. Van Gend & Loos filed objections and eventually sued the relevant Dutch financial authorities (*Nederlandse administratie der belastingen*) before the appropriate tribunal, the *Tariefcommissie.* Van Gend & Loos claimed that the rise in import duty violated Article 12 of the Treaty of Rome which provides that Member States shall refrain from introducing between themselves any new customs duties on imports or exports or any charges having equivalent effect, and from increasing those which they already apply to their trade with each other.

The *Tariefcommissie* suspended the proceedings and, under Article 177 of the EEC Treaty, referred the following two questions to the European Court of Justice:

> 1. Whether Article 12 of the EEC Treaty has direct application within the territory of a Member State, in other words, whether nationals of such a State can, on the basis of the Article in question, lay claim to individual rights which the court must protect, and

> 2. In the event of an affirmative reply, whether the application of an import duty of 8% to the import into the Netherlands by the applicant in the main action * * * represented an unlawful increase within the meaning of Article 12 of the EEC Treaty. * * *

The Dutch, Belgian, and German governments as well the EEC Commission submitted their arguments, and the Court of Justice eventually decided the case.

In reading the following case, note that the text has three main parts. First, the Court lays out the "Arguments and Observations" of the parties. Second, the Court presents the "Opinion of the Advocate General." The Advocate General is an official of the Court who holds the rank of a judge but does not participate in making the decision. While his "Opinion" is thus merely a suggestion of how to decide, it often carries great weight, and reading it helps to understand the reasoning of the Court even if the Court does not follow the suggestion. Finally, there is the actual "Judgment of the Court."

What are the main positions taken by the participating governments and by the Commission? What does the Court's ruling mean for the relationship between Community law and Member State law? How does this relationship compare to the rules normally governing the relationship between a treaty and domestic law?

NV ALGEMENE TRANSPORT–EN EXPEDITIE ONDERNEMING VAN GEND & LOOS V. NETHERLANDS INLAND REVENUE ADMINISTRATION

European Court of Justice
Case 2–26/62, 1963 E.C.R. 585

* * *

11. Pursuant to Article 20 of the Protocol on the Statute of the Court of Justice of the EEC written observations were submitted to the Court by the parties to the main action, by the Government of the Kingdom of Belgium, the Government of the Federal Republic of Germany, the Commission of the EEC and the Government of the Kingdom of the Netherlands.

* * *

II. ARGUMENTS AND OBSERVATIONS

The arguments contained in the observations submitted * * * may be summarized as follows:

A. THE FIRST QUESTION—ADMISSIBILITY

* * *

The *Netherlands Government* disputes whether an alleged infringement of the Treaty by a Member State can be submitted to the judgment of the Court by a procedure other than that laid down by Article 169 or 170,[7] that is to say on the initiative of another Member State or of the Commission. It maintains in particular that the matter cannot be brought before the Court by means of the procedure of reference for a preliminary ruling under Article 177.

The Court, according to the Netherlands Government, cannot, in the context of the present proceedings, decide a problem of this nature, since it

---

[7] Authors' note: these Articles provided:

Article 169: If the Commission considers that a Member State has failed to fulfil an obligation under this Treaty, it shall deliver a reasoned opinion on the matter after giving the State concerned the opportunity to submit its observations.

If the State concerned does not comply with the opinion within the period laid down by the Commission, the latter may bring the matter before the Court of Justice.

Article 170: A Member State which considers that another Member State has failed to fulfil an obligation under this Treaty may bring the matter before the Court of Justice.

Before a Member State brings an action against another Member State for an alleged infringement of an obligation under this Treaty, it shall bring the matter before the Commission.

The Commission shall deliver a reasoned opinion after each of the States concerned has been given the opportunity to submit its own case and its observations on the other party's case both orally and in writing.

If the Commission has not delivered an opinion within three months of date on which the matter was brought before it, the absence of such opinion shall not prevent the matter from being brought before the Court of Justice.

does not relate to the interpretation but to the application of the Treaty in a specific case.

The *Belgian Government* maintains that the first question is a reference to the Court of a problem of constitutional law, which falls exclusively within the jurisdiction of the Netherlands court.

That court is confronted with two international treaties both of which are part of the national law. It must decide under national law—assuming that they are in fact contradictory—which treaty prevails over the other or more exactly whether a prior national law of ratification prevails over a subsequent one.

This is a typical question of national constitutional law which has nothing to do with the interpretation of an Article of the EEC Treaty and is within the exclusive jurisdiction of the Netherlands court, because it can only be answered according to the constitutional principles and jurisprudence of the national law of the Netherlands.

The *Belgian Government* also points out that a decision on the first question referred to the Court is not only unnecessary to enable the Tarief-commissie to give its judgment but cannot even have any influence on the solution to the actual problem which it is asked to resolve.

In fact, whatever answer the Court may give, the Tariefcommissie has to solve the same problem: Has it the right to ignore the law of 16 December 1959 ratifying the Brussels protocol, because it conflicts with an earlier law of 5 December 1957 ratifying the Treaty establishing the EEC?

The question raised is not therefore an appropriate question for a preliminary ruling, since its answer cannot enable the court which has to adjudicate upon the merits of the main action to make a final decision in the proceedings pending before it.

The *Commission of the EEC*, on the other hand, observes that the effect of the provisions of the Treaty on the national law of Member States cannot be determined by the actual national law of each of them but by the Treaty itself. The problem is therefore without doubt one of interpretation of the Treaty.

Further the Commission calls attention to the fact that a finding of inadmissibility would have the paradoxical and shocking result that the rights of individuals would be protected in all cases of infringement of Community law except in the case of an infringement by a Member State.

* * *

According to the Commission an analysis of the legal structure of the Treaty and of the legal system which it establishes shows on the one hand that the Member States did not only intend to undertake mutual commitments but to establish a system of Community law, and on the other hand that they did not wish to withdraw the application of this law from the ordinary jurisdiction of the national courts of law.

However, Community law must be effectively and uniformly applied throughout the whole of the Community.

The result is first that the effect of Community law on the internal law of Member States cannot be determined by this internal law but only by Community law, further that the national courts are bound to apply directly the rules of Community law and finally that the national court is bound to ensure that the rules of Community law prevail over conflicting national laws even if they are passed later.

The Commission observes in this context that the fact that a Community rule is, as regards its form, directed to the states does not of itself take away from individuals who have an interest in it the right to require it to be applied in the national courts.

As regards more particularly the question referred to the Court, the Commission is of the opinion that Article 12 contains a rule of law capable of being effectively applied by the national court.

It is a provision which is perfectly clear in the sense that it creates for Member States a specific unambiguous obligation relating to the extension of their internal law in a matter which directly affects their nationals and it is not affected or qualified by any other provision of the Treaty.

It is also a complete and self-sufficient provision in that it does not require on a Community level any new measure to give concrete form to the obligation which it defines.

The *Netherlands Government* draws a distinction between the question of the internal effect and that of the direct effect (or direct applicability), the first, according to it, being a pre-condition of the second.

It considers that the question whether a particular provision of the Treaty has an internal effect can only be answered in the affirmative, if all the essential elements, namely the intention of the contracting parties and the material terms of the provision under consideration, allows such a conclusion.

With regard to the intention of the parties to the Treaty the Netherlands Government maintains that an examination of the actual wording is sufficient to establish that Article 12 only places an obligation on Member States, who are free to decide how they intend to fulfil its obligation. A comparison with other provisions of the Treaty confirms this finding.

As Article 12 does not have internal effect it cannot, *a fortiori*, have direct effect.

Even if the fact that Article 12 places an obligation on Member States were to be considered as an internal effect, it cannot have direct effect in the sense that it permits the nationals of Member States to assert subjective rights which the courts must protect.

Alternatively the Netherlands Government argues that, so far as the necessary conditions for its direct application are concerned, the EEC Treaty does not differ from a standard international treaty. The conclusive factors in this respect are the intention of the parties and the provisions of the Treaty.

However the question whether under Netherlands constitutional law Article 12 is directly applicable is one concerning the interpretation of Netherlands law and does not come within the jurisdiction of the Court of Justice.

* * *

Opinion of Advocate General Karl Roemer

* * *

II.   The first question

   1.   Admissibility

[The Netherlands and Belgian Governments have thus drawn attention to two points bearing on the admissibility of the first question:]

1. It is not concerned with the interpretation of an Article of the Treaty, but with a problem under Netherlands constitutional law.

2. The answer to the first question has no effect upon the solution of the real difficulties in the Dutch case. Even if an affirmative reply is given to the question, the Netherlands court is still faced with the problem of deciding to which law of ratification (that relating to the EEC Treaty or that relating to the Brussels Agreement) it should give precedence.

* * *

With regard to the question whether the Tariefcommissie has submitted to the Court a problem of Dutch constitutional law the following observations may be made: it seems clear to me that the wording of the first question ("whether Article 12 * * * has direct application") gives the impression that the Court is faced with a task which goes beyond its jurisdiction under Article 177. It is impossible to clarify exhaustively the real legal effects of an international agreement on the nationals of a Member State without having regard to the constitutional law of that Member State.

But, on the other hand, it is clear that the question does not refer exclusively to problems of constitutional law. The effect of an international treaty depends in the first place on the legal force which its authors intended its individual provisions to have, whether they are to be merely programmes or declarations of intent, or obligations to act on the international plane or whether some of them are to have a direct effect on the legal system of Member States. If the examination is limited to this aspect, without reaching a conclusion on the question how national constitutional law incorporates the intended effects of the treaty into the national legal system, it comes within the field of interpretation of the Treaty. In spite of the unfortunate wording of the first question, it is possible to recognize in it an admissible request for an interpretation which the Court can extract without difficulty from the facts put forward and can deal with under Article 177.

* * *

2.   EXAMINATION OF THE FIRST QUESTION

I have already mentioned that the question is not happily phrased. But its meaning appears clear when looked at in the light of the constitutional law of the Netherlands. Article 66 of the Netherlands Constitution—according to its interpretation in cases decided by its courts—gives international agreements precedence over national law, if the provisions of such agreements have a general binding effect, that is, when they are directly applicable ("self-executing"). The question is, therefore, whether it can be inferred from the EEC Treaty that Article 12 has this legal effect or whether it only contains an obligation on the part of Member States not to enact laws to the contrary, the infringement of which would not result in the national laws being ineffective.

* * *

Anyone familiar with Community law knows that in fact it does not just consist of contractual relations between a number of States considered as subjects of the law of nations. The Community has its own institutions, independent of the Member States, endowed with the power to take administrative measures and to make rules of law which directly create rights in favour of and impose duties on Member States as well as their authorities and citizens. This can be clearly deduced from Articles 187, 189, 191 and 192 of the Treaty.

The EEC Treaty contains in addition provisions which are clearly intended to be incorporated in national law and to modify or supplement it. Examples of such provisions are Articles 85 and 86 relating to competition (prohibition of certain agreements, prohibition of the abuse of dominant position in the Common Market States (Article 88)), and the duty of national courts to cooperate with the Community institutions as regards decisions and their enforcement (Articles 177 and 192 of the Treaty; Articles 26 and 27 of the Protocol on the Statute of the Court of Justice). In this connection mention can be made of the provisions which are designed to produce direct effects at a later stage, for example the provisions under the Title of the Treaty devoted to the Free Movement of Persons, Services and Capital (Articles 48 and 60).

But on the other hand it must not be forgotten that many of the Treaty's provisions expressly refer to the obligations of Member States.

* * *

The first conclusion we can draw from this analysis is that large parts of the Treaty clearly contain only obligations of Member States, and do not contain rules having a direct internal effect.

* * *

If we consider the place which Article 12 can occupy in this system, in this range of legal possibilities, it is useful to begin by recalling its wording. It reads as follows:

> Member States shall refrain from introducing between themselves any new customs duties or imports or exports or any charges having equivalent effect and from increasing those which they already apply in their trade with each other.

It seems to me beyond doubt that the form of words chosen—which moreover no one has called into question—no more precludes the assumption of a legal obligation than does the similar wording of other Articles of the Treaty. To give Article 12 a lower legal status would not be in keeping with its importance in the framework of the Treaty. Further, I consider that the implementation of this obligation does not depend on other legal measures of the Community institutions, which allows us in a certain sense to speak of the direct legal effect of Article 12.

However, the crucial issue according to the question raised by the Tariefcommissie is whether this direct effect stops at the Governments of the Member States, or whether it should penetrate into the national legal field and lead to its direct application by the administrative authorities and courts of Member States. It is here that the real difficulties of interpretation begin.

* * *

IV. CONCLUSION

I propose that the Court should restrict its judgment to the first question and hold that Article 12 only contains an obligation on the part of the Member States.

JUDGMENT OF THE COURT OF JUSTICE

* * *

II. THE FIRST QUESTION

A. JURISDICTION OF THE COURT

2. The Government of the Netherlands and the Belgian Government challenge the jurisdiction of the Court on the ground that the reference relates not to the interpretation but to the application of the Treaty in the context of the constitutional law of the Netherlands, and that in particular the Court has no jurisdiction to decide, should the occasion arise, whether the provisions of the EEC Treaty prevail over Netherlands legislation or over other agreements entered into by the Netherlands and incorporated into Dutch national law. The solution of such a problem, it is claimed, falls within the exclusive jurisdiction of the national courts, subject to an application in accordance with the provisions laid down by Articles 169 and 170 of the Treaty.

3. However in this case the Court is not asked to adjudicate upon the application of the Treaty according to the principles of the national law of the Netherlands, which remains the concern of the national courts, but is asked, in conformity with subparagraph (a) of the first paragraph of Article 177 of the Treaty, only to interpret the scope of Article 12 of the said Treaty within the context of Community law and with reference to its effect on individuals. This argument has therefore no legal foundation.

4. The Belgian Government further argues that the Court has no jurisdiction on the ground that no answer which the Court could give to the first question of the Tariefcommissie would have any bearing on the result of the proceedings brought in that court.

5. However, in order to confer jurisdiction on the Court in the present case it is necessary only that the question raised should clearly be concerned with the interpretation of the Treaty. The considerations which may have led a national court or tribunal to its choice of questions as well as the relevance which it attributes to such questions in the context of a case before it are excluded from review by the Court of Justice.

6. It appears from the wording of the questions referred that they relate to the interpretation of the Treaty. The Court therefore has the jurisdiction to answer them.

7. This argument, too, is therefore unfounded.

B. ON THE SUBSTANCE OF THE CASE

8. The first question of the Tariefcommissie is whether Article 12 of the Treaty has direct application in national law in the sense that nationals

of Member States may on the basis of this Article lay claim to rights which the national court must protect.

9. To ascertain whether the provisions of an international treaty extend so far in their effects it is necessary to consider the spirit, the general scheme and the wording of those provisions.

10. The objective of the EEC Treaty, which is to establish a Common Market, the functioning of which is of direct concern to interested parties in the Community, implies that this Treaty is more than an agreement which merely creates mutual obligations between the contracting states. This view is confirmed by the preamble to the Treaty which refers not only to governments but to peoples. It is also confirmed more specifically by the establishment of institutions endowed with sovereign rights, the exercise of which affects Member States and also their citizens. Furthermore, it must be noted that the nationals of the states brought together in the Community are called upon to cooperate in the functioning of this Community through the intermediary of the European Parliament and the Economic and Social Committee.

11. In addition the task assigned to the Court of Justice under Article 177, the object of which is to secure uniform interpretation of the Treaty by national courts and tribunals, confirms that the states have acknowledged that Community law has an authority which can be invoked by their nationals before those courts and tribunals.

12. The conclusion to be drawn from this is that the Community constitutes a new legal order of international law for the benefit of which the states have limited their sovereign rights, albeit within limited fields, and the subjects of which comprise not only Member States but also their nationals. Independently of the legislation of Member States, Community law therefore not only imposes obligations on individuals but is also intended to confer upon them rights which become part of their legal heritage. These rights arise not only where they are expressly granted by the Treaty, but also by reason of obligations which the Treaty imposes in a clearly defined way upon individuals as well as upon the Member States and upon the institutions of the Community.

* * *

14. The wording of Article 12 contains a clear and unconditional prohibition which is not a positive but a negative obligation. This obligation, moreover, is not qualified by any reservation on the part of states which would make its implementation conditional upon a positive legislative measure enacted under national law. The very nature of this prohibition makes it ideally adapted to produce direct effects in the legal relationship between Member States and their subjects.

15. The implementation of Article 12 does not require any legislative intervention on the part of the states. The fact that under this Article it is the Member States who are made the subject of the negative obligation does not imply that their nationals cannot benefit from this obligation.

16. In addition the argument based on Articles 169 and 170 of the Treaty put forward by the three Governments which have submitted observations to the Court in their statements of case is misconceived. The fact that these Articles of the Treaty enable the Commission and the Member States to bring before the Court a State which has not fulfilled its obligations does not mean that individuals cannot plead these obligations, should the occasion arise, before a national court, any more than the fact that the Treaty places at the disposal of the Commission ways of ensuring that obligations imposed upon those subject to the Treaty are observed, precludes the possibility, in actions between individuals before a national court, of pleading infringements of these obligations.

17. A restriction of the guarantees against an infringement of Article 12 by Member States to the procedures under Article 169 and 170 would remove all direct legal protection of the individual rights of their nationals. There is the risk that recourse to the procedure under these Articles would be ineffective if it were to occur after the implementation of a national decision taken contrary to the provisions of the Treaty.

18. The vigilance of individuals concerned to protect their rights amounts to an effective supervision in addition to the supervision entrusted by Articles 169 and 170 to the diligence of the Commission and of the Member States.

19. It follows from the foregoing considerations that, according to the spirit, the general scheme and the wording of the Treaty, Article 12 must be interpreted as producing direct effects and creating individual rights which national courts must protect.

* * *

THE COURT in answer to the questions referred to it for a preliminary ruling by the Tariefcommissie by decision of 16 August 1962, hereby rules:

1. Article 12 of the Treaty establishing the European Economic Community produces direct effects and creates individual rights which national courts must protect.

* * *

The next year, the Court returned to the question of the relationship between Community and Member State law in *Costa v. ENEL.*

In 1962, the Italian Republic nationalized the production and distribution of electric energy and created the *Ente Nazionale per l'Energia Elettrica* (ENEL), a state-owned energy concern. Flaminio Costa, a Milanese attorney, had been a shareholder of one of the nationalized companies and owed ENEL 1,925 lire—at the time about three dollars. He refused to pay and challenged the nationalization statute by taking the government to court in Milan. He argued, inter alia, that the nationalization violated the Italian constitution as well as various provisions in the EEC Treaty.

The Italian judge referred the constitutional question to the Italian Constitutional Court and the EEC law question to the European Court of Justice. The Italian Constitutional Court rejected the challenge and held, inter alia:

> Nor is there any validity to the other argument, according to which the State, once it has agreed to limitations [upon] its own sovereignty, could not pass [a] Law withdrawing such limitations and restoring its freedom of action, without [violating] the Constitution. Against this can be set our foregoing remarks * * * that the violation of a treaty, even if it results in [liability of the State under international law] does not detract from the [internal] validity of [the] conflicting law.

> There is no doubt that the State is bound to honor its obligations, just as there is no doubt that an international treaty is fully effective in so far as a Law has given execution to it. But with regard to such a Law * * * [it is also true that] subsequent laws [must prevail] in accordance with the principles governing the succession of laws in time; it follows that any conflict between the one and the other cannot give rise to [a] constitutional [question].

The European Court of Justice subsequently handed down the following decision. Regarding the relationship between EC/EU law and national law, exactly what does it add to *Van Gend & Loos?*

Flaminio Costa v. E.N.E.L.

European Court of Justice
Case 6/64, 1964 E.C.R. 585

* * *

By order dated 16 January 1964, duly sent to the Court, the Giudice, Conciliatore of Milan, "having regard to Article 177 of the Treaty of 25 March 1957 establishing the EEC," * * * stayed the proceedings and ordered that the file be transmitted to the Court of Justice.

ON THE APPLICATION OF ARTICLE 177

ON THE SUBMISSION REGARDING THE WORKING OF THE QUESTION

The complaint is made that the intention behind the question posed was to obtain, by means of Article 177, a ruling on the compatibility of a national law with the Treaty.

By the terms of this Article, however, national courts against whose decisions, as in the present case, there is no judicial remedy, must refer the matter to the Court of Justice so that a preliminary ruling may be given upon the "interpretation of the Treaty" whenever a question of interpretation is raised before them. This provision gives the court no jurisdiction either to apply the Treaty to a specific case or to decide upon the validity of a provision of domestic law in relation to the Treaty, as it would be possible for it to do under Article 169.

Nevertheless, the Court has power to extract from a question imperfectly formulated by the national court those questions which alone pertain to the interpretation of the Treaty. Consequently a decision should be given by the court not upon the validity of an Italian law in relation to the Treaty, but only upon the interpretation of the abovementioned Articles in the context of the points of law stated by the Giudice Conciliatore.

* * *

ON THE SUBMISSION THAT THE COURT WAS OBLIGED TO APPLY THE NATIONAL LAW

The Italian government submits that the request of the Giudice Conciliatore is "absolutely inadmissible," inasmuch as a national court which is obliged to apply a national law cannot avail itself of Article 177.

By contrast with ordinary international treaties, the EEC Treaty has created its own legal system which, on the entry into force of the Treaty, became an integral part of the legal systems of the Member States and which their courts are bound to apply.

By creating a Community of unlimited duration, having its own institutions, its own personality, its own legal capacity and capacity of representation on the international plane and, more particularly, real powers stemming from a limitation of sovereignty or a transfer of powers from the States to the Community, the Member States have limited their sovereign rights, albeit within limited fields, and have thus created a body of law which binds both their nationals and themselves.

The integration into the laws of each Member State of provisions which derive from the Community, and more generally the terms and the spirit of the Treaty, make it impossible for the States, as a corollary, to accord precedence to a unilateral and subsequent measure over a legal system accepted by them on a basis of reciprocity. Such a measure cannot therefore be inconsistent with that legal system. The executive force of Community law cannot vary from one state to another in deference to subsequent domestic laws, without jeopardizing the attainment of the objectives of the Treaty set out in Article 5 (2) and giving rise to the discrimination prohibited by Article 7.

The obligations undertaken under the Treaty establishing the Community would not be unconditional, but merely contingent, if they could be called in question by subsequent legislative acts of the signatories. Wherever the Treaty grants the States the right to act unilaterally, it does this by clear and precise provisions. Applications, by Member States for authority to derogate from the Treaty are subject to a special authorization procedure which would lose their purpose if the Member States could renounce their obligations by means of an ordinary law.

The precedence of Community law is confirmed by Article 189, whereby a regulation "shall be binding" and "directly applicable in all Member States." This provision, which is subject to no reservation, would be quite meaningless if a state could unilaterally nullify its effects by means of a legislative measure which could prevail over Community law.

It follows from all these observations that the law stemming from the Treaty, an independent source of law, could not, because of its special and original nature, be overridden by domestic legal provisions, however framed, without being deprived of its character as Community law and without the legal basis of the Community itself being called into question.

The transfer by the States from their domestic legal system to the Community legal system of the rights and obligations arising under the Treaty carries with it a permanent limitation of their sovereign rights, against which a subsequent unilateral act incompatible with the concept of the Community cannot prevail. Consequently Article 177 is to be applied regardless of any domestic law, whenever questions relating to the interpretation of the Treaty arise.

* * *

After *Costa*, what is the force of EU law in member states? How does this compare to ordinary principles pertaining to the effect of treaties?

More than a decade later, the European Court of Justice faced another request from an Italian court for a "preliminary ruling." What does this ruling add to *Van Gend & Loos* and *Costa*? In particular, who gets to decide conflicts between EU and national law?

AMMINISTRAZIONE DELLE FINANZE DELLO STATO V. SIMMENTHAL

European Court of Justice
Case No. 106/77, 1978 E.C.R. 629

* * *

1. By an order of 28 July 1977, received at the Court on 29 August 1977, the Pretore di Susa referred to the Court for a ruling pursuant to Article 177 of the EEC Treaty, two questions relating to the principle of the direct applicability of Community law as set out in Article 189 of the Treaty for the purpose of determining the effects of that principle when a rule of Community law conflicts with a subsequent provision of national law.

2. It is appropriate to draw attention to the fact that at a previous stage of the proceedings the Pretore referred to the Court for a preliminary ruling questions designed to enable him to determine whether veterinary and public health fees levied on imports of beef and veal under the consolidated text of the Italian veterinary and public health laws * * * were compatible with the Treaty and with certain regulations—in particular Regulation (EEC) No 805/68 of the Council of 27 June 1968 on the common organization of the market in beef and veal.

3. Having regard to the answers given by the Court in its judgment of 15 December 1976 [*Simmenthal s.p.a. v. Italian Minister for Finance* (1976) ECR1871] the Pretore held that the levying of the fees in question was incompatible with the provisions of Community law and ordered the Amministrazione delle Finanze dello Stato (Italian Finance Administration) to repay the fees unlawfully charged, together with interest.

4. The Amministrazione appealed against that order.

5. The Pretore, taking into account the arguments put forward by the parties during the proceedings arising out of this appeal, held that the issue before him involved a conflict between certain rules of Community law and a subsequent national law, namely the said Law No. 1239/70.

6. He pointed out that to resolve an issue of this kind, according to recently decided cases of the Italian Constitutional Court, the question whether the law in question was unconstitutional under Article 11 of the constitution must be referred to the Constitutional Court itself.

7. The Pretore, having regard, on the one hand, to the well-established case-law of the Court of Justice relating to the applicability of Community law in the legal systems of the Member States and, on the other hand, to the disadvantages which might arise if the national Court, instead of declaring of its own motion that a law impeding the full force and effect of Community law was inapplicable, were required to raise the issue of constitutionality, referred to the Court two questions framed as follows:

(a) since, in accordance with Article 189 of the EEC Treaty and the established case-law of the Court of Justice of the European Communities, directly applicable Community provisions must, notwithstanding any internal rule or practice whatsoever of the Member States, have full, complete and uniform effect in their legal systems in order to protect subjective legal rights created in favour of individuals, is the scope of the said provisions to be interpreted to the effect that any subsequent national measures which conflict with those provisions must be forthwith disregarded without waiting until those measures have been eliminated by action on the part of the national legislature concerned (repeal) or of other constitutional authorities (declaration that they are unconstitutional) especially, in the case of the latter alternative, where, since the national law continues to be fully effective pending such declaration, it is impossible to apply the Community provisions and, in consequence, to ensure that they are fully, completely and uniformly applied and to protect the legal rights created in favour of individuals?

* * *

THE SUBSTANCE OF THE CASE

13. The main purpose of the *first question* is to ascertain what consequences flow from the direct applicability of a provision of Community law in the event of incompatibility with a subsequent legislative provision of a Member State.

14. Direct applicability in such circumstances means that rules of Community law must be fully and uniformly applied in all the Member States from the date of their entry into force and for so long as they continue in force.

15. These provisions are therefore a direct source of rights and duties for all those affected thereby, whether Member States or individuals, who are parties to legal relationships under Community law.

16. This consequence also concerns any national Court whose task it is as an organ of a Member State to protect, in a case within its jurisdiction, the rights conferred upon individuals by Community law.

17. Furthermore, in accordance with the principle of the precedence of Community law, the relationship between provisions of the Treaty and directly applicable measures of the institutions on the one hand and the national law of the Member States on the other is such that those provisions and measures not only by their entry into force render automatically inapplicable any conflicting provision of current national law but—in so far as they are an integral part of, and take precedence in, the legal order applicable in the territory of each of the Member States—also preclude

the valid adoption of new national legislative measures to the extent to which they would be incompatible with Community provisions.

18. Indeed any recognition that national legislative measures which encroach upon the field within which the Community exercises its legislative power or which are otherwise incompatible with the provisions of Community law had any legal effect would amount to a corresponding denial of the effectiveness of obligations undertaken unconditionally and irrevocably by Member States pursuant to the Treaty and would thus imperil the very foundations of the Community.

19. The same conclusion emerges from the structure of Article 177 of the Treaty which provides that any Court or tribunal of a Member State is entitled to make a reference to the Court whenever it considers that a preliminary ruling on a question of interpretation or validity relating to Community law is necessary to enable it to give judgment.

20. The effectiveness of that provision would be impaired if the national Court were prevented from forthwith applying Community law in accordance with the Decision or the case-law of the Court.

21. It follows from the foregoing that every national court must, in a case within its jurisdiction, apply Community law in its entirety and protect rights which the latter confers on individuals and must accordingly set aside any provision of national law which may conflict with it, whether prior or subsequent to the Community rule.

22. Accordingly any provision of a national legal system and any legislative, administrative or judicial practice which might impair the effectiveness of Community law by withholding from the national court having jurisdiction to apply such law the power to do everything necessary at the moment of its application to set aside national legislative provisions which might prevent Community rules from having full force and effect are incompatible with those requirements which are the very essence of Community law.

23. This would be the case in the event of a conflict between a provision of Community law and a subsequent national law if the solution of the conflict were to be reserved for an authority with a discretion of its own, other than the court called upon to apply Community law, even if such an impediment to the full effectiveness of Community law were only temporary.

24. The first question should therefore be answered to the effect that a national court which is called upon, within the limits of its jurisdiction, to apply provisions of Community law is under a duty to give full effect to those provisions, if necessary refusing of its own motion to apply any conflicting provision of national legislation, even if adopted subsequently,

and it is not necessary for the Court to request or await the prior setting aside of such provision by legislative or other constitutional means.

* * *

What does all this mean for the sovereignty of the EU member states? Could the UN (through the Security Council or otherwise) bind its members in a way comparable to the effect of EU law?

The Evolution of the European Regime of Civil Jurisdiction and Judgments Recognition

As we have seen, European integration was originally driven primarily by the European Court of Justice through a gradual constitutionalization of the Treaty of Rome. More recently, integration has also been reflected in the increasing accumulation of lawmaking power in the Union institutions, i.e., the Commission and the Parliament. The story of the European regime of Civil Jurisdiction and Judgments Recognition provides an illustration of that phenomenon.

In its original form, Article 220 of the Treaty of Rome of 1957 provided:

> Member States shall, so far as is necessary, enter into negotiations with each other with a view to securing for the benefit of their nationals:
>
> * * *
>
> the simplification of formalities governing the reciprocal recognition and enforcement of judgments of courts or tribunals and of arbitration awards.

The member states acted on this instruction in 1968 by making the following agreement.

BRUSSELS CONVENTION ON JURISDICTION AND THE ENFORCEMENT OF JUDGMENTS IN CIVIL AND COMMERCIAL MATTERS

(Adopted 1968; in force 1973)

PREAMBLE

The High Contracting Parties to the Treaty Establishing the European Economic Community

DESIRING to implement the provisions of Article 220 of that Treaty by virtue of which they undertook to secure the simplification of formalities governing the reciprocal recognition and enforcement of judgments of courts or tribunals;

ANXIOUS to strengthen in the Community the legal protection of persons therein established;

CONSIDERING that it is necessary for this purpose to determine the international jurisdiction of their courts, to facilitate recognition and to introduce an expeditious procedure for securing the enforcement of judgments, authentic instruments and court settlements;

HAVE DECIDED to conclude this Convention and to this end have designated as their Plenipotentiaries:

[Designations of Plenipotentiaries of the original six Contracting States]

WHO, meeting within the Council, having exchanged their Full Powers, found in good and due form;

HAVE AGREED AS FOLLOWS:

Title I—Scope

Article 1

This Convention shall apply in civil and commercial matters whatever the nature of the court or tribunal. It shall not extend, in particular, to revenue, customs or administrative matters.

The Convention shall not apply to:

1. the status or legal capacity of natural persons, rights in property arising out of a matrimonial relationship, wills and succession;
2. bankruptcy, proceedings relating to the winding-up of insolvent companies or other legal persons, judicial arrangements, compositions and analogous proceedings;
3. social security;
4. arbitration.

* * *

This so-called Brussels Convention provided uniform rules on the civil jurisdiction of member state courts and on the mutual recognition of judgments for more than thirty years. Many of its provisions were interpreted by the European Court of Justice (which had jurisdiction to do so under a separate Protocol). In 1988, the Brussels Convention was supplemented by an almost identical agreement between the member states and other (non-member) countries in Europe, the Lugano Convention.

In 1993, the Treaty of Maastricht (Treaty on the European Union) expanded, modified, and superceded the Treaty of Rome. It considerably extended the powers of the Community institutions. Inter alia, it added Article 61:

> In order to establish progressively an area of freedom, security and justice, the Council shall adopt:
>
> * * *
>
> (c) measures in the field of judicial cooperation in civil matters as provided in Article 65;
>
> * * *

Article 65, in turn, provides:

> Measures in the field of judicial cooperation in civil matters, having cross-border implications * * * shall include:
>
> * * *
>
> (a) improving and simplifying:
>
> * * *
>
> —the recognition and enforcement of decisions in civil and commercial cases;
>
> * * *

Consequently, in 2000, the Council issued the following document and adopted a regulation on jurisdiction:

COUNCIL REGULATION (EC) NO 44/2001 ON JURISDICTION AND THE RECOGNITION AND ENFORCEMENT OF JUDGMENTS IN CIVIL AND COMMERCIAL MATTERS

(Adopted 2000)

THE COUNCIL OF THE EUROPEAN UNION,

Having regard to the Treaty establishing the European Community, and in particular Article 61(c) and Article 67(1) thereof,

Having regard to the proposal from the Commission,

Having regard to the opinion of the European Parliament,

Having regard to the opinion of the Economic and Social Committee,

Whereas:

1. The Community has set itself the objective of maintaining and developing an area of freedom, security and justice, in which the free movement of persons is ensured. In order to establish progressively such an area, the Community should adopt, amongst other things, the measures relating to judicial cooperation in civil matters which are necessary for the sound operation of the internal market.

2. Certain differences between national rules governing jurisdiction and recognition of judgments hamper the sound operation of the internal market. Provisions to unify the rules of conflict of jurisdiction in civil and commercial matters and to simplify the formalities with a view to rapid and simple recognition and enforcement of judgments from Member States bound by this Regulation are essential.

3. This area is within the field of judicial cooperation in civil matters within the meaning of Article 65 of the Treaty.

4. In accordance with the principles of subsidiarity and proportionality as set out in Article 5 of the Treaty, the objectives of this Regulation cannot be sufficiently achieved by the Member States and can therefore be better achieved by the Community. This Regulation confines itself to the minimum required in order to achieve those objectives and does not go beyond what is necessary for that purpose.

5. On 27 September 1968 the Member States, acting under Article 293, fourth indent, of the Treaty, concluded the Brussels Convention on Jurisdiction and the Enforcement of Judgments in Civil and Commercial Matters, as amended by Conventions on the Accession of the New Member States to that Convention (hereinafter referred to as the "Brussels Convention"). On 16 September 1988 Member States and EFTA States concluded the Lugano Convention on Jurisdiction and the Enforcement of Judgments in Civil and Commercial Matters, which is a parallel Convention to the 1968 Brussels Convention. Work has been undertaken for the

revision of those Conventions, and the Council has approved the content of the revised texts. Continuity in the results achieved in that revision should be ensured.

6. In order to attain the objective of free movement of judgments in civil and commercial matters, it is necessary and appropriate that the rules governing jurisdiction and the recognition and enforcement of judgments be governed by a Community legal instrument which is binding and directly applicable.

* * *

In substance and structure, Regulation No. 44/2001 is largely similar to the Brussels Convention. Its nature, however, is radically different. Article 249 section 2 of the Treaty of Maastricht (formerly Article 189 section 2 of the Treaty of Rome) provides:

> A regulation shall have general application. It shall be binding in its entirety and directly applicable in all Member States.

What does the shift from a convention to a regulation tell us about the integration of Europe?

The three core ECJ cases we have seen—*Van Gend*, *Costa*, and *Simmenthal*—all concern the relationship between the state and private individuals or entities. Does European law also have an effect on the relationship between private parties themselves?

GABRIELLE DEFRENNE V. SOCIÉTÉ ANONYME BELGE DE NAVIGATION AÉRIENNE SABENA

European Court of Justice
Case 43/75 1976 E.C.R. 455

* * *

I.   FACTS AND WRITTEN PROCEDURE

Miss Gabrielle Defrenne was engaged as an air hostess by the Société Anonyme Belge de Navigation Aérienne (hereinafter referred to as Sabena) on 10 December 1951. On 1 October 1963 her employment was confirmed by a new contract of employment which gave her the duties of "Cabin Steward and Air Hostess—Principal Cabin Attendant."

Miss Defrenne gave up her duties on 15 February 1968 in pursuance of the sixth paragraph of Article 5 of the contract of employment entered into by air crew employed by Sabena, which stated that contracts held by women members of the crew shall terminate on the day on which the employee in question reaches the age of 40 years.

When Miss Defrenne left she received an allowance on termination of service.

On 9 February 1970 Miss Defrenne brought an action before the Conseil d'État of Belgium for the annulment of the Royal Decree of 3 November 1969 which laid down special rules governing the acquisition of the right to a pension by air crew in civil aviation.

This action gave rise, following a request for a preliminary ruling, to a judgment of the Court of Justice of 25 May 1971. The Conseil d'État dismissed the application by a judgment of 10 December 1971.

Miss Defrenne had previously brought an action before the Tribunal du travail of Brussels on 13 March 1968 for compensation for the loss she had suffered in terms of salary, allowance on termination of service and pension as a result of the fact that air hostesses and male members of the air crew performing identical duties did not receive equal pay.

In a judgment given on 17 December 1970 the Tribunal du travail of Brussels dismissed all Miss Defrenne's claims as unfounded.

On 11 January 1971 Miss Defrenne appealed from this judgment to the Cour du Travail of Brussels.

In a judgment given on 23 April 1975 the Fourth Chamber B of the Cour du Travail of Brussels upheld the judgment at first instance on the second and third heads of claim.

As regards the first head of claim (arrears of salary) the court decided, in pursuance of Article 177 of the EEC Treaty, to stay the proceedings until the Court of Justice had given a preliminary ruling on the following questions:

> 1. Does Article 119 of the Treaty of Rome introduce directly into the national law of each Member State of the European Community the principle that men and women should receive equal pay for equal work and does it, therefore, independently of any national provision, entitle workers to institute proceedings before national courts in order to ensure its observance, and if so as from what date?

> 2. Has Article 119 become applicable in the internal law of the Member States by virtue of measures adopted by the authorities of the European Economic Community (if so, which, and as from what date?) or must the national legislature be regarded as alone competent in this matter?

* * *

THE FIRST QUESTION (DIRECT EFFECT OF ARTICLE 119):

* * *

7. The question of the direct effect of Article 119 must be considered in the light of the nature of the principle of equal pay, the aim of this provision and its place in the scheme of the Treaty.

8. Article 119 pursues a double aim.

9. First, in the light of the different stages of the development of social legislation in the various Member States, the aim of Article 119 is to avoid a situation in which undertakings established in States which have actually implemented the principle of equal pay suffer a competitive disadvantage in intra-Community competition as compared with undertakings established in States which have not yet eliminated discrimination against women workers as regards pay.

10. Secondly, this provision forms part of the social objectives of the Community, which is not merely an economic union, but is at the same time intended, by common action, to ensure social progress and seek the constant improvement of the living and working conditions of their peoples, as is emphasized by the Preamble to the Treaty.

11. This aim is accentuated by the insertion of Article 119 into the body of a chapter devoted to social policy whose preliminary provision, Article 117, marks "the need to promote improved working conditions and an improved standard of living for workers, so as to make possible their harmonization while the improvement is being maintained."

12. This double aim, which is at once economic and social, shows that the principle of equal pay forms part of the foundations of the Community.

* * *

15. In particular, since Article 119 appears in the context of the harmonization of working conditions while the improvement is being maintained, the objection that the terms of this article may be observed in other ways than by raising the lowest salaries may be set aside.

16. Under the terms of the first paragraph of Article 119, the Member States are bound to ensure and maintain "the application of the principle that men and women should receive equal pay for equal work."

* * *

18. For the purposes of the implementation of these provisions a distinction must be drawn within the whole area of application of Article 119 between, first, direct and overt discrimination which may be identified solely with the aid of the criteria based on equal work and equal pay referred to by the article in question and, secondly, indirect and disguised

discrimination which can only be identified by reference to more explicit implementing provisions of a Community or national character.

19. It is impossible not to recognize that the complete implementation of the aim pursued by Article 119, by means of the elimination of all discrimination, direct or indirect, between men and women workers, not only as regards individual undertakings but also entire branches of industry and even of the economic system as a whole, may in certain cases involve the elaboration of criteria whose implementation necessitates the taking of appropriate measures at Community and national level.

* * *

21. Among the forms of direct discrimination which may be identified solely by reference to the criteria laid down by Article 119 must be included in particular those which have their origin in legislative provisions or in collective labour agreements and which may be detected on the basis of a purely legal analysis of the situation.

22. This applies even more in cases where men and women receive unequal pay for equal work carried out in the same establishment or service, whether public or private.

23. As is shown by the very findings of the judgment making the reference, in such a situation the court is in a position to establish all the facts which enable it to decide whether a woman worker is receiving lower pay than a male worker performing the same tasks.

24. In such situation, at least, Article 119 is directly applicable and may thus give rise to individual rights which the courts must protect.

25. Furthermore, as regards equal work, as a general rule, the national legislative provisions adopted for the implementation of the principle of equal pay as a rule merely reproduce the substance of the terms of Article 119 as regards the direct forms of discrimination.

26. Belgian legislation provides a particularly apposite illustration of this point, since Article 14 of Royal Decree No 40 of 24 October 1967 on the employment of women merely sets out the right of any female worker to institute proceedings before the relevant court for the application of the principle of equal pay set out in Article 119 and simply refers to that article.

27. The terms of Article 119 cannot be relied on to invalidate this conclusion.

28. First of all, it is impossible to put forward an argument against its direct effect based on the use in this article of the word "principle," since, in the language of the Treaty, this term is specifically used in order to indicate the fundamental nature of certain provisions, as is shown, for ex-

ample, by the heading of the first part of the Treaty which is devoted to "Principles" and by Article 113, according to which the commercial policy of the Community is to be based on "uniform principles."

29. If this concept were to be attenuated to the point of reducing it to the level of a vague declaration, the very foundations of the Community and the coherence of its external relations would be indirectly affected.

30. It is also impossible to put forward arguments based on the fact that Article 119 only refers expressly to "Member States."

31. Indeed, as the Court has already found in other contexts, the fact that certain provisions of the Treaty are formally addressed to the Member States does not prevent rights from being conferred at the same time on any individual who has an interest in the performance of the duties thus laid down.

32. The very wording of Article 119 shows that it imposes on States a duty to bring about a specific result to be mandatorily achieved within a fixed period.

33. The effectiveness of this provision cannot be affected by the fact that the duty imposed by the Treaty has not been discharged by certain Member States and that the joint institutions have not reacted sufficiently energetically against this failure to act.

34. To accept the contrary view would be to risk raising the violation of the right to the status of a principle of interpretation, a position the adoption of which would not be consistent with the task assigned to the Court by Article 164 of the Treaty.

35. Finally, in its reference to "Member States," Article 119 is alluding to those States in the exercise of all those of their functions which may usefully contribute to the implementation of the principle of equal pay.

36. Thus, contrary to the statements made in the course of the proceedings this provision is far from merely referring the matter to the powers of the national legislative authorities.

37. Therefore, the reference to "Member States" in Article 119 cannot be interpreted as excluding the intervention of the courts in direct application of the Treaty.

38. Furthermore it is not possible to sustain any objection that the application by national courts of the principle of equal pay would amount to modifying independent agreements concluded privately or in the sphere of industrial relations such as individual contracts and collective labour agreements.

39. In fact, since Article 119 is mandatory in nature, the prohibition on discrimination between men and women applies not only to the action of public authorities, but also extends to all agreements which are intended

to regulate paid labour collectively, as well as to contracts between individuals.

40. The reply to the first question must therefore be that the principle of equal pay contained in Article 119 may be relied upon before the national courts and that these courts have a duty to ensure the protection of the rights which this provision vests in individuals, in particular as regards those types of discrimination arising directly from legislative provisions or collective labour agreements, as well as in cases in which men and women receive unequal pay for equal work which is carried out in the same establishment or service, whether private or public.

THE SECOND QUESTION (IMPLEMENTATION OF ARTICLE 119 AND POWERS OF THE COMMUNITY AND OF THE MEMBER STATES):

41. The second question asks whether Article 119 has become "applicable in the internal law of the Member States by virtue of measures adopted by the authorities of the European Economic Community," or whether the national legislature must "be regarded as alone competent in this matter."

42. In accordance with what has been set out above, it is appropriate to join to this question the problem of the date from which Article 119 must be regarded as having direct effect.

* * *

44. Article 119 itself provides that the application of the principle of equal pay was to be uniformly ensured by the end of the first stage of the transitional period at the latest.

45. The information supplied by the Commission reveals the existence of important differences and discrepancies between the various States in the implementation of this principle.

* * *

47. In the light of this situation, on 30 December 1961, the eve of the expiry of the time-limit fixed by Article 119, the Member States adopted a Resolution concerning the harmonization of rates of pay of men and women which was intended to provide further details concerning certain aspects of the material content of the principle of equal pay, while delaying its implementation according to a plan spread over a period of time.

48. Under the terms of that Resolution all discrimination, both direct and indirect, was to have been completely eliminated by 31 December 1964.

49. The information provided by the Commission shows that several of the original Member States have failed to observe the terms of that Resolution and that, for this reason, within the context of the tasks entrusted to it by Article 155 of the Treaty, the Commission was led to bring togeth-

er the representatives of the governments and the two sides of industry in order to study the situation and to agree together upon the measures necessary to ensure progress towards the full attainment of the objective laid down in Article 119.

* * *

53. For its part, in order to hasten the full implementation of Article 119, the Council on 10 February 1975 adopted Directive No 75/117 on the approximation of the laws of the Member States relating to the application of the principle of equal pay for men and women.

* * *

56. It follows from the express terms of Article 119 that the application of the principle that men and women should receive equal pay was to be fully secured and irreversible at the end of the first stage of the transitional period, that is, by 1 January 1962.

* * *

59. Moreover, it follows from the foregoing that, in the absence of transitional provisions, the principle contained in Article 119 has been fully effective in the new Member States since the entry into force of the Accession Treaty, that is, since 1 January 1973.

* * *

61. Although Article 119 is expressly addressed to the Member States in that it imposes on them a duty to ensure, within a given period, and subsequently to maintain the application of the principle of equal pay, that duty assumed by the States does not exclude competence in this matter on the part of the Community.

* * *

63. In the absence of any express reference in Article 119 to the possible action to be taken by the Community for the purposes of implementing the social policy, it is appropriate to refer to the general scheme of the Treaty and to the courses of action for which it provided, such as those laid down in Articles 100, 155 and, where appropriate, 235.

64. As has been shown in the reply to the first question, no implementing provision, whether adopted by the institutions of the Community or by the national authorities, could adversely affect the direct effect of Article 119.

65. The reply to the second question should therefore be that the application of Article 119 was to have been fully secured by the original Member

States as from 1 January 1962, the beginning of the second stage of the transitional period, and by the new Member States as from 1 January 1973, the date of entry into force of the Accession Treaty.

* * *

68. Even in the areas in which Article 119 has no direct effect, that provision cannot be interpreted as reserving to the national legislature exclusive power to implement the principle of equal pay since, to the extent to which such implementation is necessary, it may be relieved by a combination of Community and national measures.

THE TEMPORAL EFFECT OF THIS JUDGMENT

69. The Governments of Ireland and the United Kingdom have drawn the Court's attention to the possible economic consequences of attributing direct effect to the provisions of Article 119, on the ground that such a decision might, in many branches of economic life, result in the introduction of claims dating back to the time at which such effect came into existence.

70. In view of the large number of people concerned, such claims, which undertakings could not have [been] foreseen, might seriously affect the financial situation of such undertakings and even drive some of them to bankruptcy.

71. Although the practical consequences of any judicial decision must be carefully taken into account, it would be impossible to go so far as to diminish the objectivity of the law and compromise its future application on the ground of the possible repercussions which might result, as regards the past, from such a judicial decision.

* * *

74. In these circumstances, it is appropriate to determine that, as the general level at which pay would have been fixed cannot be known, important considerations of legal certainty affecting all the interests involved, both public and private, make it impossible in principle to reopen the question as regards the past.

75. Therefore, the direct effect of Article 119 cannot be relied on in order to support claims concerning pay periods prior to the date of this judgment, except as regards those workers who have already brought legal proceedings or made an equivalent claim.

* * *

On those grounds,

THE COURT

in answer to the questions referred to it by the Cour du travail, Brussels, by judgment dated 23 April 1975 hereby rules:

1. The principle that men and women should receive equal pay, which is laid down by Article 119, may be relied on before the national courts. These courts have a duty to ensure the protection of the rights which that provision vests in individuals, in particular in the case of those forms of discrimination which have their origin in legislative provisions or collective labour agreements, as well as where men and women receive unequal pay for equal work which is carried out in the same establishment or service, whether private or public.

2. The application of Article 119 was to have been fully secured by the original Member States as from 1 January 1962, the beginning of the second stage of the transitional period, and by the new Member States as from 1 January 1973, the date of entry into force of the Accession Treaty. The first of these time-limits was not modified by the Resolution of the Member States of 30 December 1961.

3. Council Directive No 75/117 does not prejudice the direct effect of Article 119 and the period fixed by that Directive for compliance therewith does not affect the time-limits laid down by Article 119 of the EEC Treaty and the Accession Treaty.

4. Even in the areas in which Article 119 has no direct effect, that provision cannot be interpreted as reserving to the national legislature exclusive power to implement the principle of equal pay since, to the extent to which such implementation is necessary, it may be achieved by a combination of Community and national provisions.

5. Except as regards those workers who have already brought legal proceedings or made an equivalent claim, the direct effect of Article 119 cannot be relied on in order to support claims concerning pay periods prior to the date of this judgment.

———————

In *Defrenne*, the ECJ found that Article 119 had "direct effect" in the courts of the member states. "Effect" between (or among) whom? Does the ECJ decision create directly enforceable individual rights? What does this decision tell you about the impact of European law on private (market) relationships?

To the extent that European law does create directly enforceable private rights, where can those rights be vindicated?

D. THE DELEGATION OF SOVEREIGN POWERS AND DEMOCRATIC LEGITIMACY

If states delegate important parts of their sovereign authority to international organizations, these organizations acquire—and wield—significant decision-making power. Ultimately, this is power over people—their liberty (to act in this way or that), their property (especially its economic use), and sometimes even their lives (e.g., when the UN Security Council permits the use of force). Such power calls for some form of legitimacy. This legitimacy may come from expertise or perhaps even necessity, but in our age of democracy, legitimacy must eventually also come from popular vote. Yet, as many observers have noted, the connection between popular vote (in the various member states) and the decision-making process in international organizations is, as a rule, weak to the point of non-existence. To put it provocatively: international organizations, such as the UN and the WTO, govern innumerable important aspects of our lives today without a meaningful mandate from the people.[8] This "democratic deficit" has been a major point of discussion not only among international theorists and lawyers but also, especially in Europe with regard to the European Union, among the public at large. How can the problem be solved?

The following article presents one of the most perceptive discussions of the issue.

ERIC STEIN, INTERNATIONAL INTEGRATION AND DEMOCRACY: NO LOVE AT FIRST SIGHT
95 Am. J. Int'l Law 489 (2001)

In this essay I suggest a correlation between the integration level of an international institution and the public discourse about the lack of democracy and legitimacy in the institution's structure and functioning. This discourse includes ideas for remedial action at both the national and international levels; it also becomes inevitably intertwined with other reform proposals that may call for an incremental or—particularly in the case of a more integrated organization—a radical restructuring. Having originated in the highly integrated European Community, the debate on the "democracy-legitimacy deficit" has reached other institutions, particularly the World Trade Organization (WTO) and the international financial bodies, and has become one component of the backlash rhetoric against "globalization."

* * *

---

[8] The European Union is a partial exception because its parliament is directly elected by the people in the member states. It shares its lawmaking power, however, with the Council which is staffed by the respective executives.

CHANGES IN THE NATIONAL AND INTERNATIONAL SYSTEMS: IMPACT ON THE DISCOURSE

Two trends. First, by one count the number of intergovernmental organizations (IGOs) and regimes has increased from 123 in 1951 to 251 in 1999 (although the numbers vary according to the different criteria employed). The solution of vital problems, such as national security, protection of basic human rights, international trade and economic development, the surge of migration, environmental protection, and cross-border criminality, has moved beyond the reach of individual states and has called for institutionalized commitment and cooperation on global and regional levels.

Second, the idea and practice of democratic government has received widening acceptance, particularly in the 1990s. According to the most recent Freedom House survey, the number of "electoral" democracies increased from 69 in 1988–1989 to 120 in 1999–2000, although not all trends have been positive. Taking into account this growing acceptance and the commitment of most states under UN covenants and other global and regional treaties, as well as the extensive practice of states fostering democracy abroad, some commentators have argued that the rights to free elections and participation in public affairs are becoming—or have already become—part of the cluster of basic rights protected by general international law.

The tension. These two trends, the internationalization of decision making in IGOs and the expansion of democracy, have led to a tension that underlies discourse on the democracy-legitimacy deficit in national and international arenas.

For one thing, internationalization "almost invariably means a loss of democracy." A new level of normative activity superimposed on national democratic systems makes citizen participation more remote, and parliamentary control over the executive, notoriously loose in foreign affairs matters, becomes even less effective. This result can clearly be observed in parliamentary democracies and, perhaps less markedly, also in presidential systems where the chief executive, elected directly by the people, claims legitimacy independently of the parliament. The problem becomes even more palpable when a member state is outvoted in an IGO organ or when the law of the IGO is enforced directly in the domestic legal order without the national parliament's imprimatur (i.e., it is "self-executing," has "direct effect"). Again, the IGOs themselves are considered "undemocratic" since they operate with little transparency or public and parliamentary scrutiny. They are seen as being governed by an elite group of national officials who are instructed by their respective executives, and by international secretariats whose staffs at times act independently of the top IGO management.

In the last decade, a "third force" has emerged in the shape of proliferating nongovernmental organizations (NGOs), which are founded both on grassroots and transborder links and take full advantage of the new information technology. Depending on the criteria employed, the number of NGOs is said to have risen from 832 in 1951 to 5825 or (for "total types of NGOs") 43,958 in 1999. Some view these groups as emanations of an embryonic "international civil society" and as a possible substitute for representative democracy. Others see them as self-elected elite advocates of special causes, unrepresentative of the general public and engaged in an unholy alliance with international bureaucrats and "sympathetic states," "a romance of questionable legitimacy." At any rate, NGOs are justly credited both with raising national and international awareness and with opening the IGOs to the scrutiny of public opinion. They have left a deep imprint on a number of significant UN acts.

A caveat is in order. There is no assurance that the two trends noted above will continue in a linear mode, as shown by the rise of "illiberal democracies." Moreover, the disputed impact of liberalization of trade and investment on developing economies, the environment, health, workers' rights, and human rights generally, as well as constraints on states' social policies, has stood at the core of the backlash movement against internationalization and globalization.

* * *

Despite their usefulness, national procedures alone can hardly be expected to meet the democracy-legitimacy requirement appropriate to the integration level of an IGO. Measures must also be sought at the level of the organization:

- Most sessions of the institutions, particularly rule-making sessions, should be open to the public and documents, including draft proposals, should be placed on the Internet.

- In organizations at higher levels of integration, a standing consultative body composed of members of national parliaments might be established to assure greater accountability.

- Actual decision making should not be confined to major powers acting in a clublike setting; the broad membership should have an opportunity for genuine participation.

- Nongovernmental organizations and interest groups should be given adequate and fair access to the institutions for exchange of data and consultation. A normative framework should be devised for such participation.

- An inspection panel (such as that created by the World Bank) and an ombudsman should be appointed to receive citizen complaints of maladministration.

- At low integration levels such as that of the WHO, remedial measures should focus on transparency, openness to the outside world, accountable and effective management, and policy results that gain the constituency's acceptance in terms of empirical-social legitimacy.

- Some of the discrete features of the European Union may be transferable to international institutions, such as phased development, the vigorous use of institutional powers, the ombudsman mentioned above, the procedures and precedent building of the EU judiciary, the consultation system and advisory organs, measures to improve transparency, cooperation with national parliaments, and—depending on the level of integration—the efforts to advance the sense of common good and expectations.

- Particularly at a higher level of integration, dispersion of the organization's central power should be sought through reliance on regional and local authorities, and the principle of subsidiarity should be honored.

- In the interest of legitimacy, if for no other reasons, IGOs and regimes should explore the ways of protecting the core of fundamental human rights within the confines of their competence.

Several observations regarding this list are in order. The new information technology, including the Internet, has already contributed to greater transparency and to enhancing the role of NGOs. A major problem has been finding a way to open the preparatory proceeding that precedes final action, while protecting genuinely confidential information and allowing space for confidential bargaining. The protesters against the WTO "club system" of decision making included not only NGOs but also government delegates from less developed countries—a signal to the WTO establishment. Generally, NGOs play a useful role, provided that they shun violence and are themselves democratic in their organization and transparent in respect of their constituency, internal proceedings, and sources of funding.

The institution of the ombudsman has proved highly popular in the European Union and should be considered for other international structures. In principle, however, the transfer of any feature of one organization to another succeeds only if the basic contexts of both are roughly comparable.

Regionalism has figured prominently, if not uncontroversially, in the WHO, but in the Union it appears only in the form of an advisory committee with limited influence. Both regionalism and subsidiarity should be kept in mind in connection with all international institutions since only those powers that are necessary to deal with international problems should be centralized in IGOs.

Some participants in the discourse see the currently feasible measures as palliatives. They believe that nothing short of a radical restructuring of the international and regional systems can cure the democracy-legitimacy gap. Thus, in the WTO, private individuals and firms are to replace the member governments as the principal actors. In the European Union, voices in the judiciary and high political circles call for a federation (often not meaningfully defined) based on a European constitution as the only effective remedy.

All of these "radical" measures are designed to inject the voice of individual citizens into the exclusively state-based structures. This could be accomplished in two major ways. First, individuals could be recognized as stakeholders with individual rights derived from the constituent treaty and broadly enforceable by the domestic or supranational judiciary. A less intrusive alternative would be to enable a private party to pursue a specific claim in an arbitration proceeding, as in the NAFTA chapter on investment. In this context, I have noted the vital differences between the European Union and the WTO, which at this stage of integration make transfers of the basic features of the European Union difficult to envision.

A second avenue toward broadening citizen participation would enlarge the structure by adding an assembly, elected directly by the people in the member states, with powers to recommend norms and policy; such an assembly would eventually replace the organs of general membership represented by states and obtain lawmaking powers. As globalization progresses and democracy spreads worldwide, a "cosmopolitan" democracy could make possible—so goes the argument—the direct election by universal suffrage of a Global Peoples Assembly, with general competence to legislate where worldwide action is called for and to coordinate the work of international institutions.

* * *

Stein lays out a problem that cannot be solved easily. How should a country like the United States react to it when making decisions about the impact of the law produced by international organizations on domestic law?

3. MODERN VARIATIONS ON SOVEREIGN IMMUNITY

Domestic lawsuits involving foreign governments, their officials, acts or property normally present issues of immunity from suit or judicial scrutiny. Since such lawsuits are numerous, immunity is probably the most frequently litigated international law issue in domestic courts. There are essentially three kinds of immunity.

The first form of immunity is that of foreign *sovereigns*, particularly states, but also their organs and subdivisions. There are several treaties on this subject; for states not party to them, the field is governed by customary international law. This is true for the United States. In the United States, the rules governing sovereign immunity are codified in a domestic (federal) statute, the Foreign Sovereign Immunities Act of 1976. The Act by and large codifies, but to some extent also modifies, the generally recognized rules of international law. Note that there is also the (functional) immunity of international organizations, which is usually based on international agreements and implementing legislation.

Second, there is the immunity of certain *persons* charged with governmental functions, in particular heads of state, diplomats, consular officers and civil servants of intergovernmental organizations. Like the immunity of foreign sovereigns, this area is governed by a combination of various international conventions (especially with regard to diplomatic and consular personnel) and customary international law (especially with regard to heads of state).

Third, the *acts* of certain foreign sovereigns may be immune from judicial scrutiny. Unlike the two forms of immunity discussed above, immunity of foreign sovereign acts is not based on international law; instead, it is purely a matter of domestic law in the United States and some other common law countries. (Most other countries in the world do not recognize it.) This form of immunity is expressed in the so-called Act of State Doctrine. It provides that domestic courts cannot question the validity of certain foreign governmental acts. Unlike the immunity of foreign sovereigns and certain officials, the Act of State Doctrine does not provide immunity from jurisdiction but only from judicial scrutiny on the merits.

As you will see, immunity, like other aspects of sovereignty, is not quite what it used to be. Most notably, a foreign state's sovereign immunity has been severely curtailed in the last half-century. The immunity of former heads of state is no longer absolute either. And even the Act of State Doctrine has come under pressure.

A. FOREIGN SOVEREIGN IMMUNITY

The immunity of foreign sovereigns is governed by both international and domestic law. While they are by and large in sync, there can be some variations when domestic laws address details in idiosyncratic ways. You will be able to observe some of these idiosyncrasies when we turn to the law of the United States.

Sovereign Immunity on the International Level

On the international level, there are, as mentioned, several conventions, especially the United Nations Convention on Jurisdictional Immunities of States and Their Property (which has not yet entered into force) and the European Convention on State Immunity (which entered into force in 1976). Outside of these conventions, the field is governed by customary international law. Under customary international law, foreign sovereigns are in principle immune from the jurisdiction of another state's courts, which means that they cannot be sued at all. Today, many exceptions from that principle are recognized. They are better addressed when we look at sovereign immunity on the domestic level (i.e., the law of the United States) below.

While the international law rules on sovereign immunity are by and large fairly well-settled, recently, a major issue has arisen: are foreign sovereigns immune even when they are being sued for massive human rights violations (especially of *jus cogens*)? In other words, is there, or should there be, a human rights exception to foreign sovereign immunity? After several years of debate, this issue finally came before the International Court of Justice.

NOTE ON RECENT ICJ JURISPRUDENCE ON THE JURISDICTIONAL IMMUNITIES OF STATES

On December 23, 2008, Germany instituted proceedings against Italy in the International Court of Justice alleging that Italian courts, particularly the Corte di Cassazione (Italy's highest court in civil matters), had infringed Germany's sovereign immunity. Italian citizens who were victimized by the Third Reich during World War II and their family members sued Germany in various Italian courts. In the *Ferrini* decision (Sentenza 5044, March 21, 2004), the Corte di Cassazione declared that Italy had jurisdiction over a claim by an Italian plaintiff who had been deported to Germany by the German government during World War II and had been subjected to forced labor in the armaments industry. According to Germany's submission before the ICJ, as of June 2009, approximately 500 claimants had initiated actions against Germany in 24 Italian courts.

Germany emphasized that while it took responsibility for atrocities committed by the Third Reich, as a sovereign state it enjoyed immunity from the jurisdiction of foreign courts. Additionally, Germany argued that a 1947 Peace Treaty between Italy and the Allied Powers contained a waiver of claims on behalf of Italy and Italian citizens regarding World War II atrocities (although subsequently, in 1961, Germany agreed to pay a total of 80 million marks—more than $20 million dollars at the time and approximately $150 million today—in reparation to Italy as a final settlement, with an additional waiver). Ultimately, Germany demanded that "the Italian Republic must, by means of its own choosing, take any and all steps to ensure that all the decisions of its courts * * * infringing Germany's sovereign immunity become unenforceable."

Italy responded that the principle of sovereign immunity is not absolute when the state in question has breached international law (as Germany had by committing atrocities against Italian citizens). Moreover, Italy argued that Germany had continued to breach its obligation to provide reparations and had misinterpreted the waiver clauses in the post-war agreements.

On July 4, 2011, the ICJ granted Greece permission to intervene as a nonparty in the case. Greek victims of a German massacre in the Greek village of Distomo in 1944 had won a judgment against Germany in a Greek court in 1997. This judgment could not be enforced because the Greek justice minister refused to authorize enforcement against a foreign state. The victims subsequently took the judgment to an Italian court which held the judgment enforceable in Italy. Germany considered this decision an additional violation of its sovereignty.

In 2012, the ICJ decided that Italy had violated the sovereign immunity of Germany by allowing individuals to pursue civil claims in Italy's domestic courts; three judges concurred, while three others dissented. The ICJ also held that Italy had further violated Germany's sovereign immunity by considering the decisions against Germany issued by the Greek courts to be enforceable in Italy. The ICJ found that, since the acts by Germany were performed by German armed forces, the acts were sovereign in nature rather than commercial and were therefore covered by immunity.

The more contested question was whether customary international law allowed an exception from sovereign immunity for state acts that violated peremptory (*jus cogens*) norms of international law. According to the ICJ, there is no such exception because there is no consistent state practice to support it. While some countries' courts had denied sovereign immunity for *jus cogens* violations, this did not amount to consistent state practice. The ICJ expressed concern that such an exception would open the gateway for plaintiffs to plead *jus cogens* violations in order to overcome sovereign immunity.

The Court also noted that, even though the states themselves were immune from suit, state officials may not be. The ICJ expressed "surprise" and "regret" that Germany had denied relief to the victims under its forced labor compensation scheme—signaling the Court's expectation that the plaintiffs should have other avenues for redress, including through diplomatic means.

Three judges dissented from the Court's judgment. Judge Gaja, an ad hoc judge designated by Italy, dissented in part. He argued that a tort exception (under which foreign sovereigns are not immune with regard to torts committed in the territory of the forum state) should have applied to Germany's acts. Judge Cançado Trindade of Brazil, the former president of the Inter–American Court of Human Rights, also dissented, arguing that states do not have immunity for *jus cogens* violations. Judge Yusuf of Somalia, who wrote the third dissent, argued that Italy did not violate Germany's sovereignty by allowing civil claims against Germany in Italian courts, where the victims had no other means to get reparations for the injuries they had suffered. According to Judge Yusuf, "[t]he assertion of jurisdiction by domestic courts in those exceptional circumstances where there is a failure to make reparations, and where the responsible State has admitted to the commission of serious violations of humanitarian law, without providing a contextual remedy for the victims, does not, in my view, upset the harmonious relations between States, but contributes to a better observance of international human rights and humanitarian law."

Should states be immune from suits for violations of *jus cogens* norms? If so, do *jus cogens* norms really matter? If not, is the ICJ's concern justified that plaintiffs could bring more suits against sovereign states by pleading violations of *jus cogens* norms?

In light of what you have learned in *The Paquete Habana*, how would one go about pleading a violation of customary international law? What additional steps are required for pleading a violation of *jus cogens*?

The European Convention on State Immunity, to which both Germany and Italy are parties, includes a tort exception to sovereign immunity. The Convention also provides an exception to this exception: states are *always* immune for acts committed by their armed forces, even if those acts constitute torts and even if the acts were committed in the territory of another state. Had this second-order exception for acts by armed forces not existed, could Italy have allowed the civil suits, relying on the treaty rather than on customary international law?

The issue of whether sovereign immunity should be denied in a case of massive (uncontested) human rights violations has also come before the courts of the United States. In *Princz v. Federal Republic of Germany*, 26 F.3d 1166 (D.C. Cir. 1994), a U.S. citizen who was a Holocaust survivor sued Germany in Federal District Court for compensation primarily for the slave labor he had been forced to perform during World War II. Germany acknowledged the truth of his allegations, pointed to the massive reparations programs it had funded in the past, and invoked sovereign immunity. The District Court denied Germany the protection of sovereign immunity in a highly emotional opinion essentially on grounds of fundamental fairness. 813 F. Supp. 22 (D.D.C. 1992). The Court of Appeals for the District of Columbia Circuit reversed the decision and granted Germany sovereign immunity over a strong dissent by Judge Patricia Wald. Is this decision consistent with the ICJ's ruling in *Germany v. Italy*? In any event, would such a decision now be required?

Sovereign Immunity on the Domestic Level

Most countries have specific domestic rules on foreign sovereign immunity; domestic courts primarily look to these rules. Sometimes the rules are codified; sometimes they come from case law. An example of a codification is the U.S. Foreign Sovereign Immunities Act of 1976 (FSIA), which will be our primary focus in this section. For comparative purposes, we will also look at a recent case from the Supreme Court of India.

Prior to 1976, U.S. courts had decided foreign sovereign immunity on a case-by-case basis. Foreign sovereigns could apply for a statement of support from the State Department, which could issue a "suggestion of immunity." The State Department took into account diplomatic considerations, among other factors. Courts consistently abided by the State Department's suggestions. Where the foreign sovereign had failed to apply for a suggestion of immunity, courts made decisions following the prior practice of the State Department. In the absence of firm guidelines, this practice sometimes rendered inconsistent and contradictory results.

The FSIA transferred the primary responsibility for decisions about foreign sovereign immunity from the State Department to the courts according to a set of statutory rules.

On the one hand, this means there is now a clear and conclusive statutory basis in a relatively short act. In particular, the Supreme Court has held that in all cases against foreign sovereigns, jurisdiction must be based on the FSIA. In *Argentine Republic v. Amerada Hess Shipping Corp.*, 488 U.S. 428 (1989), the Court decided that plaintiffs cannot circumvent the FSIA by invoking other bases for jurisdiction, such as the Alien Tort Claims Act or general maritime law.

On the other hand, the FSIA is complex, and its application by courts has proven difficult, leading to uneven and sometimes problematic results. Here, we will not explore most of these complexities, focusing instead on the overall structure and approach of the FSIA. In reading its provisions, pay particular attention to the following three questions:

First, what is the Act's scope? In particular, who counts as a "foreign sovereign"? What about the Swiss canton of Unterwalden, Air Madagascar (Madagascar's national airline), the Ministry of Culture of the Russian Federation, a private computer company majority owned by the French government, and the European Union (as such)?

Second, what is the ground rule established by the Act, and what is its effect? Are state courts bound by the FSIA as well?

Third, the FSIA codifies what is commonly known as the "restrictive theory of sovereign immunity" because it recognizes a list of exceptions.

Which exceptions from sovereign immunity does the Act provide? Capture the gist of each of these exceptions by putting them in your own words.

FOREIGN SOVEREIGN IMMUNITIES ACT
(Enacted 1976, as amended), 28 U.S.C. § 1602 et seq.

§ 1602. Findings and declaration of purpose

§ 1603. Definitions

§ 1604. Immunity of a foreign state from jurisdiction

§ 1605. General exceptions to the jurisdictional immunity of a foreign state

§ 1605A. Terrorism exception to the jurisdictional immunity of a foreign state

§ 1606. Extent of liability

§ 1607. Counterclaims

§ 1608. Service; time to answer; default

§ 1609. Immunity from attachment and execution of property of a foreign state

§ 1610. Exceptions to the immunity from attachment or execution

§ 1611. Certain types of property immune from execution

§ 1602. FINDINGS AND DECLARATION OF PURPOSE

The Congress finds that the determination by United States courts of the claims of foreign states to immunity from the jurisdiction of such courts would serve the interests of justice and would protect the rights of both foreign states and litigants in United States courts. Under international law, states are not immune from the jurisdiction of foreign courts insofar as their commercial activities are concerned, and their commercial property may be levied upon for the satisfaction of judgments rendered against them in connection with their commercial activities. Claims of foreign states to immunity should henceforth be decided by courts of the United States and of the States in conformity with the principles set forth in this chapter.

§ 1603. DEFINITIONS

For purposes of this chapter—

(a) A "foreign state," except as used in section 1608 of this title, includes a political subdivision of a foreign state or an agency or instrumentality of a foreign state as defined in subsection (b).

(b) An "agency or instrumentality of a foreign state" means any entity—

(1) which is a separate legal person, corporate or otherwise, and

(2) which is an organ of a foreign state or political subdivision thereof, or a majority of whose shares or other ownership interest is owned by a foreign state or political subdivision thereof, and

(3) which is neither a citizen of a State of the United States as defined in section 1332(c) and (e) of this title, nor created under the laws of any third country.

(c) The "United States" includes all territory and waters, continental or insular, subject to the jurisdiction of the United States.

(d) A "commercial activity" means either a regular course of commercial conduct or a particular commercial transaction or act. The commercial character of an activity shall be determined by reference to the nature of the course of conduct or particular transaction or act, rather than by reference to its purpose.

(e) A "commercial activity carried on in the United States by a foreign state" means commercial activity carried on by such state and having substantial contact with the United States.

§ 1604.   IMMUNITY OF A FOREIGN STATE FROM JURISDICTION

Subject to existing international agreements to which the United States is a party at the time of enactment of this Act a foreign state shall be immune from the jurisdiction of the courts of the United States and of the States except as provided in sections 1605 to 1607 of this chapter.

§ 1605.   GENERAL EXCEPTIONS TO THE JURISDICTIONAL IMMUNITY OF A
           FOREIGN STATE

(a) A foreign state shall not be immune from the jurisdiction of courts of the United States or of the States in any case:

(1) in which the foreign state has waived its immunity either explicitly or by implication, notwithstanding any withdrawal of the waiver which the foreign state may purport to effect except in accordance with the terms of the waiver;

(2) in which the action is based upon a commercial activity carried on in the United States by the foreign state; or upon an act performed in the United States in connection with a commercial activity of the foreign state elsewhere; or upon an act outside the territory of the United States in connection with a commercial activity of the foreign state elsewhere and that act causes a direct effect in the United States;

(3) in which rights in property taken in violation of international law are in issue and that property or any property exchanged for such property is present in the United States in connection with a commercial activity carried on in the United States by the foreign state; or that property or any property exchanged for such property is owned or operated by an agency or instrumentality of the for-

eign state and that agency or instrumentality is engaged in a commercial activity in the United States;

(4) in which rights in property in the United States acquired by succession or gift or rights in immovable property situated in the United States are in issue;

(5) not otherwise encompassed in paragraph (2) above, in which money damages are sought against a foreign state for personal injury or death, or damage to or loss of property, occurring in the United States and caused by the tortious act or omission of that foreign state or of any official or employee of that foreign state while acting within the scope of his office or employment; except this paragraph shall not apply to:

(A) any claim based upon the exercise or performance or the failure to exercise or perform a discretionary function regardless of whether the discretion be abused, or

(B) any claim arising out of malicious prosecution, abuse of process, libel, slander, misrepresentation, deceit, or interference with contract rights; or

(6) in which the action is brought, either to enforce an agreement made by the foreign state with or for the benefit of a private party to submit to arbitration all or any differences which have arisen or which may arise between the parties with respect to a defined legal relationship, whether contractual or not, concerning a subject matter capable of settlement by arbitration under the laws of the United States, or to confirm an award made pursuant to such an agreement to arbitrate, if:

(A) the arbitration takes place or is intended to take place in the United States,

(B) the agreement or award is or may be governed by a treaty or other international agreement in force for the United States calling for the recognition and enforcement of arbitral awards,

(C) the underlying claim, save for the agreement to arbitrate, could have been brought in a United States court under this section or section 1607, or

(D) paragraph (1) of this subsection is otherwise applicable.

* * *

§ 1605A. TERRORISM EXCEPTION TO THE JURISDICTIONAL IMMUNITY OF A FOREIGN STATE

(a) In General.

(1) No immunity. A foreign state shall not be immune from the jurisdiction of courts of the United States or of the States in any case not otherwise covered by this chapter in which money damages

are sought against a foreign state for personal injury or death that was caused by an act of torture, extrajudicial killing, aircraft sabotage, hostage taking, or the provision of material support or resources for such an act if such act or provision of material support or resources is engaged in by an official, employee, or agent of such foreign state while acting within the scope of his or her office, employment, or agency.

(2) Claim heard. The court shall hear a claim under this section if

(A)(i) (I) the foreign state was designated as a state sponsor of terrorism at the time the act described in paragraph (1) occurred, or was so designated as a result of such act, and, subject to subclause (II), either remains so designated when the claim is filed under this section or was so designated within the 6-month period before the claim is filed under this section;

* * *

(ii) the claimant or the victim was, at the time the act described in paragraph (1) occurred—

(I)   a national of the United States;

(II)   a member of the armed forces; or

(III)   otherwise an employee of the Government of the United States, or of an individual performing a contract awarded by the United States Government, acting within the scope of the employee's employment; and

(iii) in a case in which the act occurred in the foreign state against which the claim has been brought, the claimant has afforded the foreign state a reasonable opportunity to arbitrate the claim in accordance with the accepted international rules of arbitration;

* * *

(c) Private Right of Action. A foreign state that is or was a state sponsor of terrorism as described in subsection (a)(2)(A)(i), and any official, employee, or agent of that foreign state while acting within the scope of his or her office, employment, or agency, shall be liable to—

(1) a national of the United States,

(2) a member of the armed forces,

(3) an employee of the Government of the United States, or of an individual performing a contract awarded by the United States Government, acting within the scope of the employee's employment, or

(4) the legal representative of a person described in paragraph (1), (2), or (3),

for personal injury or death caused by acts described in subsection (a)(1) of that foreign state, or of an official, employee, or agent of that foreign state, for which the courts of the United States may maintain jurisdiction under this section for money damages. In any such action, damages may include economic damages, solatium, pain and suffering, and punitive damages. In any such action, a foreign state shall be vicariously liable for the acts of its officials, employees, or agents.

(d) Additional Damages. After an action has been brought under subsection (c), actions may also be brought for reasonably foreseeable property loss, whether insured or uninsured, third party liability, and loss claims under life and property insurance policies, by reason of the same acts on which the action under subsection (c) is based.

* * *

(h) Definitions. For purposes of this section—

   (1) the term "aircraft sabotage" has the meaning given that term in Article 1 of the Convention for the Suppression of Unlawful Acts Against the Safety of Civil Aviation;

   (2) the term "hostage taking" has the meaning given that term in Article 1 of the International Convention Against the Taking of Hostages;

* * *

§ 1606.   EXTENT OF LIABILITY

As to any claim for relief with respect to which a foreign state is not entitled to immunity under section 1605 or 1607 of this chapter, the foreign state shall be liable in the same manner and to the same extent as a private individual under like circumstances; but a foreign state except for an agency or instrumentality thereof shall not be liable for punitive damages; if, however, in any case wherein death was caused, the law of the place where the action or omission occurred provides, or has been construed to provide, for damages only punitive in nature, the foreign state shall be liable for actual or compensatory damages measured by the pecuniary injuries resulting from such death which were incurred by the persons for whose benefit the action was brought.

§ 1607.   COUNTERCLAIMS

In any action brought by a foreign state, or in which a foreign state intervenes, in a court of the United States or of a State, the foreign state shall not be accorded immunity with respect to any counterclaim—

(a) for which a foreign state would not be entitled to immunity under section 1605 or 1605A of this chapter had such claim been brought in a separate action against the foreign state; or

(b) arising out of the transaction or occurrence that is the subject matter of the claim of the foreign state; or

(c) to the extent that the counterclaim does not seek relief exceeding in amount or differing in kind from that sought by the foreign state.

§ 1608. SERVICE; TIME TO ANSWER; DEFAULT

* * *

(e) No judgment by default shall be entered by a court of the United States or of a State against a foreign state, a political subdivision thereof, or an agency or instrumentality of a foreign state, unless the claimant establishes his claim or right to relief by evidence satisfactory to the court. A copy of any such default judgment shall be sent to the foreign state or political subdivision in the manner prescribed for service in this section.

§ 1609. IMMUNITY FROM ATTACHMENT AND EXECUTION OF PROPERTY OF A
         FOREIGN STATE

* * *

§ 1610. EXCEPTIONS TO THE IMMUNITY FROM ATTACHMENT OR EXECUTION

* * *

§ 1611. CERTAIN TYPES OF PROPERTY IMMUNE FROM EXECUTION

* * *

———————

Note that there is also no jury trial in lawsuits against foreign sovereigns. See 28 USC § 1330(a).

The FSIA has generated a significant amount of case law in U.S. courts, including several decisions by the Supreme Court. Most of this case law involves the application of the various exceptions to the presumption of immunity. Practically, the most important, and most litigated, exception pertains to "commercial activity" under § 1605(a)(2). The following case is a leading example. What does the characterization of the activities involved turn on? Exactly which part of § 1605(a)(2) is involved here?

REPUBLIC OF ARGENTINA V. WELTOVER, INC.

United States Supreme Court
504 U.S. 607 (1992)

JUSTICE SCALIA:

This case requires us to decide whether the Republic of Argentina's default on certain bonds issued as part of a plan to stabilize its currency was an act taken "in connection with a commercial activity" that had a "direct effect in the United States" so as to subject Argentina to suit in an American court under the Foreign Sovereign Immunities Act of 1976, 28 U.S.C. § 1602 et seq.

I

Since Argentina's currency is not one of the mediums of exchange accepted on the international market, Argentine businesses engaging in foreign transactions must pay in United States dollars or some other internationally accepted currency. In the recent past, it was difficult for Argentine borrowers to obtain such funds, principally because of the instability of the Argentine currency. To address these problems, petitioners, the Republic of Argentina and its central bank, Banco Central (collectively Argentina), in 1981 instituted a foreign exchange insurance contract program (FEIC), under which Argentina effectively agreed to assume the risk of currency depreciation in cross-border transactions involving Argentine borrowers. This was accomplished by Argentina's agreeing to sell to domestic borrowers, in exchange for a contractually predetermined amount of local currency, the necessary United States dollars to repay their foreign debts when they matured, irrespective of intervening devaluations.

Unfortunately, Argentina did not possess sufficient reserves of United States dollars to cover the FEIC contracts as they became due in 1982. The Argentine Government thereupon adopted certain emergency measures, including refinancing of the FEIC-backed debts by issuing to the creditors government bonds. These bonds, called "Bonods," provide for payment of interest and principal in United States dollars; payment may be made through transfer on the London, Frankfurt, Zurich, or New York market, at the election of the creditor. Under this refinancing program, the foreign creditor had the option of either accepting the Bonods in satisfaction of the initial debt, thereby substituting the Argentine Government for the private debtor, or maintaining the debtor/creditor relationship with the private borrower and accepting the Argentine Government as guarantor.

When the Bonods began to mature in May 1986, Argentina concluded that it lacked sufficient foreign exchange to retire them. Pursuant to a Presidential Decree, Argentina unilaterally extended the time for payment and offered bondholders substitute instruments as a means of rescheduling the debts. Respondents, two Panamanian corporations and a Swiss bank who hold, collectively, $1.3 million of Bonods, refused to accept the rescheduling and insisted on full payment, specifying New York as the place where payment should be made. Argentina did not pay, and respondents then brought this breach-of-contract action in the United States District Court for the Southern District of New York, relying on the Foreign Sovereign Immunities Act of 1976 as the basis for jurisdiction. Petitioners moved to dismiss for lack of subject-matter jurisdiction, lack of personal jurisdiction, and *forum non conveniens*. The District Court denied these motions, and the Court of Appeals affirmed. We granted Argentina's petition for certiorari, which challenged the Court of Appeals' determination that, under the Act, Argentina was not immune from the jurisdiction of the federal courts in this case.

II

The Foreign Sovereign Immunities Act of 1976 (FSIA) establishes a comprehensive framework for determining whether a court in this country, state or federal, may exercise jurisdiction over a foreign state. Under the Act, a "foreign state *shall* be immune from the jurisdiction of the courts of the United States and of the States" unless one of several statutorily defined exceptions applies. § 1604 (emphasis added). The FSIA thus provides the "sole basis" for obtaining jurisdiction over a foreign sovereign in the United States. See *Argentine Republic v. Amerada Hess Shipping Corp.*, 488 U.S. 428, 434–439 (1989). The most significant of the FSIA's exceptions—and the one at issue in this case—is the "commercial" exception of § 1605(a)(2), which provides that a foreign state is not immune from suit in any case

> "in which the action is based upon a commercial activity carried on in the United States by the foreign state; or upon an act performed in the United States in connection with a commercial activity of the foreign state elsewhere; or upon an act outside the territory of the United States in connection with a commercial activity of the foreign state elsewhere and that act causes a direct effect in the United States." § 1605(a)(2).

In the proceedings below, respondents relied only on the third clause of § 1605(a)(2) to establish jurisdiction, and our analysis is therefore limited to considering whether this lawsuit is (1) "based * * * upon an act outside the territory of the United States"; (2) that was taken "in connection with a commercial activity" of Argentina outside this country; and (3) that "cause[d] a direct effect in the United States." The complaint in this case alleges only one cause of action on behalf of each of the respondents, viz., a breach-of-contract claim based on Argentina's attempt to refinance the Bonods rather than to pay them according to their terms. The fact that the cause of action is in compliance with the first of the three requirements—that it is "based upon an act outside the territory of the United States" (presumably Argentina's unilateral extension)—is uncontested. The dispute pertains to whether the unilateral refinancing of the Bonods was taken "in connection with a commercial activity" of Argentina, and whether it had a "direct effect in the United States." We address these issues in turn.

A

Respondents and their *amicus*, the United States, contend that Argentina's issuance of, and continued liability under, the Bonods constitute a "commercial activity" and that the extension of the payment schedules was taken "in connection with" that activity. The latter point is obvious enough, and Argentina does not contest it; the key question is whether the activity is "commercial" under the FSIA.

The FSIA defines "commercial activity" to mean:

> "[E]ither a regular course of commercial conduct or a particular commercial transaction or act. The commercial character of an activity shall be determined by reference to the nature of the course of conduct or particular transaction or act, rather than by reference to its purpose." 28 U.S.C. § 1603(d).

This definition, however, leaves the critical term "commercial" largely undefined: The first sentence simply establishes that the commercial nature of an activity does *not* depend upon whether it is a single act or a regular course of conduct; and the second sentence merely specifies what element of the conduct determines commerciality (*i.e.,* nature rather than purpose), but still without saying what "commercial" means. Fortunately, however, the FSIA was not written on a clean slate. As we have noted, the Act (and the commercial exception in particular) largely codifies the so-called "restrictive" theory of foreign sovereign immunity first endorsed by the State Department in 1952. The meaning of "commercial" is the meaning generally attached to that term under the restrictive theory at the time the statute was enacted.

* * *

* * * [W]e conclude that when a foreign government acts, not as regulator of a market, but in the manner of a private player within it, the foreign sovereign's actions are "commercial" within the meaning of the FSIA. Moreover, because the Act provides that the commercial character of an act is to be determined by reference to its "nature" rather than its "purpose," 28 U.S.C. § 1603(d), the question is not whether the foreign government is acting with a profit motive or instead with the aim of fulfilling uniquely sovereign objectives. Rather, the issue is whether the particular actions that the foreign state performs (whatever the motive behind them) are the *type* of actions by which a private party engages in "trade and traffic or commerce," Black's Law Dictionary 270 (6th ed. 1990). Thus, a foreign government's issuance of regulations limiting foreign currency exchange is a sovereign activity, because such authoritative control of commerce cannot be exercised by a private party; whereas a contract to buy army boots or even bullets is a "commercial" activity, because private companies can similarly use sales contracts to acquire goods.

The commercial character of the Bonods is confirmed by the fact that they are in almost all respects garden-variety debt instruments: They may be held by private parties; they are negotiable and may be traded on the international market (except in Argentina); and they promise a future stream of cash income. We recognize that, prior to the enactment of the FSIA, there was authority [in *Victory Transport*] suggesting that the issuance of public debt instruments did not constitute a commercial activity. There is, however, nothing distinctive about the state's assumption of debt (other than perhaps its purpose) that would cause it always to be classified as *jure imperii*, and in this regard it is significant that *Victory Transport* expressed confusion as to whether the "nature" or the "purpose" of a transaction was controlling in determining commerciality. Because the FSIA has now clearly established that the "nature" governs, we perceive no basis for concluding that the issuance of debt should be treated as categorically different from other activities of foreign states.

Argentina contends that, although the FSIA bars consideration of "purpose," a court must nonetheless fully consider the *context* of a transaction in order to determine whether it is "commercial." Accordingly, Argentina claims that the Court of Appeals erred by defining the relevant conduct in what Argentina considers an overly generalized, acontextual manner and by essentially adopting a *per se* rule that all "issuance of debt instruments" is "commercial." We have no occasion to consider such a *per se* rule, because it seems to us that even in full context, there is nothing about the issuance of these Bonods (except perhaps its purpose) that is not analogous to a private commercial transaction.

Argentina points to the fact that the transactions in which the Bonods were issued did not have the ordinary commercial consequence of raising capital or financing acquisitions. Assuming for the sake of argument that this is not an example of judging the commerciality of a transaction by its purpose, the ready answer is that private parties regularly issue bonds, not just to raise capital or to finance purchases, but also to refinance debt. That is what Argentina did here: By virtue of the earlier FEIC contracts, Argentina was *already* obligated to supply the United States dollars needed to retire the FEIC-insured debts; the Bonods simply allowed Argentina to restructure its existing obligations. Argentina further asserts (without proof or even elaboration) that it "received consideration [for the Bonods] in no way commensurate with [their] value." Assuming that to be true, it makes no difference. Engaging in a commercial act does not require the receipt of fair value, or even compliance with the common-law requirements of consideration.

Argentina argues that the Bonods differ from ordinary debt instruments in that they "were created by the Argentine Government to fulfill its obligations under a foreign exchange program designed to address a domestic credit crisis, and as a component of a program designed to control that nation's critical shortage of foreign exchange." In this regard, Argentina relies heavily on *De Sanchez v. Banco Central de Nicaragua*, in which the Fifth Circuit took the view that "[o]ften, the essence of an act is defined by its purpose;" that unless "we can inquire into the purposes of such acts, we cannot determine their nature;" and that, in light of its purpose to control its reserves of foreign currency, Nicaragua's refusal to honor a check it had issued to cover a private bank debt was a sovereign act entitled to immunity. Indeed, Argentina asserts that the line between "nature" and "purpose" rests upon a "formalistic distinction [that] simply is neither useful nor warranted." We think this line of argument is squarely foreclosed by the language of the FSIA. However difficult it may be in some cases to separate "purpose" (*i.e.*, the *reason* why the foreign state engages in the activity) from "nature" (*i.e.*, the outward form of the conduct that the foreign state performs or agrees to perform), the statute unmistakably commands that to be done, 28 U.S.C. § 1603(d). We agree with the Court of Appeals that it is irrelevant *why* Argentina participated in the bond market in the manner of a private actor; it matters only that it did so. We conclude that Argentina's issuance of the Bonods was a "commercial activity" under the FSIA.

B

The remaining question is whether Argentina's unilateral rescheduling of the Bonods had a "direct effect" in the United States, 28 U.S.C. § 1605(a)(2). In addressing this issue, the Court of Appeals rejected the suggestion in the legislative history of the FSIA that an effect is not "direct" unless it is both "substantial" and "foreseeable." That suggestion is found in the House Report, which states that conduct covered by the third clause of § 1605(a)(2) would be subject to the jurisdiction of American courts "consistent with principles set forth in section 18, Restatement of the Law, Second, Foreign Relations Law of the United States (1965)." * * *

The Court of Appeals concluded that the rescheduling of the maturity dates obviously had a "direct effect" on respondents. It further concluded that that effect was sufficiently "in the United States" for purposes of the FSIA, in part because "Congress would have wanted an American court to entertain this action" in order to preserve New York City's status as "a preeminent commercial center." The question, however, is not what Congress "would have wanted" but what Congress enacted in the FSIA.

Although we are happy to endorse the Second Circuit's recognition of "New York's status as a world financial leader," the effect of Argentina's rescheduling in diminishing that status (assuming it is not too speculative to be considered an effect at all) is too remote and attenuated to satisfy the "direct effect" requirement of the FSIA.

We nonetheless have little difficulty concluding that Argentina's unilateral rescheduling of the maturity dates on the Bonods had a "direct effect" in the United States. Respondents had designated their accounts in New York as the place of payment, and Argentina made some interest payments into those accounts before announcing that it was rescheduling the payments. Because New York was thus the place of performance for Argentina's ultimate contractual obligations, the rescheduling of those obligations necessarily had a "direct effect" in the United States: Money that was supposed to have been delivered to a New York bank for deposit was not forthcoming. We reject Argentina's suggestion that the "direct effect" requirement cannot be satisfied where the plaintiffs are all foreign corporations with no other connections to the United States. We expressly stated in *Verlinden* that the FSIA permits "a foreign plaintiff to sue a foreign sovereign in the courts of the United States, provided the substantive requirements of the Act are satisfied."

* * *

We conclude that Argentina's issuance of the Bonods was a "commercial activity" under the FSIA; that its rescheduling of the maturity dates on those instruments was taken in connection with that commercial activity and had a "direct effect" in the United States; and that the District Court therefore properly asserted jurisdiction, under the FSIA, over the breach-of-contract claim based on that rescheduling. Accordingly, the judgment of the Court of Appeals is

Affirmed.

Was there in fact a "direct effect" in New York? If so what was that effect according to the Second Circuit and the Supreme Court respectively? If there is a "direct effect" wherever the bond-holders request payment, doesn't that put foreign sovereign immunity at the mercy of creditors?

One year after *Weltover*, the Supreme Court struggled with the "commercial activity" exception once again. In *Saudi Arabia v. Nelson*, 507 U.S. 349 (1993), Scott Nelson, a U.S. citizen, brought a tort suit against the Kingdom of Saudi Arabia claiming damages for personal injuries suffered while under arrest in Saudi Arabia. Nelson had moved to Saudi Arabia for employment as a monitoring systems engineer at a government owned hospital in Riyadh. Within a few months of employment, Nelson had identified significant safety issues at the hospital and repeatedly urged the hospital authorities to address those concerns. The hospital's administrators initially told Nelson to ignore the safety concerns. Eventually the administrators had him arrested and taken to jail where he was allegedly tortured, beaten, and subjected to inhumane conditions. The Saudi government eventually released Nelson after the intervention of a U.S. Senator.

The district court dismissed the case for lack of subject matter jurisdiction under the Foreign Sovereign Immunities Act. It rejected Nelson's claim that Saudi Arabia's actions were subject to the § 1605(a)(2) "commercial activities" exception—an exception which states that a foreign sovereign's commercial activities "carried on" in the United States are not subject to jurisdictional immunity. The district court did not find a sufficient nexus between Nelson's recruitment in the United States and the injuries he suffered in Saudi Arabia. The Court of Appeals reversed, finding that a sufficient nexus did exist. Ultimately, the Supreme Court reversed the Court of Appeals decision. The Court observed that, while Nelson's recruitment in the United States eventually led to actions that caused his injuries, the employment contract was not the basis of his suit. The Court found that Saudi Arabia's abusive actions (unlawful detention, torture, etc.) were not commercial in nature. Instead, these actions entailed the exercise of Saudi Arabia's police power, a type of authority that is "peculiarly sovereign in nature."

––––––––––––––

The Supreme Court has also taken up the FSIA in contexts other than the "commercial activity" exception. In *Republic of Austria v. Altmann*, 541 U.S. 677 (2004), Maria Altmann, a Jewish Holocaust survivor and naturalized U.S. citizen, sued Austria over six valuable paintings confiscated by the Nazis in Austria in 1938. The question of Austria's sovereign immunity turned, inter alia, on whether any of the exceptions provided by the FSIA applied. This, in turn, depended on whether the Act applied retroactively, i.e., to cases involving events before 1976.

Austria claimed sovereign immunity because, in 1938, the U.S. State Department had endorsed absolute immunity of foreign states. Austria noted that the State Department had first adopted the theory of restrictive immunity in 1952 (in the "Tate Letter"), more than ten years after the confiscation. The United States, Mexico and Japan filed amicus briefs in support of Austria, arguing that applying the FSIA (and in particular its exceptions) retroactively to pre-1976 conduct would threaten reasonable and settled expectations of foreign states. The Supreme Court disagreed and held that the FSIA does apply retroactively.

Sovereign immunity is also an issue with regard to international organizations. In *Waite & Kennedy v. Germany*, App. No. 26083/94, 30 Eur. H.R. Rep. 261 (1999), employees of the European Space Agency (the ESA, an international organization), sued their employer in German courts for violations of German labor law. Among other defenses, the ESA asserted sovereign immunity. The plaintiffs claimed that granting immunity violated their right of access to the courts under the European Convention of Human Rights and Fundamental Freedoms. The European Court of Human Rights held that if an international organization does not provide effective remedies, granting immunity to that international organization in national courts may constitute a violation of Article 6 of the European Convention on Human Rights. In the end, the Court rejected the claim because the employees had such remedies within the ESA.

In the United States, are international organizations covered by the FSIA?

For a comparative perspective, consider the following decision from the Supreme Court of India. What is the statutory basis for the decision? Why does the court deny Ethiopia sovereign immunity? In particular, what sources does the court invoke? What exact role do these sources play in the outcome of the case?

ETHIOPIAN AIRLINES V. GANESH NARAIN SABOO

Supreme Court of India
Civil Appeal No. 7037 of 2004 (2011)

JUSTICE BHANDARI:

* * *

3. The respondent booked a consignment of Reactive Dyes with the appellant Ethiopian Airlines to be delivered at the Dar Es Salaam, Tanzania on 30.9.1992. The airway bills were duly issued by the appellant from its office in Bombay at the Taj Mahal Hotel for the said consignment. According to the respondent there was gross delay in arrival of the consignment at the destination, which led to deterioration of the goods.

4. The respondent filed a complaint on 11.5.1993 before the Maharashtra State Consumer Dispute Redressal Commission (hereinafter referred to as 'the State Commission'). Pursuant to the notice issued by the State Commission, the appellant filed a written statement in which the appellant raised a preliminary objection regarding maintainability of the complaint.

* * *

8. The appellant * * * has preferred this appeal on the ground that a foreign State or its instrumentality cannot be proceeded against * * * without obtaining prior permission from the Central Government. The appellant contends that a foreign State or its instrumentality can legitimately claim sovereign immunity from being proceeded against * * * in respect of a civil claim.

9. It is submitted that, in India, it is clear that there is a presumption that sovereign immunity is absolute, but that a foreign sovereign can still be sued in India under certain circumstances with the permission of the Government of India. The Central Government may give consent for such a suit if:

(a) the foreign State has instituted a suit in the Court against the person desiring to sue it; or

(b) the foreign State trades within the legal limits of the jurisdiction of the Court or;

(c) the foreign State is in possession of immovable property situated within those limits and is to be sued with reference to such property or for money charged thereon or;

(d) the foreign State has expressly or impliedly waived the privilege of immunity.

* * *

11. Reliance was also placed on another judgment of this Court in the case of *Veb Deutfracht Seereederei Rostock (D.S.R. Lines) a Department of the German Democratic Republic v. New Central Jute Mills Co. Ltd. and Another* (1994). In para 5 of the judgment this Court held that:

* * *

The object of Section 86 of the Code is to give effect to the principles of International Law. But, in India it is only a qualified privilege because a suit can be brought with the consent of the Central Government in certain circumstances. Just as an independent sovereign State may statutorily provide for its own rights and liabilities to sue and be sued so can it provide rights and liabilities of foreign States to sue and be sued in its Courts. It can be said that effect of Section 86 thus is to modify the extent of doctrine of immunity recognised by the International Law. If a suit is filed in Indian Courts with the consent of the Central Government as required by Section 86, it shall not be open to any foreign State to rely on the doctrine of immunity. Sub-section (1) of Section 86 says in clear and unambiguous terms that no foreign State may be sued in any court, except with the consent of the Central Government certified in writing by the Secretary to that Government. Sub-section (2) prescribes that such consent shall not be given unless it appears to the Central Government that the case falls within any of the clauses (a) to (d) of sub-section (2) of Section 86. Sub-section (6) enjoins that where a request is made to the Central Government for the grant of any consent referred to in sub-section (1), the Central Government shall before refusing to accede to the request in whole or in part, give to the person making the request a reasonable opportunity of being heard.

On a plain reading of different sub-sections of Section 86, it is apparent that no foreign State may be sued in any court in India, except with the consent of the Central Government which has to be certified in writing by the Secretary to that Government. In view of the provisions aforesaid, before any action is launched or a suit is filed against a foreign State, person concerned has to make a request to the Central Government for grant of the necessary consent as required by sub-section (1) of Section 86 and the Central Government has to accede to the said request or refuse the same after taking into consideration all the facts and circumstances of the case.

12. It was submitted by the learned counsel for the appellant, Mr. K.G. Presswala, that when interpreting Section 86 of the CPC, it should always be kept in view that the said Section gives effect to the principles of international law.

* * *

51. We have heard learned counsel for the parties and carefully perused relevant cases cited at the Bar. The Central Question which requires adjudication is whether the appellant Ethiopian Airlines is entitled to sovereign immunity in this case?

* * *

68. In effect, by signing onto the Warsaw Convention [Convention for the Unification of Certain Rules Relating to International Carriage by Air (1929), the predecessor to the Montreal Convention, which we encountered in our introduction], Ethiopia had expressly waived its Airlines' right to immunity in cases such as that sub judice. Therefore, the Central Governments of both India and Ethiopia have waived that right by passing the Carriage by Air Act, 1972 and by signing onto the Warsaw Convention.

69. In accordance with the interpretation set forth above, the Bombay High Court has noted that Section 86 is of only limited applicability and can be overcome in cases of even implied waiver. For example, in *The German Democratic Republic v. The Dynamic Industrial Undertaking Ltd.*, the Bombay High Court found that Section 86 does not supplant the relevant doctrine under International Law. Rather, Section 86 "creates

another exception" to immunity, in addition to those exceptions recognized under International Law. Likewise, in *Kenya Airways v. Jinibai B. Kheshwala*, AIR 1998 Bombay 287, the Bombay High Court found that, while Kenya Airways was a state entity prima facie entitled to immunity under Section 86, it had nevertheless waived that immunity by, in its written statements, failing to raise a plea of sovereign immunity under Section 86 of the CPC. Therefore, in that case, the Bombay High Court found that Kenya Airways was not entitled to sovereign immunity and could be subjected to suit in an Indian court.

70. Ethiopian Airlines is not entitled to sovereign immunity with respect to a commercial transaction is also consonant with the holdings of other countries' courts and with the growing International Law principle of restrictive immunity. For instance, in England, in *Rahimtoola v. H.E.H. The Nizam of Hyderabad and Others* (1957) 3 All E.R. 441, Lord Denning found that "there was no reason why [a country] should grant to the departments or agencies of foreign governments an immunity which [the country does] not grant [its] own, provided always that the matter in dispute arises within the jurisdiction of [the country's] courts and is properly cognizable by them." Lord Denning also held that "if the dispute concerns * * * the commercial transactions of a foreign government * * * and it arises properly within the territorial jurisdiction of [a country's] courts, there is no ground for granting immunity," finding implicitly that it would not "offend the dignity of a foreign sovereign to have the merits of such a dispute canvassed in the domestic courts of another country."

71. Likewise, in *Trendtex Trading Corporation Ltd. v. Central Bank of Nigeria* (1977) 1 All E.R. 881, the Court held that the Central Bank of Nigeria was not entitled to plead sovereign immunity because, according to International Law Principle of restrictive immunity, a state-owned entity is not entitled to immunity for acts of a commercial nature, *jure gestionis*. The Court noted that "if a government department goes into the market places of the world and buys boots or cement—as a commercial transaction—that government department should be subject to all the rules of the market place." The Court also noted an "important practical consideration," stating that foreign sovereign immunity, "in protecting sovereign bodies from the indignities and disadvantages of that process, operates to deprive other persons of the benefits and advantages of [the judicial] process in relation to rights which they posses and which would otherwise be susceptible to enforcement." As the court stated, the principle of restrictive immunity is "manifestly better in accord with practical good sense and with justice."

72. On careful analysis of the American, English and Indian cases, it is abundantly clear that the appellant Ethiopian Airlines must be held accountable for the contractual and commercial activities and obligations that it undertakes in India.

73. * * * In the modern era, where there is close interconnection between different countries as far as trade, commerce and business are concerned, the principle of sovereign immunity can no longer be absolute in the way that it much earlier was. Countries who participate in trade, commerce and business with different countries ought to be subjected to normal rules of the market. If State owned entities would be able to operate with impunity, the rule of law would be degraded and international trade, commerce and business will come to a grinding halt. Therefore, we have no hesitation in coming to the conclusion that the appellant cannot claim sovereign immunity. The preliminary objection raised by the appellant before the court is devoid of any merit and must be rejected.

* * *

76. This appeal is accordingly disposed of, leaving the parties to bear their own costs.

How would the *Ethiopian Airlines* case have been decided under the FSIA?

B. HEAD OF STATE IMMUNITY

We must distinguish the immunity of sovereigns (especially states) from the immunity of state officials. There are essentially three groups of such officials. The first are the members of the diplomatic and consular corps. Their immunity is the subject of two treaties to which the vast majority of countries in the world (including the United States) are parties—the Vienna Convention on Diplomatic Relations of 1961 (which we already encountered in the Teheran Embassy Case in Chapter I) and the Vienna Convention on Consular Relations of 1963 (which we will encounter in Chapter X). We will not further discuss this group here. The second group consists of civil servants of intergovernmental organizations. It is regulated by various agreements about these IOs, such as the Convention on the Privileges and Immunities of the United Nations of 1946 and the Agreement Relating to the Headquarters of the United Nations of 1947. We also will not address this group in any detail. The third group consists of the so-called heads of state (such as the U.S. President), but also cabinet-level government officials (such as a country's foreign minister). This group is the subject of the cases below.

The immunity of heads of state (in courts outside of their own country) continues to be based on customary international law. Below you find three important recent decisions on this issue—one from an international court (the ICJ), the others from two domestic courts (the U.S. Supreme Court and the U.K. House of Lords). Do they strike the right balance between the needs of the international system and the protection of victims of human rights violations? Can the cases be reconciled? Where do they leave the law of head of state immunity?

Head of State Immunity in International Tribunals

In the case below, on what basis does Belgium issue an arrest warrant for the Congolese foreign minister? Why does the Court come down on the Congo's side? What concerns do the three judges in the separate opinion raise?

Note that the Court distinguishes between two types of immunity for heads of state. In your own words, what are these types and what are the main differences between them? Why does this distinction matter in the context of the case?

CASE CONCERNING THE ARREST WARRANT OF APRIL 2000 (DEMOCRATIC REPUBLIC OF THE CONGO V. BELGIUM)

International Court of Justice
2002 I.C.J. 3 (2002)

* * *

13. On 11 April 2000 an investigating judge of the Brussels tribunal de première instance issued "an international arrest warrant *in absentia*" against Mr. Abdulaye Yerodia Ndombasi, charging him, as perpetrator or co-perpetrator, with offences constituting grave breaches of the Geneva Conventions of 1949 and of the Additional Protocols thereto, and with crimes against humanity.

At the time when the arrest warrant was issued Mr. Yerodia was the Minister for Foreign Affairs of the Congo.

14. The arrest warrant was transmitted to the Congo on 7 June 2000, being received by the Congolese authorities on 12 July 2000. According to Belgium, the warrant was at the same time transmitted to the International Criminal Police Organization (Interpol), an organization whose function is to enhance and facilitate cross-border criminal police co-operation worldwide; through the latter, it was circulated internationally.

15. In the arrest warrant, Mr. Yerodia is accused of having made various speeches inciting racial hatred during the month of August 1998. The crimes with which Mr. Yerodia was charged were punishable in Belgium under the Law of 16 June 1993 "concerning the Punishment of Grave Breaches of the International Geneva Conventions of 12 August 1949 and of Protocols I and II of 8 June 1977 Additional Thereto", as amended by the Law of 19 February 1999 "concerning the Punishment of Serious Vio-

lations of International Humanitarian Law" (hereinafter referred to as the "Belgian Law").

Article 7 of the Belgian Law provides that "The Belgian courts shall have jurisdiction in respect of the offences provided for in the present Law, wheresoever they may have been committed". In the present case, according to Belgium, the complaints that initiated the proceedings as a result of which the arrest warrant was issued emanated from 12 individuals all resident in Belgium, five of whom were of Belgian nationality. It is not contested by Belgium, however, that the alleged acts to which the arrest warrant relates were committed outside Belgian territory, that Mr. Yerodia was not a Belgian national at the time of those acts, and that Mr. Yerodia was not in Belgian territory at the time that the arrest warrant was issued and circulated. That no Belgian nationals were victims of the violence that was said to have resulted from Mr. Yerodia's alleged offences was also uncontested.

Article 5, paragraph 3, of the Belgian Law further provides that "[i]mmunity attaching to the official capacity of a person shall not prevent the application of the present Law".

* * *

17. On 17 October 2000, the Congo filed in the Registry an Application instituting the present proceedings (see paragraph 1 above), in which the Court was requested "to declare that the Kingdom of Belgium shall annul the international arrest warrant issued on 11 April 2000". The Congo relied in its Application on two separate legal grounds. First, it claimed that "[t]he *universal jurisdiction* that the Belgian State attributes to itself under Article 7 of the Law in question" constituted a

> "[v]iolation of the principle that a State may not exercise its authority on the territory of another State and of the principle of sovereign equality among all Members of the United Nations, as laid down in Article 2, paragraph 1, of the Charter of the United Nations".

Secondly, it claimed that "[t]he non-recognition, on the basis of Article 5 * * * of the Belgian Law, of the immunity of a Minister for Foreign Affairs in office" constituted a "[v]iolation of the diplomatic immunity of the Minister for Foreign Affairs of a sovereign State, as recognized by the jurisprudence of the Court and following from Article 41, paragraph 2, of the Vienna Convention of 18 April 1961 on Diplomatic Relations".

* * *

51. The Court would observe at the outset that in international law it is firmly established that, as also diplomatic and consular agents, certain holders of high-ranking office in a State, such as the Head of State, Head of Government and Minister for Foreign Affairs, enjoy immunities from

jurisdiction in other States, both civil and criminal. For the purposes of the present case, it is only the immunity from criminal jurisdiction and the inviolability of an incumbent Minister for Foreign Affairs that fall for the Court to consider.

52. A certain number of treaty instruments were cited by the Parties in this regard. These included, first, the Vienna Convention on Diplomatic Relations of 18 April 1961, which states in its preamble that the purpose of diplomatic privileges and immunities is "to ensure the efficient performance of the functions of diplomatic missions as representing States". It provides in Article 32 that only the sending State may waive such immunity. On these points, the Vienna Convention on Diplomatic Relations, to which both the Congo and Belgium are parties, reflects customary international law. The same applies to the corresponding provisions of the Vienna Convention on Consular Relations of 24 April 1963, to which the Congo and Belgium are also parties.

The Congo and Belgium further cite the New York Convention on Special Missions of 8 December 1969, to which they are not, however, parties. They recall that under Article 21, paragraph 2, of that Convention:

"The Head of the Government, the Minister for Foreign Affairs and other persons of high rank, when they take part in a special mission of the sending State, shall enjoy in the receiving State or in a third State, in addition to what is granted by the present Convention, the facilities, privileges and immunities accorded by international law".

These conventions provide useful guidance on certain aspects of the question of immunities. They do not, however, contain any provision specifically defining the immunities enjoyed by Ministers for Foreign Affairs. It is consequently on the basis of customary international law that the Court must decide the questions relating to the immunities of such Ministers raised in the present case.

53. In customary international law, the immunities accorded to Ministers for Foreign Affairs are not granted for their personal benefit, but to ensure the effective performance of their functions on behalf of their respective States. In order to determine the extent of these immunities, the Court must therefore first consider the nature of the functions exercised by a Minister for Foreign Affairs. He or she is in charge of his or her Government's diplomatic activities and generally acts as its representative in international negotiations and intergovernmental meetings. Ambassadors and other diplomatic agents carry out their duties under his or her authority. His or her acts may bind the State represented, and there is a presumption that a Minister for Foreign Affairs, simply by virtue of that office, has full powers to act on behalf of the State (see, for example, Article 7, Paragraph 2 (a), of the 1969 Vienna Convention on the Law of Treaties). In the performance of these functions, he or she is frequently re-

quired to travel internationally, and thus must be in a position freely to do so whenever the need should arise. He or she must also be in constant communication with the Government, and with its diplomatic missions around the world, and be capable at any time of communicating with representatives of other States. The Court further observes that a Minister for Foreign Affairs, responsible for the conduct of his or her State's relations with all other States, occupies a position such that, like the Head of State or the Head of Government, he or she is recognized under international law as representative of the State solely by virtue of his or her office. * * *

54. The Court accordingly concludes that the functions of a Minister for Foreign Affairs are such that, throughout the duration of his or her office, he or she when abroad enjoys full immunity from criminal jurisdiction and inviolability. That immunity and that inviolability protect the individual concerned against any act of authority of another State which would hinder him or her in the performance of his or her duties.

55. In this respect, no distinction can be drawn between acts performed by a Minister for Foreign Affairs in an "official" capacity, and those claimed to have been performed in a "private capacity", or, for that matter, between acts performed before the person concerned assumed office as Minister for Foreign Affairs and acts committed during the period of office. Thus, if a Minister for Foreign Affairs is arrested in another State on a criminal charge, he or she is clearly thereby prevented from exercising the functions of his or her office. The consequences of such impediment to the exercise of those official functions are equally serious, regardless of whether the Minister for Foreign Affairs was, at the time of arrest, present in the territory of the arresting State on an "official" visit or a "private" visit, regardless of whether the arrest relates to acts allegedly performed before the person became the Minister for Foreign Affairs or to acts performed while in office, and regardless of whether the arrest relates to alleged acts performed in an "official" capacity or a "private" capacity. Furthermore, even the mere risk that, by travelling to or transiting another State a Minister for Foreign Affairs might be exposing himself or herself to legal proceedings could deter the Minister from travelling internationally when required to do so for the purposes of the performance of his or her official functions. * *

56. The Court will now address Belgium's argument that immunities accorded to incumbent Ministers for Foreign Affairs can in no case protect them where they are suspected of having committed war crimes or crimes against humanity. In support of this position, Belgium refers in its Counter-Memorial to various legal instruments creating international criminal tribunals, to examples from national legislation, and to the jurisprudence of national and international courts.

Belgium begins by pointing out that certain provisions of the instruments creating international criminal tribunals state expressly that the official capacity of a person shall not be a bar to the exercise by such tribunals of their jurisdiction.

Belgium also places emphasis on certain decisions of national courts, and in particular on the judgments rendered on 24 March 1999 by the House of Lords in the United Kingdom and on 13 March 2001 by the Court of Cassation in France in the *Pinochet* and *Qaddafi* cases respectively, in which it contends that an exception to the immunity rule was accepted in the case of serious crimes under international law. Thus, according to Belgium, the *Pinochet* decision recognizes an exception to the immunity rule when Lord Millett stated that "[i]nternational law cannot be supposed to have established a crime having the character of a *jus cogens* and at the same time to have provided an immunity which is co-extensive with the obligation it seeks to impose", or when Lord Phillips of Worth Matravers said that "no established rule of international law requires state immunity *ratione materiae* to be accorded in respect of prosecution for an international crime". As to the French Court of Cassation, Belgium contends that, in holding that, "under international law as it currently stands, the crime alleged [acts of terrorism], irrespective of its gravity, does not come within the exceptions to the principle of immunity from jurisdiction for incumbent foreign Heads of State", the Court explicitly recognized the existence of such exceptions.

57. The Congo, for its part, states that, under international law as it currently stands, there is no basis for asserting that there is any exception to the principle of absolute immunity from criminal process of an incumbent Minister for Foreign Affairs where he or she is accused of having committed crimes under international law.

In support of this contention, the Congo refers to State practice, giving particular consideration in this regard to the *Pinochet* and *Qaddafi* cases, and concluding that such practice does not correspond to that which Belgium claims but, on the contrary, confirms the absolute nature of the immunity from criminal process of Heads of State and Ministers for Foreign Affairs. Thus, in the *Pinochet* case, the Congo cites Lord Browne-Wilkinson's statement that "[t]his immunity enjoyed by a head of state in power and an ambassador in post is a complete immunity attached to the person of the head of state or ambassador and rendering him immune from all actions or prosecutions * * * ". According to the Congo, the French Court of Cassation adopted the same position in its *Qaddafi* judgment, in affirming that "international custom bars the prosecution of incumbent Heads of State, in the absence of any contrary international provision binding on the parties concerned, before the criminal courts of a foreign State".

As regards the instruments creating international criminal tribunals and the latter's jurisprudence, these, in the Congo's view, concern only those tribunals, and no inference can be drawn from them in regard to criminal proceedings before national courts against persons enjoying immunity under international law.

58. The Court has carefully examined State practice, including national legislation and those few decisions of national higher courts, such as the House of Lords or the French Court of Cassation. It has been unable to deduce from this practice that there exists under customary international law any form of exception to the rule according immunity from criminal jurisdiction and inviolability to incumbent Ministers for Foreign Affairs, where they are suspected of having committed war crimes or crimes against humanity.

The Court has also examined the rules concerning the immunity or criminal responsibility of persons having an official capacity contained in the legal instruments creating international criminal tribunals, and which are specifically applicable to the latter (see Charter of the International Military Tribunal of Nuremberg, Art. 7; Charter of the International Military Tribunal of Tokyo, Art. 6; Statute of the International Criminal Tribunal for the former Yugoslavia, Art. 7, para. 2; Statute of the International Criminal Tribunal for Rwanda, Art. 6, para. 2; Statute of the International Criminal Court, Art. 27). It finds that these rules likewise do not enable it to conclude that any such an exception exists in customary international law in regard to national courts.

Finally, none of the decisions of the Nuremberg and Tokyo international military tribunals, or of the International Criminal Tribunal for the former Yugoslavia, cited by Belgium deal with the question of the immunities of incumbent Ministers for Foreign Affairs before national courts where they are accused of having committed war crimes or crimes against humanity. The Court accordingly notes that those decisions are in no way at variance with the findings it has reached above.

* * *

60. The Court emphasizes, however, that the *immunity* from jurisdiction enjoyed by incumbent Ministers for Foreign Affairs does not mean that they enjoy *impunity* in respect of any crimes they might have committed, irrespective of their gravity. Immunity from criminal jurisdiction and individual criminal responsibility are quite separate concepts. While jurisdictional immunity is procedural in nature, criminal responsibility is a question of substantive law. Jurisdictional immunity may well bar prosecution for a certain period or for certain offences; it cannot exonerate the person to whom it applies from all criminal responsibility.

61. Accordingly, the immunities enjoyed under international law by an incumbent or former Minister for Foreign Affairs do not represent a bar to criminal prosecution in certain circumstances.

First, such persons enjoy no criminal immunity under international law in their own countries, and may thus be tried by those countries' courts in accordance with the relevant rules of domestic law.

Secondly, they will cease to enjoy immunity from foreign jurisdiction if the State which they represent or have represented decides to waive that immunity.

Thirdly, after a person ceases to hold the office of Minister for Foreign Affairs, he or she will no longer enjoy all of the immunities accorded by international law in other States. Provided that it has jurisdiction under international law, a court of one State may try a former Minister for Foreign Affairs of another State in respect of acts committed prior or subsequent to his or her period of office, as well as in respect of acts committed during that period of office in a private capacity.

Fourthly, an incumbent or former Minister for Foreign Affairs may be subject to criminal proceedings before certain international criminal courts, where they have jurisdiction. Examples include the International Criminal Tribunal for the former Yugoslavia, and the International Criminal Tribunal for Rwanda, established pursuant to Security Council resolutions under Chapter VII of the United Nations Charter, and the future International Criminal Court created by the 1998 Rome Convention. The latter's Statute expressly provides, in Article 27, paragraph 2, that "[i]mmunities or special procedural rules which may attach to the official capacity of a person, whether under national or international law, shall not bar the Court from exercising its jurisdiction over such a person".

* * *

70. The Court notes that the *issuance*, as such, of the disputed arrest warrant represents an act by the Belgian judicial authorities intended to enable the arrest on Belgian territory of an incumbent Minister for Foreign Affairs on charges of war crimes and crimes against humanity. * * * The Court notes that the warrant did admittedly make an exception for the case of an official visit by Mr. Yerodia to Belgium, and that Mr. Yerodia never suffered arrest in Belgium. The Court is bound, however, to find that, given the nature and purpose of the warrant, its mere issue violated the immunity which Mr. Yerodia enjoyed as the Congo's incumbent Minister for Foreign Affairs. The Court accordingly concludes that the issue of the warrant constituted a violation of an obligation of Belgium towards the Congo, in that it failed to respect the immunity of that Minister and, more particularly, infringed the immunity from criminal jurisdiction and the inviolability then enjoyed by him under international law.

* * *

78. For these reasons,

THE COURT,

* * *

(2) By thirteen votes to three,

Finds that the issue against Mr. Abdulaye Yerodia Ndombasi of the arrest warrant of 11 April 2000, and its international circulation, constituted violations of a legal obligation of the Kingdom of Belgium towards the Democratic Republic of the Congo, in that they failed to respect the immunity from criminal jurisdiction and the inviolability which the incumbent Minister for Foreign Affairs of the Democratic Republic of the Congo enjoyed under international law;

* * *

Joint Separate Opinion of JUDGES HIGGINS [United Kingdom], KOOIJMANS [Netherlands] and BUERGENTHAL [United States]:

1. We generally agree with what the Court has to say on the issues of jurisdiction and admissibility and also with the conclusions it reaches. There are, however, reservations that we find it necessary to make, both on what the Court has said and what it has chosen not to say when it deals with the merits. * * *

74. The increasing recognition of the importance of ensuring that the perpetrators of serious international crimes do not go unpunished has had its impact on the immunities which high State dignitaries enjoyed under traditional customary law. Now it is generally recognized that in the case of such crimes, which are often committed by high officials who make use of the power invested in the State, immunity is never substantive and thus cannot exculpate the offender from personal criminal responsibility. It has also given rise to a tendency, in the case of international crimes, to grant procedural immunity from jurisdiction only for as long as the suspected State official is in office.

75. These trends reflect a balancing of interests. On the one scale, we find the interest of the community of mankind to prevent and stop impunity for perpetrators of grave crimes against its members; on the other, there is the interest of the community of States to allow them to act freely on the inter-State level without unwarranted interference. A balance therefore must be struck between two sets of functions which are both valued by the international community. Reflecting these concerns, what is regarded as a permissible jurisdiction and what is regarded as the law on immunity are in constant evolution. The weights on the two scales are not

set for all perpetuity. Moreover, a trend is discernible that in a world which increasingly rejects impunity for the most repugnant offences, the attribution of responsibility and accountability is becoming firmer, the possibility for the assertion of jurisdiction wider and the availability of immunity as a shield more limited. The law of privileges and immunities, however, retains its importance since immunities are granted to high State officials to guarantee the proper functioning of the network of mutual inter-State relations, which is of paramount importance for a well-ordered and harmonious international system.

* * *

78. In the Judgment, the Court diminishes somewhat the significance of Belgium's arguments. After having emphasized—and we could not agree more—that the immunity from jurisdiction enjoyed by incumbent Ministers for Foreign Affairs does not mean that they enjoy impunity in respect of any crimes they might have committed (para. 60), the Court goes on to say that these immunities do not represent a bar to criminal prosecution in certain circumstances (para. 61). We feel less than sanguine about examples given by the Court of such circumstances. The chance that a Minister for Foreign Affairs will be tried in his own country in accordance with the relevant rules of domestic law or that his immunity will be waived by his own State is not high as long as there has been no change of power, whereas the existence of a competent international criminal court to initiate criminal proceedings is rare; moreover, it is quite risky to expect too much of a future international criminal court in this respect. The only credible alternative therefore seems to be the possibility of starting proceedings in a foreign court after the suspected person ceases to hold the office of Foreign Minister. This alternative, however, can also be easily forestalled by an uncooperative government that keeps the Minister in office for an as yet indeterminate period.

79. We wish to point out, however, that the frequently expressed conviction of the international community that perpetrators of grave and inhuman international crimes should not go unpunished does not *ipso facto* mean that immunities are unavailable whenever impunity would be the outcome. The nature of such crimes and the circumstances under which they are committed, usually by making use of the State apparatus, makes it less than easy to find a convincing argument for shielding the alleged perpetrator by granting him or her immunity from criminal process. But immunities serve other purposes which have their own intrinsic value and to which we referred in paragraph 77 above. International law seeks the accommodation of this value with the fight against impunity, and not the triumph of one norm over the other. A State may exercise the criminal jurisdiction which it has under international law, but in doing so it is subject to other legal obligations, whether they pertain to the non-

exercise of power in the territory of another State or to the required respect for the law of diplomatic relations or, as in the present case, to the procedural immunities of State officials. In view of the worldwide aversion to these crimes, such immunities have to be recognized with restraint, in particular when there is reason to believe that crimes have been committed which have been universally condemned in international conventions. It is, therefore, necessary to analyse carefully the immunities which under customary international law are due to high State officials and, in particular, to Ministers for Foreign Affairs.

80. Under traditional customary law the Head of State was seen as personifying the sovereign State. The immunity to which he was entitled was therefore predicated on status, just like the State he or she symbolized. Whereas State practice in this regard is extremely scarce, the immunities to which other high State officials (like Heads of Government and Ministers for Foreign Affairs) are entitled have generally been considered in the literature as merely functional.

81. We have found no basis for the argument that Ministers for Foreign Affairs are entitled to the same immunities as Heads of State. * * *

83. We agree, therefore, with the Court that the purpose of the immunities attaching to Ministers for Foreign Affairs under customary international law is to ensure the free performance of their functions on behalf of their respective States. During their term of office, they must therefore be able to travel freely whenever the need to do so arises. * * *

85. Nonetheless, that immunity prevails only as long as the Minister is in office and continues to shield him or her after that time only for "official" acts. It is now increasingly claimed in the literature that serious international crimes cannot be regarded as official acts because they are neither normal State functions nor functions that a State alone (in contrast to an individual) can perform (Goff, J. (as he then was) and Lord Wilberforce articulated this test in the case of *1° Congreso del Partido* (1978) QB 500 at 528 and (1983) AC 244 at 268, respectively). This view is underscored by the increasing realization that State-related motives are not the proper test for determining what constitutes public State acts. The same view is gradually also finding expression in State practice, as evidenced in judicial decisions and opinions. (For an early example, see the judgment of the Israel Supreme Court in the *Eichmann* case.) * * *

At the core, what policies are competing in the *Arrest Warrant* case? Why does the Court distinguish between immunity and impunity, and what measures does it believe are available to protect against impunity? What concerns do you have regarding the effectiveness of these measures?

Head of State Immunity in Domestic Courts

Over the last twenty years, heads of state have been sued repeatedly in domestic courts for alleged human rights violations. In some cases, states have brought criminal charges; in others, private plaintiffs have sought civil damages. Where these cases were brought in domestic courts outside of the defendant's home country, they have raised the issue of whether the courts of one country can exercise jurisdiction over the head of state (past or present) of another.

The case below is widely regarded as a milestone. The *Pinochet Case*, as it is generally known, is such an important event in the development of immunity (and of international criminal jurisdiction more generally) that even those who will never read the actual opinion should know the basic issue, decision and reasoning—as well as its (often ignored) limits. In the words of Lord Browne-Wilkinson, who penned the leading opinion, it was "the first time * * * when a local court * * * refused to afford immunity to a head of state or former head of state on the grounds that there can be no immunity against prosecution for certain international crimes."

In 1973, Augusto Pinochet led a military coup in Chile. It violently over-threw the socialist government of Salvador Allende, who was killed in the process. Pinochet then governed the country for seventeen years as president and head of a military junta, at least initially with the support of the United States (provided largely through the CIA). Undeniably, the Pinochet regime committed massive human rights violations in Chile, including murder and torture on a large scale. In 1990, the country made a transition to democracy. Pinochet stepped down as president, although he remained commander in chief of the armed forces until 1998 and a "senator for life," thus enjoying immunity in the Chilean courts.

In 1998, Pinochet traveled to London for medical treatment. At that point, a Spanish judge issued an arrest warrant against him for the torture of Spanish citizens in Chile and for the assassination of a Spanish diplomat. Spain requested that the United Kingdom extradite Pinochet to stand trial in Spain. Pinochet, who was placed under house arrest in London, claimed immunity from prosecution under the British State Immunity Act (of 1978). Chile, where Pinochet still enjoyed considerable political support even under the new, democratic regime, also resisted his extradition to Spain and claimed immunity for its former president.

The case occupied the British courts for more than a year and worked its way up to the country's highest tribunal at the time, the House of Lords (replaced in that role by the Supreme Court of the United Kingdom in 2009). The House of Lords issued its final decision in March of 1999. This decision is difficult to summarize because—in the manner typical for the House of Lords—each of the seven Law Lords sitting in the case issued his own, separate opinion (called a "speech"). As a result, the whole decision is so complex and long-winded that a careful reading requires the better part of a day. Six of the Law Lords eventually agreed that Pinochet was not entitled to immunity, although they did not fully agree on which crimes he could be prosecuted for. The seventh Law Lord (Goff of Chieveley) disagreed and considered Pinochet entitled to full immunity. The decision was also complex because it involved specific issues pertaining to extradition beyond the immunity problem. The following summary is limited to the immunity question and is based on what can be considered the lead opinion (by Lord Browne-Wilkinson).

Since at the time of the decision, Pinochet was no longer in office as a head of state, he was not—outside of Chile—entitled to immunity *ratione personae*. But was he immune from prosecution *ratione materiae*, i.e., because the alleged crimes (of at least orchestrating murder and torture) were official acts? It is important to note that Lord Browne-Wilkinson (and his colleagues) accepted that even crimes (committed in office) can be official acts for which immunity must be granted. The crucial question was whether torture was an exception. Lord Browne-Wilkinson veered in that direction because torture was now generally condemned as an international crime, and because universal jurisdiction over torture was now firmly established. Yet his crucial argument against allowing immunity for Pinochet was much more narrowly circumscribed: it ultimately turned on the United Nations Convention against Torture (adopted in 1984, in force 1987), which all the countries involved in the case had ratified (Spain in 1987, Chile and the United Kingdom in 1988).

Under Article 1 of the Convention, "torture" requires that the perpetrator act "in an official capacity"—which seems to suggest that the infliction of torture actually is an official act. At the same time, however, the Convention's very purpose is to ensure that torturers can find no refuge from prosecution anywhere in the world. (It creates universal jurisdiction, obligates member states to arrest torturers found on their territory, and then requires either prosecution or extradition to countries (e.g., of the victim's nationality) willing to prosecute, a principle known as *aut dedere aut punire*.) If torture counted as an official act for immunity purposes, this regime would be entirely undermined: perpetrators would—virtually by definition—enjoy immunity for torture as an official act and could thus never be effectively prosecuted (unless their home countries specifically waived their immunity—which Chile clearly had not done here). In other words, the Torture Convention would have no traction. In the view of Lord Browne-Wilkinson, such an absurd result had to be avoided. Consequently, the very nature and purpose of the Torture Convention excluded the characterization of torture as an official act for immunity purposes.

This implied, however, that Pinochet could be prosecuted only for acts of torture (not other crimes) and only for those acts committed after the Torture Convention had entered into force for the countries involved here, i.e., for acts after 1988. Thus the denial of immunity not only depended on the particular circumstances of the case, it was also very narrowly circumscribed. Still, it was sufficient to clear the path for extradition to Spain.

Once the House of Lords had issued its ruling, the decision on whether to extradite Pinochet was in the hands of the government. In 2000, the British Home Secretary (the cabinet member in charge of the matter) decided not to grant Spain's extradition request, allegedly on grounds of Pinochet's poor health. Pinochet returned to Chile where he was triumphantly greeted by supporters. He lived out his days in his home country, though not entirely peacefully. When the political tide turned more decisively against his former regime, he was subjected to a barrage of criminal investigations and eventually charged with more than 300 counts of human rights violations, tax evasion, passport forgery, etc., and he was eventually put under house arrest. For many years, the Chilean courts struggled with issues of his immunity (under Chilean law) and his fitness to stand trial. When Augusto Pinochet died in 2006 (aged 96), he had not yet been convicted of a single crime.

The following excerpts from the House of Lords decision are limited to three of the opinions issued and present only a very small part of a very long case.

REGINA V. EVANS AND ANOTHER AND THE COMMISSIONER OF POLICE FOR THE METROPOLIS AND OTHERS EX PARTE PINOCHET

House of Lords, 1 A.C. 147 (2000)

LORD BROWNE-WILKINSON:

My Lords,

As is well known, this case concerns an attempt by the Government of Spain to extradite Senator Pinochet from this country to stand trial in Spain for crimes committed (primarily in Chile) during the period when Senator Pinochet was head of state in Chile. The interaction between the various legal issues which arise is complex. I will therefore seek, first, to give a short account of the legal principles which are in play in order that my exposition of the facts will be more intelligible.

OUTLINE OF THE LAW

In general, a state only exercises criminal jurisdiction over offences which occur within its geographical boundaries. If a person who is alleged to have committed a crime in Spain is found in the United Kingdom, Spain can apply to the United Kingdom to extradite him to Spain. The power to extradite from the United Kingdom for an "extradition crime" is now contained in the Extradition Act 1989. For the purposes of the present case, the most important requirement is that the conduct complained of must constitute a crime under the law of both Spain and of the United Kingdom. This is known as the double criminality rule.

* * *

THE FACTS

* * *

There is no real dispute that during the period of the Senator Pinochet regime appalling acts of barbarism were committed in Chile and elsewhere in the world: torture, murder and the unexplained disappearance of individuals, all on a large scale. Although it is not alleged that Senator Pinochet himself committed any of those acts, it is alleged that they were done in pursuance of a conspiracy to which he was a party, at his instigation and with his knowledge. He denies these allegations. None of the conduct alleged was committed by or against citizens of the United Kingdom or in the United Kingdom.

In 1998 Senator Pinochet came to the United Kingdom for medical treatment. The judicial authorities in Spain sought to extradite him in order to stand trial in Spain on a large number of charges. Some of those charges had links with Spain. But most of the charges had no connection with Spain. The background to the case is that to those of left-wing political convictions Senator Pinochet is seen as an arch-devil: to those of right-wing persuasions he is seen as the saviour of Chile. It may well be thought that the trial of Senator Pinochet in Spain for offences all of which related to the state of Chile and most of which occurred in Chile is not calculated to achieve the best justice. But I cannot emphasise too strongly that that is no concern of your Lordships. Although others perceive our task as being to choose between the two sides on the grounds of personal preference or political inclination, that is an entire misconception. Our job is to decide two questions of law: are there any extradition crimes and, if so, is Senator Pinochet immune from trial for committing those crimes. If, as a matter of law, there are no extradition crimes or he is entitled to immunity in relation to whichever crimes there are, then there is no legal right to extradite Senator Pinochet to Spain or, indeed, to stand in the way of his return to Chile. If, on the other hand, there are extradition crimes in relation to which Senator Pinochet is not entitled to state immunity then it will be open to the Home Secretary to extradite him. The task of this House is only to decide those points of law.

* * *

I must therefore consider whether * * * Senator Pinochet enjoys sovereign immunity. But first it is necessary to consider the modern law of torture.

TORTURE

Apart from the law of piracy, the concept of personal liability under international law for international crimes is of comparatively modern growth. The traditional subjects of international law are states not human beings. But consequent upon the war crime trials after the 1939–45 World War, the international community came to recognise that there could be criminal liability under international law for a class of crimes such as war crimes and crimes against humanity. Although there may be legitimate doubts as to the legality of the Charter of the Nuremberg Tribunal, in my judgment those doubts were stilled by the Affirmation of the Principles of International Law recognised by the Charter of Nuremberg Tribunal adopted by the United Nations General Assembly on 11 December 1946. That Affirmation affirmed the principles of international law recognised by the Charter of the Nuremberg Tribunal and the judgment of the Tribunal and directed the Committee on the codification of international law to treat as a matter of primary importance plans for the formulation of the principles recognised in the Charter of the Nuremberg Tribunal. At least from that date onwards the concept of personal liability for a crime in international law must have been part of international law. In the early years state torture was one of the elements of a war crime. In consequence torture, and various other crimes against humanity, were linked to war or at least to hostilities of some kind. But in the course of time this linkage with war fell away and torture, divorced from war or hostilities, became an international crime on its own: see *Oppenheim's International Law* (Jennings and Watts edition) vol. 1, 996; note 6 to Article 18 of the *I.L.C. Draft Code of Crimes Against Peace*; *Prosecutor v. Furundzija* Tribunal for Former Yugoslavia, Case No. 17–95–17/1–T. Ever since 1945, torture on a large scale has featured as one of the crimes against humanity: see, for example, U.N. General Assembly Resolutions 3059, 3452 and 3453 passed in 1973 and 1975; Statutes of the International Criminal Tribunals for former Yugoslavia (Article 5) and Rwanda (Article 3).

Moreover, the Republic of Chile accepted before your Lordships that the international law prohibiting torture has the character of *jus cogens* or a peremptory norm, i.e. one of those rules of international law which have a particular status. * * *

The *jus cogens* nature of the international crime of torture justifies states in taking universal jurisdiction over torture wherever committed. International law provides that offences [against] *jus cogens* may be punished by any state because the offenders are "common enemies of all mankind and all nations have an equal interest in their apprehension and prosecution": *Demjanjuk v. Petrovsky* (1985) 603 F. Supp. 1468; 776 F. 2d. 571.

It was suggested by Miss Montgomery, for Senator Pinochet, that although torture was contrary to international law it was not strictly an international crime in the highest sense. In the light of the authorities to which I have referred (and there are many others) I have no doubt that long before the Torture Convention of 1984 state torture was an international crime in the highest sense.

But there was no tribunal or court to punish international crimes of torture. Local courts could take jurisdiction: see *Demjanjuk* (supra); *Attorney–General of Israel v. Eichmann* (1962) 36 I.L.R.S. But the objective was to ensure a general jurisdiction so that the torturer was not safe wherever he went. For example, in this case it is alleged that during the Pinochet regime torture was an official, although unacknowledged, weapon of government and that, when the regime was about to end, it passed legislation designed to afford an amnesty to those who had engaged in institutionalised torture. If these allegations are true, the fact that the local court had jurisdiction to deal with the international crime of torture was nothing to the point so long as the totalitarian regime remained in power: a totalitarian regime will not permit adjudication by its own courts on its own shortcomings. Hence the demand for some international machinery to repress state torture which is not dependent upon the local courts where the torture was committed. In the event, over 110 states (including Chile, Spain and the United Kingdom) became state parties to the Torture Convention. But it is far from clear that none of them practised state torture. What was needed therefore was an international system which could punish those who were guilty of torture and which did not permit the evasion of punishment by the torturer moving from one state to another. The Torture Convention was agreed not in order to create an international crime which had not previously existed but to provide an international system under which the international criminal—the torturer—could find no safe haven. Burgers and Danelius (respectively the chairman of the United Nations Working Group on the 1984 Torture Convention and the draftsmen of its first draft) say, at p. 131, that it was "an essential purpose [of the Convention] to ensure that a torturer does not escape the consequences of his act by going to another country."

THE TORTURE CONVENTION

Article 1 of the Convention defines torture as the intentional infliction of severe pain and of suffering with a view to achieving a wide range of purposes "when such pain or suffering is inflicted by or at the instigation of or with the consent or acquiesence of a public official or other person acting in an official capacity." Article 2(1) requires each state party to prohibit torture on territory within its own jurisdiction and Article 4 requires each state party to ensure that "all" acts of torture are offences under its criminal law. Article 2(3) outlaws any defence of superior orders. Under Article 5(1) each state party has to establish its jurisdiction over torture

(a) when committed within territory under its jurisdiction (b) when the alleged offender is a national of that state, and (c) in certain circumstances, when the victim is a national of that state. Under Article 5(2) a state party has to take jurisdiction over any alleged offender who is found within its territory. Article 6 contains provisions for a state in whose territory an alleged torturer is found to detain him, inquire into the position and notify the states referred to in Article 5(1) and to indicate whether it intends to exercise jurisdiction. Under Article 7 the state in whose territory the alleged torturer is found shall, if he is not extradited to any of the states mentioned in Article 5(1), submit him to its authorities for the purpose of prosecution. Under Article 8(1) torture is to be treated as an extraditable offence and under Article 8(4) torture shall, for the purposes of extradition, be treated as having been committed not only in the place where it occurred but also in the state mentioned in Article 5(1).

WHO IS AN "OFFICIAL" FOR THE PURPOSES OF THE TORTURE CONVENTION?

The first question on the Convention is to decide whether acts done by a head of state are done by "a public official or a person acting in an official capacity" within the meaning of Article 1. * * *

It became clear during the argument that both the Republic of Chile and Senator Pinochet accepted that the acts alleged against Senator Pinochet, if proved, were acts done by a public official or person acting in an official capacity within the meaning of Article 1. In my judgment these concessions were correctly made. Unless a head of state authorising or promoting torture is an official or acting in an official capacity within Article 1, then he would not be guilty of the international crime of torture even within his own state. That plainly cannot have been the intention. In my judgment it would run completely contrary to the intention of the Convention if there was anybody who could be exempt from guilt. The crucial question is not whether Senator Pinochet falls within the definition in Article 1: he plainly does. The question is whether, even so, he is procedurally immune from process. To my mind the fact that a head of state can be guilty of the crime casts little, if any, light on the question whether he is immune from prosecution for that crime in a foreign state.

UNIVERSAL JURISDICTION

There was considerable argument before your Lordships concerning the extent of the jurisdiction to prosecute torturers conferred on states other than those mentioned in Article 5(1). I do not find it necessary to seek an answer to all the points raised. It is enough that it is clear that in all circumstances, if the Article 5(1) states do not choose to seek extradition or to prosecute the offender, other states must do so. The purpose of the Convention was to introduce the principle *aut dedere aut punire*—either you extradite or you punish. * * *

I gather the following important points from the Torture Convention:

1) Torture within the meaning of the Convention can only be committed by "a public official or other person acting in an official capacity," but these words include a head of state. A single act of official torture is "torture" within the Convention;

2) Superior orders provide no defence;

3) If the states with the most obvious jurisdiction (the Article 5(1) states) do not seek to extradite, the state where the alleged torturer is found must prosecute or, apparently, extradite to another country, i.e. there is universal jurisdiction.

4) There is no express provision dealing with state immunity of heads of state, ambassadors or other officials.

5) Since Chile, Spain and the United Kingdom are all parties to the Convention, they are bound under treaty by its provisions whether or not such provisions would apply in the absence of treaty obligation. Chile ratified the Convention with effect from 30 October 1988 and the United Kingdom with effect from 8 December 1988.

STATE IMMUNITY

This is the point around which most of the argument turned. It is of considerable general importance internationally since, if Senator Pinochet is not entitled to immunity in relation to the acts of torture alleged to have occurred after 29 September 1988, it will be the first time so far as counsel have discovered when a local domestic court has refused to afford immunity to a head of state or former head of state on the grounds that there can be no immunity against prosecution for certain international crimes.

Given the importance of the point, it is surprising how narrow is the area of dispute. There is general agreement between the parties as to the rules of statutory immunity and the rationale which underlies them. The issue is whether international law grants state immunity in relation to the international crime of torture and, if so, whether the Republic of Chile is entitled to claim such immunity even though Chile, Spain and the United Kingdom are all parties to the Torture Convention and therefore "contractually" bound to give effect to its provisions from 8 December 1988 at the latest.

* * *

[Like an ambassador under the Vienna Convention on Diplomatic Relations] a former head of state enjoys similar immunities, *ratione materiae*, once he ceases to be head of state. He too loses immunity *ratione personae* on ceasing to be head of state. As ex head of state he cannot be sued in respect of acts performed whilst head of state in his public capacity. Thus, at common law, the position of the former ambassador and the former head of state appears to be much the same: both enjoy immunity for acts done in performance of their respective functions whilst in office.

* * * Accordingly, in my judgment, Senator Pinochet as former head of state enjoys immunity *ratione materiae* in relation to acts done by him as head of state as part of his official functions as head of state.

The question then which has to be answered is whether the alleged organisation of state torture by Senator Pinochet (if proved) would constitute an act committed by Senator Pinochet as part of his official functions as head of state. It is not enough to say that it cannot be part of the functions of the head of state to commit a crime. Actions which are criminal under the local law can still have been done officially and therefore give rise to immunity *ratione materiae*. The case needs to be analysed more closely.

Can it be said that the commission of a crime which is an international crime against humanity and *jus cogens* is an act done in an official capacity on behalf of the state? I believe there to be strong ground for saying that the implementation of torture as defined by the Torture Convention cannot be a state function. * * *

I have doubts whether, before the coming into force of the Torture Convention, the existence of the international crime of torture as *jus cogens* was enough to justify the conclusion that the organisation of state torture could not rank for immunity purposes as performance of an official function. At that stage there was no international tribunal to punish torture and no general jurisdiction to permit or require its punishment in domestic courts. Not until there was some form of universal jurisdiction for the punishment of the crime of torture could it really be talked about as a fully constituted international crime. But in my judgment the Torture Convention did provide what was missing: a worldwide universal jurisdiction. Further, it required all member states to ban and outlaw torture: Article 2. How can it be for international law purposes an official function to do something which international law itself prohibits and criminalises? Thirdly, an essential feature of the international crime of torture is that it must be committed "by or with the acquiesence of a public official or other person acting in an official capacity." As a result all defendants in torture cases will be state officials. Yet, if the former head of state has immunity, the man most responsible will escape liability while his inferiors (the chiefs of police, junior army officers) who carried out his orders will be liable. I find it impossible to accept that this was the intention.

Finally, and to my mind decisively, if the implementation of a torture regime is a public function giving rise to immunity *ratione materiae*, this produces bizarre results. Immunity *ratione materiae* applies not only to ex-heads of state and ex-ambassadors but to all state officials who have been involved in carrying out the functions of the state. Such immunity is

necessary in order to prevent state immunity being circumvented by
prosecuting or suing the official who, for example, actually carried out the
torture when a claim against the head of state would be precluded by the
doctrine of immunity. If that applied to the present case, and if the implementation of the torture regime is to be treated as official business sufficient to found an immunity for the former head of state, it must also be
official business sufficient to justify immunity for his inferiors who actually did the torturing. Under the Convention the international crime of torture can only be committed by an official or someone in an official capacity. They would all be entitled to immunity. It would follow that there can
be no case outside Chile in which a successful prosecution for torture can
be brought unless the State of Chile is prepared to waive its right to its
officials [sic] immunity. Therefore the whole elaborate structure of universal jurisdiction over torture committed by officials is rendered abortive
and one of the main objectives of the Torture Convention—to provide a
system under which there is no safe haven for torturers—will have been
frustrated. In my judgment all these factors together demonstrate that
the notion of continued immunity for ex-heads of state is inconsistent
with the provisions of the Torture Convention.

For these reasons in my judgment if, as alleged, Senator Pinochet organised and authorised torture after 8 December 1988, he was not acting in
any capacity which gives rise to immunity *ratione materiae* because such
actions were contrary to international law, Chile had agreed to outlaw
such conduct and Chile had agreed with the other parties to the Torture
Convention that all signatory states should have jurisdiction to try official
torture (as defined in the Convention) even if such torture were committed in Chile.

As to the charges of murder and conspiracy to murder, no one has advanced any reason why the ordinary rules of immunity should not apply
and Senator Pinochet is entitled to such immunity.

* * *

LORD GOFF of Chieveley:

* * *

Before the Divisional Court, and again before the first Appellate Committee, it was argued on behalf of the Government of Spain that Senator Pinochet was not entitled to the benefit of state immunity basically on two
grounds, viz. first, that the crimes alleged against Senator Pinochet are so
horrific that an exception must be made to the international law principle
of state immunity; and second, that the crimes with which he is charged
are crimes against international law, in respect of which state immunity
is not available. Both arguments were rejected by the Divisional Court,
but a majority of the first Appellate Committee accepted the second ar-

gument. The leading opinion was delivered by Lord Nicholls of Birken-head, whose reasoning was of great simplicity. He said (see [1998] 3 W.L.R. 1456 at p. 1500C-F):

> In my view, article 39(2) of the Vienna Convention, as modified and applied to former heads of state by section 20 of the Act of 1978, is apt to confer immunity in respect of functions which international law recognises as functions of a head of state, irrespective of the terms of his domestic constitution. This formulation, and this test for determining what are the functions of a head of state for this purpose, are sound in principle and were not the subject of controversy before your Lordships. International law does not require the grant of any wider immunity. And it hardly needs saying that torture of his own subjects, or of aliens, would not be regarded by international law as a function of a head of state. All states disavow the use of torture as abhorrent, although from time to time some still resort to it. Similarly, the taking of hostages, as much as torture, has been outlawed by the international community as an offence. International law recognises, of course, that the functions of a head of state may include activities which are wrongful, even illegal, by the law of his own state or by the laws of other states. But international law has made plain that certain types of conduct, including torture and hostage-taking, are not acceptable conduct on the part of anyone. This applies as much to heads of state, or even more so, as it does to everyone else; the contrary conclusion would make a mockery of international law.

Lord Hoffmann agreed, and Lord Steyn delivered a concurring opinion to the same effect.

Lord Slynn of Hadley and Lord Lloyd of Berwick, however, delivered substantial dissenting opinions. * * *

* * *

IV. STATE IMMUNITY

Like my noble and learned friend Lord Browne-Wilkinson, I regard the principles of state immunity applicable in the case of heads of state and former heads of state as being relatively non-controversial * * *.

* * *

However, a question arises whether any limit is placed on the immunity in respect of criminal offences. Obviously the mere fact that the conduct is criminal does not of itself exclude the immunity, otherwise there would be little point in the immunity from criminal process; and this is so even where the crime is of a serious character. It follows, in my opinion, that the mere fact that the crime in question is torture does not exclude state immunity. It has however been stated by Sir Arthur Watts (op. cit. at pp. 81-84) that a head of state may be personally responsible:

> "for acts of such seriousness that they constitute not merely international wrongs (in the broad sense of a civil wrong) but rather international crimes which offend against the public order of the international community."

He then referred to a number of instruments, including the Charter of the Nuremberg Tribunal (1946), the Charter of the Tokyo Tribunal (1948), the International Law Commission's Draft Code of Crimes Against the Peace and Security of Mankind (provisionally adopted in 1988), and the Statute of the War Crimes Tribunal for former Yugoslavia (1993), all of which expressly provide for the responsibility of heads of state, apart from the Charter of the Tokyo Tribunal which contains a similar provision regarding the official position of the accused. He concluded, at p. 84, that:

> "It can no longer be doubted that as a matter of general customary international law a head of state will personally be liable to be called to account if there is sufficient evidence that he authorised or perpetrated such serious international crimes."

* * * [But] these instruments are all concerned with international responsibility before international tribunals, and not with the exclusion of state immunity in criminal proceedings before national courts. This supports the conclusion of Lord Slynn ([1998] 3 W.L.R. 1456 at p. 1474H) that "except in regard to crimes in particular situations before international tribunals these measures did not in general deal with the question whether otherwise existing immunities were taken away," with which I have already expressed my respectful agreement.

It follows that, if state immunity in respect of crimes of torture has been excluded at all in the present case, this can only have been done by the Torture Convention itself.

V.   TORTURE CONVENTION

I turn now to the Torture Convention of 1984, which lies at the heart of the present case. This is concerned with the jurisdiction of national courts, but its "essential purpose" is to ensure that a torturer does not escape the consequences of his act by going to another country * * *.

* * *

It is to be observed that no mention is made of state immunity in the Convention. Had it been intended to exclude state immunity, it is reasonable to assume that this would have been the subject either of a separate article, or of a separate paragraph in Article 7, introduced to provide for that particular matter. This would have been consistent with the logical framework of the Convention, under which separate provision is made for each topic, introduced in logical order.

* * *

In the light of the foregoing it appears to me to be clear that, in accordance both with international law, and with the law of this country which on this point reflects international law, a state's waiver of its immunity by treaty must, as Dr. Collins submitted, always be express. Indeed, if this was not so, there could well be international chaos as the courts of different state parties to a treaty reach different conclusions on the question whether a waiver of immunity was to be implied.

* * *

For the above reasons, I am of the opinion that * * * Senator Pinochet is entitled to the benefit of state immunity *ratione materiae* as a former head of state. I would therefore dismiss the appeal of the Government of Spain from the decision of the Divisional Court.

LORD HOPE of Craighead:

* * *

[E]ven in the field of such high crimes as have achieved the status of *jus cogens* under customary international law there is as yet no general agreement that they are outside the immunity to which former heads of state are entitled from the jurisdiction of foreign national courts. There is plenty of source material to show that war crimes and crimes against humanity have been separated out from the generality of conduct which customary international law has come to regard as criminal. These developments were described by Lord Slynn of Hadley [1998] 3 W.L.R. 1456, 1474D–H and I respectfully agree with his analysis. As he said, at p. 1474H, except in regard to crimes in particular situations where international tribunals have been set up to deal with them and it is part of the arrangement that heads of state should not have any immunity, there is no general recognition that there has been a loss of immunity from the jurisdiction of foreign national courts. This led him to sum the matter up in this way at p. 1475B-E:

> "So it is necessary to consider what is needed, in the absence of a general international convention defining or cutting down head of state immunity, to define or limit the former head of state immunity in particular cases. In my opinion it is necessary to find provision in an international convention to which the state asserting, and the state being asked to refuse, the immunity of a former head of state for an official act is a party; the convention must clearly define a crime against international law and require or empower a state to

prevent or prosecute the crime, whether or not committed in its jurisdiction and whether or not committed by one of its nationals; it must make it clear that a national court has jurisdiction to try a crime alleged against a former head of state, or that having been a head of state is no defence and that expressly or impliedly the immunity is not to apply so as to bar proceedings against him. The convention must be given the force of law in the national courts of the state; in a dualist country like the United Kingdom that means by legislation, so that with the necessary procedures and machinery the crime may be prosecuted there in accordance with the procedures to be found in the convention."

That is the background against which I now turn to the Torture Convention. As all the requirements which Lord Slynn laid out in the passage at p. 1475B-E save one are met by it, when read with the provisions of sections 134 and 135 of the Criminal Justice Act 1988 which gave the force of law to the Convention in this country, I need deal only with the one issue which remains. Did it make it clear that a former head of state has no immunity in the courts of a state which has jurisdiction to try the crime?

THE TORTURE CONVENTION AND LOSS OF IMMUNITY

* * * The Torture Convention does not contain any provision which deals expressly with the question whether heads of state or former heads of state are or are not to have immunity from allegations that they have committed torture.

But there remains the question whether the effect of the Torture Convention was to remove the immunity by necessary implication. * * *

The preamble to the Torture Convention explains its purpose. After referring to Article 5 of the Universal Declaration of Human Rights which provides that no one shall be subjected to torture or other cruel, inhuman or degrading treatment and to the United Nations Declaration of 9 December 1975 regarding torture and other cruel, inhuman or degrading treatment or punishment, it states that it was desired "to make more effective the struggle against torture and other cruel, inhuman or degrading treatment or punishment throughout the world." There then follows in Article 1 a definition of the term "torture" for the purposes of the Convention. It is expressed in the widest possible terms. It means "any act by which severe pain or suffering, whether physical or mental, is intentionally inflicted" for such purposes as obtaining information or a confession, punishment, intimidation or coercion or for any reason based on discrimination of any kind. It is confined however to official torture by its concluding words, which require such pain or suffering to have been "inflicted by or at the instigation of or with the consent or acquiescence of a public official or other person acting in an official capacity."

This definition is so broadly framed as to suggest on the one hand that heads of state must have been contemplated by its concluding words, but to raise the question on the other hand whether it was also contemplated that they would by necessary implication be deprived of their immunity. The words "public official" might be thought to refer to someone of lower rank than the head of state. Other international instruments suggest that where the intention is to include persons such as the head of state or diplomats they are mentioned expressly in the instrument: see Article 27 of the Rome Statute of the International Criminal Court which was adopted on 17 July 1998. But a head of state who resorted to conduct of the kind described in the exercise of his function would clearly be "acting in an official capacity." It would also be a strange result if the provisions of the Convention could not be applied to heads of state who, because they themselves inflicted torture or had instigated the carrying out of acts of torture by their officials, were the persons primarily responsible for the perpetration of these acts.

* * *

* * * [I]t would be wrong to regard the Torture Convention as having by necessary implication removed the immunity *ratione materiae* from former heads of state in regard to every act of torture of any kind which might be alleged against him falling within the scope of Article 1. * * *

Nevertheless there remains the question whether the immunity can survive Chile's agreement to the Torture Convention if the torture which is alleged was of such a kind or on such a scale as to amount to an international crime. Sir Arthur Watts in his Hague Lectures, p. 82 states that the idea that individuals who commit international crimes are internationally accountable for them has now become an accepted part of international law. The international agreements to which states have been striving in order to deal with this problem in international criminal courts have been careful to set a threshold for such crimes below which the jurisdiction of those courts will not be available. The Statute of the International Tribunal for the Former Yugoslavia (1993) includes torture in article 5 as one of the crimes against humanity. In paragraph 48 of his Report to the United Nations the Secretary–General explained that crimes against humanity refer to inhuman acts of a very serious nature, such as willful killing, torture or rape, committed as part of a widespread or systematic attack against any civilian population. Similar observations appear in paragraphs 131 to 135 of the Secretary–General's Report of 9 December 1994 on the Rwanda conflict. Article 3 of the Statute of the International Tribunal for Rwanda (1994) included torture as one of the crimes against humanity "when committed as part of a widespread or systematic attack against any civilian population" on national, political, ethnic or other grounds. Article 7 of the Rome Statute contains a similar limitation to acts of widespread or systematic torture.

The allegations which the Spanish judicial authorities have made against Senator Pinochet fall into that category. As I sought to make clear in my analysis of the draft charges, we are not dealing in this case—even upon the restricted basis of those charges on which Senator Pinochet could lawfully be extradited if he has no immunity—with isolated acts of official torture. We are dealing with the remnants of an allegation that he is guilty of what would now, without doubt, be regarded by customary international law as an *international* crime. This is because he is said to have been involved in acts of torture which were committed in pursuance of a policy to commit systematic torture within Chile and elsewhere as an instrument of government. On the other hand it is said that, for him to lose his immunity, it would have to be established that there was a settled practice for crime of this nature to be so regarded by customary international law at the time when they were committed. I would find it hard to say that it has been shown that any such settled practice had been established by 29 September 1988. But we must be careful not to attach too much importance to this point, as the opportunity for prosecuting such crimes seldom presents itself.

Despite the difficulties which I have mentioned, I think that there are sufficient signs that the necessary developments in international law were in place by that date. * * *

I would not regard this as a case of waiver. Nor would I accept that it was an implied term of the Torture Convention that former heads of state were to be deprived of their immunity *ratione materiae* with respect to all acts of official torture as defined in article 1. It is just that the obligations which were recognized by customary international law in the case of such serious international crimes by the date when Chile ratified the Convention are so strong as to override any objection by it on the ground of immunity *ratione materiae* to the exercise of the jurisdiction over crimes committed after that date which the United Kingdom had made available.

I consider that the date as from which the immunity *ratione materiae* was lost was 30 October 1988, which was the date when Chile's ratification of the Torture Convention on 30 September 1988 took effect. Spain had already ratified the Convention. It did so on 21 October 1987. The Convention was ratified by the United Kingdom on 8 December 1988 following the coming into force of section 134 of the Criminal Justice Act 1988. On the approach which I would take to this question the immunity *ratione materiae* was lost when Chile, having ratified the Convention to which section 134 gave effect and which Spain had already ratified, was deprived of the right to object to the extra-territorial jurisdiction which the

United Kingdom was able to assert over these offences when the section came into force. * * *

[The speeches (opinions) by Lords Hutton, Saville of Newdigate, Millett, and Phillips of Worth Matravers are omitted.]

———————

How do the three Law Lords' opinions excerpted above differ from one another with regard both to result and rationale? As you see, the outcome in the case turns in large part on the Torture Convention and the number of states that have ratified it. How would the case have come out in the absence of that Convention?

In the United States, a foreign head of state would understandably try to seek refuge under the FSIA. Why does this strategy fail in the case below?

SAMANTAR V. YOUSUF

United States Supreme Court
130 S. Ct. 2278 (2010)

[Victims of torture and other human rights violations brought a case under the Torture Victim Protection Act (TVPA) and the Alien Tort Claims Act (ATCA) against Mohamed Ali Samantar, the former vice president, minister of defense and prime minister of Somalia. The plaintiffs alleged that Samantar had exercised command and control over the Somali military forces when the human rights violations occurred, that he had known about the on-going abuses committed by members of the military, and that he had aided and abetted the acts of torture and other atrocities. Samantar had fled to the United States after the Somali military regime was overthrown in 1991.

In the district court proceedings, Samantar asked the U.S. State Department for a statement of interest, but received no response. The district court nonetheless dismissed the case, holding that it lacked subject matter jurisdiction. The court interpreted the FSIA to grant immunity to foreign government members acting in their official capacity. The Fourth Circuit Court of Appeals reversed, holding that the FSIA does not apply to individual officials of foreign states, and that, therefore, Samantar was not immune.]

JUSTICE STEVENS:

* * *

What we must now decide is whether the Act also covers the immunity claims of foreign officials. We begin with the statute's text and then consider petitioner's reliance on its history and purpose.

III

The FSIA provides that "a foreign state shall be immune from the jurisdiction of the courts of the United States and of the States" except as provided in the Act. § 1604. Thus, if a defendant is a "foreign state" within the meaning of the Act, then the defendant is immune from jurisdiction unless one of the exceptions in the Act applies. The Act, if it applies, is the "sole basis for obtaining jurisdiction over a foreign state in federal court." The question we face in this case is whether an individual sued for conduct undertaken in his official capacity is a "foreign state" within the meaning of the Act.

* * *

The term "foreign state" on its face indicates a body politic that governs a particular territory. See, *e.g.*, Restatement § 4 (defining "state" as "an entity that has a defined territory and population under the control of a government and that engages in foreign relations"). In § 1603(a), however, the Act establishes that "foreign state" has a broader meaning, by mandating the inclusion of the state's political subdivisions, agencies, and instrumentalities. Then, in § 1603(b), the Act specifically delimits what counts as an agency or instrumentality. Petitioner argues that either "foreign state," § 1603(a), or "agency or instrumentality," § 1603(b), could be read to include a foreign official. Although we agree that petitioner's interpretation is literally possible, our analysis of the entire statutory text persuades us that petitioner's reading is not the meaning that Congress enacted.

We turn first to the term "agency or instrumentality of a foreign state," § 1603(b). It is true that an individual official could be an "agency or instrumentality," if that term is given the meaning of "any thing or person through which action is accomplished." But Congress has specifically defined "agency or instrumentality" in the FSIA, and all of the textual clues in that definition cut against such a broad construction.

First, the statute specifies that " 'agency or instrumentality * * * ' means any *entity*" matching three specified characteristics, § 1603(b) (emphasis added), and "entity" typically refers to an organization, rather than an individual. Furthermore, several of the required characteristics apply awkwardly, if at all, to individuals. The phrase "separate legal person, corporate or otherwise," § 1603(b)(1), could conceivably refer to a natural person, solely by virtue of the word "person." But the phrase "separate legal person" typically refers to the legal fiction that allows an entity to hold personhood separate from the natural persons who are its shareholders or officers. It is similarly awkward to refer to a person as an "organ" of the foreign state. See § 1603(b)(2). And the third part of the definition could not be applied at all to a natural person. A natural person cannot be a citizen of a State "as defined in section 1332(c) and (e)," § 1603(b)(3), because those subsections refer to the citizenship of corporations and estates. Nor can a natural person be "created under the laws of any third country." Thus, the terms Congress chose simply do not evidence the intent to include individual officials within the meaning of "agency or instrumentality."

Petitioner proposes a second textual route to including an official within the meaning of "foreign state." He argues that the definition of "foreign state" in § 1603(a) sets out a nonexhaustive list that "includes" political subdivisions and agencies or instrumentalities but is not so limited. It is true that use of the word "include" can signal that the list that follows is meant to be illustrative rather than exhaustive. And, to be sure, there are fewer textual clues within § 1603(a) than within § 1603(b) from which to interpret Congress' silence regarding foreign officials. But even if the list in § 1603(a) is merely illustrative, it still suggests that "foreign state" does not encompass officials, because the types of defendants listed are all entities.

Moreover, elsewhere in the FSIA Congress expressly mentioned officials when it wished to count their acts as equivalent to those of the foreign state, which suggests that officials are not included within the unadorned term "foreign state." For example, Congress provided an exception from the general grant of immunity for cases in which "money damages are sought against a foreign state" for an injury in the United States "caused by the tortious act or omission of that foreign state or of any official or employee of that foreign state while acting within the scope of his office." § 1605(a)(5). * * *

Other provisions of the statute also point away from reading "foreign state" to include foreign officials. Congress made no express mention of service of process on individuals in § 1608(a), which governs service upon a foreign state or political subdivision. Although some of the methods listed could be used to serve individuals—for example, by delivery "in accordance with an applicable international convention," § 1608(a)(2)—the methods specified are at best very roundabout ways of serving an individual official. Furthermore, Congress made specific remedial choices for different types of defendants. See § 1606 (allowing punitive damages for an agency or instrumentality but not for a foreign state); § 1610 (affording a plaintiff greater rights to attach the property of an agency or instrumentality as compared to the property of a foreign state). By adopting petitioner's reading of "foreign state," we would subject claims against officials to the more limited remedies available in suits against states, without so much as a whisper from Congress on the subject. (And if we were instead to adopt petitioner's other textual argument, we would subject those claims to the different, more expansive, remedial scheme for agencies). The Act's careful calibration of remedies among the listed types of defendants suggests that Congress did not mean to cover other types of defendants never mentioned in the text.

In sum, "[w]e do not * * * construe statutory phrases in isolation; we read statutes as a whole." Reading the FSIA as a whole, there is nothing to suggest we should read "foreign state" in § 1603(a) to include an official acting on behalf of the foreign state, and much to indicate that this meaning was not what Congress enacted. The text does not expressly foreclose petitioner's reading, but it supports the view of respondents and the United States that the Act does not address an official's claim to immunity.

IV

Petitioner argues that the FSIA is best read to cover his claim to immunity because of its history and purpose. As discussed at the outset, one of the primary purposes of the FSIA was to codify the restrictive theory of sovereign immunity, which Congress recognized as consistent with extant international law. See § 1602. We have observed that a related purpose was "codification of international law at the time of the FSIA's enactment," and have examined the relevant common law and international practice when interpreting the Act. Because of this relationship between the Act and the common law that it codified, petitioner argues that we should construe the FSIA consistently with the common law regarding individual immunity, which—in petitioner's view—was coextensive with the law of state immunity and always immunized a foreign official for acts taken on behalf of the foreign state. Even reading the Act in light of Congress' purpose of codifying state sovereign immunity, however, we do not think that the Act codified the common law with respect to the immunity of individual officials.

The canon of construction that statutes should be interpreted consistently with the common law helps us interpret a statute that clearly covers a field formerly governed by the common law. But the canon does not help us to decide the antecedent question whether, when a statute's coverage is ambiguous, Congress intended the statute to govern a particular field—in this case, whether Congress intended the FSIA to supersede the common law of official immunity.

Petitioner argues that because state and official immunities are coextensive, Congress must have codified official immunity when it codified state immunity. But the relationship between a state's immunity and an official's immunity is more complicated than petitioner suggests, although we need not and do not resolve the dispute among the parties as to the precise scope of an official's immunity at common law. * * *

Petitioner urges that a suit against an official must always be equivalent to a suit against the state because acts taken by a state official on behalf of a state are acts of the state. We have recognized, in the context of the act of state doctrine, that an official's acts can be considered the acts of the foreign state, and that "the courts of one country will not sit in judgment" of those acts when done within the territory of the foreign state. Although the act of state doctrine is distinct from immunity, and instead "provides foreign states with a substantive defense on the merits," we do not doubt that in some circumstances the immunity of the foreign state extends to an individual for acts taken in his official capacity. But it does not follow from this premise that Congress intended to codify that immunity in the FSIA. It hardly furthers Congress' purpose of "clarifying the rules that judges should apply in resolving sovereign immunity claims" to lump individual officials in with foreign states without so much as a word spelling out how and when individual officials are covered.

Petitioner would have a stronger case if there were any indication that Congress' intent to enact a comprehensive solution for suits against states extended to suits against individual officials. But to the extent Congress contemplated the Act's effect upon officials at all, the evidence points in the opposite direction. * * *

[The Supreme Court affirmed the Fourth Circuit Court's decision. Justices Alito and Thomas concurred, opining that the Court's consideration of the legislative history of the FSIA, omitted from this excerpt of the majority opinion, was not necessary to decide the case. Justice Scalia concurred in the judgment, stating, more strongly, that the legislative history should not have been considered.

The case was remanded to the District Court for consideration of common law immunity and other defenses Samantar could assert. In the District Court, when Samantar argued for common law immunity, participation by the State Department proved crucial to the resolution of the case. The State Department filed a statement of interest recommending that Samantar not be granted immunity. The District Court denied common law immunity on the following day. At trial in February 2012, Samantar appeared in person and, surprisingly, conceded his liability for torture, extrajudicial killing, crimes against humanity, war crimes, and other human rights abuses and also conceded that plaintiffs are entitled to recover damages for these violations.]

Samantar has been perceived as a major human rights victory: it was the first time that anyone had admitted responsibility for the atrocities committed by the Somali military regime in the 1980s.

Does it make a difference whether the plaintiffs recover from the state directly or from a (former) official in his personal capacity? In light of this decision, can a former head of state ever enjoy immunity from suit?

What if Augusto Pinochet had come to New York instead of London and was served with process in a suit brought by former victims of his regime under the Alien Tort Claims Act for civil damages? Are the arguments against immunity in a civil suit stronger or weaker than in the context of criminal prosecution?

C. THE ACT OF STATE DOCTRINE

At the end of the 19th century, the U.S. Supreme Court officially adopted an idea with roots in earlier English law: the Act of State Doctrine (*Underhill v. Hernandez*, 168 U.S. 250 (1897)). During the next century, the Court returned to the Doctrine more than a dozen times. Although the Doctrine's exact contours remained unclear, the Court took an increasingly expansive view that culminated in its most widely known Act of State Doctrine decision, *Banco Nacional de Cuba v. Sabbatino*, a long case, which is excerpted below.

The Act of State Doctrine is often confused with sovereign immunity, from which it should be carefully distinguished. What exactly does the Doctrine mean? What are the reasons for it? What is the effect of invoking it in court?

BANCO NACIONAL DE CUBA V. SABBATINO

United States Supreme Court
376 U.S. 398 (1964)

[In 1960 relations grew increasingly strained between the United States and Fidel Castro's revolutionary regime in Cuba. In July of that year, in response to a U.S. reduction of Cuba's quota for sugar imports into the United States, Cuba nationalized most property in Cuba belonging to U.S. nationals. In expropriating U.S. property, the government declared that "Cuba must be a luminous and stimulating example for the sister nations of America and all the underdeveloped countries of the world to follow in their struggle to free themselves from the brutal claws of Imperialism." Among the companies whose property was nationalized was Compania Azucarera Vertientes (CAV), which had contracted to sell a shipload of sugar to Farr, Whitlock, a U.S. commodities broker. After nationalization of CAV's sugar, Farr, Whitlock entered into a second contract for the sugar with the Cuban government, the new "owner" of the sugar. Farr, Whitlock then took delivery of the sugar and, after receiving payment from its customers, turned the proceeds over not to the Cuban government but rather to the receiver for CAV (Sabbatino). Banco Nacional de Cuba, which had been assigned the Cuban government's right to payment under Farr, Whitlock's second contract, then filed suit against Farr, Whitlock and against Sabbatino in U.S. courts. The defendants argued that the shipload of sugar never belonged to Cuba because the Cuban seizure of the sugar violated international law.]

JUSTICE HARLAN:

* * *

The classic American statement of the act of state doctrine * * * is found in *Underhill v. Hernandez*, where Chief Justice Fuller said for a unanimous Court:

> "Every sovereign state is bound to respect the independence of every other sovereign state, and the courts of one country will not sit in judgment on the acts of the government of another, done within its own territory. Redress of grievances by reason of such acts must be obtained through the means open to be availed of by sovereign powers as between themselves."

Following this precept the Court in that case refused to inquire into acts of Hernandez, a revolutionary Venezuelan military commander whose government had been later recognized by the United States, which were made the basis of a damage action in this country by Underhill, an American citizen, who claimed that he had been unlawfully assaulted, coerced, and detained in Venezuela by Hernandez.

* * *

The outcome of this case, therefore, turns upon whether any of the contentions urged by respondents against the application of the act of state doctrine in the premises is acceptable: (1) that the doctrine does not apply to acts of state which violate international law, as is claimed to be the case here; (2) that the doctrine is inapplicable unless the Executive specifically interposes it in a particular case; and (3) that, in any event, the doctrine may not be invoked by a foreign government plaintiff in our courts.

V.

Preliminarily, we discuss the foundations on which we deem the act of state doctrine to rest, and more particularly the question of whether state or federal law governs its application in a federal diversity case.

We do not believe that this doctrine is compelled either by the inherent nature of sovereign authority, as some of the earlier decisions seem to imply or by some principle of international law. If a transaction takes place in one jurisdiction and the forum is in another, the forum does not by dismissing an action or by applying its own law purport to divest the first jurisdiction of its territorial sovereignty; it merely declines to adjudicate or makes applicable its own law to parties or property before it. The refusal of one country to enforce the penal laws of another is a typical example of an instance when a court will not entertain a cause of action arising in another jurisdiction. While historic notions of sovereign authority do bear upon the wisdom of employing the act of state doctrine, they do not dictate its existence.

That international law does not require application of the doctrine is evidenced by the practice of nations. Most of the countries rendering decisions on the subject fail to follow the rule rigidly. No international arbitral or judicial decision discovered suggests that international law prescribes recognition of sovereign acts of foreign governments, and apparently no claim has ever been raised before an international tribunal that failure to apply the act of state doctrine constitutes a breach of international obligation. * * *

Despite the broad statement in *Oetjen* that "The conduct of the foreign relations of our government is committed by the Constitution to the executive and legislative * * * departments," it cannot of course be thought that "every case or controversy which touches foreign relations lies beyond judicial cognizance." The text of the Constitution does not require the act of state doctrine; it does not irrevocably remove from the judiciary the capacity to review the validity of foreign acts of state.

The act of state doctrine does, however, have "constitutional" underpinnings. It arises out of the basic relationships between branches of government in a system of separation of powers. It concerns the competency of dissimilar institutions to make and implement particular kinds of decisions in the area of international relations. The doctrine as formulated in past decisions expresses the strong sense of the Judicial Branch that its engagement in the task of passing on the validity of foreign acts of state may hinder rather than further this country's pursuit of goals both for itself and for the community of nations as a whole in the international sphere. * * *

VI.

If the act of state doctrine is a principle of decision binding on federal and state courts alike but compelled by neither international law nor the Constitution, its continuing vitality depends on its capacity to reflect the proper distribution of functions between the judicial and political branches of the Government on matters bearing upon foreign affairs. It should be apparent that the greater the degree of codification or consensus concerning a particular area of international law, the more appropriate it is for the judiciary to render decisions regarding it, since the courts can then focus on the application of an agreed principle to circumstances of fact rather than on the sensitive task of establishing a principle not inconsistent with the national interest or with international justice. It is also evident that some aspects of international law touch much more sharply on national nerves than do others; the less important the implications of an issue are for our foreign relations, the weaker the justification for exclusivity in the political branches. The balance of relevant considerations may also be shifted if the government which perpetrated the challenged act of state is no longer in existence, as in the Bernstein case, for the political interest of this country may, as a result, be measurably altered. Therefore, rather than laying down or reaffirming an inflexible and all-encompassing rule in this case, we decide only that the Judicial Branch will not examine the validity of a taking of property within its own territory by a foreign sovereign government, extant and recognized by this country at the time of suit, in the absence of a treaty or other unambiguous agreement regarding controlling legal principles, even if the complaint alleges that the taking violates customary international law.

[As a result, the Court did not question the Cuban expropriation of the American company, and the National Bank of Cuba won the case.]

* * *

In a spirited dissent, Justice White argued that the Act of State Doctrine should not apply to acts in violation of international law. What are the arguments for and against his position?

How does the Doctrine differ from sovereign immunity? Consider its origins, purpose, effects, and who can invoke it.

After *Sabbatino*, Congress amended the Foreign Assistance Act as follows:

HICKENLOOPER AMENDMENT

(2) Notwithstanding any other provision of law, no court in the United States shall decline on the ground of the federal act of state doctrine to make a determination on the merits giving effect to the principles of international law in a case in which a claim of title or other right to property is asserted by any party including a foreign state (or a party claiming through such state) based upon (or traced through) a confiscation or other taking after January 1, 1959, by an act of that state in violation of the principles of international law, including the principles of compensation and the other standards set out in this subsection: *Provided*, That this subparagraph shall not be applicable (1) in any case in which an act of a foreign state is not contrary to international law or with respect to a claim of title or other right to property acquired pursuant to an irrevocable letter of credit of not more than 180 days duration issued in good faith prior to the time of the confiscation or other taking, or (2) in any case with respect to which the President determines that application of the act of state doctrine is required in that particular case by the foreign policy interests of the United States and a suggestion to this effect is filed on his behalf in that case with the court.

Note that this so-called (Second) Hickenlooper Amendment (named after the Senator who introduced the legislation) has been narrowly construed by courts. According to the majority view, it applies only to the expropriation of personal property (later) physically present in the United States. Thus, it has little effect in practice.

Here is how the Restatement (Third) of the Foreign Relations Law of the United States summarizes the Act of State Doctrine.

§ 443   Act of State Doctrine: Law of the United States

(1) In the absence of a treaty or other unambiguous agreement regarding controlling legal principles, courts in the United States will generally refrain from examining the validity of a taking by a foreign state of property within its own territory, or from sitting in judgment on other acts of a governmental character done by a foreign state within its own territory and applicable there.

(2) The doctrine set forth in Subsection (1) is subject to modification by act of Congress. See § 444.

In its latest pronouncement on the Act of State Doctrine, the Supreme Court took a more restrictive view than in earlier cases. A company obtained a construction contract from the Nigerian government by bribing Nigerian officials in violation of Nigerian law. A competitor sued the company in U.S. District Court under various federal (anti-corruption and other) statutes. The district court dismissed the case under the Act of State Doctrine. It found that the Doctrine forbade the imputation of unlawful motivations underlying the foreign governmental act (to award the contract) because that could embarrass a foreign sovereign and interfere with U.S. foreign policy. The Court of Appeals reversed, and the Supreme Court affirmed.

Writing for a unanimous Court in *W.S. Kirkpatrick & Co. v. Environmental Tectonics Corp., International*, 493 U.S. 400, 409–410 (1990), Justice Scalia unequivocally rejected the application of the Act of State Doctrine in this case:

> The short of the matter is this: Courts in the United States have the power, and ordinarily the obligation, to decide cases and controversies properly presented to them. The act of state doctrine does not establish an exception for cases and controversies that may embarrass foreign governments, but merely requires that, in the process of deciding, the acts of foreign sovereigns taken within their own jurisdictions shall be deemed valid. That doctrine has no application to the

present case because the validity of no foreign sovereign act is at issue.

In other words, while comity and foreign policy considerations underlie the Act of State Doctrine, it is not a general means of abstention based on those grounds. It merely prohibits courts from holding that certain foreign governmental acts are actually invalid. The general tone of the opinion suggests that the Supreme Court prefers a minimalist view of the Doctrine and would not look kindly at expansive interpretation.

Is there a "commercial exception" to the Act of State Doctrine just like to foreign sovereign immunity? In other words, does a foreign state enjoy deference if the act in question was of a purely commercial nature? The answer is not clear. In *Alfred Dunhill of London v. Republic of Cuba*, 425 U.S. 682 (1976), four Justices on the Supreme Court endorsed such an exception and refused to apply the doctrine to the simple repudiation and non-payment of a commercial debt—but four does not make a majority. *Should* the Act of State Doctrine apply to purely commercial acts?

Should it apply to blatant violations of human rights on foreign soil? For example, in the *Kadic* case (supra VI.5.), should Karadzic have been allowed to argue that the acts of the Serbian government could not be scrutinized in a U.S. court?

4. THE EXPANSION OF JURISDICTION

As we have seen, state sovereignty has become "weaker" over the last half-century in the sense of more diffuse (especially through the delegation of power to the international or even supranational level) and more porous (especially through the erosion of immunity). At the same time, however, sovereignty has become "stronger" in the sense that states assert power more broadly, particularly in the area of jurisdiction: today, states claim regulatory, adjudicatory and enforcement power beyond the traditional bases.

Under the classic approach, as illustrated by the *Lotus* case (Chapter II.2.C.), the two generally accepted bases for jurisdiction under international law were territoriality and nationality (of the defendant). Today, other doctrines of jurisdiction play an increasing role. The "effects doctrine" is the most widely recognized, but the "protective principle" is often invoked nowadays in the fight against terrorism. Other bases are subject to more intense debate, especially the "passive personality principle" and the "universality principle." All of these bases for jurisdiction will be discussed below.

With regard to jurisdiction to prescribe (i.e., to legislate and regulate), the Restatement (Third) of Foreign Relations Law of the United States summarizes the situation in the following terms:

RESTATEMENT (THIRD) OF THE FOREIGN RELATIONS LAW OF THE UNITED STATES

American Law Institute (1986)

§ 402.   BASES OF JURISDICTION TO PRESCRIBE

Subject to § 403, a state has jurisdiction to prescribe law with respect to

(1) (a) conduct that, wholly or in substantial part, takes place within its territory;

   (b) the status of persons, or interests in things, present within its territory;

   (c) conduct outside its territory that has or is intended to have a substantial effect within its territory;

(2) the activities, interests, status, or relations of its nationals outside as well as within its territory; and

(3) certain conduct outside its territory by persons not its nationals that is directed against the security of the state or against a limited class of other state interests.

The following cases illustrate various aspects of the four major jurisdictional bases going beyond territoriality and personality. Is the exercise of jurisdiction in these cases justified by legitimate state interests? As you read through the cases, ask yourself what happened to the *Lotus* Presumption.

A. THE EFFECTS DOCTRINE

In the case below, why could jurisdiction not be predicated on traditional grounds? How does the court overcome this problem? Is the court's approach a paradigm shift or merely a modification of traditional principles?

UNITED STATES V. ALUMINUM CO. OF AMERICA

United States Circuit Court
148 F.2d 416 (2d Cir. 1945)

[Several foreign corporations (incorporated abroad) formed a cartel on foreign soil to limit aluminum production, creating the potential for impact on aluminum prices worldwide. The United States sued them for violating U.S. antitrust law. Recall that in *American Banana Company v. United Fruit Company* (Chapter II.2.C.) the application of U.S. statutes was territorially restricted to acts within the United States. Acting under this precedent, the District Court dismissed the action. The United States then appealed directly to the Supreme Court. That court, however, was unable to muster a quorum to hear the case and thus referred it to the Court of Appeals for the Second Circuit—which was then sitting as a court of last resort.

The Court of Appeals sustained some of the lower court's findings. Judge Learned Hand then turned to the question whether (some of) the defendants had actually violated the Sherman Act. In reading his opinion, ask yourself how it compares to Justice Holmes' views in *American Banana*.]

L. HAND, CIRCUIT JUDGE:

* * *

Did either the agreement of 1931 or that of 1936 violate § 1 of the Act? The answer does not depend upon whether we shall recognize as a source of liability a liability imposed by another state. On the contrary we are concerned only with whether Congress chose to attach liability to the conduct outside the United States of persons not in allegiance to it. That being so, the only question open is whether Congress intended to impose the liability, and whether our own Constitution permitted it to do so: as a court of the United States, we cannot look beyond our own law. Nevertheless, it is quite true that we are not to read general words, such as those in this Act, without regard to the limitations customarily observed by nations upon the exercise of their powers; limitations which generally correspond to those fixed by the "Conflict of Laws." We should not impute to Congress an intent to punish all whom its courts can catch, for conduct which has no consequences within the United States. On the other hand, it is settled law—as "Limited" itself agrees—that any state may impose liabilities, even upon persons not within its allegiance, for conduct outside its borders that has consequences within its borders which the state reprehends; and these liabilities other states will ordinarily recognize. It may be argued that this Act extends further. Two situations are possible. There may be agreements made beyond our borders not intended to affect imports, which do affect them, or which affect exports. Almost any limitation of the supply of goods in Europe, for example, or in South America, may have repercussions in the United States if there is trade between the two. Yet when one considers the international complications likely to arise from an effort in this country to treat such agreements as unlawful, it is safe to assume that Congress certainly did not intend the Act to cover them. Such agreements may on the other hand intend to include imports into the United States, and yet it may appear that they had no effect upon them. * * *

Both agreements would clearly have been unlawful, had they been made within the United States; and it follows from what we have just said that both were unlawful, though made abroad, if they were intended to affect imports and did affect them. * * * The first of the conditions which we mentioned was therefore satisfied; the intent was to set up a quota system for imports.

* * *

* * * We shall dispose of the matter therefore upon the assumption that, although the shareholders intended to restrict imports, it does not appear whether in fact they did so. Upon our hypothesis the plaintiff would therefore fail, if it carried the burden of proof upon this issue as upon others. We think, however, that, after the intent to affect imports was proved, the burden of proof shifted to "Limited." In the first place a depressant upon production which applies generally may be assumed, certeris paribus, to distribute its effect evenly upon all markets. Again, when the parties took the trouble specifically to make the depressant apply to a given market, there is reason to suppose that they expected that it would have some effect, which it could have only by lessening what would otherwise have been imported. * * * Moreover, there is an especial propriety in demanding this of "Limited," because it was "Limited" which procured the inclusion in the agreement of 1936 of imports in the quotas.

There remains only the question whether this assumed restriction had any influence upon prices. To that, *Socony–Vacuum Oil Co. v. United States* is an entire answer. It will be remembered that, when the defendants in that case protested that the prosecution had not proved that the "distress" gasoline had affected prices, the court answered that that was not necessary, because an agreement to withdraw any substantial part of the supply from a market would, if carried out, have some effect upon prices, and was as unlawful as an agreement expressly to fix prices. The underlying doctrine was that all factors which contribute to determine prices, must be kept free to operate unhampered by agreements. For these reasons we think that the agreement of 1936 violated Sec. 1 of the Act.

* * *

Is the effects doctrine just a variation of the territoriality principle? In an integrated world market, does the effects doctrine tend to give states jurisdiction over business decisions taken anywhere in the world?

In 1982, the Sherman Act (15 U.S.C. § 1) was amended by adding § 6a. The provision is very difficult to understand, mainly because its drafting leaves a lot to be desired. For now, just state its basic thrust in a single sentence.

15 United States Code § 6a Conduct Involving Trade Or Commerce With Foreign Nations

Sections 1 to 7 of this title shall not apply to conduct involving trade or commerce (other than import trade or import commerce) with foreign nations unless—

(1) such conduct has a direct, substantial, and reasonably foreseeable effect—

    (A) on trade or commerce which is not trade or commerce with foreign nations, or on import trade or import commerce with foreign nations; or

    (B) on export trade or export commerce with foreign nations, of a person engaged in such trade or commerce in the United States; and

(2) such effect gives rise to a claim under the provisions of sections 1 to 7 of this title, other than this section.

If sections 1 to 7 of this title apply to such conduct only because of the operation of paragraph (1)(B), then sections 1 to 7 of this title shall apply to such conduct only for injury to export business in the United States.

In the excerpts below, how do Germany and the European Union, respectively, deal with the extraterritorial application of antitrust law?

GERMAN ANTITRUST STATUTE

(Gesetz gegen Wettbewerbsbeschränkungen, Gwb, Germany)

* * *

Art. 130 (2)

This Act shall apply to all restraints of competition having an effect within the [territorial] scope of application of this Act, also if they were caused outside of the [territorial] scope of application of this Act.

* * *

Regulation (EC) No. 864/2007 of the European Parliament and of the Council of 11 July 2007 on the Law Applicable to Non-contractual Obligations (Rome II)

(Adopted 2007)

* * *

Art. 6

Unfair competition and acts restricting free competition

1. The law applicable to a non-contractual obligation arising out of an act of unfair competition shall be the law of the country where competitive relations or the collective interests of consumers are, or are likely to be, affected.

2. * * *

3. (a) The law applicable to a non-contractual obligation arising out of a restriction of competition shall be the law of the country where the market is, or is likely to be, affected.

* * *

B. THE PROTECTIVE PRINCIPLE

In the case below, the court relies on yet another basis of jurisdiction. Why weren't the traditional bases, or at least the effects doctrine, sufficient?

UNITED STATES v. YOUSEF

327 F.3d 56 (2d Cir. 2003)

INTRODUCTION

Defendants-appellants Ramzi Yousef, Eyad Ismoil, and Abdul Hakim Murad appeal from judgments of conviction entered in the United States District Court for the Southern District of New York. * * *

GENERAL BACKGROUND

I.   WORLD TRADE CENTER BOMBING

The conspiracy to bomb the World Trade Center began in the Spring of 1992, when Yousef met Ahmad Mohammad Ajaj at a terrorist training camp on the border of Afghanistan and Pakistan. After formulating their terrorist plot, Yousef and Ajaj traveled to New York together in September 1992. In Ajaj's luggage, he carried a "terrorist kit" that included, among other things, bomb-making manuals. After Yousef and Ajaj arrived at John F. Kennedy International Airport, inspectors of the Immigration and Naturalization Service ("INS") discovered the "terrorist kit" in Ajaj's luggage and arrested him. Although Yousef was also stopped, he and Ajaj did not disclose their connection to one another, and INS officials allowed Yousef to enter the United States.[2]

Once in New York, Yousef began to put together the manpower and the supplies that he would need to carry out his plan to bomb the World Trade Center. Yousef assembled a group of co-conspirators to execute his plan, including defendants Mohammad Salameh, Nidal Ayyad, Mahmud Abouhalima, and Abdul Rahman Yasin. Next, Yousef began accumulating the necessary ingredients for the bomb. He ordered the required chemicals, and his associates rented a shed in which to store them. Yousef and Salameh established their headquarters at an apartment they rented in Jersey City, New Jersey, an urban center located across the Hudson River from Manhattan. The apartment also functioned as their bomb-making factory.

In December 1992, Yousef contacted Ismoil, who was then living in Dallas, Texas. On February 22, 1993, Ismoil joined Yousef and the others in New York to help complete the bomb preparations.

On February 26, 1993, Yousef and Ismoil drove a bomb-laden van onto the B-2 level of the parking garage below the World Trade Center. They then set the bomb's timer to detonate minutes later. At approximately 12:18 p.m. that day, the bomb exploded, killing six people, injuring more than a thousand others, and causing widespread fear and more than $500 million in property damage.

Soon after the bombing, Yousef and Ismoil fled from the United States. Yousef and Ismoil were indicted for their participation in the bombing on March 31, 1993 and August 8, 1994, respectively. Yousef was captured in Pakistan nearly two years after the bombing, and Ismoil was arrested in Jordan a little over two years after the attack. Both were returned to the United States to answer the charges in the indictment.

II. AIRLINE BOMBING

A year and a half after the World Trade Center bombing, Yousef entered Manila, the capital of the Philippines, under an assumed name. By September 1994, Yousef had devised a plan to attack United States airliners. According to the plan, five individuals would place bombs aboard twelve United States-flag aircraft that served routes in Southeast Asia. The conspirators would board an airliner in Southeast Asia, assemble a bomb on

---

[2] Yousef told the INS that he was traveling alone and presented INS officials with a passport from Iraq in the name of Ramzi Yousef. To explain his lack of the required visa, Yousef stated that a contact from Iraq's consulate in Pakistan helped him to get on the plane to New York without a visa. Yousef requested political asylum in the United States, claiming that he was in danger from Iraq because its Government believed that he was aligned with the Kuwaiti Government. Yousef filled out the applicable asylum application forms and made a sworn statement to support his claim. He was then released into the United States with an asylum hearing appointment.

the plane, and then exit the plane during its first layover. As the planes continued on toward their next destinations, the time-bombs would detonate. Eleven of the twelve flights targeted were ultimately destined for cities in the United States.

Yousef and his co-conspirators performed several tests in preparation for the airline bombings. In December 1994, Yousef and Wali Khan Amin Shah placed one of the bombs they had constructed in a Manila movie theater. The bomb exploded, injuring several patrons of the theater. Ten days later, Yousef planted another test bomb under a passenger's seat during the first leg of a Philippine Airlines flight from Manila to Japan. Yousef disembarked from the plane during the stopover and then made his way back to Manila. During the second leg of the flight, the bomb exploded, killing one passenger, a Japanese national, and injuring others.

The plot to bomb the United States-flag airliners was uncovered in January 1995, only two weeks before the conspirators intended to carry it out. Yousef and Murad were burning chemicals in their Manila apartment and accidentally caused a fire. An apartment security guard saw the smoke coming from the apartment and called the fire department. After the firemen left, the Philippine police arrived at the apartment, where they discovered chemicals and bomb components, a laptop computer on which Yousef had set forth the aircraft bombing plans, and other incriminating evidence. Philippine authorities arrested Murad and Shah, though Shah escaped and was not recaptured until nearly a year later. Yousef fled the country, but was captured in Pakistan the next month.

* * *

On February 21, 1996, a grand jury in the Southern District of New York filed a twenty-count superseding indictment against the defendants and others. Counts One through Eleven charged Yousef and Ismoil with various offenses arising from their participation in the February 26, 1993 bombing of the World Trade Center. Counts Twelve through Nineteen charged Yousef, Murad, and Shah with various crimes relating to their conspiracy to bomb United States airliners in Southeast Asia in 1994 and 1995.

The trial of Yousef, Murad, and Shah on the airline bombing charges began on May 29, 1996 and ended on September 5, 1996, when the jury found all three defendants guilty on all counts. Yousef and Ismoil's trial on charges relating to the World Trade Center bombing began on July 15, 1997 and concluded on November 12, 1997, when the jury found both defendants guilty on all counts.

Yousef was sentenced for both convictions on January 8, 1998. For the World Trade Center convictions he was sentenced principally to a total of 240 years of imprisonment: 180 years on Counts One through Eight, plus two 30-year terms on Counts Nine and Ten for violations of 18 U.S.C. § 924(c), to be served consecutively to the 180-year sentence and to each other. For the airline bombing convictions, Yousef was sentenced principally to a term of life imprisonment, to be served consecutively to his 240-year sentence for the World Trade Center bombing.

* * *

c.   IN ANY EVENT, JURISDICTION OVER COUNT NINETEEN IS
     PROPER UNDER THE PROTECTIVE PRINCIPLE OF CUSTOMARY
     INTERNATIONAL LAW

Although the government is not required to prove that its prosecution of Yousef comported with any of the customary international law bases of criminal jurisdiction, we note that, in fact, Yousef's prosecution by the United States *is* consistent with the "protective principle" of international law. The protective (or "security") principle permits a State to assume jurisdiction over non-nationals for acts done abroad that affect the security of the State. The protective principle generally is invoked to obtain jurisdiction over politically motivated acts but is not limited to acts with a political purpose. *In re Marc Rich & Co.*, 707 F.2d 663, 666 (2d Cir. 1983) (stating that the protective principle provides jurisdiction over acts committed outside of a State's territory that are directed at interfering with the State's "governmental funcitons," provided that the act also is contrary to the laws of the host State, if such State has a "reasonably developed" legal system); *see also United States v. Pizzarusso*, 338 F.2d 8, 10 (2d Cir. 1968) (same).

The stated purpose of Yousef's plot to destroy United States commercial aircraft was to influence United States foreign policy, the making of which clearly constitutes a "governmental function." The bombing of the Philippine Airlines flight at issue in Count Nineteen, which killed one Japanese national and maimed another, was merely a test-run that Yousef executed to ensure that the tactics and devices the conspirators planned to use on United States aircraft operated properly.

Documentation stored on Yousef's laptop computer and adduced at trial demonstrates that the Philippine Airlines bombing constituted part of the co-conspirators' plan to detonate numerous bombs on United States-flag aircraft. A letter, with a file date of November 19, 1994, found in Yousef's laptop states, in pertinent part:

> We, the Fifth Division of the Liberation Army * * * declare our responsibility for striking at some American targets in the near future in retaliation for the financial, political, and military support extended by the American government to the Jewish State. * * * [T]he Jewish State continues its massacres * * * with American money, weapons, and ammunition, in addition to the support and blessing given

* * * by the U.S. Congress. The American people are quite aware of all this. [Therefore] [we] *will consider all American nationals as part of our legitimate targets because they are responsible for the behavior of their government and its foreign policies*, for the policy of the government represents the will of the people.

Letter from Fifth Division of the Liberation Army (Nov. 19, 1994) (emphasis added).

Extensive additional documentation was found on Yousef's laptop and presented at trial. These documents, which set forth, *inter alia*, the flight schedules and paths of United States-flag aircraft and detailed plans for planting bombs on these flights, confirmed that the co-conspirators intended to bomb United States-flag aircraft using a *modus operandi* identical to that which permitted them to place the bomb on Philippine Airlines flight 434. All of these flights were scheduled to depart from cities in Southeast Asia where the bomber would board the plane, make a stopover in that region where the bomber would disembark, and then continue on to a United States destination, at which point the previously-planted explosive device would detonate. This is more than enough to permit the United States to claim jurisdiction over Yousef under the protective principle.

* * *

What does the protective principle add to the effects doctrine? Note that we hardly need the principle if someone detonates a bomb in downtown New York. In what sense (and in which cases) does it expand the jurisdiction of the U.S. courts?

C. THE PASSIVE PERSONALITY PRINCIPLE

Can a state ever assert jurisdiction based solely on the basis of a connection between it and the victims of an alleged wrong? Before reading the next two cases, turn back to the PCIJ decision in the *Lotus* case (Chapter II.2.C.). What did that Court say about a state's assertion of jurisdiction based on such a connection?

ATTORNEY GENERAL OF THE GOVERNMENT OF ISRAEL V. ADOLF EICHMANN
36 Int'l Law Reports 9,277 (1962)

[In May 1960, fifteen years after the end of World War II, the Israeli Secret Service abducted Adolf Eichmann, Hitler's architect of the Holocaust, from a suburb of Buenos Aires and flew him to Israel. Eichmann was tried in Jerusalem for crimes against humanity, sentenced to death, and executed in 1962. For a full account, see the classic book by Hannah Arendt, EICHMANN IN JERUSALEM—A STUDY IN THE BANALITY OF EVIL (1963). On appeal, the Supreme Court of Israel had to deal with the argument that it lacked jurisdiction over Eichmann because he had committed his acts as a German national and completely outside of Israel (which did not even exist at the time). The Court rejected that argument.]

* * *

[CRIMINAL JURISDICTION OVER ACTS COMMITTED BY FOREIGN NATIONALS ABROAD]

9.   The same applies to the second argument also. As will be recalled, this argument is to the effect that the enactment of a criminal law applicable to an act committed in a foreign country by a foreign national conflicts with the principle of territorial sovereignty. But here too we must hold that there is no such rule in customary international law, and that to this day it has not obtained general international agreement. Evidence of this is to be found in the Judgment of the Permanent Court of International Justice in the *Lotus* case. There the majority of the Judges recognized the competence of the State of Turkey to enact a criminal statute covering the negligent conduct of a French citizen while on duty as officer-of-the-watch of a French ship at the time of her collision on the high seas—and therefore outside Turkey's territorial waters—with a ship flying the Turkish flag. The collision caused the sinking of the Turkish ship and also the death of eight of her passengers who were of Turkish nationality. It was held in that case that the principle of territorial sovereignty merely requires that a State exercise its penal power within its own borders and not outside them; that subject to this restriction every state has a wide discretion as to the application of its laws and the jurisdiction of its courts in respect of acts committed outside the State; and that only in so far as it is possible to point to a specific rule prohibiting the exercise of this discretion—a rule agreed upon by international treaty—is a State prevented from exercising it. That view was based on the following two grounds: (a) it is precisely the conception of State sovereignty which demands the preclusion of any presumption that there is a restriction on its independence; and (b) even if it is true that the principle of the territorial character of criminal law is firmly established, in various States it is no less true that in almost all such States penal jurisdiction has been extended, in ways that vary from State to State, so as to embrace offences committed outside its territory. * * *

[THE "PROTECTIVE" AND "PASSIVE PERSONALITY" PRINCIPLES]

We wish to add one further observation. In regard to the crimes directed against the Jews the District Court found additional support for its jurisdiction in the connecting link between the State of Israel and the Jewish people—including that between the State of Israel and the Jewish victims of the holocaust—and the National Home in Palestine, as is explained in its judgment. It therefore upheld its criminal and penal jurisdiction by virtue also of the "protective" principle and the principle of "passive personality." It should be made clear that we fully agree with every word said by the Court on this subject in paragraphs 31–38 of its judgment. If in our judgment we have concentrated on the international and universal character of the crimes of which the appellant has been convicted, one of the reasons for our so doing is that some of them were directed against non-Jewish groups (Poles, Slovenes, Czechs and gipsies).

* * *

How can the state of Israel claim jurisdiction under the passive personality principle if the victims of the Holocaust couldn't possibly have been Israeli citizens because there was no State of Israel before 1948? In a similar vein, can the protective principle be invoked in favor of an (as-yet) non-existent state?

What does the case below add to our understanding of the passive personality principle beyond *Eichmann*? Is it a stronger or weaker case for asserting jurisdiction based on this principle?

UNITED STATES V. YUNIS

United States District Court
681 F. Supp. 896 (D.D.C. 1988)

JUDGE PARKER:

* * *

I.   BACKGROUND

This criminal proceeding and indictment arise from the hijacking of a Jordanian civil aircraft, Royal Jordanian Airlines ("ALIA") Flight 402, on June 11, and 12, 1985. There is no dispute that the only nexus to the United States was the presence of several American nationals on board the flight. The airplane was registered in Jordan, flew the Jordanian flag and never landed on American soil or flew over American airspace.

* * *

* * * Yunis has moved to dismiss the entire indictment, arguing that no United States federal court has jurisdiction to prosecute a foreign national for crimes committed in foreign airspace and on foreign soil. He further claims that the presence of the American nationals on board the aircraft is an insufficient basis for exercising jurisdiction under principles of international law.

Defendant's motion raises several threshold inquiries: whether or not there is a basis for jurisdiction under international law, and if so, whether Congress intended to and had authority to extend jurisdiction of our federal courts over criminal offenses and events which were committed and occurred overseas and out of the territorial jurisdiction of such courts.

II. ANALYSIS

A. JURISDICTION UNDER INTERNATIONAL LAW

The parties agree that there are five traditional bases of jurisdiction over extraterritorial crimes under international law:

> *Territorial*, wherein jurisdiction is based on the place where the offense is committed;

> *National*, wherein jurisdiction is based on the nationality of the offender;

> *Protective*, wherein jurisdiction is based on whether the national interest is injured;

> *Universal*, wherein jurisdiction is conferred in any forum that obtains physical custody of the perpetuator of certain offenses considered particularly heinous and harmful to humanity[;]

> *Passive personal*, wherein jurisdiction is based on the nationality of the victim.

* * *

The Universal and the Passive Personal principle appear to offer potential bases for asserting jurisdiction over the hostage-taking and aircraft piracy charges against Yunis. However, his counsel argues that the Universal principle is not applicable because neither hostage-taking nor aircraft piracy are heinous crimes encompassed by the doctrine. He urges further, that the United States does not recognize Passive Personal as a legitimate source of jurisdiction. The government flatly disagrees and maintains that jurisdiction is appropriate under both.

1. UNIVERSAL PRINCIPLE

[See Section D. below]

2. PASSIVE PERSONAL PRINCIPLE

This principle authorizes states to assert jurisdiction over offenses committed against their citizens abroad. It recognizes that each state has a legitimate interest in protecting the safety of its citizens when they journey outside national boundaries. Because American nationals were on board the Jordanian aircraft, the government contends that the Court may exercise jurisdiction over Yunis under this principle. Defendant argues that this theory of jurisdiction is neither recognized by the international community nor the United States and is an insufficient basis for sustaining jurisdiction over Yunis.

Although many international legal scholars agree that the principle is the most controversial of the five sources of jurisdiction, they also agree that the international community recognizes its legitimacy. Most accept that "the extraterritorial reach of a law premised upon the * * * principle would not be in doubt as a matter of international law." Paust, *Jurisdiction and Nonimmunity*, 23 Va.J. of Int'l Law, 191, 203 (1983). More importantly, the international community explicitly approved of the principle as a basis for asserting jurisdiction over hostage takers. As noted above, the Hostage Taking Convention set forth certain mandatory sources of jurisdiction. But it also gave each signatory country discretion to exercise extraterritorial jurisdiction when the offense was committed "with respect to a hostage who is a national of that state if that state considers it appropriate." Art. 5(a)(d). Therefore, even if there are doubts regarding the international community's acceptance, there can be no doubt concerning the application of this principle to the offense of hostage taking, an offense for which Yunis is charged.

Defendant's counsel correctly notes that the Passive Personal principle traditionally has been an anathema to United States lawmakers. But his reliance on the Restatement (Revised) of Foreign Relations Laws for the claim that the United States can never invoke the principle is misplaced. In the past, the United States has protested any assertion of such jurisdiction for fear that it could lead to indefinite criminal liability for its own citizens. This objection was based on the belief that foreigners visiting the United States should comply with our laws and should not be permitted to carry their laws with them. Otherwise Americans would face criminal prosecutions for actions unknown to them as illegal. However, in the most recent draft of the Restatement, the authors noted that the theory "has been increasingly accepted when applied to terrorist and other organized attacks on a state's nationals by reason of their nationality, or to assassinations of a state's ambassadors, or government officials." Restatement (Revised) § 402, comment g (Tent.Draft No. 6). The authors retreated from their wholesale rejection of the principle, recognizing that perpetrators of crimes unanimously condemned by members of the international community, should be aware of the illegality of their actions. Therefore, qualified application of the doctrine to serious and universally condemned crimes will not raise the specter of unlimited and unexpected criminal liability.

Finally, this case does not present the first time that the United States has invoked the principle to assert jurisdiction over a hijacker who seized an American hostage on foreign soil. The government relied on this very principle when it sought extradition of Muhammed Abbas Zaiden, the leader of the terrorists who hijacked the Achillo Lauro vessel in Egyptian waters and subsequently killed Leon Klinghoffer, an American citizen. As here, the only connection to the United States was Klinghoffer's American citizenship. Based on that link, an arrest warrant was issued charging Abbas with hostage taking, conspiracy and piracy.

Thus the Universal and the Passive Personal principles together, provide ample grounds for this Court to assert jurisdiction over Yunis. In fact, reliance on both strengthens the basis for asserting jurisdiction. Not only is the United States acting on behalf of the world community to punish alleged offenders of crimes that threaten the very foundations of world order, but the United States has its own interest in protecting its nationals.

[The decision was affirmed in *United States v. Yunis*, 924 F.2d. 1086 (D.C. Cir. 1991).]

––––––––––––

The passive personality principle was widely embraced in 19th-century European penal codes that provided for criminal jurisdiction on the basis of the victim's nationality. An example is the French Penal Code, Article 113–7, which provides (even today) that "French Criminal law is applicable to any felony, as well as to any misdemeanor punished by imprisonment committed by a French or foreign national outside the territory of the French Republic, where the victim is a French national at the time the offense took place."

Compare the French Penal Code provision to the court's opinion in *Yunis*. The court in *Yunis* recognizes that, at least in the past, the passive personality principle "traditionally has been an anathema to United States lawmakers." Why is that? What concerns does the passive personality principle raise? In the *Yunis* case, does it matter whether the hijackers knew that there were American citizens onboard the airplane? Does it matter whether they hijacked the plane at least in part for that reason?

A perhaps curious case of passive personality jurisdiction is Article 14 of the French Code civil (1804), which, as we have seen before (Ch. II.1.C.), provides for *civil* jurisdiction of the French courts in all cases involving obligations resulting from contracts made with a French citizen. As a result, a French plaintiff can always pursue a remedy for breach of contract in French court, regardless of where and with whom that contract was made and where it was to be performed.

The passive personality principle also led to a famous conflict between Mexico and the United States in *Cutting's Case* in 1886, when Mexican authorities brought criminal charges against an American citizen (Mr. Cutting) for having published an allegedly libelous article in a Texan newspaper about a Mexican citizen (2 Moore International Law Digest 228 (1906)). Cutting was eventually arrested in Mexico, leading the United States to protest Mexico's assertion of passive personality jurisdiction. Mexico dropped the case against Cutting and released him for diplomatic reasons.

D. THE UNIVERSALITY PRINCIPLE

In order to help orient you, some of the text from the Eichmann and Yunis decisions has been repeated, but the discussions of passive personality have been replaced now by the courts' discussions of the principle of universality.

ATTORNEY GENERAL OF THE GOVERNMENT OF ISRAEL V. ADOLF EICHMANN

36 Int'l Law Reports 9,277 (1962)

* * *

[UNIVERSAL JURISDICTION]

12. *The second proposition.* It will be recalled that according to this proposition it is the universal character of the crimes in question which vests in every State the authority to try and punish those who participated in their commission. This proposition is closely linked with the one advanced in the preceding paragraph, from which indeed it follows as a logical outcome. The grounds upon which it rests are as follows:

(a) One of the principles whereby States assume in one degree or another the power to try and punish a person for an offence is the principle of universality. Its meaning is substantially that such power is vested in every State regardless of the fact that the offence was committed outside its territory by a person who did not belong to it, provided he is in its custody when brought to trial. This principle has wide currency and is universally acknowledged with respect to the offence of piracy *jure gentium*. But while general agreement exists as to this offence, the question of the scope of its application is in dispute (see *Harvard Research* (1935), pp. 503 ff). Thus, one school of thought holds that it cannot be applied to any offence other than the one mentioned above, lest it involve excessive interference with the competence of the State in which the offence was committed. This view is reflected in the following extract from the judgment of Judge Moore in the *Lotus* case:

> It is important to bear in mind the foregoing opinions of eminent authorities as to the essential nature of piracy by law of nations, especially for the reason that nations have shown the strongest repug-

nance to extending the scope of the offence, because it carried with it
* * * the principle of universal jurisdiction. * * *

What is more:

> "Piracy by law of nations, in its jurisdictional aspects, is *sui generis*."

A second school of thought—represented by the authors of the draft convention on this subject in *Harvard Research*—agrees, it is true, to the extension of the principle to all manner of extra-territorial offences committed by foreign nationals, but regards it as only an auxiliary principle "to be employed in circumstances in which no resort can be had to the principle of territorial sovereignty or to the nationality principle, two principles on which all are agreed." The authors of this draft therefore variously restrict the application of the principle of universal jurisdiction with the object of avoiding opposition by those States who find the need to punish the offender under one of the other two principles mentioned. One of these restrictions—to which we shall revert—is that the State contemplating the exercise of the power in question must first offer the extradition of the offender to the State within whose territory the offence was committed (*forum delicti commissi*). The justification found by this school of thought, as distinct from the first, for adopting the said principle, albeit as a purely auxiliary one, is the consideration that it is calculated to prove useful in circumstances in which the offender is likely to escape punishment if it is not applied.

A third school of thought holds that the rule of universal jurisdiction, which is valid in cases of piracy, is logically applicable also to all such criminal acts of commission or omission which constitute offences under the law of nations (*delicta juris gentium*), without any reservation whatever or at most subject to a reservation of the kind mentioned above. (See the quotation in paragraph 14 of the judgment of the District Court from Wheaton's *Elements of International Law*, 5th English ed. (1916); also proposals in this spirit referred to in *Harvard Research*.) This view has been opposed in the past because of the difficulty of securing general agreement as to the offences to be included in the above-mentioned class.

A fourth view is that expressed *de lege ferenda* by Lauterpacht in 1949 in the *Cambridge Law Journal*:

> It would be in accordance with an enlightened principle of justice—a principle which has not yet become part of the law of nations—if, in the absence of effective extradition, the courts of a State were to assume jurisdiction over common crimes, by whomsoever and wherever committed, of a heinous character.

(b) The brief survey of views set out above shows that, notwithstanding the differences between them, there is full justification for applying here the principle of universal jurisdiction since the international character of "crimes against humanity" (in the wide meaning of the term) dealt with in this case is no longer in doubt, while the unprecedented extent of their injurious and murderous effects is not to be disputed at the present time. In other words, the basic reason for which international law recognizes the right of each State to exercise such jurisdiction in piracy offences—notwithstanding the fact that its own sovereignty does not extend to the scene of the commission of the offence (the high seas) and the offender is a national of another State or is stateless—applies with even greater force to the above-mentioned crimes.

* * *

The Restatement (Third) of Foreign Relations Law states the universality principle as follows:

§ 404.   Universal Jurisdiction to Define and Punish Certain Offenses

A state has jurisdiction to define and prescribe punishment for certain offenses recognized by the community of nations as of universal concern, such as piracy, slave trade, attacks on or hijacking of aircraft, genocide, war crimes, and perhaps certain acts of terrorism, even where none of the bases of jurisdiction indicated in § 402 is present.

As you saw earlier, the prosecution in *Yunis* also relied on the universality principle.

UNITED STATES V. YUNIS

United States District Court
681 F. Supp. 896 (D.D.C. 1988)

* * *

1.   UNIVERSAL PRINCIPLE

The Universal principle recognizes that certain offenses are so heinous and so widely condemned that "any state if it captures the offender may prosecute and punish that person on behalf of the world community regardless of the nationality of the offender or victim or where the crime was committed." M. Bassiouini, II International Criminal Law, Ch. 6 at 298 (ed. 1986). The crucial question for purposes of defendant's motion is how crimes are classified as "heinous" and whether aircraft piracy and hostage taking fit into this category.

Those crimes that are condemned by the world community and subject to prosecution under the Universal princip[le] are often a matter of international conventions or treaties. See *Demjanjuk v. Petrovsky*, 776 F.2d 571, 582 (6th Cir.1985) (Treaty against genocide signed by a significant number of states made that crime heinous; therefore, Israel had proper jurisdiction over nazi war criminal under the Universal principle).

Both offenses are the subject of international agreements. A majority of states in the world community including Lebanon, have signed three treaties condemning aircraft piracy: The Tokyo Convention,[2] The Hague Convention,[3] and The Montreal Convention.[4] The Hague and Montreal Conventions explicitly rely on the principle of Universal jurisdiction in mandating that all states "take such measures as may be necessary to establish its jurisdiction over the offences * * * where the alleged offender is present in its territory." Hague Convention Art. 4 § 2; Montreal Convention Art. 5 § 2. Further, those treaties direct that all "contracting states * * * of which the alleged offender is found, * * * shall, be obliged, *without exception whatsoever and whether or not the offense was committed in its territory*, to submit the case to its competent authorities for the purpose of prosecution." Hague Convention Art. 7; Montreal Convention Art. 7. (emphasis added) These two provisions together demonstrate the international community's strong commitment to punish aircraft hijackers irrespective of where the hijacking occurred.

The global community has also joined together and adopted the International Convention for the Taking of Hostages[5] an agreement which condemns and criminalizes the offense of hostage taking. Like the conventions denouncing aircraft piracy, this treaty requires signatory states to prosecute any alleged offenders "present in its territory."[6]

In light of the global efforts to punish aircraft piracy and hostage taking, international legal scholars unanimously agree that these crimes fit within the category of heinous crimes for purposes of asserting universal jurisdiction. In The Restatement (Revised) of Foreign Relations Law of the United States, a source heavily relied upon by the defendant, aircraft hijacking is specifically identified as a universal crime over which all states should exercise jurisdiction.

---

[2] Convention on Offenses and Certain Other Acts Committed on Board Aircraft, Sept. 14, 1963 T.I.A.S. No. 159.

[3] Convention for the Suppression of Unlawful Seizure of Aircraft, Dec. 16, 1970, T.I.A.S. No. 7192.

[4] Convention for the Suppression of Unlawful Acts against the Safety of Civil Aviation, Sept. 23, 1971. T.I.A.S. No. 7570.

[5] 34 U.N. GAOR Supp. (No. 39) at 23, UN. Doc. A/34/39 (1979), reprinted in 18 I.L.M. 1456 (1979) [hereinafter Hostage Taking Convention].

[6] Art. V. § 2 states "each state shall establish jurisdiction in cases where the alleged offender is present in its territory."

Our Circuit has cited the Restatement with approval and determined that the Universal principle, standing alone, provides sufficient basis for asserting jurisdiction over an alleged offender. See *Tel-Oren v. Libyan Arab Republic*, 726 F.2d at 781, n. 7, ("The premise of universal jurisdiction is that a state "may exercise jurisdiction to define and punish certain offenses recognized by the community of nations as of universal concern," * * * even where no other recognized basis of jurisdiction is present.") Therefore, under recognized principles of international law, and the law of this Circuit, there is clear authority to assert jurisdiction over Yunis for the offenses of aircraft piracy and hostage taking.

* * *

Would "terrorism" count as a "heinous" crime under international law triggering universal jurisdiction?

For a more recent American case invoking the universality principle, *see United States v. Shi*, 525 F. 3d 709 (9th Cir. 2008) (cert. denied, 129 S. Ct. 324, 2008). The Ninth Circuit Court of Appeals considered this a case of piracy—almost certainly wrongly. *See* Eugene Kontorovich, 103 Am. J. Int'l L. 734-740 (2009). *See also United States v. Hassan et al.*, 747 F. Supp. 2d 599 (E.D. Va 2010)—where pirates found themselves a bit outgunned: to their surprise the ship they went to hijack (at night) turned out to be the USS *Nicholas*, a naval frigate (which promptly returned fire).

The universality principle is also recognized in the Statute of the International Criminal Court and thus in countries that incorporate the Statute into their domestic law. The excerpt below shows how Germany implemented it.

GERMAN CODE OF CRIMES AGAINST INTERNATIONAL LAW
(2002)

Section 1

The Act shall apply to all criminal offenses against international law designated under this Act, to serious criminal offenses designated therein even when the offense was committed abroad and bears no relation to Germany.

[The Code then incorporates the major substantive provisions of the Rome Statute on genocide, crimes against humanity, war crimes, etc., which you have already seen in Chapter VI.4.B.]

Addendum: *Erga Omnes* (Universal) Obligations

The concept of universal jurisdiction is based on the idea that the violation of certain norms of international law is the concern of all members of the world community of states. In other words, there are norms that apply not only between those states which have agreed on them but rather among all. As a result, all states can take jurisdiction over such violations.

The idea that some norms apply universally is related to the notion that, in international law, states may have certain obligations vis-à-vis all others, in Latin, *erga omnes*. The concept of *erga omnes* norms has its (at least modern) origins in the *Barcelona Traction Case* (Chapter VI.5.).

To be sure, the *Barcelona Traction Case* did not involve any heinous crimes that would allow a (domestic) court to assert universal (criminal) jurisdiction. As you will recall, the case instead involved the question of whether a particular country had standing to sue before the ICJ. Belgium sued Spain claiming that Spain had essentially ruined a Canadian corporation and thereby violated Spain's obligations to diplomatic protection (herein of a foreign enterprise). A crucial issue was whether Belgium could invoke diplomatic protection with regard to the Canadian corporation at all. Normally, a state can claim diplomatic protection only with regard to its own citizens (or corporations).

The ICJ began its analysis by making "an essential distinction * * * between the obligations of a State towards the international community as a whole, and those arising vis-à-vis another State in the field of diplomatic protection." The former obligations are, "[b]y their very nature * * * the concern of all States. In view of the importance of the rights involved, all States can be held to have a legal interest in their protection; they are obligations *erga omnes*." The latter, however, are obligations only with regard to particular States, i.e., those who can claim a specific status or interest.

If the obligations of diplomatic protection belonged to the former category (i.e., had *erga omnes* effect), Belgium could invoke them without further ado—just like any other state in the world. Yet the ICJ found that these obligations had no *erga omnes* effect. In order to bring suit, Belgium thus had to show a specific concern. It claimed such a concern because a large number of investors in the ruined corporation were Belgian. The ICJ, however, considered that insufficient and held that only the state of incorporation (here Canada) could bring a claim (which Canada chose not to do).

On the one hand, the idea that some norms have *erga omnes* effects while others do not is fairly straightforward—just like the idea that some private rights, e.g., in property, can be invoked against all comers while others, e.g., those arising from contract, can be made only within a particular relationship. (This is the notion of privity.) On the other hand, the concept of *erga omnes* norms has, to put it mildly, not been entirely worked out in international law—as the following text emphasizes.

BRUNO SIMMA, DOES THE UN CHARTER PROVIDE AN ADEQUATE LEGAL BASIS FOR INDIVIDUAL OR COLLECTIVE RESPONSES TO VIOLATIONS OF OBLIGATIONS ERGA OMNES?

In THE FUTURE OF INTERNATIONAL LAW ENFORCEMENT (J. Delbrück ed. 1993)

In earlier times, cartographers used to fill blank spots on their maps with the words *hic sunt leones:* here is where the lions roam. The treatment of obligations *erga omnes* in international legal literature reminds me of this description for two different reasons. First, although the notion of obligations *erga omnes* appears to be here to stay, we are still far from having a clear picture of its precise ramifications and implications for an international law traditionally viewed from a strictly individualist—or bilateralist—perspective. But *hic sunt leones* would also be fitting with regard to the use, or non-use, of the concept of obligations *erga omnes* and of the faculties which it entails in actual state practice: like chunks of meat thrown to the lions, such legal constructs are either devoured or neglected by states, depending on their political "appetite" or lack thereof at a given time. Just compare the readiness of the United States in resorting to the pipeline embargo against the Soviet Union in 1982 as a reaction against the declaration of martial law in Poland, or the energy displayed in countering the Iraqi invasion of Kuwait, with the absolute lack of interest in doing anything that could have forced Indonesia to have second thoughts about its annexation of East Timor.

Thus, any observer entering the terrain of obligations *erga omnes* should be aware that one will be moving on largely uncharted and dangerous grounds, where the animals whose actions we will observe rarely display the tameness—or the willingness to perform—which some academic guidebooks so readily foresee. Viewed realistically, the world of obligations *erga omnes* is still the world of the "ought" rather than of the "is;" the concept marks the direction in which international law will have to move rather than a clear course already steered today. * * *

If taken seriously, acceptance of obligations *erga omnes,* as conceived by the International Court, asks for a lot. Such obligations presuppose not only universal agreement on certain values to be protected by and enshrined in international law (which, in a certain sense, is the case with all norms of universal international law, also with those that are then left to bilateral application). The concept of obligations *erga omnes* requires, in addition, universal agreement to the effect that the enforcement of the rules embodying these values is not to be left—or at least not totally—to the discretion or power of individual states, and, further, that the principle *volenti non fit iniuria* ought not to apply to infringements of such rules. But does a consensus on the values and norms that are to enjoy such superiority or on the means by which the international community may take action actually exist? How are we to perceive the achievement of such universal agreement? As to the *substance* of the obligations *erga omnes* claimed by the ICJ and others, of course everyone will accept the broad principles—the prohibition of the use of force, respect for human rights, the duty not to stand in the way of self-determination, and the like. But most cases out there in the real world will be "hard cases" where principles conflict or where we have to find our way through a normative penumbra. For instance, is a state employing military force abroad to protect its own nationals, the human rights of nationals of the target state, or democracy pure and simple, violating an obligation *erga omnes?* Michael Reisman or Tony D'Amato would never agree with me on such issues. Is the execution of minors or mentally retarded criminals to be seen as contrary to an obligation *erga omnes* to respect the fundamental human right to life? Or would non-recognition of Croatia and Slovenia have to be considered in violation of these peoples' right to self-determination?

One can say that states have essentially recognized the *erga omnes* effect of certain fundamental human rights norms. As a result, states have standing, so to speak, to prosecute individuals accused of having violated these rights by asserting universal jurisdiction. In that sense, universal jurisdiction can be regarded as the practically most relevant manifestation of *erga omnes* effect. In fact, the ICJ may have had that in mind when it decided the *Barcelona Traction* case in 1970: as examples of obligations *erga omnes*, it mentioned those that derive "from the outlawing of acts of aggression, and of genocide, as also from the principles and rules concerning the basic rights of the human person, including protection from slavery and racial discrimination."

If the obligations not to violate fundamental human rights norms are indeed *erga omnes*, can every state in the world not only prosecute the perpetrator but also bring a claim for reparations against every (alleged) perpetrator state regardless of the nationality of the victims? In other words, if the Sudanese government violates the human rights of its own people, can Belgium (or the United States) seek reparations from Sudan (and on behalf of whom)?

5. COMITY LIMITATIONS ON THE EXERCISE OF JURISDICTION

In a world of coexisting bases of state jurisdiction, many international events can be subject to the legitimate jurisdiction of more than one state. This creates potential conflicts if the involved states have different laws. Such conflicts can be avoided, or at least alleviated, if the states involved impose limitations on their own jurisdiction under the principle of "comity." Sometimes they do so, sometimes they don't.

Although the concept of comity arises in the context of international law, comity-based restrictions on jurisdiction generally are imposed by domestic courts as a matter of domestic law. The following materials illustrate this phenomenon in the area of antitrust and securities law, which are two of the primary battlefields in transnational disputes.

The courts in the cases below approach comity in a different way. How does the Ninth Circuit Court of Appeals in *Timberlane* address the problem? How does the Supreme Court react in *Hartford*, both in the majority opinion and in the dissent? What approach does the European Court of Justice take in the *Wood Pulp* case?

TIMBERLANE V. BANK OF AMERICA

United States Circuit Court
549 F.2d 597 (9th Cir. 1976)

JUDGE CHOY:

Four separate actions, arising from the same series of events, were dismissed by the same district court and are consolidated here on appeal. The principal action is *Timberlane Lumber Co. v. Bank of America* (Timberlane action), an antitrust suit alleging violations of sections 1 and 2 of the Sherman Act (15 U.S.C. §§ 1, 2) and the Wilson Tariff Act (15 U.S.C. § 8). This action raises important questions concerning the application of American antitrust laws to activities in another country, including actions of foreign government officials. The district court dismissed the Timberlane action under the act of state doctrine and for lack of subject matter jurisdiction. * * *

I.   THE TIMBERLANE ACTION

The basic allegation of the Timberlane plaintiffs is that officials of the Bank of America and others located in both the United States and Honduras conspired to prevent Timberlane, through its Honduras subsidiaries, from milling lumber in Honduras and exporting it to the United States, thus maintaining control of the Honduran lumber export business in the hands of a few select individuals financed and controlled by the Bank. The intent and result of the conspiracy, they contend, was to interfere with the exportation to the United States, including Puerto Rico, of Honduran lumber for sale or use there by the plaintiffs, thus directly and substantially affecting the foreign commerce of the United States.

* * *

CAST OF CHARACTERS

There are three affiliated plaintiffs in the Timberlane action. Timberlane Lumber Company is an Oregon partnership principally involved in the purchase and distribution of lumber at wholesale in the United States and the importation of lumber into the United States for sale and use. Danli Industrial, S.A., and Maya Lumber Company, S. de R.L., are both Honduras corporations, incorporated and principally owned by the general partners of Timberlane. Danli held contracts to purchase timber in Honduras, and Maya was to conduct the milling operations to produce the lumber for export. (Timberlane, Danli, and Maya will be collectively referred to as "Timberlane.")

The primary defendants are Bank of America Corporation (Bank), a California corporation, and its wholly-owned subsidiary, Bank of America National Trust and Savings Association, which operates a branch in Tegucigalpa, Honduras. Several employees of the Bank have also been named and served as defendants. * * *

FACTS AS ALLEGED

[The facts are complex and it is not necessary to remember all the details; just get the general picture.]

The conspiracy sketched by Timberlane actually started before the plaintiffs entered the scene. The Lima family operated a lumber mill in Honduras, competing with Lamas and Casanova, in both of which the Bank had significant financial interests. The Lima enterprise was also indebted to the Bank. By 1971, however, the Lima business was in financial trouble. Timberlane alleges that driving Lima under was the first step in the conspiracy which eventually crippled Timberlane's efforts, but the particulars do not matter for this appeal. What does matter is that various interests in the Lima assets, including its milling plant, passed to Lima's creditors: Casanova, the Bank, and the group of Lima employees who had not been paid the wages and severance pay due them. Under Honduran law, the employees' claim had priority.

Enter Timberlane, with a long history in the lumber business, in search of alternative sources of lumber for delivery to its distribution system on the East Coast of the United States. After study, it decided to try Honduras. In 1971, Danli was formed, tracts of forest land were acquired, plans for a modern log-processing plant were prepared, and equipment was purchased and assembled for shipment from the United States to Danli in

Honduras. Timberlane became aware that the Lima plant might be available and began negotiating for its acquisition. Maya was formed, purchased the Lima employees' interest in the machinery and equipment in January 1972, despite opposition from the conspirators, and re-activated the Lima mill.

Realizing that they were faced with better-financed and more vigorous competition from Timberlane and its Honduran subsidiaries, the defendants and others extended the anti-Lima conspiracy to disrupt Timberlane's efforts. The primary weapons employed by the conspirators were the claim still held by the Bank in the remaining assets of the Lima enterprise under the all-inclusive mortgage Lima had been forced to sign and another claim held by Casanova. Maya made a substantial cash offer for the Bank's interest in an effort to clear its title, but the Bank refused to sell. Instead, the Bank surreptitiously conveyed the mortgage to Casanova for questionable consideration, Casanova paying nothing and agreeing only to pay the Bank a portion of what it collected. Casanova immediately assigned the Bank's claim and its own on similar terms to Caminals, who promptly set out to disrupt the Timberlane operation.

Caminals is characterized as the "front man" in the campaign to drive Timberlane out of Honduras, with the Bank and other defendants intending and carrying responsibility for his actions. Having acquired the claims of Casanova and the Bank, Caminals went to court to enforce them, ignoring throughout Timberlane's offers to purchase or settle them. Under the laws of Honduras, an "embargo" on property is a court-ordered attachment, registered with the Public Registry, which precludes the sale of that property without a court order. Honduran law provides, upon embargo, that the court appoint a judicial officer, called an "interventor" to ensure against any diminution in the value of the property. In order to paralyze the Timberlane operation, Caminals obtained embargoes against Maya and Danli. Acting through the interventor, since accused of being on the payroll of the Bank, guards and troops were used to cripple and, for a time, completely shut down Timberlane's milling operation. The harassment took other forms as well: the conspirators caused the manager of Timberlane's Honduras operations, Gordon Sloan Smith, to be falsely arrested and imprisoned and were responsible for the publication of several defamatory articles about Timberlane in the Honduran press.

As a result of the conspiracy, Timberlane's complaint claimed damages then estimated in excess of $5,000,000. Plaintiffs also allege that there has been a direct and substantial effect on United States foreign commerce, and that defendants intended the results of the conspiracy, including the impact on United States commerce.

* * *

EXTRATERRITORIAL REACH OF THE UNITED STATES ANTITRUST LAWS

There is no doubt that American antitrust laws extend over some conduct in other nations. There was language in the first Supreme Court case in point, *American Banana Co. v. United Fruit Co.*, 213 U.S. 347 (1909), casting doubt on the extension of the Sherman Act to acts outside United States territory. But subsequent cases have limited *American Banana* to its particular facts, and the Sherman Act and with it other antitrust laws has been applied to extraterritorial conduct. * * *

That American law covers some conduct beyond this nation's borders does not mean that it embraces all, however. Extraterritorial application is understandably a matter of concern for the other countries involved. Those nations have sometimes resented and protested, as excessive intrusions into their own spheres, broad assertions of authority by American courts. Our courts have recognized this concern and have, at times, responded to it, even if not always enough to satisfy all the foreign critics. In any event, it is evident that at some point the interests of the United States are too weak and the foreign harmony incentive for restraint too strong to justify an extraterritorial assertion of jurisdiction.

What that point is or how it is determined is not defined by international law. Nor does the Sherman Act limit itself. In the domestic field the Sherman Act extends to the full reach of the commerce power. To define it somewhat more modestly in the foreign commerce area courts have generally, and logically, fallen back on a narrower construction of congressional intent * * *.

* * *

* * * American courts have firmly concluded that there is some extraterritorial jurisdiction under the Sherman Act.

Even among American courts and commentators, however, there is no consensus on how far the jurisdiction should extend. The district court here concluded that a "direct and substantial effect" on United States foreign commerce was a prerequisite, without stating whether other factors were relevant or considered. * * *

A tripartite analysis seems to be indicated. As acknowledged above, the antitrust laws require in the first instance that there be *some* effect actual or intended on American foreign commerce before the federal courts may legitimately exercise subject matter jurisdiction under those statutes. Second, a greater showing of burden or restraint may be necessary to demonstrate that the effect is sufficiently large to present a cognizable injury to the plaintiffs and, therefore, a civil violation of the antitrust laws. Third, there is the additional question which is unique to the international setting of whether the interests of, and links to, the United States including the magnitude of the effect on American foreign commerce are sufficiently strong, vis-á-vis those of other nations, to justify an assertion of extraterritorial authority.

* * *

* * * We believe that the field of conflict of laws presents the proper approach, as was suggested, if not specifically employed, in *Alcoa* in expressing the basic limitation on application of American laws:

> [W]e are not to read general words, such as those in this Act, without regard to the limitations customarily observed by nations upon the exercise of their powers; limitations which generally correspond to those fixed by the "Conflict of Laws."

The same idea is reflected in Restatement (Second) of Foreign Relations Law of the United States § 40:

> Where two states have jurisdiction to prescribe and enforce rules of law and the rules they may prescribe require inconsistent conduct upon the part of a person, each state is required by international law to consider, in good faith, moderating the exercise of its enforcement jurisdiction * * *.

The act of state doctrine discussed earlier demonstrates that the judiciary is sometimes cognizant of the possible foreign implications of its action. Similar awareness should be extended to the general problems of extraterritoriality. Such acuity is especially required in private suits, like this one, for in these cases there is no opportunity for the executive branch to weigh the foreign relations impact, nor any statement implicit in the filing of the suit that that consideration has been outweighed.

What we prefer is an evaluation and balancing of the relevant considerations in each case—in the words of Kingman Brewster, a "jurisdictional rule of reason." * * *

The elements to be weighed include the degree of conflict with foreign law or policy, the nationality or allegiance of the parties and the locations or principal places of businesses or corporations, the extent to which enforcement by either state can be expected to achieve compliance, the relative significance of effects on the United States as compared with those elsewhere, the extent to which there is explicit purpose to harm or affect American commerce, the foreseeability of such effect, and the relative importance to the violations charged of conduct within the United States as compared with conduct abroad. A court evaluating these factors should identify the potential degree of conflict if American authority is asserted. A difference in law or policy is one likely sore spot, though one which may not always be present. Nationality is another; though foreign governments may have some concern for the treatment of American citizens and business residing there, they primarily care about their own nationals.

Having assessed the conflict, the court should then determine whether in the face of it the contacts and interests of the United States are sufficient to support the exercise of extraterritorial jurisdiction.[34]

We conclude, then, that the problem should be approached in three parts: Does the alleged restraint affect, or was it intended to affect, the foreign commerce of the United States? Is it of such a type and magnitude so as to be cognizable as a violation of the Sherman Act? As a matter of international comity and fairness, should the extraterritorial jurisdiction of the United States be asserted to cover it? The district court's judgment found only that the restraint involved in the instant suit did not produce a direct and substantial effect on American foreign commerce. That holding does not satisfy any of these inquiries.

The Sherman Act is not limited to trade restraints which have both a direct and substantial effect on our foreign commerce. Timberlane has alleged that the complained of activities were intended to, and did, affect the export of lumber from Honduras to the United States—the flow of United States foreign commerce, and as such they are within the jurisdiction of the federal courts under the Sherman Act. Moreover, the magnitude of the effect alleged would appear to be sufficient to state a claim.

The comity question is more complicated. From Timberlane's complaint it is evident that there are grounds for concern as to at least a few of the defendants, for some are identified as foreign citizens: Laureano Gutierrez Falla, Michael Casanova and the Casanova firms, of Honduras, and Patrick Byrne, of Canada. Moreover, it is clear that most of the activity took place in Honduras, though the conspiracy may have been directed from San Francisco, and that the most direct economic effect was probably on Honduras. However, there has been no indication of any conflict with the law or policy of the Honduran government, nor any comprehensive analysis of the relative connections and interests of Honduras and the United States. Under these circumstances, the dismissal by the district court cannot be sustained on jurisdictional grounds.

We, therefore, vacate the dismissal and remand the Timberlane action.

* * *

---

[34] In requiring district courts to assess the conflicting contacts and interests of those nations involved, we do not thereby assign them the same task which the "act of state" doctrine prohibits them from undertaking. As the quotation from *comment d.* to § 41 of the Restatement, Second, Foreign Relations Law of the United States (1965), *see* pp. 607-08, supra, makes clear, there is an important distinction between examining the validity of the "public interests" which are involved in a sovereign policy decision amounting to an "act of state" and evaluating the relative "interests" which each state may have "in providing the means of adjudicating disputes or claims that arise within its territory." Our "jurisdictional rule of reason" does not in any way require the court to question the "validity" of "foreign law or policy." Rather, the legitimacy of each nation's interests is assumed. It is merely the relative involvement and concern of each state with the suit at hand that is to be evaluated in determining whether extraterritorial jurisdiction should be exercised by American courts as a matter of comity and fairness.

[On remand, the federal District Court decided not to exercise jurisdiction (574 F. Supp. 1453 (N.D. Cal. 1983)), the Court of Appeals affirmed (749 F.2d 1378 (9th Cir. 1984)), and the Supreme Court denied certiorari (472 U.S. 1032 (1985)).]

How does Section 403 of the Restatement (Third) of Foreign Relations Law compare to *Timberlane*?

§ 403.   Limitations on Jurisdiction to Prescribe

(1) Even when one of the bases for jurisdiction under § 402 is present, a state may not exercise jurisdiction to prescribe law with respect to a person or activity having connections with another state when the exercise of such jurisdiction is unreasonable.

(2) Whether exercise of jurisdiction over a person or activity is unreasonable is determined by evaluating all relevant factors, including, where appropriate:

   (a) the link of the activity to the territory of the regulating state, i.e. the extent to which the activity takes place within the territory, or has substantial, direct, and foreseeable effect upon or in the territory;

   (b) the connections, such as nationality, residence, or economic activity, between the regulating state and the person principally responsible for the activity to be regulated, or between that state and those whom the regulation is designed to protect;

   (c) the character of the activity to be regulated, the importance of regulation to the regulating state, the extent to which other states regulate such activities, and the degree to which the desirability of such regulation is generally accepted;

   (d) the existence of justified expectations that might be protected or hurt by the regulation

   (e) the importance of the regulation to the international political, legal, or economic system;

   (f) the extent to which the regulation is consistent with the traditions of the international system;

   (g) the extent to which another state may have an interest in regulating the activity; and

   (h) the likelihood of conflict with regulation by another state.

(3) When it would not be unreasonable for each of two states to exercise jurisdiction over a person or activity, but the prescriptions by the two states are in conflict, each state has an obligation to evaluate its own as well as the other state's interest in exercising jurisdiction, in light

of all the relevant factors, including those set out in Subsection (2); a state should defer to the other state if that state's interest is clearly greater.

———————

If you thought "comity" is too vague to do any real (law) work, think again: the result in *Timberlane* was, after all, dismissal of an otherwise fairly promising antitrust action brought by an American plaintiff against an American defendant with an alleged impact on the American market. Where can the plaintiffs take their grievances now?

How does the Supreme Court handle comity in the case below? How does its analysis compare to the Ninth Circuit's approach in *Timberlane*? How does Justice Scalia's dissenting opinion square with the Ninth Circuit's approach?

HARTFORD FIRE INSURANCE CO. V. CALIFORNIA
United States Supreme Court
509 U.S. 764 (1993)

Syllabus

Nineteen States and many private plaintiffs filed complaints alleging that the defendants—four domestic primary insurers, domestic companies who sell reinsurance to insurers, two domestic trade associations, a domestic reinsurance broker, and reinsurers based in London—violated the Sherman Act by engaging in various conspiracies aimed at forcing certain other primary insurers to change the terms of their standard domestic commercial general liability insurance policies to conform with the policies the defendant insurers wanted to sell. After the actions were consolidated for litigation, the District Court granted the defendants' motions to dismiss. The Court of Appeals reversed, rejecting the District Court's conclusion that the defendants were entitled to antitrust immunity under § 2(b) of the McCarran–Ferguson Act, which exempts from federal regulation "the business of insurance," except "to the extent that such business is not regulated by State Law." * * * [The Court of Appeals also] rejected the District Court's conclusion that the principle of international comity barred it from exercising Sherman Act jurisdiction over the three claims brought solely against the London reinsurers.

* * *

JUSTICE SOUTER announced the judgment of the Court and delivered * * * the opinion of the Court with respect to Parts III and IV, in which CHIEF JUSTICE REHNQUIST and JUSTICES WHITE, BLACKMUN, and STEVENS joined. * * * JUSTICE SCALIA delivered * * * a dissenting opinion with respect to Part II, in which JUSTICES O'CONNOR, KENNEDY, and THOMAS joined.

* * *

III

Finally, we take up the question * * * whether certain claims against the London reinsurers should have been dismissed as improper applications of the Sherman Act to foreign conduct. The Fifth Claim for Relief in the California Complaint alleges a violation of § 1 of the Sherman Act by certain London reinsurers who conspired to coerce primary insurers in the United States to offer CGL coverage on a claims-made basis, thereby making "occurrence CGL coverage * * * unavailable in the State of California for many risks." The Sixth Claim for Relief in the California Complaint alleges that the London reinsurers violated § 1 by a conspiracy to limit coverage of pollution risks in North America, thereby rendering "pollution liability coverage * * * almost entirely unavailable for the vast majority of casualty insurance purchasers in the State of California." The Eighth Claim for Relief in the California Complaint alleges a further § 1 violation by the London reinsurers who, along with domestic retrocessional reinsurers, conspired to limit coverage of seepage, pollution, and property contamination risks in North America, thereby eliminating such coverage in the State of California. * * *

At the outset, we note that the District Court undoubtedly had jurisdiction of these Sherman Act claims, as the London reinsurers apparently concede. See Tr. of Oral Arg. 37 ("Our position is not that the Sherman Act does not apply in the sense that a minimal basis for the exercise of jurisdiction doesn't exist here. Our position is that there are certain circumstances, and that this is one of them, in which the interests of another State are sufficient that the exercise of that jurisdiction should be restrained"). Although the proposition was perhaps not always free from doubt, see *American Banana Co. v. United Fruit Co.*, 213 U.S. 347 (1909), it is well established by now that the Sherman Act applies to foreign conduct that was meant to produce and did in fact produce some substantial effect in the United States. Such is the conduct alleged here: that the London reinsurers engaged in unlawful conspiracies to affect the market for insurance in the United States and that their conduct in fact produced substantial effect.

According to the London reinsurers, the District Court should have declined to exercise such jurisdiction under the principle of international comity. The Court of Appeals agreed that courts should look to that principle in deciding whether to exercise jurisdiction under the Sherman Act. This availed the London reinsurers nothing, however. To be sure, the Court of Appeals believed that "application of [American] antitrust laws to the London reinsurance market 'would lead to significant conflict with English law and policy,'" and that "[s]uch a conflict, unless outweighed by other factors, would by itself be reason to decline exercise of jurisdiction." But other factors, in the court's view, including the London reinsurers' express purpose to affect United States commerce and the substantial nature of the effect produced, outweighed the supposed conflict and required the exercise of jurisdiction in this litigation.

When it enacted the FTAIA, Congress expressed no view on the question whether a court with Sherman Act jurisdiction should ever decline to exercise such jurisdiction on grounds of international comity. See H.R.Rep. No. 97-686, p. 13 (1982) ("If a court determines that the requirements for subject matter jurisdiction are met, [the FTAIA] would have no effect on the court['s] ability to employ notions of comity * * * or otherwise to take account of the international character of the transaction"). We need not decide that question here, however, for even assuming that in a proper case a court may decline to exercise Sherman Act jurisdiction over foreign conduct (or, as Justice SCALIA would put it, may conclude by the employment of comity analysis in the first instance that there is no jurisdiction), international comity would not counsel against exercising jurisdiction in the circumstances alleged here.

The only substantial question in this litigation is whether "there is in fact a true conflict between domestic and foreign law." *Société Nationale Industrielle Aérospatiale v. United States Dist. Court for Southern Dist. of Iowa*, 482 U.S. 522, 555, (1987) (BLACKMUN, J., concurring in part and dissenting in part). The London reinsurers contend that applying the Act to their conduct would conflict significantly with British law, and the British Government, appearing before us as *amicus curiae*, concurs. They assert that Parliament has established a comprehensive regulatory regime over the London reinsurance market and that the conduct alleged here was perfectly consistent with British law and policy. But this is not to state a conflict. "[T]he fact that conduct is lawful in the state in which it took place will not, of itself, bar application of the United States antitrust laws," even where the foreign state has a strong policy to permit or encourage such conduct. Restatement (Third) Foreign Relations Law § 415, Comment *j*. No conflict exists, for these purposes, "where a person subject to regulation by two states can comply with the laws of both." Restatement (Third) Foreign Relations Law § 403, Comment *e*. Since the London reinsurers do not argue that British law requires them to act in some fashion prohibited by the law of the United States or claim that their compliance with the laws of both countries is otherwise impossible, we see no conflict with British law. See Restatement (Third) Foreign Relations Law § 403, Comment *e*, § 415, Comment *j*. We have no need in this litigation to address other considerations that might inform a decision to refrain from the exercise of jurisdiction on grounds of international comity.

IV

The judgment of the Court of Appeals is affirmed in part and reversed in part, and the cases are remanded for further proceedings consistent with this opinion.

It is so ordered.

JUSTICE SCALIA * * * delivered a dissenting opinion with respect to Part II in which JUSTICE O'CONNOR, JUSTICE KENNEDY, and JUSTICE THOMAS have joined.

* * *

II

* * *

* * * There is no doubt, of course, that Congress possesses legislative jurisdiction over the acts alleged in this complaint: Congress has broad power under Article I, § 8, cl. 3, "[t]o regulate Commerce with foreign Nations," and this Court has repeatedly upheld its power to make laws applicable to persons or activities beyond our territorial boundaries where United States interests are affected. But the question in this litigation is whether, and to what extent, Congress *has* exercised that undoubted legislative jurisdiction in enacting the Sherman Act.

Two canons of statutory construction are relevant in this inquiry. The first is the "longstanding principle of American law 'that legislation of Congress, unless a contrary intent appears, is meant to apply only within the territorial jurisdiction of the United States.' "*Aramco*, 499 U.S., at 248. Applying that canon in *Aramco*, we held that the version of Title VII of the Civil Rights Act of 1964 then in force, 42 U.S.C. §§ 2000e to 2000e–17 (1988 ed.), did not extend outside the territory of the United States even though the statute contained broad provisions extending its prohibitions to, for example, " 'any activity, business, or industry in commerce.' " *Id.*, 499 U.S., at 249. We held such "boilerplate language" to be an insufficient indication to override the presumption against extraterritoriality. The Sherman Act contains similar "boilerplate language," and if the question were not governed by precedent, it would be worth considering whether that presumption controls the outcome here. We have, however, found the presumption to be overcome with respect to our antitrust laws; it is now well established that the Sherman Act applies extraterritorially.

But if the presumption against extraterritoriality has been overcome or is otherwise inapplicable, a second canon of statutory construction becomes relevant: "[A]n act of congress ought never to be construed to violate the law of nations if any other possible construction remains." *Murray v. Schooner Charming Betsy*, 118, 2 L.Ed. 208 (1804) (Marshall, C.J.). This canon is "wholly independent" of the presumption against extraterritoriality. *Aramco*, 499 U.S., at 264. It is relevant to determining the substantive reach of a statute because "the law of nations," or customary international law, includes limitations on a nation's exercise of its jurisdiction to prescribe. See Restatement (Third) §§ 401–416. Though it clearly has constitutional authority to do so, Congress is generally presumed not to have exceeded those customary international-law limits on jurisdiction to prescribe.

* * *

More recent lower court precedent has also tempered the extraterritorial application of the Sherman Act with considerations of "international comity." See *Timberlane Lumber Co. v. Bank of America, N.T. & S.A.*, 549 F.2d 597, 608–615 (CA9 1976) * * *. The "comity" they refer to is not the comity of courts, whereby judges decline to exercise jurisdiction over matters more appropriately adjudged elsewhere, but rather what might be termed "prescriptive comity": the respect sovereign nations afford each other by limiting the reach of their laws. That comity is exercised by legislatures when they enact laws, and courts assume it has been exercised when they come to interpreting the scope of laws their legislatures have enacted. It is a traditional component of choice-of-law theory. See J. Story, Commentaries on the Conflict of Laws § 38 (1834) (distinguishing between the "comity of the courts" and the "comity of nations," and defining the latter as "the true foundation and extent of the obligation of the laws of one nation within the territories of another"). Comity in this sense includes the choice-of-law principles that, "in the absence of contrary congressional direction," are assumed to be incorporated into our substantive laws having extraterritorial reach. Considering comity in this way is just part of determining whether the Sherman Act prohibits the conduct at issue.

In sum, the practice of using international law to limit the extraterritorial reach of statutes is firmly established in our jurisprudence. In proceeding to apply that practice to the present cases, I shall rely on the Restatement (Third) for the relevant principles of international law. Its standards appear fairly supported in the decisions of this Court construing international choice-of-law principles and in the decisions of other federal courts, especially *Timberlane*. Whether the Restatement precisely reflects international law in every detail matters little here, as I believe this litigation would be resolved the same way under virtually any conceivable test that takes account of foreign regulatory interests.

Under the Restatement, a nation having some "basis" for jurisdiction to prescribe law should nonetheless refrain from exercising that jurisdiction "with respect to a person or activity having connections with another state when the exercise of such jurisdiction is unreasonable." Restatement (Third) § 403(1). The "reasonableness" inquiry turns on a number of factors including, but not limited to: "the extent to which the activity takes place within the territory [of the regulating state]," § 403(2)(a); "the connections, such as nationality, residence, or economic activity, between the regulating state and the person principally responsible for the activity to be regulated," § 403(2)(b); "the character of the activity to be regulated, the importance of regulation to the regulating state, the extent to which other states regulate such activities, and the degree to which the desirability of such regulation is generally accepted," § 403(2)(c); "the extent to which another state may have an interest in regulating the activity," § 403(2)(g); and "the likelihood of conflict with regulation by another state," § 403(2)(h). Rarely would these factors point more clearly against application of United States law. The activity relevant to the counts at issue here took place primarily in the United Kingdom, and the defendants in these counts are British corporations and British subjects having their principal place of business or residence outside the United States. Great Britain has established a comprehensive regulatory scheme governing the London reinsurance markets, and clearly has a heavy "interest in regulating the activity," § 403(2)(g). Finally, § 2(b) of the McCarran–Ferguson Act allows state regulatory statutes to override the Sherman Act in the insurance field, subject only to the narrow "boycott" exception set forth in § 3(b)—suggesting that "the importance of regulation to the [United States]," Restatement (Third) § 403(2)(c), is slight. Considering these factors, I think it unimaginable that an assertion of legislative jurisdiction by the United States would be considered reasonable, and therefore it is inappropriate to assume, in the absence of statutory indication to the contrary, that Congress has made such an assertion.

* * *

What are the consequences of the majority position? Of the dissent? Can elements of the majority and dissent be combined to reach a more reasonable result?

Note that it is Justice Scalia who waves the international flag here. Is his position internally consistent? Do you see any problems with how he combines the *Charming Betsy* principle and international comity? Is he right when he says that this is actually an easy case (for deference)?

A few years earlier, the European Court of Justice had faced more or less the same issue. There was an alleged international conspiracy among American, Canadian, Finnish, and Swedish firms that exported wood pulp, either themselves or through export associations (especially the

Kraft Export Association, KEA), to the European Community (among others). Under American law, export associations were exempt from the antitrust laws under the Webb–Pomerene Act (the idea being that anticompetitive behavior with an effect solely on foreign markets is not the business of American law).

The Commission of the European Community charged the wood pulp exporters with price fixing. At the time, Article 85 of the Treaty of Rome[9] provided:

> 1. The following shall be prohibited as incompatible with the common market: all agreements between undertakings, decisions by associations of undertakings and concerted practices which may affect trade between Member States and which have as their object or effect the prevention, restriction or distortion of competition within the common market. * * *

> 2. Any agreements or decisions prohibited pursuant to this Article shall be automatically void.

The Commission found infringements of this provision and imposed fines. The wood pulp exporters took the case before the European Court of Justice, arguing, inter alia, that the EC Commission had no jurisdiction. Here is the answer they received from the Court.

AHLSTRÖM OSAKEYHTIÖ v. COMMISSION (WOOD PULP, JURISDICTION)
European Court of Justice
1988 E.C.R. 5193

* * *

11. In so far as the submission concerning the infringement of Article 85 of the Treaty itself is concerned, it should be recalled that that provision prohibits all agreements between undertakings and concerted practices which may affect trade between Member States and which have as their object or effect the restriction of competition within the common market.

12. It should be noted that the main sources of supply of wood pulp are outside the Community, in Canada, the United States, Sweden and Finland and that the market therefore has global dimensions. Where wood pulp producers established in those countries sell directly to purchasers established in the Community and engage in price competition in order to win orders from those customers, that constitutes competition within the common market.

---

[9] The matter is now addressed in Article 101 of the Treaty of the Functioning of the European Union (TFEU).

13. It follows that where those producers concert on the prices to be charged to their customers in the Community and put that concertation into effect by selling at prices which are actually coordinated, they are taking part in concertation which has the object and effect of restricting competition within the common market within the meaning of Article 85 of the Treaty.

14. Accordingly, it must be concluded that by applying the competition rules in the Treaty in the circumstances of this case to undertakings whose registered offices are situated outside the Community, the Commission has not made an incorrect assessment of the territorial scope of Article 85.

15. The applicants have submitted that the decision is incompatible with public international law on the grounds that the application of the competition rules in this case was founded exclusively on the economic repercussions within the common market of conduct restricting competition which was adopted outside the Community.

16. It should be observed that an infringement of Article 85, such as the conclusion of an agreement which has had the effect of restricting competition within the common market, consists of conduct made up of two elements, the formation of the agreement, decision or concerted practice and the implementation thereof. If the applicability of prohibitions laid down under competition law were made to depend on the place where the agreement, decision or concerted practice was formed, the result would obviously be to give undertakings an easy means of evading those prohibitions. The decisive factor is therefore the place where it is implemented.

17. The producers in this case implemented their pricing agreement within the common market. It is immaterial in that respect whether or not they had recourse to subsidiaries, agents, sub-agents, or branches within the Community in order to make their contacts with purchasers within the Community.

18. Accordingly the Community's jurisdiction to apply its competition rules to such conduct is covered by the territoriality principle as universally recognized in public international law.

19. As regards the argument based on the infringement of the principle of non-interference, it should be pointed out that the applicants who are members of KEA have referred to a rule according to which where two States have jurisdiction to lay down and enforce rules and the effect of those rules is that a person finds himself subject to contradictory orders as to the conduct he must adopt, each State is obliged to exercise its jurisdiction with moderation. The applicants have concluded that by disregarding that rule in applying its competition rules the Community has infringed the principle of non-interference.

20. There is no need to enquire into the existence in international law of such a rule since it suffices to observe that the conditions for its application are in any event not satisfied. There is not, in this case, any contradiction between the conduct required by the United States and that required by the Community since the Webb Pomerene Act merely exempts the conclusion of export cartels from the application of United States antitrust laws but does not require such cartels to be concluded.

21. It should further be pointed out that the United States authorities raised no objections regarding any conflict of jurisdiction when consulted by the Commission pursuant to the OECD Council Recommendation of 25 October 1979 concerning cooperation between member countries on restrictive business practices affecting international trade (*Acts of the organization*, Vol. 19, p. 376).

22. As regards the argument relating to disregard of international comity, it suffices to observe that it amounts to calling in question the Community's jurisdiction to apply its competition rules to conduct such as that found to exist in this case and that, as such, that argument has already been rejected.

23. Accordingly it must be concluded that the Commission's decision is not contrary to Article 85 of the Treaty or to the rules of public international law relied on by the applicants.

* * *

Of the various approaches taken by U.S. courts in *Timberlane* and *Hartford*, which does this decision resemble most?

The battle about the "extraterritorial" reach of antitrust law continued in the following case. What precisely was the issue? How does the Supreme Court resolve it?

F. HOFFMANN–LA ROCHE LTD. V. EMPAGRAN S. A.

United States Supreme Court
542 U.S. 155 (2004)

JUSTICE BREYER:

* * *

* * * The issue before us concerns (1) significant foreign anticompetitive conduct with (2) an adverse domestic effect and (3) an independent foreign effect giving rise to the claim. In more concrete terms, this case involves vitamin sellers around the world that agreed to fix prices, leading to higher vitamin prices in the United States and independently leading to higher vitamin prices in other countries such as Ecuador. We conclude that, in this scenario, a purchaser in the United States could bring a Sherman Act claim under the FTAIA based on domestic injury, but a purchaser in Ecuador could not bring a Sherman Act claim based on foreign harm.

I

The plaintiffs in this case originally filed a class-action suit on behalf of foreign and domestic purchasers of vitamins under, *inter alia*, § 1 of the Sherman Act and §§ 4 and 16 of the Clayton Act. Their complaint alleged that petitioners, foreign and domestic vitamin manufacturers and distributors, had engaged in a price-fixing conspiracy, raising the price of vitamin products to customers in the United States and to customers in foreign countries.

As relevant here, petitioners moved to dismiss the suit as to the *foreign* purchasers (the respondents here), five foreign vitamin distributors located in Ukraine, Australia, Ecuador, and Panama, each of which bought vitamins from petitioners for delivery outside the United States. Respondents have never asserted that they purchased any vitamins in the United States or in transactions in United States commerce, and the question presented assumes that the relevant "transactions occurr[ed] entirely outside U.S. commerce." * * *

II

The FTAIA seeks to make clear to American exporters (and to firms doing business abroad) that the Sherman Act does not prevent them from entering into business arrangements (say, joint-selling arrangements), however anticompetitive, as long as those arrangements adversely affect only foreign markets. It does so by removing from the Sherman Act's reach, (1) export activities and (2) other commercial activities taking place abroad, *unless* those activities adversely affect domestic commerce, imports to the United States, or exporting activities of one engaged in such activities within the United States.

The FTAIA says:

> "Sections 1 to 7 of this title [the Sherman Act] shall not apply to conduct involving trade or commerce (other than import trade or import commerce) with foreign nations unless—

> "(1) such conduct has a direct, substantial, and reasonably foreseeable effect—

> "(A) on trade or commerce which is not trade or commerce with foreign nations [*i.e.*, domestic trade or commerce], or on import trade or import commerce with foreign nations; or

"(B) on export trade or export commerce with foreign nations, of a person engaged in such trade or commerce in the United States [*i.e.*, on an American export competitor]; and

(2) such effect gives rise to a claim under the provisions of *sections 1 to 7* of this title, other than this section.

* * *

This technical language initially lays down a general rule placing *all* (non-import) activity involving foreign commerce outside the Sherman Act's reach. It then brings such conduct back within the Sherman Act's reach *provided that* the conduct *both* (1) sufficiently affects American commerce, *i.e.*, it has a "direct, substantial, and reasonably foreseeable effect" on American domestic, import, or (certain) export commerce, *and* (2) has an effect of a kind that antitrust law considers harmful, *i.e.*, the "effect" must "giv[e] rise to a [Sherman Act] claim." §§ 6a(1), (2).

We ask here how this language applies to price-fixing activity that is in significant part foreign, that has the requisite domestic effect, and that also has independent foreign effects giving rise to the plaintiff's claim.

* * *

IV

We turn now to the basic question presented, that of the exception's application. Because the underlying antitrust action is complex, potentially raising questions not directly at issue here, we reemphasize that we base our decision upon the following: The price-fixing conduct significantly and adversely affects both customers outside the United States and customers within the United States, but the adverse foreign effect is independent of any adverse domestic effect. In these circumstances, we find that the FTAIA exception does not apply (and thus the Sherman Act does not apply) for two main reasons.

First, this Court ordinarily construes ambiguous statutes to avoid unreasonable interference with the sovereign authority of other nations. This rule of construction reflects principles of customary international law—law that (we must assume) Congress ordinarily seeks to follow. See Restatement (Third) of Foreign Relations Law of the United States §§ 403(1), 403(2) (1986) (hereinafter Restatement) (limiting the unreasonable exercise of prescriptive jurisdiction with respect to a person or activity having connections with another State); *Murray v. Schooner Charming Betsy*, 6 U.S. 64 (1804) ("[A]n act of Congress ought never to be construed to violate the law of nations if any other possible construction remains"); *Hartford Fire Insurance Co. v. California*, 509 U.S. 764, 817 (1993) (Scalia, J., dissenting) (identifying rule of construction as derived from the principle of " 'prescriptive comity' ").

This rule of statutory construction cautions courts to assume that legislators take account of the legitimate sovereign interests of other nations when they write American laws. It thereby helps the potentially conflicting laws of different nations work together in harmony—a harmony particularly needed in today's highly interdependent commercial world.

No one denies that America's antitrust laws, when applied to foreign conduct, can interfere with a foreign nation's ability independently to regulate its own commercial affairs. But our courts have long held that application of our antitrust laws to foreign anticompetitive conduct is nonetheless reasonable, and hence consistent with principles of prescriptive comity, insofar as they reflect a legislative effort to redress *domestic* antitrust injury that foreign anticompetitive conduct has caused. See *United States v. Aluminum Co. of America*, 148 F.2d 416, 443–444 (CA2 1945) (L. Hand, J.).

But why is it reasonable to apply those laws to foreign conduct *insofar as that conduct causes independent foreign harm and that foreign harm alone gives rise to the plaintiff's claim?* Like the former case, application of those laws creates a serious risk of interference with a foreign nation's ability independently to regulate its own commercial affairs. But, unlike the former case, the justification for that interference seems insubstantial. See Restatement § 403(2) (determining reasonableness on basis of such factors as connections with regulating nation, harm to that nation's interests, extent to which other nations regulate, and the potential for conflict). Why should American law supplant, for example, Canada's or Great Britain's or Japan's own determination about how best to protect Canadian or British or Japanese customers from anticompetitive conduct engaged in significant part by Canadian or British or Japanese or other foreign companies?

We recognize that principles of comity provide Congress greater leeway when it seeks to control through legislation the actions of *American* companies, see Restatement § 402; and some of the anticompetitive price-fixing conduct alleged here took place in *America*. But the higher foreign prices of which the foreign plaintiffs here complain are not the consequence of any domestic anticompetitive conduct *that Congress sought to forbid*, for Congress did not seek to forbid any such conduct insofar as it is here relevant, *i.e.*, insofar as it is intertwined with foreign conduct that causes independent foreign harm. Rather Congress sought to *release* domestic (and foreign) anticompetitive conduct from Sherman Act constraints when that conduct causes foreign harm. Congress, of course, did make an exception where that conduct also causes domestic harm. See House Report 13 (concerns about American firms' participation in international cartels addressed through "domestic injury" exception). But any independent domestic harm the foreign conduct causes here has, by definition, little or nothing to do with the matter.

We thus repeat the basic question: Why is it reasonable to apply this law to conduct that is significantly foreign *insofar as that conduct causes independent foreign harm and that foreign harm alone gives rise to the plaintiff's claim?* We can find no good answer to the question.

* * *

[E]ven where nations agree about primary conduct, say price fixing, they disagree dramatically about appropriate remedies. The application, for example, of American private treble-damages remedies to anticompetitive conduct taking place abroad has generated considerable controversy. And several foreign nations have filed briefs here arguing that to apply our remedies would unjustifiably permit their citizens to bypass their own less generous remedial schemes, thereby upsetting a balance of competing considerations that their own domestic antitrust laws embody. * * *

These briefs add that a decision permitting independently injured foreign plaintiffs to pursue private treble-damages remedies would undermine foreign nations' own antitrust enforcement policies by diminishing foreign firms' incentive to cooperate with antitrust authorities in return for prosecutorial amnesty. Brief for Federal Republic of Germany et al. as *Amici Curiae* 28–30; Brief for Government of Canada as *Amicus Curiae* 11–14. See also Brief for United States as *Amicus Curiae* 19–21 (arguing the same in respect to American antitrust enforcement).

* * *

We conclude that principles of prescriptive comity counsel against the Court of Appeals' interpretation of the FTAIA. Where foreign anticompetitive conduct plays a significant role and where foreign injury is independent of domestic effects, Congress might have hoped that America's antitrust laws, so fundamental a component of our own economic system, would commend themselves to other nations as well. But, if America's antitrust policies could not win their own way in the international marketplace for such ideas, Congress, we must assume, would not have tried to impose them, in an act of legal imperialism, through legislative fiat.

Second, the FTAIA's language and history suggest that Congress designed the FTAIA to clarify, perhaps to limit, but not *to expand* in any significant way, the Sherman Act's scope as applied to foreign commerce. And we have found no significant indication that at the time Congress wrote this statute courts would have thought the Sherman Act applicable in these circumstances.

* * *

V

Respondents point to several considerations that point the other way. For one thing, the FTAIA's language speaks in terms of the Sherman Act's *applicability* to certain kinds of *conduct*. The FTAIA says that the Sherman Act applies to foreign "conduct" with a certain kind of harmful domestic effect. Why isn't that the end of the matter? How can the Sherman Act both *apply to the conduct* when one person sues but *not apply to the same conduct* when another person sues? The question of who can or cannot sue is a matter for other statutes (namely, the Clayton Act) to determine.

Moreover, the exception says that it applies if the conduct's domestic effect gives rise to "*a* claim," not to "*the plaintiff's* claim" or "*the* claim *at issue.*" 15 U.S.C. § 6a(2) [15 USCS § 6a(2)] (emphasis added). The alleged conduct here did have domestic effects, and those effects were harmful enough to give rise to "a" claim. Respondents concede that this claim is not their own claim; it is someone else's claim. But, linguistically speaking, they say, that is beside the point. Nor did Congress place the relevant words "gives rise to a claim" in the FTAIA to suggest any geographical limitation; rather it did so for a here neutral reason, namely, in order to make clear that the domestic effect must be an *adverse* (as opposed to a beneficial) effect.

Despite their linguistic logic, these arguments are not convincing. Linguistically speaking, a statute can apply and not apply to the same conduct, depending upon other circumstances; and those other circumstances may include the nature of the lawsuit (or of the related underlying harm). It also makes linguistic sense to read the words "a claim" as if they refer to the "plaintiff's claim" or "the claim at issue."

At most, respondents' linguistic arguments might show that respondents' reading is the more natural reading of the statutory language. But those arguments do not show that we *must* accept that reading. And that is the critical point. The considerations previously mentioned—those of comity and history—make clear that the respondents' reading is not consistent with the FTAIA's basic intent. If the statute's language reasonably permits an interpretation consistent with that intent, we should adopt it. And, for the reasons stated, we believe that the statute's language permits the reading that we give it.

* * *

JUSTICE O'CONNOR took no part in the consideration or decision of this case.

JUSTICE SCALIA, with whom JUSTICE THOMAS joins, concurring in the judgment.

I concur in the judgment of the Court because the language of the statute is readily susceptible of the interpretation the Court provides and because only that interpretation is consistent with the principle that statutes should be read in accord with the customary deference to the application of foreign countries' laws within their own territories.

After *Empagran*, are we back (from *Hartford*) to *Timberlane*?

Is the result in *Empagran* not merely a matter of comity but actually required by international law? If exercising jurisdiction in this case would violate international law, what does the *Charming Betsy* principle require?

In 2010, the Supreme Court continued its restrictive course with regard to the "extraterritorial" application of U.S. (federal) economic legislation. In some ways, the case was similar to *Empagran*, but it involved the antifraud provisions of the securities laws (Section 10(b) of the Securities Exchange Act of 1934).

Many lower courts had relied on the so-called "conduct" and "effects" test and thus applied these provisions whenever either fraudulent conduct or its effect took place in the United States. That could include so called "f-cubed" cases: claims by *foreign* plaintiffs against *foreign* defendants based on fraud in connection with transactions on *foreign* exchanges. Many lower courts had then engaged in a *Timberlane* balancing analysis to decide whether actually to exercise jurisdiction and to apply these provisions.

In *Morrison* below, the Supreme Court had to react to this practice. What is the core disagreement between Justice Scalia and Justice Stevens?

MORRISON V. NATIONAL AUSTRALIA BANK LTD.

United States Supreme Court
130 S. Ct. 2869 (2010)

JUSTICE SCALIA:

We decide whether § 10(b) of the Securities Exchange Act of 1934 provides a cause of action to foreign plaintiffs suing foreign and American defendants for misconduct in connection with securities traded on foreign exchanges.

I

Respondent National Australia Bank Limited (National) was, during the relevant time, the largest bank in Australia. Its Ordinary Shares—what in America would be called "common stock"—are traded on the Australian

Stock Exchange Limited and on other foreign securities exchanges, but not on any exchange in the United States. There are listed on the New York Stock Exchange, however, National's American Depositary Receipts (ADRs), which represent the right to receive a specified number of National's Ordinary Shares.

The complaint alleges the following facts, which we accept as true. In February 1998, National bought respondent HomeSide Lending, Inc., a mortgage servicing company headquartered in Florida. HomeSide's business was to receive fees for servicing mortgages (essentially the administrative tasks associated with collecting mortgage payments). The rights to receive those fees, so-called mortgage-servicing rights, can provide a valuable income stream. How valuable each of the rights is depends, in part, on the likelihood that the mortgage to which it applies will be fully repaid before it is due, terminating the need for servicing. HomeSide calculated the present value of its mortgage-servicing rights by using valuation models designed to take this likelihood into account. It recorded the value of its assets, and the numbers appeared in National's financial statements.

From 1998 until 2001, National's annual reports and other public documents touted the success of HomeSide's business, and respondents Frank Cicutto (National's managing director and chief executive officer), Kevin Race (HomeSide's chief operating officer), and Hugh Harris (HomeSide's chief executive officer) did the same in public statements. But on July 5, 2001, National announced that it was writing down the value of HomeSide's assets by $450 million; and then again on September 3, by another $1.75 billion. The prices of both Ordinary Shares and ADRs slumped. After downplaying the July write-down, National explained the September write-down as the result of a failure to anticipate the lowering of prevailing interest rates (lower interest rates lead to more refinancings, *i.e.*, more early repayments of mortgages), other mistaken assumptions in the financial models, and the loss of goodwill. According to the complaint, however, HomeSide, Race, Harris, and another HomeSide senior executive who is also a respondent here had manipulated HomeSide's financial models to make the rates of early repayment unrealistically low in order to cause the mortgage-servicing rights to appear more valuable than they really were. The complaint also alleges that National and Cicutto were aware of this deception by July 2000, but did nothing about it.

As relevant here, petitioners Russell Leslie Owen and Brian and Geraldine Silverlock, all Australians, purchased National's Ordinary Shares in 2000 and 2001, before the write-downs. They sued National, HomeSide, Cicutto, and the three HomeSide executives in the United States District Court for the Southern District of New York for alleged violations of §§ 10(b) and 20(a) of the Securities and Exchange Act of 1934, 15 U.S.C. §§ 78j(b) and 78t(a), and SEC Rule 10b–5, 17 CFR § 240.10b–5 (2009), promulgated pursuant to § 10(b). They sought to represent a class of foreign purchasers of National's Ordinary Shares during a specified period up to the September write-down.

Respondents moved to dismiss for lack of subject-matter jurisdiction under Federal Rule of Civil Procedure 12(b)(1) and for failure to state a claim under Rule 12(b)(6). The District Court granted the motion on the former ground, finding no jurisdiction because the acts in this country were, "at most, a link in the chain of an alleged overall securities fraud scheme that culminated abroad." The Court of Appeals for the Second Circuit affirmed on similar grounds. The acts performed in the United States did not "compris[e] the heart of the alleged fraud." We granted certiorari.

* * *

III

A

It is a "longstanding principle of American law 'that legislation of Congress, unless a contrary intent appears, is meant to apply only within the territorial jurisdiction of the United States.'" *EEOC* v. *Arabian American Oil Co.*, 499 U.S. 244, 248 (1991) (*Aramco*). This principle represents a canon of construction, or a presumption about a statute's meaning, rather than a limit upon Congress's power to legislate, see *Blackmer* v. *United States*, 284 U.S. 421, 437 (1932). It rests on the perception that Congress ordinarily legislates with respect to domestic, not foreign matters. Thus, "unless there is the affirmative intention of the Congress clearly expressed" to give a statute extraterritorial effect, "we must presume it is primarily concerned with domestic conditions." *Aramco, supra*, at 248. The canon or presumption applies regardless of whether there is a risk of conflict between the American statute and a foreign law. When a statute gives no clear indication of an extraterritorial application, it has none.

Despite this principle of interpretation, long and often recited in our opinions, the Second Circuit believed that, because the Exchange Act is silent as to the extraterritorial application of § 10(b), it was left to the court to "discern" whether Congress would have wanted the statute to apply. This disregard of the presumption against extraterritoriality did not originate with the Court of Appeals panel in this case. It has been repeated over many decades by various courts of appeals in determining the application of the Exchange Act, and § 10(b) in particular, to fraudulent schemes that involve conduct and effects abroad. That has produced a collection of tests for divining what Congress would have wanted, complex in formulation and unpredictable in application.

* * *

The Second Circuit had * * * established that application of § 10(b) could be premised upon either some effect on American securities markets or investors or significant conduct in the United States, It later formalized these two applications into (1) an "effects test," "whether the wrongful conduct had a substantial effect in the United States or upon United States citizens," and (2) a "conduct test," "whether the wrongful conduct occurred in the United States." These became the north star of the Second Circuit's § 10(b) jurisprudence, pointing the way to what Congress would have wished. Indeed, the Second Circuit declined to keep its two tests distinct on the ground that "an admixture or combination of the two often gives a better picture of whether there is sufficient United States involvement to justify the exercise of jurisdiction by an American court." The Second Circuit never put forward a textual or even extratextual basis for these tests. As early as [1975], it confessed that "if we were asked to point to language in the statutes, or even in the legislative history, that compelled these conclusions, we would be unable to respond."

As they developed, these tests were not easy to administer. * * *

At least one Court of Appeals has criticized this line of cases and the interpretive assumption that underlies it. In *Zoelsch* v. *Arthur Andersen & Co.*, 824 F. 2d 27, 32 (1987) (Bork, J.), the District of Columbia Circuit observed that rather than courts' "divining what 'Congress would have wished' if it had addressed the problem[, a] more natural inquiry might be what jurisdiction Congress in fact thought about and conferred." Although tempted to apply the presumption against extraterritoriality and be done with it, that court deferred to the Second Circuit because of its "preeminence in the field of securities law," *id.*, at 32.

Commentators have criticized the unpredictable and inconsistent application of § 10(b) to transnational cases. * * *

The criticisms seem to us justified. The results of judicial-speculation-made-law—divining what Congress would have wanted if it had thought of the situation before the court—demonstrate the wisdom of the presumption against extraterritoriality. Rather than guess anew in each case, we apply the presumption in all cases, preserving a stable background against which Congress can legislate with predictable effects.

B

Rule 10b–5, the regulation under which petitioners have brought suit, was promulgated under § 10(b), and "does not extend beyond conduct encompassed by § 10(b)'s prohibition." Therefore, if § 10(b) is not extraterritorial, neither is Rule 10b–5.

On its face, § 10(b) contains nothing to suggest it applies abroad:

> "It shall be unlawful for any person, directly or indirectly, by the use of any means or instrumentality of interstate commerce or of the

mails, or of any facility of any national securities exchange * * * [t]o use or employ, in connection with the purchase or sale of any security registered on a national securities exchange or any security not so registered, * * * any manipulative or deceptive device or contrivance in contravention of such rules and regulations as the [Securities and Exchange] Commission may prescribe * * *."

* * *

The concurrence claims we have impermissibly narrowed the inquiry in evaluating whether a statute applies abroad, citing for that point the dissent in *Aramco*. But we do not say, as the concurrence seems to think, that the presumption against extraterritoriality is a "clear statement rule," if by that is meant a requirement that a statute say "this law applies abroad." Assuredly context can be consulted as well. But whatever sources of statutory meaning one consults to give "the most faithful reading" of the text, there is no clear indication of extraterritoriality here. The concurrence does not even try to refute that conclusion, but merely puts forward the same (at best) uncertain indications relied upon by petitioners and the Solicitor General. As the opinion *for the Court* in *Aramco* (which we prefer to the dissent) shows, those uncertain indications do not suffice.

In short, there is no affirmative indication in the Exchange Act that § 10(b) applies extraterritorially, and we therefore conclude that it does not.

IV

A

Petitioners argue that the conclusion that § 10(b) does not apply extraterritorially does not resolve this case. They contend that they seek no more than domestic application anyway, since Florida is where HomeSide and its senior executives engaged in the deceptive conduct of manipulating HomeSide's financial models; their complaint also alleged that Race and Hughes made misleading public statements there. This is less an answer to the presumption against extraterritorial application than it is an assertion—a quite valid assertion—that that presumption here (as often) is not self-evidently dispositive, but its application requires further analysis. For it is a rare case of prohibited extraterritorial application that lacks *all* contact with the territory of the United States. But the presumption against extraterritorial application would be a craven watchdog indeed if it retreated to its kennel whenever *some* domestic activity is involved in the case. The concurrence seems to imagine just such a timid sentinel, but our cases are to the contrary. In *Aramco*, for example, the Title VII plaintiff had been hired in Houston, and was an American citizen. The Court concluded, however, that neither that territorial event nor that relationship was the "focus" of congressional concern, but rather domestic employment.

Applying the same mode of analysis here, we think that the focus of the Exchange Act is not upon the place where the deception originated, but upon purchases and sales of securities in the United States. * * *

Finally, we reject the notion that the Exchange Act reaches conduct in this country affecting exchanges or transactions abroad for the same reason that *Aramco* rejected overseas application of Title VII to all domestically concluded employment contracts or all employment contracts with American employers: The probability of incompatibility with the applicable laws of other countries is so obvious that if Congress intended such foreign application "it would have addressed the subject of conflicts with foreign laws and procedures." Like the United States, foreign countries regulate their domestic securities exchanges and securities transactions occurring within their territorial jurisdiction. And the regulation of other countries often differs from ours as to what constitutes fraud, what disclosures must be made, what damages are recoverable, what discovery is available in litigation, what individual actions may be joined in a single suit, what attorney's fees are recoverable, and many other matters. The Commonwealth of Australia, the United Kingdom of Great Britain and Northern Ireland, and the Republic of France have filed *amicus* briefs in this case. So have (separately or jointly) such international and foreign organizations as the International Chamber of Commerce, the Swiss Bankers Association, the Federation of German Industries, the French Business Confederation, the Institute of International Bankers, the European Banking Federation, the Australian Bankers' Association, and the Association Française des Entreprises Privées. They all complain of the interference with foreign securities regulation that application of § 10(b) abroad would produce, and urge the adoption of a clear test that will avoid that consequence. The transactional test we have adopted— whether the purchase or sale is made in the United States, or involves a security listed on a domestic exchange—meets that requirement.

* * *

The Solicitor General points out that the "significant and material conduct" test is in accord with prevailing notions of international comity. If so, that proves that *if* the United States asserted prescriptive jurisdiction pursuant to the "significant and material conduct" test it would not violate customary international law; but it in no way tends to prove that that is what Congress has done.

* * *

Section 10(b) reaches the use of a manipulative or deceptive device or contrivance only in connection with the purchase or sale of a security listed on an American stock exchange, and the purchase or sale of any other security in the United States. This case involves no securities listed on a domestic exchange, and all aspects of the purchases complained of by those petitioners who still have live claims occurred outside the United States. Petitioners have therefore failed to state a claim on which relief can be granted. We affirm the dismissal of petitioners' complaint on this ground.

It is so ordered.

* * *

[The concurring opinion of JUSTICE BREYER is omitted.]

JUSTICE STEVENS, with whom JUSTICE GINSBURG joins, concurring in the judgment.

While I agree that petitioners have failed to state a claim on which relief can be granted, my reasoning differs from the Court's. I would adhere to the general approach that has been the law in the Second Circuit, and most of the rest of the country, for nearly four decades.

I

Today the Court announces a new "transactional test," for defining the reach of § 10(b) of the Securities Exchange Act of 1934 (Exchange Act): Henceforth, those provisions will extend only to "transactions in securities listed on domestic exchanges * * * and domestic transactions in other securities." If one confines one's gaze to the statutory text, the Court's conclusion is a plausible one. But the federal courts have been construing § 10(b) in a different manner for a long time, and the Court's textual analysis is not nearly so compelling, in my view, as to warrant the abandonment of their doctrine.

* * *

II

The Court's other main critique of the Second Circuit's approach—apart from what the Court views as its excessive reliance on functional considerations and reconstructed congressional intent—is that the Second Circuit has "disregard[ed]" the presumption against extraterritoriality. It is the Court, however, that misapplies the presumption, in two main respects.

First, the Court seeks to transform the presumption from a flexible rule of thumb into something more like a clear statement rule. We have been here before. In the case on which the Court primarily relies, *EEOC* v. *Arabian American Oil Co.*, 499 U.S. 244 (1991) *(Aramco)*, Chief Justice Rehnquist's majority opinion included a sentence that appeared to make the same move. ("Congress' awareness of the need to make a clear state-

ment that a statute applies overseas is amply demonstrated by the numerous occasions on which it has expressly legislated the extraterritorial
application of a statute"). Justice Marshall, in dissent, vigorously objected. ("[C]ontrary to what one would conclude from the majority's analysis,
this canon is *not* a 'clear statement' rule, the application of which relieves
a court of the duty to give effect to all available indicia of the legislative
will").

Yet even *Aramco*—surely the most extreme application of the presumption against extraterritoriality in my time on the Court—contained numerous passages suggesting that the presumption may be overcome without a clear directive. * * *

Second, and more fundamentally, the Court errs in suggesting that the
presumption against extraterritoriality is fatal to the Second Circuit's
test. For even if the presumption really were a clear statement (or "clear
indication") rule, it would have only marginal relevance to this case.

It is true, of course, that "this Court ordinarily construes ambiguous statutes to avoid unreasonable interference with the sovereign authority of
other nations," *F. Hoffmann–La Roche Ltd* v. *Empagran S. A.*, 542 U.S.
155, 164 (2004), and that, absent contrary evidence, we presume "Congress is primarily concerned with domestic conditions." Accordingly, the
presumption against extraterritoriality "provides a sound basis for concluding that Section 10(b) does not apply when a securities fraud with no
effects in the United States is hatched and executed entirely outside this
country." Brief for United States as *Amicus Curiae* 22. But that is just
about all it provides a sound basis for concluding. And the conclusion is
not very illuminating, because no party to the litigation disputes it. No
one contends that § 10(b) applies to wholly foreign frauds.

Rather, the real question in this case is how much, and what kinds of,
domestic contacts are sufficient to trigger application of § 10(b). * * *

Imagine, for example, an American investor who buys shares in a company listed only on an overseas exchange. That company has a major American subsidiary with executives based in New York City; and it was in
New York City that the executives masterminded and implemented a
massive deception which artificially inflated the stock price—and which
will, upon its disclosure, cause the price to plummet. Or, imagine that
those same executives go knocking on doors in Manhattan and convince
an unsophisticated retiree, on the basis of material misrepresentations, to
invest her life savings in the company's doomed securities. Both of these
investors would, under the Court's new test, be barred from seeking relief
under § 10(b).

The oddity of that result should give pause. For in walling off such individuals from § 10(b), the Court narrows the provision's reach to a degree
that would surprise and alarm generations of American investors—and, I

am convinced, the Congress that passed the Exchange Act. Indeed, the Court's rule turns § 10(b) jurisprudence (and the presumption against extraterritoriality) on its head, by withdrawing the statute's application from cases in which there is *both* substantial wrongful conduct that occurred in the United States *and* a substantial injurious effect on United States markets and citizens.

* * *

State the rule of the case according to the majority opinion in a single sentence. Now state the rule according to Justice Stevens' concurring opinion. What does this tell you about the current Supreme Court position on extraterritoriality?

At one level, *Morrison* is primarily a case about statutory construction. What role does that leave for comity to play?

Note that in the Dodd–Frank Act, Congress partially revived the applicability of the antifraud provisions, but only in actions brought by the SEC; private actions in f-cubed cases remain closed. See 15 U.S.C. § 77v(c).

We have just seen five cases (four American, one European) struggling with whether to restrict their jurisdiction as a matter of international comity. Is there a way to reconcile them? Can you identify a single, coherent approach underlying them all (or at least the American cases)?

CHAPTER 8

LAW: DIVERSIFICATION OF SOURCES

■ ■ ■

Under the classic approach, international law consisted mainly of custom and treaties, both being about equally relevant, while general principles, court decisions and scholarly writings played a lesser role in practice. This line-up continues to make up most public international law, even today. We will not revisit the entire line-up in this chapter. Instead, we will focus on six major developments that have significantly changed the traditional picture over the last half-century.

First, treaties have become arguably the most important source, relegating even custom to a secondary role. Second, the role of custom and the process of creating it have evolved in various ways. Third, general principles have become more difficult to identify and defend. Fourth, UN Security Council resolutions have sometimes taken the form of binding quasi-legislation. Fifth, international organizations have issued myriad regulations, creating a regime of international administrative law. Sixth, non-binding resolutions or statements, often called "soft law," have come to play an increasingly important role. In most of these contexts, international law is no longer limited to rules governing the relationship between states; increasingly, it also includes international private law, i.e., rules dealing with the interaction between market actors. All of this has, again, made the picture much more complex than it used to be.

1. THE NEW GENERATION OF TREATIES

In Chapter III, we saw that, under the traditional rules codified in the Vienna Convention on the Law of Treaties, treaties were dealt with pretty much like contracts (between states). This is still true today in many instances. Yet, as Abram Chayes and Antonia Handler Chayes explain, the world of treaties has changed significantly since the middle of the 20th century:

> In an increasingly complex and interdependent world, the negotiation, adoption, and implementation of international agreements are major elements of the foreign policy activity of every state. In earlier times, the principal function of treaties was to record bilateral (or sometimes regional) political settlements and arrangements. But in recent decades, the main focus of treaty practice has moved to multilateral regulatory agreements addressing complex economic, politi-

cal, and social problems that require cooperative action among states over time. Chief among the areas of concern are trade, monetary policy, resource management, security, environmental degradation, and human rights. * * *

The agreements vary widely in scope, number of parties, and degree of specificity, as well as in subject matter. Some are little more than statements of principle or agreements to agree. Others contain detailed prescriptions for behavior in a defined field. Still others may be umbrella agreements for consensus building in preparation for more specific regulation later. Often they create international organizations to oversee the enterprise.

Abram Chayes & Antonia Handler Chayes, The New Sovereignty, at 3 (1995).

A. WORLDWIDE MULTI–PARTY CONVENTIONS

The rise of a new generation of multilateral treaties aiming at worldwide adoption began immediately after World War II. The first prominent example was the Genocide Convention below. How does it differ from, say, the United States–Mexico extradition treaty that was at stake in the *Alvarez-Machain* case (Chapter III.3.)?

CONVENTION ON THE PREVENTION AND PUNISHMENT OF THE CRIME OF GENOCIDE
(Adopted 1948; in force 1951)

The Contracting Parties,

Having considered the declaration made by the General Assembly of the United Nations in its resolution 96 (I) dated 11 December 1946 that genocide is a crime under international law, contrary to the spirit and aims of the United Nations and condemned by the civilized world,

Recognizing that at all periods of history genocide has inflicted great losses on humanity, and

Being convinced that, in order to liberate mankind from such an odious scourge, international cooperation is required,

Hereby agree as hereinafter provided:

Article I

The Contracting Parties confirm that genocide, whether committed in time of peace or in time of war, is a crime under international law which they undertake to prevent and to punish.

Article II

In the present Convention, genocide means any of the following acts committed with intent to destroy, in whole or in part, a national, ethnical, racial or religious group, as such:

(a) Killing members of the group;

(b) Causing serious bodily or mental harm to members of the group;

(c) Deliberately inflicting on the group conditions of life calculated to bring about its physical destruction in whole or in part;

(d) Imposing measures intended to prevent births within the group;

(e) Forcibly transferring children of the group to another group.

Article III

The following acts shall be punishable:

(a) Genocide;

(b) Conspiracy to commit genocide;

(c) Direct and public incitement to commit genocide;

(d) Attempt to commit genocide;

(e) Complicity in genocide.

Article IV

Persons committing genocide or any of the other acts enumerated in article III shall be punished, whether they are constitutionally responsible rulers, public officials or private individuals.

Article V

The Contracting Parties undertake to enact, in accordance with their respective Constitutions, the necessary legislation to give effect to the provisions of the present Convention, and, in particular, to provide effective penalties for persons guilty of genocide or any of the other acts enumerated in article III.

Article VI

Persons charged with genocide or any of the other acts enumerated in article III shall be tried by a competent tribunal of the State in the territory of which the act was committed, or by such international penal tribunal as may have jurisdiction with respect to those Contracting Parties which shall have accepted its jurisdiction.

Article VII

Genocide and the other acts enumerated in article III shall not be considered as political crimes for the purpose of extradition.

The Contracting Parties pledge themselves in such cases to grant extradition in accordance with their laws and treaties in force.

Article VIII

Any Contracting Party may call upon the competent organs of the United Nations to take such action under the Charter of the United Nations as they consider appropriate for the prevention and suppression of acts of genocide or any of the other acts enumerated in article III.

Article IX

Disputes between the Contracting Parties relating to the interpretation, application or fulfilment of the present Convention, including those relating to the responsibility of a State for genocide or for any of the other acts enumerated in article III, shall be submitted to the International Court of Justice at the request of any of the parties to the dispute.

Article X

The present Convention, of which the Chinese, English, French, Russian and Spanish texts are equally authentic, shall bear the date of 9 December 1948.

Article XI

The present Convention shall be open until 31 December 1949 for signature on behalf of any Member of the United Nations and of any nonmember State to which an invitation to sign has been addressed by the General Assembly.

The present Convention shall be ratified, and the instruments of ratification shall be deposited with the Secretary–General of the United Nations.

After 1 January 1950, the present Convention may be acceded to on behalf of any Member of the United Nations and of any non-member State which has received an invitation as aforesaid. Instruments of accession shall be deposited with the Secretary–General of the United Nations.

Article XII

Any Contracting Party may at any time, by notification addressed to the Secretary–General of the United Nations, extend the application of the present Convention to all or any of the territories for the conduct of whose foreign relations that Contracting Party is responsible.

Article XIII

On the day when the first twenty instruments of ratification or accession have been deposited, the Secretary–General shall draw up a *proces-verbal* and transmit a copy thereof to each Member of the United Nations and to each of the non-member States contemplated in article XI.

The present Convention shall come into force on the ninetieth day following the date of deposit of the twentieth instrument of ratification or accession.

Any ratification or accession effected subsequent to the latter date shall become effective on the ninetieth day following the deposit of the instrument of ratification or accession.

Article XIV

The present Convention shall remain in effect for a period of ten years as from the date of its coming into force.

It shall thereafter remain in force for successive periods of five years for such Contracting Parties as have not denounced it at least six months before the expiration of the current period.

Denunciation shall be effected by a written notification addressed to the Secretary–General of the United Nations.

Article XV

If, as a result of denunciations, the number of Parties to the present Convention should become less than sixteen, the Convention shall cease to be in force as from the date on which the last of these denunciations shall become effective.

Article XVI

A request for the revision of the present Convention may be made at any time by any Contracting Party by means of a notification in writing addressed to the Secretary–General.

The General Assembly shall decide upon the steps, if any, to be taken in respect of such request.

Article XVII

The Secretary–General of the United Nations shall notify all Members of the United Nations and the non-member States contemplated in article XI of the following:

(a) Signatures, ratifications and accessions received in accordance with article XI;

(b) Notifications received in accordance with article XII;

(c) The date upon which the present Convention comes into force in accordance with article XIII;

(d) Denunciations received in accordance with article XIV;

(e) The abrogation of the Convention in accordance with article XV;

(f) Notifications received in accordance with article XVI.

Article XVIII

The original of the present Convention shall be deposited in the archives of the United Nations.

A certified copy of the Convention shall be transmitted to each Member of the United Nations and to each of the non-member States contemplated in article XI.

Article XIX

The present Convention shall be registered by the Secretary–General of the United Nations on the date of its coming into force.

What is the object and purpose of this treaty? How does the Treaty purport to achieve its object and purpose?

NOTE ON THE GENOCIDE CASE

The ICJ was presented with its first opportunity to interpret the text of the Genocide Convention in a contentious case—*The Application of the Convention on the Prevention and Punishment of the Crime of Genocide (Bosnia and Herzegovina v. Serbia and Montenegro)*, [2007] ICJ 108. In the *Genocide Case* (as it came to be called), Bosnia and Herzegovina attempted to invoke the international legal responsibility of Serbia for its participation in and support for the acts of the Bosnian Serb Army (VRS) committed on Bosnian territory during the 1992–1995 Bosnian War. Because the Court's jurisdiction was founded solely on the 1948 Genocide Convention, the Court's mandate was limited. For example, the actions of Serbia were investigated only for those acts proscribed by the Geneva Convention, not for other crimes against humanity. Furthermore, while the popular and perhaps legal conception of genocide had evolved since 1948, the Court was bound by the language of the 1948 Convention in rendering its decision. The opinion's narrow compass led to disappointment within Bosnian and international human rights circles.

The Court held that Serbia was not legally responsible for *committing* the Srebrenica genocide, but that Serbia had violated its obligation to *prevent* genocide. The Court pointed to Serbia's knowledge of the likely consequences of a VRS occupation of Srebrenica and to Serbia's demonstrated ability to exercise control over the VRS in establishing Serbia's responsibility. Under the test enunciated by the Court, in order for a State to be held liable for violating its obligation to prevent genocide, a litigant need not prove that the State definitely had the power to prevent the genocide, but rather that the State had the means to do so and "manifestly refrained" from using them. The Court also noted that Serbia's continued failure to prosecute the perpetrators of the genocide and to extradite war criminals for trial at the International Criminal Tribunal for the Former Yugoslavia (ICTY) constituted a further violation of the Genocide Convention.

As compensation for Serbia's breach of its obligation to prevent genocide, the ICJ did not award money damages, but rather satisfaction in the form of a declaration that Serbia has failed to comply with its obligations under the Genocide Convention. With regard to Serbia's ongoing failure to prosecute those responsible for genocide and cooperate with the ICTY, the ICJ decided that Serbia must take immediate steps to comply with these obligations.

B. THE COMPLEXITY OF MULTILATERAL AGREEMENTS

Modern, multilateral treaties often involve dozens of parties. This raises several complex issues rarely faced under the traditional approach. Can a state, for example, ratify the basic text only in part, i.e., can it make reservations or object to certain elements?

More than 140 states are parties to the Genocide Convention. However, 32 of the state parties have filed reservations, understandings or declarations to the Convention (of which five states have subsequently withdrawn their reservations). A substantial number of state parties have made objections to some of those reservations.

The most common reservations were to Article IX (ICJ jurisdiction) and Article XII (applicability of the convention to non-self-governing territories). Eighteen states made a reservation to the ICJ's jurisdiction; most of them reserved the right to give their express consent in each case that might be brought in the ICJ by any state party. Eleven states thought that the Convention should apply to non-self-governing territories, contrary to the text of Article XII. Two states considered that the treaty should be open for accession by all states, not merely by members of the UN (Article XI), and that limiting prospective membership to UN countries rendered the treaty discriminatory.

One state, Myanmar, made a reservation to Article VIII (regarding the right of other parties to call upon UN organs to take action to prevent genocide). Another state, the Philippines, made a reservation to Article IV, purporting to preserve immunity of heads of state as guaranteed under the Constitution of the Philippines.

Here are the U.S. reservations to and understandings of the Convention as well as the objections by Italy, the Netherlands and the United Kingdom to the U.S. reservations.

The United States

Reservations:

(1) That with reference to article IX of the Convention, before any dispute to which the United States is a party may be submitted to the jurisdiction of the International Court of Justice under this article, the specific consent of the United States is required in each case.

(2) That nothing in the Convention requires or authorizes legislation or other action by the United States of America prohibited by the Constitution of the United States as interpreted by the United States.

Understandings:

(1) That the term "intent to destroy, in whole or in part, a national, ethnical, racial, or religious group as such" appearing in article II means the specific intent to destroy, in whole or in substantial part, a national, ethnical, racial or religious group as such by the acts specified in article II.

(2) That the term "mental harm" in article II (b) means permanent impairment of mental faculties through drugs, torture or similar techniques.

(3) That the pledge to grant extradition in accordance with a state's laws and treaties in force found in article VII extends only to acts which are criminal under the laws of both the requesting and the requested state and nothing in article VI affects the right of any state to bring to trial before its own tribunals any of its nationals for acts committed outside a state.

(4) That acts in the course of armed conflicts committed without the specific intent required by article II are not sufficient to constitute genocide as defined by this Convention.

(5) That with regard to the reference to an international penal tribunal in article VI of the Convention, the United States declares that it reserves the right to effect its participation in any such tribunal only by a treaty entered into specifically for that purpose with the advice and consent of the Senate.

Italy

29 December 1989

The Government of the Republic of Italy objects to the second reservation entered by the United States of America. It creates uncertainty as to the extent of the obligations which the Government of the United States of America is prepared to assume with regard to the Convention.

The Netherlands

27 December 1989

With regard to the reservations made by the United States of America:

As concerns the first reservation, the Government of the Kingdom of the Netherlands recalls its declaration, made on 20 June 1966 on the occasion of the accession of the Kingdom of the Netherlands to the Convention [* * *] stating that in its opinion the reservations in respect of article IX of the Convention, made at that time by a number of states, were incompatible with the object and purpose of the Convention, and that the Government of the Kingdom of the Netherlands did not consider states making such reservations parties to the Convention. Accordingly, the Government of the Kingdom of the Netherlands does not consider the United States of America a party to the Convention. Similarly, the Government of the Kingdom of the Netherlands does not consider parties to the Convention other states which have made such reservations, i.e., in addition to the states mentioned in the aforementioned declaration, the People's Republic of China, Democratic Yemen, the German Democratic Republic, the Mongolian People's Republic, the Philippines, Rwanda, Spain, Venezuela, and Viet Nam, on the other hand, the Government of the Kingdom of the Netherlands does consider parties to the Convention those states that have since withdrawn their reservations, i.e., the Union of Soviet Socialist Republics, the Byelorussian Soviet Socialist Republic, and the Ukrainian Soviet Socialist Republic.

As the Convention may come into force between the Kingdom of the Netherlands and the United States of America as a result of the latter withdrawing its reservation in respect of article IX, the Government of the Kingdom of the Netherlands deems it useful to express the following position on the second reservation of the United States of America:

The Government of the Kingdom of the Netherlands objects to this reservation on the ground that it creates uncertainty as to the extent of the obligations the Government of the United States of America is prepared to assume with regard to the Convention. Moreover, any failure by the United States of America to act upon the obligations contained in the Convention on the ground that such action would be prohibited by the constitution of the United States would be contrary to the generally accepted rule of international law, as laid down in article 27 of the Vienna Convention on the law of treaties (Vienna, 23 May 1969).

United Kingdom of Great Britain and Northern Ireland

22 December 1989

The Government of the United Kingdom have consistently stated that they are unable to accept reservations to article IX. Accordingly, in conformity with the attitude adopted by them in previous cases, the Government of the United Kingdom do not accept the first reservation entered by the United States of America.

The Government of the United Kingdom object to the second reservation entered by the United States of America. It creates uncertainty as to the extent of the obligations which the Government of the United States of America is prepared to assume with regard to the Convention.

———————

Are all reservations allowed?

RESERVATIONS TO THE CONVENTION ON THE PREVENTION AND PUNISHMENT OF THE CRIME OF GENOCIDE

International Court of Justice
1951 I.C.J. 15

THE COURT,

composed as above,

gives the following Advisory Opinion:

On November 16th, 1950, the General Assembly of the United Nations adopted the following resolution:

> The General Assembly,

* * *

> 1. Requests the International Court of Justice to give an Advisory Opinion on the following questions:

> In so far as concerns the Convention on the Prevention and Punishment of the Crime of Genocide in the event of a State ratifying or acceding to the Convention subject to a reservation made either on ratification or on accession, or on signature followed by ratification:

> I. Can the reserving State be regarded as being a party to the Convention while still maintaining its reservation if the reservation is objected to by one or more of the parties to the Convention but not by others?

* * *

The Court recognizes that an understanding was reached within the General Assembly on the faculty to make reservations to the Genocide Convention and that it is permitted to conclude therefrom that States becoming parties to the Convention gave their assent thereto. It must now determine what kind of reservations may be made and what kind of objections may be taken to them.

The solution of these problems must be found in the special characteristics of the Genocide Convention. The origins and character of that Convention, the objects pursued by the General Assembly and the contracting parties, the relations which exist between the provisions of the Convention, *inter se*, and between those provisions and these objects, furnish elements of interpretation of the will of the General Assembly and the parties. The origins of the Convention show that it was the intention of the United Nations to condemn and punish genocide as "a crime under international law" involving a denial of the right of existence of entire human groups, a denial which shocks the conscience of mankind and results in great losses to humanity, and which is contrary to moral law and to the spirit and aims of the United Nations (Resolution 96 (I) of the General Assembly, December 11th 1946). The first consequence arising from this conception is that the principles underlying the Convention are principles which are recognized by civilized nations as binding on States, even without any conventional obligation. A second consequence is the universal character both of the condemnation of genocide and of the co-operation required "in order to liberate mankind from such an odious scourge" (Preamble to the Convention). The Genocide Convention was therefore intended by the General Assembly and by the contracting parties to be definitely universal in scope. It was in fact approved on December 9th, 1948, by a resolution which was unanimously adopted by fifty-six States.

The objects of such a convention must also be considered. The Convention was manifestly adopted for a purely humanitarian and civilizing purpose. It is indeed difficult to imagine a convention that might have this dual character to a greater degree, since its object on the one hand is to safeguard the very existence of certain human groups and on the other to confirm and endorse the most elementary principles of morality. In such a convention the contracting States do not have any interests of their own; they merely have, one and all, a common interest, namely, the accomplishment of those high purposes which are the *raison d'être* of the convention. Consequently, in a convention of this type one cannot speak of individual advantages or disadvantages to States, or of the maintenance of a perfect contractual balance between rights and duties. The high ideals which inspired the Convention provide, by virtue of the common will of the parties, the foundation and measure of all its provisions.

The foregoing considerations, when applied to the question of reservations, and more particularly to the effects of objections to reservations, lead to the following conclusions.

The object and purpose of the Genocide Convention imply that it was the intention of the General Assembly and of the States which adopted it that as many States as possible should participate. The complete exclusion from the Convention of one or more States would not only restrict the scope of its application, but would detract from the authority of the moral and humanitarian principles which are its basis. It is inconceivable that the contracting parties readily contemplated that an objection to a minor reservation should produce such a result. But even less could the contracting parties have intended to sacrifice the very object of the Convention in favour of a vain desire to secure as many participants as possible. The object and purpose of the Convention thus limit both the freedom of making reservations and that of objecting to them. It follows that it is the compatibility of a reservation with the object and purpose of the Convention that must furnish the criterion for the attitude of a State in making the reservation on accession as well as for the appraisal by a State in objecting to the reservation. Such is the rule of conduct which must guide every State in the appraisal which it must make, individually and from its own standpoint, of the admissibility of any reservation.

Any other view would lead either to the acceptance of reservations which frustrate the purposes which the General Assembly and the contracting parties had in mind, or to recognition that the parties to the Convention have the power of excluding from it the author of a reservation, even a minor one, which may be quite compatible with those purposes.

It has nevertheless been argued that any State entitled to become a party to the Genocide Convention may do so while making any reservation it chooses by virtue of its sovereignty. The Court cannot share this view. It is obvious that so extreme an application of the idea of State sovereignty could lead to a complete disregard of the object and purpose of the Convention.

On the other hand, it has been argued that there exists a rule of international law subjecting the effect of a reservation to the express or tacit assent of all the contracting parties. This theory rests essentially on a contractual conception of the absolute integrity of the convention as adopted. This view, however, cannot prevail if, having regard to the character of the convention, its purpose and its mode of adoption, it can be established that the parties intended to derogate from that rule by admitting the faculty to make reservations thereto.

* * *

What are the competing policies considered by the ICJ? Why are they (at least to some extent) in conflict? How does the ICJ seek to balance them to produce an optimal compromise? State the basic rule that results from this balancing act.

Today, the Vienna Convention on the Law of Treaties provides fairly clear, and widely accepted, rules on the permissibility and effect of reservations (and objections). Does the VCLT codify the holding in the *Reservations Case*? According to the VCLT, under what circumstances can a state make a reservation to a treaty?

VIENNA CONVENTION ON THE LAW OF TREATIES
(Adopted 1969; in force 1980)

* * *

Section 2. Reservations

Article 19
Formulation of reservations

A State may, when signing, ratifying, accepting, approving or acceding to a treaty, formulate a reservation unless:

(a) the reservation is prohibited by the treaty;

(b) the treaty provides that only specified reservations, which do not include the reservation in question, may be made; or

(c) in cases not falling under sub-paragraphs (a) and (b), the reservation is incompatible with the object and purpose of the treaty.

Article 20
Acceptance of and objection to reservations

1. A reservation expressly authorized by a treaty does not require any subsequent acceptance by the other contracting States unless the treaty so provides.

2. When it appears from the limited number of the negotiating States and the object and purpose of a treaty that the application of the treaty in its entirety between all the parties is an essential condition of the consent of each one to be bound by the treaty, a reservation requires acceptance by all the parties.

3. When a treaty is a constituent instrument of an international organization and unless it otherwise provides, a reservation requires the acceptance of the competent organ of that organization.

4. In cases not falling under the preceding paragraphs and unless the treaty otherwise provides:

(a) acceptance by another contracting State of a reservation constitutes the reserving State a party to the treaty in relation to that other State if or when the treaty is in force for those States;

(b) an objection by another contracting State to a reservation does not preclude the entry into force of the treaty as between the objecting and reserving States unless a contrary intention is definitely expressed by the objecting State;

(c) an act expressing a State's consent to be bound by the treaty and containing a reservation is effective as soon as at least one other contracting State has accepted the reservation.

5. For the purposes of paragraphs 2 and 4 and unless the treaty otherwise provides, a reservation is considered to have been accepted by a

State if it shall have raised no objection to the reservation by the end of a period of twelve months after it was notified of the reservation or by the date on which it expressed its consent to be bound by the treaty, whichever is later.

Article 21
Legal effects of reservations and of objections to reservations

1. A reservation established with regard to another party in accordance with articles 19, 20 and 23:

   (a) modifies for the reserving State in its relations with that other party the provisions of the treaty to which the reservation relates to the extent of the reservation; and

   (b) modifies those provisions to the same extent for that other party in its relations with the reserving State.

2. The reservation does not modify the provisions of the treaty for the other parties to the treaty inter se.

3. When a State objecting to a reservation has not opposed the entry into force of the treaty between itself and the reserving State, the provisions to which the reservation relates do not apply as between the two States to the extent of the reservation.

* * *

Article 23
Procedure regarding reservations

1. A reservation, an express acceptance of a reservation and an objection to a reservation must be formulated in writing and communicated to the contracting States and other States entitled to become parties to the treaty.

2. If formulated when signing the treaty subject to ratification, acceptance or approval, a reservation must be formally confirmed by the reserving State when expressing its consent to be bound by the treaty. In such a case the reservation shall be considered as having been made on the date of its confirmation.

3. An express acceptance of, or an objection to, a reservation made previously to confirmation of the reservation does not itself require confirmation.

4. The withdrawal of a reservation or of an objection to a reservation must be formulated in writing.

* * *

In light of Article 21(3), what good does an objection to a reservation do? Doesn't the reserving state still get its way (not to be bound by the clauses to which it made the reservation)? Is there any way other states can prevent that?

Note that in 2011 the International Law Commission published a *Guide to Practice on Reservations to Treaties*. The Guide contains detailed (but non-binding) rules to supplement the relevant provisions of the VCLT.

Despite all this potential complexity, there is some good news: most treaties in the areas of private, business or procedural law do not allow many reservations. They either explicitly forbid them (i.e., come on a take-it-or-leave-it basis) or, more often, explicitly list permissible reservations, thereby excluding others (see Art. 19(a) and (b) of the VCLT). You will see an example in the Hague Convention on Service Abroad shortly (infra. Section 6.A.). As a result, most treaties that are relevant for international business practice and litigation are not susceptible to much variation.

Another major issue regarding modern multilateral treaties is how to change (especially amend) them. Obviously, the more parties are involved, the more problematic this issue can be. Some of the modern human rights treaties have well over a hundred members. Do they all have to agree on every amendment? Look again at the Vienna Convention:

VIENNA CONVENTION ON THE LAW OF TREATIES
(Adopted 1969; in force 1980)

* * *

Part IV. Amendment and Modification of Treaties

Article 30
Application of successive treaties relating to the same subject matter

1. Subject to Article 103 of the Charter of the United Nations, the rights and obligations of States Parties to successive treaties relating to the same subject matter shall be determined in accordance with the following paragraphs.

2. When a treaty specifies that it is subject to, or that it is not to be considered as incompatible with, an earlier or later treaty, the provisions of that other treaty prevail.

3. When all the parties to the earlier treaty are parties also to the later treaty but the earlier treaty is not terminated or suspended in operation under article 59, the earlier treaty applies only to the extent that its provisions are compatible with those of the later treaty.

4. When the parties to the later treaty do not include all the parties to the earlier one:

(a) as between States Parties to both treaties the same rule applies as in paragraph 3;

(b) as between a State party to both treaties and a State party to only one of the treaties, the treaty to which both States are parties governs their mutual rights and obligations.

5. Paragraph 4 is without prejudice to article 41, or to any question of the termination or suspension of the operation of a treaty under article 60 or to any question of responsibility which may arise for a State from the conclusion or application of a treaty the provisions of which are incompatible with its obligations towards another State under another treaty.

* * *

Article 39
General rule regarding the amendment of treaties

A treaty may be amended by agreement between the parties. The rules laid down in Part II apply to such an agreement except insofar as the treaty may otherwise provide.

Article 40
Amendment of multilateral treaties

1. Unless the treaty otherwise provides, the amendment of multilateral treaties shall be governed by the following paragraphs.

2. Any proposal to amend a multilateral treaty as between all the parties must be notified to all the contracting States, each one of which shall have the right to take part in:

(a) the decision as to the action to be taken in regard to such proposal;

(b) the negotiation and conclusion of any agreement for the amendment of the treaty.

3. Every State entitled to become a party to the treaty shall also be entitled to become a party to the treaty as amended.

4. The amending agreement does not bind any State already a party to the treaty which does not become a party to the amending agreement; article 30, paragraph 4(b), applies in relation to such State.

5. Any State which becomes a party to the treaty after the entry into force of the amending agreement shall, failing an expression of a different intention by that State:

(a) be considered as a party to the treaty as amended; and

(b) be considered as a party to the unamended treaty in relation to any party to the treaty not bound by the amending agreement.

Article 41
Agreements to modify multilateral treaties between certain of the parties only

1. Two or more of the parties to a multilateral treaty may conclude an agreement to modify the treaty as between themselves alone if:

   (a) the possibility of such a modification is provided for by the treaty; or

   (b) the modification in question is not prohibited by the treaty and:

      (i) does not affect the enjoyment by the other parties of their rights under the treaty or the performance of their obligations;

      (ii) does not relate to a provision, derogation from which is incompatible with the effective execution of the object and purpose of the treaty as a whole.

2. Unless in a case falling under paragraph 1(a) the treaty otherwise provides, the parties in question shall notify the other parties of their intention to conclude the agreement and of the modification to the treaty for which it provides.

* * *

_____

If some (let's say ten) out of all (let's say one hundred) parties to a multilateral agreement decide to amend it in accordance with Article 41, doesn't that mean that there will then be two versions of the same treaty—the amended version applying among all amending members and the original version among the rest? What if then ten other parties (or, to make matters worse, five of the amendment group and five of the rest) decide to amend the treaty in a different way? Will we not pretty soon have various versions of the same treaty in force between various combinations of parties? Obviously, this would be quite a mess. Can it be prevented?

The UN Charter, like many treaties, has specific provisions addressing amendment. How do the Charter's provisions differ from the amendment procedure under the Vienna Convention?

CHARTER OF THE UNITED NATIONS
(Adopted 1945; in force 1945)

* * *

Article 108

Amendments to the present Charter shall come into force for all Members of the United Nations when they have been adopted by a vote of two thirds of the members of the General Assembly and ratified in accordance with their respective constitutional processes by two thirds of the Members of the United Nations, including all the permanent members of the Security Council.

Article 109

1. A General Conference of the Members of the United Nations for the purpose of reviewing the present Charter may be held at a date and place to be fixed by a two-thirds vote of the members of the General Assembly and by a vote of any nine members of the Security Council. Each Member of the United Nations shall have one vote in the conference.

2. Any alteration of the present Charter recommended by a two-thirds vote of the conference shall take effect when ratified in accordance with their respective constitutional processes by two thirds of the Members of the United Nations including all the permanent members of the Security Council.

3. If such a conference has not been held before the tenth annual session of the General Assembly following the coming into force of the present Charter, the proposal to call such a conference shall be placed on the agenda of that session of the General Assembly, and the conference shall be held if so decided by a majority vote of the members of the General Assembly and by a vote of any seven members of the Security Council.

* * *

C. INTERPRETING MULTILATERAL CONVENTIONS

In Chapter III, we saw two cases where courts were called on to interpret bilateral treaties—*Asakura v. City of Seattle* and *United States v. Alvarez-Machain*. The interpretation of multilateral treaties presents additional challenges. What might those challenges be? How does the Supreme Court try to meet them in the case below?

ABBOTT V. ABBOTT

United States Supreme Court
130 S. Ct. 1983 (2010)

* * *

[JUSTICE KENNEDY delivered the opinion of the Court, in which CHIEF JUSTICE ROBERTS and JUSTICES SCALIA, GINSBURG, ALITO, and SOTOMAYOR joined. JUSTICE STEVENS filed a dissenting opinion, in which JUSTICES THOMAS and BREYER joined.]

This case presents, as it has from its inception in the United States District Court, a question of interpretation under the Hague Convention on the Civil Aspects of International Child Abduction (Convention). The United States is a contracting state to the Convention; and Congress has implemented its provisions through the International Child Abduction Remedies Act (ICARA). The Convention provides that a child abducted in violation of "rights of custody" must be returned to the child's country of habitual residence, unless certain exceptions apply. The question is whether a parent has a "righ[t] of custody" by reason of that parent's *ne exeat* right: the authority to consent before the other parent may take the child to another country.

I

Timothy Abbott and Jacquelyn Vaye Abbott married in England in 1992. He is a British citizen, and she is a citizen of the United States. Mr. Abbott's astronomy profession took the couple to Hawaii, where their son A.J. A. was born in 1995. The Abbotts moved to La Serena, Chile, in 2002. There was marital discord, and the parents separated in March 2003. The Chilean courts granted the mother daily care and control of the child, while awarding the father "direct and regular" visitation rights, including visitation every other weekend and for the whole month of February each year.

Chilean law conferred upon Mr. Abbott what is commonly known as a *ne exeat* right: a right to consent before Ms. Abbott could take A.J. A. out of Chile. In effect a *ne exeat* right imposes a duty on one parent that is a right in the other. After Mr. Abbott obtained a British passport for A.J. A., Ms. Abbott grew concerned that Mr. Abbott would take the boy to Britain. She sought and obtained a *"ne exeat* of the minor" order from the Chilean family court, prohibiting the boy from being taken out of Chile.

In August 2005, while proceedings before the Chilean court were pending, the mother removed the boy from Chile without permission from either the father or the court. A private investigator located the mother and the child in Texas. In February 2006, the mother filed for divorce in Texas state court. Part of the relief she sought was a modification of the father's rights, including full power in her to determine the boy's place of residence and an order limiting the father to supervised visitation in Texas. This litigation remains pending.

Mr. Abbott brought an action in Texas state court, asking for visitation rights and an order requiring Ms. Abbott to show cause why the court should not allow Mr. Abbott to return to Chile with A.J. A. In February 2006, the court denied Mr. Abbott's requested relief but granted him "liberal periods of possession" of A.J. A. throughout February 2006, provided Mr. Abbott remained in Texas.

In May 2006, Mr. Abbott filed the instant action in the United States District Court for the Western District of Texas. He sought an order requiring his son's return to Chile pursuant to the Convention and enforcement provisions of the ICARA. In July 2007, after holding a bench trial during which only Mr. Abbott testified, the District Court denied relief. The court held that the father's *ne exeat* right did not constitute a right of custody under the Convention and, as a result, that the return remedy was not authorized.

The United States Court of Appeals for the Fifth Circuit affirmed on the same rationale. The court held the father possessed no rights of custody under the Convention because his *ne exeat* right was only "a veto right over his son's departure from Chile." The court expressed substantial agreement with the Court of Appeals for the Second Circuit in *Croll v. Croll*. Relying on American dictionary definitions of "custody" and noting that *ne exeat* rights cannot be " 'actually exercised' " within the meaning of the Convention, *Croll* held that *ne exeat* rights are not rights of custody. A dissenting opinion in *Croll* was filed by then-Judge Sotomayor. The dissent maintained that a *ne exeat* right is a right of custody because it "provides a parent with decisionmaking authority regarding a child's international relocation."

The Courts of Appeals for the Fourth and Ninth Circuits adopted the conclusion of the *Croll* majority. The Court of Appeals for the Eleventh Circuit has followed the reasoning of the *Croll* dissent. Certiorari was granted to resolve the conflict.

II

The Convention was adopted in 1980 in response to the problem of international child abductions during domestic disputes. The Convention seeks "to secure the prompt return of children wrongfully removed to or retained in any Contracting State," and "to ensure that rights of custody and of access under the law of one Contracting State are effectively respected in the other Contracting States."

The provisions of the Convention of most relevance at the outset of this discussion are as follows:

"Article 3: The removal or the retention of the child is to be considered wrongful where—

"[a] it is in breach of rights of custody attributed to a person, an institution or any other body, either jointly or alone, under the law of the State in which the child was habitually resident immediately before the removal or retention; and

"[b] at the time of removal or retention those rights were actually exercised, either jointly or alone, or would have been so exercised but for the removal or retention.

* * *

"Article 5: For the purposes of this Convention—

"[a] 'rights of custody' shall include rights relating to the care of the person of the child and, in particular, the right to determine the child's place of residence;

"[b] 'rights of access' shall include the right to take a child for a limited period of time to a place other than the child's habitual residence.

* * *

"Article 12: Where a child has been wrongfully removed or retained in terms of Article 3 * * * the authority concerned shall order the return of the child forthwith."

The Convention's central operating feature is the return remedy. When a child under the age of 16 has been wrongfully removed or retained, the country to which the child has been brought must "order the return of the child forthwith," unless certain exceptions apply. A removal is "wrongful" where the child was removed in violation of "rights of custody." The Convention defines "rights of custody" to "include rights relating to the care of the person of the child and, in particular, the right to determine the child's place of residence." A return remedy does not alter the pre-abduction allocation of custody rights but leaves custodial decisions to the courts of the country of habitual residence. The Convention also recognizes "rights of access," but offers no return remedy for a breach of those rights.

The United States has implemented the Convention through the ICARA. The statute authorizes a person who seeks a child's return to file a petition in state or federal court and instructs that the court "shall decide the case in accordance with the Convention." If the child in question has been "wrongfully removed or retained within the meaning of the Convention," the child shall be "promptly returned," unless an exception is applicable.

III

As the parties agree, the Convention applies to this dispute. A.J. A. is under 16 years old; he was a habitual resident of Chile; and both Chile and the United States are contracting states. The question is whether A.J. A. was "wrongfully removed" from Chile, in other words, whether he was removed in violation of a right of custody. This Court's inquiry is shaped by the text of the Convention; the views of the United States Department of State; decisions addressing the meaning of "rights of custody" in courts of other contracting states; and the purposes of the Convention. After considering these sources, the Court determines that Mr. Abbott's *ne exeat* right is a right of custody under the Convention.

A

"The interpretation of a treaty, like the interpretation of a statute, begins with its text." *Medellín v. Texas,* 552 U.S. 491, 506 (2008). This Court consults Chilean law to determine the content of Mr. Abbott's right, while following the Convention's text and structure to decide whether the right at issue is a "righ[t] of custody."

* * *

That a *ne exeat* right does not fit within traditional notions of physical custody is beside the point. The Convention defines "rights of custody," and it is that definition that a court must consult. This uniform, text-based approach ensures international consistency in interpreting the Convention. It forecloses courts from relying on definitions of custody confined by local law usage, definitions that may undermine recognition of custodial arrangements in other countries or in different legal traditions, including the civil-law tradition. * * *

B

This Court's conclusion that Mr. Abbott possesses a right of custody under the Convention is supported and informed by the State Department's view on the issue. The United States has endorsed the view that *ne exeat* rights are rights of custody. In its brief before this Court the United States advises that "the Department of State, whose Office of Children's Issues serves as the Central Authority for the United States under the Convention, has long understood the Convention as including *ne exeat* rights among the protected 'rights of custody.'" It is well settled that the Executive Branch's interpretation of a treaty "is entitled to great weight." There is no reason to doubt that this well-established canon of deference is appropriate here. The Executive is well informed concerning the diplomatic consequences resulting from this Court's interpretation of "rights of custody," including the likely reaction of other contracting states and the impact on the State Department's ability to reclaim children abducted from this country.

C

This Court's conclusion that *ne exeat* rights are rights of custody is further informed by the views of other contracting states. In interpreting any treaty, "[t]he 'opinions of our sister signatories' * * * are 'entitled to considerable weight.'" The principle applies with special force here, for Congress has directed that "uniform international interpretation of the Convention" is part of the Convention's framework.

A review of the international case law confirms broad acceptance of the rule that *ne exeat* rights are rights of custody. In an early decision [*C. v. C.*], the English High Court of Justice explained that a father's "right to ensure that the child remain[ed] in Australia or live[d] anywhere outside Australia only with his approval" is a right of custody requiring return of the child to Australia. Lords of the House of Lords have agreed, noting that *C. v. C.*'s conclusion is "settled, so far as the United Kingdom is concerned" and "appears to be the majority [view] of the common law world."

The Supreme Court of Israel follows the same rule, concluding that "the term 'custody' should be interpreted in an expansive way, so that it will apply [i]n every case in which there is a need for the consent of one of the parents to remove the children from one country to another." The High Courts of Austria, South Africa, and Germany are in accord. See Oberster Gerichtshof [O.G.H.] [Supreme Court] Feb. 5, 1992, (Austria) ("Since the English Custody Court had ordered that the children must not be removed from England and Wales without the father's written consent, both parents had, in effect, been granted joint custody concerning the children's place of residence"); *Sonderup v. Tondelli*, 2001(1) SA 1171, 1183 (Constitutional Ct. of South Africa 2000) ("[The mother's] failure to return to British Columbia with the child * * * was a breach of the conditions upon which she was entitled to exercise her rights of custody and * * * therefore constituted a wrongful retention * * * as contemplated by [Article 3] of the Convention"); Bundesverfassungsgericht [BVerfG] [Federal Constitutional Court of Germany] July 18, 1997, 2 BvR 1126/97, ¶ 15 (the Convention requires a return remedy for a violation of the "right to have a say in the child's place of residence"). Appellate courts in Australia and Scotland agree. See *In the Marriage of Resina* [1991] FamCA 33 (Austl., May 22, 1991), ¶¶ 18–27; *A.J. v. F. J.*, [2005] CSIH 36, 2005 1 S.C. 428, 435–436.

It is true that some courts have stated a contrary view, or at least a more restrictive one. The Canadian Supreme Court has said *ne exeat* orders are "usually intended" to protect access rights. *Thomson v. Thomson*, [1994] 3 S.C.R. 551, 589–590; see *D.S. v. V. W.*, [1996] 2 S.C.R. 108. But the Canadian cases are not precisely on point here. *Thomson* ordered a return remedy based on an interim *ne exeat* order, and only noted in dicta that it may not order such a remedy pursuant to a permanent *ne exeat* order. See [1994] 3 S.C. R., at 589–590. *D.S.* involved a parent's claim based on an implicit *ne exeat* right and, in any event, the court ordered a return remedy on a different basis.

French courts are divided. A French Court of Appeals held that "the right to accept or refuse the removal of the children's residence" outside of a region was "a joint exercise of rights of custody." *Public Ministry v. M. B.,* [CA] Aix-en-Provence, 6e ch., Mar. 23, 1989, Rev. crit. dr. internat. Prive 79(3), July–Sept.1990, 529, 533–535. A trial court in a different region of France rejected this view, relying on the mother's "fundamental liberty" to establish her domicil[e].

See *Attorney for the Republic at Perigueux v. Mrs. S.,* [T.G.I.] Perigueux, Mar. 17, 1992, Rev. cr. dr. internat. Prive 82(4) Oct.–Dec.1993, 650, 651–653, note Bertrand Ancel, D.1992, note G. C.

Scholars agree that there is an emerging international consensus that *ne exeat* rights are rights of custody, even if that view was not generally formulated when the Convention was drafted in 1980. At that time, joint custodial arrangements were unknown in many of the contracting states, and the status of *ne exeat* rights was not yet well understood. See 1980 Conference de La Haye de droit international prive, Enlévement d'enfants, morning meeting of Wed., Oct. 8, 1980 (discussion by Messrs. Leal & van Boeschoten), in 3 Actes et Documents de la Quatorziéme session, pp. 263–266 (1982) (Canadian and Dutch delegates disagreeing whether the Convention protected *ne exeat* rights, while agreeing that it should protect such rights). Since 1980, however, joint custodial arrangements have become more common. And, within this framework, most contracting states and scholars now recognize that *ne exeat* rights are rights of custody. * * *

A history of the Convention, known as the Perez–Vera Report, has been cited both by the parties and by Courts of Appeals that have considered this issue. See 1980 Conference de La Haye de droit international prive, Enlévement d'enfants, E. Perez–Vera, Explanatory Report (Perez–Vera Report or Report), in 3 Actes et Documents de la Quatorziéme session, pp. 425–473 (1982). We need not decide whether this Report should be given greater weight than a scholarly commentary. Compare Hague International Child Abduction Convention; Text and Legal Analysis, 51 Fed.Reg. 10503–10506 (1986) (identifying the Report as the "official history" of the Convention and "a source of background on the meaning of the provisions of the Convention"), with Perez–Vera Report ¶ 8, at 427–428 ("[the Report] has not been approved by the Conference, and it is possible that, despite the Rapporter's *[sic]* efforts to remain objective, certain passages reflect a viewpoint which is in part subjective"). It suffices to note that the Report supports the conclusion that *ne exeat* rights are rights of custody. The Report explains that rather than defining custody in precise terms or referring to the laws of different nations pertaining to parental rights, the

Convention uses the unadorned term "rights of custody" to recognize "*all* the ways in which custody of children can be exercised" through "a flexible interpretation of the terms used, which allows the greatest possible number of cases to be brought into consideration." *Id.*, ¶¶ 67, 71, at 446, 447–448. Thus the Report rejects the notion that because *ne exeat* rights do not encompass the right to make medical or some other important decisions about a child's life they cannot be rights of custody. Indeed, the Report is fully consistent with the conclusion that *ne exeat* rights are just one of the many "ways in which custody of children can be exercised." *Id.*, ¶ 71, at 447.

D

Adopting the view that the Convention provides a return remedy for violations of *ne exeat* rights accords with its objects and purposes. The Convention is based on the principle that the best interests of the child are well served when decisions regarding custody rights are made in the country of habitual residence. See Convention Preamble, Treaty Doc., at 7. Ordering a return remedy does not alter the existing allocation of custody rights, but does allow the courts of the home country to decide what is in the child's best interests. It is the Convention's premise that courts in contracting states will make this determination in a responsible manner.

* * *

To interpret the Convention to permit an abducting parent to avoid a return remedy, even when the other parent holds a *ne exeat* right, would run counter to the Convention's purpose of deterring child abductions by parents who attempt to find a friendlier forum for deciding custodial disputes. Ms. Abbott removed A.J. A. from Chile while Mr. Abbott's request to enhance his relationship with his son was still pending before Chilean courts. After she landed in Texas, the mother asked the state court to diminish or eliminate the father's custodial and visitation rights. The Convention should not be interpreted to permit a parent to select which country will adjudicate these questions by bringing the child to a different country, in violation of a *ne exeat* right. Denying a return remedy for the violation of such rights would "legitimize the very action—removal of the child—that the home country, through its custody order [or other provision of law], sought to prevent" and would allow "parents to undermine the very purpose of the Convention." *Croll*, 229 F.3d, at 147 (Sotomayor, J., dissenting). This Court should be most reluctant to adopt an interpretation that gives an abducting parent an advantage by coming here to avoid a return remedy that is granted, for instance, in the United Kingdom, Israel, Germany, and South Africa.

Requiring a return remedy in cases like this one helps deter child abductions and respects the Convention's purpose to prevent harms resulting from abductions. An abduction can have devastating consequences for a child. "Some child psychologists believe that the trauma children suffer from these abductions is one of the worst forms of child abuse." H.R.Rep. No. 103–390, p. 2 (1993), U.S.Code Cong & Admin.News 1993, pp. 2419, 2420. A child abducted by one parent is separated from the second parent and the child's support system. Studies have shown that separation by abduction can cause psychological problems ranging from depression and acute stress disorder to posttraumatic stress disorder and identity-formation issues. A child abducted at an early age can experience loss of community and stability, leading to loneliness, anger, and fear of abandonment. Abductions may prevent the child from forming a relationship with the left-behind parent, impairing the child's ability to mature.

* * *

The judgment of the Court of Appeals is reversed, and the case is remanded for further proceedings consistent with this opinion.

It is so ordered.

* * *

[The dissenting opinion by JUSTICES STEVENS, THOMAS, and BREYER is omitted.]

———————

The Court notes that its interpretation is supported by the object and purpose of the treaty, the position of the executive branch, and the majority of foreign courts it consults. What if one or more of these factors pointed towards a different outcome? How much weight should the interpretation by foreign courts carry in such a case? At what point should the Court yield to foreign views for the sake of uniformity even though it would prefer a different interpretation?

2. THE CHANGING FACE OF CUSTOMARY INTERNATIONAL LAW

A. THE MODERN IMPORTANCE OF CUSTOM

In a world of rapidly proliferating treaties, it is tempting to think of customary international law as having been relegated to a marginal position. The following excerpt argues that this would be a mistake. According to Alvarez, why has custom not only remained an important source but actually experienced a comeback in recent decades? In his opinion, what is the relationship between customary international law and treaties today? Is a prominent role for custom to be welcomed, especially in light of how (and by whom) it is made?

JOSE E. ALVAREZ, THE INTERNATIONALIZATION
OF U.S. LAW
47 Colum. J. Transnat'l L. 537 (2009)

* * *

There is yet another reason for the internationalization of U.S. law beyond the mission creep of our favored institutions: the reemergence of customary law. Now at this point, I expect several of you to conclude that I really must be hallucinating. Haven't I heard from well-known U.S. revisionist scholars that customary international law is of no real relevance to the behavior of states; that it ought to have no status as federal common law; that it is subject to hopeless circularity in terms of definition; and that in game-theoretic terms it is a collective delusion routinely ignored when not consistent with the national interests of states? Well yes, actually I have heard these arguments by Curtis Bradley, Jack Goldsmith, and Eric Posner, among others. I just think they need to get out more and take a stroll, for example, in the real world of practicing lawyers where real cases are won or lost. They need to take a close look at, for example, U.S. government or U.S. investor briefs in NAFTA arbitrations.

My foreign investment students have a difficult time understanding those who say that customary law does not exist or cannot bind. They certainly do not understand how such arguments can be made by those who simultaneously defend—in preference to supposedly "imprecise," "ineffectual" customary law—the "hard" or more binding rules and institutions of international economic law such as bilateral investment treaties, free trade agreements such as the NAFTA or the WTO.

They have a tough time understanding such contentions because even a cursory examination of the abundant case law of BIT and NAFTA tribunals reveal considerable reliance on rules of custom as well as general principles of law. The substantive guarantees provided in even relatively precise investment agreements anticipate, indeed require, reliance on these other sources of general international law outside the four corners of international trade or investment law narrowly construed. As the emerging arbitral case law suggests, provisions requiring investors to receive "fair and equitable treatment," "full protection and security," treatment that is not less than required "under international law," or requiring states to respect investor-state contracts are recipes for dredging through hoary cases dealing with state responsibility to aliens (such as *Chattin* or *Neer*); more recent considerations of what constitutes fair or equitable procedures (as in human rights tribunals that apply both treaty and customary standards); and comparative analyses of the general principles of law that can be drawn from national law (such as national law protecting the legitimate expectations of rights holders). The customary "denial of justice" standard is being used in many of these investment disputes, as are general principles of estoppel, unclean hands and acquiescence. States trying to defend themselves from investors' claims, such as Argentina, find themselves parsing the customary international law defenses of distress, necessity or force majeure, as well as the rules concerning attribution. Despite recent Argentine threats not to abide by ICSID rulings, no one questions that such arbitral awards are among the most effectively enforceable in the international system, even when these decisions are contrary to what states originally contemplated or currently desire. The emerging "international common law" relating to the handling of evidentiary and procedural questions among our proliferating international judiciary is also a resurgent form of customary international law.

The re-emergence of customary law in these contexts is in turn affecting the treaty obligations of the United States. Our government's latest model bilateral investment treaty now takes a more nuanced position on such matters as the meaning of "fair and equitable treatment" and the scope of permissible treaty exceptions because of these developments. And it is as yet unknown whether, for example, the customary law of permissible countermeasures, including traditional remedies canvassed in the rules of state responsibility such as reparations and the principle of proportionality, may yet play a role even with respect to the *lex specialis* remedial scheme contained in the WTO's Dispute Settlement Understanding.

While it may be true that customary norms are generally consistent with U.S. national interests, to conclude from that banal point that the United States is therefore unconstrained by the product of investor-state and WTO dispute settlement insofar as it incorporates custom is a non sequitur. As is suggested by the huge efforts expended by the U.S. government to win NAFTA (and WTO) cases, the interpretations of customary and treaty law by such tribunals are of deep interest to us—because our federal and state laws or enforcement efforts could be undermined by the precedents established. That the United States has a national interest in, for example, having its investors be compensated for an expropriation, does not mean that NAFTA arbitrators will necessarily take the same view as a state of the United States about what an "indirect expropriation" means.

The revival of custom is occurring in more than the investment and trade regimes. As Ted Meron has recently pointed out, customary international law is undergoing a renaissance in part because all of our proliferating international dispute settlers face comparable needs to avoid a finding of *non liquet*—even when faced with questions over which no treaty rules apply or with respect to questions left open by vague or porous treaties. They too regularly turn to general principles and custom. Thus, the Iran–U.S. Claims Tribunal revived and gave more specific content to a range of customary rules, such as those governing the wrongful expulsion of aliens. That Tribunal, which continues to operate today, along with other ad hoc bodies such as the UN Compensation Commission and the Eritrea–Ethiopia Claims Commission, have also applied and helped to refine the state responsibility rules recently issued by the ILC. Those rules, as well as customary human rights such as the ban on torture, continue to be emphasized in our regional human rights courts—as in the *Velasquez–Rodriguez* decision by the Inter–American Court of Human Rights and numerous decisions issued by the European Court of Human Rights.

As Meron also points out, despite the strictures of *nullum crimen sine lege,* the ad hoc war crimes tribunals have also applied and developed customary rules about command responsibility, what constitutes participation in a "joint criminal enterprise," and the requisites of the crime of complicity. As he indicates, those tribunals have developed customary law concerning "the nexus of such crimes to armed conflict, the distinction between the concepts of 'attack' and 'armed conflict,' the requirement of discriminatory intent, the elements of the crime, such as the existence of a plan or policy, the relevance of personal motives, and the actus reus of the crime of persecution." As Meron also indicates, with respect to the treaty-based crime of genocide, these tribunals have turned to, and in turn developed, the customary law with respect to genocidal intent, and the meaning of aiding and abetting or complicity. The treaty-based category of war crimes has also been subject to considerable customary law elaboration—as with respect to the crimes of torture and rape or the defense of duress. Like other international adjudicators mentioned here that have had to resolve evidentiary and procedural disputes, the ad hoc war crimes tribunals have addressed (and developed) customary rules regarding the issuance of subpoenas to state officials, the examination of documents raising national security concerns, and arrest, abduction and international transfer. Most of this law is relatively precise and none of it can be disparaged as unenforceable.

Note that much of the customary international law revival has occurred in the shadow of, and been spurred on by, a considerable number of multilateral treaties across a range of topics, from the regulation of trade and investment to rules governing combatants. Those who predicted that the proliferation of such treaties would bring about the demise of customary law overestimated the ability of treaty drafters to anticipate the needs of states—or of their dispute settlers.

* * *

B. NEW MODES OF CUSTOMARY INTERNATIONAL LAW MAKING

Traditionally, customary international law required consistent state practice combined with an understanding that this practice is followed as a matter of legal obligation (*opinio juris*), not just of comity. Since the middle of the 20th century, however, new (additional) forms of creating customary international law have emerged—or have at least been suggested. They have not much affected the *opinio juris* element, but they have challenged the traditional understanding of state practice.

To begin with, can states "make" customary international law by unilateral "proclamation" that they have certain rights (from now on)? You might think not, but at least in the document below, the United States tried to do exactly that. Perhaps amazingly, it "got away with it," so to speak. No other country seriously contested its claim and, today, the jurisdiction of states over the continental shelf beyond their coasts is generally accepted.

TRUMAN PROCLAMATION ON THE CONTINENTAL SHELF
Presidential Proclamation No. 2667
10 Fed. Reg. 12,305 (Sept. 28, 1945)

POLICY OF THE UNITED STATES WITH RESPECT TO THE NATURAL RESOURCES OF THE SUBSOIL AND SEA BED OF THE CONTINENTAL SHELF

Whereas the Government of the United States of America, aware of the long range world-wide need for new sources of petroleum and other minerals, holds the view that efforts to discover and make available new supplies of these resources should be encouraged; and

Whereas its competent experts are of the opinion that such resources underlie many parts of the continental shelf off the coasts of the United States of America, and that with modern technological progress their utilization is already practicable or will become so at any early date; and

Whereas recognized jurisdiction over these resources is required in the interest of their conservation and prudent utilization when and as development is undertaken; and

Whereas it is the view of the Government of the United States that the exercise of jurisdiction over the natural resources of the subsoil and sea bed of the continental shelf by the contiguous nation is reasonable and just, since the effectiveness of measures to utilize or conserve these resources would be contingent upon cooperation and protection from shore, since the continental shelf may be regarded as an extension of the land mass of the coastal nation and thus naturally appurtenant to it, since these resources frequently form a seaward extension of a pool or deposit lying within the territory, and since self-protection compels the coastal nation to keep close watch over activities off its shores which are of their nature necessary for utilization of these resources;

NOW THEREFORE I, HARRY S. TRUMAN, President of the United States of America, do hereby proclaim the following policy of the United

States of America with respect to the natural resources of the subsoil and sea bed of the continental shelf.

Having concern for the urgency of conserving and prudently utilizing its natural resources, the Government of the United States regards the natural resources of the subsoil and sea bed of the continental shelf beneath the high seas but contiguous to the coasts of the United States as appertaining to the United States, subject to its jurisdiction and control. In cases where the continental shelf extends to the shores of another States, or is shared with an adjacent State, the boundary shall be determined by the United States and the State concerned in accordance with equitable principles. The character as high seas of the waters above the continental shelf and the right to their free and unimpeded navigation are in no way thus affected.

Within a few years, the principle proclaimed by President Truman has been widely accepted by other states. What may explain that? Was it simply because the United States was the most powerful country in the world at the time? Would, for example, Venezuela have "gotten away with it"?

Customary international law also played a major role in the *Nicaragua Case* decided by the ICJ in 1986. In 1979, the regime led by Anasatasio Somoza Debayle in Nicaragua, which had been supported by the United States, was overthrown by the socialist Sandanista National Liberation Front. The Sandanista regime that came to power after 1979 was supported by Cuba and the Soviet Union at the height of the Cold War.

The Sandinista regime was opposed by a loose affiliation of rebel groups, known as the *contras*, operating both in Nicaragua and out of neighboring states. The United States supported the *contras* as part of its Cold War strategy during the 1980s by providing military support in various forms. Nicaragua considered this an illegal interference with its sovereignty and ultimately challenged the actions of the United States in the ICJ. The United States claimed that its actions were justified as an act of support of El Salvador's self-defense (under Article 51 of the UN Charter) against Nicaragua. In a landmark decision in 1986, the ICJ ruled that the United States had indeed violated international law.

For jurisdictional reasons too complex to go into here, the ICJ could not (directly) apply the UN Charter to decide on the legitimacy of the United States' use of force. Instead, it had to rely on customary international law, which therefore came to play a crucial rule.

How does the Court approach customary international law in the following case excerpt? To what extent is this approach traditional or novel? What exactly is the basis for finding customary international law here?

CASE CONCERNING MILITARY AND PARAMILITARY ACTIVITIES IN AND AGAINST NICARAGUA (NICARAGUA V. UNITED STATES)

International Court of Justice
1986 I.C.J. 14

* * *

183. * * * [T]he Court has next to consider what are the rules of customary international law applicable to the present dispute. For this purpose, it has to direct its attention to the practice and *opinio juris* of States; as the Court recently observed,

> "It is of course axiomatic that the material of customary international law is to be looked for primarily in the actual practice and *opinio juris* of States, even though multilateral conventions may have an important role to play in recording and defining rules deriving from custom, or indeed in developing them." (*Continental Shelf (Libyan Arab Jamahiriya/Malta), I.C.J. Reports 1985*, pp. 29–30, para. 27.)

In this respect the Court must not lose sight of the Charter of the United Nations and that of the Organization of American States, notwithstanding the operation of the multilateral treaty reservation. Although the Court has no jurisdiction to determine whether the conduct of the United States constitutes a breach of those conventions, it can and must take them into account in ascertaining the content of the customary international law which the United States is also alleged to have infringed.

184. The Court notes that there is in fact evidence, to be examined below, of a considerable degree of agreement between the Parties as to the content of the customary international law relating to the non-use of force and non-intervention. This concurrence of their views does not however dispense the Court from having itself to ascertain what rules of customary international law are applicable. The mere fact that States declare their recognition of certain rules is not sufficient for the Court to consider these as being part of customary international law, and as applicable as such to those States. Bound as it is by Article 38 of its Statute to apply, *inter alia*, international custom "as evidence of a general practice accepted as law", the Court may not disregard the essential role played by general practice. Where two States agree to incorporate a particular rule in a treaty, their agreement suffices to make that rule a legal one, binding upon them; but in the field of customary international law, the shared view of the Parties as to the content of what they regard as the rule is not enough. The Court must satisfy itself that the existence of the rule in the *opinio juris* of States is confirmed by practice.

185. In the present dispute, the Court, while exercising its jurisdiction only in respect of the application of the customary rules of non-use of force and non-intervention, cannot disregard the fact that the Parties are

bound by these rules as a matter of treaty law and of customary international law. Furthermore, in the present case, apart from the treaty commitments binding the Parties to the rules in question, there are various instances of their having expressed recognition of the validity thereof as customary international law in other ways. It is therefore in the light of this "subjective element"—the expression used by the Court in its 1969 Judgment in the *North Sea Continental Shelf* cases—that the Court has to appraise the relevant practice.

186. It is not to be expected that in the practice of States the application of the rules in question should have been perfect, in the sense that States should have refrained, with complete consistency, from the use of force or from intervention in each other's internal affairs. The Court does not consider that, for a rule to be established as customary, the corresponding practice must be in absolutely rigorous conformity with the rule. In order to deduce the existence of customary rules, the Court deems it sufficient that the conduct of States should, in general, be consistent with such rules, and that instances of State conduct inconsistent with a given rule should generally have been treated as breaches of that rule, not as indications of the recognition of a new rule. If a State acts in a way prima facie incompatible with a recognized rule, but defends its conduct by appealing to exceptions or justifications contained within the rule itself, then whether or not the State's conduct is in fact justifiable on that basis, the significance of that attitude is to confirm rather than to weaken the rule.

187. The Court must therefore determine, first, the substance of the customary rules relating to the use of force in international relations, applicable to the dispute submitted to it. The United States has argued that, on this crucial question of the lawfulness of the use of force in inter-State relations, the rules of general and customary international law, and those of the United Nations Charter, are in fact identical. In its view this identity is so complete that, as explained above, it constitutes an argument to prevent the Court from applying this customary law, because it is indistinguishable from the multilateral treaty law which it may not apply. In its Counter-Memorial on jurisdiction and admissibility the United States asserts that "Article 2(4) of the Charter is customary and general international law". It quotes with approval an observation by the International Law Commission to the effect that

> "the great majority of international lawyers today unhesitatingly hold that Article 2, paragraph 4, together with other provisions of the Charter, authoritatively declares the modern customary law regarding the threat or use of force".

The United States points out that Nicaragua has endorsed this view, since one of its counsel asserted that "indeed it is generally considered by publicists that Article 2, paragraph 4, of the United Nations Charter is in this respect an embodiment of existing general principles of international law". And the United States concludes:

> "In sum, the provisions of Article 2(4) with respect to the lawfulness of the use of force are 'modern customary law' and the 'embodiment of general principles of international law'. There is no other 'customary and general international law' on which Nicaragua can rest its claims."

> "It is, in short, inconceivable that this Court could consider the lawfulness of an alleged use of armed force without referring to the principal source of the relevant international law—Article 2(4) of the United Nations Charter."

As for Nicaragua, the only noteworthy shade of difference in its view lies in Nicaragua's belief that

> "in certain cases the rule of customary law will not necessarily be identical in content and mode of application to the conventional rule".

188. The Court thus finds that both Parties take the view that the principles as to the use of force incorporated in the United Nations Charter correspond, in essentials, to those found in customary international law. The Parties thus both take the view that the fundamental principle in this area is expressed in the terms employed in Article 2, paragraph 4, of the United Nations Charter. They therefore accept a treaty-law obligation to refrain in their international relations from the threat or use of force against the territorial integrity or political independence of any State, or in any other manner inconsistent with the purposes of the United Nations. The Court has however to be satisfied that there exists in customary international law an *opinio juris* as to the binding character of such abstention. This *opinio juris* may, though with all due caution, be deduced from, *inter alia*, the attitude of the Parties and the attitude of States towards certain General Assembly resolutions, and particularly resolution 2625 (XXV) entitled "Declaration on Principles of International Law concerning Friendly Relations and Co-operation among States in accordance with the Charter of the United Nations". The effect of consent to the text of such resolutions cannot be understood as merely that of a "reiteration or elucidation" of the treaty commitment undertaken in the Charter. On the contrary, it may be understood as an acceptance of the validity of the rule or set of rules declared by the resolution by themselves. The principle of non-use of force, for example, may thus be regarded as a principle of customary international law, not as such conditioned by provisions relating to collective security, or to the facilities or armed contingents to be provided under Article 43 of the Charter. It would therefore seem apparent that the attitude referred to expresses an *opinio juris* respecting such rule (or set of rules), to be thenceforth treated separately

from the provisions, especially those of an institutional kind, to which it is subject on the treaty-law plane of the Charter.

189. As regards the United States in particular, the weight of an expression of *opinio juris* can similarly be attached to its support of the resolution of the Sixth International Conference of American States condemning aggression (18 February 1928) and ratification of the Montevideo Convention on Rights and Duties of States (26 December 1933), Article 11 of which imposes the obligation not to recognize territorial acquisitions or special advantages which have been obtained by force. Also significant is United States acceptance of the principle of the prohibition of the use of force which is contained in the declaration on principles governing the mutual relations of States participating in the Conference on Security and Co-operation in Europe (Helsinki, 1 August 1975), whereby the participating States undertake to "refrain in their mutual relations, *as well as in their international relations in general*," (emphasis added) from the threat or use of force. Acceptance of a text in these terms confirms the existence of an *opinio juris* of the participating States prohibiting the use of force in international relations.

190. A further confirmation of the validity as customary international law of the principle of the prohibition of the use of force expressed in Article 2, paragraph 4, of the Charter of the United Nations may be found in the fact that it is frequently referred to in statements by State representatives as being not only a principle of customary international law but also a fundamental or cardinal principle of such law. The International Law Commission, in the course of its work on the codification of the law of treaties, expressed the view that "the law of the Charter concerning the prohibition of the use of force in itself constitutes a conspicuous example of a rule in international law having the character of *jus cogens*". Nicaragua in its Memorial on the Merits submitted in the present case states that the principle prohibiting the use of force embodied in Article 2, paragraph 4, of the Charter of the United Nations "has come to be recognized as *jus cogens*." The United States, in its Counter-Memorial on the questions of jurisdiction and admissibility, found it material to quote the views of scholars that this principle is a "universal norm," a "universal international law," a "universally recognized principle of international law," and a "principle of *jus cogens*".

* * *

_____

Is the Court's attempt to show consistent state practice successful? What evidence of such practice does the Court present?

The following text describes three models of customary international law-making. (It is true that it deals primarily with two models, but it then adds on a third in the last paragraph). What are these models and which of the texts above reflect which?

ENZO CANNIZZARO & PAOLO PALCHETTI (EDS.), CUSTOMARY INTERNATIONAL LAW ON THE USE OF FORCE
(2005)

* * *

As international law textbooks almost uniformly repeat, the coming into being of a customary rule requires the concomitance of an established practice plus *opinio iuris*. Despite this apparent unanimity, however, authors are much divided on the identification of customary law's creating factor, and a variety of opinions has been suggested, ranging from spontaneism to voluntarism.

Beyond the obvious differences among such views, there is an overarching tendency to present each approach as exclusive, i.e., as a theoretical model capturing all the subtleties of the law-making or, respectively, of the law-determining process. This claim to exclusivity probably lies at the origin of the weaknesses and shortcomings of each approach: while these models might address how a particular category of rules comes into being, they fail to fully explain the coming into existence of the plethora of customary rules.

Instead of insisting on the unity of the process of creating customary law, the idea has at times been put forward that a multiplicity of law-making processes are hidden under the general and facile formula of customary international law. Following this approach, different categories of customary rules may be identified. Thus, while certain customary rules have slowly emerged over the centuries, through conduct which gradually proved to serve most appropriately the needs of the international community, and to balance accordingly the respective interests of the various actors, others appear to be the product of the claims of certain actors, usually the most powerful among them, implicitly or expressly put forward in order to provoke a change in the law which better accommodates their interests, and which is accepted, or acquiesced to by other actors convinced of the necessity or of the ineluctable character of such change.

Rules of the first type are the expression of the more or less spontaneous convergence of the conduct of relevant actors towards certain behavioural schemes; they emerge and evolve slowly, through a process of mutual adjustment of conduct and reaction thereto, and which, comprehensively considered, continuously adapt the law to the changing social needs. For these rules, traditional modes of ascertaining the law, based on the lengthy and patient research of practice and *opinio iuris*, remain the most appropriate. This category of rules mirrors the communitarian spirit of customary international law. On the other hand, rules falling within the other category are more the product of an act of law-making in strict sense than an expression of *opinio iuris*, and the process of their formation resembles a consensualist scheme more than any other theoretical one. This process of creating law is therefore one which emphasises the antagonistic character of the process of customary law-making.

These two categories do not exhaust the variety of the law-making processes. Many authors have, in the past, underlined the existence of a further category of customary law, whose coming into being is not explained by the existence of a well settled practice, nor by the will of states. These rules, whose creation may be very rapid indeed, can be ascertained by way of a deductive process, looking at the *opinio iuris* of the actors of international law, at the structure of the international system, or at a combination of principles and values in this legal order. Whereas some might find it more appropriate to refer to them as principles rather than customary rules, they are not rarely labelled as such, perhaps in order to escape the difficult task of explaining their establishment.

* * *

As you may have noticed, there has been a modern tendency to dilute the "consistent state practice requirement" by looking not only (or even primarily) at what states are actually doing but (also) at what they are saying, declaring or intending. The following text takes a critical view of this trend. What are the primary concerns expressed in it? In particular, what dangers does it see?

* * *

JAMES C. HATHAWAY, LEVERAGING ASYLUM

45 Tex. Int'l L.J. 503 (2010)

* * *

* * * The essence of the argument is that a very broad reading of "state practice" is justified under which words alone may amount to "practice." The proponents of this position look to many of the same statements relied upon to show *opinio juris* as the relevant practice in support of the norm, and thereby arrive at the conclusion that consistent state "practice" can be located despite the evidence of non-conforming "practice on the ground" previously identified.

It is in regard to this issue that the rules of customary law formation are most contested. As Kammerhofer explains, there is a tendency among

many academics to define "practice" in a way that obviates the distinction
between practice and *opinio juris*:

> Behind the apparent dichotomy of "acts" and "statements" lies a more
> important distinction: that between one argument that sees practice
> as the exercise of the right claimed and the other that includes the
> claims themselves and thus blurs the border between the concept of
> "state practice" and "*opinio juris.*"

This is indeed the nub of the controversy: despite the continued insistence
of the ICJ that there are two, not one, essential elements to the formation
of customary international law, there seems to be a determined academic
effort to downplay that requirement. The Final Report of the International Law Association (ILA) Committee on Formation of Customary (General) International Law provides a classic example of this propensity to
confuse:

> The Court has not in fact said in so many words that just because
> there are (allegedly) distinct elements in customary law the same
> conduct cannot manifest both. It is in fact often difficult or even im-
> possible to disentangle the two elements.

The language used is quite extraordinary. The ILA does *not* say that the
International Court of Justice *has* held that both elements of custom may
be manifested by the same, presumably purely verbal, evidence, but rather simply that it "has not * * * said in so many words" that it cannot!

This cautious, if convoluted, framing is warranted given the actual state
of ICJ jurisprudence. The decision in *Nicaragua*, while often cited as the
leading source of the notion that words alone can constitute state practice, did not actually reach that conclusion. The focus of the dispute was
whether there was a customary norm prohibiting the threat or use of
force against the territorial integrity or political independence of a state
that parallels the treaty-based rule in Article 2(4) of the UN Charter. The
Court was insistent that a customary norm could arise only upon proof of
"the actual practice and *opinio juris* of States." For good measure, it added:

> The mere fact that States declare their recognition of certain rules is
> not sufficient for the Court to consider these as being part of custom-
> ary international law. * * * [I]n the field of customary international
> law, the shared view of the Parties as to the content of what they re-
> gard as the rule is not enough. The Court must satisfy itself that the
> existence of the rule in the *opinio juris* of States is confirmed by prac-
> tice.

The common confusion about just what the Court decided arises from the
fact that it took what can only be described as a fairly slipshod approach
to the assessment of state practice before focusing on the issue of *opinio*

juris. Implicit in its analysis that "[i]t is not to be expected that the application of the rules in question should have been perfect" and that "rigorous conformity" is too high a standard is an assumption, though an empirically suspect one, that there was evidence on the facts of the case of relatively consistent state practice of non-intervention other than as authorized by the Charter. Because the parties chose not to contest the issue of state practice, the Court understandably focused its analysis on the opinio juris question, finding that a wide-ranging set of verbal acts could give rise to *opinio juris*.

However, the Court is explicit that these verbal acts are approved strictly as forms of *opinio juris*, not state practice. As such, and despite the failure of the Court to interrogate clearly the state practice dimension of the claim, it is disingenuous to suggest that its lack of precision in this regard amounts to an endorsement of a new theory of customary international law formation in which state practice is rendered virtually identical to *opinio juris*. If this had been the Court's intention, why would it have been at such pains to confirm the traditional two-part test and address the sufficiency of imperfect state practice?

It follows that the notion that verbiage without concordant state practice gives rise to customary law is at best *de lege ferenda* rather than settled law. Four main arguments favor this approach: plain meaning allows it; it avoids a detrimental reliance concern; states want it; and it promotes international order and human values.

On the first point, Villiger argues that "the term 'practice' is general enough—thereby corresponding with the flexibility of customary law itself—to cover *any act or behaviour of a State*, and it is not * * * entirely clear in what respect verbal acts originating from a State would be lacking." While linguistically plausible and with at least some support in the jurisprudence, the double-counting of the same words as both *opinio juris* and relevant practice is difficult to square with the ICJ's continued insistence on *both* evidence of state practice and *opinio juris*. If words evincing acceptance as law are the essence of *opinio juris*, a court inclined to view words as sufficient state practice ought simply to have dispensed with the dual requirement—which the ICJ has not.

Villiger advances a second argument for treating words alone as practice that is grounded in the importance of avoiding detrimental reliance. He writes that "whatever a State feels or believes when making a statement, at least other States may come to rely on this statement, and the original State may even be estopped from altering its position." This is a circular argument. If it is clear that only practical actions "on the ground" count as relevant state practice, then the risk of detrimental reliance is disposed of because there is no reasonable basis for other states to put stock in statements standing alone.

A third argument, advanced by Oscar Schachter, is that in at least some circumstances states seem to want statements standing alone to be treated as practice relevant to the formation of custom:

> [In] the contemporary international milieu governments have felt a need for new law which, for one reason or another, could not be fully realized through multilateral treaties. * * * For one thing, the processes of treaty negotiation are often slow and cumbersome. * * * In these circumstances, it has been natural for States to turn to law-declaring resolutions of the General Assembly.

In Schachter's view, there is implied consent for treating at least this one form of "words alone"—namely, law-declaring resolutions adopted unanimously or without significant dissent—as instant customary international law.

This is, of course, a narrower point than the general argument in favor of treating words generally as state practice. Schachter is far from alone in wishing to see at least some resolutions of international organizations, in particular resolutions of the General Assembly, treated as a special example of "state practice." As Jennings and Watt opine, "the concentration of state practice now developed and displayed in international organisations and the collective decisions and activities of the organisations themselves may be valuable evidence of general practice accepted as law in the fields in which those organisations operate." There are nonetheless several concerns.

First, the fact that the General Assembly is explicitly denied the right to engage in general lawmaking activities should give pause before attributing special lawmaking force to its resolutions. Second, it seems contradictory to argue that governments have effectively consented to use of the General Assembly as a lawmaking forum in order to overcome the (presumably overly demanding) procedural requirements of lawmaking by treaty when those same governments have declined either to amend the rules of treaty-making or the Charter to provide for the speedy process Schachter assumes they want. And finally, where precisely is the evidence that states, rather than scholars, want a speedy, less formal lawmaking process? The only example Schachter provides in support of his thesis is the adoption in 1946 of resolutions condemning genocide as a crime and approving the Nuremberg Principles. Both the paucity of examples and the fact that Schachter's cited instances led to subsequent codification in treaty form suggest that support for the "states want it" thesis is modest at best.

This leaves us with one final argument for treating verbal statements as practice: that the world needs a lawmaking process capable of generating results in some core areas, even if state consent cannot be located through one of the general modes, including via consistent practice in the case of custom. In advancing this thesis, Schachter forthrightly acknowledges its instrumentalist tenor, writing that "[t]he problem of inconsistent practice (i.e. violations) comes up sharply in respect of declared norms of international human rights. * * * In the face of these facts, it is hard to conclude that the declared norms are confirmed by general and consistent practice." He is equally candid in noting that "[m]ost international lawyers seek to minimize the violations by emphasizing strong verbal condemnations and denials. * * * [But] [t]he notion that contrary practice should yield to *opinio juris* challenges the basic premise of customary law."

Schachter's solution is to endorse that contradiction in relation to only a subset of customary lawmaking, where putative norms "are strongly supported and important to international order and human values." He argues that in this context "the norm has to be maintained despite violations" because "they are brittle in the sense that violations are likely." A more systematized version of this approach is offered by Frederic Kirgis, who asserts that the two elements of customary lawmaking—*opinio juris* and consistent state practice—should be viewed "not as fixed and mutually exclusive, but as interchangeable along a sliding scale":

> The more destabilizing or morally distasteful the activity—for example, the offensive use of force or the deprivation of fundamental human rights—the more readily international decision makers will substitute one element for the other, provided that the asserted restrictive rule seems reasonable.

Despite the fact that Kirgis speaks of what international decision makers do, his analysis relies only on the *Nicaragua* case to support the claim that "a clearly demonstrated *opinio juris* establishes a customary rule without much (or any) affirmative showing that governments are consistently behaving in accordance with the asserted rule." For reasons previously given, this is not in my view an accurate interpretation of the *Nicaragua* case. Even if advanced simply as a thesis *de lege ferenda*, there are good reasons not to endorse the proposed instrumentalist "gloss over" of the duty to show relatively consistent state practice in support of the putative customary norm.

Most fundamentally, this view of custom is a disingenuous circumvention of the requirements of lawmaking by treaty. If words alone are to evince state consent to be bound, then those words are required to be formalized as treaty. To treat a wide variety of words uttered in less exacting circumstances not simply as *opinio juris* but as binding in and of themselves would, as Kelly rightly asserts, be to "constitute a new legislative form of lawmaking, not [customary international law] based on state behavior accepted as law." Proponents of an exaggerated definition of state "practice" deny the most elementary distinction between treaties and custom: custom is not simply a matter of words, wherever or by whomever uttered, but is a function of what is happening in the real world. Custom, as distinguished from treaty, is about negotiation via practice. The effective obliteration of the consistent practice requirement advocated by many scholars is thus conceptually flawed. As Wolfke has acerbically observed, "[R]epeated verbal acts are also acts of conduct * * * but only to customs of making such declarations * * * and not to customs of the conduct described in the content of the verbal acts."

This is not a purely formalist point. The huge variation in theories of which words count as practice makes clear that the risk of subjectivity and political distortion inherent in the transmutation of words into practice is extreme. Kelly rightly points to the likelihood of cultural bias in the selection of which norms are "important to international order and human values," "important [to] the common interests of states or humanity," or which address concerns that are "destabilizing or morally distasteful":

> Powerful states use "non-empirical" [customary international law] to justify the exercise of power without actual acceptance. Environmental and human rights activists, on the other hand, envision [customary international law] as an instrument for progressive change. * * * [Customary international law] is an inapt instrument for all of these uses. The clever use of arbitral decisions, general *dicta* from a few ICJ cases, the glorification of general and ambiguous non-binding instruments, or the reconceptualization of [customary international law] do not establish either requirement of customary law. Custom takes its authority from the belief in the normative quality of resolved experience, not the manipulation of legal instruments.

In sum, "[t]his impressionistic disarray allows the scholar, advocate, or judge in the few cases that are adjudicated to subjectively arrive at a conclusion affected by normative predilection. The [customary international law] of human rights is a product of the normative perspective of academics and advocates practicing human rights law, not the social facts of states accepting legal norms."

Given the inherent subjectivity of treating some, but not all, words as customary law without need for concordant practice, it should come as little surprise that relevant assertions of customary duty rarely attract compliance by states. It is surely true that "[t]he less powerful nations * * * would be unlikely to accept the 'claims' approach of D'Amato or the New Haven school because it would diminish their role in law formation." It is equally clear that the view favored by many in less powerful nations that "the accumulation of non-binding international instruments creates binding legal obligations is," as Kelly notes, "not one which is widely shared by [more powerful] states and has been specifically rejected by the United States." This is the critical answer to scholars, such as Schachter, who argue for the revaluation of words as practice based on the need to secure critical social ends. If compliance is not in fact advanced by the assertion of words alone as customary international law, and there is little evidence that it is, then on what basis does the appeal to necessity really stand? And if the alleged necessity really does exist in the context of a shared assumption of critical need, as most theorists assume it should, then there will in any event be little difficulty proceeding to a treaty to concretize that agreement.

* * *

Should we stick to the traditional concept of customary international law and thus require a showing of *actual* state *practice* (i.e., on the ground)? If so, what would be the price of such a restrictive approach?

In the previous excerpt, Hathaway criticizes the Final Report of a committee of the International Law Association (issued in 2000) for having mischaracterized the reasoning of the ICJ in order to push for an exaggerated view of customary international law that does not require evidence of any actual state practice (that is, in which words alone can count as both state practice and *opinio juris*). How convincing do you find the ILA's reasoning in the excerpt below that words alone can, at least in some situations, substitute for real practice on the ground in the formation of customary international law?

STATEMENT OF PRINCIPLES APPLICABLE TO THE FORMATION OF GENERAL CUSTOMARY INTERNATIONAL LAW

International Law Association (2000)

* * *

19. *It appears that, in the conduct of States and international courts and tribunals, a substantial manifestation of acceptance (consent or belief) by States that a customary rule exists may compensate for a relative lack of practice, and vice versa.*

COMMENTARY.

(a) The view has already been expressed in this Statement that the subjective element is not in fact usually a *necessary* ingredient in the formation of customary international law—certainly on the part of any given State which is allegedly bound by the putative customary rule. But whether or not this approach is accepted, what seems clear is that, if there is a good deal of State practice, the need (if such there be) also to demonstrate the presence of the subjective element is likely to be dispensed with. There are, for instance, numerous examples where the ICJ has simply referred to the constant and uniform practice of States, with-

out any reference to the subjective element. For voluntarists, this is because, the more widespread the practice, the easier it is to infer the requisite consent. *Mutatis mutandis*, this is also the case for supporters of the
belief approach. For Mendelson, it is simply because it is a misconception
to think that the subjective element is invariably (or perhaps even usually) necessary. But whatever the theory, the result is the same: the more
the practice, the less the need for the subjective element.

(b) More controversial is the converse proposition, that if there is a great
deal of evidence of consent or *opinio juris*, less proof of practice is required. Some would question it on the grounds that customary law without custom (practice) is a contradiction in terms. The answer to this could
be that terminology is not the key issue. It could also be recalled that, as
stated in Section 4, statements are a form of State practice. Others would
have reservations on the grounds that, to put it crudely, "talk is cheap"
and only practice represents a sufficiently serious *prise de position* by
States. But it has already been suggested that this is something of an
over-simplification: see Sections 3 and 4. In particular, verbal acts can
constitute a form of State practice, and not all verbal acts carry little
weight. For those who, like Cheng, consider that *opinio juris* is the key
element in customary law, there is no need to attach excessive importance
to State practice anyway. And for voluntarists, consent is the key ingredient. Even though this Statement does not endorse either of these positions in an unqualified form, it has already been stated (in Section 18)
that, if an individual State *does* consent to a rule, that State will normally
be bound by it. It follows that, if the generality of States consent, they will
all be bound. Consequently, this assertion in this Section appear[s] to be
correct as a matter of theory. It also seems to correspond to current
trends in the practice of international courts and tribunals. For instance,
in the *Nicaragua case (Merits)*, the International Court of Justice, whilst
re-emphasizing the need for both the objective and the subjective elements, in fact demanded very little evidence of actual practice in the face
of what it apparently considered to be clear-cut proof of the *opinio juris* of
the international community embodied in such instruments as the Declaration on Principles of International Law concerning Friendly Relations
and Co-operation among States in Accordance with the Charter of the
United Nations. On the basis of this case in particular, Kirgis has specu-
lated that there might be a "sliding scale":

> On the sliding scale, very frequent, consistent state practice estab-
> lishes a customary rule without much (or any) affirmative showing of
> an *opinio juris* so long as it is not negated by evidence of non-
> normative intent. As the frequency and consistency of the practice
> decline in any series of cases, a stronger showing of an *opinio juris* is
> required. At the other end of the scale a clearly demonstrated *opinio
> juris* establishes a customary rule without much (or any) affirmative

showing that governments are consistently behaving in accordance with the asserted rule.

But if this approach is to be accepted, it can only be with the clear proviso that the evidence of States' intentions or opinio juris must be clear-cut and unequivocal. This is a very high threshold. * * *

C. CUSTOMARY INTERNATIONAL LAW IN HUMAN RIGHTS CASES IN AMERICAN COURTS

In the following two cases, different judges on the same court (writing 23 years apart) display different attitudes towards the plaintiffs' claims that the defendants violated customary international law in the human rights context.

Filartiga is the case that revived the Alien Tort Claims Act after nearly two centuries of hibernation. What is the role of customary international law in this case, and how does the court establish it?

FILARTIGA V. PEÑA–IRALA
United States Circuit Court
630 F.2d 876 (2d Cir. 1980)

JUDGE KAUFMAN:

* * *

I

The appellants, plaintiffs below, are citizens of the Republic of Paraguay. Dr. Joel Filartiga, a physician, describes himself as a longstanding opponent of the government of President Alfredo Stroessner, which has held power in Paraguay since 1954. His daughter, Dolly Filartiga, arrived in the United States in 1978 under a visitor's visa, and has since applied for permanent political asylum. The Filartigas brought this action in the Eastern District of New York against Americo Norberto Peña-Irala (Peña), also a citizen of Paraguay, for wrongfully causing the death of Dr. Filartiga's seventeen-year old son, Joelito. Because the district court dismissed the action for want of subject matter jurisdiction, we must accept as true the allegations contained in the Filartigas' complaint and affidavits for purposes of this appeal.

The appellants contend that on March 29, 1976, Joelito Filartiga was kidnapped and tortured to death by Peña, who was then Inspector General of Police in Asuncion, Paraguay. Later that day, the police brought Dolly Filartiga to Peña's home where she was confronted with the body of her brother, which evidenced marks of severe torture. As she fled, horrified, from the house, Peña followed after her shouting, "Here you have what you have been looking for for so long and what you deserve. Now shut up." The Filartigas claim that Joelito was tortured and killed in retaliation for his father's political activities and beliefs.

In July of 1978, Peña sold his house in Paraguay and entered the United States under a visitor's visa. He was accompanied by Juana Bautista Fernandez Villalba, who had lived with him in Paraguay. The couple remained in the United States beyond the term of their visas, and were living in Brooklyn, New York, when Dolly Filartiga, who was then living in Washington, D. C., learned of their presence. Acting on information provided by Dolly the Immigration and Naturalization Service arrested Peña and his companion, both of whom were subsequently ordered deported on April 5, 1979 following a hearing. They had then resided in the United States for more than nine months.

Almost immediately, Dolly caused Peña to be served with a summons and civil complaint at the Brooklyn Navy Yard, where he was being held pending deportation. The complaint alleged that Peña had wrongfully caused Joelito's death by torture and sought compensatory and punitive damages of $10,000,000. The Filartigas also sought to enjoin Peña's deportation to ensure his availability for testimony at trial. The cause of action is stated as arising under "wrongful death statutes; the U. N. Charter; the Universal Declaration on Human Rights; the U. N. Declaration Against Torture; the American Declaration of the Rights and Duties of Man; and other pertinent declarations, documents and practices constituting the customary international law of human rights and the law of nations," as well as 28 U.S.C. § 1350, Article II, sec. 2 and the Supremacy Clause of the U. S. Constitution. Jurisdiction is claimed under the general federal question provision, 28 U.S.C. § 1331 and, principally on this appeal, under the Alien Tort Statute, 28 U.S.C. § 1350.

* * * The Filartigas submitted the affidavits of a number of distinguished international legal scholars, who stated unanimously that the law of nations prohibits absolutely the use of torture as alleged in the complaint.[4] Peña, in support of his motion to dismiss on the ground of *forum non conveniens,* submitted the affidavit of his Paraguayan counsel, Jose Emilio Gorostiaga, who averred that Paraguayan law provides a full and adequate civil remedy for the wrong alleged. Dr. Filartiga has not com-

---

[4] Richard Falk, the Albert G. Milbank Professor of International Law and Practice at Princeton University, and a former Vice President of the American Society of International Law, avers that, in his judgment, "it is now beyond reasonable doubt that torture of a person held in detention that results in severe harm or death is a violation of the law of nations." Thomas Franck, professor of international law at New York University and Director of the New York University Center for International Studies offers his opinion that torture has now been rejected by virtually all nations, although it was once commonly used to extract confessions. Richard Lillich, the Howard W. Smith Professor of Law at the University of Virginia School of Law, concludes, after a lengthy review of the authorities, that officially perpetrated torture is "a violation of international law (formerly called the law of nations)." Finally, Myres MacDougal, a former Sterling Professor of Law at the Yale Law School, and a past President of the American Society of International Law, states that torture is an offense against the law of nations, and that "it has long been recognized that such offenses vitally affect relations between states."

menced such an action, however, believing that further resort to the courts of his own country would be futile.

* * *

II

Appellants rest their principal argument in support of federal jurisdiction upon the Alien Tort Statute, 28 U.S.C. § 1350, which provides: "The district courts shall have original jurisdiction of any civil action by an alien for a tort only, committed in violation of the law of nations or a treaty of the United States." Since appellants do not contend that their action arises directly under a treaty of the United States[7], a threshold question on the jurisdictional issue is whether the conduct alleged violates the law of nations. In light of the universal condemnation of torture in numerous international agreements, and the renunciation of torture as an instrument of official policy by virtually all of the nations of the world (in principle if not in practice), we find that an act of torture committed by a state official against one held in detention violates established norms of the international law of human rights, and hence the law of nations.

The Supreme Court has enumerated the appropriate sources of international law. The law of nations "may be ascertained by consulting the works of jurists, writing professedly on public law; or by the general usage and practice of nations; or by judicial decisions recognizing and enforcing that law." *United States v. Smith*, 18 U.S. (5 Wheat.) 153, 160–61 (1820). In *Smith*, a statute proscribing "the crime of piracy [on the high seas] as defined by the law of nations," 3 Stat. 510(a) (1819), was held sufficiently determinate in meaning to afford the basis for a death sentence. The *Smith* Court discovered among the works of Lord Bacon, Grotius, Bochard and other commentators a genuine consensus that rendered the crime "sufficiently and constitutionally defined." *Smith, supra,* 18 U.S. (5 Wheat.) at 162.

The Paquete Habana, 175 U.S. 677 (1900), reaffirmed that

> where there is no treaty, and no controlling executive or legislative act or judicial decision, resort must be had to the customs and usages of civilized nations; and, as evidence of these, to the works of jurists and commentators, who by years of labor, research and experience, have made themselves peculiarly well acquainted with the subjects of which they treat. Such works are resorted to by judicial tribunals, not for the speculations of their authors concerning what the law ought to be, but for trustworthy evidence of what the law really is.

---

[7] Appellants "associate themselves with" the argument of some of the *amici curiae* that their claim arises directly under a treaty of the United States, but nonetheless primarily rely upon treaties and other international instruments as evidence of an emerging norm of customary international law, rather then independent sources of law.

Id. at 700. Modern international sources confirm the propriety of this approach.

* * *

The requirement that a rule command the "general assent of civilized nations" to become binding upon them all is a stringent one. Were this not so, the courts of one nation might feel free to impose idiosyncratic legal rules upon others, in the name of applying international law. Thus, in *Banco Nacional de Cuba v. Sabbatino*, 376 U.S. 398 (1964), the Court declined to pass on the validity of the Cuban government's expropriation of a foreign-owned corporation's assets, noting the sharply conflicting views on the issue propounded by the capital-exporting, capital-importing, socialist and capitalist nations.

The case at bar presents us with a situation diametrically opposed to the conflicted state of law that confronted the *Sabbatino* Court. Indeed, to paraphrase that Court's statement, there are few, if any, issues in international law today on which opinion seems to be so united as the limitations on a state's power to torture persons held in its custody.

The United Nations Charter makes it clear that in this modern age a state's treatment of its own citizens is a matter of international concern. It provides:

> With a view to the creation of conditions of stability and well-being which are necessary for peaceful and friendly relations among nations * * * the United Nations shall promote * * * universal respect for, and observance of, human rights and fundamental freedoms for all without distinctions as to race, sex, language or religion.

And further:

> All members pledge themselves to take joint and separate action in cooperation with the Organization for the achievement of the purposes set forth in Article 55.

While this broad mandate has been held not to be wholly self-executing, this observation alone does not end our inquiry. For although there is no universal agreement as to the precise extent of the "human rights and fundamental freedoms" guaranteed to all by the Charter, there is at present no dissent from the view that the guaranties include, at a bare minimum, the right to be free from torture. This prohibition has become part of customary international law, as evidenced and defined by the Universal Declaration of Human Rights, General Assembly Resolution 217 (III)(A) (Dec. 10, 1948) which states, in the plainest of terms, "no one shall be subjected to torture." The General Assembly has declared that the Charter precepts embodied in this Universal Declaration "constitute basic principles of international law." G.A.Res. 2625 (XXV) (Oct. 24, 1970).

Particularly relevant is the Declaration on the Protection of All Persons from Being Subjected to Torture, General Assembly Resolution 3452, 30 U.N. GAOR Supp. (No. 34) 91, U.N.Doc. A/1034 (1975) * * *. The Declaration expressly prohibits any state from permitting the dastardly and totally inhuman act of torture. Torture, in turn, is defined as "any act by which severe pain and suffering, whether physical or mental, is intentionally inflicted by or at the instigation of a public official on a person for such purposes as * * * intimidating him or other persons." The Declaration goes on to provide that "[w]here it is proved that an act of torture or other cruel, inhuman or degrading treatment or punishment has been committed by or at the instigation of a public official, the victim shall be afforded redress and compensation, in accordance with national law." This Declaration, like the Declaration of Human Rights before it, was adopted without dissent by the General Assembly.

These U.N. declarations are significant because they specify with great precision the obligations of member nations under the Charter. Since their adoption, "[m]embers can no longer contend that they do not know what human rights they promised in the Charter to promote." Moreover, a U.N. Declaration is, according to one authoritative definition, "a formal and solemn instrument, suitable for rare occasions when principles of great and lasting importance are being enunciated.," Accordingly, it has been observed that the Universal Declaration of Human Rights "no longer fits into the dichotomy of 'binding treaty' against 'non-binding pronouncement,' but is rather an authoritative statement of the international community." Thus, a Declaration creates an expectation of adherence, and "insofar as the expectation is gradually justified by State practice, a declaration may by custom become recognized as laying down rules binding upon the States." Indeed, several commentators have concluded that the Universal Declaration has become, *in toto,* a part of binding, customary international law.

Turning to the act of torture, we have little difficulty discerning its universal renunciation in the modern usage and practice of nations. The international consensus surrounding torture has found expression in numerous international treaties and accords. *E. g., American Convention on Human Rights*, Art. 5, OAS Treaty Series No. 36 at 1, OAS Off. Rec. OEA/Ser 4 v/II 23, doc. 21, rev. 2 (English ed., 1975) ("No one shall be subjected to torture or to cruel, inhuman or degrading punishment or treatment"); International Covenant on Civil and Political Rights, U.N. General Assembly Res. 2200 (XXI)A, U.N. Doc. A/6316 (Dec. 16, 1966) (identical language); *European Convention for the Protection of Human Rights and Fundamental Freedoms,* Art. 3, Council of Europe, European Treaty Series No. 5 (1968), 213 U.N.T.S. 211 *(semble).* The substance of these international agreements is reflected in modern municipal—i. e., national—law as well. Although torture was once a routine concomitant of criminal interrogations in many nations, during the modern and hopefully more enlightened era it has been universally renounced. According to one survey, torture is prohibited, expressly or implicitly, by the constitutions of over fifty-five nations, including both the United States and Paraguay. Our State Department reports a general recognition of this principle:

> There now exists an international consensus that recognizes basic human rights and obligations owed by all governments to their citizens. * * * There is no doubt that these rights are often violated; but virtually all governments acknowledge their validity.

We have been directed to no assertion by any contemporary state of a right to torture its own or another nation's citizens. Indeed, United States diplomatic contacts confirm the universal abhorrence with which torture is viewed:

> In exchanges between United States embassies and all foreign states with which the United States maintains relations, it has been the Department of State's general experience that no government has asserted a right to torture its own nationals. Where reports of torture elicit some credence, a state usually responds by denial or, less frequently, by asserting that the conduct was unauthorized or constituted rough treatment short of torture.[15]

Having examined the sources from which customary international law is derived the usage of nations, judicial opinions and the works of jurists we conclude that official torture is now prohibited by the law of nations. The prohibition is clear and unambiguous, and admits of no distinction between treatment of aliens and citizens. Accordingly, we must conclude that the dictum in *Dreyfus v. von Finck*, 534 F.2d at 31, to the effect that "violations of international law do not occur when the aggrieved parties are nationals of the acting state," is clearly out of tune with the current usage and practice of international law. The treaties and accords cited above, as well as the express foreign policy of our own government, all make it clear that international law confers fundamental rights upon all people vis-a-vis their own governments. While the ultimate scope of those rights will be a subject for continuing refinement and elaboration, we hold that the right to be free from torture is now among them. * * *

* * *

---

[15] The fact that the prohibition of torture is often honored in the breach does not diminish its binding effect as a norm of international law. As one commentator has put it, "The best evidence for the existence of international law is that every actual State recognizes that it does exist and that it is itself under an obligation to observe it. States often violate international law, just as individuals often violate municipal law; but no more than individuals do States defend their violations by claiming that they are above the law." J. Brierly, *The Outlook for International Law* 4–5 (Oxford 1944).

In the twentieth century the international community has come to recognize the common danger posed by the flagrant disregard of basic human rights and particularly the right to be free of torture. Spurred first by the Great War, and then the Second, civilized nations have banded together to prescribe acceptable norms of international behavior. From the ashes of the Second World War arose the United Nations Organization, amid hopes that an era of peace and cooperation had at last begun. Though many of these aspirations have remained elusive goals, that circumstance cannot diminish the true progress that has been made. In the modern age, humanitarian and practical considerations have combined to lead the nations of the world to recognize that respect for fundamental human rights is in their individual and collective interest. Among the rights universally proclaimed by all nations, as we have noted, is the right to be free of physical torture. Indeed, for purposes of civil liability, the torturer has become like the pirate and slave trader before him *hostis humani generis,* an enemy of all mankind. Our holding today, giving effect to a jurisdictional provision enacted by our First Congress, is a small but important step in the fulfillment of the ageless dream to free all people from brutal violence.

In reading the next case, watch how the Court defines and then tries to ascertain customary international law.

FLORES V. SOUTHERN PERU COPPER CORP.

United States Circuit Court
343 F.3d 140 (2d Cir. 2003)

JUDGE CABRANES:

* * *

I.   STATEMENT OF THE CASE

* * *

Plaintiffs in this case are residents of Ilo, Peru, and the representatives of deceased Ilo residents. Defendant, SPCC, is a United States corporation headquartered in Arizona with its principal place of operations in Peru. It is majority-owned by Asarco Incorporated ("Asarco"), a Delaware corporation with its principal place of business in Peru. Asarco is a wholly-owned subsidiary of Grupo Mexico, S.A. de C.V., which is a Mexican corporation with its principal place of business in Mexico City. SPCC has operated copper mining, refining, and smelting operations in and around Ilo since 1960.

SPCC's operations emit large quantities of sulfur dioxide and very fine particles of heavy metals into the local air and water. Plaintiffs claim that these emissions have caused their respiratory illnesses and that this "egregious and deadly" local pollution constitutes a customary international law offense because it violates the "right to life," "right to health," and right to "sustainable development."[3]

SPCC's activities, as well as their environmental impact, are regulated by the government of Peru. Since 1960, commissions of the Peruvian government have conducted annual or semi-annual reviews of the impact of SPCC's activities on the ecology and agriculture of the region. These commissions have found that SPCC's activities have inflicted environmental damage affecting agriculture in the Ilo Valley and have required SPCC to pay fines and restitution to area farmers. In addition to imposing fines and permitting area residents to seek restitution, the government of Peru also has required SPCC to modify its operations in order to abate pollution and other environmental damage. Under the direction of Peru's Ministry of Energy and Mines ("MEM"), SPCC has conducted studies to ascertain the environmental impact of its operations and the technical and economic feasibility of abating that impact. SPCC is required to meet levels of emissions and discharges set by the MEM under Peruvian environmental laws enacted in 1993, and is subject to the jurisdiction of the courts of Peru.

* * *

[II. THE ALIEN TORT CLAIMS ACT]

    B.   THE "LAW OF NATIONS"

        1.   DEFINITION OF "LAW OF NATIONS," OR "CUSTOMARY INTERNATIONAL LAW," FOR PURPOSES OF THE ATCA

The ATCA permits an alien to assert a cause of action in tort for violations of a treaty of the United States and for violations of "the law of nations," which, as used in this statute, refers to the body of law known as customary international law. 28 U.S.C. § 1350. The determination of what offenses violate customary international law, however, is no simple task. Customary international law is discerned from myriad decisions made in numerous and varied international and domestic arenas. Furthermore, the relevant evidence of customary international law is widely dispersed and generally unfamiliar to lawyers and judges. These difficulties are compounded by the fact that customary international law—as the term itself implies—is created by the general customs and practices of nations and therefore does not stem from any single, definitive, readily-

---

[3] On appeal, plaintiffs only pursue their claims that defendant's conduct violates customary international law rights to life and health; they no longer base their argument on a right to "sustainable development."

identifiable source. All of these characteristics give the body of customary international law a "soft, indeterminate character," Louis Henkin, *International Law: Politics and Values* 29 (1995), that is subject to creative interpretation. *See Amerada Hess Shipping Corp. v. Argentine Republic*, 830 F.2d 421, 429 (2d Cir.1987) (Kearse, J., dissenting) (noting the problem of allowing jurisdiction to "ebb and flow with the vicissitudes of 'evolving standards of international law' "), *rev'd*, 488 U.S. 428. Accordingly, in determining what offenses violate customary international law, courts must proceed with extraordinary care and restraint.

In short, customary international law is composed only of those rules that States universally abide by, or accede to, out of a sense of legal obligation and mutual concern.

* * *

III. PLAINTIFFS HAVE FAILED TO ALLEGE A VIOLATION OF CUSTOMARY INTERNATIONAL LAW

Having established the proper framework for analyzing ATCA claims, we must now decide whether plaintiffs have alleged a violation of customary international law.

A. THE RIGHTS TO LIFE AND HEALTH ARE INSUFFICIENTLY DEFINITE TO CONSTITUTE RULES OF CUSTOMARY INTERNATIONAL LAW

As an initial matter, we hold that the asserted "right to life" and "right to health" are insufficiently definite to constitute rules of customary international law. As noted above, in order to state a claim under the ATCA, we have required that a plaintiff allege a violation of a "clear and unambiguous" rule of customary international law. *Filartiga*, 630 F.2d at 884 (holding that the prohibition on official torture is "clear and unambiguous" and, as such, can serve as a basis for suit under the ATCA); *see id.* at 888 (stating that in order to state a claim, a plaintiff must allege a violation of "well-established, universally recognized norms of international law"); *Kadic*, 70 F.3d at 239 (holding that federal jurisdiction lies under the ATCA if "the defendant's alleged conduct violates 'well-established, universally recognized norms of international law' * * * as opposed to 'idiosyncratic legal rules' " (quoting *Filartiga*, 630 F.2d at 888, 881)).

Far from being "clear and unambiguous," the statements relied on by plaintiffs to define the rights to life and health are vague and amorphous. For example, the statements that plaintiffs rely on to define the rights to life and health include the following:

> Everyone has the right to a standard of living adequate for the health and well-being of himself and of his family. * * *

Universal Declaration of Human Rights, Art. 25, G.A. Res. 217A(III), U.N. GAOR, 3d Sess., U.N. Doc. A/810, at 71 (1948).

> The States Parties to the present Covenant recognize the right of everyone to the enjoyment of the highest attainable standard of physical and mental health.

International Covenant on Economic, Social, and Cultural Rights, Art. 12, *opened for signature* Dec. 19, 1966, 993 U.N.T.S. 3, 6 I.L.M. 360.

> Human beings are * * * entitled to a healthy and productive life in harmony with nature.

Rio Declaration on Environment and Development ("Rio Declaration"), United Nations Conference on Environment and Development, Rio de Janeiro, Brazil, June 13, 1992, Principle 1, 31 I.L.M. 874.

These principles are boundless and indeterminate. They express virtuous goals understandably expressed at a level of abstraction needed to secure the adherence of States that disagree on many of the particulars regarding how actually to achieve them. But in the words of a sister circuit, they "state abstract rights and liberties devoid of articulable or discernable standards and regulations." *Beanal*, 197 F.3d at 167. The precept that "[h]uman beings are * * * entitled to a healthy and productive life in harmony with nature," Rio Declaration, Principle 1, 31 I.L.M. 874, for example, utterly fails to specify what conduct would fall within or outside of the law. Similarly, the exhortation that all people are entitled to the "highest attainable standard of physical and mental health," International Covenant on Economic, Social, and Cultural Rights, Art. 12, 993 U.N.T.S. 3, proclaims only nebulous notions that are infinitely malleable.

In support of plaintiffs' argument that the statements and instruments discussed above are part of customary international law, plaintiffs attempt to underscore the universality of the principles asserted by pointing out that they "contain *no limitations as to how or by whom these rights may be violated.*" However, this assertion proves too much; because of the conceded absence of any "limitations" on these "rights," they do not meet the requirement of our law that rules of customary international law be clear, definite, and unambiguous.

For the foregoing reasons, plaintiffs have failed to establish the existence of a customary international law "right to life" or "right to health."

    B.   Plaintiffs Have Not Submitted Evidence Sufficient to Establish that Customary International Law Prohibits Intranational Pollution

Although customary international law does not protect a right to life or right to health, plaintiffs' complaint may be construed to assert a claim under a more narrowly-defined customary international law rule against *intranational* pollution. However, the voluminous documents and the affidavits of international law scholars submitted by plaintiffs fail to demonstrate the existence of any such norm of customary international law.

In support of their claims, plaintiffs have submitted the following types of evidence: (i) treaties, conventions, and covenants; (ii) non-binding declarations of the United Nations General Assembly, (iii) other non-binding multinational declarations of principle; (iv) decisions of multinational tribunals, and (v) affidavits of international law scholars. We analyze each type of evidence submitted by the plaintiffs in turn.

1.   TREATIES, CONVENTIONS, AND COVENANTS

Plaintiffs rely on numerous treaties, conventions, and covenants in support of their claims.[31] Although these instruments are proper evidence of customary international law to the extent that they create legal obligations among the States parties to them, plaintiffs have not demonstrated that the particular instruments on which they rely establish a legal rule prohibiting intranational pollution.

Treaties, which sometimes are entitled "conventions" or "covenants," are proper evidence of customary international law because, and insofar as, they create *legal obligations* akin to contractual obligations on the States parties to them. Like contracts, these instruments are legally binding only on States that become parties to them by consenting to be bound.

All treaties that have been ratified by at least two States provide *some* evidence of the custom and practice of nations. However, a treaty will only constitute *sufficient proof* of a norm of customary international law if an overwhelming majority of States have ratified the treaty, *and* those States uniformly and consistently act in accordance with its principles. The evidentiary weight to be afforded to a given treaty varies greatly depending on (i) how many, and which, States have ratified the treaty, and (ii) the degree to which those States actually implement and abide by the principles set forth in the treaty.

With respect to the first of these factors, the more States that have ratified a treaty, and the greater the relative influence of those States in international affairs, the greater the treaty's evidentiary value. With respect to the second of these factors—the degree to which States parties actually implement and abide by the principles set forth in the treaty— the evidentiary value of a treaty increases if the States parties have taken tangible action to implement the principles embodied in the treaty. For example, in the United States, a treaty that is self-executing or that has been executed through an Act of Congress—and therefore gives rise to rights legally enforceable in our courts—provides greater evidence of the

---

[31] Although the ATCA provides a cause of action to aliens for torts "committed in violation of * * * a treaty of the United States," 28 U.S.C. § 1350, as well as for violations of the law of nations, plaintiffs do not contend that defendant's actions violate a United States treaty. Instead, they rely on various multilateral treaties, conventions, and covenants as evidence of the "law of nations," or customary international law.

customs and practices of the United States than a treaty that has not been executed. Similarly, the evidentiary weight of a treaty increases if States parties have taken official action to enforce the principles set forth in the treaty either internationally or within their own borders.

The treaties on which plaintiffs principally rely include: the International Covenant on Civil and Political Rights, *opened for signature* Dec. 19, 1966 (ratified by the United States June 8, 1992); the American Convention on Human Rights, Nov. 22, 1969; the International Covenant on Economic, Social and Cultural Rights, *opened for signature* Dec. 19, 1966; and the United Nations Convention on the Rights of the Child.

The only treaty relied on by plaintiffs that the United States has ratified is the non-self-executing International Covenant on Civil and Political Rights ("ICCPR"). In addition to the United States, 148 nations have ratified the ICCPR. Plaintiffs rely on Article 6(1) of the ICCPR, which states that "[e]very human being has the inherent right to life" that "shall be protected by law," and that "[n]o one shall be arbitrarily deprived of his life." As noted above, the "right to life" is insufficiently definite to give rise to a rule of customary international law. Because no other provision of the ICCPR so much as suggests an international law norm prohibiting intranational pollution, the ICCPR does not provide a basis for plaintiffs' claim that defendant has violated a rule of customary international law.

Similarly, the American Convention on Human Rights ("American Convention") does not assist plaintiffs because, while it notes the broad and indefinite "[r]ight to [l]ife," it does not refer to the more specific question of environmental pollution, let alone set parameters of acceptable or unacceptable limits. Moreover, the United States has declined to ratify the American Convention for more than three decades, indicating that this document has not even been universally embraced by all of the prominent States within the region in which it purports to apply.

Plaintiffs also rely on the unratified International Covenant on Economic, Social and Cultural Rights ("ICESCR"). This instrument arguably refers to the topic of pollution in article 12, which "recognize[s] the right of everyone to the enjoyment of the highest attainable standard of physical and mental health," and instructs the States parties to take the steps necessary for "[t]he improvement of all aspects of environmental and industrial hygiene." Although article 12(2)(b) instructs States to take steps to abate environmental pollution within their borders, it does not mandate particular measures or specify what levels of pollution are acceptable. Instead, it is vague and aspirational, and there is no evidence that the States parties have taken significant uniform steps to put it into practice. *See, e.g.,* Oona A. Hathaway, *Do Human Rights Treaties Make a Difference?*, 111 Yale L.J. 1935, 1965 & n.14 (2002) (noting the absence of data indicating compliance of States parties with their obligations under the ICESCR).

Finally, even if this provision were sufficient to create a rule of customary international law, the rule would apply only to state actors because the provision addresses only "the steps to be taken *by the States Parties*," ICESCR art. 12(2) (emphasis added), and does not profess to govern the conduct of private actors such as defendant SPCC.

The last treaty on which plaintiffs principally rely is the United Nations Convention on the Rights of the Child (1989), which has not been ratified by the United States. Plaintiffs rely on two sections of the Convention in support of their claims. First, they cite Article 24, section 1, of the Convention, which "recognize[s] the right of the child to the enjoyment of the highest attainable standard of health." This provision does not address the issue of intranational pollution. Moreover, it is extremely vague, clearly aspirational in nature, and does not even purport to reflect the actual customs and practices of States. Plaintiffs also cite Article 24, section 2(c) of the Convention, which instructs States to "take appropriate measures * * * [t]o combat disease and malnutrition * * * through * * * the provision of adequate nutritious foods and clean drinking water, taking into consideration the dangers and risks of environmental pollution." While Article 24 of the Convention expressly addresses environmental pollution, it does not attempt to set its parameters or regulate it, let alone to proscribe it. Rather, it instructs States themselves to "consider the dangers and risks of environmental pollution" in determining what measures they deem to be "appropriate" to combat disease and malnutrition. Accordingly, instead of articulating, reflecting, or governing the actual customs and practices of States, the Convention defers to the States' own practices regarding pollution control. Moreover, as with Article 12 of the ICESCR, this provision only addresses concerns as to which "appropriate measures" are to be taken *by States themselves*, and does not profess to govern the conduct of private parties such as defendant SPCC.

For the foregoing reasons, the treaties, conventions or covenants relied on by plaintiffs do not support the existence of a customary international law rule against intranational pollution.

* * *

Are *Filartiga* and *Flores* reconcilable? What explains the different outcomes? Differences in the law pertaining to torture on the one hand and to environmental degradation on the other hand? Or rather differences in the degree of judicial activism? Reconsider the latter question in light of the following two texts:

IAN BROWNLIE, PRINCIPLES OF INTERNATIONAL LAW
(7th ed. 2008)

* * *

The vast majority of States and authoritative writers would now recognize that the fundamental principles of human rights form part of customary or general international law, although they would not necessarily agree on the identity of the fundamental principles. In 1970 the International Court, delivering judgment in the *Barcelona Traction* case, referred to obligations *erga omnes* in contemporary international law and these were stated to include "the principles and rules concerning the basic rights of the human person, including protection from slavery and racial discrimination." The Final Act of the Helsinki Conference of 1975 included a "Declaration of Principles Guiding Relations between Participating States." This Declaration includes a section on human rights and the following paragraph appears in that section:

> In the field of human rights and fundamental freedoms, the participating States will act in conformity with the purposes and principles of the Charter of the United Nations and with the Universal Declaration of Human Rights. They will also fulfil their obligations as set forth in the international declarations and agreements in this field, including *inter alia* the International Covenants on Human Rights, by which they may be bound.

It is evident that the participating States recognize that human rights standards form part of general international law: thus the *Digest of United States Practice in International Law* (United States Department of State, 1975, p. 7) sets forth the Declaration referred to in the previous paragraph under the heading: "Rights and Duties of States."

The significance of the role of the "customary international law of human rights" is recognized in the most recent edition of the *Restatement of the Law: The Third*. Under the rubric just quoted the following proposition appears:

> A State violates international law if, as a matter of State policy, it practices, encourages, or condones
>
> > (1) genocide,
> >
> > (2) slavery or slave trade,
> >
> > (3) the murder or causing the disappearance of individuals,
> >
> > (4) torture or other cruel, inhuman or degrading treatment or punishment,
> >
> > (5) prolonged arbitrary detention,
> >
> > (6) systematic racial discrimination, or

(7) a consistent pattern of gross violations of internationally recognised human rights.

The literature of human rights tends to neglect the role, or potential role,
of customary law. * * *

JAMES C. HATHAWAY, THE RIGHTS OF REFUGEES UNDER INTERNATIONAL LAW

(2005)

* * *

It must be acknowledged * * * that the very nature of customary international law sits uncomfortably with the search for universal norms of human rights. Customary law exists to formalize interstate practice that
has come to represent an agreed benchmark of acceptable relations between and among states. Custom has legitimacy as law only because interstate behavior is accepted by states as an ongoing medium of negotiation. It is clearly understood by governments that there is no customary
law until there is both agreement on "terms" signaled by constant and
relatively uniform interstate practice, and a sufficient expression of the
willingness of states to be bound by that agreement. This structure is
highly unlikely to produce universal human rights norms, as was observed by Lord Hoffmann in the House of Lords:

> I do not think it is possible to apply the rules for the development of
> rules of international law concerning the relations of states with each
> other (for example, as to how boundaries should be drawn) to the
> fundamental human rights of citizens against the state. There are
> unhappily many fundamental rights which would fail such a test of
> state practice, and the Refugee Convention is itself a recognition of
> this fact. In my opinion, a different approach is needed. Fundamental
> human rights are the minimum rights which a state ought to concede
> to its citizens. For the purpose of deciding what these minimum
> rights are, international instruments are important even if many
> states in practice disregard them * * * [because they] show recogni-
> tion that such rights ought to exist.

The essential problem with reliance on custom is that human rights will
only rarely be subject to the kind of interstate give and take that is the
essence of customary lawmaking. The requisite pattern of dealing may,
for example, be observed in regard to the rights of aliens, where the mutual self-interest of states of nationality and the states in which aliens are
located has produced observable patterns of affirmative protection and
forbearance. Relevant interaction between and among states regarding
the rights of human beings generally, however, is rare.

Schachter made a creative effort to overcome this problem by counting the willingness of states to condemn particular forms of human rights abuse as a relevant form of interstate dealing. His argument is that consistent censure of invidious conduct is a sufficiently clear pattern of interaction to render the condemned conduct contrary to customary law. The problem with this approach, however, is that the activity consistently engaged in by states (study and condemnation) is not the subject of the putative customary norm (for example, freedom from arbitrary detention). Because the basis of customary law formation is concrete performance or self-restraint *in regard to* the matter said to acquire binding force, the behavior relied upon by Schachter can at best reinforce as customary law the Charter-derived *droit de regard*. But it is not authority for the existence of new substantive norms of universal human rights law.

* * *

According to Brownlie and Hathaway, what is special about customary international law in the human rights context? In particular, should customary international law be treated differently here as opposed to other fields? How do the approaches taken by Brownlie and Hathaway relate to the fundamental conceptions of international law discussed at the beginning of Chapter III?

3. GENERAL PRINCIPLES IN A NEW WORLD ORDER

Just like treaties and custom, general principles continue to play an important role today. In fact, they have experienced something of a renaissance in the last several decades. As the range of international disputes has grown, so too has the need to resort to such principles because more specific sources of international law are often lacking. This is true for a broad variety of decisionmakers, ranging from international criminal courts to arbitral panels and the WTO Appellate Body. (We will see some of this in Chapter IX below).

Yet in the new (post-World War II) global order, "general principles recognized by civilized nations" have also become more problematic. Two particular challenges have presented themselves. The first challenge is due to the increasing number and diversity of nation states (Chapter VI.1.) and to the fact that the club of "civilized nations" can no longer be limited to Western countries; this has made it much more difficult to ascertain principles that are generally shared. The second modern challenge involves the broader question of whether the traditional view of principles has become too narrow.

The excerpt below captures the first of these challenges. Does Judge Simma's effort to ascertain a general principle meet this challenge?

THE CASE CONCERNING OIL PLATFORMS
(IRAN V. UNITED STATES)

International Court of Justice
2003 I.C. J. 161

[The *Case Concerning Oil Platforms* resulted from allegations that both Iran and the United States had violated provisions of a 1955 treaty guaranteeing unimpeded commerce between the two countries. Iranian allegations of breach by the United States were based on U.S. attacks on three Iranian offshore oil platforms. They were dismissed on the ground that the attacks did not in fact impede commerce since the platforms were under repair and non-operational at the time of the attacks. Similarly, the U.S. counter-claim that Iranian attacks on U.S. ships violated the commerce provisions of the treaty was dismissed on the basis that none of the ships was engaged in commercial activities at the time.

Judge Simma, writing a Separate Opinion in the case, took up the question whether Iran could be held liable under the 1955 treaty by reason of mine-laying activities in the Persian Gulf during Iran's war with Iraq. He noted in particular that "[b]y laying mines without warning commercial shipping of all nationalities in the Persian Gulf * * * Iran created dangerous and more onerous conditions for commercial shipping also between the two Parties [i.e. between Iran and the United States]" (para. 59). Yet it was also true that not only Iran, but also Iraq had engaged in mine-laying activities. The question, then, was whether Iran was responsible to make reparations to the U.S. under the treaty since not all of the harm caused by the mine-laying was attributable to Iran's actions. Indeed, Judge Simma clearly acknowledged that it was "difficult—if not impossible—to measure with an exactitude the negative impact of individual Iraqi or Iranian actions on the economic conditions of commerce, let alone on American commerce specifically" (para.64).

To resolve the question of attribution of responsibility, Judge Simma turned to an analysis based on general principles of international law.]

SEPARATE OPINION OF JUDGE SIMMA

* * *

65. Responsibility, however, is another matter. It is clear that a series of actions taken by each party to the war necessarily disturbed the economic environment (even if unintentionally). But what conclusion is to be drawn from this? Should we hold both States equally responsible for the impediments caused to commerce and navigation? Or can neither of the two

States be held responsible because it is impossible to determine precisely who did what?

66. In order to find a solution to our dilemma, I have engaged in some research in comparative law to see whether anything resembling a "general principle of law" within the meaning of Article 38, paragraph 1 (c), of the Statute of the Court can be developed from solutions arrived at in domestic law to come to terms with the problem of multiple tortfeasors. I submit that we find ourselves here in what I would call a textbook situation calling for such an exercise in legal analogy. To state its result forthwith: research into various common law jurisdictions as well as French, Swiss and German tort law indicates that the question has been taken up and solved by these legal systems with a consistency that is striking.

67. To begin with common law jurisprudence, in a well-known case heard by the Supreme Court of California, the plaintiff sued two defendants for injury to his right eye and face as a result of having been struck by birdshot discharged from a shotgun while the two defendants had been hunting in an open range. It was admitted that both defendants had fired at a quail, and that one piece of birdshot had hit the plaintiff's eye and another his lip. However, there was no means of determining which injury had been caused by which defendant. The defendants argued that they were not joint tortfeasors because they had not been acting in concert, and that there was not sufficient evidence to show which of the two was guilty of the negligence that caused the injuries.

The trial court had determined that "the negligence of both defendants was the legal cause of the injury—or that both were responsible," even though "the court was unable to ascertain whether the shots were from the gun of one defendant or the other or one shot from each of them." The California Supreme Court went on to quote Dean Wigmore, a United States authority on tort law:

> "When two or more persons by their acts are possibly the sole cause of a harm * * * and the plaintiff has introduced evidence that the one of the two persons * * * is culpable, then the defendant has the burden of proving that the other person * * * was the sole cause of the harm. The real reason for the rule that each joint tortfeasor is responsible for the whole damage is the practical unfairness of denying the injured person redress simply because he cannot prove how much damage each did, when it is certain that between them they did all."

As a matter of fairness to the plaintiff, the court then reversed the burden of proof: each defendant had to prove that he had not caused the injury. Since such proof could not be put forward, the court held both defendants liable. The court dismissed the defendants' argument that causation was lacking between their acts and the plaintiff's damage. Most importantly, the court also dismissed the argument that the plaintiff should establish the portion of the damage caused by each tortfeasor in cases where there is a plurality of tortfeasors and where the damage cannot be apportioned among them.

68. This solution, which has since been embodied in the Restatement of Torts, is interesting in many ways. On the one hand, it recognizes the difficulty of a finding of responsibility where apportionment is impossible. On the other hand, it excludes as unfair a solution in which no one would be held responsible. Finally, this provides an answer by shifting the burden of proof on to each defendant. The solution provides the wrongdoer a way out—acknowledging the peculiarity of a situation where facts cannot be ascertained with certainty—while at the same time ensuring the plaintiff recovery for his injury if the defendant fails to show his innocence.

69. The same solution was adopted by Canadian courts in *Cook v. Lewis*. According to Markesinis and Deakin, English courts faced with the question of multiple tortfeasors are likely to take a similar approach.

70. In French law, too, multiple tortfeasors (irrespective of whether they are acting in concert) causing an indivisible damage are each responsible for the entirety of such damage. Each tortfeasor is considered as having caused the entire prejudice to the victim, who can recover in full from any of them. In any event, when French courts dealt with this question in the past, they typically discussed the *extent* of each tortfeasor's responsibility (partial or total) rather than responsibility as such. When unable to hold each defendant liable on the basis of a specific damage, French courts resorted to interpretations such as "collective breach of duty" or "collective duty to look after the object which caused the damage" even when tortfeasors had evidently not been acting with a common motive, merely out of fairness for the injured plaintiff. In fact, this solution had already been adopted in Roman law in the form of the cause of action concerning *"effusis et dejectis"* (things spilled or thrown out): whenever someone was injured by an object that had fallen from the unidentified window of an apartment building, all residents of such building were considered liable for the damage caused.

71. The same principles can be found in Swiss law, where Article 51 of the Code des Obligations states that, when multiple tortfeasors acting independently of each other cause a damage that cannot be divided among them, any of the tortfeasors can be held responsible in full—just like in the case of tortfeasors acting in concert. * * *

72. The way, finally, in which German tort law addresses our issue is virtually identical with the domestic solutions hitherto outlined. The pertinent provision of the German Civil Code (Bürgerliches Gesetzbuch), § 830, reads as follows:

> "1. If several persons through a jointly committed delict have caused damage, each is responsible for the damage. The same applies

if it cannot be discovered which of several participants has caused the damage through his action.

2. Instigators and accomplices are in the same position as joint actors."

The first sentence of § 830, paragraph 1, is not relevant to our case because it presupposes the pursuance of a common design by the tortfeasors. The same is valid regarding the provision's paragraph 2. However, the rule contained in the second sentence of § 830, paragraph 1, is to the point: its function is precisely to spare the victim the difficult, indeed impossible, task of proving which one of several tortfeasors actually caused the damage. The rule's applicability depends upon three conditions: first, each of the participants must have engaged in the activity leading to loss or damage (irrespective of causality); second, one of the participants must necessarily have caused such loss or damage; but, third, it is impossible to determine which one of the participants did so, in whole or in part.

73. Elevating the joint-and-several liability doctrine thus described to the level of international law in the present case would lead to a finding that Iran is responsible for damages, or impediments, that it did not directly cause. Personally, I would find it more objectionable not to hold Iran liable than to hold Iran liable for the entire damage caused to the United States as a result of actions taken during the Iran–Iraq war. In fact, I see no objection to holding Iran responsible for the entire damage even though it did not directly cause it all. * * *

74. On the basis of the (admittedly modest) study of comparative tort law thus provided, I venture to conclude that the principle of joint-and-several responsibility common to the jurisdictions that I have considered can properly be regarded as a "general principle of law" within the meaning of Article 38, paragraph 1 (c), of the Court's Statute. I submit that this principle should have been applied in our present case to the effect that, even though responsibility for the impediment caused to United States commerce with Iran cannot (and ought not) be apportioned between Iran and Iraq, Iran should nevertheless have been held in breach of its treaty obligations.

* * *

Should Iran be bound by what American, French, Swiss or German domestic courts have decided? If the answer is yes, would such "principles" also apply against China or Botswana? If the answer is no, what would it take to establish such general principles—a survey of the laws of all (nearly 200) countries in the world? Who should bear the burden of presenting the evidence? The tribunal? The party relying on the general principle?

As mentioned above, the second modern challenge regarding general principles is the question of whether the traditional monolithic conception has become too narrow. Just like treaties and custom, principles have arguably diversified. In the excerpt below, Oscar Schachter, one of the great American international law scholars of the late 20th century, suggests several types of principles.

OSCAR SCHACHTER, INTERNATIONAL LAW IN THEORY AND PRACTICE
(1991)

* * *

We can distinguish five categories of general principles that have been invoked and applied in international law discourse and cases. Each has a different basis for its authority and validity as law. They are:

(1) The principles of municipal law "recognized by civilized nations".

(2) General principles of law "derived from the specific nature of the international community".

(3) Principles "intrinsic to the idea of law and basic to all legal systems".

(4) Principles "valid through all kinds of societies in relationships of hierarchy and co-ordination".

(5) Principles of justice founded on "the very nature of man as a rational and social being".

Although these five categories are analytically distinct, it is not unusual for a particular general principle to fall into more than one of the categories. For example, the principle that no one shall be a judge in his own cause or that a victim of a legal wrong is entitled to reparation are considered part of most, if not all, systems of municipal law and as intrinsic to the basic idea of law.

Our first category, general principles of municipal law, has given rise to a considerable body of writing and much controversy. Article 38 (1) (c) of the Statute of the Court does not expressly refer to principles of national law but rather general principles "recognized by civilized nations".

* * *

Despite the eloquent arguments made for using national law principles as an independent source of international law, it cannot be said that either courts or the political organs of States have significantly drawn on municipal law principles as an autonomous and distinct ground for binding rules of conduct. It is true that the International Court and its predecessor the Permanent Court of International Justice have made reference on a number of occasions to "generally accepted practice" or "all systems of law" as a basis for its approval of a legal rule. (But curiously the Court has done so without explicit reference to its own statutory authority in Article 38 (I) (*c*).) Those references to national law have most often been to highly general ideas of legal liability or precepts of judicial administration. In the former category, we find the much-quoted principles of the *Chorzów Factory* case that "every violation of an engagement involves an obligation to make reparation" and that "a party cannot take advantage of his own wrong". These maxims and certain maxims of legal interpretation, as for example, *lex specialis derogat generalis*, and "no one may transfer more than he has", are also regarded as notions intrinsic to the idea of law and legal reasoning. As such they can be (and have been) accepted not as municipal law, but as general postulates of international law, even if not customary law in the specific sense of that concept.

* * *

The second category of general principles included in our list comprises principles derived from the specific character of the international community. The most obvious candidates for this category of principles are those mentioned in the last section of Chapter II as the necessary principles of co-existence. They include the principles of *pacta sunt servanda*, non-intervention, territorial integrity, self-defence and the legal quality of States. Some of these principles are in the United Nations Charter and therefore part of treaty law, but others might appropriately be treated as principles required by the specific character of a society of sovereign independent members.

Our third category is even more abstract but not infrequently cited: principles "intrinsic to the idea of law and basic to all legal systems". As stated it includes an empirical element—namely, the ascertainment of principles found in "all" legal systems. It also includes a conceptual criterion—"intrinsic to the idea of law". Most of the principles cited in World Court and arbitral decisions as common in municipal law are also referred to as "basic" to all law. In this way, the tribunals move from a purely empirical municipal law basis to "necessary" principles based on the logic of the law.

* * *

[Let us turn] to the next two categories of general principles. The idea of principles "*jus rationale*" "valid through all kinds of human societies" (in Judge Tanaka's words) is associated with traditional natural law doctrine. At the present time its theological links are mainly historical as far as international law is concerned, but its principal justification does not depart too far from the classic natural law emphasis on the nature of "man", that is, on the human person as a rational and social creature.

The universalist implication of this theory—the idea of the unity of the human species—has had a powerful impetus in the present era. This is evidenced in at least three significant political and legal developments. The first is the global movements against discrimination on grounds of race, colour and sex. The second is the move toward general acceptance of human rights. The third is the increased fear of nuclear annihilation. These three developments strongly reinforce the universalistic values inherent in natural law doctrine. They have found expression in numerous international and constitutional law instruments as well as in popular movements throughout the world directed to humanitarian ends. Clearly, they are a "material source" of much of the new international law manifested in treaties and customary rules.

In so far as they are recognized as general principles of law, many tend to fall within our fifth category—the principles of natural justice. This concept is well known in many municipal law systems (although identified in diverse ways). "Natural justice" in its international legal manifestation has two aspects. One refers to the minimal standards of decency and respect for the individual human being that are largely spelled out in the human rights instruments. We can say that in this aspect, "natural justice" has been largely subsumed as a source of general principles by the human rights instruments. The second aspect of "natural justice" tends to be absorbed into the related concept of equity which includes such elements of "natural justice" as fairness, reciprocity, and consideration of the particular circumstances of a case.

* * *

How do Schachter's categories differ from the traditional conception of general principles? What changes from the traditional to the modern global order do his categories reflect? In particular, who produces the principles in his various categories, and what authority do those producers have?

4. THE EMERGENCE OF INTERNATIONAL "LEGISLATION"?

Under the traditional (Westphalian) system, legislation was not among the recognized sources of international law as evidenced by its absence from the catalog of sources in Article 38(1) of the ICJ Statute. In recent years, however, the UN Security Council may have changed that.

Virtually since its inception, the Security Council has passed Resolutions as contemplated by Article 24 of the UN Charter:

> In order to ensure prompt and effective action by the United Nations, its Members confer upon the Security Council primary responsibility for the maintenance of international peace and security, and agree that in carrying out its duties under this responsibility the Security Council acts on their behalf.

In addition, Article 25 provides:

> The Members of the United Nations agree to accept and carry out the decisions of the Security Council in accordance with the present Charter.

We saw the Security Council (and its Resolutions) in action under Chapter VII of the UN Charter in the context of "The Delegation of Sovereign Powers" (to international organizations) (Chapter VII.2.).

In 2001, the Security Council adopted Resolution 1373. How does it differ from the Resolutions you have seen before, in particular with regard to its scope and timeframe?

UNITED NATIONS SECURITY COUNCIL RESOLUTION 1373
(Adopted by Security Council 2001)

The Security Council,

Reaffirming its resolutions 1269 (1999) of 19 October 1999 and 1368 (2001) of 12 September 2001,

Reaffirming also its unequivocal condemnation of the terrorist attacks which took place in New York, Washington, D.C. and Pennsylvania on 11 September 2001, and expressing its determination to prevent all such acts,

Reaffirming further that such acts, like any act of international terrorism, constitute a threat to international peace and security,

Reaffirming the inherent right of individual or collective self-defence as recognized by the Charter of the United Nations as reiterated in resolution 1368 (2001),

Reaffirming the need to combat by all means, in accordance with the Charter of the United Nations, threats to international peace and security caused by terrorist acts,

Deeply concerned by the increase, in various regions of the world, of acts of terrorism motivated by intolerance or extremism,

Calling on States to work together urgently to prevent and suppress terrorist acts, including through increased cooperation and full implementation of the relevant international conventions relating to terrorism,

Recognizing the need for States to complement international cooperation by taking additional measures to prevent and suppress, in their territories through all lawful means, the financing and preparation of any acts of terrorism,

Reaffirming the principle established by the General Assembly in its declaration of October 1970 (resolution 2625 (XXV)) and reiterated by the Security Council in its resolution 1189 (1998) of 13 August 1998, namely that every State has the duty to refrain from organizing, instigating, assisting or participating in terrorist acts in another State or acquiescing in organized activities within its territory directed towards the commission of such acts,

Acting under Chapter VII of the Charter of the United Nations,

1. *Decides* that all States shall:

    (a) Prevent and suppress the financing of terrorist acts;

    (b) Criminalize the wilful provision or collection, by any means, directly or indirectly, of funds by their nationals or in their territories with the intention that the funds should be used, or in the knowledge that they are to be used, in order to carry out terrorist acts;

    (c) Freeze without delay funds and other financial assets or economic resources of persons who commit, or attempt to commit, terrorist acts or participate in or facilitate the commission of terrorist acts; of entities owned or controlled directly or indirectly by such persons; and of persons and entities acting on behalf of, or at the direction of such persons and entities, including funds derived or generated from property owned or controlled directly or indirectly by such persons and associated persons and entities;

    (d) Prohibit their nationals or any persons and entities within their territories from making any funds, financial assets or economic resources or financial or other related services available, directly or indirectly, for the benefit of persons who commit or attempt to commit or facilitate or participate in the commission of terrorist acts, of entities owned or controlled, directly or indirectly, by such persons and of persons and entities acting on behalf of or at the direction of such persons;

2. *Decides also* that all States shall:

    (a) Refrain from providing any form of support, active or passive, to entities or persons involved in terrorist acts, including by suppressing recruitment of members of terrorist groups and eliminating the supply of weapons to terrorists;

(b) Take the necessary steps to prevent the commission of terrorist acts, including by provision of early warning to other States by exchange of information;

(c) Deny safe haven to those who finance, plan, support, or commit terrorist acts, or provide safe havens;

(d) Prevent those who finance, plan, facilitate or commit terrorist acts from using their respective territories for those purposes against other States or their citizens;

(e) Ensure that any person who participates in the financing, planning, preparation or perpetration of terrorist acts or in supporting terrorist acts is brought to justice and ensure that, in addition to any other measures against them, such terrorist acts are established as serious criminal offences in domestic laws and regulations and that the punishment duly reflects the seriousness of such terrorist acts;

(f) Afford one another the greatest measure of assistance in connection with criminal investigations or criminal proceedings relating to the financing or support of terrorist acts, including assistance in obtaining evidence in their possession necessary for the proceedings;

(g) Prevent the movement of terrorists or terrorist groups by effective border controls and controls on issuance of identity papers and travel documents, and through measures for preventing counterfeiting, forgery or fraudulent use of identity papers and travel documents;

* * *

6. *Decides* to establish, in accordance with rule 28 of its provisional rules of procedure, a Committee of the Security Council, consisting of all the members of the Council, to monitor implementation of this resolution, with the assistance of appropriate expertise, and *calls upon* all States to report to the Committee, no later than 90 days from the date of adoption of this resolution and thereafter according to a timetable to be proposed by the Committee, on the steps they have taken to implement this resolution;

7. *Directs* the Committee to delineate its tasks, submit a work programme within 30 days of the adoption of this resolution, and to consider the support it requires, in consultation with the Secretary–General;

8. *Expresses* its determination to take all necessary steps in order to ensure the full implementation of this resolution, in accordance with its
responsibilities under the Charter;

9. *Decides* to remain seized of this matter.

––––––––––––––––

Is this a form of "legislation"? Specifically, what are the main characteristics of legislation and does this Resolution meet them? If it does meet
them, does the Security Council have the power to legislate for the world?
Should it have such power, especially given its composition?

To better understand the impact of UN Security Council Resolutions, consider the case of Security Council Resolution 1267 of 1999, which preceded Resolution 1373. In 1999, concerned about the impact of the Taliban
within and beyond Afghanistan's borders, the Security Council passed
this resolution, requiring all UN member states to impose economic, arms
and aircraft sanctions against the Taliban. The Resolution also created a
special body, the so-called Sanctions Committee, tasked with ensuring
that the regulations were enforced.

In the years that followed, the role of the Sanctions Committee expanded
significantly as the Committee was given additional responsibilities, including the right to add additional names to the sanctions list. Eventually, the list (known as the "Consolidated List") came to include Osama Bin
Laden and his associates and a wide array of other suspected terrorists or
financiers of terrorism. While the United States and other major countries maintain their own lists of suspected terrorists that sometimes overlap with and at other times go beyond the suspects on the Consolidated
List, for many states, the Consolidated List is the lone basis for imposing
sanctions against these suspected terrorists.

As a result, the regime initiated by Resolution 1267 has now created binding legal obligations across the globe—obligations that many states had
no role in creating, and over persons whom those same states may not
have been involved in vetting and including on the list of potential suspects.

Over time, the UN sanctions regime encountered increasing resistance
from both individuals and states because it provided little or no due process rights for those blacklisted and thus subjected to sanctions. In a
landmark decision rendered in 2008, the European Court of Justice (ECJ)
nullified the implementation of the UN regime in the European Union
(and thus its member states) because the regime violated various fundamental rights, such as the right to legal defense, effective judicial protection, and the right to property. *Kadi & Al Barakaat Int'l Foundation v.
Council of the EU and Comm'n of the E.C.* (joined cases C-402/05 & C-
415/05, 3 C.M.L.R. 41 (2008)). In effect, the ECJ subjected the respective

Security Council regime to judicial review and found it wanting under European law. This amounted to an outright clash between the global legal order of the United Nations and the regional order of the European Union with the latter defying the former.

5. ADMINISTRATIVE REGULATIONS

Today, a significant part of the law relevant in international practice comes in the form of regulations and standards, which form an emerging international administrative regime. Some of them are binding, others are mere recommendations. They derive what force they have not directly from state consent (like treaties) nor from consistent state practice (like customary international law), but primarily from the authority of the bodies that issue them. Such bodies, in turn, are usually either governmental organizations created through international agreements or agencies of existing governmental organizations (such as the United Nations). There is a large number and variety of such bodies, ranging from the International Postal and Telecommunications Union to the International Labor Organization (ILO) and the International Civil Aviation Organization (ICAO).

International regulatory regimes are among the most understudied and under-researched areas of international law. In fact, most works on international law barely mention them. Part of the reason may be that they are a thicket formidable to penetrate.

In the following case, you see an international administrative regime (based on a multilateral treaty) in action. What exactly are the plaintiffs complaining about and why are they so upset? How does the Federal Aviation Administration (FAA) defend its action? What is the relationship between the Chicago Convention on International Civil Aviation and administrative regulations on aircraft safety?

BRITISH CALEDONIAN AIRWAYS LTD. V. BOND

United States Circuit Court
665 F.2d 1153 (D.C. Cir. 1981)

JUDGE ROBB:

The petitioners in these consolidated actions are foreign airlines challenging "Special Federal Aviation Regulation No. 40" (SFAR 40) which was issued on June 6, 1979, by the Federal Aviation Administration in the aftermath of the catastrophic crash of a domestic DC–10 airliner on May 25, 1979. SFAR 40 prohibited the operation of all Model DC–10 airplanes within the airspace of the United States, including those aircraft registered in other nations. The Administrator of the FAA terminated the effectiveness of SFAR 40 on July 13, 1979, five weeks after it was issued.

The petitioners contend that the Administrator's actions in issuing SFAR 40 violated the provisions of several international agreements, and in particular Article 33 of the Convention on International Civil Aviation (the Chicago Convention) (ratified by the United States August 9, 1946). The petitioners say this in turn constituted a violation of section[ ] 1102 of the Federal Aviation Act of 1958. We agree.

I.   FACTUAL BACKGROUND

* * *

D.   THE RESPONSE OF FOREIGN CARRIERS TO SFAR 40

After the Administrator suspended the DC–10 type certificate, a number of foreign governments, including those of the petitioners in the present case, provisionally suspended the individual airworthiness certificates for each of their DC–10 aircraft. During the week of June 11, 1979, European aviation authorities and European DC–10 operators conferred to determine whether and under what conditions the aircraft could be returned to service, consistent with the highest safety standards. * * *

On June 25, 1979, representatives of member states of the European Civil Aviation Conference met in Paris with a delegation from the United States and requested rescission of SFAR 40 as to those DC–10 aircraft for which certificates of airworthiness had been re-issued. In a statement issued June 25 the representatives of the European States took the position that

> According to Article 33 of the Chicago Convention, certificates of airworthiness issued by the State of registry have to be recognized by the other Contracting States. There is no doubt that the requirements under which these certificates were issued are equal to or above the minimum standards established under the Chicago Convention. * * * No evidence has been presented by the United States authorities to the effect that the requirements under which European States have issued their certificates of airworthiness fall short of * * * minimum standards.

Citing Article 9(b) of the Chicago Convention the United States rejected the request of the Conference and maintained that its position was consistent with its international obligations and with domestic law.

E.   THE LITIGATION

On June 27, 1979, petitioner British Caledonian Airways Limited filed in this court its petition for review of SFAR 40. On the same day petitioners Belair AG, Lufthansa German Airlines, and Swissair, Swiss Air Transport Company, Ltd., filed with the FAA a petition for rulemaking in which they sought immediate adoption of a rule rescinding SFAR 40. The FAA did not act on the petition, and Belair, Lufthansa, and Swissair filed their petition for review in this court on July 11, 1979. Jurisdiction was based on 49 U.S.C. § 1486 (1976).

The United States and the member states of the European Civil Aviation Conference continued to confer but were unable to resolve the dispute over the United States' refusal to rescind SFAR 40. However on July 13, 1979, the FAA terminated its suspension of the DC–10 type certificate and at the same time rescinded SFAR 40. * * *

II. JUSTICIABILITY

[The Government first contended that the petitioners' claim was moot— and thus not subject to judicial review—because the FAA had already withdrawn SFAR 40. The Court rejected this argument because it was reasonable to expect that the FAA would subject the petitioners to the same action in the future.]

* * *

B.   A NON–SELF–EXECUTING TREATY RAISING POLITICAL QUES-
      TIONS?

[In the alternative, the] petitioners contend that the FAA Administrator's refusal to rescind SFAR 40, after the foreign aviation authorities revalidated the airworthiness certificates of their DC–10s, violated various multilateral and bilateral agreements between the United States and the petitioners' governments, and that the refusal was in turn a violation of section 1102 of the Federal Aviation Act of 1958. The government argues, however, that the petitioners may not seek judicial enforcement of rights and obligations under these international agreements because the agreements in question are not "self-executing" and present non-justiciable political questions.

* * *

* * * In general, courts in the United States have exclusive authority to interpret an international agreement to which the United States is a party for the purpose of applying it in litigation as the domestic law of the United States. Similarly, whether a given treaty is self-executing or requires special implementing legislation to give force and effect to its provisions is primarily a domestic question of construction for the courts. Apart from those few instances in which the language of the treaty provision expressly calls for legislative implementation or the subject matter is within the exclusive jurisdiction of Congress, such as the appropriation of money, the question is one of interpretation. In such cases the courts must "look to the intent of the signatory parties as manifested by the language of the instrument, and, if the instrument is uncertain, recourse must be had to the circumstances surrounding its execution."

The pertinent treaty provision in the present case is Article 33 of the Chicago Convention. Article 33 provides as follows:

> Certificates of airworthiness and certificates of competency and licenses issued or rendered valid by the contracting State in which the aircraft is registered, shall be recognized as valid by the other contracting States, provided that the requirements under which such certificates or licenses were issued or rendered valid are equal to or above the minimum standards which may be established from time to time pursuant to this Convention.

Thus, under Article 33, the judgment of the country of registry that an aircraft is airworthy must be respected, unless the country of registry is not observing the "minimum standards." Annex 8 to the Chicago Convention contains the international standards of airworthiness contemplated by Article 33 and specifically provided for in Article 37. Annex 8 was adopted and is periodically amended by the Council of the International Civil Aviation Organization (ICAO), pursuant to Article 90 of the Chicago Convention.

Because the Chicago Convention itself provides that the ICAO, and not the individual contracting states, will adopt the airworthiness standards now contained in Annex 8, we cannot say that Article 33 requires legislative implementation by Congress. In contrast, several provisions of the Chicago Convention clearly require the contracting states, as distinguished from ICAO, to take the necessary steps under national law to implement the purposes of those provisions. * * * We think these provisions state rules that may not be qualified or modified through legislation or administrative regulations enacted by the individual signatory nations, consistent with the international obligations undertaken by each nation that is a party to the Convention. Article 33 is such a provision and we therefore hold that it was intended to operate upon ratification of the Convention and promulgation of the minimum airworthiness standards—that is, we conclude that Article 33 is self-executing.

[The court rejected the Government's political question doctrine claim because the question at issue involved a legal inquiry.]

* * *

III. THE LEGALITY OF SFAR 40

Section 1102 of the Federal Aviation Act of 1958, 49 U.S.C. § 1502 (1976), requires the Administrator, in exercising and performing his powers and duties, to "do so consistently with any obligation assumed by the United States in any treaty, convention, or agreement that may be in force between the United States and any foreign country or foreign countries." As we have said, Article 33 of the Chicago Convention requires each contracting state, including the United States, to recognize as valid the certificates of airworthiness issued by the other contracting states, as long as those certificates are issued under requirements that are equal to or above the minimum standards established by the International Civil Aviation Organization. Section 1102 of the FAA requires the Administrator to discharge his duties consistently with the obligation assumed by the United States in Article 33. Because the Administrator at no time questioned whether the foreign governments met the minimum safety standards set by the ICAO, his issuance of SFAR 40 and his refusal to rescind the order after the foreign governments had revalidated the airworthiness certificates for aircraft flying under their flags would appear to have violated Article 33 and, therefore, section 1102. The Administrator now maintains, however, that there are provisions in the Chicago Convention and the bilateral agreements which override Article 33 and recognize his authority to issue SFAR 40. In addition, when he promulgated SFAR 40 the Administrator cited four sections of the Federal Aviation Act as a statutory basis for the regulation.

* * *

[The court rejected the FAA Administrator's arguments.]

IV. CONCLUSION

For the foregoing reasons we conclude that the Administrator's action in issuing SFAR 40 violated various multilateral and bilateral civil aviation agreements, which in turn violated section 1502 of the Federal Aviation Act of 1958. Accordingly, that action must be set aside under 49 U.S.C. § 1486(d) (1976).

What body adopts the international standards of airworthiness contemplated in the Convention? Who is responsible for maintaining aircraft safety under these standards? What concerns does this arrangement raise?

The following text is an attempt to structure the types of international administrative regimes. You should get a good sense of the "structure of the global administrative space" and of its complexity. Which of the categories suggested by the authors does the aircraft safety regime you saw in the previous case fall into?

BENEDICT KINGSBURY, NICO KRISCH, RICHARD B. STEWART, THE EMERGENCE OF GLOBAL ADMINISTRATIVE LAW

68 Law & Contemporary Problems 15 (2005)

I. INTRODUCTION: THE UNNOTICED RISE OF GLOBAL ADMINISTRATIVE LAW

Emerging patterns of global governance are being shaped by a little-noticed but important and growing body of global administrative law. This body of law is not at present unified—indeed, it is not yet an organized field of scholarship or of practice. * * *

Underlying the emergence of global administrative law is the vast increase in the reach and forms of transgovernmental regulation and administration designed to address the consequences of globalized interdependence in such fields as security, the conditions on development and financial assistance to developing countries, environmental protection, banking and financial regulation, law enforcement, telecommunications, trade in products and services, intellectual property, labor standards, and cross-border movements of populations, including refugees. Increasingly, these consequences cannot be addressed effectively by isolated national regulatory and administrative measures. As a result, various transnational systems of regulation or regulatory cooperation have been established through international treaties and more informal intergovernmental networks of cooperation, shifting many regulatory decisions from the national to the global level. Further, much of the detail and implementation of such regulation is determined by transnational administrative bodies—including international organizations and informal groups of officials—that perform administrative functions but are not directly subject to control by national governments or domestic legal systems or, in the case of treaty-based regimes, the states party to the treaty. These regulatory decisions may be implemented directly against private parties by the global regime or, more commonly, through implementing measures at the national level. Also increasingly important are regulation by private international standard-setting bodies and by hybrid public-private organizations that may include, variously, representatives of businesses, NGOs, national governments, and intergovernmental organizations.

This situation has created an accountability deficit in the growing exercise of transnational regulatory power, which has begun to stimulate two different types of responses: first, the attempted extension of domestic administrative law to intergovernmental regulatory decisions that affect a nation; and second, the development of new mechanisms of administrative law at the global level to address decisions and rules made within the intergovernmental regimes.

A somewhat different but related issue arises when regulatory decisions by a domestic authority adversely affect other states, designated categories of individuals, or organizations, and are challenged as contrary to that government's obligations under an international regime to which it is a party. Here one response has been the development by intergovernmental regimes of administrative law standards and mechanisms to which national administrations must conform in order to assure their compliance and accountability with the international regime. In order to boost their legitimacy and effectiveness, a number of regulatory bodies not composed exclusively of states—hybrid public-private, and purely private bodies—have also begun to adopt administrative law decisionmaking and rulemaking procedures.

These developments lead us to define global administrative law as comprising the mechanisms, principles, practices, and supporting social understandings that promote or otherwise affect the accountability of global administrative bodies, in particular by ensuring they meet adequate standards of transparency, participation, reasoned decision, and legality, and by providing effective review of the rules and decisions they make. Global administrative bodies include formal intergovernmental regulatory bodies, informal intergovernmental regulatory networks and coordination arrangements, national regulatory bodies operating with reference to an international intergovernmental regime, hybrid public-private regulatory bodies, and some private regulatory bodies exercising transnational governance functions of particular public significance.

* * *

II.   The Structure of the Global Administrative Space

The conceptualization of global administrative law presumes the existence of global or transnational administration. We argue that enough global or transnational administration exists that it is now possible to identify a multifaceted "global administrative space" (a concept to which we will return shortly), populated by several distinct types of regulatory administrative institutions and various types of entities that are the subjects of regulation, including not only states but also individuals, firms, and NGOs. But this view is certainly contested. Many international lawyers still view administration largely as the province of the state or of exceptional interstate entities with a high level of integration, such as the European Union. In this view, which is complemented by what has hitherto been the largely domestic or E.U. focus of administrative lawyers, international action might coordinate and assist domestic administration, but given the lack of international executive power and capacity, does not constitute administrative action itself. This view, however, is contradicted by the rapid growth of international and transnational regulatory regimes with administrative components and functions. Some of the most dense regulatory regimes have arisen in the sphere of economic regulation: the OECD networks and committees, the administration and the committees of the WTO, the committees of the G–7/G–8, structures of antitrust cooperation, and financial regulation performed by, among others, the IMF, the Basle Committee and the Financial Action Task Force. Environmental regulation is partly the work of non-environmental administrative bodies such as the World Bank, the OECD, and the WTO, but increasingly far-reaching regulatory structures are being established in specialized regimes such as the prospective emissions trading scheme and the Clean Development Mechanism in the Kyoto Protocol. Administrative action is now an important component of many international security regimes, including work of the U.N. Security Council and its committees, and in related fields such as nuclear energy regulation (the IAEA) or the supervision mechanism of the Chemical Weapons Convention. Reflection on these illustrations immediately indicates that the extraordinarily varied landscape of global administration results not simply from the highly varied regulatory subject areas and correlative functional differentiations among institutions, but also from the multi-layered character of the administration of global governance. * * *

A.   FIVE TYPES OF GLOBAL ADMINISTRATION

Five main types of globalized administrative regulation are distinguishable: (1) administration by formal international organizations; (2) administration based on collective action by transnational networks of cooperative arrangements between national regulatory officials; (3) distributed administration conducted by national regulators under treaty, network, or other cooperative regimes; (4) administration by hybrid intergovernmental-private arrangements; and (5) administration by private institutions with regulatory functions. In practice, many of these layers overlap or combine, but we propose this array of ideal types to facilitate further inquiry.

In *international administration*, formal inter-governmental organizations established by treaty or executive agreement are the main administrative actors. A central example is the U.N. Security Council and its committees, which adopt subsidiary legislation, take binding decisions related to particular countries (mostly in the form of sanctions), and even act directly on individuals through targeted sanctions and the associated listing of persons deemed to be responsible for threats to international peace. Similarly, the United Nations High Commissioner for Refugees has assumed numerous regulatory and other administrative tasks, such as conducting refugee status determinations and administering refugee camps in many countries. Other examples include the World Health Organization's assessing global health risks and issuing warnings, the Financial Action Task Force's assessing policies against money-laundering and sanctioning violations by specific states of the standards it has adopted, the compliance mechanisms of the Montreal Protocol under which subsidiary bodies of an administrative character deal with non-compliance by Parties to the Protocol, and the World Bank's setting standards for "good governance" for specific developing countries as a condition for financial aid.

Transnational networks and coordination arrangements, by contrast, are characterized by the absence of a binding formal decisionmaking structure and the dominance of informal cooperation among state regulators. This horizontal form of administration can, but need not, take place in a treaty framework. For example, the Basle Committee brings together the heads of various central banks, outside any treaty structure, so they may coordinate on policy matters like capital adequacy requirements for banks. The agreements are non-binding in legal form but can be highly effective. A different example is the pressure WTO law exerts for mutual recognition of regulatory rules and decisions among member states, thus establishing a strong form of horizontal cooperation through which regulatory acts of one state automatically gain validity in another. National regulators also develop, on a bilateral basis, arrangements for mutual recognition of national regulatory standards or conformity procedures and other forms of regulatory coordination, such as regulatory equivalence determinations.

In *distributed administration*, domestic regulatory agencies act as part of the global administrative space: they take decisions on issues of foreign or global concern. An example is in the exercise of extraterritorial regulatory jurisdiction, in which one state seeks to regulate activity primarily occurring elsewhere. In some circumstances, such regulation is subject to substantive limitations and even procedural requirements established internationally, as has become evident from the WTO Appellate Body's 1998 ruling in *United States—Import Prohibition of Certain Shrimp and Shrimp Products (Shrimp–Turtle)*. But even domestic administration without immediate extraterritorial effects may be part of the global administrative space, especially when it is charged with implementing an international regime. National environmental regulators concerned with biodiversity conservation or greenhouse gas emissions are today often part of a global administration, as well as part of a purely national one: they are responsible for implementing international environmental law for the achievement of common objectives, and their decisions are thus of concern to governments (and publics) in other states, as well as to the international environmental regime they are implementing. Arrangements for mutual recognition of standards and certifications between particular national regulators might also have some of the qualities of distributed administration, although opinions vary sharply as to how best to understand the mosaic of mutual recognition agreements and comparable cooperative approaches.

A fourth type of global administration is *hybrid intergovernmental-private administration*. Bodies that combine private and governmental actors take many different forms and are increasingly significant. An example is the Codex Alimentarius Commission, which adopts standards on food safety through a decisional process that now includes significant participation by non-governmental actors as well as by government representatives, and produces standards that gain a quasi-mandatory effect via the SPS Agreement under WTO law. Another example is the Internet address protocol regulatory body, the Internet Corporation for Assigned Names and Numbers (ICANN), which was established as a non-governmental body, but which has come to include government representatives who have gained considerable powers, often via service on ICANN's Governmental Advisory Committee, since the 2002 reforms. Determining how administrative law can be shaped or made operational in relation to such bodies is difficult. The involvement of state actors, subject to national and international public law constraints, alongside private actors who are not, and who may indeed have conflicting duties such as commercial confidentiality, threatens a very uneven and potentially disruptive set of controls. The challenge is nevertheless an important one, and sufficiently distinctive that we treat these hybrid bodies as a separate category.

Fifth and finally, many regulatory functions are carried out by *private* bodies. For example, the private International Standardization Organization (ISO) has adopted over 13,000 standards that harmonize product and process rules around the world. On a smaller scale, NGOs have come to develop standards and certification mechanisms for internationally traded products, for example fair-trade coffee and sustainably harvested timber. Business organizations have set up rules and regulatory regimes in numerous industries, ranging from the Society for Worldwide Interstate Financial Telecommunications (SWIFT) system for letters of credit, to Fair Labor Association standards for sports apparel production. In national law, such private bodies are typically treated as clubs rather than as administrators, unless they exercise public power by explicit delegation. But in the global sphere, due to the lack of international public institutions, they often have greater power and importance. Their acts may not be much different in kind from many non-binding intergovernmental public norms, and may often be more effective. We cautiously suggest that the margins of the field of global administration be extended to the activities of some of these non-governmental bodies. The ISO provides a good example: not only do its decisions have major economic impacts, but they are also used in regulatory decisions by treaty-based authorities such as the WTO. An example of a private regulatory body that is less connected with state or inter-state action is the World Anti-Doping Agency, an organization connected with the International Olympic Committee, which applies careful due process standards in dealing with athletes suspected of using banned substances, culminating in the review system of the private International Court of Arbitration for Sport. Significant normative and practical problems arise in proposals to extend administrative law approaches to such bodies, although these problems are context-specific rather than uniform. We believe it is desirable to study such bodies as part of global administration, and to trace similarities as well as differences in mechanisms of accountability developed for public and private bodies.

* * *

———————————

The authors note "an accountability deficit in the growing exercise of transnational regulatory power" as a consequence of the emergence of global administrative regimes. Even if the governments involved in the respective rule-making bodies as well as the industries regulated by them (such as manufacturers, airlines or banks) participate in the rule-making process, consumers (such as buyers of manufactured goods, passengers or bank clients) rarely do so. Yet they have to live (or, in the case of safety rules, possibly die) with the result.

6. NON–BINDING SOURCES: "SOFT LAW"?

Beyond treaties, customary international law, general principles of law, case decisions, and regulatory rules, there are myriad forms of non-binding "declarations," "recommendations," "statements," "principles," etc., adopted and published by a large variety of bodies such as the UN General Assembly, specialized agencies, private and semi-private organizations, etc. The status and relevance of these sources is much debated. On the one hand, they clearly do not have the force of law; on the other hand, they are frequently invoked by advocates and often considered by tribunals.

How much weight, if any, they carry is impossible to generalize and difficult to gauge because it depends very much on the circumstances of the case. Experienced international lawyers often develop a feel for how to use these sources of "soft law" (an oxymoron of sorts). In this section, we will look at three examples of such "soft law" sources—one created domestically and the other two drafted by international bodies.

A. THE RESTATEMENT (THIRD) OF FOREIGN RELATIONS LAW

In the United States, and sometimes beyond, provisions of the *Restatement (Third) of the Foreign Relations Law* of the United States (1986) are frequently cited by scholars, counsel and courts in debates about the content of international law. Like its counterparts in other areas, this Restatement aims to reflect the status quo of the law but also expresses the views of its drafters, who are leading international law scholars, and of the American Law Institute (ALI) which published it. It thus enjoys a certain academic and institutional authority but it is, of course, not binding law, and one must be careful not to use it as such. How much persuasive force it enjoys in the courts varies a great deal. The two excerpts below, taken from cases we have encountered before, illustrate somewhat different positions in this regard. Are they reconcilable?

HARTFORD FIRE INSURANCE CO. V. CALIFORNIA
United States Supreme Court
509 U.S. 764 (1993)

* * *

Dissenting opinion by JUSTICE SCALIA * * * in which JUSTICES O'CONNOR, KENNEDY, and THOMAS have joined * * *

[T]he practice of using international law to limit the extraterritorial reach of statutes is firmly established in our jurisprudence. In proceeding to apply that practice to the present cases, I shall rely on the Restatement (Third) for the relevant principles of international law. Its standards appear fairly supported in the decisions of this Court construing international choice-of-law principles (*Lauritzen*, *Romero*, and *McCulloch*) and in the decisions of other federal courts, especially *Timberlane*. Whether the Restatement precisely reflects international law in every detail matters little here, as I believe this litigation would be resolved the same way under virtually any conceivable test that takes account of foreign regulatory interests.

* * *

UNITED STATES V. YOUSEF
United States Circuit Court
327 F.3d 56 (2d Cir. 2003)

* * *

The Restatement (Third), a kind of treatise or commentary, is not a *primary* source of authority upon which, standing alone, courts may rely for propositions of customary international law. Such works at most provide evidence of the practice of States, and then only insofar as they rest on factual and accurate descriptions of the past practices of states, not on projections of future trends or the advocacy of the "better rule." * * *[31]

---

[31] * * * The American Law Institute ("ALI") began its project of preparing comprehensive "restatements" of the laws of the United States in order " 'to promote the clarification and simplification of the law and its better adaptation to social needs.' " Accordingly, the Restatements do not merely (or necessarily) "restate" the law as it is; the ALI handbook for reporters instructs

B. UN GENERAL ASSEMBLY DECLARATIONS AND RESOLUTIONS IN THE COURTS

What use can one make of UN General Assembly Declarations and Resolutions especially in U.S. courts? Let us begin with another look at *Flores v. South-Peru Copper Corporation*, a case we have seen several times already. In the excerpt below, the Second Circuit Court of Appeals addressed the impact of these sources. How does the court treat them?

that reporters are "not compelled to adhere to * * * a preponderating balance of authority but [are] instead expected to *propose the better rule* and provide the rationale for choosing it."

The ALI published its first Restatement of the Foreign Relations Law of the United States in 1965 * * *. The Restatement (Third) is a "comprehensive revision" of the Restatement (Second). The Director of the ALI notes in the foreword to the Restatement (Third) that it is "in no sense an official document of the United States," and that "[i]n a number of particulars the formulations in this Restatement are at variance with positions that have been taken by the United States Government." These variations presumably are intentional because, although the ALI extended the Restatement (Third) project by a year to consider "communications received * * * from the Department of State and from the Justice Department," it did not fully conform the Restatement to the positions expressed in those communications. The Restatement (Third) addresses for the first time the central subject of the sources of international law, which the Restatement (Second) had relegated to the comments of section 1.

The Restatement (Third)'s innovations on the subject of customary international law have been controversial. For example, the Restatement (Third) suggests that customary international law might trump prior inconsistent statutory law, binding the executive branch. This proposition is without foundation or merit. Indeed, other commentators have called the Restatement (Third)'s view that customary international law could supersede federal statutory law "pure bootstrapping," noting that the only authority cited for that proposition in the Restatement (Third) is a single article by the Restatement (Third)'s own Reporter—that is, the citation is without external authority. Curtis A. Bradley & Jack L. Goldsmith, *Customary International Law as Federal Common Law: A Critique of the Modern Position*, 110 Harv. L. Rev. 815, 835–36 & nn. 142–43 (1997). Even the current President of the ALI notes that this rule was "much debated when the Restatement (Third) was under discussion in the Institute * * * [and is] not completely free from controversy now." Michael Traynor, *That's Debatable: The ALI as a Public Policy Forum, Part II*, 25 The ALI Reporter 1, 2 (2002).

Inasmuch as the Restatement (Third) notes that certain of its positions are "at variance" with the practice and customs followed by the United States in its international relations, and incorrectly asserts that customary international law may trump United States statutory law, courts must be vigilant and careful in adopting the statements of the Restatement (Third) as evidence of the customs, practices, or laws of the United States and/or evidence of customary international law.

FLORES V. SOUTHERN PERU COPPER CORP.

United States Circuit Court
414F.3d 233 (2d Cir. 2003)

JUDGE CABRANES:

* * *

2. NON–BINDING GENERAL ASSEMBLY DECLARATIONS

Plaintiffs rely on several resolutions of the United Nations General Assembly in support of their assertion that defendant's conduct violated a rule of customary international law. These documents are not proper sources of customary international law because they are merely aspirational and were never intended to be binding on member States of the United Nations.

The General Assembly has been described aptly as "the world's most important political discussion forum," but it is not a law-making body. *The Charter of the United Nations: A Commentary* 248, 269 (Bruno Simma ed., 2d ed. 2002). General Assembly resolutions and declarations do not have the power to bind member States because the member States specifically denied the General Assembly that power after extensively considering the issue * * *.

* * *

* * * Because General Assembly documents are at best merely advisory, they do not, on their own and without proof of uniform state practice, evidence an intent by member States to be legally bound by their principles, and thus cannot give rise to rules of customary international law.

* * *

In the instant case, the General Assembly documents relied on by plaintiffs do not describe the actual customs and practices of States. Accordingly, they cannot support plaintiffs' claims.

3. OTHER MULTINATIONAL DECLARATIONS OF PRINCIPLE

In addition to General Assembly documents, plaintiffs rely on numerous other multinational "declarations" to substantiate their position that defendant's intranational pollution in Peru violated customary international law. A declaration, which may be made by a multinational body, or by one or more States, customarily is a "mere general statement of policy [that] is unlikely to give rise to * * * obligation[s] in any strict sense." In undertaking the difficult task of determining the contours of customary international law, a court is not granted a roving commission to pick and choose among declarations of public and private international organizations that have articulated a view on the matter at hand. Such declarations are almost invariably political statements—expressing the sensibilities and the asserted aspirations and demands of some countries or organizations—rather than statements of universally-recognized legal obligations. Accordingly, such declarations are not proper evidence of customary international law.

Occasionally, a document entitled a "declaration" may actually be a binding treaty because the document uses language indicating the parties' intent to be bound and sets forth "definite rules of conduct." *[S]ee, e.g., Iran v. United States (Case A/1), 68 I.L.R. 523, 525* (Iran–U.S. Claims Trib. 1982) (noting that the agreements between the United States and Iran that concluded the hostage crisis were termed "declarations," even though they created legally binding obligations). Only in such rare instances—where the States joining in the self-styled "declaration" intended it to be legally binding—may a party rely on a document entitled a "declaration" as evidence of the customs and practices of the States joining the declaration.

Apart from the General Assembly documents addressed above, plaintiffs principally rely on two multinational declarations in support of their claims. First, they draw our attention to the American Declaration of the Rights and Duties of Man ("American Declaration") promulgated by the Organization of American States ("OAS"). As one of our sister Circuits has correctly observed, the American Declaration "is an aspirational document which * * * did not on its own create any enforceable obligations on the part of any of the OAS member nations." *Garza v. Lappin*, 253 F.3d 918, 925 (7th Cir. 2001).

Plaintiffs also rely on Principle 1 of the Rio Declaration, which sets forth broad, aspirational principles regarding environmental protection and sustainable development. The Rio Declaration includes no language indicating that the States joining in the Declaration intended to be legally bound by it.

Because neither of these declarations created enforceable legal obligations, they do not provide reliable evidence of customary international law.

* * *

If such "declarations" are neither binding nor evidence of customary international law, what are they good for anyway? Can one make *any* (legal) use of them? Compare the *Flores* court's reaction to UN General Assembly resolutions with the treatment they received in *Filartiga*, supra Ch. VIII.2.B.

How does the arbitrator in the following case treat UN resolutions? What types of markers is he looking for to determine their value? Is his assessment correct of which resolutions count and which ones do not?

TEXACO V. LIBYAN ARAB REPUBLIC

Ad Hoc Arbitration Award
53 I.L.R. 389 (1977)

[The arbitration arose from several contracts made by the Libyan government with Texaco Overseas Petroleum Company and California Asiatic Oil Company (the "Companies") between 1955 and 1968. The contracts were subject to modification only by consent of both parties and contained an arbitration clause. In 1973–1974, the Libyan government nationalized all of the assets, rights and properties of the Companies created by the contracts. The Companies initiated arbitration of the dispute.]

DUPUY, SOLE ARBITRATOR:

* * *

III. AWARD ON THE MERITS

* * *

The arbitrator declared that he would refer on the one hand to the principle of the binding force of contracts recognized by Libyan law and on the other to the principle of *pacta sunt servanda* which is a general principle of law constituting an essential foundation of international law. The arbitrator found therefore on this point that the principles of Libyan law were in conformity with international law and concluded that the [contracts] in dispute had a binding force.

* * *

C. THE PRESENT STATE OF INTERNATIONAL LAW AND THE RESOLUTIONS CONCERNING NATURAL RESOURCES AND WEALTH ADOPTED BY THE UNITED NATIONS

In the Memorandum of July 26, 1974, Libya raised the objection that, according to Resolutions of the General Assembly of the United Nations, nationalization was recognized as a legitimate and internationally recognized method to ensure the sovereignty of the State upon its natural resources, and that nationalization or its consequences should be settled in accordance with provisions of domestic law of the State. In this connection Libya relied on Resolutions 3171 (XXVII) of December 13, 1973 and 3201 (S–VI) of May 1, 1974, entitled "Declaration on the Establishment of a New International Economic Order." Although it was adopted after the date of the Memorandum the arbitrator also took account of Resolution

3281 (XXIX) of December 12, 1974, entitled "Charter of Economic Rights and Duties of the States," in support of the contention of Libya.

As regards the role of international law in the exercise of permanent sovereignty over natural resources, the arbitrator noted substantial differences between the recent Resolutions relied upon by Libya, and Resolution 1803 (XVII) of December 14, 1962 entitled "Permanent Sovereignty over Natural Resources." Whilst the more recent Resolutions refer only to domestic law of the State, Resolution 1803 of 1962 also makes allowance for international law. The arbitrator then appraised the legal validity of the Resolutions, taking account of two criteria: the examination of the voting conditions and the analysis of the provisions concerned.

With respect to the voting conditions, the arbitrator observed that only Resolution 1803 of 1962 was supported by a majority of Member States representing all the various groups. In contrast, the other Resolutions, mentioned above, were supported by a majority of States but not by any of the developed countries with market economies which carry on the major part of international trade.

With respect to the analysis of the provisions concerned, the arbitrator distinguished between those provisions stating the existence of a right on which the generality of States had expressed agreement and those provisions introducing new principles which were rejected by certain representative groups of States. The latter types of provisions have a *de lege ferenda* value only in the eyes of the States which adopted them, whilst as far as the others are concerned, the rejection implies that they consider these provisions as *contra legem*. The former types of provisions can be considered as an *opinio juris communis* reflecting the state of customary law. This was the case with Resolution 1803 of 1962 which expressed the consensus of a majority of States belonging to the various representative groups, but cannot be said of the other Resolutions. The provisions of the latter do not make any connection between the procedure of compensation and international law, the absence of which appeared *contra legem* in the eyes of many developed countries. The arbitrator noted in addition that this attitude was confirmed by the general practice of relations between States with respect to investments, referring to the Convention on the Settlement of Investment Disputes between States and Nationals of other States, done at Washington, March 18, 1965, which, as of October 31, 1974, no fewer than 65 States had ratified.

* * *

5.   DECISION

For the reasons stated above the arbitrator decided:

(1) that the Deeds of Concession are binding on the parties;

(2) that by adopting the measures of nationalization, the Libyan Government breached its obligations under the Deeds of Concession;

(3) that the Libyan Government is legally bound to perform the Deeds of Concession and to give them full force and effect;

(4) to grant the Libyan Government a time period of 5 months running from February 1, 1977 to June 30, 1977, to inform the arbitrator of the measures taken by it with a view to complying with the present award;

(5) that if the present award were not to be implemented within the period of time, the matter of further proceedings is reserved and that the costs and expenses of the arbitration shall be borne, for the present, wholly by the plaintiffs; and

(6) that the award shall be filed with the Registry of the I.C.J. within 6 months from February 1, 1977.

The case was settled after the award was issued. The parties agreed that Libya would provide the companies with $152 million of Libyan crude oil over the following 15 months and that, in exchange, the companies would terminate the arbitration proceedings.

The following excerpt provides a scholarly perspective on the question of when soft law instruments can be transformed into hard law. According to Chinkin, under what conditions can such a transformation take place?

Christine M. Chinkin, The Challenge of Soft Law: Development and Change in International Law
38 Int'l & Comp. L.Q. 850 (1989)

* * *

Claims * * * that the principles contained in a soft law instrument have become transformed into hard law, rest upon an assertion that subsequent State practice has changed the status of the principles. It may also be urged that this very transformation was a major goal of the formulation of the principles. The requisite State practice may be the inclusion of principles originally expressed in soft law forms into treaties, although it is likely that the language would have to be adapted to create hard obligations. Such action represents a deliberate choice on the part of States parties to the treaty to change the status of the principles.

Far more problematic is the * * * claim, that soft law principles have come to represent customary international law. Such principles do not and cannot *per se* be regarded as customary international law for a number of reasons. There must be sufficient evidence of State practice and *opinio juris.* "The elements of the formation of the rules of general international law—international custom—are not some esoteric invention but rather they provide criteria by which the actual expectations and commitments of States can be tested." State practice is evidenced by what States do, as well as by what they say. Before a decision-maker accepts such a claim, evidence should be produced that an instrument of soft law has been consistently acted upon. Even where there is evidence of a consistent and uniform body of State practice, there is the need to establish *opinio juris* and the conceptual problem as to whether action taken in compliance with an instrument specifically denied to be legally binding and asserted to be voluntary can be evidence of *opinio juris*. The required intention to be bound may be denied, either expressly by the words of the instrument, or implicitly by the choice of a soft law form. The interests of States in voting for the adoption of a soft law instrument will differ along with their expectations and intentions as to implementation. This is not to deny that soft law can become customary international law or be declaratory of it. It can clearly do so, and the relevant soft law instruments may well have a catalytic effect. Since soft law is used in international economic relations precisely where there is an intention in at least some of the participants to develop and change the law it cannot be expected that this will happen instantly or readily: the notion of instant customary law appears incompatible with the revolutionary content of much soft law.

* * *

C. A BROADER VIEW

The excerpt below, taken from the same article by Christine Chinkin that you just saw, deals with two broader questions pertaining to "soft law". First, it asks why parties opt for it. How does Chinkin answer that question? Can you think of additional reasons? Second, it asks how "soft law" can be made effective even without (formal) adjudication. Consider what costs an international actor incurs if it defies these modes of "soft enforcement."

CHRISTINE M. CHINKIN, THE CHALLENGE OF SOFT LAW: DEVELOPMENT AND CHANGE IN INTERNATIONAL LAW

38 Int'l & Comp. L.Q. 850 (1989)

* * *

IV. CHOICE OF SOFT LAW FORMS

Both treaties and international customary law have inadequacies for the regulation of this area of international relations so that it is not surprising that new techniques were sought for the projection of a New International Economic Order. The success of the development of human rights law from the Universal Declaration on Human Rights was an encouraging model to adopt.

Multilateral treaties are slow to be concluded, slower still to come into force, and bind only the parties to them. The avoidance of the treaty form means that States are not bound by either domestic or international rules relating to treaties. There may be domestic constitutional technicalities to be satisfied before a treaty can be ratified; the growth of executive agreements in United States domestic law was a national response to this while the evolution of soft law forms is an international one. The Vienna Convention aimed at hardening the rules regulating those treaties that come within its terms. For example, the rules regulating the termination and amendment of treaties are restrictive; a fundamental change of circumstances is a ground for termination but only within tightly drawn limits and is not a basis for amendment within the terms of the Convention. It is possibly no coincidence that the trend towards concluding international soft law instruments gained momentum within a very short time after the finalising of the Vienna Convention, which hardened the rules governing treaties.

* * *

The use of a soft law form is often a compromise between those States which did not favour any regulatory instrument and those which would have preferred the conclusion of a treaty. Although it is the substantive claims of the newly independent States that challenge the international legal order, those States often favour the use of the traditional sources to bestow the required certain legality upon their claims. However, a soft law form is preferable to either no outcome at all to negotiations, or to a treaty with diluted and vague provisions. In the light of the requirement of the International Court of Justice "that the provision concerned should, at all events potentially be of a fundamentally norm-creating character," such a treaty may be less likely to evolve as customary international law than a more precisely worded resolution. Even if such a provision cannot be shown to have become customary international law it may in practice be harder to discount than a treaty which has failed to come into force.

The increasing use of soft law forms also reflects the present importance of the organised international and regional, specialised and general institutional bodies for the negotiation, formulation and propagation of principles of international law. Despite this widespread reliance upon multilateral negotiation, however, an essential element of international economic relations remains the bilateral barter or trade-off which cannot easily be incorporated within multipartite institutional resolutions. Although soft law instruments have a high profile a large number of bilateral treaties and international contracts are still regularly concluded between States in the conduct of their economic affairs. Further, the multilateral treaty is still the preferred instrumentality where formal rights and obligations need to be specified. Soft law is well suited for the specification of interests and values but does not provide the required precision for such matters as the passing of title or of risk. There is a continuing process of treaty-making in the formation of international economic relations which runs parallel to and supplements the developments in soft law. This emphasises the deliberate choice made between hard law and soft law forms and reinforces the view that they are not intended to be equated.

V.   CLAIMS AS TO OUTCOMES

A.   SOFT MEANS OF ENFORCEMENT

Claims may also be made about the outcome of non-compliance with soft law and its use in the settlement of disputes. Much of the substantive content of soft law is subjective and discretionary and is inherently unsuited to adjudication. What it is pre-eminently suitable for is avoiding the need for adjudication by providing a framework for negotiation and other non-adjudicative forms of dispute resolution by creating expectations as to the frame of reference for the conduct of negotiations. This process is well illustrated by the Badger and Hertz incidents where the Organisation for Economic Cooperation and Development Guidelines on Restrictive Business Practices were used to reach an adjustment of the respective disputes, although the Guidelines were not directly applicable and could have been discounted in an adjudication.

Soft law has an informative and educative role which is well suited to non-judicial means of dispute settlement and to self-regulation between interested participants. Domestic alternative dispute resolution procedures are being increasingly promoted in a number of jurisdictions as the disadvantages of litigation for dispute resolution become ever more apparent. Again the international developments mirror domestic ones. Soft means of enforcement through the role of monitoring or follow-up agencies can assist in this role. Monitoring and watchdog bodies can be established domestically or internationally which can lobby governments and corporations as well as document violations. They can also further the development and reform process by suggesting amendments based upon their experience of examining the operation of the instruments. Since adjudication has never been the primary means of resolving international disputes, especially those involving economic matters, the unsuitability of soft law for adjudication should not be viewed as a major disadvantage.

* * *

7. SOURCES REGULATING PRIVATE LITIGATION AND TRANSACTIONS

In the first half of the 20th century, international law was seen as concerned with the law of nations. Thus, it was understood to be first and foremost *public* international law. The relationships among private actors were by and large left to law on the domestic level.

This was not always so. In the early 19th century, writers like Joseph Story thought that international law had two sides: public (the law of nations) and private (the law governing international issues between private parties). By the late 19th century, however, this tradition had been mostly lost. The nationalism of the early 20th century led to an increasing absorption of private international law into domestic law so that, in a sense, the law of nations remained the only object of international law. Thus international law by and large came to mean public international law (only), and this is often still true today. Of course, there were still rules dealing with international issues among private actors, but they were no longer part of international (and thus, at least in principle, uniform) law; instead, each country decided for itself how it wanted to deal with transboundary relationships and disputes between private parties.

In the second half of the 20th century, the pendulum began to swing back. Private law returned, so to speak, to the international plane. Today, however, it comes no longer mainly in the form of generally shared principles but rather, as we shall see, in the garb of actual treaties. Before we get under way, some terminological issues need to be addressed.

The law governing transnational private relationships and disputes could well be called *private international law*. But that is, perhaps surprisingly, not the common usage of that term. Instead, it has acquired a narrower, more technical meaning: *private international law* is used synonymously with *conflict of laws* and thus comprises the rules about international civil jurisdiction, choice of law, judgments recognition and ancillary procedural issues arising in international cases (such as service of process or the taking of evidence abroad) (infra. A.). Thus, *private international law* does not encompass any *substantive* private law on the international level. The reason for that is mainly that until quite recently, there was virtually no such thing, as all substantive private law was left to the domestic level. Today, however, there actually are *substantive private law rules* on the international plane, for example in the form of treaties governing international sales transactions (infra. B.).

In addition, there are various sources of non-state private law. The most important categories are Restatement-like (i.e., non-binding) "Principles" drafted by non-governmental bodies (infra. C.) and, of course, (business) contracts through which the parties establish their own law for their specific transactions (infra. D.).

A. PRIVATE INTERNATIONAL LAW ("CONFLICT OF LAWS")

Private international law ("Conflict of Laws") is concerned mainly with how to handle international civil disputes and is thus closely related to civil procedure. The concept of private international law is premised on several assumptions.

First, it assumes that there are no international courts available for private litigation, which is true (although there are, as we shall see, international arbitral tribunals). Thus private international law asks in which country's *domestic* courts private parties to an international dispute can sue. This is the question of international jurisdiction. Second, private international law assumes that substantive private law is located on the domestic level, which is mostly, though not always, true. Thus it asks which of the national laws involved will be applied in the case. This is the question of choice of law (normally considered the core of the field). Third, private international law assumes that there are no international law rules determining whether courts in one country must recognize judgments reached in another country, which is true in principle, although there are many exceptions. Thus it asks under what circumstances one country will accept (and, if need be, execute) a court decision reached in another country. This is the question of judgments recognition. (See Chapter IV.2.)

In addition, private international law also deals with certain procedural issues, such as how to serve process abroad, how to take evidence outside of the jurisdiction state or what to do if lawsuits are being filed in more than one country. All these issues are covered in separate, more specialized courses, and we will not discuss most of them here in any detail.[1]

What is significant for our purposes, however, is how private international law has become increasingly re-internationalized in the last couple of decades. This may sound like an absurd statement but it is nonetheless

---

[1] As taught in U.S. law schools, *Conflict of Laws* addresses jurisdiction, choice of law, and judgments recognition (not necessarily in that order), mainly on the domestic level, i.e., among the states of the Union. The international dimension as well as the additional procedural issues mentioned are covered by courses normally called *International (Civil) Litigation*.

entirely true for the following reason. In the later 19th and for most of the 20th century, private international law rules were not really a matter of international law at all. Instead, they were made and applied purely as a matter of domestic law by each country for itself. Thus there were French, Brazilian, Japanese, etc. rules on (international) jurisdiction, choice of law, judgments recognition, etc., and while they were often similar, each country still had its own, often jealously guarded, private international law regime often in the form of (domestic) statutes. In other words, private international law was "international" only by virtue of its subject (because it dealt with international disputes), not by its nature. Although to a large extent this is still true today, much has changed.

Many private international rules today are enshrined in international conventions. They are thus, as treaties, truly part of international law. This is in large part due to the work of the Hague Conference on Private International Law. The Hague Conference is a (now permanent) governmental organization charged with unifying the field by drafting international conventions. It was founded in 1893 as an entirely European club with thirteen members. For the first few decades of its existence, it remained a rather small affair, and its conventions were rarely adopted by more than a dozen or so countries. Since World War II, however, it has grown into a truly worldwide organization with over 60 members, it has produced a host of conventions, and many of them have been adopted by dozens of countries around the globe. As a result, private international law is no longer merely a matter of varying domestic regimes but increasingly the subject of an extensive global treaty network.

Most of the Hague Conventions concern issues of choice of law, and the United States is not a party to any of these. Others, however, regulate important procedural issues in private ligation. Perhaps the most frequently used is the *Hague Service Convention* below. Read it straight through at first and try to understand what its principal idea is. How does the mechanism it establishes work? Then apply it to the following problem:

EXERCISE IN PRIVATE INTERNATIONAL LAW

Let us return for a moment to a hypothetical we first saw in Chapter 3. The American–Russian Cultural Cooperation Foundation (the Foundation), an entity organized by the United States federal government, negotiated an agreement with the Organizing Committee for the Goodwill Mission (the Organizing Committee), a group under the auspices of the Russian Ministry of Culture. Under the agreement, the Russian Royal Jewels of the Romanov (Tsar) family were going to be shown in various museums in the United States.

Following several preliminary agreements, members of the American Foundation flew to Moscow to negotiate the final deal with the Russian Organizing Committee. The agreement was signed in Moscow. While in Moscow, one of the Foundation's representatives, Carl Valenstein, secretly paid undisclosed sums of money to key government officials in the Russian Ministry of Culture to secure their cooperation.

While the Romanov Jewels Exhibition was on tour in the United States, the Austrian newspaper *Die Presse* published an article about corruption in international business practices. It mentioned the bribery committed by Mr. Valenstein as a prominent recent example and alleged that he had acted with the knowledge and approval of the American–Russian Cultural Cooperation Foundation. The Foundation then sued *Die Presse* in New York (where the newspaper is widely available) for libel. It wants to know how to serve the summons and complaint.

What if the story had been published by *Le Monde* in Paris, and the Foundation wanted to sue the paper in New York?

HAGUE CONVENTION ON THE SERVICE ABROAD OF JUDICIAL AND EXTRAJUDICIAL DOCUMENTS IN CIVIL OR COMMERCIAL MATTERS
(Adopted 1965; in force 1969)

The States signatory to the present Convention,

Desiring to create appropriate means to ensure that judicial and extrajudicial documents to be served abroad shall be brought to the notice of the addressee in sufficient time,

Desiring to improve the organisation of mutual judicial assistance for that purpose by simplifying and expediting the procedure,

Have resolved to conclude a Convention to this effect and have agreed upon the following provisions:

Article 1

The present Convention shall apply in all cases, in civil or commercial matters, where there is occasion to transmit a judicial or extrajudicial document for service abroad.

This Convention shall not apply where the address of the person to be served with the document is not known.

Chapter I. Judicial Documents

Article 2

Each Contracting State shall designate a Central Authority which will undertake to receive requests for service coming from other Contracting States and to proceed in conformity with the provisions of Articles 3 to 6.

Each State shall organise the Central Authority in conformity with its own law.

Article 3

The authority or judicial officer competent under the law of the State in which the documents originate shall forward to the Central Authority of the State addressed a request conforming to the model annexed to the present Convention, without any requirement of legalisation or other equivalent formality.

The document to be served or a copy thereof shall be annexed to the request. The request and the document shall both be furnished in duplicate.

Article 4

If the Central Authority considers that the request does not comply with the provisions of the present Convention it shall promptly inform the applicant and specify its objections to the request.

Article 5

The Central Authority of the State addressed shall itself serve the document or shall arrange to have it served by an appropriate agency, either—

   a) by a method prescribed by its internal law for the service of documents in domestic actions upon persons who are within its territory, or

   b) by a particular method requested by the applicant, unless such a method is incompatible with the law of the State addressed.

Subject to sub-paragraph (b) of the first paragraph of this Article, the document may always be served by delivery to an addressee who accepts it voluntarily.

If the document is to be served under the first paragraph above, the Central Authority may require the document to be written in, or translated into, the official language or one of the official languages of the State addressed.

That part of the request, in the form attached to the present Convention, which contains a summary of the document to be served, shall be served with the document.

Article 6

The Central Authority of the State addressed or any authority which it may have designated for that purpose, shall complete a certificate in the form of the model annexed to the present Convention.

The certificate shall state that the document has been served and shall include the method, the place and the date of service and the person to whom the document was delivered. If the document has not been served, the certificate shall set out the reasons which have prevented service.

The applicant may require that a certificate not completed by a Central Authority or by a judicial authority shall be countersigned by one of these authorities.

The certificate shall be forwarded directly to the applicant.

Article 7

The standard terms in the model annexed to the present Convention shall in all cases be written either in French or in English. They may also be written in the official language, or in one of the official languages, of the State in which the documents originate.

The corresponding blanks shall be completed either in the language of the State addressed or in French or in English.

Article 8

Each Contracting State shall be free to effect service of judicial documents upon persons abroad, without application of any compulsion, directly through its diplomatic or consular agents.

Any State may declare that it is opposed to such service within its territory, unless the document is to be served upon a national of the State in which the documents originate.

Article 9

Each Contracting State shall be free, in addition, to use consular channels to forward documents, for the purpose of service, to those authorities of another Contracting State which are designated by the latter for this purpose.

Each Contracting State may, if exceptional circumstances so require, use diplomatic channels for the same purpose.

Article 10

Provided the State of destination does not object, the present Convention shall not interfere with—

a) the freedom to send judicial documents, by postal channels, directly to persons abroad,

b) the freedom of judicial officers, officials or other competent persons of the State of origin to effect service of judicial documents directly through the judicial officers, officials or other competent persons of the State of destination,

c) the freedom of any person interested in a judicial proceeding to effect service of judicial documents directly through the judicial officers, officials or other competent persons of the State of destination.

Article 11

The present Convention shall not prevent two or more Contracting States from agreeing to permit, for the purpose of service of judicial documents, channels of transmission other than those provided for in the preceding Articles and, in particular, direct communication between their respective authorities.

Article 12

The service of judicial documents coming from a Contracting State shall not give rise to any payment or reimbursement of taxes or costs for the services rendered by the State addressed.

The applicant shall pay or reimburse the costs occasioned by—

   a)   the employment of a judicial officer or of a person competent under the law of the State of destination,

   b)   the use of a particular method of service.

Article 13

Where a request for service complies with the terms of the present Convention, the State addressed may refuse to comply therewith only if it deems that compliance would infringe its sovereignty or security.

It may not refuse to comply solely on the ground that, under its internal law, it claims exclusive jurisdiction over the subject-matter of the action or that its internal law would not permit the action upon which the application is based.

The Central Authority shall, in case of refusal, promptly inform the applicant and state the reasons for the refusal.

Article 14

Difficulties which may arise in connection with the transmission of judicial documents for service shall be settled through diplomatic channels.

* * *

Chapter II. Extrajudicial Documents

Article 17

Extrajudicial documents emanating from authorities and judicial officers of a Contracting State may be transmitted for the purpose of service in another Contracting State by the methods and under the provisions of the present Convention.

Chapter III. General Clauses

Article 18

Each Contracting State may designate other authorities in addition to the Central Authority and shall determine the extent of their competence.

The applicant shall, however, in all cases, have the right to address a request directly to the Central Authority.

Federal States shall be free to designate more than one Central Authority.

Article 19

To the extent that the internal law of a Contracting State permits methods of transmission, other than those provided for in the preceding Articles, of documents coming from abroad, for service within its territory, the present Convention shall not affect such provisions.

* * *

Currently, more than 60 countries are members of the Hague Service Convention, among them most of the important trading partners of the United States. Note that the United States has also ratified the Interamerican Convention on Letters Rogatory (1975) which several Latin American countries have joined as well. But many other countries are parties to neither convention.

In 1988, the U.S. Supreme Court had occasion to interpret the Hague Service Convention. Is the majority decision correct? Is it prudent? How does the Court approach the interpretation of an international agreement? Can you guess how other member states of the Convention reacted to the decision?

VOLKSWAGENWERK AG v. SCHLUNK

United States Supreme Court
486 U.S. 694 (1988)

JUSTICE O'CONNOR:

This case involves an attempt to serve process on a foreign corporation by serving its domestic subsidiary which, under state law, is the foreign corporation's involuntary agent for service of process. We must decide whether such service is compatible with the Convention on Service Abroad of Judicial and Extrajudicial Documents in Civil and Commercial Matters, Nov. 15, 1965 (Hague Service Convention).

I

The parents of respondent Herwig Schlunk were killed in an automobile accident in 1983. Schlunk filed a wrongful death action on their behalf in the Circuit Court of Cook County, Illinois. Schlunk alleged that Volkswagen of America, Inc. (VWoA), had designed and sold the automobile that his parents were driving, and that defects in the automobile caused or contributed to their deaths. Schlunk also alleged that the driver of the other automobile involved in the collision was negligent; Schlunk has since obtained a default judgment against that person, who is no longer a party to this lawsuit. Schlunk successfully served his complaint on VWoA, and VWoA filed an answer denying that it had designed or assembled the automobile in question. Schlunk then amended the complaint to add as a defendant Volkswagen Aktiengesellschaft (VWAG), which is the petitioner here. VWAG, a corporation established under the laws of the Federal Republic of Germany, has its place of business in that country. VWoA is a wholly owned subsidiary of VWAG. Schlunk attempted to serve his amended complaint on VWAG by serving VWoA as VWAG's agent.

VWAG filed a special and limited appearance for the purpose of quashing service. VWAG asserted that it could be served only in accordance with the Hague Service Convention, and that Schlunk had not complied with the Convention's requirements. The Circuit Court denied VWAG's motion. It first observed that VWoA is registered to do business in Illinois and has a registered agent for receipt of process in Illinois. The court then reasoned that VWoA and VWAG are so closely related that VWoA is VWAG's agent for service of process as a matter of law, notwithstanding VWAG's failure or refusal to appoint VWoA formally as an agent. The court relied on the facts that VWoA is a wholly owned subsidiary of VWAG, that a majority of the members of the board of directors of VWoA are members of the board of VWAG, and that VWoA is by contract the exclusive importer and distributor of VWAG products sold in the United States. The court concluded that, because service was accomplished within the United States, the Hague Service Convention did not apply.

* * *

II

The Hague Service Convention is a multilateral treaty that was formulated in 1964 by the Tenth Session of the Hague Conference of Private International Law. * * *

The primary innovation of the Convention is that it requires each state to establish a central authority to receive requests for service of documents from other countries. Art. 2. Once a central authority receives a request in the proper form, it must serve the documents by a method prescribed by the internal law of the receiving state or by a method designated by the requester and compatible with that law. Art. 5. The central authority must then provide a certificate of service that conforms to a specified model. Art. 6. A state also may consent to methods of service within its boundaries other than a request to its central authority. Arts. 8–11, 19. The remaining provisions of the Convention that are relevant here limit the circumstances in which a default judgment may be entered against a defendant who had to be served abroad and did not appear, and provide some means for relief from such a judgment. Arts. 15, 16.

Article 1 defines the scope of the Convention, which is the subject of controversy in this case. It says: "The present Convention shall apply in all cases, in civil or commercial matters, where there is occasion to transmit a judicial or extrajudicial document for service abroad." * * * By virtue of the Supremacy Clause, U.S. Const., Art. VI, the Convention pre-empts inconsistent methods of service prescribed by state law in all cases to which it applies. Schlunk does not purport to have served his complaint on VWAG in accordance with the Convention. Therefore, if service of process in this case falls within Article 1 of the Convention, the trial court should have granted VWAG's motion to quash.

* * *

The Convention does not specify the circumstances in which there is "occasion to transmit" a complaint "for service abroad." But at least the term "service of process" has a well-established technical meaning. Service of process refers to a formal delivery of documents that is legally sufficient to charge the defendant with notice of a pending action. The legal sufficiency of a formal delivery of documents must be measured against some standard. The Convention does not prescribe a standard, so we almost necessarily must refer to the internal law of the forum state. If the internal law of the forum state defines the applicable method of serving process as requiring the transmittal of documents abroad, then the Hague Service Convention applies.

* * *

VWAG protests that it is inconsistent with the purpose of the Convention to interpret it as applying only when the internal law of the forum requires service abroad. One of the two stated objectives of the Convention is "to create appropriate means to ensure that judicial and extrajudicial documents to be served abroad shall be brought to the notice of the addressee in sufficient time." The Convention cannot assure adequate notice, VWAG argues, if the forum's internal law determines whether it applies. VWAG warns that countries could circumvent the Convention by defining methods of service of process that do not require transmission of documents abroad. * * *

* * * One important objective of the Convention is to provide means to facilitate service of process abroad. Thus the first stated purpose of the Convention is "to create" appropriate means for service abroad, and the second stated purpose is "to improve the organization of mutual judicial assistance for that purpose by simplifying and expediting the procedure." By requiring each state to establish a central authority to assist in the service of process, the Convention implements this enabling function. Nothing in our decision today interferes with this requirement.

* * *

Furthermore, nothing that we say today prevents compliance with the Convention even when the internal law of the forum does not so require. The Convention provides simple and certain means by which to serve process on a foreign national. Those who eschew its procedures risk discovering that the forum's internal law required transmittal of documents for service abroad, and that the Convention therefore provided the exclusive means of valid service. In addition, parties that comply with the Convention ultimately may find it easier to enforce their judgments abroad. For these reasons, we anticipate that parties may resort to the Convention voluntarily, even in cases that fall outside the scope of its mandatory application.

III

In this case, the Illinois long-arm statute authorized Schlunk to serve VWAG by substituted service on VWoA, without sending documents to Germany. VWAG has not petitioned for review of the Illinois Appellate Court's holding that service was proper as a matter of Illinois law. VWAG contends, however, that service on VWAG was not complete until VWoA transmitted the complaint to VWAG in Germany. According to VWAG, this transmission constituted service abroad under the Hague Service Convention.

VWAG explains that, as a practical matter, VWoA was certain to transmit the complaint to Germany to notify VWAG of the litigation. Indeed, as a legal matter, the Due Process Clause requires every method of service to provide "notice reasonably calculated, under all the circumstances, to apprise interested parties of the pendency of the action and afford them an opportunity to present their objections." VWAG argues that, because of this notice requirement, every case involving service on a foreign national will present an "occasion to transmit a judicial * * * document for service abroad" within the meaning of Article 1. VWAG emphasizes that in this case, the Appellate Court upheld service only after determining that "the relationship between VWAG and VWoA is so close that it is certain that VWAG 'was fully apprised of the pendency of the action' by delivery of the summons to VWoA."

We reject this argument. Where service on a domestic agent is valid and complete under both state law and the Due Process Clause, our inquiry ends and the Convention has no further implications. Whatever internal, private communications take place between the agent and a foreign principal are beyond the concerns of this case. The only transmittal to which the Convention applies is a transmittal abroad that is required as a necessary part of service. And, contrary to VWAG's assertion, the Due Process Clause does not require an official transmittal of documents abroad every time there is service on a foreign national. Applying this analysis, we conclude that this case does not present an occasion to transmit a judicial document for service abroad within the meaning of Article 1. Therefore the Hague Service Convention does not apply, and service was proper. The judgment of the Appellate Court is

Affirmed.

JUSTICE BRENNAN, with whom JUSTICE MARSHALL and JUSTICE BLACKMUN join, concurring in the judgment.

We acknowledged last Term, and the Court reiterates today, that the terms of the Convention on Service Abroad of Judicial and Extrajudicial Documents in Civil or Commercial Matters are "mandatory," not "optional" with respect to any transmission that Article 1 covers. *Société Nationale Industrielle Aérospatiale v. United States District Court*, 482 U.S. 522, 534, and n. 15, (1987). Even so, the Court holds, and I agree, that a litigant may, consistent with the Convention, serve process on a foreign corporation by serving its wholly owned domestic subsidiary, because such process is not "service abroad" within the meaning of Article 1. The Court reaches that conclusion, however, by depriving the Convention of any mandatory effect, for in the Court's view the "forum's internal law" defines conclusively whether a particular process is "service abroad," which is covered by the Convention, or domestic service, which is not. I do not join the Court's opinion because I find it implausible that the Convention's framers intended to leave each contracting nation, and each of the 50 States within our Nation, free to decide for itself under what circumstances, if any, the Convention would control. Rather, in my view, the words "service abroad," read in light of the negotiating history, embody a substantive standard that limits a forum's latitude to deem service complete domestically.

* * *

My difference with the Court does not affect the outcome of this case, and, given that any process emanating from our courts must comply with due process, it may have little practical consequence in future cases that come before us. But cf. S.Exec.Rep. No. 6, at 15 (statement by Philip W. Amram suggesting that Convention may require "a minor change in the practice of some of our States in long-arm and automobile accident cases" where "service on the appropriate official need be accompanied only by a minimum effort to notify the defendant"). Our Constitution does not, however, bind other nations haling our citizens into their courts. Our citizens rely instead primarily on the forum nation's compliance with the Convention, which the Senate believed would "provide increased protection (due process) for American Citizens who are involved in litigation abroad." Id., at 3. And while other nations are not bound by the Court's pronouncement that the Convention lacks obligatory force, after today's decision their courts will surely sympathize little with any United States national pleading that a judgment violates the Convention because (notwithstanding any local characterization) service was "abroad."

It is perhaps heartening to "think that [no] countr[y] will draft its internal laws deliberately so as to circumvent the Convention in cases in which it would be appropriate to transmit judicial documents for service abroad," although from the defendant's perspective "circumvention" (which, according to the Court, entails no more than exercising a prerogative not to be bound) is equally painful whether deliberate or not. The fact remains, however, that had we been content to rely on foreign notions of fair play and substantial justice, we would have found it unnecessary, in the first place, to participate in a Convention "to ensure that judicial * * * documents to be served abroad [would] be brought to the notice of the addressee in sufficient time."

Does the Supreme Court's reading of the Convention comply with the rules on treaty interpretation in Articles 31–32 of the Vienna Convention on the Law of Treaties (Chapter III.4.)? If service of process abroad—and thus the mechanism established by the Hague Service Convention—can be circumvented so easily, doesn't that gut the whole idea of such an agreement?

What are the risks, if any, for the plaintiff of circumventing the Hague Service Convention mechanism? Think about how the Germans will view the proceedings in the United States. Should the plaintiff care?

Note that the United States is also a party to the Hague Convention on the Taking of Evidence Abroad in Civil and Commercial Matters (1970). The Supreme Court interpreted this Convention narrowly as well in *Société Nationale Industrielle Aérospatiale v. U.S. District Court*, 482 U.S. 522 (1987). The Convention provides rules for the taking of evidence in member states other than the forum. The issue was whether, in cases before U.S. courts, the use of these rules was mandatory with regard to evidence located in another member state. The Court held that it was not, so the litigants were still free to use American discovery rules. In short, in a manner that foreshadowed *Schlunk*, the Court read the Hague Convention as an optional regime.

B. SUBSTANTIVE PRIVATE LAW RULES

In contrast to private international law (in the sense of Conflict of Laws), substantive private law rules on the international level are a more recent phenomenon. Since private law rules had been incorporated into the laws of the modern nation states (beginning in the 17th century and culminating with the great civil codes in the 19th and early 20th centuries), there was virtually no such private law on the international level. Even today, the vast majority of private law rules are of a purely domestic character (raising the choice-of-law issues addressed by private international law).

Beginning in the first half of the 20th century, many jurists considered this state of affairs unfortunate as they saw a need to harmonize, and possibly even to unify, at least the law of international market transactions. Thus efforts towards a uniform international sales law began as early as the 1930s under the auspices of the International Institute for the Unification of Private Law. They never bore fruit, in part because World War II made the requisite international cooperation temporarily impossible. In the postwar years, the Hague Conference adopted two conventions pertaining to international sales; they entered into force in 1972, but neither was widely ratified, and the United States did not become a party to either.

In 1980, however, an international conference convened by the UN General Assembly in Vienna, adopted the *United Nations Convention on Contracts for the International Sale of Goods (CISG)*. It was the fruit of many years of labor by the *United Nations Commission on International Trade Law (UNCITRAL)*. The CISG entered into force in 1988 with the United States among the first group of countries to ratify it. Since that time, the Convention has been ratified by over 75 countries that account for three quarters of world trade, although some commercially important countries, notably the United Kingdom and India, are not members. Still, in terms of ratification, the Convention is easily the most successful project of international unification of private law. Today, its practical importance is enormous since thousands of international sales transactions take place under its regime every day in the United States alone.

Beware that the Convention has several commonly used names, and insiders often assume that everybody else understands what they mean. In the English-speaking world, it is generally known by the acronym CISG. It is often also called the UN Sales Convention or even the Vienna Convention. (The latter term is infelicitous since there are so many other "Vienna Conventions," such as those on the Law of Treaties, on Diplomatic Relations, and on Consular Relations.)

Note also that in 1994, its minor sister, the UN Convention on the Limitation Period in the International Sale of Goods entered into force in the

United States as well. It provides uniform limitation periods that displace the state rules where the Convention applies.

When reading the following excerpts from the CISG, ask yourself three questions: (1) What does the Convention really cover (and what does it leave to purely domestic law)? (2) Where do its rules resemble, and where do they differ from, American sales law? Make a list of the articles you find most surprising—or even disconcerting. (3) What is the potential impact of Article 6 on the practical relevance of the Convention?

UNITED NATIONS CONVENTION ON CONTRACTS FOR THE INTERNATIONAL SALE OF GOODS
(Adopted 1980; in force 1988)

The States Parties to this Convention,

Bearing in mind the broad objectives in the resolutions adopted by the sixth special session of the General Assembly of the United Nations on the establishment of a New International Economic Order,

Considering that the development of international trade on the basis of equality and mutual benefit is an important element in promoting friendly relations among States,

Being of the opinion that the adoption of uniform rules which govern contracts for the international sale of goods and take into account the different social, economic and legal systems would contribute to the removal of legal barriers in international trade and promote the development of international trade,

Have decreed as follows:

Part I
Sphere of Application and General Provisions

Chapter I
Sphere of Application

Article 1

(1) This Convention applies to contracts of sale of goods between parties whose places of business are in different States:

   (a) when the States are Contracting States; or

   (b) when the rules of private international law lead to the application of the law of a Contracting State.

(2) The fact that the parties have their places of business in different States is to be disregarded whenever this fact does not appear either from the contract or from any dealings between, or from information disclosed by, the parties at any time before or at the conclusion of the contract.

(3) Neither the nationality of the parties nor the civil or commercial character of the parties or of the contract is to be taken into consideration in determining the application of this Convention.

Article 2

This Convention does not apply to sales:

(a) of goods bought for personal, family or household use, unless the seller, at any time before or at the conclusion of the contract, neither knew nor ought to have known that the goods were bought for any such use;

(b) by auction;

(c) on execution or otherwise by authority of law;

(d) of stocks, shares, investment securities, negotiable instruments or money;

(e) of ships, vessels, hovercraft or aircraft;

(f) of electricity.

Article 3

(1) Contracts for the supply of goods to be manufactured or produced are to be considered sales unless the party who orders the goods undertakes to supply a substantial part of the materials necessary for such manufacture or production.

(2) This Convention does not apply to contracts in which the preponderant part of the obligations of the party who furnishes the goods consists in the supply of labour or other services.

Article 4

This Convention governs only the formation of the contract of sale and the rights and obligations of the seller and the buyer arising from such a contract. In particular, except as otherwise expressly provided in this Convention, it is not concerned with:

(a) the validity of the contract or of any of its provisions or of any usage;

(b) the effect which the contract may have on the property in the goods sold.

Article 5

This Convention does not apply to the liability of the seller for death or personal injury caused by the goods to any person.

Article 6

The parties may exclude the application of this Convention or, subject to article 12, derogate from or vary the effect of any of its provisions.

Chapter II
General Provisions

Article 7

(1) In the interpretation of this Convention, regard is to be had to its international character and to the need to promote uniformity in its application and the observance of good faith in international trade.

(2) Questions concerning matters governed by this Convention which are not expressly settled in it are to be settled in conformity with the general principles on which it is based or, in the absence of such principles, in conformity with the law applicable by virtue of the rules of private international law.

Article 8

(1) For the purposes of this Convention statements made by and other conduct of a party are to be interpreted according to his intent where the other party knew or could not have been unaware what that intent was.

(2) If the preceding paragraph is not applicable, statements made by and other conduct of a party are to be interpreted according to the understanding that a reasonable person of the same kind as the other party would have had in the same circumstances.

(3) In determining the intent of a party or the understanding a reasonable person would have had, due consideration is to be given to all relevant circumstances of the case including the negotiations, any practices which the parties have established between themselves, usages and any subsequent conduct of the parties.

Article 9

(1) The parties are bound by any usage to which they have agreed and by any practices which they have established between themselves.

(2) The parties are considered, unless otherwise agreed, to have impliedly made applicable to their contract or its formation a usage of which the parties knew or ought to have known and which in international trade is widely known to, and regularly observed by, parties to contracts of the type involved in the particular trade concerned.

Article 10

For the purposes of this Convention:

(a) If a party has more than one place of business, the place of business is that which has the closest relationship to the contract and its performance, having regard to the circumstances known to or contemplated by the parties at any time before or at the conclusion of the contract;

(b) if a party does not have a place of business, reference is to be made to his habitual residence.

Article 11

A contract of sale need not be concluded in or evidenced by writing and is not subject to any other requirement as to form. It may be proved by any means, including witnesses.

Article 12

Any provision of article 11, article 29 or Part II of this Convention that allows a contract of sale or its modification or termination by agreement or any offer, acceptance or other indication of intention to be made in any form other than in writing does not apply where any party has his place of business in a Contracting State which has made a declaration under article 96 of this Convention. The parties may not derogate from or vary the effect or this article.

Article 13

For the purposes of this Convention "writing" includes telegram and telex.

Part II
Formation of the Contract

Article 14

(1) A proposal for concluding a contract addressed to one or more specific persons constitutes an offer if it is sufficiently definite and indicates the intention of the offeror to be bound in case of acceptance. A proposal is sufficiently definite if it indicates the goods and expressly or implicitly fixes or makes provision for determining the quantity and the price.

(2) A proposal other than one addressed to one or more specific persons is to be considered merely as an invitation to make offers, unless the contrary is clearly indicated by the person making the proposal.

Article 15

(1) An offer becomes effective when it reaches the offeree.

(2) An offer, even if it is irrevocable, may be withdrawn if the withdrawal reaches the offeree before or at the same time as the offer.

Article 16

(1) Until a contract is concluded an offer may be revoked if the revocation reaches the offeree before he has dispatched an acceptance.

(2) However, an offer cannot be revoked:

(a) if it indicates, whether by stating a fixed time for acceptance or otherwise, that it is irrevocable; or

(b) if it was reasonable for the offeree to rely on the offer as being ir-revocable and the offeree has acted in reliance on the offer.

Article 17

An offer, even if it is irrevocable, is terminated when a rejection reaches the offeror.

Article 18

(1) A statement made by or other conduct of the offeree indicating assent to an offer is an acceptance. Silence or inactivity does not in itself amount to acceptance.

(2) An acceptance of an offer becomes effective at the moment the indica-tion of assent reaches the offeror. An acceptance is not effective if the indication of assent does not reach the offeror within the time he has fixed or, if no time is fixed, within a reasonable time, due account be-ing taken of the circumstances of the transaction, including the rapid-ity of the means of communication employed by the offeror. An oral of-fer must be accepted immediately unless the circumstances indicate otherwise.

(3) However, if, by virtue of the offer or as a result of practices which the parties have established between themselves or of usage, the offeree may indicate assent by performing an act, such as one relating to the dispatch of the goods or payment of the price, without notice to the of-feror, the acceptance is effective at the moment the act is performed, provided that the act is performed within the period of time laid down in the preceding paragraph.

Article 19

(1) A reply to an offer which purports to be an acceptance but contains additions, limitations or other modifications is a rejection of the offer and constitutes a counter-offer.

(2) However, a reply to an offer which purports to be an acceptance but contains additional or different terms which do not materially alter the terms of the offer constitutes an acceptance, unless the offeror, without undue delay, objects orally to the discrepancy or dispatches a notice to that effect. If he does not so object, the terms of the contract are the terms of the offer with the modifications contained in the ac-ceptance.

(3) Additional or different terms relating, among other things, to the price, payment, quality and quantity of the goods, place and time of delivery, extent of one party's liability to the other or the settlement of disputes are considered to alter the terms of the offer materially.

Article 20

(1) A period of time for acceptance fixed by the offeror in a telegram or a letter begins to run from the moment the telegram is handed in for dispatch or from the date shown on the letter or, if no such date is shown, from the date shown on the envelope. A period of time for acceptance fixed by the offeror by telephone, telex or other means of instantaneous communication, begins to run from the moment that the offer reaches the offeree.

(2) Official holidays or non-business days occurring during the period for acceptance are included in calculating the period. However, if a notice of acceptance cannot be delivered at the address of the offeror on the last day of the period because that day falls on an official holiday or a non-business day at the place of business of the offeror, the period is extended until the first business day which follows.

Article 21

(1) A late acceptance is nevertheless effective as an acceptance if without delay the offeror orally so informs the offeree or dispatches a notice to that effect.

(2) If a letter or other writing containing a late acceptance shows that it has been sent in such circumstances that if its transmission had been normal it would have reached the offeror in due time, the late acceptance is effective as an acceptance unless, without delay, the offeror orally informs the offeree that he considers his offer as having lapsed or dispatches a notice to that effect.

Article 22

An acceptance may be withdrawn if the withdrawal reaches the offeror before or at the same time as the acceptance would have become effective.

Article 23

A contract is concluded at the moment when an acceptance of an offer becomes effective in accordance with the provisions of this Convention.

Article 24

For the purposes of this Part of the Convention, an offer, declaration of acceptance or any other indication of intention "reaches" the addressee when it is made orally to him or delivered by any other means to him personally, to his place of business or mailing address or, if he does not have a place of business or mailing address, to his habitual residence.

Part III
Sale of Goods

Chapter I
General Provisions

Article 25

A breach of contract committed by one of the parties is fundamental if it results in such detriment to the other party as substantially to deprive him of what he is entitled to expect under the contract, unless the party in breach did not foresee and a reasonable person of the same kind in the same circumstances would not have foreseen such a result.

Article 26

A declaration of avoidance of the contract is effective only if made by notice to the other party.

Article 27

Unless otherwise expressly provided in this Part of the Convention, if any notice, request or other communication is given or made by a party in accordance with this Part and by means appropriate in the circumstances, a delay or error in the transmission of the communication or its failure to arrive does not deprive that party of the right to rely on the communication.

Article 28

If, in accordance with the provisions of this Convention, one party is entitled to require performance of any obligation by the other party, a court is not bound to enter a judgement for specific performance unless the court would do so under its own law in respect of similar contracts of sale not governed by this Convention.

Article 29

(1) A contract may be modified or terminated by the mere agreement of the parties.

(2) A contract in writing which contains a provision requiring any modification or termination by agreement to be in writing may not be otherwise modified or terminated by agreement. However, a party may be precluded by his conduct from asserting such a provision to the extent that the other party has relied on that conduct.

Chapter II
Obligations of the Seller

* * *

Chapter III
Obligations of the Buyer

* * *

Chapter IV
Passing of Risk

* * *

Chapter V
Provisions Common to the Obligations of the Seller
and the Buyer

* * *

Part IV
Final Provisions

Article 95

Any State may declare at the time of the deposit of its instrument of ratification, acceptance, approval or accession that it will not be bound by subparagraph (1)(b) of article 1 of this Convention.

Article 96

A Contracting State whose legislation requires contracts of sale to be concluded in or evidenced by writing may at any time make a declaration in accordance with article 12 that any provision of article 11, article 29, or Part II of this Convention, that allows a contract of sale or its modification or termination by agreement or any offer, acceptance, or other indication of intention to be made in any form other than in writing, does not apply where any party has his place of business in that State.

* * *

The CISG can be a pitfall—especially because you may not realize (in time) that your (client's) contract is actually governed by it—rather than by more familiar sources such as the Uniform Commercial Code. The following case illustrates this—and other—dangers. What lessons does it teach?

ASANTE TECHNOLOGIES, INC. v. PMC–SIERRA, INC.

United States District Court
164 F. Supp. 2d 1142 (N.D. Cal. 2001)

* * *

Order Denying Motion to Remand and Request for
Attorneys' Fees

JUDGE WARE:

I.   INTRODUCTION

This lawsuit arises out of a dispute involving the sale of electronic components. Plaintiff, Asante Technologies Inc., filed the action in the Superior Court for the State of California, Santa Clara County, on February 13, 2001. Defendant, PMC–Sierra, Inc., removed the action to this Court, asserting federal question jurisdiction pursuant to 28 U.S.C. section 1331. Specifically, Defendant asserts that Plaintiff's claims for breach of contract and breach of express warranty are governed by the United Nations Convention on Contracts for the International Sale of Goods ("CISG"). Plaintiff disputes jurisdiction and filed this Motion To Remand And For Attorneys' Fees. The Court conducted a hearing on June 18, 2001. Based upon the submitted papers and oral arguments of the parties, the Court DENIES the motion to remand and the associated request for attorneys' fees.

II.   BACKGROUND

The Complaint in this action alleges claims based in tort and contract. Plaintiff contends that Defendant failed to provide it with electronic components meeting certain designated technical specifications. Defendant timely removed the action to this Court on March 16, 2001.

Plaintiff is a Delaware corporation having its primary place of business in Santa Clara County, California. Plaintiff produces network switchers, a type of electronic component used to connect multiple computers to one another and to the Internet. Plaintiff purchases component parts from a number of manufacturers. In particular, Plaintiff purchases application-specific integrated circuits ("ASICs"), which are considered the control center of its network switchers, from Defendant.

Defendant is also a Delaware corporation. Defendant asserts that, at all relevant times, its corporate headquarters, inside sales and marketing office, public relations department, principal warehouse, and most design and engineering functions were located in Burnaby, British Columbia, Canada. Defendant also maintains an office in Portland, Oregon, where many of its engineers are based. Defendant's products are sold in California through Unique Technologies, which is an authorized distributor of Defendant's products in North America. It is undisputed that Defendant directed Plaintiff to purchase Defendant's products through Unique, and that Defendant honored purchase orders solicited by Unique. Unique is located in California. Determining Defendant's "place of business" with respect to its contract with Plaintiff is critical to the question of whether the Court has jurisdiction in this case.

Plaintiff's Complaint focuses on five purchase orders. Four of the five purchase orders were submitted to Defendant through Unique as directed by Defendant. However, Plaintiff does not dispute that one of the purchase orders, dated January 28, 2000, was sent by fax directly to Defendant in British Columbia, and that Defendant processed the order in British Columbia. Defendant shipped all orders to Plaintiff's headquarters in California. Upon delivery of the goods, Unique sent invoices to Plaintiff, at which time Plaintiff tendered payment to Unique either in California or in Nevada.

The Parties do not identify any single contract embodying the agreement pertaining to the sale. Instead, Plaintiff asserts that acceptance of each of its purchase orders was expressly conditioned upon acceptance by Defendant of Plaintiff's "Terms and Conditions," which were included with each Purchase Order. Paragraph 20 of Plaintiff's Terms and Conditions provides "APPLICABLE LAW. The validity [and] performance of this [purchase] order shall be governed by the laws of the state shown on Buyer's address on this order." The buyer's address as shown on each of the Purchase Orders is in San Jose, California. Alternatively, Defendant suggests that the terms of shipment are governed by a document entitled "PMC–Sierra TERMS AND CONDITIONS OF SALE." Paragraph 19 of Defendant's Terms and conditions provides "APPLICABLE LAW: The contract between the parties is made, governed by, and shall be construed in accordance with the laws of the Province of British Columbia and the laws of Canada applicable therein, which shall be deemed to be the proper law hereof * * * ."

* * *

B.   THE CONTRACT IN QUESTION IS BETWEEN PARTIES FROM DIFFERENT STATES

The CISG only applies when a contract is "between parties whose places of business are in different States."[4] Art. 1(1)(a). If this requirement is not satisfied, Defendant cannot claim jurisdiction under the CISG. It is undisputed that Plaintiff's place of business is Santa Clara County, California, U.S.A. It is further undisputed that during the relevant time period, Defendant's corporate headquarters, inside sales and marketing office, public relations department, principal warehouse, and most of its design

---

[4] In the context of the CISG, "different States" refers to different countries. U.S. Ratification of 1980 United Nations Convention on Contracts for the International Sale of Goods: Official English Text, 15 U.S.C.App. at 52 (1997).

and engineering functions were located in Burnaby, British Columbia, Canada. However, Plaintiff contends that, pursuant to Article 10 of the CISG, Defendant's "place of business" having the closest relationship to the contract at issue is the United States.[5]

The Complaint asserts *inter alia* two claims for breach of contract and a claim for breach of express warranty based on the failure of the delivered ASICS to conform to the agreed upon technical specifications. * * *

Plaintiff's claims concern breaches of representations made by Defendant from Canada. Moreover, the products in question are manufactured in Canada, and Plaintiff knew that Defendant was Canadian, having sent one purchase order directly to Defendant in Canada by fax. Plaintiff supports its position with the declaration of Anthony Contos, Plaintiff's Vice President of Finance and Administration, who states that Plaintiff's primary contact with Defendant "during the development and engineering of the ASICs at issue * * * was with [Defendant's] facilities in Portland, Oregon." The Court concludes that these contacts are not sufficient to override the fact that most if not all of Defendant's alleged representations regarding the technical specifications of the products emanated from Canada. Moreover, Plaintiff directly corresponded with Defendant at Defendant's Canadian address. Plaintiff relies on all of these alleged representations at length in its Complaint. In contrast, Plaintiff has not identified any specific representation or correspondence emanating from Defendant's Oregon branch. For these reasons, the Court finds that Defendant's place of business that has the closest relationship to the contract and its performance is British Columbia, Canada. Consequently, the contract at issue in this litigation is between parties from two different Contracting States, Canada and the United States. This contract therefore implicates the CISG.

C.   THE EFFECT OF THE CHOICE OF LAW CLAUSES

Plaintiff next argues that, even if the Parties are from two nations that have adopted the CISG, the choice of law provisions in the "Terms and Conditions" set forth by both Parties reflect the Parties' intent to "opt out" of application of the treaty. Article 6 of the CISG provides that "[t]he parties may exclude the application of the Convention or, subject to Article 12, derogate from or vary the effect of any of its provisions." 15 U.S.C.App., Art. 6. Defendant asserts that merely choosing the law of a jurisdiction is insufficient to opt out of the CISG, absent express exclusion of the CISG. The Court finds that the particular choice of law provisions

---

[5] Article 10 of the CISG states *inter alia:*

For the purposes of this Convention:

(a) If a party has more than one place of business, the place of business is that which has the closest relationship to the contract and its performance, having regard to the circumstances known to or contemplated by the parties at any time before or at the conclusion of the contract.

in the "Terms and Conditions" of both parties are inadequate to effectuate an opt out of the CISG.

Although selection of a particular choice of law, such as "the California Commercial Code" or the "Uniform Commercial Code" *could* amount to implied exclusion of the CISG, the choice of law clauses at issue here do not evince a clear intent to opt out of the CISG. For example, Defendant's choice of applicable law adopts the law of British Columbia, and it is undisputed that the CISG *is* the law of British Columbia. (International Sale of Goods Act ch. 236, 1996 S.B.C. 1 *et seq.* (B.C.).) Furthermore, even Plaintiff's choice of applicable law generally adopts the "laws of" the State of California, and California is bound by the Supremacy Clause to the treaties of the United States. U.S. Const. art. VI, cl. 2 ("This Constitution, and the laws of the United States which shall be made in pursuance thereof; and all treaties made, or which shall be made, under the authority of the United States, shall be the supreme law of the land.") Thus, under general California law, the CISG is applicable to contracts where the contracting parties are from different countries that have adopted the CISG. In the absence of clear language indicating that both contracting parties intended to opt out of the CISG, and in view of Defendant's Terms and Conditions which would apply the CISG, the Court rejects Plaintiff's contention that the choice of law provisions preclude the applicability of the CISG.

* * *

Compare the District Court's opinion in *Asante* with the decision below.

JUDGMENT OF THE AUSTRIAN SUPREME COURT (OBERSTER GERICHTSHOF)

CISG Online 614 (Oct. 22, 2001)
(translation from the German by the authors)

[In their contract, a Hungarian seller and an Austrian buyer agreed that their transaction was governed by Austrian law. The defendant then argued that, as a result, the CISG did not apply.]

* * *

At the time of concluding the contract, the CISG was in force both in Hungary and in Austria. The parties, which have their seats in different countries, concluded a contract on the delivery of goods (Art. 1 lit. a CISG). In principle, the CISG is thus included in their choice of law as part of Austrian law. If the CISG applies, parties who do not want it to apply must agree on its exclusion; this exclusion can be explicit or implied. An explicit exclusion is not even claimed by the defendant; contrary to the appellant's argument, there is no reason to assume an implied exclusion either since such an assumption requires a sufficiently clear intention of the parties. If it is not sufficiently clear, according to the standards announced in CISG Art. 8 on the interpretation of the declarations and conduct of the parties, that such an exclusion was intended, the CISG remains applicable. According to the clearly prevailing view, the general choice of the law of a (CISG) member state cannot, in and of itself and without additional indications (which are missing here), lead to the exclusion of the CISG.

* * *

Is the conclusion that the parties did not effectively opt out of the CISG in these cases correct? In both cases, isn't it clear that the parties wanted some other law to apply and even agreed on that score? If the parties to an international sales contract wanted to be sure to avoid the CISG, what exactly should their clause say?

C. INTERNATIONAL PRINCIPLES OF PRIVATE LAW

Towards the end of the 20th century, several private or semi-private institutions created international Principles in various areas of private law. This trend has been particularly strong in Europe, where such Principles are considered steps on the path towards the harmonization of European private law, possibly even leading to a European civil code. (See especially the so-called *Principles of European Contract Law*, often called *Lando Principles* because they were drafted by an expert commission convened and chaired by Danish law professor Ole Lando.) Such Principles are related to two other phenomena.

First, they are often seen as the modern version of a much older tradition: the *lex mercatoria* (law merchant). The whole phenomenon is highly contested, but many scholars believe that this *lex mercatoria* developed in the middle ages as a body of law governing commercial transactions between merchants from different countries or regions. Its principles and rules were, at least by and large, recognized by merchants, their courts (see Chapter IV.2.) and often even the general tribunals throughout Europe as a special kind of law, coexisting with (and influenced by) Roman private law, ecclesiastical law, local custom and ordinances. The *lex mercatoria* lost its force as a quasi-international regime when it was absorbed by the legislation of the rising nation states beginning in the 17th century. Whether the various Principles drafted and published in recent decades can justly be regarded as a revival of the medieval *lex mercatoria* is subject to debate. They do, however, pursue a similar goal: to create a uniform set of rules for international transactions independent of national laws.

Second, these Principles have often been likened to the Restatements of domestic American law published by the American Law Institute since the 1930s. Both endeavors are similar in form: they consist of blackletter rules organized into a quasi-code. They also have similar aims in that they restate principles and rules accepted across jurisdictions—one on the international, the other on the interstate level. While they are not legally binding, both aim to guide (and perhaps persuade) decision-makers in real cases by providing a kind of common denominator above and beyond the particularities of local rules.

The most notable recent endeavor on a global scale resulted in the *Principles of International Commercial Contracts* produced by the *International Institute for the Unification of Private Law (Institut International pour l'unification du droit privé—UNIDROIT)*. UNIDROIT is an independent intergovernmental organization originally founded in 1926 (as an auxiliary organ of the League of Nations) and has its seat in Rome. Today, it has over sixty member states. It has also promulgated a considerable variety of international private law conventions. The UNIDROIT Principles were originally published in 1994 with enlarged editions following in 2004 and 2010.

You should not focus on the details of the Principles, but should instead strive to get a sense of the nature of such projects. What are the avowed goals of these Principles? Also, make a list of the provisions you find surprising or even troublesome from an American lawyer's perspective. In light of this list, would you advise your American client to adopt the UNIDROIT principles as the law governing its contract with a foreign partner?

PRINCIPLES OF INTERNATIONAL COMMERCIAL CONTRACTS

International Institute for the Unification of Private Law (3d ed. 2010)

Preamble

(Purpose of the Principles)

These Principles set forth general rules for international commercial contracts.

They shall be applied when the parties have agreed that their contract be governed by them.

They may be applied when the parties have agreed that their contracts be governed by general principles of law, the *lex mercatoria* or the like.

They may be applied when the parties have not chosen any law to govern their contract.

They may be used to interpret or supplement international uniform law instruments.

They may be used to interpret or supplement domestic law.

They may serve as a model for national and international legislators.

Chapter 1. General Provisions

Article 1.1
Freedom of Contract

The parties are free to enter into a contract and to determine its content.

Article 1.2
No Form Required

Nothing in these Principles requires a contract, statement or any other act to be made or evidenced by a particular form. It may be proved by any means, including witnesses.

Article 1.3
Binding Character of Contract

A contract validly entered into is binding upon the parties. It can only be modified or terminated in accordance with its terms or by agreement or as otherwise provided in these Principles.

Article 1.4
Mandatory Rules

Nothing in these Principles shall restrict the application of mandatory rules, whether of national, international or supranational origin, which are applicable in accordance with the relevant rules of private international law.

Article 1.5
Exclusion or Modification by the Parties

The parties may exclude the application of these Principles or derogate from or vary the effect of any of their provisions, except as otherwise provided in the Principles.

Article 1.6
Interpretation and supplementation of the Principles

(1) In the interpretation of these Principles, regard is to be had to their international character and to their purposes including the need to promote uniformity in their application.

(2) Issues within the scope of these Principles but not expressly settled by them are as far as possible to be settled in accordance with their underlying general principles.

Article 1.7
Good Faith and Fair Dealing

(1) Each party must act in accordance with good faith and fair dealing in international trade.

(2) The parties may not exclude or limit this duty.

Article 1.8
Inconsistent Behaviour

A party cannot act inconsistently with an understanding it has caused the other party to have and upon which that other party reasonably has acted in reliance to its detriment.

Article 1.9
Usages and Practices

(1) The parties are bound by any usage to which they have agreed and by any practices which they have established between themselves.

(2) The parties are bound by a usage that is widely known to and regularly observed in international trade by parties in the particular trade concerned except where the application of such usage would be unreasonable.

Article 1.10
Notice

(1) Where notice is required it may be given by any means appropriate to the circumstances.

(2) A notice is effective when it reaches the person to whom it is given.

(3) For the purpose of paragraph (2) a notice "reaches" a person when given to that person orally or delivered at that person's place of business or mailing address.

(4) For the purpose of this article "notice" includes a declaration, demand, request or any other communication of intention.

* * *

Chapter 2. Formation and Authority of Agents

Section 1. Formation

Article 2.1.1
Manner of Formation

A contract may be concluded either by the acceptance of an offer or by conduct of the parties that is sufficient to show agreement.

Article 2.1.2
Definition of Offer

A proposal for concluding a contract constitutes an offer if it is sufficiently definite and indicates the intention of the offeror to be bound in case of acceptance.

Article 2.1.3
Withdrawal of Offer

(1) An offer becomes effective when it reaches the offeree.

(2) An offer, even if it is irrevocable, may be withdrawn if the withdrawal reaches the offeree before or at the same time as the offer.

Article 2.1.4
Revocation of Offer

(1) Until a contract is concluded an offer may be revoked if the revocation reaches the offeree before it has dispatched an acceptance.

(2) However, an offer cannot be revoked

   (a) if it indicates, whether by stating a fixed time for acceptance or otherwise, that it is irrevocable; or

   (b) if it was reasonable for the offeree to rely on the offer as being irrevocable and the offeree has acted in reliance of the offer.

Article 2.1.5
Rejection of Offer

An offer is terminated when a rejection reaches the offeror.

Article 2.1.6
Mode of Acceptance

(1) A statement made by or other conduct of the offeree indicating assent to an offer is an acceptance. Silence or inactivity does not in itself amount to acceptance.

(2) An acceptance of an offer becomes effective when the indication of assent reaches the offeror.

(3) However, if, by virtue of the offer or as a result of practices which the parties have established between themselves or of usage, the offeree may indicate assent by performing an act without notice to the offeror, the acceptance is effective when the act is performed.

Article 2.1.7
Time of Acceptance

An offer must be accepted within the time the offeror has fixed or, if no time is fixed, within a reasonable time having regard to the circumstances, including the rapidity of the means of communication employed by the offeror. An oral offer must be accepted immediately unless the circumstances indicate otherwise.

* * *

Article 2.1.12
Writings in Confirmation

If a writing which is sent within a reasonable time after the conclusion of the contract and which purports to be a confirmation of the contract contains additional or different terms, such terms become part of the contract unless they materially alter the contract or the recipient, without undue discrepancy.

* * *

Article 2.1.15
Negotiations in Bad Faith

(1) A party is free to negotiate and is not liable for failure to reach an agreement.

(2) However, a party who negotiates or breaks off negotiations in bad faith is liable for the losses caused to the other party.

* * *

Article 2.1.20
Surprising Terms

(1) No term contained in standard terms which is of such a character that the other party could not reasonably have expected it, is effective unless it has been expressly accepted by that party.

(2) In determining whether a term is of such a character regard shall be had to its content, language and presentation.

* * *

Article 2.1.22
Battle of Forms

Where both parties use standard terms and reach agreement except on those terms, a contract is concluded on the basis of the agreed terms and of any standard terms which are common in substance unless one party clearly indicates in advance, or later and without undue delay informs the other party, that it does not intend to be bound by such a contract.

* * *

Chapter 3. Validity

Section 2. Grounds for Avoidance

* * *

Article 3.2.7
Gross Disparity

(1) A party may avoid the contract or an individual term of it if, at the time of the conclusion of the contract, the contract term unjustifiably gave the other party an excessive advantage. Regard is to be had, among other factors, to

    (a) the fact that the other party has taken unfair advantage of the first party's dependence, economic distress or urgent needs, or of its improvidence, ignorance, inexperience or lack of bargaining skill; and

    (b) the nature and purpose of the contract.

(2) Upon the request of the party entitled to avoidance, a court may adapt the contract or term in order to make it accord with reasonable commercial standards of fair dealing.

(3) A court may also adapt the contract or term upon the request of the party receiving notice of avoidance, provided that that party informs the other party of its request promptly after receiving such notice and before the other party has reasonably acted in reliance on it. Article 3.2.10(2) applies accordingly.

* * *

Chapter 4. Interpretation

Article 4.6
Contra Proferentem Rule

If contract terms supplied by one party are unclear, an interpretation against that party is preferred.

* * *

Article 4.8
Supplying an Omitted Term

(1) Where the parties to a contract have not agreed with respect to a term which is important for a determination of their rights and duties, a term which is appropriate in the circumstances shall be supplied.

(2) In determining what is an appropriate term regard shall be had, among other factors, to

    (a) the intention of the parties;

(b) the nature and purpose of the contract;

(c) good faith and fair dealing;

(d) reasonableness.

Chapter 5. Content, Third Party Rights and Conditions

Section 1. Content

Article 5.1.1
Express and Implied Obligations

The contractual obligations of the parties may be express or implied.

Article 5.1.2
Implied Obligations

Implied obligations stem from

(a) the nature and purpose of the contract;

(b) practices established between the parties and usages;

(c) good faith and fair dealing;

(d) reasonableness.

Article 5.1.3
Co-operation between the Parties

Each party shall co-operate with the other party when such co-operation may reasonably be expected for the performance of that party's obligations.

* * *

Chapter 6. Performance

Section 2. Hardship

Article 6.2.1
Contract to be Observed

Where the performance of a contract becomes more onerous for one of the parties, that party is nevertheless bound to perform its obligations subject to the following provisions on hardship.

Article 6.2.2
Definition of Hardship

There is hardship where the occurrence of events fundamentally alters the equilibrium of the contract either because the cost of a party's performance has increased or because the value of the performance a party receives has diminished, and

(a) the events occur or become known to the disadvantaged party after the conclusion of the contract;

(b) the events could not reasonably have been taken into account by the disadvantaged party at the time of the conclusion of the contract;

(c) the events are beyond the control of the disadvantaged party; and

(d) the risk of the events was not assumed by the disadvantaged party.

Article 6.2.3
Effects of Hardship

(1) In case of hardship the disadvantaged party is entitled to request renegotiations. The request shall be made without undue delay and shall indicate the grounds on which it is based.

(2) The request for renegotiation does not itself entitle the disadvantaged party to withhold performance.

(3) Upon failure to reach agreement within a reasonable time either party may resort to the court.

(4) If the court finds hardship it may, if reasonable,

    (a) terminate the contract at a date and on terms to be fixed; or

    (b) adapt the contract with a view to restoring its equilibrium.

* * *

The practical impact of the UNIDROIT Principles is a matter of some debate. It is clear however, that these (and similar) Principles play a considerable role primarily in international commercial arbitration (which we survey in Chapter IX.2.), often because arbitral tribunals rely on them as a neutral source not tied to any of the parties' national laws. Here is an example. Note that this is a very small excerpt from an opinion totaling 88 single-spaced pages. What is the effect of the UNIDROIT Principle provision employed here?

PETROBART LIMITED (CLAIMANT) V. THE KYRGYZ REPUBLIC (RESPONDENT)

Arbitration Institute of the Stockholm Chamber of Commerce SCC Institute
SCC Case No. 126/2003 (2005)

Arbitrators: Hans Danelius; Ove Bring; Jeroen Smets

Place: Stockholm, Sweden

Language: English

I.   THE CONTRACT

Petrobart Limited (hereinafter called *"Petrobart"*) is a company registered in Gibraltar. On 23 February 1998, Petrobart as Supplier and the state joint stock company Kyrgyzgazmunaizat (hereinafter called *"KGM"*) as Purchaser concluded Goods Supply Contract No. 1/98–PB (hereinafter called *"the Contract"*) the subject-matter of which was defined as follows:

"1. Subject-Matter of the Contract

1.1 SUPPLIER shall supply and transfer ownership of two hundred thousand (200,000) tons of stable gas condensate (the "goods") to PURCHASER over the course of one year on a monthly basis.

1.2 PURCHASER shall accept the supplied goods and make payment under the conditions of this agreement.

1.3 The goods shall be delivered on the terms CIF Kant station. The station of destination shall be Kant station."

As regards the price of the goods, Section 4 of the Contract provided as follows:

"4. Price and Payments

4.1 The price of the goods shall be established in United States dollars and shall not be subject to change: one hundred forty-three US dollars and fifty cents (US$143.50) per metric ton of gas condensate.

4.2 The price is given inclusive of VAT.

4.3 PURCHASER shall make payments according to the details pursuant to the invoice presented by SUPPLIER in relation to each separate consignment of goods, within ten days of the date of the goods' arrival at the station of destination."

* * *

F.   CONCLUSION

In light of the above, Petrobart is entitled to receive:

(a) compensatory damages in the amount of USD 1,507,812.60 (the total sum awarded by the Bishkek Court) together with interest thereon at an annual rate determined in accordance with Article 7.4.9 of the UNIDROIT Principles of International Commercial Contracts[2] from 25 December 1998 (the date of the Bishkek Court's award) until payment has been made;

---

[2] Note by the authors: Article 7.4.9. provides:

Interest for Failure to Pay Money

(1) If a party does not pay a sum of money when it falls due the aggrieved party is entitled to interest upon that sum from the time when payment is due to the time of payment whether or not the non-payment is excused.

(2) The rate of interest shall be the average bank short-term lending rate to prime borrowers prevailing for the currency of payment at the place for payment, or where no such rate exists at that place, then the same rate in the State of the currency of payment. In the absence of such a rate at either place the rate of interest shall be the appropriate rate fixed by the law of the State of the currency of payment.

(b) an amount of USD 2,376,339.60 in lost future profits arising as a consequence of the Republic's breach of its obligations under both the Treaty and international law, together with interest thereon at an annual rate determined in accordance with Article 7.4.9 of the UNIDROIT Principles of International Commercial Contracts from 4 March 1999 (the date when the Government Decree No. 11 was executed at the extraordinary shareholders' meeting in KGM) until payment has been made;

(c) an amount of USD 200,500.00 for outlays and related expenses together with interest thereon at the annual rate determined in accordance with Article 7.4.9 of the UNIDROIT Principles of International Commercial Contracts from 1 September 2003 (the date of the Request for Arbitration) until payment has been made;

(d) a declaration that all costs, as between the parties, of this arbitral proceeding, including legal fees, are to be borne by the Republic; and

(e) such other relief as the Arbitral Tribunal may deem appropriate.

————————

Note that according to the Preamble, the parties can agree that their contract be governed by the UNIDROIT Principles. That would mean making *non-state law* binding by consent. Should courts allow that? Wouldn't that enable parties to contract out of the states' legal orders altogether?

D. INTERNATIONAL BUSINESS CONTRACTS

If a dispute arises out of an international business transaction, a threshold question will be to identify the law that applies to the dispute. In the absence of any contractual provisions, that question will be decided under the choice-of-law rules of the state where the litigation takes place. Parties can also choose the applicable law in their contract, and such choice-of-law clauses are usually enforced in business transactions. For example, Article 3 of the Law of the People's Republic of China on the Laws Applicable to Foreign-Related Civil Relations (2010), provides that "[t]he parties may explicitly choose the law applicable to their foreign-related civil relations in accordance with the provisions of this law."

Parties to international transactions often create their own substantive private law rules by drafting extensive contracts. This may be particularly important where the law is otherwise unclear, not specific enough or where it does not fit the parties' particular needs. By creating their own legal regimes, parties can also largely avoid the choice-of-law question. Of course, the parties will still include a choice-of-forum (or arbitration) clause—and even a choice-of-law clause to cover unforeseen issues.

Due to the commercial importance of the United States, the dominance of the English banking, shipping, and insurance industries, and the influence of American and English global law firms (or of international firms modeled after them), the majority of such international business contracts are currently drafted in English. This may change as China and the Pacific Rim emerge as robust markets in which (Mandarin) Chinese is gradually becoming a dominant language.

The details of business contracts between parties from different countries are ordinarily covered by an advanced course (or seminar) called *International Business Transactions* (in insider lingo, IBT) or, with regard to particular areas, in other specialized courses. We will focus here on only one, frequently observed and widely discussed, phenomenon: the traditional differences in drafting-style between civil law countries (especially in continental Europe, but also on the Pacific Rim and in Latin America) and common law countries (especially the United States, but also England). The former have usually preferred shorter contracts, limited to the essentials. The latter have tended to produce much longer and more prolix documents (although the influence of American and British law firms has gradually pulled civilian practice in the Anglo–American direction).

How would you react if you were an American lawyer faced with the shorter ("civilian") version? What if you were a European or Japanese lawyer confronted with the American-style document? Which version do you prefer personally? Why?

What can explain the differences in drafting styles? In the article below, John Langbein rejects several explanations and then proffers another. Is his view convincing, or at least plausible? What other explanations can you think of (in terms of cultural differences, the styles of legal practice, the role of law in business more generally, etc.)?

JOHN H. LANGBEIN, COMPARATIVE CIVIL PROCEDURE AND THE STYLE OF COMPLEX CONTRACTS
35 Am. J. Comp. L. 381 (1987)

Among businessmen and lawyers familiar with commercial practice in complex transactions on both sides of the Atlantic, it is a common observation that a contract drafted in the United States is typically vastly more detailed than a contract originating in Germany or elsewhere on the Continent. My purpose in this paper is to inquire into the causes of that notable difference in the style of contracting.

The Belgian legal writer Georges van Hecke discussed this subject in a stimulating paper that is now a quarter-century old. He illustrated the phenomenon with an anecdote. He told of a transaction in which an American company and a European company were planning to affiliate by exchanging shares. The lawyers for the American firm drafted two contracts to embrace the transaction. The combined drafts ran about 10,000 words in length. The European businessman had no prior experience with

American lawyers, and when presented with the elephantine American drafts he was so shocked that he nearly renounced the deal. Thereupon it was decided to start over, and the European businessman arranged for his lawyer to prepare a counterdraft. "The result was a document of 1400 words. It was found by the American party to include all the substance that was really needed, and it was readily executed by both parties and adequately performed."[1]

I.   VAN HECKE'S ACCOUNT

Why are American contracts so much more detailed than European?[2] Van Hecke's article supplies a convenient starting point for that inquiry. He offered three explanations.

1. *Perfectionism.* Van Hecke attributed to the American lawyer a drive "for perfection that is not commonly to be found in Europe. The average American businessman is prepared to pay for this perfection in the form of high fees," while his European counterpart is not. But why? Why does "[t]he average European businessman" seem to think "that a perfectly watertight contract cannot be achieved and that it is not worthwhile to pay unreasonably high fees for an objective that is not within reach"? To speak of differing prospensities for perfectionism merely restates the problem, which is to understand why the Americans strive for contractual terms that are, in van Hecke's apt phrase, "perfectly watertight."

2. *Federalism.* Van Hecke directed attention to the multiplicity of American jurisdictions. "An American lawyer, when drafting a contract, does not know in what jurisdiction litigation will arise. He must make a contract that will achieve its purpose in any American jurisdiction." By contrast, the European lawyer "always has in mind the law of one country where the contract is being localized by both choice of law and choice of forum."

I think this argument is considerably overstated. European states are comparatively small, and European deals must frequently entail multi-state dimensions. Further, the degree of diversity among the American states in matters of contract and commercial law is relatively slight—certainly less than among the states of Europe. Although there are 50-odd American jurisdictions, all but Louisiana and Puerto Rico have a law of

---

[1] Van Hecke, "A Civilian Looks at the Common–Law Lawyer," *International Contracts: Choice of Law and Language* 5, 10 (Parker School of Foreign and Comparative Law, Columbia University, ed. 1962).

[2] At some level the tension between "going short" and "going long"—between capturing the essentials and enumerating the details—is endemic to legal drafting in any legal system. Nor is the choice confined to styles of contracting; it can be seen in statutory drafting as well. Contrast the gargantuan and pedantic Prussian civil code of 1794 with the compressed and reticulated civil code (the BGB) that emerged on the same soil a century later. Or notice the difference in aspiration between the American antitrust statutes (the Sherman and Clayton acts) that "went short", on the one hand, and the pension law (ERISA) that "went long." The point being asserted in text is not that Europeans always "go short," but that Americans are comparatively more disposed than Europeans to "go long."

contracts based on English common law; and all except Louisiana now adhere to the Uniform Commercial Code for commercial transactions.

I do concede the point at which van Hecke hints when he speaks of choice of law. The movements that have dominated American choice-of-law thinking in recent decades have materially impaired the predictability of our conflicts rules. Yet, if the sponginess of American conflicts law were the factor driving American lawyers to particularize the terms of complex contracts, we would expect to see Americans drafting skimpier, more European-style documents in real estate contracts, trust instruments, and other fields where choice-of-law problems are slight or can be easily avoided. As a trust lawyer, I assure you that such is not the case. Gargantuan, massively detailed instruments are a hallmark of routine trust drafting.

3. *Code law versus case law.* The most intriguing of van Hecke's suggestions is that the different American style of contracting is a manifestation of that seemingly profound difference between Continental and Anglo–American legal systems: The European private law is codified whereas the American is not. Codification, especially in Germany and in the German-influenced legal systems, entailed not only a reorganization of the law, but a scientific recasting of legal concepts. "The European lawyer has at his command a store of synthetic concepts, such as 'force majeure' [an odd example, since equivalent notions exist in the common law]. Their exact meaning may not always be perfectly clear, but they do save a lot of space-consuming enumeration." By contrast, American lawyers draft to combat "the lawless science of their law, that code-less myriad of precedent, that wilderness of single instances." Thus, van Hecke observes, "when a European and an American lawyer want to express the same thing, an American lawyer needs far more words." American contracts are prolix because American substantive law is primitive.

The way to test this beguiling notion is to ask whether it fairly describes what the American draftsman is doing with his boilerplate. Is he really using his instrument to compensate for the lesser precision of his substantive law? Van Hecke supplies a single (and not very typical) example of American boilerplate—he found it in a contract and could not resist quoting it. The term read: "Except where otherwise indicated by the context, singular terminology shall indicate the plural and neuter terminology shall include the masculine and feminine." Van Hecke then remarked dryly: "I do not know in what American jurisdiction such a clause is considered to be necessary * * *." The answer, of course, is that it is not necessary in any American jurisdiction, but neither do Continental codes contain such drivel. Whatever may be the purpose of such a clause, it hardly seems to have much to do with that "store of synthetic concepts" that distinguish the best codes.

I do not mean to deny the bearing that the gulf between case-law and code-law legal cultures may have on the contrast between American- and Continental-style contracting. I would agree to reckon this difference in legal cultures as a predisposing factor. American lawyers, reared in the case method, may indeed be more sensitive to the nuances of factual detail than Continental lawyers, whose training emphasizes doctrinal principles. Sometimes American boilerplate can be traced to a particular decided case, whose result the draftsman is trying to avoid. But comparative law long ago recognized how much case law was being generated in the code systems, indeed, how strongly the forces of convergence were narrowing the code law/case law contrast. Accordingly, it seems unrealistic to attribute a practical difference as fundamental as the discrepancy between American- and Continental-style contracting to that tired contrast between code law and case law.

II. THE OBJECTS OF PROLIXITY

Broadly speaking, the provisions that lengthen most American contracts serve either of two purposes.

1. *Transaction-specific foresight clauses.* Van Hecke ascribed to perfectionism the American lawyer's effort to "handle all eventualities in the contract rather than leave them to the decision of the judge." Much of the detail in an American contract is tailored to the particular transaction, and is designed to foresee ever more remote contingencies. But human foresight has major limits, as anyone who follows the stock market will attest. Today's price changes reflect failures of foresight by half of yesterday's traders. Since it is so intrinsically difficult to foresee future turns of events, the question is why the Americans bother. Why should Americans be so much more reluctant than Europeans to leave future events "to the decision of the judge"?

2. *Incorporating default rules.* Even more curious than the striving of the American draftsman to foresee the unforeseeable is his propensity for incorporating into a contract numerous well-settled principles of law ("black letter rules") and canons of interpretation (such as van Hecke's illustration about construing number and gender). To be sure, some boilerplate varies the subsidiary law, but most boilerplate imposes rules whose applicability should be easily ascertainable if not instantly obvious. In current legal-academic parlance, these are "default rules"—the rules that would routinely apply if the contract had neglected to govern the matter. The puzzle about American practice is to understand why, when the default rules are obvious, the draftsman nevertheless wants to internalize them in the instrument.

Notice that neither the foresight clauses nor the clauses incorporating default rules have much to do with the relative merits of American and European substantive law. As regards foresight clauses, the arguably superior Continental substantive law has no advantage. The limits of foresight arise from the human condition; European lawyers do no better at prophecy than American. The question is why the Americans strain so much harder against the limits of foresight. When, on the other hand, the contract is incorporating a default rule, the relative sophistication of the rule is beside the point. The rule would govern, whatever its quality. The phenomenon that needs explaining is why Americans put the rule in the deal for the offchance that it is needed, rather than leave it on the statute book or in the case law.

III. PROCEDURE AND PROCEDURAL INSTITUTIONS

I wish to offer a suggestion about the causes of American-style contracting that points away from substantive law and toward procedure. I locate the problem in another of the grand contrasts of comparative law: not code law versus case law, but in the gulf between Continental and American civil procedure and procedural institutions.

If you are a businessman (or the legal advisor to a businessman) and you are contemplating a complex transaction, one of your decisions is how much time, effort, and money you want to invest in contracting precisely. To be sure, the clarity of the underlying substantive law will strongly affect your decision, but as I have said, there is little reason to think that American law is so consistently and markedly underdeveloped by comparison with the law in all the European states that differences in the quality of the substantive law could explain the differing propensities of American and European businessmen to invest in contracting precisely.

Far more important, in my view, is your perception of the efficiency and predictability of the procedural system through which you would have to work in order to vindicate your substantive rights. The point is not that most deals breed lawsuits—in truth few do—but that, *ex ante,* every complex written contract contemplates the risk of a lawsuit in the event of a breach. If the procedural system that would process such a lawsuit is reasonably efficient, you will have less to fear from litigation than if it is not. For reasons that I shall summarize below, American civil procedure is inefficient. It is expensive, protracted, and unpredictable, and it does a poor job of discouraging frivolous suits (or frivolous defenses). The European systems are markedly more efficient and more predictable (some, to be sure, more so than others).

A businessman aware that his transaction would be subject to litigation under the American system would have a materially greater incentive to invest in contracting precision. His object would be to prevent the lawsuit, by foreseeing the claim and stipulating against it; or, should litigation nevertheless arise, to reduce the range and complexity of the issues.

Consider, therefore, some of the most prominent shortcomings of American civil procedure:

1. *Who decides.* Recall van Hecke's formulation of our problem: "[T]he American lawyer tries to handle all eventualities in the contract rather than to leave them to the decision of the judge." Then recall who judges in American courts. The bench is composed of politically selected (sometimes politically elected) ex-lawyers, as opposed to the career magistrates who staff European courts. The range of quality within the American judiciary is notoriously broad, especially in the state courts that handle most commercial business. The best American judges are splendid figures, but what must concern a transaction planner is the risk that his contract will fall to a judge drawn from the bottom of the American deck. A prudent transaction planner assumes the reasonable worst case, and in the United States in a matter of potential litigation that means reckoning on a judge of the meanest ability and disposition.

Contrast in this regard the litigation prospects of the European businessman. If his contract should give rise to litigation, the matter will be decided by a trustworthy career judiciary whose members have been selected and promoted on criteria of ability, learning, and diligence. If the case cannot be clarified and resolved by settlement, the first instance court decides the dispute by means of a written judgment containing findings of fact and rulings of law.

The conclusory general verdict of an American jury is, by contrast, the antithesis of a reasoned judgment; nor does American procedure require much better when the judge decides without a jury. The failure of American procedure to require effective disclosure of the grounds of decision at first instance greatly hampers appellate review.

The European transaction planner knows that if he is dissatisfied with the first-instance decision, he can obtain review *de novo* (that is, full retrial on all issues of fact and law, with no presumption of correctness attaching to the first-instance decision). The reviewing court will be composed of seasoned judges who have been promoted to the appellate bench in recognition of the quality of their performance in lower-court adjudication. Particularly in commercial matters, it is common for European legal systems to employ specialized courts or divisions, sometimes even at first-instance, and routinely at the appellate level. Thus, on the Continent, a complex transaction that results in litigation will be decided by people who are expert in the law governing such affairs—a notable contrast to the amateurs who populate the American generalist judiciary.

And, of course, the grotesque amateurism of the American civil jury system will not bedevil the European businessman. It is conceivable that there is merit in having laymen adjudicate civil cases that partake of ordinary experience; but no prudent businessman would want to delegate to randomly selected laymen the power to pass upon complex commercial and technological questions. Historically, the law/fact distinction (reinforced by the reductionism of common law pleading) limited jurors to deciding issues of "mere" fact. In today's circumstances, however, issues of fact can be vastly more difficult than those of law. If a legal system puts unsophisticated laymen in charge of deciding issues of advanced finance and technology, transaction planners will strain to avoid litigating in that legal system.

2. *Trial: adversary distortions.* American procedure can function with a bench of uncertain quality in part because the judicial role is narrower. In the American adversary system, the lawyers for the parties gather evidence in advance of trial with virtually no judicial involvement. The lawyers also dominate American trial procedure. Each side decides what evidence to present and in what sequence. Continental procedure lacks the pretrial/trial distinction, and the judge has the primary responsibility for eliciting the facts.

The truth-defeating excesses of American trial practice are well known: coaching of witnesses, abusive cross-examination, and the use of party-selected, litigation-biased experts. Civil procedure in a system like the German quite effectively prevents these abuses. Because the lawyers are forbidden to have pretrial contact with non-party witnesses, trial testimony is undistorted. The judge does most of the examining of witnesses at trial, which largely eliminates partisanship and trickery in examination and cross-examination. Perhaps most important for the businessman concerned about the possibility that a complex commercial transaction might give rise to litigation, the German court has the help of neutral experts chosen for their ability to assist the court in deciding correctly, rather than (as in American practice) hirelings selected for their willingness to reach preordained results favorable to the adversaries who hired them.

From the standpoint of the transaction planner, these truth-defeating excesses of American procedure all trend in the same direction: They reduce the predictability of litigation by increasing the chance that adversary trickery will wrest an advantage over orderly disclosure and consideration of relevant information.

3. *Runaway pretrial.* A corollary of the principle of the concentrated trial that dominates American civil procedure is that there must be a separate pretrial process for the parties to gather the evidence that they may need at trial. The judge customarily has little contact with this pretrial investigation, although, especially in large multi-party litigation, the prototype of strict judicial passivity is softening. The parties' lawyers employ the compulsory powers of the discovery system largely without judicial supervision. They gather documents from each other, and they create fresh evidence by propounding interrogatories and by deposing witnesses.

This system is immensely expensive and wasteful. It suffers two fundamental flaws. It is intrinsically duplicative: Witnesses are prepared, examined, and cross-examined during pretrial, then prepared, examined, and cross-examined again at trial. But worse, the want of judicial direction of pretrial all but guarantees that discovery proceedings will be overbroad. In any legal system, a lawsuit arising from a complex transaction can have many endings. Only rarely can a litigator tell at the beginning precisely what issues and what facts will prove important in the end. In a legal system such as the German, the judge controls what issues will be investigated and in what sequence. He limits the fact-gathering to the most promising issues—those most likely to clarify the case and hence to promote settlement or adjudication. Much of what could be investigated does not have to be. By contrast, the American pre-trial/trial division requires that discovery take place for the entire case before the trier has the opportunity to signal what information he thinks relevant to the decision. American lawyers thus strain to investigate everything that could possibly arise at trial, because once the trial commences there is no opportunity to go back and search for further information.

The basic incentives of the American discovery system make for waste and duplication. Discovery is the main activity of the American litigator. An experienced American transaction planner knows that a central risk of having his contract enmeshed in litigation is having to pay for so much legal makework.

4. *Costs: subsidizing losers.* Unique among the legal systems of the world's advanced states, American civil procedure lacks the general principle that the loser pays the winner's legal expenses. The world's most expensive legal system is also the least sensitive about allocating the cost burden in a fair and rational manner. While not all the ramifications of the American no-cost-shifting rule trend in the same direction, the most important consequence of the American rule is to encourage contumacy. In a loser-pays system, the party with a bleak or hopeless case has a strong incentive to foresake or abandon litigation. Under the American rule, by contrast, litigating a losing case can be a strategic way of inflicting costs on the other side. The American transaction planner knows that if he has to litigate to enforce his deal, he cannot be made whole.

5. *The planner's response.* I have assembled this catalogue of procedural horrors with a view to showing why a rational businessman should be terrified of having to litigate about a complex contract under the American civil procedural system. Unfortunately, it is very hard to contract out of a procedural system entirely. Two contracting parties located, say, in Pennsylvania would have a hard time under the applicable choice-of-law rule devising an enforceable term that litigation arising under the contract should be processed in Germany. Nor would they want to. There are enormous difficulties and costs associated with litigating offshore: the inconvenience and expense of a distant forum, the translations across language and culture, the limits of foreign writ in such matters as compulsory process and execution of judgment. Reasons such as these explain why,

even when an American firm engages in a transnational transaction that could plausibly invoke foreign law and a foreign forum, the American firm will often seek to impose American law. Convenience and familiarity supply formidable economies.

The much-heralded growth of arbitration and of other modes of alternative dispute resolution (ADR) in American commercial practice is, of course, consistent with the thesis I have been advancing in this paper. ADR represents another kind of contractual response to the defects of ordinary civil justice. Whereas contracting precision aims to foresee the problems, ADR tries to avoid the courts. If anything, the puzzle is to understand why Americans do not make greater use of arbitration clauses than is now common. I sense that the American lawyer does not fully trust arbitration agreements, at least not enough to surrender his boilerplate. He may fear that the court that adjudicates his contract will prove hostile to arbitration—that the court will dust off the old theory that arbitration offends public policy because it ousts the jurisdiction of the courts; or that, despite a good deal of contrary legislation and decisional law restricting judicial review of arbitration awards, a reviewing court may still find a way to subvert the award.

Because it is so hard for the American transaction planner to escape the shortcomings of his legal system, he is left to concentrate on contracting precision for the purpose of narrowing his exposure to the system. This motivation is clearest in those provisions that I have called transaction-specific foresight clauses. To quote van Hecke's formulation yet again, "the American lawyer tries to handle all eventualities in the contract rather than leave them to the decision of the judge."

The other great source of prolixity in American-style contracting—general boilerplate incorporating the law that should apply even without the contractual term—is also to be explained by fear of the litigation system. Why trust a judicial lightweight to find his way in the law to the right rule when you can impose it on him in the contract? Why should you risk a jury trial and its attendant pretrial abuses over the question of whether you meant for some ordinary principle of commercial or legal common sense to apply? The instinctive response is to spell it all out. Remember in this regard that, unlike transaction-specific clauses,[33] general boilerplate is cheap to use. Formbooks collect the stuff, and businesses and law firms

---

[33] The smaller the deal, the more likely is the American lawyer to overcome his instinct for contracting precision. The client will not pay $20,000 for legal services to implement a $10,000 deal. American and Continental contracting styles diverge least in the realm of the small deal, for which an exchange of relatively simple letters would be as nearly as routine on one side of the Atlantic as on the other.

An experienced American draftsman has remarked to me that he senses a difference in the predilection for contracting precision according to whether his client is an independent entrepreneur or a large corporation. Corporate officers are more likely to want to "cover themselves," to show superiors that the attempt was made to "think of everything."

tend to develop and carry forward their own sets of it. Boilerplate becomes habit—the *mos Americanus*.

To be sure, the effort at greater precision in contracting is sometimes counterproductive. Detail is not synonymous with certainty. Because the risks of ambiguity and of missed connections increase with the complexity of an instrument, the draftsman may breed litigation where he meant to prevent it. Alas, American practice seems to show that the draftsman will respond by producing yet more boilerplate for the next contract, hoping for the future to cover the contingency that surprised him the last time.

* * *

V.   BEYOND PROCEDURE

In emphasizing the shortcomings of American civil procedure and procedural institutions as the primary explanation for American-style contracting, I do not mean to exclude other factors. * * *

American-style contracting is related to the broader use of lawyers throughout American business. In areas as diverse as taxation, regulatory compliance, and transaction planning, European businessmen are more likely than Americans to act without counsel. Some of this greater lawyerization of American life simply recapitulates my theme (preventive law is the reaction to deficient legal procedures and institutions), but the phenomenon is surely deeper.

Another suggestion that I find plausible although hardly cogent is that cultural differences in the conduct of commercial affairs play a role in American-style contracting. Business in the United States has not been the preserve of the gentle elite. Commercial dealings in Europe may have been conducted within a smaller and more socially homogeneous group, and hence may have had more of the considerate overtones that Americans think are confined to long-term (that is, relational or repeat-player) contracts.

I have no doubt that a much longer list of such possibilities can be assembled. I doubt, however, that anything on that list will explain as much about the difference in the style of complex contracts as does comparative civil procedure.

———————

Now that you have a better understanding of the differences in drafting styles, and of their possible reasons, how would you approach a business partner or lawyer from a civil law system when it comes to drafting a contract? What can you do to avoid misunderstanding and potential failure of the agreement? In particular, how would you react if the other side rejected your (probably extensive) draft and insisted on its own (probably much shorter) version?

CHAPTER 9

DISPUTE RESOLUTION: PROLIFERATION OF INSTITUTIONS

■ ■ ■

In Chapter IV, we saw that under the classic regime of international law there were virtually no permanent international tribunals. If states wanted to settle their disputes through a legal proceeding, they had to set up their own arbitration panel and process, and if private individuals wanted to assert claims, they by and large had to sue each other in domestic courts.

Today, a wide array of international dispute resolution mechanisms exists. States can now go to the International Court of Justice (ICJ) in The Hague, bring their trade disputes before the WTO in Geneva, or resort to various regional tribunals, such as the Court of Justice of the European Union (CJEU) in Luxembourg or to specialized courts, such as the International Tribunal on the Law of the Sea (ITLOS) in Hamburg. Private parties still have to sue each other in domestic courts, but if they wish to pursue human rights claims against states, they can so do in several places, such as the UN Human Rights Committee, the European Court of Human Rights (ECHR) or the Inter–American Commission on Human Rights (IACHR). In addition, both private parties and states have increasingly resorted to international arbitration in all sorts of contexts. Finally, several international criminal tribunals have been created, especially the International Criminal Court (ICC) in the Hague but also various specialized courts such as the International Tribunal for the former Yugoslavia (ICTY).

In this chapter, we will first look at dispute resolution among states in the International Court of Justice, then consider two major issues pertaining to international litigation among private parties in the modern age, discuss the current regime of international arbitration, and finally survey the dispute resolution process in the WTO. This will lead to the concluding question whether we actually have too many international fora today.

1. INTERNATIONAL LITIGATION

A. BETWEEN STATES:
THE INTERNATIONAL COURT OF JUSTICE

Under the traditional Westphalian system, there was no permanent judicial forum in which sovereign states could resolve their disputes. States had to settle their quarrels diplomatically, establish an arbitral process— or go to war. Even today, the vast majority of disagreements between states are settled on the political and diplomatic level, and even today, some result in the use of force. But the 20th century has also created a judicial option in the form of a permanent court for international dispute resolution. The first such institution was the Permanent Court of International Justice (PCIJ, the court that decided the *Lotus* case), established by the League of Nations in 1921. With the foundation of the United Nations, it was succeeded by the International Court of Justice (ICJ). In 2009, the ICJ decided its 100th case.

While reading the following account and the selection of provisions from the UN Charter and the Statute of the International Court of Justice, make a list of the major differences between the ICJ and the national (domestic) courts you are familiar with. What explains these differences?

DAVID BEDERMAN, INTERNATIONAL LAW FRAMEWORKS
(3d ed. 2006)

* * *

B.   THE WORLD COURT

Proposals for the creation of an international adjudicatory body were first made in earnest at the Hague Peace Conferences of 1899 and 1907. In spite of the relative allure of international arbitration, many States believed that international law could not truly be effectively followed and enforced until there was a permanent institution for settling inter-State disputes. Plans for the creation of such a court foundered in 1907 when some nations objected to a tribunal with a limited number of judges (these States wanted a judge appointed for every member nation, making for an unwieldy bench), and Germany generally opposed a tribunal with anything but optional jurisdiction. As already noted, the establishment of the Permanent Court of Arbitration (PCA) was a middling consolation prize—it was merely a facilitation center for arbitration, not a permanent judicial body. It was only in 1920, with the end of World War One and the creation of the League of Nations that the Permanent Court of International Justice (PCIJ) was founded at The Peace Palace, in The Hague in The Netherlands. The PCIJ (as noted in Chapter 6) was conceived as a separate institution from the League, with potentially different memberships. A Commission of Jurists drafted the PCIJ Statute in 1920, and the text of that effort is largely reflected in the current Statute of the ICJ. Indeed, for all practical purposes, the ICJ (created as part of the U.N. in 1945) is the successor to the PCIJ, and they are together referred to as the "World Court."

1. *Organization of the World Court.* The structure and operating procedures of the ICJ are fairly straight-forward. The current Court consists of 15 members, each of whom serve 9-year terms. By tradition (and that is all it is), each of the permanent members of the Security Council has a national on the Court. The remaining 10 seats are distributed by region, in order to give the Court as wide a perspective of the world's legal systems as possible. Judges are picked in their individual capacity. They are not political appointees by their respective governments. Actually, the method of nominating and electing ICJ judges can be fairly called byzantine. The national groups of four PCA arbitrators each nominate outstanding international lawyers from government ministries, law faculties, the bench and bar. Judges are elected when they receive a majority vote in each of the U.N. Security Council and the General Assembly.

Despite what has sometimes been suggested by commentators, the judges of the ICJ are rarely politicized. Even at the height of the Cold War, judges from Eastern Europe and the Socialist bloc did not always vote with what were perceived to be Soviet interests in some cases. (Manfred Lachs, a judge from Poland who served over 26 years on the Court, routinely voted in surprising ways.) According to the Court's Statute, however, in any case where one (or more) of the parties are not represented on the bench by a judge of its nationality, then that litigant can appoint a judge *ad hoc*. A holdover of the practice of "party-appointed arbitrators," *ad hoc* judges almost invariably vote in favor of the legal arguments advanced by the State which named them. This has come to be expected, although judges *ad hoc* may exercise some subtle influence on the Court's deliberations, especially in cases where the legal issues may turn on the interpretation of treaties written in an arcane language or on a fuller understanding of particular local laws or customs.

The World Court traditionally hears cases in plenary sessions, with a full bench of 15 judges (or 16 or 17, if there are *ad hoc* judges appointed). A majority vote determines the case. (In case of a tie, the President gets to cast the deciding ballot.) Because the Court hears cases in full benches, the proceedings can be exceedingly slow, and it can take some time for the Court to render a decision. (The fact that proceedings consist of long speeches read laboriously from scripts, and then simultaneously translated into French and English, does not help.) Proposals to utilize *chambers* of the Court, consisting (usually) of 5 hand-picked judges to hear cases, has received mixed reviews. A decision of a Court chamber has the same binding effect as one made by the full bench, and (presumably) the same "precedential" weight (although remember there is no strict doctrine of *stare dccisis* in international law). Recent plans to inaugurate a special chamber on international environmental disputes, as well as one for summary procedures have yet to bear fruit. Likewise, the Court has rarely agreed to revise an earlier judgment, although parties may request such action under the Court's rules.

The operating procedures of the World Court would hardly matter if its docket consisted of one or two cases a year. Like all international arbitration, the Court has gone through periods of dizzying popularity and profound irrelevance. The PCIJ was heavily employed during the inter-War years, as was the ICJ from 1945 to 1960. But from 1960 to about 1985, the Court went on the skids, the result of a premeditated boycott of developing nations from the Third World who believed that the ICJ did not (and could not) represent or reflect their interests. But, slowly, the Court regained its stature. In a series of wise rulings on border disputes (both land and maritime), the Court acquired the trust of many nations around the world.

In early 2010, the Court's docket consisted of a quite large number of 15 cases. Of these, 2 were boundary cases (maritime delimitation or territorial rights). But of the remainder, three involved environmental issues, four concerned treatment of aliens or jurisdictional immunities, one raised enforcement of commercial judgment issues, one involved State recognition, and the rest implicated State responsibility for genocide, use of force, or war crimes in the Balkans, the Caucuses, and central Africa. The Court had never been as busy and as much needed as it was at the beginning of the new Millennium.

2. *The Court's Jurisdiction.* How, then, does the Court get its cases? It is vital to realize that every matter which comes before the ICJ does so because of the consent of the litigants. The only question is how that consent is manifested. The Court does not—and cannot—exercise a mandatory form of jurisdiction over States. And, remember, only States may be parties before the Court. Article 36(1) of the Statute of the Court thus provides that: "The jurisdiction of the Court comprises all cases which the parties refer to it and all matters specially provided for in the Charter of the United Nations or in treaties and conventions in force."

The most common, and uncontroversial, way for the Court to receive a case is by the special agreement of the parties to submit it specially by *compromis.* This is an especially popular vehicle for seizing the Court in boundary or other territorial disputes. In such circumstances, the parties have each concluded that the political costs of losing the case are less than escalating the dispute. Both sides are prepared to lose, in effect, so submitting it to the adjudication of the Court provides a valuable, "face-saving" device for an embattled government. When cases are submitted by *compromis,* the Court proceeds immediately to briefing on the merits since there is no conceivable jurisdictional concern. The Court can, very occasionally, infer consent to jurisdiction, based on the acts of the parties (what is known as *forum prorogatum*).

An increasingly accepted way to invoke the ICJ's jurisdiction is through *compromissory clauses* included in bilateral and multilateral conventions. Such provisions allow, in the event of a dispute arising under the treaty, that the matter will be submitted to the Court. Although a compromissory clause need not be formally drafted, it must unambiguously indicate that the ICJ has been selected to resolve any future disputes that might arise under the treaty. Equivocal undertakings to have the ICJ settle a dispute are insufficient. At last count, there are approximately 300 conventions with clauses that raise the Court's jurisdiction. Of these, the United States is party to a few dozen, including the Friendship, Commerce and Navigation (FCN) treaties that the U.S. concludes with many nations. FCN Treaties were the basis of the U.S. suit against Iran in the Hostage Crisis, and Nicaragua's suit against the U.S. arising from the *Contra* Affair and a later suit regarding U.S. military actions in the Persian Gulf. In the event that a respondent State objects to the jurisdiction of the Court, it is up to the ICJ (under Article 36(6) of its Statute) to decide the jurisdictional matter. In cases involving compromissory clauses, the inquiry is usually limited to the question of whether the dispute before the Courts falls within the relevant treaty containing the clause.

Aside from special agreements and compromissory clauses, the ICJ can also acquire, in exceptional cases, matters on appeal from other bodies. While it would be incorrect to regard the Court as having appellate jurisdiction in any real sense, a handful of treaties or agreements give the Court the power to review decisions by other bodies. Until recently, the ICJ was the court of final recourse for decisions from the U.N. Administrative Tribunal (UNAT), a staff grievance body. The World Court periodically reviews decisions from the International Civil Aviation Organization (ICAO), often in relation to aerial incidents. The possibility that the U.N. Security Council could mandatorily refer disputes to the Court for legal determination has never been accepted.

That leaves, as a final basis of the Court's authority, what is rather misleadingly called its "compulsory jurisdiction." This is premised on Statute Article 36, paragraphs 2 and 3:

> 2. The states parties to the present Statute may at any time declare that they recognize as compulsory ipso facto and without special agreement, in relation to any other state accepting the same obligation, the jurisdiction of the Court in all legal disputes concerning:
>
> a. the interpretation of a treaty;
>
> b. any question of international law;

c. the existence of any fact which, if established, would constitute a breach of an international obligation;

d. the nature or extent of the reparation to be made for the breach of an international obligation.

3. The declarations referred to above may be made unconditionally or on condition of reciprocity on the part of several or certain states, or for a certain time.

Of the nearly 190 nations that are parties to the Court's Statute only about 65 currently have made "optional clause" declarations under Article 36. Of the five permanent members of the Security Council, only the United Kingdom today accepts the compulsory jurisdiction of the Court. The United States had an optional clause declaration in force from 1946 until 1985, when it was withdrawn in the heat of the *Nicaragua* litigation.

One need not look far for the reason for the relative unpopularity of optional clause jurisdiction. Filing an Article 36 declaration exposes States to suits brought by any other nation that has filed a similar declaration. That would invoke the Court's jurisdiction over disputes that may not even be in the contemplation of a State when it makes its declaration, and, in many cases, countries have been quite queasy about making such broad, advance concessions. Virtually none of the States that have made an Article 36 declaration have accepted the ICJ's jurisdiction unconditionally. Article 36(2) establishes an incredibly broad ambit for disputes covered by a declaration—virtually anything involving the content of international law obligations (including treaty interpretations) and remedies for the breach of such a duty. Most countries have, therefore, applied substantial reservations to their acceptances. It is worth reviewing the scope of these typical reservations, if for no other reason tha[n] to examine the relative failure of the Court's "compulsory" jurisdiction.

Many countries, for example, exclude any matter from the Court's jurisdiction which is being handled by an alternative dispute resolution mechanism. This makes good sense; there is no point to triggering the Court's involvement if another arbitration is handling the case, or if the dispute is in negotiation or mediation. Other declarations specifically exclude certain kinds of disputes. (Canada's, for example, withdraws jurisdiction for any matter involving law of the sea issues, and particularly any matters involving Arctic claims or fisheries enforcement.)

Many optional clause reservations also place time limits on the filing of claims. The United Kingdom's 1969 Declaration, for example, provides that the Court will *not* have jurisdiction where

Any other party to the dispute has accepted the compulsory jurisdiction of the [Court] only in relation to or for the purpose of the dispute;

or where the acceptance of the Court's compulsory jurisdiction * * *
was deposited or ratified less than twelve months prior to the filing of
the application bringing the dispute before the Court.

This was intended to avoid what is known as the "hit-and-run" tactic. All
the Court requires, under Statute Article 36, is that the two litigating
States have in force, *on the same day*, a declaration. But for Britain's reservation, it would have been conceivable for another State, on Day 1, to
file an optional clause declaration, to sue Britain before the Court on Day
2, and then to withdraw its declaration (before any other nation could file
an Application) on Day 3. Britain's craftily-drafted Declaration requires
that a potential applicant State expose itself to litigation for at least a
year prior to filing against the U.K.

By far and away, the two most controversial reservations to optional
clause jurisdiction were those appended by the United States to its 1946
Declaration. The first, known as the Connally Reservation (for the Senator who proposed it), simply provided that the Court would not have jurisdiction over "disputes with regard to matters which are essentially
within the domestic jurisdiction of the United States of America as determined by the United States." This was essentially seen as an escape
valve; the U.S. would accept the Court's compulsory jurisdiction (thereby
setting a good example), but it always had the option to take it back if it
decided that a case was in its "domestic jurisdiction." Had this reservation simply required that the Court could not rule on domestic matters
and still let the Court decide the issue (as Statute Article 36(6) allows),
then it would have been unobjectionable. It was the self-judging character
of the Connally Reservation that was so corrosive of international expectations.

These provisions were challenged as reservations that were inconsistent
with the object and purpose of an optional clause declaration * * *. In the
Norwegian Loans Case, which featured an identical clause in France's
Declaration, the Court could have struck it out on that ground. But, instead, the ICJ came up with a positively fiendish response to the use of
these clauses. The Court permitted States to make such a reservation,
but also allowed respondent States to invoke the reservation *against* an
applicant. Because optional clause declarations must be read reciprocally
under Statute Article 36(3), a defendant State before the Court may pick-
and-choose among its opponent's reservations and use them. Norway thus
invoked France's self-judging reservation and declared that France's case
involved a matter within Norway's "domestic jurisdiction," as decided by
Norway. That was the end of the case. In fact, it was the end of every case
brought by the United States against another State with an optional
clause. Every time the U.S. sued, the other nation simply invoked the
Connally Reservation. What was intended as the ultimate "shield" to be
used by the United States to avoid embarrassing World Court litigation

was consistently used as "sword" by its opponents. Ironically, in the one dispute where the U.S. would have most like to have invoked the reservation—in the *Nicaragua* Case—it did not.

If the Connally Reservation is proof positive that the most important rule of all in international affairs is the law of unintended consequences, the second reservation made by the 1946 U.S. Declaration was equally equivocal. The multilateral treaty exception (or "Vandenburg Amendment") excluded disputes arising under such treaties "unless (1) all parties to the treaty affected by the decision are also parties to the case before the Court, or (2) the United States specially agrees to jurisdiction." The purpose of this was to prevent the U.S. from getting in the middle of a whipsaw situation. The Court could conceivably make a ruling on treaty interpretation in a case involving one of our treaty partners. But because such a ruling is not necessarily binding in disputes with other parties to the treaty, there was a risk that the U.S. would be obliged to take contrary positions or perform mutually contradictory actions. While the Vandenburg Amendment was successfully invoked by the United States in the *Nicaragua* Case, its only effect was to force the ICJ into premising its rulings on uses of force * * * on customary law, and not the U.N. Charter.

All in all, the ICJ's compulsory jurisdiction has been regarded as a failure. It is very unlikely that the United States will ever again file an optional clause declaration. With the advent of many treaties containing compromissory clauses, and with the willingness of States to submit disputes by special agreement, optional clause cases may become a rarity. Those countries that traditionally have been the most vociferous supporters of compulsory jurisdiction are now vexed with its application. Those States that have active declarations are regarded as targets of opportunity. (Australia recently has been hit with a number of suits that can only charitably be described as ill-conceived.) Lastly, the Court itself does not seem to like premising its jurisdiction on this basis. Compulsory jurisdiction cases are usually bitterly-contested. After all, if a respondent State had really wanted to be before the Court, it would have consented by other means.

3. *Admissibility, Provisional Measures and Interventions.* Just because the Court has jurisdiction with some basis under the Statute—*compromis,* compromissory clause or optional clause—does not necessarily mean that the ICJ will actually hear the case. Over nearly ninety years, the World Court has developed a number of prudential grounds for finding a case *inadmissible,* and thus declining to decide it. These grounds are analogous to the prudential reasons that U.S. federal courts often refuse to hear cases, even though jurisdiction is otherwise proper. For example, the Court will dismiss a case if its subject-matter has become moot, as when in the *Nuclear Test* Cases France unilaterally declared that it would no longer conduct atmospheric testing. Although the

Court was careful to say that it would remain seized of the issue (just in case the French decided to change their minds), the dispute was, for all intents and purposes, concluded. Likewise, the ICJ will not decide a case if the dispute is not sufficiently ripe, or well-developed.

Somewhat more controversially, the Court will dismiss a case because of failure to exhaust local remedies, a rule borrowed from the international law of diplomatic protection * * *. Likewise, the ICJ will not hear a case if there are indispensable parties that are missing in the litigation. In what was probably its nadir, the Court refused to adjudicate a dispute involving South Africa's illegal occupation of South West Africa (Namibia) because the applicant countries lacked standing to bring the claim. This was despite the fact that both Ethiopia and Liberia had been members of the League of Nations which had issued the original mandate for South West Africa, that South Africa had allegedly violated. As it turned out, it was only the Court's standing that was damaged by this decision, and, because of it, countries from the developing world avoided the ICJ for nearly two decades. Perhaps as a consequence of this, the Court has flatly rejected other forms of admissibility challenges, most notably arguments that certain forms of "political questions" should be avoided by the Court.

Among other aspects of the World Court's procedures, it is important to note the ICJ's power to indicate provisional measures. These are interim measures of protection, ensuring the equality of the parties while the proceedings are underway. If the issue in the case is a border conflict, the Court might order provisional measures for a cease-fire and no further aggressive action to be taken by the two sides while the case is pending. While the ostensible standard for the Court to indicate provisional measures is irreparable prejudice, the ICJ will often grant measures even when the underlying jurisdiction of the Court looks doubtful. What this means is that many cases are split into three procedural phases before the Court: (1) an order about provisional measures; (2) a ruling about jurisdiction; and (3) a judgment on the merits. Some of the ICJ's orders for provisional measures have been ignored by the parties—such as Iran's refusal to release the U.S. hostages in 1979, and the United States' later refusal to stay executions in cases involving the Vienna Convention on Consular Relations.

Traditionally, the World Court has been parsimonious in granting leave for third parties to intervene in cases before the Court. The ICJ Statute, in Articles 62 and 63, provides authority for such interventions, and (one would have thought) such would be desirable in order to promote wider settlement of disputes. The Court's refusal to allow El Salvador to intervene in the *Nicaragua* Case was savaged by critics. Although the Court is correct to be concerned about intervention being used as a ruse to introduce new parties and issues into pending cases, and it has therefore established a high level of showing for prejudice, this procedural bar has lately been lowered. In three recent cases, the ICJ has allowed interventions by third States that would be affected by maritime delimitation findings.

4. *Advisory Jurisdiction.* The foregoing has considered the World Court's contentious jurisdiction—cases involving States as opposing litigants. But as has been considered in substantial detail in this volume, many of the Court's most significant rulings have come in advisory opinions requested by an organ of the United Nations or one of its specialized agencies. Almost all of the critical decisions as to the "constitutional law" of the U.N. have come through the ICJ's advisory rulings * * *.

Under the Court's Statute, the U.N. General Assembly, Security Council, and Economic and Social Council can each request advisory opinions, as can certain specialized agencies. The Court will not answer a request for an advisory opinion if it is propounded by an inappropriate body. For example, the ICJ refused to answer a request for an advisory opinion by the World Health Organization (WHO) on the legality of the use of nuclear weapons in armed conflict, since such a question had nothing to do with the WHO's central mission of disease prevention and public health. (As was noted in the previous Chapter, the ICJ did reply to a similar request made by the U.N. General Assembly, which is charged with disarmament questions.)

Nor will the Court allow a request for an advisory opinion be used as a way to force it to render a decision in what is really a contentious dispute between nations, where one or more of the States interested are not inclined to accept the Court's jurisdiction in the matter. For example, in the *Eastern Carelia* Opinion, the PCIJ refused to entertain a request for an advisory opinion on the legal status of disputed territory claimed both by Finland and the Soviet Union when it was manifest that the Soviets would not participate. The Court will issue an opinion, even if States have an interest in the matter, so long as their rights and duties under international law are not being directly adjudicated. Nonetheless, in a very controversial 2004 decision, the ICJ issued an advisory opinion declaring that Israel's construction of a barrier on the occupied West Bank (separating Jewish settlements from Arab populations) violated international law. Currently before the Court is a request (by the U.N. General Assembly) for an advisory opinion on the legality of Kosovo's 2008 unilateral declaration of independence from Serbia.

* * *

As you read the following excerpts from the UN Charter and the Statute of the ICJ, make a list of the ways in which the ICJ differs from domestic courts. In addition, think back on the course to date and consider what provisions we have seen in action in ICJ cases.

CHARTER OF THE UNITED NATIONS
(Adopted 1945; in force 1945)

* * *

Chapter XIV
The International Court of Justice
Article 92

The International Court of Justice shall be the principal judicial organ of the United Nations. It shall function in accordance with the annexed Statute which is based upon the Statute of the Permanent Court of International Justice and forms an integral part of the present Charter.

Article 93

1. All Members of the United Nations are *ipso facto* parties to the Statute of the International Court of Justice.

2. A state which is not a Member of the United Nations may become a party to the Statute of the International Court of Justice on conditions to be determined in each case by the General Assembly upon the recommendation of the Security Council.

Article 94

1. Each Member of the United Nations undertakes to comply with the decision of the International Court of Justice in any case to which it is a party.

2. If any party to a case fails to perform the obligations incumbent upon it under a judgment rendered by the Court, the other party may have recourse to the Security Council, which may, if it deems necessary, make recommendations or decide upon measures to be taken to give effect to the judgment.

Article 95

Nothing in the present Charter shall prevent Members of the United Nations from entrusting the solution of their differences to other tribunals by virtue of agreements already in existence or which may be concluded in the future.

Article 96

a. The General Assembly or the Security Council may request the International Court of Justice to give an advisory opinion on any legal question.

b. Other organs of the United Nations and specialized agencies, which may at any time be so authorized by the General Assembly, may also request advisory opinions of the Court on legal questions arising within the scope of their activities.

* * *

STATUTE OF THE INTERNATIONAL COURT OF JUSTICE

June 26, 1945, 59 Stat. 1055, T.S. No. 993

Article 1

The International Court of Justice established by the Charter of the United Nations as the principal judicial organ of the United Nations shall be constituted and shall function in accordance with the provisions of the present Statute.

Chapter I

Organization of the Court

Article 2

The Court shall be composed of a body of independent judges, elected regardless of their nationality from among persons of high moral character, who possess the qualifications required in their respective countries for appointment to the highest judicial offices, or are jurisconsults of recognized competence in international law.

Article 3

1. The Court shall consist of fifteen members, no two of whom may be nationals of the same state.

* * *

Article 4

1. The members of the Court shall be elected by the General Assembly and by the Security Council from a list of persons nominated by the national groups in the Permanent Court of Arbitration, in accordance with the following provisions.

* * *

Article 13

1. The members of the Court shall be elected for nine years and may be re-elected.

* * *

Article 19

The members of the Court, when engaged on the business of the Court, shall enjoy diplomatic privileges and immunities.

* * *

Article 22

1. The seat of the Court shall be established at The Hague. This, however, shall not prevent the Court from sitting and exercising its functions elsewhere whenever the Court considers it desirable.

* * *

Article 25

1. The full Court shall sit except when it is expressly provided otherwise in the present Statute.

* * *

3. A quorum of nine judges shall suffice to constitute the Court.

Article 26

1. The Court may from time to time form one or more chambers, composed of three or more judges as the Court may determine, for dealing with particular categories of cases; for example, labour cases and cases relating to transit and communications.

2. The Court may at any time form a chamber for dealing with a particular case. The number of judges to constitute such a chamber shall be determined by the Court with the approval of the parties.

3. Cases shall be heard and determined by the chambers provided for in this article if the parties so request.

* * *

Article 31

1. Judges of the nationality of each of the parties shall retain their right to sit in the case before the Court.

2. If the Court includes upon the Bench a judge of the nationality of one of the parties, any other party may choose a person to sit as judge. Such person shall be chosen preferably from among those persons who have been nominated as candidates as provided in Articles 4 and 5.

3. If the Court includes upon the Bench no judge of the nationality of the parties, each of these parties may proceed to choose a judge as provided in paragraph 2 of this Article.

* * *

Chapter II

Competence of the Court

Article 34

1. Only states may be parties in cases before the Court.

2. The Court, subject to and in conformity with its Rules, may request of public international organizations information relevant to cases before it, and shall receive such information presented by such organizations on their own initiative.

3. Whenever the construction of the constituent instrument of a public international organization or of an international convention adopted thereunder is in question in a case before the Court, the Registrar shall so notify the public international organization concerned and shall communicate to it copies of all the written proceedings.

Article 35

1. The Court shall be open to the states parties to the present Statute.

2. The conditions under which the Court shall be open to other states shall, subject to the special provisions contained in treaties in force, be laid down by the Security Council, but in no case shall such conditions place the parties in a position of inequality before the Court.

* * *

Article 36

1. The jurisdiction of the Court comprises all cases which the parties re-fer to it and all matters specially provided for in the Charter of the United Nations or in treaties and conventions in force.

2. The states parties to the present Statute may at any time declare that they recognize as compulsory *ipso facto* and without special agreement, in relation to any other state accepting the same obligation, the juris-diction of the Court in all legal disputes concerning:

   a. the interpretation of a treaty;

   b. any question of international law;

   c. the existence of any fact which, if established, would constitute a breach of an international obligation;

   d. the nature or extent of the reparation to be made for the breach of an international obligation.

3. The declarations referred to above may be made unconditionally or on condition of reciprocity on the part of several or certain states, or for a certain time.

* * *

Article 38

1. The Court, whose function is to decide in accordance with international law such disputes as are submitted to it, shall apply:

   a. international conventions, whether general or particular, establishing rules expressly recognized by the contesting states;
   b. international custom, as evidence of a general practice accepted as law;
   c. the general principles of law recognized by civilized nations;
   d. subject to the provisions of Article 59, judicial decisions and the teachings of the most highly qualified publicists of the various nations, as subsidiary means for the determination of rules of law.

2. This provision shall not prejudice the power of the Court to decide a case *ex aequo et bono*, if the parties agree thereto.

Chapter III

Procedure

Article 39

1. The official languages of the Court shall be French and English. If the parties agree that the case shall be conducted in French, the judgment shall be delivered in French. If the parties agree that the case shall be conducted in English, the judgment shall be delivered in English.

* * *

Article 41

1. The Court shall have the power to indicate, if it considers that circumstances so require, any provisional measures which ought to be taken to preserve the respective rights of either party.

2. Pending the final decision, notice of the measures suggested shall forthwith be given to the parties and to the Security Council.

Article 42

1. The parties shall be represented by agents.

2. They may have the assistance of counsel or advocates before the Court.

3. The agents, counsel, and advocates of parties before the Court shall enjoy the privileges and immunities necessary to the independent exercise of their duties.

Article 43

1. The procedure shall consist of two parts: written and oral.

2. The written proceedings shall consist of the communication to the Court and to the parties of memorials, counter-memorials and, if necessary, replies; also all papers and documents in support.

* * *

5. The oral proceedings shall consist of the hearing by the Court of witnesses, experts, agents, counsel, and advocates.

* * *

Article 46

The hearing in Court shall be public, unless the Court shall decide otherwise, or unless the parties demand that the public be not admitted.

* * *

Article 50

The Court may, at any time, entrust any individual, body, bureau, commission, or other organization that it may select, with the task of carrying out an enquiry or giving an expert opinion.

* * *

Article 53

1. Whenever one of the parties does not appear before the Court, or fails to defend its case, the other party may call upon the Court to decide in favour of its claim.

2. The Court must, before doing so, satisfy itself, not only that it has jurisdiction in accordance with Article[ ] 36 * * * but also that the claim is well founded in fact and law.

* * *

Article 55

1. All questions shall be decided by a majority of the judges present.

2. In the event of an equality of votes, the President or the judge who acts in his place shall have a casting vote.

Article 56

1. The judgment shall state the reasons on which it is based.

2. It shall contain the names of the judges who have taken part in the decision.

Article 57

If the judgment does not represent in whole or in part the unanimous opinion of the judges, any judge shall be entitled to deliver a separate opinion.

* * *

Article 59

The decision of the Court has no binding force except between the parties and in respect of that particular case.

Article 60

The judgment is final and without appeal. In the event of dispute as to the meaning or scope of the judgment, the Court shall construe it upon the request of any party.

* * *

Chapter IV

Advisory Opinions

Article 65

1. The Court may give an advisory opinion on any legal question at the request of whatever body may be authorized by or in accordance with the Charter of the United Nations to make such a request.

2. Questions upon which the advisory opinion of the Court is asked shall be laid before the Court by means of a written request containing an exact statement of the question upon which an opinion is required, and accompanied by all documents likely to throw light upon the question.

* * *

The excerpt below revisits the ICJ decision in the dispute between the United States and Nicaragua over the role of the United States in supporting forces opposing the Nicaraguan government in the 1980s. The judgment resolved the United States' arguments that the ICJ lacked jurisdiction over the case. (We have already seen excerpts of the ICJ's later judgment on the merits of the dispute in Chapters VII.1. and VIII.2.) What is the core of the U.S. government's argument presented here? How does Nicaragua respond? Why does the Court agree with Nicaragua?

CASE CONCERNING MILITARY AND PARAMILITARY ACTIVITIES IN AND AGAINST NICARAGUA (NICARAGUA V. UNITED STATES)

International Court of Justice
1984 I.C.J. 392 Preliminary Objections Judgment of May 10, 1984

* * *

84. The Court now turns to the question of the admissibility of the Application of Nicaragua. The United States of America contended in its Counter–Memorial that Nicaragua's Application is inadmissible on five separate grounds, each of which, it is said, is sufficient to establish such inadmissibility, whether considered as a legal bar to adjudication or as "a matter requiring the exercise of prudential discretion in the interest of the integrity of the judicial function". * * *

85. In its Application instituting proceedings, Nicaragua asserts that:

> "The United States of America is using military force against Nicaragua and intervening in Nicaragua's internal affairs, in violation of Nicaragua's sovereignty, territorial integrity and political independence and of the most fundamental and universally accepted principles of international law. The United States has created an 'army' of more than 10,000 mercenaries * * * installed them in more than ten base camps in Honduras along the border with Nicaragua, trained them, paid them, supplied them with arms, ammunition, food and medical supplies, and directed their attacks against human and economic targets inside Nicaragua",

and that Nicaragua has already suffered and is now suffering grievous consequences as a result of these activities. The purpose of these activities is claimed to be

> "to harass and destabilize the Government of Nicaragua so that ultimately it will be overthrown, or, at a minimum, compelled to change those of its domestic and foreign policies that displease the United States".

* * *

89. [T]he United States regards the Application as inadmissible because each of Nicaragua's allegations constitutes no more than a reformulation and restatement of a single fundamental claim, that the United States is engaged in an unlawful use of armed force, or breach of the peace, or acts of aggression against Nicaragua, a matter which is committed by the Charter and by practice to the competence of other organs, in particular the United Nations Security Council. All allegations of this kind are confided to the political organs of the Organization for consideration and determination; the United States quotes Article 24 of the Charter, which

confers upon the Security Council "primary responsibility for the mainte-nance of international peace and security". The provisions of the Charter dealing with the ongoing use of armed force contain no recognition of the possibility of settlement by judicial, as opposed to political, means. * * *

90. Nicaragua contends that the United States argument fails to take ac-count of the fundamental distinction between Article 2, paragraph 4, of the Charter which defines a legal obligation to refrain from the threat or use of force, and Article 39, which establishes a political process. The re-sponsibility of the Security Council under Article 24 of the Charter for the maintenance of international peace and security is "primary", not exclu-sive. Until the Security Council makes a determination under Article 39, a dispute remains to be dealt with by the methods of peaceful settlement provided under Article 33, including judicial settlement; and even after a determination under Article 39, there is no necessary inconsistency be-tween Security Council action and adjudication by the Court. From a ju-ridical standpoint, the decisions of the Court and the actions of the Secu-rity Council are entirely separate.

91. It will be convenient to deal with this alleged ground of inadmissibil-ity together with the third ground advanced by the United States namely that the Court should hold the Application of Nicaragua to be inadmissi-ble in view of the subject-matter of the Application and the position of the Court within the United Nations system, including the impact of proceed-ings before the Court on the ongoing exercise of the "inherent right of in-dividual or collective self-defence" under Article 51 of the Charter. * * *

93. The United States is thus arguing that the matter was essentially one for the Security Council since it concerned a complaint by Nicaragua in-volving the use of force. However, having regard to the *United States Dip-lomatic and Consular Staff in Tehran* case, the Court is of the view that the fact that a matter is before the Security Council should not prevent it being dealt with by the Court and that both proceedings could be pursued *pari passu*. In that case the Court held:

> "In the preamble to this second resolution the Security Council ex-pressly took into account the Court's Order of 15 December 1979 in-dicating provisional measures; and it does not seem to have occurred to any member of the Council that there was or could be anything ir-regular in the simultaneous exercise of their respective functions by the Court and the Security Council. Nor is there in this any cause for surprise." (*I.C.J. Reports* 1980, p. 21, para. 40.)

The Court in fact went further, to say:

> "Whereas Article 12 of the Charter expressly forbids the General As-sembly to make any recommendation with regard to a dispute or sit-uation while the Security Council is exercising its functions in re-spect of that dispute or situation, no such restriction is placed on the

functioning of the Court by any provision of either the Charter or the Statute of the Court. The reasons are clear. It is for the Court, the principal judicial organ of the United Nations, to resolve any legal questions that may be in issue between parties to the dispute; and the resolution of such legal questions by the Court may be an important, and sometimes decisive, factor in promoting the peaceful settlement of the dispute. This is indeed recognized by Article 36 of the Charter, paragraph 3 of which specifically provides that:

> 'In making recommendations under this Article the Security Council should also take into consideration that legal disputes should as a general rule be referred by the parties to the International Court of Justice in accordance with the provisions of the Statute of the Court.'" (*I.C.J. Reports* 1980, p. 22, para. 40.)

94. The United States argument is also founded on a construction, which the Court is unable to share, of Nicaragua's complaint about the United States use, or threat of the use, of force against its territorial integrity and national independence, in breach of Article 2, paragraph 4, of the United Nations Charter. The United States argues that Nicaragua has thereby invoked a charge of aggression and armed conflict envisaged in Article 39 of the United Nations Charter, which can only be dealt with by the Security Council in accordance with the provisions of Chapter VII of the Charter, and not in accordance with the provisions of Chapter VI. This presentation of the matter by the United States treats the present dispute between Nicaragua and itself as a case of armed conflict which must be dealt with only by the Security Council and not by the Court which, under Article 2, paragraph 4, and Chapter VI of the Charter, deals with pacific settlement of all disputes between member States of the United Nations. But, if so, it has to be noted that, while the matter has been discussed in the Security Council, no notification has been given to it in accordance with Chapter VII of the Charter, so that the issue could be tabled for full discussion before a decision were taken for the necessary enforcement measures to be authorized. It is clear that the complaint of Nicaragua is not about an ongoing armed conflict between it and the United States, but one requiring, and indeed demanding, the peaceful settlement of disputes between the two States. Hence, it is properly brought before the principal judicial organ of the Organization for peaceful settlement.

95. It is necessary to emphasize that Article 24 of the Charter of the United Nations provides that

> "In order to ensure prompt and effective action by the United Nations, its Members confer on the Security Council *primary* responsibility for the maintenance of international peace and security * * * "

The Charter accordingly does not confer *exclusive* responsibility upon the Security Council for the purpose. * * *

96. It must also be remembered that, as the *Corfu Channel* case shows, the Court has never shied away from a case brought before it merely because it had political implications or because it involved serious elements of the use of force. * * * What is also significant is that the Security Council itself in that case had "undoubtedly intended that the whole dispute should be decided by the Court".

97. It is relevant also to observe that while the United States is arguing today that because of the alleged ongoing armed conflict between the two States the matter could not be brought to the International Court of Justice but should be referred to the Security Council, in the 1950s the United States brought seven cases to the Court involving armed attacks by military aircraft of other States against United States military aircraft; the only reason the cases were not dealt with by the Court was that each of the Respondent States indicated that it had not accepted the jurisdiction of the Court, and was not willing to do so for the purposes of the case. * * * In the view of the Court, this argument is not relevant.

98. Nor can the Court accept that the present proceedings are objectionable as being in effect an appeal to the Court from an adverse decision of the Security Council. The Court is not asked to say that the Security Council was wrong in its decision, nor that there was anything inconsistent with law in the way in which the members of the Council employed their right to vote. The Court is asked to pass judgment on certain legal aspects of a situation which has also been considered by the Security Council, a procedure which is entirely consonant with its position as the principal judicial organ of the United Nations. As to the inherent right of self-defence, the fact that it is referred to in the Charter as a "right" is indicative of a legal dimension; if in the present proceedings it becomes necessary for the Court to judge in this respect between the Parties—for the rights of no other State may be adjudicated in these proceedings—it cannot be debarred from doing so by the existence of a procedure for the States concerned to report to the Security Council in this connection.

* * *

112. In its above-mentioned Order of 10 May 1984, the Court indicated provisional measures "pending its final decision in the proceedings instituted on 9 April 1984 by the Republic of Nicaragua against the United States of America". It follows that the Order of 10 May 1984, and the provisional measures indicated therein, remain operative until the delivery of the final judgment in the present case.

113. For these reasons,

THE COURT,

(1)(a) *finds*, by eleven votes to five, that it has jurisdiction to entertain the Application filed by the Republic of Nicaragua on 9 April 1984, on the basis of Article 36, paragraphs 2 and 5, of the Statute of the Court;

> IN FAVOUR: *President* Elias; *Vice-President* Sette-Camara; *Judges* Lachs, Morozov, Nagendra Singh, Ruda, El-Khani, de Lacharriere, Mbaye, Bedjaoui; Judge *ad hoc* Colliard;

> AGAINST: *Judges* Mosler, Oda, Ago, Schwebel and Sir Robert Jennings.

(b) *finds*, by fourteen votes to two, that it has jurisdiction to entertain the Application filed by the Republic of Nicaragua on 9 April 1984, in so far as that Application relates to a dispute concerning the interpretation or application of the Treaty of Friendship, Commerce and Navigation between the United States of America and the Republic of Nicaragua signed at Managua on 21 January 1956, on the basis of Article XXIV of that Treaty;

> IN FAVOUR: *President* Elias; *Vice-President* Sette-Camara; *Judges* Lachs, Morozov, Nagendra Singh, Mosler, Oda, Ago, El-Khani, Sir Robert Jennings, de Lacharriere, Mbaye, Bedjaoui; Judge *ad hoc* Colliard;

> AGAINST: *Judges* Ruda and Schwebel.

(c) *finds*, by fifteen votes to one, that it has jurisdiction to entertain the case;

> IN FAVOUR: *President* Elias; *Vice-President* Sette-Camara; *Judges* Lachs, Morozov, Nagendra Singh, Ruda, Mosler, Oda, Ago, El-Khani, Sir Robert Jennings, de Lacharriere, Mbaye, Bedjaoui; Judge *ad hoc* Colliard;

> AGAINST: *Judge* Schwebel.

(2) *finds*, unanimously, that the said Application is admissible.

———————

How does the Court view the roles of the Security Council and the ICJ, respectively? What should those roles be in light of the institutions' designs and power structures?

———————

B. BETWEEN PRIVATE PARTIES: DOMESTIC COURT JURISDICTION IN INTERNATIONAL CASES

While there are international courts today in which states can litigate their disputes, most notably the ICJ, there is still no international court in which private parties can sue each other. As a result, international civil and commercial litigation continues to take place in domestic courts, as in *Hilton v. Guyot* more than a hundred years ago (see Chapter IV.2.). Private parties, like states, can also avoid litigation altogether and resort to arbitration instead, thus sidestepping the domestic court systems. We will turn to that option in the next subchapter.

The threshold question in private international litigation is: in which country's (domestic) courts can the case proceed? The answer depends on which courts have adjudicatory power over the parties, i.e., personal jurisdiction. (Note that the issue of what law can be applied is a different question altogether.) The general principles of public international law pertaining to jurisdiction (Chapters II.2.C. and VII.4.) have little to contribute here, mainly because they are so permissive (especially under the *Lotus* principle) that they impose almost no limits in practice. As a result, each country has traditionally decided for itself—as a matter of its domestic law—over which parties its courts shall exercise jurisdiction.

Typically, such jurisdiction is predicated either on the parties' *consent* or on *contacts* between them or their dispute and the forum state.

Jurisdiction by Consent: Choice of Forum Agreements

It is virtually undisputed that parties may agree to a so-called forum selection clause under which they designate a particular situs for potential litigation. Under what conditions they may do so, as well as the precise effect of such a clause, is, again, for the domestic law of the respective forum state to decide. *M/S Bremen v. Zapata Offshore Company* is the seminal American case on the matter. In reading the case, consider: (1) What exactly is the issue? (2) What did the German party get out of litigating in London rather than Tampa? (3) Why does the Court enforce the clause here? (4) What would it take for the clause to be struck down?

M/S BREMEN V. ZAPATA OFF–SHORE CO.

United States Supreme Court
407 U.S. 1 (1972)

CHIEF JUSTICE BURGER:

We granted certiorari to review a judgment of the United States Court of Appeals for the Fifth Circuit declining to enforce a forum-selection clause governing disputes arising under an international towage contract between petitioners and respondent. The circuits have differed in their approach to such clauses. For the reasons stated hereafter, we vacate the judgment of the Court of Appeals.

In November 1967, respondent Zapata, a Houston-based American corporation, contracted with petitioner Unterweser, a German corporation, to tow Zapata's ocean-going, self-elevating drilling rig *Chaparral* from Louisiana to a point off Ravenna, Italy, in the Adriatic Sea, where Zapata had agreed to drill certain wells.

Zapata had solicited bids for the towage, and several companies including Unterweser had responded. Unterweser was the low bidder and Zapata requested it to submit a contract, which it did. The contract submitted by Unterweser contained the following provision, which is at issue in this case:

> "Any dispute arising must be treated before the London Court of Justice."

In addition the contract contained two clauses purporting to exculpate Unterweser from liability for damages to the towed barge.

After reviewing the contract and making several changes, but without any alteration in the forum-selection or exculpatory clauses, a Zapata vice president executed the contract and forwarded it to Unterweser in Germany, where Unterweser accepted the changes, and the contract became effective.

On January 5, 1968, Unterweser's deep sea tug *Bremen* departed Venice, Louisiana, with the *Chaparral* in tow bound for Italy. On January 9, while the flotilla was in international waters in the middle of the Gulf of Mexico, a severe storm arose. The sharp roll of the *Chaparral* in Gulf waters caused its elevator legs, which had been raised for the voyage, to break off and fall into the sea, seriously damaging the *Chaparral*. In this emergency situation Zapata instructed the *Bremen* to tow its damaged rig to Tampa, Florida, the nearest port of refuge.

On January 12, Zapata, ignoring its contract promise to litigate "any dispute arising" in the English courts, commenced a suit in admiralty in the United States District Court at Tampa, seeking $3,500,000 damages against Unterweser *in personam* and the *Bremen in rem*, alleging negligent towage and breach of contract. Unterweser responded by invoking the forum clause of the towage contract, and moved to dismiss for lack of jurisdiction or on *forum non conveniens* grounds, or in the alternative to stay the action pending submission of the dispute to the "London Court of Justice." Shortly thereafter, in February, before the District Court had ruled on its motion to stay or dismiss the United States action, Unterweser commenced an action against Zapata seeking damages for breach of the towage contract in the High Court of Justice in London, as the contract provided. Zapata appeared in that court to contest jurisdiction, but its challenge was rejected, the English courts holding that the contractual forum provision conferred jurisdiction.

* * *

* * * [T]he District Court denied Unterweser's January motion to dismiss or stay Zapata's initial action. In denying the motion, that court relied on the prior decision of the Court of Appeals in *Carbon Black Export, Inc. v. The Monrosa.* In that case the Court of Appeals had held a forum-selection clause unenforceable, reiterating the traditional view of many American courts that "agreements in advance of controversy whose object is to oust the jurisdiction of the courts are contrary to public policy and will not be enforced." Apparently concluding that it was bound by the *Carbon Black* case, the District Court gave the forum-selection clause little, if any, weight. Instead, the court treated the motion to dismiss under normal *forum non conveniens* doctrine applicable in the absence of such a clause, citing *Gulf Oil Corp. v. Gilbert.* Under that doctrine "unless the balance is strongly in favor of the defendant, the plaintiff's choice of forum should rarely be disturbed." The District Court concluded: "the balance of conveniences here is not strongly in favor of [Unterweser] and [Zapata's] choice of forum should not be disturbed."

Thereafter, on January 21, 1969, the District Court denied another motion by Unterweser to stay the limitation action pending determination of the controversy in the High Court of Justice in London and granted Zapata's motion to restrain Unterweser from litigating further in the London court. The District Judge ruled that, having taken jurisdiction in the limitation proceeding, he had jurisdiction to determine all matters relating to the controversy. He ruled that Unterweser should be required to "do equity" by refraining from also litigating the controversy in the London court, not only for the reasons he had previously stated for denying Unterweser's first motion to stay Zapata's action, but also because Unterweser had invoked the United States court's jurisdiction to obtain the benefit of the Limitation Act.

* * *

We hold, with the six dissenting members of the Court of Appeals, that far too little weight and effect were given to the forum clause in resolving this controversy. For at least two decades we have witnessed an expansion of overseas commercial activities by business enterprises based in the United States. The barrier of distance that once tended to confine a business concern to a modest territory no longer does so. Here we see an American company with special expertise contracting with a foreign company to tow a complex machine thousands of miles across seas and oceans. The expansion of American business and industry will hardly be encouraged if, notwithstanding solemn contracts, we insist on a parochial concept that all disputes must be resolved under our laws and in our courts. Absent a contract forum, the considerations relied on by the Court of Appeals would be persuasive reasons for holding an American forum convenient in the traditional sense, but in an era of expanding world trade and commerce, the absolute aspects of the doctrine of the *Carbon Black* case have little place and would be a heavy hand indeed on the future development of international commercial dealings by Americans. We cannot have trade and commerce in world markets and international waters exclusively on our terms, governed by our laws, and resolved in our courts.

Forum-selection clauses have historically not been favored by American courts. Many courts, federal and state, have declined to enforce such clauses on the ground that they were "contrary to public policy," or that their effect was to "oust the jurisdiction" of the court. Although this view apparently still has considerable acceptance, other courts are tending to adopt a more hospitable attitude toward forum-selection clauses. This view, advanced in the well-reasoned dissenting opinion in the instant case, is that such clauses are prima facie valid and should be enforced unless enforcement is shown by the resisting party to be "unreasonable" under the circumstances. We believe this is the correct doctrine to be followed by federal district courts sitting in admiralty. It is merely the other side of the proposition recognized by this Court in *National Equipment Rental, Ltd. v. Szukhent,* holding that in federal courts a party may validly consent to be sued in a jurisdiction where he cannot be found for service of process through contractual designation of an "agent" for receipt of process in that jurisdiction. In so holding, the Court stated:

> "[I]t is settled * * * that parties to a contract may agree in advance to submit to the jurisdiction of a given court to permit notice to be served by the opposing party, or even to waive notice altogether."

This approach is substantially that followed in other common-law countries including England. It is the view advanced by noted scholars and that adopted by the Restatement [Second] of the Conflict of Laws. It accords with ancient concepts of freedom of contract and reflects an appreciation of the expanding horizons of American contractors who seek business in all parts of the world. Not surprisingly, foreign businessmen prefer, as do we, to have disputes resolved in their own courts, but if that choice is not available, then in a neutral forum with expertise in the subject matter. Plainly, the courts of England meet the standards of neutrality and long experience in admiralty litigation. The choice of that forum was made in an arm's-length negotiation by experienced and sophisticated businessmen, and absent some compelling and countervailing reason it should be honored by the parties and enforced by the courts.

The argument that such clauses are improper because they tend to "oust" a court of jurisdiction is hardly more than a vestigial legal fiction. It appears to rest at core on historical judicial resistance to any attempt to reduce the power and business of a particular court and has little place in an era when all courts are overloaded and when businesses once essentially local now operate in world markets. It reflects something of a provincial attitude regarding the fairness of other tribunals. No one seriously contends in this case that the forum selection clause "ousted" the District Court of jurisdiction over Zapata's action. The threshold question is whether that court should have exercised its jurisdiction to do more than give effect to the legitimate expectations of the parties, manifested in their freely negotiated agreement, by specifically enforcing the forum clause.

There are compelling reasons why a freely negotiated private international agreement, unaffected by fraud, undue influence, or overweening bargaining power, such as that involved here, should be given full effect. In this case, for example, we are concerned with a far from routine transaction between companies of two different nations contemplating the tow of a extremely costly piece of equipment from Louisiana across the Gulf of Mexico and the Atlantic Ocean, through the Mediterranean Sea to its final destination in the Adriatic Sea. In the course of its voyage, it was to traverse the waters of many jurisdictions. The *Chaparral* could have been damaged at any point along the route, and there were countless possible ports of refuge. That the accident occurred in the Gulf of Mexico and the barge was towed to Tampa in an emergency were mere fortuities. It cannot be doubted for a moment that the parties sought to provide for a neutral forum for the resolution of any disputes arising during the tow. Manifestly much uncertainty and possibly great inconvenience to both parties could arise if a suit could be maintained in any jurisdiction in which an accident might occur or if jurisdiction were left to any place where the *Bremen* or Unterweser might happen to be found.[15] The elimination of all such uncertainties by agreeing in advance on a forum acceptable to both parties is an indispensable element in international trade, commerce, and contracting. There is strong evidence that the forum clause was a vital part of the agreement, and it would be unrealistic to think that the parties did not conduct their negotiations, including fixing the monetary terms, with the consequences of the forum clause figuring prominently in their calculations. Under these circumstances, as Justice Karminski reasoned in sustaining jurisdiction over Zapata in the High Court of Justice,

---

[15] At the very least, the clause was an effort to eliminate all uncertainty as to the nature, location, and outlook of the forum in which these companies of differing nationalities might find themselves. Moreover, while the contract here did not specifically provide that the substantive law of England should be applied, it is the general rule in English courts that the parties are assumed, absent contrary indication, to have designated the forum with the view that it should apply its own law. * * *

"[t]he force of an agreement for litigation in this country, freely entered into between two competent parties, seems to me to be very powerful."

Thus, in the light of present-day commercial realities and expanding international trade we conclude that the forum clause should control absent a strong showing that it should be set aside. Although their opinions are not altogether explicit, it seems reasonably clear that the District Court and the Court of Appeals placed the burden on Unterweser to show that London would be a more convenient forum than Tampa, although the contract expressly resolved that issue. The correct approach would have been to enforce the forum clause specifically unless Zapata could clearly show that enforcement would be unreasonable and unjust, or that the clause was invalid for such reasons as fraud or overreaching. Accordingly, the case must be remanded for reconsideration.

We note, however, that there is nothing in the record presently before us that would support a refusal to enforce the forum clause. The Court of Appeals suggested that enforcement would be contrary to the public policy of the forum under *Bisso v. Inland Waterways Corp.*, because of the prospect that the English courts would enforce the clauses of the towage contract purporting to exculpate Unterweser from liability for damages to the *Chaparral*. A contractual choice-of-forum clause should be held unenforceable if enforcement would contravene a strong public policy of the forum in which suit is brought, whether declared by statute or by judicial decision. It is clear, however, that whatever the proper scope of the policy expressed in *Bisso*, it does not reach this case. *Bisso* rested on considerations with respect to the towage business strictly in American waters, and those considerations are not controlling in an international commercial agreement. * * *

Courts have also suggested that a forum clause, even though it is freely bargained for and contravenes no important public policy of the forum, may nevertheless be "unreasonable" and unenforceable if the chosen forum is *seriously* inconvenient for the trial of the action. Of course, where it can be said with reasonable assurance that at the time they entered the contract, the parties to a freely negotiated private international commercial agreement contemplated the claimed inconvenience, it is difficult to see why any such claim of inconvenience should be heard to render the forum clause unenforceable. We are not here dealing with an agreement between two Americans to resolve their essentially local disputes in a remote alien forum. In such a case, the serious inconvenience of the contractual forum to one or both of the parties might carry greater weight in determining the reasonableness of the forum clause. The remoteness of the forum might suggest that the agreement was an adhesive one, or that the parties did not have the particular controversy in mind when they made their agreement; yet even there the party claiming should bear a heavy burden of proof. Similarly, selection of a remote forum to apply differing foreign law to an essentially American controversy might contravene an important public policy of the forum. For example, so long as *Bisso* governs American courts with respect to the towage business in American waters, it would quite arguably be improper to permit an American tower to avoid that policy by providing a foreign forum for resolution of his disputes with an American towee.

This case, however, involves a freely negotiated international commercial transaction between a German and an American corporation for towage of a vessel from the Gulf of Mexico to the Adriatic Sea. As noted, selection of a London forum was clearly a reasonable effort to bring vital certainty to this international transaction and to provide a neutral forum experienced and capable in the resolution of admiralty litigation. Whatever "inconvenience" Zapata would suffer by being forced to litigate in the contractual forum as it agreed to do was clearly foreseeable at the time of contracting. In such circumstances it should be incumbent on the party seeking to escape his contract to show that trial in the contractual forum will be so gravely difficult and inconvenient that he will for all practical purposes be deprived of his day in court. Absent that, there is no basis for concluding that it would be unfair, unjust, or unreasonable to hold that party to his bargain.

* * *

JUSTICE DOUGLAS, dissenting:

* * *

The Limitation Court [i.e., district court] is a court of equity and traditionally an equity court may enjoin litigation in another court where equitable considerations indicate that the other litigation might prejudice the proceedings in the Limitation Court. Petitioners' petition for limitation subjects them to the full equitable powers of the Limitation Court.

Respondent is a citizen of this country. Moreover, if it were remitted to the English court, its substantive rights would be adversely affected. Exculpatory provisions in the towage control provide (1) that petitioners, the masters and the crews "are not responsible for defaults and/or errors in the navigation of the tow" and (2) that "[d]amages suffered by the towed object are in any case for account of its Owners."

Under our decision in *Dixilyn Drilling Corp. v. Crescent Towing & Salvage Co.*, "a contract which exempts the tower from liability for its own negligence" is not enforceable, though there is evidence in the present record that it is enforceable in England. That policy was first announced in *Bisso v. Inland Waterways Corp.* Although the casualty occurred on the high seas, the *Bisso* doctrine is nonetheless applicable.

Moreover, the casualty occurred close to the District Court, a number of potential witnesses, including respondent's crewmen, reside in that area, and the inspection and repair work were done there. The testimony of the tower's crewmen, residing in Germany, is already available by way of depositions taken in the proceedings.

All in all, the District Court judge exercised his discretion wisely in enjoining petitioners from pursuing the litigation in England.

I would affirm the judgment below.

In most countries (particularly in civil law jurisdictions), forum selection clauses are governed by statute. How do the Swiss and Turkish statutes compare to each other?

SWISS FEDERAL STATUTE ON PRIVATE INTERNATIONAL LAW (1987)

Jean-Claude Cornu, Stephane Hankins & Symeon Symeonides, transl.
37 Am. J. Comp. Law 193 (1989)

* * *

Chapter One: Common Provisions

Section 2: Jurisdiction

IV. Choice of forum

Article 5

(1) In patrimonial matters, the parties may agree on the court that will have jurisdiction to adjudicate a present or future dispute arising out of a particular legal relationship. The agreement may be executed in writing, by telegram, telex, telecopier or by any other medium of communication allowing proof of the agreement by means of a text. In the absence of contrary stipulation, the choice of forum is exclusive.

(2) A choice of forum has no legal force if it results in depriving one party, in an abusive manner, of the protection accorded him by a forum provided by Swiss law.

* * *

TURKISH CODE ON PRIVATE INTERNATIONAL LAW AND INTERNATIONAL CIVIL PROCEDURE

Law No. 5718 of Nov. 27, 2007

* * *

Article 47

1. In cases where the local jurisdiction is not determined on the basis of exclusive jurisdiction, the parties may agree on having a suit between them with a foreign element and arising from obligational relationships heard before the court of a foreign state. The agreement shall be valid on the condition that it may be proven by written evidence. * * *

2. The jurisdiction of the courts as determined in articles 44 [employment contracts], 45 [consumer contracts] and 46 [insurance contracts] may not be set aside by the agreement of the parties.

* * *

———————————

Are the Swiss and Turkish provisions more or less permissive than the *Bremen* test?

Like other aspects of private international law (Chapter VIII.5.A.), the law governing choice of forum clauses is in the process of becoming "internationalized": it is no longer exclusively a matter of the respective states' domestic law but is sometimes determined (uniformly) through supranational or international instruments. Most importantly, all EU member states are bound by regulations.

(EC) COUNCIL REGULATION NO. 44/2001 ON JURISDICTION AND THE RECOGNITION AND ENFORCEMENT OF JUDGMENTS IN CIVIL AND COMMERCIAL MATTERS

(22 December 2000)

* * *

Article 23

1. If the parties, one or more of whom is domiciled in a Member State, have agreed that a court or the courts of a Member State are to have jurisdiction to settle any disputes which have arisen or which may arise in connection with a particular legal relationship, that court or those courts shall have jurisdiction. Such jurisdiction shall be exclusive unless the parties have agreed otherwise. Such an agreement conferring jurisdiction shall be either:

(a) in writing or evidenced in writing; or

(b) in a form which accords with practices which the parties have established between themselves; or

(c) in international trade or commerce, in a form which accords with a usage of which the parties are or ought to have been aware and which in such trade or commerce is widely known to, and regularly observed by, parties to contracts of the type involved in the particular trade or commerce concerned.

2. Any communication by electronic means which provides a durable record of the agreement shall be equivalent to "writing."

* * *

How does Article 23 of the EU Regulation compare to the Swiss and Turkish provisions?

NOTE ON THE HAGUE CONVENTION ON CHOICE OF FORUM AGREEMENTS

A Convention on Choice of Court Agreements was adopted by the Hague Conference on Private International Law in 2005. It is not yet in force, but its prospects are good: both the United States and the European Union have signed, and Mexico has already ratified it. The Convention provides that exclusive international forum selection clauses (in the commercial, i.e., non-consumer, context) are binding and enforceable. The chosen court must accept jurisdiction, and all other courts must defer (i.e., dismiss or stay an action filed in them). The Convention also provides that judgments based on exclusive forum selection clauses must be enforced. Of course, there are a lot of strings attached and the devil is, as usual, in the details.

Note that, in addition to choosing a forum, the parties to a contract can also designate the law applicable to their dispute in a so-called choice of law clause. Especially in international contracts, this is advisable and often routinely done for the sake of predictability. It is by and large permitted although the limits depend, again, on the respective forum's law. In particular, choice of law clauses must not violate a forum's public policy and, especially in Europe, special limits are imposed in order to protect consumers and employees.

Jurisdiction by Contacts:
Fairness Limitations in International Cases

If the parties have not chosen a forum, for example because they had no contractual relationship, jurisdiction in civil and commercial matters is usually based on the fact that either the parties or the underlying events are somehow connected with the forum state. What exactly that requires varies significantly among national laws, but there are also considerable commonalities. For example, virtually everywhere courts have jurisdiction over those individuals or enterprises who have their home in the forum (their domicile, place of incorporation or headquarters). Also, there usually is jurisdiction in cases of breach of contract where the agreement had to be performed, in tort suits where the wrong was committed, and in property disputes where the item in question is located, etc.

In U.S. law in particular, jurisdiction in civil cases typically requires not only a connection between the defendant or the dispute and the forum[1] but also, more generally, compliance with due process under the Fourteenth (or, in federal courts, the Fifth) Amendment. According to the United States Supreme Court, this requires that the defendant "if he be not present within the territory of the forum, * * * have certain minimum contacts with it such that the maintenance of the suit does not offend 'traditional notions of fair play and substantial justice.'" *International Shoe v. Washington*, 326 U.S. 310, 154 (1945).

In other words, there must be (minimum) contacts, and the exercise of jurisdiction must be fair—obviously a very vague standard that invites litigation of the jurisdictional issue in cases involving out-of-state defendants sued in U.S. courts.

The details of U.S. law on personal jurisdiction are covered (mainly with regard to interstate cases) either in courses on civil procedure or on conflict of laws; they are not our concern here. For transnational law purposes, we are mainly interested in a specific question arising in international cases: should it make a difference if the defendant is not just from another American state but from a foreign country altogether? In other words, are there special concerns in international cases that warrant special jurisdictional analysis?

For a long time, American courts happily ignored the fact that the defendant was from a foreign country. In the wake of the Supreme Court's decision in *The Bremen*, this began to change. In the case below, the Court explicitly recognized for the first time that foreign defendants sued in American courts may require special treatment.

---

[1] The plaintiff typically submits to jurisdiction by bringing suit in a particular court, i.e., is subject to jurisdiction by consent.

ASAHI METAL INDUSTRY CO., LTD. V. SUPERIOR COURT OF CALIFORNIA

United States Supreme Court
480 U.S. 102 (1987)

JUSTICE O'CONNOR announced the judgment of the Court and delivered the unanimous opinion of the Court with respect to Part I, the opinion of the Court with respect to Part II–B, in which THE CHIEF JUSTICE, JUSTICE BRENNAN, JUSTICE WHITE, JUSTICE MARSHALL, JUSTICE BLACKMUN, JUSTICE POWELL, and JUSTICE STEVENS join. * * *

This case presents the question whether the mere awareness on the part of a foreign defendant that the components it manufactured, sold, and delivered outside the United States would reach the forum State in the stream of commerce constitutes "minimum contacts" between the defendant and the forum State such that the exercise of jurisdiction "does not offend 'traditional notions of fair play and substantial justice.'" *International Shoe Co. v. Washington*, 326 U.S. 310, 316 (1945), quoting *Milliken v. Meyer*, 311 U.S. 457, 463 (1940).

I

On September 23, 1978, on Interstate Highway 80 in Solano County, California, Gary Zurcher lost control of his Honda motorcycle and collided with a tractor. Zurcher was severely injured, and his passenger and wife, Ruth Ann Moreno, was killed. In September 1979, Zurcher filed a product liability action in the Superior Court of the State of California in and for the County of Solano. Zurcher alleged that the 1978 accident was caused by a sudden loss of air and an explosion in the rear tire of the motorcycle, and alleged that the motorcycle tire, tube, and sealant were defective. Zurcher's complaint named, *inter alia*, Cheng Shin Rubber Industrial Co., Ltd. (Cheng Shin), the Taiwanese manufacturer of the tube. Cheng Shin in turn filed a cross-complaint seeking indemnification from its codefendants and from petitioner, Asahi Metal Industry Co., Ltd. (Asahi), the manufacturer of the tube's valve assembly. Zurcher's claims against Cheng Shin and the other defendants were eventually settled and dismissed, leaving only Cheng Shin's indemnity action against Asahi.

California's long-arm statute authorizes the exercise of jurisdiction "on any basis not inconsistent with the Constitution of this state or of the United States." Cal. Civ. Proc. Code Ann. § 410.10 (West 1973). Asahi moved to quash Cheng Shin's service of summons, arguing the State could not exert jurisdiction over it consistent with the Due Process Clause of the Fourteenth Amendment.

In relation to the motion, the following information was submitted by Asahi and Cheng Shin. Asahi is a Japanese corporation. It manufactures tire valve assemblies in Japan and sells the assemblies to Cheng Shin, and to several other tire manufacturers, for use as components in finished tire tubes. Asahi's sales to Cheng Shin took place in Taiwan. The shipments from Asahi to Cheng Shin were sent from Japan to Taiwan. Cheng Shin bought and incorporated into its tire tubes 150,000 Asahi valve assemblies in 1978; 500,000 in 1979; 500,000 in 1980; 100,000 in 1981; and 100,000 in 1982. Sales to Cheng Shin accounted for 1.24 percent of Asahi's income in 1981 and 0.44 percent in 1982. Cheng Shin alleged that approximately 20 percent of its sales in the United States are in California. Cheng Shin purchases valve assemblies from other suppliers as well, and sells finished tubes throughout the world.

* * *

The Supreme Court of the State of California * * * observed: "Asahi has no offices, property or agents in California. It solicits no business in California and has made no direct sales [in California]." Moreover, "Asahi did not design or control the system of distribution that carried its valve assemblies into California." Nevertheless, the court found the exercise of jurisdiction over Asahi to be consistent with the Due Process Clause. It concluded that Asahi knew that some of the valve assemblies sold to Cheng Shin would be incorporated into tire tubes sold in California, and that Asahi benefited indirectly from the sale in California of products incorporating its components. The court considered Asahi's intentional act of placing its components into the stream of commerce—that is, by delivering the components to Cheng Shin in Taiwan—coupled with Asahi's awareness that some of the components would eventually find their way into California, sufficient to form the basis for state court jurisdiction under the Due Process Clause.

We granted certiorari and now reverse.

* * *

II

* * *

B

The strictures of the Due Process Clause forbid a state court to exercise personal jurisdiction over Asahi under circumstances that would offend "'traditional notions of fair play and substantial justice.'" *International Shoe Co. v. Washington*, 326 U.S., at 316, quoting *Milliken v. Meyer*, 311 U.S., at 463.

We have previously explained that the determination of the reasonableness of the exercise of jurisdiction in each case will depend on an evaluation of several factors. A court must consider the burden on the defendant, the interests of the forum State, and the plaintiff's interest in obtaining relief. It must also weigh in its determination "the interstate judicial system's interest in obtaining the most efficient resolution of controversies; and the shared interest of the several States in furthering fundamental substantive social policies."

A consideration of these factors in the present case clearly reveals the unreasonableness of the assertion of jurisdiction over Asahi, even apart from the question of the placement of goods in the stream of commerce.

Certainly the burden on the defendant in this case is severe. Asahi has been commanded by the Supreme Court of California not only to traverse the distance between Asahi's headquarters in Japan and the Superior Court of California in and for the County of Solano, but also to submit its dispute with Cheng Shin to a foreign nation's judicial system. The unique burdens placed upon one who must defend oneself in a foreign legal system should have significant weight in assessing the reasonableness of stretching the long arm of personal jurisdiction over national borders.

When minimum contacts have been established, often the interests of the plaintiff and the forum in the exercise of jurisdiction will justify even the serious burdens placed on the alien defendant. In the present case, however, the interests of the plaintiff and the forum in California's assertion of jurisdiction over Asahi are slight. All that remains is a claim for indemnification asserted by Cheng Shin, a Taiwanese corporation, against Asahi. The transaction on which the indemnification claim is based took place in Taiwan; Asahi's components were shipped from Japan to Taiwan. Cheng Shin has not demonstrated that it is more convenient for it to litigate its indemnification claim against Asahi in California rather than in Taiwan or Japan.

Because the plaintiff is not a California resident, California's legitimate interests in the dispute have considerably diminished. * * *

WorldWide Volkswagen also admonished courts to take into consideration the interests of the "several States," in addition to the forum State, in the efficient judicial resolution of the dispute and the advancement of substantive policies. In the present case, this advice calls for a court to consider the procedural and substantive policies of other *nations* whose interests are affected by the assertion of jurisdiction by the California court. The procedural and substantive interests of other nations in a state court's assertion of jurisdiction over an alien defendant will differ from case to case. In every case, however, those interests, as well as the Federal interest in Government's foreign relations policies, will be best served by a careful inquiry into the reasonableness of the assertion of jurisdiction in the particular case, and an unwillingness to find the serious burdens on an alien defendant outweighed by minimal interests on the part of the plaintiff or the forum State. "Great care and reserve should be exercised when extending our notions of personal jurisdiction into the international field."

Considering the international context, the heavy burden on the alien defendant, and the slight interests of the plaintiff and the forum State, the exercise of personal jurisdiction by a California court over Asahi in this instance would be unreasonable and unfair.

* * *

————————

Notice the odd procedural posture of the case when it reached the United States Supreme Court: the plaintiff had settled the case and the only remaining litigants were two foreign parties, one an original defendant, the other a third-party defendant. Would or should the case have come out differently if the original plaintiff had still been involved in the litigation?

In 2011, on the same day, the U.S. Supreme Court decided two further cases raising the issue of personal jurisdiction over foreign defendants in product liability actions. The Court denied jurisdiction in both instances. *J. McIntyre Machinery, Ltd. v. Nicastro*, 131 S. Ct. 2780 (2011); *Goodyear Dunlop Tires Operation, S.A. v. Brown*, 131 S. Ct. 2846 (2011).

The Court's opinion in *Asahi* can be read to suggest that foreign defendants receive greater due process protection in light of the particular burdens they face. What exactly are those burdens? Is it really true that foreign defendants face greater burdens? In all cases? Even if they do face such burdens, is a court justified in taking those burdens into account at all or should they be considered the price for having acted in the United States or for having used its markets?

In thinking about these questions, consider the arguments by Gary Born in the excerpt below.

GARY BORN, REFLECTIONS ON JUDICIAL JURISDICTION IN INTERNATIONAL CASES
17 Ga. J. Int'l & Comp. L. 1 (1987)

* * *

IV. FASHIONING A STANDARD OF JUDICIAL JURISDICTION FOR INTERNATIONAL CASES

* * *

* * * The following section considers whether international cases possess special characteristics requiring application of a different Due Process standard. The section concludes that international assertions of jurisdiction do implicate special concerns that call for modification of traditional Due Process standards. The second section of this Part provides a sketch of an appropriate Due Process standard for judicial jurisdiction in international cases.

A.   SPECIAL CONSIDERATIONS IN INTERNATIONAL CASES

Assertions of judicial jurisdiction in international cases raise a number of concerns that are absent from purely domestic cases. This section first discusses three differences between domestic and international cases that, upon analysis, do not provide a legitimate basis for modifying traditional Due Process standards. The section then discusses two other differences that do provide sound justifications for treating judicial jurisdiction in international cases differently from domestic cases.

1.   INAPPROPRIATE REASONS FOR TREATING INTERNATIONAL CASES DIFFERENTLY FROM DOMESTIC CASES

First, and most obviously, international cases involve defendants who are not citizens or residents of the United States. Arguably, United States constitutional limitations on the exercise of judicial jurisdiction over non-resident aliens should be less restrictive than the limits on jurisdiction over United States citizens or residents. This result might seek support in the diminished constitutional protections that nonresident aliens receive in various other contexts. For example, several decisions have held that nonresident aliens seeking admittance to the United States may not invoke the procedural protections of the Due Process Clause. Similarly, other decisions have refused to subject the substantive requirements imposed on immigration by nonresident aliens to constitutional review. Finally, reduced Due Process protection also might seek support in notions that the Constitution has no extraterritorial effect, at least for noncitizens.

Although reduced constitutional protection may be appropriate for non-resident foreigners in some instances, it is plainly inappropriate when determining limits on the exercise of judicial jurisdiction. As most courts have concluded, the full protection of the Due Process Clause should be available to foreign citizens summoned to defend themselves in United States courts. It would be unfair and ironic to hale an alien into an unfamiliar United States court, forcing him to litigate according to our procedures and laws, yet deny him the protections of the Due Process Clause on the grounds that he is an alien.

A second difference between international and domestic cases that may bear on judicial jurisdiction involves the recognition and enforcement of United States judgments by foreign courts. In the domestic context the Constitution's Full Faith and Credit Clause generally compels recognition of judgments issued in the courts of sister states. In the international context judgments rendered by United States courts are given considerably less deference than provided by the Full Faith and Credit Clause. While practice varies between countries, foreign courts often recognize United

States judgments only in limited circumstances. Most important, many foreign courts will refuse to recognize United States judgments based on assertions of jurisdiction under long-arm statutes.

Some commentators have reasoned that the difficulties United States plaintiffs face in enforcing United States judgments against foreign defendants argues for more restrictive limits on judicial jurisdiction in international cases. The better view, however, is that foreign nonrecognition of United States judgments does not point decisively towards any special Due Process treatment of judicial jurisdiction in international cases. It is unclear how frequently foreign recognition of judgments is necessary, even in international cases. Some foreign defendants may voluntarily pay judgments rendered against them, perhaps because they wish to continue or expand their United States business activities. Other defendants may have assets in the United States, may bring assets here in the future, or may have assets in countries that will liberally enforce United States judgments, even if rendered on the basis of long-arm jurisdiction. For these reasons, there is no way to predict accurately whether a particular plaintiff will actually need to enforce a long-arm judgment rendered in a United States court, and if so whether he will be successful. Without these determinations, however, a rule restricting judicial jurisdiction in international cases on the ground that resulting judgments may be unenforceable, would have unjustifiable effects. Such a rule would foreclose litigation in the United States by some plaintiffs who could collect on judgments they obtained. In addition, the rule would encourage foreign states to limit recognition of United States judgments, and penalize nationals of countries with liberal recognition policies. Finally, if a particular assertion of United States long-arm judicial jurisdiction over foreigners is regarded as fair and reasonable by United States courts and legislatures, it would be anomalous to forego such assertions solely because foreign states took a different view.

A third way in which assertions of judicial jurisdiction in international cases differ from those in domestic cases involves the burden of litigation. In general, litigation by a foreign defendant in international cases involves comparatively greater hardships than litigation by a United States resident in another state or region of the United States. In many international cases one party will be required to follow procedural rules that differ markedly from those in its home jurisdiction. In addition, one litigant will generally be a significantly greater distance from the forum than in purely domestic cases, and time differences, language barriers, mail delays, transportation difficulties, and other logistical obstacles which impede efficient communications will create further hardships. Furthermore, while the United States is a relatively homogeneous legal, economic, cultural, social and political unit, the domestic institutions and attitudes within this country often differ markedly from those in foreign states. Litigation in this unfamiliar environment often will create a host of hardships not encountered in the domestic context. Finally, local decision-makers may hold prejudices or parochial biases against foreign litigants not held against persons from other sections of the nation.

In virtually all international cases, an increased litigation burden will exist for the parties regardless of the forum. As a result, resolving personal jurisdiction disputes usually will not involve avoiding litigation burdens, but instead, deciding which party will bear the unavoidable inconvenience of litigating abroad. Moreover, as one court observed, "many of the inconvenience burdens in [international cases] are symmetrical." In general, both parties would suffer roughly the same level of inconvenience if forced to litigate abroad.

The implications of the differences in litigation burdens in international cases are unclear. As we have seen, prevailing Due Process doctrine teaches that the "primary concern" of the Due Process Clause is the "burden on the defendant." [T]he "plaintiff's interest in obtaining convenient and effective relief" is also a "relevant factor," but current doctrine places greater weight on protecting defendants from burdensome litigation than on ensuring plaintiffs a convenient forum. In the words of one court of appeals, "the law of personal jurisdiction * * * is asymmetrical. The primary concern is for the burden on a defendant."

Under this view of the Due Process Clause, assertions of judicial jurisdiction in international cases generally should be more restrained than such assertions in purely domestic cases. Since litigation burdens are greater in international cases, and since the burden on the defendant is the primary concern of Due Process analysis, assertions of United States jurisdiction will more frequently impose unacceptable burdens on foreign defendants than on domestic defendants. This result does not appear to turn on a special constitutional standard for judicial jurisdiction in international cases. Instead, more restrained jurisdictional claims arguably would follow from the fact that litigation burdens in international cases are, as a factual matter, usually more significant than those in domestic cases, and from the significance that existing Due Process analysis places on burdens imposed on defendants.

On the other hand, it is at least arguable that existing Due Process formulations do not take adequate account of the greater hardships that exist in the international context. Current Due Process analysis generally permits jurisdiction when the defendant's contacts with the forum are "such that he should reasonably anticipate being haled into court there." Because of its focus on foreseeability and prelitigation contacts with the forum, this formulation may not give adequate weight to the greater litigation burdens that exist in international cases. The better view, however, is that current Due Process analysis is sufficiently flexible to take account of the comparatively greater litigation burdens on private parties in international cases. The Supreme Court's *World-Wide Volkswagen* decision, as well as better-reasoned lower court decisions, appear to take the defendant's litigation burdens into account in deciding foreseeability questions. Likewise, the lack of suggestions for a special Due Process standard for domestic cases involving great litigation inconvenience suggests that existing Due Process formulations are able to deal with varying levels of litigation burdens. In short, although current Due Process analysis suggests that jurisdiction in international cases should be more restrained than in domestic cases because of the increased litigation burdens faced by foreign defendants, existing formulations appear able to produce the requisite degree of restraint.

2. REASONS FOR TREATING INTERNATIONAL CASES DIFFERENTLY FROM DOMESTIC CASES

There are, however, legitimate reasons for taking different approaches to the exercise of judicial jurisdiction in domestic and international cases. Treating jurisdiction differently in domestic and international cases would be entirely consistent with existing United States constitutional and common law doctrine in a number of other areas. As Judge Jessup observed in the International Court of Justice's *Barcelona Traction* decision, jurisdictional rules that are "valid enough for interstate conflicts within the constitutional system of the United States, may be improper when placing a burden on international commerce."

The first reason for different treatment of judicial jurisdiction in international cases is that assertions of jurisdiction over foreigners can affect United States foreign relations in ways that domestic claims of jurisdiction cannot. The exercise of judicial jurisdiction over foreign defendants by United States courts plainly implicates the sovereign interests of foreign states. In the words of one English court, "service out of the jurisdiction at the instance of our courts is necessarily prima facie an interference with the exclusive jurisdiction of the sovereignty of the foreign country where service is to be effected." As a result, assertions of United States judicial jurisdiction over foreigners can readily arouse foreign resentment. This risk is heightened because, although United States principles of judicial jurisdiction are generally consistent with international law, they are not always so. Moreover, the imprecision of the international law requirement that assertions of judicial jurisdiction be "reasonable" creates further possibilities for dispute.

Because exorbitant assertions of judicial jurisdiction by United States courts may offend foreign sovereigns, these claims can provoke diplomatic protests, trigger commercial or judicial retaliation, and threaten friendly relations in unrelated fields. Equally important, exorbitant jurisdictional claims can frustrate diplomatic initiatives by the United States, particularly in the private international law field. Most significantly, these claims can interfere with United States efforts to conclude international agreements providing for mutual recognition and enforcement of judgments or restricting exorbitant jurisdictional claims by foreign states.

An appropriate way to deal with the risk that assertions of judicial jurisdiction by United States courts will interfere with the nation's foreign relations is to subject these claims to heightened constitutional scrutiny. As discussed in detail below, heightened scrutiny would place a check on exorbitant jurisdictional claims, thereby reducing the risks of offending foreign sovereigns and interfering with United States foreign relations. This approach to judicial jurisdiction finds strong support in constitutional and common law principles in other international contexts, where heightened scrutiny is used to minimize the risk that United States courts will infringe foreign sovereign interests or interfere with national foreign relations.

* * *

B. A STANDARD OF JUDICIAL JURISDICTION

1. THE LEVEL OF DUE PROCESS SCRUTINY IN INTERNATIONAL CASES

The contours of heightened scrutiny of judicial jurisdiction in international cases are dictated by the justifications for such scrutiny: preventing friction with foreign sovereigns, avoiding foreign retaliation or interference with United States foreign relations, and minimizing unfairness to persons engaged in foreign commerce. To accomplish these objectives, the Due Process Clause should impose two related requirements on assertions of judicial jurisdiction in international cases. First the Clause should require United States courts to use particular caution in asserting long-arm jurisdiction over foreigners; second, it should require closer connections between the forum and the defendant than are necessary in domestic cases.

In the words of one English judge, "as a matter of international comity it seems to me important to make sure that no * * * service [outside the jurisdiction] shall be allowed unless it is clearly within both the letter and spirit" of applicable English jurisdictional statutes. Or, as Justice Harlan explained, "great care and reserve should be exercised when extending our notions of personal jurisdiction into the international field." As both comments suggest, before asserting jurisdiction over foreign persons, United States courts should give careful scrutiny to the defendant's relationship to the forum, paying especial attention to jurisdictional claims likely to offend foreign sovereigns.

One benefit of heightened constitutional scrutiny is that it would reduce the risk of exorbitant United States jurisdictional claims caused by misapplications of personal jurisdictional standards. Because the consequences of exorbitant jurisdictional claims in international cases are more serious than in domestic cases, it is appropriate to use greater care to ensure that such claims are not made. By focusing on offense to foreign sovereigns, the suggested analysis also would seek to reduce the likelihood that United States jurisdictional assertions would be inconsistent with emerging norms of international law and thus objectionable to foreign states. For example, under the suggested analysis, the Due Process Clause would likely preclude the exercise of "tag" jurisdiction in international cases based on a foreigner's fleeting presence in the forum. Although jurisdiction based on transitory presence within the forum is often permitted in domestic cases, it is inconsistent with emerging principles of international law. Moreover, in most commentator's eyes, "tag" jurisdiction is inconsistent with the premises underlying *International Shoe*'s minimum contacts test. Under the heightened scrutiny proposed above, "tag" jurisdiction should not be available in international cases.

Due Process analysis in international cases also should require closer pre-litigation contacts between the defendant and the forum than would be necessary in domestic cases. Specifying exactly how much closer a foreign defendant's connections with the forum should be admittedly is difficult, and perhaps unwise. As in the domestic context, "the criteria by which we mark the boundary line between those activities which justify the subjection of a [foreign] corporation to suit, and those which do not, cannot be simply mechanical or quantitative." Although precision is difficult and perhaps undesirable, however, the appropriate Due Process standard in international cases should require more substantial, direct, or foreseeable distribution of products into the forum, or more pervasive and sustained business contacts with the forum, than that required in domestic cases. As we already have seen, this would reduce the risks of offending foreign sovereigns, provoking retaliatory responses, interfering with United States foreign affairs, and imposing unfairness on foreign defendants.

2. THE FOCUS OF DUE PROCESS ANALYSIS IN INTERNATIONAL CASES

International cases not only require a different level of Due Process scrutiny from that applicable in domestic cases, but also demand a different focus of Due Process analysis. For purposes of international law and foreign relations, the separate identities of individual states of the Union are generally irrelevant. In the Supreme Court's words, "[f]or local interests, the several states of the Union exist, but for national purposes, embracing our relations with foreign nations, we are but one people, one nation, one power."

Under this basic principle of international law, foreign nations may properly complain when a United States court asserts jurisdiction over a national who has no reasonable connection to the United States. A foreign nation, however, has no basis for complaint under international law when a United States court asserts jurisdiction over a national who has a reasonably close relationship to the United States, even if the foreign national has no connections with the state of the Union asserting jurisdiction. "International law addresses the reasonableness of an exercise of jurisdiction to adjudicate by a nation-state; it does not concern itself with the allocation of jurisdiction among domestic courts, for example between national and state courts in a federal system."

The de minimis importance of individual states of the Union for purposes of international law and foreign relations has important implications for defining Due Process limitations on exercises of judicial jurisdiction in international cases. It suggests inquiring into a foreign defendant's contacts with the United States as a whole, rather than into contacts with a particular state. A Due Process test which looks to "national contacts" would be consistent with international law. As we have seen, international law is not concerned with allocations of jurisdiction among national sub-units. Instead, international law looks only to the propriety of a nation-state's assertion of jurisdiction over foreigners. Indeed, a national contacts test would be in closer keeping with the practice of other nations than the current Due Process analysis employed by United States courts.

Putting aside questions of international law, a Due Process standard for jurisdiction which looked to national contacts would serve important public policy goals. First, a national contacts test would permit United States courts to exercise jurisdiction to the fullest extent permitted under international law. This would relieve United States plaintiffs of the burden of litigating in foreign forums, without giving foreign governments basis for offense.

Second, a national contacts test would provide a better method for dealing with foreign defendants who have significant United States contacts spread evenly, but thinly, over a number of individual states. Jurisdiction in some United States forum would clearly be desirable in such cases, but current Due Process analysis would generally preclude any individual state from asserting jurisdiction. A test looking at least in part to national contacts would improve on current law by facilitating suits by United States plaintiffs against foreign defendants with significant, but widely dispersed contacts with this country.

Third, considering a foreign defendant's national contacts and his expectations about being required to litigate in United States courts would provide a reasonably well-tailored measure of inconvenience to foreign defendants. "[C]orporations * * * headquartered in foreign lands will usually be no more inconvenienced by a trip to one state [of the Union] than another." Similarly, there are relatively minor differences among the several states of the Union in procedural rules, including discovery, legal ethics, including treatment of legal fees, or in the quantum of damages likely to be recovered. In contrast, United States rules and practices in these areas often differ dramatically from rules and practices in other countries. Finally, the United States social, cultural, and political environment will be equally foreign to non-citizens, regardless of the particular state the parties choose as the forum.

For these reasons, requiring a foreign defendant to litigate in the United States, rather than in another country, has major consequences and can impose significant hardship. The risk of unfairly imposing these hardships on foreigners can be minimized by requiring closer contacts with the United States forum than would be necessary in an interstate context. Once it is clear that litigation will be required in some United States forum, however, it often will be relatively unimportant which United States forum is selected. Unlike the existing "state" contacts test, a test looking at least in part to national contacts, would more accurately reflect this proposition.

* * *

Why is Born skeptical of permitting the "greater burden" argument? Consider the *Asahi* facts and assume, for a moment, that the case had not been settled with the principal plaintiff. What would you say as Gary Zurcher's counsel if the court dismissed your complaint against Asahi for the death of his wife on the ground that it is too burdensome for Asahi to defend in the United States?

Both the Court in *Asahi* and Gary Born in his article suggest that foreign policy considerations should influence jurisdictional decisions in international cases. What kinds of considerations are these exactly? Again, how would you react as counsel to the plaintiff in *Asahi* if the court dismissed your case, explaining that unfortunately, entertaining the lawsuit would alienate the Japanese government and thus cause undue tensions in our trade relations with Japan?

Should it matter if the United States government had filed an amicus brief urging the court to dismiss the case for foreign policy reasons? If the Japanese government had filed an amicus brief expressing its anger about the lawsuit?

C. BETWEEN PRIVATE PARTIES AND STATES: REDRESS OPTIONS IN INTERNATIONAL TRIBUNALS

Litigation between private parties and states is frequent, of course, in domestic courts, although sovereign immunity can be an obstacle. Such litigation is much more limited, however, in international courts. This is mainly because there are few tribunals in which states have made themselves subject to jurisdiction in suits brought by private parties. The main area of such litigation is the field of human rights. As we saw in Chapter VI.4., there are now various human rights regimes with tribunals in which victims can pursue remedies against states. On the whole, it is fair to say that the global (UN) system gives little access to particularized and enforceable remedies, while regional systems often provide more powerful redress options (see Chapter IV.4.A.). Some of these regional regimes are widely known, such as the European and the Inter–American systems. Others, however, are usually overlooked because they operate in the developing world, such as in Africa. The following case demonstrates that these regional regimes may still provide redress against states—not only with regard to violations of the integrity of the person, but also in cases involving property rights.

Who is suing whom here and who is deciding the case? What is the gist of the plaintiffs' complaint? What sources does the court rely on in making its decision?

MIKE CAMPBELL (PVT) LTD., WILLIAM MICHAEL CAMPBELL, GIDEON STEPHANUS THERON, DOUGLAS STUART TAYLOR–FREEME, MERLE TAYLOR–FREEME, KONRAD VAN DER MERWE, LOUIS KAREL FICK, ANDREW PAUL ROSSLYN STIDOLPH, R.J VAN RENSBURG AND SONS (PVT) LTD., REINIER JANSE VAN RENSBURG (SENIOR), HARLEN BROTHERS (PVT) LTD., RAYMOND FINAUGHTY, BOUNCHCAP (PVT) LTD., DIRK VISAGIE, SABAKI (PVT) LTD., WILLIAM BRUCE ROGERS, J.B.W ARDEN & SONS (PVT) LTD., WILLIAM GILCHRIST NICOLSON, RICHARD THOMAS ETHEREDGE, JOHN NORMAN EASTWOOD, JOHANNES FREDERICK FICK, W.R SEAMAN (PVT) LTD, WAYNE REDVERS SEAMAN, PETRUS STEPHANUS MARTIN, ISMAEL CAMPHER PASQUES, CLAREMONT ESTATES (PVT) LTD, GRAMARA (PVT) LTD., COLIN BAILLIE CLOETE, BLAKLE STANLEY NICOLLE, NEWMARCH FARM (PVT) LTD., JOHN MCCLEARY BEATIE, HERMANUS GERHARDUS GROVE, FREDERICK WILLEM BIUTENDAG, L.M. FARMING (PVT) LTD., BART HARVEY MCCLELLAND WILDE, P. N. STIDOLPH (PVT) LTD., NEVILLE STIDOLPH, KATAMBORA ESTATES (PVT) LTD., ANDREW ROY FERREIRA, HERBST ESTATE (PVT) LTD., ANDREW MARC FERANGCON HERBST,

IZAK DANIEL NEL, JOHANNES HENDRIK OOSTHUIZEN,
MURRAY HUNTER POTT, GARY BRUCE HENSMAN,
CHARLES THOMAS SCHOULTZ, JACK WALTER HALL, BUSI
COFFEE ESTATE (PVT) LTD., ALGERNAN TRACY TAFF,
ELSJE HESTER HERBST, CRISTOFFEL GIDEON HERBST,
JACOBUS ADRIAAN SMIT, PALM RIVER RANCH (PVT) LTD.,
JOHN ROBERT CAUDREY BEVERLEY, ROBERT ANTHONY
MCKERSIE, S.C. SHAW (PVT) LTD., GRANT IAN LOCKE,
PETER FOSTER BOOTH, ARISTIDES PETER LANDOS, ANN
LOURENS, N & B HOLDINGS (PVT) LTD., DIGBY SEAN
NESBITT, KENNETH CHARLES ZIEHL, KENYON GARTH
BAINES ZIEHL, MLEME ESTATE (PVT) LTD., JEAN DANIEL
CECIL DE ROBBILARD, ANGLESEA FARM (PVT) LTD.,
GAMESTON ENTERPRISES (PVT) LTD., MALUNDI
RANCHING CO (PVT) LTD., GWELMID PROPERTY
HOLDINGS (PVT) LTD., TAMBA FARM (PVT) LTD.,
R.H.GREAVES (PVT) LTD., HEANY JUNCTION FARMS (PVT)
LTD., RUDOLF ISAAC DU PREEZ, WALTER BRYAN LAWRY,
DEREK ALFRED ROCHAT, CHRISTOPHER MELLISH
JARRETT, TENGWE ESTATE (PVT) LTD., FRANCE FARM
(PVT) LTD. V. THE REPUBLIC OF ZIMBABWE

Southern African Development Community (SADC) Tribunal, Windhoek, NamibiaSADC
(T) Case No. 2/2007 (Main Decision)

CORAM:

H.E. JUSTICE ARIRANGA GOVINDASAMY PILLAY

H.E. JUSTICE SSAAC JAMU MTAMBO, SC

H.E. JUSTICE DR. LUIS ANTONIO MONDLANE

H.E. DR. RIGOBERTO KAMBOVO

H.E. DR. ONKEMETSE B. TSHOSA

JUDGEMENT

Delivered by H. E. JUSTICE DR. LUIS ANTONIO MONDLANE:

I.   FACTUAL BACKGROUND

On 11 October, 2007, Mike Campbell (Pvt) Limited and William Michael
Campbell filed an application with the Southern African Development
Community Tribunal (the Tribunal) challenging the acquisition by the
Respondent of agricultural land known as Mount Carmell in the District
of Chegutu in the Republic of Zimbabwe. Simultaneously, they filed an
application in terms of Article 28 of the Protocol on Tribunal (the Protocol), as read with Rule 61 (2)–(5) of the Rules of Procedure of the SADC
Tribunal (the Rules), for an interim measure restraining the Respondent
from removing or allowing the removal of the Applicants from their land,
pending the determination of the matter.

On 13 December, 2007, the Tribunal granted the interim measure through its ruling which in the relevant part stated as follows:

> "[T]he Tribunal grants the application pending the determination of the main case and orders that the Republic of Zimbabwe shall take no steps, or permit no steps to be taken, directly or indirectly, whether by its agents or by orders, to evict from or interfere with the peaceful residence on, and beneficial use of, the farm known as Mount Carmell of Railway 19, measuring 1200.6484 hectares held under Deed of Transfer No. 10301/99, in the District of Chegutu in the Republic of Zimbabwe, by Mike Campbell (Pvt) Limited and William Michael Campbell, their employees and the families of such employees and of William Michael Campbell".

Subsequently, 77 other persons applied to intervene in the proceedings, pursuant to Article 30 of the Protocol, as read with Rule 70 of the Rules. [Those cases were all consolidated into a single case.]

* * *

On 20 June, 2008, the Applicants referred to the Tribunal the failure on the part of the Respondent to comply with the Tribunal's decision regarding the interim reliefs granted. The Tribunal, having established the failure, reported its finding to the Summit, pursuant to Article 32 (5) of the Protocol.

In the present case, the Applicants are, in essence, challenging the compulsory acquisition of their agricultural lands by the Respondent. The acquisitions were carried out under the land reform programme undertaken by the Respondent.

We note that the acquisition of land in Zimbabwe has had a long history. However, for the purposes of the present case, we need to confine ourselves only to acquisitions carried out under section 16B of the Constitution of Zimbabwe (Amendment No. 17, 2005), hereinafter referred to as Amendment 17.

* * *

Amendment 17 effectively vests the ownership of agricultural lands compulsorily acquired under Section 16B (2) (a) (i) and (ii) of Amendment 17 in the Respondent and ousts the jurisdiction of the courts to entertain any challenge concerning such acquisitions. It is on the basis of these facts that the present matter is before the Tribunal.

* * *

III. ISSUES FOR DETERMINATION

After due consideration of the facts of the case, in the light of the submissions of the parties, the Tribunal settles the matter for determination as follows:

- whether or not the Tribunal has jurisdiction to entertain the application;
- whether or not the Applicants have been denied access to the courts in Zimbabwe;
- whether or not the Applicants have been discriminated against on the basis of race, and
- whether or not compensation is payable for the lands compulsorily acquired from the Applicants by the Respondent.

IV. JURISDICTION

Before considering the question of jurisdiction, we note first that the Southern African Development Community is an international organization established under the Treaty of the Southern African Development Community, hereinafter referred to as "the Treaty." The Tribunal is one of the institutions of the organization which are established under Article 9 of the Treaty. The functions of the Tribunal are stated in Article 16. They are to ensure adherence to, and the proper interpretation of, the provisions of the Treaty and the subsidiary instruments made thereunder, and to adjudicate upon such disputes as may be referred to it.

The bases of jurisdiction are, among others, all disputes and applications referred to the Tribunal, in accordance with the Treaty and the Protocol, which relate to the interpretation and application of the Treaty—vide Article 14 (a) of the Protocol. The scope of the jurisdiction, as stated in Article 15 (1) of the Protocol, is to adjudicate upon *"disputes between States, and between natural and legal persons and States."* In terms of Article 15 (2), no person may bring an action against a State before, or without first, exhausting all available remedies or unless is unable to proceed under the domestic jurisdiction of such State. For the present case such are, indeed, the bases and scope of the jurisdiction of the Tribunal.

The first and the second Applicants first commenced proceedings in the Supreme Court of Zimbabwe, the final court in that country, challenging the acquisition of their agricultural lands by the Respondent.

The claim in that court, among other things, was that Amendment 17 obliterated their right to equal treatment before the law, to a fair hearing before an independent and impartial court of law or tribunal, and their right not to be discriminated against on the basis of race or place of origin, regarding ownership of land.

On October 11, 2007, before the Supreme Court of Zimbabwe had delivered its judgment, the first and second Applicants filed an application for an interim relief, as mentioned earlier in this judgement.

At the hearing of the application, the Respondent raised the issue as to whether the Tribunal has jurisdiction to hear the matter considering that the Supreme Court of Zimbabwe had not yet delivered the judgement and, therefore, that the Applicants had not *"exhausted all available remedies or were unable to proceed under the domestic jurisdiction,"* in terms of Article 15 (2) of the Protocol.

The concept of exhaustion of local remedies is not unique to the Protocol. It is also found in other regional international conventions. The European Convention on Human Rights provides in Article 26 as follows:

> *"The Commission* (of Human Rights) *may only deal with a matter after all domestic remedies have been exhausted, according to the generally recognized rules of international law * * * "*

Similarly, the African Charter on Human and Peoples' Rights states in Article 50 as follows:

> *"The Commission can only deal with a matter submitted to it after making sure that all local remedies, if they exist, have been exhausted, unless it is obvious to the Commission that the procedure of achieving the remedies would have been unduly prolonged".*

Thus, individuals are required to exhaust local remedies in the municipal law of the state before they can bring a case to the Commissions. * * *

However, where the municipal law does not offer any remedy or the remedy that is offered is ineffective, the individual is not required to exhaust the local remedies. Further, where, as the African Charter on Human and Peoples' Rights states, *" * * * it is obvious * * * that the procedure of achieving the remedies would have been unduly prolonged,"* the individual is not expected to exhaust local remedies. These are circumstances that make the requirement of exhaustion of local remedies meaningless, in which case the individual can lodge a case with the international tribunal.

In deciding this issue, the Tribunal stressed the fact that Amendment 17 has ousted the jurisdiction of the courts of law in Zimbabwe from any case related to acquisition of agricultural land and that, therefore, the first and second Applicants were unable to institute proceedings under the domestic jurisdiction. This position was subsequently confirmed by the decision of the Supreme Court given on February 22, 2008 in Mike Campbell (Pty) Ltd v Minister of National Security Responsible for Land, Land Reform and Resettlement (SC 49/07).

* * *

It is clear to us that the Tribunal has jurisdiction in respect of any dispute concerning human rights, democracy and the rule of law, which are the very issues raised in the present application. Moreover, the Respondent cannot rely on its national law, namely, Amendment 17 to avoid its legal obligations under the Treaty. As Professor Shaw Malcolm in his treatise entitled International Law at pages 104–105 aptly observed:

> *"It is no defence to a breach of an international obligation to argue that the state acted in such a manner because it was following the dictates of is own municipal laws. The reason for this inability to put forward internal rules as an excuse to evade international obligation are obvious. Any other situation would permit international law to be evaded by the simple method of domestic legislation".*

This principle is also contained in the Vienna Convention on the Law of Treaties, in which it is provided in Article 27 as follows:

> *"A party may not invoke provisions of its own internal law as justification for failure to carry out an international agreement".*

V. ACCESS TO JUSTICE

The next issue to be decided is whether or not the Applicants have been denied access to the courts and whether they have been deprived of a fair hearing by Amendment 17.

It is settled law that the concept of the rule of law embraces at least two fundamental rights, namely, the right of access to the courts and the right to a fair hearing before an individual is deprived of a right, interest or legitimate expectation. As indicated already, Article 4 (c) of the Treaty obliges Member States of SADC to respect principles of *"human rights, democracy and the rule of law"* and to undertake under Article 6 (1) of the Treaty *"to refrain from taking any measure likely to jeopardize the sustenance of its principles, the achievement of its objectives and the implementation of the provisions of the Treaty."* Consequently, Member States of SADC, including the Respondent, are under a legal obligation to respect, protect and promote those twin fundamental rights.

* * *

Moreover, the European Court of Human Rights, in *Golder v UK* (1975) 1 EHRR 524, at paragraph 34 of its judgement stated as follows:

> *"And in civil matters one can scarcely conceive of the rule of law without there being a possibility of having access to the courts".*

The same Court held, in *Philis v. Greece* (1991), at paragraph 59 of its judgement that:

> *"Article 6, paragraph 1 (art. 6–1) secured to everyone the right to have any claim relating to his civil rights and obligations brought before a*

court or tribunal; in this way the Article embodies the "right to a court," of which the right of access, that is the right to institute proceedings before courts in civil matters, constitutes one aspect. * * * "

The Inter–American Court of Human Rights, in its *Advisory Opinion OC–9/87 of 6 October, 1987, Judicial Guarantees in States of Emergency* (Articles 27 (2), 25 and 8 of the *American Convention on Human Rights*), construed Article 27 (2) of the Convention as requiring Member States to respect essential judicial guarantees, such as *habeas corpus* or any other effective remedy before judges or competent tribunals—vide paragraph 41. The Court also considered that Member States were under a duty to provide effective judicial remedies to those alleging human rights violations under Article 25 of the Convention. * * *

The Court also, at paragraph 35 of its judgement, pointed out that the rule of law, representative democracy and personal liberty are essential for the protection of human rights and that *"in a democratic society, the rights and freedoms inherent in the human person, the guarantees applicable to them and the rule of law form a triad. Each component thereof defines itself, complements and depends on the others for its meaning"*.

The right of access to the courts is also enshrined in international human rights treaties. For instance, the African Charter on Human and Peoples' Rights provides in Article 7 (1) (a) as follows:

"Every individual shall have the right to have his cause heard. This comprises:

(a) The right to an appeal to competent national organs against acts violating his fundamental rights * * * "

The African Commission on Human and Peoples' Rights in its decision in *Constitutional Rights Project, Civil Liberties Organisation and Media Rights Agenda v. Nigeria*, Comm.No. 140/94, 141/94 145/95 (1999), held at paragraph 29 of its judgement that the ouster clauses introduced by the Nigerian military government which prevented Nigerian courts from hearing cases initiated by publishers against the search of their premises and the suppression of their newspapers *"render local remedies non-existent, ineffective or illegal. They create a legal situation in which the judiciary can provide no check on the executive branch of the government"*.

The African Commission on Human and Peoples' Right also in its decision in *Zimbabwe Human Rights NGO Forum / Zimbabwe,* Comm.No.245 (2002), found that the complainant had been denied access to judicial remedies since the clemency order introduced to pardon *"every person liable for any politically motivated crime"* had prevented in effect the complainant from bringing criminal action against the perpetrators of such crimes. * * *

It is useful, finally, to refer to the decision of the *Constitutional Court of South Africa in Zondi v MEC for Traditional and Local Government Affairs and Others* 2005 (3) SA 589 (CC). The Court found that certain provisions of the Pound Ordinance of 1947 of KwaZulu–Natal which allowed landowners to bypass the courts and recover damages against the owners of trespassing animals were inconsistent with section 34 of the Constitution which guarantees the right of access to courts.

* * *

We are, therefore, satisfied that the Applicants have established that they have been deprived of their agricultural lands without having had the right of access to the courts and the right to a fair hearing, which are essential elements of the rule of law, and we consequently hold that the Respondent has acted in breach of Article 4 (c) of the Treaty.

VI. RACIAL DISCRIMINATION

The other issue raised by the Applicants is that of racial discrimination. They contended that the land reform programme is based on racial discrimination in that it targets white Zimbabwean farmers only. The Applicants further argue that Amendment 17 was intended to facilitate or implement the land reform policy of the Government of Zimbabwe based on racial discrimination. * * *

The Tribunal has to determine whether or not Amendment 17 discriminates against the Applicants and as such violates the obligation that the Respondent has undertaken under the Treaty to prohibit discrimination.

It should first be noted that discrimination of whatever nature is outlawed or prohibited in international law. There are several international instruments and treaties which prohibit discrimination based on race, the most important one being the United Nations Charter, which provides in Article 1 (3) that one of its purposes is:

> *"To achieve international corporation in solving international problems of an economic, social, cultural or humanitarian character, and in promoting and encouraging respect for human rights and fundamental freedoms for all without distinction as to **race**, sex, language or religion". (emphasis supplied).*

There is also the Universal Declaration of Human Rights which provides in Article 2 as follows:

> *"Everyone is entitled to all the rights and freedoms set forth in this Declaration without distinction of any kind, such as **race**, colour, sex, language, religion, political or other opinion, national or social origin, property, birth or other status". (emphasis supplied).*

Moreover, Article 2 (1) of the International Covenant on Civil and Political Rights and Article 2 (2) of the International Covenant on Economic, Social and Cultural Rights prohibit racial discrimination, respectively, as follows:

> "*Each State party to the present Covenant undertakes to respect and ensure to all individuals within its territory without distinction of any kind such as **race**, colour, sex, language, religion, political or other opinion, national or social origin, property, birth or other status*".

> "*The States parties to the present Covenant undertake to guarantee that the rights enunciated in the present Covenant will be exercised without discrimination of any kind as to **race**, colour, sex, language, religious, political or other opinion, national or social origin, property, birth or other status*". (*emphasis supplied*).

The above provisions are similar to Article 2 of the African Charter on Human and Peoples' Rights (African Charter) and Article 14 of the European Convention on Human Rights.

Discrimination on the basis of race is also outlawed by the Convention On the Elimination of All Forms of Racial Discrimination (the Convention). It is worth noting that the Respondent has acceded to both Covenants, the African Charter and the Convention and, by doing so, is under an obligation to respect, protect and promote the principle of non-discrimination and must, therefore, prohibit and outlaw any discrimination based on the ground of race in its laws, policies and practices.

Apart from all the international human rights instruments and treaties, the Treaty also prohibits discrimination. Article 6 (2) states as follows:

> "*SADC and Member States shall not discriminate against any person on grounds of gender, religion, political views, **race**, ethnic origin, culture, ill health, disability or such other ground as may be determined by the Summit*". (*emphasis supplied*).

This Article, therefore, enjoins SADC and Member States, including the Respondent, not to discriminate against any person on the stated grounds, one of which is race.

* * *

The question that arises is whether Amendment 17 subjects the Applicants to any racial discrimination, as defined above. It is clear that the Amendment affected all agricultural lands or farms occupied and owned by the Applicants and all the Applicants are white farmers. Can it then be said that, because all the farms affected by the Amendment belong to white farmers, the Amendment and the land reform programme are racially discriminatory?

We note here that there is no explicit mention of race, ethnicity or people of a particular origin in Amendment 17 as to make it racially discriminatory. If any such reference were made, that would make the provision expressly discriminatory against a particular race or ethnic group. The effect of such reference would be that the Respondent would be in breach of its obligations under the Article 6 (2) of the Treaty.

The question is whether, in the absence of the explicit mention of the word "race" in Amendment 17, that would be the end of the matter. It should be recalled that the Applicants argued that, even if Amendment could be held not to be racially discriminatory in itself, its effects make it discriminatory because the targeted agricultural lands are all owned by white farmers and that the purpose of Amendment 17 was to make it apply to white farmers only, regardless of any other factors such as the proper use of their lands, their citizenship, their length of residence in Zimbabwe or any other factor other than the colour of their skin.

Since the effects of the implementation of Amendment 17 will be felt by the Zimbabwean white farmers only, we consider it, although Amendment 17 does not explicitly refer to white farmers, as we have indicated above, its implementation affects white farmers only and consequently constitutes indirect discrimination or *de facto* or substantive inequality.

In examining the effects of Amendment 17 on the applicants, it is clear to us that those effects have had an unjustifiable and disproportionate impact upon a group of individuals distinguished by race such as the Applicants.

We consider that the differentiation of treatment meted out to the Applicants also constitutes discrimination as the criteria for such differentiation are not reasonable and objective but arbitrary and are based primarily on considerations of race. The aim of the Respondent in adopting and implementing a land reform programme might be legitimate if and when all lands under the programme were indeed distributed to poor, landless and other disadvantaged and marginalized individuals or groups.

We, therefore, hold that, implementing Amendment 17, the Respondent has discriminated against the Applicants on the basis of race and thereby violated its obligation under Article 6 (2) of the Treaty.

We wish to observe here that if: (a) the criteria adopted by the Respondent in relation to the land reform programme had not been arbitrary but reasonable and objective; (b) fair compensation was paid in respect of the expropriated lands, and (c) the lands expropriated were indeed distributed to poor, landless and other disadvantaged and marginalized individuals or groups, rendering the purpose of the programme legitimate, the differential treatment afforded to the Applicants would not constitute racial discrimination.

We can do no better than quote in this regard what the Supreme Court of Zimbabwe stated in *Commercial Farmers Union v Minister of Lands* 2001 (2) SA 925 (ZSC) at paragraph 9 where it dealt with the history of land injustice in Zimbabwe and the need for a land reform programme under the rule of law:

> *"We are not entirely convinced that the expropriation of white farmers, if it is done lawfully and fair compensation is paid, can be said to be discriminatory. But there can be no doubt that it is unfair discrimination * * * to award the spoils of expropriation primarily to ruling party adherents".*

* * *

VII. COMPENSATION

We hold, therefore, that fair compensation is due and payable to the Applicants by the Respondent [Zimbabwe] in respect of their expropriated lands.

VIII. CONCLUSIONS

For the reasons given, the Tribunal holds and declares that:

(a) by unanimity, the Tribunal has jurisdiction to entertain the application;

(b) by unanimity, the Applicants have been denied access to the courts in Zimbabwe;

(c) by a majority of four to one, the Applicants have been discriminated against on the ground of race, and

(d) by unanimity, fair compensation is payable to the Applicants for their lands compulsorily acquired by the Respondent.

The Tribunal further holds and declares that:

(1) by unanimity, the Respondent is in breach of its obligations under Article 4 (c) and, by a majority of four to one, the Respondent is in breach of its obligations under Article 6 (2) of the Treaty;

(2) by unanimity, Amendment 17 is in breach of Article 4 (c) and, by a majority of four to one, Amendment 17 is in breach of Article 6 (2) of the Treaty;

(3) by unanimity, the Respondent is directed to take all necessary measures, through its agents, to protect the possession, occupation and ownership of the lands of the Applicants, except for Christopher Mellish Jarret, Tengwe Estates (Pvt) Ltd. and France Farm (Pvt) Ltd. that have already been evicted from their lands, and to take all appropriate measures to ensure that no action is taken, pursuant to Amendment 17, directly or indirectly, whether by its agents or by

others, to evict from, or interfere with, the peaceful residence on, and of those farms by, the Applicants, and

(4) by unanimity, the Respondent is directed to pay fair compensation, on or before 30 June 2009, to the three Applicants, namely, Christopher Mellish Jarret, Tengwe Estates (Pvt) Ltd. and France Farm (Pvt) Ltd.

By a majority of four to one, the Tribunal makes no order as to costs in the circumstances.

[The dissenting opinion by Justice Dr Onkemetse B. Tshosa is omitted.]

As you see in the opinion, this Southern African regional tribunal relies on a wide variety of sources, including decisions of national and regional courts from all over the world. What does this tell you about the role of judicial decisions in the formation of international law?

What do the plaintiffs gain by their victory in court?

WILLIAM MICHAEL CAMPBELL AND RICHARD THOMAS ETHEREDGE v. THE REPUBLIC OF ZIMBABWE

Southern African Development Community Tribunal
Case No. SADC (T): 03/2009 (SADC, June 5, 2009)

Ruling

Delivered by the President of the Tribunal, H.E. JUSTICE A.G. PILLAY:

This is an urgent application filed by the applicants on 7 May 2009 seeking, in substance, a declaration to the effect that the respondent is in breach, and contempt, of the decision of the Tribunal of the 28th November 2008 in the matter of *Mike Campbell (Pvt) Ltd and 78 Others v The Republic of Zimbabwe.*

The decision of the Tribunal was to the effect, in substance, that "the Respondent is directed to take all necessary measures, through its agents, to protect the possession, occupation and ownership of the land of the applicants * * * and to take all appropriate measures to ensure that no action is taken * * * directly or indirectly whether by its agents or others, to evict from, or interfere with, the peaceful residence on, and of these farms, by the applicants."

We note that the respondent has not taken part in the proceedings since, as learned Counsel for the respondent has put it, he lacks instructions from the respondent.

We hold that the applicants have adduced enough material to show that the existence of a failure on the part of the respondent and its agents to comply with the decision of the Tribunal has been established. In this regard, we need only, inter alia, to refer to—

(1) the Deputy Attorney–General's letter addressed to Messrs Gollop and Blank, Legal Practitioners dated 18 December 2008 which says: " * * * that the policy position taken by the Government to the judgment handed down by the SADC Tribunal on the 28th November, 2008 is that all prosecutions of defaulting farmers under the provisions of the Gazetted Lands (Consequential Provisions) Act should now be resumed";

(2) the speech delivered in Bulawayo, Zimbabwe by the Deputy Chief Justice on 12 January 2009 at the opening of the 2009 legal year in the course of which he stated, among other things, that the Tribunal lacked jurisdiction to hear and determine the *Campbell* case;

(3) President Robert Mugabe in the course of his birthday celebrations qualified the Tribunal's decision as "nonsense" and "of no consequence".

We note further that all those statements were followed by invasion of the lands of the applicants and their intimidation and prosecution.

Consequently, pursuant to Article 32(5) of the Protocol on Tribunal, the Tribunal will report its finding to the Summit for the latter to take appropriate action.

We order costs in favour of the applicants, pursuant to Rule 78(2) of the Rules of Procedure of the SADC Tribunal. The costs are to be agreed by the parties. In case of disagreement, the Registrar shall determine the costs to be awarded.

Delivered in open court this 05th day of June 2009, at Windhoek in the Republic of Namibia.

Mike Campbell, the lead plaintiff in the case, and members of his family were allegedly abducted from their home in mid-2008 (after his case had been filed but before a judgment had been issued). They were taken to a remote location where they were beaten and forced to sign a document promising to dismiss the SADC Tribunal case. Nonetheless, the case continued in the Tribunal with Campbell and his co-plaintiffs emerging victorious as you see above. However, the Government of Zimbabwe never paid the plaintiffs as ordered in the judgment. Campbell died at the age of 78 in April 2011. The story of Campbell and his use of the SADC Tribunal to vindicate his property rights formed the central narrative of the award-winning documentary *Mugabe and the White African* (2009).

2. INTERNATIONAL ARBITRATION: NOT JUST FOR STATES

A dispute resolution method available both to states and private parties is international arbitration. Today both states and private parties use it more frequently than litigation to resolve international cases. As a result, the practical importance of international arbitration is simply enormous. It occurs in three basic configurations: between states, between private parties, and between states and private parties. We will address these three forms in the subchapters below. First, however, we must turn to the general framework of international arbitration, i.e., the UN (New York) Convention of 1958.

Introduction: The General Framework of The New York Convention

While there is no worldwide treaty regime governing international litigation (there are many bilateral or regional regimes, but the United States is not a party to any of them), there *is* a global convention on international arbitration: the United Nations Convention on the Recognition and Enforcement of Foreign Arbitral Awards of 1958. Since it was concluded in New York, it is also variously known as the "New York Convention" or the "UN Convention" (of course, since there are scores of "UN Conventions," only the context can tell which one is meant). It is a widely adopted treaty, binding on more than 140 countries, including the United States and virtually all its important trading partners. The United States executed it by making it Chapter 2 of the United States Arbitration Act (9 U.S.C. §§ 201–208).

The United States has also ratified and executed the Inter–American Convention on International Commercial Arbitration (found in Chapter 3 of the U.S. Arbitration Act, 9 U.S.C. §§ 301–307). In addition, a number of states have adopted the (European) Geneva Convention on International Commercial Arbitration, which is not binding on the United States. These regional regimes, however, do not play nearly the same role in practice as the New York (UN) Convention.

The New York Convention is mercifully short—it consists of merely sixteen articles and all the important substance is contained in the first six. Note exactly what it regulates: it addresses the validity and enforcement of arbitration *clauses* (Article II) and the recognition and enforcement of arbitration *awards* (Articles III–VI). What exactly do its provisions say? In particular, how do they compare to the basic rules governing the recognition of foreign judgments (Chapter IV.2.)?

UNITED NATIONS CONVENTION ON THE RECOGNITION AND ENFORCEMENT OF FOREIGN ARBITRAL AWARDS (NEW YORK CONVENTION)

(Adopted 1958; in force 1959)

Article I

1. This Convention shall apply to the recognition and enforcement of arbitral awards made in the territory of a State other than the State where the recognition and enforcement of such awards are sought, and arising out of differences between persons, whether physical or legal. It shall also apply to arbitral awards not considered as domestic awards in the State where their recognition and enforcement are sought.

2. The term "arbitral awards" shall include not only awards made by arbitrators appointed for each case but also those made by permanent arbitral bodies to which the parties have submitted.

3. When signing, ratifying or acceding to this Convention, or notifying extension under article X hereof, any State may on the basis of reciprocity declare that it will apply the Convention to the recognition and enforcement of awards made only in the territory of another Contracting State. It may also declare that it will apply the Convention only to differences arising out of legal relationships, whether contractual or not, which are considered as commercial under the national law of the State making such declaration.

Article II

1. Each Contracting State shall recognize an agreement in writing under which the parties undertake to submit to arbitration all or any differences which have arisen or which may arise between them in respect of a defined legal relationship, whether contractual or not, concerning a subject matter capable of settlement by arbitration.

2. The term "agreement in writing" shall include an arbitral clause in a contract or an arbitration agreement, signed by the parties or contained in an exchange of letters or telegrams.

3. The court of a Contracting State, when seized of an action in a matter in respect of which the parties have made an agreement within the meaning of this article, shall, at the request of one of the parties, refer the parties to arbitration, unless it finds that the said agreement is null and void, inoperative or incapable of being performed.

Article III

Each Contracting State shall recognize arbitral awards as binding and enforce them in accordance with the rules of procedure of the territory where the award is relied upon, under the conditions laid down in the following articles. There shall not be imposed substantially more onerous conditions or higher fees or charges on the recognition or enforcement of arbitral awards to which this Convention applies than are imposed on the recognition or enforcement of domestic arbitral awards.

Article IV

1. To obtain the recognition and enforcement mentioned in the preceding article, the party applying for recognition and enforcement shall, at the time of the application, supply:

   (a) The duly authenticated original award or a duly certified copy thereof;

   (b) The original agreement referred to in article II or a duly certified copy thereof.

2. If the said award or agreement is not made in an official language of the country in which the award is relied upon, the party applying for recognition and enforcement of the award shall produce a translation of these documents into such language. The translation shall be certified by an official or sworn translator or by a diplomatic or consular agent.

Article V

1. Recognition and enforcement of the award may be refused, at the request of the party against whom it is invoked, only if that party furnishes to the competent authority where the recognition and enforcement is sought, proof that:

   (a) The parties to the agreement referred to in article II were, under the law applicable to them, under some incapacity, or the said agreement is not valid under the law to which the parties have subjected it or, failing any indication thereon, under the law of the country where the award was made; or

   (b) The party against whom the award is invoked was not given proper notice of the appointment of the arbitrator or of the arbitration proceedings or was otherwise unable to present his case; or

   (c) The award deals with a difference not contemplated by or not falling within the terms of the submission to arbitration, or it contains decisions on matters beyond the scope of the submission to arbitration, provided that, if the decisions on matters submitted to arbitration can be separated from those not so submitted, that part of the award which contains decisions on matters submitted to arbitration may be recognized and enforced; or

   (d) The composition of the arbitral authority or the arbitral procedure was not in accordance with the agreement of the parties, or, failing such agreement, was not in accordance with the law of the country where the arbitration took place; or

(e) The award has not yet become binding on the parties, or has been set aside or suspended by a competent authority of the country in which, or under the law of which, that award was made.

2. Recognition and enforcement of an arbitral award may also be refused if the competent authority in the country where recognition and enforcement is sought finds that:

(a) The subject matter of the difference is not capable of settlement by arbitration under the law of that country; or

(b) The recognition or enforcement of the award would be contrary to the public policy of that country.

Article VI

If an application for the setting aside or suspension of the award has been made to a competent authority referred to in article V (1) (e), the authority before which the award is sought to be relied upon may, if it considers it proper, adjourn the decision on the enforcement of the award and may also, on the application of the party claiming enforcement of the award, order the other party to give suitable security.

* * *

By ordering the member states (and their courts) to enforce arbitration clauses, the New York Convention regulates the exit from the "normal" judicial process: if a party still files suit despite a valid arbitration clause, the New York Convention mandates that a court not proceed in the matter, but rather refer the parties to arbitration. The Convention also addresses what may be called the re-entry into the judicial system: courts must in principle enforce a valid arbitration award.

The Convention does not, however, say anything about the actual arbitration procedure. That is left for the parties to determine and for the arbitrators to run. It is sometimes also regulated by the national laws of the place of arbitration. These laws now often follow the *UNCITRAL Model Law on International Commercial Arbitration* of 1985 or its newer version of 2002. There are also the *UNICTRAL Arbitration Rules* of 1976 which are widely adopted by parties as a quasi-procedural code.

A. BETWEEN STATES: AN ALTERNATIVE TO THE INTERNATIONAL COURT OF JUSTICE

As we saw in Chapter IV, states arbitrated many of their disputes long before there was an option to litigate in a permanent international court. Even today, despite the establishment of the ICJ and other international courts and tribunals, states often resort to arbitration rather than litigation for various reasons—because they may not want to submit a dispute to an international court since they do not trust the court, because they want to pick their own arbitrators, because they want to by-pass often lengthy and ritualistic procedures, etc. Today, states sometimes still arbitrate under an ad hoc regime created, as in the *Alabama Arbitration*, just to resolve a current dispute. That said, states have increasingly turned to the preexisting framework of the Permanent Court of Arbitration in The Hague (PCA) (see Chapter IV.1.C.).

The PCA was founded in 1899. After being fairly active in the first third of the 20th century, it lay essentially dormant for the rest of it. Since the turn of the 21st century, however, it has experienced an impressive revival. In the last decade, it has assisted in resolving about 20 cases, and currently more than a dozen disputes are pending under its auspices. Today, over 100 states are members of the organization.

The enforcement of resulting awards is largely left to the political process, however, since states typically enjoy immunity in each other's courts.

B. BETWEEN PRIVATE PARTIES: WHAT GOES TO ARBITRATION?

Private parties have increasingly resorted to arbitration over the last few decades. Today, the majority of international commercial disputes, especially among businesses, are resolved not in courts but before arbitral tribunals. The basis is normally a clause in a contract in which the parties agree to submit disputes that arise between them to arbitration. Courts (especially in the United States) enforce such clauses almost routinely and with few exceptions. If a party still brings a lawsuit, the court will normally dismiss it and, upon application by the other party, compel arbitration. In short, by agreeing to arbitrate, a party gives up its right to litigate.

Like states, private parties sometimes arbitrate under ad hoc regimes. An advantage is that the parties save the fee they would have to pay to a preestablished arbitral institution for its services; of course, the parties also forego the benefits of the assistance of such an institution in selecting arbitrators and in administering the proceedings. Normally, however, international commercial arbitration proceeds in a prefabricated manner under the auspices of a private organization providing arbitral services for a fee. Probably the most important of these organizations are the International Chamber of Commerce (ICC) in Paris, the London Court of Arbitration (LCA), and the international center of the American Arbitration Association (AAA) in New York. There are also many trade-specific arbitration regimes. These organizations provide their own personnel and rule frameworks. Arbitral institutions furnish the parties with a list of arbitrators (which is usually not binding). The parties then either jointly pick one arbitrator or each side picks one, whereupon the two select a third as the chairman of the tribunal.

In the business world, arbitration is popular because it has considerable advantages over litigation. It is forum neutral (nobody gets a home game) and more specialized. It can be held anywhere and anytime. One can choose arbitrators who are experts in the commercial sector involved, have greater business sense than most judges, and represent all countries (or legal cultures) involved. Arbitration avoids jury trials and is procedurally more flexible; in particular, the parties can design a procedure that focuses on their main concerns, establish their own disclosure rules, and agree about the means of evidence. Arbitration is perceived as less hostile than litigation and thus less disruptive of business relationships, in part because its proceedings and results can be kept confidential. It also used to be cheaper and faster than litigation, although that is no longer necessarily true as American-style lawyering has led to more discovery which tends to be expensive. Foreign arbitral awards are often more easily enforced than foreign judgments, at least as long as the countries involved are members of the UN (New York) Convention.

Arbitration, however, also entails considerable risks. Due process rights are weaker than in most courts. Arbitrators may be more partisan than judges, and their services cost a lot of money. Discovery is usually more limited, and it is more difficult to compel the attendance of unwilling witnesses. Interim measures are often harder to obtain and more difficult to enforce. Perhaps most importantly, there is no appeal; while there are ways to set aside an arbitral award, the grounds for doing so are very limited and attempts are rarely successful.

In legal practice, international commercial arbitration has become a specialty in its own right. In law teaching, it is established as a separate field as well, with its own courses, casebooks, and scholarly literature. Its relationship with international litigation is complex because of the many opportunities for courts and arbitral tribunals to interact.

Under the New York Convention, a threshold issue is whether the dispute can be arbitrated at all. In both Article II and Article V the subject matter must be "capable of settlement by arbitration." In other words, there are certain types of disputes which may not be settled by arbitration, e.g., for consumer protection or other public policy reasons. Countries in the world differ widely about exactly what can be arbitrated. The United States is perhaps the most liberal in that regard.

The development of the law of arbitrability in the United States is an interesting story in its own right. Originally, many claims involving a strong public interest element, such as claims arising under the antitrust and securities laws, were considered non-arbitrable. The Supreme Court then held that these claims could in fact be arbitrated *in international cases* (though not in purely domestic ones), mainly because of the need for flexibility in international dispute resolution. Later, the Court extended this liberal construction to purely domestic cases as well. In this manner, international cases took the lead, so to speak, and domestic cases followed.

The case below is the perhaps most widely noted step in that process. What are the major arguments against subjecting antitrust claims to arbitration? Why does the majority nonetheless allow them to be arbitrated?

MITSUBISHI MOTORS CORPORATION V. SOLER CHRYSLER–PLYMOUTH, INC.

United States Supreme Court
473 U.S. 614 (1985)

JUSTICE BLACKMUN:

The principal question presented by these cases is the arbitrability, pursuant to the Federal Arbitration Act and the [New York] Convention on the Recognition and Enforcement of Foreign Arbitral Awards (Convention), of claims arising under the Sherman Act and encompassed within a valid arbitration clause in an agreement embodying an international commercial transaction.

I

Petitioner-cross-respondent Mitsubishi Motors Corporation (Mitsubishi) is a Japanese corporation which manufactures automobiles and has its principal place of business in Tokyo, Japan. Mitsubishi is the product of a joint venture between, on the one hand, Chrysler International, S.A. (CISA), a Swiss corporation registered in Geneva and wholly owned by Chrysler Corporation, and, on the other, Mitsubishi Heavy Industries, Inc., a Japanese corporation. The aim of the joint venture was the distribution through Chrysler dealers outside the continental United States of vehicles manufactured by Mitsubishi and bearing Chrysler and Mitsubishi trademarks. Respondent-cross-petitioner Soler Chrysler–Plymouth, Inc. (Soler), is a Puerto Rico corporation with its principal place of business in Pueblo Viejo, Guaynabo, Puerto Rico.

On October 31, 1979, Soler entered into a Distributor Agreement with CISA which provided for the sale by Soler of Mitsubishi-manufactured vehicles within a designated area, including metropolitan San Juan. On the same date, CISA, Soler, and Mitsubishi entered into a Sales Procedure Agreement (Sales Agreement) which, referring to the Distributor Agreement, provided for the direct sale of Mitsubishi products to Soler and governed the terms and conditions of such sales. Paragraph VI of the Sales Agreement, labeled "Arbitration of Certain Matters," provides:

> "All disputes, controversies or differences which may arise between [Mitsubishi] and [Soler] out of or in relation to Articles I–B through V of this Agreement or for the breach thereof, shall be finally settled by arbitration in Japan in accordance with the rules and regulations of the Japan Commercial Arbitration Association."

Initially, Soler did a brisk business in Mitsubishi-manufactured vehicles. As a result of its strong performance, its minimum sales volume, specified by Mitsubishi and CISA, and agreed to by Soler, for the 1981 model year was substantially increased. In early 1981, however, the new-car market slackened. Soler ran into serious difficulties in meeting the expected sales volume, and by the spring of 1981 it felt itself compelled to request that Mitsubishi delay or cancel shipment of several orders. About the same time, Soler attempted to arrange for the transshipment of a quantity of its vehicles for sale in the continental United States and Latin America. Mitsubishi and CISA, however, refused permission for any such diversion, citing a variety of reasons, and no vehicles were transshipped. Attempts to work out these difficulties failed. Mitsubishi eventually withheld shipment of 966 vehicles, apparently representing orders placed for May, June, and July 1981 production, responsibility for which Soler disclaimed in February 1982.

The following month, Mitsubishi brought an action against Soler in the United States District Court for the District of Puerto Rico under the Federal Arbitration Act and the Convention. Mitsubishi sought an order * * * to compel arbitration in accord with ¶ VI of the Sales Agreement. Shortly after filing the complaint, Mitsubishi filed a request for arbitration before the Japan Commercial Arbitration Association.

Soler denied the allegations and counterclaimed against both Mitsubishi and CISA. It alleged numerous breaches by Mitsubishi of the Sales Agreement * * * and asserted causes of action under the Sherman Act. In the counterclaim premised on the Sherman Act, Soler alleged that Mitsubishi and CISA had conspired to divide markets in restraint of trade. To effectuate the plan, according to Soler, Mitsubishi had refused to permit Soler to resell to buyers in North, Central, or South America vehicles it had obligated itself to purchase from Mitsubishi; had refused to ship ordered vehicles or the parts, such as heaters and defoggers, that would be necessary to permit Soler to make its vehicles suitable for resale outside Puerto Rico; and had coercively attempted to replace Soler and its other Puerto Rico distributors with a wholly owned subsidiary which would serve as the exclusive Mitsubishi distributor in Puerto Rico.

[The District Court ordered Mitsubishi and Soler to arbitrate the issues raised in the complaint and the antitrust counterclaims. The United

States Court of Appeals for the First Circuit affirmed as to the issues in the complaint but reversed as to the antitrust counterclaims, holding them nonarbitrable.]

II

[The Court addressed and rejected Soler's contention that the arbitration clause could not be read to encompass the statutory antitrust claims stated in its answer to the complaint.]

III

We now turn to consider whether Soler's antitrust claims are nonarbitrable even though it has agreed to arbitrate them. In holding that they are not, the Court of Appeals followed the decision of the Second Circuit in *American Safety Equipment Corp. v. J.P. Maguire & Co.* Notwithstanding the absence of any explicit support for such an exception in either the Sherman Act or the Federal Arbitration Act, the Second Circuit there reasoned that "the pervasive public interest in enforcement of the antitrust laws, and the nature of the claims that arise in such cases, combine to make * * * antitrust claims * * * inappropriate for arbitration." We find it unnecessary to assess the legitimacy of the *American Safety* doctrine as applied to agreements to arbitrate arising from domestic transactions. As in *Scherk v. Alberto-Culver Co.*, 417 U.S. 506 (1974), we conclude that concerns of international comity, respect for the capacities of foreign and transnational tribunals, and sensitivity to the need of the international commercial system for predictability in the resolution of disputes require that we enforce the parties' agreement, even assuming that a contrary result would be forthcoming in a domestic context.

* * *

* * * [A]t least since this Nation's accession in 1970 to the [New York] Convention and the implementation of the Convention in the same year by amendment of the Federal Arbitration Act, that federal policy applies with special force in the field of international commerce. Thus, we must weigh the concerns of *American Safety* against a strong belief in the efficacy of arbitral procedures for the resolution of international commercial disputes and an equal commitment to the enforcement of freely negotiated choice-of-forum clauses.

At the outset, we confess to some skepticism of certain aspects of the *American Safety* doctrine. As distilled by the First Circuit, the doctrine comprises four ingredients. First, private parties play a pivotal role in aiding governmental enforcement of the antitrust laws by means of the private action for treble damages. Second, "the strong possibility that contracts which generate antitrust disputes may be contracts of adhesion militates against automatic forum determination by contract." Third, antitrust issues, prone to complication, require sophisticated legal and economic analysis, and thus are "ill-adapted to strengths of the arbitral process, i.e., expedition, minimal requirements of written rationale, simplicity, resort to basic concepts of common sense and simple equity." Finally, just as "issues of war and peace are too important to be vested in the generals, * * * decisions as to antitrust regulation of business are too important to be lodged in arbitrators chosen from the business community—particularly those from a foreign community that has had no experience with or exposure to our law and values."

Initially, we find the second concern unjustified. The mere appearance of an antitrust dispute does not alone warrant invalidation of the selected forum on the undemonstrated assumption that the arbitration clause is tainted. A party resisting arbitration of course may attack directly the validity of the agreement to arbitrate. Moreover, the party may attempt to make a showing that would warrant setting aside the forum-selection clause—that the agreement was "[a]ffected by fraud, undue influence, or overweening bargaining power;" that "enforcement would be unreasonable and unjust;" or that proceedings "in the contractual forum will be so gravely difficult and inconvenient that [the resisting party] will for all practical purposes be deprived of his day in court." *The Bremen*, 407 U.S., at 12, 15, 18. But absent such a showing—and none was attempted here—there is no basis for assuming the forum inadequate or its selection unfair.

Next, potential complexity should not suffice to ward off arbitration. We might well have some doubt that even the courts following *American Safety* subscribe fully to the view that antitrust matters are inherently insusceptible to resolution by arbitration, as these same courts have agreed that an undertaking to arbitrate antitrust claims entered into *after* the dispute arises is acceptable. And the vertical restraints which most frequently give birth to antitrust claims covered by an arbitration agreement will not often occasion the monstrous proceedings that have given antitrust litigation an image of intractability. In any event, adaptability and access to expertise are hallmarks of arbitration. The anticipated subject matter of the dispute may be taken into account when the arbitrators are appointed, and arbitral rules typically provide for the participation of experts either employed by the parties or appointed by the tribunal. Moreover, it is often a judgment that streamlined proceedings and expeditious results will best serve their needs that causes parties to agree to arbitrate their disputes; it is typically a desire to keep the effort and expense required to resolve a dispute within manageable bounds that prompts them mutually to forgo access to judicial remedies. In sum, the factor of potential complexity alone does not persuade us that an arbitral tribunal could not properly handle an antitrust matter.

For similar reasons, we also reject the proposition that an arbitration panel will pose too great a danger of innate hostility to the constraints on business conduct that antitrust law imposes. International arbitrators frequently are drawn from the legal as well as the business community; where the dispute has an important legal component, the parties and the arbitral body with whose assistance they have agreed to settle their dispute can be expected to select arbitrators accordingly.[18] We decline to indulge the presumption that the parties and arbitral body conducting a proceeding will be unable or unwilling to retain competent, conscientious, and impartial arbitrators.

We are left, then, with the core of the *American Safety* doctrine—the fundamental importance to American democratic capitalism of the regime of the antitrust laws. Without doubt, the private cause of action plays a central role in enforcing this regime. * * * The treble-damages provision wielded by the private litigant is a chief tool in the antitrust enforcement scheme, posing a crucial deterrent to potential violators.

* * *

There is no reason to assume at the outset of the dispute that international arbitration will not provide an adequate mechanism. To be sure, the international arbitral tribunal owes no prior allegiance to the legal norms of particular states; hence, it has no direct obligation to vindicate their statutory dictates. The tribunal, however, is bound to effectuate the intentions of the parties. Where the parties have agreed that the arbitral body is to decide a defined set of claims which includes, as in these cases, those arising from the application of American antitrust law, the tribunal therefore should be bound to decide that dispute in accord with the national law giving rise to the claim.[19] And so long as the prospective liti-

---

[18] We are advised by Mitsubishi and *amicus* International Chamber of Commerce, without contradiction by Soler, that the arbitration panel selected to hear the parties' claims here is composed of three Japanese lawyers, one a former law school dean, another a former judge, and the third a practicing attorney with American legal training who has written on Japanese antitrust law. * * *

[19] In addition to the clause providing for arbitration before the Japan Commercial Arbitration Association, the Sales Agreement includes a choice-of-law clause which reads: "This Agreement is made in, and will be governed by and construed in all respects according to the laws of the Swiss Confederation as if entirely performed therein." The United States raises the possibility that the arbitral panel will read this provision not simply to govern interpretation of the contract terms, but wholly to displace American law even where it otherwise would apply. The International Chamber of Commerce opines that it is "[c]onceivabl[e], although we believe it unlikely, [that] the arbitrators could consider Soler's affirmative claim of anticompetitive conduct by CISA and Mitsubishi to fall within the purview of this choice-of-law provision, with the result that it would be decided under Swiss law rather than the U.S. Sherman Act." At oral argument, however, counsel for Mitsubishi conceded that American law applied to the antitrust claims and represented that the claims had been submitted to the arbitration panel in Japan on that basis. The record confirms that before the decision of the Court of Appeals the arbitral panel had taken these claims under submission.

We therefore have no occasion to speculate on this matter at this stage in the proceedings, when Mitsubishi seeks to enforce the agreement to arbitrate, not to enforce an award. Nor need we consider now the effect of an arbitral tribunal's failure to take cognizance of the statutory cause of action on the claimant's capacity to reinitiate suit in federal court. We merely note that in the event the choice-of-forum and choice-of-law clauses operated in tandem as a prospective

gant effectively may vindicate its statutory cause of action in the arbitral forum, the statute will continue to serve both its remedial and deterrent function.

Having permitted the arbitration to go forward, the national courts of the United States will have the opportunity at the award-enforcement stage to ensure that the legitimate interest in the enforcement of the antitrust laws has been addressed. The Convention reserves to each signatory country the right to refuse enforcement of an award where the "recognition or enforcement of the award would be contrary to the public policy of that country." Art. V(2)(b). While the efficacy of the arbitral process requires that substantive review at the award-enforcement stage remain minimal, it would not require intrusive inquiry to ascertain that the tribunal took cognizance of the antitrust claims and actually decided them.

As international trade has expanded in recent decades, so too has the use of international arbitration to resolve disputes arising in the course of that trade. * * * If [arbitral tribunals] are to take a central place in the international legal order, national courts will need to "shake off the old judicial hostility to arbitration," and also their customary and understandable unwillingness to cede jurisdiction of a claim arising under domestic law to a foreign or transnational tribunal. To this extent, at least, it will be necessary for national courts to subordinate domestic notions of arbitrability to the international policy favoring commercial arbitration.

Accordingly, we "require this representative of the American business community to honor its bargain," *Alberto–Culver Co. v. Scherk*, 484 F.2d 611, 620 (CA7 1973) (Stevens, J., dissenting), by holding this agreement to arbitrate "enforce[able] * * * in accord with the explicit provisions of the Arbitration Act."

The judgment of the Court of Appeals is affirmed in part and reversed in part, and the cases are remanded for further proceedings consistent with this opinion.

It is so ordered.

JUSTICE POWELL took no part in the decision of these cases.

JUSTICE STEVENS, with whom JUSTICE BRENNAN joins, and with whom JUSTICE MARSHALL joins except as to Part II, dissenting.

[Justice Stevens first argued in Part II that the arbitration clause should not be construed to include antitrust claims. In Part III he stressed the importance of antitrust policy. ("Antitrust laws in general, and the Sherman Act in particular, are the magna carta of free enterprise. They are as important to the preservation of economic freedom and our free-

---

waiver of a party's right to pursue statutory remedies for antitrust violations, we would have little hesitation in condemning the agreement as against public policy.

enterprise system as the Bill of Rights is to the protection of our funda-mental personal freedoms.") He stressed also that the mandatory treble damages provisions of the United States antitrust law signal the im-portance Congress attached to the private-attorney-general role of private litigants who in pursuing private antitrust claims are at the same time protecting the broad public interest in the proper functioning of the free market. The opinion continues with the following quote from the Second Circuit opinion in *American Safety*.]

> " * * * Antitrust violations can affect hundreds of thousands—perhaps millions—of people and inflict staggering economic damage. * * * We do not believe that Congress intended such claims to be re-solved elsewhere than in the courts. * * * [I]t is also proper to ask whether contracts of adhesion between alleged monopolists and their customers should determine the forum for trying antitrust viola-tions."

* * *

* * * Arbitration awards are only reviewable for manifest disregard of the law, 9 U.S.C. §§ 10, 207, and the rudimentary procedures which make arbitration so desirable in the context of a private dispute often mean that the record is so inadequate that the arbitrator's decision is virtually unreviewable.[31] Despotic decisionmaking of this kind is fine for parties who are willing to agree in advance to settle for a best approximation of the correct result in order to resolve quickly and inexpensively any con-tractual dispute that may arise in an ongoing commercial relationship. Such informality, however, is simply unacceptable when every error may have devastating consequences for important businesses in our national economy and may undermine their ability to compete in world markets. Instead of "muffling a grievance in the cloakroom of arbitration," the pub-lic interest in free competitive markets would be better served by having the issues resolved "in the light of impartial public court adjudication."

[Justice Stevens stressed that the New York Convention would allow the United States to refuse to order arbitration of antitrust claims on the ground of nonarbitrability, citing Articles II(1) and II(3).]

* * * The courts of other nations * * * have applied the exception provided in the Convention, and refused to enforce agreements to arbitrate specific subject matters of concern to them.[35]

---

[31] The arbitration procedure in this case does not provide any right to evidentiary discovery or a written decision, and requires that all proceedings be closed to the public. Moreover, Japa-nese arbitrators do not have the power of compulsory process to secure witnesses and documents, nor do witnesses who are available testify under oath. Cf. 9 U.S.C. § 7 (arbitrators may summon witnesses to attend proceedings and seek enforcement in a district court).

[35] For example, the Cour de Cassation in Belgium has held that disputes arising under a Belgian statute limiting the unilateral termination of exclusive distributorships are not arbitra-

It may be that the subject-matter exception to the Convention ought to be reserved—as a matter of domestic law—for matters of the greatest public interest which involve concerns that are shared by other nations. The Sherman Act's commitment to free competitive markets is among our most important civil policies. This commitment, shared by other nations which are signatory to the Convention, is hardly the sort of parochial concern that we should decline to enforce in the interest of international comity. * * *

V

* * *

In my opinion, the elected representatives of the American people would not have us dispatch an American citizen to a foreign land in search of an uncertain remedy for the violation of a public right that is protected by the Sherman Act. This is especially so when there has been no genuine bargaining over the terms of the submission, and the arbitration remedy provided has not even the most elementary guarantees of fair process. Consideration of a fully developed record by a jury, instructed in the law by a federal judge, and subject to appellate review, is a surer guide to the competitive character of a commercial practice than the practically unreviewable judgment of a private arbitrator.

Unlike the Congress that enacted the Sherman Act in 1890, the Court today does not seem to appreciate the value of economic freedom. I respectfully dissent.

According to the majority, are all antitrust claims arbitrable under all circumstances? What protections does the majority envisage against the risk that arbitrators might misapply antitrust laws or ignore fundamental antitrust policies?

In recent years, the Supreme Court has allowed arbitration in a great variety of contexts. The lower federal courts have by and large taken similar positions. As a result, in American law today, non-arbitrable cases have become a rare species. In its most recent decision, the Supreme Court held 5–4 that, even in consumer contracts (in this case with a cell phone service provider), mandatory arbitration clauses are valid, even if they exclude class proceedings. Accordingly, the court held that California (state) consumer protection legislation, which forbade such clauses, was preempted by the Federal Arbitration Act. Providers can thus not only exclude access to court but also force a consumer to arbitrate his or her

---

ble under the Convention in that country, and the Corte di Cassazione in Italy has held that labor disputes are not arbitrable under the Convention in that country.

individual claim—which is rarely, if ever, a viable option. *AT & T Mobility, LLC v. Concepcion*, 131 S. Ct. 1740 (2011).

By contrast, arbitration clauses in consumer contracts are presumed to be invalid under European (Union) Law, see Council Directive 93/13/EEC of April 5, 1003 on unfair terms in consumer contracts, Article 3, Annex 1(q). Generally speaking, foreign countries, notably in Europe, take a more conservative position and view arbitration critically (often refusing to allow it) if it takes place between parties of greatly different bargaining power.

Another major issue is the validity of the arbitration clause itself. What arguments does the American party in the case below advance as a basis for invalidating the clause? How do these arguments fare in court?

TENNESSEE IMPORTS, INC. v. P.P. FILIPPI & PRIX ITALIA S.R.L.

United States District Court
745 F. Supp. 1314 (M.D. Tenn. 1990)

[In 1985, Prix Italia, an Italian corporation that manufactured sequential pricing and labeling machines, appointed Tennessee Imports, a Tennessee corporation, as its exclusive distributor of the machines for the U.S., Canada and Mexico. In August 1989, as required by their contract, Prix gave notice to terminate the exclusive contract, but Tennessee Imports alleged that the contract remained in effect until August 1, 1990. Tennessee Imports further alleged that in May 1989, while the exclusive distribution contract was still in effect and before the termination notice had been given, the export manager of Prix, Paulo Filippi, traveled to New York City and Miami and "made false, misleading, and intentionally incorrect statements by advising individuals at the meeting that Prix had no relationship with Tennessee Imports * * * [and] that Prix would not in the future sell any of its products to Tennessee Imports." Tennessee Imports alleged that Mr. Filippi told these individuals that they were free to import and resell the Prix machines that were then the subject of Prix's exclusive contract with Tennessee Imports. Tennessee Imports alleged that these and other actions by Mr. Filippi were "grossly negligent;" that they destroyed "the valuable dealer network, advertising, and other exclusive trade developed by Tennessee Imports," and that they "induced and procured a breach of the contract between Prix and Tennessee Imports." Based on these allegations, Tennessee Imports brought an action against Prix and Mr. Filippi in a U.S. federal district court in Tennessee for breach of contract and tortious interference with contract.]

JUDGE DIXON:

* * *

In response to the plaintiff's complaint, the defendants moved to dismiss for lack of proper venue or, alternatively, for lack of subject matter jurisdiction. In support of their motion, the defendants point to Article 8 of the contract between Prix and Tennessee Imports which provides:

> Should any dispute arise between the contractual parties or in connection with the relations stipulated by this contract and no settlement can be achieved, then both parties agree to the competence of [the] Arbitration Court of [the] Chamber of Commerce in Venice (Italy).

The defendants claim that this forum selection clause renders venue in this Court improper and thus that this action should be dismissed.

Tennessee Imports filed a memorandum in opposition to Defendants' Motion to Dismiss ("Plaintiff's Memo") making the following arguments:

> 1) That Article 8 of the contract is not a forum selection clause because the Arbitration Court of the Chamber of Commerce in Venice is not a "judicial institution" listed in the *Martindale–Hubb[ell] Italy Law Digest* and therefore is a "non-judicial and possibly non-existent forum;"

> 2) That enforcement of Article 8 would result in substantial inconvenience to Tennessee Imports and would deny Tennessee Imports effective relief;

> 3) That, because the sequential machines manufactured by Prix are a unique product and unavailable from other free-world sources, the bargaining position of the two parties was unequal. Thus, Tennessee Imports argues, Prix used its economic power to obtain Tennessee Imports' agreement to Article 8 without negotiation and, as such, Article 8 is adhesive and unconscionable;

> 4) That Mr. Filippi's conduct in inducing and procuring Prix's breach of contract was tortious and, therefore, that its claim against Mr. Filippi is not within the scope of the forum selection clause found in Article 8 of the contract; and

> 5) That the public policy of the State of Tennessee and the State's interest in protecting its citizens and in providing them with an equitable forum warrant the Court's retention of this action.

Darrell Johnson, CEO of Tennessee Imports, attests that, after inquiry by Tennessee Imports regarding the "availability of [Prix's] machines for import and distribution into the State of Tennessee," Prix drew up the contract at issue and forwarded it to Tennessee Imports; that "there was no bargaining at all concerning the forum selection clause;" that the sequential machines manufactured by Prix were unavailable from any other source in the free world; and that upon receiving the contract from Prix, Mr. Johnson executed it. Mr. Johnson also attests that "all of the evidence and witnesses except [Mr.] Filippi * * * are found in the United States."

The defendants have responded to the plaintiff's arguments as follows:

> 1) That the Arbitration Court referred to in Article 8 is the Arbitration Court of the International Chamber of Commerce (the "ICC Arbitration Court"), a well-recognized and competent arbitral body which may conduct proceedings at the Venice location specified in the contract. The defendants maintain that the ICC Arbitration Court is "specifically tailored to handle international disputes" such as that between Prix and Tennessee Imports and will afford Tennessee Imports an effective forum in which to seek relief;

> 2) That Tennessee Imports has failed to show that arbitration in Italy would cause Tennessee Imports sufficient inconvenience to justify a refusal by this Court to enforce Article 8 of the contract;

> 3) That the contract between Prix and Tennessee Imports was the result of "arms length negotiations by experienced and sophisticated business entities;"

> 4) That Tennessee Imports' claim of tortious interference falls within the scope of Article 8 and thus should be resolved through arbitration; and

> 5) That, because of the expansion of American trade and commerce in world markets, public policy now supports upholding forum selection clauses such as Article 8 of the contract.

In support, Prix has submitted the affidavit of Deborah Enix-Ross, the Manager of Legal Affairs for the United States Council for International Business (the United States Affiliate of the ICC) attesting to the expertise of the ICC Arbitration Court in settling international commercial disputes and to the availability of ICC arbitration in Venice. The defendants have also submitted the sworn declaration of Mr. Filippi stating that although Tennessee Imports did not bargain about Article 8, neither did it raise any objections to its inclusion in the contract. * * *

    C.   TENNESSEE IMPORTS' CLAIMS AGAINST PRIX ITALIA

        1.   CLAIMS AT LAW

The contract between Tennessee Imports and Prix clearly evidences a commercial relationship between the parties: the sale and purchase of goods by corporate entities. This transaction is also an international one. Prix manufactures sequential machines in Italy. Tennessee Imports purchased them for sale in the United States, Canada, and Mexico. Each of the two parties is incorporated and has its principal place of business in a different signatory country; Tennessee Imports in the United States and Prix in Italy. Article 8 of the sales contract contains an express agreement to arbitrate and provides for arbitration in Italy, a signatory to the Convention. Clearly, the arbitration agreement between Tennessee Imports and Prix is the type of agreement contemplated by the Convention. Thus, if the disputes between these parties fall within the scope of their arbitration agreement, this Court must enforce that agreement unless the Court finds that it falls within the meaning of the "null and void" clause of the Convention.

In Article 8, the parties agree to arbitrate *"any dispute aris[ing] between the contractual parties or in connection with the relations stipulated* by the contract [for which] no settlement can be achieved. * * * "* (emphasis added). The emphasized language gives this clause a very broad scope. Indeed, the Second Circuit has observed that "[i]t is difficult to imagine broader general language than contained in the * * * arbitration clause, 'any dispute' * * * " When the language of an arbitration clause is broad, the court should "focus on the factual allegations in the complaint rather than the legal causes asserted. If the allegations underlying the claims 'touch matters' covered by the parties' [contract], then those claims must be arbitrated, whatever the legal labels attached to them."

Tennessee Imports has made no claims at law against Prix which do not touch in some way upon the exclusive agreement between the parties. First, Tennessee Imports claims a breach of contract. There can be no doubt that this claim falls within the scope of Article 8. Tennessee Imports' claim of inducing and procuring breach cannot be directed at Prix. "A party cannot tortiously induce a breach of its own contract." Although Tennessee Imports has alleged some facts which might give rise to other tort claims (misrepresentation of bad faith, e.g.), Tennessee Imports cannot escape arbitration merely by characterizing these claims as sounding in tort. Courts have consistently held that broad arbitration clauses encompass contract-based tort claims. The Court finds no basis for any claims against Prix that fall outside the scope of Article 8 which encompasses virtually any dispute which touches upon the parties' contractual relationship. Thus, all of Tennessee Imports' claims against Prix are arbitrable ones, and only if the Court finds, in accordance with Article II(3) of the Convention, that the arbitration clause is "null and void, inoperative, or incapable of being performed" may it refuse to refer the parties to arbitration.

Here, Tennessee Imports has made several relevant arguments. First, Tennessee Imports argues that Article 8 is not a forum selection clause because the Arbitration Court of the Chamber of Commerce in Venice is not a "judicial institution" listed in the *Martindale–Hubb[ell] Italy Law Digest* and therefore is a "non-judicial and possibly non-existent forum."

Considering this argument in light of the Arbitration Act, the Court takes this as an argument that the clause is "incapable of being performed."

Tennessee Imports' argument that the Arbitration Court of the Chamber of Commerce in Venice is a non-judicial forum completely ignores the quasi-judicial nature of arbitral bodies. The omission of an arbitral body from the Martindale–Hubb[ell] listing of Italy's judicial institutions provides no support at all for Tennessee Imports' half-hearted contention that the Arbitration Court is a "*possibly* non-existent forum." There is no reason for a quasi-judicial body to be listed among judicial institutions, and such an omission is neither surprising nor dispositive in any way.

Furthermore, Tennessee Imports has offered no reply to the defendants' assertion that Article 8 refers to the ICC arbitration court. The ICC Arbitration Court is, as the affidavit of Ms. Enix-Ross attests, a well-recognized and highly-regarded arbitral institution specializing in the field of international commercial disputes. There is little doubt that the ICC Arbitration Court can offer Tennessee Imports an effective forum. Even absent the defendants' assertion, however, Tennessee Imports has offered this Court no substantive evidence that enforcement of Article 8 would in fact deprive it of a forum in which to seek redress for its grievances.

Tennessee Imports' argument that enforcing Article 8 would cause it substantial inconvenience, presumably by forcing it to transport witnesses and to incur the expense and risk of seeking redress in a distant and foreign forum, is equally without merit. As the Second Circuit has observed, the:

> inability to produce one's witnesses before an arbitral tribunal is a risk inherent in an agreement to submit to arbitration. By agreeing to submit disputes to arbitration, a party relinquishes his courtroom rights—including that to subpoena witnesses—in favor of arbitration "with all of its well know [sic] advantages and drawbacks."

The frequency with which depositions and affidavits are used in international litigation and arbitration further detracts from the Tennessee Imports argument. See *M/S Bremen v. Zapata Off–Shore Co.*, 407 U.S. 1, 19 (1972) (noting that "[i]t is not unusual for important issues in international admiralty cases to be dealt with by deposition"). The Court agrees with the defendants that Tennessee Imports has failed to demonstrate that it will be inconvenienced and prejudiced so significantly as to overcome the strong presumption in favor of arbitration mandated by the Arbitration Act and the Convention.

In *Mitsubishi Motors*, the Supreme Court observed that, while honoring this strong presumption in favor of arbitrability, courts must still "remain attuned to *well-supported* claims that the *agreement to arbitrate* resulted from the sort of fraud or overwhelming economic power that would provide grounds for 'the revocation of any contract.' " In the case of a broad arbitration clause, the court's inquiry is limited to whether the arbitration clause itself, as opposed to the entire contract, was obtained through such means.

Mr. Johnson attests that he "would not have executed the contract * * * [had he] known that [the defendants] would take the action which is described in the Complaint." Mr. Johnson maintains that the defendants' failure "to reveal in advance that they would take such action * * * was false and misleading." Certainly, not every breach of contract rises to the level of fraud or misrepresentation. Nevertheless, assuming arguendo that [P]rix entered into or renewed its contract with Tennessee Imports intending to breach that contract, such actions would call into question the formation of and obligations arising under the entire contract, not simply the arbitration agreement. Such claims would fall within the broad scope of the parties' arbitration agreement.

* * *

Finally, Tennessee Imports argues that public policy dictates against enforcement of Article 8. Tennessee Imports argues that innocent parties should not be forced to seek redress in distant, foreign forums. Whether or not Tennessee Imports is in fact an innocent party, this argument demonstrates the type of parochialism which the Arbitration Act and the Convention have sought to overcome. The Act, the Convention, and the case law interpreting them clearly establish a strong federal policy favoring arbitration. "The utility of the Convention in promoting the process of international commercial arbitration depends upon the willingness of national courts to let go of matters they normally would think of as their own." *Mitsubishi Motors*, 473 U.S. at 639, n. 21. Absent any reason to except Tennessee Imports from this policy, this Court has no choice but to refer Tennessee Imports' claims against Prix to arbitration.

* * *

[The court concluded that the claim against Paulo Filippi should not be dismissed; Filippi, as an individual, was not a party to the agreement and therefore not a party to the arbitration agreement. The claim against Filippi, however, was closely related to, and in part dependent upon, the claim against Prix. To succeed against Filippi, for example, Tennessee Imports would have to show that Prix did in fact breach the contract, and any such breach would, in all likelihood, involve the actions of Filippi as agent for Prix. Also to prevent double recovery, any damages collected against Prix would have to be subtracted from the claim against Filippi. For these reasons the court stayed the action against Filippi to await the result of the arbitration.]

III. SUMMARY

In summary, as to Prix Italia, S.R.L., the Court GRANTS the defendants' motion to dismiss. The parties are hereby referred to arbitration. As to Pier Paulo Filippi, the Court DENIES the defendants' motion to dismiss, but the Court ORDERS that further proceedings against Pier Paulo Filippi be STAYED and placed on the Retired Docket pending the completion of arbitration between Tennessee Imports and Prix Italia, S.R.L.

* * *

What is the take-away lesson from *Mitsubishi* and *Tennessee Imports* when you consider whether to agree to a contract that includes an arbitration clause?

C. BETWEEN PRIVATE PARTIES AND STATES: DISPUTE RESOLUTION BETWEEN EQUALS?

Finally, arbitration also can take place between states and private parties. This form of dispute resolution has become increasingly frequent in recent years. It typically comes in two basic forms.

Often, arbitration between private parties and states is simply a variation of international commercial arbitration where the primary difference is that one of the parties to the dispute happens to be a sovereign state. States routinely buy services or goods from foreign businesses (banks, shipping companies, manufacturers of military equipment, etc.). The underlying contract typically contains an arbitration clause. For the state, such a clause has the advantage that it will not be asked to submit to the jurisdiction of a foreign country. For the private party, it avoids running headlong into a (foreign) sovereign immunity problem as states normally enjoy no immunity if they have agreed to arbitration.

Increasingly, however, arbitration between states and private parties is not based on contractual agreements, but on treaties. Some of these treaties address special crises, and we will see an example in sub-section (d) when we look at the Algiers Accords. Currently, the most important basis for arbitration between private parties and states are bilateral investment treaties (BITs). They supplemented and sometimes replaced an older generation of so-called *Treaties of Friendship, Commerce, and Navigation* (FCNs), some of which still exist between the United States and several other countries but do not contain arbitration clauses for disputes between private parties and governments. Today, there are thousands of BITs in the world, and the United States has concluded them with dozens of countries.

Foreign investment disputes typically occur when a private enterprise from one country makes an investment in another country and then runs into problems there because the host government infringes the value of the investment through taxation, regulation or outright expropriation. Resulting arbitration thus straddles the private/public law boundary not only because one party is a private business while the other is a public entity, but also because it is based on a full-fledged treaty that protects private interests.

Most of the BITs follow a fairly standard pattern with some variations. Here are the pertinent provisions of the BIT between the United States and Argentina, which we saw earlier in a different context (see Chapter VI.5.A.). What options for dispute resolution does the Treaty create (1) between the state parties and (2) between a private party (foreign investor) and a (host) state? What benefits do investors and states, respectively, get from these provisions?

TREATY BETWEEN THE UNITED STATES OF AMERICA AND THE ARGENTINE REPUBLIC CONCERNING THE RECIPROCAL ENCOURAGEMENT AND PROTECTION OF INVESTMENT
(Adopted 1991; in force 1994)

* * *

Article VI

The Parties agree to consult promptly, on the request of either, to resolve any disputes in connection with the Treaty, or to discuss any matter relating to the interpretation or application of the Treaty.

Article VII

1. For purposes of this Article, an investment dispute is a dispute between a Party and a national or company of the other Party arising out of or relating to (a) an investment agreement between that Party and such national or company; (b) an investment authorization granted by that Party's foreign investment authority (if any such authorization exists) to such national or company; or (c) an alleged breach of any right conferred or created by this Treaty with respect to an investment.

2. In the event of an investment dispute, the parties to the dispute should initially seek a resolution through consultation and negotiation. If the dispute cannot be settled amicably, the national or company concerned may choose to submit the dispute for resolution:

   (a) to the courts or administrative tribunals of the Party that is a party to the dispute; or

   (b) in accordance with any applicable, previously agreed dispute-settlement procedures; or

(c) in accordance with the terms of paragraph 3.

3. (a) Provided that the national or company concerned has not submitted the dispute for resolution under paragraph 2(a) or (b) and that six months have elapsed from the date on which the dispute arose, the national or company concerned may choose to consent in writing to the submission of the dispute for settlement by binding arbitration:

   (i) to the International Centre for the Settlement of Investment Disputes ("Centre") established by the Convention on the Settlement of Investment Disputes between States and Nationals of other States, done at Washington, March 18, 1965 ("ICSID Convention"), provided that the Party is a party to such Convention; or

   (ii) to the Additional Facility of the Centre, if the Centre is not available; or

   (iii) in accordance with the Arbitration Rules of the United Nations Commission on International Trade Law (UNICTRAL); or

   (iv) to any other arbitration institution, or in accordance with any other arbitration rules, as may be mutually agreed between the parties to the dispute.

   (b) Once the national or company concerned has so consented, either party to the dispute may initiate arbitration in accordance with the choice so specified in the consent.

4. Each Party hereby consents to the submission of any investment dispute for settlement by binding arbitration in accordance with the choice specified in the written consent of the national or company under paragraph 3. Such consent, together with the written consent of the national or company when given under paragraph 3 shall satisfy the requirement for:

   (a) written consent of the parties to the dispute for purposes of Chapter II of the ICSID Convention (Jurisdiction of the Centre) and for purposes of the Additional Facility Rules; and

   (b) an "agreement in writing" for purposes of Article II of the United Nations Convention on the Recognition and Enforcement of Foreign Arbitral Awards, done at New York, June 10, 1958 ("New York Convention").

5. Any arbitration under paragraph 3(a)(ii), (iii) or (iv) of this Article shall be held in a state that is a party to the New York Convention.

6. Any arbitral award rendered pursuant to this Article shall be final and binding on the parties to the dispute. Each Party undertakes to carry out without delay the provisions of any such award and to provide in its territory for its enforcement.

7. In any proceeding involving an investment dispute, a Party shall not assert, as a defense, counterclaim, right of set-off or otherwise, that the national or company concerned has received or will receive, pursuant to an insurance or guarantee contract, indemnification or other compensation for all or part of its alleged damages.

8. For purposes of an arbitration held under paragraph 3 of this Article, any company legally constituted under the applicable laws and regulations of a Party or a political subdivision thereof but that, immediately before the occurrence of the event or events giving rise to the dispute, was an investment of nationals or companies of the other Party, shall be treated as a national or company of such other Party in accordance with Article 25(2)(b) of the ICSID Convention.

Article VIII

1. Any dispute between the Parties concerning the interpretation or application of the Treaty which is not resolved through consultations or other diplomatic channels, shall be submitted, upon the request of either Party, to an arbitral tribunal for binding decision in accordance with the applicable rules of international law. In the absence of an agreement by the Parties to the contrary, the arbitration rules of the United Nations Commission on International Trade Law (UNCITRAL), except to the extent modified by the Parties or by the arbitrators, shall govern.

2. Within two months of receipt of a request, each Party shall appoint an arbitrator. The two arbitrators shall select a third arbitrator as Chairman, who is a national of a third State. The UNCITRAL Rules for appointing members of three member panels shall apply mutatis mutandis to the appointment of the arbitral panel except that the appointing authority referenced in those rules shall be the Secretary General of the Permanent Court of Arbitration.

3. Unless otherwise agreed, all submissions shall be made and all hearings shall be completed within six months of the date of selection of the third arbitrator, and the Tribunal shall render its decisions within two months of the date of the final submissions or the date of the closing of the hearings, whichever is later.

4. Expenses incurred by the Chairman, the other arbitrators, and other costs of the proceedings shall be paid for equally by the Parties.

* * *

The following case shows investment dispute arbitration in action. The decision is difficult to understand without some knowledge of the background of the dispute.

Like many South American countries post-World War II, Argentina had slowly evolved into both a democracy and a free market economy. Indeed, by the late 1980s and early '90s, as the government made sweeping economic changes, Argentina was singled out by many as a favorable environment for foreign investment. The government instituted free market policies, pegged the local currency (the Argentine peso) to the U.S. dollar, privatized state-owned enterprises and put in place a host of other "Washington solutions." Inflation dropped sharply, the economy grew at a respectable annual rate, and foreign companies were satisfied with their investments.

Among the measures adopted to attract foreign investments, Argentina entered into bilateral investment treaties with more than 50 countries. Those treaties provided investors with important guarantees: no taking would be carried out without adequate compensation, foreign investment would be treated on a "fair and equitable" and non-discriminatory basis, and any dispute between an investor and the government could be arbitrated through the World Bank's ICSID process. Finally, the treaties typically included an umbrella clause, designed to raise further provisions to the level of treaty protections.

While the Argentine government reforms actually led to a significant increase in foreign investment and a drop in inflation, some negative consequences also emerged. For various reasons, by the late 1990s the economy lapsed into a steep recession. The fiscal deficit, the artificially inflated value of the local currency and other external factors deepened Argentina's economic woes. Capital inflows were reduced and economic turmoil resulted in significant capital flight, which exacerbated the fiscal crisis, increased unemployment, and brought about a serious political crisis.

When the crisis intensified (from December 2001 through the early part of 2002), the government passed a series of emergency laws and decrees intended to avoid a run on the banks and allowing the government to suspend any payments on its foreign debt. The Emergency Law of 2002 introduced a reform of the foreign exchange system and an end of the dollar/peso peg. And, on top of all of this, the government froze tariff rates that were charged to consumers for gas and other government-regulated services. In 2002, the peso fell against the dollar to almost 3:1 when allowed to float freely.

Several investors, including CMS (the claimant in the case below), took their grievances through the ICSID process, challenging the government's authority to issue the emergency decrees set out above. They claimed that the governments' actions violated various protections afforded to them under the BIT, claiming that the government's actions: 1) were tantamount to expropriation (since the government had effectively bankrupted their in-country operations); 2) failed to provide "fair and equitable" treatment for foreign investors; 3) discriminated against foreign investors because the laws unfairly targeted them over local businesses; and 4) violated the umbrella clause of the BIT.

In 2005 (several years after the government's actions), the first ICSID award was issued relating to the Argentine crisis. In the CMS case, the tribunal issued an opinion of 147 pages, in which it examined in an exhaustive manner each of CMS' claims and the government's response. As you read the excerpt, consider carefully how the tribunal approached both CMS's allegations and the government's responses. Why did the tribunal reject certain arguments of CMS while accepting others? Did the government put forward its best case on all fronts? Did CMS have a realistic chance of recovering under all of its theories?

IN THE PROCEEDING BETWEEN CMS GAS TRANSMISSION COMPANY (CLAIMANT) AND THE ARGENTINE REPUBLIC (RESPONDENT)

Investment Centre for Settlement of Investment Disputes
Case No. Arb/01/8 Award of May 12, 2005

Members of the Tribunal

Professor Francisco Orrego Vicuña, President

The Honorable Marc Lalonde P.C., O.C., Q.C., Arbitrator

H.E. Judge Francisco Rezek, Arbitrator

* * *

C. CONSIDERATIONS

    3. THE PRIVATIZATION PROGRAM AS THE BACKGROUND TO THE DISPUTE

53. As had been observed by the Tribunal in its Decision on Jurisdiction, the Argentine Republic embarked in 1989 on economic reforms, which included the privatization of important industries and public utilities as well as the participation of foreign investment. Gas transportation was one of the significant sectors to be included under this reform program. The basic instruments governing these economic reforms were Law No. 23.696 on the Reform of the State of 1989, Law No. 23.928 on Currency Convertibility of 1991 and Decree No. 2128/91 fixing the Argentine peso at par with the United States dollar.

54. Within this broad framework specific instruments were enacted to govern the privatization of the main industries. As far as the Gas sector

was concerned, Law No. 24.076 of 1992, or Gas Law, established the basic rules for the transportation and distribution of natural gas. This instrument was implemented the same year by Decree No. 1738/92 or Gas Decree.

55. As a consequence of the new legislation, Gas del Estado, a State-owned entity, was divided into two transportation companies and eight distribution companies. Transportadora de Gas del Norte (TGN) was one of the companies created for gas transportation. The privatization of the new company was opened to investors by means of a public tender offer and a related Information Memorandum was prepared by consultant and investment firms in 1992 at the request of the Government.

56. A Model License approved by Decree No. 2255/92 established the basic terms and conditions for the licenses that each new company would be granted by the Argentine Government. TGN's license was granted by Decree No. 2457/92 for a period of thirty-five years, subject to extension for another ten years on the fulfillment of certain conditions.

57. In the Claimant's view, the legislation and regulations enacted, as well as the license, resulted in a legal regime under which tariffs were to be calculated in dollars, conversion to pesos was to be effected at the time of billing and tariffs would be adjusted every six months in accordance with the United States Producer Price Index (US PPI). As will be examined further below, the Respondent has a different understanding of the nature and legal effects of these various instruments.

58. CMS's participation in TGN began in 1995 under a 1995 Offering Memorandum leading to the purchase of the shares still held by the government. CMS's acquisition represented 25% of the company, later supplemented by the purchase of an additional 4.42%, thus totaling 29.42% of TGN's shares. This new Offering Memorandum was modeled on the 1992 Information Memorandum and the license.

4.   ARGENTINA'S MEASURES IN THE PERIOD 1999–2002 AND THE EMERGENCE OF THE DISPUTE

59. Towards the end of the 1990's a serious economic crisis began to unfold in Argentina, which eventually had profound political and social ramifications. The nature and extent of this crisis will be discussed below.

* * *

67. On February 13, 2002 CMS notified an ancillary dispute [in addition to its original dispute over tariffs] concerning the measures enacted under the Emergency Law and related decisions. In its Decision on Jurisdiction, the Tribunal considered that the disputes arising from the one as well as the other types of measures were sufficiently closely related and thus proceeded to the merits phase in respect of both.

5. CMS'S CLAIM FOR BUSINESS AND FINANCIAL LOSSES

68. The Claimant explains that it decided to undertake important investments in the gas transportation sector in reliance on the Argentine
Government's promises and guarantees, particularly those that offered a
real return in dollar terms and the adjustment of tariffs according to the
US PPI. The Claimant asserts that it invested almost US$ 175 million in
the purchase of shares in TGN and that TGN invested more than US$ 1
billion in the renovation and expansion of the gas pipeline network.

69. The Claimant further argues that the measures undertaken by the
Government in the period 1999–2002 and in the aftermath have had devastating consequences. The effects relate in part to the loss of income and
in part to the fact that the Claimant's ability to pay its debt has been reduced by a factor of more than three because the debt is denominated in
US dollars and there has been an intervening devaluation of the peso.
The Claimant also asserts that the value of its shares in TGN has
dropped by 92%, falling from US$ 261.1 million to US$ 21.2 million, this
last figure having later been revised to US$ 23.7 million and later yet to
US$ 17.5 million.

70. Because no adjustment of tariffs has taken place since January 1,
2000 and because tariffs may no longer be calculated in US dollars, the
Claimant explains that TGN's domestic tariff revenue has decreased by
nearly 75%. Only export revenues have been kept in US dollars. In the
Claimant's view the situation has been aggravated by the assertion by
some Provincial governments of the right to pay gas and other invoices in
bonds.

71. It is further explained that the devaluation has also had an adverse
impact on TGN's costs: taking into account an exchange rate of 3.6 pesos
to the dollar, the rate used by the Claimant in its Memorial, it now takes
3.6 times as much revenue as before to pay existing debt. As a result, it is
claimed, TGN has defaulted on certain dollar-denominated obligations
and on its foreign and domestic debt, thus having been excluded from international capital markets. Dollar-denominated operating costs, it is asserted, have also been affected.

72. In addition to the losses that CMS has suffered as a result of the specific measures referred to above, the Claimant argues that the broader
economic implications of the Emergency Law have led to an artificial depression of consumer gas prices in Argentina, particularly as a result of
the tariff freeze. Because Argentine gas prices are among the lowest in
the world, an effective subsidy benefiting the rest of the Argentine economy has had a negative impact on the regulated gas sector, amounting to
several billion dollars for the energy sector as a whole.

73. The end result of these measures, in the Claimant's view, has led to
the suspension of investments in new expansion projects and the collapse

of the pipeline network. This, in turn, it is argued, has brought about serious gas shortages both in the domestic market and in the supply of neighboring countries, such as Brazil, Chile and Uruguay. A fiduciary fund was established in 2004 to channel investment, in conjunction with private participation, in gas transportation infrastructure, particularly with a view to importing gas from Bolivia to compensate for the domestic shortages. While the Respondent argues that this is evidence of the normal operation of companies and TGN in the gas market, the Claimant is of the view that TGN's participation in this arrangement has not been voluntary.

6. THE RESPONDENT'S ARGUMENTS IN RESPECT OF BUSINESS AND FINANCIAL LOSSES

74. The Government of Argentina argues that the losses incurred by the Claimant are not attributable to the Respondent and that any such losses arise from business decisions of TGN. The effects of the measures on TGN's costs are in the Respondent's view very different from what CMS claims.

* * *

81. The Respondent also argues that the License did not guarantee the profitability of the business because, as stated in Article 2.4 of the Basic Rules of the License, "the Licensor does not guarantee or ensure the profitability of exploitation." Nor, it is argued, can credit rating deterioration be attributed to the Government. It is further asserted that TGN is free to renegotiate its debt in the international financial market at discounts ranging from 55% to 90%, just as other businesses have done.

* * *

7. CMS'S LEGAL JUSTIFICATION OF ITS CLAIMS

84. The Claimant is of the view that the measures adopted by the Argentine Government are in violation of the commitments that the Government made to foreign investors in the offering memoranda, relevant laws and regulations and the License itself.

85. Such commitments, it is asserted, included the calculation of tariffs in US dollars, the semi-annual adjustment in accordance with the US PPI and general adjustment of tariffs every five years, all with the purpose of maintaining the real dollar value of the tariffs.

86. The Claimant argues that Argentina further agreed expressly not to freeze the tariff structure or subject it to further regulation or price controls; and that in the event that price controls were introduced, TGN would be entitled to compensation for the difference between the tariff it

was entitled to and the tariff actually charged. Moreover, the basic rules governing the License could not be altered without TGN's consent.

87. The Claimant is of the view that these guarantees constituted essential conditions for CMS's investment and that it has an acquired right to the application of the agreed tariff regime. The Claimant says that the Government of Argentina itself confirmed this in Decree No. 669/2000 by explaining the adjustment mechanism of the licenses as a "legitimately acquired right."

88. It is further argued that the measures adopted are all attributable to the Argentine Government and result in the violation of all the major investment protections owed to CMS under the Treaty. It is claimed in particular that Argentina has wrongfully expropriated CMS's investment without compensation in violation of Article IV of the Treaty; that Argentina has failed to treat CMS's investment in accordance with the standard of fair and equitable treatment of Article II(2)(a) of the Treaty; that the passing of arbitrary and discriminatory measures violates Article II(2)(b); and that it has also failed to observe the many obligations entered into with regard to the investment in violation of the standard of Article II(2)(c) of that Treaty. Unlawful restrictions to the free transfer of funds in violation of Article V of the Treaty were also invoked in the Claimant's memorial, a claim that was later withdrawn.

89. On the basis of its understanding of the measures adopted, their economic impact on the company and the legal violations invoked the Claimant requests compensation in the amount of US$ 261.1 million for Treaty breaches plus interest and costs.

90. The specific arguments invoked by the Claimant in support of its legal contentions will be examined by the Tribunal separately when discussing each of the claims made.

8. THE RESPONDENT'S LEGAL DEFENSE

91. In the view of the Argentine Government, the License, and the legal and regulatory framework governing it, provide only for the right of the licensee to a fair and reasonable tariff, encompassing costs of operation, taxes, amortizations, and a reasonable return on investments, but excluding altogether financial costs. It is further asserted that no guarantees were offered in respect of convertibility and currency devaluation and the risk inherent to the investment in these respects was expressly brought to the attention of the company.

92. The Respondent is of the view that any consequences arising from CMS's decision to rely on the report of private consultants for its investment strategies cannot be assigned to the Government. That report was not made by the Government and all responsibility for its contents was the subject of an express disclaimer.

93. The Respondent argues in addition that, under the Gas Law, transportation and distribution of gas is a national public service which must take into account particular needs of social importance. To this end, the Government is under an obligation to ensure the efficient operation of the service and must control the implementation of the contract, including the alternative of amendment or unilateral termination. Thus, the regulation of tariffs is a discretionary power of the Government insofar as it must take social and other public considerations into account.

94. In the Respondent's view, it follows that no commitments could have been made by the Government to maintain a certain economic or exchange rate policy and that the State is free to change such policies, a right which cannot be subject to claims by individuals or corporations. In this respect, the argument follows, CMS could not have ignored the public law of Argentina and the risks involved in investing in that country.

95. In this context, it is further asserted, tariffs must ensure to consumers the minimum cost compatible with the certainty of supply, as long as the provision of the service is efficient. Because Argentina was characterized by an unstable economy, the tariffs took into account the added risk of investing in that country and were therefore higher than would normally have been the case. As a result profits were also higher.

* * *

97. As a result of the above considerations, the Respondent argues that there has been no violation of the commitments made, explaining that the loss of value of CMS's shares is the result of recession and deflation, of a major social and economic crisis and the currency devaluation that followed. This devaluation, it is asserted, had already occurred in other important international financial markets. All the measures adopted by the Government, it is further argued, were needed for the normalization of the country and the continuous operation of public services. Had tariffs been adjusted by 300% as CMS would have wanted, public services would have been paralyzed, the income of licensees would have dramatically decreased and public reaction would have been beyond control.

98. The Respondent further explains that, in this legal and regulatory context, there could be no violation of the Treaty and objects, in that regard, particularly to the legal claims of CMS. In the Respondent's view, none of the requirements under international law of indirect expropriation are met. The guarantees invoked by CMS are not the property of the company protected under the Treaty and TGN continues to operate normally. Nor was there a violation of the standard of fair and equitable treatment, or a case of arbitrariness or discrimination. The umbrella clause of the Treaty, the argument follows, cannot be invoked as no obligations were undertaken by Argentina in respect of CMS, only in respect

of TGN, and the latter has not made any claim for contractual violation under the License.

99. In the alternative, the Republic of Argentina has invoked national emergency, brought about by the above-mentioned economic and social crisis, as grounds for exemption of liability under international law and the Treaty.

* * *

11. APPLICABLE LAW: THE TRIBUNAL'S FINDINGS

115. Much discussion has surrounded the meaning of Article 42(1) of the Convention[2] and the interpretations have ranged from a restricted application of international law in a complementary or corrective role, to be relied upon only in case of domestic *lacunae* or where the law of the Contracting State is inconsistent with international law, to a role that calls for the application of international law only to safeguard principles of *jus cogens*.

116. More recently, however, a more pragmatic and less doctrinaire approach has emerged, allowing for the application of both domestic law and international law if the specific facts of the dispute so justifies. It is no longer the case of one prevailing over the other and excluding it altogether. Rather, both sources have a role to play. The Annulment Committee in *Wenci v. Egypt* held in this respect:

> "Some of these views have in common the fact that they are aimed at restricting the role of international law and highlighting that of the law of the host State. Conversely, the view that calls for a broad application of international law aims at restricting the role of the law of the host State. There seems not to be a single answer as to which of these approaches is the correct one. The circumstances of each case may justify one or another solution * * * What is clear is that the sense and meaning of the negotiations leading to the second sentence of Article 42(1) allowed for both legal orders to have a role. The law of the host State can indeed be applied in conjunction with international law if this is justified. So too international law can be applied by itself if the appropriate rule is found in this other ambit."

117. This is the approach this Tribunal considers justified when taking the facts of the case and the arguments of the parties into account. Indeed, there is here a close interaction between the legislation and the regulations governing the gas privatization, the License and international

---

[2] Authors' Note: Article 42(1) of the ICSID Convention provides: The Tribunal shall decide a dispute in accordance with such rules of law as may be agreed by the parties. In the absence of such agreement, the Tribunal shall apply the law of the Contracting State party to the dispute (including its rules on the conflict of laws) and such rules of international law as may be applicable.

law, as embodied both in the Treaty and in customary international law. All of these rules are inseparable and will, to the extent justified, be applied by the Tribunal.

118. It is also necessary to note that the parties themselves, in spite of their doctrinal differences, have in fact invoked the role of both legal orders. The Republic of Argentina relies for its arguments heavily on provisions of domestic law, but also resorts to international law, for example in respect of treaty clauses on national security and customary law on state of necessity and other matters. Similarly, the Claimant invokes provisions of domestic law, regulations and the License to explain the rights TGN has under these instruments and the measures affecting them. But also the Claimant invokes Treaty guarantees and customary law on various issues.

* * *

16. WAS THE ECONOMIC BALANCE OF THE LICENSE ALTERED IN LIGHT OF CHANGING REALITIES?

152. While the legal meaning of the governing legal framework and the License is quite straightforward and granted rights that are now invoked by the Claimant, the reality of the Argentine economy is more difficult to assess. It may be recalled that the privatization program was conceived to overcome the crisis of the late 1980's. This crisis was characterized by hyper inflation, the inefficient operation of many publicly-owned companies, including those responsible for public utilities, and a dramatic shortage of investments. The privatization program was very successful but the late 1990's witnessed the emergence of another major crisis.

153. This crisis will be discussed further below, but it should be mentioned at this point that it stemmed basically from economic conditions that made it impossible to maintain the fixed exchange rate and which gradually led to the greatest default on foreign debt in history and the collapse of the Argentine financial markets. Some tend to fault foreign investors and put the blame on excessive privatization and globalization, while others see in it the result of not having carried out the liberalization program in its entirety and having allowed major governmental interferences in the functioning of the economy.

154. Justice, however, is not as blind as it is often thought and this Tribunal acknowledges that changing realities had an impact on the operation of the industry and the governing legal and contractual arrangements.

* * *

165. The question for the Tribunal is then how does one weigh the significance of a legal guarantee in the context of a collapsing economic situa-

tion. It is certainly not an option to ignore the guarantee, as the Respondent has advocated and done, but neither is it an option to disregard the economic reality which underpinned the operation of the industry.

* * *

24. HAS THERE BEEN EXPROPRIATION OF THE INVESTMENT?

252. Having established that the Respondent did not keep the commitments and obligations it had undertaken under its own legislation, regulations and the Licence to TGN, the question is then what is the legal situation in terms of the protection granted by the Treaty to the investor.

253. The Claimant's first major allegation in this respect is that there has been an expropriation in breach of the express provision of Article IV(1) of the Treaty. This Article provides as follows:

> "Investments shall not be expropriated or nationalized either directly or indirectly through measures tantamount to expropriation or nationalization ('expropriation') except for a public purpose; in a nondiscriminatory manner; upon payment of prompt, adequate and effective compensation; and in accordance with due process of law and the general principles of treatment provided for in Article II (2)."

* * *

260. The Tribunal has examined with great attention the views expounded by the parties on the issue. Both parties are in agreement that no direct expropriation has taken place. The issue for the Tribunal to determine is then whether the measures adopted constitute an indirect or regulatory expropriation. The answer is of course not quite simple for indeed the measures have an important effect on the business of the Claimant.

261. The Tribunal in the *Lauder* case rightly explained that

> "The concept of indirect (or "*de facto*", or "*creeping*") expropriation is not clearly defined. Indirect expropriation or nationalization is a measure that does not involve an overt taking, but that effectively neutralized the enjoyment of the property."

262. The essential question is therefore to establish whether the enjoyment of the property has been effectively neutralized. The standard that a number of tribunals have applied in recent cases where indirect expropriation has been contended is that of substantial deprivation. In the *Metalclad* case the tribunal held that this kind of expropriation relates to incidental interference with the use of property which has "the effect of depriving the owner, in whole or in significant part, of the use or reasonable-to-be-expected economic benefit of property even if not necessarily to the obvious benefit of the host State." Similarly, the Iran–United States Claims Tribunal has held that deprivation must affect "fundamental

rights of ownership," a criteria reaffirmed in the *CME v. Czech Republic* case. The test of interference with present uses and prevention of the realization of a reasonable return on investments has also been discussed by the Respondent in this context.

263. Substantial deprivation was addressed in detail by the tribunal in the *Pope & Talbot* case. The Government of Argentina has convincingly argued that the list of issues to be taken into account for reaching a determination on substantial deprivation, as discussed in that case, is not present in the instant dispute. In fact, the Respondent has explained, the investor is in control of the investment; the Government does not manage the day-to-day operations of the company; and the investor has full ownership and control of the investment.

264. The Tribunal is persuaded that this is indeed the case in this dispute and holds therefore that the Government of Argentina has not breached the standard of protection laid down in Article IV(1) of the Treaty.

265. It remains necessary to examine the extent of the interference caused by the measures on the Claimant's business operations under the other standards of the Treaty. This question will be addressed next by the Tribunal.

25. HAS THERE BEEN A BREACH OF FAIR AND EQUITABLE TREATMENT?

266. The second substantive standard of protection provided to investors under the Treaty is that of fair and equitable treatment. Article II(2)(a) provides:

> "Investment shall at all times be accorded fair and equitable treatment, shall enjoy full protection and security and shall in no case be accorded treatment less than that required by international law."

267. Under this provision, the Claimant asserts that Argentina has breached the fair and equitable treatment standard and has not ensured full protection and security to the investment, particularly insofar as it has profoundly altered the stability and predictability of the investment environment, an assurance that was key to its decision to invest. The Claimant cites a number of distinguished writers and decisions pointing out the significance of this particular requirement, with particular reference to the CME case, where it was held that

> "[The Government] breached its obligation of fair and equitable treatment by evisceration of the arrangements in reliance upon [which] the foreign investor was induced to invest."

268. The Claimant also relies on the following finding of the tribunal in the *Técnicas Medioambientales Tecmed, S.A. v. Mexico* case to the effect that fair and equitable treatment:

" * * * requires the Contracting Parties to provide to international investments treatment that does not affect the basic expectations that were taken into account by the foreign investor to make the investment * * * "

269. According to the Claimant's argument, the uncertainty characterizing the period 2000–2002 and the final determinations under the Emergency Law that dismantled all the arrangements in reliance on which the investment had been made, are the main events that resulted in the breach of this standard.

270. In the Respondent's view, the standard of fair and equitable treatment is too vague to allow for any clear identification of its meaning and, in any event, it only provides for a general and basic principle found in the law of the host State which at the same time is compatible with an international minimum standard. A deliberate intention to ignore an obligation or even bad faith would be required to breach the standard, the argument adds.

* * *

273. The key issue that the Tribunal has to decide is whether the measures adopted in 2000–2002 breached the standard of protection afforded by Argentina's undertaking to provide fair and equitable treatment. The Treaty, like most bilateral investment treaties, does not define the standard of fair and equitable treatment and to this extent Argentina's concern about it being somewhat vague is not entirely without merit.

274. The Treaty Preamble makes it clear, however, that one principal objective of the protection envisaged is that fair and equitable treatment is desirable "to maintain a stable framework for investments and maximum effective use of economic resources." There can be no doubt, therefore, that a stable legal and business environment is an essential element of fair and equitable treatment.

275. The measures that are complained of did in fact entirely transform and alter the legal and business environment under which the investment was decided and made. The discussion above, about the tariff regime and its relationship with a dollar standard and adjustment mechanisms unequivocally shows that these elements are no longer present in the regime governing the business operations of the Claimant. It has also been established that the guarantees given in this connection under the legal framework and its various components were crucial for the investment decision.

276. In addition to the specific terms of the Treaty, the significant number of treaties, both bilateral and multilateral, that have dealt with this standard also unequivocally shows that fair and equitable treatment is

inseparable from stability and predictability. Many arbitral decisions and scholarly writings point in the same direction.

* * *

281. The Tribunal, therefore, concludes against the background of the present dispute that the measures adopted resulted in the objective breach of the standard laid down in Article II(2)(a) of the Treaty.

* * *

26. HAS THERE BEEN ARBITRARINESS AND/OR DISCRIMINATION?

285. Article II(2)(b) of the Treaty provides that

"Neither Party shall in any way impair by arbitrary or discriminatory measures the management, operation, maintenance, use, enjoyment, acquisition, expansion, or disposal of investments."

286. The Claimant invokes the test defined in the *Pope and Talbot* case, and asserts that because the measures adopted are opposed to the rule of law or surprise a sense of judicial propriety, it follows that there has been arbitrary treatment of the investor and hence the Treaty standard has been breached. In the Claimant's view, dismantling the whole legal framework of the gas industry is contrary to any reasonable expectation.

* * *

290. The standard of protection against arbitrariness and discrimination is related to that of fair and equitable treatment. Any measure that might involve arbitrariness or discrimination is in itself contrary to fair and equitable treatment. The standard is next related to impairment: the management, operation, maintenance, use, enjoyment, acquisition, expansion, or disposal of the investment must be impaired by the measures adopted.

291. In the *Lauder* case, an equivalent provision of the pertinent investment treaty was explained in accordance with the definition of "arbitrary" in Black's Law Dictionary, which states that an arbitrary decision is one "depending on individual discretion; * * * founded on prejudice or preference rather than on reason or fact."

292. This Tribunal is not persuaded by the Claimant's view about arbitrariness because there has been no impairment, for example, in respect of the management and operation of the investment. Admittedly, some adverse effects can be noted in respect of other matters, such as the use, expansion or disposal of the investment, which since the measures were adopted have been greatly limited. To the extent that such effects might endure, the test applied in the *Lauder* case becomes relevant and could result in a factor reinforcing the related finding of a breach of fair and equitable treatment.

293. The situation in respect of discrimination is somewhat similar. The Respondent's argument about discrimination existing only in similarly situated groups or categories of people is correct, and no discrimination can be discerned in this respect. Admittedly, it is quite difficult to establish whether that similarity exists only in the context of the gas transportation and distribution industry or extends to other utilities as well.

294. Be that as it may, the fact is that to the extent that the measures persisted beyond the crisis, the differentiation between various categories or groups of businesses becomes more difficult to explain. Indeed, the Government of Argentina has successfully concluded renegotiations and other arrangements with a number of industries and businesses equally protected by guarantees of investment treaties. This includes the gas producers, but not the transportation and distribution side of the industry. The gas producers have been allowed to proceed to a gradual tariff adjustment to be completed by mid-2005. The longer the differentiation is kept the more evident the issue becomes, thus eventually again reinforcing the related finding about the breach of fair and equitable treatment.

295. The Tribunal, therefore, cannot hold that arbitrariness and discrimination are present in the context of the crisis noted, and to the extent that some effects become evident they will relate rather to the breach of fair and equitable treatment than to the breach of separate standards under the Treaty.

* * *

31.   THE EMERGENCY CLAUSE OF THE TREATY

332. The discussion on necessity and emergency is not confined to customary international law as there are also specific provisions of the Treaty dealing with this matter. Article XI of the Treaty provides:

> "This Treaty shall not preclude the application by either Party of measures necessary for the maintenance of public order, the fulfillment of its obligations with respect to the maintenance or restoration of international peace or security, or the protection of its own essential security interests."

333. Article IV(3) of the Treaty reads as follows:

> "Nationals or companies of either Party whose investments suffer losses in the territory of the other Party owing to war or other armed conflict, revolution, state of national emergency, insurrection, civil disturbance or other similar events shall be accorded treatment by such other Party no less favorable than that accorded to its own nationals or companies or to nationals or companies of any third country, whichever is the more favorable treatment, as regards any measures it adopts in relation to such losses."

* * *

34. THE TRIBUNAL'S FINDINGS IN RESPECT OF THE TREATY'S CLAUSES ON EMERGENCY

353. The first issue the Tribunal must determine is whether the object and purpose of the Treaty exclude necessity. There are of course treaties designed to be applied precisely in the case of necessity or emergency, such as those setting out humanitarian rules for situations of armed conflict. In those cases, as rightly explained in the Commentary to Article 25 of the Articles on State Responsibility, the plea of necessity is excluded by the very object and purpose of the treaty.

354. The Treaty in this case is clearly designed to protect investments at a time of economic difficulties or other circumstances leading to the adoption of adverse measures by the Government. The question is, however, how grave these economic difficulties might be. A severe crisis cannot necessarily be equated with a situation of total collapse. And in the absence of such profoundly serious conditions it is plainly clear that the Treaty will prevail over any plea of necessity. However, if such difficulties, without being catastrophic in and of themselves, nevertheless invite catastrophic conditions in terms of disruption and disintegration of society, or are likely to lead to a total breakdown of the economy, emergency and necessity might acquire a different meaning.

355. As stated above, the Tribunal is convinced that the Argentine crisis was severe but did not result in total economic and social collapse. When the Argentine crisis is compared to other contemporary crises affecting countries in different regions of the world it may be noted that such other crises have not led to the derogation of international contractual or treaty obligations. Renegotiation, adaptation and postponement have occurred but the essence of the international obligations has been kept intact.

356. As explained above, while the crisis in and of itself might not be characterized as catastrophic and while there was therefore not a situation of *force majeure* that left no other option open, neither can it be held that the crisis was of no consequence and that business could have continued as usual, as some of the Claimant's arguments seem to suggest. Just as the Tribunal concluded when the situation under domestic law was considered, there were certain consequences stemming from the crisis. And while not excusing liability or precluding wrongfulness from the legal point of view they ought nevertheless to be considered by the Tribunal when determining compensation.

357. A second issue the Tribunal must determine is whether, as discussed in the context of Article 25 of the Articles on State Responsibility, the act in question does not seriously impair an essential interest of the State or States towards which the obligation exists. If the Treaty was made to pro-

tect investors it must be assumed that this is an important interest of the States parties. Whether it is an essential interest is difficult to say, particularly at a time when this interest appears occasionally to be dwindling.

358. However, be that as it may, the fact is that this particular kind of treaty is also of interest to investors as they are specific beneficiaries and for investors the matter is indeed essential. For the purpose of this case, and looking at the Treaty just in the context of its States parties, the Tribunal concludes that it does not appear that an essential interest of the State to which the obligation exists has been impaired, nor have those of the international community as a whole. Accordingly, the plea of necessity would not be precluded on this count.

359. The third issue the Tribunal must determine is whether Article XI of the Treaty can be interpreted in such a way as to provide that it includes economic emergency as an essential security interest. While the text of the Article does not refer to economic crises or difficulties of that particular kind, as concluded above, there is nothing in the context of customary international law or the object and purpose of the Treaty that could on its own exclude major economic crises from the scope of Article XI.

360. It must also be kept in mind that the scope of a given bilateral treaty, such as this, should normally be understood and interpreted as attending to the concerns of both parties. If the concept of essential security interests were to be limited to immediate political and national security concerns, particularly of an international character, and were to exclude other interests, for example, major economic emergencies, it could well result in an unbalanced understanding of Article XI. Such an approach would not be entirely consistent with the rules governing the interpretation of treaties.

361. Again, the issue is then to establish how grave an economic crisis must be so as to qualify as an essential security interest, a matter discussed above.

* * *

366. The fourth issue the Tribunal must determine is whether the rule of Article XI of the Treaty is self-judging, that is if the State adopting the measures in question is the sole arbiter of the scope and application of that rule, or whether the invocation of necessity, emergency or other essential security interests is subject to some form of judicial review.

* * *

370. The Tribunal is convinced that when States intend to create for themselves a right to determine unilaterally the legitimacy of extraordinary measures importing non-compliance with obligations assumed in a

treaty, they do so expressly. The examples of the GATT and bilateral investment treaty provisions offered above are eloquent examples of this approach. The first does not preclude measures adopted by a party "which it considers necessary" for the protection of its security interests. So too, the U.S.–Russia treaty expressly confirms in a Protocol that the non-precluded measures clause is self-judging.

371. The International Court of Justice has also taken a clear stand in respect of this issue, twice in connection with the *Nicaragua* case and again in the *Oil Platforms* case noted above. * * *

372. As explained above, in the *Gabcikovo–Nagymaros* case the International Court of Justice, referring to the work and views of the International Law Commission, notes the strict and cumulative conditions of necessity under international law and that "the State concerned is not the sole judge of whether those conditions have been met."

373. In light of this discussion, the Tribunal concludes first that the clause of Article XI of the Treaty is not a self-judging clause. Quite evidently, in the context of what a State believes to be an emergency, it will most certainly adopt the measures it considers appropriate without requesting the views of any court. However, if the legitimacy of such measures is challenged before an international tribunal, it is not for the State in question but for the international jurisdiction to determine whether the plea of necessity may exclude wrongfulness. It must also be noted that clauses dealing with investments and commerce do not generally affect security as much as military events do and, therefore, would normally fall outside the scope of such dramatic events.

374. The Tribunal must conclude next that this judicial review is not limited to an examination of whether the plea has been invoked or the measures have been taken in good faith. It is a substantive review that must examine whether the state of necessity or emergency meets the conditions laid down by customary international law and the treaty provisions and whether it thus is or is not able to preclude wrongfulness.

* * *

376. As noted above, the Tribunal is satisfied that the measures adopted by the Respondent have not adversely discriminated against the Claimant.

* * *

378. The Tribunal must finally conclude in this section that the umbrella clauses invoked by the Claimant do not add anything different to the overall Treaty obligations which the Respondent must meet if the plea of necessity fails.

* * *

38. THE STANDARDS OF REPARATION UNDER INTERNATIONAL LAW

399. It is broadly accepted in international law that there are three main standards of reparation for injury: restitution, compensation and satisfaction. As this is not a case of reparation due to an injured State, satisfaction can be ruled out at the outset.

400. Restitution is the standard used to reestablish the situation which existed before the wrongful act was committed, provided this is not materially impossible and does not result in a burden out of proportion as compared to compensation. The Permanent Court of International Justice concluded in the landmark *Chorzow Factory* case that

> "restitution in kind, or, if this is not possible, payment of a sum corresponding to the value which a restitution in kind would bear; the award, if need be, of damages for loss sustained which would not be covered by restitution in kind or payment in place of it—such are the principles which should serve to determine the amount of compensation due for an act contrary to international law."

* * *

402. The loss suffered by the claimant is the general standard commonly used in international law in respect of injury to property, including often capital value, loss of profits and expenses. The methods to provide compensation, a number of which the parties have discussed, are not unknown in international law. Depending on the circumstances, various methods have been used by tribunals to determine the compensation which should be paid but the general concept upon which commercial valuation of assets is based is that of "fair market value." That concept has an internationally recognized definition which reads as follows:

> "the price, expressed in terms of cash equivalents, at which property would change hands between a hypothetical willing and able buyer and a hypothetical willing and able seller, acting at arms length in an open and unrestricted market, when neither is under compulsion to buy or sell and when both have reasonable knowledge of the relevant facts."

403. In the case of a business asset which is quoted on a public market, that process can be a fairly easy one, since the price of the shares is determined under conditions meeting the above mentioned definition. However, it happens frequently that the assets in question are not publicly traded and it is then necessary to find other methods to establish fair market value. Four ways have generally been relied upon to arrive at such value. (1) The "asset value" or the "replacement cost" approach which evaluates the assets on the basis of their "break-up" or their re-

placement cost; (2) the "comparable transaction" approach which reviews comparable transactions in similar circumstances; (3) the "option" approach which studies the alternative uses which could be made of the assets in question, and their costs and benefits; (4) the "discounted cash flow" ("DCF") approach under which the valuation of the assets is arrived at by determining the present value of future predicted cash flows, discounted at a rate which reflects various categories of risk and uncertainty. The Tribunal will determine later which method it has chosen and why.

* * *

43. THE VALUATION OF DAMAGES

418. This leaves the Tribunal with the assessment of the damages claimed. In this task, the Tribunal was greatly helped by the submissions and the testimonies of the experts produced by the Parties in this case. As will be seen below, the Tribunal however is of the view that certain assumptions and arguments of those experts require some adjustments. In its study of those submissions and testimonies, the Tribunal was ably assisted by its own experts, Professors Jacques Fortin and Alix Mandron of the Ecole des Hautes Etudes Commerciales de Montreal. The Parties were informed of their appointment and given an opportunity to comment on their analysis of the parties' expert submissions. Those comments were the subject of careful review by the Tribunal. The Tribunal wishes to express its gratitude to all the experts for their contribution.

* * *

[The Tribunal extensively discussed various valuation methods, chose one and applied it to the present case.]

NOW THEREFORE THE ARBITRAL TRIBUNAL DECIDES AND AWARDS AS FOLLOWS:

1. The Respondent breached its obligations to accord the investor the fair and equitable treatment guaranteed in Article II (2) (a) of the Treaty and to observe the obligations entered into with regard to the investment guaranteed in Article II (2) (c) of the Treaty.

2. The Respondent shall pay the Claimant compensation in the amount of US$ 133.2 million.

3. Upon payment of the compensation decided in this Award, the Claimant shall transfer to the Respondent the ownership of its shares in TGN upon payment by the Respondent of the additional sum of US$ 2,148,100. The Respondent shall have up to one year after the date this Award is dispatched to the parties to accept such transfer.

4. The Respondent shall pay the Claimant simple interest at the annualized average rate of 2.51% of the United States Treasury Bills for the period August 18, 2000 to 60 days after the date of this Award, or the date of effective payment if before, applicable to both the value loss suffered by the Claimant and the residual value of its shares established in 2 and 3 above. * * *

5. Each party shall pay one half of the arbitration costs and bear its own legal costs.

6. All other claims are herewith dismissed.

––––––––––––

Is the outcome of the case a victory for CMS? For Argentina? Arbitral tribunals are often criticized for simply "splitting the baby" in their awards so that both parties can claim victory; is that true here?

Following the award, Argentina filed an annulment application on the grounds that (1) the Tribunal had manifestly exceeded its authority on a number of issues, (2) CMS did not have standing to bring its claim, and (3) the tribunal had inadequately explained its findings. The Annulment Committee (see Chapter VII of the ICSID Convention for the rules applicable to the annulment process and the grounds for annulment) criticized the Tribunal's findings in a number of areas but noted that it did not have jurisdiction to reverse most of the findings of the Tribunal. Nevertheless, the Committee set aside the Award with respect to the Argentinean violations of the umbrella clause of the BIT, although this did not impact the amount of the Tribunal's award.

The CMS arbitration and the dozens of other international arbitrations that resulted from Argentina's economic meltdown in 2001–2002 initiated a wave of legal developments that challenged prior assumptions about both the utility of BITs (and the investment chapters of Free Trade Agreements) as well as arbitration awards that emanate from those investment treaties.

These treaties were based on the assumption that they would bolster foreign direct investment, bring comfort to investors by providing a neutral forum to vindicate their rights directly against sovereign states and, ultimately, develop a larger body of international law upon which private parties could rely. These assumptions have come under sharp challenge. For example, as of the spring of 2013, Argentina had not paid a single arbitration award (ICSID or otherwise) issued against it arising out of the Argentine economic crisis of 2001–2002. Moreover, Bolivia, Ecuador and Venezuela have withdrawn from ICSID, and some Latin American countries have repudiated certain BITs.

If Argentina's current stance with respect to arbitration awards continues, it will never pay any award issued against it. Thus, the very premise of investment protection treaties—that aggrieved private investors will be afforded compensation in a timely manner—is now being challenged by a major debtor state.

So where does this take us? What can be done to ensure, within the existing system of international law, that investor rights will be protected by the sovereign states that ratify investment protection treaties? Would more powerful enforcement mechanisms for arbitration awards provide more certainty of result? Are there mechanisms that can be built into the international arbitration system that would provide greater certainty so that arbitration awards will be viewed as more valid and therefore respected? For example, some commentators advocate an appellate mechanism to review arbitral awards. Would such a mechanism be helpful or simply create more delays? Or is the problem deeper because the entire BIT system is somehow biased against less-developed states?

Below is an example of one of the options available to push states like Argentina to fulfill their international obligations. What does this proclamation by President Obama accomplish? Does this approach take us back to the classic (Westphalian) mechanisms of state-to-state dispute resolution?

PRESIDENTIAL PROCLAMATION—TO MODIFY DUTY–FREE TREATMENT UNDER THE GENERALIZED SYSTEM OF PREFERENCES AND FOR OTHER PURPOSES

Presidential Proclamation No. 8788
77 Fed. Reg. 18,899 (March 26, 2012)

1. Section 502(b)(2)(E) of the Trade Act of 1974, as amended (the "1974 Act") (19 U.S.C. 2462(b)(2)(E)), provides that the President shall not designate any country a beneficiary developing country under the Generalized System of Preferences (GSP) if such country fails to act in good faith in recognizing as binding or in enforcing arbitral awards in favor of United States citizens or a corporation, partnership, or association that is 50 percent or more beneficially owned by United States citizens, which have been made by arbitrators appointed for each case or by permanent arbitral bodies to which the parties involved have submitted their dispute. Section 502(d)(2) (19 U.S.C. 2462(d)(2)) provides that, after complying with the requirements of section 502(f)(2) (19 U.S.C. 2462(f)(2)), the President shall withdraw or suspend the designation of any country as a beneficiary developing country if, after such designation, the President determines that as the result of changed circumstances such country would be barred from designation as a beneficiary developing country under section 502(b)(2). Section 502(f)(2) requires the President to notify the Congress and the country concerned at least 60 days before terminating the coun-

try's designation as a beneficiary developing country for purposes of the GSP.

2. Having considered the factors set forth in section 502(b)(2)(E) of the 1974 Act, I have determined pursuant to section 502(d) that it is appropriate to suspend Argentina's designation as a GSP beneficiary developing country because it has not acted in good faith in enforcing arbitral awards in favor of United States citizens or a corporation, partnership, or association that is 50 percent or more beneficially owned by United States citizens, and I will so notify the Congress. In order to reflect the suspension of Argentina's status as a beneficiary developing country under the GSP, I have determined that it is appropriate to modify general note 4(a) of the Harmonized Tariff Schedule of the United States (HTS).

* * *

D. ARBITRATION ON ALL FRONTS: THE ALGIERS ACCORDS

Tribunals may be set up to resolve political crises among different kinds and various combinations of parties. The so-called Algiers Accords is an example of such an arrangement. These agreements created a special arbitral tribunal for claims between Iran and the United States and their respective businesses.

The Algiers Accords helped to end the Iranian Hostage Crisis in 1981. (We saw another aspect of this crisis in Chapter II.3.B. when we studied the ICJ decision in the *Case Concerning United States Diplomatic and Consular Staff in Tehran.*) The Accords consisted of two primary agreements: the Algiers Accords and the Claim Settlement Declaration. The Algiers Accords set forth the terms of the release of the American hostages. The Claim Settlement Declaration established the Iran–United States Claim Tribunal. It sits in The Hague and has decided claims worth billions of dollars since its creation. It is still active, although its business is winding down.

What do the United States and Iran commit themselves to in the agreements below? What do they commit their citizens to? On the U.S. side, who exactly is making the agreement?

THE DECLARATION OF THE GOVERNMENT OF THE DEMOCRATIC AND POPULAR REPUBLIC OF ALGERIA CONCERNING THE SETTLEMENT OF CLAIMS BY THE GOVERNMENT OF THE UNITED STATES OF AMERICA AND THE GOVERNMENT OF THE ISLAMIC REPUBLIC OF IRAN

75 Am. J. Int'l L. 422, 1 Iran–U.S. Cl. Trib. Rep. 9 (January 19, 1981).

The Government of the Democratic and Popular Republic of Algeria, having been requested by the Governments of the Islamic Republic of Iran and the United States of America to serve as an intermediary in seeking a mutually acceptable resolution of the crisis in their relations arising out of the detention of the 52 United States nationals in Iran, has consulted extensively with the two governments as to the commitments which each is willing to make in order to resolve the crisis within the framework of the four points stated in the resolution of November 2, 1980, of the Islamic Consultative Assembly of Iran. On the basis of formal adherences received from Iran and the United States, the Government of Algeria now declares that the following interdependent commitments have been made by the two governments:

General Principles

The undertakings reflected in this Declaration are based on the following general principles:

A. Within the framework of and pursuant to the provisions of the two Declarations of the Government of the Democratic and Popular Republic of Algeria, the United States will restore the financial position of Iran, in so far as possible, to that which existed prior to November 14, 1979. In this context, the United States commits itself to ensure the mobility and free transfer of all Iranian assets within its jurisdiction, as set forth in Paragraphs 4–9.

B. It is the purpose of both parties, within the framework of and pursuant to the provisions of the two Declarations of the Government of the Democratic and Popular Republic of Algeria, to terminate all litigation as between the Government of each party and the nationals of the other, and to bring about the settlement and termination of all such claims through binding arbitration. Through the procedures provided in the Declaration, relating to the Claims Settlement Agreement, the United States agrees to terminate all legal proceedings in United States courts involving claims of United States persons and institutions against Iran and its state enterprises, to nullify all attachments and judgments obtained therein, to prohibit all further litigation based on such claims, and to bring about the termination of such claims through binding arbitration.

* * *

POINT IV:
RETURN OF THE ASSETS OF THE FAMILY OF THE FORMER SHAH

12. Upon the making by the Government of Algeria of the certification described in Paragraph 3 above, the United States will freeze, and prohibit any transfer of, property and assets in the United States within the control of the estate of the former Shah or of any close relative of the former Shah served as a defendant in U.S. litigation brought by Iran to recover such property and assets as belonging to Iran. As to any such defendant, including the estate of the former Shah, the freeze order will remain in effect until such litigation is finally terminated. Violation of the freeze order shall be subject to the civil and criminal penalties prescribed by U.S. law.

* * *

15. As to any judgment of a U.S. court which calls for the transfer of any property or assets to Iran, the United States hereby guarantees the enforcement of the final judgment to the extent that the property or assets exist within the United States.

16. If any dispute arises between the parties as to whether the United States has fulfilled any obligation imposed upon it by Paragraphs 12–15, inclusive, Iran may submit the dispute to binding arbitration by the tribunal established by, and in accordance with the provisions of, the claims settlement agreement. If the tribunal determines that Iran has suffered a loss as a result of a failure by the United States to fulfill such obligation, it shall make an appropriate award in favor of Iran which may be enforced by Iran in the courts of any nation in accordance with its laws.

Settlement of Disputes

17. If any other dispute arises between the parties as to the interpretation or performance of any provision of this declaration, either party may submit the dispute to binding arbitration by the tribunal established by, and in accordance with the provisions of, the claims settlement agreement. Any decision of the tribunal with respect to such dispute, including any award of damages to compensate for a loss resulting from a breach of this declaration or the claims settlement agreement, may be enforced by the prevailing party in the courts of any nation in accordance with its laws.

Claims Settlement Declaration

The Government of the Democratic and Popular Republic of Algeria, on the basis of formal notice of adherence received from the Government of the Islamic Republic of Iran and the Government of the United States of

America, now declares that Iran and the United States have agreed as follows:

Article I

Iran and the United States will promote the settlement of the claims described in Article II by the parties directly concerned. Any such claims not settled within six months from the date of entry into force of this agreement shall be submitted to binding third-party arbitration in accordance with the terms of this agreement. The aforementioned six months' period may be extended once by three months at the request of either party.

Article II

1. An International Arbitral Tribunal (the Iran–United States Claims Tribunal) is hereby established for the purpose of deciding claims of nationals of the United States against Iran and claims of nationals of Iran against the United States, and any counterclaim which arises out of the same contract, transaction or occurrence that constitutes the subject matter of that national's claim, if such claims and counterclaims are outstanding on the date of this agreement, whether or not filed with any court, and arise out of debts, contracts (including transactions which are the subject of letters of credit or bank guarantees), expropriations or other measures affecting property rights, excluding claims described in Paragraph 11 of the Declaration of the Government of Algeria of January 19, 1981, and claims arising out of the actions of the United States in response to the conduct described in such paragraph, and excluding claims arising under a binding contract between the parties specifically providing that any disputes thereunder shall be within the sole jurisdiction of the competent Iranian courts in response to the Majlis position.

2. The Tribunal shall also have jurisdiction over official claims of the United States and Iran against each other arising out of contractual arrangements between them for the purchase and sale of goods and services.

3. The Tribunal shall have jurisdiction, as specified in Paragraphs 16–17 of the Declaration of the Government of Algeria of January 19, 1981, over any dispute as to the interpretation or performance of any provision of that declaration.

Article III

1. The Tribunal shall consist of nine members or such larger multiple of three as Iran and the United States may agree are necessary to conduct its business expeditiously. Within ninety days after the entry into force of this agreement, each government shall appoint one-third of the members. Within thirty days after their appointment, the members so appointed shall by mutual agreement select the remaining third of the

members and appoint one of the remaining third President of the Tribunal. Claims may be decided by the full Tribunal or by a panel of three members of the Tribunal as the President shall determine. Each such panel shall be composed by the President and shall consist of one member appointed by each of the three methods set forth above.

2. Members of the Tribunal shall be appointed and the Tribunal shall conduct its business in accordance with the arbitration rules of the United Nations Commission on International Trade Law (UNCITRAL) except to the extent modified by the parties or by the Tribunal to ensure that this agreement can be carried out. The UNCITRAL rules for appointing members of three-member Tribunals shall apply *mutatis mutandis* to the appointment of the Tribunal.

3. Claims of nationals of the United States and Iran that are within the scope of this agreement shall be presented to the Tribunal either by claimants themselves or, in the case of claims of less than $250,000, by the Government of such national.

4. No claim may be filed with the Tribunal more than one year after the entry into force of this agreement or six months after the date the President is appointed, whichever is later. These deadlines do not apply to the procedures contemplated by Paragraphs 16 and 17 of the Declaration of the Government of Algeria of January 19, 1981.

Article IV

1. All decisions and awards of the Tribunal shall be final and binding.

2. The President of the Tribunal shall certify, as prescribed in Paragraph 7 of the Declaration of the Government of Algeria of January 19, 1981, when all arbitral awards under this agreement have been satisfied.

3. Any award which the Tribunal may render against either government shall be enforceable against such government in the courts of any nation in accordance with its laws.

Article V

The Tribunal shall decide all cases on the basis of respect for law, applying such choice of law rules and principles of commercial and international law as the Tribunal determines to be applicable, taking into account relevant usages of the trade, contract provisions and changed circumstances.

Article VI

1. The seat of the Tribunal shall be The Hague, the Netherlands, or any other place agreed by Iran and the United States.

2. Each government shall designate an agent at the seat of the Tribunal to represent it to the Tribunal and to receive notices or other communi-

cations directed to it or to its nationals, agencies, instrumentalities, or entities in connection with proceedings before the Tribunal.

3. The expenses of the Tribunal shall be borne equally by the two governments.

4. Any question concerning the interpretation or application of this agreement shall be decided by the Tribunal upon the request of either Iran or the United States.

* * *

What is the effect of awards made under this regime?

In *Dames & Moore v. Regan*, 453 U.S. 654 (1981), a private party challenged the constitutionality of the Accords, arguing that the President lacked the authority to release funds to Iran and to transfer private rights of action from U.S. courts to the newly created Tribunal. In a unanimous decision that speaks above all to the extent of presidential powers under the U.S. Constitution, the Supreme Court upheld the Accords.

3. DISPUTE RESOLUTION IN THE WTO: ADJUDICATION OR ARBITRATION?

Beginning in 1947, international trade had operated under the GATT (General Agreement of Tariffs and Trade) with an unwieldy system of resolving disputes. When the WTO (World Trade Organization) was founded in 1995, one of the most important innovations was the establishment of a new (much more formalized) dispute resolution process.

Below, you will see the WTO's official description of this process (on its website at wto.org). The process is governed by the Understanding on Rules and Procedures Governing the Settlement of Disputes, which is Annex 2 of the WTO Agreement. The Understanding is essentially a code of procedure, detailing how disputes are initiated, processed, decided and enforced.

The point of our looking at the WTO dispute settlement process is not to study any of its details but to compare it with other forms of international dispute resolution. Is it more like litigation before the ICJ? Like international arbitration? To what extent have the member states of the WTO given up their sovereignty when it comes to settling trade disputes?

Here is how the WTO presented itself in late 2012.

UNDERSTANDING THE WTO:
SETTLING DISPUTES
(WTO Website, 2012)

A UNIQUE CONTRIBUTION

Dispute settlement is the central pillar of the multilateral trading system, and the WTO's unique contribution to the stability of the global economy. Without a means of settling disputes, the rules-based system would be less effective because the rules could not be enforced. The WTO's procedure underscores the rule of law, and it makes the trading system more secure and predictable. The system is based on clearly-defined rules, with timetables for completing a case. First rulings are made by a panel and endorsed (or rejected) by the WTO's full membership. Appeals based on points of law are possible.

However, the point is not to pass judgement. The priority is to settle disputes, through consultations if possible. By January 2008, only about 136 of the nearly 369 cases had reached the full panel process. Most of the rest have either been notified as settled "out of court" or remain in a prolonged consultation phase—some since 1995.

PRINCIPLES: EQUITABLE, FAST, EFFECTIVE, MUTUALLY ACCEPTABLE

Disputes in the WTO are essentially about broken promises. WTO members have agreed that if they believe fellow-members are violating trade rules, they will use the multilateral system of settling disputes instead of taking action unilaterally. That means abiding by the agreed procedures, and respecting judgements.

A dispute arises when one country adopts a trade policy measure or takes some action that one or more fellow-WTO members considers to be breaking the WTO agreements, or to be a failure to live up to obligations. A third group of countries can declare that they have an interest in the case and enjoy some rights.

A procedure for settling disputes existed under the old GATT, but it had no fixed timetables, rulings were easier to block, and many cases dragged on for a long time inconclusively. The Uruguay Round agreement introduced a more structured process with more clearly defined stages in the procedure. It introduced greater discipline for the length of time a case should take to be settled, with flexible deadlines set in various stages of the procedure. The agreement emphasizes that prompt settlement is essential if the WTO is to function effectively. It sets out in considerable detail the procedures and the timetable to be followed in resolving disputes. If a case runs its full course to a first ruling, it should not normally take more than about one year—15 months if the case is appealed. The agreed time limits are flexible, and if the case is considered urgent (e.g. if perishable goods are involved), it is accelerated as much as possible.

The Uruguay Round agreement also made it impossible for the country losing a case to block the adoption of the ruling. Under the previous GATT procedure, rulings could only be adopted by consensus, meaning that a single objection could block the ruling. Now, rulings are automatically adopted unless there is a consensus to reject a ruling—any country wanting to block a ruling has to persuade all other WTO members (including its adversary in the case) to share its view.

Although much of the procedure does resemble a court or tribunal, the preferred solution is for the countries concerned to discuss their problems and settle the dispute by themselves. The first stage is therefore consultations between the governments concerned, and even when the case has progressed to other stages, consultation and mediation are still always possible.

* * *

How are disputes settled?

Settling disputes is the responsibility of the Dispute Settlement Body (the General Council in another guise), which consists of all WTO members. The Dispute Settlement Body has the sole authority to establish "panels" of experts to consider the case, and to accept or reject the panels' findings or the results of an appeal. It monitors the implementation of the rulings and recommendations, and has the power to authorize retaliation when a country does not comply with a ruling.

- First stage: consultation (up to 60 days). Before taking any other actions the countries in dispute have to talk to each other to see if they can settle their differences by themselves. If that fails, they can also ask the WTO director-general to mediate or try to help in any other way.

- Second stage: the panel (up to 45 days for a panel to be appointed, plus 6 months for the panel to conclude). If consultations fail, the complaining country can ask for a panel to be appointed. The country "in the dock" can block the creation of a panel once, but when the Dispute Settlement Body meets for a second time, the appointment can no longer be blocked (unless there is a consensus against appointing the panel).

Officially, the panel is helping the Dispute Settlement Body make rulings or recommendations. But because the panel's report can only be rejected by consensus in the Dispute Settlement Body, its conclusions are difficult to overturn. The panel's findings have to be based on the agreements cited.

The panel's final report should normally be given to the parties to the dispute within six months. In cases of urgency, including those concerning perishable goods, the deadline is shortened to three months.

The agreement describes in some detail how the panels are to work. The main stages are:

- Before the first hearing: each side in the dispute presents its case in writing to the panel.

- First hearing: the case for the complaining country and defence: the complaining country (or countries), the responding country, and those that have announced they have an interest in the dispute, make their case at the panel's first hearing.

- Rebuttals: the countries involved submit written rebuttals and present oral arguments at the panel's second meeting.

- Experts: if one side raises scientific or other technical matters, the panel may consult experts or appoint an expert review group to prepare an advisory report.

- First draft: the panel submits the descriptive (factual and argument) sections of its report to the two sides, giving them two weeks to comment. This report does not include findings and conclusions.

- Interim report: The panel then submits an interim report, including its findings and conclusions, to the two sides, giving them one week to ask for a review.

- Review: The period of review must not exceed two weeks. During that time, the panel may hold additional meetings with the two sides.

- Final report: A final report is submitted to the two sides and three weeks later, it is circulated to all WTO members. If the panel decides that the disputed trade measure does break a WTO agreement or an obligation, it recommends that the measure be made to conform with WTO rules. The panel may suggest how this could be done.

- The report becomes a ruling: The report becomes the Dispute Settlement Body's ruling or recommendation within 60 days unless a consensus rejects it. Both sides can appeal the report (and in some cases both sides do).

APPEALS

Either side can appeal a panel's ruling. Sometimes both sides do so. Appeals have to be based on points of law such as legal interpretation—they cannot reexamine existing evidence or examine new issues.

Each appeal is heard by three members of a permanent seven-member Appellate Body set up by the Dispute Settlement Body and broadly representing the range of WTO membership. Members of the Appellate Body have four-year terms. They have to be individuals with recognized standing in the field of law and international trade, not affiliated with any government.

The appeal can uphold, modify or reverse the panel's legal findings and conclusions. Normally appeals should not last more than 60 days, with an absolute maximum of 90 days.

The Dispute Settlement Body has to accept or reject the appeals report within 30 days—and rejection is only possible by consensus.

THE CASE HAS BEEN DECIDED: WHAT NEXT?

Go directly to jail. Do not pass Go, do not collect. * * * Well, not exactly. But the sentiments apply. If a country has done something wrong, it should swiftly correct its fault. And if it continues to break an agreement, it should offer compensation or suffer a suitable penalty that has some bite.

Even once the case has been decided, there is more to do before trade sanctions (the conventional form of penalty) are imposed. The priority at this stage is for the losing "defendant" to bring its policy into line with the ruling or recommendations. The dispute settlement agreement stresses that "prompt compliance with recommendations or rulings of the DSB [Dispute Settlement Body] is essential in order to ensure effective resolution of disputes to the benefit of all Members."

If the country that is the target of the complaint loses, it must follow the recommendations of the panel report or the appeals report. It must state its intention to do so at a Dispute Settlement Body meeting held within 30 days of the report's adoption. If complying with the recommendation immediately proves impractical, the member will be given a "reasonable period of time" to do so. If it fails to act within this period, it has to enter into negotiations with the complaining country (or countries) in order to determine mutually-acceptable compensation—for instance, tariff reductions in areas of particular interest to the complaining side.

If after 20 days, no satisfactory compensation is agreed, the complaining side may ask the Dispute Settlement Body for permission to impose limited trade sanctions ("suspend concessions or obligations") against the other side. The Dispute Settlement Body must grant this authorization within 30 days of the expiry of the "reasonable period of time" unless there is a consensus against the request.

In principle, the sanctions should be imposed in the same sector as the dispute. If this is not practical or if it would not be effective, the sanctions can be imposed in a different sector of the same agreement. In turn, if this is not effective or practicable and if the circumstances are serious enough, the action can be taken under another agreement. The objective is to minimize the chances of actions spilling over into unrelated sectors while at the same time allowing the actions to be effective.

In any case, the Dispute Settlement Body monitors how adopted rulings are implemented. Any outstanding case remains on its agenda until the issue is resolved.

* * *

CASE STUDY: THE TIMETABLE IN PRACTICE

On 23 January 1995, Venezuela complained to the Dispute Settlement Body that the United States was applying rules that discriminated against gasoline imports, and formally requested consultations with the United States. Just over a year later (on 29 January 1996) the dispute panel completed its final report. (By then, Brazil had joined the case, lodging its own complaint in April 1996. The same panel considered both complaints.) The United States appealed. The Appellate Body completed its report, and the Dispute Settlement Body adopted the report on 20 May 1996, one year and four months after the complaint was first lodged.

The United States and Venezuela then took six and a half months to agree on what the United States should do. The agreed period for implementing the solution was 15 months from the date the appeal was concluded (20 May 1996 to 20 August 1997).

The case arose because the United States applied stricter rules on the chemical characteristics of imported gasoline than it did for domestically-refined gasoline. Venezuela (and later Brazil) said this was unfair because US gasoline did not have to meet the same standards—it violated the "national treatment" principle and could not be justified under exceptions to normal WTO rules for health and environmental conservation measures. The dispute panel agreed with Venezuela and Brazil. The appeal report upheld the panel's conclusions (making some changes to the panel's legal interpretation). The United States agreed with Venezuela that it would amend its regulations within 15 months and on 26 August 1997 it reported to the Dispute Settlement Body that a new regulation had been signed on 19 August.

* * *

_____

As a lawyer, what is your reaction to this process? How might your reaction differ if you were a politician or economist?

4. THE PROLIFERATION OF TRIBUNALS

Over the course of this chapter and throughout the casebook, we have encountered decisions from a wide array of international courts and tribunals. At this point, it would be worthwhile to take stock by compiling a list of them.

The following article by Thomas Buergenthal, the United States judge on the ICJ from 2000 to 2010, provides an overview of international courts and tribunals and poses some challenging questions. What are Buergenthal's primary concerns and hopes, in particular with regard to the tension between the growing multitude of tribunals and the unity of international law?

THOMAS BUERGENTHAL, PROLIFERATION OF INTERNATIONAL COURTS AND TRIBUNALS: IS IT GOOD OR BAD?

14 Leiden J. Int'l L. 267 (2001)

* * *

The topic of my talk today is: "Proliferation of International Courts and Tribunals: Is It Good or Bad?" Much has been written on the subject, so I am unlikely to say anything new or profound about it. I selected this topic because we are in fact witnessing such a proliferation. It has practical implications for students of international law and raises the question whether this proliferation is to be welcomed or to be regretted by those of us who are interested in seeing international law become a vibrant and politically relevant legal system in international relations. Moreover, even if one were to believe that there is nothing really wrong with the creation of an ever increasing number of international judicial institutions, one will still have to address questions relating to their interaction and how to delimit their respective roles. I shall attempt to deal with some of these questions.

For the moment, I will keep you in suspense and not tell you whether I believe that the proliferation of international courts is good or bad. Instead, I would first like to provide you with an inventory of existing international courts and tribunals. I will not attempt to be exhaustive, since the complete list is long and would put you all to sleep. I am offering this inventory to provide the context for my talk. It occurs to me, however, that it might also benefit the many law students in this audience who are no doubt thinking of their future careers in international law and wondering what jobs are available in the field. To you I can say, things certainly look much more promising career-wise than in my day—you are the real beneficiaries of the inflationary tendency as far as the creation of international tribunals is concerned.

As you know, besides the International Court of Justice ("ICJ"), we now have the following major international regional judicial and specialized tribunals: the International Tribunal for the Law of the Sea, the European Court of Human Rights, the Court of Justice of the European Union and its first-instance tribunal, and the Inter–American Court of Human Rights and its Commission, which is a quasi-judicial institution. The African Court of Human and Peoples' Rights is also in the process of coming into being. There also exists the Andean Court of Justice, designed to serve the Andean common market. It is modeled on its European counterpart but it is not very active. Equally inactive is the new Central American Court of Justice. Not to be forgotten are the *ad hoc* International Criminal Tribunals for the Former Yugoslavia and for Rwanda— they are really two separate courts with one appellate tribunal—and the Iran–United States Claims Tribunal. This *ad hoc* body has now been in existence for about 20 years, and will no doubt continue for some years to come. The two existing *ad hoc* international criminal courts will soon be followed by a permanent International Criminal Court. It will most likely come into existence in two to three years. In the meantime, an *ad hoc* criminal tribunal for Sierra Leone is in the making and there is talk of one for East Timor. Mention should also be made of the World Trade Organization's ("WTO") dispute settlement mechanism, which provides for the resolution of trade law disputes between member states of the WTO. A similar mechanism for the North American Free Trade Agreement ("NAFTA") also exists.

Not to be forgotten in making our inventory are the many international administrative tribunals in existence today. International administrative tribunals are established to enable employees of inter-governmental international organizations to sue their employers, which they could not do in national courts because these organizations are immune as a general rule from suit in domestic courts. These administrative tribunals have a very interesting jurisprudence that deserves more scholarly attention than it has received. * * *

The fact that leading international law practitioners and judges serve on these administrative tribunals contributes to the cross-fertilization of international jurisprudence and thus to the enrichment of international law in general. Let me emphasize, in this connection, that it is a mistake to assume that these tribunals deal only with narrow questions relating to the interpretation of employment contracts and pension rights. They do that too, but, in addition, they deal more and more with human rights issues, particularly due process of law questions and various forms of discrimination, whether it be racial, religious, or sexual, as well as with sexual harassment claims. I regard them therefore as specialized human rights tribunals whose jurisprudence deserves more attention from those interested in international human rights law.

There is yet another ever-expanding group of tribunals that belong on our inventory list of international judicial and quasi-judicial institutions. These are the various types of international arbitral tribunals. First, there are those that deal only with disputes involving private parties of different nationalities and frequently concern transnational commercial disputes. They are not inter-governmental or inter-state in character, and the law they apply is generally not public international law, but national law, private international law, and international commercial law.

At the other extreme are the types of *ad hoc* arbitration tribunals that are set up when two states have a dispute and decide to settle it by arbitration instead of going to an existing international court. Such *ad hoc* tribunals have a long history and for centuries were the only institutions that provided the world with international law jurisprudence. They continue to be established. Of course, as a theoretical matter, the Iran–United States Claims Tribunal probably falls into this category, as do the various mixed arbitral commissions that existed before and between the two World Wars. The United States and Mexico had such a body, and, if I remember correctly, it was in business even longer than the Iran–United States Claims Tribunal. There is of course also the Permanent Court of Arbitration ("PCA"), the grandparent of modern inter-state arbitration, which has its seat in The Hague. It is not a court as such and is permanent only in the sense that it has a permanent secretariat and a list of panels of arbitrators to which the parties to a dispute may resort when they agree to establish their arbitral tribunal. While initially set up to deal only with inter-state disputes, the PCA is today available as an arbitration facility that private parties and states may also utilize.

The third category of arbitral mechanisms consists of international arbitral institutions that provide dispute settlement facilities to states and private persons to resolve disputes between them. The modern prototype of such institutions, in addition to the PCA, is the International Centre for Settlement of Investment Disputes ("ICSID"), which is a World Bank institution. It was established by the 1965 International Convention on the Settlement of Investment Disputes between States and Nationals of Other States and has more than a hundred member states. As its name indicates, ICSID is the forum for the resolution of disputes between private investors and governments. The proliferation of so-called Bilateral Investment Treaties ("BITS"), which frequently confer dispute resolution jurisdiction on ICSID, has in recent years dramatically increased the ICSID caseload.

Here you should keep in mind that the law which applies to most of ICSID arbitrations and similar types of arbitrations is a mixture of public international law, private international law, and national law, with all three types of law relevant to the resolution of a particular dispute. Public international law tends to play an important role in these arbitrations because at least one party to the dispute is a state and because the outcome of some disputes turn on the interpretation of treaties. What you have here is confirmation to a certain extent of the thesis, which is gaining support among international lawyers, that the traditional dividing line between public and private international law, including international commercial and economic law, is gradually becoming less pronounced and relevant. This is the result, of course, of the fact that bilateral and multilateral treaties and conventions deal increasingly with subjects that regulate and facilitate private cross-boundary conduct and transnational commercial relations of all kinds. The entire process is driven by the globalization and privatization revolution. Globalization and privatization can function effectively only within a legal infrastructure consisting of an amalgam of different national and international laws and institutions in which the academic distinctions between international public and private law gradually lose significance. Whether one likes it or not, privatization and globalization are transforming the role and character of international law and, with it, the function of international dispute settlement mechanisms.

But ICSID and the PCA are not alone in providing arbitral facilities for the settlement of disputes between private parties and states. There are various private institutions, such as the London Court of International Arbitration ("LCIA") and the International Court of Arbitration of the International Chamber of Commerce ("ICC") in Paris, which also provide arbitral facilities for the adjudication of disputes between states and private parties, although most of their caseload consists of disputes between private parties only. The jurisdiction of these institutions to deal with disputes involving governments and private parties is based on arbitration clauses found in numerous international commercial agreements concluded by states and private commercial enterprises. The number of these agreements and the arbitrations giving rise to them are also increasing dramatically. What is particularly interesting, in this connection, is that a treaty drawn up under the auspices of the United Nations, the so-called New York Convention, which has now been ratified by more than a hundred countries, has proved to be an effective mechanism for the enforcement of international arbitral awards by the national courts of the states party to the New York Convention. This enforcement mechanism can be invoked by and against states and private parties.

What this by no means complete inventory of international judicial, quasi-judicial, and arbitral institutions and mechanisms suggests is that an increasing number of disputes involving states are dealt with by third-party adjudication of one form or another, traditional and non-traditional. As a consequence, international law plays an ever-increasing role in the resolution of such disputes, whether or not they are adjudicated or settled by negotiations. That is to say, the availability of these dispute-resolution mechanisms and institutions, even if they are not resorted to in a particular case, increases the role law plays in bilateral and multilateral negotiations. The more such institutions exist in the background, the more the law they apply provides the normative context for negotiated settlements. This law, of course, also influences the contents of international conventions, domestic legislation, and national jurisprudence applicable to international transactions and international relations.

Much more important is the very special effect that the existence and proliferation of these judicial, quasi-judicial, and arbitral institutions have on states. They socialize states, in my opinion, to the idea of international adjudication; that is, they tend to make states less reluctant of and more agreeable to the idea of settling their disputes by adjudication or arbitration. Put another way, the proliferation of international tribunals is both the consequence of and a major factor contributing to the acceptance by states of international adjudication, as a viable and effective option for the resolution of disputes between them. This phenomenon contributes, in turn, to the development and application of international law and its increased relevance in international relations. The proliferation of international tribunals with specialized and regional competence has in recent decades enabled governments to experiment with and observe the effects of international adjudication involving states and their acceptance of the jurisdiction of international tribunals. That is why I believe that in general the proliferation of international tribunals has been beneficial. It has contributed to the development of international law and increased its relevance to the conduct of contemporary international relations to a much greater extent than in the past, and that is certainly a welcome development.

It is clear, at the same time, that the proliferation of international tribunals can also have adverse consequences for the development of international law. A major risk, and one that is frequently noted by commentators, is that the jurisprudence of the different international tribunals can erode the unity of international law, lead to the development of conflicting or mutually exclusive legal doctrines, and thus eventually threaten the universality of international law.

Let me give you one example of the type of problems that are already beginning to emerge. Recently, the Inter–American Court of Human Rights rendered an Advisory Opinion in which it interpreted the scope of Article 36 of the Vienna Convention on Consular Relations, which deals with the right of consular officials of one state to communicate with and render assistance to their nationals detained or arrested in another State. The Court was asked to decline to comply with the request or delay acting on it because some of the same issues were raised in a contentious case pending before the International Court of Justice. That is the *LaGrand* case, brought by Germany against the United States, which will be heard by the ICJ in November. The Inter–American Court did not see the pending ICJ case as an obstacle to proceeding, and rendered a very extensive Advisory Opinion. It is, of course, impossible to say at this time whether the ICJ will in fact reach a conclusion different from that of the Inter–American Court, but such a conflict is theoretically possible. Similar conflicts can also arise, for example, between decisions of the ICJ and those of the International Criminal Tribunal for the Former Yugoslavia ("ICTY") or the Law of the Sea Tribunal. In fact, one such conflict involving the holding of the ICTY in the *Tadi* case and the Judgment of the ICJ in the *Nicaragua* case has already arisen.

I must say, I do not see the likelihood of these conflicts as major risks, at this time, to the unity of the international legal system, provided the various tribunals stay within their respective spheres of competence, apply traditional international legal reasoning, show judicial restraint by seeking to avoid unnecessary conflicts, and remain open to reconsider their prior legal pronouncements in order to take account of the case-law of other international courts. Such attitudes, if they become the *modus operandi* of international courts, would go a long way in recognizing that they are all part of the same legal system.

The Inter–American Court, for example, could substantially reduce the possibility of an irreconcilable conflict between its holding and a possible contrary judgment of the ICJ if it limited its interpretation of Article 36 of the Consular Convention to the context of the inter-American human rights system. It must be kept in mind, however, that if the ICJ were to reach a different conclusion regarding the obligations of states under the Vienna Consular Convention than the Inter–American Court, states parties to inter-American human rights instruments would be deemed to have different obligations among themselves under the Vienna Convention than vis-à-vis states not members of the inter-American system. This problem would not be serious as long as the Inter–American Court recognized that its interpretation of universal treaties would have to be reconsidered if it were to conflict with subsequent judgments of the ICJ. Unless regional and specialized courts adopt such a policy of judicial deference with regard to the interpretation of universal treaties, serious practical problems will arise for states. These, in turn, would detract from the legitimacy and efficacy of international judicial pronouncements in general, besides leading to unseemly forum shopping. The same deference would have to be shown by such tribunals with regard to ICJ pronouncements regarding the contents of specific customary international law principles or with determinations relating to the competence or authority of universal international organizations, where the ICJ may rightly be deemed to have the last word on the subject. Judicial deference must not be a one-way street, however. There will be situations where the ICJ will have to reconsider or modify some of its holdings to avoid conflicts with pronouncements of regional or specialized tribunals within their primary jurisdiction.

It is clear, of course, that conflicts cannot always be avoided and that they will arise as long as there does not exist within the international legal system a court with authority to render final decisions binding on all other courts within the system. No such court is likely to be established in the near future, nor is it realistic at this time to assume that the jurisdiction of the ICJ will be expanded to give it the same power that the Court of Justice of the European Union has and give such a court the power to render preliminary decisions interpreting treaties and customary international law.

Short of the existence of such institutional mechanisms, conflicts will arise. Here it is important for all international tribunals, the ICJ as well as the other specialized and regional courts, to recognize that they are all part of the same legal system and that this fact imposes certain obligations. Of these, the most basic one is the obligation to accept the methodological and doctrinal unity of the international legal system. This means, among other things, that each tribunal has an obligation to respect the general and special competence of the other judicial and quasi-judicial institutions which comprise the system, to recognize that it has an obligation, when rendering judgments, to take account of the case-law of other judicial institutions that have pronounced on the same subject and, most importantly, to promote and be open to jurisprudential interaction or cross-fertilization.

Let me illustrate what I mean by jurisprudential interaction. As you know, the European and Inter–American Human Rights Courts, but particularly the European Court, has very creatively expanded the international law concept of the exhaustion of domestic remedies doctrine. It seems to me that other international courts, including the ICJ cannot simply disregard this body of law, when they have to deal with exhaustion of domestic remedies issues. This does not mean that these courts need necessarily follow the precedents set by the European or Inter–American Courts, since some of the precedents may be appropriate only for human rights cases. But if other courts decide not to follow these precedents, they have an obligation, in my opinion, to distinguish these precedents, that is, to explain why they cannot or need not follow them, and do so by reference to generally accepted methods of international legal analysis and discourse. Not irrelevant, in this connection, is the regrettable tendency of some international tribunals to cite only their own decisions as if other courts did not exist. The ICJ is not the only culprit in this regard. I believe that this tendency is bad and needs to be reversed, if only because it sends the wrong message regarding the conceptual unity of the international legal system. The vitality and creativity of contemporary international law can be greatly enhanced, I believe, if international courts and judges recognize that they are part of the same legal system. This means, among other things, that they should look to the jurisprudence of their sister institutions as sources from which to draw judicial inspiration and not to view the other institutions as competitors to be treated with disdain or to act as if they did not exist.

Finally, it should be asked whether we should continue to support the establishment of more and more regional and specialised international tribunals. To me the answer depends on the needs of the international community. For example, there was a real need for a permanent international criminal court, and its establishment met that need. In the future, there may be a need for additional specialized courts. There certainly is a need for additional human rights courts in other regions of the world. In short, I do not see the problem as one of mere numbers, although I believe that there may come a time when the creation of too many specialized courts will gradually diminish the relevance of the ICJ and, with it, its capacity to contribute to the development of universal international law. This problem could of course be avoided if a way were found to relate such courts to the ICJ in a hierarchical relationship that would give the ICJ the final word on the subject, but this is not likely to happen soon. In the meantime, though, I do not believe that we have too many international courts and that they pose a serious threat to the international system.

Moreover, if I am right in believing that the proliferation of international judicial institutions has a socializing effect on states that leads to the ever greater acceptance by them of the jurisdiction and role of international tribunals, then it can be assumed that states will, in the future, be more willing to resort to the ICJ instead of creating more specialized tribunals to settle their disputes. The current increased caseload of the ICJ suggests that this development is beginning to take place. To take full advantage of it, the ICJ may have to reform or restructure its procedure and judicial *modus operandi,* but that is another topic. It is certainly not a topic that I, as the most junior in seniority member of the Court, dare to touch.

Buergenthal argues that a multitude of international tribunals have the advantage that they will "socialize states * * * to the idea of international adjudication." Doesn't that depend entirely on their experience, e.g., on whether they win or lose? As you will see in Chapter X, the reaction of the United States to losing two highly similar cases under the Vienna Convention on Consular Relations in the International Court of Justice was to withdraw from the Optional Protocol (to the Convention) that provided for ICJ jurisdiction. Note also that we would normally not expect private litigants to become more "agreeable to the idea of settling their disputes by adjudication" because they get sued more often. Is there any merit in Buergenthal's argument?

Another alleged advantage is the "cross fertilization" between the various tribunals. That is often considered an upside of a multitude of courts in a federal system. But in a federal system, we expect courts to take notice of, and cite, each others' decisions. As Buergenthal admits, however, international tribunals have a tendency to cite only their own cases. So how would such "cross-fertilization" occur? Think about how the SADC Tribunal in *Campbell et al. v. Zimbabwe* (Chapter IX.1.C.) used the decisions of other courts and tribunals.

One of the downsides is the risk of conflicting case law. Should that be a concern at all since none of these tribunal's decisions is binding on other tribunals and (as under Article 59 of the ICJ statute) often not even on the judgment-rendering court itself? In other words, who (except an academic) cares if the ICJ decides an issue one way while the International Tribunal for the Law of the Sea or the Court of Justice of the European Union decides it in another (as long as each tribunal stays within its jurisdictional limits)?

Buergenthal repeatedly invokes the "methodological and doctrinal" (or "conceptual") "unity of the international legal system," and he urges the various tribunals never to forget that "they are all part of the same legal system." Is the notion of such unity an old-fashioned, outdated and somewhat romantic idea? In light of the complexities of the modern global legal order, the multitude and variety of its actors (including tribunals), sources, and specialized areas, should we simply admit that the centrifugal force is predominant and that we have an increasingly decentralized system? Or is at least striving for "unity" still important? Why?

In the excerpt below, Anne-Marie Slaughter presents a different perspective on courts and judges in the current global environment. What is her main point? How does the picture she presents fit with Buergenthal's conception? Do the cases we have read to date in this course support or undermine her position?

ANNE–MARIE SLAUGHTER, A NEW WORLD ORDER

(2004)

* * *

Globalization is generally thought of in terms of corporations more than courts, global markets more than global justice. Yet judges around the world are talking to one another: exchanging opinions, meeting face to face in seminars and judicial organizations, and even negotiating with one another over the outcome of specific cases. The Federal Judicial Conference established a Committee on International Judicial Relations in

1993 to conduct a wide variety of exchanges and training programs with foreign courts. The U.S. Supreme Court has regular summits with its counterpart in the European Union, the ECJ; it has also visited the House of Lords, the German Federal Constitutional Court, the French Conseil d'Etat, the Indian Supreme Court, and the Mexican Supreme Court. Beyond the United States, to take only one recent example, the United Nations Environment Programme (UNEP) and the INECE—itself a regulators network—organized a Global Judges Symposium in conjunction with the UN Conference on Sustainable Development in Johannesburg. The symposium brought together over one hundred of the world's most senior judges from over eighty countries to discuss improving the adoption and implementation of environment-related laws.

One result of this judicial globalization is an increasingly global constitutional jurisprudence, in which courts are referring to each other's decisions on issues ranging from free speech to privacy rights to the death penalty. To cite a recent example from our own Supreme Court, Justice Stephen Breyer recently cited cases from Zimbabwe, India, South Africa, and Canada, most of which in turn cite one another. A Canadian constitutional court justice, noting this phenomenon, observes that unlike past legal borrowings across borders, judges are now engaged not in passive reception of foreign decisions, but in active and ongoing dialogue. She chides the United States Supreme Court for lagging behind, but in recent speeches Justices Sandra Day O'Connor and Stephen Breyer have urged American lawyers to know and cite more foreign and international law in their arguments and briefs to U.S. courts.

This growing judicial interaction is not only transnational. Judges are also forging relationships with their regional and international counterparts. Constitutional courts frequently cite the European Court of Human Rights alongside the decisions of foreign courts, not only within Europe but also around the world. Opportunities to build such "vertical" relationships can only increase; a wave of new international courts and tribunals has followed in the wake of economic globalization. For instance, both NAFTA and the Rome Statute establishing an international criminal court envision direct relationships between national and international tribunals. These relationships are likely to have important consequences far beyond the intentions of their creators. To take the most prominent example, the catalyst for the creation and implementation of the EU legal system was a set of relationships developed between the ECJ and lower national courts in EU member states, relationships largely unanticipated by the diplomats negotiating the Treaty of Rome.

Another set of examples of direct and at least quasi-autonomous judicial interaction comes from the realm of private litigation. In a breach-of-contract case in 1983, Lord Denning observed that he was faced with a situation in which "one [court] or another must give way. I wish that we could sit together to discuss it." Twenty years later courts are sitting together to discuss it, at least virtually. Judges are increasingly entering into various forms of "international judicial negotiation." In transnational bankruptcy disputes, for instance, national courts are concluding "Cross-Border Insolvency Cooperation Protocols," which are essentially mini treaties setting forth each side's role in resolving the dispute. More generally, at least in the United States, judges are beginning to develop a distinct doctrine of "judicial comity": a set of principles designed to guide courts in giving deference to foreign courts as a matter of respect owed judges by judges, rather than of the more general respect owed by one nation to another.

Taken together, these wide-ranging examples represent the gradual construction of a global legal system. It is a far different kind of system than has traditionally been envisaged by international lawyers. That vision has always assumed a global legal hierarchy, with a world supreme court such as the International Court of Justice resolving disputes between states and pronouncing on rules of international law that would then be applied by national courts around the world. What is in fact emerging is messier and much more complex. It is a system composed of both horizontal and vertical networks of national and international judges, usually arising from jurisdiction over a common area of the law or a particular region of the world. The judges who are participating in these networks are motivated not out of respect for international law per se, or even out of any conscious desire to build a global system. They are instead driven by a host of more prosaic concerns, such as judicial politics, the demands of a heavy caseload, and the new impact of international rules on national litigants.

What these judges share above all is the recognition of one another as participants in a common judicial enterprise. They see each other not only as servants and representatives of a particular government or polity, but also as fellow members of a profession that transcends national borders. They face common substantive and institutional problems; they learn from one another's experience and reasoning. They cooperate directly to resolve specific disputes. And they conceive of themselves as capable of independent action in both the international and domestic realms. Indeed, a 1993 resolution by the French Institute of International Law calls upon national courts to become independent actors in the international arena and to apply international norms impartially, without deferring to their governments.

The system these judges are creating is better described as a community of courts than as a centralized hierarchy. Nevertheless, it is emerging as a community with identifiable organizing principles. Recognition and elaboration of these principles is critical to understanding the full scope, implications, and potential of the examples set forth in this chapter. They include, first, a rough conception of checks and balances, both vertical and horizontal. In the most developed set of vertical networks, the EU legal system, neither national nor international tribunals hold the definitive upper hand. Horizontally as well, national courts remain acutely conscious of their prerogatives as representatives of independent and interdependent sovereigns, even as they recognize the need for cooperation and even deference to one another.

Second, and relatedly, is a principle of positive conflict, in which judges do not shy from arguing with one another, even acrimoniously, yet do not fear a fundamental rupture in their relations. In this sense, judges are drawing on a domestic understanding of transjudicial relations rather than a diplomatic one. Conflict in domestic politics is to be expected and even embraced; conflict in traditional unitary state diplomacy is to be avoided or quickly resolved.

Third is a principle of pluralism and legitimate difference, whereby judges acknowledge the validity of a wide variety of different approaches to the same legal problem. This pluralism is not unbounded, however. It operates within a framework of common fundamental values, such as recognition of the necessity of judicial independence and basic due process.

Fourth, and finally, is acceptance of the value of persuasive, rather than coercive, authority. Judges from different legal systems acknowledge the possibility of learning from one another based on relative experience with a particular set of issues and on the quality of reasoning in specic decisions.

NOTE ON ENFORCEMENT BEYOND COURTS AND TRIBUNALS

Even as we study the proliferation of tribunals and the benefits and costs of such proliferation, it is important to remain realistic: the truth is that, in the absence of a global enforcement mechanism, many international disputes, even when adjudicated, do not lead to actual compensation or other effective remedies. In a course focused on the mechanisms for lawmaking and adjudication in an increasingly global world, it is easy to forget that transnational law often is enforced through means that are outside the typical legal process.

Much as the past 60 years have witnessed a proliferation in the number and types of courts and tribunals, they have also seen the growth of other means of enforcement through political, economic or other means. In the United States, the executive branch (as the central player in foreign affairs) often employs diplomacy to resolve international disputes or to cajole parties into compliance with judgments or awards. The political branches can also use, or at least threaten, economic sanctions, political retaliation or even military pressure. In addition, they can use their influence in international organizations or on other governments to induce these players to exert pressure, e.g., by withholding aid, denying loans or withdrawing political favors.

In particular, international organizations themselves offer a range of processes—from treaty drafting conferences to regularized commissions to ad hoc measures—through which international disputes can be resolved and decisions enforced. For example, the UN Secretary–General (or his or her designate) is on occasion asked by parties to assist in arbitration, mediation or negotiation of contentious disputes. Similarly, NGOs can prove effective at pushing resolution—often through publicity in the form of negative reports and other mechanisms that can serve to shame the wrongdoer and thus to inflict political costs.

To illustrate the importance of non-judicial mechanisms in vindicating rights on the transnational level, let us consider the case of Orlando Letelier. Letelier served as ambassador to the United States, foreign minister, interior minister and minister of defense of Chile in the early 1970s under President Salvador Allende. When Allende was overthrown by Augusto Pinochet (see Chapter VII.3.B.), Letelier was imprisoned for over a year, tortured and eventually exiled from Chile after a great deal of political pressure for his release was exerted by a number of countries, including the United States.

After his release in 1974, Letelier settled in Washington, D.C. On September 21, 1976, as he was driving to work with his assistant (Ronni Moffitt) and her husband, Letelier's car exploded while rounding Sheridan Circle on Embassy Row in the heart of Washington. Letelier and Ms. Moffitt were killed, while her husband survived. A subsequent investigation revealed that Letelier had been assassinated by agents connected to the Chilean government who had placed a bomb under his car.

Survivors of Letelier and Moffitt sued Chile in a U.S. Federal District Court, claiming that the Chilean government had directed and assisted its agents in the assassination. The Chilean government defended on a variety of grounds, prime among them that the FSIA did not provide jurisdiction over it. Chile lost, with the court finding that the tort exception to sovereign immunity applied (the first time that exception had been employed against a state). Subsequently, the Chilean government refused to participate in the proceedings, leading the court to issue a default judgment against Chile for more than $5 million.

Not surprisingly, the Chilean government refused to pay. In response, the survivors sought to execute the judgment by attaching property of LAN Chile, the Chilean state-owned airline, which had assets in New York. The District Court issued an order allowing attachment of the assets, but the Second Circuit Court of Appeals reversed, finding that LAN Chile had a separate legal personality from the Republic of Chile. Its property could thus not be attached. At this point, the plaintiffs were left without effective recourse against the Republic of Chile.

In 1990, a decade after the plaintiffs had prevailed in their lawsuit and after the end of the Pinochet regime, the executive branch of the United States succeeded in persuading the government of Chile actually to pay $5 million to the survivors of the assassination, though that payment came without any admission of liability and without interest for the decade since the court had ruled in favor of the families.

Without the political intervention of the U.S. government and the strong pressure it placed on Chile, the survivors would never have been compensated. It is tempting therefore to see the judgment against Chile as an empty victory—a vindication of rights without compensation. After all, it was the political process that ultimately brought the families compensation. It is important to recognize, however, that the judicial and the political processes went hand in hand: the judgment provided the basis for the U.S. government to pressure Chile to pay.

CHAPTER 10

DOMESTIC EFFECTS: BLURRING OF LINES

■ ■ ■

The traditional approach to international law was based on the assumption that there was a fundamental difference between international and domestic law as well as a categorical distinction between public and private international law. Of course, there were many points of contact and perhaps even some overlaps, especially in practice. But at least in theory, these distinctions were considered essential, if not indispensible.

As many observers have recognized, and as the previous four chapters in this book have repeatedly indicated, the traditional boundaries between international law and domestic law have become more and more blurred in recent years, and they sometimes break down entirely. Of course, these boundaries can still provide a sense of orientation. But, in an era increasingly characterized by hybrids, the traditional categories can also become obstacles to our understanding of transnational legal problems.

The following materials deal with the changing relationship between the established categories. We begin with an essay providing an overview of the marked internationalization of U.S. law. We then turn to three illustrations of more particular aspects. The first shows the interplay especially between international and domestic law. The second focuses on the blending of public and private law in international disputes. The third looks at the much-debated question of the extent to which U.S. courts should look to international and foreign law for guidance in difficult cases.

JOSE E. ALVAREZ, THE INTERNATIONALIZATION OF U.S. LAW

47 Colum. J. Transnat'l L. 537 (2009)

* * *

* * * I want to suggest how the "evolving world of international law" is turning U.S. law inside-out. I will suggest that as never before in U.S. history, all three branches of the federal government, as well as the citizenry, media, and representatives of civil society—from the world of NGOs and from the private sector—are now perennially engaged with international and foreign law, despite bills in Congress that seek to halt this phenomenon, at least with respect to federal judges. I will address

only a few current realities to make my point and to suggest that legal internationalization is likely to accelerate, not decline. * * *

I.

The internationalization of U.S. law is occurring because of the mission creep of those international regimes that we are very much a part of and from which we are unlikely to detach because they support the United States' national interest: namely, the UN system, the international financial institutions and the World Trade Organization (WTO). All of these institutions are, to greater and lesser extents, expanding their domain beyond what was originally intended by those who entered into the original treaties establishing them.

Today's UN General Assembly and Security Council have eroded the core non-interference norm of Art. 2(7) of the Charter. Nothing today is considered immune, on the basis of sacred "domestic jurisdiction," from consideration by either body and in the case of the Security Council, even legally binding Chapter VII enforcement action. Thanks in substantial part to the United States' very own revolution on behalf of human rights, it is impossible to suggest (as some still try) that the U.S. treaty power is confined by subject matter to foreign affairs. At a time when the U.S. government itself sometimes insists that international norms supplement the Constitution's dormant Commerce and Takings Clauses, that we have the right to examine how other nations treat their own nationals, and that there may even be international limits on how others choose to rule themselves, it is impossible to contain the sphere of international law. Try as we might, the General Assembly is no longer constrained (if it ever was) from making recommendations even with respect to matters being examined by the Council—from the legality of the Israeli security wall to the due process rights of alleged terrorists. The human rights genie that we helped to breed is out of its bottle. It is being used by all, including by domestic NGOs and the government—for instance, in criticizing the selectivity of the UN's own human rights actions. Human rights now make a prominent appearance in the ICJ, at the World Bank and even indirectly at the WTO—and in street demonstrations protesting against some of these institutions themselves.

A panoply of UN experts and assorted others—from human rights treaty bodies to the special rapporteur on torture—now routinely make ever more specific legal pronouncements about such things as the propriety or consequences of "invalid" treaty reservations, specific interrogation techniques or states' reliance on diplomatic assurances when engaging in the foreign rendition of suspects. While the U.S. executive branch has contested many of these pronouncements, even the one hundred plus lawyers of the U.S. State Department are no match for the sheer quantity and variety of this institutionalized output, which—as amplified by the voice of organizations like Human Rights Watch—may achieve a legitimacy greater than the views of any single nation, including the United States.

It is impossible for even the United States to register its persistent objection—if that is what it is—to the sheer multitude of today's international lawmakers. And the United States' "soft power" now has to contend with those of activist NGOs around the world who often serve as the "bad cop" to those international organizations too meek to serve as anything other than "good cop." Inevitably, some of this legal output—whose content not even the United States can control—whether incorporated in Alien Tort Claims Act-based plaintiffs' briefs or in *amici* before appellate courts, has begun to influence even relatively nativist judges. Such judges sometimes find themselves citing, as never before, "soft" law such as General Assembly resolutions, reports of human rights rapporteurs, judgments issued by international criminal courts or guidelines for multinational corporations, at least by way of interpreting U.S. law and even in some rare cases, the U.S. Constitution.

As the UN High Commissioner on Human Rights Louise Arbour has suggested, the global war on terror has also played a part in the internationalization of U.S. law. As American judges and law enforcers increasingly deal with legal issues involving others' citizens and others' territory, they find an increasing need to work with those others and to examine both international rules and foreign law. Global and common justice concerns—and not merely those under U.S. law—are implicated by the detention and treatment pending trial of detainees in a war subject to no evident temporal or geographical boundaries or by, for example, the transnational privacy implications posed by internet and satellite communications and governments' efforts to regulate them.

Of course, the same war on terror has facilitated the legislative turn of the UN's Security Council, which has now adopted legally binding action directed at the world as a whole and not merely a single target rogue nation. Largely at the United States' behest, the Security Council has become a global law-maker and not just a sporadic collective enforcer of the peace. Apart from repeated, and now increasingly routine, collective sanctions efforts and the occasional authorization to use force, that body has settled a boundary dispute, created a standing dispute settlement mechanism to settle post-war interstate disputes, established two ad hoc war crimes tribunals and influenced prosecutions in a third, is embarking on the creation of another (hybrid) tribunal to deal with a terrorist act, enhanced its own authority as well as powers of the International Atomic Energy Agency ("IAEA") over weapons inspections, expanded the range of peacekeepers' authority—including as de facto administrators of territory, repeatedly authorized election assistance and supervision, criminalized for the world a range of terrorist activity (including financial transactions that facilitate terrorism), imposed smart sanctions on designated individuals and groups allegedly connected to the Taliban and Al Qaeda, developed "best practices" for the world's law enforcement agencies with respect to counter-terrorism and the non-proliferation of weapons of mass destruction, and supervised the military occupation of a state.

The Security Council's mission creep is having dramatic effects on the law—on the interpretation of UN Charter article 39, on the law of self defense, particularly with respect to states that "acquiesce" in terrorist activity within their borders, on the jurisdiction of states over a variety of activity and persons (including reviving notions of universal civil and criminal jurisdiction), on alleged norms such as the right to democratic governance or an alleged "responsibility to protect," on the law of occupation, on the legality of certain weapons and on the expanding scope of international criminal law. And though the United States has been a principal mover and participant in the Council's normative activity, even the United States has not been able to control the resulting legal implications and today faces, for example, the broader legal ripples brought about by the consequent revival of international criminal law, including enhanced interest in command responsibility and universal jurisdiction.

The mission creep of international financial institutions—and the ever-expanding range of law affected by their activities—is ever more evident. The World Bank no longer sees itself as confined to financing infrastructure projects; its operational policies include such matters as the rights of those displaced by the projects that it funds. The IMF—freed from patrolling fixed exchange rates—imposes structural adjustment loans that incorporate normative values, such as respect for the rule of law and property rights, and even for an entitlement to "democratic governance." And a funny thing happens when such institutions are used to encourage "democracy" along Western lines: people begin to demand that those institutions themselves respect the rights of the governed by adapting techniques from national administrative law. All of these institutions—including UN specialized agencies and the WTO—find themselves under pressure, including by our government, to adopt mechanisms to encourage transparency, accountability, greater access for NGOs and legal responsibility. There is even today an effort by the International Law Commission (ILC) to elaborate articles of responsibility for international organizations comparable to those it promulgated recently for state responsibility. The international community is encouraging these organizations to become more legalized even as these organizations attempt to legalize others.

All of this suggests that international law is deepening both horizontally—as particular treaty regimes evolve with ever greater specificity—and vertically, as ever more intrusive forms for the national incorporation of its rules evolve, including within the United States itself.

To be sure, the U.S. government tries to confine these developments to those regimes that it believes serve its interests—such as trade and investment and their intrusive forms of dispute settlement—but it is becoming ever clearer that those regimes, which at our behest have developed some space for autonomous action, are not self-contained. As many have noticed, the emerging law of the WTO now deals with, and in turn has influenced, such matters as the rules of treaty interpretation and the status of the precautionary principle in environmental law. The WTO also serves to harden "soft" standards elaborated by the International Organization for Standardization (ISO) (through the TBT Agreement) and the FAO–WHO's (Food and Agriculture Organization; World Health Organization) Codus Alimentarius (through the SPS Agreement, among others), thereby triggering the attention of both business and consumer groups. The result is that those treaty regimes are now part of our domestic politics. The sunk costs that the United States has incurred in establishing the WTO and constructing a web of investment agreements has not merely tied the hands of subsequent administrations, Democrat and Republican, but it also created domestic audiences for supranational regulation and supervision. The genie of supranational scrutiny over U.S. law is now out of its bottle as well and will prove difficult to contain.

* * *

1. THE MODERN INTERPLAY BETWEEN INTERNATIONAL AND DOMESTIC LAW: A CASE STUDY

The modern interplay between domestic and international law is vividly illustrated by several recent developments involving the United States. Perhaps the most striking example is the series of court battles arising from the failure of officials in the United States to advise arrested foreign citizens of their right to seek assistance from their home country's consulate. The following materials show the development of this "Consular Rights Saga" over more than a decade.

In the 1990s, it became increasingly evident that police officers and prosecutors in the United States often, if not regularly, failed to comply with the Vienna Convention on the Law of Consular Relations of 1963 (VCCR, in force for the United States in 1969) which provides in Article 36:

> 1.   (b) If he so requests, the competent authorities of the receiving state shall, without delay, inform the consular post of the sending State if, within its consular district, a national of that State is arrested or committed to prison or to custody pending trial or is detained in any other manner. Any communication addressed to the consular

post by the person arrested, in prison, custody or detention shall also be forwarded by the said authorities without delay. The said authorities shall inform the person concerned without delay of his rights under this sub-paragraph.

* * *

2. The rights referred to in paragraph 1 of this article shall be exercised in conformity with the laws and regulations of the receiving State, subject to the proviso, however, that the said laws and regulations must enable full effect to be given to the purposes for which the rights accorded under this article are intended.

Foreign citizens arrested (and later convicted) in the United States were often not informed about their right to seek assistance from their home country's consulate and thus failed to do so, arguably to the detriment of their defense in criminal court.

A. SETTING THE STAGE: THE CASE OF ANGEL BREARD

The legal saga began in 1998 with the case of Angel Breard, a Paraguayan citizen, who had not been advised of his consular rights upon arrest for murder and whose fate was decided by the United States Supreme Court literally an hour before his scheduled execution. The factual saga had begun six years earlier, in 1992, when Breard was arrested by Virginia authorities and charged with a murder committed in Arlington, just outside Washington, D.C. Breard was convicted and sentenced to death in 1993. All challenges to his conviction (in state and federal court) proved unsuccessful, and his execution was scheduled for April 14, 1998.

On April 3, 1998, the state of Paraguay filed suit against the United States in the International Court of Justice in The Hague, requesting that Breard's conviction be voided and asking for provisional measures preventing his execution. Paraguay argued that the United States had breached its international obligations when it had failed to advise Breard upon his arrest of his rights under the VCCR to which both Paraguay and the United States are parties.

The purpose of Article 36 of the VCCR is to provide a detainee with access to consular assistance and to provide the consular authorities with an opportunity to render it. The United States admitted that Breard had not been advised of his rights under the Convention.

The ICJ unanimously issued a provisional order stating that the "United States should take all measures at its disposal to ensure that Angel Francisco Breard is not executed pending the final decision in these proceedings."

Immediately thereafter, the U.S. Secretary of State asked the Governor of Virginia to halt the execution. At the same time, Breard and the State of Paraguay, as well as its Ambassador and its Consul–General to the United States, all sought relief from the United States Supreme Court. Why did they all lose?

BREARD V. GREENE
United States Supreme Court
523 U.S. 371 (1998)

PER CURIAM.

Angel Francisco Breard is scheduled to be executed by the Commonwealth of Virginia this evening at 9 p.m. Breard, a citizen of Paraguay, came to the United States in 1986, at the age of 20. In 1992, Breard was charged with the attempted rape and capital murder of Ruth Dickie. At his trial in 1993, the State presented overwhelming evidence of guilt, including semen found on Dickie's body matching Breard's DNA profile and hairs on Dickie's body identical in all microscopic characteristics to hair samples taken from Breard. Breard chose to take the witness stand in his defense. During his testimony, Breard confessed to killing Dickie, but explained that he had only done so because of a Satanic curse placed on him by his father-in-law. Following a jury trial in the Circuit Court of Arlington County, Virginia, Breard was convicted of both charges and sentenced to death. On appeal, the Virginia Supreme Court affirmed Breard's convictions and sentences. State collateral relief was subsequently denied as well.

Breard then filed a motion for habeas relief under 28 U.S.C. § 2254 in Federal District Court on August 20, 1996. In that motion, Breard argued for the first time that his convictions and sentences should be overturned because of alleged violations of the Vienna Convention on Consular Relations (Vienna Convention), April 24, 1963, [1970] at the time of his arrest. Specifically, Breard alleged that the Vienna Convention was violated when the arresting authorities failed to inform him that, as a foreign national, he had the right to contact the Paraguayan Consulate. The District Court rejected this claim, concluding that Breard procedurally defaulted the claim when he failed to raise it in state court and that Breard could not demonstrate cause and prejudice for this default. The Fourth Circuit affirmed. Breard has petitioned this Court for a writ of certiorari.

In September 1996, the Republic of Paraguay, the Ambassador of Paraguay to the United States, and the Consul General of Paraguay to the United States (collectively Paraguay) brought suit in Federal District Court against certain Virginia officials, alleging that their separate rights under the Vienna Convention had been violated by the Commonwealth's failure to inform Breard of his rights under the treaty and to inform the Paraguayan Consulate of Breard's arrest, convictions, and sentences. In addition, the Consul General asserted a parallel claim under Rev.Stat. § 1979, 42 U.S.C. § 1983, alleging a denial of his rights under the Vienna Convention. * * *

On April 3, 1998, nearly five years after Breard's convictions became final, the Republic of Paraguay instituted proceedings against the United States in the International Court of Justice (ICJ), alleging that the United States violated the Vienna Convention at the time of Breard's arrest. On April 9, the ICJ noted jurisdiction and issued an order requesting that the United States "take all measures at its disposal to ensure that Angel Francisco Breard is not executed pending the final decision in these proceedings. * * * " The ICJ set a briefing schedule for this matter, with oral argument likely to be held this November. Breard then filed a petition for an original writ of habeas corpus and a stay application in this Court in order to "enforce" the ICJ's order. Paraguay filed a motion for leave to file a bill of complaint in this Court, citing this Court's original jurisdiction over cases "affecting Ambassadors * * * and Consuls." U.S. Const., Art. III, § 2.

It is clear that Breard procedurally defaulted his claim, if any, under the Vienna Convention by failing to raise that claim in the state courts. Nevertheless, in their petitions for certiorari, both Breard and Paraguay contend that Breard's Vienna Convention claim may be heard in federal court because the Convention is the "supreme law of the land" and thus trumps the procedural default doctrine. This argument is plainly incorrect for two reasons.

First, while we should give respectful consideration to the interpretation of an international treaty rendered by an international court with jurisdiction to interpret such, it has been recognized in international law that, absent a clear and express statement to the contrary, the procedural rules of the forum State govern the implementation of the treaty in that State. This proposition is embodied in the Vienna Convention itself, which provides that the rights expressed in the Convention "shall be exercised in conformity with the laws and regulations of the receiving State," provided that "said laws and regulations must enable full effect to be given to the purposes for which the rights accorded under this Article are intended." Article 36(2), [1970] 21 U.S. T., at 101. It is the rule in this country that assertions of error in criminal proceedings must first be raised in state court in order to form the basis for relief in habeas. Claims not so raised are considered defaulted. By not asserting his Vienna Convention claim in state court, Breard failed to exercise his rights under the Vienna Convention in conformity with the laws of the United States and the Commonwealth of Virginia. Having failed to do so, he cannot raise a claim of violation of those rights now on federal habeas review.

Second, although treaties are recognized by our Constitution as the supreme law of the land, that status is no less true of provisions of the Constitution itself, to which rules of procedural default apply. We have held "that an Act of Congress * * * is on a full parity with a treaty, and that when a statute which is subsequent in time is inconsistent with a treaty, the statute to the extent of conflict renders the treaty null." *Reid v. Covert*, 354 U.S. 1, 18, 77 S.Ct. 1222, 1231 (1957) (plurality opinion); see also *Whitney v. Robertson*, 124 U.S. 190, 194 (1888) (holding that if a treaty and a federal statute conflict, "the one last in date will control the other"). The Vienna Convention—which arguably confers on an individual the right to consular assistance following arrest—has continuously been in effect since 1969. But in 1996, before Breard filed his habeas petition raising claims under the Vienna Convention, Congress enacted the Antiterrorism and Effective Death Penalty Act (AEDPA), which provides that a habeas petitioner alleging that he is held in violation of "treaties of the United States" will, as a general rule, not be afforded an evidentiary hearing if he "has failed to develop the factual basis of [the] claim in State court proceedings." 28 U.S.C. § 2254(a), (e)(2) (1994 ed., Supp. IV). Breard's ability to obtain relief based on violations of the Vienna Convention is subject to this subsequently enacted rule, just as any claim arising under the United States Constitution would be. This rule prevents Breard from establishing that the violation of his Vienna Convention rights prejudiced him. Without a hearing, Breard cannot establish how the Consul would have advised him, how the advice of his attorneys differed from the advice the Consul could have provided, and what factors he considered in electing to reject the plea bargain that the State offered him. That limitation, Breard also argues, is not justified because his Vienna Convention claims were so novel that he could not have discovered them any earlier. Assuming that were true, such novel claims would be barred on habeas review under *Teague v. Lane*, 489 U.S. 288 (1989).

Even were Breard's Vienna Convention claim properly raised and proved, it is extremely doubtful that the violation should result in the overturning of a final judgment of conviction without some showing that the violation had an effect on the trial. In this action, no such showing could even arguably be made. Breard decided not to plead guilty and to testify at his own trial contrary to the advice of his attorneys, who were likely far better able to explain the United States legal system to him than any consular official would have been. Breard's asserted prejudice—that had the Vienna Convention been followed, he would have accepted the State's offer to forgo the death penalty in return for a plea of guilty—is far more speculative than the claims of prejudice courts routinely reject in those cases were [sic] an inmate alleges that his plea of guilty was infected by attorney error.

* * *

It is unfortunate that this matter comes before us while proceedings are pending before the ICJ that might have been brought to that court earlier. Nonetheless, this Court must decide questions presented to it on the basis of law. The Executive Branch, on the other hand, in exercising its authority over foreign relations may, and in this case did, utilize diplomatic discussion with Paraguay. Last night the Secretary of State sent a letter to the Governor of Virginia requesting that he stay Breard's execution. If the Governor wishes to wait for the decision of the ICJ, that is his prerogative. But nothing in our existing case law allows us to make that choice for him.

* * *

JUSTICE BREYER, dissenting.

In my view, several of the issues raised here are of sufficient difficulty to warrant less speedy consideration. Breard argues, for example, that the novelty of his Vienna Convention claim is sufficient to create "cause" for his having failed to present that claim to the Virginia state courts. He might add that the nature of his claim, were we to accept it, is such as to create a "watershed rule of criminal procedure," which might overcome the bar to consideration otherwise posed by *Teague v. Lane*. He additionally says that what the Solicitor General describes as Virginia's violation of the Convention "prejudiced" him by isolating him at a critical moment from Consular Officials who might have advised him to try to avoid the death penalty by pleading guilty. I cannot say, without examining the record more fully, that these arguments are obviously without merit. Nor am I willing to accept without fuller briefing and consideration the positions taken by the majority on all of the sometimes difficult issues that the majority addresses.

At the same time, the international aspects of the cases have provided us with the advantage of additional briefing even in the short time available. More time would likely mean additional briefing and argument, perhaps, for example, on the potential relevance of proceedings in an international forum.

Finally, as Justice STEVENS points out, Virginia is now pursuing an execution schedule that leaves less time for argument and for Court consideration than the Court's Rules provide for ordinary cases. Like Justice STEVENS, I can find no special reason here to truncate the period of time that the Court's Rules would otherwise make available.

* * *

[Dissenting opinions by JUSTICES SOUTER, STEVENS, and GINSBURG are omitted.]

———————

The Governor of Virginia refused to stay Breard's execution because, as he wrote, such a stay would "have the practical effect of transferring responsibility from the courts of the Commonwealth and the United States to the International Court," while also noting that the "International Court of Justice has no authority to interfere with our criminal justice system." Breard was executed the same day.

The next day, the Secretary of State wrote to the ICJ that the United States, through its request to the governor of Virginia, had taken all measures lawfully at the disposal of the United States to implement the Court's order as required by the ICJ.

In November 1998, Paraguay withdrew its request for an ICJ ruling on the merits and the case was removed from the docket. About two years later, Germany sued the United States in the ICJ on virtually the same grounds, resulting in the decision below.

The Supreme Court majority is right, of course, that, as a matter of domestic law, Breard had forfeited his right to raise his consular rights by failing to raise the issue in the original state court proceedings. It is also right that the Antiterrorism and Effective Death Penalty Act (AEDPA) was enacted after the ratification of the Vienna Convention so that, again as a matter of domestic law, the statute won under the later-in-time rule (see Chapter V.2.A.). Still, does that really solve the problem? Should the United States be allowed to invoke the procedural default rule under these circumstances? What is the major argument in favor of permitting that? What is the major argument against?

Does the Supreme Court's decision mean that the United States was now in breach of its international obligations (i.e., under the Vienna Convention vis-à-vis Paraguay)? What are the main arguments for and against that position?

B. THE SECOND ROUND: THE BROTHERS LAGRAND

The saga continued with the case of the LaGrand brothers. A few months after the *Breard* case, Arizona executed two German brothers who had also not been advised of their consular rights until long after their conviction. All court action in the United States to stay their executions as well as all diplomatic intervention proved useless as Arizona executed the first of the brothers, Karl LaGrand, on February 24, 1999.

Germany then instituted proceedings against the United States in the International Court of Justice, both to seek compensation for the alleged breach of Article 36 of the Vienna Convention and in order to prevent the execution of the second brother, Walter.

Germany presented four claims (submissions) against the United States. What were those claims? What were the parties' arguments with regard to each? And how did the Court decide them?

LA GRAND CASE
(GERMANY V. UNITED STATES)
International Court of Justice
2001 I.C.J. 466

* * *

13. Walter LaGrand and Karl LaGrand were born in Germany in 1962 and 1963 respectively, and were German nationals. In 1967, when they were still young children, they moved with their mother to take up permanent residence in the United States. They returned to Germany only once, for a period of about six months in 1974. Although they lived in the United States for most of their lives, and became the adoptive children of a United States national, they remained at all times German nationals, and never acquired the nationality of the United States. However, the United States has emphasized that both had the demeanour and speech of Americans rather than Germans, that neither was known to have spoken German, and that they appeared in all respects to be native citizens of the United States.

14. On 7 January 1982, Karl LaGrand and Walter LaGrand were arrested in the United States by law enforcement officers on suspicion of having been involved earlier the same day in an attempted armed bank robbery in Marana, Arizona, in the course of which the bank manager was murdered and another bank employee seriously injured. They were subsequently tried before the Superior Court of Pima County, Arizona, which, on 17 February 1984, convicted them both of murder in the first degree, attempted murder in the first degree, attempted armed robbery and two counts of kidnapping. On 14 December 1984, each was sentenced to death for first degree murder and to concurrent sentences of imprisonment for the other charges.

15. At all material times, Germany as well as the United States were parties to both the Vienna Convention on Consular Relations and the Optional Protocol to that Convention. Article 36, paragraph 1 (*b*), of the Vienna Convention provides that:

> "if he so requests, the competent authorities of the receiving State shall, without delay, inform the consular post of the sending State if, within its consular district, a national of that State is arrested or committed to prison or to custody pending trial or is detained in any other manner. Any communication addressed to the consular post by the person arrested, in prison, custody or detention shall be forward-

ed by the said authorities without delay. The said authorities shall inform the person concerned without delay of his rights under this subparagraph."

It is not disputed that at the time the LaGrands were convicted and sentenced, the competent United States authorities had failed to provide the LaGrands with the information required by this provision of the Vienna Convention, and had not informed the relevant German consular post of the LaGrands' arrest. The United States concedes that the competent authorities failed to do so, even after becoming aware that the LaGrands were German nationals and not United States nationals, and admits that the United States has therefore violated its obligations under this provision of the Vienna Convention.

* * *

17. At their trial, the LaGrands were represented by counsel assigned by the court, as they were unable to afford legal counsel of their own choice. Their counsel at trial did not raise the issue of non-compliance with the Vienna Convention, and did not themselves contact the German consular authorities.

18. The convictions and sentences pronounced by the Superior Court of Pima County, Arizona, were subsequently challenged by the LaGrands in three principal sets of legal proceedings.

19. The first set of proceedings consisted of appeals against the convictions and sentences to the Supreme Court of Arizona, which were rejected by that court on 30 January 1987. The United States Supreme Court, in the exercise of its discretion, denied applications by the LaGrands for further review of these judgments on 5 October 1987.

20. The second set of proceedings involved petitions by the LaGrands for post-conviction relief, which were denied by an Arizona state court in 1989. Review of this decision was denied by the Supreme Court of Arizona in 1990, and by the United States Supreme Court in 1991.

21. At the time of these two sets of proceedings, the LaGrands had still not been informed by the competent United States authorities of their rights under Article 36, paragraph 1 (*b*), of the Vienna Convention, and the German consular post had still not been informed of their arrest. The issue of the lack of consular notification, which had not been raised at trial, was also not raised in these two sets of proceedings.

22. The relevant German consular post was only made aware of the case in June 1992 by the LaGrands themselves, who had learnt of their rights from other sources, and not from the Arizona authorities. In December 1992, and on a number of subsequent occasions between then and February 1999, an official of the Consulate–General of Germany in Los Angeles visited the LaGrands in prison. Germany claims that it subsequently

helped the LaGrands' attorneys to investigate the LaGrands' childhood in Germany, and to raise the issue of the omission of consular advice in further proceedings before the federal courts.

23. The LaGrands commenced a third set of legal proceedings by filing applications for writs of *habeas corpus* in the United States District Court for the District of Arizona, seeking to have their convictions—or at least their death sentences—set aside. In these proceedings they raised a number of different claims, which were rejected by that court in orders dated 24 January 1995 and 16 February 1995. One of these claims was that the United States authorities had failed to notify the German consulate of their arrest, as required by the Vienna Convention. This claim was rejected on the basis of the "procedural default" rule. According to the United States, this rule:

> "is a federal rule that, before a state criminal defendant can obtain relief in federal court, the claim must be presented to a state court. If a state defendant attempts to raise a new issue in a federal *habeas corpus* proceeding, the defendant can only do so by showing cause and prejudice. Cause is an external impediment that prevents a defendant from raising a claim and prejudice must be obvious on its face. One important purpose of this rule is to ensure that the state courts have an opportunity to address issues going to the validity of state convictions before the federal courts intervene."

The United States District Court held that the LaGrands had not shown an objective external factor that prevented them from raising the issue of the lack of consular notification earlier. On 16 January 1998, this judgment was affirmed on appeal by the United States Court of Appeals, Ninth Circuit, which also held that the LaGrands' claim relating to the Vienna Convention was "procedurally defaulted", as it had not been raised in any of the earlier proceedings in state courts. On 2 November 1998, the United States Supreme Court denied further review of this judgment.

24. On 21 December 1998, the LaGrands were formally notified by the United States authorities of their right to consular access.

25. On 15 January 1999, the Supreme Court of Arizona decided that Karl LaGrand was to be executed on 24 February 1999, and that Walter LaGrand was to be executed on 3 March 1999. Germany claims that the German Consulate learned of these dates on 19 January 1999.

26. In January and early February 1999, various interventions were made by Germany seeking to prevent the execution of the LaGrands. In particular, the German Foreign Minister and German Minister of Justice wrote to their respective United States counterparts on 27 January 1999; the German Foreign Minister wrote to the Governor of Arizona on the same day; the German Chancellor wrote to the President of the United

States and to the Governor of Arizona on 2 February 1999; and the President of the Federal Republic of Germany wrote to the President of the United States on 5 February 1999. These letters referred to German opposition to capital punishment generally, but did not raise the issue of the absence of consular notification in the case of the LaGrands. The latter issue was, however, raised in a further letter, dated 22 February 1999, two days before the scheduled date of execution of Karl LaGrand, from the German Foreign Minister to the United States Secretary of State.

27. On 23 February 1999, the Arizona Board of Executive Clemency rejected an appeal for clemency by Karl LaGrand. Under the law of Arizona, this meant that the Governor of Arizona was prevented from granting clemency.

28. On the same day, the Arizona Superior Court in Pima County rejected a further petition by Walter LaGrand, based *inter alia* on the absence of consular notification, on the ground that these claims were "procedurally precluded".

29. On 24 February 1999, certain last-minute federal court proceedings brought by Karl LaGrand ultimately proved to be unsuccessful. In the course of these proceedings the United States Court of Appeals, Ninth Circuit, again held the issue of failure of consular notification to be procedurally defaulted. Karl LaGrand was executed later that same day.

30. On 2 March 1999, the day before the scheduled date of execution of Walter LaGrand, at 7.30 p.m. (The Hague time), Germany filed in the Registry of this Court the Application instituting the present proceedings against the United States (see paragraph 1 above), accompanied by a request for the following provisional measures:

> "The United States should take all measures at its disposal to ensure that Walter LaGrand is not executed pending the final decision in these proceedings, and should inform the Court of all the measures which it has taken in implementation of that Order."

By a letter of the same date, the German Foreign Minister requested the Secretary of State of the United States "to urge [the] Governor [of Arizona] for a suspension of Walter LaGrand's execution pending a ruling by the International Court of Justice".

31. On the same day, the Arizona Board of Executive Clemency met to consider the case of Walter LaGrand. It recommended against a commutation of his death sentence, but recommended that the Governor of Arizona grant a 60-day reprieve having regard to the Application filed by Germany in the International Court of Justice. Nevertheless, the Governor of Arizona decided, "in the interest of justice and with the victims in mind", to allow the execution of Walter LaGrand to go forward as scheduled.

32. In an Order of 3 March 1999, this Court found that the circumstances required it to indicate, as a matter of the greatest urgency and without any other proceedings, provisional measures in accordance with Article 41 of its Statute and with Article 75, paragraph 1, of its Rules (*I.C.J. Reports 1999*, p. 9, para. 26); it indicated provisional measures in the following terms:

> "(*a*) The United States of America should take all measures at its disposal to ensure that Walter LaGrand is not executed pending the final decision in these proceedings, and should inform the Court of all the measures which it has taken in implementation of this Order;
>
> (*b*) The Government of the United States of America should transmit this Order to the Governor of the State of Arizona."

33. On the same day, proceedings were brought by Germany in the United States Supreme Court against the United States and the Governor of Arizona, seeking *inter alia* to enforce compliance with this Court's Order indicating provisional measures. In the course of these proceedings, the United States Solicitor–General as counsel of record took the position, *inter alia*, that "an order of the International Court of Justice indicating provisional measures is not binding and does not furnish a basis for judicial relief". On the same date, the United States Supreme Court dismissed the motion by Germany, on the ground of the tardiness of Germany's application and of jurisdictional barriers under United States domestic law.

34. On that same day, proceedings were also instituted in the United States Supreme Court by Walter LaGrand. These proceedings were decided against him. Later that day, Walter LaGrand was executed.

35. The Court must as a preliminary matter deal with certain issues, which were raised by the Parties in these proceedings, concerning the jurisdiction of the Court in relation to Germany's Application, and the admissibility of its submissions.

* * *

64. Having determined that the Court has jurisdiction, and that the submissions of Germany are admissible, the Court now turns to the merits of each of these four submissions.

65. Germany's first submission requests the Court to adjudge and declare:

> "that the United States, by not informing Karl and Walter LaGrand without delay following their arrest of their rights under Article 36 subparagraph 1 (*b*) of the Vienna Convention on Consular Relations, and by depriving Germany of the possibility of rendering consular assistance, which ultimately resulted in the execution of Karl and Walter LaGrand, violated its international legal obligations to Germany,

in its own right and in its right of diplomatic protection of its nationals, under Articles 5 and 36 paragraph 1 of the said Convention".

66. Germany claims that the United States violated its obligation under Article 36, paragraph 1 (*b*) to "inform a national of the sending state without delay of his or her right to inform the consular post of his home State of his arrest or detention". Specifically, Germany maintains that the United States violated its international legal obligation to Germany under Article 36, paragraph 1 (*b*), by failing to inform the German nationals Karl and Walter LaGrand "without delay" of their rights under that subparagraph.

67. The United States acknowledges, and does not contest Germany's basic claim, that there was a breach of its obligation under Article 36, paragraph 1 (*b*), of the Convention "promptly to inform the LaGrand brothers that they could ask that a German consular post be notified of their arrest and detention".

68. Germany also claims that the violation by the United States of Article 36, paragraph 1 (*b*), led to consequential violations of Article 36, paragraph 1 (*a*) and (*c*). It points out that, when the obligation to inform the arrested person without delay of his or her right to contact the consulate is disregarded, "the other rights contained in Article 36, paragraph 1, become in practice irrelevant, indeed meaningless". Germany maintains that, "[b]y informing the LaGrand brothers of their right to inform the consulate more than 16 years after their arrest, the United States * * * clearly failed to meet the standard of Article 36 [1 (*c*)]." It concludes that, by not preventing the execution of Karl and Walter LaGrand, and by "making irreversible its earlier breaches of Art. 5 and 36 (1) and (2) and causing irreparable harm, the United States violated its obligations under international law".

* * *

71. Germany further contends that there is a causal relationship between the breach of Article 36 and the ultimate execution of the LaGrand brothers. Germany's inability to render prompt assistance was, in its view, a "direct result of the United States' breach of its Vienna Convention obligations". It is claimed that, had Germany been properly afforded its rights under the Vienna Convention, it would have been able to intervene in time and present a "persuasive mitigation case" which "likely would have saved" the lives of the brothers. Germany believes that, "[h]ad proper notification been given under the Vienna Convention, competent trial counsel certainly would have looked to Germany for assistance in developing this line of mitigating evidence". Moreover, Germany argues that, due to the doctrine of procedural default and the high post-conviction threshold for proving ineffective counsel under United States law, Germany's intervention at a stage later than the trial phase could not "reme-

dy the extreme prejudice created by the counsel appointed to represent the LaGrands".

* * *

74. Article 36, paragraph 1, establishes an interrelated régime designed to facilitate the implementation of the system of consular protection. It begins with the basic principle governing consular protection: the right of communication and access (Art. 36, para. 1 (*a*)). This clause is followed by the provision which spells out the modalities of consular notification (Art. 36, para. 1 (*b*)). Finally Article 36, paragraph 1 (*c*), sets out the measures consular officers may take in rendering consular assistance to their nationals in the custody of the receiving State. It follows that when the sending State is unaware of the detention of its nationals due to the failure of the receiving State to provide the requisite consular notification without delay, which was true in the present case during the period between 1982 and 1992, the sending State has been prevented for all practical purposes from exercising its rights under Article 36, paragraph 1. It is immaterial for the purposes of the present case whether the LaGrands would have sought consular assistance from Germany, whether Germany would have rendered such assistance, or whether a different verdict would have been rendered. It is sufficient that the Convention conferred these rights, and that Germany and the LaGrands were in effect prevented by the breach of the United States from exercising them, had they so chosen.

75. Germany further contends that "the breach of Article 36 by the United States did not only infringe upon the rights of Germany as a State party to the [Vienna] Convention but also entailed a violation of the individual rights of the LaGrand brothers". Invoking its right of diplomatic protection, Germany also seeks relief against the United States on this ground.

Germany maintains that the right to be informed of the rights under Article 36, paragraph 1 (*b*), of the Vienna Convention, is an individual right of every national of a State party to the Convention who enters the territory of another State party. It submits that this view is supported by the ordinary meaning of the terms of Article 36, paragraph 1 (*b*), of the Vienna Convention, since the last sentence of that provision speaks of the "rights" under this subparagraph of "the person concerned", i.e., of the foreign national arrested or detained. * * *

76. * * * The United States contends * * * that rights of consular notification and access under the Vienna Convention are rights of States, and not of individuals, even though these rights may benefit individuals by permitting States to offer them consular assistance. It maintains that the treatment due to individuals under the Convention is inextricably linked to and derived from the right of the State, acting through its consular of-

ficer, to communicate with its nationals, and does not constitute a fundamental right or a human right. * * *

77. The Court notes that Article 36, paragraph 1 (*b*), spells out the obligations the receiving State has towards the detained person and the sending State. It provides that, at the request of the detained person, the receiving State must inform the consular post of the sending State of the individual's detention "without delay". It provides further that any communication by the detained person addressed to the consular post of the sending State must be forwarded to it by authorities of the receiving State "without delay". Significantly, this subparagraph ends with the following language: "The said authorities shall inform the person concerned without delay of *his rights* under this subparagraph" (emphasis added). Moreover, under Article 36, paragraph 1 (*c*), the sending State's right to provide consular assistance to the detained person may not be exercised "if he expressly opposes such action". The clarity of these provisions, viewed in their context, admits of no doubt. It follows, as has been held on a number of occasions, that the Court must apply these as they stand. Based on the text of these provisions, the Court concludes that Article 36, paragraph 1, creates individual rights, which, by virtue of Article I of the Optional Protocol, may be invoked in this Court by the national State of the detained person. These rights were violated in the present case.

78. At the hearings, Germany further contended that the right of the individual to be informed without delay under Article 36, paragraph 1, of the Vienna Convention was not only an individual right, but has today assumed the character of a human right. In consequence, Germany added, "the character of the right under Article 36 as a human right renders the effectiveness of this provision even more imperative". The Court having found that the United States violated the rights accorded by Article 36, paragraph 1, to the LaGrand brothers, it does not appear necessary to it to consider the additional argument developed by Germany in this regard.

79. The Court will now consider Germany's second submission, in which it asks the Court to adjudge and declare:

> "that the United States, by applying rules of its domestic law, in particular the doctrine of procedural default, which barred Karl and Walter LaGrand from raising their claims under the Vienna Convention on Consular Relations, and by ultimately executing them, violated its international legal obligation to Germany under Article 36, paragraph 2, of the Vienna Convention to give full effect to the purposes for which the rights accorded under Article 36 of the said Convention are intended".

80. Germany argues that, under Article 36, paragraph 2, of the Vienna Convention

"the United States is under an obligation to ensure that its municipal "laws and regulations * * * enable full effect to be given to the purposes for which the rights accorded under this article are intended" [and that it] is in breach of this obligation by upholding rules of domestic law which make it impossible to successfully raise a violation of the right to consular notification in proceedings subsequent to a conviction of a defendant by a jury".

81. Germany points out that the "procedural default" rule is among the rules of United States domestic law whose application make it impossible to invoke a breach of the notification requirement. According to Germany, this rule "is closely connected with the division of labour between federal and state jurisdiction in the United States * * * [where] [c]riminal jurisdiction belongs to the States except in cases provided for in the Constitution". This rule, Germany explains, requires "exhaustion of remedies at the State level before a *habeas corpus* motion can be filed with federal Courts".

Germany emphasizes that it is not the "procedural default" rule as such that is at issue in the present proceedings, but the manner in which it was applied in that it "deprived the brothers of the possibility to raise the violations of their right to consular notification in U.S. criminal proceedings".

82. Furthermore, having examined the relevant United States jurisprudence, Germany contends that the procedural default rule had "made it impossible for the LaGrand brothers to effectively raise the issue of the lack of consular notification after they had at last learned of their rights and established contact with the German consulate in Los Angeles in 1992".

83. Finally, Germany states that it seeks

"[n]othing * * * more than compliance, or, at least, a system in place which does not automatically reproduce violation after violation of the Vienna Convention, only interrupted by the apologies of the United States Government".

84. The United States objects to Germany's second submission, since it considers that "Germany's position goes far beyond the wording of the Convention, the intentions of the parties when it was negotiated, and the practice of States, including Germany's practice".

* * *

88. Article 36, paragraph 2, of the Vienna Convention reads as follows:

"The rights referred to in paragraph 1 of this article shall be exercised in conformity with the laws and regulations of the receiving State, subject to the proviso, however, that the said laws and regulations must enable full effect to be given to the purposes for which the rights accorded under this article are intended."

* * *

90. Turning now to the "procedural default" rule, the application of which in the present case Germany alleges violated Article 36, paragraph 2, the Court emphasizes that a distinction must be drawn between that rule as such and its specific application in the present case. In itself, the rule does not violate Article 36 of the Vienna Convention. The problem arises when the procedural default rule does not allow the detained individual to challenge a conviction and sentence by claiming, in reliance on Article 36, paragraph 1, of the Convention, that the competent national authorities failed to comply with their obligation to provide the requisite consular information "without delay", thus preventing the person from seeking and obtaining consular assistance from the sending State.

91. In this case, Germany had the right at the request of the LaGrands "to arrange for [their] legal representation" and was eventually able to provide some assistance to that effect. By that time, however, because of the failure of the American authorities to comply with their obligation under Article 36, paragraph 1 (*b*), the procedural default rule prevented counsel for the LaGrands to effectively challenge their convictions and sentences other than on United States constitutional grounds. As a result, although United States courts could and did examine the professional competence of counsel assigned to the indigent LaGrands by reference to United States constitutional standards, the procedural default rule prevented them from attaching any legal significance to the fact, *inter alia*, that the violation of the rights set forth in Article 36, paragraph 1, prevented Germany, in a timely fashion, from retaining private counsel for them and otherwise assisting in their defence as provided for by the Convention. Under these circumstances, the procedural default rule had the effect of preventing "full effect [from being] given to the purposes for which the rights accorded under this article are intended", and thus violated paragraph 2 of Article 36.

92. The Court will now consider Germany's third submission, in which it asks the Court to adjudge and declare:

> "that the United States, by failing to take all measures at its disposal to ensure that Walter LaGrand was not executed pending the final decision of the International Court of Justice on the matter, violated its international legal obligation to comply with the Order on Provisional Measures issued by the Court on 3 March 1999, and to refrain from any action which might interfere with the subject matter of a dispute while judicial proceedings are pending".

93. In its Memorial, Germany contended that "[p]rovisional [m]easures indicated by the International Court of Justice [were] binding by virtue of the law of the United Nations Charter and the Statute of the Court". * * *

94. Germany claims that the United States committed a threefold violation of the Court's Order of 3 March 1999:

"(1) Immediately after the International Court of Justice had rendered its Order on Provisional Measures, Germany appealed to the U.S. Supreme Court in order to reach a stay of the execution of Walter LaGrand, in accordance with the International Court's Order to the same effect. In the course of these proceedings—and in full knowledge of the Order of the International Court—the Office of the Solicitor General, a section of the U.S. Department of Justice—in a letter to the Supreme Court argued once again that: 'an order of the International Court of Justice indicating provisional measures is not binding and does not furnish a basis for judicial relief'.

This statement of a high-ranking official of the Federal Government * * * had a direct influence on the decision of the Supreme Court.

* * *

(2) In the following, the U.S. Supreme Court—an agency of the United States—refused by a majority vote to order that the execution be stayed. In doing so, it rejected the German arguments based essentially on the Order of the International Court of Justice on Provisional Measures * * *

(3) Finally, the Governor of Arizona did not order a stay of the execution of Walter LaGrand although she was vested with the right to do so by the laws of the State of Arizona. Moreover, in the present case, the Arizona Executive Board of Clemency—for the first time in the history of this institution—had issued a recommendation for a temporary stay, not least in light of the international legal issues involved in the case * * * "

95. The United States argues that it "did what was called for by the Court's 3 March Order, given the extraordinary and unprecedented circumstances in which it was forced to act". It points out in this connection that the United States Government "immediately transmitt[ed] the Order to the Governor of Arizona", that "the United States placed the Order in the hands of the one official who, at that stage, might have had legal authority to stop the execution" and that by a letter from the Legal Counsellor of the United States Embassy in The Hague dated 8 March 1999, it informed the International Court of Justice of all the measures which had been taken in implementation of the Order.

The United States further states that:

> "[t]wo central factors constrained the United States ability to act. The first was the extraordinarily short time between issuance of the Court's Order and the time set for the execution of Walter LaGrand * * *

> The second constraining factor was the character of the United States of America as a federal republic of divided powers."

* * *

101. * * * The Court will therefore now consider the object and purpose of the Statute together with the context of Article 41.

102. The object and purpose of the Statute is to enable the Court to fulfil the functions provided for therein, and in particular, the basic function of judicial settlement of international disputes by binding decisions in accordance with Article 59 of the Statute. The context in which Article 41 has to be seen within the Statute is to prevent the Court from being hampered in the exercise of its functions because the respective rights of the parties to a dispute before the Court are not preserved. It follows from the object and purpose of the Statute, as well as from the terms of Article 41 when read in their context, that the power to indicate provisional measures entails that such measures should be binding, inasmuch as the power in question is based on the necessity, when the circumstances call for it, to safeguard, and to avoid prejudice to, the rights of the parties as determined by the final judgment of the Court. The contention that provisional measures indicated under Article 41 might not be binding would be contrary to the object and purpose of that Article.

103. A related reason which points to the binding character of orders made under Article 41 and to which the Court attaches importance, is the existence of a principle which has already been recognized by the Permanent Court of International Justice when it spoke of

> "the principle universally accepted by international tribunals and likewise laid down in many conventions * * * to the effect that the parties to a case must abstain from any measure capable of exercising a prejudicial effect in regard to the execution of the decision to be given, and, in general, not allow any step of any kind to be taken which might aggravate or extend the dispute" (*Electricity Company of Sofia and Bulgaria, Order of 5 December 1939, P.C.I.J, Series A/B, No. 79*, p. 199).

* * *

109. In short, it is clear that none of the sources of interpretation referred to in the relevant Articles of the Vienna Convention on the Law of Treaties, including the preparatory work, contradict the conclusions drawn

from the terms of Article 41 read in their context and in the light of the object and purpose of the Statute. Thus, the Court has reached the conclusion that orders on provisional measures under Article 41 have binding effect.

110. The Court will now consider the Order of 3 March 1999. This Order was not a mere exhortation. It had been adopted pursuant to Article 41 of the Statute. This Order was consequently binding in character and created a legal obligation for the United States.

111. * * * The United States authorities have * * * limited themselves to the mere transmission of the text of the Order to the Governor of Arizona. This certainly met the requirement of the second of the two measures indicated. As to the first measure, the Court notes that it did not create an obligation of result, but that the United States was asked to "take all measures at its disposal to ensure that Walter LaGrand is not executed pending the final decision in these proceedings". The Court agrees that due to the extremely late presentation of the request for provisional measures, there was certainly very little time for the United States authorities to act.

112. The Court observes, nevertheless, that the mere transmission of its Order to the Governor of Arizona without any comment, particularly without even so much as a plea for a temporary stay and an explanation that there is no general agreement on the position of the United States that orders of the International Court of Justice on provisional measures are non-binding, was certainly less than could have been done even in the short time available. The same is true of the United States Solicitor General's categorical statement in his brief letter to the United States Supreme Court that "an order of the International Court of Justice indicating provisional measures is not binding and does not furnish a basis for judicial relief" (see paragraph 33 above). This statement went substantially further than the amicus brief referred to in a mere footnote in his letter, which was filed on behalf of the United States in earlier proceedings before the United States Supreme Court in the case of Angel Francisco Breard (see *Breard* v. *Greene*, United States Supreme Court, 14 April 1998, *International Legal Materials*, Vol. 37 (1988), p. 824; Memorial of Germany, Ann. 34). In that amicus brief, the same Solicitor General had declared less than a year earlier that "there is substantial disagreement among jurists as to whether an ICJ order indicating provisional measures is binding * * * The better reasoned position is that such an order is not binding."

113. It is also noteworthy that the Governor of Arizona, to whom the Court's Order had been transmitted, decided not to give effect to it, even though the Arizona Clemency Board had recommended a stay of execution for Walter LaGrand.

114. Finally, the United States Supreme Court rejected a separate application by Germany for a stay of execution, "[g]iven the tardiness of the pleas and the jurisdictional barriers they implicate". Yet it would have been open to the Supreme Court, as one of its members urged, to grant a preliminary stay, which would have given it "time to consider, after briefing from all interested parties, the jurisdictional and international legal issues involved * * * " (*Federal Republic of Germany et al.* v. *United States et al.*, United States Supreme Court, 3 March 1999).

115. The review of the above steps taken by the authorities of the United States with regard to the Order of the International Court of Justice of 3 March 1999 indicates that the various competent United States authorities failed to take all the steps they could have taken to give effect to the Court's Order. The Order did not require the United States to exercise powers it did not have; but it did impose the obligation to "take all measures at its disposal to ensure that Walter LaGrand is not executed pending the final decision in these proceedings * * * ". The Court finds that the United States did not discharge this obligation.

Under these circumstances the Court concludes that the United States has not complied with the Order of 3 March 1999.

116. The Court observes finally that in the third submission Germany requests the Court to adjudge and declare only that the United States violated its international legal obligation to comply with the Order of 3 March 1999; it contains no other request regarding that violation. Moreover, the Court points out that the United States was under great time pressure in this case, due to the circumstances in which Germany had instituted the proceedings. The Court notes moreover that at the time when the United States authorities took their decision the question of the binding character of orders indicating provisional measures had been extensively discussed in the literature, but had not been settled by its jurisprudence. The Court would have taken these factors into consideration had Germany's submission included a claim for indemnification.

117. Finally, the Court will consider Germany's fourth submission, in which it asks the Court to adjudge and declare

> "that the United States shall provide Germany an assurance that it will not repeat its unlawful acts and that, in any future cases of detention of or criminal proceedings against German nationals, the United States will ensure in law and practice the effective exercise of the rights under Article 36 of the Vienna Convention on Consular Relations. In particular in cases involving the death penalty, this requires the United States to provide effective review of and remedies for criminal convictions impaired by a violation of the rights under Article 36."

118. Germany states that:

> "[c]oncerning the requested assurances and guarantees of non-repetition of the United States, they are appropriate because of the existence of a real risk of repetition and the seriousness of the injury suffered by Germany. Further, the choice of means by which full conformity of the future conduct of the United States with Article 36 of the Vienna Convention is to be ensured, may be left to the United States."

Germany explains that:

> "the effective exercise of the right to consular notification embodied in [Article 36,] paragraph 2, requires that, where it cannot be excluded that the judgment was impaired by the violation of the right to consular notification, appellate proceedings allow for a reversal of the judgment and for either a retrial or a re-sentencing".

Finally, Germany points out that its fourth submission has been so worded "as to * * * leave the choice of means by which to implement the remedy [it seeks] to the United States".

119. In reply, the United States argues as follows:

> "Germany's fourth submission is clearly of a wholly different nature than its first three submissions. Each of the first three submissions seeks a judgment and declaration by the Court that a violation of a stated international legal obligation has occurred. Such judgments are at the core of the Court's function, as an aspect of reparation.
>
> * * *
>
> In contrast, however, to the character of the relief sought in the first three submissions, the requirement of assurances of non-repetition sought in the fourth submission has no precedent in the jurisprudence of this Court and would exceed the Court's jurisdiction and authority in this case. It is exceptional even as a non-legal undertaking in State practice, and it would be entirely inappropriate for the Court to require such assurances with respect to the duty to inform undertaken in the Consular Convention in the circumstances of this case."

It points out that "U.S. authorities are working energetically to strengthen the regime of consular notification at the state and local level throughout the United States, in order to reduce the chances of cases such as this recurring" and adds that:

> "the German request for an assurance as to the duty to inform foreign nationals without delay of their right to consular notification * * * seeks to have the Court require the United States to assure that it will never again fail to inform a German foreign national of his or her right to consular notification",

and that "the Court is aware that the United States is not in a position to provide such an assurance." The United States further contends that it "has already provided appropriate assurances to Germany on this point".

* * *

120. The Court observes that in its fourth submission Germany seeks several assurances. First it seeks a straightforward assurance that the United States will not repeat its unlawful acts. This request does not specify the means by which non-repetition is to be assured.

Additionally, Germany seeks from the United States that

> "in any future cases of detention of or criminal proceedings against German nationals, the United States will ensure in law and practice the effective exercise of the rights under Article 36 of the Vienna Convention on Consular Relations".

This request goes further, for, by referring to the law of the United States, it appears to require specific measures as a means of preventing recurrence.

Germany finally requests that

> "[i]n particular in cases involving the death penalty, this requires the United States to provide effective review of and remedies for criminal convictions impaired by a violation of the rights under Article 36".

This request goes even further, since it is directed entirely towards securing specific measures in cases involving the death penalty.

121. Turning first to the general demand for an assurance of non-repetition, the Court observes that it has been informed by the United States of the "substantial measures [which it is taking] aimed at preventing any recurrence" of the breach of Article 36, paragraph 1 (*b*). Throughout these proceedings, oral as well as written, the United States has insisted that it "keenly appreciates the importance of the Vienna Convention's consular notification obligation for foreign citizens in the United States as well as for United States citizens travelling and living abroad"; that "effective compliance with the consular notification requirements of Article 36 of the Vienna Convention requires constant effort and attention"; and that

> "the Department of State is working intensively to improve understanding of and compliance with consular notification and access requirements throughout the United States, so as to guard against future violations of these requirements".

The United States points out that

> "[t]his effort has included the January 1998 publication of a booklet entitled "Consular Notification and Access: Instructions for Federal,

State and Local Law Enforcement and Other Officials Regarding Foreign Nationals in the United States and the Rights of Consular Officials to Assist Them," and development of a small reference card designed to be carried by individual arresting officers".

According to the United States, it is estimated that until now over 60,000 copies of the brochure as well as over 400,000 copies of the pocket card have been distributed to federal, state and local law enforcement and judicial officials throughout the United States. The United States is also conducting training programmes reaching out to all levels of government. In the Department of State a permanent office to focus on United States and foreign compliance with consular notification and access requirements has been created.

* * *

123. The Court notes that the United States has acknowledged that, in the case of the LaGrand brothers, it did not comply with its obligations to give consular notification. The United States has presented an apology to Germany for this breach. The Court considers however that an apology is not sufficient in this case, as it would not be in other cases where foreign nationals have not been advised without delay of their rights under Article 36, paragraph 1, of the Vienna Convention and have been subjected to prolonged detention or sentenced to severe penalties.

In this respect, the Court has taken note of the fact that the United States repeated in all phases of these proceedings that it is carrying out a vast and detailed programme in order to ensure compliance by its competent authorities at the federal as well as at the state and local levels with its obligation under Article 36 of the Vienna Convention.

124. The United States has provided the Court with information, which it considers important, on its programme. If a State, in proceedings before this Court, repeatedly refers to substantial activities which it is carrying out in order to achieve compliance with certain obligations under a treaty, then this expresses a commitment to follow through with the efforts in this regard. The programme in question certainly cannot provide an assurance that there will never again be a failure by the United States to observe the obligation of notification under Article 36 of the Vienna Convention. But no State could give such a guarantee and Germany does not seek it. The Court considers that the commitment expressed by the United States to ensure implementation of the specific measures adopted in performance of its obligations under Article 36, paragraph 1 (*b*), must be regarded as meeting Germany's request for a general assurance of non-repetition.

125. * * * The Court considers in this respect that if the United States, notwithstanding its commitment referred to in paragraph 124 above,

should fail in its obligation of consular notification to the detriment of German nationals, an apology would not suffice in cases where the individuals concerned have been subjected to prolonged detention or convicted and sentenced to severe penalties. In the case of such a conviction and sentence, it would be incumbent upon the United States to allow the review and reconsideration of the conviction and sentence by taking account of the violation of the rights set forth in the Convention. This obligation can be carried out in various ways. The choice of means must be left to the United States.

* * *

128. For these reasons,

THE COURT,

(1) By fourteen votes to one,

Finds that it has jurisdiction, on the basis of Article I of the Optional Protocol concerning the Compulsory Settlement of Disputes to the Vienna Convention on Consular Relations of 24 April 1963, to entertain the Application filed by the Federal Republic of Germany on 2 March 1999;

* * *

(2) (*a*) By thirteen votes to two,

Finds that the first submission of the Federal Republic of Germany is admissible;

* * *

(*b*) By fourteen votes to one,

Finds that the second submission of the Federal Republic of Germany is admissible;

* * *

(*c*) By twelve votes to three,

Finds that the third submission of the Federal Republic of Germany is admissible;

* * *

(*d*) By fourteen votes to one,

Finds that the fourth submission of the Federal Republic of Germany is admissible;

* * *

(3) By fourteen votes to one,

Finds that, by not informing Karl and Walter LaGrand without delay following their arrest of their rights under Article 36, paragraph 1 (*b*), of the Convention, and by thereby depriving the Federal Republic of Germany of the possibility, in a timely fashion, to render the assistance provided for by the Convention to the individuals concerned, the United States of America breached its obligations to the Federal Republic of Germany and to the LaGrand brothers under Article 36, paragraph 1;

* * *

(4) By fourteen votes to one,

Finds that, by not permitting the review and reconsideration, in the light of the rights set forth in the Convention, of the convictions and sentences of the LaGrand brothers after the violations referred to in paragraph (3) above had been established, the United States of America breached its obligation to the Federal Republic of Germany and to the LaGrand brothers under Article 36, paragraph 2, of the Convention;

* * *

(5) By thirteen votes to two,

Finds that, by failing to take all measures at its disposal to ensure that Walter LaGrand was not executed pending the final decision of the International Court of Justice in the case, the United States of America breached the obligation incumbent upon it under the Order indicating provisional measures issued by the Court on 3 March 1999;

* * *

(6) Unanimously,

Takes note of the commitment undertaken by the United States of America to ensure implementation of the specific measures adopted in performance of its obligations under Article 36, paragraph 1 (*b*), of the Convention; and *finds* that this commitment must be regarded as meeting the Federal Republic of Germany's request for a general assurance of non-repetition;

(7) By fourteen votes to one,

Finds that should nationals of the Federal Republic of Germany nonetheless be sentenced to severe penalties, without their rights under Article 36, paragraph 1 (*b*), of the Convention having been respected, the United States of America, by means of its own choosing, shall allow the review and reconsideration of the conviction and sentence by taking account of the violation of the rights set forth in that Convention.

* * *

Done in English and in French, the English text being authoritative, at the Peace Palace, The Hague, this twenty-seventh day of June, two thousand and one, in three copies, one of which will be placed in the archives of the Court and the others transmitted to the Government of the Federal Republic of Germany and the Government of the United States of America, respectively.

What exactly was the United States required to do to comply with the ICJ's judgment? Which actors within the United States could or were required to ensure such compliance?

In paragraph 121 of the *LaGrand* decision, the Court refers to a pocket card created by the State Department and distributed to law enforcement agencies throughout the United States. Below, find the current version of the pocket card on VCCR notification. Should distributing this card count as a sufficient effort by the United States to prevent further violations of Article 36 of the Vienna Convention?

Consular Notification and Access Reference Card: Instructions for Arrests and Detentions of Foreign Nationals

This card summarizes for law enforcement officials the basic consular notification procedures to follow upon the arrest or detention of a foreign national. For more detailed instructions and legal material, see the Department of State publication *Consular Notification and Access*. The complete publication is available at http://travel.state.gov/consularnotification.

Questions may be addressed to:

Office of Policy Coordination & Public Affairs
CA/P, Room 4800 HST
U.S. Department of State
Washington, DC 20520
Telephone: 202-647-4415
Fax: 202-736-7559
Email: consnot@state.gov

Urgent after-hours inquiries may be directed to 202-647-1512
(State Department Operations Center.)

"Mandatory Notification" ("List") Countries

Albania	Malta
Algeria	Mauritius
Antigua and Barbuda	Moldova
Armenia	Mongolia
Azerbaijan	Nigeria
Bahamas	Philippines
Barbados	Poland[2]
Belarus	Romania
Belize	Russia
Brunei	Saint Kitts and Nevis
Bulgaria	Saint Lucia
China[1] (Including Macau and Hong Kong)	Saint Vincent and
Costa Rica	the Grenadines
Cyprus	Seychelles
Czech Republic	Sierra Leone
Dominica	Singapore
Fiji	Slovakia
Gambia	Tajikistan
Georgia	Tanzania
Ghana	Tonga
Grenada	Trinidad and Tobago
Guyana	Tunisia
Hungary	Turkmenistan
Jamaica	Tuvalu
Kazakhstan	Ukraine
Kiribati	United Kingdom[3]
Kuwait	Uzbekistan
Kyrgyzstan	Zambia
Malaysia	Zimbabwe

[1]Does not include Republic of China (Taiwan) passport holders.
[2]Mandatory for non-permanent residents only.
[3]U.K. includes Anguilla, Bermuda, the British Virgin Islands, the Cayman Islands, Montserrat, and the Turks and Caicos Islands. Residents' passports bear the name of their territory and may also bear the name "United Kingdom."

Steps To Follow When a Foreign National Is Arrested or Detained[1]

1. Determine the foreign national's country of nationality. In the absence of other information, assume this is the country on whose passport or other document the national is traveling.

2. If the foreign national's country is **not** on the list of mandatory notification countries:

   a) Use Statement 1 on the back of this card to inform the national, without delay, that he or she may have his or her consular officers notified and may communicate with them.

   b) If the national requests that the consular officers be notified, notify the nearest consulate of the national's country without delay.

   c) Forward any communication from the national to the consulate without delay.

3. If the foreign national's country is on the list of mandatory notification countries:

   a) Notify the national's nearest consulate, without delay, of the arrest or detention.

   b) Use Statement 2 on the back of this card to tell the national, without delay, that you are making this notification and that he or she may communicate with the consulate.

   c) Forward any communication from the national to the consulate without delay.

4. Keep a written record of:

   • What information you provided to the foreign national and when.

   • The foreign national's requests, if any.

   • Whether you notified consular officers and, if so, the date and time and how you notified them (e.g., fax or phone). Keep any fax confirmation in your records.

   • Any other relevant actions taken.

[1]These steps should be followed for all foreign nationals, regardless of their immigration status.

Suggested Statements to Arrested or Detained Foreign Nationals

Statement 1:
For All Foreign Nationals Except Those From Mandatory Notification Countries

As a non-U.S. citizen who is being arrested or detained, you may request that we notify your country's consular officers here in the United States of your situation. You may also communicate with your consular officers. A consular officer may be able to help you obtain legal representation, and may contact your family and visit you in detention, among other things. If you want us to notify your consular officers, you can request this notification now, or at any time in the future. Do you want us to notify your consular officers at this time?

Statement 2:
For Foreign Nationals From Mandatory Notification Countries

Because of your nationality, we are required to notify your country's consular officers here in the United States that you have been arrested or detained. We will do this as soon as possible. In addition, you may communicate with your consular officers. You are not required to accept their assistance, but your consular officers may be able to help you obtain legal representation, and may contact your family and visit you in detention, among other things. Please sign to show that you have received this information.

GPS Printed by Global Publishing Solutions (A/GIS/GPS) © (10-2396-E-1.0)

C. ROUND THREE: THE AVENA GROUP

Perhaps encouraged by Germany's resounding victory in the *LaGrand* case, Mexico brought suit against the United States in the ICJ in January 2003 because over 50 of its nationals, who were on death row in various U.S. states and who were thus threatened with execution, had not been informed of their consular rights either. The ICJ again issued a provisional measure seeking to prevent executions while the case was pending; this time, no executions took place during that interim period. In its final decision in *Avena*, the ICJ handed the United States another defeat.

What exactly does *Avena* add to *LaGrand*? Do the obligations of the United States under the Vienna Convention become more stringent or precise? In particular, according to the ICJ, what must the United States do regarding the "procedural default" rule?

CASE CONCERNING AVENA
AND OTHER MEXICAN NATIONALS
(MEXICO V. UNITED STATES)

International Court of Justice
2001 I.C.J. 1

[The International Court of Justice first found the United States had breached its obligations under Article 36 paragraph 1 of the Vienna Convention on Consular Relations by failing to inform the arrested Mexican nationals of their rights thereunder as well as by failing to inform the Mexican consular posts of the arrests. It then turned to the harder questions arising from the procedural default rule and to the issue of the appropriate remedy.]

* * *

107. In its third final submission Mexico asks the Court to adjudge and declare that "the United States violated its obligations under Article 36 (2) of the Vienna Convention by failing to provide meaningful and effective review and reconsideration of convictions and sentences impaired by a violation of Article 36 (1)".

108. Article 36, paragraph 2, provides:

"The rights referred to in paragraph 1 of this article shall be exercised in conformity with the laws and regulations of the receiving State, subject to the proviso, however, that the said laws and regulations must enable full effect to be given to the purposes for which the rights accorded under this article are intended."

* * *

112. The Court has already considered the application of the "procedural default" rule, alleged by Mexico to be a hindrance to the full implementation of the international obligations of the United States under Article 36, in the *LaGrand* case, when the Court addressed the issue of its implications for the application of Article 36, paragraph 2, of the Vienna Convention. The Court emphasized that "a distinction must be drawn between that rule as such and its specific application in the present case". The Court stated:

> "In itself, the rule does not violate Article 36 of the Vienna Convention. The problem arises when the procedural default rule does not allow the detained individual to challenge a conviction and sentence by claiming, in reliance on Article 36, paragraph 1, of the Convention, that the competent national authorities failed to comply with their obligation to provide the requisite consular information 'without delay', thus preventing the person from seeking and obtaining consular assistance from the sending State." (*I.C.J. Reports 2001*, p. 497, para. 90.)

On this basis, the Court concluded that "the procedural default rule prevented counsel for the LaGrands to effectively challenge their convictions and sentences other than on United States constitutional grounds" (*I.C.J. Reports 2001*, p. 497, para. 91). This statement of the Court seems equally valid in relation to the present case, where a number of Mexican nationals have been placed exactly in such a situation.

113. The Court will return to this aspect below, in the context of Mexico's claims as to remedies. For the moment, the Court simply notes that the procedural default rule has not been revised, nor has any provision been made to prevent its application in cases where it has been the failure of the United States itself to inform that may have precluded counsel from being in a position to have raised the question of a violation of the Vienna Convention in the initial trial. It thus remains the case that the procedural default rule may continue to prevent courts from attaching legal significance to the fact, *inter alia*, that the violation of the rights set forth in Article 36, paragraph 1, prevented Mexico, in a timely fashion, from retaining private counsel for certain nationals and otherwise assisting in their defence. In such cases, application of the procedural default rule would have the effect of preventing "full effect [from being] given to the purposes for which the rights accorded under this article are intended", and thus violate paragraph 2 of Article 36. The Court notes moreover that in several of the cases cited in Mexico's final submissions the procedural default rule has already been applied, and that in others it could be applied at subsequent stages in the proceedings. However, in none of the cases, save for the three mentioned in paragraph 114 below, have the criminal proceedings against the Mexican nationals concerned already reached a stage at which there is no further possibility of judicial reexam-

ination of those cases; that is to say, all possibility is not yet excluded of "review and reconsideration" of conviction and sentence, as called for in the *LaGrand* case, and as explained further in paragraphs 128 and following below. It would therefore be premature for the Court to conclude at this stage that, in those cases, there is already a violation of the obligations under Article 36, paragraph 2, of the Vienna Convention.

114. By contrast, the Court notes that in the case of three Mexican nationals, Mr. Fierro (case No. 31), Mr. Moreno (case No. 39), and Mr. Torres (case No. 53), conviction and sentence have become final. Moreover, in the case of Mr. Torres the Oklahoma Court of Criminal Appeals has set an execution date. The Court must therefore conclude that, in relation to these three individuals, the United States is in breach of the obligations incumbent upon it under Article 36, paragraph 2, of the Vienna Convention.

LEGAL CONSEQUENCES OF THE BREACH

115. Having concluded that in most of the cases brought before the Court by Mexico in the 52 instances, there has been a failure to observe the obligations prescribed by Article 36, paragraph 1 (*b*), of the Vienna Convention, the Court now proceeds to the examination of the legal consequences of such a breach and of what legal remedies should be considered for the breach.

* * *

119. The general principle on the legal consequences of the commission of an internationally wrongful act was stated by the Permanent Court of International Justice in the Factory at Chorzów case as follows: "It is a principle of international law that the breach of an engagement involves an obligation to make reparation in an adequate form." (*Factory at Chorzów, Jurisdiction, 1927, P.C.I.J., Series A, No. 9*, p. 21.) What constitutes "reparation in an adequate form" clearly varies depending upon the concrete circumstances surrounding each case and the precise nature and scope of the injury, since the question has to be examined from the viewpoint of what is the "reparation in an adequate form" that corresponds to the injury. In a subsequent phase of the same case, the Permanent Court went on to elaborate on this point as follows:

> "The essential principle contained in the actual notion of an illegal act—a principle which seems to be established by international practice and in particular by the decisions of arbitral tribunals—is that reparation must, as far as possible, wipe out all the consequences of the illegal act and reestablish the situation which would, in all probability, have existed if that act had not been committed." (*Factory at Chorzów, Merits, 1928, P.C.I.J., Series A, No. 17*, p. 47.)

120. In the *LaGrand* case the Court made a general statement on the principle involved as follows:

> "The Court considers in this respect that if the United States, notwithstanding its commitment [to ensure implementation of the specific measures adopted in performance of its obligations under Article 36, paragraph 1 (*b*)], should fail in its obligation of consular notification to the detriment of German nationals, an apology would not suffice in cases where the individuals concerned have been subjected to prolonged detention or convicted and sentenced to severe penalties. In the case of such a conviction and sentence, it would be incumbent upon the United States to allow the review and reconsideration of the conviction and sentence by taking account of the violation of the rights set forth in the Convention. This obligation can be carried out in various ways. The choice of means must be left to the United States." (*I.C.J. Reports 2001*, pp. 513–514, para. 125.)

121. Similarly, in the present case the Court's task is to determine what would be adequate reparation for the violations of Article 36. It should be clear from what has been observed above that the internationally wrongful acts committed by the United States were the failure of its competent authorities to inform the Mexican nationals concerned, to notify Mexican consular posts and to enable Mexico to provide consular assistance. It follows that the remedy to make good these violations should consist in an obligation on the United States to permit review and reconsideration of these nationals' cases by the United States courts, as the Court will explain further in paragraphs 128 to 134 below, with a view to ascertaining whether in each case the violation of Article 36 committed by the competent authorities caused actual prejudice to the defendant in the process of administration of criminal justice.

122. The Court reaffirms that the case before it concerns Article 36 of the Vienna Convention and not the correctness as such of any conviction or sentencing. The question of whether the violations of Article 36, paragraph 1, are to be regarded as having, in the causal sequence of events, ultimately led to convictions and severe penalties is an integral part of criminal proceedings before the courts of the United States and is for them to determine in the process of review and reconsideration. In so doing, it is for the courts of the United States to examine the facts, and in particular the prejudice and its causes, taking account of the violation of the rights set forth in the Convention.

* * *

131. In stating in its Judgment in the *LaGrand* case that "the United States of America, *by means of its own choosing*, shall allow the review and reconsideration of the conviction and sentence" (*I.C.J. Reports 2001*,

p. 516, para. 128 (7); emphasis added), the Court acknowledged that the concrete modalities for such review and reconsideration should be left primarily to the United States. It should be underlined, however, that this freedom in the choice of means for such review and reconsideration is not without qualification: as the passage of the Judgment quoted above makes abundantly clear, such review and reconsideration has to be carried out "by taking account of the violation of the rights set forth in the Convention" (*I.C.J. Reports 2001*, p. 514, para. 125), including, in particular, the question of the legal consequences of the violation upon the criminal proceedings that have followed the violation.

132. The United States argues (1) "that the Court's decision in *LaGrand* in calling for review and reconsideration called for a process to re-examine a conviction and sentence in light of a breach of Article 36"; (2) that, "in calling for a process of review, the Court necessarily implied that one legitimate result of that process might be a conclusion that the conviction and sentence should stand"; and (3) "that the relief Mexico seeks in this case is flatly inconsistent with the Judgment in *LaGrand*: it seeks precisely the award of a substantive outcome that the *LaGrand* Court declined to provide".

133. However, the Court wishes to point out that the current situation in the United States criminal procedure, as explained by the Agent at the hearings, is that

> "If the defendant alleged at trial that *a failure of consular information resulted in harm to a particular right essential to a fair trial*, an appeals court can *review how the lower court handled that claim of prejudice*,"

but that

> "*If the foreign national did not raise his Article 36 claim at trial, he may face procedural constraints* [i.e., the application of the procedural default rule] on raising that particular claim in direct or collateral judicial appeals" (emphasis added).

As a result, a claim based on the violation of Article 36, paragraph 1, of the Vienna Convention, however meritorious in itself, could be barred in the courts of the United States by the operation of the procedural default rule (see paragraph 111 above).

134. * * * The crucial point in this situation is that, by the operation of the procedural default rule as it is applied at present, the defendant is effectively barred from raising the issue of the violation of his rights under Article 36 of the Vienna Convention and is limited to seeking the vindication of his rights under the United States Constitution.

* * *

136. Against this contention of Mexico, the United States claims that it "gives 'full effect' to the 'purposes for which the rights accorded under [Article 36, paragraph 1,] are intended' through executive clemency". It argues that "[t]he clemency process * * * is well suited to the task of providing review and reconsideration". The United States explains that "Clemency * * * is more than a matter of grace; it is part of the overall scheme for ensuring justice and fairness in the legal process" and that "Clemency procedures are an integral part of the existing 'laws and regulations' of the United States through which errors are addressed".

137. Specifically in the context of the present case, the United States contends that the following two points are particularly noteworthy:

> "First, these clemency procedures allow for broad participation by advocates of clemency, including an inmate's attorney and the sending state's consular officer * * * Second, these clemency officials are not bound by principles of procedural default, finality, prejudice standards, or any other limitations on judicial review. They may consider any facts and circumstances that they deem appropriate and relevant, including specifically Vienna Convention claims."

138. The Court would emphasize that the "review and reconsideration" prescribed by it in the *LaGrand* case should be effective. Thus it should "tak[e] account of the violation of the rights set forth in [the] Convention" (*I.C.J. Reports 2001*, p. 516, para. 128 (7)) and guarantee that the violation and the possible prejudice caused by that violation will be fully examined and taken into account in the review and reconsideration process. Lastly, review and reconsideration should be both of the sentence and of the conviction.

139. Accordingly, in a situation of the violation of rights under Article 36, paragraph 1, of the Vienna Convention, the defendant raises his claim in this respect not as a case of "harm to a particular right essential to a fair trial"—a concept relevant to the enjoyment of due process rights under the United States Constitution—but as a case involving the infringement of his rights under Article 36, paragraph 1. The rights guaranteed under the Vienna Convention are treaty rights which the United States has undertaken to comply with in relation to the individual concerned, irrespective of the due process rights under United States constitutional law. In this regard, the Court would point out that what is crucial in the review and reconsideration process is the existence of a procedure which guarantees that full weight is given to the violation of the rights set forth in the Vienna Convention, whatever may be the actual outcome of such review and reconsideration.

140. As has been explained in paragraphs 128 to 134 above, the Court is of the view that, in cases where the breach of the individual rights of Mexican nationals under Article 36, paragraph 1 (*b*), of the Convention

has resulted, in the sequence of judicial proceedings that has followed, in the individuals concerned being subjected to prolonged detention or convicted and sentenced to severe penalties, the legal consequences of this breach have to be examined and taken into account in the course of review and reconsideration. The Court considers that it is the judicial process that is suited to this task.

* * *

151. The Court would now re-emphasize a point of importance. In the present case, it has had occasion to examine the obligations of the United States under Article 36 of the Vienna Convention in relation to Mexican nationals sentenced to death in the United States. Its findings as to the duty of review and reconsideration of convictions and sentences have been directed to the circumstance of severe penalties being imposed on foreign nationals who happen to be of Mexican nationality. To avoid any ambiguity, it should be made clear that, while what the Court has stated concerns the Mexican nationals whose cases have been brought before it by Mexico, the Court has been addressing the issues of principle raised in the course of the present proceedings from the viewpoint of the general application of the Vienna Convention, and there can be no question of making an *a contrario* argument in respect of any of the Court's findings in the present Judgment. In other words, the fact that in this case the Court's ruling has concerned only Mexican nationals cannot be taken to imply that the conclusions reached by it in the present Judgment do not apply to other foreign nationals finding themselves in similar situations in the United States.

* * *

153. For these reasons,

The Court,

* * *

(8) By fourteen votes to one,

Finds that, by not permitting the review and reconsideration, in the light of the rights set forth in the Convention, of the conviction and sentences of Mr. César Roberto Fierro Reyna, Mr. Roberto Moreno Ramos and Mr. Osvaldo Torres Aguilera, after the violations referred to in subparagraph (4) above had been established in respect of those individuals, the United States of America breached the obligations incumbent upon it under Article 36, paragraph 2, of the Convention;

* * *

(9) By fourteen votes to one,

Finds that the appropriate reparation in this case consists in the obligation of the United States of America to provide, by means of its own choosing, review and reconsideration of the convictions and sentences of the Mexican nationals referred to in subparagraphs (4), (5), (6) and (7) above, by taking account both of the violation of the rights set forth in Article 36 of the Convention and of paragraphs 138 to 141 of this Judgment;

* * *

(10) Unanimously,

Takes note of the commitment undertaken by the United States of America to ensure implementation of the specific measures adopted in performance of its obligations under Article 36, paragraph 1 (*b*), of the Vienna Convention; and finds that this commitment must be regarded as meeting the request by the United Mexican States for guarantees and assurances of non-repetition;

* * *

(11) Unanimously,

Finds that, should Mexican nationals nonetheless be sentenced to severe penalties, without their rights under Article 36, paragraph 1 (*b*), of the Convention having been respected, the United States of America shall provide, by means of its own choosing, review and reconsideration of the conviction and sentence, so as to allow full weight to be given to the violation of the rights set forth in the Convention, taking account of paragraphs 138 to 141 of this Judgment.

* * *

In order to comply, would the United States have to abandon the procedural default rule in cases in which the state authorities had failed to inform the arrested foreign nationals of their consular rights?

Whom does the ICJ try to bind with its decision? Is paragraph 151 of the opinion consistent with Article 59 of the ICJ Statute?

D. ROUND FOUR: IMPLEMENTING AVENA?

Having had a brush with defeat in Paraguay's suit and having suffered two beatings in the cases brought by Germany and Mexico, the United States attempted to ensure that no more cases would be brought against it in the ICJ for breach of the Vienna Convention on Consular Relations:

it withdrew from the Optional Protocol which contains the promissory clause giving the ICJ jurisdiction over claims under the Convention.

Can the United States just withdraw from the Optional Protocol, which is a treaty in its own right, at will? If so, when does the withdrawal become effective? Where would you go to look for an answer? What does the United States' move mean for other foreigners arrested *before* the withdrawal?

The United States' withdrawal notwithstanding, the consular rights issue continued to occupy the domestic courts. In December of 2004, the United States Supreme Court granted certiorari in the case of José Medellín— one of the convicts on death row covered by the *Avena* case—and several other Mexican death row inmates who argued that their convictions and sentences should be reexamined in light of the ICJ's holding. The two questions presented to the Supreme Court were:

> 1. In a case brought by a Mexican national whose rights were adjudicated in the *Avena* judgment, must a court in the United States apply as the rule of decision, notwithstanding any inconsistent United States precedent, the *Avena* holding that the United States courts must review and reconsider the national's conviction and sentence, without resort to procedural default doctrines?

> 2. In a case brought by a foreign national of a State party to the Vienna Convention, should a court in the United States give effect to the *LaGrand* and *Avena* judgments as a matter of international judicial comity and in the interest of uniform treaty interpretation?

The Supreme Court heard oral argument, but then dismissed the petition for certiorari as improvidently granted. It thus avoided a decision on the merits. The 5–4 decision is complex (there were three dissenting opinions), and there were several (official) reasons for the dismissal. Perhaps the most important consideration was that after *Avena*, Medellín had filed a new petition for rehearing in the Texas state courts. If that petition was successful, the issue would become moot; if it was not, the Supreme Court could still review the denial. Thus, the Court decided to stay out of the fray, at least for the time being.

However, the question of the impact of *Avena* (and *LaGrand*) on domestic law, especially on the procedural default rule, could ultimately not be ducked. Pretty soon, the United States Supreme Court faced it in a similar case (i.e., not Medellín's). This time, the Court grabbed the bull by the horns.

SANCHEZ–LLAMAS V. OREGON
BUSTILLO V. JOHNSON
United States Supreme Court
548 U.S. 331 (2006)

CHIEF JUSTICE ROBERTS delivered the opinion of the Court, in which JUS-
TICES SCALIA, KENNEDY, THOMAS, and ALITO joined. JUSTICE GINSBURG
filed an opinion concurring in the judgment. JUSTICE BREYER filed a dissenting opinion, in which JUSTICES STEVENS and SOUTER joined, and in
which JUSTICE GINSBURG joined as to Part II.

* * *

Article 36 of the Vienna Convention on Consular Relations (Vienna Convention or Convention), addresses communication between an individual
and his consular officers when the individual is detained by authorities in
a foreign country. These consolidated cases concern the availability of judicial relief for violations of Article 36. We are confronted with three
questions. *First,* does Article 36 create rights that defendants may invoke
against the detaining authorities in a criminal trial or in a postconviction
proceeding? *Second*, does a violation of Article 36 require suppression of a
defendant's statements to police? *Third*, may a State, in a postconviction
proceeding, treat a defendant's Article 36 claim as defaulted because he
failed to raise the claim at trial? We conclude, even assuming the Convention creates judicially enforceable rights, that suppression is not an appropriate remedy for a violation of Article 36, and that a State may apply
its regular rules of procedural default to Article 36 claims. We therefore
affirm the decisions below.

* * *

Bustillo argues that *LaGrand* and *Avena* warrant revisiting the procedural default holding of *Breard*. In a similar vein, several *amici* contend
that "the United States is *obligated* to comply with the Convention, *as
interpreted by the ICJ*." We disagree. Although the ICJ's interpretation
deserves "respectful consideration," we conclude that it does not compel
us to reconsider our understanding of the Convention in *Breard*.

Under our Constitution, "[t]he judicial Power of the United States" is
"vested in one supreme Court, and in such inferior Courts as the Congress may from time to time ordain and establish." Art. III, § 1. That "judicial Power * * * extend[s] to * * * Treaties." *Id., §* 2. And, as Chief Justice Marshall famously explained, that judicial power includes the duty
"to say what the law is." *Marbury v. Madison,* 1 Cranch 137, 177 (1803). If
treaties are to be given effect as federal law under our legal system, determining their meaning as a matter of federal law "is emphatically the
province and duty of the judicial department," headed by the "one supreme Court" established by the Constitution. It is against this back-

ground that the United States ratified, and the Senate gave its advice and consent to, the various agreements that govern referral of Vienna Convention disputes to the ICJ.

Nothing in the structure or purpose of the ICJ suggests that its interpretations were intended to be conclusive on our courts. The ICJ's decisions have *"no binding force* except between the parties and in respect of that particular case,"* Statute of the International Court of Justice, Art. 59 (1945) (emphasis added). Any interpretation of law the ICJ renders in the course of resolving particular disputes is thus not binding precedent *even as to the ICJ itself*; there is accordingly little reason to think that such interpretations were intended to be controlling on our courts. The ICJ's principal purpose is to arbitrate particular disputes between national governments. While each member of the United Nations has agreed to comply with decisions of the ICJ "in any case to which it is a party," United Nations Charter, Art. 94(1) (1945), the Charter's procedure for noncompliance—referral to the Security Council by the aggrieved state—contemplates quintessentially *international* remedies, Art. 94(2).

In addition, "[w]hile courts interpret treaties for themselves, the meaning given them by the departments of government particularly charged with their negotiation and enforcement is given great weight." Although the United States has agreed to "discharge its international obligations" in having state courts give effect to the decision in *Avena,* it has not taken the view that the ICJ's interpretation of Article 36 is binding on our courts. President Bush, Memorandum for the Attorney General (Feb. 28, 2005). Moreover, shortly after *Avena,* the United States withdrew from the Optional Protocol concerning Vienna Convention disputes. Whatever the effect of *Avena* and *LaGrand* before this withdrawal, it is doubtful that our courts should give decisive weight to the interpretation of a tribunal whose jurisdiction in this area is no longer recognized by the United States.

LaGrand and *Avena* are therefore entitled only to the "respectful consideration" due an interpretation of an international agreement by an international court. Even according such consideration, the ICJ's interpretation cannot overcome the plain import of Article 36. As we explained in *Breard,* the procedural rules of domestic law generally govern the implementation of an international treaty. In addition, Article 36 makes clear that the rights it provides "shall be exercised in conformity with the laws and regulations of the receiving State" provided that "full effect * * * be given to the purposes for which the rights accorded under this Article are intended." In the United States, this means that the rule of procedural default—which applies even to claimed violations of our Constitution—applies also to Vienna Convention claims. Bustillo points to nothing in the drafting history of Article 36 or in the contemporary practice of other signatories that undermines this conclusion.

The ICJ concluded that where a defendant was not notified of his rights under Article 36, application of the procedural default rule failed to give "full effect" to the purposes of Article 36 because it prevented courts from attaching "legal significance" to the Article 36 violation. *LaGrand,* 2001 I.C.J., at 497–498, ¶¶ 90–91. This reasoning overlooks the importance of procedural default rules in an adversary system, which relies chiefly on the *parties* to raise significant issues and present them to the courts in the appropriate manner at the appropriate time for adjudication. Procedural default rules are designed to encourage parties to raise their claims promptly and to vindicate "the law's important interest in the finality of judgments." The consequence of failing to raise a claim for adjudication at the proper time is generally forfeiture of that claim. As a result, rules such as procedural default routinely deny "legal significance"—in the *Avena* and *LaGrand* sense—to otherwise viable legal claims.

Procedural default rules generally take on greater importance in an adversary system such as ours than in the sort of magistrate-directed, inquisitorial legal system characteristic of many of the other countries that are signatories to the Vienna Convention. "What makes a system adversarial rather than inquisitorial is * * * the presence of a judge who does not (as an inquisitor does) conduct the factual and legal investigation himself, but instead decides on the basis of facts and arguments pro and con adduced by the parties." In an inquisitorial system, the failure to raise a legal error can in part be attributed to the magistrate, and thus to the state itself. In our system, however, the responsibility for failing to raise an issue generally rests with the parties themselves.

The ICJ's interpretation of Article 36 is inconsistent with the basic framework of an adversary system. Under the ICJ's reading of "full effect," Article 36 claims could trump not only procedural default rules, but any number of other rules requiring parties to present their legal claims at the appropriate time for adjudication. If the State's failure to inform the defendant of his Article 36 rights generally excuses the defendant's failure to comply with relevant procedural rules, then presumably rules such as statutes of limitations and prohibitions against filing successive habeas petitions must also yield in the face of Article 36 claims. This sweeps too broadly, for it reads the "full effect" proviso in a way that leaves little room for Article 36's clear instruction that Article 36 rights "shall be exercised in conformity with the laws and regulations of the receiving State."

* * * In this regard, a comparison of Article 36 and a suspect's rights under *Miranda* disposes of Bustillo's claim. Bustillo contends that applying procedural default rules to Article 36 rights denies such rights "full effect" because the violation itself—*i.e.*, the failure to inform defendants of their right to consular notification—prevents them from becoming aware of their Article 36 rights and asserting them at trial. Of course, precisely the

same thing is true of rights under *Miranda*. Police are required to advise suspects that they have a right to remain silent and a right to an attorney. If police do not give such warnings, and counsel fails to object, it is equally true that a suspect may not be "aware he even *had* such rights until well after his trial had concluded." Nevertheless, it is well established that where a defendant fails to raise a *Miranda* claim at trial, procedural default rules may bar him from raising the claim in a subsequent postconviction proceeding.

* * *

Although these cases involve the delicate question of the application of an international treaty, the issues in many ways turn on established principles of domestic law. Our holding in no way disparages the importance of the Vienna Convention. The relief petitioners request is, by any measure, extraordinary. Sanchez-Llamas seeks a suppression remedy for an asserted right with little if any connection to the gathering of evidence; Bustillo requests an exception to procedural rules that is accorded to almost no other right, including many of our most fundamental constitutional protections. It is no slight to the Convention to deny petitioners' claims under the same principles we would apply to an Act of Congress, or to the Constitution itself.

The judgments of the Supreme Court of Oregon and the Supreme Court of Virginia are affirmed.

It is so ordered.

JUSTICE GINSBURG, concurring in the judgment.

I agree that Article 36 of the Vienna Convention grants rights that may be invoked by an individual in a judicial proceeding, and therefore join Part II of Justice BREYER's dissenting opinion. As to the suppression and procedural default issues, I join the Court's judgment. The dissenting opinion veers away from the two cases here for review, imagining other situations unlike those at hand. In neither of the cases before us would I remand for further proceedings.

* * *

Critical for me, Bustillo has conceded that his "attorney at trial was aware of his client's rights under the Vienna Convention." Given the knowledge of the Vienna Convention that Bustillo's lawyer possessed, this case fails to meet the dissent's (and the International Court of Justice's) first condition for overriding a State's ordinary procedural default rules: "[T]he [Vienna] Convention forbids American States to apply a procedural default rule to bar assertion of a Convention violation claim 'where it has been the failure of the United States [or of a State] itself to inform that may have precluded counsel from being in a position to have raised the

question of a violation of the Vienna Convention in the initial trial.'"
Nothing the State did or omitted to do here "precluded counsel from * * *
rais[ing] the question of a violation of the Vienna Convention in the initial trial." Had counsel done so, the trial court could have made "appropriate accommodations to ensure that the defendant secure[d], to the extent possible, the benefits of consular assistance."

In short, if there are some times when a Convention violation, standing
alone, might warrant suppression, or the displacement of a State's ordinarily applicable procedural default rules, neither Sanchez-Llamas' case
nor Bustillo's belongs in that category.

For the reasons stated, I would not disturb the judgments of the Supreme
Court of Oregon and the Supreme Court of Virginia.

JUSTICE BREYER, with whom JUSTICE STEVENS and JUSTICE SOUTER join,
and with whom JUSTICE GINSBURG joins as to Part II, dissenting.

* * *

II

The first question presented is whether a criminal defendant may raise a
claim (at trial or in a postconviction proceeding) that state officials violated Article 36 of the Convention. The Court assumes that the answer to
this question is "yes," but it does not decide the matter because it concludes in any event that the petitioners are not entitled to the remedies
they seek. As explained below, I would resolve those remedial questions
differently. Hence, I must decide, rather than assume, the answer to the
first question presented.

* * *

In answering the question it is common ground that the Convention is
"self-executi[ng]." * * *

Accordingly, I would allow the petitioners to raise their claims based on
violations of the Convention in their respective state-court proceedings.

III

The more difficult issue, I believe, concerns the nature of the Convention's
requirements as to remedy. In particular, Bustillo's case concerns a state
procedural default rule. When, if ever, does the Convention require a
state court to set aside such a rule in order to hear a criminal defendant's
claim that the police did not "inform" him of his "right" to communicate
with his "consular post"? The Court says that the answer is "never." In its
view, the Convention does not under any circumstances trump a State's
ordinary procedural rules requiring a defendant to assert his claims at
trial or lose them forever.

In my view, Article 36 of the Convention requires a less absolute answer. Article 36 says that the rights it sets forth "shall be exercised in conformity with the laws and regulations of the receiving State," but it instantly adds, "subject to the proviso * * * that the said laws and regulations must enable *full effect* to be given to the purposes for which the [Article 36] rights are * * * intended." The proviso means that a State's ordinary procedural default rules apply *unless* (1) the defendant's failure to raise a Convention matter (*e.g.,* that police failed to inform him of his Article 36 rights) can itself be traced to the failure of the police (or other governmental authorities) to inform the defendant of those Convention rights, *and* (2) state law does not provide any other effective way for the defendant to raise that issue (say, through a claim of ineffective assistance of counsel).

* * *

I will assume that the ICJ's interpretation does not bind this Court in this case. Statute of the International Court of Justice, Art. 59 (1945) (ICJ decisions have "binding force" only "between the parties and in respect of that particular case"). But as the majority points out, the ICJ's decisions on this issue nonetheless warrant our " 'respectful consideration.' " That "respectful consideration" reflects the understanding that uniformity is an important goal of treaty interpretation. And the ICJ's position as an international court specifically charged with the duty to interpret numerous international treaties (including the Convention) provides a natural point of reference for national courts seeking that uniformity. * * *

That "respectful consideration" also reflects an understanding of the ICJ's expertise in matters of treaty interpretation, a branch of international law. The ICJ's opinions "are persuasive evidence" of what "[international] law is." 1 Restatement § 103, comment *b*, at 37; see also *The Paquete Habana*, 175 U.S. 677, 700 (1900) ("[T]rustworthy evidence of what [international] law really is" can be found in "the works of jurists and commentators, who by years of labor, research and experience have made themselves peculiarly well acquainted with the subjects of which they treat").

Thus, this Court has repeatedly looked to the ICJ for guidance in interpreting treaties and in other matters of international law.

The lower courts have done the same.

Today's decision interprets an international treaty in a manner that conflicts not only with the treaty's language and history, but also with the ICJ's interpretation of the same treaty provision. In creating this last-mentioned conflict, as far as I can tell, the Court's decision is unprecedented.

* * *

The majority's argument * * * overlooks what the ICJ actually said, over-states what it actually meant, and is inconsistent with what it actually did. In *Avena* and *LaGrand,* the ICJ did not say that the Convention nec-essarily trumps any, let alone all, procedural rules that would otherwise bar assertion of a Convention violation claim. Nor did it say that the Con-vention necessarily trumps all procedural default rules. Rather, it said that the Convention prohibits application of those rules to a Convention violation claim only "where it has been the *failure* of the United States [or of a State] itself *to inform* that may have precluded counsel from being in a position to have raised the question of a violation of the Vienna Conven-tion in the initial trial." *Avena,* 2004 I.C.J., at 57, ¶ 113 (emphasis added). Thus, Article 36(2) precludes procedural default only *where the defend-ant's failure to bring his claim sooner is the result of the underlying viola-tion.* Since procedural default rules themselves typically excuse defaults where a defendant shows "cause and prejudice," it is difficult to see how this statement "overlooks the importance of procedural default rules in an adversary system," or is "inconsistent with the basic framework" of that "system."

Moreover, *Avena* and *LaGrand* make clear what the ICJ's language taken in context means: The Convention requires effective national remedies; hence local procedural rules must give way (to the Convention's "full ef-fect" requirement) when, but only when, it is the failure of the arresting authorities to inform the defendant of his Convention rights that prevent-ed the defendant from bringing his claim sooner. The opinions nowhere suggest that a State must provide a procedural remedy to a defendant who, for example, sleeps on his rights.

* * *

Moreover, the ICJ decided *Avena* and *LaGrand* after this Court decided *Breard.* And it is not difficult to reconcile those cases with *Breard* because they do not directly conflict with *Breard's* result. Rather, they interpret Article 36(2) to require state procedural default rules *sometimes* to give way to the Convention, namely, when those rules prevent effective reme-dy by barring assertion of a claim because of a delay caused by the Con-vention violation itself. I would read *Breard* as consistent with this inter-pretation, *i.e.,* as not saying that the Convention *never* trumps any proce-dural default rule.

* * *

And there are other reasons not to place too much reliance on the breadth of *Breard's* language. *Breard* is a *per curiam* decision that the Court had to reach within the few hours available between the time a petition for certiorari was filed and a scheduled execution, the decision is fairly re-cent, and the modification to which I refer requires no more than reading an exception into *Breard's* language, language that in any event was not central to the Court's holding.

* * *

Finally, the Court says it would be odd to treat Convention rights more favorably than rights protected by the U.S. Constitution. But "[a] treaty is in its nature a contract between two nations," and nations are of course free to agree to grant one another's citizens protections that differ from the protections enjoyed by citizens at home, particularly when circumstances call for differential treatment.

In sum, I find strong reasons for interpreting the Convention as sometimes prohibiting a state court from applying its ordinarily [applicable] procedural default rule to a Convention violation claim. The fact that the ICJ reached a similar conclusion in *LaGrand* and *Avena* adds strength to those reasons. And I cannot agree with the majority's arguments to the contrary.

Consequently, I would remand No. 05–51 so that Bustillo can argue to the Virginia state courts that they should modify their ordinary procedural default requirements. I would leave it to the state courts to determine in the first instance whether state law has provided Bustillo the effective remedy that the Convention requires and how it has done so (whether through "cause and prejudice" exceptions, ineffective-assistance-of-counsel claims, or other ways).

* * *

Accordingly, I respectfully dissent.

———————

It seems that everybody on the Court agrees—or is at least ready to "assume"—that the ICJ's judgment in *Avena* is not binding on U.S. courts. But isn't that entirely wrong? At least one state judge thought so. When the Oklahoma Court of Criminal Appeals halted the execution of Osbaldo Torres, one of the death row inmates covered by the *Avena* judgment, in response to the ICJ's decision, Judge Chapel wrote a special concurrence.

> As this Court is bound by the treaty itself, we are bound to give full faith and credit to the *Avena* decision. I am not suggesting that the International Court of Justice has jurisdiction over this Court—far from it. However, in these unusual circumstances the issue of whether this Court must abide by the court's opinion in Torres's case is not ours to determine. The United States Senate and the President have made that decision for us. The Optional Protocol, an integral part of the treaty, provides that the International Court of Justice is the forum for resolution of disputes under the Vienna Convention. The ne-

gotiation and administration of treaties is reserved to the Executive Branch, with Senate ratification. Therefore, when interpreting a treaty, we give great weight to the opinion and practice of the government department primarily responsible for it. The State Department has consistently taken the position that the only remedies under the Vienna Convention are diplomatic, political, or exist between states under international law. * * * [T]he State Department has also consistently turned to the International Court of Justice to provide a binding resolution of disputes under the Vienna Convention, and has relied on the binding nature of International Court of Justice decisions to enforce United States rights under the Convention. The *Avena* decision mandates a remedy for a particular violation of Torres's, and Mexico's rights under the Vienna Convention.

Judge Chapel further noted that:

> *Avena* directs the United States to review and reconsider Torres's conviction and sentence in light of the consequences of the treaty violation. That review and reconsideration falls to this Court. This is the first state pleading in which Torres has raised his Vienna Convention claim, and normally this Court would consider it procedurally barred. However, while leaving the particular method of review and reconsideration up to the United States, *Avena* states that a complete application of procedural bar will not fulfill the mandate to review and reconsider the conviction, if procedural bar prevents the Vienna Convention claim from being heard. In order to give full effect to *Avena*, we are bound by its holding to review Torres's conviction and sentence in light of the Vienna Convention violation, without recourse to procedural bar. * * * Torres's Vienna Convention claim was generated by the State of Oklahoma's initial failure to comply with a treaty. I believe we cannot fulfill the goal of a fair and just review of Torres's case if we refuse to look at his Vienna Convention claims on the merits.

Torres v. Oklahoma, 43 I.L.M. 1227 (2004).

The same day, the governor of Oklahoma followed the Oklahoma Board of Clemency and Parole's recommendation and commuted Torres' death sentence into prison for life. Having rejected earlier recommendations of that nature, this was the first time he had commuted a death sentence. He did so citing the ICJ's ruling in *Avena* and stating that the ICJ's rulings are binding on U.S. courts.

Do Judge Chapel's arguments show that the Supreme Court majority's reliance on Article 59 of the ICJ Statute is misplaced?

As in *Breard*, the Supreme Court majority in *Bustillo* relies, inter alia, on Congressional legislation (regarding the procedural default rule) and especially on the fact that, as the rule later in time, it trumps Article 27 of the Vienna Convention on Consular Relations. Does that argument violate the well-established principle that a country cannot invoke its internal law to justify the breach of an international obligation (see Article 27 of the Vienna Convention on the Law of Treaties)?

Is the majority's argument convincing (that the ICJ decisions regarding the Vienna Convention on Consular Relations should carry less weight) now that the United States has withdrawn from the ICJ's jurisdiction in that regard?

One might have thought that after *Sanchez-Llamas*, the Consular Rights Saga had come to an end given that the Supreme Court had decided that the ICJ decisions in *LaGrand* and *Avena* did not bind the (U.S.) state courts. Yet the effect of the ICJ's decisions on domestic proceedings in the United States came up again—now in the Texas state courts and in the case of the very José Ernesto Medellín whose petition for certiorari had first been granted and then denied by the U.S. Supreme Court back in 2006 (because the Court wanted to give the Texas state courts a chance to decide the matter).

In 2006, the Texas Criminal Court of Appeals decided that the ICJ decision was not binding in Medellín's case because the U.S. Supreme Court had said so:

> Our decision is controlled by the Supreme Court's recent opinion in *Sanchez-Llamas v. Oregon*, and accordingly, we hold that *Avena* is not binding federal law and therefore does not preempt [Texas law].
>
> * * *
>
> In this case, we are bound by the Supreme Court's determination that ICJ decisions are not binding on United States courts. As a result, Medellín, even as one of the named individuals in the decision, cannot show that *Avena* requires us to set aside [Texas law] and review and reconsider his Vienna Convention claim.

Ex parte Jose Ernesto Medellín, 223 S.W. 3d 315 (Tex. 2006).

Is the court's conclusion correct? What is the main difference between the situation in *Sanchez-Llamas* and *Bustillo* on the one hand, and *Medellín* on the other? Does that difference matter? Why/why not?

Predictably, this case also ended up before the U.S. Supreme Court. Just after oral argument (held October 10, 2007), Roger Alford's post on *Opinio Juris* described the options of the Court with regard to the effect of the ICJ's *Avena* judgment:

ROGER ALFORD, MEDILLÍN AND THE CONTINUUM OF DEFERENCE TO INTERNATIONAL TRIBUNALS

Opinio Juris, October 10, 2007

[F]ederal courts have adopted varying degrees of deference to decisions of international tribunals. As for direct enforcement and recognition between the parties, it largely depends on what federal law says the federal courts should do with the international judgment. Here is a brief outline of the "continuum of deference" that federal courts have shown to decisions of international tribunals.

At one extreme is the full and faith and credit model, in which a federal statute (22 U.S.C. 1650a) mandates that "the pecuniary obligations imposed by an [ICSID tribunal] award shall be given the same full faith and credit as if the award were a final judgment of a court of general jurisdiction of one of the several States." It is possible that Article 94 of the U.N. Charter and Article 59–60 of the ICJ Statute could be interpreted in a similar manner as a federal mandate to recognize the ICJ decision as between the parties.

A second approach is the arbitration model, in which a federal statute (the FAA) implementing the New York Convention requires recognition of international tribunal judgments (like the Iran–U.S. Claims Tribunal), unless one of the procedural errors outlined in Article V of the treaty are present. A third model is the foreign judgment model, in which international court judgments are recognized subject to the *Hilton v. Guyot* limitations. The Supreme Court has treated decisions of one international tribunal, the U.S.–Mexican Claims Commission, in a manner similar to foreign judgments. As the Court put it in *La Abra*, "an award by a tribunal acting under joint authority of two countries is conclusive between the governments concerned and must be executed in good faith unless there be ground to impeach the integrity of the tribunal itself."

The last significant model for direct enforcement is the *Charming Betsy* model. In the WTO context, the implementing legislation (the Uruguay Round Agreements Act) authorizes the executive branch to decide whether to enforce the WTO decision and precludes private parties from directly enforcing the decision (See 19 U.S.C. 3512(c)). Nonetheless, under *Charming Betsy*, courts try to read federal statutes in a manner consistent with international law obligations as interpreted by the WTO.

How the Supreme Court resolves *Medellín* should depend on how they interpret the federal mandate to recognize decisions of the International Court of Justice. If they determine that there are no federal law requirements on what effect to give to ICJ decisions, then the Court should at a minimum treat an ICJ decision no worse than it would a foreign court judgment using principles similar to *Hilton v. Guyot*. Unless there is some ground to impeach the integrity of the decision, or there is some binding federal mandate requiring a contrary result, the Court should recognize the ICJ decision as having no precedential weight, but nonetheless binding as between the parties to the judgment.[1]

The U.S. Supreme Court handed down its decision in 2008.

MEDELLÍN V. TEXAS
United States Supreme Court
552 U.S. 491 (2008)

CHIEF JUSTICE ROBERTS delivered the opinion of the Court, in which JUSTICES SCALIA, KENNEDY, THOMAS, and ALITO joined. JUSTICE STEVENS filed an opinion concurring in the judgment. JUSTICE BREYER filed a dissenting opinion, in which JUSTICES SOUTER and GINSBURG joined. * * *

Petitioner José Ernesto Medellín, who had been convicted and sentenced in Texas state court for murder, is one of the 51 Mexican nationals named in the *Avena* decision. Relying on the ICJ's decision and the President's Memorandum, Medellín filed an application for a writ of habeas corpus in state court. The Texas Court of Criminal Appeals dismissed Medellín's application as an abuse of the writ under state law, given Medellín's failure to raise his Vienna Convention claim in a timely manner under state law. We granted certiorari to decide [whether] the ICJ's judgment in *Avena* [is] directly enforceable as domestic law in a state court in the United States? * * *

Under Article 94(1) of the U.N. Charter, "[e]ach Member of the United Nations undertakes to comply with the decision of the [ICJ] in any case to which it is a party." The ICJ's jurisdiction in any particular case, however, is dependent upon the consent of the parties. The ICJ Statute delineates two ways in which a nation may consent to ICJ jurisdiction: It may consent generally to jurisdiction on any question arising under a treaty or general international law, or it may consent specifically to jurisdiction over a particular category of cases or disputes pursuant to a separate treaty. The United States originally consented to the general jurisdiction of the ICJ when it filed a declaration recognizing compulsory jurisdiction under Art. 36(2) in 1946. The United States withdrew from general ICJ jurisdiction in 1985. By ratifying the Optional Protocol to the Vienna Convention, the United States consented to the specific jurisdiction of the ICJ with respect to claims arising out of the Vienna Convention. On March 7, 2005, subsequent to the ICJ's judgment in *Avena*, the United States gave notice of withdrawal from the Optional Protocol to the Vienna Convention.

---

[1] http://www.opiniojuris.org/2007/10/11/medellin-and-the-continuum-of-deference-to-international-tribunals/

II

Medellín first contends that the ICJ's judgment in *Avena* constitutes a "binding" obligation on the state and federal courts of the United States. He argues that "by virtue of the Supremacy Clause, the treaties requiring compliance with the *Avena* judgment are *already* the 'Law of the Land' by which all state and federal courts in this country are 'bound.'" Accordingly, Medellín argues, *Avena* is a binding federal rule of decision that preempts contrary state limitations on successive habeas petitions.

No one disputes that the *Avena* decision—a decision that flows from the treaties through which the United States submitted to ICJ jurisdiction with respect to Vienna Convention disputes—constitutes an *international* law obligation on the part of the United States. But not all international law obligations automatically constitute binding federal law enforceable in United States courts. The question we confront here is whether the *Avena* judgment has automatic *domestic* legal effect such that the judgment of its own force applies in state and federal courts.

This Court has long recognized the distinction between treaties that automatically have effect as domestic law, and those that—while they constitute international law commitments—do not by themselves function as binding federal law. * * *

Medellín and his *amici* nonetheless contend that the Optional Protocol, United Nations Charter, and ICJ Statute supply the "relevant obligation" to give the *Avena* judgment binding effect in the domestic courts of the United States. Because none of these treaty sources creates binding federal law in the absence of implementing legislation, and because it is uncontested that no such legislation exists, we conclude that the *Avena* judgment is not automatically binding domestic law.

A

* * *

As a signatory to the Optional Protocol, the United States agreed to submit disputes arising out of the Vienna Convention to the ICJ. The Protocol provides: "Disputes arising out of the interpretation or application of the [Vienna] Convention shall lie within the compulsory jurisdiction of the International Court of Justice." Art. I, 21. Of course, submitting to jurisdiction and agreeing to be bound are two different things. A party could, for example, agree to compulsory nonbinding arbitration. Such an agreement would require the party to appear before the arbitral tribunal without obligating the party to treat the tribunal's decision as binding. See, *e.g.,* North American Free Trade Agreement, U.S.–Can.–Mex., Art.2018(1), Dec. 17, 1992, 32 I.L.M. 605, 697 (1993) ("On receipt of the final report of [the arbitral panel requested by a Party to the agreement], the disputing Parties shall agree on the resolution of the dispute, which normally shall conform with the determinations and recommendations of the panel").

The most natural reading of the Optional Protocol is as a bare grant of jurisdiction. It provides only that "[d]isputes arising out of the interpretation or application of the [Vienna] Convention shall lie within the compulsory jurisdiction of the International Court of Justice" and "may accordingly be brought before the [ICJ] * * * by any party to the dispute being a Party to the present Protocol." The Protocol says nothing about the effect of an ICJ decision and does not itself commit signatories to comply with an ICJ judgment. The Protocol is similarly silent as to any enforcement mechanism.

The obligation on the part of signatory nations to comply with ICJ judgments derives not from the Optional Protocol, but rather from Article 94 of the United Nations Charter—the provision that specifically addresses the effect of ICJ decisions. Article 94(1) provides that "[e]ach Member of the United Nations *undertakes to comply* with the decision of the [ICJ] in any case to which it is a party." The Executive Branch contends that the phrase "undertakes to comply" is not "an acknowledgement that an ICJ decision will have immediate legal effect in the courts of U.N. members," but rather "a *commitment* on the part of U.N. Members to take *future* action through their political branches to comply with an ICJ decision."

We agree with this construction of Article 94. The Article is not a directive to domestic courts. It does not provide that the United States "shall" or "must" comply with an ICJ decision, nor indicate that the Senate that ratified the U.N. Charter intended to vest ICJ decisions with immediate legal effect in domestic courts. Instead, "[t]he words of Article 94 * * * call upon governments to take certain action." See also *Foster,* 2 Pet., at 314, 315 (holding a treaty non-self-executing because its text—"all * * * grants of land * * * shall be ratified and confirmed" —did not "act directly on the grants" but rather "pledge[d] the faith of the United States to pass acts which shall ratify and confirm them"). In other words, the U.N. Charter reads like a "compact between independent nations" that "depends for the enforcement of its provisions on the interest and the honor of the governments which are parties to it."

The remainder of Article 94 confirms that the U.N. Charter does not contemplate the automatic enforceability of ICJ decisions in domestic courts. Article 94(2)—the enforcement provision—provides the sole remedy for noncompliance: referral to the United Nations Security Council by an aggrieved state.

The U.N. Charter's provision of an express diplomatic—that is, nonjudicial—remedy is itself evidence that ICJ judgments were not meant to be enforceable in domestic courts. And even this "quintessentially *international* remed[y]" is not absolute. First, the Security Council must "dee[m] necessary" the issuance of a recommendation or measure to effectuate the judgment. Art. 94(2). (Second,) as the President and Senate were undoubtedly aware in subscribing to the U.N. Charter and Optional Protocol, the United States retained the unqualified right to exercise its veto of any Security Council resolution.

This was the understanding of the Executive Branch when the President agreed to the U.N. Charter and the declaration accepting general compulsory ICJ jurisdiction. * * *

If ICJ judgments were instead regarded as automatically enforceable domestic law, they would be immediately and directly binding on state and federal courts pursuant to the Supremacy Clause. Mexico or the ICJ would have no need to proceed to the Security Council to enforce the judgment in this case. Noncompliance with an ICJ judgment through exercise of the Security Council veto—always regarded as an option by the Executive and ratifying Senate during and after consideration of the U.N. Charter, Optional Protocol, and ICJ Statute—would no longer be a viable alternative. There would be nothing to veto. In light of the U.N. Charter's remedial scheme, there is no reason to believe that the President and Senate signed up for such a result.

In sum, Medellín's view that ICJ decisions are automatically enforceable as domestic law is fatally undermined by the enforcement structure established by Article 94. His construction would eliminate the option of noncompliance contemplated by Article 94(2), undermining the ability of the political branches to determine whether and how to comply with an ICJ judgment. Those sensitive foreign policy decisions would instead be transferred to state and federal courts charged with applying an ICJ judgment directly as domestic law. And those courts would not be empowered to decide whether to comply with the judgment—again, always regarded as an option by the political branches—any more than courts may consider whether to comply with any other species of domestic law. This result would be particularly anomalous in light of the principle that "[t]he conduct of the foreign relations of our Government is committed by the Constitution to the Executive and Legislative—'the political'—Departments."

The ICJ Statute, incorporated into the U.N. Charter, provides further evidence that the ICJ's judgment in *Avena* does not automatically constitute federal law judicially enforceable in United States courts. To begin with, the ICJ's "principal purpose" is said to be to "arbitrate particular disputes between national governments." Accordingly, the ICJ can hear disputes only between nations, not individuals. Art. 34(1). More important, Article 59 of the statute provides that "[t]he decision of the [ICJ] has *no binding force* except between the parties and in respect of that particular case." The dissent does not explain how Medellín, an individual, can be a party to the ICJ proceeding.

Medellín argues that because the *Avena* case involves him, it is clear that he—and the 50 other Mexican nationals named in the *Avena* decision—should be regarded as parties to the *Avena* judgment. But cases before the ICJ are often precipitated by disputes involving particular persons or entities, disputes that a nation elects to take up as its own. See, *e.g., Case Concerning the Barcelona Traction, Light & Power Co. (Belg.v.Spain),* 1970 I.C.J. 3 (Judgment of Feb. 5) (claim brought by Belgium on behalf of Belgian nationals and shareholders). * * * That has never been understood to alter the express and established rules that only nation-states may be parties before the ICJ, and—contrary to the position of the dissent—that ICJ judgments are binding only between those parties, Art. 59.

It is, moreover, well settled that the United States' interpretation of a treaty is entitled to great weight. The Executive Branch has unfailingly adhered to its view that the relevant treaties do not create domestically enforceable federal law.

The pertinent international agreements, therefore, do not provide for implementation of ICJ judgments through direct enforcement in domestic courts, and "where a treaty does not provide a particular remedy, either expressly or implicitly, it is not for the federal courts to impose one on the States through lawmaking of their own."

B

The dissent faults our analysis because it "looks for the wrong thing (explicit textual expression about self-execution) using the wrong standard (clarity) in the wrong place (the treaty language)." Given our obligation to interpret treaty provisions to determine whether they are self-executing, we have to confess that we do think it rather important to look to the treaty language to see what it has to say about the issue. That is after all what the Senate looks to in deciding whether to approve the treaty.

The interpretive approach employed by the Court today—resorting to the text—is hardly novel. In two early cases involving an 1819 land-grant treaty between Spain and the United States, Chief Justice Marshall found the language of the treaty dispositive. In *Foster,* after distinguishing between self-executing treaties (those "equivalent to an act of the legislature") and non-self-executing treaties ("those the legislature must execute"), Chief Justice Marshall held that the 1819 treaty was non-self-executing. Four years later, the Supreme Court considered another claim under the same treaty, but concluded that the treaty was self-executing. The reason was not because the treaty was sometimes self-executing and sometimes not, but because the language of the Spanish translation (brought to the Court's attention for the first time) indicated the parties' intent to ratify and confirm the land-grant by force of the instrument itself.

As against this time-honored textual approach, the dissent proposes a multifactor, judgment-by-judgment analysis that would "jettiso[n] relative predictability for the open-ended rough-and-tumble of factors." The dissent's novel approach to deciding which (or, more accurately, when) treaties give rise to directly enforceable federal law is arrestingly indeterminate. Treaty language is barely probative. Determining whether treaties themselves create federal law is sometimes committed to the political branches and sometimes to the judiciary. Of those committed to the judiciary, the courts pick and choose which shall be binding United States law—trumping not only state but other federal law as well—and which shall not. They do this on the basis of a multifactor, "context-specific" inquiry. Even then, the same treaty sometimes gives rise to United States law and sometimes does not, again depending on an ad hoc judicial assessment.

Our Framers established a careful set of procedures that must be followed before federal law can be created under the Constitution—vesting that decision in the political branches, subject to checks and balances. U.S. Const., Art. I, § 7. They also recognized that treaties could create federal law, but again through the political branches, with the President making the treaty and the Senate approving it. Art. II, § 2. The dissent's understanding of the treaty route, depending on an ad hoc judgment of the judiciary without looking to the treaty language—the very language negotiated by the President and approved by the Senate—cannot readily be ascribed to those same Framers.

The dissent's approach risks the United States' involvement in international agreements. It is hard to believe that the United States would enter into treaties that are sometimes enforceable and sometimes not. Such a treaty would be the equivalent of writing a blank check to the judiciary. Senators could never be quite sure what the treaties on which they were voting meant. Only a judge could say for sure and only at some future date. This uncertainty could hobble the United States' efforts to negotiate and sign international agreements.

* * *

C

Our conclusion that *Avena* does not by itself constitute binding federal law is confirmed by the "postratification understanding" of signatory nations. There are currently 47 nations that are parties to the Optional Protocol and 171 nations that are parties to the Vienna Convention. Yet neither Medellín nor his *amici* have identified a single nation that treats ICJ judgments as binding in domestic courts. * * *

Our conclusion is further supported by general principles of interpretation. To begin with, we reiterated in *Sanchez–Llamas* what we held in

Breard, that " 'absent a clear and express statement to the contrary, the procedural rules of the forum State govern the implementation of the treaty in that State.' " Given that ICJ judgments may interfere with state procedural rules, one would expect the ratifying parties to the relevant treaties to have clearly stated their intent to give those judgments domestic effect, if they had so intended. Here there is no statement in the Optional Protocol, the U.N. Charter, or the ICJ Statute that supports the notion that ICJ judgments displace state procedural rules.

Moreover, the consequences of Medellín's argument give pause. An ICJ judgment, the argument goes, is not only binding domestic law but is also unassailable. As a result, neither Texas nor this Court may look behind a judgment and quarrel with its reasoning or result. (We already know, from *Sanchez-Llamas,* that this Court disagrees with both the reasoning and result in *Avena.*) Medellín's interpretation would allow ICJ judgments to override otherwise binding state law; there is nothing in his logic that would exempt contrary federal law from the same fate. And there is nothing to prevent the ICJ from ordering state courts to annul criminal convictions and sentences, for any reason deemed sufficient by the ICJ. Indeed, that is precisely the relief Mexico requested.

* * *

* * * We do not suggest that treaties can never afford binding domestic effect to international tribunal judgments—only that the U.N. Charter, the Optional Protocol, and the ICJ Statute do not do so. And whether the treaties underlying a judgment are self-executing so that the judgment is directly enforceable as domestic law in our courts is, of course, a matter for this Court to decide.

D

Our holding does not call into question the ordinary enforcement of foreign judgments or international arbitral agreements. Indeed, we agree with Medellín that, as a general matter, "an agreement to abide by the result" of an international adjudication—or what he really means, an agreement to give the result of such adjudication domestic legal effect—can be a treaty obligation like any other, so long as the agreement is consistent with the Constitution. The point is that the particular treaty obligations on which Medellín relies do not of their own force create domestic law.

* * *

In addition, Congress is up to the task of implementing non-self-executing treaties, even those involving complex commercial disputes. The judgments of a number of international tribunals enjoy a different status because of implementing legislation enacted by Congress. See, *e.g.,* 22 U.S.C. § 1650a(a) ("An award of an arbitral tribunal rendered pursuant to chapter IV of the [Convention on the Settlement of Investment Disputes] shall create a right arising under a treaty of the United States. The pecuniary obligations imposed by such an award shall be enforced and shall be given the same full faith and credit as if the award were a final judgment of a court of general jurisdiction of one of the several States"); 9 U.S.C. §§ 201–208 ("The [U.N.] Convention on the Recognition and Enforcement of Foreign Arbitral Awards of June 10, 1958, shall be enforced in United States courts in accordance with this chapter, § 201"). Such language demonstrates that Congress knows how to accord domestic effect to international obligations when it desires such a result.

Further, Medellín frames his argument as though giving the *Avena* judgment binding effect in domestic courts simply conforms to the proposition that domestic courts generally give effect to foreign judgments. But Medellín does not ask us to enforce a foreign-court judgment settling a typical commercial or property dispute. See, *e.g., Hilton v. Guyot,* 159 U.S. 113 (1895); see also Uniform Foreign Money-Judgments Recognition Act § 1(2), 13 U.L. A., pt. 2, p. 44 (2002) ("[F]oreign judgment means any judgment of a foreign state granting or denying recovery of a sum of money"). Rather, Medellín argues that the *Avena* judgment has the effect of enjoining the operation of state law. What is more, on Medellín's view, the judgment would force the State to take action to "review and reconside[r]" his case. The general rule, however, is that judgments of foreign courts awarding injunctive relief, even as to private parties, let alone sovereign States, are not generally "entitled to enforcement."

The judgment of the Texas Court of Criminal Appeals is affirmed.

It is so ordered.

JUSTICE STEVENS, concurring in the judgment.

There is a great deal of wisdom in Justice BREYER's dissent. I agree that the text and history of the Supremacy Clause, as well as this Court's treaty-related cases, do not support a presumption against self-execution. I also endorse the proposition that the Vienna Convention on Consular Relations "is itself self-executing and judicially enforceable." Moreover, I think this case presents a closer question than the Court's opinion allows. In the end, however, I am persuaded that the relevant treaties do not authorize this Court to enforce the judgment of the International Court of Justice (ICJ) in *Case Concerning Avena and Other Mexican Nationals* (*Mex.v.U.S.*), 2004 I.C.J. 12 (Judgment of Mar. 31).

JUSTICE BREYER, with whom JUSTICE SOUTER and JUSTICE GINSBURG join, dissenting.

* * *

The United States has signed and ratified a series of treaties obliging it to comply with ICJ judgments in cases in which it has given its consent to the exercise of the ICJ's adjudicatory authority. Specifically, the United States has agreed to submit, in this kind of case, to the ICJ's "compulsory jurisdiction" for purposes of "compulsory settlement." Optional Protocol Concerning the Compulsory Settlement of Disputes (Optional Protocol or Protocol). And it agreed that the ICJ's judgments would have "binding force * * * between the parties and in respect of [a] particular case." United Nations Charter, Art. 59 (1945). President Bush has determined that domestic courts should enforce this particular ICJ judgment. Memorandum to the Attorney General (Feb. 28, 2005). And Congress has done nothing to suggest the contrary. Under these circumstances, I believe the treaty obligations, and hence the judgment, resting as it does upon the consent of the United States to the ICJ's jurisdiction, bind the courts no less than would "an act of the [federal] legislature."

I

* * *

In a word, for present purposes, the absence or presence of language in a treaty about a provision's self-execution proves nothing at all. At best the Court is hunting the snark. At worst it erects legalistic hurdles that can threaten the application of provisions in many existing commercial and other treaties and make it more difficult to negotiate new ones.

seems contrary to everything we've been taught

2

The case law also suggests practical, context-specific criteria that this Court has previously used to help determine whether, for Supremacy Clause purposes, a treaty provision is self-executing. * * *

Such questions, drawn from case law stretching back 200 years, do not create a simple test, let alone a magic formula. But they do help to constitute a practical, context-specific judicial approach, seeking to separate run-of-the-mill judicial matters from other matters, sometimes more politically charged, sometimes more clearly the responsibility of other branches, sometimes lacking those attributes that would permit courts to act on their own without more ado. And such an approach is all that we need to find an answer to the legal question now before us.

C

Applying the approach just described, I would find the relevant treaty provisions self-executing as applied to the ICJ judgment before us (giving that judgment domestic legal effect) for the following reasons, taken together.

First, the language of the relevant treaties strongly supports direct judicial enforceability, at least of judgments of the kind at issue here. * * *

Second, the Optional Protocol here applies to a dispute about the meaning of a Vienna Convention provision that is itself self-executing and judicially enforceable. The Convention provision is about an individual's "rights," namely, his right upon being arrested to be informed of his separate right to contact his nation's consul. See Art. 36(1)(b), 21. The provision language is precise. The dispute arises at the intersection of an individual right with ordinary rules of criminal procedure; it consequently concerns the kind of matter with which judges are familiar. The provisions contain judicially enforceable standards. See Art. 36(2) (providing for exercise of rights "in conformity with the laws and regulations" of the arresting nation provided that the "laws and regulations * * * enable full effect to be given to the purposes for which the rights accorded under this Article are intended"). And the judgment itself requires a further hearing of a sort that is typically judicial.

* * *

Third, logic suggests that a treaty provision providing for "final" and "binding" judgments that "settl[e]" treaty-based disputes is self-executing insofar as the judgment in question concerns the meaning of an underlying treaty provision that is itself self-executing. * * *

To put the same point differently: What sense would it make (1) to make a self-executing promise and (2) to promise to accept as final an ICJ judgment interpreting that self-executing promise, yet (3) to insist that the judgment itself is not self-executing (*i.e.,* that Congress must enact specific legislation to enforce it)?

I am not aware of any satisfactory answer to these questions. It is no answer to point to the fact that in *Sanchez-Llamas v. Oregon,* 548 U.S. 331 (2006), this Court interpreted the relevant Convention provisions differently from the ICJ in *Avena.* This Court's *Sanchez-Llamas* interpretation binds our courts with respect to individuals whose rights were not espoused by a state party in *Avena.* Moreover, as the Court itself recognizes, and as the President recognizes, the question here is the very different question of applying the ICJ's *Avena* judgment to the very parties whose interests Mexico and the United States espoused in the ICJ *Avena* proceeding. It is in respect to these individuals that the United States has promised the ICJ decision will have binding force.

Contrary to the majority's suggestion, that binding force does not disappear by virtue of the fact that Mexico, rather than Medellín himself, presented his claims to the ICJ. Mexico brought the *Avena* case in part in "the exercise of its right of diplomatic protection of its nationals," including Medellín. Such derivative claims are a well-established feature of international law, and the United States has several times asserted them on behalf of its own citizens. * * *

Nor does recognition of the ICJ judgment as binding with respect to the individuals whose claims were espoused by Mexico in any way derogate from the Court's holding in *Sanchez–Llamas*. This case does not implicate the general interpretive question answered in *Sanchez–Llamas:* whether the Vienna Convention displaces state procedural rules. We are instead confronted with the discrete question of Texas' obligation to comply with a binding judgment issued by a tribunal with undisputed jurisdiction to adjudicate the rights of the individuals named therein. "It is inherent in international adjudication that an international tribunal may reject one country's legal position in favor of another's—and the United States explicitly accepted this possibility when it ratified the Optional Protocol."

Fourth, the majority's very different approach has seriously negative practical implications. The United States has entered into at least 70 treaties that contain provisions for ICJ dispute settlement similar to the Protocol before us. Many of these treaties contain provisions similar to those this Court has previously found self-executing—provisions that involve, for example, property rights, contract and commercial rights, trademarks, civil liability for personal injury, rights of foreign diplomats, taxation, domestic-court jurisdiction, and so forth. If the Optional Protocol here, taken together with the U.N. Charter and its annexed ICJ Statute, is insufficient to warrant enforcement of the ICJ judgment before us, it is difficult to see how one could reach a different conclusion in any of these other instances. And the consequence is to undermine longstanding efforts in those treaties to create an effective international system for interpreting and applying many, often commercial, self-executing treaty provisions. I thus doubt that the majority is right when it says, "We do not suggest that treaties can never afford binding domestic effect to international tribunal judgments." In respect to the 70 treaties that currently refer disputes to the ICJ's binding adjudicatory authority, some multilateral, some bilateral, that is just what the majority has done.

* * *

Fifth, other factors, related to the particular judgment here at issue, make that judgment well suited to direct judicial enforcement. The specific issue before the ICJ concerned " 'review and reconsideration' " of the "possible prejudice" caused in each of the 51 affected cases by an arresting State's failure to provide the defendant with rights guaranteed by the Vienna Convention. This review will call for an understanding of how criminal procedure works, including whether, and how, a notification failure may work prejudice. As the ICJ itself recognized, "it is the judicial process that is suited to this task." Courts frequently work with criminal procedure and related prejudice. Legislatures do not. Judicial standards are readily available for working in this technical area. Legislative standards are not readily available. Judges typically determine such matters, deciding, for example, whether further hearings are necessary, after reviewing a record in an individual case. Congress does not normally legislate in respect to individual cases. Indeed, to repeat what I said above, what kind of special legislation does the majority believe Congress ought to consider?

Sixth, to find the United States' treaty obligations self-executing as applied to the ICJ judgment (and consequently to find that judgment enforceable) does not threaten constitutional conflict with other branches; it does not require us to engage in nonjudicial activity; and it does not require us to create a new cause of action. The only question before us concerns the application of the ICJ judgment as binding law applicable to the parties in a particular criminal proceeding that Texas law creates independently of the treaty. * * *

Seventh, neither the President nor Congress has expressed concern about direct judicial enforcement of the ICJ decision. To the contrary, the President favors enforcement of this judgment. Thus, insofar as foreign policy impact, the interrelation of treaty provisions, or any other matter within the President's special treaty, military, and foreign affairs responsibilities might prove relevant, such factors *favor,* rather than militate against, enforcement of the judgment before us.

For these seven reasons, I would find that the United States' treaty obligation to comply with the ICJ judgment in *Avena* is enforceable in court in this case without further congressional action beyond Senate ratification of the relevant treaties. The majority reaches a different conclusion because it looks for the wrong thing (explicit textual expression about self-execution) using the wrong standard (clarity) in the wrong place (the treaty language). Hunting for what the text cannot contain, it takes a wrong turn. It threatens to deprive individuals, including businesses, property owners, testamentary beneficiaries, consular officials, and others, of the workable dispute resolution procedures that many treaties, including commercially oriented treaties, provide. In a world where commerce, trade, and travel have become ever more international, that is a step in the wrong direction.

Were the Court for a moment to shift the direction of its legal gaze, looking instead to the Supremacy Clause and to the extensive case law interpreting that Clause as applied to treaties, I believe it would reach a better supported, more felicitous conclusion. That approach, well embedded in Court case law, leads to the conclusion that the ICJ judgment before us is judicially enforceable without further legislative action.

II

A determination that the ICJ judgment is enforceable does not quite end the matter, for the judgment itself requires us to make one further decision. It directs the United States to provide further judicial review of the 51 cases of Mexican nationals "by means of its own choosing." As I have explained, I believe the judgment addresses itself to the Judicial Branch. This Court consequently "must choose" the means. And rather than, say, conducting the further review in this Court, or requiring Medellín to seek the review in another federal court, I believe that the proper forum for review would be the Texas-court proceedings that would follow a remand of this case.

* * *

Even if one is willing to concede that each of Justice Breyer's arguments has considerable merit, isn't a seven-factor test for the self-executing nature of a treaty inherently indeterminate and a sure ticket to prolonged litigation? If you had to choose the strongest argument, which would you pick?

For an in-depth discussion of the consular right saga (and for more data on how American courts have reacted to the ICJ's decisions in *LaGrand* and *Avena*), see Bruno Simma & Carsten Hoppe, *From* LaGrand *and* Avena *to* Medellín—*A Rocky Road Towards Implementation*, 14 Tul. J. Int'l & Comp. L. 1 (2005).

NOTE ON THE GERMAN CONSTITUTIONAL COURT DECISION

In September of 2006, the German Constitutional Court (Bundesverfassungsgericht) decided that the failure by the police to inform an arrested foreign citizen of his rights under Article 36 of the Vienna Convention on Consular Relations can amount to a violation of the constitutional right to a fair trial (derived under the German Constitution from the principle of the rule of law, *Rechtsstaatsprinzip*). The issue was whether evidence obtained from the defendants after the failure to inform them of their rights could be used to support their conviction. The Criminal Division of the German Supreme Court had held that it could, affirming the convictions. The Constitutional Court reversed the decision and ordered the Supreme Court to determine the appropriate remedy in the case before it.

The Constitutional Court emphasized that German courts have to interpret and apply national law in conformity with the country's international obligations. While it did not consider the ICJ's decisions in *LaGrand* and *Avena* strictly binding on the German judiciary, the Constitutional Court decided that domestic courts should prefer interpretations of international law by international tribunals over other possible readings. Courts should follow these interpretations even if Germany was not a party to the proceedings before the ICJ (as in *Avena*).

Note that German criminal procedure does not have a strict "procedural default rule." Thus, the defendants' failure to raise the issue at trial did not exclude them from raising it at the appellate level.

See *Decisions of the German Constitutional Court of September 19, 2006* (2 BvR 2115/01, 2132/01, 348/03), 60 Neue Juristische Wochenschrift 499 (2007). For a summary and (critical) discussion in English, see Klaus Ferdinand Gärditz, *Article 36, Vienna Convention on Consular Relations—Treaty Interpretation and Enforcement,* 101 Am. J. Int'l. L. 627 (2007).

CAN THE PRESIDENT FIX IT?

In *Medellín*, the Texas courts faced another thorny issue that arose from a peculiar action by President George W. Bush. In response to the ICJ's *Avena* judgment (and perhaps in order to help avoid a decision by the Supreme Court in that case), President Bush issued a "Memorandum to the Attorney General" in February of 2004, which read in part:

> I have determined, pursuant to the authority vested in me as President by the Constitution and the laws of the United States of America, that the United States will discharge its international obligation under the decision of the International Court of Justice in the *Case Concerning Avena and Other Mexican Nationals" (Mexico v. United States of America) (Avena)* * * *, by having State courts give effect to the decision in accordance with general principles of comity in cases filed by the 51 Mexican nationals addressed in that decision.

Brief for the United States as Amicus Curiae Respondent, *Medellín v. Dretke,* 544 U.S. 660, 2005 WL 504490, app. 2.

Thus the Texas courts had to deal not only with the question whether they were bound to abide by ICJ decisions—a question the Supreme Court had just answered in the negative for itself—but also whether the President of the United States could just tell them (and under which provisions of the Constitution or which "laws of the United States") to comply with the ICJ anyway. After all, one could have doubts whether the head of the federal executive could issue orders to a state's judiciary. Can he do so because it was ultimately the *President's* call whether to comply with ICJ decisions?

The Texas Court of Criminal Appeals was not amused by the action of the President (and former Texas governor). It held that President Bush had no constitutional (or other) authority to tell the state courts what to do:

> [T]he President has exceeded his constitutional authority by intruding into the independent powers of the judiciary. * * * [T]he President cannot dictate to the judiciary what law to apply or how to interpret the applicable law. * * * [T]he President has violated the separation of powers doctrine. * * *

Ex parte Medellín, 223 S.W. 3d, 315, 334, 349 (Tex. Crim. App. 2006).

This issue was also taken up by the U.S. Supreme Court in *Medellín v. Texas*. The Court sided with the Texas judges. What were the President's best arguments, and why did they fail?

MEDELLÍN V. TEXAS
United States Supreme Court
552 U.S. 491 (2008)

* * *

III

Medellín next argues that the ICJ's judgment in *Avena* is binding on state courts by virtue of the President's February 28, 2005 Memorandum. The United States contends that while the *Avena* judgment does not of its own force require domestic courts to set aside ordinary rules of procedural default, that judgment became the law of the land with precisely that effect pursuant to the President's Memorandum and his power "to establish binding rules of decision that preempt contrary state law." Accordingly, we must decide whether the President's declaration alters our conclusion that the *Avena* judgment is not a rule of domestic law binding in state and federal courts.

A

The United States maintains that the President's constitutional role "uniquely" qualifies him to resolve the sensitive foreign policy decisions that bear on compliance with an ICJ decision and "to do so expeditiously." We do not question these propositions. In this case, the President seeks to vindicate United States interests in ensuring the reciprocal observance of the Vienna Convention, protecting relations with foreign governments, and demonstrating commitment to the role of international law. These interests are plainly compelling.

Such considerations, however, do not allow us to set aside first principles. The President's authority to act, as with the exercise of any governmental power, "must stem either from an act of Congress or from the Constitution itself."

Justice Jackson's familiar tripartite scheme provides the accepted framework for evaluating executive action in this area. First, "[w]hen the President acts pursuant to an express or implied authorization of Congress, his authority is at its maximum, for it includes all that he possesses in his own right plus all that Congress can delegate." *Youngstown Sheet & Tube Co. v. Sawyer*, 343 U.S. 579, 635 (1952) (Jackson, J, concurring). Second, "[w]hen the President acts in absence of either a congressional grant or denial of authority, he can only rely upon his own independent powers, but there is a zone of twilight in which he and Congress may have concurrent authority, or in which its distribution is uncertain." *Id.*, at 637. In this circumstance, Presidential authority can derive support from "congressional inertia, indifference or quiescence." *Ibid.* Finally, "[w]hen the President takes measures incompatible with the expressed or implied will of Congress, his power is at its lowest ebb, and the Court can sustain his actions only by disabling the Congress from acting upon the subject." *Id.,* at 637–638.

B

The United States marshals two principal arguments in favor of the President's authority "to establish binding rules of decision that preempt contrary state law." The Solicitor General first argues that the relevant treaties give the President the authority to implement the *Avena* judgment and that Congress has acquiesced in the exercise of such authority. The United States also relies upon an "independent" international dispute-resolution power wholly apart from the asserted authority based on the pertinent treaties. Medellín adds the additional argument that the President's Memorandum is a valid exercise of his power to take care that the laws be faithfully executed.

1

The United States maintains that the President's Memorandum is authorized by the Optional Protocol and the U.N. Charter. That is, because the relevant treaties "create an obligation to comply with *Avena*," they "*implicitly* give the President authority to implement that treaty-based obligation." As a result, the President's Memorandum is well grounded in the first category of the *Youngstown* framework.

We disagree. The President has an array of political and diplomatic means available to enforce international obligations, but unilaterally converting a non-self-executing treaty into a self-executing one is not among them. The responsibility for transforming an international obligation arising from a non-self-executing treaty into domestic law falls to Congress. As this Court has explained, when treaty stipulations are "not self-executing they can only be enforced pursuant to legislation to carry them into effect." Moreover, "[u]ntil such act shall be passed, the Court is not at liberty to disregard the existing laws on the subject."

* * *

The United States nonetheless maintains that the President's Memorandum should be given effect as domestic law because "this case involves a valid Presidential action in the context of Congressional 'acquiescence'." Under the *Youngstown* tripartite framework, congressional acquiescence is pertinent when the President's action falls within the second category—that is, when he "acts in absence of either a congressional grant or denial of authority." Here, however, as we have explained, the President's effort to accord domestic effect to the *Avena* judgment does not meet that prerequisite.

In any event, even if we were persuaded that congressional acquiescence could support the President's asserted authority to create domestic law pursuant to a non-self-executing treaty, such acquiescence does not exist here. The United States first locates congressional acquiescence in Congress's failure to act following the President's resolution of prior ICJ controversies. A review of the Executive's actions in those prior cases, however, cannot support the claim that Congress acquiesced in this particular exercise of Presidential authority, for none of them remotely involved transforming an international obligation into domestic law and thereby displacing state law. * * *

The United States also directs us to the President's "related" statutory responsibilities and to his "established role" in litigating foreign policy concerns as support for the President's asserted authority to give the ICJ's decision in *Avena* the force of domestic law. Congress has indeed authorized the President to represent the United States before the United Nations, the ICJ, and the Security Council, 22 U.S.C. § 287, but the authority of the President to represent the United States before such bodies speaks to the President's *international* responsibilities, not any unilateral authority to create domestic law. The authority expressly conferred by Congress in the international realm cannot be said to "invite" the Presidential action at issue here. At bottom, none of the sources of authority identified by the United States supports the President's claim that Congress has acquiesced in his asserted power to establish on his own federal law or to override state law.

None of this is to say, however, that the combination of a non-self-executing treaty and the lack of implementing legislation precludes the President from acting to comply with an international treaty obligation. It is only to say that the Executive cannot unilaterally execute a non-self-executing treaty by giving it domestic effect. That is, the non-self-executing character of a treaty constrains the President's ability to comply with treaty commitments by unilaterally making the treaty binding on domestic courts. The President may comply with the treaty's obligations by some other means, so long as they are consistent with the Constitution. But he may not rely upon a non-self-executing treaty to "establish binding rules of decision that preempt contrary state law."

2

We thus turn to the United States' claim that—independent of the United States' treaty obligations—the Memorandum is a valid exercise of the President's foreign affairs authority to resolve claims disputes with foreign nations. * * *

* * * [T]he limitations on this source of executive power are clearly set forth and the Court has been careful to note that "[p]ast practice does not, by itself, create power."

The President's Memorandum is not supported by a "particularly longstanding practice" of congressional acquiescence, but rather is what the United States itself has described as "unprecedented action." Indeed, the Government has not identified a single instance in which the President has attempted (or Congress has acquiesced in) a Presidential directive issued to state courts, much less one that reaches deep into the heart of the State's police powers and compels state courts to reopen final criminal judgments and set aside neutrally applicable state laws. The Executive's narrow and strictly limited authority to settle international claims disputes pursuant to an executive agreement cannot stretch so far as to support the current Presidential Memorandum.

3

Medellín argues that the President's Memorandum is a valid exercise of his "Take Care" power. The United States, however, does not rely upon the President's responsibility to "take Care that the Laws be faithfully executed." U.S. Const., Art. II, § 3. We think this a wise concession. This authority allows the President to execute the laws, not make them. For the reasons we have stated, the *Avena* judgment is not domestic law; accordingly, the President cannot rely on his Take Care powers here.

* * *

Doesn't the Court's decision mean that (even) the President is powerless to enforce the ICJ judgment? If so, how can that judgment be enforced at all? If it can't be, hasn't the United States locked itself into an impossible position?

José Ernesto Medellín was executed on August 5, 2008, 9:57 p.m. Central Time. What is the moral of this saga and its ultimate significance for the effect of international law in the United States?

E. AFTERMATH: BACK IN THE HAGUE!

In the summer of 2008, Mexico and the United States found themselves in the ICJ once again, burning up more taxpayer dollars and pesos.

ICJ REJECTS MEXICO'S REQUEST TO INTERPRET AVENA BUT FINDS UNITED STATES VIOLATED PROVISIONAL MEASURES ORDER

103 Am. J. Int'l. L. 362 (2009)

[Order at Request for Interpretation of the Judgment of 31 March 2004, Case Concerning Avena and Other Mexican Nationals (Mexico v. United States), 2009 I.C.J. 1]

In January 2009, the International Court of Justice decided Mexico's June 2008 suit against the United States under Article 60 of the ICJ Statute seeking an interpretation of paragraph 153(9) of the Court's March 2004 judgment in *Avena*. The ICJ rejected Mexico's request for interpretation. The Court also found, however, that the United States violated its July 2008 provisional measures order directing that José Ernesto Medellín not be executed while the case was under consideration, unless he first received review and reconsideration of his conviction pursuant to paragraph 153(9). * * *

Mexico contended that there was a dispute between the parties regarding the meaning or scope of the ICJ's directive in *Avena*'s paragraph 153(9), requiring the United States to "provide, by means of its own choosing, review and reconsideration of the convictions and sentences of the Mexican nationals." As evidence, Mexico cited the disagreement between the U.S. federal government and the State of Texas regarding the obligation to comply with the *Avena* judgment, as well as the U.S. Supreme Court's decision that the judgment did not operate directly in U.S. law.

In accordance with its usual practice in cases under Article 60, the Court decided the case without a hearing. By a vote of 11–1, it rejected Mexico's request for an interpretation.

> 44. The *Avena* Judgment nowhere lays down or implies that the courts in the United States are required to give direct effect to paragraph 153(9). The obligation laid down in that paragraph is indeed an obligation of result which clearly must be performed unconditionally; non-performance of it constitutes internationally wrongful conduct. However, the Judgment leaves it to the United States to choose the means of implementation, not excluding the introduction within a reasonable time of appropriate legislation, if deemed necessary under domestic constitutional law. Nor moreover does the *Avena* Judgment prevent direct enforceability of the obligation in question, if such an effect is permitted by domestic law. In short, the question is not decided in the Court's original Judgment and thus cannot be submitted to it for interpretation under Article 60 of the Statute (Request for Interpretation of the Judgment of 20 November 1950 in the Asylum Case (Colombia v. Peru), Judgment, I.C.J. Reports 1950, p. 402).

45. Mexico's argument * * * concerns the general question of the effects of a judgment of the Court in the domestic legal order of the States parties to the case in which the judgment was delivered, not the "meaning or scope" of the *Avena* Judgment, as Article 60 of the Court's Statute requires. By virtue of its general nature, the question underlying Mexico's Request for interpretation is outside the jurisdiction specifically conferred upon the Court by Article 60. Whether or not there is a dispute, it does not bear on the interpretation of the *Avena* Judgment, in particular of paragraph 153(9).

46. For these reasons, the Court cannot accede to Mexico's Request for interpretation.

The ICJ also found, however, that the United States violated its July 2008 provisional measures order directing the United States to "take all measures necessary to ensure" that Medellín and four other Mexican nationals convicted of murder in U.S. state courts "are not executed pending judgment on the Request for interpretation * * * unless and until these five Mexican nationals receive review and reconsideration" as required by *Avena*.

52. Mr. Medellín was executed in the State of Texas on 5 August 2008 after having unsuccessfully filed an application for a writ of habeas corpus and applications for stay of execution and after having been refused a stay of execution through the clemency process. Mr. Medellín was executed without being afforded the review and reconsideration provided for by paragraphs 138 to 141 of the *Avena* Judgment, contrary to what was directed by the Court in its Order indicating provisional measures of 16 July 2008.

53. The Court thus finds that the United States did not discharge its obligation under the Court's Order of 16 July 2008, in the case of Mr. José Ernesto Medellín Rojas.

The Court also affirmed the United States' continuing obligation under *Avena* to provide for review and reconsideration of the individual Mexicans' convictions, as acknowledged by the United States in the proceedings. It declined to act on Mexico's request that the United States be ordered to provide assurances against repetition.

---

2. THE BLENDING OF PUBLIC AND PRIVATE ELEMENTS IN INTERNATIONAL LAW

The following case was part of the wave of litigation in U.S. courts resulting from claims brought by victims of the Nazi regime, especially by people who had been used as slave laborers in the German armaments industry. In reading the excerpt below, ask yourself whether the plaintiff's claim is based on private or public (international?) law. In a similar vein, are the defendants' arguments derived from public or private law? Are the reasons for the court's decision primarily drawn from domestic or international law?

IWANOWA v. FORD MOTOR COMPANY AND FORD WERKE A.G.

United States District Court
67 F. Supp. 2d 424 (D.N.J. 1999)

JUDGE GREENAWAY, JR.:

INTRODUCTION

This matter comes before the Court on the motion of defendants Ford Motor Company ("Ford") and its German subsidiary, Ford Werke A.G. ("Ford Werke") (collectively "Defendants"), seeking to dismiss plaintiff Elsa Iwanowa's ("Iwanowa" or "Plaintiff") Complaint, pursuant to Federal Rule of Civil Procedure 12(b)(1) and 12(b)(6). Before this Court ruled on the above-mentioned motion, Defendants filed a second motion to dismiss on the grounds of nonjusticiability and international comity. This Court shall consider each of Defendants' motions.

This action arises out of Iwanowa's allegations that Ford Werke coerced her, and thousands of other persons, to perform forced labor under inhuman conditions during World War II without compensation. The Complaint asserts causes of action against Defendants (1) for restitution/unjust enrichment and quantum meruit/quasi-contract under Michigan and Delaware law [Ford is incorporated in Delaware, and its principal place of business is in Michigan]; (2) for restitution/unjust enrichment under German law; and (3) for violations of the law of nations. Iwanowa seeks disgorgement of all economic benefits which have accrued to Defendants as a result of her forced labor, compensation for the reasonable value of her services and damages for the inhuman conditions Ford Werke inflicted upon her.

For the reasons set forth below, Defendants' motion to dismiss the claims under international law for lack of subject matter jurisdiction, pursuant to Rule 12(b)(l), is denied. Defendants' motion to dismiss all of the claims, pursuant to Rule 12(b)(6), is granted. Defendants' motion to dismiss on the grounds of nonjusticiability and international comity is also granted. Accordingly, the Complaint is dismissed in its entirety, with prejudice.

BACKGROUND

NAZI GERMANY

Ford established its German subsidiary, Ford Werke, in 1925. In 1931, Ford Werke moved its headquarters and manufacturing plant to Cologne,

Germany. Ford Werke's Cologne plant produced passenger vehicles until 1938, when it began manufacturing tracked vehicles for the German government to be used to transport troops and military equipment during World War II. By 1941, Ford Werke had ceased production of passenger vehicles and had begun to devote its entire production capacity to the manufacture of military trucks. The Complaint alleges that Ford Werke produced approximately sixty percent (60%) of the three-ton tracked vehicles the German army used during World War II.

By December, 1941, the German National Socialist Party (the "Nazis") had achieved domination over territories, in Europe and elsewhere, with an aggregate population of 350,000,000 people. The Nazi juggernaut required more labor than the voluntary labor the German people could provide. In order to support its war effort, the Nazi regime turned to unpaid, forced labor. Specifically, the Nazis used forced labor from the captive population, inmates of concentration camps and prisoners of war.

On March 21, 1942, the Nazi Party appointed Fritz Sauckel ("Sauckel") as Nazi Plenipotentiary General for the Allocation of Labor, with explicit authority over all available manpower, including workers recruited from abroad and prisoners of war. After Sauckel's appointment, the Nazi regime obtained forced laborers by conducting manhunts in the streets, movie houses and churches. The Nazi regime forcibly deported over 7,500,000 persons from occupied territories to Germany to support its war effort.

Sauckel encouraged German industries to bid for forced laborers in order to meet production quotas and to increase their profits. The Complaint alleges that Ford Werke began utilizing French prisoners of war as forced laborers in 1941 and continued utilizing thousands of forced laborers throughout World War II. The Complaint further alleges that by 1942, unpaid, forced laborers comprised twenty-five percent (25%) of Ford Werke's work force. By 1943, that percentage had risen to fifty percent (50%), where it remained until the end of the war. The forced laborers at Ford Werke's Cologne plant included French prisoners of war; Russian, Ukrainian, Italian and Belgian civilians; and concentration camp inmates from Buchenwald.

The Complaint alleges that Ford Werke profited from the use of forced laborers because, although it paid the Nazi government for its use of the prisoners, it did not compensate the laborers for their work. Consequently, Ford Werke's annual profits doubled between 1939 and 1943. The Complaint further alleges that Ford Werke placed its wartime profits in a growing reserve account or reinvested them in the company through the building of additional production capacity. In the years succeeding the war, as a result of its economic reserves and increased production capacity, Ford Werke continued producing trucks at a substantial profit, even though most of Europe, and specifically the German economy, was devastated. Iwanowa alleges that Ford Werke's internal reserves and large production capacity resulted from the work of unpaid, forced laborers.

In addition to bringing suit against Ford Werke, Iwanowa has also named Ford, Ford Werke's parent company, as a defendant. Ford is a party based on its ownership of between fifty-two percent (52%) to seventy-five percent (75%) of Ford Werke's outstanding shares during World War II. Although the Nazi party nationalized or confiscated many American companies in Germany, the Nazis did not confiscate Ford Werke as enemy property; instead, the Nazis allowed Ford to continue its controlling ownership of Ford Werke. Indeed, the Nazis named Robert H. Schmidt ("Schmidt"), Ford Werke's CEO, *Wehrwirtschaftsfuehrer,* meaning Military Economic Leader. In addition to his duties as Military Economic Leader, Schmidt continued to manage Ford Werke on Ford's behalf until the end of the War.

IWANOWA

Plaintiff Iwanowa was born in 1925, in Rostov, Russia. Starting in November, 1941, the Nazi army occupied Rostov. In June, 1942, the Nazi army began abducting adolescents as young as fourteen (14) years of age for transportation to Germany as forced laborers. On October 6, 1942, Nazi troops abducted Iwanowa and transported her to Germany with approximately 2,000 other adolescents. When Iwanowa arrived in Wuppertal, Germany, a representative of Ford Werke purchased her, along with thirty-eight (38) other adolescents from Rostov. Ford Werke's representative had Iwanowa, and the other adolescents, transported to Ford Werke's plant in Cologne. Once in Cologne, Ford Werke placed Iwanowa with approximately sixty-five Ukrainian deportees in a wooden hut, without heat, running water or sewage facilities. They slept in three-tiered bunks without bedding and were locked in at night.

From 1942–1945, Ford Werke required Iwanowa to perform heavy labor at its Cologne plant. Iwanowa's assignment consisted of drilling holes into the motor blocks of engines for military trucks. Ford Werke security officials supervised the forced laborers, at times using rubber truncheons to beat those who failed to meet production quotas.

Iwanowa continued to perform forced labor for Ford Werke until 1945, when the victorious Allied Powers liberated her, and thousands of other slave laborers, in 1945. After the War, she became a citizen of Belgium, where she presently resides. Ford Werke's forced laborers, including Iwanowa, have never received compensation for their years of forced labor.

On March 8, 1998, Iwanowa filed the instant suit on her own behalf and on behalf of a class of thousands of persons who were compelled to perform forced labor for Ford Werke between 1941–1945. Iwanowa seeks compensation for the reasonable value of her services, restitution of un-just enrichment flowing to Defendants, as a consequence of her labor, and damages for the pain and suffering that Defendants' imposition of inhu-man working conditions caused her.

Defendants moved to dismiss on the grounds that (1) this Court lacks subject matter jurisdiction over the claims under the law of nations; (2) all of the claims are barred by the applicable statute of limitations; (3) the Complaint fails to state a cognizable cause of action; (4) the claims are nonjusticiable; and (5) consideration of the instant claims would violate principles of international comity. This Court heard oral argument on De-fendants' motions on March 8, 1999 and August 5, 1999.

DISCUSSION

I.   OVERVIEW OF GERMAN JUDICIAL SYSTEM

* * *

II. CLAIMS UNDER THE LAW OF NATIONS

Iwanowa asserts that "by knowingly utilizing unpaid, forced labor under inhuman conditions, [Defendants] violated the law of nations, including the Hague Convention and the Geneva Convention." Defendants have moved to dismiss Iwanowa's claims under the law of nations based on (1) lack of subject matter jurisdiction; (2) failure to state a claim; and (3) ex-piration of the applicable limitations period.

A. MOTION TO DISMISS FOR LACK OF SUBJECT MATTER JURISDICTION

1. STANDARD FOR DISMISSAL

* * *

Upon consideration of the Complaint, the relevant case and statutory law and the declarations the parties have submitted to the Court, this Court finds that Defendants' motion to dismiss the claims under the law of na-tions for lack of subject matter jurisdiction is without merit. As shown below, this Court has jurisdiction over the instant claims, pursuant to the Alien Tort Claims Act, 28 U.S.C. § 1350.

2. ALIEN TORT CLAIMS ACT

Iwanowa claims that the Alien Tort Claims Act ("ATCA"), 28 U.S.C. § 1350, grants this Court subject matter jurisdiction over her claims un-der customary international law. Originally promulgated as part of the Judiciary Act of 1789, the ATCA provides that

> [t]he district courts shall have original jurisdiction of any civil action by an alien for a tort only, committed in violation of the law of na-tions or a treaty of the United States.

28 U.S.C. § 1350.

The Complaint alleges that Defendants' use of forced labor violated both the Hague Convention and the Geneva Convention. At oral argument, however, Iwanowa's attorneys clarified that Iwanowa is not asserting a claim under either of those treaties. Rather, she is asserting a claim under the law of nations and is merely relying on the Hague and the Geneva Conventions as evidence of an emerging norm of customary international law. Thus, this Court need only address Iwanowa's claim under the law of nations.

As stated above, Iwanowa contends that Defendants' use of forced labor during World War II violates the law of nations. The ATCA confers federal subject matter jurisdiction when: "(1) an alien sues (2) for a tort (3) committed in violation of the law of nations (i.e., international law)." *Kadic*, 70 F.3d at 238. The ATCA grants district courts subject matter jurisdiction to entertain "suits alleging torts committed anywhere in the world against aliens in violation of the law of nations." Id. at 236.

As a citizen and resident of Belgium, Iwanowa is an alien. She alleges that Defendants committed a tort by forcing her to perform unpaid, forced labor under inhuman conditions. Thus, she has satisfied the first and second requirements for jurisdiction under the ATCA. * * *

[The Court, citing inter alia *Doe v. Unocal* and *Kadic v. Karadzic*, then concluded that (1) the use of unpaid, forced labor during World War II violated clearly established norms of customary international law; (2) the ATCA provides both subject matter jurisdiction and a private right of action for violations of the law of nations; (3) private entities using slave labor are liable under the law of nations; (4) in any event the defendants were de facto state actors.]

* * * [T]he Complaint pleads sufficient facts to support a claim that from 1942–1945, Defendants were acting as *de facto* state actors. The Complaint alleges that the Nazi army abducted adolescents in occupied territories, including Iwanowa, and transported them to Germany to work as slave laborers. The Complaint also asserts that Sauckel, the Nazi Plenipotentiary General for the Allocation of Labor, encouraged German industries to bid for forced laborers in order to meet production quotas and to increase their profits. The Complaint further alleges that as a result of Sauckel's solicitation, Ford Werke purchased forced laborers, including Iwanowa, from the Nazis.

Hence, the Complaint alleges that Defendants acted in close cooperation with Nazi officials in compelling civilians to perform forced labor. This constitutes an allegation that Defendants were *de facto* state actors and are therefore, liable under all possible interpretations of the ATCA.

The allegation that Ford Werke pursued its own economic interests, or that its own employees (as opposed to Nazi officials), mistreated

Iwanowa, does not preclude a determination that Ford Werke acted as an agent of, or in concert with, the German Reich. *See* BGH [Supreme Court], NJW 1973, 1549, at 9–10 (F.R.G.) ["BGH (1973)"]. Indeed, German courts have held that private companies using forced labor as a result of Nazi directives, acted as agents of the German Reich. *See id.*; *Staucher v. I.G. Farben*, BGH [Supreme Court], RzW 1963, 525, at 4–5 (F.R.G.) ["*Staucher*, BHG (1963)"].

* * * Accordingly, Defendants' motion to dismiss Iwanowa's claims under international law for lack of subject matter jurisdiction is denied.

B.   MOTION TO DISMISS FOR FAILURE TO STATE A CLAIM

Defendants have moved, pursuant to Federal Rule of Civil Procedure 12(b)(6), to dismiss Iwanowa' s claims under the law of nations on three separate grounds: (1) the Paris Reparations Treaty subsumed all individual claims arising out of World War II into each nation's reparations claims against Germany; (2) the claims are time-barred; and (3) the U.S.S.R. waived Iwanowa's claims. The Court shall address each argument separately.

1.   STANDARD FOR DISMISSAL FOR FAILURE TO STATE A CLAIM

* * *

A complete comprehension of the context of this litigation and the parties' arguments cannot be attained without an overview of post-war Germany and four relevant treaties: (1) Agreement on Reparations From Germany, on the Establishment of an Inter–Allied Reparation Agency and on the Restitution of Monetary Gold, Jan 14, 1946 ("Paris Reparations Treaty"); (2) Convention Between the United Kingdom of Great Britain and Northern Ireland, France, the United States of America and the Federal Republic of Germany on the Settlement of Matters Arising Out of the War and the Occupation, May 26, 1952 ("Transition Agreement") (as amended by Schedule IV to the Protocol on the Termination of the Occupation Regime in the Federal Republic of Germany, Oct. 23, 1954); (3) Agreement on German External Debts, Feb. 27, 1953 ("London Debt Agreement"); and (4) Treaty on the Final Settlement with Respect to Germany, Sept. 12, 1990 ("Two-Plus-Four Treaty").

2.   POST-WAR GERMANY

On May 8, 1945, the Nazi army surrendered unconditionally. The Allied Powers' immediate objective was to completely demilitarize, disarm and dismember Germany to the extent deemed necessary for future peace and security in Europe. To implement this plan, the Allied Powers divided Germany into four occupation zones, American, British, French and Soviet, and assumed government control in their respective occupation zones. The most senior military commanders for each of the Allied Powers, Eisenhower (U.S.), Zhukov (U.S.S.R.), Montgomery (U.K.) and De-Latttre de Tassigny (France), formed the Inter–Allied Control Council with legislative authority over Germany. Although Berlin was situated in the Soviet zone, all four Allied Powers occupied and governed Berlin by inter-allied authority.

The occupying powers could not agree on Germany's political and economic future. The U.S., France and the U.K. ("Western Powers") intended to create a democratic German state. In furtherance of this end, they (1) gave the Germans substantial administrative responsibility beginning in 1946, (2) set up state *(Länder)* governments with state parliaments in their zones of occupation (the "Western Zones") and (3) helped the Germans draft a constitution, the Basic Law, in 1948. The Soviets objected to the Western Powers' goals regarding the future political status of Germany, specifically, their efforts to create a fully sovereign Germany. As shown *infra*, the U.S.S.R. and the Western Powers also disagreed on the issue of reparations. Consequently, in March, 1948, the U.S.S.R. left the Inter–Allied Control Council, thus initiating the division of Germany.

On May 23, 1949, the Western Powers established the F.R.G. in the Western Zones. In response to the creation of the F.R.G., the Soviets formed the G.D.R. in the Soviet Zone that same year. In 1954, the Western Powers ended the occupation regime in the F.R.G. However, the Western Powers explicitly reserved their rights with respect to Berlin and Germany as a whole, and to participate in the conclusion of a final peace treaty.

a.   YALTA AND POTSDAM

In February, 1945, prior to Germany's surrender, Roosevelt, Churchill and Stalin, the heads of the U.S., the U.K. and the U.S.S.R., respectively, met in Yalta to decide post-war policies. They agreed that "Germany must pay in kind for the losses caused by her to the Allied nations in the course of the war." The U.S. the U.K. and the U.S.S.R. agreed that the Allied nations which bore the main burden of the war, suffered the greatest losses and organized the victory over Germany, would receive reparations from Germany.

Shortly after the war, the U.S., the U.K. and the U.S.S.R. met again, this time in Potsdam, and reiterated their Yalta understanding—to make Germany pay reparations. They decided to extract reparations from Germany in the form of machines, other industrial equipment and German external assets, rather than in monetary payments. * * *

b.   PARIS REPARATIONS TREATY

In January, 1946, the U.K. and the U.S., along with the governments of sixteen other nations, met in Paris to decide upon the method of distributing reparations between those nations as to whom no decision had been reached at the Potsdam Conference. The Paris conference culminated in the enactment of the Paris Reparations Treaty, which provided that each signatory nation would receive a percentage of the total reparations the Western Powers collected based on their war related damages and contribution to the Allied war effort. The signatory nations agreed that Germany would pay reparations in the form of industrial and capital equipment, merchants ships, German external assets and monetary gold. Further, the Western Powers agreed to dismantle and transfer Germany's industrial plants located in their respective zones, along with any other German assets, to the Inter–Allied Reparation Agency by the end of 1947, for redistribution as war reparations.

Pursuant to the Paris Reparations Treaty, each signatory nation's share of reparations was supposed to satisfy any and all claims held by a nation, or its nationals, against the German government or German companies. Specifically, the Paris Reparations Treaty provided that:

> The Signatory Governments agree among themselves that their respective shares of reparation, as determined by the present Agreement, *shall be regarded by each of them as covering all its claims and those of its nationals against the former German Government and its Agencies, of a governmental or private nature arising out of the war* * * *

In sum, the Paris Reparations Treaty authorized the Western Powers to seize Germany's assets for distribution to the signatory nations in accordance with the Treaty, thereby satisfying any claims the signatory nations, or their nationals, might have against the German government or its "Agencies."

The German Supreme Court has held that the term "Agencies" encompasses private corporations using forced laborers, such as Defendants. Thus, the parties agree that Article 2.A of the Paris Reparations Treaty subsumed the claims of the signatory nations, and their nationals, thereby precluding nationals of the signatory nations from bringing forced labor claims against the German government or German companies. As stated by Professor Neuborne at oral argument, it would have been illogical to allow "private litigation against corporations all of whose assets were being seized, dismantled and taken and literally distributed to the people on whose behalf the litigation would have been brought."

* * *

c.   HALT OF REPARATIONS

Tensions between the Western Powers and the U.S.S.R. developed over the issue of reparations. The Soviets felt that they were entitled to seize as much of Germany's industrial equipment as possible as compensation for the Nazis' destruction and ravaging of the U.S.S.R. Accordingly, they dismantled and shipped entire factories, motor vehicles and railroad rails from the Soviet Zone to the U.S.S.R. In addition, they seized a portion of the current production of German factories in the Soviet Zone and shipped it to the U.S.S.R.

These actions were unacceptable to the Western Powers. First, because the Soviets never shipped food and raw materials to the Western Zones, as agreed in Potsdam, those Zones (which did not produce enough food to feed their population) had to export industrial products to pay for the cost of importing food. Second, the reduction in Germany's industrial productivity as a result of reparations to the Soviets shifted the cost of feeding the Germans to the Western Powers. The Western Powers feared that the extraction of reparations would destroy Germany's economy, and that they, specifically the U.S., would have had to bear responsibility for providing relief to the Germans.

Pursuant to the Potsdam Conference and the Paris Reparations Treaty, the Western Powers were supposed to complete the removal of industrial equipment from their respective Zones by the end of 1947 so that the Inter–Allied Reparation Agency could complete distribution of reparations by June, 1948. However, taxpayers in the U.S., the U.K. and France began pressuring their governments to reduce costly shipments of food to the Germans in the Western Zones. Consequently, in May, 1946, the U.S. halted the dismantling of German industries in its Zone and halted reparation shipments to the Soviet Zone. Shortly thereafter, the U.K. and France did the same * * * Consequently, the Allies never received their respective share of reparations, as negotiated in the Paris Reparations Treaty.

d.   TRANSITION AGREEMENT

The German Reich's military and political collapse in 1945 resulted in state bankruptcy such that the amount of debt precluded complete satisfaction of all liabilities. By 1952, the F.R.G. had not paid its war debts, including the reparations set forth in the Paris Reparations Treaty. Furthermore, as stated above, the Western Powers feared that the payment of reparations would continue to hinder the F.R.G.'s ability to rebuild its economy. Consequently, on May 26, 1952, the Western Powers and the F.R.G. entered into the Transition Agreement, whereby the Western Powers agreed to defer payment of their share of reparations until a later date. Specifically, the Transition Agreement provides that:

> The problem of reparation shall be settled by the peace treaty between Germany and its former enemies or by earlier agreements concerning this matter. The Three Powers undertake that they will at no time assert any claim for reparation against the current production of the Federal Republic [of Germany].

Further, in addition to deferring payment of reparations, by agreeing to never seek reparations from the F.R.G.'s current production, the Western

Powers gave the F.R.G. the encouragement and freedom it needed to rebuild its industries and stabilize its economy.

e.   LONDON DEBT AGREEMENT

Many of the signatories to the Paris Reparations Treaty agreed with the Western Powers' philosophy, as evidenced by the Transition Agreement—that allowing West Germany to rebuild its economy was more important than collecting their respective shares of reparations. Thus, on February 27, 1953, Belgium, Canada, Ceylon, Denmark, France, Greece, Iran, Ireland, Italy, Liechtenstein, Luxembourg, Norway, Pakistan, Spain, Sweden, Switzerland, South Africa, the U.K., the U.S. and Yugoslavia, on the one hand, and the F.R.G., on the other, entered into the London Debt Agreement.

* * *

* * * As stated by the Preamble, the London Debt Agreement's main purpose was to enable the F.R.G. to establish normal economic relations with other nations and to settle its external debts. In order to allow the F.R.G. to settle its external debts, the London Debt Agreement established a list of the debts that the Agreement would settle, along with a schedule of payments.

The London Debt Agreement's objective, "to achieve the reestablishment of orderly and normal economic relations with foreign [nations], could only be accomplished" if the F.R.G. could avoid excessive claims for wartime and pre-war debt. To relieve the F.R.G. from excessive claims, the signatories to the London Debt Agreement agreed to defer the collection of reparations, as defined and scheduled by the Paris Reparations Treaty, until the F.R.G. rebuilt its economy. In effect, the London Debt Agreement established the equivalent of a bankruptcy workout plan designed to defer consideration of certain private liabilities until the bankrupt entity (the F.R.G.) regained its financial health.

Article 5 of the London Debt Agreement sets forth the claims that would be deferred. Article 5(2) titled *Claims Excluded from the Agreement* is particularly relevant to Iwanowa's claims. Article 5(2) provides:

> Consideration of claims arising out of the Second World War by countries which were at war with or were occupied by Germany during that war, and by nationals of such countries, against the Reich [or] agencies of the Reich * * * shall be deferred until the final settlement of the problem of reparations.

Thus, Article 5(2) defers consideration of the war related claims of the Allies, or their nationals, against the German government or its agencies.

Although Article 5(2) of the London Debt Agreement only addressed claims "against the Reich or agencies of the Reich," the Supreme Court has interpreted the London Debt Agreement as covering claims against private corporations such as Defendants. Specifically, German courts have held that, pursuant to Article 5(2) of the London Debt Agreement, private corporations that utilized unpaid labor during World War II were entitled to the same deferral defense as the German government.

f.   TWO–PLUS–FOUR TREATY

The London Debt Agreement precluded adjudication of any war related claims by the Allies, and their nationals, against German defendants "until the final settlement of the problem of reparations." Although the London Debt Agreement was silent as to when this "final settlement" would occur, as stated *supra*, the Transition Agreement specifically dictated that "the problem of reparation shall be settled by the peace treaty between Germany and its former enemies or by earlier agreements concerning this matter."

On September 12, 1990, the F.R.G. and the G.D.R. on one side and the U.S., the U.K., France and the U.S.S.R. on the other, entered into the Two-Plus-Four Treaty, effective March 15, 1991. The Two-Plus-Four Treaty reunified West and East Germany and terminated the occupying Allied Powers' rights and responsibilities over Germany. In accordance with the Transition Agreement, the Two-Plus-Four Treaty, a peace treaty between a unified Germany and its former adversaries, settled the problem of reparations. See Transition Agreement, Ch. 6, Art. 1; see also OVG Muenster (1998), at 12 (stating that the final settlement of the reparations issue within the context of Article 5(2) of the London Debt Agreement was necessarily linked to Germany's reunification "because only a government which represented all of Germany [could] assert or waive German counterclaims.").

In Article 7 of the Two-Plus-Four Treaty, the Allied Powers relinquished the rights and responsibilities concerning Berlin and all of Germany that they expressly had reserved in Potsdam. Although the Two-Plus-Four Treaty does not expressly state that the phase of German reparations has ended, it is clear from Article 7 that the Allied nations can demand no further reparations payments from Germany. Further, the Two-Plus-Four Treaty's silence on the issue of reparations can be explained, in part, by the fact that between 1953 and 1990, the F.R.G. resolved the issue of reparations by way of international agreements with the individual Allied nations. Indeed, the F.R.G.'s Federal Government has stated that "45 years after the war, the reparations issue is de facto finished with, owing to the lack of concrete, contractually agreed upon obligations, owing to the renunciations of our former enemies, and owing to already completed efforts of Germany."

Thus, German courts have held that the signing of the Two-Plus-Four Treaty constitutes the "final settlement of the problem of [World War II] reparations" for purposes of the London Debt Agreement. Since the Two-

Plus-Four Treaty is the final settlement of the reparations issue, the London Debt Agreement no longer bars review of the war related claims of the Allies or their nationals against the German government or German companies. As stated by the Administrative Court of Appeals:

> [T]he Two Plus Four Treaty causes the lapse of the postponement agreed upon in [the London Debt Agreement] because the issue of reparations in connection with World War II will no longer arise after the conclusion of this Treaty. It is apparent from the preamble that the Treaty was concluded with the goal of agreeing upon the definite settlement with regard to Germany. This makes it clear that there will be no additional (peace) treaty settlements concerning legal questions in connection with World War II and the occupation of Germany.

The Administrative Court of Appeals concluded that "it was the intent of the signatory parties that there be no future treaty settlement of the reparation issue with regard to Germany; thus, the reparations issue was 'settled.'" In short, the Two-Plus-Four Treaty lifted the London Debt Agreement's moratorium on consideration of the Allies', or their nationals', claims against the German government or German companies.

3. London Debt Agreement Contemplates Individual Claims

Defendants argue that the Paris Reparations Treaty permanently subsumed all private claims arising out of World War II, thereby precluding the instant claims. Iwanowa agrees that the intent of the Paris Reparations Treaty was to subsume government and individual claims arising out of the war into the Treaty and preclude private litigation. She asserts, however, that "the entire structure of the Paris [Reparations] Agreement was axed * * * because it was self-defeating, and we moved instead to the London Debt Agreement." Iwanowa argues:

> If, in fact, the [Paris Reparations Treaty] subsumed [private] claims once and for all, and there were no individual claims left, why was it necessary to say [in the London Debt Agreement] that the individual claims would be postponed?

> It was because the people who were drafting the London Debt Agreement knew that this was a new regime, that the old regime, in which these claims would have been subsumed, because there was no room for them, was simply over, and that there was a new regime in which these claims had to be thought about, but they wanted to postpone them to give the German corporations a chance to regain their economic health.

In effect, Iwanowa argues that the London Debt Agreement superseded the Paris Reparations Treaty.

Defendants assert that the London Debt Agreement could not have deferred consideration of individual claims because such claims were subsumed into the governmental claims of the signatories to the Paris Reparations Treaty. Defendants assert that the London Debt Agreement only deferred consideration of the claims of governments. German courts have rejected this argument and held that the London Debt Agreement deferred consideration of private claims against the German government and its agencies, including German companies. Specifically, German courts have held that forced labor claims "are to be viewed as claims arising from World War II within the meaning of [the London Debt Agreement], the review of which must be postponed until the final settlement of the reparations issue." Until recently, German courts have denied forced labor claims as "unfounded at the time" or "invalid at the present time;" in each instance, the courts have cited Article 5(2) of the London Debt Agreement.

As shown above, the German Supreme Court has repeatedly held that the London Debt Agreement deferred individual forced labor claims until the final settlement of the reparations issue. However, the German Supreme Court has never held that these deferred claims were cognizable. The German Supreme Court refused to address the merits of forced labor claims and merely held that courts could not consider forced labor claims for the time being. As such, the issue before this Court is not whether the London Debt Agreement deferred consideration of private claims—the German Supreme Court has already answered that question in the affirmative—but whether such claims are cognizable versus being permanently barred by the Paris Reparations Treaty. For the reasons discussed below, this Court finds that individual claims are cognizable under the London Debt Agreement; however, only the government of the country of which the forced laborer was a national at the time the forced labor claims arose can pursue such claims. In short, Iwanowa must press her individual claims through the governments of the successor states to the U.S.S.R.

* * *

d.   LONDON DEBT AGREEMENT SUPERSEDES PARIS REPARATIONS TREATY

The language of the London Debt Agreement is inconsistent with the language of the Paris Reparations Treaty. Article 2.A of the Paris Reparations Treaty subsumed the individual claims of the nationals of the Allied nations into their respective country's share of reparations. However, Article 5(2) of the London Debt Agreement contemplates that nationals of the Allied nations may have individual claims arising out of World War II, separate from the claims held by their respective nations. Iwanowa reconciles the inconsistency between Article 2.A of the Paris Reparations

Treaty and Article 5(2) of the London Debt Agreement by arguing that the drafters of the London Debt Agreement recognized that the old regime providing for reparations to the Allied nations pursuant to the Paris Reparations Treaty and subsuming individual claims, "was simply over, and that there was a new regime in which [individual] claims had to be thought about." This Court finds that to the extent the Paris Reparations Treaty and the London Debt Agreement conflict, the London Debt Agreement is controlling.

A later statute or treaty must be harmonized with existing treaties to the extent possible. However, it has long been the rule that when a subsequent inconsistent law cannot be reconciled with a prior treaty, the subsequent law is deemed to abrogate the treaty to the extent of the inconsistency, without specific words of abrogation. See *Breard v. Greene*, 523 U.S. 371, 376, (1998) ("when a statute which is subsequent in time is inconsistent with a treaty, the statute to the extent of conflict, renders the treaty null."). By the same token, if there is an irreconcilable conflict between a subsequent treaty and a prior treaty between the same nations, relating to the same subject matter, the new treaty is controlling and must be deemed to abrogate the prior inconsistent treaty or provision therein.

* * *

Article 2.A of the Paris Reparations Treaty bars individual claims against Germany or its agencies. Article 5(2) of the London Debt Agreement defers individuals' claims against Germany or its agencies. Thus, there exists an irreconcilable conflict between Article 2.A. of the Paris Reparations Treaty and Article 5(2) of the London Debt Agreement. As such, the canons of statutory interpretation dictate that Article 5(2) of the London Debt Agreement, as a provision in the later treaty, supersedes Article 2.A of the Paris Reparations Treaty.

> e. Iwanowa Cannot Press Individual Claims in a Judicial Forum

As further discussed in *infra* Part V, the fact that the London Debt Agreement contemplates individual claims is not tantamount to a finding that such claims may be asserted in a judicial forum. Indeed, the London Debt Agreement indicates that all claims arising out of World War II, including individual claims, may only be pursued through government-to-government negotiations.

* * *

> 4. Statute of Limitations

Defendants assert, in the alternative, that even if the Paris Reparations Treaty does not permanently bar Iwanowa's claims, the applicable statute of limitations for claims alleging violations of customary international law has run.

* * *

Defendants have failed to show that the Paris Reparations Treaty or the U.S.S.R. Waiver permanently barred individual forced labor claims. However, Iwanowa's claims against Ford, for violations of international law, are time-barred. Furthermore, although Iwanowa's claims against Ford Werke, for violations of the law of nations, are timely, they must be dismissed on the ground that the London Debt Agreement contemplated that individual claims would be pursued by way of government-to-government negotiations, not private litigation. Consequently, Defendants' motion to dismiss Iwanowa's claims for violations of the law of nations is granted.

III. CLAIMS UNDER U.S. LAW

Iwanowa asserts that "[b]y taking and receiving economic benefits from unpaid, forced labor without making any effort to compensate the laborers, [Defendants] have been unjustly enriched and are obliged under the laws of * * * Michigan and Delaware to disgorge to plaintiff, and the Class, all profits and other economic benefits earned or derived from the forced labor of plaintiff and the Class." She further attests that "[b]y knowingly utilizing unpaid, forced labor to generate enormous profits, [Defendants] are obliged under the laws of * * * Michigan and Delaware to pay to plaintiff, and the Class, the reasonable value of their services." In sum, Iwanowa asserts claims for restitution/unjust enrichment and quantum meruit.

Defendants have moved to dismiss Iwanowa's claims under U.S. law, pursuant to Federal Rule of Civil Procedure 12(b)(6), on the ground that they are time-barred.

* * *

Even if this Court were to find that the London Debt Agreement's moratorium on forced labor claims precluded claims under U.S. law, Iwanowa's claims would nevertheless be time-barred. * * * [T]he Two-Plus-Four Treaty lifted the London Debt Agreement's moratorium on forced labor claims. The Two-Plus-Four Treaty became effective on March 15, 1991. The longest applicable limitations period for quantum meruit or restitution/unjust enrichment claims under New Jersey, Michigan or Delaware law is six years. Because Iwanowa did not file the instant action until March, 1998, seven years after the effective date of the Two-Plus-Four Treaty, her claims under U.S. law are time-barred. Defendants' motion to dismiss the claims under U.S. law is granted.

IV. CLAIMS UNDER GERMAN LAW

Iwanowa asserts that "[b]y taking and receiving economic benefits from unpaid, forced labor without making any effort to compensate the laborers, [Defendants] have been unjustly enriched and are obliged under the laws of Germany * * * to disgorge to plaintiff and the Class all profits and other economic benefits earned or derived from the forced labor of plaintiff and the Class." She further alleges that "[b]y knowingly utilizing unpaid, forced labor to generate enormous profits, [Defendants] are obliged under the laws of Germany * * * to pay to plaintiff and the Class the reasonable value of their services."

* * *

* * * [T]he Two-Plus-Four Treaty lifted the London Debt Agreement's moratorium on foreign nationals' forced labor claims against German companies. The Two-Plus-Four Treaty became effective on March 15, 1991. The statute of limitations on the claims under German law expired, at the latest, three years later. Because Iwanowa filed her Complaint on March 5, 1998, seven years after the enactment of the Two–Plus–Four Treaty, Defendants' motion to dismiss Iwanowa's claims under German law as time-barred is granted.

V. NONJUSTICIABILITY

Defendants have moved to dismiss the Complaint on the ground that Plaintiff's claims are nonjusticiable. This Court has dismissed Iwanowa's claims under U.S. law and German law as time-barred. This Court has also dismissed Iwanowa's claims under international law on the ground that the London Debt Agreement intended that Nazi era forced laborers pursue their claims by way of government-to-government negotiations, not through individual litigation in multiple fora. This Court is also compelled to dismiss Iwanowa's claims on the ground that forced labor claims arising out of World War II raise nonjusticiable political questions.

* * *

[T]his Court cannot sit as the ultimate judge of foreign policy issues falling outside the ambit of proper judicial review. As stated by the Federal Circuit in upholding President Ronald Reagan's extinguishment of any claims the Iran hostages may have had against Iran in exchange for their release:

> [t]he determination whether and upon what terms to settle the dispute with Iran over its holding of the hostages and obtain their release, necessarily was for the President to make in his foreign relations role. That determination was "of a kind clearly for nonjudicial discretion," and there are no "judicially discoverable and manageable standards" for reviewing such a Presidential decision. A judicial in-

quiry into whether the President could have extracted a more favorable settlement would seriously interfere with the President's ability to conduct foreign relations.

Thus, adjudication of Nazi era forced labor claims when the executive branch has rejected the notion that such claims are justiciable, would embarrass the executive branch in the eyes of the international community.

* * *

VI. International Comity

International comity also counsels that this Court abstain from hearing the instant claims. The principle of international comity mandates the "proper level of respect for the acts of our fellow sovereign nations." *Turner Entertainment Co. v. Degeto Film GmbH*, 25 F.3d 1512, 1518 (11th Cir. 1994).

* * *

The German Federal Government has taken the position that foreign citizens may not assert direct claims for war-time forced labor against private companies. First, in a letter to Chancellor Helmut Kohl, the German Ministerial Director, Horst Teltschik, wrote that "under international law, the concept of reparations claims encompasses all international law claims for compensation related to war [including] individual claims by injured citizens of victorious powers." Second, in its report to the German Federal Diet (the German legislative body), the German Federal Government stated:

> To the extent that foreign forced laborers were obligated and employed during the Second World War, they cannot make direct claims applicable against the state waging war or its enterprises. Such claims cannot, according to generally acknowledged international law fundamentals, be made applicable by individual persons and also cannot be made applicable against individual persons or civil law legal persons but rather be made applicable from state to state as reparations claims. Civil law agreements between the affected states are required for regulating such claims. German private enterprises are therefore not able to be laid claim to by foreign forced laborers. German laws as well do not provide for such claims.

Thus, according to the German Federal Government, Iwanowa may not assert forced labor claims against Ford Werke; such claims must be pursued by way of agreements between nations.

Although courts are not bound by a foreign government's pronouncement of which claims are cognizable, the principles of international comity dictate that a court not interfere with a foreign sovereign's pronouncement of its law. Furthermore, courts generally give great weight to a signatory nation's interpretation of a treaty.

International comity dictates that this Court follow the pronouncements of the German Federal Government as to individual claims. As such, this Court must also dismiss the instant claims on the ground that consideration of these claims violates principles of international comity.

CONCLUSION

For the reasons set forth above, Defendants' motion to dismiss, pursuant to Federal Rule of Civil Procedure 12(b)(1), for lack of subject matter jurisdiction, is denied. Defendants' motion to dismiss the claims against Ford, for violations of international law, pursuant to Federal Rule of Civil Procedure 12(b)(6), is granted on the ground that the claims are time-barred. Defendants' motion to dismiss the claims against Ford Werke, for violations of international law, is granted based on the London Debt Agreement's contemplation that individual claims against German companies would be pursued by way of government-to-government negotiations, not private litigation. Defendants' motion to dismiss the claims under German law and U.S. common law is granted on the ground that the claims are time-barred by the applicable statute of limitations. Finally, Defendants' motion to dismiss on the grounds of nonjusticiability and international comity is also granted.

––––––––––

Why did the plaintiff lose here? Does the Court ultimately deny her claims for political reasons? Is the outcome fair? If not, could it have been avoided?

Is the court right that the case must be dismissed as a "non-justiciable political question"? Is it correct that the case should be dismissed as a matter of comity vis-à-vis Germany (i.e., the original perpetrator nation)?

If you answer either of these questions in the affirmative, then why does the long and complex story involving a thicket of potentially inconsistent treaties made over the course of almost half a century even matter?

Eventually, claims arising from slave labor for the Nazi regime were comprehensively settled on the political level. First, the German government established a Foundation named "Rememberance, Responsibility and Future" ("Erinnerung, Verantwortung und Zukunft") in 2000. The government and members of German industry each contributed 10 billion Deutschmarks (approximately 7 billion dollars at the time), which were then paid out to more than 1.6 million former slave laborers.

Second, in the same year, Germany and the United States entered into an agreement, which provided that the exclusive compensation for those forced into slave labor in World War II would be the German Foundation.

As part of the agreement, the United States Government sent a "Statement of Interest" to U.S. courts informing them that all Nazi slave labor cases must be dismissed and referred to the Foundation for settlement. The Agreement thus ended all litigation in U.S. courts about World War II slave labor claims. See Agreement between the Government of the Federal Republic of Germany and the Government of the United States of America concerning the Foundation "Remembrance, Responsibility, and the Future," F.R.G.–U.S., Berlin, 17 July 2000, T.I.A.S. No. 13104.

What gives the United States executive branch the power to abrogate otherwise potentially meritorious private claims for compensation in U.S. courts? What if these claims are brought by foreign citizens? Are the courts bound by the government's "Statement of Interest"?

3. INTERNATIONAL AND FOREIGN LAW ARGUMENTS IN DOMESTIC COURTS

In the last several years, there have been extensive and intensive debates about the degree to which international and foreign law should be considered by American courts in deciding cases.

International and foreign law can provide binding rules of decision. International law may be binding if contained in a treaty ratified by the United States or through custom that is accepted as applicable in domestic courts (as famously stated in the *Paquete Habana*). Foreign law can be binding when U.S. choice of law rules designate it as governing a transboundary dispute, e.g., because the parties to a contract decided to subject their agreement to the law of a foreign country (choice of law clause), or because a tort was committed abroad. None of these propositions is seriously controversial.

The bone of contention has rather been whether international or foreign law should be consulted by U.S. courts as a model, an inspiration, or as a source of arguments for a particular result. We have seen one example of the use of foreign law in *Abbott v. Abbott* (Ch. VIII.1.C.) in the context of treaty interpretation, where the use of international and foreign law has not stirred a great deal of debate.

That debate was triggered mainly in the context of constitutional interpretation. In several opinions, some justices on the Supreme Court derived arguments from international or foreign law in support of a particular outcome, an approach to which other justices vigorously objected. The disagreement among the justices presented itself starkly in the following highly publicized case. What role does Justice Kennedy see for foreign and international law in interpreting the United States Constitution? What is Justice Scalia's view on their proper function?

LAWRENCE V. TEXAS

United States Supreme Court
539 U.S. 558 (2003)

JUSTICE KENNEDY delivered the opinion of the Court.

* * *

I

The question before the Court is the validity of a Texas statute making it a crime for two persons of the same sex to engage in certain intimate sexual conduct.

In Houston, Texas, officers of the Harris County Police Department were dispatched to a private residence in response to a reported weapons disturbance. They entered an apartment where one of the petitioners, John Geddes Lawrence, resided. The right of the police to enter does not seem to have been questioned. The officers observed Lawrence and another man, Tyron Garner, engaging in a sexual act. The two petitioners were arrested, held in custody overnight, and charged and convicted before a Justice of the Peace.

* * *

II

We conclude the case should be resolved by determining whether the petitioners were free as adults to engage in the private conduct in the exercise of their liberty under the Due Process Clause of the Fourteenth Amendment to the Constitution. For this inquiry we deem it necessary to reconsider the Court's holding in *Bowers*. [In *Bowers v. Hardwick*, 478 U.S. 186 (1986), the Court had upheld the constitutionality of a Georgia statute criminalizing sodomy.]

* * *

Chief Justice Burger joined the opinion for the Court in *Bowers* and further explained his views as follows: "Decisions of individuals relating to homosexual conduct have been subject to state intervention throughout the history of Western civilization. Condemnation of those practices is firmly rooted in Judeao–Christian moral and ethical standards." As with Justice White's assumptions about history, scholarship casts some doubt on the sweeping nature of the statement by Chief Justice Burger as it pertains to private homosexual conduct between consenting adults. In all events we think that our laws and traditions in the past half century are of most relevance here. These references show an emerging awareness that liberty gives substantial protection to adult persons in deciding how to conduct their private lives in matters pertaining to sex. "[H]istory and tradition are the starting point but not in all cases the ending point of the substantive due process inquiry."

* * *

The sweeping references by Chief Justice Burger to the history of Western civilization and to Judeo–Christian moral and ethical standards did not take account of other authorities pointing in an opposite direction. A committee advising the British Parliament recommended in 1957 repeal of laws punishing homosexual conduct. Parliament enacted the substance of those recommendations 10 years later. Sexual Offences Act 1967, § 1.

Of even more importance, almost five years before *Bowers* was decided the European Court of Human Rights considered a case with parallels to *Bowers* and to today's case. An adult male resident in Northern Ireland alleged he was a practicing homosexual who desired to engage in consensual homosexual conduct. The laws of Northern Ireland forbade him that right. He alleged that he had been questioned, his home had been searched, and he feared criminal prosecution. The court held that the laws proscribing the conduct were invalid under the European Convention on Human Rights. *Dudgeon v. United Kingdom,* 45 Eur. Ct. H.R. (1981) & ¶ 52. Authoritative in all countries that are members of the Council of Europe (21 nations then, 45 nations now), the decision is at odds with the premise in *Bowers* that the claim put forward was insubstantial in our Western civilization.

* * *

To the extent *Bowers* relied on values we share with a wider civilization, it should be noted that the reasoning and holding in *Bowers* have been rejected elsewhere. The European Court of Human Rights has followed not *Bowers* but its own decision in *Dudgeon v. United Kingdom.* See *P.G. & J.H. v. United Kingdom*; *Modinos v. Cyprus*; *Norris v. Ireland.* Other nations, too, have taken action consistent with an affirmation of the protected right of homosexual adults to engage in intimate, consensual conduct. The right the petitioners seek in this case has been accepted as an integral part of human freedom in many other countries. There has been no showing that in this country the governmental interest in circumscribing personal choice is somehow more legitimate or urgent.

* * *

Bowers was not correct when it was decided, and it is not correct today. It ought not to remain binding precedent. *Bowers v. Hardwick* should be and now is overruled.

* * *

The judgment of the Court of Appeals for the Texas Fourteenth District is reversed, and the case is remanded for further proceedings not inconsistent with this opinion.

It is so ordered.

[The concurring opinion of JUSTICE O'CONNOR is omitted.]

JUSTICE SCALIA, with whom THE CHIEF JUSTICE and JUSTICE THOMAS join, dissenting.

* * *

Today's approach to *stare decisis* invites us to overrule an erroneously decided precedent (including an "intensely divisive" decision) *if:* (1) its foundations have been "ero[ded]" by subsequent decisions; (2) it has been subject to "substantial and continuing" criticism; and (3) it has not induced "individual or societal reliance" that counsels against overturning. * * *

* * * Constitutional entitlements do not spring into existence because some States choose to lessen or eliminate criminal sanctions on certain behavior. Much less do they spring into existence, as the Court seems to believe, because *foreign nations* decriminalize conduct. The *Bowers* majority opinion *never* relied on "values we share with a wider civilization," but rather rejected the claimed right to sodomy on the ground that such a right was not " 'deeply rooted in *this Nation's* history and tradition,' " 478 U.S., at 193–194 (emphasis added). *Bowers'* rational-basis holding is likewise devoid of any reliance on the views of a "wider civilization." The Court's discussion of these foreign views (ignoring, of course, the many countries that have retained criminal prohibitions on sodomy) is therefore meaningless dicta. Dangerous dicta, however, since "this Court * * * should not impose foreign moods, fads, or fashions on Americans."

* * *

The tendency of some Justices to invoke foreign and international law to support a certain interpretation of the U.S. Constitution has led to something like a (miniature) culture war among the members of the Court. See, e.g., *Princz v. United States*, 521 U.S. 898, 921 n.11 (1997) (commenting on dissent) and 976–877 (Breyer, J., dissenting); *Roper v. Simmons*, 543 U.S. 551, 575–578 and 622–628 (2005) (Scalia, J., dissenting).

During her days on the Court, former Supreme Court Justice Sandra Day O'Connor long and openly advocated the use of international and foreign law by American courts as the excerpt below demonstrates.

SANDRA DAY O'CONNOR, AMERICAN SOCIETY OF INTERNATIONAL LAW PROCEEDINGS—KEYNOTE ADDRESS
March 16, 2002

* * *

Although international law and the law of other nations are rarely binding upon our decisions in U.S. courts, conclusions reached by other countries and by the international community should at times constitute persuasive authority in American courts. This is sometimes called "transjudicialism."

American courts have not, however, developed as robust a transnational jurisprudence as they might. Many scholars have documented how the decisions of the court on which I sit have had an influence on the opinions of foreign tribunals. One scholar has even said that, when life or liberty is at stake, the landmark judgments of the Supreme Court of the United States, giving fresh meaning to the principles of the Bill of Rights, are studied with as much attention in New Delhi or Strasbourg as they are in Washington, DC or the state of Washington or Springfield, Illinois.

This reliance, unfortunately, has not been reciprocal. There has been a reluctance on our current Supreme Court to look to international or foreign law in interpreting our own Constitution and related statutes. While ultimately we must bear responsibility for interpreting our own laws, there is much to learn from other distinguished jurists who have given thought to the same difficult issues that we face here.

The court on which I sit has held, for more than two hundred years, that acts of Congress should be construed to be consistent with international law, absent clear expression to the contrary. Somewhat surprisingly, however, this doctrine is rarely utilized in our court's contemporary jurisprudence. I can think of only two cases during my more than twenty years on the Supreme Court that have relied upon this interpretive principle.

* * *

Although our reliance on international and foreign law is rare, it is not nonexistent. For instance, we have looked to international law notions of sovereignty when shaping our federalism jurisprudence and to international law norms in boundary disputes between American states. In areas such as these, it would be a mistake to ignore the rich resources developed in the law of nations. I suspect that, with time, we will rely increasingly on international and foreign law in resolving what now appear to be purely domestic issues.

I have not even scratched the surface of the issues and areas of application of foreign and international law in U.S. courts. The fact is that international and foreign law are being raised in our courts more often and in more areas than our courts have the knowledge and experience to deal with. There is a great need for expanded knowledge in the field, and the need is now.

According to Justice O'Connor, what are the primary benefits of considering international and foreign law in deciding questions of domestic law?

The following case demonstrates how Canadian courts have approached similar questions. What is the issue here? How is it resolved? Who has the better arguments—Justice L'Heureux–Dubé or Justice Iacobucci?

BAKER V. CANADA

Supreme Court of Canada
2 S.C.R. 817 (1999)

[Mavis Baker was a Jamaican citizen who had entered Canada on a visitor visa in 1981 and had then remained in the country illegally. When she was about to be deported in 1993, she applied for an exemption from the rule that applications for permanent residency status must be made from outside of Canada. Such an exemption is possible for, inter alia, humanitarian and compassionate reasons. Baker had four minor children, all of whom were Canadian citizens and two of whom were dependent on her for support. She also suffered from mental illness but was on the road to recovery. The immigration officer denied her petition, and she sued. The trial court judge certified the following question for appeal: "Given that the Immigration Act does not expressly incorporate the language of Canada's international obligations with respect to the International Convention on the Rights of the Child, must federal immigration authorities treat the best interests of the Canadian child as a primary consideration in assessing an applicant under s. 114(2) of the Immigration Act?" The federal court of appeal answered in the negative and decided against Ms. Baker. The Supreme Court of Canada "allowed the appeal," i.e., reversed.]

JUSTICE L'HEUREUX–DUBÉ:

* * *

(b) INTERNATIONAL LAW

69. Another indicator of the importance of considering the interests of children when making a compassionate and humanitarian decision is the ratification by Canada of the Convention on the Rights of the Child, and the recognition of the importance of children's rights and the best interests of children in other international instruments ratified by Canada. International treaties and conventions are not part of Canadian law un-

less they have been implemented by statute. I agree with the respondent and the Court of Appeal that the Convention has not been implemented by Parliament. Its provisions therefore have no direct application within Canadian law.

70. Nevertheless, the values reflected in international human rights law may help inform the contextual approach to statutory interpretation and judicial review. As stated in R. Sullivan, *Driedger on the Construction of Statutes* (3rd ed. 1994), at p. 330:

> [T]he legislature is presumed to respect the values and principles enshrined in international law, both customary and conventional. These constitute a part of the legal context in which legislation is enacted and read. *In so far as possible, therefore, interpretations that reflect these values and principles are preferred.* [Emphasis added.]

The important role of international human rights law as an aid in interpreting domestic law has also been emphasized in other common law countries: see, for example, *Tavita v. Minister of Immigration*, [1994] 2 N.Z.L.R. 257 (C.A.), at p. 266; *Vishaka v. Rajasthan*, [1997] 3 L.R.C. 361 (S.C. India), at p. 367. It is also a critical influence on the interpretation of the scope of the rights included in the *Charter*: *Slaight Communications, supra; R. v. Keegstra,* [1990] 3 S.C.R. 697.

71. The values and principles of the Convention recognize the importance of being attentive to the rights and best interests of children when decisions are made that relate to and affect their future. In addition, the preamble, recalling the *Universal Declaration of Human Rights*, recognizes that "childhood is entitled to special care and assistance." A similar emphasis on the importance of placing considerable value on the protection of children and their needs and interests is also contained in other international instruments. The United Nations *Declaration of the Rights of the Child* (1959), in its preamble, states that the child "needs special safeguards and care." The principles of the Convention and other international instruments place special importance on protections for children and childhood, and on particular consideration of their interests, needs, and rights. They help show the values that are central in determining whether this decision was a reasonable exercise of the H & C power.

(c) THE MINISTERIAL GUIDELINES

72. Third, the guidelines issued by the Minister to immigration officers recognize and reflect the values and approach discussed above and articulated in the Convention. * * *

73. The above factors indicate that emphasis on the rights, interests, and needs of children and special attention to childhood are important values that should be considered in reasonably interpreting the "humanitarian" and "compassionate" considerations that guide the exercise of the discre-

tion. I conclude that because the reasons for this decision do not indicate that it was made in a manner which was alive, attentive, or sensitive to the interests of Ms. Baker's children, and did not consider them as an important factor in making the decision, it was an unreasonable exercise of the power conferred by the legislation, and must, therefore, be overturned. In addition, the reasons for decision failed to give sufficient weight or consideration to the hardship that a return to Jamaica might cause Ms. Baker, given the fact that she had been in Canada for 12 years, was ill and might not be able to obtain treatment in Jamaica, and would necessarily be separated from at least some of her children.

* * *

E.   Conclusions and Disposition

76. Therefore, both because there was a violation of the principles of procedural fairness owing to a reasonable apprehension of bias, and because the exercise of the H & C discretion was unreasonable, I would allow this appeal.

* * *

The reasons of [Justices] CORY and IACOBUCCI were delivered by

78. [Justice] IACOBUCCI—I agree with L'Heureux–Dubé J.'s reasons and disposition of this appeal, except to the extent that my colleague addresses the effect of international law on the exercise of ministerial discretion pursuant to s. 114(2) of the *Immigration Act*. The certified question at issue in this appeal concerns whether federal immigration authorities must treat the best interests of the child as a primary consideration in assessing an application for humanitarian and compassionate consideration under s. 114(2) of the Act, given that the legislation does not implement the provisions contained in the *Convention on the Rights of the Child*, a multilateral convention to which Canada is party. In my opinion, the certified question should be answered in the negative.

79. It is a matter of well-settled law that an international convention ratified by the executive branch of government is of no force or effect within the Canadian legal system until such time as its provisions have been incorporated into domestic law by way of implementing legislation. I do not agree with the approach adopted by my colleague, wherein reference is made to the underlying values of an unimplemented international treaty in the course of the contextual approach to statutory interpretation and administrative law, because such an approach is not in accordance with the Court's jurisprudence concerning the status of international law within the domestic legal system.

80. In my view, one should proceed with caution in deciding matters of this nature, lest we adversely affect the balance maintained by our Par-

liamentary tradition, or inadvertently grant the executive the power to bind citizens without the necessity of involving the legislative branch. I do not share my colleague's confidence that the Court's precedent in *Capital Cities,* survives intact following the adoption of a principle of law which permits reference to an unincorporated convention during the process of statutory interpretation. Instead, the result will be that the appellant is able to achieve indirectly what cannot be achieved directly, namely, to give force and effect within the domestic legal system to international obligations undertaken by the executive alone that have yet to be subject to the democratic will of Parliament.

* * *

Appeal allowed with costs.

Would Justice Iacobucci's reasons be equally valid in the United States?

In the United States, the role of foreign and international law in domestic courts has actually spilled over into the political arena as well. There have been several successive efforts in Congress to introduce legislation limiting the extent to which U.S courts can use international and foreign law in deciding cases. The sentiment underlying such efforts was expressed by Representative Sandy Adams of Florida who, upon sponsoring one such bill in 2011, released a statement explaining that

> [w]e have an American judicial system for a reason and my bill aims to protect it. Over the years, Supreme Court justices have interjected international law into their rulings, creating precedent for national sovereignty and our Constitution. Not only does using international precedent chip away at our nation's founding principles, but it could be used to promote a judge's personal political agenda instead of what's best for the country. My bill protects the integrity of our Constitution and U.S. laws by clarifying that our courts should follow and uphold our laws—not defer to those of foreign nations.

> Every case that cites foreign law is another opportunity for precedent to be set and the Constitution to be challenged or overrun. Policy should be decided through the American policy-making process prescribed by our Constitution, not by foreign courts or the preferences of the judges who happened to be serving at the time. We have an American judicial system for a reason, and it is time we protect our Constitution and the system that was put in place over 200 years ago[2].

---

[2] Except on file with authors.

In addition, recently several states have either enacted legislation or are considering bills purporting to restrict or prohibit the application of foreign or international law by their courts. Going beyond the legislative level, in November 2010, Oklahoma voters approved the "Save Our State" amendment to the Oklahoma state constitution. That amendment sought to bar the state courts from referring to international and Shari'a law in deciding cases. The amendment was challenged in federal court and struck down by the 10th Circuit Court of Appeals on first amendment grounds. *Awad v. Ziriax*, 670 F.3d 1111 (10th Cir. 2012).

If you were a state legislator, would you vote in favor of these efforts? What are the main arguments for or against them? In particular, consider how these efforts would affect the United States' international law obligations.

By contrast, many other countries' judiciaries are very open to international and foreign law arguments in constitutional and other, more routine, adjudication. Perhaps the most impressive commitment to such considerations is contained in the South African Constitution:

SOUTH AFRICAN CONSTITUTION
(1996)

Article 39   Interpretation of Bill of Rights

(1) When interpreting the Bill of Rights, a court tribunal or forum:

  (a) must promote the values that underlie an open and democratic society based on human dignity, equality and freedom;

  (b) must consider international law; and

  (c) may consider foreign law.

The following article discusses the use of foreign and international law in constitutional adjudication. What are the main distinctions it draws? What does Larson mean by "moral fact-finding"? Why does she find that particular use of international and foreign law problematic?

JOAN L. LARSEN, IMPORTING CONSTITUTIONAL NORMS FROM A "WIDER CIVILIZATION": *LAWRENCE* AND THE REHNQUIST COURT'S USE OF FOREIGN AND INTERNATIONAL LAW DOMESTIC CONSTITUTIONAL INTERPRETATION

65 Ohio St. L.J. 1283 (2004)

* * *

Lawrence was not the first case in recent memory in which the Justices relied upon international or comparative law sources to decide a constitutional case. In 2002, the Court pointed to the opinion of the "world community" in support of its conclusion that the Constitution prohibited executing the mentally retarded. And individual Justices of the Court recently have invoked international and comparative law norms in opinions supporting the constitutionality of practices as diverse as race-based affirmative action in higher education and federal commandeering of state executive officials. All this comes despite the fact that only seven years ago a majority of the Court endorsed the proposition that "comparative analysis [is] inappropriate to the task of interpreting a constitution, though it was of course quite relevant to the task of writing one."

Given the Court's recent rejection of foreign and international law as aids to domestic constitutional interpretation, one would expect the proponents of the practice to offer a thoughtful and thorough justification for their adoption of this technique. But they have given none. The majorities in *Lawrence* and *Atkins*, for example, simply cited international conventions and the opinions of foreign and international bodies as if they were well-accepted sources of domestic constitutional interpretation, no more controversial than citations of the Court's own precedent. Yet, as we have seen, such is not the case.

This lack of reflection should alarm us. New forms of constitutional argument have a way of perpetuating themselves. As Professor Vicki Jackson has observed, "if Justices refer more to the constitutional decisions of other courts, this practice to some extent will become self-legitimating, a phenomenon that is already occurring around the world." But before embracing any innovative form of constitutional argument, we should consider whether and how it improves upon our current modes of constitutional decision-making and whether it can be reconciled with our constitutional traditions.

Although the Court's opinions have failed to justify the invocation of international and foreign norms in constitutional interpretation, the extrajudicial speeches and writings of some of the Justices, and scholarly works by several academics, have attempted to fill the void. The Justices and commentators typically suggest that it is appropriate for American judges to look to foreign sources in search of persuasive legal reasoning. That is, just as a U.S. Court of Appeals might find persuasive the opinion of a court in a sister circuit, domestic courts might also look abroad in search of persuasive legal argument. In Justice Ginsburg's words, when it comes to constitutional interpretation, "[w]e are the losers if we do not both share our experience with and learn from others."

Whether and when domestic courts can profitably and legitimately borrow legal reasoning from foreign jurisdictions addressing foreign constitutional questions is an important question, which I hope to address elsewhere. Yet, even if one were to conclude that American courts could profitably borrow constitutional reasoning from foreign jurisdictions, that still would not explain or justify the Justices' actual use of foreign and international law in cases like *Lawrence*. Reason-borrowing simply does not describe what members of the Rehnquist Court have done. None of the recent opinions invoking international or comparative law sources has explicitly looked to the reasoning of a foreign decision-maker. Instead, the opinions have used comparative and international law norms for three distinct purposes, which I have labeled expository, empirical, and substantive. Each of these uses requires its own justification, but none, at least as it has actually been employed by the Justices of the Rehnquist Court, can be justified as a form of constitutional reason-borrowing.

The purpose of this Article is two-fold: to describe the Rehnquist Court's actual uses of foreign and international law in domestic constitutional interpretation and to examine the existing attempts to justify these uses. In Part II, I describe the different uses to which the Justices of the Rehnquist Court have put comparative and international law in constitutional decision-making. Not until we have a coherent description of such uses can we begin to frame a normative evaluation of them. In Part III, I explore whether any of these uses has a present justification. I conclude that both the expository and empirical uses of foreign and international materials are easily justified. Yet the Rehnquist Court's approach to using foreign and international law to supply substantive meaning to the Constitution (which I call "moral fact-finding") is more problematic. The Court has offered no justification for employing this technique. Nor have scholars provided explanations that satisfy. Ultimately, I conclude that the moral fact-finding approach remains without constitutional justification.

II.   THE USES OF COMPARATIVE AND INTERNATIONAL LAW: A TYPOLOGY

* * *

A.   EXPOSITORY

The "expository" use of comparative or international law is relatively straightforward. A court uses comparative or international law in this sense when it uses the foreign law rule to contrast and thereby explain a domestic constitutional rule.

A classic example of the expository model is found in Chief Justice Rehnquist's opinion for the Court in *Raines v. Byrd*. The question presented in Raines was whether certain Members of Congress had standing to challenge the alleged dilution of their legislative votes brought about by the Line Item Veto Act. Finding neither precedent nor history to support the Congressmen's claim, the Court held that they lacked standing. The Chief Justice acknowledged that "[t]here would be nothing irrational about a system that granted standing in these cases," and noted that "some European constitutional courts operate under one or another variant of such a regime." Nonetheless, the Chief Justice explained, such "is obviously not the regime that has obtained under our Constitution to date. Our regime contemplates a more restricted role for Article III courts * * *."

Why did the Chief Justice cite the standing practices of foreign constitutional courts? Perhaps he simply found them interesting. More likely, he offered these foreign practices as an example of the "expository" approach; that is, as a way of explaining what the United States law of standing is by contrasting it with an example of what it is not.

B.   EMPIRICAL

The empirical use of comparative and international law norms is more complex than the expository use, but no more problematic in principle. The Justices sometimes use comparative (or, less frequently, international) norms in an empirical sense when the answer to the ultimate constitutional question before the Court is contingent upon the answer to an empirical question. In such situations, the Court may look to a foreign law source for its practical effect. The Court does not rely on the foreign law to supply the rule of decision, *per se*; instead it derives the general rule of decision from domestic sources. But the Court looks abroad to see what the effect of the proposed rule might be in the context of a particular legal system and to ascertain whether the effect of the specific ruling urged upon the Court will comply with the constitutional principle the Court has derived through domestic sources.

The Supreme Court's decision in *Washington v. Glucksberg* exemplifies the "empirical" use of comparative experience. In *Glucksberg*, the Court was asked to decide whether the State of Washington's ban on physician-assisted suicide violated the Due Process Clause of the Fourteenth Amendment. After "examining our Nation's history, legal traditions, and practices," the Court concluded that the right to physician-assisted suicide was not a fundamental liberty interest protected by the Fourteenth Amendment. That left the Court to determine whether the State's ban on physician-assisted suicide could survive the rational basis review. It was in answering this question that the Court turned to comparative sources.

Washington had claimed an interest in banning physician-assisted suicide to prevent euthanasia and asserted a fear that "permitting assisted suicide w[ould] start it down the path to voluntary and perhaps even involuntary euthanasia." To determine whether this fear was fanciful, the Court looked to the Netherlands, "the only place where experience with physician-assisted suicide and euthanasia has yielded empirical evidence." Turning to the "Dutch government's own study," the Court discovered that

> in 1990, there were 2,300 cases of voluntary euthanasia * * * 400 cases of assisted suicide, and more than 1,000 cases of euthanasia without an explicit request. In addition, * * * the study found an additional 4,941 cases where physicians administered lethal morphine overdoses without the patients' explicit consent.

These data, the Court concluded,

> suggest that, despite the existence of various reporting procedures, euthanasia in the Netherlands has not been limited to competent, terminally ill adults who are enduring physical suffering, and that regulation of the practice may not have prevented abuses in cases involving vulnerable persons. * * *

Washington, the Court held, was therefore reasonable in "ensur[ing] against this risk by banning, rather than regulating assisting suicide."

The Court's reliance on the Dutch experience in *Glucksberg* is a good example of the empirical use of foreign law. The Court did not rely on the fact of Dutch toleration for physician assisted suicide as a *reason in itself* why the United States should constitutionalize a principle allowing the practice. Nor did it consider the *reasons* articulated by Dutch policymakers for allowing the practice as reasons why the United States Constitution should incorporate a similar rule. Rather, the Court simply looked to the *effect* of the Dutch rule to provide it with an empirical basis for answering the question posed by the domestic constitutional standard: whether Washington's statute bore a rational relationship to the interest it sought to protect. In other words, the Court took evidence, from the only source available, of the likely effect of Washington's legislation to test its conformity with the domestic constitutional rule.

C. SUBSTANTIVE

There is yet a third type of domestic constitutional question to which international and comparative law might be relevant. This type of question asks not what the factual *consequences* of a particular rule might be, but rather what the *substantive content* of the constitutional rule is or ought to be. A court using comparative and international law rules in this substantive sense does not derive the constitutional rule exclusively from domestic sources and look outward for factual information bearing upon whether a state rule or action comports with the domestic constitutional norm; it instead reaches out at the first stage—to seek foreign and international guidance in defining the content of the domestic constitutional rule.

One can imagine two ways in which a court might go about using comparative and international law to help formulate a domestic constitutional norm. The first would be to read the opinions of foreign and international courts that have addressed questions similar to the question facing the domestic court and use the foreign courts' reasoning to help shape the domestic constitutional rule. This approach, widely advocated by jurists and scholars, I will call the "reason-borrowing" approach.

Alternatively, a court looking abroad in search of the content of a domestic constitutional rule might look simply to the *fact* that foreign or international jurisdictions have adopted a particular rule as a reason to conform the U.S. constitutional rule to the foreign or international norm. I will call this approach "moral fact-finding."

1.   REASON–BORROWING

The reason-borrowing approach, although widely advocated by jurists and scholars, has played no discernible role in the Rehnquist Court's recent embrace of foreign and international law as aids to domestic constitutional interpretation. To my knowledge, no opinion of a Supreme Court Justice in the Rehnquist Court years has actually looked to the *reasons given* by a foreign or international decision-maker to support a domestic constitutional interpretation. To find an example of the reason-borrowing approach, I will have to reach back in time.

* * *

2.   MORAL FACT–FINDING

The "moral fact-finding" variant of the substantive use of comparative and international law is much more sweeping and perhaps more problematic than any of the approaches I have discussed previously. Moreover, it is the only approach that Justices of the Rehnquist Court have applied when using comparative or international law to give substantive content to the Constitution, and it was the one applied, without explanation, in *Lawrence*.

* * *

* * * Recall that the Court in *Lawrence* began its discussion of comparative and international law by suggesting that *Bowers* was wrong, both at the time of decision and now, to suggest that prohibitions on homosexual sodomy reflected "values we share with a wider civilization." As evidence, the Court noted that the European Court of Human Rights had held, both before and after *Bowers*, that laws forbidding homosexual conduct violated the European Convention on Human Rights. Although one might question whether the European Court of Human Rights is actually synony-

mous with the "wider civilization," the jurisprudential move of criticizing the prior reliance on such perceived shared values with evidence to the contrary is unremarkable.

But the Court did not stop there. Instead, it went on to note that "[o]ther nations, too, have taken action consistent with an affirmation of the protected right of homosexual adults to engage in intimate, consensual conduct." And, finally, the Court announced, "[t]he right the petitioners seek in this case has been accepted as an integral part of human freedom in many other countries. There has been no showing that in this country the governmental interest in circumscribing personal choice is somehow more legitimate or urgent." It is in these last three sentences that the Court embraces the moral fact-finding approach. For it was the mere *fact* that other nations (and, presumably, the European Court of Human Rights) had accepted the right the petitioners sought that the Court deemed important. Indeed, the Court's last sentence goes so far as to suggest a standard governing the incorporation of international moral facts into the domestic Constitution: if many other nations of the world have recognized a right, and there is no showing of a domestic need to restrict the right that is greater than the need of foreign governments to restrict the right, the right recognized by the foreign community is, at least potentially, a part of domestic constitutional law.

III. JUSTIFICATIONS FOR THE VARIOUS USES OF COMPARATIVE AND INTERNATIONAL LAW IN CONSTITUTIONAL INTERPRETATION

* * * In this Part, I examine whether any well-accepted theory of constitutional interpretation licenses the various uses of comparative and international law that the Justices of the Rehnquist Court have actually employed in their written opinions. I quickly conclude that the expository use fits easily within conventional constitutional interpretation. Likewise, the empirical use is easily defended, at least from a theoretical perspective. Finding a justification for the one variant of the substantive use that the Justices of the Rehnquist Court have actually employed—the moral fact-finding approach—is harder. * * *

C.   CONSTITUTIONAL JUSTIFICATIONS FOR THE MORAL FACT–FINDING APPROACH

* * *

The Justices do not stand alone in their enthusiasm for moral fact-finding. For years, some legal academics have proposed using international or foreign legal norms to give meaning to discrete provisions of the U.S. Constitution. * * *

Yet looking for a legitimating theory in the literature advocating moral fact-finding produces disappointing results. Many proponents of this use ignore the licensing question altogether. Those who have attempted to engage the question have touched on it only briefly and have failed to produce a convincing answer. This section will discuss the shortcomings of the four principal arguments advanced in favor of moral fact-finding: that importing foreign and international law norms avoids the problem of judicial subjectivity in constitutional interpretation; that such a practice is consistent with original intent or understanding; that it will aid U.S. foreign policy; and that it will produce good results.

1.   THE OBJECTIVITY THEORY

The legitimating theory that scholars most commonly offer is what I call the "objectivity theory." The objectivity theory holds that judges should look to comparative and international law for substantive constitutional content because foreign and international law rules are readily ascertainable and are formulated by sources external to the judiciary itself. Thus, the theory asserts, importing such rules avoids the problem of judicial subjectivity in constitutional interpretation.

* * *

The first difficulty with the objectivity theory is that it rests on a flawed premise: that comparative and international law norms, particularly as they relate to human rights, are, in fact, determinate, and readily-ascertainable by American judges. That premise appears not to hold true for at least one [of] the two major sources of international human rights norms—customary international law.

* * *

Not surprisingly, these uncertainties have lead [sic] to divergent views about the actual content of customary international human rights law. As Justice Bruno Simma of the International Court of Justice explained before his elevation to the bench:

> The theory of a customary law of human rights is presented with varying degrees of sophistication—or lack thereof. Some writers state flatly that international human rights law in its entirety or, at least, the whole range of rights enumerated in the 1948 Universal Declaration is now to be regarded as customary law. * * * Then there are more moderate, "middle-of-the-road" views * * * according to which something like a "hard core" of human rights obligations is said to exist as customary law. * * *
>
> Against the proponents of such a broad-based customary law of human rights stands a group of writers who declare themselves unable to verify the existence of the prerequisites of true custom in presence of so much hypocrisy, double-standards, and second thoughts.

Thus, it is far from clear that international human rights norms, at least in the form of CIL ["customary international law"], actually produce the set of "readily-ascertainable" and "particularized" principles the proponents of the objectivity theory would ascribe to them. To the contrary, the swarm of unanswered questions surrounding the content of CIL has led one commentator to call the specification of customary international human rights norms in American courts a "highly creative process" and another to call it "a matter of taste." The major premise of the objectivity theory appears, therefore, to be untrue.

* * * But, even if international human rights norms were perfectly determinate, the objectivity theory would still fall short of providing the requisite grounding for the moral fact-finding approach. That is because the objectivity theory fails to appreciate the other central reason why constitutional scholars are concerned about judicial subjectivity: countermajoritarianism.

As the well-known story goes, legitimate government in America must be premised on the consent of the governed. Ordinarily, that consent is reflected through enactments of legislatures composed of elected representatives of the people. Judicial review of legislative decision-making sets the judgment of unaccountable courts against the judgment of accountable legislatures, and is, thus, inherently "countermajoritarian." This "countermajoritarian difficulty" is alleviated, of course, when the Constitution clearly commands a particular result; then judges are simply enforcing against current majorities the value judgments previously made by a supermajority of the people. But constitutional interpretation that invites judicial discretion threatens self-governance because it allows the unaccountable judiciary to substitute its own policy preferences for those of the representatives of the people. Relying on even perfectly determinate pronouncements of foreign governments and international bodies cannot solve the countermajoritarian difficulty, for it merely replaces one domestically unaccountable decision-maker (the judiciary) with another (foreign governments, foreign or international courts, or the international community, as the case may be). Indeed, reliance on foreign and international law, "over which the American people have no control—either directly through the power of election or even indirectly through the process of judicial appointment," may actually exacerbate the countermajoritarian problem. One cannot purport to solve the countermajoritarian difficulty by substituting a new form of countermajoritarianism. It is this fact that deprives the "objectivity theory" of its legitimating force.

2. THE ORIGINALIST ARGUMENT

Some commentators have argued that comparative or international law, especially in the field of human rights, should supply substantive content to the Constitution because the Framers intended or understood that it would be so. This argument typically begins with the proposition that the

Founders of the Constitution believed in natural law and intended to constitutionalize its precepts. * * *

* * * But even accepting that supposition would not get the proponents of the originalist theory where they aim to go. Many scholars and jurists have theories about where the judiciary should look for specifications of the content of unenumerated constitutional norms. Indeed, not long ago a majority of the Supreme Court in *Washington v. Glucksberg* held that the Court would only recognize unenumerated "fundamental rights and liberties which are, objectively, 'deeply rooted in the Nation's history and tradition,' and 'implicit in the concept of ordered liberty' such that 'neither liberty nor justice would exist if they were sacrificed.' " And in deciding whether to recognize such an unenumerated right, the Court directed that "[o]*ur Nation's* history, legal traditions, and practices * * * provide the crucial 'guideposts for responsible decisionmaking.' "

* * * [H]ow are we to know that the true content of these rights is to be found in the laws of other nations, the pronouncements of foreign or international courts, or the dictates of international human rights law?

* * *

3.   THE ARGUMENT FROM FOREIGN POLICY

Proponents of the moral fact-finding approach sometimes support their position by arguing that U.S. courts' continued failure to rely on comparative and international norms in deciding constitutional questions could damage U.S. foreign policy. They note the risk of perceived hypocrisy, as the United States acts on the one hand as an outspoken champion of human rights, criticizing, and sometimes sanctioning, foreign governments for failing to respect their citizens' basic human rights, while on the other hand refusing to employ the full measure of international human rights law at home. The consequence, scholars predict, is that the United States will lose its moral authority in the field of human rights and thus its ability to foster human rights abroad.

Of course, the core of rights protected by international human rights law is already protected by the United States Constitution. Nonetheless, critics charge, the United States still falls short of international standards in important areas. This non-compliance is accomplished domestically through a number of mechanisms. First, the United States has failed to ratify a number of significant human rights treaties—for example, the Convention on the Rights of the Child and the Convention on the Elimination of All Forms of Discrimination against Women. Second, even when it does ratify human rights treaties, it routinely attaches reservations to them that render the treaties unenforceable as a matter of domestic law. Constitutionalization of comparative or international law norms could alleviate this problem since, under the Supremacy Clause, any state or federal legislation or government action contrary to the constitutional norm would not survive. Thus, it is sometimes argued that the courts, interpreting the U.S. Constitution, should do for the United States' position in the world what the political branches have failed to do by their refusal fully to embrace international human rights norms.

But it is not clear by what authority the federal courts are licensed to rehabilitate the foreign policy of the United States. Foreign policy decisions have always been understood to be the domain of the political branches, and matters of foreign affairs are traditionally questions in which the courts are reluctant to intervene. That a decision by the federal courts to decide a case in a particular way may produce happy consequences for U.S. foreign relations is, of course, not objectionable. The political branches might even urge the courts to accept or reject a particular constitutional rule because of the effect they believe that rule will have in the global arena. But for the courts to decide at the urging of private parties or on their own initiative that the political branches have failed adequately to protect the nation's position in the world, and to seek to rectify that policy failing of their own accord, would work a fundamental reallocation of the Constitution's distribution of powers.

4.   THE ARGUMENT FROM RESULT

Finally, there are those who argue that comparative and international law norms should become domestic constitutional law because such an approach would produce substantive outcomes that the authors view as good. This argument is sometimes augmented by what might be called an argument from broad consensus. This argument posits that a norm that has achieved a high degree of international support—either through adoption in international treaties with numerous signatories, or through its reflection "in widely shared practices around the world"—is more reliable as an indicator of "true" human rights (or, presumably of "good" governmental structure) than the decisions of an individual nation. This is because a norm's acceptance, and perhaps even its incorporation into international law, under these circumstances "requires the acquiescence of numerous societies."

This argument might be deemed a constitutional application of the old maxim that "two heads are better than one." And, as with many old maxims, there is a good deal of sense behind it. If the world's nations, save the United States, have uniformly adopted a particular structural constitutional rule, or have guaranteed their citizens a particular constitutional right, there is some reason to question whether the United States' position is correct as a matter of morality or good public policy—certainly more reason than if the decks were not so unevenly stacked. But, as far as our search for a legitimating constitutional theory goes, this observation is largely beside the point. For the "broad consensus" theory to have any sway with respect to that question, it must attach itself to some theory of constitutional interpretation that both equates the constitutional rule with the "right" or "best" rule and authorizes the courts to be the institution that imposes this rule. I have previously discussed the counter-majoritarian concerns raised by deference to the international community in constitutional interpretation. It remains here to discuss whether the moral fact-finding approach can be justified by the good results it will produce.

* * *

To take seriously the notion of deference to the international community in constitutional interpretation would mean, for example, vast restrictions on the constitutional right to abortion as currently recognized in the United States. Or, to put it another way, deference to the international community would require far greater constitutional protection for fetal life. According to statistics published by the Center for Reproductive Rights, the United States is one of only six countries in the world that allows abortion, without restriction as to reason, until the point of viability. The vast majority of the world's countries (187 of 195) forbid abortion after 12 weeks gestation, and require, at a minimum, that the pregnant woman make some showing of "good reason" to terminate a pregnancy (141 of 195). Indeed, half the countries of the world (98 of 195) either forbid abortion altogether or allow abortions only to save the woman's life or physical health, or in cases of rape or incest. World opinion on abortion thus appears much more restrictive of abortion rights than domestic constitutional law.

Or consider the First Amendment. Deference to the world community here would probably result in abridgment of currently recognized constitutional rights to freedom of speech. Many nations restrict speech far more than is constitutionally permissible in the United States. For example, in the United States, hate speech generally is constitutionally protected unless it amounts to an "incitement of violence." By contrast, many nations, including those that typically recognize some measure of protection for the freedom of expression, substantially restrict hate speech. Indeed, most Western democracies prohibit such speech and subject it to criminal sanction. In addition, both the International Covenant on Civil and Political Rights ("ICCPR") and the Convention on the Elimination of All Forms of Racial Discrimination ("Race Convention") contain restrictions on hate speech that are widely thought to be inconsistent with current interpretations of the First Amendment. Although the United States has ratified these treaties, it has attached reservations to them indicating that the United States does not agree to the restrictions on hate speech to the extent that they are inconsistent with First Amendment protections. If, however, the hate speech provisions of the ICCPR or the Race Convention were deemed to represent the consensus of the world community, as indeed they might, given the number of signatories to these conventions who have not reserved against the hate speech provisions, and the prevalence of hate speech restrictions in the laws of other nations, the moral fact-finding approach to constitutional interpretation might suggest (or require) the Court to re-examine current First Amendment doctrine.

Of course, deference to the international community in constitutional interpretation would also suggest or require other outcomes. Deference to world opinion might suggest that the Eighth Amendment be re-interpreted to forbid the execution of persons who were minors at the time they committed a capital crime; and might someday require abolition of the death penalty altogether. For some, this mix of substantive constitutional outcomes would be optimal. Others would undoubtedly disagree. My point is simply that true deference to international opinion would fundamentally alter the constitutional path we have forged for ourselves in the United States, and not all change would point in one direction.

* * *

———————————

After having surveyed what we call Transnational Law, and particularly after having looked at the changing interplay between international and domestic law, should American courts consider international and foreign law when they interpret the U.S. Constitution or even regular statutes? Does the answer depend on the kind of international or foreign law? Does the nature of the case or issue matter? What are the advantages of taking such foreign and international sources into account? What are the costs and risks?

EPILOGUE

TWO VIEWS OF THE NEW WORLD ORDER

■ ■ ■

In this course, we have seen the world order evolve through several stages. In Part One, we observed the transition (in Europe) from the medieval world of fragmented and constantly contested political authority to the "Westphalian" system of modern nation states characterized by (at least claims of) internal and external sovereignty and coexisting under a regime of (largely consent-based) international law. In Part Two, we observed the emergence of a more complex global order shaped by a diversification of actors, sources, dispute resolution mechanisms, and forms of legal and political power. Taking a broad view of this evolution, one can say that we saw the rise (in the early modern period) and the "decline" (since the later 20th century) of the Westphalian system.

Where does that leave the global order today? Below, two authors present different views on the current state of affairs. In comparing their views, begin by asking yourself what they agree on. Then consider how their views differ. Finally, relate their views of the modern world to what you have learned in this course as well as to your own experience of living in the early 21st century. (Note that these articles were written at the close of the 20th century.)

What are the implications of these two views? Are the modern orders described by these authors to be preferred to the traditional Westphalian system? If so, which of the two modern orders promises better governance? "Better" in what sense?

JESSICA T. MATTHEWS, POWER SHIFT
76 Foreign Affairs 50 (Jan–Feb 1997)

THE RISE OF GLOBAL CIVIL SOCIETY

The end of the Cold War has brought no mere adjustment among states but a novel redistribution of power among states, markets, and civil society. National governments are not simply losing autonomy in a globalizing economy. They are sharing powers—including political, social, and security roles at the core of sovereignty—with businesses, with international organizations, and with a multitude of citizens groups, known as nongovernmental organizations (NGOs). The steady concentration of power in the hands of states that began in 1648 with the Peace of Westphalia is over, at least for a while.

The absolutes of the Westphalian system—territorially fixed states where everything of value lies within some state's borders; a single, secular authority governing each territory and representing it outside its borders; and no authority above states—are all dissolving. Increasingly, resources and threats that matter, including money, information, pollution, and popular culture, circulate and shape lives and economies with little regard for political boundaries. International standards of conduct are gradually beginning to override claims of national or regional singularity. Even the most powerful states find the marketplace and international public opinion compelling them more often to follow a particular course.

The state's central task of assuring security is the least affected, but still not exempt. War will not disappear, but with the shrinkage of U.S. and Russian nuclear arsenals, the transformation of the Nuclear Nonproliferation Treaty into a permanent covenant in 1995, agreement on the long-sought Comprehensive Test Ban treaty in 1996, and the likely entry into force of the Chemical Weapons Convention in 1997, the security threat to states from other states is on a downward course. Nontraditional threats, however, are rising—terrorism, organized crime, drug trafficking, ethnic conflict, and the combination of rapid population growth, environmental decline, and poverty that breeds economic stagnation, political instability, and, sometimes, state collapse. The nearly 100 armed conflicts since the end of the Cold War have virtually all been intrastate affairs. Many began with governments acting against their own citizens, through extreme corruption, violence, incompetence, or complete breakdown, as in Somalia.

* * *

The most powerful engine of change in the relative decline of states and the rise of nonstate actors is the computer and telecommunications revolution, whose deep political and social consequences have been almost completely ignored. Widely accessible and affordable technology has broken governments' monopoly on the collection and management of large amounts of information and deprived governments of the deference they enjoyed because of it. In every sphere of activity, instantaneous access to information and the ability to put it to use multiplies the number of players who matter and reduces the number who command great authority. The effect on the loudest voice—which has been governments—has been the greatest.

* * *

Above all, the information technologies disrupt hierarchies, spreading power among more people and groups. In drastically lowering the costs of communication, consultation, and coordination, they favor decentralized networks over other modes of organization. In a network, individuals or groups link for joint action without building a physical or formal institutional presence. Networks have no person at the top and no center. Instead, they have multiple nodes where collections of individuals or groups interact for different purposes. Businesses, citizen's organizations, ethnic groups, and crime cartels have all readily adopted the network model. Governments, on the other hand, are quintessential hierarchies, wedded to an organizational form incompatible with all that the new technologies make possible.

Today's powerful nonstate actors are not without precedent. The British East India Company ran a subcontinent, and a few influential NGOs go back more than a century. But these are exceptions. Both in numbers and in impact, nonstate actors have never before approached their current strength. And a still larger role likely lies ahead.

* * *

LEAPS OF IMAGINATION

After three and a half centuries, it requires a mental leap to think of world politics in any terms other than occasionally cooperating but generally competing states, each defined by its territory and representing all the people therein. Nor is it easy to imagine political entities that could compete with the emotional attachment of a shared landscape, national history, language, flag, and currency.

Yet history proves that there are alternatives other than tribal anarchy. Empires, both tightly and loosely ruled, achieved success and won allegiance. In the Middle Ages, emperors, kings, dukes, knights, popes, archbishops, guilds, and cities exercised overlapping secular power over the same territory in a system that looks much more like a modern, three-dimensional network than the clean-lined, hierarchical state order that replaced it. The question now is whether there are new geographic or functional entities that might grow up alongside the state, taking over some of its powers and emotional resonance.

The kernels of several such entities already exist. The European Union is the most obvious example. Neither a union of states nor an international organization, the EU leaves experts groping for inadequate descriptions like "post-sovereign system" or "unprecedented hybrid." It respects members' borders for some purposes, particularly in foreign and defense policy, but ignores them for others. The union's judiciary can override national law, and its Council of Ministers can overrule certain domestic executive decisions. In its thousands of councils, committees, and working groups, national ministers increasingly find themselves working with their counterparts from other countries to oppose colleagues in their own government; agriculture ministers, for example, ally against finance ministers. In this sense the union penetrates and to some extent weakens the internal bonds of its member states. Whether Frenchmen, Danes, and Greeks will ever think of themselves first as Europeans remains to be seen, but the EU has already come much further than most Americans realize.

Meanwhile, units below the national level are taking on formal international roles. Nearly all 50 American states have trade offices abroad, up from four in 1970, and all have official standing in the World Trade Organization (WTO). German *Länder* and British local governments have offices at EU headquarters in Brussels. France's Rhone–Alpes region, centered in Lyon, maintains what it calls "embassies" abroad on behalf of a regional economy that includes Geneva, Switzerland, and Turin, Italy.

Emerging political identities not linked to territory pose a more direct challenge to the geographically fixed state system. The WTO is struggling to find a method of handling environmental disputes in the global commons, outside all states' boundaries, that the General Agreement on Tariffs and Trade, drafted 50 years ago, simply never envisioned. Proposals have been floated for a Parliamentary Assembly in the United Nations, parallel to the General Assembly, to represent the people rather than the states of the world. Ideas are under discussion that would give ethnic nations political and legal status, so that the Kurds, for example, could be legally represented as a people in addition to being Turkish, Iranian, or Iraqi citizens.

* * *

The realm of most rapid change is hybrid authorities that include state and nonstate bodies such as the International Telecommunications Union, the International Union for the Conservation of Nature, and hundreds more. In many of these, businesses or NGOs take on formerly public roles. The Geneva-based International Standards Organization, essentially a business NGO, sets widely observed standards on everything from products to internal corporate procedures. The International Securities Markets Association, another private regulator, oversees international trade in private securities markets—the world's second-largest capital market after domestic government bond markets. In another crossover, markets become government enforcers when they adopt treaty standards as the basis for market judgments. States and NGOs are collaborating ad hoc in large-scale humanitarian relief operations that involve both military and civilian forces. Other NGOs have taken on standing operational roles for international organizations in refugee work and development assistance. Almost unnoticed, hybrids like these, in which states are often the junior partners, are becoming a new international norm.

* * *

Dissolving and Evolving

Might the decline in state power prove transitory? Present disenchantment with national governments could dissipate as quickly as it arose. Continuing globalization may well spark a vigorous reassertion of economic or cultural nationalism. By helping solve problems governments cannot handle, business, NGOs, and international organizations may actually be strengthening the nation-state system.

These are all possibilities, but the clash between the fixed geography of states and the nonterritorial nature of today's problems and solutions, which is only likely to escalate, strongly suggests that the relative power of states will continue to decline. Nation-states may simply no longer be the natural problem-solving unit. Local government addresses citizens' growing desire for a role in decision-making, while transnational, regional, and even global entities better fit the dimensions of trends in economics, resources, and security.

The evolution of information and communications technology, which has only just begun, will probably heavily favor nonstate entities, including those not yet envisaged, over states. The new technologies encourage noninstitutional, shifting networks over the fixed bureaucratic hierarchies that are the hallmark of the single-voiced sovereign state. They dissolve issues' and institutions' ties to a fixed place. And by greatly empowering individuals, they weaken the relative attachment to community, of which the preeminent one in modern society is the nation-state.

If current trends continue, the international system 50 years hence will be profoundly different. During the transition, the Westphalian system and an evolving one will exist side by side. States will set the rules by which all other actors operate, but outside forces will increasingly make decisions for them. In using business, NGOs, and international organizations to address problems they cannot or do not want to take on, states will, more often than not, inadvertently weaken themselves further. Thus governments' unwillingness to adequately fund international organizations helped NGOs move from a peripheral to a central role in shaping multilateral agreements, since the NGOs provided expertise the international organizations lacked. At least for a time, the transition is likely to weaken rather than bolster the world's capacity to solve its problems. If states, with the overwhelming share of power, wealth, and capacity, can do less, less will get done.

Whether the rise of nonstate actors ultimately turns out to be good news or bad will depend on whether humanity can launch itself on a course of rapid social innovation, as it did after World War II. Needed adaptations include a business sector that can shoulder a broader policy role, NGOs that are less parochial and better able to operate on a large scale, international institutions that can efficiently serve the dual masters of states and citizenry, and, above all, new institutions and political entities that match the transnational scope of today's challenges while meeting citizens' demands for accountable democratic governance.

ANNE–MARIE SLAUGHTER, THE REAL NEW WORLD ORDER
76 Foreign Affairs 183 (Sept.–Oct. 1997)

THE STATE STRIKES BACK

Many thought that the new world order proclaimed by George Bush was the promise of 1945 fulfilled, a world in which international institutions, led by the United Nations, guaranteed international peace and security with the active support of the world's major powers. That world order is a chimera. Even as a liberal internationalist ideal, it is infeasible at best and dangerous at worst. It requires a centralized rule-making authority, a hierarchy of institutions, and universal membership. Equally to the point, efforts to create such an order have failed. The United Nations cannot function effectively independent of the major powers that compose it, nor will those nations cede their power and sovereignty to an international institution. Efforts to expand supranational authority, whether by the U.N. secretary–general's office, the European Commission, or the World Trade Organization (WTO), have consistently produced a backlash among member states.

The leading alternative to liberal internationalism is "the new medievalism," a back-to-the-future model of the 21st century. Where liberal internationalists see a need for international rules and institutions to solve states' problems, the new medievalists proclaim the end of the nation-state. Less hyperbolically, in her article, "Power Shift," in the January/February 1997 *Foreign Affairs*, Jessica T. Mathews describes a shift away from the state—up, down, and sideways—to supra-state, sub-state, and, above all, nonstate actors. These new players have multiple allegiances and global reach.

Mathews attributes this power shift to a change in the structure of organizations: from hierarchies to networks, from centralized compulsion to voluntary association. The engine of this transformation is the information technology revolution, a radically expanded communications capacity that empowers individuals and groups while diminishing traditional authority. The result is not world government, but global governance. If government denotes the formal exercise of power by established institutions, governance denotes cooperative problem-solving by a changing and often uncertain cast. The result is a world order in which global governance networks link Microsoft, the Roman Catholic Church, and Amnesty International to the European Union, the United Nations, and Catalonia.

The new medievalists miss two central points. First, private power is still no substitute for state power. Consumer boycotts of transnational corporations destroying rain forests or exploiting child labor may have an impact on the margin, but most environmentalists or labor activists would prefer national legislation mandating control of foreign subsidiaries. Second, the power shift is not a zero-sum game. A gain in power by nonstate actors does not necessarily translate into a loss of power for the state. On the contrary, many of these nongovernmental organizations (NGOs) network with their foreign counterparts to apply additional pressure on the traditional levers of domestic politics.

A new world order is emerging, with less fanfare but more substance than either the liberal internationalist or new medievalist visions. The state is not disappearing, it is disaggregating into its separate, functionally distinct parts. These parts—courts, regulatory agencies, executives, and even legislatures—are networking with their counterparts abroad, creating a dense web of relations that constitutes a new, transgovernmental order. Today's international problems—terrorism, organized crime, environmental degradation, money laundering, bank failure, and securities fraud—created and sustain these relations. Government institutions have formed networks of their own, ranging from the Basle Committee of Central Bankers to informal ties between law enforcement agencies to legal networks that make foreign judicial decisions more and more familiar. While political scientists Robert Keohane and Joseph Nye first observed its emergence in the 1970s, today transgovernmentalism is rapidly becoming the most widespread and effective mode of international governance.

Compared to the lofty ideals of liberal internationalism and the exuberant possibilities of the new medievalism, transgovernmentalism seems mundane. Meetings between securities regulators, antitrust or environmental officials, judges, or legislators lack the drama of high politics. But for the internationalists of the 1990s—bankers, lawyers, businesspeople, public-interest activists, and criminals—transnational government networks are a reality. Wall Street looks to the Basle Committee rather than the World Bank. Human rights lawyers are more likely to develop transnational litigation strategies for domestic courts than to petition the U.N. Committee on Human Rights.

* * *

An offspring of an increasingly borderless world, transgovernmentalism is a world order ideal in its own right, one that is more effective and potentially more accountable than either of the current alternatives. Liberal internationalism poses the prospect of a supranational bureaucracy answerable to no one. The new medievalist vision appeals equally to states' rights enthusiasts and supranationalists, but could easily reflect the worst of both worlds. Transgovernmentalism, by contrast, leaves the control of government institutions in the hands of national citizens, who must hold their governments as accountable for their transnational activities as for their domestic duties.

* * *

A NEW WORLD ORDER IDEAL

Transgovernmentalism offers its own world order ideal, less dramatic but more compelling than either liberal internationalism or the new medievalism. It harnesses the state's power to find and implement solutions to global problems. International institutions have a lackluster record on such problem-solving; indeed, NGOs exist largely to compensate for their inadequacies. Doing away with the state, however, is hardly the answer. The new medievalist mantra of global governance is "governance without government." But governance without government is governance without power, and government without power rarely works. Many pressing international and domestic problems result from states' insufficient power to establish order, build infrastructure, and provide minimum social services. Private actors may take up some slack, but there is no substitute for the state.

Transgovernmental networks allow governments to benefit from the flexibility and decentralization of nonstate actors. Jessica T. Mathews argues that "businesses, citizens' organizations, ethnic groups, and crime cartels have all readily adopted the network model," while governments "are quintessential hierarchies, wedded to an organizational form incompatible with all that the new technologies make possible." Not so. Disaggregating the state into its functional components makes it possible to create networks of institutions engaged in a common enterprise even as they represent distinct national interests. Moreover, they can work with their subnational and supranational counterparts, creating a genuinely new world order in which networked institutions perform the functions of a world government—legislation, administration, and adjudication—without the form.

These globe-spanning networks will strengthen the state as the primary player in the international system. The state's defining attribute has traditionally been sovereignty, conceived as absolute power in domestic affairs and autonomy in relations with other states. But as Abram and Antonia Chayes observe in *The New Sovereignty* (1995), sovereignty is actually "status—the vindication of the state's existence in the international system." More importantly, they demonstrate that in contemporary international relations, sovereignty has been redefined to mean "membership * * * in the regimes that make up the substance of international life." Disaggregating the state permits the disaggregation of sovereignty as well, ensuring that specific state institutions derive strength and status from participation in a transgovernmental order.

Transgovernmental networks will increasingly provide an important anchor for international organizations and nonstate actors alike. U.N. officials have already learned a lesson about the limits of supranational authority; mandated cuts in the international bureaucracy will further tip the balance of power toward national regulators. The next generation of international institutions is also likely to look more like the Basle Committee, or, more formally, the Organization of Economic Cooperation and Development, dedicated to providing a forum for transnational problem-solving and the harmonization of national law. The disaggregation of the state creates opportunities for domestic institutions, particularly courts, to make common cause with their supranational counterparts against their fellow branches of government. Nonstate actors will lobby and litigate wherever they think they will have the most effect. Many already realize that corporate self-regulation and states' promises to comply with vague international agreements are no substitute for national law.

The spread of transgovernmental networks will depend more on political and professional convergence than on civilizational boundaries. Trust and awareness of a common enterprise are more vulnerable to differing political ideologies and corruption than to cultural differences. Government networks transcend the traditional divide between high and low politics. National militaries, for instance, network as extensively as central bankers with their counterparts in friendly states. Judicial and regulatory networks can help achieve gradual political convergence, but are unlikely to be of much help in the face of a serious economic or military threat. If the coming conflict with China is indeed coming, transgovernmentalism will not stop it.

The strength of transgovernmental networks and of transgovernmentalism as a world order ideal will ultimately depend on their accountability to the world's peoples. To many, the prospect of transnational government by judges and bureaucrats looks more like technocracy than democracy. Critics contend that government institutions engaged in policy coordination with their foreign counterparts will be barely visible, much less accountable, to voters still largely tied to national territory.

Citizens of liberal democracies will not accept any form of international regulation they cannot control. But checking unelected officials is a familiar problem in domestic politics. As national legislators become increasingly aware of transgovernmental networks, they will expand their oversight capacities and develop networks of their own. Transnational NGO networks will develop a similar monitoring capacity. It will be harder to monitor themselves.

Transgovernmentalism offers answers to the most important challenges facing advanced industrial countries: loss of regulatory power with economic globalization, perceptions of a "democratic deficit" as international institutions step in to fill the regulatory gap, and the difficulties of engaging nondemocratic states. Moreover, it provides a powerful alternative to a liberal internationalism that has reached its limits and to a new medievalism that, like the old Marxism, sees the state slowly fading away. The new medievalists are right to emphasize the dawn of a new era, in which information technology will transform the globe. But government networks are government for the information age. They offer the world a blueprint for the international architecture of the 21st century.

INDEX

References are to Pages
